THE INTELLIGENCE COMMUNITY

PUBLIC DOCUMENTS SERIES

Series Editors: Tyrus G. Fain, with Katharine C. Plant and Ross Milloy

Federal Reorganization: The Executive Branch
The Intelligence Community: History, Organization, and Issues
National Health Insurance

THE INTELLIGENCE COMMUNITY
History, Organization, and Issues

Public Documents Series

Compiled and Edited by
Tyrus G. Fain
in collaboration with
Katharine C. Plant and Ross Milloy

With an Introduction by
Senator Frank Church

R. R. BOWKER COMPANY
New York & London, 1977

Published by R. R. Bowker Company
1180 Avenue of the Americas, New York, N.Y. 10036
Copyright © 1977 by Xerox Corporation
All rights reserved
Printed and bound in the United States of America

Library of Congress Cataloging in Publication Data
Main entry under title:
The Intelligence community.

  (Public documents series)
  Bibliography: p.
  Includes index.
    1. United States.   Central Intelligence Agency.
I. Fain, Tyrus G.   II. Plant, Katharine C.
III. Milloy, Ross.   IV. Series.
JK468.I6I57   353.008'92   77-5854
ISBN 0-8352-0959-8

CONTENTS

PART I
HISTORY AND STRUCTURE OF THE U.S. FOREIGN
INTELLIGENCE COMMUNITY

PART II
COMPONENTS OF THE FOREIGN INTELLIGENCE COMMUNITY

PART III
THE PUBLIC ISSUES

10. Accountability and Oversight

PREFACE

This edited collection of contemporary government documents on United States foreign intelligence represents the first title in the Public Documents Series, a publishing effort seeking to make government documents more accessible to the public. The series addresses itself to matters of major and topical public policy concern, on which a considerable quantity of information has been generated and released by government sources.

The effectiveness and the morality of U.S. foreign intelligence activities has indeed been the subject of widespread controversy, discussion, and debate over the past decade. Highly significant revelations on intelligence functions are contained in the investigative hearings, studies, and reports issued from 1970 to 1976. And it is these inquiries, made by various commissions and congressional committees, which have necessitated further reflection of the purposes and direction of the entire intelligence community. Never before in the nation's history has the clandestine aspect of foreign intelligence been so thoroughly scrutinized in the public forum. The documentary record of that scrutiny provides a fertile resource for understanding the operations of the intelligence community and the international and domestic ramifications of those operations.

That documentary record, however, is a vast and cumbersome body of information, which is often inaccessible or out of print. The material was written, edited, published, and distributed for the use of government officials. It consists of over 30,000 pages from 124 sources in varying styles and formats; some of the material was indexed, bound, and placed on sale through the Government Printing Office, but a large portion was issued without indexes or other bibliographic controls. A diligent researcher could assemble this data, but the time spent and the cost would be considerable. The documents are in the "public domain." They are free of the restraints of copyright, but they lack any promotional sponsorship which might bring them to the attention of the scholar and layperson alike. So, it is the purpose of the Public Documents Series to compile an orderly "file" of excerpts from key documents, place them under bibliographic controls, and give them a sponsor in the private publishing community.

The scope of *The Intelligence Community* encompasses that body of official reports, hearings, and studies concerning the U.S. foreign intelligence establishment, released by the government from 1970 to 1976. The decision to begin the Public Documents Series with the intelligence literature was prompted by the unprecedented, intellectually rich, and provocative output of government sources during the early and mid 1970s. These years represent a period of revelation and reform in the history of intelligence activity. The political climate of the nation, and its morale, were influenced by the war in Southeast Asia, by the scandal associated with the Watergate affair, and by the downfall of the Nixon administration. All of these experiences led to a reexamination and reassessment of the purposes, organization, and operations of the agencies and programs associated with intelligence and espionage. Reports of possible CIA involvement in Watergate, plots encouraging the overthrow of particular governments, complicity in assassinations of foreign leaders, and evidence of extensive domestic spying and abuse by the intelligence agencies have had serious consequences for American citizens and their elected representatives in government.

The focus of the book is on U.S. intelligence activities directed at other nations. The counterespionage activities of the FBI, directed against foreign agents in their attempts to penetrate and disrupt U.S. agencies, are dealt with briefly. There is also documentation on illegal involvement of American foreign intelligence agencies in efforts to thwart specific U.S. political activities. Clandestine, but legal, domestic activities related to internal security and crime are outside the scope of the book and are not addressed.

The volume is organized into three parts. Part I deals with the legal and historical underpinnings of the U.S. foreign intelligence effort and its place within the formation and conduct of foreign policy. The notion of a "community" of coordinated intelligence agencies, operating in pursuit of U.S. policy interests, is also examined. Part II treats the principal agencies of the intelligence community: the Central Intelligence Agency, the Department of Defense, the National Security Agency, the Federal Bureau of Investigation's counterespionage programs, and the Department of State's Bureau of Intelligence and Research. The documentation of the National Security Agency is rather limited because its activities were not examined in detail by congressional committees and investigative commissions, according to the available hearings and reports. The chapter on the FBI is restricted to documents describing its counterespionage programs against foreign agents and to an examination of some of its domestic intelligence activities.

Part III examines three broad public policy issues: public accountability and congressional oversight; the ethics of covert action; and intrusion by the intelligence agencies into domestic affairs. Public accountability is a fundamental element in any democratic society, and in America it can best be assured by the effective oversight of Congress. The problem, then, is how to conduct clandestine operations while, at the same time, guaranteeing public accountability. Covert action is the combative side of intelligence in that it involves undercover operations designed to influence the outcome of events. The ethical limits and procedures to control such activities are discussed in policy-oriented documents and case material related to Chile and alleged U.S. involvement in assassination plots against foreign leaders. Finally, the operation of intelligence agencies in the domestic area is considered. Documents from the Watergate experience, such as the Huston Plan, are reprinted, along with the recommendations of the Senate Select Committee to Study Governmental Operations with Respect to Intelligence Activities (Church Committee).

Preparation of this compilation began with the assemblage of a bibliographic team, coordinated by Alice Keefer, a librarian with the Library of Congress, and comprised of the volume's three editors. Their task was to locate pertinent and available public documents, review the documents and bibliographies, and interview committee and commission staffs. Each document was considered on its merit as either being representative or particularly illuminating. Consultation with intelligence experts was part of the team's research in order to gain additional perspective on the value of specific information.

Acknowledgment for making this publication possible must begin with a tribute to the dozens of government officials who created this body of information. Regretfully, most government authors remain anonymous, by long-standing custom, but to them we owe a debt of gratitude. To any who should come across their work here, we wish to thank you. Those who led the investigations into the intelligence field should also be recognized with appreciation, especially Senator Frank Church and Representatives Otis Pike and Lucien Nedzi. The careful analysis and attention to detail reflected in the Church Committee hearings and reports is indeed a valuable contribution to government literature.

The R. R. Bowker staff who supported this publishing effort and who are continuing to develop the Public Documents Series are due special thanks. Bob Asleson, Bowker's president, and his able colleagues, Desmond Reaney and Judy Garodnick, offered encouragement from the beginning. Nancy Volkman, of R. R. Bowker, guided the entire editorial process with skill, diligence, patience, and good humor. Her belief in the project inspired everyone. Alice Keefer located the documents, cataloged them, and constructed the bibliographies. Her ability to locate information and impose order on the material was remarkable. Many others made contributions of note, among them: Richard Grimmett of the Congressional Research Service, James Klick, Keneth Fain, David Phillips, Jack Tacke, Paul Fain, and Edmund Wise. My special thanks go to Katharine Plant and Ross Milloy, the two key collaborators in the overall work. They spent months on this compilation, bringing to it dedication, skill, and judgment, without which the job would never have begun nor been accomplished.

TYRUS G. FAIN

GUIDE TO USE

The documents in this volume were edited and, at times, abridged; where abridgement occurs, it is because of space limitations or because the editors sought to reduce redundancy—in an attempt to offer the most apposite information. Like the sources from which the text was drawn, there are inevitably gaps and inconsistencies in the style and format of the book. The editors have provided explanatory bridging narrative to facilitate transition between the documents, to lend continuity, and to elucidate the material. This narrative is set apart from the documents by horizontal lines. The editors have also provided notes and references at the end of each chapter, to give background on and perspective to the documents. The boldface numbers in the margin of the text (e.g., **N1**, **N2**, **N3**) refer to these notes and references.

The source of each document has been identified by the bracketed number appearing with the headings in chapters. The number, which is followed by the page numbers in the original source, refers to the numbered documents listed in the bibliography. This number is cited whenever a document changes. Ellipses points have been inserted by the editors to indicate deletions of nonpertinent material from the original document. Because of these deletions, there are gaps in the numbering of the original documents' footnotes.

The volume concludes with a bibliography; appendixes containing a list of acronyms, a glossary, reprints of legislation, Executive actions, and abstracts of documents; an index of included documents; and a subject and name index.

INTRODUCTION

I welcome this opportunity to contribute an introduction to this documentary volume on foreign intelligence. I believe it is important to make government documents as accessible as possible to the public. As the reader will see, the topics in this volume extend over the vast range of foreign intelligence activities. From this array, I have chosen to write about one subject in particular: covert action. For it is in this area where the abuses have been most far-reaching and the moral and policy issues are especially controversial.

Two hundred years ago, at the founding of this nation, Thomas Paine observed that "Not a place upon earth might be so happy as America. Her situation is remote from all the wrangling world . . . ." I still believe America remains the best place on earth, but it has long since ceased to be "remote from all the wrangling world." On the contrary, even our internal economy now depends on events far beyond our shores. The energy crisis, which exposed our vulnerable dependence upon foreign oil, makes the point vividly.

It is also tragic, but true, that our own people can no longer be made safe from the threat of savage destruction, hurled down upon them from the most hidden and remote regions on earth. Russian submarines silently traverse the ocean floors, carrying transcontinental missiles with the capacity to strike at our heartland. The nuclear arms race between the United States and the Soviet Union threatens to continue its deadly spiral toward Armageddon. In this dangerous setting, it is imperative for the United States to maintain a strong and effective intelligence service. We have no choice other than to gather, analyze, and assess—to the best of our abilities—vital information on the intent and capability of foreign adversaries, present or potential. Without an adequate intelligence-gathering apparatus, we would be unable to gauge with confidence our defense requirements—unable to control, through satellite surveillance, a runaway nuclear arms race. "The winds and waves are always on the side of the ablest navigators," wrote Gibbon. Those nations without a skillful intelligence service must navigate beneath a clouded sky.

With this truth in mind, the United States established, by the National Security Act of 1947, a Central Intelligence Agency to collect and evaluate intelligence and provide for its proper dissemination within the government. The CIA was to be a clearinghouse for other American intelligence agencies, including those of the State Department and the various military services. It was to be an independent, civilian intelligence agency whose duty it was, in the words of Allen Dulles, CIA director from 1953 to 1961:

> To weigh facts, and to draw conclusions from those facts, without having either the facts
> or the conclusions warped by the inevitable and even proper prejudices of the men whose
> duty it is to determine policy and who, having once determined a policy are too likely to be
> blind to any facts which might tend to prove the policy to be faulty.

"The Central Intelligence Agency," concluded Dulles, "should have nothing to do with policy." In this way, neither the president nor the Congress would be left to rely upon any of the frequently self-interested intelligence assessments afforded by the Pentagon and the State Department.

While one may debate the quality of the agency's performance, there has never been any question about the propriety and necessity of its evolvement in the process of gathering and evaluating foreign intelligence. Nor have serious questions been raised about the means used to acquire such information, whether from overt sources, technical devices, or by clandestine methods. What has become controversial is quite unrelated to intelligence, but has to do instead with the so-called covert operations of the CIA, those secret efforts to manipulate events within foreign countries in ways presumed to serve the interests of the United States. The legal basis for this political action arm of the CIA is very much open to question. Certainly the legislative history of the 1947 Act fails to indicate that Congress anticipated the CIA would ever engage in covert political warfare abroad.

The CIA points to a catch-all phrase contained in the 1947 Act as a rationalization for its covert operations. A clause in the statute permits the agency "to perform such other functions and duties related to intelligence affecting the national security as the National Security Council may, from time to time, direct." These vague and seemingly innocuous words have been seized upon as the green light for CIA intervention around the world. Moreover, these interventions into the political affairs of foreign countries soon came to overshadow the agency's original purpose of gathering and evaluating information. Just consider how far afield we strayed. For example:

> We deposed the government of Guatemala when its leftist leanings displeased us;
>
> We attempted to ignite a civil war against Sukarno in Indonesia;
>
> We intervened to restore the Shah to his throne in Iran, after Mossadegh broke the monopoly grip of British petroleum over Iranian oil;
>
> We attempted to launch a counterrevolution in Cuba through the abortive landing of an army of exiles at the Bay of Pigs;
>
> We even conducted a secret war in Laos, paying Meo tribesmen and Thai mercenaries to do our fighting there.

All these engagements were initiated without the knowledge or consent of Congress.

No country was too small, no foreign leader too trifling, to escape our attention:

> We sent a deadly toxin to the Congo with the purpose of injecting Lumumba with a fatal disease;
>
> We armed local dissidents in the Dominican Republic, knowing their purpose to be the assassination of Trujillo;
>
> We participated in a military coup, overturning the very government we were pledged to defend in South Vietnam; and when Premier Diem resisted, he and his brother were murdered by the very generals to whom we gave money and support;
>
> For years, we attempted to assassinate Fidel Castro and other Cuban leaders. The various plots spanned three administrations and involved an extended collaboration between the CIA and the Mafia.

Whatever led the United States to such extremes? Assassination is nothing less than an act of war, and our targets were leaders of small, weak countries that could not possibly threaten the United States. Only once did Castro become an accessory to a threat, by permitting the Russians to install missiles on Cuban soil within range of the United States; and this was the one time when the CIA called off all attempts against his life.

The roots of these malignant plots grew out of the obsessions of the cold war. When the CIA succeeded the Office of Strategic Services of World War II, Stalin replaced Hitler as the devil incarnate. Wartime methods were routinely adopted for peacetime use. In those myopic years, the world was seen as up for grabs between the United States and the Soviet Union. Castro's Cuba raised the spectre of a Soviet outpost at America's doorstep. Events in the Dominican Republic appeared to offer an additional opportunity for the Russians and their allies. The Congo, freed from Belgian rule, occupied the strategic center of the African continent, and the prospect of Soviet penetration there was viewed as a threat to American interests in emerging Africa. There was a great concern that a Communist takeover in Indochina would have a "domino effect" throughout Asia. Even the lawful election in 1970 of a Marxist president in Chile was still seen by some as the equivalent of Castro's conquest of Cuba.

In the words of a former secretary of state, "A desperate struggle [was] going on in the back alleys of world politics." Every upheaval, wherever it occurred, was likened to a pawn on a global chessboard, to be moved this way or that, by the two principal players. This led the CIA to plunge into a full range of covert activities, designed to counteract the competitive efforts of the KGB. Thus, the United States came to adopt the methods and accept the value system of the "enemy." In the secret world of covert action, we threw off all restraints. Not content merely to discreetly subsidize foreign political parties, labor unions, and newspapers, the Central Intelligence Agency soon began to directly manipulate the internal politics of other countries. Spending many millions of dollars annually, the CIA filled its bag with dirty tricks—ranging from bribery and false propaganda to schemes to "alter the health" of unfriendly foreign leaders and undermine their regimes.

Nowhere is this imitation of KGB tactics better demonstrated than in the directives sent to CIA agents in the Congo in 1960. Instructions to kill the African leader Lumumba were sent via diplomatic pouch, along with rubber gloves, a mask, syringe, and a lethal biological material. The poison was to be injected into some substance that Lumumba would ingest, whether food or toothpaste. Before this plan was implemented, Lumumba was killed by Congolese rivals. But, nevertheless, our actions had fulfilled the prophesy of George Williams, an eminent theologian at the Harvard Divinity School, who once warned: "Be cautious when you choose your enemy, for you will grow more like him."

The imperial view from the White House reached its arrogant summits during the adminstration of Richard Nixon. On September 15, 1970, following the election of Allende to be president of Chile, Richard Nixon summoned to the White House Henry Kissinger, Richard Helms, and John Mitchell. The topic was Chile. Allende, Nixon stated, was unacceptable to the president of the United States. In his handwritten notes for this meeting, Nixon indicated that he was "not concerned" with the risks involved. As Director Helms recalled in testimony before the Senate Committee, "The president came down very hard that he wanted something done, and he didn't care how . . . ." To Helms, the order had been all inclusive. "If I ever carried a marshal's baton in my knapsack out of the Oval Office," he recalled, "it was that day." Thus, the president of the United States had given orders to the CIA to prevent the popularly elected president of Chile from entering office.

To bar Allende from the presidency, a military coup was organized, with the CIA playing a direct role in the planning. One of the major obstacles to the success of the mission was the strong opposition to a coup by the commander in chief of the Chilean army, General René Schneider, who insisted that Chile's Constitution be upheld. As a result of his stand, the removal of General Schneider became a necessary ingredient in the coup plans. Unable to get General Schneider to resign, conspirators in Chile decided to kidnap him. Machine guns and ammunition were passed by the CIA to a group of kidnappers on October 22, 1970. That same day, General Schneider was mortally wounded on his way to work in an attempted kidnap, apparently by a group affiliated with the one provided weapons by the CIA.

The plot to kidnap General Schneider was but one of many efforts to subvert the Allende regime. The United States sought also to bring the Chilean economy, under Allende, to its knees. In a situation report to Dr. Kissinger, our ambassador wrote that:

> Not a nut or bolt will be allowed to reach Chile under Allende. Once Allende comes to power, we shall do all within our power to condemn Chile and the Chileans to utmost deprivation and poverty, a policy designed for a long time to come to accelerate the hard features of a Communist society in Chile.

The ultimate outcome, as you know, of these and other efforts to destroy the Allende government, was a bloodbath which included the death of Allende and the installation, in his place, of a repressive military dictatorship.

Why Chile? What can possibly explain or justify such an intrusion upon the right of the Chilean people to self-determination? The country itself was no threat to us. It has been aptly characterized as a "dagger pointed straight at the heart of Antarctica." Was it to protect American-owned big business? We know that I.T.T. offered the CIA a million dollars to prevent the ratification of Allende's election by the Chilean Congress. Quite properly, this offer was rejected. But the CIA then spent much more on its own, in an effort to accomplish the same general objective. Yet, if our purpose was to save the properties of large American corporations, that cause had already been lost. The nationalization of the mines was decided well before Allende's election; and the question of compensation was tempered by insurance against confiscatory losses issued to the companies by the U.S. government itself.

No, the only plausible explanation for our intervention in Chile is the persistence of the myth that Communism is a single, hydra-headed serpent, and that it remains our duty to cut off each ugly head—wherever and however it may appear. Ever since the end of World War II, we have justified our mindless meddling in the affairs of others on the ground that since the Russians do it, we must do it, too. The time is at hand to reexamine that thesis.

Before Chile, we insisted that Communism had never been freely chosen by any people, but forced upon them against their will. The Communists countered that they resorted to revolution because the United States would never permit the establishment of a Communist regime by peaceful means. In Chile, President Nixon confirmed the Communist thesis. Like Caesar peering into the colonies from distant Rome, Nixon said the choice of government by the Chileans was unacceptable to the president of the United States. The attitude of our chief executive seemed to be: If—in the wake of Vietnam—I can no longer send the Marines, then I will send in the CIA.

But, what have we gained by our policy of consummate intervention?

> A "friendly" Iran and Indonesia, members of the OPEC cartel, which imposes extortionate prices on the Western world for indispensable oil?
>
> A hostile Laos that preferred the indigenous forces of communism to control imposed by Westerners, which smacked of the hated colonialism, against which they had fought so long to overthrow?
>
> A fascist Chile, with thousands of political prisoners languishing in its jails, mocking the professed ideals of the United States throughout the Hemisphere?

If we have gained little, what then have we lost? I suggest we have lost—or grievously impaired—the good name and reputation of the United States, from which we once drew a unique capacity to exercise matchless moral leadership. In the eyes of millions of once friendly foreign people, the United States is today regarded with grave suspicion and distrust. What else can account for the startling decline in American prestige? Certainly not the collapse of our military strength; for our firepower has grown immensely since the end of World War II. Of course, our eagerness, since then, to enter Asian wars, at the very time Western colonialism was being driven out of the Orient, has cost us dearly. But, on the whole, we welcomed the emergence of the newly independent governments of the Third World, and gave them aid in the most generous measure.

I must lay the blame, in large part, to the fantasy that it lay within our power to control other countries through the covert manipulation of their affairs. It formed part of a greater illusion that entrapped and enthralled our presidents—the illusion of American omnipotence. Nevertheless, I do not draw the conclusion of those who now argue that all American covert operations must be banned in the future. I can conceive of a dire emergency when timely clandestine action on our part might avert a nuclear holocaust and save an entire civilization. But for such extraordinary events, certainly we do not need a regiment of cloak and dagger men, earning their campaign ribbons—and, indeed, their promotions—by planning new exploits throughout the world. Theirs is a self-generating enterprise. Once the capability for covert activity is established, the pressures brought to bear on the president to use it are immense.

I, myself, believe that all covert activity unrelated with the gathering of essential information should be severed entirely from the CIA. If some circumstance in the future should require a secret operation in a foreign land, let it be done under the direct aegis of the State Department. And if the covert activity is not impelled by the imperative of survival itself, then let it be directly connected with legitimate security interests of the United States in a way that conforms with our traditional belief in freedom. Then, if our hand were exposed, we could scorn the cynical doctrine of "plausible denial," and say openly, "Yes, we were there—and proud of it!"

We were there in Western Europe, helping to restore democratic governments in the aftermath of the Second World War. It was only after our faith gave way to fear that we began to act as a self-appointed sentinel of the status quo. Then it was that all the dark arts of secret intervention—bribery, blackmail, abduction, assassination—were put to the service of reactionary and repressive regimes that can never, or for long, escape or withstand the volcanic forces of change. And the United States, as a result, became even more identified with the claims of the older order, instead of the aspirations of the new.

The remedy is clear. American foreign policy must be made to conform, once more, to our historic ideals, to conform to the same fundamental belief in freedom and popular government that once made us a beacon of hope for the downtrodden and oppressed throughout the world.

SENATOR FRANK CHURCH

PART I

HISTORY AND STRUCTURE OF THE U.S. FOREIGN INTELLIGENCE COMMUNITY

Chapter 1
Development of the
Intelligence Community

THE CONSTITUTIONAL FRAMEWORK FOR
INTELLIGENCE ACTIVITIES

"The necessity of procuring good intelligence is apparent and need not be further urged—all that remains for me to add, is, that you keep the whole matter as secret as possible. For upon Secrecy, Success depends in most Enterprizes of the kind, and for want of it, they are generally defeated, however well planned and promising a favourable issue." So wrote General George Washington to Colonel Elias Dayton, a chief of intelligence, on July 26, 1777. Since that time, U.S. presidents, in varying degrees, have employed the techniques of clandestine operations in their dealings with other nations.

It was the eleventh president of the United States, James K. Polk, who provoked one of the first domestic crises over the use of the Executive branch for covert activities when he denied to the House Foreign Affairs Committee information concerning Secretary of State Daniel Webster's expenditures from "Secret Service Funds." His message to the House of Representatives on April 20, 1846, read in part: "The experience of every nation on earth has demonstrated that emergencies may arise in which it becomes absolutely necessary for the public safety or the public good to make expenditures the very object of which would be defeated by publicity. . . . In no nation is the application of such sums ever made public. In time of war or impending danger, the situation of the country may make it necessary to employ individuals for the purpose of obtaining information or rendering other important services who could never be prevailed upon to act if they entertained the least apprehension that their names or their agency would in any contingency be divulged. So it may often become necessary to incur an expenditure for an object highly useful to the country. . . . But this object might be altogether defeated by the intrigues of other powers if our purposes were to be made known by the exhibition of the original papers and vouchers to the accounting officers of the Treasury. It would be easy to specify other cases which may occur in the history of a great nation, in its intercourse with other nations, wherein it might become absolutely necessary to incur expenditures for objects which could never be accomplished if it were suspected in advance that the items of expenditure and the agencies employed would be made public."

While the concept of clandestine operations on behalf of national security may not have changed much over the 130 years that have elapsed since Polk confronted an angry congressional committee, the size and complexity of the instrumentalities employed certainly have. The editors of this volume, however, do not have the space available to treat the historical antecedents of the public policy issues involved in the present state of the U.S. intelligence community.*

In Chapter 1 there has been an attempt to trace the evolution of the intelligence community since the end of World War II and the beginning of the cold war and to draw together the materials that set forth the legal foundations upon which present U.S. intelligence is based. The shaping of the modern intelligence community has indeed been influenced by two world wars and by the ensuing struggle for power and rank in the world order between the postwar superpowers.

Public documents, such as the 1947 Kermit Roosevelt study of the OSS period or the CIA's detailed, but still classified, history of American intelligence, provide additional perspectives.† These and other post–World War II documents relating to the evolution of the espionage establishment undoubtedly touch on some of the same problems that confronted the congressional committees and presidential commissions of the 1970s.

Reprinted text in this chapter has been drawn from Book I of the 1976 Senate Church Committee Report on Foreign and Military Intelligence ([45A]). As is the custom with most congressional staff reports, the authors are not specifically identified. Further treatment of legal and historical matters is provided in Part II, where the specific components of the new intelligence community are described, and in Part III, where there is a discussion of the legal basis for covert action.

*Henry Merritt Wriston, *Executive Agents in American Foreign Relations* (Baltimore: Johns Hopkins Press, 1929; reprinted Gloucester, Mass.: Peter Smith Publishers, 1967).

†Department of War, Strategic Services Unit, *War Report: Office of Strategic Services* (Washington, D.C. 1947), 3 vols.

The Joint Responsibilities of the Legislative and Executive Branches— Separation of Powers and Checks and Balances ([45A], pp. 31–40)

While the Constitution contains no provisions expressly allocating authority for intelligence activity, the Constitution's provisions regarding foreign affairs and national defense are directly relevant. From the beginning, U.S. foreign intelligence activity [1] has been conducted in connection with our foreign relations and national defense.

In these areas, as in all aspects of our Government, the Constitution provides for a system of checks and balances under the separation of powers doctrine. In foreign affairs and national defense, Congress and the President were both given important powers. The Constitution, as Madison explained in *The Federalist*, established "a partial mixture of powers." [2] Unless the branches of government, Madison said, "be so far connected and blended as to give each a constitutional control over the others, the degree of separation which the maxim requires, as essential to a free government, can never in practice be maintained." [3] The framers' underlying purpose, as Justice Brandeis pointed out, was "to preclude the exercise of arbitrary power." [4]

This pattern of checks and balances is reflected in the constitutional provisions with respect to foreign affairs and national defense. In foreign affairs, the President has the power to make treaties and to appoint Ambassadors and envoys, but this power is subject to the "advice and consent" of the Senate. [5] While the President has the exclusive power to receive ambassadors from foreign states, [6] the Congress has important powers of its own in foreign affairs, most notably the power to regulate foreign commerce and to lay duties. [7]

[1] A definition of the term "foreign intelligence activity" is necessary in order to properly assess the constitutional aspects of foreign intelligence activity. Foreign intelligence activity is now understood to include secret information gathering and covert action. Covert action is defined by the CIA as secret action designed to influence events abroad, including the use of political means or varying degrees of force. The political means can range from the employment of propaganda to large-scale efforts to finance foreign political parties or groups so as to influence elections or overthrow governments; covert action involving the use of force may include U.S. paramilitary operations or the support of military operations by foreign conventional or unconventional military organizations. (Memorandum from Mitchell Rogovin, Special Counsel to the Director of Central Intelligence, House Select Committee on Intelligence, Hearings, 12/9/75, p. 1730.)

[2] *The Federalist*, No. 47 (J. Madison).
[3] *The Federalist*, No. 48 (J. Madison).
[4] *Meyers* v. *United States*, 272 U.S. 52, 292 (1926).
[5] United States Constitution, Article II, Section 2.
[6] *Ibid.*, Sec. 3.
[7] *Ibid.*, Art. I, Sec. 8.

In national defense, the President is made Commander-in-Chief, thereby having the power to command the armed forces, to direct military operations once Congress has declared war, and to repel sudden attacks.[8] Congress, however, has the exclusive power to declare war, to raise and support the armed forces, to make rules for their government and regulation, to call forth the militia, to provide for the common defense, and to make appropriations for all national defense activities.[9]

Moreover, under the Necessary and Proper clause, the Constitution specifies that Congress shall have the power "to make all laws necessary and proper for carrying into execution" not only its own powers but also "all other powers vested by [the] Constitution in the Government of the United States, or in any Department or Officer thereof." [10]

This constitutional framework—animated by the checks and balances concept—makes clear that the Constitution contemplates that the judgment of both the Congress and the President will be applied to major decisions in foreign affairs and national defense. The President, the holder of "the executive power," conducts daily relations with other nations through the State Department and other agencies. The Senate, through its "advice and consent" power and through the work of its appropriate committees participates in foreign affairs. As Hamilton observed in *The Federalist*, foreign affairs should not be left to the "sole disposal" of the President:

> The history of human conduct does not warrant that exalted opinion of human virtue which would make it wise to commit interests of so delicate and momentous a kind, as those which concern its intercourse with the rest of the world, to the sole disposal of a magistrate created and circumstanced as would be a President of the United States.[11]

Similarly, in national defense. the constitutional framework is a "partial mixture of powers," calling for collaboration between the executive and the legislative branches. The Congress, through its exclusive power to declare war, alone decides whether the nation shall move from a state of peace to a state of war. While as Commander-in-Chief the President commands the armed forces, Congress is empowered "to make rules" for their "government and regulation." [12]

Moreover, in both the foreign affairs and defense fields, while the President makes executive decisions, the Congress with its exclusive power over the purse is charged with authority to determine whether, or to what extent, government activities in these areas shall be funded. [13]

The Constitution. while containing no express authority for the conduct of foreign intelligence activity, clearly endowed the Federal Government (i.e., Congress and the President jointly) with all the power necessary to conduct the nation's foreign affairs and national

---

[8] *Ibid.*, Art. II, Sect. 2.
[9] *Ibid.*, Sect. 8.
[10] *Ibid.*
[11] *The Federalist*. No. 75 (A. Hamilton).
[12] United States Constitution, Article I, Section 8.
[13] *Ibid.*, Art. II, Sect. 8.

defense and to stand on an equal basis with other sovereign states.[14] Inasmuch as foreign intelligence activity is a part of the conduct of the United States' foreign affairs and national defense, as well as part of the practice of sovereign states, the Federal Government has the constitutional authority to undertake such activity in accordance with applicable norms of international law.[14a]

We discuss below the manner in which Congress and the Executive branch have undertaken to exercise this federal power, and the consistency of their action with the Constitution's framework and system of checks and balances.

The Historical Practice

The National Security Act of 1947[14b] was a landmark in the evolution of United States foreign intelligence. In the 1947 Act, Congress created the National Security Council and the CIA, giving both of these entities a statutory charter.

N1

Prior to 1947, Congress, despite its substantial authority in foreign affairs and national defense, did not legislate directly with respect to foreign intelligence activity. Under the Necessary and Proper Clause, and its power to make rules and regulations for the Armed Forces, Congress might have elaborated specific statutes authorizing and regulating the conduct of foreign intelligence. In the absence of such statutes, Presidents conducted foreign intelligence activity prior to the 1947 National Security Act on their own authority.

In wartime, the President's power as Commander-in-Chief provided ample authority for both the secret gathering of information and covert action.[15] The authority to collect foreign intelligence information before 1947 in peacetime can be viewed as implied from the Presi-

---

[14] As the Supreme Court has declared, "the United States, in their relation to foreign countries . . . are invested with the powers which belong to independent nations. . . ." [*Chinese Exclusion Case*, 130 U.S. 581, 604 (1889).]

[14a] There are a number of international agreements which the United States has entered into which prohibit certain forms of intervention in the domestic affairs of foreign states. The Nations Charter in Article 2(4) obligates all U.N. members to 'refrain in their international relations from the threat or use of force against the territorial integrity of any state." The Charter of the Organization of American States (OAS) in Article 18 provides:

"No State or group of States has the right to intervene, directly or indirectly for any reason whatever, in the internal or external affairs of any other State. The foregoing principle prohibits not only armed force but also any other form of interference or attempted threat against the personality of the State or against its political, economic, and cultural elements."

Under the Supremacy Clause of the Constitution (Art. VI, Sec. 2), treaty obligations of the United States are part of the law of the land. While the general principles of such treaties have not been spelled out in specific rules of application, and much depends on the facts of particular cases as well as other principles of international law (including the right of self-preservation, and the right to assist states against prior foreign intervention) it is clear that the norms of international law are relevant in assessing the legal and constitutional aspects of covert action.

[14b] 50 U.S.C. 430.

[15] In *Totten* v. *United States*, 92 U.S. 105 (1875), the Supreme Court upheld the authority of the President to hire, without statutory authority, a secret agent for intelligence purposes during the Civil War. Authority for wartime covert action can be implied from the President's powers as Commander-in-Chief to conduct military operations in a war declared by Congress. Compare, *Totten* v. *United States*.

dent's power to conduct foreign affairs.[16] In addition to the more or less discreet gathering of information by the regular diplomatic service, the President sometimes used specially-appointed "executive agents" to secretly gather information abroad.[17] In addition, executive agents were on occasion given secret political missions that were similar to modern day political covert action.[18] These, however, tended to be in the form of relatively small-scale responses to particular concerns, rather than the continuous, institutionalized activity that marked the character of covert action in the period after the passage of the 1947 National Security Act. There were no precedents for the peacetime use of covert action involving the use of armed force of the type conducted after 1947.

1. Foreign Intelligence and the President's Foreign Affairs Power

Although the Constitution provides that the President "shall appoint ambassadors, other public ministers and consuls" only "by and with the advice and consent of the Senate," beginning with Washington Presidents have appointed special envoys to carry out both overt diplomatic functions and foreign intelligence missions.[19] The great majority of these envoys were sent on overt missions, such as to negotiate treaties or to represent the United States at international conferences. Some, however, were sent in secrecy to carry out the near equivalent of modern-day intelligence collection and covert political action. For example, in connection with U.S. territorial designs on central and western Canada in 1869, President Grant's Secretary of State sent a private citizen to that area to investigate and promote the possibility of annexation to the United States.[20]

Presidential discretion as to the appointment of such executive agents derived from the President's assumption of the conduct of foreign relations. From the beginning, the President represented the United States to the world and had exclusive charge of the channels and processes of communication. The President's role as "sole organ" of the nation in dealing with foreign states was recognized by John Marhall in 1816 [21] and reflected the views expressed in *The Federalist*

---

[16] Compare, *United States* v. *Butenko.* 494 F.2d 593 (3d Cir. 1974) : "Decisions affecting the United States' relationship with other sovereign states are more likely to advance our national interests if the President is apprised of the intentions. capabilities and possible responses of other countries."

[17] Henry Wriston, *Executive Agents in American Foreign Relations*, (1929, 1967).

[18] *Ibid.*, pp. 693, *et. seq.*

[19] The first such specially-appointed individual was Governeur Morris, sent by President Washington in 1789 as a "private agent" to Britain to explore the possibilities for opening normal diplomatic relations. Morris was appointed in October 1789 because Washington's Secretary of State, Jefferson, was not yet functioning. The mission was not reported to the Congress until February 1791. Henry Wriston. "The Special Envoy," *Foreign Affairs*, 38 (1960), pp. 219, 220)

[20] Wriston. *Executive Agents in American Foreign Relations*, p. 739.

[21] Marshall spoke, not as Chief Justice in an opinion of the Supreme Court, but rather in a statement to the House of Representatives. The House of Representatives was engaged in a debate as to whether a demand by the British Government for the extradition of one Robbins was a matter for the courts or for the President, acting upon an extradition treaty. Marshall argued that the case involved "a national demand made upon the nation." Since the President is the "sole organ of the nation in its external relations." Marshall said. "of consequence, the demand can only be made upon him." [10 Annals of Congress 613 (1800), reprinted in 5 Wheat, Appendix, Note 1, at 26 (U.S. 1820).]

that the characteristics of the Presidency—unity, secrecy, decision, dispatch—were especially suited to the conduct of diplomacy.[22] As a consequence, historical development saw the President take charge of the daily conduct of foreign affairs, including the formulation of much of the nation's foreign policy. But "sole organ" as to communications with foreign governments and historical practice did not amount to "sole disposal" in a constitutional sense over foreign affairs; as Hamilton declared, the Constitution did not grant that degree of power to the President in foreign affairs.[23] Moreover, Marshall's reference to the President as "sole organ" did not purport to mean that the President was not subject to congressional regulation, should Congress wish to act. For Marshall, in addition to speaking of the President as "sole organ," went on to point out that "Congress, unquestionably, may prescribe the mode" by which such power to act was to be exercised.[24] Congress, with its own constitutional powers in foreign affairs, its power over the purse, and under the authority contained in the Necessary and Proper Clause, had the option of regulating the practice of using executive agents on foreign intelligence missions, as well as the conduct of foreign intelligence activity by other means.[25]

2. The Use of Force in Covert Action

Covert action may include the use of armed force. In modern times, the President's authorization of the CIA–financed and directed invasion of Cuba at the Bay of Pigs and paramilitary operations in Laos are examples of this type of covert action.

N2

---

[22] Nor did Marshall intend to say that "sole organ" meant the power of "sole disposal." As the eminent constitutional expert Edward S. Corwin wrote, "Clearly, what Marshall had foremost in mind was simply the President's role as instrument of communication with other governments." (Edward S. Corwin, *The President's Control of Foreign Relations*, p. 216.)

[23] *The Federalist*, No. 75 (A. Hamilton).

[24] Citing Marshall's expression, the Supreme Court has recognized the President as "sole organ" of communication and negotiation in foreign affairs. [*United States* v. *Curtiss-Wright Export Corp.*, 299 U.S. 304 (1952).] Although dicta of Justice Sutherland in the *Curtiss-Wright* opinion put forward a broad view of "inherent" Presidential power in foreign affairs, the case and the holding of the court involved, as Justice Jackson stated in his opinion in the *Steel Seizure* case, "not the question of the President's power to act without congressional authority, but the question of his right to act under and in accord with an Act of Congress." [*Youngstown Steel & Tube Co.* v. *Sawyer*, 343 U.S. 579, 635–636 (1952) (consurring opinion).]

In *Curtiss-Wright* a joint resolution of Congress had authorized the President to embargo weapons to countries at war in the Chaco, and imposed criminal sanctions for any violation. After President Franklin D. Roosevelt proclaimed an embargo, the Curtiss-Wright Corporation, indicted for violating the embargo, challenged the congressional resolution and the President's proclamation, claiming Congress had made an improper delegation of legislative power to the President. Speaking for six justices, Justice Sutherland sustained the indictment, holding only, as Justice Jackson later noted, "that the strict limitation upon Congressional delegations of power to the President over internal affairs does not apply with respect to delegations of power in external affairs." (343 U.S. at 636.)

[25] In 1793. for example, Congress established a procedure for the financing of secret foreign affairs operations. It enacted a statute providing for expenses of "intercourse or treaty" with foreign nations. The Act required the President to report all such expenditures, but granted him the power to give a certificate in lieu of a report for those payments the President deemed should be kept secret. (Act of February 9, 1973, 1 Stat. 300.

The executive branch relies in large part on the President's own constitutional powers for authority to conduct such covert action.[26] After the failure of the Bay of Pigs operation in 1961, the CIA asked the Justice Department for an analysis of the legal authority for **N3**   covert actions. In its response, the Justice Department's Office of Legislative Council stated:

> It would appear that the executive branch, under the direction of the President, has been exercising without express statutory authorization a function which is within the constitutional powers of the President, and that the CIA was the agent selected by the President to carry out these functions.[27]

The Justice Department memorandum pointed to the President's foreign relations power and his responsibility for national security.[28] Arguing by analogy from the President's power as Commander-in-Chief to conduct a declared war, the memorandum contended that the President could conduct peacetime covert actions involving armed force without authority from Congress. The memorandum argued that there was no limit to the means the President might employ in exercising his foreign affairs power:

> Just as "the power to wage war is the power to wage war successfully," so the power of the President to conduct foreign relations should be deemed to be the power to conduct foreign relations successfully, *by any means necessary* to combat the measures taken by the Communist bloc, including both open and covert measures.[29] [Emphasis added.]

In view of the Constitution's grant of concurrent jurisdiction to the Congress in foreign affairs and Congress' exclusive constitutional authority to declare war, there is little to support such an extravagant claim of Presidential power in peacetime. The case which prompted the Justice Department's argument—the invasion of Cuba at the Bay

---

[26] In September 1947, the CIA General Counsel expressed the opinion that activity such as "black propaganda, ranger and commando raids, behind-the-lines sabotage, and support of guerrilla warfare" would constitute "an unwarranted extension of the functions authorized" by the 1947 Act. (Memorandum from the CIA General Counsel to Director, 9/25/47.) And, in 1969, the CIA General Counsel wrote that the 1947 Act provided "rather doubtful statutory authority" for at least those covert actions—such as paramilitary operations—which were not related to intelligence gathering. (Memorandum from CIA General Counsel to Director, 10/30/69.) The Agency's General Counsel took the position that the authority for covert action rested on the President's delegation of his own constitutional authority to CIA through various National Security Council Directives. (Ibid.)

[27] Memorandum, Office of Legislative Counsel, Department of Justice, 1/17/62, p. 11.

[28] *Ibid.*, p. 7. The memorandum stated:

"Under modern conditions of 'cold war,' the President can properly regard the conduct of covert activities . . . as necessary to the effective and successful conduct of foreign relations and the protection of the national security. When the United States is attacked from without or within, the President may 'meet force with force' . . . In wagering a worldwide contest to strengthen the free nations and contain the Communist nations, and thereby to preserve the existence of the United States, the President should be deemed to have comparable authority to meet covert activities with covert activities if he deems such action necessary and consistent with our national objectives."

[29] *Ibid.*

of Pigs—illustrates the serious constitutional questions which arise. In that operation, the President in effect authorized the CIA to secretly direct and finance the military invasion of a foreign country. This action approached, and may have constituted, an act of war. At the least, it seriously risked placing the United States in a state of war *vis-á-vis* Cuba on the sole authority of the President. Absent the threat of sudden attack or a grave and immediate threat to the security of the country, only Congress, under the Constitution, has such authority. As James Madison declared, Congress' power to declare war includes the "power of judging the causes of war." [30] Madison wrote:

> Every just view that can be taken of the subject admonishes the public of the necessity of a rigid adherence to the simple, the received, and the fundamental doctrine of the constitution, that the power to declare war, including the power of judging the causes of war, is fully and exclusively vested in the legislature. . . ." [31]

This view was also affirmed by Hamilton who, although a principal exponent of expansive Presidential power, wrote that it is the

> exclusive province of Congress, when the nation is at peace, to change that state into a state of war . . . it belongs to Congress only, to go to war.[32]

Nor is there much support in historical practice prior to 1950 for the use of armed force to achieve foreign policy objectives on the sole authority of the President. The 1962 Justice Department memorandum argued that the practice of Presidents in using force to protect American citizens and property abroad was authority for covert action involving armed force.[33] Before the post-World War II era, Presidents on occasion asserted their own authority to use armed force short of war, but as the Senate Committee on Foreign Relations noted in 1973, these operations were for "limited, minor, or essentially non-political purposes." As the Foreign Relations Committee stated:

> During the course of the nineteenth century it became accepted practice, if not strict constitutional doctrine, for Presidents acting on their own authority to use the armed forces for such limited purposes as the suppression of piracy and the slave trade, for "hot pursuit" of criminals across borders, and for the protection of American lives and property in places abroad where local government was not functioning effectively. An informal, operative distinction came to be accepted between the use of the armed forces for limited, minor or essentially nonpolitical purposes and the use of the armed forces for "acts of war" in the sense of large-scale military operations against sovereign states.[34]

That these operations were, as the Committee on Foreign Relations noted, for "limited, minor, or essentially non-political purposes" is also

---

[30] *Letters of Helvidius* (1793), Madison, *Writings*, Vol. 6, p. 174 (Hunt ed.).
[31] *Ibid.*
[32] Hamilton, *Works*, Vol. 8, pp. 249–250 (Lodge ed.)
[33] Justice Department Memorandum, 1/17/62, p. 2.
[34] Senate Report No. 220, 93d Cong., 1st Sess. (1973).

affirmed by the eminent authority on constitutional law, Edward Corwin. Prior to the Korean War, the "vast majority" of such cases, Corwin wrote, "involved fights with pirates, landings of small naval contingents on barbarous coasts [to protect American citizens], the dispatch of small bodies of troops to chase bandits or cattle rustlers across the Mexican border." [35]

To stretch the President's foreign relations power so far as to authorize the secret use of armed force against foreign states without congressional authorization or at least "advice and consent," appears to go well beyond the proper scope of the Executive's power in foreign affairs under the Constitution. Moreover, where Congress is not informed prior to the initiation of such armed covert action—as it was not, for example, in the Bay of Pigs operation—the constitutional system of checks and balances can be frustrated. Without prior notice, there can be no effective check on the action of the executive branch. Once covert actions involving armed force, such as the invasion of Cuba at the Bay of Pigs or paramilitary operations, are begun, it may be difficult if not impossible for practical reasons to stop them. In such circumstances, covert action involving armed intervention in the affairs of foreign states may be inconsistent with our constitutional system and its principle of checks and balances.

The Constitutional Power of Congress to Regulate the Conduct of Foreign Intelligence Activity

Prior to the 1947 National Security Act, Congress did not seek to expressly authorize or regulate foreign intelligence activity by statute.

Congress' decision not to act, however, did not reduce or eliminate its constitutional power to do so in the future. The Necessary and Proper Clause and its power to "make rules for the government and regulation" of the armed forces, along with Congress' general powers in the fields of foreign affairs and national defense, were always available.

In this light, the question of the legal authority for the conduct of foreign intelligence activity in the absence of express statutory authorization can be viewed in the manner set forth by Justice Jackson in the *Steel Seizure* case. He wrote:

> When the President acts in absence of either a congressional grant or denial of authority, he can only rely upon his own independent powers, but there is a zone of twilight in which he and Congress may have concurrent authority, or in which its distribution is uncertain. Therefore, congressional inertia, indifference or quiescence may sometimes, at least as a practical matter, enable, if not invite, measures on independent Presidential responsibility.[36]

Foreign intelligence activity, particularly political covert action not involving the use of force, can be seen as lying in such a "zone of twilight" in which both the President and the Congress have concurrent authority and responsibilities. (As discussed above, the use of covert

---

[35] Edward S. Corwin, "The President's Power," in Haight and Johnson, eds. *The President's Role and Powers*, (1965), p. 361.

[36] *Youngstown Co.* v. *Sawyer*, 343 U.S. 579, 637 (1952) (concurring opinion).

action involving armed force raises serious constitutional problems where it is not authorized by statute, particularly if Congress is not informed.) When Congress does not act, the President may in certain circumstances exercise authority on the basis of his own constitutional powers.

Congress can, however, choose to exercise its legislative authority to regulate the exercise of that authority. In view of the President's own constitutional powers, Congress may not deprive the President of the function of foreign intelligence. But, as Chief Justice Marshall stated, Congress can "prescribe the mode" by which the President carries out that function. And the Congress may apply certain limits or controls upon the President's discretion.

The Supreme Court has affirmed this constitutional power of Congress. In *Little* v. *Barreme*,[37] Chief Justice Marshall, speaking for the Court, found the seizure by the U.S. Navy of a ship departing a French port to be unlawful, even though the Navy acted pursuant to Presidential order. By prior statute, Congress had authorized the seizure of ships by the Navy, but limited the types of seizures that could be made. The President's orders to the Navy disregarded the limits set out in the law. If Congress had been silent, Chief Justice Marshall stated, the President's authority as Commander-in-Chief might have been sufficient to permit the seizure. But, Marshall declared, once Congress had "prescribed . . . the manner in which this law shall be carried into execution," the President was bound to respect the limitations imposed by Congress.[38]

There have been at least as many conceptions of the range of the President's own power as there have been holders of the office of the President. In the case of foreign intelligence activity, Justice Jackson's statement that "comprehensive and undefined Presidential powers hold both practical advantages and grave dangers for the country"[39] is particularly relevant, especially in view of the tension between the need for secrecy and the constitutional principle of checks and balances. Yet, as Justice Brandeis declared, "checks and balances were established in order that this should be a government of laws and not of men."[40]

The 1947 National Security Act represented the exercise of Congress' constitutional power to order the conduct of foreign intelligence activity under law. By placing the authority for foreign intelligence activity on a statutory base, Congress sought to reduce the reliance on "comprehensive and undefined" Presidential power that had previously been the principal source of authority. However, the language of the 1947 Act did not expressly authorize the conduct of covert action and, as discussed earlier, Congress apparently did not intend to grant such authority. As a result, inherent Presidential power has continued to serve as the principal source of authority for covert action.

Congress continued to exercise this constitutional power in subsequent legislation. In the Central Intelligence Act of 1949,[41] Congress

N4

---

[37] 2 Cranch 170 (1805).
[38] 2 Cranch 170, 178 (1805).
[39] *Youngstown Co.* v. *Sawyer*, 343 U.S. 579. 634 (1952) (concurring opinion).
[40] *Myers* v. *United States*, 272 U.S. 52, 292 (1926) (dissenting opinion).
[41] 50 U.S.C. 403a–403j.

set out the administrative procedures governing CIA activities. The 1949 Act regulated the CIA's acquisition of material, the hiring of personnel and its accounting for funds expended.

In 1974, Congress imposed a reporting requirement for the conduct of certain foreign intelligence activities. In an amendment to the Foreign Assistance Act,[42] Congress provided that no funds may be expended by or on behalf of the CIA for operations abroad "other than activities intended solely for obtaining necessary intelligence" unless two conditions were met: a) the President must make a finding that "each such operation is important to the national security of the United States", and b) the President must report "in a timely fashion" a description of such operation and its scope to congressional committees.[43]

In short, the Constitution provides for a system of checks and balances and interdependent power as between the Congress and the executive branch with respect to foreign intelligence activity. Congress, with its responsibility for the purse and as the holder of the legislative power, has the constitutional authority to regulate the conduct of foreign intelligence activity.

EVOLUTION OF THE U.S. INTELLIGENCE COMMUNITY ([45A], pp. 19–29)

The evolution of the United States intelligence community since World War II is part of the larger history of America's effort to come to grips with the spread of communism and the growing power of the Soviet Union. As the war ended, Americans were torn by hopes for peace and fear for the future. The determination to return the nation promptly to normal was reflected in demobilization of our wartime military establishment. In the field of intelligence, it was clear in President Truman's decision to dismantle the Office of Strategic Services, scattering its functions to the military departments and the Department of State.

The Second World War saw the defeat of one brand of totalitarianism. A new totalitarian challenge quickly arose. The Soviet Union, a major ally in war, became America's principal adversary in peace. The power of fascism was in ruin but the power of communism was mobilized. Not only had the communist parties in France, Italy, and Greece emerged politically strengthened by their roles in the Resistance, but the armies of the Soviet Union stretched across the center of Europe. And, within four years, America's nuclear monopoly would end.

American military intelligence officers were among the first to perceive the changed situation. Almost immediately after the fall of Berlin to the Red Army, U.S. military intelligence sought to determine Soviet objectives. Harry Rositzke, later to become chief of the CIA's Soviet Division, but at the time a military intelligence officer, was despatched to Berlin by jeep. Although the Soviet Union was still an ally, Rositzke was detained, interrogated, then ordered expelled by the Soviet occupying forces. He managed, however, to escape his Soviet "escort" and arrive in Berlin. He described his experience to the Committee:

> We got on the outskirts of Berlin and yelled out "Amerikanski," and were highly welcomed. And as we went over the

---

[42] 22 U.S.C. 2422.
[43] *Ibid.*

Autobahn the first basic impression I got, since I had known Germany well before the war, was a long walking group of German males under 16 and over 60 who were being shepherded to the east by four-foot-ten, five-foot Mongolian soldiers with straw shoes.

The Russians also had been looting. With horses and farm wagons they were taking away mattresses, wall fixtures, plumbing fixtures, anything other than the frame of the houses.

We then made our way through the rubble of Berlin—most were one-way streets—identifying every shoulder patch we could, and passed the Siemans-Halske works, in front of which were 40 or 50 lend-lease trucks, on each of which was a large shiny lathe, drill press, et cetera.

When we had seen enough and were all three extremely nervous, we headed straight west from Berlin to the British Zone. When we arrived we had an enormous amount of exuberance and a real sense of relief, for the entire 36 hours had put us in another world. The words that came to my mind then were, "Russia moves west." [3]

At home, the Truman Administration was preoccupied by the transition from war to an uncertain peace. Though dispersed, and in some cases disbanded, America's potential capabilities in the field of intelligence were considerable. There were a large number of well-trained former OSS operation officers; the military had developed a remarkable capacity for cryptologic intelligence (the breaking of codes) and communications intelligence (COMINT); there was also a cadre of former OSS intelligence analysts both within the government and in the academic community.

The Origins of the Postwar Intelligence Community

With the experiences of World War II and particularly Pearl Harbor still vivid, there was a recognition within the government that, notwithstanding demobilization, it was essential to create a centralized body to collate and coordinate intelligence information. There was also a need to eliminate frictions between competing military intelligence services. Although there was disagreement about the structure and authority of the postwar intelligence service, President Truman and his senior advisers concluded that, unlike the OSS, this centralized body should be civilian in character.

The military resisted this judgment. Virtually all of America's competing intelligence assets were in the armed services. Then, as now, the military considered an intelligence capability essential in wartime and equally important in time of peace to be prepared for military crises. Thus, the services were strongly opposed to having their authority over intelligence diminished. In contrast, factions within the State Department were reluctant to accept any greater responsibility or role in the field of clandestine intelligence.

Six months after V–J Day, and three months after he had disbanded OSS, President Truman established the Central Intelligence

N8

---

[3] Harry Rozitzke testimony, 10/31/75, p. 7.

Group (CIG). CIG was the direct predecessor of the CIA. It reported to the National Intelligence Authority, a body consisting of the Secretaries of State, War and Navy and their representatives. CIG had a brief existence. It never was able to overcome the constraints and institutional resistances found in the Department of State and the armed services.

N9   The National Security Act of 1947 was passed on July 26, 1947. The Act included, in large part, the recommendations of a report prepared for Secretary of the Navy James Forrestal by New York investment broker Ferdinand Eberstadt. Though largely concerned with the creation of the National Security Council (NSC) and the unification of the military services within the Department of Defense, the Act also created a Director of Central Intelligence (DCI) and a Central Intelligence Agency (CIA). The powers of the DCI and the CIA were an amalgam of careful limits on the DCI's authority over the intelligence community and an open-ended mission for the CIA itself. The power of the DCI over military and diplomatic intelligence was confined to "coordination." At the same time, however, the Agency was authorized to carry out unspecified "services of common concern" and, more importantly, could "carry out such other functions and duties" as the National Security Council might direct.

Nowhere in the 1947 Act was the CIA explicitly empowered to collect intelligence or intervene secretly in the affairs of other nations. But the elastic phrase, "such other functions," was used by successive presidents to move the Agency into espionage, covert action, paramilitary operations, and technical intelligence collection. Often conceived as having granted significant peacetime powers and flexibility to the CIA and the NSC, the National Security Act actually legislated
N10   that authority to the President.

The 1947 Act provided no explicit charter for military intelligence. The charter and mission of military intelligence activities was established either by executive orders, such as the one creating the National Security Agency in 1952, or various National Security Council directives. These National Security Council Intelligence Directives (NSCID's) were the principal means of establishing the roles and functions of all the various entities in the intelligence community. They composed the so-called "secret charter" for the CIA. However, most of them also permitted "departmental" intelligence activities, and in this way also provided the executive charter for the intelligence activities of the State Department and the Pentagon. However, the intelligence activities of the Department of Defense remained with the military rather than with the new Defense Department civilians. At the end of the war, the Joint Chiefs of Staff decided to continue the inter-Service coordinating mechanism—the Joint Intelligence Committee—which had been created in 1942. With the 1947 Act and the establishment of the Joint Chiefs of Staff, a working level intelligence operation was created in the Joint Staff, known as the Joint Intelligence Group, or J-2.

The structure created by the 1947 Act and ensuing NSCID's was highly decentralized. The task of the CIA and the Director of Central Intelligence was to "coordinate" the intelligence output of all the various intelligence collection programs in the military and the Department of State. The CIA and its Director had little power to act itself, but the potential was there.

The Response to the Soviet Threat

Immediately after its establishment, the CIA and other elements of the intelligence community responded to the external threats facing the United States.

—*The threat of war in Europe.* Following the war there was a distinct possibility of a Soviet assault on Western Europe. Communist regimes had been established in Poland, Hungary, Romania and Bulgaria. Czechoslovakia went Communist in 1948 through a coup supported by the Russian Army. There was a Russian-backed civil war in Greece. And, above all, there was the presence of the Soviet Army in Eastern Europe and the pressure on Berlin.

N11

In light of these developments, U.S. policymakers came to the conclusion that outright war with the Soviet Union was possible. The U.S. intelligence community responded accordingly. The CIA assumed the espionage task, running agents and organizing "stay-behind networks" in the event the Soviets rolled west. Agents, mostly refugees, were sent into the East to report on Soviet forces and, in particular, any moves that signalled war. The U.S. went so far as to establish contact with Ukrainian guerrillas—a relationship that was maintained until the guerrillas were finally wiped out in the early 1950s by Soviet security forces. CIA activities, however, were outnumbered by the clandestine collection operations of the military, particularly in Western Europe, where the Army maintained a large covert intelligence and paramilitary capability.

—*Turmoil in the West.* The Soviets had powerful political resources in the West—the Communist parties and trade unions. Provided with financial and advisory support from the Soviet Union, the Communist parties sought to exploit and exacerbate the economic and political turmoil in postwar Europe. As the elections in 1948 and 1949 in Italy and France approached, the democratic parties were in disarray and the possibility of a Communist takeover was real. Coordinated Communist political unrest in western countries combined with extremist pressure from the Soviet Union, confirmed the fears of many that America faced an expansionist Communist monolith.

The United States responded with overt economic aid—the Truman Doctrine and the Marshall Plan—and covert political assistance. This latter task was assigned to the Office of Special Projects, later renamed the Office of Policy Coordination (OPC). The Office was housed in the CIA but was directly responsible to the Departments of State and Defense. Clandestine support from the United States for European democratic parties was regarded as an essential response to the threat of "international communism." OPC became the fastest growing element in the CIA. To facilitate its operations, as well as to finance CIA espionage activities, the Congress passed the Central Intelligence Agency Act of 1949, which authorized the Director of CIA to spend funds on his voucher without having to account for disbursements.

—*Nuclear weapons.* The advent of nuclear weapons and the Soviet potential in this field led to efforts to ascertain the status of the Soviet Union's nuclear program. By the time of the Soviet's first atomic explosion in 1949, the U.S. Air Force and Navy had begun a peripheral reconnaissance program to monitor other aspects of Soviet nuclear development and Soviet military capabilities. As the Soviet strategic nuclear threat grew, America's efforts to contain it would grow in scale and sophistication until it would overshadow the classic tools of espionage.

Korea: The Turning Point

The Communist attack, feared in Europe, took place in Asia. The Korean War, following less than a year after the fall of China to the Communists, marked a turning point for the CIA. The requirements of that war, the involvement of China, the concern that war in Europe might soon follow, led to a fourfold expansion of the CIA—particularly in the paramilitary field. This period was characterized by efforts to infiltrate agents into mainland China, which led to the shoot-down and capture of a number of Americans.

The CIA's activities elsewhere in Asia also expanded. Instrumental in helping Ramon Magsaysay defeat the communist Hukbalahaps in the Philippines, the CIA also assisted the French in their losing struggle against the Viet Minh in Indochina.

The failure to anticipate the attack on Korea was regarded as a major intelligence failure. The new Director of the CIA, General Bedell Smith, was determined to improve CIA's estimating and forecasting capabilities. He called on William Langer, formerly chief of the Research and Analysis section of the OSS, to come to Washington from Harvard, in 1950, to head a small staff for analysis and the production of intelligence. An Office of National Estimates (ONE) was established to produce finished intelligence estimates. ONE drew on the intelligence information resources of the entire U.S. intelligence community and was aided by a Board of National Estimates composed of leading statesmen and academic experts.

By the end of the Korean War and the naming of Allen Dulles as DCI, the powers, responsibilities and basic structure of the CIA were established. The Agency had assumed full responsibility for covert operations in 1950, and by 1952 covert action had exceeded the money and manpower allotted to the task of espionage—a situation that would persist until the early 1970s.

Paramilitary actions were in disrepute because of a number of failures during the Korean War. However, the techniques of covert military assistance in training had been developed, and the pattern of CIA direction of Special Forces and other unconventional components of the U.S. Armed Forces in clandestine operations had been established.

In the field of espionage, the CIA had become the predominant, but by no means the exclusive operator. Clandestine human collection of intelligence by the military services continued at a relatively high rate. The military also had a large stake in clandestine technical collection of intelligence.

Major structural changes in the intelligence community were brought about by the consolidation of cryptanalysis and related functions. Codebreaking is a vital part of technical intelligence collection and has had an important role in the history of U.S. intelligence efforts. The American "Black Chamber" responsible for breaking German codes in WWI was abolished in the 1920s. As WWII approached, cryptanalysis received increased attention in the military. Both the Army and Navy had separate cryptologic services which had combined to break the Japanese code. Known as "the magic" this information signalled the impending attack on Pearl Harbor but the intelligence and alert system as a whole failed to respond.

In order to unify and coordinate defense cryptologic and communications security functions, President Truman created the National Security Agency by Executive Order on November 4, 1952. Prior to this time, U.S. cryptological capabilities resided in the separate agencies of the Army, Navy, and Air Force. The very existence of still the most secret of all U.S. intelligence agencies, NSA, was not acknowledged until 1957.

The "Protracted Conflict"

With the end of the Korean conflict and as the mid–1950s approached, the intelligence community turned from the desperate concern over imminent war with the U.S.S.R. to the long-term task of containing and competing with communism. In the "struggle for men's minds," covert action developed into a large-scale clandestine psychological and political program aimed at competing with Soviet propaganda and front organizations in international labor and student activities. Specific foreign governments considered antithetical to the United States and its allies or too receptive to the influence of the Soviet Union, such as Mosedegh in Iran in 1953 and Arbenz in Guatemala in 1954, were toppled with the help of the CIA. Anticommunist parties and groups were given aid and encouragement such as the Sumatran leaders who, in 1958, sought the overthrow of President Sukarno of Indonesia.

At the same time, the CIA was moving into the field of technical intelligence and reconnaissance in a major way. The U.S. military had recognized the value of aerial reconnaissance within a few short years after the Wright brothers' successful flight in 1903 and had borne major responsibility for reconnaissance against Communist bloc countries. But it was the CIA in 1959 that began work on the U–2.

It proved to be a technical triumph. The U–2 established that the Soviet Union was not, as had been feared, about to turn the tables of the strategic balance. It gained more information about Soviet military developments than had been acquired in the previous decade of espionage operations. But there were risks in this operation. Despite the effort to minimize them with a special system of high-level NSC review and approval, Francis Gary Powers was shot down in a U–2 over the Soviet Union on the eve of the Paris summit conference in 1960. President Eisenhower's acceptance of responsibility and Nikita Khrushchev's reaction led to the collapse of the conference before it began.

Nonetheless the U–2 proved the value of exotic and advanced technical means of intelligence collection. It was followed by a transformation of the intelligence community. As the 1950s gave way to the 1960s, large budgets for the development and operation of technical collection systems created intense competition among the military services and the CIA and major problems in management and condensation.

To support the Director of Central Intelligence's task of coordinating the activities of the intelligence community, the United States Intelligence Board (USIB) was established in 1958. Made up of senior representatives of the State Department, the Department of Defense, the military services, Treasury (since 1973) and the FBI, USIB was to coordinate the setting of requirements for intelligence, approve National Intelligence Estimates and generally supervise the operations of the intelligence agencies. However, the real power to set requirements and allocate resources to intelligence programs remained decentralized and in the hands of the principal collectors—the military services, the Foreign Service and the clandestine service of the CIA. As collection programs mushroomed, USIB proved unequal to the task of providing centralized management and eliminating duplication.

Third World Competition and Nuclear Crisis

While the United States' technical, military and intelligence capabilities advanced, concern intensified over the vulnerability of the newly independent nations of Africa and Asia to communist subversion. And in the Western Hemisphere the establishment of a communist Cuba by Fidel Castro was seen as presaging a major incursion of revolutionary communism to the Western Hemisphere.

At his inauguration in January, 1961, President Kennedy proclaimed that America would "pay any price and bear any burden" so that liberty might prevail in the world over the "forces of communist totalitarianism." Despite the catastrophe of the CIA-sponsored Bay of Pigs invasion only four months later, the covert action and paramilitary operations staffs of the CIA were to shoulder a significant part of that burden. In Latin America the Alliance for Progress, the overt effort to help modernize the southern half of the hemisphere, was accompanied by a significant expansion of covert action and internal security operations aimed at blocking the spread of Castro's influence or ideology. This was accompanied by an intense paramilitary campaign of harassment, sabotage, propaganda against Cuba, and attempted assassination against Castro.

Nearby, in the Dominican Republic, the United States had already supported the assassins of Dictator Raphael Trujillo in order to preempt a Castro-type takeover. In Africa, significant paramilitary aid was given in support of anti-Soviet African leaders. In Asia, American intelligence had been involved for a long time in the Indochina struggle. The CIA, along with the rest of the United States government, was drawn ever deeper into the Vietnamese conflict.

Early in the decade the United States faced its most serious postwar crisis affecting its security—the Cuban Missile Crisis of October 1962. It illustrated a number of important facts concerning the nature and structure of American intelligence.

During the summer of 1962 overhead reconnaissance confirmed agent intelligence reports that some form of unusual military installation was being placed in Cuba. By October 16 it was clear that these were medium and intermediate-range ballistic missile sites capable of handling nuclear weapons that could strike targets throughout significant areas of the United States.

As the United States moved towards a confrontation with the Soviet Union, U.S. intelligence played a significant role at every turn. Overhead reconnaissance of the Soviet strategic posture was vastly superior to that of the Russians. Reports from Col. Oleg Penkovsky, the U.S. agent in the Kremlin, kept the United States abreast of the Soviet military response to the crisis. U.S. tactical reconnaissance of Cuba not only prepared the United States for possible invasion but signalled the earnestness of our intention to do so should the situation deteriorate. Naval reconnaissance kept close tabs on Soviet ships bearing ballistic missile components. As the crisis neared its showdown with a quarantine, the President demanded and received the most detailed tactical intelligence, including the distance in yards between American naval vessels and the Soviet transport ships.

This crisis dramatized the importance of integrated intelligence collection and production in times of crisis. It also clearly illustrated the difficulty in distinguishing between national and so-called tactical intelligence. This distinction has been a central feature of the structure of the American intelligence community with the military services maintaining control over tactical intelligence and the so-called national intelligence assets subject to varying degrees of control by the Director of Central Intelligence or the Secrtary of Defense and the National Security Council. Cuba proved that in time of crisis these distinctions evaporate.

Technology and Tragedy

During the 1960s the U.S. intelligence community was dominated by two developments: First, the enormous explosion in the volume of technical intelligence as the research and development efforts of the previous period came to fruition; second, the ever-growing involvement of the United States in the war in Vietnam.

The increase in the quantity and quality of technically acquired information on Soviet military forces, in particular strategic forces, made possible precise measurement of the existing level of Soviet strategic deployments. However, it did not answer questions about the ultimate scale of Soviet strategic deployments, nor did it provide firm information on the quality of their forces. While it provided an additional clue as to Soviet intentions, it did not offer any definitive answers.

In the Pentagon disparate estimates of future Soviet strategic power from each of the Armed Services led Secretary Robert McNamara to establish the Defense Intelligence Agency. The Secretary of Defense was in the ironic position of being responsible for the bulk of American intelligence collection activity but lacking the means to coordinate either the collection programs or the intelligence produced. The DIA was to fulfill this need, but in a compromise with the military services the DIA was made to report to the Secretary of Defense through the Joint Chiefs of Staff. The DIA has never fulfilled its promise.

In the CIA the analysts confronted by the new mass of technical intelligence information underestimated the ultimate scale of Soviet deployments while tending to overestimate the qualitative aspects of Soviet weapons systems. Previously, intelligence analysts had to build up their picture of Soviet capability from fragmentary information, inference and speculation, particularly as to Soviet purposes. Confronted with the challenge to exploit the new sources of intelligence on Soviet programs, the analysts in the intelligence community turned away from the more speculative task of understanding Soviet purposes and intentions, even though insight into these questions was central to a greater understanding of the technical information being acquired in such quantity.

The war in Vietnam also posed serious problems in the analysis and production of intelligence. In effect, the analysts were continually in the position of having to bring bad news to top policymakers. The result produced some serious anomalies in the nature of intelligence estimates concerning the Vietnam conflict. For example, the CIA continually flew in the face of the Pentagon and the evident desires of the White House by denigrating the effectiveness of the bombing campaigns over North Vietnam, but as American involvement deepened from 1965 onward, the CIA was unwilling to take on the larger and more important task of assessing the possibility for the success of the overall U.S. effort in Vietnam.

The increase in technical collection capabilities of the United States were also brought to bear on that conflict, creating in its turn important questions about the application of such resources to tactical situations. As one intelligence officer put it, local military commanders in Vietnam "were getting SIGINT (signals intelligence) with their orange juice every morning and have now come to expect it everywhere." This involves two problems: first, whether "national" intelligence resources aimed at strategic problems should be diverted to be used for local combat application and, second, whether this might not lead to a compromise of the technical collection systems and the elimination of their effectiveness for broader strategic missions.

The 1970s

Together, the advent of increased technical capabilities and the Vietnam War brought to a climax concerns within the Government over the centralized management of intelligence resources. This coincided with increased dissatisfaction in the Nixon Administration over the quality of intelligence produced on the war and on Soviet strategic developments.

In the nation as a whole, the impact of the Vietnam War destroyed the foreign policy consensus which had underpinned America's intelligence activities abroad. Starting with the disclosures of CIA involvement with the National Student Association of 1967, there were a series of adverse revelations concerning the activities of the Central Intelligence Agency and the military intelligence agencies.

Concern over the secret war in Laos, revulsion at the Phoenix program which took at least 20,000 lives in South Vietnam, army spying on U.S. civilians, U.S. "destabilization" efforts in Chile, and finally the revelations concerning Operation CHAOS and the CIA's domestic intelligence role created a climate for a thorough Congressional investigation.

During this same period, the Executive moved to initiate certain management reforms. Beginning as early as 1968, there were cutbacks in the scale of the overall intelligence community. These cutbacks deepened by 1970, both in the size of the overall intelligence budget in real terms and in the manpower devoted to intelligence activities. CIA covert activities were sharply reduced with a few notable exceptions such as Chile. The internal security mission in foreign countries was dropped. There was a re-emphasis on collecting covert intelligence on the Soviet Union. Terrorism and narcotics were added to the list of intelligence requirements for our clandestine espionage services.

In 1971 James Schlesinger, then serving in the Office of Management and Budget, was asked to do a sweeping analysis of the intelligence community. That study led to an effort to increase the authority of the Director of Central Intelligence over the management of the intelligence community. However, President Nixon limited the scope of reform to that which could be accomplished without legislation.

Congress also took an increased interest in the activities of the intelligence community. The role of the CIA in the Watergate affair was examined in the Senate Watergate Committee's investigation. At the close of 1974 a rider, the Hughes-Ryan amendment, was added to the Foreign Assistance Act which required the President to certify that covert actions were important to the national interest and directed that the Congress be fully informed of them. In this connection, the responsibility to inform the Congress was broadened beyond the traditional Armed Services and Appropriations Committees of the Congress to include the Senate Foreign Relations Committee and the House Foreign Affairs Committee. However, the first real effort of the Congress to come to grips with the challenge posed to the American democratic form of government by necessarily secret foreign and military intelligence activities came with the establishment of the Senate Select Committee on Intelligence in January of 1975. The results of its inquiry are set forth in the following chapters of this report.

The Task Ahead

The American intelligence community has changed markedly from the early postwar days, yet some of the major problems of that period persist. The intelligence community is still highly decentralized; the problem of maintaining careful command and control over risky secret activities is still great. There is a continuing difficulty in drawing a line between national intelligence activities, which should be closely supervised by the highest levels of government, and tactical intelligence, which are the province of the military services and the departments.

The positive steps undertaken by President Ford in his recent Executive Order have not diminished the need for a new statutory framework for American intelligence activities. Only through the legislative process can the broad political consensus be expressed which is necessary for the continuing conduct of those intelligence activities essential to the nation's security and diplomacy.

Clark M. Clifford, who was one of the authors of the 1947 National Security Act that established the present legislative framework for America's intelligence activities, made these comments in open session before the Committee:

As one attempts to analyze the difficulty and hopefully offer constructive suggestions for improvement, he finds much confusion existing within the system. It is clear that lines of authority and responsibility have become blurred and indistinct.

The National Security Council under the Act of 1947 is given the responsibility of directing our country's intelligence activities. My experience leads me to believe that this function has not been effectively performed. . . .

The 1947 law creating the CIA should be substantially amended and a new law should be written covering intelligence functions. We have had almost thirty years of experience under the old law and have learned a great deal. I believe it has served us reasonably well but its defects have become increasingly apparent. A clear, more definitive bill can be prepared that can accomplish our purposes by creating clear lines of authority and responsibility and by carefully restricting certain activities we can hopefully prevent the abuses of the past.

And Mr. Clifford concluded:

We have a big job to do in this country. Our people are confused about our national goals and cynical about our institutions. Our national spirit seems to have been replaced by a national malaise. It is my conviction that the efforts of this committee will assist us in regaining confidence in our national integrity, and in helping to restore to our nation its reputation in the world for decency, fair dealing, and moral leadership.[6]

---

[6] Clifford, 12/5/75, Hearings, p. 53.

NOTES AND REFERENCES

1. The National Security Act of 1947 is reprinted in the Appendix.
2. "Covert action" is referred to by the CIA as any clandestine operation or activity designed to influence foreign governments, organizations, persons, or events in support of U.S. foreign policy. This CIA policy tool is examined in Chapter 11.
3. The text of a heretofore secret memorandum on the constitutional and legal basis of covert operations is reprinted in Chapter 11. It was prepared on January 17, 1962 by the Office of Legislative Counsel of the Department of Justice.
4. A legislative history of the National Security Act of 1947 appears in [104], p. 62.
5. The CIA Act of 1949 appears in the Appendix.
6. This view of the constitutional authority of Congress, as expressed by the Church Committee report, is subject to differing interpretations. See Chapter 10, Congressional Oversight.
7. A history of the CIA appears in [45D]. Prepared by Church Committee staff member Anne Karalekas, it is derived from the agency's own classified history and offers further details on the development of the current CIA structure.
8. OSS refers to the Office of Strategic Services, the U.S. intelligence agency from 1942 to 1945. See the Appendix for a list of commonly used acronyms and their meanings.
9. For selected debate on the passage of the National Security Act of 1947 and the role of the NSC, see *Congressional Record,* July 9, 1947; or [13], pp. 37–40; or [22], pp. 39–41.
10. A detailed legislative history of the CIA containing reprinted pages from congressional documents is provided in [101].
11. A previously secret report, prepared by NSC Executive Secretary James Lay, Jr., is now available, providing a view as to how the threat of Soviet expansion into Europe was perceived at high policymaking levels in 1950 ([110]).

Chapter 2
Structure and Organization

COLBY TESTIMONY ON ORGANIZATION
([84A], pp. 109–116)

The intelligence community is an administrative apparatus composed of specialized agencies with roles circumscribed by both statute and policy control. Some elements of it have evolved somewhat independently (such as the Department of Defense, the State Department, and the CIA) and have overlapping jurisdictions and capabilities. This framework exists and is encouraged to promote a "healthy competition" and "diversity of views" among the various elements of the community. Presided over in theory by a "director of Central Intelligence" and subjected to continuing review by four different coordinating bodies, plus the president's own staff, the various intelligence agencies are supposed to unify on matters of supreme importance. Four organizations comprise the principal operating elements of the community:

Central Intelligence Agency. Established in 1947, the CIA was to correlate and evaluate foreign intelligence relating to the national security; to recommend to the NSC methods for the coordination of intelligence; and to perform those services that the NSC determined could be more efficiently accomplished centrally. It was authorized "to perform such other functions and duties as the NSC may from time to time direct," language often interpreted to authorize covert action. Police, subpoena, law enforcement powers, and internal security functions were forbidden. The CIA has authority to expend funds solely on the certification of its director, to negotiate purchases without publicly soliciting bids, and to transfer funds and people among government agencies. The CIA Act of 1949 exempted the CIA from existing federal laws, which required disclosure of its organization, functions, and budgets and the identity of its employees. The CIA is headed by a director and deputy director, both appointed by the president and confirmed by the Senate. The director of Central Intelligence is responsible for all activities of the CIA, but is also the principal intelligence adviser to the president and NSC, and thereby responsible for coordinating the activities of the entire intelligence community.

Bureau of Intelligence and Research. This State Department bureau is devoted to the assessment rather than the collection of intelligence. Serving policymakers in the State Department, INR manages the department's external research and provides departmental policy guidance for intelligence operations conducted by other agencies.

Department of Defense and the Defense Intelligence Agency. The DIA supports the Joint Chiefs of Staff and the secretary of defense with its own intelligence assessments and coordinates Department of Defense involvement in national intelligence. It manages the Defense Attache system in U.S. embassies. A semiautonomous program within the Defense Department is the Program for Overhead Reconnaissance, which operates overhead reconnaissance programs for the entire intelligence community under general direction of the DCI and the assistant secretary of defense for intelligence. In addition, it responds to specific requirements determined by a committee of the U.S. Intelligence Board. (The USIB, created in 1958, includes representatives from all the intelligence agencies and is instrumental in coordinating and managing the national intelligence effort.) Each of the armed services maintains sizable intelligence organizations and conducts its own cryptology. All participate in the production of national intelligence but concentrate on the security of installations and personnel and on the weaponry of their counterpart services in other countries.

National Security Agency. NSA is the largest of the intelligence agencies in personnel despite considerable contraction in recent years. It is responsible for monitoring foreign communications and other signals for analysis by other agencies. NSA is also responsible for protecting the security of U.S. communications and is technically part of DOD.

The intelligence units of the FBI, Treasury Department, and Energy Research and Development Administration are also formally part of the intelligence community, contributing specialized foreign intelligence on matters within their jurisdiction. However, they are not dealt with in any detail in this collection since their mandates are principally domestic.

Chapter 2 begins with a statement by DCI William Colby, made before the House Select Committee on Intelligence, chaired by Otis Pike, in August 1975. Colby sets forth the scope and purposes of the intelligence community. His testimony is followed by reprinted portions of the Senate Church Committee report, which elaborates on the structures that coordinate and control the activities of various agencies within the community. Following his initial statement is a response to questions and further discussion, which portion has not been reprinted here. The Church Committee text addresses problems as to the manner in which the CIA community is organized, reflecting that committee's investigatory mandate. Following this material is a partially reprinted 1974 study by William J. Barnds, one of the principal authors of the Murphy Commission reports. Barnds traces the origins and evolution of the intelligence function within the postwar U.S. government, and discusses organizational and procedural issues raised by changing international political and economic realities. It should be noted that the detailed information later developed and used by the Church Committee writers was not available to Barnds.

STATEMENT OF W. E. COLBY, DIRECTOR OF CENTRAL INTELLIGENCE, ACCOMPANIED BY MITCHELL ROGOVIN, SPECIAL COUNSEL TO THE DIRECTOR OF CENTRAL INTELLIGENCE

Mr. COLBY. Mr. Chairman and members of the committee, I am pleased to have this opportunity to present to you today the structure of the U.S. intelligence community, and to provide what I hope will N1 prove to be insight into how it is organized and how it operates. I understand that you ask that I focus today on the community as a whole, and turn to CIA specifically on Wednesday. I also understand that you wish especially to cover our budget procedures and the budgets themselves, as a way of investigating the degree of what might be called the command and control of this important activity. I will cover as much as I believe possible in this open session; I will then seek your agreement to cover the remainder in executive session.

I know we will debate the need for such a step, but I would hope we could proceed first with the open part.

"Community" is a particularly apt phrase to describe the structure that performs the important task of providing intelligence to our Government. The intelligence community exists in the same sense as does any other group of people involved in a common endeavor. It is a set of bodies (in this case, Governmental ones) operating within a fairly well understood procedural framework which enables its members to pursue a common objective: Providing intelligence to those who need it.

COMMUNITY MEMBERS

The intelligence community involves all or part of the activities of several departments and agencies of the executive branch:

The Central Intelligence Agency, Defense Intelligence Agency, the Bureau of Intelligence and Research, Department of State, National Security Agency, Army, Navy, and Air Force military intelligence organizations, Federal Bureau of Investigation, Treasury Department, and Energy Research and Development Administration.

There are, in addition, a variety of intelligence-related activities which, while not a part of the community as such, nonetheless make significant contributions to information available to the overall U.S. intelligence effort. Among these are general reporting from our embassies abroad and the intelligence activities integral to our military force structure, referred to as tactical intelligence.

N2   This community reflects the basic intelligence concept contained in the National Security Act of 1947. This established the Central Intelligence Agency under the National Security Council to advise the National Security Council concerning foreign intelligence activities of the other governmental departments and agencies, to recommend to the National Security Council the coordination of the intelligence activities of other departments and agencies, and to perform services of common concern centrally. It was provided, however, that other departments and agencies should continue to collect, evaluate, correlate, and disseminate what was identified as departmental intelligence, that is, intelligence for department purposes.

The act clearly contemplates the present structure of the agencies and departments working on their own on matters of individual interest but coordinating and collaborating with the Central Intelligence Agency to provide the best service to the National Security Council. . . .

THE DCI'S ROLE

Under the provisions of a Presidential memorandum issued in November 1971, which was reaffirmed by President Ford, I have been charged to report to the President and the Congress on "all U.S. intelligence programs." Specifically, I am under instructions to assume leadership of the intelligence community; improve the intelligence product; review all intelligence activities and recommend the appropriate allocation of resources.

CONGRESSIONAL OVERSIGHT

The community keeps the Congress informed of its activities through the mechanism the Congress has established: The designated subcommittees of both the House and Senate Armed Services and Appropriations Committees. We appear before these subcommittees to discuss and report on U.S. foreign intelligence programs and to support the detailed budgetary aspects of the programs. Through formal executive session presentations, testimony, and question and answer sessions, senior intelligence officers provide information to the appropriate level of detail desired by committee members. For example, in considering the fiscal year 1976 intelligence community program now before Congress, I appeared before the Defense Subcommittee of the House Appropriations Committee on six separate occasions—four times on the community program and twice on the CIA budget. In addition, I provided written responses to over 200 committee questions. In addition, Dr. Hall, the Assistant Secretary of Defense for Intelligence, testified on the DOD portions of the community programs and provided written responses to about 200 committee questions.

Various individual program managers provided similar extensive testimony.

I also appear regularly before various congressional committees and subcommittees—in addition to these oversight groups—to provide briefings and intelligence analyses on world affairs. I also maintain daily liaison with the Congress through my legislative counsel and provide substantive inputs to questions as they are raised in the normal course of business.

GUIDANCE

Within the executive branch, there are a number of sources of guidance to the intelligence community. I have direct contact with the President and the Assistant to the President for National Security Affairs. In addition to this personal contact, several organizational mechanisms exist which provide direction or guidance to me as leader of the intelligence community and as the Director of the Central Intelligence Agency:

The National Security Council, consisting of the President, the Vice President, the Secretaries of State and Defense, and, as adviser, the Chairman, JCS—military adviser—and myself as intelligence adviser;

The various committees and groups of the NSC, particularly the NSC Intelligence Committee—NSCIC;

The President's Foreign Intelligence Advisory Board; and

The Office of Management and Budget.

THE NSC MECHANISM

In addition to being an adviser to the National Security Council itself, I am a member of, or am represented on, various NSC groups and committees. In these, I provide information and judgments about foreign developments which impact on national security policy. While my participation is involved primarily with the substance of intelligence, I also receive guidance and important insights concerning the management of the U.S. intelligence effort.

The NSC Intelligence Committee is charged directly with providing direction and guidance on national intelligence needs, and with evaluation of intelligence products from the viewpoint of the user. This committee is chaired by the Assistant to the President for National Security Affairs. Members are the Under Secretary of State for

Political Affairs, the Deputy Secretary of Defense, the Under Secretary of the Treasury, the Chairman, JCS, and myself.

The 40 Committee of the National Security Council provides policy guidance and approval for any CIA activity abroad other than intelligence collection and production—the so-called covert action mission. It is chaired by the Assistant to the President for National Security Affairs. Its members are the Deputy Secretary of State, the Deputy Secretary of Defense, the Chairman, Joint Chiefs of Staff, and me.

THE PRESIDENT'S FOREIGN INTELLIGENCE ADVISORY BOARD (PFIAB)

This Board is the direct descendant of the board of consultants recommended by the second Hoover Commission in 1955. President Eisenhower created the President's Board of Consultants on Foreign Intelligence Activities by Executive Order in 1956. It has been continued by all Presidents since then. The Board, now known as the President's Foreign Intelligence Advisory Board (PFIAB), was most recently continued by President Nixon's Executive Order 11460, dated March 20, 1969. It consists of prominent Americans from outside the Government appointed by the President: Adm. George W. Anderson, Jr., U.S. Navy, Retired, Chairman, Dr. William O. Baker, Bell Labs; Mr. Leo Cherne, Research Institute of America; Dr. John S. Foster, Jr., TRW; Mr. Robert W. Galvin, Motorola; Mr. Gordon Gray; Dr. Edward Land, Polaroid; Mrs. Clare Boothe Luce; Dr. Edward Teller, University of California; and Mr. George P. Shultz, Bechtel. Vice President Rockefeller was a member of the Board until he assumed his present office. Its purpose is to strengthen the collection, evaluation, production, and timely dissemination of reliable intelligence by both military and civilian Government agencies and to assure the President of the quality, responsiveness, and reliability of intelligence provided to policymaking personnel.

The Board operates under a very broad charter which directs it to review all significant aspects of foreign intelligence and related activities in which the Central Intelligence Agency and other elements of the intelligence community are engaged. It reports periodically to the President and makes appropriate recommendations.

THE BUDGET PROCESS

Now, with respect to the budgetary processes, the national foreign intelligence program (NFIP) is formulated on the basis of substantive and fiscal guidance provided by the President, through the Office of Management and Budget. The individual intelligence program budgets which make up the NFIP are developed in accordance with the same guidelines applicable to other Government agency programs—Office of Management and Budget Circular A-11, "Preparation and Submission of Budget Estimates."

Program plans are developed and reviewed by each agency of the intelligence community during the spring and early summer to ensure that the general scope, size, and direction of the plan are in accordance with the objectives and priorities contained in the overall guidance.

These plans are reviewed and approved at the various levels of the member agencies up to the head. They then form the basis against which detailed budget estimates are developed and submitted to the Office of Management and Budget in the fall.

These budget requests are then reviewed in detail by the Office of Management and Budget; by my intelligence community staff; by the Staff of the Assistant Secretary of Defense (Intelligence); and the Comptrollers of Defense and of CIA. Based on these reviews, the approved budget requests for the individual intelligence programs are included within their parent department and agency budgets and form an integral part of the President's overall Federal budget. After consulting with the member agencies, I then provide to the President my independent assessment of the intelligence community resource requests, along with my overall recommendations for the national foreign intelligence program.

My annual recommendations do not constitute a budget in the traditional sense, as I have statutory authority only for the CIA. Rather, in accordance with the President's November 5, 1971 directive, these recommendations represent my view as to the appropriate substantive focus and allocation of resources for the U.S. intelligence effort during the coming 5-year period. The Director has presented three such sets of consolidated community program recommendations to the President and the Congress—for fiscal years 1974, 1975, and 1976.

Once the national foreign intelligence program recommendations are submitted (in early December), they are considered by the President. I then defend the community's portion of the President's budget before the congressional committees, in addition to CIA's, as outlined above.

The national foreign intelligence program is contained in about 20 Department of Defense appropriation accounts and 1 Department of State appropriation account; all of which require annual appropriation by congressional appropriations committees. Of these, about half require annual authorization, which falls under the purview of the Armed Services Committees. I have also participated in these reviews, speaking for the community.

THE INTELLIGENCE COMMUNITY MANAGEMENT STRUCTURE

President Nixon's memorandum of November 5, 1971 was reaffirmed by President Ford's memorandum of October 9, 1974. The President's guidance and direction, enunciated in his November 5, 1971 memorandum, were incorporated into National Security Council Intelligence Directives (NSCID's) in an extensive update and revision of NSCID 1 (basic duties and responsibilities); all other NSCID's were also reexamined, and the entire set was reissued on February 17, 1972. These NSCID's are supplemented by Director of Central Intelligence Directives, or DCID's issued after consultation with the community members, which specify in greater detail the policies and procedures established by the NSCID's. Each agency then develops its internal regulations in conformity with these policies. In addition to creating the NSC Intelligence Committee, the 1971 memorandum directed the creation of an Intelligence Resources Advisory Committee (IRAC).

This committee, chaired by the Director, consists of senior representatives of the Departments of State and Defense, the Central Intelligence Agency, and the Office of Management and Budget. The Director, since IRAC's inception, has invited the Director, NSA and the Director, DIA to participate regularly in the IRAC as observers in their capacity as national intelligence program managers. A representative of the NSC staff also participates regularly as an observer. Other community program managers are invited as appropriate.

The IRAC meets approximately once each quarter, except at the end of the calendar year, when more frequent meetings are needed to formulate the annual budget.

The principal role of IRAC is to advise the Director on (1) the allocation and use of intelligence resources and (2) the formulation of the DCI's national foreign intelligence program recommendations to the president.

Another board, the United States Intelligence Board (USIB) is responsible for providing advice to the DCI on matters of substantive intelligence. It is designed to assist me in the production of national intelligence, establishing requirements and setting priorities, supervising dissemination and security of intelligence, and protecting intelligence sources and methods.

The Board is chaired by the Director and meets weekly. Members include the Deputy Director of Central Intelligence (vice chairman); Director of Intelligence and Research, Department of State; Director, National Security Agency; Director, DIA; and representatives of the Secretary of the Treasury, the Director, FBI, and the Administrator of the Energy Research and Development Administration. The intelligence chiefs of the military services have observer status on USIB and participate in its meetings.

USIB is supported by 14 subordinate committees, organized along functional lines and drawing upon all elements of the intelligence community for membership. These committees also serve IRAC as required.

To assist in assuming the more comprehensive management of the intelligence community called for in the November 5, 1971 presidential memorandum, the President directed that the DCI strengthen his personal staff. This has led to the formation of two groups: The National Intelligence Officer structure and the intelligence community staff.

THE NIO STRUCTURE

The National Intelligence Officers were established in October 1973, replacing the former Board of National Estimates. The group is headed by a deputy to me for NIO's. Each National Intelligence Officer has a specific area of geographic or functional responsibility for which he or she is responsible. Each NIO's raison d'etre is to provide substantive expertise to support me and to be responsible for insuring that the community is doing everything it can to meet consumer needs. The NIO staff has been kept deliberately austere—each NIO is limited to an assistant and a secretary—on the philosophy that it is the NIO's job to stimulate the community to produce the intelligence, not to do it himself. There are presently eleven NIO's dealing with subjects as diverse as strategic forces, the Middle East, and international economics and energy. The NIO's identify the key intelligence questions needing action in their area, review and develop our collection and production strategy, insure that our intelligence is responsive to our customers' needs, and evaluate how well we are performing against our objectives.

THE INTELLIGENCE COMMUNITY STAFF

The IC Staff provides management and evaluation support to the DCI. It is headed by an active duty military officer at the three-star level and is a composite of individuals drawn from CIA, NSA, DIA, active duty military—from all services—and private industry. It is organized into three main divisions: management, planning and resources review; product review; and collection and processing assessment. The titles are descriptive of the functions performed.

MANAGEMENT VEHICLES

Since I do not exercise command authority over the component organizations of the intelligence community—other than the CIA—I rely on a family of management devices to provide guidance, stimulate the proper program direction and balance, and provide a basis for evaluation.

Each year, I issue Perspectives for Intelligence, a document intended to provide a broad framework to guide program development over the next 5 years. Perspectives provide the community with my views of the environment within which the community must prepare to operate. It attempts to identify, in broad terms, where the heaviest demands on the community will come from.

I have also asked that the three major collection programs develop plans to portray the direction each is taking over the next 5 years and to serve to identify major strengths and weaknesses.

Each year, following a very extensive and detailed program development and review cycle, I submit to the President my national foreign intelligence program recommendations. Because of the large concentration of community resources within the Defense Department—over 80 percent—the process leading up to the NFIPR is dovetailed carefully with the defense planning, programing and budgeting process. This document provides the President with my independent view of the national intelligence aspects of the budget he submits to the Congress. The NFIPR is prepared by the IC staff working closely with all members of the community.

Each year I also issue a set of national intelligence objectives and submit them for NSCIC approval. At the end of the year, I submit an annual report to the President on community performance against these objectives.

These are supplemented by key intelligence questions issued by me after consultation with the U.S. Intelligence Board and the national intelligence officers. These focus the national intelligence effort on the main problems the Nation faces in the world.

This extensive management structure focuses, of course, on the objectives and programs of the intelligence community. It also provides a basis for evaluation of the effectiveness of the community on a regular basis. The detailed financial auditing and controls are conducted within the member agencies of the community, however, according to their specific departmental regulations.

DIRECTION OF THE INTELLIGENCE COMMUNITY

The President's Office ([45A], pp. 41–48, 60–65, 73–95)

Intelligence has been the province of the President. It has informed his decisions and furthered his purposes. Intelligence information has been seen as largely belonging to the President, as being his to classify or declassify, his to withhold or share. The instruments of U.S. intelligence have been the Presidents' to use and sometimes to abuse.

The President is the only elected official in the chain of command over the United States intelligence community. It is to him the Constitution and the Congress have granted authority to carry out intelligence activities. It is the President who is ultimately accountable to the Congress and the American people.

The Committee focused its investigation on the instruments available to the President to control, direct, and supervise the U.S. intelligence community. As the result of controversy as to whether the intelligence community has been "out of control," Senate Resolution 21 directed the Committee to determine the "nature and extent of executive branch oversight of all United States intelligence activities."

This involves three Presidential instrumentalities:
—The National Security Council;
—The Office of Management and Budget;
N3 —The President's Foreign Intelligence Advisory Board.

The Committee sought to establish whether these mechanisms, as they have evolved, provide effective control over the entire range of U.S. intelligence activities. Particular attention was given to the subject of covert action, in part because it has been a major object of presidential-level review. In addition, the Committee considered the adequacy of high-level supervision of espionage, counterintelligence, and the overall management of the U.S. intelligence community. For the first time in the history of congressional oversight, the Committee had access to records of the proceedings of the National Security Council and its subcommittees. It reviewed the NSC directives related to intelligence and the files of other agencies' participation in the NSC's intelligence-related activities. The Committee conducted extensive interviews with current and former White House, NSC, and cabinet-level officials dealing with intelligence matters. It took sworn testimony on these issues from a number of them, including the present Secretary of State. Officials of the Office of Management and Budget and former members and staff of the President's Foreign Intelligence Advisory Board were also interviewed.

This report presents the results of that investigation and the Committee's findings with respect to the central question of Presidential accountability and control of the foreign intelligence activities of the United States Government.

The National Security Council

1. Overview

The National Security Council was created by the National Security Act of 1947. According to the Act, the NSC is "to advise the President with respect to the integration of domestic, foreign, and military policies relating to national security" and "assess and appraise the objectives, commitments, and risks of the United States in relation to our actual and potential military power." Over the years, the principal functions of the NSC have been in the field of policy formulation and the coordination and monitoring of overseas operations. Among its responsibilities, the NSC has provided policy guidance and direction for United States intelligence activities.

The National Security Council is an extremely flexible instrument. It has only four statutory members: the President, the Vice President, and the Secretaries of State and Defense. At the discretion of the President, others may be added to the list of attendees; NSC subcommittees may be created or abolished, and the NSC staff given great N4 power or allowed to wither.

Thus, the operation of the NSC has reflected the personal style of each President. The Council's role and responsibilities have varied according to personalities, changing policies and special circumstances. Presidents Truman, Kennedy and Johnson found a loose and informal NSC structure to their liking. Others have set up more formal and elaborate structures—President Eisenhower's NSC system is the best example.[2] At times, particularly during crises, Presidents have bypassed the formal NSC mechanisms. President Kennedy set up an Executive Committee (EXCOM) to deal with the Cuban Missile Crisis; President Johnson had his Tuesday Lunch group to discuss Viet Nam and other high level concerns. As a result, over the years the NSC has undergone major changes, from the elaborate Planning Board/Operations Coordination Board structure under Eisenhower to its dismantlement by Kennedy and the creation of a centralized system of NSC subcommittees under President Nixon and his Assistant for National Security Affairs, Dr. Kissinger.

Today, in addition to the four statutory members, the National Security Council is attended by the Director of Central Intelligence (DCI) and the Chairman of the Joint Chiefs of Staff as advisers. From time to time, others, such as the Director of the Arms Control N5 and Disarmament Agency, also attend.

Prior to President Ford's reorganization, the NSC was served by seven principal committees: the Senior Review Group, the Under Secretary's Committee, the Verification Panel, the Washington Special Actions Group (WSAG), the Defense Program Review Committee, the 40 Committee, and the National Security Council Intelligence

---

[2] For a full treatment of the evolution of the National Security Council and its place within the national security decisionmaking process, see Keith Clark and Laurence Legere, *The President and the Management of National Security* (1969); Stanley Falk and Theodore Bauer, *National Security Management: The National Security Structure* (1972); and Inquiries of the Subcommittee on National Policy Machinery for the Senate Committee on Government Operations, *Organizing for National Security* (1961).

Committee (NSCIC).[3] The latter two committees had direct intelligence responsibilities. The 40 Committee has now been replaced by the Operations Advisory Group. No successor for NSCIC has been designated. The current NSC structure is shown below.

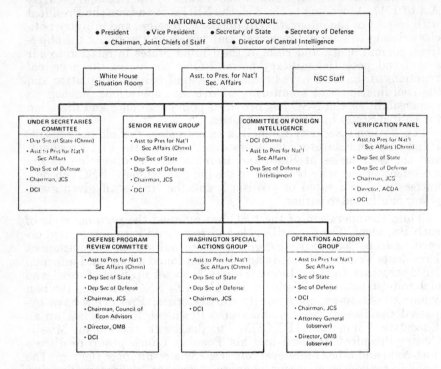

Each of the current NSC subcommittees are "consumers" of the intelligence community product. The DCI sits on all of them. In most cases, the DCI briefs the subcommittees and the full NSC before agenda items are considered. CIA representatives sit on working and ad hoc groups of the various subcommittees. The CIA's Area Division Chiefs are the Agency's representatives on the NSC Interdepartmental Groups (IGs).[4] In all of these meetings there is a constant give and take. Policymakers are briefed on current intelligence and they, in turn, levy intelligence priorities on the CIA's representatives.

---

[3] The Senior Review Group, under the direction of the President's Assistant for National Security Affairs defines NSC issues; determines whether alternatives, costs, and consequences have been fully considered; and forwards recommendations to the full Council and/or the President. The Under Secretaries Committee seeks to ensure effective implementation of NSC decisions. The Verification Panel monitors arms control agreements and advises on SALT and MBFR negotiations. WASG coordinates activities during times of crises, such as the Middle East and Southeast Asia. The Defense Program Review Committee, now nearly defunct, assesses the political, military and economic implications of defense policies and programs.

[4] NSC Interdepartmental Groups (IGs) are made up of representatives from State, Defense, CIA, the Joint Chiefs of Staff and the National Security Council. IGs are chaired by the State representative, an Assistant Secretary, and they prepare working papers for the Senior Review Group.

2. The NSC and Intelligence

The 1947 National Security Act established the CIA as well as the NSC. The Act provided that the CIA was "established under the National Security Council" and was to carry out its prescribed functions "under the direction of the National Security Council." Five broad functions were assigned to the CIA:

(1) *to advise* the National Security Council in matters concerning such intelligence activities of the Government departments and agencies as relate to national security.

(2) *to make recommendations* to the National Security Council for the coordination of such intelligence activities of the departments and agencies of the Government as relate to the national security;

(3) *to correlate and evaluate* intelligence relating to the national security, and provide for the appropriate dissemination of such intelligence within the Government using where appropriate existing agencies and facilities.

(4) *to perform*, for the benefit of the existing intelligence agencies, *such additional services of common concern* as the National Security Council determines can be more efficiently accomplished centrally.

(5) *to perform such other functions and duties* related to intelligence affecting the national security as the National Security Council may from time to time direct.

The Director of Central Intelligence is responsible for seeing that these functions are performed, and is to serve as the President's principal foreign intelligence officer.

The NSC sets overall policy for the intelligence community. It does not, however, involve itself in day-to-day management activities. The task of coordinating intelligence community activities has been delegated to the DCI, who, until President Ford's reorganization, sought to accomplish it through the United States Intelligence Board (USIB). USIB was served by 15 inter-agency committees and a variety of ad hoc groups. It provided guidance to the intelligence community on requirements and priorities, coordinated community activities and issued, through the DCI, National Intelligence Estimates (NIEs). The DCI was also assisted by the Intelligence Resources Advisory Committee (IRAC). IRAC assisted the DCI in the preparation of a consolidated intelligence budget and sought to assure that intelligence resources were being used efficiently.

As a result of President Ford's Executive Order, management of the intelligence community will now be vested in the Committee on Foreign Intelligence (CFI). USIB and IRAC are abolished. Membership on the new committee will include the DCI, as Chairman, the Deputy Secretary of Defense for Intelligence and the Deputy Assistant to the President for National Security Affairs. Staff support will be provided by the DCI's Intelligence Community (IC) staff. The new committee will report directly to the NSC.

The CFI will have far-ranging responsibilities. It will oversee the budget and resources, as well as establish management policies, for the CIA, the National Security Agency, the Defense Intelligence Agency, and United States reconnaissance programs. Further, it will establish policy priorities for the collection and production of national intelligence. The DCI will be responsible for producing national intelligence, including NIEs. To assist him in this task, the DCI will set up whatever boards and committees (similar to the now defunct USIB) are necessary.

The President's Executive Order also directed the NSC to review, on a semi-annual basis, certain foreign intelligence activities. Prepared by the President's Assistant for National Security Affairs, these reviews will focus on the quality, scope and timeliness of the intelligence product; the responsiveness of the intelligence community to policymakers' needs; the allocation of intelligence collection resources; and the continued appropriateness of ongoing covert operations and sensitive intelligence collection missions.

One of the functions the NSC has assigned to the CIA is the conduct of foreign covert operations. These operations began in 1948 and have continued to the present, uninterrupted. Authority to conduct covert operations has usually been ascribed to the "such other functions and duties" provision of the 1947 Act.[5]

N7

The NSC uses National Security Council Intelligence Directives (NSCIDs) to set policy for the CIA and the intelligence community. NSCIDs are broad delegations of responsibility, issued under the authority of the 1947 Act.[6] They may assign duties not explicitly stated in the 1947 Act to the CIA or other intelligence departments or agencies. NSCIDs, sometimes referred to by critics as the intelligence community's "secret charter," are executive directives and, therefore, not subject to congressional review. Until recently, Congress has not seen the various NSCIDs issued by the NSC.

N8

3. Overview: 40 Committee and NSCIC

Prior to President Ford's reorganization, two NSC committees, the 40 Committee and the National Security Council Intelligence Committee, had special intelligence duties. Their functions and responsibilities will be discussed in turn.

Throughout its history, the 40 Committee and its direct predecessors—the 303 Committee, the 5412 or Special Group, the 10/5 and 10/2 Panels—have been charged by various NSC directives with exercising political control over foreign covert operations.[7] Now this task will be the responsibility of the Operations Advisory Group. The Committees have considered the objectives of any proposed activity,

---

[5] Three possible legal bases for covert operations are most often cited: the National Security Act of 1947, the "inherent powers" of the President in foreign affairs and as Commander-in-Chief, and the Foreign Assistance Act of 1974. Congressional acquiescence and ratification through the appropriations process is a fourth possibility. . . .

[6] For example, NSCIDs are used to spell out the duties and responsibilities of the DCI, the coordination of covert intelligence collection activities, and the production and dissemination of the intelligence community product.

[7] Covert operations encompass a wide range of programs. These include political and propaganda programs designed to influence or support foreign political parties, groups, and specific political and military leaders; economic action programs; paramilitary operations; and some counterinsurgency programs. Human intelligence collection, or spying, and counterespionage programs are not included under the rubric of covert operations.

whether the activity would accomplish those aims, how likely it would be to succeed, and in general whether the activity would be in the American interest. In addition, the Committees have attempted to insure that covert operations were framed in such a way that they later could be "disavowed" or "plausibly denied" by the United States Government. President Ford's Executive Order included the concept of "plausible denial." Using the euphemism "special activities" to describe covert operations, the Order stated:

> Special activities in support of national foreign policy objectives [are those] activities . . . designed to further official United States programs and policies abroad which are planned and executed so that the role of the United States Government is not apparent or publicly acknowledged.[7a]

The concept of "plausible denial" is intended not only to hide the hand of the United States Government, but to protect the President from the embarrassment of a "blown" covert operation. In the words of former CIA Director Richard Helms:

> . . . [the] Special Group was the mechanism . . . set up . . . to use as a circuit-breaker so that these things did not explode in the President's face and so that he was not held responsible for them.[7b]

In the past, it appears that one means of protecting the President from embarrassment was not to tell him about certain covert operations, at least formally. According to Bromley Smith, an official who served on the National Security Council staff from 1958 to 1969, the concept of "plausible denial" was taken in an almost literal sense: "The government was authorized to do certain things that the President was not advised of." [7c] According to Secretary of State Kissinger, however, this practice was not followed during the Nixon Administration and he doubted it ever was. In an exchange with a member of the House Select Committee on Intelligence, Secretary Kissinger stated:

> Mr. KASTEN. Mr. Secretary, you said that the President personally, directly approved all of the covert operations during that period of time [1972 to 1974] and, in your knowledge, during all periods of time. Is that correct?
>
> Secretary KISSINGER. I can say with certainty during the period of time that I have been in Washington and to my almost certain knowledge at every period of time, yes.[8]

Four senior officials who deal almost exclusively with foreign affairs have been central to each of the sequence of committees charged with considering covert operations: The President's Assistant for National Security Affairs, the Deputy Secretary of Defense, the Under Secretary of State for Political Affairs (formerly the Deputy Under Secretary), and the Director of Central Intelligence. These four officials, plus the Chairman of the Joint Chiefs of Staff, made up the 40 Com-

---

[7a] Executive Order No. 11905, 2/18/76.
[7b] Richard Helms testimony, 6/13/75, pp. 28–29.
[7c] Staff summary of Bromley Smith interview, 5/5/75.
[8] Henry Kissinger testimony, House Select Committee on Intelligence, Hearings, 10/31/75, p. 3341.

mittee. At certain times the Attorney General also sat on the Committee. President Ford's reorganization will significantly alter this membership. The new Operations Advisory Group will consist of the President's Assistant for National Security Affairs, the Secretaries of State and Defense, the Chairman of the JCS, and the DCI. The Attorney General and the Director of OMB will attend meetings as observers. The Chairman of the Group will be designated by the President. Staff support will be provided by the NSC staff.

The formal composition of the Operations Group breaks with tradition. The Secretaries of State and Defense will now be part of the approval process for covert operations, rather than the Under Secretary of State for Political Affairs and Deputy Secretary of Defense. The Operations Advisory Group appears to be, therefore, an up-graded 40 Committee. Whether this proves to be the case remains to be seen. President Ford's Executive Order contained a provision, Section 3(c)(3), which allows Group members to send a "designated representative" to meetings in "unusual circumstances."

The National Security Council Intelligence Committee (NSCIC) was established in November 1971 as part of a far-reaching reorganization of the intelligence community ordered by President Nixon.[9] The Presidential directive stated:

> The Committee will give direction and guidance on national intelligence needs and provide for a continuing evaluation of intelligence products from the viewpoint of the intelligence user.

One reason cited for creating NSCIC was a desire to make the intelligence community more responsive to the needs of policy makers. According to a news report at the time:

> "The President and Henry [Kissinger] have felt that the intelligence we were collecting wasn't always responsive to their needs," said one source. "They suspected that one reason was because the intelligence community had no way of knowing day to day what the President and Kissinger needed. This is a new link between producers and consumers. We'll have to wait and see if it works."[10]

Prior to NSCIC no formal structure existed for addressing the major questions concerning intelligence priorities rather than specific operations: Do "producers" in the intelligence community perform analyses which are useful to "consumers"—the policymakers at various levels of government; are intelligence resources allocated wisely among agencies and types of collection? NSCIC was a structural response to these issues as well as part of the general tendency at that

---

[9] For over a year, the intelligence community had been under study by the Office of Management and Budget, then headed by James Schlesinger. In addition to NSCIC, the President's reorganization included an enhanced leadership role for the DCI, the establishment of a Net Assessment Group within the NSC staff, the creation of an Intelligence Resources Advisory Committee (IRAC), and a reconstitution of the United States Intelligence Board (USIB). The Net Assessment Group was headed by a senior NSC staff member and was responsible for reviewing and evaluating all intelligence products and for producing net assessments. When James Schlesinger was named Secretary of Defense in June, 1973, the NSC Net Assessment Group was abolished. Its staff member joined Schlesinger at the Defense Department and set up a similar office.

[10] "Helms Told to Cut Global Expenses," *New York Times*, 11/7/71, p. 55.

time to centralize a greater measure of control in the White House for national security affairs.

NSCIC's mission was to give direction and policy guidance to the intelligence community. It was not, and was not intended to be, a channel for transmitting substantive intelligence from the intelligence community to policymakers nor for levying specific requirements in the opposite direction. Neither was NSCIC involved in the process of allocating intelligence resources. Its membership included the Assistant to the President for National Security Affairs, who chaired the Committee, the DCI, the Deputy Secretaries of State and Defense, the Chairman of the JCS, and the Under Secretary of the Treasury for Monetary Affairs.

NSCIC was abolished by Executive Order 11905. No successor body was created. The task of providing policy guidance and direction to the intelligence community now falls to the Committee on Foreign Intelligence. According to the President's Executive Order, the CFI will "establish policy priorities for the collection and production of national intelligence." In addition, the full NSC is now required to conduct policy reviews twice a year on the quality, scope and timeliness of intelligence and on the responsiveness of the intelligence community to the needs of policymakers. . . .

N9

Role of OMB

In order to meet unanticipated needs, the CIA maintains a Contingency Reserve Fund. The fund is replenished by annual appropriations as well as unobligated funds from previous CIA appropriations. More often than not, the unanticipated needs of the CIA relate to covert operations.

The Director of Central Intelligence has the authority, under the Central Intelligence Agency Act of 1949, to spend reserve funds without consulting OMB. However, due to an arrangement among OMB, the CIA, and the Appropriations Committees of Congress, the CIA has agreed not to use reserve funds without OMB approval. There is no evidence that the DCI has ever violated this agreement. In practice. OMB holds a double key to this reserve fund: first, it approves additions to the reserve fund and, second, it approves the amounts to be released from the fund, upon CIA request and justification. OMB holds a careful review of each proposed release. Turndowns are rare, but reductions in amounts requested occur often enough to prompt a careful CIA presentation of its case.

Despite these levers of control, OMB has faced several handicaps which render its control of the Contingency Reserve Fund less effective than it might be. First, OMB has not, in the past, been represented on the National Security Council or the 40 Committee.[29] Much of the dollar volume of reserve releases originates in 40 Committee action. Thus, OMB resistance to reserve release requests were often in the face of policy determinations already made. Second, although the chairmen of the appropriations subcommittees of Congress are notified of drawdowns from the fund, these notifications occur *after* the release action, even though the release is conceptually the same as a supplemental appropriation. Thus, OMB does not have the leverage in regard to

---

[29] Under President Ford's Executive Order, the Director of OMB will sit as an observer on the Operations Arvisory Group, the successor to the 40 Committee.

Contingency Reserve Fund releases that it does in regard to supplemental appropriatitons requests (where OMB is a party to recommending supplementals to the President and Congress).

OMB suffers other limitations with respect to the use of CIA funds for covert operations. First, CIA's budget submission to OMB has, in the past, neglected some aspects of clandestine spending, notably proprietary activities. Second, current ground rules allow the reprogramming of CIA's regular appropriations to meet unanticipated needs; no OMB approval is required for this reprogramming. To the extent that the above funds are used for covert operations, OMB has no control over their use. . . .

The PFIAB and Intelligence Oversight Board

1. Overview

The President needs an independent body to assess the quality and effectiveness of our foreign intelligence effort. Since 1956 the President's Foreign Intelligence Advisory Board (PFIAB) has served this function. Numerous proposals have recently been made to make PFIAB an executive "watchdog" over United States foreign intelligence activities. Some have suggested that a joint presidential/congressional intelligence board be established or, at the least, Senate confirmation of members of the President's board be required. The Rockefeller Commission recommended that the Board's functions be expanded to include oversight of the CIA with responsibility for assessing CIA compliance with its statutory authority. The Murphy Commission commented favorably on the Rockefeller Commission recommendations. Whether PFIAB should adopt this oversight or "watchdog" function, or whether Congress should be involved in the activities of the Board is open to question. President Ford, in his Executive Order, decided against transforming the Board into a CIA watchdog. Instead, he created a new three-member Intelligence Oversight Board to monitor the activities of the intelligence community.

2. History of PFIAB

On February 6, 1956, President Eisenhower created, by Executive Order, the Board of Consultants on Foreign Intelligence Activities. The Board was established in response to a recommendation by the second Hoover Commission, calling for the President to appoint a committee of private citizens who would report to him on United States foreign intelligence activities. Creation of the Board was also intended to preempt a move in Congress at the time, led by Senator Mike Mansfield, to establish a Joint Congressional Committee on Intelligence.

The Board ceased functioning when President Eisenhower left office in 1961, but was reactivated by President Kennedy following the Bay of Pigs failure. It was renamed the President's Foreign Intelligence Advisory Board (PFIAB) and has functioned, uninterrupted, since that time.

3. PFIAB Today

The Board currently operates under Executive Order 11460, issued by President Nixon on March 20, 1969. The Board is responsible for reviewing and assessing United States foreign intelligence activities. It reports to the President periodically on its findings and recommendations for improving the effectiveness of the nation's foreign intelligence effort.

N10 The Board presently has seventeen members, all drawn from private life and all appointed by the President. It is chaired by Leo Cherne, and holds formal meetings two days every other month. It has a staff of two, headed by an executive secretary.

As its name indicates, the Board is advisory. Board reports and recommendations have contributed to the increased effectiveness and efficiency of our foreign intelligence effort. For example, the Board played a significant role in the development of our overhead reconnaissance program. It has made recommendations on coordinating American intelligence activities; reorganizing Defense intelligence; applying science and technology to the National Security Agency, and rewriting the National Security Council Intelligence Directives (NSCIDs). The Board has conducted post-mortems on alleged intelligence failures and, since 1969, made a yearly, independent assessment of the Soviet strategic threat, thereby supplementing regular community intelligence assessments. Most recently, it has reported to the President on economic intelligence and human clandestine intelligence collection.

The Board has not served a "watchdog" function. As the Rockefeller Commission noted, the Board does not exercise control over the CIA, which is, in fact, the Board's only source of information about Agency activities. When the Board has occasionally inquired into areas of possible illegal or improper CIA activity, it has met resistance. For example, when the Board became aware of the so-called Huston Plan and asked the FBI and the Attorney General for a copy, the request was refused. The Board did not pursue the matter with the White House. In 1970, the Board was asked by Henry Kissinger, then the President's National Security Advisor, to examine Allende's election victory in Chile to determine whether the CIA had failed to foresee, and propose appropriate actions, to prevent Allende's taking office. The Board requested 40 Committee and NSC minutes to determine the facts. Its request was refused and its inquiry was dropped.

The President needs an independent body to assess the quality and effectiveness of our foreign intelligence effort. In the words of its Executive Secretary, the Board has "looked at intelligence through the eyes of the President." PFIAB has served, in effect, as an intelligence "Kitchen Cabinet." The Board has been useful, in part, because its advice and recommendations have been *for* the President. As such, the executive nature of this relationship should be maintained.

Over the years, many of PFIAB's recommendations have been adopted, and others have served as a basis for later reform or reorganization. The Board has not been an executive "watchdog" of the CIA. To make it so would be to place the Board in an untenable position: adviser to the President on the quality and effectiveness of intelligence on the one hand and "policeman" of the intelligence community on the other. These two roles conflict and should be performed separately.

4. Intelligence Oversight Board

To assist the President, the NSC, and the Attorney General in overseeing the intelligence community, President Ford has created an Intelligence Oversight Board. The Board will consist of three private citizens appointed by the President. They will also serve on PFIAB.

The Board will be, in effect, a community-wide Inspector General of last resort. It will review reports from the Inspectors General and General Counsels of the intelligence community and report periodically to the Attorney General and the President on any activities which appear to be illegal or improper. The Board will also review the practices, procedures, and internal guidelines of the various IGs and General Counsels to ensure that they are designed to bring questionable activities to light. Finally, the Board will see to it that intelligence community IGs and General Counsels have access to any information they require.

The President's Intelligence Oversight Board should serve a useful purpose. However, the ability of a small, part-time Board to monitor the activities of the entire intelligence community is questionable. Further, the Board is a creature of the Executive and, as such, may be unable or, at times, unwilling to probe certain sensitive areas. A body independent of the Executive must also be responsible for monitoring the activities of the intelligence community, including those which may be either illegal or improper. . . .

The Director of Central Intelligence

The Pearl Harbor intelligence failure was the primary motivation for establishing a Director of Central Intelligence. President Truman desired a national intelligence organization which had access to all information and would be headed by a Director who could speak authoritatively for the whole community and could insure that the community's operation served the foreign policy needs of the President and his senior advisers.[8] President Truman and subsequent Presidents have not wanted to rely exclusively on the intelligence judgments of departments with vested interests in applying intelligence to support a particular foreign policy or to justify acquiring a new weapons system.

However, the DCI's responsibility to produce national intelligence and to coordinate intelligence activities has often been at variance with the particular interests and prerogatives of the other intelligence community departments and agencies. During the Second World War, the Department of State and the military services developed their own intelligence operations. Despite establishment of the Director of Central Intelligence in 1946, they have not wanted to give up control over their own intelligence capabilities. The military services particularly have argued that they must exercise direct control over peacetime intelligence activities in order to be prepared to conduct wartime military operations. The State and Defense Departments have steadfastly opposed centralized management of the intelligence community under the DCI.

However, over time the actual degree of conflict between the DCI's responsibility to coordinate intelligence activities and the interests of the other parts of the community has depended on how broadly each DCI chose to interpret his coordination responsibilities and how he allocated his time between his three major roles.[9] The three roles the DCI plays are: (1) the producer of national intelligence; (2) the coordinator of intelligence activities; and (3) the Director of the Central Intelligence Agency.

A. THE PRODUCER OF NATIONAL INTELLIGENCE

As the President's principal foreign intelligence adviser, the DCI's major responsibility is to produce objective and independent *national*

---

[8] Harry S. Truman, *Memoirs*, Vol. II, p. 58.

[9] QUESTION: When you were DCI, did you feel that institutionally or functionally your position was bumping heads with the DOD intelligence apparatus in different ways or not, and if not, why not, in view of the structure?

Mr. SCHLESINGER: Well, historically there have been intervening periods of open warfare and detente . . . Prior to these, one of the problems of the intelligence

intelligence for senior policymakers.[10] In so doing, he draws on a variety of collection methods and on the resources of the departmental intelligence organizations as well as CIA analysts.[11] But the DCI issues national intelligence and is alone responsible for its production.[12]

The most important national intelligence which the DCI produces is the National Intelligence Estimate (NIE). An NIE presents the intelligence community's current knowledge of the situation in a particular country or on a specific topic and then tries to estimate what is going to happen within a certain period of time. NIEs are prepared for use by those in the highest policy levels of government and represent the considered judgment of the entire community.[13] Major differences of opinion within the intelligence community are illuminated in the text or in the footnotes. When an NIE is released, however, it is the DCI's own national intelligence judgment, in theory free from departmental or agency biases.[14]

To carry out this responsibility to produce independent and objective national intelligence, DCI Walter Bedell Smith established the Board of National Estimates in 1950. The Board was comprised of senior government officials, academicians and intelligence officers and had a small staff known as the Office of National Estimates (ONE). One member of the Board would be responsible for supervising the drafting of the estimates by the ONE staff, for reviewing these judgments collectively for the DCI, and for adjudicating disputes within the community. When the United States Intelligence Board reviewed an NIE, the DCI could have confidence in the opinions expressed in the estimate because each estimate reflected the collective judgment of his own Board. According to the former chairman of the Board of National Estimates, John Huizenga:

> The Board of National Estimates in fact functioned as a kind of buffer. It provided procedures by which the departmental views could be given a full and fair hearing, while at the same time ensuring that the DCI's responsibilities to produce intelligence from a national viewpoint could be upheld.[15]

community has been the warfare that exists along jurisdictional boundaries, and this tended to erupt in the period of the 1960's, in particular when they were introducing a whole set of new technical collection capabilities; that open warfare was succeeded by a period of true detente, but the problem with such detente is that it tends to be based on marriage contracts and the principle of good fences make good neighbors, and that a mutual back-scratching and the like, so that you do not get effective resource management under those circumstances. (James Schlesinger, testimony, 2/2/76, pp. 29–30.)

[10] According to NSCID No. 1, 2/17/72, national intelligence is that intelligence required for the formulation of national security policy and concerning more than one department or agency. It is distinguished from departmental intelligence, which is that intelligence in support of the mission of a particular department.

[11] Prior to President Ford's Executive Order No. 11905, 2/18/76, the United States Intelligence Board, composed of representatives from the various agencies and departments of the intelligence community, formally reviewed the DCI's national intelligence judgments.

[12] Under President Ford's Executive Order No. 11905, 2/18/76, the DCI will have responsibility to "supervise production and dissemination of national intelligence."

[13] At present, the DCI briefs the Congress on the judgments contained in his NIEs. The Congress does not receive the DCI's NIEs on a regular basis.

[14] In his role as CIA Director, the DCI also produces current intelligence and research studies for senior policymakers. These intelligence judgments are prepared by CIA analysts who are supposed to be free from departmental preferences. Such current reporting is not formally reviewed by the other members of the intelligence community, but is often informally coordinated.

[15] John Huizenga testimony, 1/26/76, p. 11.

In 1973, Colby replaced the Board and the ONE staff with a new system of eleven National Intelligence Officers (NIOs). Each NIO has staff responsibility to the DCI for intelligence collection and production activities in his geographical or functional specialty. The NIOs coordinate the drafting of NIEs within the community. They do not, however, collectively review the final product for the DCI.[16] Director Colby testified that he thought the Board of National Estimates tended to fuzz over differences of opinion and to dilute the DCI's final intelligence judgments.[17]

In the course of its investigation, the Committee concluded that the most critical problem confronting the DCI in carrying out his responsibility to produce national intelligence is making certain that his intelligence judgments are in fact *objective* and *independent* of departmental and agency biases. However, this is often quite difficult. A most delicate relationship exists between the DCI and senior policymakers. According to John Huizenga:

> There is a natural tension between intelligence and policy, and the task of the former is to present as a basis for the decisions of policymakers as realistic as possible a view of forces and conditions in the external environment. Political leaders often find the picture presented less than congenial. . . . Thus, a DCI who does his job well will more often than not be the bearer of bad news, or at least will make things seem disagreeable, complicated, and uncertain. . . . When intelligence people are told, as happened in recent years, that they were expected to get on the team, then a sound intelligence-policy relationship has in effect broken down.[18]

In addition, the DCI must provide intelligence for cabinet officers who often have vested interests in receiving information which supports a particular foreign policy (State Department) or the acquisi-

---

[16] Under the NIO system, the Defense Intelligence Agency (DIA) and the military services have assumed greater responsibility for the initial drafting of military estimates. Because NIOs have no separate staff, they must utilize experts in the community to draft sections of the estimates. In 1975, DIA prepared the first drafts of two chapters of the NIE on Soviet offensive and defensive strategic forces. Colby contends that as a consequence, analysts throughout the community felt more involved. (William Colby testimony, 12/11/75.)

[17] According to Colby:

"A board? You say why don't you have a board also? I have some reservation at the ivory tower kind of problem that you get out of a board which is too separated from the rough and tumble of the real world. I think there is a tendency for it to intellectualize and then write sermons and appreciations. . . .

"I think there is a tendency to become institutionally committed to an approach and to an appraisal of a situation and to begin to interpret new events against the light of a predetermined approach toward those events. I think that has been a bother. I like the idea of an individual total responsibility, one man or woman totally responsible, and then you don't get any fuzz about how there was a vote, and therefore I really didn't like it but I went along and all that sort of thing, one person totally responsible, I think, is a good way to do it. That can be the Director or whatever you set up. But I do like that idea of separating out and making one individual totally responsible so there's nobody else to go to, and there's no way of dumping the responsibility onto somebody else. That really is my main problem with the board, that it diffuses responsibility, that it does get out of the main line of the movement of material. (Colby, 12/11/75, pp. 36–37.)

[18] Huizenga, 1/26/76, pp. 13–14.

tion of a new weapon system (Department of Defense).[19] The President and NSC staff want confirmation that their policies are succeeding. Moreover, each NIE has in the past been formally reviewed by other members of the intelligence community. Although CIA analysts have developed expertise on issues of critical importance to national policymakers, such as Soviet strategic programs, most DCIs have been reluctant to engage in a confrontation with members of the USIB over substantive findings in national intelligence documents.[20] According to John Huizenga:

> The truth is that the DCI, since his authority over the intelligence process is at least ambiguous, has an uphill struggle to make a sophisticated appreciation of a certain range of issues prevail in the national intelligence product over against the parochial views and interests of departments, and especially the military departments.[21]

Finally, the DCI's own analysts in CIA are sometimes accused of holding an "institutional" bias. According to James Schlesinger:

> The intelligence directorate of the CIA has the most competent, qualified people in it, just in terms of their raw intellectual capabilities, but this does not mean that they are free from error. In fact, the intelligence directorate tends to make a particular type of error systematically in that the intelligence directorate tends to be in close harmony with the prevailing biases in the intellectual community, in the university community, and as the prevailing view changes in that community, it affects the output of the intelligence directorate.[22]

In particular, CIA analysts are sometimes viewed as being predisposed to provide intelligence support for the preferences of the arms control community. According to Schlesinger:

> For many years it was said, for example, that the Air Force had an institutional bias to raise the level of the Soviet threat, and one can argue that in many cases that it did and that was a consequence.

---

[19] According to Huizenga:
"It should be recognized that the approach of an operating department to intelligence issues is not invariably disinterested. The Department of State sometimes has an interest in having intelligence take a certain view of a situation because it has a heavy investment in an ongoing line of policy, or because the Secretary has put himself on record as to how to think about a particular problem. In the Defense Department, intelligence is often seen as the servant of desired policies and programs. At a minimum there is a strong organizational interest in seeing to it that the intelligence provides a vigorous appraisal of potential threats. It is not unfair to say that because of the military leadership's understandable desire to hedge against the unexpected, to provide capabilities for all conceivable contingencies there is a natural thrust in military intelligence to maximize threats and to oversimplify the intentions of potential adversaries. It is also quite naturally true that military professionals tend to see military power as the prime determinant of the behavior of states and of the movement of events in international politics." (Huizenga, 1/26/76, pp. 11–12.)

[20] *Ibid.*, p. 11.

[21] *Ibid.*, p. 12.

[22] Schlesinger, 2/2/76, pp. 24–25.

But there developed an institutional bias amongst the analytic fraternity which ran in the opposite direction. There was an assumption that the Soviets had the same kind of arms control objectives that they wished to ascribe or persuade American leaders to adopt, and as a result there was a steady upswing of Soviet strategic capabilities, and the most serious problem, it seems to me, or the most amusing problem developed at the close of the cycle when the Soviets had actually deployed more than 1,000 ICBMs, and the NIEs, as I recall it, were still saying that they would deploy no more than 1,000 ICBMs because of the prevailing belief in the intelligence analytic fraternity that the Soviets would level off at 1,000 just as we had.

So one must be careful to balance what I will call the academic biases amongst the analysts with the operational biases amongst other elements of the intelligence community.[23]

Consequently, on the occasions when the DCI does support his own staff's recommendations over the objection of the other departments, the objectivity of the national intelligence product may still be undermined by the bias of CIA analysts.

Recognizing all these difficulties, the Select Committee has investigated two particularly difficult cases for Director Helms in an effort to illustrate the problems the DCI confronts in carrying out his responsibility to produce objective and independent national intelligence.

During the summer and fall of 1969, the White House and then the Secretary of Defense indirectly pressured the DCI to modify his judgments on the capability of the new Soviet SS–9 strategic missile system. The issues under debate were: (1) whether the SS–9 was a MIRV (Multiple Independently Targeted Re-entry Vehicle) missile; and (2) whether the Soviets were seeking to achieve a first strike capability. The intelligence judgments on these points would be critical in decisions as to whether the United States would deploy its own MIRV missiles or try to negotiate MIRV limitations in SALT (the Strategic Arms Limitation Talks), and whether the United States would deploy an Anti-Ballistic Missile (ABM) system to protect the United States Minuteman missile force against a Soviet first strike.

On the first issue, in June 1969, the President's Special Adviser for National Security Affairs, Henry Kissinger, called Director Helms to the White House to discuss an estimate on Soviet strategic forces. Kissinger and the NSC staff made clear their view that the new Soviet missile was a MIRV and asked that Helm's draft be rewritten to provide more evidence supporting the DCI's judgment that the SS–9 had *not* demonstrated a MIRV capability. In response, the Chairman of the Board of National Estimates rewrote the draft, but he did not change

---

[23] Schlesinger, 2/2/76, pp. 26–27. CIA analysts are also sometimes accused of being biased in favor of the clandestine intelligence collected by their own agency. This charge is not, however, supported by a CIA study of what kinds of reporting CIA analysts themselves find KEY in writing their intelligence memoranda. For FY 1974, while CIA analysts considered clandestine reporting to be important, overt State Department reporting on political and economic subjects was cited more frequently as KEY. (*Annual DDI Survey, FY 1974.*)

the conclusion: All seven tests of the SS–9 were MRVs (Multiple Reentry Vehicles); they were certainly not independently guided after separation from the launch vehicle.[24] According to testimony by three Board members, at the time they saw nothing improper in a White House request to redraft the estimate to include more evidence. However, in this case, they interpreted the White House request as a subtle and indirect effort to alter the DCI's national intelligence judgment.[25]

On the second issue, three months later, Helms decided to delete a paragraph in the Board of National Estimates' draft on Soviet strategic forces after an assistant to Secretary of Defense Laird informed Helms that the statement contradicted the public position of the Secretary.[26]

The deleted paragraph read:

> We believe that the Soviets recognize the enormous difficulties of any attempt to achieve strategic superiority of such order as to significantly alter the strategic balance. Consequently, we consider it highly unlikely that they will attempt within the period of this estimate to achieve a first-strike capability, i.e., a capability to launch a surprise attack against the U.S. with assurance that the USSR would not itself receive damage it would regard as unacceptable. For one thing, the Soviets would almost certainly conclude that the cost of such an undertaking along with all their other military commitments would be prohibitive. More important, they almost certainly would consider it impossible to develop and deploy the combination of offensive and defensive forces necessary to counter successfully the various elements of U.S. strategic attack forces. Finally, even if such a project were economically and technically feasible the Soviets almost certainly would calculate that the U.S. would detect and match or overmatch their efforts.[27]

Subsequently, the State Department representative on the United States Intelligence Board inserted the deleted paragraph as a footnote.

---

[24] In a memorandum to the USIB representatives, dated 6/16/69, the Director of the Office of National Estimates, Abbot Smith, stated:

"The Memorandum to Holders of NIE 11–8–68, approved by USIB on 12 June was discussed at a meeting with Dr. Kissinger and others on Saturday. Out of this meeting came requests for (a) some reordering of the paper; (b) clarification of some points; and (c) additional argument pro and con about the MRV–MIRV problem. We have accordingly redrafted the paper with these requests in mind. No changes in estimates were asked, nor (we think) have been made. But the details call for coordination."

See also, staff summary of Carl Duckett interview, 6/13/75.

[25] Staff summaries of interviews with John Huizenga, 7/9/75; Abbot Smith, 8/2/75; Williard Mathias, 7/7/75.

[26] Memorandum from Director Helms to USIB Members, 9/4/69, and staff summary of Abbot Smith interview, 8/2/75.

According to William Baroody, Secretary Laird's Special Assistant:

"I am fairly confident that I did not specifically bring pressures to bear on the Director of Central Intelligence to delete or change any particular paragraph. We did discuss the differences at the time between, as these documents refresh my memory, between the DIA concern of that particular paragraph and the CIA estimate." (William Baroody testimony, 2/27/76, p. 4.)

[27] Draft NIE 11–8–69, approved by the Board of National Estimates prior to the USIB meeting on August 28, 1969.

These are stark, and perhaps exceptional, examples of White House and Defense Department pressures on the DCI, but they illustrate the kinds of buffeting with which the DCI must contend. Director Helms testified:

> A national intelligence estimate, at least when I was Director, was considered to be the Director's piece of paper. USIB contributed to the process but anybody could contribute to the process, the estimates staff, individuals in the White House. And the fact that a paragraph or a sentence was changed or amended after USIB consideration was not extraordinary. . . .
>
> So this question which seems to have come up about somebody influencing one aspect or influencing another aspect of it, the whole process was one of influences back and forth, some in favor of this and some in favor of that. . . .
>
> So that was the system then. I don't know what is the system now, but on this issue of the first strike capability one of the things that occurred in connection with that was a battle royale over whether it was the Agency's job to decide definitively whether the Soviet Union had its first strike capability or did not have a first strike capability. And this became so contentious that it seemed almost impossible to get it resolved.
>
> I have forgotten just exactly what I decided to do about the whole thing, but I don't know, I think it was back in '69. There was a question about certain footprints and MRVs and things of this kind, and some people felt that they were very important footprints and other people thought they were unimportant footprints, and there's no question there's a battle royale about it.
>
> However, it was resolved however. If you felt that there was pressure to eliminate one thing, there was a manifold pressure to put in something else.
>
> But anyway, I don't really see an issue here.[28]

While Helms may not see an issue here, the Committee found that constant tension exists between the DCI, whose responsibility it is to produce independent and objective national intelligence, and the agencies, who are required to cooperate in this effort.

A second case investigated by the Select Committee illustrates the potential problems the DCI confronts in producing relevant national intelligence for senior policymakers planning highly sensitive military operations. In April 1970, following Prince Sihanouk's ouster, United States policymakers decided to initiate a military incursion into Cambodia to destroy North Vietnamese sanctuaries. In making this decision, these policymakers had to rely on an earlier (February) NIE and current reporting from the various departments and agencies. They never received a formal DCI national intelligence estimate or memorandum on the political conditions inside Cambodia after Sihanouk's departure or on the possible consequences of such an American incursion. Why? Because Director Helms decided in April not to send such an estimate to the NSC.

---

[28] Richard Helms testimony, 1/30/76, pp. 59–61.

In April 1970, analysts in the Office of National Estimates prepared a long memorandum entitled "Stocktaking in Indochina: Longer Term Prospects" which included discussion of the broad question of future developments in Cambodia, and addressed briefly the question of possible United States intervention: [29]

> Nevertheless, the governments of Laos and Cambodia are both fragile, and the collapse of either under Communist pressure could have a significant adverse psychological and military impact on the situation in South Vietnam. . . . Because the events in Cambodia and their impact are harder to predict, if Hanoi could be denied the use of base areas and sanctuaries in Cambodia, its strategy and objectives in South Vietnam would be endangered. Hanoi is clearly concerned over such a prospect. Cambodia, however, has no chance of being able to accomplish this by itself; to deny base areas and sanctuaries in Cambodia would require heavy and sustained bombing and large numbers of foot soldiers which could only be supplied by the U.S. and South Vietnam. Such an expanded allied effort could seriously handicap the Communists and raise the cost to them of prosecuting the war, but, however successful, it probably would not prevent them from continuing the struggle in some form.[30]

Helms received this draft memorandum 13 days before the planned United States incursion into Cambodia. Then the day before the incursion began, Helms decided not to send the memorandum to the White House. A handwritten note from Helms to the Chairman of the Board of National Estimates stated: "Let's take a look at this on June 1, and see if we would keep it or make certain revisions."

The Committee has been unable to pinpoint exactly why Director Helms made this decision.[31] One member of the Board of National Estimates recalled that Helms would have judged it "most counterproductive" to send such a negative assessment to the White House.[32] George Carver, Director Helms' Special Assistant for Vietnamese Affairs in 1970, objected to this conclusion that Helms refrained from sending the memorandum forward because he thought the message

---

[29] DCI Helms encouraged the analysts to prepare such a memorandum for the White House. On an early draft, Helms commented to Abbot Smith, Chairman of the Board of National Estimates: "O.K. Let's develop the paper as you suggest and do our best to coordinate it within the Agency. But in the end I want a good paper on this subject, even if I have to make the controversial judgments myself. We owe it to the policymakers I feel." (Richard Helms, 4/7/70.)

[30] "Stocktaking in Indochina: Longer Term Prospects," ONE memorandum, 4/17/70, para. 69.

[31] Helms told the Committee:
"Unfortunately my memory has become hazy about the reasons for decisions on the papers you identify. . . . In a more general way let me try to be helpful to you (I will assume that you have or will talk to [George] Carver and that you will give reasonable weight to his comments. In the first place, it is almost impossible at this late date to recreate all the relevant circumstances and considerations which went into decisions of the kind you are examining, made six years ago. Secondly, it is dangerous to examine exhaustively one bead to the exclusion of other beads in the necklace." (Telegram from Richard Helms to the Select Committee, 3/23/76.)

[32] Staff summary of James Graham interview, 2/5/76.

would be unpalatable or distressing to the White House.[33] Rather, Carver argued that Helms judged that it would not be appropriate to send forward a memorandum drafted by analysts who did not know about the planned U.S. military operation.

According to Carver's testimony, Helms was told in advance about the planned incursion under the strict condition that he could not inform other intelligence analysts, including the Chairman of the Board of National Estimates and the CIA intelligence analysts working on Indochina questions. Then because the analysts were not informed, Helms decided not to send forward their memorandum on Indochina.

According to Carver:

> He [Helms] thought that it might be unhelpful, it might indeed look a little fatuous, because the people who had prepared it and drafted it were not aware that the U.S. was on the verge of making a major move into Cambodia, hence their commentary was based on the kind of unspoken assumption that there was going to be no basic operational change in the situation, as they projected over the weeks and months immediately ahead.[34]

Further, Carver speculated that Helms probably felt he would not be listened to if it were immediately open to the counterattack that the analysts did not know of the planned operations.[34a] In effect, Carver argues that in carrying out the President's restriction on discussing the planned operations, Helms denied his analysts the very information he considered necessary for them to have to provide intelligence judgments for senior policymakers. Helms took this decision even though the memorandum in question included a *judgment* on the possible consequences of United States intervention in Cambodia.

Thus, for whatever combination of reasons, in the spring of 1970 prior to the Cambodia incursion, the DCI did not provide senior policymakers formally with a national intelligence memorandum which argued that the operation would not succeed in thwarting the North Vietnamese effort to achieve control in Indochina.

Six weeks later, while the Cambodia incursion was still underway, the State Department requested a Special NIE(SNIE) on North Vietnamese intentions which would include a section on the impact of the United States intervention in Cambodia. A draft estimate was prepared and coordinated within the intelligence community, just as the incursion was ending. The estimate began with a number of caveats such as: "Considerable difficulties exist in undertaking this analysis at this time. Operations in Cambodia are continuing and the data on results to date is, in the nature of things, incomplete and provisional." The draft went on to say that assessing Hanoi's intentions is always a difficult exercise but "even more complicated in a rapidly moving situ-

---

[33] George Carver testimony, 3/5/76, p. 30.

[34] *Ibid.*, p. 10. Carver told the Committee that his overall judgments were "based on what I am reasonably convinced is a recollection of a series of conversations, although I cannot cite to you a specific conversation or give you a Memorandum for the Record that says that." (*Ibid.*, p. 15.)

[34a] *Ibid.*, pp. 22–23.

ation, in which there are a number of unknown elements, particularly with respect to U.S. and Allied courses of action." With respect to the situation in Cambodia, the estimate concluded:

> Although careful analysis of these losses suggests that the Communist situation is by no means critical, it is necessary to retain a good deal of caution in judging the lasting impact of the Cambodian affair on the Communist position in Indochina.[35]

Despite all these qualifications, Helms again decided not to send the estimate to the White House. While Helms does not recall the reasons for his decision, he did tell the Committee:

> In my opinion there is no way to insulate the DCI from unpopularity at the hands of Presidents or policymakers if he is making assessments which run counter to administrative policy. That is a built-in hazard of the job. Sensible Presidents understand this. On the other hand they are human too, and in my experience they are not about to place their fate in the hands of any single individual or group of individuals. In sum, make the intelligence estimates, be sure they reach the President personally, and use keen judgment as to the quantity of intelligence paper to which he should be subjected. One does not want to lose one's audience, and this is easy to do if one overloads the circuit. No power has yet been found to force Presidents of the United States to pay attention on a continuing basis to people and papers when confidence has been lost in the originator.[36]

Nevertheless, as John Huizenga testified:

> In times of political stress on intelligence, there is more a question of invisible pressures that might cause people to feel that they were being leaned upon, even though nobody asked them to take out some words or add some words . . . When intelligence producers have a general feeling that they are working in a hostile climate, what really happens is not so much that they tailor the product to please, although that's not been unknown, but more likely, they avoid the treatment of difficult issues.[37]

In the end, the DCI must depend on his position as the President's principal intelligence adviser or on his personal relationship with the President to produce objective and independent national intelligence.[38] Organizational arrangements such as the Board of National Estimates may, nevertheless, help insulate the DCI from pressures; but

---

[35] Draft SNIE 14-3-70.
[36] Telegram from Richard Helms to the Select Committee, 3/23/76.
[37] Huizenga, 1/26/76, pp. 20–21.
[38] John Huizenga testified that "there were very few instances of gross interference." While "it's fair to say [the Cambodia and SS–9 cases] were gross, particularly the SS–9 case," objectivity and independence are difficult to uphold when political consensus breaks down over foreign policy issues. Huizenga concluded, "the experience of these years persuade me that we have yet to prove that we can have in times of deep political division over foreign policy a professional, independent, objective intelligence system." (Huizenga, 1/26/76, p. 9.)

only if they are used. In the cases of the SS–9 and Cambodia, Helms took the decisions without consulting with the Board collectively.

B. Coordinator of Intelligence Activities

1. The Intelligence Process

In theory, the intelligence process works as follows. The President and members of the NSC—as the major *consumers* of foreign intelligence—define what kinds of information they need. The Director of Central Intelligence with the advice of other members of the intelligence community establishes *requirements* for the collection of different kinds of intelligence. (An intelligence requirement is defined as a consumer statement of information need for which the information is not already at hand.) Resources are allocated both to develop new collection systems and to operate existing systems to fulfill the intelligence requirements. The collection agencies—the National Security Agency (NSA), CIA, DIA, and the military services—*manage* the actual collection of intelligence. Raw intelligence is then assembled by analysts in CIA, DIA, the State Department, and the military services and *produced* as finished intelligence for senior policymakers.

In practice, however, the process is much more complicated. The following discussion treats the Committee's findings regarding the means and methods the DCI has used to carry out his responsibility for coordinating intelligence community activities.

2. Managing Intelligence Collection

Although the responsibility of the DCI to coordinate the activities of the intelligence community is most general, the DCIs have tended to interpret their responsibility narrowly to avoid antagonizing the other departments and agencies in the intelligence community. While DCIs have sought to define the general intelligence needs of senior United States policymakers, they have not actually established intelligence collection requirements or chosen specific geographical targets.

The individual departments establish their own intelligence collection requirements to fulfill their perceived national and departmental needs. For example, DIA compiles the Defense Intelligence Objectives and Priorities document (DIOP) which is a single statement of intelligence requirements for use by all DOD intelligence components, in particular, Defense attaches, DIA production elements, the intelligence groups of the military services, and the military commands. The DIOP contains a listing by country of nearly 200 intelligence issues and assigns a numerical priority from one to eight to each country and topic. The State Department sends out ad hoc requests for information from United States missions abroad. Although the Department does not compile a formal requirements document, Foreign Service Officer reporting responds to the information needs of the Secretary of State.

In the absence of authority to establish intelligence requirements, the DCI relies on issuing general collection *guidance* to carry out his coordinating responsibilities. The DCI annually defines United States substantive intelligence priorities for the coming year in a DCI Directive. This sets out an elaborate matrix arraying each of 120 countries against 83 intelligence topics and assigning a numerical priority from 1 to 7 for each country and topic combination. Since 1973, the DCI has also distributed a memorandum called the DCI's "Perspectives" which defines the major intelligence problems policymakers will face over the next five years; a memorandum known as the DCI's "Objectives" which details the general resource management and substantive intelligence problems the community will face in the upcoming year; and the DCI's "Key Intelligence Questions" (KIQs) which identify topics of particular importance to national policymakers.

All these documents have in the past been reviewed by members of the intelligence community on USIB, but the DCI cannot compel the departments and agencies to respond to this guidance. For example, the Defense Intelligence Objectives and Priorities "express the spectrum of Defense intelligence objectives and priorities geared specifically to approved strategy" derived from the Joint Chiefs of Staff. But the DIOP does not include a large number of economic, political and sociological questions which the Defense Department considers inappropriate for it to cover. Consequently, Defense-controlled intelligence assets do not give priority to non-military questions even though such questions are established as priorities in the DCI's guidance.

In addition, through three intelligence collection committees of the United States Intelligence Board, DCIs have tried in the past to reconcile the different departmental requirements and to insure that the interests of the entire community are brought to bear in the intelligence collectors' operations.[39] The Committee on Imagery Requirements and Exploitation (COMIREX) dealt with photographic reconnaissance.[40] The SIGINT Committee coordinated the collection of signals and

---

[39] Under President Ford's Executive Order No. 11905, these three collection committees will probably continue under the DCI's responsibility to establish "such committees of collectors, producers, and users to assist in his conduct of his responsibilities."

[40] In 1955, Richard Bissell, a Special Assistant to the DCI, set up an informal Ad-Hoc Requirements Committee (ARC) to coordinate collection requirements for the U–2 reconnaissance program. Membership initially included representatives of CIA, the Army, Navy, and Air Force. Later representatives of NSA, the Joint Chiefs of Staff, and the State Department were added. In 1960, with the development of a new overhead reconnaissance system, the ARC was supplanted by a formal USIB Committee, the Committee on Overhead Reconnaissance or COMOR. COMOR's responsibilities included coordination of collection requirements for the development and operation of all overhead reconnaissance systems. As these programs grew and the volume of photographs increased, serious problems of duplication in imagery exploitation prompted the DCI and the Secretary of Defense to establish a special joint review group. Subsequently, it recommended the establishment of the National Photographic Interpretation Center (NPIC) and the creation of a new USIB Committee to coordinate both collection and exploitation of national photographic intelligence. In 1967, COMIREX was established.

communications intelligence.⁴¹ The Human Resources Committee dealt with overt and clandestine human collection.⁴²

In the collection of overhead photography and signals intelligence, the DCI through the COMIREX and SIGINT Committees provides guidance as to targets and amounts of coverage. These Committees also administer a complex accounting system designed to evaluate how well, in technical terms, the specific missions have fulfilled the various national and departmental requirements. Because of the nature of overhead collection, the whole community can participate in selecting the targets and in evaluating its success. The operating agency is responsive solely to requirements and priorities established by the USIB committees. At the same time, the DCI *alone* cannot direct which photographs to take or when to alter the scope of coverage. The role of the DCI is to make sure that the preferences of the entire community are taken into account when targets are chosen.

For example, prior to the Middle East war in 1973, the USIB SIGINT committee recommended that the Middle East be a priority target for intelligence collection if hostilities broke out, and asked NSA to evaluate the intelligence collected and to determine appropriate targets. When the war broke out, NSA implemented this USIB guidance. Later in the week, the same committee discussed and approved DIA's recommendation to change the primary target of one collector. The DCI did not order the changes or direct what intelligence to collect, but through the USIB mechanism he insured that the community agreed to the retargeting of the system.

The DCI has been less successful in involving the entire intelligence community in establishing collection guidance for NSA operations or for the clandestine operations of CIA's Directorate of Operations. These collection managers have substantial latitude in choosing which activities to pursue; and the DCI has not yet established a mechanism to monitor how well these collectors are fulfilling the DCI's community guidance.

During 1975, USIB approved a new National SIGINT Requirements System, an essential feature of which requires USIB to initiate a

---

⁴¹ During World War II, the military services controlled all communications intelligence. After the war, a U.S. Communications Intelligence Board (USCIB) was established to coordinate COMINT activities for the NSC and to advise the DCI on COMINT issues. However, in 1949 the Secretary of Defense set up a separate COMINT board under the Joint Chiefs of Staff to oversee the military's COMINT activities, and this arrangement stood for three years, despite the DCI's objections. In 1952, NSA was established with operational control over COMINT resources and the Secretary of Defense was given executive authority over all COMINT activities. At the same time, the USCIB was reconstituted under the chairmanship of the DCI to advise the Director of NSA and the Secretary of Defense. In 1958, the USCIB was merged with the Intelligence Advisory Committee to form the United States Intelligence Board. The COMINT Committee of the USIB was formed soon thereafter; this became the SIGINT Committee in 1962 when its responsibilities were extended to include ELINT.

⁴² General Bennett, Director of the Defense Intelligence Agency, proposed in 1970 the establishment of a USIB subcommittee to provide a national-level forum to coordinate the various human source collection programs, both overt and clandestine. Following objections from the CIA's Directorate of Operations, Director Helms decided instead to establish an ad hoc task force to study the whole range of HUMINT problems. After a year's study, the task force recommended the establishment of a USIB committee on a one-year trial basis. The President's Foreign Intelligence Advisory Board (PFIAB), in a separate study, also endorsed the idea. Subsequently, the Human Sources Committee was accorded permanent status in June 1974 and in 1975 its name was changed to the Human Resources Committee.

formal community review and approval of *all* SIGINT requirements. In addition, each requirement must contain a cross reference to pertinent DCI priorities and specific KIQs. However, this system does not vest in the DCI operational authority over NSA and its collection systems.[43] The Director of NSA will still determine which specific communications to monitor and which signals to intercept. In a crisis, the Secretaries of State and Defense and the military commanders will continue to be able to task NSA directly and inform the DCI and the SIGINT Committee afterwards.

In contrast to technical intelligence collection where the DCI has sought expanded community involvement in defining requirements, DCIs have not been very receptive to Defense Department interests in reviewing CIA's clandestine intelligence collection. In part, the DCIs have recognized the difficulty of viewing human collection as a whole, since it comprises many disparate kinds of collectors, some of which are not even part of the intelligence community. For example, Foreign Service Officers do not view themselves as intelligence collectors, despite the large and valuable contribution FSO reporting makes to the overall national human intelligence effort. In addition, the CIA's Clandestine Service (DDO) has lobbied against a USIB Human Sources Committee, fearing that it would compromise the secrecy of their very sensitive operations.[44]

So DCIs, as Directors of the agency responsible for collecting intelligence clandestinely, resisted establishment of a permanent USIB committee to review human collection until 1974.[45] When established, the Committee was specifically not given responsibility for reviewing the operational details or internal management of the individual departments or agencies. In the case of "sensitive" information, departments and agencies were authorized to withhold information from the Committee and report directly to the DCI.

It is not surprising, therefore, that the Human Resources Committee has only just begun to expand community influence over human collection. The Committee issues a general guidance document called the Current Intelligence Reporting List (CIRL). Although the military makes some use of this document, the DDO instructs CIA Stations that the CIRL is provided only for reference and does not constitute collection requirements for CIA operations. The Human

---

[43] William Colby testified before the Committee:
"I think it is clear I do not have command authority over the [NSA]. That is not my authority. On the other hand, the National Security Council Intelligence Directives do say that I do have the job of telling them what these priorities are and what the subjects they should be working on are." (William Colby testimony, 9/29/75, pp. 20–21.)

[44] The DCI currently exercises some control over military clandestine operations. The Chief of Station in each country is the DCI's "designated representative" and has responsibility for coordinating all military clandestine operations. In the past, the DDO has only objected if the projects were not worth the risk or duplicated a DDO operation. The Chief of Station rarely undertook to evaluate whether the military operations could be done openly or would be successful.

[45] While the DCI has final responsibility for the clandestine collection of intelligence, he still faces problems in coordinating the clandestine and technical collection programs in his own agency. Illustrative of this is the recent establishment of a National Intelligence Officer (NIO) for Special Activities to help the DCI focus DDO operations on three or four central intelligence gaps. Director Colby determined that only through a special assistant could he break down the separate cultures of DDO and technical intelligence collection and the barriers between the intelligence analysts and DDO.

Resources Committee has initiated community-wide assessments of human source reporting in individual countries which emphasize the ambassador's key role in coordinating human collection activities in the field. But the Committee has not defined a national system for establishing formal collection requirements for the various human intelligence agencies.

In summary, the DCI does not have authority to manage any collection programs outside his own agency. The DCI only issues general guidance. The departments establish their own intelligence collection requirements and the collection managers (NSA, DIA, CIA, and the military services) retain responsibility for determining precisely which intelligence targets should be covered. President Ford's Executive Order does not change the DCI role in the management of intelligence collection activities.

3. Allocating Intelligence Resources

In a 1971 directive, President Nixon asked Director Helms to plan and review all intelligence activities including tactical intelligence and the allocation of all resources to rationalize intelligence priorities within budgetary constraints.[46] Since 1971, the DCI has prepared recommendations to the President for a consolidated national intelligence program budget. Director Helms, in his first budget recommendations, proposed a lid on intelligence spending, noting that "we should rely on cross-program adjustments to assure that national interests are adequately funded." [47] However, prior to President Ford's Executive Order, the DCI has had no way to insure authoritatively that such objectives were realized.

The DCI has independent budget authority over *only* his own agency which represents only a small percentage of the overall national intelligence budget. As chairman of an Executive Committee or ExCom for special reconnaissance activities, the DCI has been involved in the preparation of the program budget for the development and management of the major United States technical collection systems. However, differences of opinion between the DCI and the other member of the ExCom, the Assistant Secretary of Defense for Intelligence, were referred to the Secretary of Defense for resolution. The Secretary of Defense in his budget allocated the remaining intelligence community resources.

The DCI's role in the Defense intelligence budget process was in effect that of an adviser. The DCI's "Perspectives," which analyze the political, economic, and military environment over the next five years, have had little impact on the formulation of Defense intelligence resource requirements. According to John Clarke, former Asso-

---

[46] "Announcement Outlining Management Steps for Improving the Effectiveness of the Intelligence Community," November 5, 1971, 7 Pres. Docs. p. 1482. Nixon sought to enhance the role of the DCI as community leader and to give the DCI responsibility to coordinate Defense Department technical collection operations with other intelligence programs. Nixon's directive followed a comprehensive study of the intelligence community by the Office of Management and Budget (known as the Schlesinger Report) which recommended a fundamental reform in the intelligence community's decisionmaking bodies and procedures.

[47] Director of Central Intelligence, *National Intelligence Program Memorandum, FY 1974*, p. 44.

ciate Deputy to the Director of Central Intelligence for the Intelligence Community, the "Perspectives" "did not have any great bearing on the formal guidances that the different departments having intelligence elements used in deciding how much they needed or how many dollars they required for future years." [48] The military services and DIA responded to the fiscal guidance issued by the Secretary of Defense.

The DCI's small staff of seven professionals in the Resource Review Office of the Intelligence Community Staff kept a low profile and spent most of its time gathering information on the various Defense intelligence activities. They did not provide an independent assessment of the various programs for the DCI. Consequently, the DCI rarely had sufficient knowledge or confidence to challenge a Defense Department recommendation. When the DCI did object, he generally focused on programs where he thought the Defense Department was not giving adequate priority to intelligence activities in which the President had a particular interest.

For example, partly as a result of the intense concern by the NSC staff, the DCI expended substantial effort to insure that two Air Force ships, initially built to operate on the Atlantic missile range monitoring Cape Canaveral firings, continued to be available to monitor foreign missile activities. When in 1970–1971, the number of United States missile tests decreased substantially, the Air Force proposed that both ships be retired. The DCI, in turn, requested an intelligence community study which concluded that the ships were essential for foreign intelligence purposes. Consequently, the DCI brokered an arrangement for a sharing of the ships' cost within the Department of Defense. Today, a little under 20 percent of the ship program is devoted to intelligence needs. The DCI had neither the authority to direct the retention of these Air Force ships nor sufficient resources to take over their funding for intelligence purposes to insure that they were not retired. Nevertheless, the DCI played a definite role in working out an arrangement whereby at least one ship will be available until the national intelligence requirement can be met by another means. [49]

In practice, the DCI only watched over the shoulder of the Assistant Secretary of Defense for Intelligence as he reviewed the budget requests of DIA, NSA, and the military services. If the DCI wished to raise a particular issue, he had a number of possible forums. He could set up an ad hoc interagency study group or discuss the question in the Intelligence Resources Advisory Committee (IRAC). [50] He could highlight resource issues in the annual fall joint OMB-Defense Department review of the Defense budget or in his December letter to the President presenting the consolidated national intelligence budget. However, the groups were only advisory to the DCI and had no authority over the Secretary of Defense. The joint review and the

[48] John Clarke testimony, 2/5/76, pp. 15–16.
[49] According to Carl Duckett, the CIA's Deputy Director of Science and Technology, "frankly we had to fight very hard the last two years to keep the ships active at all." (Carl Duckett testimony, 11/10/75, pp. 106–107.)
[50] IRAC was established in 1971 to advise the DCI in preparing a consolidated intelligence program budget for the President. Members included representatives from the Departments of State and Defense, OMB, and the CIA. IRAC was abolished by President Ford's Executive Order of 2/18/76.

DCI's letter to the President occurred so late in the Defense Department budget cycle that the DCI had little opportunity to effect any significant changes.

Thus, the DCI's national budget recommendations were for the most part the aggregate figures proposed by the various Defense agencies. The DCI did not provide an independent calculated evaluation of the entire national intelligence budget. The DCI did not present the President with broad alternative options for the allocation of national intelligence resources. The DCI was not able to effect trade-offs among the different intelligence programs or to reconcile differences over priorities. Finally, the President's decisions on the intelligence budget levels were not based upon the recommendations of the DCI, but rather upon Defense Department totals. According to John Clarke:

> I would have to submit that in my judgment I do not think the Presidents have used the Director's recommendations with respect to the intelligence budgets. There have been few exceptions where they have solidified behind the Director's appeal, but fundamentally he has looked to the Secretary of Defense to decide what level of intelligence activities there should be in the defense budget.[51]

Because the Secretary of Defense had final authority to allocate most of the intelligence budget, the DCI either had to "persuade" the Secretary to allocate Defense intelligence resources according to the Director's recommendations or take his case directly to the President. According to James Schlesinger:

> . . . the authority of whoever occupies this post, whatever it is called comes from the President. . . . To the extent that it is believed that he has the President's ear, he will find that the agencies or departments will be responsive, and if it is believed that he does not have the President's ear, they will be unresponsive.[52]

But because the DCI must expend substantial political capital in taking a Defense budget issue to the President, he rarely has sought Presidential resolution. Over the past five years, the DCI went directly to the President only twice. Both these issues involved expensive technical collection systems, and both times the DCI prevailed.

In summary, DCIs have not been able to define priorities for the allocation of intelligence resources—either among the different systems of intelligence collection or among intelligence collection, analysis, and finished intelligence. Without authority to allocate intelligence budget resources, DCIs have been unable to insure that unwarranted duplication and waste are avoided.

4. Key Intelligence Questions

As described above, DCIs have confronted major problems in seeking to carry out their coordinating responsibilities under the 1947 National Security Act. They have not had authority to establish requirements for the collection or production of national intelligence. They have not been able to institute an effective means to evaluate how well the community is carrying out their guidance. They have not had a mechanism to direct the allocation of intelligence resources to insure that the intelligence needs of national policymakers are met.

---

[51] Clarke, 2/5/76, p. 27.
[52] Schlesinger, 2/2/76, pp. 43, 45.

To help solve these problems, Director Colby instituted a new intelligence management system known as the Key Intelligence Questions (KIQs). Through formation of a limited number of KIQs, Colby tried to focus collection and production efforts on critical policymaker needs and to provide a basis for reallocating resources toward priority issues.[53] This section will briefly highlight the resistance which Colby's new management scheme provoked and the difficulties experienced in evaluating the overall community efforts.

The KIQ scheme had four stages. First the DCI issued the KIQs. Then the National Intelligence Officers (NIOs) with representatives from the various collection and production agencies developed a strategy to answer the individual KIQs. After surveying what information was currently available to answer the KIQs, the various agencies made commitments to collect and produce intelligence reports "against" the various KIQs. At the end of the year, the DCI evaluated the intelligence community's performance.

The KIQ management process has finished its first full year of operation and a beginning has been made to provide intelligence consumers with the opportunity to make known their priorities for intelligence collection and production. Collection managers have been brought together in developing a strategy to answer key questions and analysts have received guidance as to the kinds of reports they should produce. In addition, the DCI now has before him considerable information about how the intelligence community is focusing on intelligence questions which are important to senior national policymakers. He should be in a better position to show collection and production managers where they have failed to meet their commitments to work against individual KIQs or to spend a high percentage of their resources on KIQ-related activities.

However, while the KIQ concept is imaginative, the management tool has encountered serious problems. First, the KIQ system does not solve the DCI's problem of trying to establish priorities in intelligence collection and production. Few topics are not included under one KIQ or another. The KIQs have not yet been meshed with the existing requirements system. While the KIQs are supposed to establish collection and production requirements in lieu of the DCI's Directive on priorities, both continue to exist today. The Defense Department has not only continued to issue the DIOP but has produced its own Defense Key Intelligence Questions (DKIQs) which number over 1,000. Instead of providing a means for the DCI to establish priorities for the intelligence community, the KIQs to date have added another layer of requirements.

Second, Colby's management scheme has met strong resistance from the collection and the production agencies. After one year it is difficult to identify many intelligence activities that have changed because of the KIQs. The KIQ Strategy Reports were issued nine months after the KIQs and tended to list collection and production activities already under way. The DCI was not in a position to direct

---

[53] In FY 1975, there were 69 KIQs, drafted by the DCI's National Intelligence Officers in consultation with the NSC Intelligence Committee working group. Approximately one-third of the KIQs dealt with Soviet foreign policy motivations and military technology. The other KIQs dealt with such issues as the negotiating position of the Arabs and Israelis, the terrorist threat, etc.

the various members of the intelligence community to undertake commitments for different collection efforts, and the Strategy Reports rarely contained new commitments.

While all agencies participated, DIA and DDO have responded to the KIQs only insofar as they were consistent with their respective internal collection objectives. DIA's "KIQ Collection Performance Report" pointed out that "the Defense Attaché system primarily responds to the DKIQs and JSOP [Joint Strategic Objectives Plan] objectives and therefore, responses to KIQs will have to maintain consistency with the two aforementioned collection guidance vehicles." [54] In fact, DIA writes its "Intelligence Collection Requests" and "Continuing Intelligence Requirements," and they are then keyed back to the relevant KIQs, somewhat as an afterthought. [55]

The Deputy Director of Operations for the CIA issues his "Objectives" for the collection of clandestine human intelligence. While these are derived from the KIQs, these "Objectives" are in fact the collection requirements of the Clandestine Service. Since it takes so long to recruit agents, DDO considers it is not in a position to respond to specific KIQs dealing with near-term intelligence gaps unless a source is already in place. Moreover, DDO determined not to deflect or divert its effort to satisfy KIQs unless the questions happened to fall within DDO internal objectives.

DIA and DDO invoked the KIQs to justify their operations and budgets, however they did not appear to be shaping the programs to meet KIQ objectives. Without authority to direct resources to answer the specific Key Intelligence Questions, the DCI had little success in compelling the major collectors and producers of intelligence to respond to the KIQs, if they were unwilling. Only NSA has made a serious effort to insure that their collection requirements are responsive to the KIQs. In USIB meetings, NSA Director General Allen argued that the KIQs should be viewed as requirements for the intelligence community and the KIQ Strategy Reports should provide more detailed instructions to field elements for collection. [56]

Colby's new management scheme also failed to establish a workable evaluation process. NIOs provided subjective judgments as to how well the community had answered each KIQ and an assessment of the relative contribution of each agency. Although NIOs discussed their assessments with consumers, they had no staff to conduct a systematic and independent review of how well the community had answered the questions. Furthermore, NIOs did not base their evaluations on any specific kinds of information, such as all production reports or all raw intelligence collected on a particular KIQ. They commented on how well the agencies had carried out their commitments in the Strategy Reports without asking the collectors for any information about what activities they undertook or what amount of money had been spent. They merely took the collector's word that something had or had not

---

[54] DIA, "KIQ Collection Performance Report," 8/18/75.

[55] In FY 1975, only 7 percent of DIA's attaché reports responded to KIQs. Out of 2,111 attaché reports against the KIQs only 34 of the 69 were covered. According to DIA, military attachés have access to particular types of information and it would be unfair to assume they had the capability to respond to all the KIQs.

[56] Minutes of USIB meeting, 2/6/75. Approximately 70 percent of NSA's requirements for FY 1975 were KIQ-related, and about 50 percent of its operations and maintenance budget could be ascribed to the KIQs.

been done. Finally, they did not develop a method to insure that the judgments of the individual NIOs were consistent with each other.

In addition, the IC Staff aggregated the amount of resources expended by the various collection and production managers in answering each KIQ and determined what problems had been encountered. However, collection and production managers prepared cost estimates of the activities expended against individual KIQs according to an imprecisely defined process. And although the IC Staff provided guidance as to how to do the calculations, the decisions as to how best to estimate costs were left to the individual agencies. Not surprisingly, the agencies employed different methods.[57] Consequently, the cost estimates were not comparable across agencies, and the IC Staff had no way of making them comparable, since they could not change the different accounting systems in the various intelligence agencies.[58]

In summary, the evaluation process did not permit a comparison of total efforts and results against the KIQs on a community-wide basis. Colby lacked the necessary tools to use the KIQ management system to effect resource allocation decisions. The DCI at best was in a position to shame recalcitrants into action by pointing up stark failures in a particular agency's efforts against the KIQs. The KIQ process was only a surrogate for DCI authority to allocate the intelligence resources of the community.

Colby's frustrations in trying to direct intelligence community efforts via the KIQ process are indicative of the DCI's limited authority. Within the present intelligence structure, an effort to get the DDO and DIA to respond to what the DCI has defined as key policymaker intelligence questions met considerable resistance. Thus, the most important issue raised by the KIQ management experience is not how to refine the process but whether the DCI can really succeed in directing collection and production activities in the intelligence community toward critical policymaker needs without greater authority over the allocation of resources.

5. President Ford's Executive Order

On February 18, 1976, President Ford announced a reorganization of the intelligence community to "establish policies to improve the quality of intelligence needed for national security, to clarify the authority and responsibilities of the intelligence departments and agencies. . . ." The major change introduced by the President is the formation of the Committee on Foreign Intelligence (CFI) chaired by the DCI and reporting directly to the NSC. The CFI will have responsibility to: (1) "control budget preparation and resource allocation for the National Foreign Intelligence Program;" (2) "establish policy priorities for the collection and production of national intelligence;" (3) "establish policy for the management of the Na-

N12

[57] For example, DIA begins with the assumption that 60 percent of the Defense attaché budget goes for collection. This figure is then multiplied by the percentage of attaché reports which responded to KIQs and the total cost expended against the KIQs was calculated to be $1.3 million. In contrast, DDO calculates cost according to the IC Staff's recommended formula, which estimates the number of manhours devoted against the KIQs and multiplies the estimate by an average production manhour cost.

[58] In addition, while the State Department provides cost estimates of INR's intelligence production costs, it did not submit collection cost statistics, maintaining that Foreign Service reports were not intelligence collection. So the evaluation process did not provide a complete picture of intelligence collection on individual KIQs.

tional Foreign Intelligence Program;" and (4) "provide guidance on the relationship between tactical and national intelligence." [59]

It is still too soon to pass judgment as to whether the Executive Order will aid the DCI in his efforts to coordinate the activities of the intelligence community. By making the DCI chairman of the CFI, the Executive Order appears to enhance the stature of the DCI by expanding his role in the allocation of national intelligence resources. But, as in the case of the Nixon directive in 1971, the DCI appears to have been given an expanded set of responsibilities without a real reduction in the authority of other members of the intelligence community over their own operations. There exist many ambiguities in the language of the Executive Order particularly with regard to the role of the CFI.

The CFI is given responsibility to "control budget preparation and resource allocation" for national intelligence programs, but the Secretary of Defense retains responsibility to "direct, fund, and operate NSA." The CFI is asked to "review and amend" the budget prior to submission to OMB, as if the CFI will not control the preparation of the budget but rather would become involved only after the agencies and departments independently put together their own budget. Finally, the relationship is not clear between the DCI's responsibility to "ensure the development and submission of a budget" and the CFI's responsibility to "control budget preparation."

Moreover, the specific prohibition against DCI and CFI responsibility for tactical intelligence appears to be a step backward from the 1971 Nixon directive which asked the DCI to plan and review the allocation of *all* intelligence resources. While DCIs since 1971 have not become deeply involved in such tactical intelligence questions, they have reserved the right to become involved; and on several occasions they have supported efforts to transfer money from the national Defense Department intelligence budget to the budgets of the military services, or vice versa. There are, in addition, at least theoretical trade-offs to be made between tactical and national intelligence, especially since the dividing mark between all intelligence operations has become increasingly blurred with the development of large and expensive technical collection systems.

C. Director of the CIA

At the same time the DCI has responsibility for coordinating the activities of the entire community, he also has direct authority over the intelligence operations of the CIA. As Director, the DCI runs covert operations and manages the collection of clandestine human intelligence (Directorate of Operations); manages the collection of signals intelligence abroad and allocates resources for the development and operation of certain technical collection systems (Directorate of Science and Technology); and produces current intelligence and finished intelligence memoranda (Directorate of Intelligence).

The fact that the DCIs have also directed the operations of the CIA has had a variety of consequences. First, DCIs have tended to focus most of their attention on CIA operations. The first Directors were preoccupied with organizing and establishing CIA and with

N13

---

[59] Executive Order No. 11905. Other members of the CFI will be the Deputy Secretary of Defense for Intelligence and the Deputy Assistant to the President for National Security Affairs.

defining the Agency's role in relation to the other intelligence organizations. While Allen Dulles and Richard Helms were DCI, each spent considerable time running covert operations. John McCone focused on improving the CIA's intelligence product and developing new technical collection systems when he was Director. Admiral Raborn emphasized refining the Agency's budgetary procedures.[60]

Second, by having their own capabilities to collect and produce intelligence, DCIs have been able to assert their influence over the intelligence activities of the other members of the intelligence community. John Clarke, former Associate Deputy to the DCI for the Intelligence Community, testified that Helms·objected to the suggestion that CIA get rid of all its SIGINT activities because he needed "something to keep [his] foot in the door" so he could "look at the bigger problem." [61] According to Clarke:

> . . . to some degree historically, the Director's involvement has not only been based upon good, healthy competition among systems, which I think is good, but the directors have seen it as an opportunity to give them a voice at the table in judgments which have importance to their higher role, a larger role as Director of CI.[62]

However, this ability to assert influence in turn has had another consequence: DCIs have been accused of not being able to play an objective role as community leader while they have responsibility for directing one of the community's intelligence agencies. Potential conflict exists in decisions with respect to every CIA activity. For example, on each of the two occasions that the DCI went directly to the President to object to a Defense Department budget recommendation, the DCI won Presidential support for a CIA-developed technical collection system. Such DCI advocacy raises the fundamental question of whether the DCI can indeed be an objective community leader if he is also Director of the CIA which undertakes research and development on technical collection systems. According to James Schlesinger:

> There has always been concern and frequently there has been the reality that the DCI does not overlook all these assets in a balanced way . . . as long as the DCI has special responsibility for the management of clandestine activities, that it tends to affect and to some extent contaminate his ability to be a spokesman of the community as a whole involving intelligence operations which are regarded as reasonably innocent from the purview of American life.
>
> Components of the intelligence community other than the CIA have feared that the DCI would be tempted to expand the authority of the CIA in the collection activities relative to the other components of the intelligence community. And there has been some evidence that supports such suspicion. . . .
>
> What I believe is at the present time you have got inconsistent expectations of the DCI. He's supposed to be the fair judge amongst the elements of the intelligence community at the same time that CIA personnel expect him to be a special advocate for the CIA. You cannot have both roles.[63]

---

[60] Colby, 12/11/75, pp. 4–5.
[61] Clarke, 2/5/76, p. 59.
[62] *Ibid.*, pp. 59–60.
[63] Schlesinger, 2/2/76, pp. 8, 49.

President Ford's Executive Order seeks in part to reduce the conflict of interest problem by establishing two Deputies to the DCI, one for intelligence community affairs and one for CIA operations. The DCI and his Deputy for community affairs will have offices in downtown Washington. Nevertheless, the DCI will continue to have an office at CIA headquarters and to have legal responsibility for the operations of the Agency and at the same time general responsibility for coordinating the activities of the entire intelligence community.

THE POLICY CONTEXT ([90], pp. 8–20)

INTRODUCTION

The structure of the United States intelligence community as it was established in the 1940s and as it has evolved since then reflects the efforts of American political leaders to create institutions and procedures which would make available to the policy makers the information necessary for the successful conduct of foreign policy. There have been some important changes in the focus, organization, and methods of the system. However, it retains the *basic* characteristics that it acquired when it was set up, as its basic functions have not changed. In short, it has been a stable system, but not a rigid or inflexible one.

Briefly, the responsibilities of the United States intelligence community are threefold: (1) to collect, evaluate, and disseminate information on the world outside the U.S. from all types of sources ranging from facts in the public domain and reports of U.S. officials stationed abroad through those obtained by secret agents and by sophisticated technological methods; (2) to prepare studies analyzing events and trends around the world that have a bearing on U.S. security and welfare, and to convey the findings to the policy makers; and (3) to conduct covert action in support of policy decisions when so directed by appropriate U.S. officials. The first two responsibilities are inherent in the nature of an intelligence system. One can conceive of a system that has no covert action capability, although major powers have seldom been willing to forego such methods entirely.

INTELLIGENCE IN A CHANGING ENVIRONMENT

Such a textbook description of a system's basic functions tells little about its operations. The particular missions assigned and methods used depend heavily upon a country's concept of its national interests, the dangers it perceives, and the domestic values of the society. The United States intelligence community is very much a product of American experiences during the Second World War and the early years of the Cold War.[1] The trauma of Pearl Harbor, the harsh struggle with the Axis, and the even longer (though less violent) struggle with the Soviets and the Chinese have all left their mark on

---

[1] The intelligence community is composed of the Central Intelligence Agency (CIA); the Department of State's Bureau of Intelligence Research (INR); the Pentagon's Defense Intelligence Agency (DIA); the National Security Agency (NSA) which is responsible for communications intelligence; the intelligence components of the Army, Navy and Air Force, and the intelligence units of the Atomic Energy Commission, the Federal Bureau of Investigation and the Treasury Department.

the outlook of U.S. officials regarding intelligence. One effect has been that the system is very heavily focused upon military considerations and toward discovering and evaluating potential military threats. About 85 percent of the intelligence community's budget is spent by the Department of Defense, although much of this is expended on collecting information sought by the whole community. (Much information is also gathered by Foreign Service Officers, but such costs do not appear in any intelligence budget.)

The tasks and targets of the intelligence organizations of a major power are many and varied, and difficult decisions must be made regarding the assignment of priorities and fields of concentration. Perhaps even more difficult are decisions concerning areas and topics to be given little attention. Even within a particular field, such as military intelligence, new developments such as the scientific revolution create both new targets and new techniques. The advent of hydrogen weapons and intercontinental ballistic missiles made it of crucial importance that the U.S. government have a reasonably accurate knowledge of the capabilities of actual and potential enemies. Fortunately, the technological revolution which led to the development of such weapons also made it possible to develop means of penetrating the Soviet veil of secrecy. The U-2, other reconnaissance vehicles, and electronic intercept stations around the edges of the Communist world enabled the United States steadily to increase its knowledge of the Soviet military establishment. Organizationally, these developments were reflected in the creation of the Directorate of Science and Technology in CIA by John McCone in the early 1960s.

Intelligence organizations operate most easily when the international system is stable and their government is pursuing a clearly defined and well-articulated foreign policy. These conditions were characteristic of the period when the Cold War was at its height, but they have been less true for several years. The strength of America's principal adversaries and allies (except the United Kingdom) has increased relative to that of the United States. The U.S. remains in an essentially competitive relationship with the Soviet Union, but the policy of "détente" injects elements of cooperation into the relationship—elements which will grow if the policy is successful. This not only creates new intelligence requirements, such as monitoring arms control agreements, but also complicates the task of appraising Soviet policy. The same is true regarding China, with whom U.S. relations have shifted even more dramatically, and whose policies have fluctuated sharply in the past.

As Western Europe and Japan regained and then surpassed their prewar strength, they became less inclined to follow the United States lead in political matters. They also became serious challengers to the U.S. in the economic field. Their achievements represented a striking success for U.S. foreign policy, but foreign policy successes often create new problems in the process of solving old ones. As dependent allies become more independent allies —and competitors—the type and quantity of intelligence needed about them must be continually reexamined. Since their options are greater, it may be more important to follow closely the trends in their policies, but it may also be more important to exchange intelligence with them about Soviet and Chinese affairs so that a sufficient measure of common understanding and outlook is retained to keep the alliances from unravelling. The growing instability in the southern tier of Europe also poses old problems in a new setting.

As developments in—and U.S. attitudes toward —the heterogeneous group of countries labeled the Third World have fluctuated over the years, the tasks of intelligence organizations have shifted. When the Cold War became stalemated in Europe and East Asia in the 1950s, competition between the Communists and the West shifted to Asia and then to Africa and Latin America. There developed a belief that the Cold War would be won or lost in these weak, impoverished and struggling lands, which seemed so vulnerable to the power and appeal of a Communist movement possessed of apparent unity and dynamism. Eventually it became clear that the local governments had seized and maintained their hold on the nationalist banner, which remained the most potent emotional symbol in these lands. The view of many Americans began to veer toward the idea that nothing that happened in any of these areas could seriously affect U.S. security.

However, the growing dependence of not only Western Europe and Japan but also the U.S. on raw materials (especially petroleum) from one part or another of Asia or Africa soon complicated the picture. This posed the analytical problem of likely trends in U.S. dependence on imported oil, the uses likely to be made by the oil producers of their new wealth, and the ability of the international monetary system to deal with new pressures. The Shah of Iran, long close to the U.S., became the leader in the move by the Organization of Petroleum Exporting Countries (OPEC) to raise the price of petroleum several fold. The King of Saudi Arabia wanted prices lowered and had the productive capacity to force such moves if he were willing to take the political risks involved. Intelligence appraisals of the strengths and likely courses of action of these two men are of critical importance, as are judgments about how they would react to various U.S. courses of action.

The oil crisis of late 1973 serves to highlight a major shift in the focus of American foreign policy in recent years. This is the growing importance of international economic policy relative to the traditional security concerns that dominated U.S. foreign policy for nearly three decades after 1941. The decline of American economic predominance by the late 1960s as a result of more rapid Western European and Japanese economic growth was one factor in this change, and the growing dependence on imported raw materials added another element. These trends have not only undermined the structure and procedures of the international monetary and trading systems that made possible the great postwar economic progress, but have also raised serious questions about the likelihood of a world-wide depression and about the economic viability of the resource-poor underdeveloped nations.

These developments raise two important questions: (1) which organizations within the U.S. government have the responsibility for collecting economic information, and by what methods against which targets, and (2) where should the analysis of foreign economic developments and trends (and their meaning for the United States) be carried out? Much of the information needed for foreign economic policy is either unclassified or available from normal government reports, but some useful material may be obtainable only by agents or as a by-product of sophisticated technological collection methods. Moreover, there often is a need to share the results of economic research and analysis with other governments and international organizations in view of growing interdependence. Will they fear they are being given distorted information if it comes from the intelligence community, or would they feel the same way no matter where it originated within the U.S. government?

The addition of new tasks while many old responsibilities continue have led to growing financial pressures on the intelligence community, which was already faced with the increasing costs of sophisticated technological systems and of personnel in a period of rapid inflation. Since there was considerable overstaffing and duplication of efforts in the past, budget reductions have been possible despite increased costs. However, the easy cuts have been made, and future progress in eliminating duplication, unnecessary functions, and low priority activities will be much more difficult.

One other change in the "environment" of intelligence warrants mention. The declining intensity of the Cold War, domestic divisions over Vietnam, and revelations of CIA's subsidization of private American institutions have dramatically altered public attitudes toward intelligence activities. There remains widespread awareness among both public officials and the public at large of the importance of intelligence collection and analysis. However, there is widespread skepticism about the need for covert operations, and such events as the attack on the U.S.S. Liberty in 1967 and the capture of the Pueblo in 1968 have raised questions about the control over certain collection methods as well. Covert operations, by most accounts, occupy a much smaller role than a decade or so earlier. Nonetheless, the absence of a broad consensus on the appropriate policies and methods of U.S. foreign policy will make it difficult to maintain the secrecy of such activities, and this will increase their political costs at home and abroad.

ORGANIZATIONAL MODELS

There are three broad ways in which an intelligence system can be organized to fulfill its basic functions, whatever the nature of a country's foreign policy and the environment in which it operates. The first would involve a completely decentralized approach. Each department or agency concerned with the formulation or execution of foreign policy (in the broadest sense of the term) would have its own intelligence unit to secure the information and provide the analytical reports needed to enable the leaders of the department to fulfill their policy functions. Each department would tend to concentrate on a particular field, e.g., the Defense Department on military intelligence, and the State Department on political intelligence.

However, all would feel the need for some capability in fields outside their primary responsibility in order to serve their top officials when the latter were engaged in basic policy debates.

The disadvantages of such a system are obvious. There would be considerable duplication of efforts —especially collection efforts—which would be hideously expensive. Just as there would be considerable overlapping, there probably would be some important gaps in coverage on areas that no department regarded as important to its specific responsibilities. Information collected by one agency and needed by another might or might not reach the latter if no central authority required its dissemination throughout the government, and considerable confusion would result if the President and other senior officials were to act on the basis of different information. Intelligence successes often come about through piecing together information from many sources in order to understand the capabilities or intentions of another government; intelligence failures (such as Pearl Harbor) can occur from the absence of any organization with access to all the known facts. Finally, the President would not only have to make his decisions on the basis of conflicting intelligence reports and estimates— something no system can, or should, completely eliminate—but all of the intelligence organizations would be parts of agencies with policy interests of their own. Despite universal acceptance of the principle that policy positions should not color intelligence judgments, subtle (and sometimes not so subtle) pressures exist which make securing disinterested intelligence appraisals a perennial difficulty. (A decentralized structure might be appropriate for a system of policy making dominated by the State Department—especially if INR were given an enhanced role—although the lack of an independent CIA could also result in greater influence for the intelligence estimates of the Defense Department.)

If the drawbacks of a completely decentralized intelligence system are clear, there are major liabilities to a completely centralized structure. Duplication and gaps would be greatly reduced if not eliminated. However, operating agencies need tactical or departmental intelligence just as senior officials need national intelligence. Military units need tactical intelligence concerning the changing size, dispositions, and equipment of the forces of potential enemies. No military commander can operate effectively without intelligence officers who, because they are under his control, can be directed to meet his rapidly changing needs rather than those of another agency whose requirements and priorities are often quite different. The same situation applies, although in a different way, to diplomats involved in negotiations with other nations.

In a centralized system the President would receive his official intelligence reports and appraisals from an organization with no *institutional* policy interests, but he would be isolated from all but a single viewpoint.[2] At the same time, the departments coming to him with policy proposals would be basing them on *implicit* intelligence appraisals of situations and trends abroad. However, these would not be easy to discern. Thus differences in judgments would be difficult to resolve in an orderly and expeditious manner. These objections, together with the forces of bureaucratic interests and inertia, meant that there were practical—and probably insurmountable—political obstacles to any attempt to deprive the various departments of their intelligence functions and units when the Central Intelligence Agency was established in 1947.

Thus the United States set up what might be termed a "mixed" system in an attempt to combine the best features of decentralization and centralization while avoiding the obvious weaknesses of each. The compromises involved in the establishment of a "mixed" system have given rise to difficulties over the years, but attempts to deal with them have focused on modifications rather than abandonment of the basic system. The decision to continue with a mixed system probably also reflects an awareness that U.S. interests and activities in world affairs range from adversary power politics to the management of interdependence with allies, and that such different types of relationships require flexible organizational structures.

The Director of Central Intelligence (DCI) was given the task of coordinating the work of the intelligence units of the U.S. government. In terms of organization charts, the DCI reports to the National Security Council. However, since this body is advisory to the President, the DCI in practice reports to the chief executive, and this apparently has worked out satisfactorily. The United States Intelligence Board (USIB)—formerly the Intelligence Advisory Committee—is the central coordinating institution of the intelligence community. It is composed of the DCI and the top officials of DIA, NSA, INR, and the intelligence units of the FBI, the Treasury, and the Energy Research and Development Administration. USIB not only passes on National Intelligence Estimates but (with the help of its various committees) establishes collection requirements for the entire community. While the DCI as chairman of USIB has the most important voice in the substance of intelligence estimates, other members can dissent from his judgments. (The heads of the intelligence units of the military services are not members of USIB, but they attend the meetings and can dissent from its intelligence judgments.)

There have been two major changes in the organization and procedures of the intelligence community as they were established in the late 1940s and modified during the Korean war years. Both involved moves toward greater centralization in one form or another. The first has been the trend toward centralization of the intelligence activities within the Department of Defense—part of a broader trend toward unified commands and increased authority for the Department of Defense (and the Office of the Secretary) over the military departments. This involved the establishment of the Defense Intelligence Agency (DIA) in 1961, and the creation of an Assistant Secretary of Defense (Intelligence) as the senior staff advisor to the Secretary of Defense in 1971. The military services are to engage in those intelligence activities necessary for their operational missions, but national intelligence—both setting collection priorities and producing finished intelligence—is the responsibility of DIA. However, lines between tactical or department intelligence and national intelligence are

---

[2]Thus, while a centralized system would at first glance appear to strengthen the President's position, the end result could restrict his options by reducing his access to a variety of viewpoints.

easier to define than to put into effect, and considerable overlapping exists.

The second major trend involves an effort to coordinate the work of the various parts of the intelligence community more effectively. The central method adopted to further this effort has been to increase the *responsibility* of the Director of Central Intelligence (DCI) as the President's principal intelligence officer. The Presidential directive of November 5, 1971 specified that the DCI was to provide leadership to all foreign intelligence activities of the U.S. government. However, the *authority* of the DCI remains limited, a subject which will be discussed shortly.

The effort to have the DCI assume greater responsibilities is not a new one. President Kennedy directed John McCone to undertake the "coordination and effective guidance of the total United States foreign intelligence effort" in 1962. Progress was sporadic, however, and the structure of the system and the loci of power within it were much the same at the beginning of the 1970s as they were a decade earlier. Secretary of Defense Laird accepted the validity of criticisms concerning the lack of coordination and the poor quality of military intelligence activities in his 1970 Annual Message to Congress. He responded not only by consolidating responsibility for advising him about defense intelligence activities in a high-level civilian official, but also by *reducing* the role of CIA, INR, and the Office of Management and Budget in the decisions of the National Intelligence Resources Board, which allocated resources among the various defense intelligence programs.

The Nixon Administration's dissatisfaction with both the cost and quality of the U.S. intelligence effort, along with similar complaints by important elements in Congress and among the public, led to the issuance of the 1971 directive, which was prepared by James Schlesinger when he was in the Office of Management and Budget. The 1971 directive also set up two new committees: (1) the National Security Council Intelligence Committee (NSCIC),[3] which was to provide substantive *guidance* and *evaluation* from senior policy makers to the intelligence community, and (2) the Intelligence Resources Advisory Committee (IRAC),[4] which was to advise the DCI so that he could better advise the President about the allocation of tasks and resources within the intelligence community. An important tool in the latter effort has been the effort to develop annual National Foreign Intelligence Program Budget Recommendations by the DCI for submission to the President.

There has also been an effort to increase the strength and responsibilities of the Intelligence Community Staff (which is headed by a senior military officer) in order to provide the DCI with the staff support necessary to manage and coordinate the intelligence community. The establishment of IRAC and an integrated program budget reflect the general agreement in government that of the three major aspects of foreign and security policy—policy planning and policy making, resource allocation,

and the coordination and monitoring of operations —centralization is most appropriate for resource allocation. (Competitive collection would be extremely expensive, whereas the cost of competitive reporting largely involves demands on the time of busy senior officials. Competitive—or duplicative— processing and analysis stands between collection and reporting in terms of resource requirements.)

Several points need to be made about the potential and the limitations of these bodies, as well as how they operate in practice. The 1971 Presidential directive did not involve any *statutory* increase in the authority of the DCI to manage and coordinate the intelligence community. The President simply directed the DCI to do more in this area and set up the interagency mechanisms described above to help him. Yet only the CIA is under the direct line authority of the DCI. The Secretary of Defense controls the DIA and NSA, and the Secretary of State controls INR. Such powerful men are, to put it mildly, hardly likely to turn complete responsibility for assigning tasks and allocating resources to parts of their own departments to an outside official. (A key responsibility of the Secretary of Defense is to be sure that the military services have the intelligence necessary for their security and operations.) In theory, either Cabinet member can be overruled by the President, but there are practical limitations on how often this will occur. Thus the DCI's chief tool is persuasion, and the normal outcome when disputes occur is often no more than a partially satisfactory compromise.

Nonetheless, three additional points are important. First, there is general agreement that those responsible for implementing the directive are making a serious effort to do so at the present time, and this view is held even by those who stress the inherent limitations involved. Second, the compartmentalization within the intelligence community has been greatly reduced in recent years as its various components have acquired greater knowledge of and more experience working with each other. (More people have worked in more than one organization, although this has resulted as much from individual job-shifting as from any planned exchange of personnel.) Overlapping and duplication in the collection process are more visible and thus more difficult to justify, although bureaucratic interests and inertia remain powerful forces. However, duplication is a less difficult problem to deal with than deciding whether or not certain collection methods yield an adequate return—or are likely to in the future—for conflicting positions on the latter often depend ultimately on individual judgments on what risks are acceptable. Third, the requirement that the DCI prepare a consolidated program budget has led to the practice of the DCI presenting this to Congress. The fact that he must be willing to defend the programs and expenditures in it puts pressure on other departments not to include items that they know the DCI opposes.

If a measure of progress is being made in coordinated management of the collection process, the same cannot be said for the NSCIC's assignment of *guiding* and *evaluating* intelligence production from the consumer's standpoint. The NSCIC remains a paper organization, partly because of the preoccupation of the Assistant to the President for National Security Affairs (who now spends most of his time as Secretary of State) with other matters. Specific

[3]NSCIC members are the Assistant to the President for National Security Affairs (Chairman), the DCI (Vice-chairman), the Deputy Secretary of State, the Deputy Secretary of Defense, the Chairman of the Joint Chiefs of Staff, and the Under Secretary of the Treasury for Monetary Affairs.

[4]IRAC members are the DCI (Chairman), and one senior official each from the Department of State, Defense, Office of Management and Budget, and CIA.

requests for and comments on individual intelligence studies are made from time to time, but this is not done in a systematic manner. The high-level officials on the committee could hardly spare the time for detailed work in this area, but without their drive and support any task force or working group of people more directly involved can make only limited progress. This failure to utilize the NSCIC mechanism is particularly striking in view of the past expressions of dissatisfaction on the part of important policy makers with both the analytical quality of intelligence and its relevance to policy requirements.

INTELLIGENCE AND POLICY MAKING

Intelligence collection and production have become major activities of the United States government in the past few decades. Intelligence organizations employ thousands of people and cost billions of dollars, and the finished intelligence products—current intelligence reports, basic research, national estimates, and special studies—influence important policy decisions and the allocation of many additional billions of dollars. The willingness of several Administrations to devote such extensive resources to intelligence is a clear indication that the importance of the intelligence function is recognized by top U.S. officials. Even those who ordered cuts in intelligence budgets in recent years have stressed that a major intelligence effort was essential for the United States.

Yet this willingness to devote substantial sums to intelligence should not obscure the widespread feeling among policy makers in recent years (and many intelligence officers as well) that the quality and relevance of intelligence production should be significantly improved. How valid these complaints are, and what might be done about them, are difficult issues. In order to grapple with them, it is necessary to discuss briefly the tasks of intelligence officers, what types of information they use in their work, how the production process works, and the contrasting views of how intelligence officers and policy makers should relate to each other.

Simply stated, the task of the intelligence officer is to tell the policy makers what has happened throughout the world in the recent past, what is happening currently (and why), and what the future is likely to hold. Thus he must be part historian, part journalist, and part forecaster. (In reality, specialization leads some officers and units to concentrate on one or another of these tasks, but senior intelligence officers must be talented in all of them if they are to be useful to the policy maker.) The constant reinterpretation of history, the disputes about the meaning of contemporary events, and the different forecasts of such basic subjects as the outlook for the U.S. economy by economists working from an elaborate data base illustrate the difficulty the intelligence officer has in meeting the many demands placed upon him.

These difficulties are currently increasing because of two developments. The first is that the analytical tasks assigned to the intelligence community are becoming more varied as a result of the growing complexity of American foreign policy. Détente requires a more sophisticated analysis of Soviet behavior as well as a monitoring of arms control agreements. The shift from bipolarity toward multipolarity adds to the importance of some countries without detracting much from the importance of others; it also makes the pattern of international affairs more difficult to discern and predict. The growing importance of economics in world affairs requires that greater direct attention be devoted to such matters, as well as to the implications of various economic trends. For example, will the oil-producing countries be able to maintain their cartel? Are economic disturbances within the capitalist world—even in societies with high-income levels—likely to provide new opportunities for Communist gains? How loyal to—or independent of—Moscow would the Communist parties of Western Europe be if they entered governments? Increased concern over drug addiction and more recently terrorism has created new responsibilities for intelligence analysts as well as collectors. It has also heightened the importance of good working relationships between the government agencies concerned. The notoriously bad relations between the FBI and CIA, whose cooperation is important in dealing with terrorism, have fortunately been reversed in the last year or so.

The second development is the knowledge explosion. The growing interdependence of nations means that a particular event may have very serious secondary and tertiary consequences which are difficult to trace out in advance. In theory the knowledge explosion—and the development of new techniques and equipment for processing and analyzing information—should be a help to the analyst, and in some ways they are. However, they often provide a flood of information which is more than an individual can digest. Jobs are then broken up and greater specialization ensues, but this increases the dangers of parochialism in outlook and creates new problems in coordinating the work of specialists.

The producer of finished intelligence stands between the intelligence collector and the policy maker. This involves him in two rather different types of relationships and creates two different sets of issues. The first involves providing coordinated guidance to the collectors of information by setting forth requirements in a regular and systematic manner, but without letting the whole procedure become a purely mechanical process divorced from the shifting concerns of the producers. The second involves the production of intelligence that is useful as well as accurate, and involves the uneasy relationship between the reporter and the analyst on the one hand and the policy maker on the other. Success or failure in the latter centers as much if not more on the *attitudes* of the officials involved toward each other's function as on *organizational* arrangements, but the *procedures* for guiding the analyst and for the transmission of intelligence are of considerable importance in the whole process.

Open materials in the public domain form a substantial part of the information used by the intelligence producer. These include newspaper and magazine reports, speeches of foreign leaders, published reports of foreign governments and international organizations, and the published research of scientists and academics around the world. Assigning responsibility for the collection of different types of open material so as to avoid duplication and gaps, and to make sure it is distributed to those who need it, is probably the easiest part of the management process.

Overt reporting by U.S. officials stationed around the world—Foreign Service Officers, military attachés, etc.—is probably the most valuable source of information available to intelligence analysts on the non-Communist areas of the world. It is also the one that is least susceptible to control by anyone in the intelligence community. While the U.S. diplomatic posts abroad receive detailed lists of intelligence requirements, the collection of intelligence is not the primary purpose of diplomats. Their reporting ability (especially when they are junior officers) is an important factor in their performance ratings, but, since they are subordinate to policy bureaus in the State Department, the influence of those managing the intelligence collection process is limited.

One of the most recently developed but nonetheless most important types of information—especially on Communist countries—is that derived from photographic reconnaissance. It is of particular importance to the analyst trying to appraise weapons production and deployment. Information can also be gathered on mineral deposits and on developing weather patterns and crop prospects which, if properly distributed, could help in the management of global economic problems. (The photoreconnaissance effort is operated by the Air Force, but decisions on how funds will be allocated are made jointly by the Assistant Secretary of Defense [Intelligence] and the DCI.)

One of the largest and most expensive collection efforts involves communications and electronic intelligence collection (COMINT and ELINT). The latter is a product of recent decades, while the former goes back several generations in its present form—and much further if capturing messages carried by courier is included. The interception and deciphering of radio messages is one of the most controversial aspects of the collection process. It has yielded extremely valuable information at times in the past, but the development of sophisticated codes and coding machines—especially among the developed countries—has proceeded faster in recent decades than deciphering or code-breaking techniques. The military services who operate most of this program continue to defend it strongly for two reasons: (1) it provides tactical intelligence which is important in peace-time, and which would be of even greater importance in wartime; and (2) standards of communications security might decline during wartime dislocations, thereby enabling NSA to break codes that are presently unreadable. Moreover, some things can be learned about another government's activities from analysis of the pattern and frequency of unreadable messages (called traffic analysis).

The final type of information is obtained from clandestine reporting—the traditional and often romanticized spying or espionage function. The relative importance of the spy was greater a century ago than it is today, when more information is published openly and when the advanced technological collection methods discussed above are available. The individual agent remains quite useful in most less developed countries. However, the great difficulties and limited successes in penetrating closed societies such as the Soviet Union and China, and the relative ease of appraising trends in the democratic industrial societies through the use of open and overt official collection efforts, have raised important questions about the basic usefulness of espionage in today's world.

Certain points are worth keeping in mind about this subject. The first is that agent reporting—which is not an expensive method of collection—sometimes fills in important gaps on a subject. It is often more useful than technological methods in revealing the *intentions* (as distinct from the capabilities) of foreign countries, although the danger of being misled by a double agent can never be ignored. Moreover, world trends can change, and the importance of espionage in an area such as the Balkans could increase if conditions became less settled. An intelligence system, while flexible enough to respond to short-term needs, should be organized and deployed for the long haul. This requires long lead times and advance planning; a skilled and experienced clandestine service and useful networks of agents can seldom be created in a hurry.

Another point was made by Hugh Trevor-Roper in his excellent study of Kim Philby:

> To have a reliable, intelligent, highly-placed agent in the center of a potentially hostile power, with access to 'hard' evidence, is the dream of every intelligence service. . . . A well-placed agent of known fidelity and intelligence who can advise his master, answer specific questions, comment on the disjointed texts which every Secret Service picks up, correct the illusions to which it is prone, has a value which transcends the occasional questionable scoop.[5]

Important as is the collection and assembling of high quality information, its analysis and presentation to the policy makers in usable form is the focal point in the intelligence community's effort. Thus William Colby stated (in his testimony to the Commission) that his responsibility for coordinating and managing the intelligence community was important, but less so than his responsibility for producing substantive intelligence. This requires a wide variety of different types of intelligence—reporting about current political and economic events from Chile to China, so that senior policy makers will know not only what has occurred but also its implications; indications of changing orders of battle of foreign military forces along the Sino-Soviet frontier or in Vietnam that might indicate increased dangers of war; and signs of new weapons developments in Russia or China that provide an indication of their future military strength and help understand their intentions on arms control. Some of this intelligence will be conveyed on a regular daily or weekly basis, while other reports will be undertaken at the initiative of the intelligence officer or at the request of the policy maker. Some of it will represent the judgment of a single organization—such as CIA, DIA, INR, or NSA. Other reports (both daily reporting and long-range estimates) will represent the coordinated effort of the entire intelligence community. Most of the "product" of intelligence officers will be written, but some will be conveyed by briefing officers whose personal styles will influence how it is delivered and received. All of it will compete with many other demands for the time and attention of the overburdened senior policy maker.

---

[5]Hugh Trevor-Roper, "The Philby Affair: Espionage, Treason, and Secret Services," *Encounter*, April 1968.

There are two main views of the appropriate relationship between the intelligence officer and the policy maker. The traditional or classic view is that this should be an arm's-length relationship, so that the dangers of the intelligence officer's judgment being swayed by the views of the policy maker are kept to a minimum. This view stresses that intelligence should tell the policy maker what he needs to know rather than what he wants to hear. The other view agrees that the intelligence officer must be rigorously honest and independent in his relationship with the policy maker, but stresses that if the former is to tell the latter what he "needs to know" he must have considerable knowledge of the specific concerns of the policy maker. Otherwise, intelligence analysis becomes an isolated intellectual effort carried out in a vacuum—the pursuit of knowledge for its own sake—rather than a carefully focused input to the policy maker's thinking and decision-making process. Even in the latter case, of course, intelligence is but one input among many involved in a decision, for the policy maker must also be concerned with such matters as domestic needs and Congressional opinion.

In describing these differences it is important not to exaggerate them. One holding the traditional viewpoint would agree that an intelligence organization should stand ready to answer questions about likely foreign reactions to various U.S. courses of action. (How would China react to the mining of Haiphong harbor? Moscow to a naval blockade of Cuba? The world to a rise in U.S. tariffs?) A person holding the view that there must be continuing contact between intelligence officials and policy makers would agree that the former should not tell the latter which policy he should follow. Nonetheless, those holding the second viewpoint argue that intelligence officers must be prepared to take the initiative in seeking out policy makers, gaining admittance to their meetings, making known the capabilities of intelligence organizations, and in effect pushing the policy makers to explain what their aims and policies are and solicit their requests for intelligence studies. Moreover, a degree of overlap in views between the two groups does not prevent sharp and passionate arguments from arising over the remaining differences.

One step taken in recent years to bring intelligence officers and policy makers into closer contact involves the Verification Panel, which utilizes intelligence on Soviet military developments to monitor the SALT agreements. Another proposal which has been made from time to time is to remove the national estimating function from CIA and place it in the NSC structure.[6] There are several reasons why this proposal has never been accepted. First, it would weaken the links between the intelligence estimators and the bulk of the intelligence researchers and analysts, thereby reducing the claims of the estimators to be heard by the policy makers. Second, the estimators would be operating in a more politicized environment, and would find it more difficult to maintain their objectivity. Third, there has been some reluctance to expand the NSC staff still further.

However, a variation of this proposal has been adopted in an effort to bridge the intelligence officer-policy maker gap. This involves the abolition of

[6]For a statement of this view see Chester Cooper, "The CIA and Decision-Making," *Foreign Affairs*, January 1972.

the Office and the Board of National Estimates in favor of a system relying on National Intelligence Officers (NIOs) with specific area or functional responsibilities for substantive intelligence. (The NIOs also function as senior advisors to the DCI in the area of collection guidance and clandestine activities.) The NIOs are to keep in close personal touch with senior policy-making officials in order to learn of their changing needs and keep them informed of the work in process and the research and analytical capabilities of intelligence producers. NIOs operate across bureaucratic boundaries, designating the most knowledgeable person on a particular topic to prepare a National Intelligence Estimate on the subject when one is needed. This system has been in operation only a short time, and thus its performance is impossible to evaluate. It obviously is dependent upon the cooperation of the heads of the various directorates in CIA (and elsewhere in the intelligence community) whose subordinates are assigned tasks by the NIOs. Since Mr. Colby has made clear his determination that the system work, such cooperation apparently has been forthcoming to date.

CLANDESTINE ACTIVITIES

The clandestine activities of the United States intelligence community, which are concentrated in the Central Intelligence Agency, are by far the most controversial aspect of intelligence activities. These have led to charges that CIA is an invisible government which could drag the United States into war on its own initiative, that it is not controlled by elected officials or accountable to Congress, and that it has undertaken actions which have undermined the reputation of the United States around the world and thus has been a major reason for the alienation of many Americans from their government. In the eyes of its critics—and these include responsible and serious people—it has created the very problems that were feared when it was established and which had been one reason the U.S. had previously eschewed such activities in peacetime. The supporters of clandestine activities make no attempt to defend every operation or practice of the clandestine services. However, they argue that the world is and is likely to remain a dangerous place and that the U.S. cannot afford to deny itself the use of potentially valuable weapons to protect its security. While concerned with the country's democratic values, they stress that the preservation of such values is dependent upon the maintenance of national security.

Before proceeding further, it would seem useful to outline briefly the assignments of CIA's clandestine service. They are essentially fourfold. First, it is responsible for the secret collection of information—traditional espionage or spying activities. Second, it has counterintelligence responsibilities, which involve protecting the United States from the operations of foreign intelligence services, especially the Soviet KGB. (It must work closely with the FBI to operate effectively in this area.) Third, it establishes working relationships with the intelligence services of allies and—on a more restricted basis—some other nations as well. It does this for three different purposes: (1) to exchange intelligence information with them, whether in the form of individual agent reports, basic research, or intelligence estimates; (2) to run occasional joint operations with them; and (3) to help them, on occasion, to protect their own societies against foreign penetration or domestic upheaval. (Its liaison activities also provide a cover for unilateral clandestine activities.) Fourth, it conducts covert political operations, which run from the counselling of foreign political leaders, conducting covert propaganda, supporting organizations or institutions ranging from publishers through labor unions to political parties, to supporting a group that is attempting to overthrow the government of its country. Sometimes an individual CIA station in a foreign country will be involved in many or all of these activities, while on other occasions some of the operations may be controlled from nearby countries or even from the United States.

Clandestine activities raise three major issues, which can be labeled *organization, procedures,* and *policy.* The last is by far the most difficult, and its complexity requires serious study rather than the few questions raised here. The problem involves the matter of ethics, both as to the target of operations and the techniques used. It involves an evaluation of the ability of the Clandestine Services (CS) to maintain secrecy—not only in wartime or in a period when a strong national consensus discourages embarrassing revelations—but in times of domestic disagreements over foreign policy when Americans tend to revert to their traditional distrust of secrecy, and when officials (or former officials) opposed to an operation may reveal its existence to the media. It involves hard (and practical) issues as to whether the benefits the U.S. derives by the respect accorded the rule of law are undermined if it emulates its enemies and fights fire with fire.

And yet, if the U.S. ceased such activities, is there any chance its enemies would exercise similar restraint? May not U.S. activities, rather than destroying the independence of small countries, contribute to helping them maintain their independence in the face of interference by others? If the U.S. decides to maintain a clandestine action capability (and most objections, it should be noted, are directed against covert operations and helping foreign governments deal with their *domestic* enemies—which sometimes have foreign backing), how often and in what circumstances should such methods be employed? These are matters of judgment. Few have the experience or the detailed knowledge to speak with authority on the balance of gains and losses in the past, or on how they are likely to balance out in the future.

Two questions involving the issues of *organization* and *procedure* do warrant consideration. The one dealing with organization is whether CIA should be divided, with the Clandestine Services established as a separate agency apart from the intelligence research and analysis function. Before discussing the arguments for and against separating operations from analysis, one important point needs to be kept in mind. This question has generated a certain amount of emotion; many of those who have been critical of CIA as an institution or its operating methods have favored such a change as a means of cutting CIA down "to size." Many of the advocates of clandestine activities or supporters of CIA have seen such a change as reflecting an animosity toward the Agency and have accordingly been almost instinctively opposed to any division of CIA. Yet there is no logical connection between the structure of CIA and U.S. reliance on clandestine activities; a person who favored *greater* reliance on covert operations might argue that the necessary security could only be achieved if clandestine activities were placed under a separate and deeper cover. Finally, whatever organizational arrangements are most appropriate for the long run should be the ones adopted *unless* they can be shown to be disastrously disruptive in the short term.

There are several arguments for and against any division of CIA. Such a change would have both beneficial and detrimental effects, which are often opposite sides of the same coin. For example, analysts and operators benefit more from the knowledge and experience of the other than would be true if they were in separate organizations. Yet security considerations and the need for compartmentalization require that some limits be kept on this exchange of information, although these have been reduced in recent years. There are at least potential dangers if the agency that provides intelligence analysis and conclusions which influence policy may become the organization which carries out elements of the policy adopted. These functions are in separate parts of CIA, it is true, but the top leaders of the Agency are responsible for both functions. However, the Pentagon Papers indicate that CIA analysts on many occasions (even when covert operations were involved) stated that U.S. policies and programs would not be successful, which indicates this problem can be overcome.

CIA has a reputation in many circles at home and abroad as a primary instrument of "American imperialism." In this view, it undertakes activities that threaten détente, interferes in the internal affairs of other nations, and aids the forces of "reaction" to suppress movements working for "freedom and justice." It could be argued that the division of the CIA would be taken as a sign that clandestine activities were being downgraded, thereby lessening antipathy to the U.S. government at home and abroad. Yet finding a different organizational cover that offered any greater security for the present Clandestine Services would be extremely difficult. Moreover, a change of organizational structure and name would be treated as a hypocritical cosmetic change by many critics (and some foreign intelligence agencies would propagate this idea) unless the new Clandestine Service's record was either more secure or more restrained. (The various name changes of the Soviet secret police have not enhanced its reputation—or that of the Soviet Union.) Any proposed change should be evaluated primarily as to whether it benefits the United States government rather than only CIA.

A division of CIA would have one clear-cut benefit. There is still considerable suspicion of CIA in much of the academic and intellectual community, and some of the most talented people probably refuse to consider working as analysts lest their association with CIA and its operators bar them from certain jobs outside the Agency. If the research and analytical function were in a separate organization—and it were adequately funded—this handicap would be eliminated. However, this handicap is somewhat less serious than it was a few years ago because of declining personnel ceilings, a surplus of college graduates, and some improvement in the Agency's reputation because of its skeptical views on the chances for the success of U.S. policy in Vietnam.

There are two remaining arguments against dividing the agency. CIA's Directorate of Science and Technology (D/S&T), which has demonstrated considerable initiative and imagination, is involved in collection activities and analysis. Dividing D/S&T would weaken it, but assigning it to either an operational or an analytical organization would reduce its ties to other operators or analysts.

The final argument for the present arrangement involves the basic workings of the intelligence community. If the Director of Central Intelligence is to be the President's principal intelligence advisor and is to coordinate the intelligence activities of the U.S. government, he must—given the realities of politics within the U.S. government—either be the head of a major organization or be personally very close to the President (as is the Special Assistant for National Security Affairs). Dividing CIA would reduce his stature and influence. The director of the Clandestine Service would find it even more difficult than it is at present to be the coordinator, and the director of the new agency dealing with research and analysis would find it much more difficult to gain the President's ear unless he and his agency—or at least part of it—become part of the President's staff. This staff is probably already too large.

Is there any change which would maximize the benefits and reduce the liabilities of a different organizational structure? One widespread conviction among those knowledgeable about intelligence activities is that no country should have two clandestine services—one for the clandestine collection of information and the other responsible for covert operations. The latter sometimes depend upon or even grow out of information collected clandestinely. The two clandestine services would sometimes find themselves trying to recruit the same agent. Every government that has divided these two functions has found that the two services have not only stumbled over each other but spent much of their time and energies competing and intriguing against each other.

These arguments appear compelling if there is to be a *large* clandestine service with extensive reliance on covert operations. Yet the latter have declined substantially in importance over the last decade, and the number of people in the Clandestine Services with secure or deep cover—as against nominal or light cover—is not large. This suggests that it would be worth exploring the possibility of keeping the administrative and support staffs—and perhaps those in the Clandestine Services who operate with light cover (officials in U.S. embassies, etc.)—within CIA, while setting up a separate but much smaller and truly clandestine organization that might operate more securely and thus more effectively. Such an organization probably should be under the authority of the DCI as head of the intelligence community, but not as part of CIA. Many questions would arise about such a change, including the need for—and possibility of securing—new legislation, but some consideration of the pros and cons of such a reorganization would seem desirable.

The third major issue to be considered is that of *control* of CIA's clandestine activities. In short, are these adequately controlled by the White House staff, the Department of State, and the Department of Defense when its interests are involved? [7] [Even such critics as Marchetti and Marks—in their book *The CIA and the Cult of Intelligence*—explicitly reject the charge that CIA acts without proper authorization, stating (disapprovingly) that every American president has concluded that the Agency's clandestine capabilities are useful.] The procedures for securing the approval of senior policy makers were rather informal during CIA's earlier years. In time these were tightened up and regularized as regards new programs, although it was only after the widespread revelations of the mid-1960s that periodic reexamination and approval of long-established and ongoing programs became the norm. By the late 1960s covert political activities had to be approved and reviewed by a committee composed of senior members of the White House staff, the State Department, and the Defense Department. This is now known as the "Forty Committee." Its members are the Assistant to the President for National Security Affairs (Chairman), Under Secretary of State for Political Affairs, the Deputy Secretary of Defense, the Chairman of the Joint Chiefs of Staff, and the DCI. INR examines these proposals for the State Department, although the need for secrecy has led to a high degree of compartmentalization.

The problem that presently exists is that approval is obtained on an individual operation basis (sometimes by telephone) rather than by a searching and systematic examination of the potential benefits and costs of such activities in relation to the totality of U.S. foreign policy objectives and activities. (This contrasts with the control exercised over those major clandestine collection operations which involve serious political risks, which are considered in a thorough and systematic manner.) Obviously, the people who approve or disapprove proposed operations are not unaware of the need to weigh each proposal in relation to broad national concerns, but it would seem more difficult to do so on the present basis than it would under a more integrated and systematic approach.

THE CONGRESSIONAL ROLE IN INTELLIGENCE ACTIVITIES

The division of powers in the American system of government has created special problems regarding the conduct of foreign policy. If the Executive branch of government has traditionally (and increasingly in recent decades) been the moving force in foreign affairs, its predominance has been even greater in the field of intelligence activities. Disputes over the substance of American foreign policy and the authority and responsibility of Congress in foreign affairs have raised many difficult issues, and some of these are having a growing impact upon the intelligence community.

There are *four* major areas or types of activities that are involved in Congressional-intelligence community relations. The *first* is that Congress must provide legal authority for the creation of organizations (as it did for CIA in 1947) and for the activities they undertake. There has been some de-

---

[7] *Control* must be distinguished from *influence*. Many critics who argue that CIA plays too large a role in government are essentially concerned with its influence, even though they sometimes speak of it as being uncontrolled by the President or Congress.

bate over the question of whether the legislation establishing CIA it authority to undertake covert operations. Those who argue that such activities are within CIA's basic charter—and are spelled out by Presidential and NSC directives—cite the fact that the law allows CIA to undertake such other functions and duties relating to national security intelligence as the National Security Council directs. Others argue that covert operations have nothing to do with the intelligence functions—collecting information, evaluating it, and disseminating finished intelligence—assigned to CIA by Congress, and that such activities are thus carried on without statutory authority.

The *second* aspect of the Congressional role is the appropriation of funds for intelligence activities. There is no dispute over Congressional authority in this area, although some Congressmen believe the funds allotted to CIA should be clearly specified rather than hidden in the budgets of other departments. Appropriations for CIA are handled by special subcommittees of the Senate and House appropriation committees, while appropriations for the intelligence activities of other departments—such as State and Defense—are handled by the subcommittees responsible for the particular departments.

The *third* issue concerns the provision of intelligence reports and estimates to Congress. A certain amount of intelligence has always been made available, chiefly in the form of committee briefings. Some Congressmen believe this is not enough, and argue that all intelligence reports (not agent reports, but finished reports by various units of the intelligence community) should be turned over to Congress on a regular basis. They stress that they must vote on important issues regarding foreign political, economic and military policy, and they question the value of a system that spends large sums for information which is not made available to them. Complicated and politically sensitive issues are involved here. For example, would the staffs of Congressional committees—and of individual Congressmen—have access to such material? What arrangements for security would be made, and how good would they be? Would Congress have a better —and perhaps more sympathetic—understanding of the difficulties and dilemmas facing any U.S. government if it received regular intelligence reports? Would it be able to provide a valuable long-range perspective since it does not have day-to-day operational responsibilities? If all written reports automatically went to Congress, would this inhibit judgments that indirectly cast doubt upon Administration policies out of fear that such reports would be used against the Administration by Congressmen critical of its policies? Would really important estimates be made orally—and therefore often more vaguely—so that they could be kept secret? To what extent does the President have the right to

receive information and advice from his subordinates without sharing it with anyone?

The *fourth* issue concerns Congressional oversight in general and surveillance of clandestine activities in particular. Oversight (except in fiscal matters) has been the responsibility of special subcommittees of the House and Senate Armed Services Committees. (CIA, on occasion, provides economic intelligence briefings to committees dealing with economic matters.) Critics have charged that these committees do not exercise their responsibilities in a sustained and serious fashion. They say that Congress—and the public—have no assurance that U.S. intelligence activities are effective or adequately controlled.

Various proposals have been put forward to deal with this matter, and most of them call for Congress to create a Joint Committee on Intelligence in order to gain greater access to intelligence production as well as to exercise greater influence over clandestine activities—and especially over covert operations. Such proposals have never been accepted for several reasons. First, they were regarded by members of the present subcommittees as challenges to their authority. Second, the proposals called for such a Joint Committee to have jurisdiction over the intelligence activities of all government departments, which created opposition among the members of committees presently responsible for matters affecting those departments. Third, every Administration has opposed such a change, fearing it would impose new constraints on an activity that was essentially executive in character. Other arguments were that secrecy would be endangered, making foreign intelligence services less willing to cooperate with CIA, and that intelligence activities have been investigated periodically by special government commissions and regularly by the President's Foreign Intelligence Advisory Board.

The critics, while granting some force to these arguments, have not been convinced by them. What is more interesting, however, is that some people in the intelligence community—and apparently in CIA in particular—now see some merit in the establishment of a Joint Committee on Intelligence. Such a committee, were it to be responsible for maintaining the security of information provided it, might result in greater rather than less security. It might also provide reassurance to Congress—and the public—that CIA was adequately supervised, and thus place the Agency in a stronger position over the long term. Important issues—such as the extent of the Joint Committee's jurisdiction, its membership and staffing, and its methods of operation —are still matters of contention, but the differences have narrowed.

NOTES AND REFERENCES

1. The Pike hearings contain colloquy between Arthur Schlesinger, Jr. and Robert Murphy on the need to restructure the intelligence community ([84E], pp. 1847–1871). Schlesinger, an historian and author, was an intelligence officer with the OSS during World War II and an adviser to President John F. Kennedy. Robert Murphy served as chairman of the Commission on the Organization of the Government for the Conduct of Foreign Policy (Murphy Commission) and as a member of the PFIAB.

2. The National Security Act of 1947 and the CIA Act of 1949 are reprinted in the Appendix.

3. A fourth presidential instrumentality has been established as a result of President Gerald R. Ford's Executive Order 11905, February 18, 1976. This order pertains to the organization and control of the U.S. foreign intelligence community and created the Intelligence Oversight Board. See the Appendix for a reprint of the presidential message on Executive Order 11905.

4. The evolution and growth of the NSC staff is detailed in [22]. President Richard M. Nixon stated his views on the revitalization of the NSC as the principal forum for presidential consideration of foreign policy matters ([7], pp. 11–14); note also the reorganization announcements of 1969 ([13], pp. 657–661) and 1970 ([13], pp. 10–14). Henry Kissinger, special assistant to the president for National Security Affairs (and as such, head of NSC), commented on the role and structure of the NSC during the early Nixon administration and its use in presidential decision making ([32], pp. 1–3).

5. The Senate overrode President Gerald R. Ford's veto message on S. 2350, a bill providing that the secretary of the treasury be made a statutory member of the NSC (*Congressional Record*, January 22, 1976, pp. S353 ff.).

6. Testimony by NSC Staff Secretary Jeanne Davis on staffing and internal operations appears in [4], pp. 1121–1133 and [3], pp. 1805–1818. The NSC's 40 Committee, now the Operations Advisory Group, is responsible for evaluating recommended covert action for presidential approval ([104], Congressional Research Service, p. 8).

7. The subject of covert action is addressed in Chapter 11.

8. National Security Council intelligence directives (NSCIDs) are NSC directives sent to the intelligence agencies and are generally classified. Senator William Proxmire has charged that they are used to provide a "secret charter" outside the legal processes (*Congressional Record*, June 4, 1973, p. 10222). Recent court cases and FOIA requests have accounted for the release of some NSCIDs. See [125], p. 6, for a listing of NSCIDs and how to obtain them.

9. For information on authorization and control of covert action, see Chapter 11.

10. A listing of PFIAB members in 1975 appears in [25], p. 358.

11. For further details on the origins of the DCI position, see Chapter 5 and [45A], pp. 71–72.

12. President Gerald R. Ford's message on Executive Order 11905 is reprinted in the Appendix.

13. The CIA is reviewed in Chapter 5.

Chapter 3
Policy Formulation
and Executive Control

INTELLIGENCE AND POLICYMAKING IN AN
INSTITUTIONAL CONTEXT ([90], pp. 21–48)

The effective conduct of U.S. foreign policy requires an intelligence capability sensitive to the needs of policymakers in the economic, political, and military fields. The evolution of the intelligence community from the World War II OSS model and the influence exerted on it by the cold war have led to an emphasis on intelligence involving political-military matters relating to Eastern Europe, China, and those areas where cold war adversaries are engaged at the time. The emergence of OPEC (Organization of Petroleum Exporting Countries), famine in West Africa, devaluations of currency, and peasant uprisings in Mexico are matters of profound significance to U.S. policy, but some experts feel that such developments are not receiving the proper attention of the "community."

In Chapter 3, specialists associated with the Murphy Commission study on the Conduct of U.S. Foreign Policy address the interplay between the intelligence function and foreign policy, as well as the need to have a policy-responsive intelligence effort. Their papers have been drawn from Appendix U of Volume 7 in the commissions's final report. Their work was completed in the fall of 1974 and published in mid-1975, prior to the conclusion of the Church and Pike Committee hearings and the Rockefeller Commission Report on the CIA ([124]). Without access to the detailed documentation gathered by those subsequent groups, the Murphy studies tend to be more abstract than they might had they been written later.

The Commission on the Organization of the Government for the Conduct of Foreign Policy (Murphy Commission) was chaired by Robert Murphy, an executive of Corning Glass and a diplomatic troubleshooter for Presidents John F. Kennedy and Lyndon B. Johnson. The commission was composed of congressmen, academicians, bank officers, advisers to the president, and the sitting vice-president, Nelson Rockefeller. It had been proposed in 1971 by Senator Mike Mansfield and was established in 1972 by Congress as part of its foreign relations appropriations act for fiscal year 1973. Its mandate was to "study and investigate the organization, methods of operation, and powers of all departments, agencies, independent establishments and instrumentalities of the United States Government participation in the formulation and implementation of U.S. foreign policy."* As the Watergate revelations unfolded and relations between the Congress and President Richard M. Nixon strained, the efforts to organize and staff the commission floundered. The twelve members were to be appointed by the president, the Senate, and the House of Representatives, each supplying four members. With delays in appointments, the commission did not organize until April 1973 and then had to act swiftly to meet its statutory deadline to report findings by June 1975.

Most of the Murphy Commission report is addressed to general foreign policy matters or the details of matters outside the scope of U.S. foreign intelligence effort. Selected passages in this chapter include four authors who focused on the interchange between intelligence gathering and the formation and execution of policy. The first section is by William Barnds, who titled his essay "Intelligence and Policymaking in an Institutional Context." John Huizenga, prepared a critique of the Barnds study, which is reprinted, along with a comment by Lawrence Lynn, Jr. entitled "A New Role for the Intelligence Community." The chapter concludes with a brief essay prepared by Russell Jack Smith entitled "Intelligence Support for Foreign Policy in the Future." Other Murphy report essays relating to intelligence are listed in [90].

*Foreign Relations Authorization Act of 1972, 603(a), Public Law No. 92-352, 86 Stat. 489, 497.

SUMMARY

1. The U.S. intelligence system remains heavily focused on military considerations and upon discovering and evaluating potential military threats. However, changing conditions in the world have added new tasks, particularly in the area of economic intelligence, without reducing old responsibilities significantly—a trend that presents growing problems in a time of fiscal stringency.

2. The information collected for processing and analyzing by the intelligence community comes from a variety of sources ranging from the mundane to the esoteric. There has been a rapid rise in the importance of technological collection methods in the past decade or so, especially on military matters involving Communist states. Nonetheless, material in the public domain, reports of U.S. officials stationed abroad, and reports from foreign agents continue to play an important role in the intelligence process.

3. The structure of the intelligence community reflects the basic decision made shortly after the Second World War that, while departments with policy responsibilities should have an intelligence capability of their own, there should also be a central agency to produce its own studies as well as to coordinate the work of the community as a whole. Each of the intelligence organizations has its particular strengths and weaknesses, but the basic structure of the intelligence community in the area of intelligence production is sound.

4. The functions of intelligence in the policy process are: (1) alerting policy makers to events abroad; (2) estimating future developments; (3) appraising the likely consequences of possible U.S. courses of action; and (4) monitoring conditions that affect U.S. policies or agreements with foreign governments. Both intelligence officers and policy makers must perform certain tasks if the relationship is to be successful. However, differences in viewpoint about the appropriate relationship between intelligence officers and policy makers—and between their respective organizations—remain widespread. Some stress that this should be an arm's-length relationship so as to assure objective intelligence judgments; others stress the need for continuing contact and interaction so that intelligence will be relevant to the policy maker's concerns.

5. Three broad conclusions about the performance of the tasks required for an effective intelligence-policy making relationship seem warranted. First, several of them are being performed in an inadequate manner. Second, the situation is better than it was a few years ago, when distrust and lack of confidence characterized the relationship. Third, substantial improvements are possible without major reorganizations or drastic increases in the workloads of busy men, although some changes in working styles would be required.

6. Despite recent efforts at improvement, deficiencies exist in the establishment of realistic collection requirements—a problem which will become more serious as more sophisticated technologies permit the collection of an ever-growing volume of information.

7. Policy makers do an uneven job of providing guidance to the intelligence community and evaluation of the intelligence product. The Nixon Administration's dissatisfaction with intelligence production led it to establish the National Security Council Intelligence Committee to guide and evaluate the work of the intelligence community, but this body—which could and should provide guidance and evaluation by policy makers—has remained a paper organization. The National Intelligence Officer system is one attempt to bridge this gap. The President's Foreign Intelligence Advisory Board (PFIAB) could usefully direct its attention to the problems of guidance and evaluation.

8. An even more serious weakness is the failure of high-level policy makers to keep the intelligence community informed of U.S. policies under consideration. Under such circumstances the intelligence officer must try to estimate what his own as well as foreign governments are doing. There is no satisfactory solution to this problem unless policy makers are less secretive about their activities and their longer-term priorities and goals.

9. Adequate arrangements for the organization and coordination of foreign economic policy—which involve a large number of powerful departments—have yet to be established. Policy formulation and coordination have fallen partly to the Council on International Economic Policy (CIEP) and partly to the National Security Council—a system that satisfies virtually no one. At the present time most economic intelligence reporting and analysis are done by the Central Intelligence Agency, whose work in this area is highly regarded throughout the government. In view of the lack of any consensus about the appropriate U.S. government organizational structure and procedural arrangements for dealing with foreign economic policy, it would be more sensible to build upon the present arrangements for economic intelligence than to make any major organizational changes. One procedural arrangement that might be appropriate, however, would be to make sure that there are adequate provisions for the DCI to report to the CIEP—and for the latter body (as well as departments outside the intelligence community) to have the authority to task the intelligence community.

INTRODUCTION

The development of the Cold War and the withdrawal of the European colonial powers from Asia in the late 1940s made it clear to American leaders that the United States would be drawn into a deeper and more lasting involvement in world affairs than had ever been the case in peacetime. During World War II, the hastily expanded U.S. intelligence organizations had given top priority to Germany, Italy, and Japan. Thus, little was known about America's principal adversary, the Soviet Union, or about the vast array of new nations stretching from North Africa through the Middle East and the Indian subcontinent to the South China Sea.

The confusion and uncertainty about the appropriate foreign policies to adopt regarding the bewildering series of problems facing the United States were intensified by the lack of institutions and procedures within the U.S. government necessary to formulate and execute an effective policy. President Roosevelt's highly personalized and informal style of leadership had obvious deficiencies and was, in any case, not congenial to his successors. Institutions and procedures had to be established which would enable the President to bring together the key U.S. officials who dealt with the various aspects of foreign policy to consider the relevant facts, to appraise American interests, and to weigh alternative courses of action, make the necessary policy decisions and see that they were carried out.

These needs led to the creation of the National Security Council and the Central Intelligence Agency in 1947. United States political leaders recognized the need for government departments with policy responsibilities to retain a capacity for intelligence research and analysis, but they decided that the task of providing much of the reporting and analysis needed should rest with an organization with no direct policy responsibilities and thus no departmental positions to defend. Thus the former Research and Analysis branch of OSS, which had moved into the State Department after World War II, was transferred to the CIA. A growing effort was launched to collect information of all kinds in Eastern Europe, the Soviet Union, the Far East, and the former colonial territories. Information that would be needed if war broke out received priority. However, the paucity of knowledge of the world abroad meant that almost any information seemed valuable, and thus a vast collection process was set up to gather data on everything from factory locations, road and rail networks, and trade relations to the strength and attitudes of various political forces in far-flung countries. Arrangements for basic research, current reporting, and long-range estimating were established, and extensive efforts were devoted to thinking through and working out appropriate arrangements for the utilization of intelligence in the policy-making process. Intelligence has had its successes and its failures over the years, but even its critics acknowledge that it has and will continue to play an important role in American foreign policy.

It is simple to state the formal responsibilities and to describe the work, varied and voluminous though it is, of the U.S. intelligence community in the area of intelligence production. It is to give the policy makers judgments as to what the situation actually is in the world at any given time, what it will be in the future, and (to a degree) what the implications of such judgments are. To carry out its responsibilities, the U.S. intelligence community has become one of the largest consumers and producers of information in the world—and thus in history. It gathers masses of facts, rumors, and opinions by reading everything from foreign newspapers and the translations of foreign radio broadcasts to the cables of U.S. missions abroad and the reports of secret agents, and from the reconnaissance photographs to the information in intercepted radio messages. Selected pieces of this information go directly to policy makers in their original form, but much of this data goes no farther than the intelligence analysts themselves. The intelligence organizations, after evaluating and analyzing it, regularly produce a variety of reports (National Intelligence Estimates, daily and weekly intelligence journals, special memoranda, and various studies in depth) and send them forth to compete for the attention of the overburdened and harassed policy makers. These reports deal with affairs in countries as far apart as Albania and Zambia and with subjects ranging from the prospects of an insurgency movement in Iraq to the implications of Soviet research and development efforts for Soviet weaponry a decade or more hence.

The responsibility for political analysis has grown as new nations have been born, and the need for such analysis seems unlikely to diminish. The amount of effort devoted to scientific intelligence has increased many-fold in the last fifteen years. In view of the seemingly inexorable march of science in the industrialized nations and the growth of the scientific capabilities of some of the new nations, the tasks in this area are likely to grow in importance, complexity, and volume. The need for accurate knowledge of the military forces of the major powers has always been substantial, and, despite a somewhat reduced U.S. involvement in the affairs of other continents, it remains important to know the military capabilities of dozens of countries. Even today the U.S. intelligence community's efforts are focused heavily upon military considerations and toward discovering and evaluating potential military threats.

Changing conditions in the world have added new tasks without reducing old responsibilities significantly—a trend that presents growing problems in a time of fiscal stringency. These new tasks are most striking in the area of economic intelligence, for the international trade and monetary upheaval of 1971 and the oil crisis of late 1973 highlight a major shift in the focus of American foreign policy in recent years. This is the growing importance of international economic policy relative to the traditional security concerns that dominated U.S. foreign policy for nearly three decades after 1941. The decline of American economic predominance by the late 1960s as a result of more rapid Western European and Japanese economic growth was one factor in this change, and the growing dependence on imported raw materials (especially petroleum) added another element. These trends have not only undermined the structure and procedures of the international monetary and trading systems that made possible the great postwar economic progress, but have also raised serious questions about the likelihood of a worldwide depression and about the economic viability of the resource-poor underdeveloped nations. Thus the intelligence community must grapple with the analytical problem of likely trends in U.S. dependence on imported oil, the uses likely to be made by the oil producers of their new wealth, and the ability of the international monetary system to deal with new pressures. Intelligence appraisals of the strengths and likely courses of action of such men as the Shah of Iran and the King of Saudi Arabia are of critical importance, as are judgments about how they would react to various U.S. courses of action.

Finally, intelligence organizations have the task of weaving judgments on political, economic, sociological, military, and scientific matters into an integrated and complete view of an area or an issue.

This is as difficult and complex as integrating the modes of thought and expression of the political scientists, historians, economists, military strategists, and scientists who comprise the intelligence community or the foreign policy apparatus of the government. Thus intelligence permeates the entire foreign policy process. Intelligence activities cost several billion dollars annually, and intelligence judgments influence decisions involving the spending of even larger sums and, on occasion, concerning war or peace.

Two developments have increased the difficulties facing intelligence analysts in recent years. The first is the growing complexity of American foreign policy. Intelligence organizations operate most easily when the international system is stable and their government is pursuing a clearly defined and well-articulated foreign policy. These conditions were characteristic of the period when the Cold War was at its height, but they have been less true for several years. The strength of America's principal adversaries and allies (except the United Kingdom) have increased relative to that of the United States, and so has their freedom of action in certain areas. The U.S. remains in an essentially competitive relationship with the Soviet Union, but the policy of "détente" injects elements of cooperation into the relationship—elements which will grow if the policy is successful. This not only creates new intelligence requirements, such as monitoring arms control agreements, but also complicates the task of appraising Soviet policy. The same is true regarding China, with whom U.S. relations have shifted even more dramatically, and whose policies have fluctuated sharply in the past. And the rise of terrorism and drug use has resulted in new demands on the intelligence community for analysis as well as collection of information.

The second development is the information and knowledge explosion. The growing interdependence of nations means that a particular event may have very serious secondary and tertiary consequences which are difficult to trace out in advance. New techniques and equipment for processing and analyzing information should be a help to the analyst, and in some ways they are. However, they often provide a flood of information which is more than any individual can digest. Jobs are then broken up and greater specialization ensues, but this increases the dangers of parochialism in outlook and creates new problems in coordinating the work of specialists.

Moreover, neither "intelligence" nor "policy making" exist in disembodied form. They represent the work of men and women, who are both supported and constrained by the institutions which employ them. Loyalties, ambitions, emotions, values, dedication, and vested interests are involved in ways difficult for the various individuals themselves to disentangle. Thus it is hardly surprising that the relationship between intelligence and policy making—and between intelligence officers and policy makers of various types and in many different situations—is a difficult and complex one. Major-General Sir Kenneth Strong, long a senior official in the British intelligence structure, has commented:

> The relationship between Intelligence officers and policy-makers is of course difficult and complex. The generally accepted view that it is the duty of the Intelligence officer to 'give just the facts, please' has little relevance in a modern governmental structure. In the first place, the facts

are often such that the policy-makers are unable to interpret them without expert advice. Secondly, and obviously, the choice of facts is critical, and the Intelligence officer's decision as to which facts are relevant and which should be presented to the policy-makers is often the major initial step in the decision process. This choice between the trivial and sensational, between the unpleasant and pleasing, is by no means as easy as it may appear. Intelligence officers are human, too, and the temptations to prepare a logical story or to serve personal prejudices cannot be overlooked, especially in areas where the facts themselves are often in some doubt and the interpretation of them is as much a matter of opinion as of logic.

> On the other hand, there is a frequent temptation for policy-makers to use Intelligence data selectively to suit their own preconceived judgments or political requirements.[1]

The relationship between intelligence and policy making is hardly as central as a feature of the American system as is that between Executive and Legislature, nor is it as complex as the military-civilian relationship. Nonetheless, it does raise important issues, but these have received relatively limited study. This is partly due to the fact that the relationship in its present form is only a few decades old, but also stems from the secrecy surrounding intelligence activities.

However, before examining the relationship itself and some of the problems it poses, it is useful to discuss the sources and types of data that intelligence is based upon as well as the organizations within the U.S. government responsible for intelligence production.

THE RAW MATERIAL OF INTELLIGENCE PRODUCTION

Intelligence is a term which has different meanings for different people. It has come to mean not only information on foreign countries which has been collected and evaluated, but also sometimes refers to counterespionage and covert operations as well as espionage. At times intelligence is used to describe a process, and at other times to describe a product. Perhaps the most useful definition for the purposes of this paper is a modification of the one found in the Dictionary of the United States Military Terms for Joint Usage: *Intelligence is the product resulting from the collection, evaluation, and analysis of all available information which concerns foreign nations or activities, and which is immediately or potentially significant to planning and decision-making.*

Thus intelligence is designed to provide policy makers with knowledge concerning present conditions, trends, capabilities, and intentions of foreign countries and groups within them. There are, of course, degrees of knowledge—or rather degrees of certainty about knowledge. Some matters are known. Others may be unknown but (at least theoretically) knowable with a high degree of certainty, such as the size and characteristics of the Soviet strategic forces. It is the task of the intelligence community to gather and interpret such facts. It is also possible, through studying the Soviet research and development effort, its industrial production capabilities and performance, and its general foreign policy, to provide fairly reliable estimates—i.e. those within reasonable ranges—of

[1]Major-General Sir Kenneth Strong, *Men of Intelligence*, St. Martin's Press, New York, 1972, page 140.

probable trends in Soviet military posture for the next several years. Other matters are not only unknown but unknowable. For example, it is not possible to give more than a rough estimate of the likelihood of a war between Greece and Turkey at a particular period in the future because this depends upon the interaction of many contingent events as well as on the intentions of leaders who probably have not made up their minds over what course they will follow. Thus one of the important but difficult tasks facing the intelligence officer is to indicate the degree of certainty (or uncertainty) he attaches to his conclusions.

Intelligence can also be categorized as either strategic or tactical. (Counterintelligence, or actions designed to counter the operations of foreign intelligence services, is basically a police function. Neither counterintelligence nor covert operations will be considered in this paper.) Strategic intelligence involves knowledge of the capabilities and intentions of foreign powers which is required by United States leaders for making plans and decisions regarding national security and foreign policy. This includes intelligence on current developments as well as long-range forecasts on political, military, economic, and scientific trends in foreign countries. Tactical (or departmental) intelligence is so designated because it involves, *in the first instance*, information needed by a military commander or a diplomat in order to conduct his own operations. Yet it quickly becomes clear that there is no dividing line between tactical and strategic intelligence when we see how a single fact—the placing of Soviet army units in East Germany on the alert—would be tactical intelligence to the U.S. Army commander in Germany *and* strategic intelligence to U.S. leaders in Washington. With this limitation in mind, this paper concentrates on strategic or national intelligence.

The information that is collected for processing and analyzing by the intelligence community comes from a variety of sources ranging from the mundane to the esoteric. Since the importance of different sources varies with the country being studied and the issue under consideration, it is difficult to provide a meaningful statement of the importance of each type of data in the over-all intelligence process. The comments made on this matter should thus be regarded as no more than *very rough orders of magnitude*.

A basic source of information for intelligence production is material which is open and in the public domain. This includes newspaper and magazine articles, scholarly journals, books, open radio broadcasts, and the published documents of foreign governments and international organizations. These are important sources of information on Communist as well as non-Communist countries in many fields—although seldom concerning Communist military affairs. Open sources tend to be of more importance in developed or semi-developed countries than in those parts of the world which have only rudimentary media facilities and statistics-producing systems. Perhaps 20–25 per cent of the information used by the intelligence community comes from open sources.

Another major source of information comes from the reports of civilian officials of U.S. government agencies (excluding CIA) stationed abroad. The most important of these are the reports of the Foreign Service Officers in embassies and consulates, but also included are the reports from U.S. aid missions, attachés from the Treasury, Labor, and Agricultural Departments, and USIS personnel. The cables and dispatches of Foreign Service Officers, containing as they do the results of conversations with high local government officials (as well as background studies), probably are the most important sources of political information available. Many extremely useful economic studies also come from American officials, who integrate open source material with information picked up in their discussions with local officials or provided by local governments. Official reporting probably also provides 20–25 per cent of the total material that goes into the intelligence process.

U.S. military officials stationed abroad (either as military attachés or as MAAG personnel to oversee the distribution and use of U.S. military equipment) and routine military operations of U.S. forces abroad also provide information through their official reports. Naturally, these reports deal largely with military matters. U.S. military officials provide much more information on non-Communist than Communist forces. The operations of U.S. forces abroad may provide information on the capabilities of allied forces, as when joint maneuvers are held. They may also stimulate actions on the part of Communist forces which provide useful information through technical collection methods, a matter that will be discussed shortly. Considerable tactical intelligence is obtained from these sources, but probably only about 10 per cent of strategic intelligence originates with them—although this figure increases sharply in wartime.

The final source of information collected by human as against technical means is that obtained from clandestine collection.[2] This has been declining for many decades for a variety of factors. Weapons have become so complex that few spies could evaluate a modern aircraft even if they examined it. Even a scientist watching a nuclear explosion can tell less than an acoustic-listening device thousands of miles away. Moreover, many societies have become so complex that they must publish increased amounts of information if they are to be managed. This process has gone very far in the open democratic countries, which automatically reduces the potential role of the spy. The police organizations of the Communist countries, especially the Soviet Union and China, make these societies extremely difficult to penetrate. However, the death of Stalin and the Sino-Soviet split have forced Soviet leaders to compete for the allegiance of foreign Communist parties by providing information on Soviet thinking and policies. Thus some success has been obtained against Communist countries by recruitment of agents from the Communist parties of non-Communist countries. However, there is always the danger that a seemingly good source will turn out to be a double agent, who has provided some good information to establish his credibility in order to mislead at a crucial point.

Nonetheless, agents can sometimes provide the missing pieces of information that make it possible to answer key questions. They can be an important source of information on the *intentions* as distinct from the *capabilities* of a foreign power. However, as governments become larger, more complex, and more bureaucratic, the amount of information that any single agent can provide is limited by his contacts. This is why such importance is attached to

---

[2]Some collection efforts involve both human and technical collection, as when an agent makes a physical penetration to implant a technical device.

securing an agent close to the center of power, who can provide a broader and more inclusive picture of the plans and policies of his government. The difficulty of penetrating the Communist governments and the ease of open and official contacts with the non-Communist industrial powers have made agents most useful in the Third World countries, which are usually not the primary concern of American foreign policy. Probably no more than 5 per cent of the total information used by the intelligence community comes from classical espionage operations.

Since World War II, technological collection methods have increased rapidly in scope and diversity, and together these probably account for over a third of the total information. The scientific and technological revolution of recent decades has not only made it possible to improve collection technology dramatically, but the increased power and range of modern weapons have made them more vulnerable to technological collection methods. The power of nuclear explosions can be detected around the globe, ICBM sites can be observed by aerial photography, and a missile being tested emits signals over the course of its several-thousand-mile flight that can be picked up hundreds or even thousands of miles away.

Before discussing those types of technical collection which have arisen and grown in recent decades, it should be noted that there has been some decline in the importance of the oldest form of intelligence collected by technological methods. This is communications intelligence (COMINT), which became a major source of intelligence after the advent of radio communications. The success achieved by the United States in breaking the Japanese codes before World War II was a major factor behind American success in the Pacific War—just as U.S. failure to utilize such intelligence made possible Japanese success at Pearl Harbor.

The reason for the decline in importance of this source is that the senders have come out ahead of the interceptors in the never-ending struggle to encrypt messages so that they cannot be deciphered. Secure systems have come to characterize not only the advanced nations—non-Communist as well as Communist—but some of the developing countries as well. At the same time, the volume of messages is so great that unbreakable systems are not practical for all communications, even in the military area. Human and mechanical errors are sometimes made which make not only individual messages readable but, in at least some instances, can lead to the breaking of a system. And communications security inevitably declines considerably during the disarray of war. Finally, it is not necessary to be able to read messages to obtain valuable information from them by means of traffic analysis. Communications between two points indicate there is a connection between them; if what is taking place at one point is known, this may provide a clue to the activities of the other. While most intercept activity can be carried out at a distance from the target country, it is sometimes necessary to bargain in order to secure listening posts within friendly countries adjacent to the target area. The host country quite naturally tries to extract a high price for its cooperation.

There has been a rapid rise in the importance of electronic intelligence (ELINT) in the past few decades. This involves the interception of radio waves of a non-communications type—from radars and from new and sophisticated weapons being tested. Radars must continually be in operation if they are to be useful, and there are few countermeasures that can be taken to maintain security. Locating the radars and determining their characteristics often involves sending planes or ships close to a country's borders—sometimes approaching them as if one intended to penetrate national boundaries, which can increase tensions and occasionally lead to international incidents. When certain types of new weapons are tested, they are equipped with instruments which measure their performance and transmit the data to test sites by radio telemetry. Another type of ELINT is the use of radars to monitor the actual flight of a missile (RADINT), which also provides valuable information on the pattern of test firings.

The advent of nuclear weapons with their tremendous power brought into being special types of technical receivers, which detect the shock waves carried through the earth and air and provide information on the location and size of the explosion—seismic and acoustical intelligence. Recordings of electromagnetic waves and the collection of radioactive debris provide other types of information, including the nature of the weapon. Since all tests —except those of China and France—have been carried out underground since 1962, the possibility of collecting such radioactive debris has declined.

Whatever the importance one attaches to the above technical collection methods, there is widespread agreement that all are overshadowed by imagery or photographic intelligence. This provides useful scientific, economic, and military information on the Communist countries that is not available from other sources. It can even, by detecting the pattern of weapons deployment, provide clues to political intentions. The SALT agreements signed in 1972 specifically stated that neither side would interfere with national technical means of collecting information to verify compliance with the agreements.

Photoreconnaisance, while sometimes hampered by cloud cover, also has the virtue of a high degree of reliability as long as the film is of readable quality. Arms control agreements would have been impossible without it. Both photographic and imagery intelligence also provide important information on the location of natural resources, industrial facilities, and on agricultural patterns. (New types of sensors which can detect crop troubles or failures have been installed in some satellites, and the Earth Resources Technology Satellite [ERTS] provides new capabilities for detection of raw materials of various types.)

The most striking characteristics of the raw information gathered by the collection process are its volume and its variety—both as to type and to quality. Millions of words of open source information, tremendous numbers of intercepted radio communications and telemetry signals, thousands of reports from U.S. officials abroad, seemingly endless rolls of photographs, and smaller numbers of agent reports reach Washington regularly for processing and transmission to intelligence analysts and policy makers. Some of this, such as open source material, requires only routine categorization and transmission to the appropriate analysts. Other materials, such as telemetry signals and most satellite photography, must be examined by specialists with esoteric technical skills before being sent to analysts. Material collected by one agency or department is generally distributed throughout the intelligence community, although some information that arises out of operational activities of the various departments is held much more closely.

Some critics have charged that collection drives the system, rather than the other way around, and that masses of information are collected simply because it is technically possible to do so. While this probably is an overstatement, the task of guiding and controlling the collection process is one that will become more difficult in the years ahead as more sophisticated collection systems now under development become operational and greatly increase the volume of data obtained.

An unending problem for the intelligence community is that of evaluating the quality of information collected. How reliable have a particular agent's reports been in the past, and does he have access to the type of information in a particular report? Is the foreign minister of a particular country telling the U.S. ambassador the truth when they talk or, more realistically, how is he mixing the truth with statements designed to entice or mislead? Does an upsurge of unreadable communications between two points indicate that an operation is about to begin, or is it an attempt to confuse or mislead people in the National Security Agency engaged in traffic analysis? Are the statistics of agricultural production given the U.S. by a foreign government accurate? If not, is it because their statistical techniques are inadequate or because they want to create a particular impression? Some of these questions can never be answered with certainty, but meticulous cross-checking and comparison of reports from many types of sources dealing with the same subject often enable the processor or the analyst to reduce the uncertainties substantially.

THE STRUCTURE AND PRODUCTION OF THE INTELLIGENCE COMMUNITY

The "production" of the intelligence community ranges from oral interpretations of a particular event by a single analyst in response to a policy maker's informal query to the formal process involved in drafting and coordinating National Intelligence Estimates (NIEs) and having them approved by the United States Intelligence Board (USIB).[3] Much of the production appears in written form, but oral briefings occupy an important role in the system, particularly in the Defense Department.

Primary responsibility for preparing intelligence reports and estimates for the policy makers rests with the Bureau of Intelligence Research, the De-

fense Intelligence Agency, and the Central Intelligence Agency. The effort of the National Security Agency results largely in the publication of individual messages—or collection of messages—on specific topics, although its reports sometimes combine this information with material from other sources. The intelligence units of the military services concentrate largely (though not entirely) on tactical intelligence matters of interest to their particular services. The production of the FBI and Energy Research and Development Administration consists largely of specific reports dealing with their special responsibilities, while the intelligence unit of the Treasury concentrates on collating and summarizing intelligence produced elsewhere for use by Treasury and other officials concerned with international economic matters.

The Central Intelligence Agency has the principal responsibility for producing national intelligence, especially for the President and the NSC apparatus. The National Intelligence Officers (NIOs) are technically under the DCI as head of the intelligence community rather than as director of the CIA, but they are more a part of CIA than of any other organization. (Most of the NIOs are from CIA, although State and Defense Department people are also involved.) Most of the regular current intelligence production is carried out by CIA, which produces two daily intelligence publications, a weekly intelligence review, an economic intelligence weekly, and a weekly review of international oil developments. However, much of the material published in the daily publications, and some of the weekly material, is coordinated with the other members of the intelligence community, who can register dissents from judgments with which they disagree. A large part of the responsibility for economic intelligence has come to rest with CIA. Originally its responsibilities in the economic field were confined to research and reporting on the economies of Communist countries (including their international economic activities), but over the years they have expanded to include virtually all parts of the world. CIA does extensive research on military affairs—chiefly involving Communist countries—which overlaps the work done in the Defense Intelligence Agency. Over the past two decades the Agency has become a leader in the field of scientific intelligence, both as regards analysis and reporting on scientific trends abroad and in developing new technologies for information collection.

CIA has several important strengths, but has also suffered from two weaknesses. Since intelligence activities—collection, research, analysis, and reporting—are its major function, its senior people can devote most of their attention to such matters. Its analysts are freer of policy pressures than those of other intelligence organizations, which makes it easier to maintain objectivity. It is not bound by Civil Service rules, which gives its greater flexibility on personnel matters. And it has less problems maintaining continuity of expertise than do other intelligence organizations.

Its first weakness—and it is difficult to know how serious this is—results from the unwillingness of some people to work as analysts for CIA because they do not want to be involved with an organization which carries on covert operations. The second, and perhaps more important, weakness involves its distance (both organizationally and

<hr>

[3]USIB is chaired by the Director of Central Intelligence. Its members are the Deputy Director of CIA (representing the Agency), the directors of the Defense Intelligence Agency (DIA) and the National Security Agency (NSA), the Director of the State Department's Bureau of Intelligence Research (INR), and the heads of the intelligence sections of the ERDA, the FBI, and the Treasury. The heads of the intelligence units of the Army, Navy, and Air Force are not official members of the USIB, but they attend the meetings and can dissent from its judgments.

physically in view of its location at Langley) from the policy-making process. This is a particularly serious problem in view of the lack of systematic guidance by the policymakers that has characterized the relationship for many years. The National Intelligence Officer system is one attempt to remedy this. The institution of a daily CIA briefing of President Ford should be valuable in helping CIA keep in touch with matters causing concern and likely to be the subject of important decisions.

The activities of the Defense Intelligence Agency (DIA), which was established in 1961, range from basic research to current reporting. DIA's efforts are focused principally upon the military capabilities of potential adversaries—especially the Communist countries. Yet it must be prepared to deal with many other matters as well, ranging from the outlook for Sino-Soviet relations to whether a natural disaster in a particular country is serious enough to warrant the dispatch of naval vessels or aircraft for relief operations. It devotes a major part of its effort to briefing senior civilian and military officials of the Department of Defense. It must also provide intelligence support for the Secretary of Defense, and take part in the preparation and coordination of national intelligence.

DIA faces a number of serious problems which limit its effectiveness. It can be tasked by so many separate people and organizations—the White House, the Secretary of Defense, the Joint Chiefs, the heads of the military services, and others—that it is difficult to plan its activities in an orderly and efficient manner. Intelligence still has a low status in the military services, and only the Army has designated intelligence a career track. This hampers DIA's ability to secure its share of the best officers, a problem complicated by the reluctance of many officers to serve in an organization not part of their own service. Personnel turnover is high among military officers, and civil service rules limit management's ability to raise the standards of performance. The inherently hierarchical nature of the military establishment creates a milieu in which it is difficult for specialists to press their views on officers who are their seniors, especially on issues involving service or departmental interests or policies.

A number of efforts have been made in recent years to mitigate these problems. DIA has experimented with new methodologies in some fields. A Directorate for Estimates was set up so that some analysts could concentrate on longer-term problems with less pressure to respond to current developments. Efforts are underway to give civilians greater responsibility in certain areas so as to be able to attract better people and to assure greater continuity of expertise. DIA no longer publishes its own daily intelligence bulletin (although it still produces a weekly review) but instead sends out its individual reports as they are prepared. These measures should result in some improvements, but, in view of the many problems facing DIA, it will be difficult to achieve a substantially better performance.

INR is the smallest of the major production units. Its production efforts are concentrated in two areas. The first is intelligence reports that service the specific needs of senior State Department policy makers. These are often short reports focused on very specific developments or issues of current interest. The second is its involvement in the coordination of current intelligence reports and NIEs produced in CIA. (In addition to its production activities, INR is responsible for appraising proposed covert operations and for managing the external research program of the State Department.) If the Secretary of State is a dominant figure in the making of foreign policy—and has confidence in the leadership of INR—the organization can play an important role, for its proximity to policy-making officials enables it to focus its efforts on those matters of intense concern to senior officials. However, it has two weaknesses: (1) its limited resources, which make it impossible to assemble a staff sizeable enough to deal with the range of issues confronting the U.S. government, and (2) its traditionally low status in the State Department (especially among Foreign Service officers) and its constant personnel turnover, which combine to make it difficult to obtain top quality people with experience and continuity in their jobs.

The size of the U.S. intelligence community gives it considerable capacity for research in depth, and also provides great strength for analyzing and reporting during a crisis. At the same time, size also imposes limitations, for subtlety of thought about complex issues is seldom a noteworthy trait of any large organization. This problem is compounded when various organizations come together in order to coordinate their judgments. Special efforts are constantly required to see that significant differences of views are spelled out rather than glossed over, and to make sure that unorthodox views and individual insights are encouraged rather than stifled by the system.

One other point warrants mention. The various intelligence organizations are more cognizant of the work underway, and of the strengths and weaknesses, of the others than was the case a decade or so ago. Less compartmentalization has resulted in somewhat easier and informal working relationships across bureaucratic lines, and this provides a measure of flexibility that does not show up on the organizational charts with their inevitable emphasis on boundaries and hierarchies. Organizational rivalries and loyalties have by no means disappeared, but on the whole the phrase "intelligence *community*" has more substance now than in the past. Moreover, a serious effort has been made to expand relations between intelligence analysts and scholars outside the government. Progress has been made despite the reluctance of some scholars to become involved with intelligence agencies. This effort warrants continuation, not because outside scholars are more able than government analysts, but simply because all possible sources of new ideas and different perceptions should be sought.

THE ROLE OF INTELLIGENCE IN THE POLICYMAKING PROCESS

Intelligence has *four* separate but related functions it must perform if it is to play its proper role in the foreign policy decision-making process. Its *first* and most obvious task is that of following events abroad and reporting on important developments so as to alert policy makers to impending opportunities and problems. A *second* task is estimating future developments in other parts of the world so as to reduce the uncertainties and risks facing the policy maker. A *third* function also involves estimating, but in the particular context of requests by policy makers for appraisals of likely foreign reactions to alternative U.S. policies currently under consideration. The *fourth* involves monitoring conditions that could affect U.S. policies adopted or operations underway. Verification of compliance or noncompliance by foreign governments of agreements, such as those on arms control, is an important example of this type of activity. (Conveying judgments to policy makers about when verification is and is not possible *before* agreements are made is a related aspect of this task.)

If the intelligence officer is to fulfill his essential functions, he must perform *four* separate tasks. The *first* is providing guidance for the collection process, so that information is collected on the subjects that the analyst must deal with in his reports to the policy maker. The *second* is to keep attuned to the concerns of the policy maker so that the analyst can produce intelligence that is relevant to forthcoming policy decisions. The *third* is to produce high-quality, objective, and relevant intelligence reports and appraisals, something as simple to state as it is difficult to do. The *fourth* task is to convey his reports and estimates in a persuasive manner, which is essential if the intelligence produced is to have the impact it warrants.

The policy maker also must perform several related tasks if the relationship is to be successful. *First*, he must provide guidance to intelligence officers on the types of intelligence needed lest the intelligence officer be forced to operate in the dark —both as to his own production and in his guidance of the collectors. Estimating likely developments abroad is difficult enough without having to guess at the needs of one's own government. A *second* and closely related task is to keep intelligence officers informed not only of policies under consideration but of actions and operations of the U.S. government. Intelligence officers can hardly be expected to interpret the actions of foreign governments successfully if they are unaware of U.S. actions, promises, or threats that may be influencing the decisions of other states. *Third*, the policy maker must convey his evaluations of the intelligence he receives so that the intelligence officer knows whether or not what he has produced is meeting the needs of the policy maker. There are obvious limitations on the ability of busy men to perform these tasks in a regular and systematic manner, but, if extensive resources are to be devoted to intelligence, they are too important to be ignored.

There would be widespread agreement about the appropriate tasks of intelligence officers and policy makers as long as they are set forth in the abstract, as they are above, but everyone with any experience in either aspect of the relationship would immediately add that reality is never as clear-cut as the principles would have it or as neat as the organization charts indicate. There is considerable friction and tension in the relationship, which stems from personality clashes, organizational rivalries and conflicts, and different views about how the tasks of each side should be carried out.

There are two main views of the appropriate relationship between the intelligence officer and the policy maker. The traditional view stresses that intelligence should tell the policy maker what he needs to know rather than what he wants to hear.

The relationship should be an arm's-length one, so as to keep to a minimum the dangers of the intelligence officer's judgment being swayed by the views of the policy maker. The other view agrees that the intelligence officer must be rigorously honest and independent in his judgments, but stresses that if the former is to tell the latter what he "needs to know" he must have considerable knowledge of the specific concerns of the policy maker. Otherwise, intelligence work becomes the pursuit of knowledge for its own sake rather than a carefully focused input to the policy-maker's thinking and decision-making process. Even in the latter case, of course, intelligence is but one input among many involved in a decision. The policy maker gathers facts and ideas from many sources, and must also be concerned with such matters as domestic needs and Congressional opinion in coming to his decisions.

In theory the intelligence officer does not put forward policy recommendations, but his decisions as to which facts are relevant and the way in which they are presented can make a particular policy look sensible or silly. His experiences will have led him to have committed himself to certain views of men and nations abroad, and he will have his personal views on what U.S. policy should be in particular instances. No matter how disciplined he is in trying to keep his views about foreign areas under constant scrutiny and modify them if unforeseen developments indicate he should, he will be hesitant to abandon positions to which he has committed himself lest he be regarded as inconsistent. Yet the intelligence officer who becomes predictable risks losing his audience. No matter how hard he tries to keep his personal policy preferences from influencing his intelligence judgments, he will find it extremely difficult to make the proper allowances for his own views. Similarly, policy makers sometimes exert pressures—subtle or otherwise—on intelligence officers to tailor their judgments so as to support existing policies, and they cannot always avoid the temptation to use intelligence selectively in order to secure support for their policies from the public, the Congress, and foreign governments. Even more delicate and complex strains arise when there is disagreement among individual policy makers or departments which lead some to cite intelligence reports as support for their positions and others to downplay the significance of such reports.

These differences should be kept in perspective. One holding the traditional viewpoint would agree that an intelligence organization should be prepared to answer questions about likely foreign reactions to various U.S. courses of action. (How would North Korea react to the removal of U.S. troops from South Korea? Moscow to full U.S. diplomatic relations with China? Other food-surplus countries to an increase—or the lack of an increase—in U.S. food shipments to avert famine?) A person holding the view that there must be continuing contact between intelligence officials and policy makers would agree that the former should not tell the latter which policy he should follow. Those holding the second viewpoint argue that intelligence officers must be prepared to take the initiative in seeking out policy makers, gaining admittance to their meetings, making known the capabilities of intelligence organizations, and in effect pushing the policy makers to explain what their aims and policies are and solicit their requests for intelligence reports. The areas of overlap between the two viewpoints provide the basis for a working relationship, but the differences in emphasis often produce sharp and bitter clashes. Such disputes constitute one source of continuing friction between intelligence officers and policy makers, particularly when an intelligence failure or an unsuccessful policy creates a major potential fracas.

Another problem is the tendency of some policy makers to regard themselves as their own best intelligence officers—at least on some issues. Few of the leading officials of the U.S. government would have gained such positions of influence were they not possessed of considerable self-confidence. They may still value intelligence reports, but they are much more receptive to specific facts and hard (measurable) judgments than to "soft" appraisals of trends or possible political developments. Moreover, intelligence "judgments" often seem much less significant than the policy maker's own high-level diplomatic exchanges or private conversations with foreign leaders—especially if something as dramatic as a "hot-line" is involved.

This tendency has probably been one factor behind the trend toward increased emphasis on current intelligence reporting and the downgrading (though not the elimination) of longer-range analysis and estimates. Another factor has been the increased skepticism about the utility of policy planning which, in the judgment of some critics, is usually no more than an unimaginative projection of the present into the future in a way that conveys an impression of predictability to policy that is impossible in a disorderly world.

Few people who have had any experience in estimating or planning are unaware of the limitations inherent in such activities. Nonetheless, they express serious concern about recent trends. Major resource decisions—such as new weapons programs—can only be based upon judgments, implicit if not explicit, about the future. Unless foreign policy has a sense of direction, individual decisions are likely to oscillate with the pressures of the moment rather than according to a well-thought-out frame of reference or design. The top official can easily allow himself to be overwhelmed with dramatic facts about current developments to the exclusion of the less exciting long-range think piece. Modern methods of communications allow the Secretaries of State and Defense, or even the President, to be the country desk officer in a crisis if he chooses to be. This happened in the Cuban missile crisis, the Dominican Republic intervention, and the early bombing campaign against North Vietnam. The record suggests that such a temptation should be resisted.

How successful or unsuccessful have intelligence officers and policy makers been in fulfilling their respective tasks in recent years? More important, what factors have been responsible for the achievements that one finds and for the problems that exist? The outside observer can make only tentative judgments, and runs the risk of being unduly influenced by individual successes or failures that have come to his knowledge. To generalize, however, three broad conclusions seem warranted. *First*, many of the tasks are being performed in an inadequate manner. *Second*, the situation is better than it was a few years ago. *Third*, substantial improvements are possible without major reorganizations or drastic increases in already heavy workloads, although some changes in working styles would be required.

Before expanding upon these judgments, several points—or perhaps viewpoints of the author—should be emphasized. First, success or failure in establishing a mutually beneficial intelligence officer-policy maker relationship depends as much if not more on the *attitudes* of the officials involved toward each other's role as on *organizational* arrangements, but the *procedures* governing their relationship are of considerable importance to the whole process. Poor organizations are a handicap, just as good structures are a help, but the basic structure of the intelligence community at the present time *in the area of intelligence production* is sound. Second, different working arrangements are necessary in dealing with different types of foreign policy problems. Relations with close allies in an era of increasing interdependence require the participation of a larger number of civil servants, Foreign Service officers, and military officers than do relations with adversaries; and the procedures for providing intelligence on different subjects should reflect this.

Third, the advent of a new Administration often results in particular strains on the intelligence-policy making relationship. Even public officials who have a proclivity to work through channels in an orderly fashion are affected by their personal appraisals of the individuals with whom they deal. When new public officials have an instinctive distrust of bureaucracy as such there will inevitably be serious strains between policy makers and intelligence officers. This happened during the early years of the Nixon Administration, when senior men in both groups found it difficult to establish the trust and confidence in the other necessary for a productive relationship. In this kind of atmosphere, subordinate officials in the two groups who have worked together in the past can only mitigate the damage. There are some signs of improvement during the past year, but given the foreign policy challenges facing the United States there is no room for complacency.

What follows is a brief expansion upon the conclusions regarding the state of the intelligence-policy making relationship, together with a short statement of what can be done to improve it. More detailed comments on these and other points are contained in the final section of this paper.

1. Establishing requirements for intelligence collectors—a task that falls mainly to intelligence officers, but indirectly to policy makers as well—has always been a weak point in the process. Some efforts at improvements are underway, and these are discussed and appraised below.

2. The policy makers by and large do an uneven job of providing guidance to the intelligence community and evaluation of the intelligence product. Evaluation in particular tends to be *ad hoc* rather than systematic. (Guidance varies over time; many requests for studies were made when the National Security Study Memorandum [NSSM] procedure was first initiated by the Nixon Administration.) Periodic requests for particular studies and occasional complaints or compliments for a failure or a helpful appraisal are not adequate substitutes for a systematic effort in these areas. While some studies are self-initiated, and much of the reporting of any large organization is routine, a lack of guidance can

lead to an effort to avoid risks by producing reports on every possible subject, thus, overwhelming the policy maker with paper. Policy makers complain—with some justification—that they find intelligence organizations unresponsive to some of their requests. (This is a particular complaint of middle-level policy officers.) Instances cited are requests for analysis of the personality traits of foreign leaders, the influence of bureaucratic interest groups on the policies of foreign nations, and the underlying goals and rationale behind such matters as the Soviet strategic arms build-up. Complaints are also heard from some policy makers that intelligence organizations are extremely conservative in experimenting with new methodologies or in hiring people with backgrounds in new disciplines, such as the psychology of organizational behavior. Failing to get an adequate response, some policy makers gave little attention to production guidance.

3. An even more serious weakness is the failure of high-level policy makers to keep the intelligence community informed of U.S. actions that have been taken, high-level conversations with foreign leaders, and policies under consideration. (This poses a particularly difficult problem when some of the basic conceptions about world politics and foreign policy goals held by newly-elected leaders are quite different from the ideas of their predecessors.) Under such circumstances the intelligence officer faces an extremely difficult task in keeping attuned to the concerns of the policy maker—as well as appraising actions of foreign political leaders. There are several reasons for this failure. One is simply the pressure of time on the top men in the foreign policy establishment. This is a particularly serious problem when one man, Dr. Kissinger, has more duties than any one person can handle—Special Assistant to the President, Secretary of State, chief American negotiator in a variety of situations, and major spokesman on foreign policy for the Administration in its dealings with Congress, the press, and the public. Moreover, no adequate delegation of authority is made for periods when Secretary Kissinger is out of Washington. Another reason is his fear of leaks—not only to other countries but also to elements in the U.S. government with different views on foreign policy—which would make it more difficult to carry out his policies. (This problem of inadequate knowledge of U.S. plans and actions is not unique to the intelligence community, but affects other parts of the foreign policy community as well. Indeed, it is ironic that as compartmentalization has declined among intelligence officers it has increased among policy makers.)

4. In view of these problems, it is surprising that the quality of intelligence is often quite good. There are weaknesses, to be sure, but the product often matches the work done at the better universities and private research establishments. (This does not imply that the intelligence community is more capable than the policy-making community, for one could make a case that the content of American foreign policy has also been good—even though neither group has made full use of the other.)

5. It is difficult to make any meaningful generalizations about how effectively and persuasively intelligence is presented to the policy maker. Considerable flexibility is required on such matters and some is clearly in evidence. Some policy makers are listeners and some are readers. Brevity and a few specific conclusions are required for some policy makers on certain subjects. In other cases much more detail and speculation may be appropriate. *Whatever the format and procedures, important intelligence should be presented in a way that can lead to discussion and questioning before decisions are made so that the dangers of the policy maker misunderstanding the judgments (especially those expressed as probabilities) and the implications of such intelligence are reduced to a minimum.* The lack of such opportunities when final decisions were being made—as distinct from options being set forth—was a weakness of the NSSM system. Moreover, the NSSM system was inadequate when a crisis arose, as evidenced by the establishment of the Washington Special Action Group (WSAG).

The Nixon Administration's dissatisfaction with the U.S. intelligence community led it to make a number of changes in 1971, one of which was the establishment of the National Security Council Intelligence Committee (NSCIC).[4] The NSCIC was to provide substantive guidance and evaluation from senior policy makers to the intelligence community. Despite Administration complaints about the analytic quality of intelligence production and its relevance to policy requirements, the NSCIC has remained a paper organization unused by those who created it.

Without suggesting that regular utilization of the NSCIC—or something much like it, with both consumers and producers of intelligence participating—would solve the complex problems and existing deficiencies in the intelligence-policy making relationship, it has the potential to improve conditions considerably if used intelligently. Its task is not to provide the week-by-week, study-by-study policy maker guidance to intelligence organizations. Rather, it should focus on major long-term issues, specific opportunities and deficiencies, and examination of the procedures used by each group to fulfill its functions. For example, the NSCIC might examine whether or not the intelligence community is devoting the right percentage of its resources to Soviet affairs, to international economic affairs, and to specific areas. Is a major new effort needed in Southern Europe in view of the importance—and fragility—of this area? This would require some changes in working styles. *Specifically, policy makers would need to be less secretive and more explicit about their longer-term priorities and goals.* (There are, of course, limitations as to how much precision one can expect about long-term aims given the periodic turnover at the top levels of the U.S. government, but some improvements are possible.) Similarly, periodic and systematic efforts to convey evaluations of the performance of the intelligence community would make its internal efforts at improvement more effective. The high-level officials who are members of the NSCIC would have to rely on subordinates for the detailed work necessary to make this body effective, but support and direction from the top are essential, and the amount necessary would not be unduly burdensome for busy officials.

---

[4] NSCIC members are the Assistant to the President for National Security Affairs (Chairman), the DCI (Vice-Chairman), the Deputy Secretary of State, the Deputy Secretary of Defense, the Chairman of the Joint Chiefs of Staff, and the Under Secretary of the Treasury for Monetary Affairs.

KEY ISSUES IN THE INTELLIGENCE POLICYMAKING RELATIONSHIP

Establishing Requirements for the Collectors

There is general agreement that one of the weakest—and most difficult—areas in the entire intelligence effort involves establishing requirements for collectors in a systematic, efficient and meaningful manner. There are some people familiar with the intelligence community who believe that far too much information of certain types is collected simply because it is collectible and because someone somewhere has requested it—and who see the problem getting worse as technological capabilities increase. This probably grows out of the "jigsaw puzzle" syndrome—the idea that somewhere there exists a particular fact which, if available, would provide the answer to the analyst's needs.

Procedures have been devised for levying individual specific requirements on collectors. Arrangements and procedures have also been adopted for deciding whether or not to undertake a major collection effort on a particular problem or to buy a new technological collection system. The latter types of decision require major coordinated studies involving estimates of likely trends in foreign countries and long-term American foreign policy priorities. Similar types of appraisals and decisions are necessary if difficult agent penetrations are to be attempted in a useful manner.

The essential problem regarding requirements is that of devising a systematic and periodic tasking of collectors in a way that uses increasingly scarce resources for the most important needs. There is a major dilemma involved here. If all the specific questions that the intelligence officer (and the policy maker) would like answered are put into a list, it would be so voluminous as to offer little practical guidance. At the other extreme, a short general list provides little real guidance to anyone. What is necessary is a continuous surveying of what is known to the intelligence community, what it is ignorant of, and what elements of ignorance can be reasonably eliminated. Then—most difficult of all—it is important to establish a priority regarding the importance of the facts that need to be known and how much it would cost to learn about them. A particular fact may be only of moderate importance, but if it can be learned at a low cost it may warrant a high priority. Decisions must also be made about the degree of certainty required. For example, are the intelligence community and the policy maker willing to accept 90 per cent certainty of knowing a particular set of facts? The cost of acquiring such facts will be far less than if 99 per cent certainty is required, for in many cases it is the most sophisticated and expensive technology that must be used to eliminate the last elements of uncertainty. Clearly these are decisions that should be made jointly by the intelligence community and the policy makers. An effectively operating National Security Council Intelligence Committee should be able to provide some guidance on such matters.

Major questions arise about why requirements have been a general weakness of the intelligence community and what is being done to overcome this deficiency. There are a variety of reasons for past shortcomings. Some of them involve the inherent difficulties and complexities of the problem.

The problems can never be "solved"; the most that can be hoped for is that they are minimized. Requirements staffs often have had little prestige in the intelligence community, and few of the best people have wanted to work in this area. The requirements staffs have little authority over the collectors, and must obtain high-level support on an *ad hoc* basis when they are confronted with unsatisfactory collector performance. Collection is to some degree an opportunistic affair with an element of luck involved, and collectors in the field are tempted to work on the easiest rather than the most important tasks. Moreover, the collectors themselves have a valid complaint in that they are often not given adequate lead time by the intelligence officers and the policy makers, who sometimes fail to anticipate their needs—a difficult task in an uncertain and fast-changing world.

One other structural weakness needs to be pointed out before discussing efforts that are under way to improve the situation. Requirements at present come under the general jurisdiction of a variety of committees of the U.S. Intelligence Board. Each of these committees—such as those dealing with human collection resources, communications intelligence, and overhead reconnaisance—try to collect what is possible with the technology available to them. What is needed is a more rigorous effort to organize and integrate requirements in their entirety rather than only by individual techniques.

A number of efforts are under way to improve the collection guidance process under the leadership of the DCI, who now has direct authority over the chairmen of the USIB committees. One of these efforts involves the development of the Key Intelligence Questions (KIQs), which are worked out by the intelligence community in cooperation with the USIB committees, and are revised annually. Since this method has only been recently adopted, it is too early to evaluate its usefulness. Secure telephone lines have been established between a growing number of U.S. embassies and Washington agencies, which enable the intelligence analysts and the collectors to be in direct communication. Efforts are also under way to make sure that policy makers as well as intelligence analysts and collectors understand each other better. One of the tasks of the National Intelligence Officers is to facilitate this dialogue. These efforts to short-circuit bureaucratic hierarchies are being supplemented by attempts to link collection needs and performance more closely to budgetary and fiscal planning. Finally, an effort is under way to mesh tactical and national collection capabilities and needs. All of these activities should be continued and institutionalized.

Guiding and Evaluating the Reporting of U.S. Embassies

Some of the most important information to reach the intelligence community in Washington grows out of the reporting activities of U.S. embassies around the world. This includes not only the extensive reporting by Foreign Service Officers (FSOs) on political, economic, and social developments in their respective countries and on the foreign policy of the governments they deal with, but also reports by American attachés responsible for agricultural, financial, labor, and military affairs. Other important information arises out of the reports of AID Missions, USIS posts, and Military Assistance and Advisory Groups (MAAG).

Several obstacles exist to making this reporting more useful and responsive to the needs of the intelligence community. The first is simply a problem of understanding. To the typical FSO, intelligence is basically what is collected clandestinely by an agent—or, at the other end of the technological spectrum—by advanced technological methods. The FSO seldom looks upon *his* reports as a part of the intelligence collection activities. He often points out that if he were regarded simply as an intelligence collector by the local government, many of his sources of information would dry up. Yet to an intelligence analyst the conversations of a U.S. diplomat with his foreign counterparts are a very important type of raw intelligence, just as are the studies done by the embassy personnel on conditions and trends within a particular country. There is no point in trying to obtain an agreed definition of what is or is not raw intelligence. What is needed on the part of the embassy personnel is an awareness that these reports do enter the intelligence process, and more systematic training and evaluation of such personnel in view of their inescapable role.

At the same time, intelligence organizations need to remain aware that the activities and purposes of the U.S. embassy personnel and intelligence officers only partially overlap. Embassy reporting must serve many masters. Much of the work of the embassy official will be directed toward managing routine relationships between governments or—if he is a senior official—negotiating important agreements and making foreign policy recommendations.

Even increased understanding of these points would still leave unresolved the responsibility for guiding and evaluating the efforts of U.S. embassies regarding reporting for intelligence purposes. One obvious improvement involves devising a better and more meaningful requirement system, a subject discussed in the previous section. According to many people who have served in embassies abroad, requirements lists are either so general as to be meaningless or so detailed as to impose impossible tasks. In either case, they receive little consideration.

The DCI is examining various methods designed to foster closer links between the intelligence community and U.S. embassy personnel as part of his responsibility for coordinating the intelligence collection activities of the government. He is considering the idea of sending an annual letter to each embassy evaluating its reporting in an effort to provide guidance and stimulate improvement. This is obviously a matter that raises some delicate issues concerning the relationships between the DCI and the Secretary of State. A letter stating that an embassy had done a good job in most areas but needs to improve its performance on a few matters probably would not create many difficulties. However, a really critical letter would in effect be an indirect criticism of the Secretary of State. For such a system to be acceptable to any Secretary of State, such letters probably would have to be coordinated with him—in effect, with INR—before they were sent.

If this system is adopted, it might also be useful to require embassies to make a systematic appraisal of the quality of intelligence produced on the countries to which they are accredited. Such a practice, if handled in a constructive manner, would provide one element of evaluation of intelligence production from the viewpoint of those "on the ground" and could encourage a useful Washington dialogue with the field.

Policy Guidance to the Intelligence Community

One of the striking deficiencies affecting the role of intelligence production is the inadequacy of guidance by policy makers as to their needs. This is a broad statement, and exceptions are easy to find. Nonetheless, complaints on this point are heard too often to be ignored. Requests for particular studies are made from time to time by virtually every policy maker, and regular reports (such as the National Intelligence Daily and National Intelligence Estimates) are read—at least partially. One of the responsibilities of the National Intelligence Officers is to solicit guidance. Nevertheless, guidance is too often *ad hoc* rather than systematic. The National Security Council Intelligence Committee (NSCIC), which was to provide systematic guidance by consumers to producers, has been a paper organization with no discernible impact. The busy high-level officials on this committee could hardly spare the time for detailed work in this area, but without their drive and support any task force or working group of people more directly involved can make very little progress.

(The problem of inadequate guidance, it should be emphasized, is *not* something that developed in recent years. It has been a problem ever since the regularized system of policy making through reliance on the NSC system was abolished by the Kennedy Administration. Previously, the NSC meetings began with an intelligence briefing, usually by the DCI; he then learned of the concerns of the policy makers as they discussed issues, and was tasked by the NSC if further work was required. The major flaw in the system was the attempt to present a consensus on policy to the President, which led to a muting of differences and an emphasis on the lowest common denominator. Had options or alternatives been presented to the President, the system might not have been largely ignored since 1960.)

A key factor in whether or not there is adequate guidance is likely to be the attitude of the President. If he makes a reasonable effort to provide guidance—and if he encourages the NSC staff to do the same—his example is likely to spur others to take this responsibility more seriously. The President's Foreign Intelligence Advisory Board (PFIAB) should make this subject one of its regular concerns.

Evaluating Intelligence Production

A major weakness in the field of intelligence over the years has been the lack of systematic evaluation of intelligence production by the intelligence community as well as the policy maker. Individual analysts evaluated their own performance on an informal basis, and their immediate supervisors also did so. Occasionally, major studies of the record on a particular problem or area were undertaken. At times intelligence officers received comments about their reports from senior policy makers, but this usually involved specific complaints when a mistake was made or specific praise for a particularly good report. (More frequent comments come from middle-level officials. These are helpful, but no substitute for awareness of high-level reactions.) What has been lacking is a systematic effort to evaluate performance. The various parts of the intelligence community need to evaluate their own production, not so much so that they will know what their scorecard is, but in order to devote serious study to the basic reasons why they did some things well and others poorly. The intelligence officer also needs feedback from the policy maker so that he knows when he is answering the questions the latter needs answered and when he has misdirected his effort, when he has been persuasive and when the policy maker remains unconvinced. Criticism is as important as praise, if not more so.

In the past year, a beginning has been made by the Intelligence Community (IC) staff in this area. A small evaluations staff has been established to assemble the production on certain major issues, to appraise the record, and to see what lessons can be learned. Several points need to be made about this. Evaluation is a difficult and time-consuming business when one not only looks at which forecasts were correct and which were wrong, but tries to discover the underlying reasons and the lessons to be learned. It is more difficult to judge whether intelligence was relevant than if it was correct. Some intelligence judgments are conveyed orally at high-level meetings, and even when these are recorded it is difficult to get their full flavor.

The present IC staff effort should be continued and a body of case studies built up as part of an ongoing process of training and research. More people from the policy-making parts of governments should become involved in this effort. The NSCIC could play a useful role in this process if its members would occasionally consider which types of intelligence have been least—as well as most—satisfactory, on what issues and areas intelligence has been helpful, and thus provide some guidance to the IC staff as to what matters it should study.

The area of evaluation is also one in which the President's Foreign Intelligence Advisory Board (PFIAB) can play a helpful role. There is a tendency for such outside groups to focus their efforts on intelligence "failures." Yet one of the most important contributions such a group—which, despite their part-time status, need not operate under the twin pressures of time and crisis—can make is periodically to appraise *important* parts of the record of the intelligence community when there is no immediate crisis. People are less defensive and more open to constructive suggestions at such points, and an outside body is often well-suited to taking a long view.

Coordination or Competition in Intelligence Activities

One question that often arises is the extent to which there should be competition—or duplication —in the work of the various parts of the intelligence community. This is an important question, but it is a much narrower one than is often assumed. There is general agreement that collection efforts should be centralized to the extent possible and coordinated to the extent that centralization is not feasible. There is also general agreement that where extensive processing of raw data is required—in photographic read-outs, telemetry, and communications intelligence processing, etc.—it need only be done once and should normally be done in one place. (This refers to routine data, not the occasional crucial piece of information which will be checked and rechecked.)

A strong case can also be made for establishing a central data base within the intelligence community—and to a degree within the government as a whole. However, there is considerable wariness about moving rapidly in this difficult area. Much can be done through the use of computers, but no analyst wants to give up his own filing system until he is confident that he will have fast and reliable access to a centralized data bank. The initial equipment and training costs of this are considerable. A more fundamental problem is the cataloguing of information in the system. A decision as to what category a particular piece of information falls into is often a matter of judgment, and the judgments of analysts and cataloguers may differ. A particular report may touch on many subjects, and it is important that it be retrievable by a request for any one of them.

This leaves two broad types of intelligence production to be considered. The first is current intelligence reporting, and the second is research and analysis—including the estimative function. The costs of competition or duplication are of a quite different magnitude and nature regarding intelligence production than they are for intelligence collection and processing. In the latter case, the costs are primarily measured in terms of large amounts of money, but in the former they often involve claims on the limited time of high-level leaders.

It is somewhat misleading to describe the current intelligence functions as "reporting" as if current intelligence publications do no more than report the facts about the most important events in other countries as quickly as possible after they occur. The collection of items to be reported requires judgments as to what is important. More basically, current intelligence publications include interpretation, analysis, and projection as well as reporting, although such forecasts are normally of a short-term nature. Very little duplication exists any longer in the current intelligence reporting field. DIA still publishes its own weekly intelligence report. However, DIA has phased out its daily intelligence publication as such. Current international reports are now issued item by item as the information is received in DIA. One reason for this is that the appropriateness of a single daily deadline is questionable for an organization whose consumers are not only officials in the national capital but also military commanders located in different time zones around the world. A second reason is the fact that DIA leaders are satisfied with the National Intelligence Daily published by CIA. Items in this publication are normally coordinated within the intelligence community, and those in disagreement with CIA views are permitted to express their dissents. (It is not always possible to coordinate last-minute items, but these are designated as being uncoordinated.)

Despite the statements of some senior officers that they want facts rather than opinions, they are generally desirous of having a variety of views (opinions) sent to them on basic analytical and estimative matters. Theoretically, it is not necessary to have different organizations dealing with the same issues to surface conflicting judgments. A single well-managed organization which encourages debate and open expression of differences can do so. Yet the reality, at least in many cases, is less satisfactory. Quite apart from the danger of stifling dissent, there would be periodic conflicts about which subjects were to receive top priorities for research and analysis. These considerations have repeatedly led those who have studied this issue to conclude that: (1) a reasonable amount of duplication (or competition) in terms of research and analysis is desirable and (2) that on major questions (especially those involving national intelligence estimates) the various parts of the intelligence community should coordinate their efforts by presenting them in a single document so that the agreements *and disagreements* are readily apparent to the reader. Despite the attraction of attacking the conventional wisdom, in this case it seems wise as well as conventional. It should be emphasized, however, that effective decentralization of analysis depends upon having a critical mass of specialists (which varies in number with the type of work involved) necessary to do high quality work.

The National Intelligence Officer (NIO) System

During the 1950s and the 1960s, one of the key organizations in the intelligence community was the Office of National Estimates (ONE), which was responsible for producing the National Intelligence Estimates. This covered a wide range of topics. There were short "reaction" estimates requested by the White House—How will Moscow react to the mining of Haiphong harbor?—written in a few days. There were studies of likely trends in countries or areas over the next few years, sometimes written because policy decisions were to be made, and sometimes because the previous NIE on the subject was outdated. There was also—and this was one of the most important—an annual series of NIEs dealing with various aspects of Soviet military and strategic developments. Estimates were drafted by the small regional or functional staffs of ONE (who drew on specialists throughout the government) and reviewed by the Board of National Estimates, a group composed of both generalists and specialists. All were coordinated at meetings with representatives from the intelligence community before being sent to USIB for final consideration and approval. In some cases, agreement came quickly and easily. In other cases—especially the estimates of Soviet military capabilities and plans, upon which hinged important policy decisions and budgetary allocations—there were long and sometimes acrimonious disputes between different agencies. The pace of ONE was occasionally frantic, but an effort was made to provide time for reflection as well as production.

It was seldom easy to know how much impact the NIEs had on policy decisions. This varied considerably with the topic under consideration, the other sources of information available to the policy maker, the persuasiveness of the particular document, and the extent to which the minds of top officials were opened or closed on a particular subject. NIEs were sometimes not read, sometimes read but ignored, sometimes used by those whose views they buttressed (as witness George Ball's unsuccessful use of the NIEs on Vietnam to argue against U.S. involvement there), and sometimes had a clearly discernible effect on U.S. policy.

The NIEs were originally designed to fit into the orderly processes of the NSC under Truman and Eisenhower. The more informal style of the Kennedy and Johnson Administrations somewhat reduced the status of the NIEs, though more in the political than in the military area. NIEs faced more competition from ideas generated by columnists, professors, and others outside the government. The influence they had stemmed more from the persuasiveness of their arguments than from their status as NIEs.

The Nixon Administration was not happy with the NIE process or with ONE. Its leading figures claimed that ONE was unwilling or unable to grapple with the issues that concerned it, and looked upon the NIEs as too bland and lacking in intellectual rigor. People in the Office of National Estimates felt that the Administration's displeasure arose largely because ONE was unwilling to tailor its views on developments abroad—such as on Vietnam or Soviet weapons developments—to the preconceived views of the Administration. It would probably be unfair to the Administration to dismiss the first reason, but it would be naive to exclude the second one.

The replacement of ONE by the NIO system in 1973 was an attempt to do several things. The DCI wanted a group of high-level advisors on particular areas. These were to be generalists in terms of covering all intelligence functions—collection, analysis, operations, and relations with policy makers—for their particular areas rather than generalists on world affairs. Thus the NIOs are responsible for advising the DCI on collection needs and proposed covert operations, as well as supervising the production of NIEs. The NIO seldom draft the NIEs, but assign that task to specialists on the particular topic elsewhere in CIA or the intelligence community.

It is too early to appraise the effectiveness of the NIO system in terms of the quality of NIE production. However, one can point to potential strengths and weaknesses of the new system. It probably is more responsive to consumer needs since the NIOs are in closer touch with policy makers, and this should make it possible to give the NIEs a sharper focus on the issues under consideration. The production process is more flexible; bureaucratic lines can be crossed and the most knowledgeable specialist can be given the assignment to draft an NIE.

There are also several problems and potential dangers to the new system. One involves quality control; the most knowledgeable specialist is not always an adept drafter, and the drafts are reviewed only by the individual NIO before being sent to other agencies for consideration. Another is the decline in intellectual interchange across area or functional responsibilities. This was a strong point of ONE, but the press of time and the multiple responsibilities of the NIO reduce the opportunities for this. However, the greatest potential danger —and there is no evidence that it is more than potential so far—is that the present system is inherently more vulnerable to pressure than was the old. ONE was not only fiercely proud of its independence of judgment, but as a corporate body was able to protect it. This will be more difficult for an individual NIO, and will require occasional doggedness on the part of both the NIO and the DCI. A more subtle variation of this is that responsibility for drafting some NIEs will be assigned to other agencies where the analysts are subject to more intense policy pressures. This may affect the tone more than the key judgments—which will remain the DCI's—but tone can have an effect on the impression left with the reader. It would be useful to explore ways to give the NIOs as a group more of a corporate existence so as to minimize these dangers without damaging the flexibility of the present arrangements.

Intelligence Support for U.S. Foreign Economic Policy

The growing importance of international economic affairs during recent years has brought to the fore many difficult questions regarding U.S. foreign economic policy. (In reality the U.S. does not have a foreign economic policy, but a series of policies dealing with trade, energy, finance, food, transportation, etc.) Key issues include not only the appropriate policies to be pursued but also what departments should have what responsibilities, how their efforts should be coordinated, and where the responsibility should be placed for providing economic intelligence support.

The formulation and execution of foreign economic policy are extremely complex and difficult matters. A large number of departments are involved—State, Treasury, Commerce, Agriculture, Labor, Interior—as well as organizations of various types dealing with resources, aviation, shipping, central banking, communications, and environmental issues. There is a growing awareness that many economic problems transcend national boundaries, and that the international institutions and procedures established at the end of World War II need major restructuring. Coordination within the U.S. government, which would be needed in any case, is doubly important in such circumstances. Moreover, foreign economic policy affects—and is affected by—domestic economic conditions and policies to a marked extent. Each agency and department involved has its domestic clientele, whose support gives it power and whose particular interests it strives to protect and advance. Finally, foreign economic policy is *foreign* as well as *economic*, and must be coordinated with U.S. military and diplomatic policies.

There are four broad choices available regarding the organization and coordination of foreign economic policy, and the appropriate organizational and procedural arrangements for economic intelligence are to some extent dependent upon which of the four is chosen. The first would involve the establishment of a Department of Foreign Economic Affairs, which would take over the foreign economic responsibilities of all departments. Such a change would provide a clear final point of responsibility, but would have the disadvantage of creating an artificial division between foreign and domestic economic activities at a time of increasing interdependence. (It probably would also be politically impossible to strip strong departments of part of their powers.)

A second possible arrangement would be to give the coordinating responsibility to a single department, along the lines of proposals periodically made to give the responsibility to the State Department for foreign policy. The difficulty here is that no one department has the combination of technical competence, breadth of vision, and political support necessary to play such a role.

This leaves two interdepartmental approaches. One involves the use of something like the Council of International Economic Policy with the responsibility for broad policy planning and coordination, with a small staff of its own but relying on interagency committees to deal with particular issues. Such a body would have to rely on individual departments to negotiate with foreign governments. The final possibility is to give the National Security Council responsibility in this area, with departments which are not in the NSC framework being brought into deliberations involving their areas of responsibility. A major drawback is the tremendously expanded workload this would create for the NSC. In the past, policy formulation and coordination have been undertaken partly by the CIEP and partly by the NSC—a system that satisfies virtually no one.

These difficulties raise several important questions regarding intelligence. First, which organizations within the U.S. government should have the responsibility for collecting economic information, and by what methods against which targets? Much of the information needed for foreign economic policy is either unclassified or available from normal government reports, but some useful material may be obtainable only by agents or as a by-product of sophisticated technological collection methods by such organizations as the National Security Agency. This poses a particular problem with regard to the economic activities of U.S. citizens or corporations. Is collection of information on such activities—when they have international implications—a reasonable function of intelligence organizations, or does this involve them in domestic affairs outside their jurisdictions?

Second, where should the analysis of foreign economic trends—and their implications for the United States—be carried out? At the present time, it is to some extent scattered throughout the government. Originally, CIA was responsible only for national economic intelligence on Communist countries (including their foreign economic activities). The State Department had responsibility for the non-Communist world, although other departments did some studies in their particular fields—departmental or tactical as against national intelligence. Over the years, however, State's role has diminished and that of CIA has increased. CIA's economic support is highly regarded throughout the government; its output appears to be of high quality and relevance. However, most of the departments with economic policy responsibilities are not members of USIB, and it is not clear how effectively their needs will be met by the intelligence community over the long term under the present arrangements.

A third question arises out of the need to share the results of economic research and analysis with other governments and international organizations on certain occasions. (Some of these reports are distributed by the State Department, which is a logical arrangement for the present.) But if foreigners become aware that some of these studies originate with CIA, will they fear they are being given distorted information, or is this no more of a problem at present than it would be if the reports originated elsewhere within the U.S. government? How much influence should any problems that develop along these lines have on organizational arrangements for economic intelligence production?

Fourth, how should information on the state of technology in foreign countries be made available on a systematic basis to those government agencies responsible for licensing the export of U.S. technology? Are there adequate procedures for allowing such agencies to ask the intelligence community what the security implications of such technology transfers are?

Finally, what standards and procedures should govern how commercially useful information obtained through intelligence collection efforts should be released to U.S. firms? Obviously, it should be done on a nondiscriminatory basis. But that is the easiest part of the answer. Does the intel-

ligence community decide when security overrides possible economic advantage, or should those departments with a specific responsibility for furthering U.S. economic interests have a voice in these decisions?

In view of the uncertainties about the extent and likely duration of the turmoil in the international economy—and the lack of any consensus about the appropriate U.S. government organizational structure and procedural arrangements for dealing with foreign economic policy—it would be more sensible to build upon the present arrangements for economic intelligence than to make any major organizational changes. One procedural arrangement that might be appropriate, however, would be to make sure that there are adequate provisions for the DCI to report to the CIEP—and for the latter body (as well as departments outside the intelligence community) to have the authority to task the intelligence community. If the CIEP (or a similar organization) gradually acquires something approaching the status of the NSC, there will be time enough to decide whether it should have its own intelligence research unit.

RESPONSE TO BARNDS

Comments on "Intelligence and Policymaking in an Institutional Context"

(NOTE: For ease of use, these comments, after the first paragraph, follow the order of treatment given various subjects in Mr. Barnds' paper.)

General—1) Both of Mr. Barnds' papers are well-informed and provide a useful survey of the present state of the Intelligence Community and some of its problems. 2) The papers contain a large amount of purely descriptive matter which the Commission may or may not need. This is on the whole reliable information, and issues of fact and formulation which might be argued are mainly omitted from these comments. 3) The papers devote considerable discussion to problems of internal management of the intelligence community on which the Commission probably does not need to focus. Examples will be given below. 4) On some larger policy issues with which the Commission could usefully be concerned, the treatment is something less than incisive, the author preferring instead to be even-handed and to avoid recommendations. The intention here is to sharpen some of these issues.

The first two sections are largely descriptive. As indicated, there are points here which could be argued, but this is probably not necessary for the Commission's purposes.

The Structure and Production of the Intelligence Community—Reference is made to "two weaknesses" of CIA. The first has to do with the problem of recruiting and retaining quality personnel. Though CIA officers will usually deny it, the problem is both real and broader than the paper puts it. Vietnam, unfavorable disclosures about CIA, and even "detente" have created a climate of opinion in which able young people are less attracted by careers in foreign affairs, let alone intelligence. There has also been some attrition of good and experienced people owing to internal organizational problems

which have depressed morale. The impact is probably small now, but a price in the average quality of people will be paid in 10 or 20 years. National leaders who believe that an effective CIA will be needed for the long term should do what they can to make the intelligence career respectable once again; the argument is not at all difficult to make if the intelligence function is rightly understood. An incidental point: the implication in this section that the authority of the DCI to ignore Civil Service rules has made for higher personnel standards is incorrect; except for a much earlier retirement age, actual personnel practice has not been different from the Civil Service generally.

Reference to "distance from the policy-making process" as a weakness is ill-founded, at least for the reasons given here. Intelligence has been deliberately and for good reason organizationally structured to be *separate*. The location at Langley has not been a factor of consequence in impeding effective support by intelligence to policy. This matter has far more serious aspects which the paper takes up later.

The "serious problems" of the Defense Intelligence Agency (DIA) are by no means exaggerated. The larger questions implied but not stated, and which apply equally to service intelligence, are these: 1) whether serious and objective intelligence work can be done in the present organizational environment of the military establishment, and therefore 2) whether the military intelligence agencies should have the great, and lately increasing, weight they carry in the national intelligence effort. My answer to both questions is no.

The weaknesses and problems of INR are correctly though rather mildly stated. The conclusion which the paper should draw but does not is that

INR needs considerably more money and people. "Wristonizing" was a mistake, and the Bureau should be manned in the main by Civil Service career people to provide professional continuity. A small complement of junior Foreign Service officers should be assigned for a training experience so that they will learn what intelligence is. The reason this matter is so important is that, if the confederal structure of the intelligence community is to be retained, which seems altogether likely and is probably desirable, INR should have strength and weight to represent effectively its own unique view of issues and to counterbalance Defense and CIA.

The Role of Intelligence in the Policymaking Process— This section deals in broad terms with how the relationship between intelligence producers and policy makers has worked, leaving particular issues for more detailed treatment in later sections. These comments are likewise general, intended to underline or qualify some points and to suggest additional ones.

1. The paper rightly conveys that the relationship between intelligence and policy has not been altogether satisfactory. Some of this is correctable, but only some of it. A natural tension between the two elements should be taken for granted; there would be reason for alarm if it were absent. This is so because if intelligence does its job well, i.e., with as much objectivity as possible, it will present a picture of the external world more intractable and less responsive to our view of our just interests than policy makers would have it; the latter, and especially political leaders, prefer lesser costs and simpler solutions than generally are possible. A good intelligence organization will frequently be a messenger bearing bad news.

2. In this connection, the paper does not clearly state that one of the functions of intelligence, perhaps its most important one, is to alert, i.e., to warn of developments which can generate policy problems before these become acute. This goes beyond "meeting the concerns" of policy makers of which the paper speaks, by which it means those they already have. Such intelligence contributions will not always be welcomed, but they are essential if policy is to be more than merely reactive and short-term.

3. The paper invokes a false problem, the alleged difference between a traditional or arms-length view of the intelligence-policy relationship and an apparently newer view which argues for a close embrace and continuous contact. For effective support by intelligence to policy, there must be *both* a functional separation *and* continuous, two-way dialogue. The effect of overemphasizing the latter and downplaying the former, which is now in vogue, is to risk turning intelligence into a pliant team-player. It has been advocated in recent years, in fact, that intelligence should "get on the policy team", "play on our side," etc. When this comes to mean that intelligence should not bring bad news or should not undertake analyses which appear to question the operating premises of political leadership, it ceases to do its job.

4. The right balance of independence and communication will never be easy to maintain, especially when the foreign policy consensus in the country breaks down and issues become sharply controversial. There are probably only two sustaining factors: 1) a strong tradition of professional commitment among intelligence people which their leaders should articulate and constantly nourish,

and 2) leadership at high levels on the policy side which insists on objectivity and high quality in intelligence products and actively encourages feedback from policy officers to intelligence analysts. The paper is correct in stating that in recent years the policy side has not been helpful in these ways. Morale and commitment on the intelligence side have suffered in consequence. As the paper rightly states, a sound intelligence-policy relationship "depends as much if not more on the *attitudes* of the officials involved toward each other's role as on *organizational* arrangements."

5. While the Nixon Administration did manifest unusual mistrust of the intelligence bureaucracy, this was not the first time that a change of administration caused problems in the intelligence-policy relationship. Two ways of dealing with this can be suggested. Political leadership should acquire a better understanding of intelligence as a professional service, whose reputation and usefulness depend entirely on its freedom from partisan or policy bias. Most intelligence career people do understand this. Secondly, the Commission may wish to consider whether the DCI should not be a qualified political appointee who can vouch for the performance of the Intelligence Community to his political colleagues in an administration. This arrangement would have the added advantage of making more likely ready and regular access by the DCI to the President, something which has not obtained for a long time and which can be extremely useful to both.

6. The characterization of the NSCIC as a "paper organization" is fair in the sense that the main body became moribund at once, but this did not prevent its "working" level from generating much paper. There are a number of lessons to be derived from this episode. It was a classic illustration that attitude and not organizational proliferation are the key to sound intelligence-policy relations. It also showed that, when organization as such proliferates, nonsubstantive "managers" multiply and get in the way of substantive producers. Finally, the case shows that "Administration complaints that the analytic quality of intelligence production and its relevance to policy requirements" were not necessarily straight-forward: it may simply have been saying that its policy problems were terribly difficult and that it did not trust the intelligence people to give disinterested help.

Establishing Requirements for the Collectors—The section gives a good idea of the problems associated with "requirements", but I believe this subject is an example of an internal management concern which the Commission would be well advised not to pursue. This has been the most over-bureaucratized aspect of intelligence management, and the latest reorganizing effort under the heading of "Key Intelligence Questions" has built a still larger paper mill and caused greater waste of time by substantive officers. I take a simplistic view: the larger the requirements apparatus, the less meaningful collection guidance will be; well-trained collectors mostly know what to collect; arrangements should be made for as much direct exchange as possible between collectors and analysts.

Guiding and Evaluating the Reporting of US Embassies —Here again is a matter which is an internal management problem of the intelligence community and which probably need not concern the Commission. In any case, the paper makes more of an issue of the inadequacies of mission reporting from the intelligence point of view than seems justified. Intelligence analysts generally find much value in such reporting, though this varies somewhat by country and the quality of a particular mission's work at a given period. It is true that the FSO does not, and does not like to, think of himself as an intelligence collector. Part of his problem is imagery and semantics: he does not mind reporting "information", but he does not think of it as "intelligence", though in fact it is. Also, some missions tend to emphasize reporting on operational diplomacy and neglect in-depth study of forces behind the politics and policies of their host countries. One proposal the DCI could consider would be to assign substantive analysts to stations in key countries to supplement mission reporting. Such people would also be helpful to station personnel who are generally not well informed on the problems and needs of analysis.

Policy Guidance to the Intelligence Community—Little is added here that has not been said earlier. Of course, guidance is needed. Whether or not it is provided depends primarily, as implied before, on attitudes toward and understanding of intelligence by principal policy-makers.

Evaluating Intelligence Production—There is some tendency here, and this has marked the attitude of intelligence managers also, to over-formalize and bureaucratize evaluation. What happens then is that some largely non-substantive apparatus, which cannot possibly get at how the product was really made and really used, begins to generate useless "studies". There is an analogy to the bureaucratization of the requirements effort. Effective evaluation of product, and corrective action if indicated, depends primarily on 1) adequate feedback from high-level users, and 2) a systematic effort at product review within substantive production units. Finally, it should not be overlooked that self-criticism is built into the work of the conscientious analyst, since events regularly provide a test of the quality of his judgment; he also knows that his peers and superiors are aware of this fact.

Coordination or Competition in Intelligence Activities—As the paper says, the conventional wisdom stands up: for estimative product on major issues, there should be competing centers of analysis lodged in the community agencies. Community coordination works against product quality unless there is adequate competence in the analytical effort of the participating agencies.

The National Intelligence Officer (NIO) System—These comments should acknowledge that their author was intimately involved in the argument over the abolition of the Office of National Estimates (ONE) and the creation of the NIO system, opposed the change, and continues to believe that it was a retrograde step very damaging to the quality and integrity of estimative product, and indeed, to the role of the DCI and the national intelligence effort. Mr. Barnds, formerly in ONE, attempts a balanced treatment, though his preference for the previous system shows through in his account of comparative strengths and weaknesses and in his final suggestion that the NIOs be given "more of a corporate existence," a step leading back to the ONE system.

The viewpoint that ONE should not have been abolished can be summarized as follows: 1) The charges against ONE performance lacked substance. They were in fact based, not on product quality, but on what product said on key issues, or a distorted notion of it. The NIO system, giving greater play to specialists who are not effectively controlled by a review process involving senior generalists, stands every chance of delivering a *less* "relevant" product. 2) Quality of product has suffered from the dissolution of ONE's able and experienced staff. Estimative drafting is a skill which needs to be mastered in itself, and few specialists can do so. 3) The corporate responsibility of the Board of National Estimates for product protected objectivity. An individual NIO with too many varied duties and an obligation to "serve" his policy opposites is placed under strong and unfair pressures to please, i.e., to be a team player. 4) The assignment of drafting responsibility (this happens primarily on military subjects) to a department which has policy and budget interests of its own compromises objectivity. To this can be added that analytical and drafting competence in the military agencies is lower than in CIA and often poor. 5) The NIO system, and especially this latter feature of it, reduces the ability of the DCI to guarantee product quality and objectivity, something which having his own staff element (O/NE) did assure. Resulting from this is an ebbing of the DCI's authority over substantive work, at a time when (under the Presidential directive of November, 1971) he is enjoined to give more effective leadership to the Community. If the DCI is to "issue" NIEs under his own name and authority, and, if members of USIB are to be his advisors and not equals for this purpose, as originally conceived, he must have procedures and staff arrangements to make his authority effective.

Intelligence Support for US Foreign Economic Policy—The paper is correct that the demand for economic intelligence has burgeoned in recent years and that formal Community arrangements for producing it systematically are not yet adequate. Much of the work done in CIA has rested on informal contacts with research components in other departments, including some outside the intelligence community like Agriculture and Interior which have a marginal involvement in foreign relations. It would be a mistake to continue to concentrate so much of analysis in this field in CIA. It will also be extremely important to develop the analytical talent, so far lacking, which can deal with economic issues not merely in a technical way but also with the politics of economic issues in various countries. Research and intelligence units should be built up in State and Treasury (the latter has been on USIB since 1971 but has no independent research capability) so that there can be a true community product in this field as in others. As to the policy structure, given the range of departmental interests involved, there clearly must be an effective interdepartmental coordinating organ. The wisest course would be to provide such a body with strong chairmanship in the person of a Deputy Secretary of State for Economic Affairs; this could help to insure that foreign economic policy would be thought of as a coherent part of foreign policy and not, as has sometimes happened, allowed to be at cross purposes with foreign policy aims. The intelligence community could provide support for such an interdepartmental organ in the manner that it does now for the NSC.

A New Role for the Intelligence Community

INTRODUCTION

How well does the intelligence community meet the needs for intelligence arising from the conduct of U.S. foreign policy? Are there changes in the organization of the intelligence community that would make the collection and production of intelligence more effective or more efficient? Are there changes in the institutions and procedures by which intelligence officers and foreign policy makers relate to one another that would significantly improve the usefulness of intelligence to the making of foreign policy?

The paper by William J. Barnds either implicitly or explicitly raises a number of important issues that must be faced in answering these three basic questions.

OVERALL PERFORMANCE

Barnds does not attempt to address the question of overall performance directly, and the amount of indirect evidence in the paper is limited. For example, he notes that "many of the tasks [of the intelligence officer and the policy maker] are being performed in an inadequate manner [, that] the situation is better than it was a few years ago [, and that] substantial improvements are possible. . . ." He also notes that "the quality of intelligence is often quite good," though "[t]here are weaknesses to be sure. . . ." Some specific complaints by policy makers about the non-responsiveness of the intelligence community to certain types of questions are also noted, and the difficulty of determining the impact of National Intelligence Estimates on policy decisions is mentioned as well.

INTERNAL ORGANIZATION AND MANAGEMENT

Barnds notes and discusses several problems with the internal organization and management of the intelligence community, including:

- guidance and control of the collection process —he notes the problems of parochialism in outlook and of coordination associated with the growing sophistication and specialization of collection technology and the temptation for collectors to work on the easiest rather than the most important tasks;
- establishment of collection priorities—he stresses the difficulties of establishing priorities concerning what is to be collected, why, and how in an era of increasing demands on the intelligence community, growing complexity of foreign policy, an "explosion" of available information, and "unstable" objectives;
- achievement of a quality product by a large organization;
- significant weaknesses in the Defense Intelligence Agency and the Bureau of Intelligence and Research;
- inadequate internal evaluation of community performance;
- difficulties with obtaining coherent intelligence on international economic problems;
- problems with recruiting a quality staff created by the organizational propinquity of covert operations and intelligence research and analysis.

On the whole, however, Barnds believes that "the basic structure of the intelligence community at the present time *in the area of intelligence production* is sound." With respect to a problem he regards as serious—economic intelligence—he recommends that the government "build upon the present arrangements for economic intelligence [rather than] make any major organizational changes." He urges continuation and evaluation of community-initiated efforts to improve internal management, such as evaluation efforts by the Intelligence Community (IC) Staff, current attempts to improve collection guidance, and improvement and evaluation of the National Intelligence Officer (NIO) system, as well as use of the National Security Council Intelligence Committee (NSCIC) to assist in improving internal management.

RELATIONSHIPS TO POLICY AND POLICY MAKERS

Measured against his view of the responsibilities of policy makers and of intelligence officers, Barnds cites a number of problems with how well these responsibilities are being fulfilled. Though he fixes responsibility for what he believes is the present unsatisfactory state of affairs on both intelligence officers and policy makers, both the tone and the content of his paper point to policy makers as the more culpable. It is policy makers, therefore, who bear the greater burden for achieving improvements.

In this regard, Barnds notes several key problems:

- Policy makers have failed to provide systematic guidance to the intelligence community about goals, priorities, and issues of concern.
- Policy makers have too often failed to keep the intelligence community informed when they possess information of importance to the intelligence function.
- Policy makers serve too often as their own intelligence officers or as country desk officers.
- Policy makers provide insufficient feedback and evaluation to the intelligence community about its performance.

Barnds recommends no organizational changes to deal with these problems. Rather, he urges that policy makers, starting with the President, recognize in carrying out their responsibilities that more systematic guidance, evaluation, and communication will greatly improve the performance of the intelligence community. More specifically, he recommends that the NSCIC be actively used to perform the functions for which it was established, and that its activities be personally directed by the Chairman, the Assistant to the President for National Security Affairs, rather than being delegated to subordinates. Further, he suggests that the NIO system, the daily briefing of President Ford by the CIA, and the President's Foreign Intelligence Advisory Board (PFIAB) all can be used to remedy defects in policy maker-intelligence community relationships.

ANALYSIS AND ASSESSMENT OF BARNDS' CONCLUSIONS

Barnds is unquestionably right in what seems to me to be his central conclusion: the White House, through the NSCIC, must do a better job of guiding, directing, and "working with" the intelligence community. The DCI as a public official and the CIA as an organization have at present an extremely limited constituency: the President and a small number of top administration officials, mainly the President's key national security aide and the members of the National Security Council, to which the DCI by law reports.

The intelligence community is uniquely a staff to the Presidency. Like any staff, if they are not properly supervised, if their work is not appreciated, and, if they are kept in the dark, their morale will be low and they will probably not perform well.

However, Barnds has failed to unearth, or to analyze properly, a number of important issues relating to improving the usefulness of intelligence to policymaking. Moreover, in reaching the conclusion he did as to the need for improved White House guidance, he failed to diagnose some of the reasons for the present unsatisfactory state of affairs. Because of this, he has put forward some mistaken ideas about what guidance should consist of and about what can be expected from improved intelligence community-policy maker relationships.

The problem with Barnds' treatment of the issues stems from a difference of opinion about how to conceptualize the role of the intelligence community in foreign policymaking.

"Intelligence," in Barnds' view, seems to have the same characteristics as the military's "completed staff work." The responsibility of the intelligence analyst is to give the policy maker "judgments," their "implications," and the "degree of uncertainty" the intelligence analyst attaches to them, thereby reducing "the uncertainties and risks facing the policy maker." In arriving at these judgments, the intelligence analyst must gather and "interpret" the facts, a process which itself requires "judgments" or "decisions" as to what is "important." To perform this role, he must weave "judgments on political, economic, sociological, military, and scientific matters into an integrated and complete view of an area or issue." The results of this comprehensive effort must be conveyed to policy officials "in a persuasive manner" if it is to have "the impact it warrants", or if it is to convince the policy maker. The intelligence analyst must recognize that the way facts are presented "can make a particular policy look sensible or silly," and that "tone" can influence the "impression left with the reader."

Hopefully, the results, i.e., the intelligence analyst's judgments, will be "correct" rather than "wrong." Hopefully, too, the analysts will not be "vulnerable" to "pressure" to "tailor" their views to "the preconceived views of the Administration." [1]

If intelligence analysts fulfilled this responsibility they would be by far the wisest and best informed men in government. In fact, they cannot realistically hope to fulfill it, and therein lies the source of many of the recent problems and frustrations of the intelligence community.

Consider the following argument.

1. By Barnds' own estimates, 50–60 percent of intelligence material comes from open sources and from U.S. civilian and military personnel abroad, i.e., from sources over which the intelligence community has little or no control, and access to which is not limited to or restricted by the intelligence community. As Barnds points out, should the DCI attempt to deal directly with U.S. embassy personnel concerning their role as intelligence sources, serious bureaucratic problems with the Secretary of State could result.

2. The material needed to analyze a problem is, as Barnds points out, as diverse as human knowledge itself, encompassing every area of human affairs. The competence needed to analyze and interpret these materials in a truly expert manner is scattered among a great many government agencies, offices, institutions, and individuals inside and outside of government.

3. Foreign policy goals and priorities are not established solely by the President, nor, to the extent such priorities exist, are they stable for very long. Moreover, elected, appointed, and other officials with different values, perceptions, access to information, and skills are involved in policymaking. As Barnds notes "the policy maker gathers facts and ideas from many sources. . . ."

4. The foreign policy of the U.S. is, as Barnds also notes, becoming increasingly complex as the number of nations and the number and types of issues affecting international relations multiply and change. New demands on the intelligence community and on policy makers are being created constantly; yet older missions seldom can be abandoned.

In a world this complex, I think it is foolish for the intelligence community to aspire to a comprehensive and all-encompassing grasp of the policy problems facing the policy maker and to insist upon special dominion over the necessary sources of information, including the policy maker himself. It is the President who is held accountable for making "correct judgments," not the intelligence community. The intelligence community is one, but only one, source of information, ideas, analyses, and insights that will be of help to the policy maker.

A NEW VIEW OF THE INTELLIGENCE COMMUNITY'S ROLE

What, then, is the intelligence community's role, and what are its organizational and procedural implications? [2]

The intelligence community has a valuable asset —special knowledge. The DCI, as leader of the intelligence community, has a valuable bureaucratic attribute as far as the President is concerned—objectivity or, to put it differently, a loyalty to the

---

[1] In creating this construct of Barnds' view, some phases have been taken out of context. I do not intend to distort his view, and I hope I have not done so.

[2] The remarks here are addressed to the types of functions Barnds refers to as "estimating" and not to "reporting" and "monitoring," which are relatively more straightforward, though difficult, tasks.

President relatively uncompromised by the need to satisfy special constituencies. Using these advantages, the DCI and, under his leadership, the intelligence community can create for themselves a unique opportunity: the opportunity to educate the President and his national security aides on important facts bearing on significant national security problems and on the possible implications of these facts for presidential decisions from an objective and impartial perspective. The criteria for success of intelligence analysis, however, should be, can the President make better informed decisions about national policy because of the analysis, not, are judgments "correct"?

The intelligence community got a black eye with Dr. Kissinger and President Nixon in the early days, for example, by offering as the result of its labors the judgments that the Soviets would have x ICBMs by 1974, that the United States could verify arms control agreements by national means, that the Soviets were not testing a MIRV, and so on. When questioned about these judgments, especially by analysts in the Office of Defense Research and Engineering and the NSC staff, many in the intelligence community reacted as if their professional integrity had been questioned, and as if close questioning by non-experts was improper. Moreover, the community, and especially the CIA, acquired the reputation among many of having its own preconceived notions, particularly since other smart people could reach different conclusions based on the same evidence. The resulting conflicts over *who* was right served neither the interests of the President nor of the intelligence community.

The objective of the intelligence community should be good analysis, not carefully hedged, persuasively stated summary judgments. The MIRV case illustrates this point.

It was the intelligence community's judgment, expressed with some dissenting views in National Intelligence Estimates (NIEs), that the Soviets were not testing a MIRV in 1969. Analysts in DOD, with access to the same information, believed that they were. The President's NSC staff could not tell from reading the NIE what the basis for the disagreement was. They were reluctant to choose the DCI's view over that of Pentagon officials simply on the grounds that DOD analysts had a vested interest in believing the worst about the Soviet threat. They wanted to know the basis for the two views.

Dr. Kissinger convened a MIRV panel composed of experts from State, CIA, DIA, and OSD (chosen, incidentally, for their expertise and not for their rank or status). After a series of lengthy meetings and much drafting and redrafting, the MIRV Panel produced an excellent report that precisely and in detail described the evidence, the areas of agreement about its implications, and the points of disagreement. (A similar but much more extensive process took place concerning the U.S. capability to verify arms control agreements.)

What was valuable to policy makers was the thorough and precise analysis that the community in the end provided. Yet, despite the success of this and similar analyses, it always seemed to be unreasonably difficult to get the community to produce them. If the community sets as its objective the production of analysis that is thorough, objective, and well presented, the President and his key aides cannot help but rely on it, ask for more, and invite its purveyors to be close at hand in time of need.

While this is a different view of the intelligence community's role than that offered by Barnds, it will probably lead to a much more productive and sustainable relationship between intelligence analysts and policy makers.

ORGANIZATIONAL ISSUES

The Commission on the Organization of the Government for the Conduct of Foreign Policy should begin its consideration of issues relating to the organization of the intelligence community by formulating a view on the proper role of the intelligence community in the policymaking process. The Commission should then address the following questions:

1. Does the intelligence community have the capacity to fulfill its role in the policymaking process?

In all likelihood the planning, analysis, and evaluation capacities of CIA, and DIA and INR as well, need to be strengthened substantially and linked much more closely to the processes for allocating collection resources.

2. Does the continuation of the present role of the United States Intelligence Board (USIB) make sense?

This is an important question whether intelligence output consists of judgments, analysis, or both.

The drafting, coordination, and USIB approval of NIEs seems to be a cumbersome process that sacrifices rigor and precision to committee-created blandness. Affording the individual military services a right to express views equal to that of CIA doesn't seem to serve any useful purpose; it can be quite misleading to policy makers trying to interpret the meaning of disagreements and trying to figure out the meaning of USIB approval when disagreements have been noted. If we have a DCI, do we really need a USIB (or do we need it for all the functions it now performs)? Is there overemphasis on the concept of community?

3. Should DIA and INR continue in their present roles and capabilities?

Barnds makes telling criticisms of both organizations, yet recommends no changes. The matter should be further analyzed.

4. What should be the role of the White House? Should the NSCIC be continued and, if so, with what specific responsibilities and with what resources to carry them out?

It must be recognized that the success of the NSCIC depends to a large extent on whether the President's national security aide is a powerful adviser, on his attitude toward committee arrangements, and on the President's own style of management and leadership.

The important point for the Commission to stress is the necessity for active White House guidance and evaluation of the intelligence community, whatever management system the President chooses to adopt.

Finally, the question of the proper relationship with Congress is important and sensitive. Close congressional examination of intelligence resource allocations and intelligence production could significantly change the incentives affecting the intelligence community and the community's value to the President. I would recommend no changes in present arrangements until the issues and alternatives are examined with great care.

SUMMARY: FINDINGS AND RECOMMENDATIONS OF THE CHURCH COMMITTEE ([45A], pp. 423–471)

In setting forth its recommendations with regard to Executive control, the Church Committee provided succinct descriptions of the coordinating and policymaking units of the Executive branch. Although some of the material relates to other sections of this compilation, the Church recommendations are reprinted here with little abridgment in order to preserve their continuity.

A. Introduction

The purpose of the Senate Select Committee's inquiry into the intelligence activities of the United States has been to determine what secret governmental activities are necessary and how they best can be conducted under the rule of law. There is unquestioned need to build a new consensus between the executive and legislative branches concerning the proper scope and purpose of foreign and military intelligence activities. Allegations of abuse, revelations in the press, and the results of the Committee's 15 month inquiry have underlined the necessity to restore confidence in the integrity of our nation's intelligence agencies.

The findings and recommendations which follow are presented in that spirit. They are, in essence, an agenda for remedial action by both the legislative and executive branches of the United States Government. There is an urgency to completing this schedule of action. This task is no less important to safeguarding America's future than are intelligence activities themselves.

The Committee's investigation and the body of its report seek, within the limits of prudence, to perform the crucial task of informing the American people concerning the nature and scope of their Government's foreign intelligence activities. The fundamental issue faced by the Committee in its investigation was how the requirements of American democracy can be properly balanced in intelligence matters against the need for secrecy. Secrecy is essential for the success of many important intelligence activities. At the same time, secrecy contributed to many of the abuses, excesses and inefficiencies uncovered by the Committee. Secrecy also makes it difficult to establish a public consensus for the future conduct of certain intelligence operations.

Because of secrecy, the Committee initially had difficulty gaining access to executive branch information required to carry out the investigation. It was not until the Committee became responsible for investigating allegations of assassination plots that many of the obstacles were cleared away. The resulting access by the Committee was in some cases unprecedented. But the Committee's access to documents and records was hampered nonetheless in a number of other instances either because the materials did not exist or because the executive branch was unwilling to make them available.

Secrecy was also a major issue in preparing this report. In order to safeguard what are now agreed to be necessary intelligence activities, the Committee decided not to reveal publicly the full and complete picture of the intelligence operations of the United States Government. The recommendations as a whole have not been materially affected by the requirements of secrecy, but some important findings of the Committee must remain classified in accordance with the Committee's policy of protecting valid secrets. In this connection it should be noted that some information which in the Committee's opinion the American public should know remains classified and has been excluded from the report at the request of the intelligence community agencies. Only the Senate will receive the full version of the Committee's Final Report in accordance with the standing rules of the Senate.

In trying to reconcile the requirements of secrecy and open democratic processes, the Committee found itself with a difficult dilemma. As an investigating committee, it cannot take affirmative legislative action respecting some of the matters that came to its attention. On the other hand, because of necessary secrecy, the Committee cannot publicly present the full case as to why its recommendations are essential.

N1

This experience underscores the need for an effective legislative oversight committee which has sufficient power to resolve such fundamental conflicts between secrecy and democracy. As stated previously, it is the Committee's view that effective congressional oversight requires the power to authorize the budgets of the national intelligence agencies. Without such authority, an oversight committee may find itself in possession of important secret information but unable to act effectively to protect the principles, integrity, and reputation of the United States.

The findings and recommendations which follow are organized principally by agency. There are, however, common themes in the recommendations which cut across agency lines. Some of these themes are: guarding against abuse of America's institutions and reputation; ensuring clear accountability for clandestine activities; establishing effective management of intelligence activities; and creating a framework of statutory law and congressional oversight for the agencies and activities of the United States intelligence community.

The Committee's recommendations fall into three categories: (1) recommendations that the Committee believes should be embodied in law; (2) recommendations to the executive branch concerning principles, practices, and policies which the Committee believes should be pursued within the executive's sphere of responsibilities; and (3) recommendations which should be taken into account by the executive branch in its relations with the intelligence oversight committee(s) of Congress.

N2

B. General Findings

The Committee finds that United States foreign and military intelligence agencies have made important contributions to the nation's security, and generally have performed their missions with dedication and distinction. The Committee further finds that the individual men and women serving America in difficult and dangerous intelligence assignments deserve the respect and gratitude of the nation.

The Committee finds that there is a continuing need for an effective system of foreign and military intelligence. United States interests and responsibilities in the world will be challenged, for the foreseeable future, by strong and potentially hostile powers. This requires the maintenance of an effective American intelligence system. The Committee has found that the Soviet KGB and other hostile intelligence services maintain extensive foreign intelligence operations, for both intelligence collection and covert operational purposes. These activities pose a threat to the intelligence activities and interests of the United States and its allies.

The Committee finds that Congress has failed to provide the necessary statutory guidelines to ensure that intelligence agencies carry out their missions in accord with constitutional processes. Mechanisms for, and the practice of, congressional oversight have not been adequate. Further, Congress has not devised appropriate means to effectively use the valuable information developed by the intelligence agencies. Intelligence information and analysis that exist within the executive branch clearly would contribute to sound judgments and more effective legislation in the areas of foreign policy and national security.

The Committee finds that covert action operations have not been an exceptional instrument used only in rare instances when the vital interests of the United States have been at stake. On the contrary, presidents and administrations have made excessive, and at times self-defeating, use of covert action. In addition, covert action has become a routine program with a bureaucratic momentum of its own. The long-term impact, at home and abroad, of repeated disclosure of U.S. covert action never appears to have been assessed. The cumulative effect of covert actions has been increasingly costly to America's interests and reputation. The Committee believes that covert action must be employed only in the most extraordinary circumstances.

Although there is a question concerning the extent to which the Constitution requires publication of intelligence expenditures information, the Committee finds that the Constitution at least requires public disclosure and public authorization of an annual aggregate figure for United States national intelligence activities. Congress' failure as a whole to monitor the intelligence agencies' expenditures has been a major element in the ineffective legislative oversight of the intelligence community. The permanent intelligence oversight committee(s) of Congress should give further consideration to the question of the extent to which further public disclosure of intelligence budget information is prudent and constitutionally necessary.

At the same time, the Committee finds that the operation of an extensive and necessarily secret intelligence system places severe strains on the nation's constitutional government. The Committee is convinced, however, that the competing demands of secrecy and the requirements of the democratic process—our Constitution and our laws—can be reconciled. The need to protect secrets must be balanced with the assurance that secrecy is not used as a means to hide the abuse of power or the failures and mistakes of policy. Means must and can be provided for lawful disclosure of unneeded or unlawful secrets.

The Committee finds that intelligence activities should not be regarded as ends in themselves. Rather, the nation's intelligence functions should be organized and directed to assure that they serve the needs of those in the executive and legislative branches who have responsibility for formulating or carrying out foreign and national security policy.

The Committee finds that Congress has failed to provide the necessary statutory guidelines to ensure that intelligence agencies carry out their necessary missions in accord with constitutional processes.

In order to provide firm direction for the intelligence agencies, the Committee finds that new statutory charters for these agencies must be written that take account of the experience of the past three and a half decades. Further, the Committee finds that the relationship among the various intelligence agencies and between them and the Director of Central Intelligence should be restructured in order to achieve better accountability, coordination, and more efficient use of resources.

These tasks are urgent. They should be undertaken by the Congress in consultation with the executive branch in the coming year. The recent proposals and executive actions by the President are most welcome.[1] However, further action by Congress is necessary.

C. The 1947 National Security Act and Related Legislation

The National Security Act of 1947 [2] is no longer an adequate framework for the conduct of America's intelligence activities. The 1947 Act, preoccupied as it was with the question of military unification, failed to provide an adequate statement of the broad policy and purposes to be served by America's intelligence effort. The Committee found that the 1947 Act constitutes a vague and open-ended statement of authority for the President through the National Security Council. Neither espionage, covert action, nor paramilitary warfare is explicitly authorized by the 1947 Act. Nonetheless, these have come to be major activities conducted by the Central Intelligence Agency, operating at the direction of the President through the National Security Council. In contrast, the 1947 Act's specific charge to the Director of Central Intelligence (DCI) to coordinate national intelligence has not been effectively realized.

N3

In addition to this broad concern, the Committee found that the 1947 Act does not provide an adequate charter for the Central Intelligence Agency. Moreover, no statutory charter exists for other key intelligence agencies: the National Security Agency and the Defense Intelligence Agency. Nor does the Act create an overall structure for intelligence which ensures effective accountability, management control, and legislative and executive oversight.

Finally, the 1947 Act fails to establish clear and specific limits on the operation of America's intelligence organizations which will help ensure the protection of the rights and liberties of Americans under the Constitution and the preservation of America's honor and reputation abroad. The need for such limits is a need for legislation. The need is not satisfied by the President's recent proposals and Executive Order.

---

[1] Executive Order 11905, 2/18/76.
[2] 50 U.S.C. 401 *et seq.*

Recommendations [3]

1. The National Security Act should be recast by omnibus legislation which would set forth the basic purposes of national intelligence activities, and define the relationship between the Congress and the intelligence agencies of the executive branch. This revision should be given the highest priority by the intelligence oversight committee(s) of Congress, acting in consultation with the executive branch.

2. The new legislation should define the charter of the organizations and entities in the United States intelligence community. It should establish charters for the National Security Council, the Director of Central Intelligence, the Central Intelligence Agency, the national intelligence components of the Department of Defense, including the National Security Agency and the Defense Intelligence Agency, and all other elements of the intelligence community, including joint organizations of two or more agencies.

3. This legislation should set forth the general structure and procedures of the intelligence community, and the roles and responsibilities of the agencies which comprise it.

4. The legislation should contain specific and clearly defined prohibitions or limitations on various activities carried out by the respective components of the intelligence community.

D. THE NATIONAL SECURITY COUNCIL AND THE OFFICE OF THE PRESIDENT

The National Security Council (NSC) is an instrument of the President and not a corporate entity with authority of its own. The Committee found that in general the President has had, through the National Security Council, effective means for exerting broad policy control over at least two major clandestine activities—covert action and sensitive technical collection. The covert American involvement in Angola and the operations of the *Glomar Explorer* are examples of that control in quite different circumstances, whatever conclusions one draws about the merits of the activities. The Central Intelligence Agency, in broad terms, is not "out of control."

The Committee found, however, that there were significant limits to this control:

1. Clandestine Activities

—The degree of control and accountability exercised regarding covert action and sensitive collection has been a function of each particular President's willingness to use these techniques.

—The principal NSC vehicle for dealing with clandestine activities, the 40 Committee and its predecessors, was the mechanism for reviewing and making recommendations regarding the approval of major covert action projects. However, this body also served generally to in-

N4

---

[3] See recommendations on this subject in the Committee's Report on Intelligence Activities and Rights of Americans.

sulate the President from official involvement and accountability in the approval process until 1974.[5]

—As high-level government officials, 40 Committee members have had neither the time nor inclination to adequately review and pass judgment on all of the literally hundreds of covert action projects. Indeed, only a small fraction of such projects (those which the CIA regards as major or sensitive) are so approved and/or reviewed. This problem is aggravated by the fact that the 40 Committee has had virtually no staff, with only a single officer from the Clandestine Services acting as executive secretary.

—The process of review and approval has been, at times, only general in nature. It sometimes has become *pro forma*, conducted over the telephone by subordinates.

—The President, without consulting any NSC mechanism, can exercise personal direction of clandestine activities as he did in the case of Chile in 1970.

—There is no systematic White House-level review of either sensitive foreign espionage or counterintelligence activities. Yet these operations may also have a potential for embarrassing the United States and sometimes may be difficult to distinguish from covert action operations. For example, a proposal to recruit a high foreign government official as an intelligence "asset" would not necessarily be reviewed outside the Central Intelligence Agency at the NSC level, despite the implications that recruitment might pose in conducting American foreign relations. Similarly, foreign counterintelligence operations might be conducted without any prior review at the highest government levels. The Committee found instances in the case of Chile when counterintelligence operations were related to, and even hard to distinguish from, the program of covert action.

—The President's proposals to upgrade the 40 Committee into the Operations Advisory Group and to give explicit recognition to its role in advising the President on covert activities are desirable. That upgrading, however, will strain further the Group's ability to conduct a systematic review of sensitive clandestine operations. Under the new structure, the Group members are cabinet officers who have even less time than their principal deputies, who previously conducted the 40 Committee's work. The Group's procedures must be carefully structured, so that the perspective of Cabinet officers can in fact be brought to bear.

2. Counterintelligence

—There is no NSC-level mechanism for coordinating, reviewing or approving counterintelligence activities in the United States, even those directed at United States citizens, despite the demonstrated potential for abuse. Both the FBI and the CIA are engaged in counter-

---

[5] Appendix D. Senate Select Committee Hearings, Vol. 7, p. 230.

In 1974 the Hughes-Ryan Amendment (22 USC, 2422, section 662) was enacted. It provides that no funds appropriated under the Foreign Assistance Act or any other act may be expended by or on behalf of CIA foreign operations other than for obtaining necessary intelligence "unless and until the President finds that each such operation is important to the national security of the United States and reports, in a timely fashion, a description and scope of such operation to the appropriate committees of the Congress . . ."

intelligence, with the CIA operating primarily abroad. The Committee found frictions between the two agencies over the last thirty-five years. The so-called Huston Plan, discredited because of its excessive scope and patent illegalities, was justified in part as a response to the need for improved CIA–FBI coordination. At the same time, the Huston Plan episode illustrates the questions of propriety and legality which may arise in counterintelligence operations conducted in the United States or involving American citizens.

3. Coordination and Resource Allocation

—The Director of Central Intelligence has been assigned the function of coordinating the activities of the intelligence community, ensuring its responsiveness to the requirements for national intelligence, and for assembling a consolidated national intelligence budget. Until the recent establishment of the Committee on Foreign Intelligence (CFI), there was no effective NSC-level mechanism for any of these purposes. The Committee believes that the CFI is a step in the right direction and is to be commended. However, the language of the Presidential Order is such that much will depend on how the order is in fact implemented. "Manage" and "coordinate" are terms that are general in nature and have proven to be so in matters of intelligence. Because the CFI was formed only recently, questions remain about its operation and its relation to the DCI's current responsibilities and to the existing authority of the Secretary of Defense.

Moreover, the Committee notes that a major collector and consumer of intelligence information, the Department of State, is not represented on the CFI. It should be. Other agencies with an important stake in intelligence, such as the Department of the Treasury, the Energy Resources Development Administration, and the Arms Control and Disarmament Agency should play an appropriate role in the CFI on an ad hoc basis.

4. Executive Oversight

—The Committee finds that Presidents have not established specific instruments of oversight to prevent abuses by the intelligence community. In essence, Presidents have not exercised effective oversight.

—The President's Foreign Intelligence Advisory Board (PFIAB) has served Presidents as a useful "Kitchen Cabinet" for intelligence and related matters. It has carried out studies that have resulted in useful changes in procedure and emphasis within the intelligence community, as well as in the adoption of new technologies and techniques. At the same time, the Committee has found that any expectations that PFIAB would serve as an independent watchdog have been mistaken. The PFIAB has been given neither statutory nor Presidential authority to serve such a function. For instance, when the Board became aware of the Huston Plan, it asked the Attorney General and the Director of the FBI for a copy of the plan. That request was refused, and the Board did not pursue the matter with the White House.

N5

—The Committee finds the President's recent establishment of the Intelligence Oversight Board to be long overdue. In the Committee's opinion, however, this does not eliminate the need for vigorous congressional oversight. Moreover, the Order is broadly phrased and at some points ambiguous. The effectiveness of the Oversight Board, as well as the rest of the President's reforms, will depend in large measure on the details of their implementation.

The Committee makes the following recommendations concerning the National Security Council and the Office of the President. These recommendations are designed to support and extend the measures taken recently by the President.

Recommendations

5. By statute, the National Security Council should be explicitly empowered to direct and provide policy guidance for the intelligence activities of the United States. including intelligence collection, counterintelligence, and the conduct of covert action.

6. By statute, the Attorney General should be made an advisor to the National Security Council in order to facilitate discharging his responsibility to ensure that actions taken to protect American national security in the field of intelligence are also consistent with the Constitution and the laws of the United States.

7. By statute, the existing power of the Director of Central Intelligence to coordinate the activities of the intelligence community should be reaffirmed. At the same time, the NSC should establish an appropriate committee—such as the new Committee on Foreign Intelligence—with responsibility for allocating intelligence resources to ensure efficient and effective operation of the national intelligence community. This committee should be chaired by the DCI and should include representatives of the Secretary of State, the Secretary of Defense, and the Assistant to the President for National Security Affairs.[6]

8. By statute, an NSC committee (like the Operations Advisory Group) should be established to advise the President on covert action. It would also be empowered, at the President's discretion, to approve *all* types of sensitive intelligence collection activities. If an OAG member dissented from an approval, the particular collection activity would be referred to the President for decision. The Group should consist of the Secretary of State, the Secretary of Defense, the Assistant to the President for National Security Affairs, the Director of Central Intelligence, the Attorney General, the Chairman of the Joint Chiefs of Staff, and the Director of OMB, as an observer. The President would designate a chairman from among the Group's members.

9. The chairman of the Group would be confirmed by the Senate for that position if he were an official not already subject to confirmation. In the execution of covert action and sensitive intelligence collection activities specifically approved by the President, the chairman would enter the chain of command below the President.

---

[6] In effect, this recommendation would establish the President's proposed Committee on Foreign Intelligence in law but would include a representative of the Secretary of State. It would also empower the DCI to establish intelligence requirements. See Recommendation #16. . . .

10. The Group should be provided with adequate staff to assist in conducting thorough reviews of covert action and sensitive collection projects. That staff should not be drawn exclusively from the Clandestine Service of the CIA.

11. Each covert action project should be reviewed and passed on by the Group. In addition, the Group should review all on-going projects at least once a year.

12. By statute, the Secretary of State should be designated as the principal administration spokesman to the Congress on the policy and purpose underlying covert action projects.

13. By statute, the Director of Central Intelligence should be required to fully inform the intelligence oversight committee(s) of Congress of each covert action [7] prior to its initiation. No funds should be expended on any covert action unless and until the President certifies and provides to the congressional intelligence oversight committee(s) the reasons that a covert acton is required by extraordinary circumstances to deal with grave threats to the national security of the United States. The congressional intelligence oversight committee(s) should be kept fully and currently informed on all covert action projects; and the DCI should submit a semi-annual report on all such projects to the committee(s).

14. The Committee recommends that when the Senate establishes an intelligence oversight committee with authority to authorize the national intelligence budget, the Hughes-Ryan Amendment (22 USC, 2422) should be amended so that the foregoing notifications and presidential certifications to the Senate are provided only to that committee.

15. By statute, a new NSC counterintelligence committee should be established, consisting of the Attorney General as chairman, the Deputy Secretary of Defense, the Director of Central Intelligence, the Director of the FBI, and the Assistant to the President for National Security Affairs. Its purpose would be to coordinate and review foreign counterintelligence activities conducted within the United States and the clandestine collection of foreign intelligence within the United States, by both the FBI and the CIA. The goal would be to ensure strict conformity with statutory and constitutional requirements and to enhance coordination between the CIA and FBI. This committee should review the standards and guidelines for all recruitments of agents within the United States for counterintelligence or positive foreign intelligence purposes, as well as for the recruitment of U.S. citizens abroad. This committee would consider differences between the agencies concerning the recruitment of agents, the handling of foreign assets who come to the United States, and the establishment of the bona fides of defectors. It should also treat any other foreign intelligence or counterintelligence activity of the FBI and CIA which either agency brings to that forum for presidential level consideration.

---

[7] A covert action would consist of either a major project, or an aggregation of smaller projects meeting the standards of this paragraph.

EXECUTIVE COMMAND AND CONTROL/INTELLIGENCE ACTIVITIES

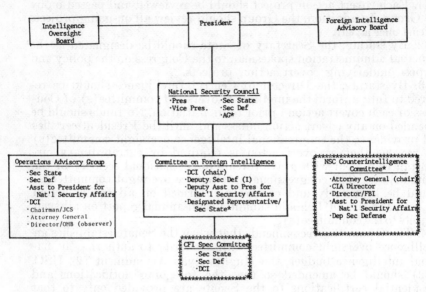

E. THE DIRECTOR OF CENTRAL INTELLIGENCE

The 1947 National Security Act gave the DCI responsibility for "coordinating the intelligence activities of the several Government departments and agencies in the interest of national security." In addition, the DCI as the President's principal foreign intelligence adviser was given responsibility for coordinating and producing national intelligence for senior policymakers. However, the Committee found that these DCI responsibilities have often conflicted with the particular interests and prerogatives of the other intelligence community departments and agencies. They have not given up control over their own intelligence operations, and in particular the Department of Defense and the military services, which allocate 80 percent of the direct costs for national intelligence, have insisted that they must exercise direct control over peacetime intelligence activities to prepare for war. Thus, while the DCI was given responsibility under the 1947 act for intelligence community activities, he was not authorized to centrally coordinate or manage the overall operations of the community.

1. *Coordinator of the Intelligence Community*

The Committee has found that the DCI in his coordinator role has been unable to ensure that waste and unnecessary duplication are avoided. Because the DCI only provides guidance for intelligence collection and production, and does not establish requirements, he is not in a position to command the intelligence community to respond to the **N6** intelligence needs of national policymakers. Where the DCI has been able to define priorities, he has lacked authority to allocate intelligence resources—either among different systems of intelligence collection or among intelligence collection, analysis and finished intelligence production.

The Committee supports President Ford's objectives of enhancing the stature of the DCI and establishing a mechanism such as the Committee on Foreign Intelligence (CFI) with the DCI as chairman to control the allocation of national intelligence programs resources. The Committee questions, however, whether the CFI can be effective without some appropriate modification of the peacetime authority of the Secretary of Defense. In order to strike an appropriate balance between the requirements of national and tactical intelligence, the intelligence collected by national means should be readily available to the military commanders and vice versa, and the Secretary of Defense and the military services should retain direct control over the operations of tactical military intelligence. Nonetheless, the DCI needs the right to review tactical military intelligence operations in order to make budget choices between tactical and national intelligence activities. Moreover, to carry out his coordinating role, the DCI needs to retain control over major technical intelligence collection systems which service both tactical and national intelligence requirements.

2. *Producer of National Intelligence*

In the area of providing finished intelligence, the Committee discovered that the DCI, in his role as intelligence adviser, has faced obstacles in ensuring that his national intelligence judgments are objective and independent of department and agency biases. The Committee has been particularly concerned with pressures from both the White House and the Defense Department on the DCI to alter his intelligence judgments. One example of such pressure investigated by the Committee occurred in the fall of 1969 when the DCI modified his judgment on the capability of the Soviet SS–9 system when it conflicted with the public position of Secretary of Defense Laird. After a meeting with staff of the Office of the Secretary of Defense, Director Helms deleted a paragraph from the draft of the National Intelligence Estimate on Soviet strategic forces which stated that within the next five years it was "highly unlikely" that the Soviets would attempt to achieve "a first strike capability, i.e., a capability to launch a surprise attack against the United States with assurance that the U.S.S.R. would not itself receive damage it would regard as unacceptable."

The Committee believes that over the past five years the DCI's ability to produce objective national intelligence and resist outside pressure has been reduced with the dissolution of the independent Board of National Estimates and the subsequent delegation of its staff to the departments with responsibility for drafting the DCI's national intelligence judgments.

In the end, the DCI must depend on his position as the President's principal intelligence adviser or on his personal relationship with the President to carry out his various responsibilities and to withstand pressures to compromise his intelligence judgments. Consequently, the Committee has been concerned that the DCI's proximity and access to the President has diminished over the years. Since 1969, at least until the confirmation of Mr. Bush, the DCI has rarely seen the President except at NSC meetings. The influence a DCI could have from a close relationship with the President has generally been lacking.

N7   While President Ford's Executive Order is a step in the right direction, the Committee believes that the DCI's responsibility over intelligence community activities should be enhanced and spelled out clearly and in detail in statute. The Executive should not continue defining these responsibilities alone as it has done since 1947 through Executive Orders and National Security Council Intelligence Directives (NSCIDs).

The Committee believes that the Congress, in carrying out its responsibilities in the area of national security policy, should have access to the full range of intelligence produced by the United States intelligence community. The Committee further believes that it should be possible to work out a means of ensuring that the DCI's national intelligence judgments are available to the appropriate Congressional committees on a regular basis without compromising the DCI's role N8   as personal adviser to the President.

Finally, the Committee has found concern that the function of the DCI in his roles as intelligence community leader and principal intelligence adviser to the President is inconsistent with his responsibility to manage one of the intelligence community agencies —the CIA. Potential problems exist in a number of areas. Because the DCI as head of the CIA is responsible for human clandestine collection overseas, interception of signals communication overseas, the development and interception of technical collection systems, there is concern that the DCI as community leader is in "a conflict of interest" situation when ruling on the activities of the overall intelligence community.

The Committee is also concerned that the DCI's new span of control—both the entire intelligence community and the entire CIA— may be too great for him to exercise effective detailed supervision of clandestine activities.

Recommendations

16. By statute, the DCI should be established as the President's principal foreign intelligence adviser, with exclusive responsibility for producing national intelligence for the President and the Congress. For this purpose, the DCI should be empowered to establish a staff directly responsible to him to help prepare his national intelligence judgments and to coordinate the views of the other members of the intelligence community. The Committee recommends that the Director establish a board to include senior outside advisers to review intelligence products as necessary, thus helping to insulate the DCI

from pressures to alter or modify his national intelligence judgments. To advise and assist the DCI in producing national intelligence, the DCI would also be empowered to draw on other elements of the intelligence community.

17. By statute, the DCI should be given responsibility and authority for establishing national intelligence requirements, preparing the national intelligence budget, and providing guidance for United States national intelligence program operations. In this capacity he should be designated as chairman of the appropriate NSC committee, such as the CFI, and should have the following powers and responsibilities:

a. The DCI should establish national intelligence requirements for the entire intelligence community. He should be empowered to draw on intelligence community representatives and others whom he may designate to assist him in establishing national intelligence requirements and determining the success of the various agencies in fulfilling them. The DCI should provide general guidance to the various intelligence agency directors for the management of intelligence operations.

b. The DCI should have responsibility for preparing the national intelligence program budget for presentation to the President and the Congress.⁹ The definition of what is to be included within that national intelligence program should be established by Congress in consultation with the Executive. In this capacity, the Director of Central Intelligence should be involved early in the budget cycle in preparing the budgets of the respective intelligence community agencies. The Director should have specific responsibility for choosing among the programs of the different collection and production agencies and departments and to insure against waste and unnecessary duplication. The DCI should also have responsibility for issuing fiscal guidance for the allocation of all national intelligence resources. The authority of the DCI to reprogram funds within the intelligence budget should be defined by statute.¹⁰

c. In order to carry out his national intelligence responsibilities the DCI should have the authority to review all foreign and military intelligence activities and intelligence resource allocations, including tactical military intelligence which is the responsibility of the armed forces.¹¹

d. The DCI should be authorized to establish an intelligence community staff to support him in carrying out his managerial responsibilities. This staff should be drawn from the best available talent within and outside the intelligence community.

---

⁹ [The DCI] shall: Ensure the development and submission of a budget for the National Foreign Intelligence Program to the CFI. (Executive Order 11905, Sec. 3(d)iii.)

¹⁰ "Reprogramming" means shifting money previously approved for one purpose to another use; for instance, from clandestine human collection to technical collection or covert action.

¹¹ In contrast to President Nixon's 1971 letter to Director Helms which asked the DCI to plan and review ". . . all intelligence activities including tactical intelligence and the allocation of all intelligence resources," President Ford's Executive Order 111905 states that ". . . neither the DCI nor the CFI shall have responsibility for tactical intelligence."

e. In addition to these provisions concerning DCI control over national intelligence operations in peacetime, the statute should require establishment of a procedure to insure that in time of war the relevant national intelligence operations come under the control of the Secretary of Defense.

18. By statute, the position of Deputy Director of Central Intelligence for the intelligence community should be established as recommended in Executive Order 11905. This Deputy Director should be subject to Senate confirmation and would assume the DCI's intelligence community functions in the DCI's absence. Current provisions regarding the status of the DCI and his single deputy should be extended to cover the DCI and both deputies. Civilian control of the nation's intelligence is important; only one of the three could be a career military officer, active or retired.

19. The Committee recommends that the intelligence oversight committee(s) of Congress consider whether the Congress should appropriate the funds for the national intelligence budget to the DCI, rather than to the directors of the various intelligence agencies and departments.

20. By statute, the Director of Central Intelligence should serve at the pleasure of the President but for no more than ten years.

21. The Committee also recommends consideration of separating the DCI from direct responsibility over the CIA.

F. The Central Intelligence Agency

1. The Charter for Intelligence Activities: Espionage, Counterintelligence and Covert Action

The Committee finds that the CIA's present charter, embodied in the National Security Act of 1947, the CIA Act of 1949, and the 1974 Hughes-Ryan amendments to the Foreign Assistance Act, is inadequate in a number of respects.

N9

While the legislative history of the 1947 Act makes clear that the CIA's mandate would be limited to "foreign intelligence," the Act itself does not so specify. Covert action, in the past a major CIA activity, is not mentioned in the 1947 Act, although the Act contains a vague and open-ended authorization for the National Security Council to direct the CIA to undertake "such other functions and duties related to the intelligence affecting the national security as the NSC may from time to time direct." [13] No explicit authority even to collect intelligence is provided the Agency.

The restrictions on domestic activities in the 1947 Act were not clearly defined, nor was the potential conflict between these limits and the Director's authority to protect "sources and methods" of intelligence gathering resolved. Neither did the 1947 Act set forth the Agency's role in conducting counterintelligence and in collecting foreign intelligence.

---

[13] Appendix B, Hearings, Vol. 7, p. 210.

The Congress' confusing and ill-defined charge to the Agency in these areas resulted in conflicts of jurisdiction with other government agencies. The lack of legislative specificity also opened the way to domestic activities such as Operation CHAOS [14] which clearly went beyond Congress' intent in enacting and amending the National

N10 Security Act. In sum, the Committee finds that a clear statutory basis is needed for the Agency's conduct abroad of covert action, espionage, counterintelligence and foreign intelligence collection and for such counterespionage operations within the United States as the Agency may have to undertake as a result of the activities abroad.[15]

Foreign Espionage

Espionage is often equated with the slightly broader category of "clandestine human collection." Although "clandestine human collection" may include collection of public information by a covert source, espionage centers on recruiting and handling agents to acquire "protected" or "denied" information.

Espionage on behalf of the United States Government is primarily the responsibility of the Central Intelligence Agency's Clandestine Service which operates on a world-wide basis. The Clandestine Service—officially, the Directorate of Operations—is responsible for CIA clandestine human collection, espionage, covert action, paramilitary operations and counterintelligence. The CIA also has special responsibilities for coordinating the military services' limited espionage activities abroad.

By CIA doctrine, espionage should be aimed at securing information others wish to conceal and not at collecting information available through diplomatic channels or from public sources, such as the press, television and radio.

The Clandestine Service regards espionage, rather than covert action and other such activities, as the essence of its mission. Indeed, the Committee found that clandestine human intelligence collection is often considered a prerequisite as well as a precursor of successful covert action, paramilitary activity, and counterintelligence.

Espionage targets vary, covering political, military and economic information wherever we perceive a national interest. Espionage involves a variety of techniques, ranging from technical surveillance, break-ins and theft, to human reporting by controlled agents, paid and unpaid of protected information. It is generally illegal in the countries against which it is aimed, but its widespread practice by nation states makes the status of espionage under international law ambiguous.

Covert action, which is designed to have an impact, differs from clandestine collection and classic espionage, which are designed to obtain intelligence without affecting the source or revealing the fact that the information has been collected. In practice, however, covert action and espionage overlap, since they rely on the same CIA officers, foreign intermediaries, and sources of information.[16]

---

[14] See the Committee's detailed report on Project CHADS.
[15] See the Committee's Report on Domestic Intelligence. Part IV, for recommended limitations on such activity.
[16] Senate Select Committee, "Covert Action in Chile," p. 6ff.

The Committee believes that the United States cannot forego clandestine human collection and expect to maintain the same quality of intelligence on matters of the highest importance to our national security. Technical collection systems do not eliminate the usefulness of espionage in denied areas (essentially the communist countries). Agent intelligence can help provide valuable insight concerning the motivations for activities or policies of potential adversaries, as well as their future intentions.

Nevertheless, the Committee found that there are certain inherent limitations to the value of clandestine sources. Espionage information tends to be fragmentary, and there is always some question as to the trustworthiness and reliability of the source.

The Committee found that over the last decade, the size of the Clandestine Service has been reduced significantly, particularly in the field. However, there remains the question of whether the complements abroad and at headquarters have been reduced sufficiently.

The Committee found that the CIA's clandestine collection effort has been reoriented towards denied areas and away from internal political and security developments in the Third World. The Committee believes that this changed emphasis is desirable and welcomes it.

The Committee found that while internal supervision of espionage within the CIA appears sufficient, there is inadequate external review and control over CIA espionage activities. There is no effective machinery to ensure that the Secretaries of States and Defense and the Assistant to the President for National Security Affairs, who are knowledgeable about the value and limitations of espionage, systematically participate directly in decisions concerning such issues as how large our espionage effort should be, the relative priorities, risk assessments, and possible duplication of effort between overt and clandestine human collection.

The Committee notes that the duplication between the CIA's Clandestine Service and the State Department's overt Foreign Service reporting appears to have diminished in recent years. However, William Colby when he was DCI voiced concern that the problem had not been solved. The Committee notes that increased collection efforts regarding economic issues may aggravate the overlap problem.

Foreign Intelligence Collection in the United States

The CIA engages in both overt and clandestine activity within the United States for the purpose of foreign intelligence collection. The Domestic Collection Division (DCD) is responsible primarily for overt collection, while the Foreign Resources Division (FRD) manages clandestine collection of foreign intelligence. Both divisions are currently within the Directorate of Operations. Formerly run and staffed by the Directorate of Intelligence, the DCD was moved to Operations in 1973 and now has many clandestine services officers assigned to it.

The Domestic Collection Division openly collects foreign intelligence information from American citizens on a wide variety of subjects, primarily of an economic and technological nature. The Domestic Collection Division currently maintains contact with tens of thousands of American citizens who, on a confidential basis, volunteer information of intelligence value to the United States. The Committee notes that the Central Intelligence Agency is *overtly* in contact with many members of the American academic community to consult with them on the subjects of their expertise. On occasion, at the request of the academic concerned, these contacts are confidential.

The Committee believes there are significant benefits to both the government and the universities in such contacts and that they should not be discouraged. The Committee sees no danger to the integrity of American academic institutions in continuing such overt contacts.

The Domestic Collection Division operates from 38 offices around the United States and lists itself in local telephone directories, although it conducts its business as discretely as possible.

The Foreign Resources Division (FRD) performs its functions in a more traditional operational manner much as it is done overseas; foreign nationals of special interest, located in the United States, are enlisted to cooperate secretly with the CIA abroad. FRD's activity, which takes place throughout the United States, is carried out by some of CIA's very best personnel. In the performance of its job, FRD maintains contact with a large number of Americans who are witting of its mission and willing to be cooperative. There are also a number of Americans who are not aware that they are participating in such CIA activities.

The Committee believes that the activities of the Foreign Resources Division and the Domestic Collection Division make an important and useful contribution to the overall intelligence effort; however, there are significant problems.

The Committee found that the Domestic Collection Division, subsidiary to its overt role, supports the clandestine components of the CIA. It provides such services as re-settling defectors, and, by drawing on DCD's extensive contacts in the U.S., reports leads regarding foreign nationals who could prove useful abroad or U.S. firms whose offices abroad could help the CIA.
The Committee is concerned that this kind of assistance provided by the Domestic Collection Division, if not closely watched, could lead to an exploitation of cooperating Americans beyond that which they, themselves, envisioned or beyond these limited CIA objectives.

The Committee notes that due to the recent revelations about CIA activities, some foreign intelligence sources are shying away from cooperation with the Domestic Collection Division, thus impeding this division's most important function, namely, the overt collection of foreign intelligence.

The Committee also questions the recruiting, for foreign espionage purposes, if immigrants desiring American citizenship, because it might be construed as coercive.

Foreign Counterintelligence [19]

Counterintelligence is defined quite broadly by the CIA. It includes the knowledge needed for the protection and preservation of the military, economic, and productive strength of the United States, as well as the government's security in domestic and foreign affairs, against or from espionage, sabotage, and subversion designed to weaken or destroy the United States.

Counterintelligence (CI) is a special form of intelligence activity, aimed at discovering hostile foreign intelligence operations and destroying their effectiveness. It involves protecting the United States Government against infiltration by foreign agents, as well as controlling and manipulating adversary intelligence operations. An effort is made to discern the plans and intentions of enemy intelligence services and to deceive them about our own.

The Committee finds that the threat from hostile intelligence services is real. In the United States alone, well over a thousand Soviet officials are on permanent assignment. Among these, over 40 percent have been identified as members of the KGB or GRU, the Soviet civilian and military intelligence units, respectively. Estimates for the number of *unidentified* Soviet intelligence officers raise this figure to over 60 percent and some defector sources have estimated that 70 percent to 80 percent of Soviet officials in the United States have some intelligence connection.

Furthermore, the number of Soviets with access to the United States his tripled since 1960, and is still increasing. In 1974, for example, over 200 Soviet ships with a total crew complement of 13,000 officers and men visited this country. Some 4,000 Soviets entered the United States as commercial or exchange visitors in 1974. In 1972–1973, for example, approximately one third of the Soviet exchange students here for the academic year under the East-West student exchange program were cooperating with the KGB, according to the Central Intelligence Agency.

Other areas of counterintelligence concern include the sharp increase in the number of Soviet immigrants to the United States (4,000 in 1974 compared to fewer than 500 in 1972) ; the rise in East-West commercial exchange visitors (from 641 in 1972 to 1,500 in 1974) ; and the growing number of officials in this country from other Communist bloc nations (from 416 in 1960 to 798 in 1975).

Both the FBI and the CIA are engaged in counterintelligence work. The CIA operates primarily abroad. Within the United States the counterintelligence mission is conducted by the FBI, except when the CIA, in consultation with the FBI, continues activities begun abroad.

Defectors are an important source of counterintelligence. Within the United States, the interrogation of defectors is primarily the responsibility of the FBI, though the CIA may also participate. Sometimes, however, the bona fides of a defector are disputed between

---

[19] See also the Select Committee Report on CHAOS and the counterintelligence recommendations in the committee's Report on Domestic Intelligence Activities and the Rights of Americans, Part IV.

the CIA and the FBI and there is no established interagency mechanism for settling such disputes—which may last for years. An incident in which a defector was held in so-called "incommunicado interrogation" for two years was, in part, a result of the lack of such a mechanism.[20]

Liaison among the various U.S. Government counterintelligence units at home is particularly important, because counterintelligence—with all its intricacies and deceptions—requires coordination among agencies and sharing of records. Unlike the totally unified KGB organization, the American intelligence service is fragmented and depends upon liaison to make operations more effective.

Coordination between CIA and FBI counterintelligence units is especially critical. The history of CIA–FBI liaison has been turbulent, though a strong undercurrent of cooperation has usually existed at the staff level since 1952 when the Bureau began sending a liaison person to the CIA on a regular basis. The sources of friction between the CIA and FBI in the early days revolved around such matters as the frequent unwillingness of the Bureau to collect positive intelligence for the CIA within the United States or to help recruit foreign officials in this country.

N11 In 1970 an essentially minor incident resulted in an order from FBI Director Hoover to discontinue FBI liaison with the Central Intelligence Agency. Although informal communications between CIA and FBI staff personnel continued, it was not until the post-Hoover era that formal liaison relations were reestablished. Today, there is still a need for closer coordination of FBI and CIA counterintelligence efforts.

The Committee believes that counterintelligence requires the direct attention of Congress and the executive for three reasons: (1) two distinct and partly incompatible approaches to counterintelligence have emerged and demand reconciliation; (2) recent evidence suggests that FBI counterespionage results have been less than satisfactory; and (3) counterintelligence has infringed on the rights and liberties of Americans.

Disagreement over the approach to counterintelligence affects all aspects of this activity—compartmentation, method of operation, security, research priorities, deception activities, and liaison. The Committee found that there has been no high-level executive branch review of the classified issues surfaced in this important disagreement.

The Committee also found that there is no system of clearance outside the CIA or FBI for sensitive counterespionage operations, despite the difficulty of distinguishing some of these operations from covert action.

On the FBI contribution to counterintelligence, testimony before the Committee reveals that the Bureau has given insufficient priority to discovering and controlling foreign agents within the United States. Insufficient manpower in the counterintelligence field, especially highly trained analysts, appears to be part of the problem.

---

[20] Recommendation 14 is based, in part, on these findings.

Recommendations

22. By statute, a charter should be established for the Central Intelligence Agency which makes clear that its activities must be related to foreign intelligence. The Agency should be given the following missions:

—The collection of denied or protected foreign intelligence information.[23]
—The conduct of foreign counterintelligence.[24]
—The conduct of foreign covert action operations.
—The production of finished national intelligence.

23. The CIA, in carrying out foreign intelligence missions, would be permitted to engage in relevant activities within the United States so long as these activities do not violate the Constitution nor any federal, state, or local laws within the United States.[25] The Committee has set forth in its Domestic Recommendations proposed restrictions on such activities to supplement restrictions already contained in the 1947 National Security Act. In addition, the Committee recommends that by statute the intelligence oversight committee(s) of Congress and the proposed counterintelligence committee of the National Security Council be required to review, at least annually, CIA foreign intelligence activities conducted within the United States.

24. By statute, the Attorney General should be required to report to the President and to the intelligence oversight committee(s) of Congress any intelligence activities which, in his opinion, violate the Constitutional rights of American citizens or any other provision of law and the actions he has taken in response. Pursuant to the Committee's Domestic Recommendations, the Attorney General should be made responsible for ensuring that intelligence activities do not violate the Constitution or any other provision of law.

25. The Committee recommends the establishment of a special committee of the Committee on Foreign Intelligence to review all foreign human intelligence collection activities. It would make recommendation activities. (See the committee's Report on Domestic Intelligence Activities and the Rights of Americans, Part IV.) U.S. clandestine human collection operations and choices between overt and clandestine human collection. This committee would be composed of a representative of the Secretary of State as chairman, the other statutory members of the CFI, and others whom the President may designate.

---

[23] This would not preclude the NSC from assigning appropriate overt collection functions to the CIA.

[24] The CIA would be excluded from any law enforcement or criminal investigation activities. (See the Committee's Report on Domestic Intelligence Activities and the Rights of Americans, Part IV.)

[25] Ibid.

26. The intelligence oversight committee(s) of Congress should carefully examine intelligence collection activities of the Clandestine Service to assure that clandestine means are used only when the information is sufficiently important and when such means are necessary to obtain the information.

27. The intelligence oversight committee(s) should consider whether:

—the Domestic Collection Division (overt collection operations) should be removed from the Directorate of Operations (the Clandestine Service), and returned to the Directorate of Intelligence;
—the CIA's regulations should require that the DCD's overt contacts be informed when they are to be used for operational support of clandestine activities;
—the CIA's regulations should prohibit recruiting as agents immigrants who have applied for American citizenship.

N12
28. The President of the United States, in consultation with the intelligence oversight committee(s) of Congress, should undertake a classified review of current issues regarding counterintelligence. This review should form the basis for a classified Presidential statement on national counterintelligence policy and objectives, and should closely examine the following issues: compartmentation, operations, security, research, accountability, training, internal review, deception, liaison and coordination, and manpower.

2. CIA Production of Finished Intelligence

Intelligence production refers to the process (coordination, collation, evaluation, analysis, research, and writing) by which "raw" intelligence is transformed into "finished" intelligence for senior policymakers. The finished intelligence product includes a daily report and summaries, as well as longer analytical studies and monographs on particular topics of policy interest. In the CIA, finished intelligence is produced by the Directorate of Intelligence and the Directorate of Science and Technology.

Certain problems and issues in the area of CIA intelligence production have come to the Committee's attention. The Committee believes thees problems deserve immediate attention by both the executive branch and future congressional intelligence oversight bodies. These problems bear directly on the resources allocated to the production of finished intelligence, the personnel system, and the organizational structure of intelligence production.

The Committee recognizes that it is not the primary purpose of intelligence to predict every world event. Rather, the principal function of intelligence is to anticipate major foreign developments and changes in policies which bear on United States interests. Intelligence should also provide a deeper understanding of the behavior, processes, and long-term trends which may underlie sudden military and political developments.

The Committee wishes to emphasize that there is an important difference between an intelligence failure and a policy failure. The United States had intelligence on the possibility of a Turkish invasion of Cyprus in 1974. The problem of taking effective action to prevent such an invasion was a policy question and not an intelligence failure.

The Committee has received evidence that on some subjects, such as the current capability of the strategic and conventional forces of potential adversaries, U.S. intelligence is considered excellent. But in other areas, U.S. finished intelligence is viewed by policymakers as far from satisfactory in light of the total resources devoted to intelligence. On balance, the Committee found that the quality, timeliness, and utility of our finished intelligence is generally considered adequate, but that major improvement is both desirable and possible.

One issue examined by the Committee is whether intelligence community elements responsible for producing finished intelligence receive adequate attention and support. Production is, in the words of one observer, "the stepchild of the intelligence community." Since finished intelligence is a principal purpose of all United States intelligence activities, the Committee finds that this neglect of finished intelligence is unacceptable for the future.

Intelligence resources are overwhelmingly devoted to intelligence collection. The system is inundated with raw intelligence. The individual analysts responsible for producing finished intelligence has difficulty dealing with the sheer volume of information. Policymakers want the latest reports, and producers of finished intelligence often have to compete with the producers of raw intelligence for policymakers' attention. In a crisis situation, analysts tend to focus on the latest piece of evidence at the expense of a longer and broader view. Intelligence Community staff saw this tendency as one reason why the Cyprus coup in July 1974 was not foreseen.

The Intelligence Community staff in its post–mortem on the 1974 Cyprus crisis noted another general analytical problem which was involved in the failure to anticipate the Cyprus coup and the Arab attack on Israeli forces in October of 1973 : "the perhaps subconscious conviction (and hope) that, ultimately, reason and rationality will prevail, that apparently irrational moves (the Arab attack, the Greek sponsored coup) will not be made by essentially rational men."

An additional area of the Committee's concern is that analysts are often not informed in a timely way of national policies and programs which affect their analyses and estimates. In its examination of cases involving Cambodia and Chile in the 1970s, the Committee encountered evidence that the analysts were so deprived.

Another issue uncovered by the Committee is whether the highest quality personnel are recruited into the CIA analytical staff. Among the problems raised :

—Analysts tend to be hired early in their careers, and stay in the Agency throughout their careers. The nature of their work tends to insulate them from other useful experiences.

—The analysts career pattern rewards most analyst by promoting them to supervisory positions thereby reducing the time available to utilize their analytical skills.

—Some analysts complain that there are too many steps in the process for reviewing finished intelligence—too much bureaucratic "layering" in the analytical components. With each successive level of review, the analysis and commentary tend to become increasingly derivative.

—There has been little lateral entry of established analysts and intelligence experts into CIA ranks to leaven the outlook, interests and skills of the Agency's intelligence analysts.[27]

A final issue raised by the Committee's investigation of intelligence production is whether the new organizational structure proposed by the President will assure the appropriate stature for the Directorate of Intelligence to help overcome existing problems in the production of finished intelligence. Instead of reporting directly to the DCI (who is still to be the President's chief intelligence adviser), CIA analysts may well report through the Deputy for the CIA. Experience indicates that the new Deputy will need to devote the bulk of his time to managing the Clandestine Services and the Directorate for Science and Technology. At the same time, the DCI may be preoccupied with greater community-wide management responsibilities. Without some further restructuring, the Committee believes that the production of finished intelligence may be lost in the shuffle.

Recommendations

29. By statute, the Director of the Directorate of Intelligence (DDI) should be authorized to continue to report directly to the Director of Central Intelligence.

30. The Committee recommends that a system be devised to ensure that intelligence analysts are better and more promptly informed about United States policies and programs affecting their respective areas of responsibility.

31. The Central Intelligence Agency and the intelligence oversight committee(s) of Congress should reexamine the personnel system of the Directorate of Intelligence with a view to providing a more flexible, less hierarchical personnel system. Super-grade positions should be available on the basis of an individual's analytical capabilities.

32. The Directorate for Intelligence should seek to bring more established analysts into the CIA at middle and upper grade levels for both career positions and temporary assignments.

33. Greater emphasis should be placed on stimulating development of new tools and methods of analysis.

34. Agency policy should continue to encourage intelligence analysts to assume substantive tours of duty on an open basis in other agencies (State, Defense, NSC staff) or in academic institutions to broaden both their analytical outlook and their appreciation for the relevance of their analysis to policymakers and operators within the Government.

---

[27] In FY 1975, only 18 out of 105 analysts hired by the DDI from outside the CIA were at grades GS-12 to GS-15.

3. Covert Action and Paramilitary Operations

Covert action is the attempt to influence the internal affairs of other nations in support of United States foreign policy in a manner that conceals the participation of the United States Government. Covert action includes political and economic action, propaganda and paramilitary activities.

N13

The basic unit of covert action is the project. Covert action "projects" can range from single assets, such as a journalist placing propaganda, through a network of assets working in the media, to major covert and military intervention such as in Laos. The Agency also maintains what it terms an "operational infrastructure" of "stand-by" assets (agents of influence or media assets) who can be used in major operations—such as in Chile. These "stand-by" assets are also part of on-going, most often routine, projects. There are no inactive assets.

Covert Action

The Committee has found that the CIA has conducted some 900 major or sensitive covert action projects plus several thousand smaller projects since 1961. The need to maintain secrecy shields covert action projects from the rigorous public scrutiny and debate necessary to determine their compatibility with established American foreign policy goals. Recently, a large-scale covert paramilitary operation in Angola was initiated without any effort on the part of the executive branch to articulate, and win public support for, its overall policy in Africa. Only public disclosure has allowed the nation to apply its standards of success or failure to covert action projects and then only in retrospect, often without the benefit of the details prompting the original choice of covert rather than overt action.

The secrecy covert action requires means that the public cannot determine whether such actions are consistent with established foreign policy goals. This secrecy also has allowed covert actions to take place which are inconsistent with our basic traditions and values.

Some covert operations have passed restrospective public judgments, such as the support given Western European democratic parties facing strong communist opposition in the late 1940s and 1950s. Others have not. In the view of the Committee, the covert harassment of the democratically elected government of Salvador Allende in Chile did not command U.S. public approval.

Even if the short-term consequences of covert action are consistent with stated policy and accepted standards, the Committee has found that the continued use of covert action techniques within or against a foreign society can have unintended consequences that sometimes subvert long-term goals. For instance, extended covert support to foreign political leaders, parties, labor unions, or the media has not always accomplished the intended objective of strengthening them against the communist challenge. In some cases, it has both encouraged a debilitating dependence on United States covert support, and made those receiving such support vulnerable to repudiation in their own society when their covert ties are exposed. Furthermore, prolonged covert relations and the resulting dependence of recipients on continued CIA support seem to encourage the CIA to extend its ties to means of controlling the recipients in other respects. Covert actions also have, over time, developed a bureaucratic momentum of their own that often surpasses the original need for covert action.

Paramilitary Operations

Covert paramilitary operations are a special, extreme form of covert action. These operations most often consist of covert military assistance and training, but occasionally have involved actual combat activities by American advisers.

Because military assistance involves foreign policy commitments, it is, with one exception, authorized by the Congress. That exception is *covert* military assistance which is channeled through the CIA without being authorized or approved by the Congress as a whole.

Covert U.S. paramilitary combat operations frequently amount to making war, but they do not come under the War Powers Act since they usually do not involve *uniformed* U.S. military officers. American military officers engaged in CIA-sponsored paramilitary operations are "sheep-dipped" for paramilitary duty—that is, they appear to resign from the military yet preserve their place for reactivation once their tour as civilian in paramilitary operations has ended.

The Committee finds that major paramilitary operations have often failed to achieve their intended objective. Most have eventually been exposed. Operations, as in Angola, recently, and Indonesia in the late 1950s are examples of such paramilitary failures. Others, such as Laos, are judged successes by the CIA and officials within the executive branch. The "success" in Laos, however, must be seen against the larger American involvement in Indochina which failed.

Paramilitary operations often have evolved into large-scale programs with a high risk of exposure (and thus embarrassment and/or failure). In some cases, the CIA has been used to undertake paramilitary operations simply because the Agency is less accountable to the public for highly visible "secret" military operations. In all cases considered by the Committee, command and control within the executive branch was rigorous. However, all such operations have been conducted without direct congressional authority or public debate. In recent years, some have been continued in the face of strong congressional disapproval.

Recently, however—apart from Angola—United States paramilitary activities have been at a very low level. The capability for these actions, residing jointly in the CIA and the Department of Defense, consists of a cadre of trained officers, stockpiles of military equipment, logistic networks and small collections of air and maritime assets.

Review and Approval of Covert Action

Given the open and democratic assumptions on which our government is based, the Committee has given serious consideration to the option of proposing a total ban on all forms of covert activity. The Committee has concluded, however, that the United States should maintain the capability to react through covert action when no other means will suffice to meet extraordinary circumstances involving grave threats to U.S. national security. Nevertheless, covert action should be considered as an exception to the normal process of government action abroad, rather than a parallel but invisible system in which covert operations are routine.

Absent some means of assuring public participation in assessing each covert action, the mechanisms of executive branch review and control and of legislative intelligence oversight must serve as the restricted arenas in which such standards are applied to covert action. The Committee's examination of the covert action record over the last 25 years has underscored the necessity for legislative reinforcement of the executive branch's internal review process. This is necessary to assure that all covert action projects are reviewed, and to establish a system of formal accountability within the executive accessible to congressional intelligence oversight bodies.

The CIA has not been free, however, to carry out covert action as it sees fit. The Committee's investigation revealed that on the whole, the Agency has been responsive to internal and external review and authorization requirements. Most of the significant covert operations have been approved by the appropriate NSC committee. At the same time, the Committee notes that approval outside the Agency does not solve all problems since the NSC committees have approved (and in some cases *initiated*) projects that involved highly improper practices or were inconsistent with declared foreign policies.

Approximately three-fourths of all covert action projects are never reviewed or approved by a high level body outside the CIA.[28] These projects which are not brought before the NSC for review are so-called "non-sensitive" projects, or part of what the CIA calls its "operational infrastructure." The Committee found that a single small project, though not reviewed by the NSC, still can be of great importance (e.g. QJWIN, the CIA "executive action" assassination capability, and AMLASH, the Cuban officer being groomed to kill Fidel Castro). Moreover, a cluster of small projects can be aggregated to form a program of significance (e.g., Chile).

Until recently, Congress, through its committees, has failed to effectively oversee CIA covert action. Much of this flowed from the legitimate desire of the congressional oversight committees to maintain the security of covert action projects, but it also resulted from a hesitancy to challenge the President or to become directly involved in projects he deemed necessary. Covert paramilitary operations pose a special problem, since they cut across several functions (and committee jurisdictions) of Congress—namely, granting military assistance and making war.

Members of the congressional oversight committees are almost totally dependent on the executive branch for information on covert operations. The secrecy needed for these covert operations allows the executive to limit the information provided to the Congress and to use covert actions to avoid the open scrutiny and debate of the normal foreign policy procedures. While the Committee believes that the

---

[28] Since 1974, the President has had to certify all covert actions as important to the national security—treating smaller projects by certain broad categories.

executive should continue to have the initiative in formulating covert action, it also strongly believes that the appropriate oversight bodies of Congress should be fully informed prior to the initiation of such actions.

Congressional power over the purse can serve as the most effective congressional oversight tool if there is the courage and the will to exercise it. In addition to the regular budget for covert action, the Agency draws on a Contingency Reserve Fund for unanticipated projects. Any withdrawals from this fund require approval from the Office of Management and Budget and notification, within 48 hours, to the appropriate congressional committees. The Committee believes that the Contingency Fund can also provide one of the mechanisms by which Congress can effectively control covert action.

Recommendations

35. The legislation establishing the charter for the Central Intelligence Agency should specify that the CIA is the only U.S. Government agency authorized to conduct covert actions. The purpose of covert actions should be to deal with grave threats to American security. Covert actions should be consistent with publicly-defined United States foreign policy goals, and should be reserved for extraordinary circumstances when no other means will suffice. The legislation governing covert action should require executive branch procedures which will ensure careful and thorough consideration of both the general policies governing covert action and particular covert action projects; such procedures should require the participation and accountability of highest level policymakers.

36. The Committee has already recommended, following its investigation of alleged assassination attempts directed at foreign leaders, a statute to forbid such activities. The Committee reaffirms its support for such a statute and further recommends prohibiting the following covert activities by statute:

— All political assassinations.[29]
— Efforts to subvert democratic governments.
— Support for police or other internal security forces which engage in the systematic violation of human rights.

37. By statute, the appropriate NSC committee (e.g., the Operations Advisory Group) should review every covert action proposal.[30]

The Committee recommends that the Operations Advisory Group review include:

—A careful and systematic analysis of the political premises underlying the recommended actions, as well as the nature, extent, purpose, risks, likelihood of success, and costs of the operation. Reasons explaining why the objective can-

---

[29] The Committee endorses Executive Order 11905, of February 18, 1976, which states: "No employee of the United States Goverment shall engage in, or conspire to engage in, political assassination."

[30] Executive Order 11905, 2/18/76, established the Operations Advisory Group and directed it to "consider and develop a policy recommendation, including any dissents, for the President prior to his decision on each special activity [e.g., covert operations] in support of national foreign policy objectives."

not be achieved by overt means should also be considered.

—Each covert action project should be formally considered at a meeting of the OAG, and if approved, forwarded to the President for final decision. The views and positions of the participants would be fully recorded. For the purpose of OAG, presidential, and congressional considerations, all so-called non-sensitive projects should be aggregated according to the extraordinary circumstances or contingency against which the project is directed.

38. By statute, the intelligence oversight committee(s) of Congress should require that the annual budget submission for covert action programs be specified and detailed as to the activity recommended. Unforeseen covert action projects should be funded from the Contingency Reserve Fund which could be replenished only after the concurrence of the oversight and any other appropriate congressional committees. The congressional intelligence oversight committees should be notified prior to any withdrawal from the Contingency Reserve Fund.

39. By statute, any covert use by the U.S. Government of American citizens as combatants should be preceded by the notification required for all covert actions. The statute should provide that within 60 days of such notification such use shall be terminated unless the Congress has specifically authorized such use. The Congress should be empowered to terminate such use at any time.[31]

40. By statute, the executive branch should be prevented from conducting any covert military assistance program (including the indirect or direct provision of military material, military or logistics advice and training, and funds for mercenaries) without the explicit prior consent of the intelligence oversight committee(s) of Congress.

G. Reorganization of the Intelligence Community

1. The Position of the DCI

The Committee recommendations regarding the Director of Central Intelligence (pages 43–45) would, if implemented, increase his authority over the entire intelligence community. Given such increased authority, the Committee believes that both the executive branch and the intelligence oversight committee(s) of Congress should give careful consideration to removing the DCI from direct management responsibility for the Central Intelligence Agency. This would free the DCI to concentrate on his responsibilities with regard to the entire intelligence community and would remove him from any conflict of interest in performing that task. It might also increase the accountability of the Central Intelligence Agency by establishing a new and separate senior position—a Director of the Central Intelligence Agency—responsible for only the CIA.

2. The Structures of the CIA

The Committee believes that several important problems uncovered in the course of this inquiry suggest that serious consideration also be given to major structural change in the CIA—in particular, sepa-

---

[31] This recommendation parallels the current provisions of the War Powers Resolution which could be so amended. (Appendix C, Hearings, Vol. 7, p. 226.)

rating national intelligence production and analysis from the clandestine service and other collection functions. Intelligence production could be placed directly under the DCI, while clandestine collection of foreign intelligence from human and technical sources and covert operations would remain in the CIA.

The advantages of such a step are several:

—The DCI would be removed from the conflict of interest situation of managing the intelligence community as a whole while also directing a collection agency.
—The concern that the DCI's national intelligence judgments are compromised by the impulse to justify certain covert action operations or by the close association of the analysts with the clandestine service would be remedied.
—The problem, seen by some in the intelligence community, of bias on the part of CIA analysts toward the collection resources of the CIA would be lessened.
—It would facilitate providing the intelligence production unit with greater priority and increased resources necessary for improving the quality of its finished intelligence.
—Tighter policy control of the Clandestine Service by the National Security Council and the Department of State would be possible.
—The Director would be able to focus increased attention on monitoring Clandestine Services.
—Internal reorganization of the Directorate for Intelligence and the remainder of the CIA could be facilitated.

There are potential drawbacks as well:

—The Director of Central Intelligence might lose the influence that is part of having command responsibility for the clandestine services.
—The increasing, though still not extensive, contact between national intelligence analysts and the Clandestine Service for the purpose of improving the espionage effort might be inhibited.
—The DCI would have managerial responsibility over the former CIA analysts which might place him in a conflict-of-interest situation in regard to the production of intelligence.
—The increased number of independent agencies would increase the DCI's coordination problems.
—If the clandestine services did not report to the DCI, there would be the problem of establishing an alternative chain of command to the President.
—The Clandestine Service might be downgraded and fail to secure adequate support.

Nonetheless, on balance, the Committee believes such a separation of functions and consequent possible realignments in authority within the intelligence community medit serious consideration.

Recommendations

41. The intelligence oversight committee(s) of Congress in the course of developing a new charter for the intelligence community should give consideration to separating the functions of the DCI and the Director of the CIA and to dividing the intelligence analysis and production functions from the clandestine collection and covert action functions of the present CIA.

H. Relations with United States Institutions and Private Citizens

In the immediate postwar period, as the communists pressed to influence and to control international organizations and movements, mass communications, and cultural institutions, the United States responded by involving American private institutions and individuals in the secret struggle over minds, institutions, and ideals. In the process, the CIA subsidized, and even helped develop "private" or non-government organizations that were designed to compete with communists around the world. The CIA supported not only foreign organizations, but also the international activities of United States student, labor, cultural, and philanthropic organizations.

These covert relationships have attracted public concern and this Committee's attention because of the importance that Americans attach to the independence of these institutions.

The Committee found that in the past the scale and diversity of these covert actions has been extensive. For operational purposes, the CIA has:

—Funded a special program of a major American business association;
—Collaborated with an American trade union federation;
—Helped to establish a research center at a major United States university;
—Supported an international exchange program sponsored by a group of United States universities;
—Made widespread use of philanthropic organizations to fund such covert action programs.

The Committee's concern about these relationships is heightened by the Agency's tendency to move from support to use of both institutions and individuals. For example, the initial purpose of the Agency's funding of the National Student Association was to permit United States students to represent their own ideas, in their own way, in the international forums of the day. Nevertheless, the Committee has found instances in which the CIA moved from general support to the "operational use" of individual students.[32] Contrary to the public's understanding, over 250 United States students were sponsored by the CIA to attend youth festivals in Moscow, Vienna and Helsinki and

N15

---

[32] Operational use, according to CIA directives, means performing services in support of the CIA Operations Directorate, and may include the recruitment, utilization, or training of any individual for such purposes as providing cover and collecting intelligence.

used for missions such as reporting on Soviet and Third World personalities or observing Soviet security practices. The CIA also used National Student Association Summer International Seminars in the United States in the 1950s and 1960s to identify and screen new leaders whom they would eventually support at the national NSA Convention.

When the CIA's relationship to NSA was publicly revealed in 1967, the Johnson Administration established the Katzenbach Committee, with a limited mandate to investigate the relationship of the CIA to "U.S. educational and private voluntary organizations which operate abroad." The Katzenbach Committee recommended that it should be the policy of the United States Government not to provide any "covert financial assistance or support, direct or indirect, to any of the nation's educational or private voluntary organizations."

The Committee found that the CIA not only carried out this Katzenbach recommendation but also terminated support for a number of other U.S.-based organizations such as publishing houses. Nevertheless, the CIA, with the approval of the appropriate NSC committee, insured the continuation of a number of high priority operations by either moving them overseas or encouraging private and non-CIA government support of domestically-based operations. More importantly, however, the CIA shifted its operational interest from institutional relationships to individuals in, or affiliated with, private institutions.

The Committee inquiry has been particularly concerned about the current operational use of United States citizens as individuals. Some academics now help the CIA by providing leads and, on occasion, making introductions to potential sources of foreign intelligence. American academics and freelance writers are occasionally used abroad to assist the CIA's clandestine mission.

1. Covert Use of the U.S. Academic Community

The Central Intelligence Agency is now using several hundred American academics,[33] who in addition to providing leads and sometimes making introductions for intelligence purposes, occasionally write books and other material to be used for propaganda purposes abroad. Beyond these, an additional few more are used in an unwitting manner for minor activities.

These academics are located in over 100 American colleges, universities, and related institutes. At the majority of institutions, no one other than the individual academic concerned is aware of the CIA link. At the others, at least one university official is aware of the operational use made of academics on his campus. In addition, there are several American academics abroad who serve operational purposes, primarily the collection of intelligence.

The CIA gives a high priority to obtaining leads on potential foreign intelligence sources especially those from communist countries. This Agency's emphasis reflects the fact that many foreign nationals in the United States are in this category. The Committee notes that American academics provide valuable assistance in this activity.

---

[33] "Academics" includes administrators, faculty members, and graduate students engaged in teaching.

The Committee is concerned, however, that American academics involved in such activities may undermine public confidence that those who train our youth are upholding the ideals, independence, and integrity of American universities.

Government Grantees

CIA regulations adopted in 1967 prohibit the "operational" use of certain narrow categories of individuals. The CIA is prohibited from using teachers, lecturers, and students receiving grants from the Board of Foreign Fellowships under the Fulbright-Hayes Act.[34] There is no prohibition on the use of individuals participating in any other federally funded exchange programs. For example, the CIA may use those grantees—artists, specialists, athletes, leaders, etc.—who do not receive their grants from the Board of Foreign Scholarships. The Committee is concerned that there is no prohibition against exploiting such open federal programs for clandestine purposes.

2. The Covert Use of Books and Publishing Houses

The Committee has found that the Central Intelligence Agency attaches a particular importance to book publishing activities as a form of covert propaganda. A former officer in the Clandestine Service stated that books are "the most important weapon of strategic (long-range) propaganda." Prior to 1967, the Central Intelligence Agency sponsored, subsidized, or produced over 1,000 books; approximately 25 percent of them in English. In 1967 alone, the CIA published or subsidized over 200 books, ranging from books on African safaris and wildlife to translations of Machiavelli's *The Prince* into Swahili and works of T. S. Eliot into Russian, to a competitor to Mao's little red book, which was entitled *Quotations from Chairman Liu.*

The Committee found that an important number of the books actually produced by the Central Intelligence Agency were reviewed and marketed in the United States:

—A book about a young student from a developing country who had studied in a communist country was described by the CIA as "developed by [two areas divisions] and produced by the Domestic Operations Division. . . and has had a high impact in the United States as well as in the [foreign area] market." This book, which was produced by the European outlet of a United States publishing house was published in condensed form in two major U.S. magazines.[36]

—Another CIA book, *The Penkovsky Papers*, was published in United States in 1965. The book was prepared and written by witting agency assets who drew on actual case materials and publication rights to the manu-

---

[34] CIA regulations also prohibit the operational use of members of ACTION and officials, employees, and grantees of the Ford, Rockefeller, and Carnegie Foundations.

[36] CBS commentator Eric Sevareid, in reviewing this book, spoke a larger truth than he knew when he suggested that "our propaganda services could do worse than flood [foreign] university towns with this volume."

script were sold to the publisher through a trust fund which was established for the purpose. The publisher was unaware of any U.S. Government interest.

In 1967, the CIA stopped publishing within the United States. Since then, the Agency has published some 250 books abroad, most of them in foreign languages. The CIA has given special attention to publication and circulation abroad of books about conditions in the Soviet Bloc. Of those targeted at audiences outside the Soviet Union and Eastern Europe, a large number has also been available in English.

3. Domestic "Fallout"

The Committee finds that covert media operations can result in manipulating or incidentally misleading the American public. Despite efforts to minimize it, CIA employees, past and present, have conceded that there is no way to shield the American public completely from "fallout" in the United States from Agency propaganda or placements overseas. Indeed, following the Katzenbach inquiry, the Deputy Director for Operations issued a directive stating: "Fallout in the United States from a foreign publication which we support is inevitable and consequently permissible."

The domestic fallout of covert propaganda comes from many sources: books intended primarily for an English-speaking foreign audience; CIA press placements that are picked up by an international wire service; and publications resulting from direct CIA funding of foreign institutes. For example, a book written for an English-speaking foreign audience by one CIA operative was reviewed favorably by another CIA agent in the *New York Times*. *The Committee also found that the CIA helped create and support various Vietnamese periodicals and publications. In at least one instance, a CIA supported Vietnamese publication was used to propagandize the American public and the members and staff of both houses of Congress. So effective was this propaganda that some members quoted from the publication in debating the controversial question of United States involvement in Vietnam.*

The Committee found that this inevitable domestic fallout was compounded when the Agency circulated its subsidized books in the United States prior to their distribution abroad in order to induce a favorable reception overseas.

The Covert Use of U.S. Journalists and Media Institutions on February 11, 1976, CIA Director George Bush announced new guidelines governing the Agency's realtionship with United States media organizations:

> *Effective immediately, CIA will not enter into any paid or contractual relationship with any full-time or part-time news correspondent accredited by any U.S. news service, newspaper, periodical, radio or television network or station.*[38]

---

[38] According to the CIA, "accredited" applies to individuals who are "formally authorized by contract or issuance of press credentials to represent themselves as correspondents.". . .

Agency officials who testified after the February 11, 1976, announcement told the Committee that the prohibition extends to non-Americans accredited to specific United States media organizations.

The CIA currently maintains a network of several hundred foreign individuals around the world who provide intelligence for the CIA and at times attempt to influence opinion through the use of covert propaganda. These individuals provide the CIA with direct access to a large number of newspapers and periodicals, scores of press services and news agencies, radio and television stations, commercial book publishers, and other foreign media outlets.

Approximately 50 of the assets are individual American journalists or employees of U.S. media organizations. Of these, fewer than half are "accredited" by U.S. media organizations and thereby affected by the new prohibitions on the use of accredited newsmen. The remaining individuals are non-accredited freelance contributors and media representatives abroad, and thus are not affected by the new CIA prohibition.

More than a dozen United States news organizations and commercial publishing houses formerly provided cover for CIA agents abroad. A few of these organizations were unaware that they provided this cover.

The Committee notes that the new CIA prohibitions do not apply to "unaccredited" Americans serving in media organizations such as representatives of U.S. media organizations abroad or freelance writers. Of the more than 50 CIA relationships with United States journalists, or employees in American media organizations, fewer than one half will be terminated under the new CIA guidelines.

The Committee is concerned that the use of American journalists and media organizations for clandestine operations is a threat to the integrity of the press. All American journalists, whether accredited to a United States news organization or just a stringer, may be suspects when any are engaged in covert activities.

4. Covert Use of American Religious Personnel

The Committee has found that over the years the CIA has used very few religious personnel for operational purposes. The CIA informed the Committee that only 21 such individuals have ever participated in either covert action projects or the clandestine collection of intelligence. On February 11, 1976, the CIA announced:

> CIA has no secret paid or contractual relationships with any American clergyman or missionary. This practice will be continued as a matter of policy.

The Committee welcomes this policy with the understanding that the prohibition against all "paid or contractual relationships" is in fact a prohibition against any operational use of all Americans following a religious vocation.

Recommendations

In its consideration of the recommendations that follow, the Committee noted the Central Intelligence Agency's concern that further restriction on the use of Americans for operational purposes will con-strain current operating programs. The Committee recognizes that there may be at least some short-term operational losses if the Committee recommendations are effected. At the same time, the Committee believes that there are certain American institutions whose integrity is critical to the maintenance of a free society and which should therefore be free of any unwitting role in the clandestine service of the United States Government.

42. The Committee is concerned about the integrity of American academic institutions and the use of individuals affiliated with such institutions for clandestine purposes. Accordingly, the Committee recommends that the CIA amend its internal directives to require that individual academics used for operational purposes by the CIA, together with the President or equivalent official of the relevant academic institutions, be informed of the clandestine CIA relationship.[41]

43. The Committee further recommends that, as soon as possible, the permanent intelligence oversight committee(s) of Congress examine whether further steps are needed to insure the integrity of American academic institutions.

44. By statute, the CIA should be prohibited from the operational use of grantees who are receiving funds through educational and/or cultural programs which are sponsored by the United States Government.

45. By statute, the CIA should be prohibited from subsidizing the writing, or production for distribution within the United States or its territories, of any book, magazine, article, publication, film, or video or audio tape unless publicly attributed to the CIA. Nor should the CIA be permitted to undertake any activity to accomplish indirectly such distribution within the United States or its territories.

46. The Committee supports the recently adopted CIA prohibitions against any paid or contractual relationship between the Agency and U.S. and foreign journalists accredited to U.S. media organizations. The CIA prohibitions should, however, be established in law.

47. The Committee recommends that the CIA prohibitions be extended by law to include the operational use of any person who regularly contributes material to, or is regularly involved directly or indirectly in the editing of material, or regularly acts to set policy or provide direction to the activities of U.S. media organizations.

48. The Committee recommends that the Agency's recent prohibition on covert paid or contractual relationship between the Agency and any American clergyman or missionary should be established by law.

I. PROPRIETARIES AND COVER

1. Proprietary Organizations

CIA proprietaries are business entities wholly-owned by the Agency which do business, or only appear to do business, under commercial guise. They are part of the "arsenal of tools" of the CIA's

---

[41] This recommendation is consistent with and would extend section 4(b)(9) of E.O. 11905 which states that CIA sponsorship of classified or unclassified research must be "known to appropriate senior officials of the academic institutions and to senior project officials."

Clandestine Services. They have been used for espionage as well as covert action. Most of the larger proprietaries have been used for paramilitary purposes. The Committee finds that too often large proprietaries have created unwarranted risks of unfair competition with private business and of compromising their cover as clandestine operations. For example, Air America, which at one time had as many as 8,000 employees, ran into both difficulties.

While internal CIA financial controls have been regular and systematic, the Committee found a need for even greater accountability both internally and externally. Generally, those auditing the CIA have been denied access to operational information, making management-oriented audits impossible. Instead, audits have been concerned only with financial security and integrity.

The Committee found that the CIA's Inspector General has, on occasion, been denied access to certain information regarding proprietaries. This has sometimes inhibited the ability of the Inspector General's office to serve the function for which it was estabished. Moreover, the General Accounting Office has not audited these operations. The lack of review, by either the GAO or the CIA Inspector General's office, means that, in essence, there has been no outside review of proprietaries.

One of the largest current proprietaries is an insurance-investment complex established in 1962 to provide pension annuities, insurance and escrow management for those who, for security reasons, could not receive them directly from the U.S. Government. The Committee determined that the Congress was not informed of the existence of this proprietary until "sometime" after it had been made operational and had invested heavily in the domestic stock markets—a practice the CIA has discontinued. Moreover, once this proprietary was removed from the Domestic Operations Division and placed under the General Counsel's office it received no annual CIA project review.

The record establishes that on occasion the insurance-investment complex had been used to provide operational support to various covert action projects. The Inspector General, in 1970, criticized this use of the complex because it threatened to compromise the security of the complex's primary insurance objectives.

In general, the Committee found that when the CIA sought to dispose of or dissolve a proprietary, considerable effort was made to avoid conflicts of interest. However, pressures were sometimes unsuccessfully brought to bear on the CIA from without, and on one or more occasions from high level Agency officials to do a favor by disposing of an entity in a manner that would benefit a particular party. In this connection, the Committee notes that the CIA is not subject to the provisions of the Federal Disposal of Property Act which ordinarily guards against such pressures.

Management and control of proprietaries frequently required, and still do, what is termed "cooperative interface" with other goverment agencies, such as the SEC and the IRS. The Committee found no evidence that these relationships involved circumventing statutory or regulatory requirements. Their purpose appears to be to enable the Agency to comply with other agencies' requirements in a secure manner. However, the nature and extent of such "interfacing" has not always been completely recorded in the CIA, making it difficult to ensure the propriety of such relationships.

2. Cover

The Committee examined cover because it is an important aspect of
N16   all CIA clandestine activities. Its importance is underscored by the
tragic murder of a CIA Station Chief in Greece, coupled with continu-
ing disclosures of CIA agents' names. The Committee sought to deter-
mine what, if anything, has been done in the past to strengthen cover,
and what should be done in the future.

The Committee found conflicting views about what constitutes cover,
what it can do, and what should be done to improve it. A 1970 CIA
Inspector General report termed the Agency's concept and use of cover
to .be lax, arbitrary, uneven, confused, and loose. The present cover
staff in the CIA considered the 1970 assessment to be simplistic and
overly harsh. There is no question, however, that some improvements
and changes are needed.

The Committee finds that there is a basic tension between maintain-
ing adequate cover and effectively engaging in overseas intelligence
activities. Almost every operational act by a CIA officer under cover in
the field—from working with local intelligence and police to attempt-
ing to recruit agents—reveals his true purpose and chips away at his
cover. Some forms of cover do not provide concealment but offer a
certain degree of deniability. Others are so elaborate that they limit
the amount of work an officer can do for the CIA. In carrying out their
responsibilities, CIA officers generally regard the maintenance of cover
as a "nuisance."

The situation of the Athens Station Chief, Richard Welch, illus-
trates the problem of striking the right balance between cover and
operations, and also the transparency of cover. As the Chief of the
CIA's Cover Staff stated, by the time a person becomes Chief of
Station, "there is not a great deal of cover left.[42] The Chief of the
Cover Staff identified terrorism as a further security problem for
officers overseas, one that is aggravated by the erosion of cover.

Recommendations

49. By statute, the CIA should be permitted to use proprietaries
subject to external and internal controls.

50. The Committee recommends that the intelligence oversight com-
mittee(s) of Congress require at least an annual report on all propri-
etaries. The report should include a statement of each proprietary's
nature and function, the results of internal annual CIA audits, a list
of all CIA intercessions on behalf of its proprietaries with any other
United States Government departments, agencies or bureaus, and such
other information as the oversight committee deems appropriate.

51. The intelligence oversight committee(s) of Congress should
require that the fiscal impact of proprietaries on the CIA's budget be
made clear in the DCI's annual report to the oversight committee. The
Commitee should also establish guidelines for creating large pro-
prietaries, should these become necessary.

---

[42] For example, the CIA was concerned about the fact that the home that Mr.
Welch moved into had been previously publicly identified as belonging to the
former Station Chief. CIA officials have testified that the Agency has no evidence
that the recent congressional inquiries into intelligence activities had any ad-
verse impact on Mr. Welch's cover or any relationship to his tragic death.
(George Bush testimony, 4/8/76, p. 41.)

52. By statute, all returns of funds from proprietaries not needed for its operational purposes or because of liquidation or termination of a proprietary, should be remitted to the United States Treasury as Miscellaneous Receipts.

The Department of Justice should be consulted during the process of the sale or disposition of any CIA proprietary.

53. By statute, former senior government officials should be prohibited from negotiating with the CIA or any other agency regarding the disposal of proprietaries. The intelligence oversight committee(s) of Congress should consider whether other activities among agencies of the intelligence community, the CIA, and former officials and employees, such as selling to or negotiating contracts with the CIA, should also be prohibitied as is the case regarding military officials under 18 U.S.C. 207.

J. Intelligence Liaison

Throughout the entire period of the CIA's history, the Agency has entered into liaison agreements with the intelligence services of foreign powers. Such arrangements are an extremely important and delicate source of intelligence and operational support. Intelligence channels can also be used to negotiate agreement outside the field of intelligence. The Committee notes that all treaties require the advice and consent of the Senate, and executive agreements must be reported to the Foreign Relations Committee of the Senate. Because of the importance of intelligence liaison agreements to national security, the Committee is concerned that such agreements have not been systematically reviewed by the Congress in any fashion.

Recommendations

54. By statute, the CIA should be prohibited from causing, funding, or encouraging actions by liaison services which are forbidden to the CIA. Furthermore, the fact that a particular project, action, or activity of the CIA is carried out through or by a foreign liaison service should not relieve the Agency of its responsibilities for clearance within the Agency, within the executive branch, or with the Congress.

55. The intelligence oversight committee(s) of Congress should be kept fully informed of agreements negotiated with other governments through intelligence channels.

K. The General Counsel and Inspector General

The General Counsel, as chief legal officer of the Central Intelligence Agency, has a special role in insuring that CIA activities are consistent with the Constitution and laws of the United States. The Committee found that, in the past, the participation of the General Counsel in determining the legality or propriety of CIA activities was limited; in many instances the General Counsel was not consulted about sensitive projects. In some cases the Director's investigative arm, the Inspector General, discovered questionable activities that often were not referred to the General Counsel for a legal opinion. Moreover, the General Counsel never had general investigatory authority.

The Inspector General not only serves as the Director's investigative arm, but he also aids the Director in attempts to increase the efficiency of Agency activities. Inspector General investigations of various Agency offices (component surveys) have been an important management tool often leading to the discovery of questionable practices. These component surveys were halted in 1973 but have recently been reinstituted.

The Committee found that there were problems with the component surveys. In some situations the Inspector General was denied access to essential information. The surveys often failed to effectively cover sensitive programs cutting across component boundaries or raising issues which affected the Agency as a whole. Finally, the Inspector General's recommendations were often disregarded particularly when the directorate being investigated opposed their implementation.

Under the President's recently issued Executive Order, the Inspector General and the General Counsel are required to report to the Intelligence Oversight Board any activities that come to their attention which raise questions of legality or propriety. The Director of the CIA is charged with assuring that those officials will have access to the information necessary to fulfill their duties under the Executive Order.

The Committee also found that while both the General Counsel and Inspector General provided valuable assistance to the Director, neither had authority to provide assistance to the congressional oversight bodies.

The Committee believes that the intelligence oversight committee(s) of Congress should examine the internal review mechanisms of foreign and military intelligence agencies and consider the feasibility of applying recommendations such as those suggested for the CIA.

Recommendations

56. Any CIA employee having information about activities which appear illegal, improper, outside the Agency's legislative charter, or in violation of Agency regulations, should be required to inform the Director, the General Counsel, or the Inspector General of the Agency. If the General Counsel is not informed, he should be notified by the other officials of such reports. The General Counsel and the Inspector General shall, except where they deem it inappropriate, be required to provide such information to the head of the Agency.[44]

57. The DCI should be required to report any information regarding employee violations of law related to their duties and the results of any internal Agency investigation to the Attorney General.[45]

---

[44] The General Counsel and Inspector General should have authority to pass the information to the Attorney General without informing the head of the Agency in extraordinary circumstances, if the employee providing the information so requests and if the General Counsel or the Inspector General deems it necessary.

The Inspector General should also regularly inform Agency employees about grievance procedures.

[45] See 28 U.S.C. 535.

58. By statute, the Director of the CIA should be required to notify the appropriate committees of the Congress of any referrals made to the Attorney General pursuant to the previous recommendation.[46]

59. The Director of the CIA should periodically require employees having any information on past, current, or proposed Agency activities which appear illegal, improper, outside the Agency's legislative charter, or in violation of the Agency's regulations, to report such information.

N17

60. By statute, the General Counsel and the Inspector General should have unrestricted access to all Agency information and should have the authority to review all of the Agency activities.

61. All significant proposed CIA activities should be reviewed by the General Counsel for legality and constitutionality.

62. The program of component inspections conducted by the Inspector General should be increased, as should the program of surveys of sensitive programs and issues which cut across component lines in the Agency.[47]

63. The Director shall, at least annually, report to the appropriate committees of the Congress on the activities of the Office of the General Counsel and the Office of the Inspector General.[48]

64. By statute, the General Counsel should be nominated by the President and confirmed by the Senate.

65. The Agency's efforts to expand and strengthen the staffs of the General Counsel and Inspector General should be continued.[49]

66. The General Counsel should be promoted to, and the Inspector General should continue to hold executive rank equal to that of the Deputy Directors of the CIA.

---

[46] Should the General Counsel or Inspector General determine that it would be inappropriate to notify the Director of an activity that appeared illegal, improper, outside the Agency's legislative charter, or in violation of Agency regulations, the General Counsel or Inspector General would be required to notify the appropriate committees of the Congress.

[47] The Inspector General's component surveys should consider not only the effectiveness of the component but should also examine the component's compliance with the legislative charter of the Agency, Agency regulations, and the law. The Director should be required to inform the Inspector General as to what actions have been taken on the recommendations made by the Inspector General.

[48] The report should include: (a) a summary of all Agency activities that raise questions of legality or propriety and the General Counsel's findings concerning these activities; (b) a summary of the Inspector General's investigations concerning any of these activities; (c) a summary of the practices and procedures developed to discover activities that raise questions of legality or propriety; (d) a summary of each component, program or issue survey, including the Inspector General's recommendations and the Director's decisions; (e) a summary of all other matters handled by the Inspector General.

The report should also include discussion of (a) major legal problems facing the Agency; (b) the need for additional statutes; (c) any cases referred to the Department of Justice.

[49] Efforts to recruit lawyers for the Office of General Counsel from outside the CIA should be increased. Efforts should also be made to provide for rotation of the attorneys in the General Counsel's Office to other governmental positions.

The Inspector General's Office should be staffed by outstanding, experienced officers drawn from inside and outside the Agency. Consideration should be given to establishing a greater number of permanent positions within the Office. Individuals rotated into the Inspector General's Office from another Agency office should not be involved in surveys of offices to which they might return.

The work of both offices would benefit from regular inspections from outside.

L. THE DEPARTMENT OF DEFENSE

The intelligence agencies of the Department of Defense make a major contribution to the development, management, and operation of intelligence systems and to the production of military and technical intelligence information. Additionally, the Department, with its major responsibility for the nation's defense is a major user of finished intelligence. The Committee's inquiry into the Department of Defense intelligence agencies focused on the Department's intelligence budget which comprises over 80 percent of the direct national United **N18** States intelligence budget.

The Committee also examined the Defense Intelligence Agency (DIA), the National Security Agency (NSA), and the intelligence activities of the military services. That portion of the investigation of NSA which centered on potential abuses is presented in detail in the Domestic Section of the Committee's report.

1. General Findings and Conclusions

The Committee finds that despite the magnitude of the tasks and the complexity of the relationships, most of the important collection activities conducted by the Defense Department (the reconnaissance and SIGINT systems) are managed relatively efficiently and are generally responsive to the needs of the military services as well as to the policymakers on the national level.

Defense intelligence must respond to a range of consumers—policymakers in Washington, defense and technical analysts, and operational commanders in the field—yet the primary mission of defense intelligence is to supply the armed services with the intelligence necessary for their operations. This overriding departmental requirement creates a major problem in the overall allocation of intelligence resources throughout the intelligence community. In promulgating Executive Order 11905, the Administration has decided on a greater centralization of authority in the Director of Central Intelligence. The Committee notes that this will require some changes in the Secretary of Defense's authority over allocating defense intelligence resources. With regard to intelligence resources management within the Department of Defense, the Committee found that the establishment of a Deputy Secretary of Defense for Intelligence should enable more effective management of defense intelligence resources and help the Defense Department play an appropriate role in the new centralized interagency structure under the Director of Central Intelligence.

Increasingly, technological intelligence systems have grown capable of serving both the interests of national policymakers and planners and of field commanders. Thus, it is often difficult to distinguish between "national" and "tactical" intelligence assets, collection, or production. It is the Committee's view that while the effect of the President's Executive Order giving the DCI more authority will be to bring national intelligence assets and budgets under the DCI's control and guidance, the defense intelligence programs which are tactical in nature and integral to the military's operational commands should remain under the control of the Secretary of Defense. The precise line drawn between the tactical and military intelligence at any given time will have a significant impact on the definition of national intelligence and on the purview of any oversight committee(s) of Congress.

2. The Defense Intelligence Agency

Even though the Defense Intelligence Agency has been the principal agency for the production of intelligence in the Defense Department, Secretaries of Defense and other key DOD officials have frequently looked to other intelligence sources rather than to DIA. For example, Robert McNamara relied heavily on the CIA; Melvin Laird sought analyses from the Defense Department's Directorate of Defense Research and Engineering; and James Schlesinger used a special Net Assessment Group. This tendency of Secretaries of Defense to rely on analytic resources outside of DIA is partly but not entirely, related to dissatisfaction with DIA's performance (see the detailed report on DIA). Another factor is the obvious difference between the role of the Defense Department as *manager* of military intelligence collection systems and the role of the Secretary of Defense as a *consumer* of intelligence products. For example, the Secretary's requirements for political and economic intelligence are considerably different from the intelligence needs of the operating forces and the Joint Chiefs of Staff, who are the primary military customers of DIA.

Historically, DOD has managed the bulk of all technical intelligence collection systems, but the CIA has managed many important national technical collection systems and has been in charge of much of the analytic function and is the primary producer of *national* intelligence. The largest proportion of intelligence needed by the military establishment, however, is *tactical*. Therefore, national intelligence is a secondary mission of DIA. Much of DIA's effort is directed toward producing intelligence needed by the JCS, the Unified and Specified Commands, and force planners and technical analysts in the services. The Secretary of Defense, on the other hand, is equally or more concerned with national intelligence. In this context, it is not surprising that DOD's civilian leadership has complemented DIA's product with analyses from sources in other agencies.

The Committee is of the view that the Secretary of Defense has a continuing need for a strong analytical intelligence capability within the Department of Defense. The Committee found that DIA has met this need better than the service intelligence organizations which preceded it, but that DIA has not fulfilled expectations that it would provide a coordinating mechanism for all defense intelligence activities and information.

The essential problem of the Defense Intelligence Agency was summed up in one study commissioned by the executive branch as "too many jobs and too many masters." [50] These problems have not

---

[50] The Report to the President and Secretary of Defense on the Department of Defense by the Blue Ribbon Defense Panel (Fitzhugh Report), 7/1/70.

been solved by the reorganizations undertaken thus far, nor has the DIA's existence led to a diminution in the size of the separate military intelligence services that was hoped for.

The Committee finds that the Defense Intelligence Agency faces serious impediments to improving the quality of, and opportunities for, its civilian and military staff. The Agency's personnel and command structure, its lack of high-level grades, and the relatively short tours for military officers are factors which make it difficult for DIA to develop and retain the high-quality analytic personnel essential for a high-quality finished product.

3. The National Security Agency

The National Security Agency is one of the largest and most technically oriented components of the United States intelligence community. Its basic function is collecting and processing foreign communications and signals for intelligence purposes. NSA is also responsible for creating and supervising the cryptography of all United States Government agencies, and has a special responsibility for supervising the military services' cryptologic agencies. Another major responsibility is protecting the security of American communications.

The Committee regards these functions as vital to American security. NSA's capability to perform these functions must be preserved. The Committee notes that despite the fact that NSA has been in existence for several decades, NSA still lacks a legislative charter. Moreover, in its extensive investigation, the Committee has identified intelligence community abuses in levying requirements on NSA and abuses by NSA itself in carrying out its functions. These abuses are detailed in the domestic portion of the Committee report. The Committee finds that there is a compelling need for an NSA charter to spell out limitations which will protect individual constitutional rights without impairing NSA's necessary foreign intelligence mission.

4. Civilian or Military Leadership

DIA and NSA have always been headed by professional military officers. In the case of DIA, Deputy Directors have also been military. This past practice should not stand in the way of appointment of any individuals, whether civilian or military, best qualified to administer these sensitive agencies.

5. Special Issues

Several important issues concerning NSA have been revealed during the course of the Committ's investigation which require regular reviews by both the intelligence oversight committee(s) of Congress and by the executive branch.

— How can the risks involved in the operations of collection systems be balanced against the value of positive intelligence information acquired through those operations?

— How far in the research/development process of collection systems should the competition between agencies continue before it leads to unwarranted duplication? Should those who develop a system also manage its acquisition and subsequent operation, or should all operations be consolidated, for example, under the Department of Defense?

—How can the technology of advanced intelligence collection systems be better utilized to assist the civilian and domestic agencies of the Government without compromising the principal mission or security of these intelligence systems, or the open character of these portions of American government?

Recommendations

67. In order to implement the Committee's and the President's recommendations for expanding the DCI's resource-allocation responsibility appropriate adjustments should be made in the Secretary of Defense's general authority regarding Defense intelligence activities and in the Department's internal budgeting procedures. At the same time, there should be provision for the transfer to the Secretary of Defense of responsibilities, particularly tasking intelligence agencies, in the event of war.

68. By statute, the intelligence oversight committee(s) of Congress, in consultation with the Executive, should establish a charter for the Defense Intelligence Agency which would clearly define its mission and relationship to other intelligence agencies. The Committee recommends that the charter include the following provisions:

A. In order to encourage close coordination between consumers and producers of national intelligence, DIA should be a part of the Office of the Secretary of Defense, and should report directly to the Deputy Secretary of Defense for Intelligence. A small J–2 staff should be reconstituted to provide intelligence support, primarily of an operational nature, to the Joint Chiefs of Staff. The Secretary of Defense should ensure full coordination and free access to information between the two groups.

B. The Director of the DIA should be appointed by the President and subject to Senate confirmation. Either the Director or Deputy Director of the Agency should be a civilian.

C. The Congress must relieve DIA from certain Civil Service regulations in order to enable the quality of DIA personnel to be upgraded. In addition, more supergrade positions must be provided for civilians in DIA.

69. By statute, a character for the National Security Agency should be established which, in addition to setting limitations on the Agency's operations (see Domestic Subcommittee Recommendations), would provide that the Director of NSA would be nominated by the President and subject to confirmation by the Senate. The Director should serve at the pleasure of the President but not for more than ten years. Either the Director or the Deputy Director should be a civilian.

70. The Department of Defense should centralize the service counterintelligence and investigative activities within the United States in the Defense Investigative Service (DIS) in order to reduce wasteful duplication.

M. The Department of State and Ambassadors

The Department of State and the Foreign Service have an important
N19 role in the intelligence operations of the United States Government.
Because of its responsibilities in formulating and conducting U.S.
foreign policy, the State Department is a principal customer for in-
telligence. Abroad, the Foreign Service, operating overtly, is the prin-
cipal collector of political intelligence and is a major collector of eco-
nomic inteligence.[51]

Because of its foreign policy responsibilities and its worldwide com-
plex of diplomatic and consular installations, the Department of State
is the only Washington agency potentially able to oversee other U.S.
N20 Government activities abroad—including those of the CIA. In the
field, this responsibility clearly falls on the Ambassador by law. In-
deed, Ambassadors are the sole mechanism available outside of the
CIA itself to assure that NSC decisions are appropriately carried out
by the Clandestine Service. The Committee found that the role of the
Department of State and the Ambassadors constitute a central ele-
ment in the control and improvement in America's intelligence
operations overseas. However, the Committee also found that Am-
bassadors are often reluctant to exercise their authority in intelli-
gence matters. The Department has not encouraged them to do so, and
the administration has not issued directives to implement existing law
covering the authority of Ambassadors.

The Committee found that in general the Department of State exer-
cised substantial high-level influence over decisions to undertake major
covert action programs. In the field, Ambassadors are generally
knowledgeable and often involved in significant covert activities proj-
ects. There were, however, notable exceptions, such as the effort to
prevent Salvador Allende from coming to power in Chile by means of
a military coup which was concealed from the Department, the Sec-
retary of State and the American Ambassador to Chile.

In contrast to covert action, the Committee found that neither the
State Department nor U.S. Ambassadors are substantially informed
about espionage or counterintelligence activities directed at foreign
governments. Such coordination as exists in this respect is at the
initiative of the Central Intelligence Agency and is infrequent. The
Committee found that there is no systematic assessment outside the
CIA of the risks of foreign espionage and counterespionage operations
and the extent to which those operations conform with overall foreign
policy.

In general, Ambassadors in the field are uninformed about specific
espionage activities within their countries of assignment. Unlike
the case of covert action, Ambassadors are not asked to appraise the
risks of espionage activities, nor to assess their benefits. Often Am-
bassadors do not want to know the specifics of such operations,
and what coordination as exists in their cases is based on a general
injunction from them to the Station Chiefs that they not be con-
fronted with any "surprises."

---

[51] The Department has often indicated in budget documents relating to intel-
ligence as having a budget of $10 million, particularly for the Bureau of Intel-
ligence and Research. However, the intelligence community staff estimates the
costs attributable to the function of overt intelligence collection by the Foreign
Service at $80 million.

That is not always enough if an Ambassador wishes to participate in policy decisions. For example, a shift of resources toward recruitment of internal targets in a Western country was under consideration between Washington and the field, and the U.S. Ambassador had not been informed. In this connection, the Committee believes it would be unrealistic to use clandestine recruitment to try to establish the kind of intimate relationship with political elites in friendly countries which we have enjoyed as a result of the shared experience of WWII and its aftermath.

The Committee finds that more than a year after enactment of a statute making Ambassadors responsible for directing, coordinating, and supervising all U.S. Government employees within their country of assignment,[52] instructions implementing this law have still not been issued by any quarter of the executive branch. A former Under Secretary of State told the Committee that the law, in effect, had been "suspended" in view of Presidential inaction. Moreover, the CIA has not modified its practices pursuant to this law. The Committee finds this thwarting of the United States law unacceptable.

The Committee finds that Ambassadors cannot effectively exercise their legal responsibilities for a wide variety of intelligence activities within their jurisdiction without State Department assistance on the Washington aspects of the activities. Such support is particularly important in the case of intelligence operations aimed at a third country. An Ambassador may be able to judge the local risks of an espionage effort, but if it is directed toward a third country the Ambassador may not be able to assess the importance or value of the effort without Washington support.

In the past, the Department of State, at least, has not had a parallel responsibility nor the right of access to information necessary to enable it to provide support to an Ambassador seeking to exercise his statutory responsibility over CIA espionage and counterespionage operations. The Committee notes section 4 in Executive Order No. 11905 of February 18, 1976 which may be intended to provide such State Department back-up for Ambassadors.

At present, the CIA handles both State Department and its own communications with overseas posts. Under this arrangement, the Ambassador's access to CIA communications is at the discretion of the CIA. The Committee finds that this is not compatible with the role assigned to the Ambassador by law; the Ambassador cannot be sure that he knows the full extent and nature of CIA operations for which he may be held accountable.

The Committee finds that Ambassadors' policies governing intelligence activities have sometimes been interpreted in a manner which vitiated their intent. For example, one Ambassador prohibited any electronic surveillance by his Embassy's CIA component. The head of the CIA component interpreted this to proscribe only CIA electronic surveillance and believed that such surveillance could be conducted in cooperation with local security services.

---

[52] 22 U.S.C. 2680a. The instructions prepared by the State Department and forwarded to the NSC have been opposed by the CIA on the grounds that the CIA still has a responsibility to protect sources and methods from unauthorized disclosure. The NSC has not acted on the proposed instructions.

The Committee found evidence that CIA Station Chiefs abroad do not always coordinate their intelligence reporting on local developments with their Ambassadors. The Committee does not believe that Ambassadors should be able to block CIA field reports. However, it found that there was no standard practice for Ambassadors to review and comment on intelligence reporting from the field.

The Committee finds that the Foreign Service is the foremost producer in the United States Government of intelligence on foreign political and economic matters. The Committee believes, however, that the State Department does not adequately train Foreign Service personnel, particularly in political reporting. Nor does the Department fund their collection operations, nor manage their activities so as to take full advantage of this extremely important intelligence capability. In effect, the Department, despite being a major source of intelligence, considers this function secondary to its principal task of diplomatic representation and negotiations.

From discussions in nearly a dozen foreign service posts, the Committee established that there is inadequate funding for Foreign Service reporting officers to carry out their responsibilities. The funds available are considered "representation funds" and must be shared with the administration and consular sections of most embassies. Such representation funds have been a favorite target for congressional cuts in the State Department budget.

Recommendations

71. The National Security Council, the Department of State, and the Central Intelligence Agency should promptly issue instructions implementing Public Law 93–475 (22 U.S.C. 2680a). These instructions should make clear that Ambassadors are authorized recipients of sources and methods information concerning all intelligence activities, including espionage and counterintelligence operations. Parallel instructions from other components of the intelligence community should be issued to their respective field organizations and operatives. Copies of all these instructions should be made available to the intelligence oversight committee(s) of Congress.

72. In the exercise of their statutory responsibilities, Ambassadors should have the personal right, which may not be delegated, of access to the operational communications of the CIA's Clandestine Service in the country to which they are assigned. Any exceptions should have Presidential approval and should be brought to the attention of the intelligence oversight committee(s) of Congress.

73. By statute, the Department of State should be authorized to take the necessary steps to assure its ability to provide effective guidance and support to Ambassadors in the execution of their responsibilities under Public Law 93–475 (22 U.S.C. Sect. 2680a).

74. Consideration should be given to increasing and earmarking funds for Foreign Service overt collection of foreign political and economic information. These funds might be administered jointly by the State Department's Bureau of Intelligence and Research and the Bureau of Economic Affairs.

75. The NSC should review the question of which U.S. Government agency should control and operate communications with over-

seas diplomatic and consular posts, including the CIA, and other civilian agencies operating abroad.

76. The Department of State should establish specific training programs for political reporting within the Foreign Service Institute, and place greater emphasis on economic reporting.

N. OVERSIGHT AND THE INTELLIGENCE BUDGET

The Committee finds that a full understanding of the budget of the intelligence community is required for effective oversight. The secrecy surrounding the budget, however, makes it impossible for Congress as a whole to make use of this valuable oversight tool.

Congress as a body has never explicitly voted on a "budget" for national intelligence activities. Congress has never voted funds specifically for CIA, NSA, and other national intelligence instrumentalities of the Department of Defense.[54]

The funding levels for these intelligence agencies are fixed by subcommittees of the Armed Services and Appropriations Committees of both Houses. Funds for these agencies are then concealed in the budget of the Department of Defense. Since this Departmental budget is the one Congress approves, Congress as a whole, and the public, have never known how much the intelligence agencies are spending or how much is spent on intelligence activities generally. Neither Congress as a whole, nor the public can determine whether the amount spent on intelligence, or by the intelligence agencies individually, is appropriate, given the priorities.

Because the funds for intelligence are concealed in Defense appropriations, those appropriations are thereby inflated. Most members of Congress and the public can neither determine which categories are inflated nor the extent to which funds in the inflated categories are being used for purposes for which they are approved.

Finally, the Committee believes there is serious question as to whether the present system of complete secrecy violates the constitutional provision that:

> No Money shall be drawn from the Treasury but in Consequence of Appropriations made by Law; and a regular Statement and Account of the Receipts and Expenditures of all public Money shall be published from time to time.[55]

The Committee believes that the overall figure for national intelligence activities can be made public annually without endangering national security or revealing sensitive programs.[56] The Committee carefully examined the possible impact of such disclosure on the sources and methods of intelligence gathering and believes it to be minimal. The Committee found that the primary concern about this

---

[54] Funds for the intelligence activities of the Department of State, ERDA, and the FBI are reviewed by the appropriate congressional committees and are voted upon by Congress as a whole, when Congress appropriates funds for these agencies.

[55] United States Constitution, Art. I. Sec. 9 Cls. 7.

[56] The Committee noted that the Special Senate Committee to Study Questions Related to Secret and Confidential Government Documents, chaired by Senators Mansfield and Scott concluded that the aggregate figure for each intelligence agency should be made public.

level of disclosure was that it would lead to pressure for even more detailed revelation which would compromise vital intelligence programs.

The Committee believes that disclosure of an aggregate figure for national intelligence is as far as it is prudent to go at this stage in reconciling the nation's constitutional and national security requirements. Public speculation about overall intelligence costs would be eliminated, the public would be assured that funds appropriated to particular government agencies were in fact intended for those agencies, and both Congress and the public would be able to assess overall priorities in governmental spending.

The Committee's analysis indicated that _____ billion constitutes the direct costs to the United States for its national intelligence program for FY 1976. This includes the total approved budgets of CIA, DIA, NSA and the national reconnaissance program.[57] If the cost of tactical intelligence by the armed services and indirect support costs [58] which may be attributed to intelligence and intelligence-related activities is added, the total cost of U.S. Government intelligence activities would be twice that amount. This represents about three percent of the total federal budget, and about eight percent of controllable federal spending.

It should be stressed that this larger estimate represents a full cost and includes activities which also fulfill other purposes. Thus the entire amount could not be "saved" if there were no intelligence activities funded by or through the Defense Department.

The CIA's budget for the fiscal year is contained in the Defense Department budget. The Committee found that the CIA spends approximately 70 percent more than it is appropriated, with the additional funds coming from advances and transfers from other agencies. These transfers and advances are made with the knowledge and approval of OMB and the appropriate congressional committees. The use of advances and transfers between agencies is a common governmental practice. In this case the CIA receives funds as the contracting agent for agencies in the Defense Department as well as other intelligence community agencies.

Recommendations

77. The intelligence oversight committee(s) of Congress should authorize on an annual basis a "National Intelligence Budget," the total amount of which would be made public. The Committee recommends that the oversight committee consider whether it is necessary, given the Constitutional requirement and the national security demands, to publish more detailed budgets.

78. The intelligence oversight committee(s) of Congress should monitor the tactical and indirect support accounts as well as the national activities of intelligence agencies in order to assure that they are kept in proper perspective and balance.

---

[57] The direct costs of the intelligence activities of the ERDA, FBI, and State Department are contained in their respective budgets.

[58] Indirect support costs include costs for personnel, operations and maintenance which support intelligence activities. Examples are the operation of training facilities, supply bases, and commissaries.

79. At the request of the intelligence oversight committee(s) of Congress and as its agent, staff members of the General Accounting Office should conduct full audits, both for compliance and for management of all components of the intelligence community. The GAO should establish such procedures, compartmentation and clearances as are necessary in order to conduct these audits on a secure basis. In conducting such audits, the GAO should be authorized to have full access to all necessary intelligence community files and records.

N23

INTELLIGENCE SUPPORT FOR FOREIGN POLICY IN THE FUTURE ([90], pp. 77–86)

SUMMARY

It is widely agreed that United States foreign policy will focus with greater intensity than before on economic and technological problems in the remaining 1970's and the 1980's. This new emphasis will require a corresponding change in intelligence support. In organizing resources to provide this support for foreign policy, one should look at existing capabilities scattered throughout the government, not only at those in the intelligence organizations.

Optimum use of U.S. intelligence agencies will require some caution not to overburden them with tasks lying outside their primary role: warning against external military and political threat to the security of the United States. On some problems now becoming urgent—like the Soviet and Chinese economies, world trade patterns, world oil production—intelligence can make a special contribution; others—like environmental studies and world food grain production—may better be assigned to departments with policy responsibilities.

Economic issues in foreign policy have great urgency at present and will retain front rank in the future. Support for economic foreign policy can be better provided in the future by organizing and coordinating those information and research facilities which now exist but are dispersed throughout the government. The creation of a central economic information authority could bring these scattered means together into "the mainstream of US international policy-making."

Research on world food and agricultural problems has been conducted intensively by commercial organizations and academic institutions as well as government departments. Like support for broader economic policy, this research can be made more responsive to policy needs through central direction.

Innovations in modes of intelligence support are at hand. Although "real-time" transmission of information directly to the desks of high level policy people, and similar futuristic concepts, appear to have limited utility, the use of electronic data processing machines can greatly improve the speed and efficiency of desk officers and intelligence analysts. Changes in format and presentation of intelligence reporting can be most effective when an active dialogue is sustained between producer and user.

INTRODUCTION

Conventional wisdom has it that, in the remaining years of the 1970's and in the 1980's, the United States will confront an array of problems in foreign policy fundamentally different from those which dominated the previous thirty years. The emphasis on military threat and related concerns will give way increasingly to policy issues centering around economic and technological problems.

There can be no serious quarrel with this contention. Indeed, the "future" as perceived here is already upon us. The great problems of energy allocation, global food supplies, and international monetary stability—to name three prime examples—have already taken the center stage away from our former main concern: the Soviet military threat against the security of the United States.

It is important to remember, however, that what is envisaged is a shift in emphasis, not an absolute change in basic U.S. foreign policy. This caveat is particularly important when considering how to focus and structure intelligence support for foreign policy in the future. It is not uncommon for those who cite the future dominance of economic and technological problems to suggest at the same time that great expansion of the intelligence establishment will be needed to explore the innumerable facets of these problems. No one can argue against the growing need for well-grounded, sophisticated studies which array the abundant economic and technical data in meaningful patterns and which guide policy toward identifying significant elements. But issue can be joined with the automatic assumption that this task should be assumed primarily by the intelligence organizations, even though a trend has already been established for intelligence to expand broadly in these fields.

Several considerations should serve as restraints. First, national security against external military threat will remain a major, if not dominant, concern for US foreign policy in the future. US intelligence has a heavy investment in guarding against this threat, and a substantial share of its energies and resources must continue to provide this protection. Second, the intelligence agencies do not invariably have something special to contribute on economic or technological problems, either in information or methodology. Instead, what they have is a tradition of service and the capacity to coordinate judgments and perform disciplined, responsive analysis.

Third, greater expertise and much of the essential information are often available outside intelligence channels, in those agencies which have line responsibilities. What is chiefly needed to bring these capabilities into the effective support of US foreign policy is machinery for coordinating and properly directing their work.

THE OPTIMUM ROLE FOR INTELLIGENCE

In surveying how US foreign policy can best be supported in the future, it is useful to consider how the intelligence organizations contribute to this support at present. It is also useful to consider briefly the forces which have pushed intelligence toward handling matters peripheral to their primary concerns, to cite constraints against furthering this trend, and to identify sample problems which are best addressed either by intelligence or by experts in Departments such as the Treasury, Justice, Agriculture, or Interior.

Intelligence organizations have steadily tended to reach further and further out from their primary tasks. In part, they have been encouraged to do so by people with policy responsibilities who desperately want help and who welcome staff studies from a source with demonstrated capability for objective study. More important, however, have been the impulses within the intelligence organizations to move outward toward recognized needs. They have frequently gone into new areas because it was clear that no one else was doing work which was useful, even essential. At the same time, they have often succumbed to the flattering notion that expertise achieved by intelligence analysis entitles them to an authoritative voice in matters related to their work chiefly by geography or academic discipline. Whatever the reasons, there is real risk that, by trying to make itself heard in a field already overcrowded by qualified experts, intelligence will seriously dilute its legitimate work.

There is a unique expertise pertaining to the use of intelligence materials. Like all evidence, these materials have their limitations and their special values, and these are not immediately apparent to every one using them. Except for the unusual instance—for example, a purloined document signed by a prime minister—intelligence evidence tends to be fragmentary, oblique, and mostly of uncertain validity. Only an art forged by prolonged, daily work in intelligence can provide the needed tool to fashion them properly into meaning and value. Intelligence analysts, examining daily the various kinds of collected information flowing through their channels, do acquire this art. Looking at the reports one by one, noting establishable connections between an item of intercepted communication, let us say, and a clandestine agent report, recalling that a recent report from this agent was verified by a frame of overhead photography, checking an embassy political officer's comments on this matter—these daily activities do, in the course of months and years, produce sharper insights and sounder judgments. They also reduce errors which result from undue reliance on a single and sometimes uncertain source. Few policy desk

officers and fewer high level policy people have this essential experience. They need guidance in threading their way through a dense maze of information and misinformation. Here, the intelligence worker can make a unique contribution.

When intelligence analysts produce reports and studies bearing a rich lode of material unique to intelligence, then they can most legitimately claim a right to be heard by policy people. They are then doing what they can do better than anyone else, and they are not basing their claim upon credentials no different from others. The exact degree of intelligence content required to establish this legitimacy is not easy to state but it becomes evident when the policy officer realizes that he is reading material pertinent to his concerns which has not been available to him in his own daily traffic. On occasion, this information may consist of a single intelligence report skilfully used to illuminate a mass of other information. More often, it will consist of several bits, or even a large number of fragments, which have been interwoven into the account in such a way as to provide greater meaning to the material surrounding it.

Intelligence organizations are able to collect uniquely valuable information and to perform special analytic tasks on many subjects of concern to policy people but certainly not on all. Traditional subjects, like military weaponry and weapons deployments or subversive political movements, come quickly to mind as their province. Others, like economic trends or international trade, have become recognized as legitimate areas for intelligence work even though the bulk of the evidence is readily and overtly available. The closed economic societies of the Communist countries, our political opponents and potential military antagonists, have made it necessary for the intelligence organizations in the years since 1945 to delve deeply into the economic underpinnings of Communist national strength. Having established expertise in advanced economic research on Eastern Europe and Communist China, it has been inevitable that intelligence would also look intensively at international economic activities where the Communist countries have important interests: food grain production and trade, gold production, international monetary transactions, and oil production.

The success intelligence has had in producing illuminating studies in these areas has gone far to persuade their clientele that the intelligence role should be broadened without much concern over the special contribution intelligence material can make. This impulse represents both opportunity and threat to the intelligence agencies: opportunity to work fruitfully on direct demand from policy people; and threat to their concentration of effort on primary tasks.

Clearly, no precise line of demarcation can—or should—be drawn between those economic studies most effectively done by intelligence and those best done by outside experts or policy staff people. What should be uppermost is how can maximum service be provided in support of foreign policy. Moreover, there are several special circumstances which give sanction to intelligence involvement in fields outside those normally their own. Having judicially determined what draining away of resources and manpower from primary tasks will be entailed by the pursuit of studies outside their top priorities, intelligence organizations will certainly be justified when those studies represent an urgent and precise need and when no other qualified group is available to do the work. This will be all the more true when unusual methodologies have been developed in intelligence studies, which have applicability to problems at hand. An example of this is the intensive work done by the Office of Economic Research in CIA on the analysis of world trade patterns, work which was originally centered on Soviet and Chinese trade but necessarily broadened in scope in order to place them in context and perspective.

Another range of studies where intelligence will be justified in directing its effort will be those which touch on the interests and concerns of several policy groups but are the primary responsibility of no single department. A good example of this is the work CIA has done—and probably in the future should concentrate even greater effort—on international production, marketing, and consumption of petroleum. Sound, objective analysis in this field is so clearly needed now and in the future that intelligence is fully justified in broadening its focus from the Soviet and Chinese fraction to the global totality.

The special objectivity which intelligence organizations can bring to policy support studies provides another justification for their involvement on problems outside their usual beat. This is delicate ground: no policy officer finds it easy to identify, let alone admit to, any persistent bias in his analysis of the problems his work addresses. Moreover, intelligence officers are frequently not aware of the distortions and bias their intelligence materials sometimes introduce into their analysis. Yet, there can be no doubt that freedom from the urgencies of solving a problem does permit a more dispassionate examination of its underlying strands and factors. Intelligence has often demonstrated that its freer perspective can provide insights and sound judgments with which to attack the problem.

Two essential elements must be present to make studies of this kind effective. First, the policy reader must be persuaded that the intelligence paper deserves his attention and earns his respect. This may be achieved by the use of unique intelligence material which enhances information otherwise available. Or, it may be obtained with fresh perspectives or new approaches to a familiar problem. Second, to be effective such studies must be pertinent to the tractable and manipulable phases of the policy problem, not merely an account of its history and prospects. Policy readers have a right to expect a high degree of pertinence to the manageable aspects of their problems. They have an accompanying responsibility to guide the intelligence officer toward those phases of the problem where their potential leverage is greatest.

Besides the traditional and established-by-custom subjects for intelligence, there are a number of others in which intelligence organizations have worked in the past or are being urged to do so in the future. These range from international narcotics traffic to climate forecasting and control. For some of these, the need to allocate intelligence resources toward them, at least for a time, has been urgent and obvious. For others, it is more difficult to find such justification.

Over the past few years, the United States has confronted urgent problems which gravely affected the lives of its citizens although they did not directly imperil the security of the nation. Two examples of these are traffic in narcotics and international terrorism. Both are areas in which intelligence organizations have been able to make immediate and valuable contributions, albeit at the cost of diverting considerable effort from their primary tasks. By turning their established agent networks overseas toward locating primary sources, main channels, and modus operandi of narcotics traffickers in foreign countries, intelligence has been highly effective in getting timely information to policy people and enforcement agencies. Similar success has been obtained in getting timely information about international terrorist organizations.

High level concern and the time urgency of these two problems provided the initial impetus to involve the intelligence agencies, but it is doubtful whether they ought to retain responsibility in the future. In the field, intelligence activity against these targets distorts their primary mission in two significant ways. First, they deflect espionage from top priority tasks: the worldwide activities and objectives of the Soviet Union and Communist China. An agent who is spending his time developing sources of information about narcotics traffic cannot at the same time widen his access to Soviet nationals working in that country. Second, espionage work in both these fields, international terrorism and narcotics, leads almost immediately to police action and enforcement activity in the country involved. Here, the overseas intelligence people find it most difficult to be helpful. In many instances, they are inhibited from sharing their information with local police for cover reasons or because they risk exposing a valuable, indigenous source contributing to their priority collection programs. Lacking police powers of their own, or the organizational relationships in some countries to assist locally, they can do little more than report the information through their channels back to Washington where its practical value is slight. On matters related to police work in these fields, it would seem preferable in the future to assign the task to US agencies already charged with action and enforcement responsibilities, such as the Bureau of Narcotics or the FBI.

It is similarly dubious whether in the future intelligence organizations can usefully continue research in international terrorism and narcotics. Once the basic papers had been done to establish broad patterns and prospects, the work that remains is highly tactical, chiefly requiring rapid communication of reports and sound arrangement with enforcement agencies for action. Like the overseas collection and action phases, the supporting staff studies essential to this work—preparation of dossiers, organization charts, and the like—are best assigned to US government organizations which have action responsibilities.

US intelligence has developed several collection techniques which have turned out to have broad utility in other fields. The most spectacular example of this, of course, is overhead photography. After the well publicized success of the U-2 in identifying Soviet missiles in Cuba, the NASA program of the past decade has probably done the most to bring attention to this new capability. Publication of photographs taken in orbit by the astronauts—hand-held shots by small cameras of vast areas of the earth, such as the entire Nile Basin—have done as much as anything to set off a scramble among government agencies and private corporations to discover ways to exploit this collection tool.

The experience of the past several years has sharpened and narrowed perceptions of the applicability and utility of reconnaissance photography. At the same time, it has become abundantly clear that this imagery can be effectively used by researchers in almost any field where rigidly controlled photographs of the earth's surface have value and where intelligence photo-interpreters are not needed. Certain mechanical phases of the exploitation of photography, such as image-enhancing or precise mensuration, have been developed to a high art by intelligence people, but these can be passed along and tailored to the specific discipline involved: meteorology, agricultural research, or mineral exploitation. Aside from that, the techniques essential for effective use of reconnaissance photography are largely peculiar to the particular area of investigation.

Historically, US intelligence agencies have put overhead photography to military uses: target identification and analysis, detecting new weapon development, locating newly deployed weapons systems. These subjects demand highly specialized backgrounds on the characteristics of weapon systems, military construction techniques, and other arcane details. Few of these have application to such subjects as weather formation or crop prospects. On the other hand, these more peaceful areas of study have their own highly specialized data bases which are already familiar to researchers in these fields.

New lines of research in environmental fields touching on foreign policy issues will certainly need to use data collected by a broad spectrum of sensors. What is being suggested here is that intelligence does not for the most part have anything special to contribute to research based on this data. Each of these fields can best be covered by experts already immersed in the study, the nature of reconnaissance imagery being such that it is most effectively used by people intensively trained and experienced, who can perceive the special, and usually supplementary, contribution photography makes to the information already in hand. Research facilities in US agencies already at work in these fields—the Departments of Agriculture and Interior among others—can be directed to pursue advanced research incorporating data from overhead sensors. Where these analyses have application to foreign policy problems, appropriate relationships with the Department of State already exist and can be expanded and extended to other departments if necessary.

SUPPORT FOR ECONOMIC PHASES OF FOREIGN POLICY

International economic developments have great urgency and significance at present and will certainly remain in the front rank of foreign policy problems in the future. The means for providing effective close support for economic policy appears to exist already within the US government, but these means, both in terms of expert personnel and research facilities, are scattered throughout various departments. The precise mechanisms essential for effective direction and coordination are lacking. Support for economic foreign policy with hard information and sound analysis represents the most urgent need for the future. At the same time, the opportunity is great to respond to that need.

Attention has been effectively focused on the need for improved support of US international economic policy by Mr. Peter G. Peterson, Assistant to the President for Economic Affairs, in a memorandum dated 31 January 1973. Mr. Peterson pointed out a number of deficiencies in current economic intelligence support and proposed new procedures for correcting those deficiencies. Among the shortcomings cited by the Peterson memorandum are the following: (a) collection of international economic data is dispersed throughout the government and both within intelligence organizations (CIA and Department of State) and outside (Treasury, Commerce, Labor, Federal Reserve, and others); (b) both data collection and analysis tend to be parochial and departmental in scope and emphasis, not "in the mainstream of US international economic policy-making;" (c) no "early warning" capability exists in economic intelligence work, thus leaving US policy people inadequately informed of forthcoming developments and "forced to react on an ad hoc basis;" and (d) proper mechanisms and procedures are lacking for bringing data and judgments together in format and scope appropriate for top-level policy people.

The deficiencies noted by the Peterson memorandum are just, and Mr. Peterson has performed timely service by focusing attention upon them just when questions of international economic interdependence have surged to the fore and every problem of foreign policy presents an economic face. It is noteworthy that aside from a reference to "important holes" in the information available, little stress is put upon a shortage of data. No only is this refreshing in a critique of government intelligence work, but it appears to be accurate. Close on the heels of the usual caveat—"we can always use more information on specifics"—the admission comes generally that by and large there is more than enough data available. The greater need is for sound, well-conceived and directed analysis, closely keyed to the immediate needs of policy people.

The existence of the "holes" ought not to be dismissed entirely, however, because they sometimes come at vital points. Some of these gaps offer good possibilities for being filled; others present problems of great and enduring difficulty. Gaps in economic information essential to sound analysis come for the most part in the following three categories: (a) national economic data of countries who deny public access to such data as a matter of national policy—the U.S.S.R., the Warsaw Pact countries, Communist China, and the other Asian Communist countries; (b) economic data of those underdeveloped countries which lack adequate bureaucratic facilities for collecting and generating such data; and (c) information about individual economic decisions or intended actions which is deliberately concealed in order to assure success for such actions.

The first of these categories, economic data for "denied areas," has been vigorously and systematically addressed by US intelligence, especially the Office of Economic Research in CIA, for more than a decade. The performance record is good, and the methodology and expertise well established. If economic policy people find significant gaps of information in this area, either now or in the future, it is fair to say that the means for filling those gaps do exist and only precise direction is needed for mounting a highly professional effort against them.

The second category, national economic data for underdeveloped and inept governments, obviously presents problems of greater difficulty. CIA and the State Department's Bureau of Intelligence and Research (INR) have done intensive work on individual problems of this kind from time to time in response to specific requests, but the results have been sometimes skimpy. When data do not exist it cannot be created, but frequently analog models and constructs can be provided which offer considerable assistance. Here again, the means exists for dealing with a shortage in a professional manner.

The third category, deliberately concealed information about individual decisions, presents the greatest difficulty. Unfortunately, it also includes information which often has most direct value for policy people, particularly for "early warning" as cited by Mr. Peterson. Clearly, when information is withheld about a specific decision for tactical advantage, the persons involved will do their best to protect that information. In the living world of human beings, however, this ability is uneven. Leaks or inspired confidences do occur. The intelligence organizations and the Department of State are already charged with responsibility for getting this kind of information by clandestine means or otherwise. What can be done further is to consolidate and streamline the mechanism by which policy people make known their exact requirements for specific information.

It will be noted that each of the categories cited above concerns information already being sought by intelligence organizations. It ought also to be noted that these categories represent a relatively small percentage of the total volume of economic data needed for a solid informational and analytic base in support of international economic policy. This becomes significant when considering how best to structure a new economic analytic effort to meet the urgent needs of the future.

The distinction is sometimes drawn between economic intelligence and economic information. Like all distinctions, it shatters when pressed too hard, but it has some utility for thinking about this particular matter. Taking as a point of departure the view that intelligence people ought to concentrate on those tasks they alone can do, or at least can do best, and accepting the need for some counterpart among the policy agencies to the established intelligence coordination mechanisms, then a basis for allocating future economic research effort and for assigning roles in a national economic support apparatus does emerge.

The Departments of State, Treasury, Commerce, Agriculture, and Labor, as well as the Federal Reserve Board and elements of other agencies, all acquire volumes of data pertaining to the economic phases of foreign policy. Most of these agencies also have analytic elements. Nearly all problems of economic policy fall within the purview of one or more of these agencies, but their natural tendency is to address only those aspects of the problem which fall within the jurisdiction of their department. Seldom is an economic issue of foreign policy analyzed and displayed in all its national policy ramifications. It is rare that an economic problem is treated with the thorough coordination of information and judgment that characterizes the national intelligence estimates process under the direction of the United States Intelligence Board (USIB). What is needed to make this kind of procedure routine and systematic is the creation of an author-

ity in the economic information and policy area analogous to the USIB in intelligence.

There are two distinct but interrelated functions to be undertaken under the aegis of an economic information and policy authority: (a) the gathering, collating, and storing in one central storehouse of economic and related data bearing on economic foreign policy; and (b) the preparation of analytic studies and estimates which explore basic factors and dynamics of international economic issues in a manner appropriate for high level consideration.

A model for the first of these functions may exist in the Legislative Reference Service. An Economic Reference Service, staffed by economic analysts, could centrally perform the task of storing economic data and could respond to requests throughout the government for collated data and reports. The main requirements for the creation of such an Economic Reference Service are the assembling of a top flight corps of analysts and issuance of a directive ensuring that all information pertinent to their mission would be systematically provided by all government agencies.

Some provision would need to be made for handling materials which carry security classification by reason of their clandestine source. This could be accomplished with a special section within the Economic Reference Service, possibly an outpost office of CIA. Alternatively, CIA could be directed to store and collate the classified material and to make it available upon request. This is roughly what happens in actual practice now. Although such a procedure can continue to work and would be greatly improved if there were a central economic reference facility with which it could cooperate, the establishment of a special classified section with the Reference Service has several advantages, including a tighter meshing of classified and open materials and firmer responsiveness through the spectrum of economic foreign policy.

It is important to recognize that what is envisaged is not merely a reference library but an economic information and analysis production center. Such a facility would ease the difficulty policy people now have in locating economic analysts to provide staff studies. In particular, by providing a central place for such work it would clarify the confusion which sometimes arises as to the role appropriately played by the intelligence agencies. A good example of this might be the work needed to support US trade and monetary policy, such as the construction of models which display the effect that changes in German or Japanese exchange rates produce on US international trade and how this effect in turn would impact upon US balance of payments. Such a task would logically fall to the Economic Reference Center for primary responsibility, while CIA's Office of Economic Research, which has done intensive work on such models, could assist with methodology and supplementary analysis.

The second function which a national economic information and policy authority would oversee would be the preparation of high level economic estimates and studies. Two approaches are suggested. The first would be to create a high level board within the authority, somewhat on the model of the former Board of National Estimates in CIA, and charge it with responsibility for coordinating staff contributions from each agency with an economic policy mission. The second would be to use the already existing mechanisms of the National Security Council for assembling and presenting such policy support papers. Such work would be considerably improved over the present by the participation of the Economic Reference Service. Both these suggestions have drawbacks and merits, and further study would be required to make an informed choice between them.

What remains is to determine just where in the executive branch of the US government such a national economic authority could best be placed. If the authority is to centralize activities now dispersed throughout the government, it would seem wise to make it independent of the line agencies. The Council on International Economic Policy comes immediately to mind as a natural choice. A presidential directive could assign it the missions and authorities described above. On the other hand, if other considerations militate against this choice, a wholly new authority could be created, again by presidential directive. The chief requirement is that the economic information and policy authority be supra-departmental.

SUPPORT FOR FOOD AND AGRICULTURE PROBLEMS

The availability of food world-wide and a host of related problems involving distribution, marketing, and financing, loom large among the foreign policy issues awaiting the US over the next decade. Policy people will need sound data and expert judgment to guide them in dealing with these issues.

Thanks to some pioneer work over the past seven or eight years, the US government can readily assemble resources and expertise for providing a solid informational and analytic base to support foreign policy formulation in this field. In the Department of Agriculture, the Economic Research Service has invested intensive effort in developing techniques for estimating forthcoming yields of food grain crops. Data for these estimates were derived largely from foreign national statistics, current planning reports, long range weather forecasts, and records of previous crop yields. The accuracy and predictive value of this array of information was greatly enhanced when overhead photography and other sensor data became available over the past half dozen years. The Department of Agriculture did considerable early work which was helpful in determining both the contribution and technical limitations of this medium.

The photographic interpretation and economic research shops of CIA were in this field at the outset, seeking to use overhead photography to penetrate the closed realms of agricultural production within the USSR and Communist China. CIA soon recognized the limitations of reconnaissance photography in identifying grain crops and their status and set to work on improving methodologies and models which would establish the correct interaction between the imagery, meteorological data, and status reports.

Outside government, interest in using overhead sensors for research in agriculture and other earth resources fields was greatly stimulated by the public availability of photography and other data from the Earth Resources Technology Satellite systems. A number of commercial aerial photography companies, already possessed of considerable experience and equipment, turned to this new field. An even larger number of academic institutions directed research and training activities toward exploiting this new and abundant data.

The consequence of the varied and broadly dispersed activity is that the US government can call upon a large number of organizations, both private and governmental, to provide technical services and data bases for work in food crop forecasting and related studies. The technology and expertise are now at hand to provide policy people with solid support in these fields.

As in the broader effort to support international economic policy, the key to success will lie largely in the organization and management of existing capabilities. Also, as in the support of the broad aspects of foreign policy, the nature of the data and its ready availability suggest that the role of the intelligence agencies can be largely supplementary, and the main burden can be carried by departments with line responsibilities: State and Agriculture.

A good case can be made for lodging primary responsibility for this support work in the Department of Agriculture, with the Economic Research Service providing the central storehouse for information and responding to policy requests for forecasts and studies. The Office of Economic Research in CIA, which already has highly effective working relationships with Agriculture, could continue to contribute both analysis and methodology pertaining to Soviet and Chinese Communist agricultural and food production activities, including weather data, much of which has applicability to other areas. Broad policy studies could be directed by INR, utilizing the information base provided by CIA and Agriculture.

Alternatively, this work could be viewed as merely a part of the whole, a significant segment of the broad field of international economic policy, and responsibility for information and analytic support could be assigned to the central economic authority described in the preceding section. Perhaps the chief advantage of this approach would be that the national economic information and policy authority could assume a commanding position in dealing with broad international economic policy in a fashion not easily available to the Department of Agriculture.

INNOVATIONS IN INTELLIGENCE SUPPORT

Both within the intelligence agencies and outside among their customers there is a constant desire to improve the ways in which intelligence information is transmitted. Intelligence people are constantly experimenting with new ways to convey the printed word, new uses for graphic displays, new devices for getting and holding the attention of the policy reader. On the other end, policy desk people are always looking for greater impact from intelligence reports; they ask for some means to alert them more fully or inform them more thoroughly. Because the techniques by which policy people ingest information are highly individualistic and because novelty in presentation has inherent appeal, albeit relatively short-lived, a continuous program of experiment and change seems both inevitable and desirable.

Among the avenues for improvement, the use of electronic data processors and video tube display devices have been most thoroughly explored. It has been expected by some that these modern machines will soon displace typewritten reports and the printed word. It has been urged that in this age of instant communication and high speed decision, policy people can no longer be served adequately with printed reports but must be provided with "real time" information relayed directly from the scene of action to their desks. It has also been suggested that government has been laggard in recognizing the advance of modern technology in this field.

The intelligence agencies, spurred both by this criticism and by their own recognition of the need for greater speed in handling their information, have been experimenting with a variety of machines for processing and transmitting information for over a decade and have been conducting intensive research and development for five years or so. Also, they have called in top experts from the national communications media to study ways of improving their procedures. By so doing they have established some guiding concepts for present and future applications, and they have reached the stage where pragmatic use of machine processing on a large scale can begin.

Among the guiding concepts that have emerged from these studies are these: (a) people currently in top policy positions are not prepared either by background or training to receive essential information by visual display or computer read-out instead of the printed word; (b) the information essential to the support of policy—intensively worked data, reasoned and modulated judgments, interlocking analyses of causes and dynamics—do not lend themselves to electronics and are better transmitted in printed paragraphs; and (c) tremendous advances can be made in the speed and efficiency with which information is processed by intelligence analysts using machines precisely designed to their needs.

Difficult as it is to generalize about the backgrounds of people in top foreign policy positions, it is still probably fair to say that generally their training has been more in economics, political science, and law than it has been in mathematics and the physical sciences. They have formed twin habits of acquiring information from the printed page and expressing themselves in written papers. Although they may have had some experience with modern computers, they usually have not performed serious work directly with the machines, as have their counterparts in the hard sciences. The information they customarily handle consists largely of approximations, generalizations, and judgments—not the discrete, quantitative data which adapts readily to digital expression. They have been trained to think in words, not numbers, and the policy work they do finds expression in words.

Moreover, except when they are dealing with a sharp crisis—say, an invasion of the Middle East—their work does not call for a steady series of high speed decisions. Most policy determinations require deliberate and intensive study before action. It is largely a myth that modern communications demand instant decisions and a twenty-four hourly readiness to react. Modern communications permit, or facilitate, quick response but they do not in themselves require it.

Crisis situations, on the other hand, do usually require rapid decision and response, and here the intelligence agencies must be prepared to use all the resources of modern technology to assist that process. For the most part, the technology already exists and what is needed is the investment of resources. Among future means of speeding the decision-making process will be video relays from television cameras on the site of crucial meetings or other key developments and televised briefings by intelligence experts who are interpreting information as fast as it arrives.

But even here, only a little reflection is needed to realize that these situations will be the exception, not the rule. Top policy people seldom have the need, and even more seldom have the time, to follow a crisis step by step as it unfolds. They must instead rely on summarized and gisted information from assistants while they spend much of their time in policy meetings and discussions with their fellow policy makers.

Although the need is clear for occasional availability of "real time" service for top policy people, the greater need is for electronic passage of information to desk officers in policy organizations and for machine processing of information for intelligence analysts. It is here that the future looks most promising for effective work.

Over the past three years substantial progress has been made in identifying precisely which phases of analytic work are adaptable to machines and in designing machines to do that work. The key to this substantial progress has been that the machines have been patterned around the work analysts actually do, not the other way around. Very often the advocates for machine data processing have lacked any intimate understanding of the work being done. They have known that machines can perform a great variety of high speed operations and they have assumed that the work can be readily adapted to the specific requirements of the machines. Prolonged experimentation has demonstrated that this is not always true. Most of the materials which intelligence analysts handle resist strict codification or digitalization. More often it is descriptive, approximative, or judgmental.

One task which intelligence analysts perform daily is to read "the traffic," the flow of cables, reports, and telegrams which reach their desk in staggering volume. A great deal of effort has been expended on speeding up this process with electronic machines, and it is now clear that in the future analysts will use text processing machines for this chore. One such system would display incoming cables on the analyst's desk, machine-sorted appropriately for his individual mission and coded by number. Scanning these cables on the video tube before him, the analyst could select those items he would like to have delivered to his desk for more intensive study and comparison with other material. This system will not only speed the process of moving innumerable bits of information around the organization, but it will also sharply reduce the consumption of paper and facilitate a corresponding reduction in the size of analysts' files.

Another system just coming into use which will be widely available for broad application in the future is a text searching machine. This system stores information in such a way that it is retrievable by key phrases punched on a console on an analyst's desk. It can provide the sentence in which the key phrase, or proper name, appears, and can provide sentences both immediately preceding and succeeding. This context enables the analyst to decide whether he needs to see the full report or can reject it. This system has the greatest utility for handling information which is easily codified, such as tabulated election results or lists of targets covered by photographic reconnaissance. Because material of this kind tends to have a high proportion of dross to metal and also comes in prodigious batches, this system will go a long way toward freeing the analyst for more useful work.

These are two examples of the adaptation of electronic machines to analytic intelligence work. Their number could be added to now and certainly will be multiplied in the future. It is fair to say that automatic data processing, appropriately designed for the specific tasks and specialized materials of intelligence work, can be a widespread reality in the next five years.

Other innovations in intelligence support are most likely to come in new formats and new conceptual approaches. Aside from those employing electronics, however, it is difficult to predict their exact shape. There has always been a steady series of adjustments and accommodations by intelligence to the expressed desires of the policy readers. The morning current intelligence report for President Kennedy moved through a steady progression from a simple listing of new reports to a highly literate account of the developments interspersed with analytic judgments, all changes being made in response to direct suggestion by the President. Similarly, the daily report was made a late afternoon publication for President Johnson who liked his ready at the end of the day. Again, the daily summary was returned to a morning timing for President Nixon, and a sharp line was drawn between fact and judgment in response to his request.

National estimates have recently undergone redesign in response to criticism by high level readers. There has been a move away from the broad consensus approach and treatment which was developed to meet the needs of the National Security Council under President Eisenhower. In its place has developed a national intelligence estimate more directed toward the delineations of issues and options, a change largely responsive to current modes and procedures introduced by Secretary of State Kissinger to the National Security Council.

As suggested above, the outlook is for a continuing series of such changes, made in response to the changing shape and texture of problems policy confronts. What will be required to ensure that intelligence provides optimum support for policy in the future is the sustaining of a dialogue which will permit precise tailoring of intelligence to needs. Both parties need to take an aggressive posture in this respect. The experience of the past, which has sound application for the future, is that policy people are often unaware that intelligence has something highly pertinent to say about their current concerns, while intelligence is unwittingly pursuing strands and facets of lesser value. There is a remedy for this. It consists of regular, frequent, and frank discussion between intelligence and policy people about present and emergent policy problems and the available or obtainable information which can be brought to bear on those problems.

NOTES AND REFERENCES

1. Secrecy and Executive privilege are addressed in Chapter 10.

2. Other recommendations for reform and redirection of the intelligence community are found in the reports of the following: the Commission on the Organization of the Government for the Conduct of Foreign Policy (Murphy Commission), authorized by Law 92-352 on July 13, 1972 ([90]); the Commission on CIA Activities Within the United States (Rockefeller Commission), created by President Gerald R. Ford on January 4, 1975 ([124]); and the House Select Committee on Intelligence (Pike Committee), established by House Resolution 591 on July 17, 1975 ([85]). Only part of the Pike reports has been released. Some was reprinted in *The Village Voice* ([175] and [176]).

3. The 1947 National Security Act is reprinted in the Appendix and its legislative history appears in [104], p. 62. The Congressional Research Service of the Library of Congress has compiled a listing of all legislation introduced from 1947 to 1972 pertaining to the intelligence community for use by members and staff in the Congress ([100]).

4. For further information on the purposes and operations of the NSC, refer to the statements of Henry Kissinger, then assistant to the president for National Security Affairs ([32], pp. 1–3); extracts from President Richard M. Nixon's February 18, 1970 report to Congress on U.S. foreign policy for the 1970s ([7], pp. 11–14); and the testimony of former NSC Staff Secretary William Watts ([84B], pp. 813–819).

5. On June 5, 1970, President Richard M. Nixon established the Ad Hoc Intergency Committee on Intelligence, chaired by FBI Director J. Edgar Hoover and composed of members representing the CIA, DIA, NSA, FBI, and the White House (represented by attorney and aide Tom Charles Huston, though not officially a committee member). The committee's special report, commonly known as the Huston Plan, is a significant document in the history of the intelligence community. It was an unprecedented, coordinated, illegal attempt to use the weapons of the U.S. espionage community against American citizens. It was authored in the White House, endorsed by the heads of the intelligence community, and approved by the president. This plan is reprinted in Chapter 12.

6. Additional insights into the functions of the director of Central Intelligence are provided by the testimony of former directors ([25]). See John McCone, p. 187; Richard Helms, p. 221; and William Colby, p. 236. George Bush, DCI during the final year of the Ford administration, discusses his conception of the job in [8], pp. 15 ff.

7. President Gerald R. Ford's message on Executive Order 11905 is reprinted in the Appendix.

8. The subject of congressional oversight is addressed in Chapter 10.

9. Chapter 5, devoted exclusively to the CIA, provides details on the operations of that agency.

10. Operation CHAOS was established in August 1967 and terminated in March 1974. Its purpose was to determine if American political dissidents were receiving foreign support. This and other domestic activities of the CIA are dealt with in more detail in Chapter 12; for additional information on Operation CHAOS itself, note also Chapter 5 and [25]; [45C], pp. 688–721; and [124], pp. 130–150.

11. The withdrawal of FBI liaison from the CIA is further discussed in [17], p. 35.

12. A variety of viewpoints on counterintelligence and overall operations are provided in the testimony of attorney and former secretary of defense, Clark Clifford; president of the Association of Retired Intelligence Officers, David Phillips; writer and former NSC staff member, Morton Halperin; and attorney and former DOD and State Department official, Cyrus Vance. Other viewpoints are found in [44G].

13. Covert action is addressed in Chapter 11.

14. For dissenting views on covert action by members of the Church Committee, see [45A].

15. The involvement of private institutions and private citizens in intelligence activities is taken up in Chapter 12.

16. A "cover" is the use of a false identity to hide an intelligence agent's activities. It may involve a change of name and/or physical identity, but it is more commonly associated with the use of a diplomatic or consular title to hide the identity of a CIA official. This subject is further discussed in Chapter 11.

17. Unpublished internal memoranda from CIA directors James Schlesinger and William Colby on the subject of the responsibility of CIA employees to report misdeeds are available, by request, from the CIA itself on payment of the FOIA copying charge.

18. Further details on Defense and NSA intelligence activities are found in Chapter 7.

19. The Bureau of Intelligence and Research (INR), a division of the Department of State, is reviewed in Chapter 9.

20. An accounting of the Department of State's objectives in the oversight of U.S. government activities abroad is found in Secretary of State William Rogers' 1969 message to officers and employees ([13], pp. 658–661).

21. Efforts to ensure ambassadorial command of CIA field activities are reflected in President John F. Kennedy's letter to American ambassadors in 1961 (reprinted in [44G], p. 137) and reiterated by President Richard M. Nixon in 1969 ([13], pp. 89–96). Further efforts are recounted by Ambassador to Iran and former DCI, Richard Helms, before the Senate Fulbright Committee on Foreign Relations ([18], p. 4).

22. A section on the budget of the foreign intelligence community follows in Chapter 4.

23. Additional oversight recommendations of the Church Committee appear in Chapter 12 in the sections dealing with domestic activities of U.S. foreign intelligence agencies.

Chapter 4

Intelligence Costs and Budget Processes

CHAIRMAN PIKE'S OPENING REMARKS ([84A], pp. 1–2)

Chapter 4 begins with Chairman Otis Pike's opening remarks at the first hearing of the House Select Committee on Intelligence on July 31, 1975. Only enough of that day's hearings is reprinted to demonstrate mounting frustrations as congressional investigators addressed government witnesses unwilling to provide facts and figures on intelligence expenditures.

The constitutional basis for concealing budgetary information from the public and Congress, an important issue raised by Chairman Pike, is discussed in this chapter under The Disclosure of Budget Information on the Intelligence Community. It is pursued further in the reprinted testimony of retired Senate parliamentarian Floyd Riddick, a protegé of Senator Mike Mansfield, well versed in the intricacies of both the appropriations process and the foreign policy establishment.

Mechanics of the budgetary process are revealed in this chapter through an examination of the Office of Management and Budget's role in the formulation of intelligence budget requests, but little substantive material on "how much for what" is provided. A recurring theme throughout the congressional investigations was the allocation of intelligence resources, an issue discussed in the final sections of this chapter under Issues on Intelligence Resource Management and Allocating Intelligence Resources. Additional resource allocation data can be found in the Murphy Commission report ([90], pp. 97–105) and the Church Committee recommendations ([45A], pp. 423–474), portions of which are reprinted in Chapter 3. An insight into CIA budgetary and resource targeting operations is found in DCI William Colby's testimony before the House Appropriations Committee on February 20, 1975 ([46], pp. 127–188). Finally, further budget information on individual intelligence agencies is included in Part II of this volume.

When making appropriations' requests of the Congress, intelligence community officials generally obtain an executive (closed) session for any detailed discussion of programs or operations. Classified transcripts of those sessions are made available on a limited basis to members of Congress (refer to [60] for a review of rules and practices). Since there is no automatic declassification system for congressional documents, it is unclear when they will become available. (The National Archives maintains an ongoing declassification program for Executive branch documents; see reprinted Executive Order 11652 on declassification procedures [117].) When open committee testimony covers a combination of declassified and classified information, it is usually printed with bracketed blanks, indicating selective deletions. Defense weapons figures and cryptological data, for example, are routinely deleted from printed transcripts of committee hearings.

It should be noted that reliable cost and budget information on the intelligence community cannot be found in public documents. Even congressional investigators are sometimes forced to rely more upon nongovernment sources than on official government statements. In terms of specific amounts spent by the individual intelligence agencies, the best unclassified source continues to be *The CIA and the Cult of Intelligence* ([158], p. 95). Researchers with sustained

155

interest in the subject of financing intelligence are well advised to follow congressional oversight hearings and privately published sources, since pressure is mounting for increased public disclosure and accountability.

The committee met, pursuant to notice, at 10 a.m., in room 2118, Rayburn House Office Building, the Honorable Otis G. Pike [chairman], presiding.

Present: Representatives Pike, Giaimo, Stanton, Dellums, Murphy, Aspin, Milford, Hayes, Lehman, McClory, Treen, Johnson, and Kasten.

Also present: A. Searle Field, staff director; Aaron B. Donner, general counsel; John L. Boos, counsel; James B. F. Oliphant, counsel; Richard S. Vermeire, counsel; Jeffrey R. Whieldon, counsel; Roger Carroll, investigator; Charles Mattox, investigator; and Jacqueline Hess, investigator.

Chairman PIKE. The committee will come to order.

After some slight delay the House Select Committee on Intelligence today opens its hearings.

Our instructions from the House of Representatives are broad and they are clear. We are to investigate the intelligence gathering activities of the U.S. Government. We are to complete our investigation by January 31 and by that date report to the House our conclusions and recommendations.

It is a huge order and the only way we can get there is by starting. We start by looking at the cost. It is not easy. The Constitution of the United States, article I, section 9, says, "No money shall be drawn from the Treasury but in consequence of appropriations made by law and a regular statement and account of the receipts and expenditures of all public money shall be published from time to time."

It does not say "some public money." It says "all public money." It would seem to me that a reasonable place to look for such a statement and account of the receipts and expenditures of the intelligence-gathering communities would be the four books provided to Congress and the American people entitled "The Budget of the United States Government." Here are the books.

I have looked hard, but the results are spotty. We have, according to the budget, an FBI, but I can find no CIA, no NSA, no DIA. There is a line item on page 73 of this book under the Department of Defense for $7.3 billion for intelligence and communications. But I don't know what that means.

I get the uneasy feeling I am not supposed to know what it means. We shall find out.

As we learn what the costs are, we will look at the benefits achieved as well as the risks created by gaining this intelligence.

What benefits have we the right to expect? Abroad we should have a good idea of what other nations, especially large nations, are doing in weapons research and development. We should be aware of the political and economic climate throughout the nations of the world.

At home we should be able to learn how organized crime is operating, who is getting rich on drugs and how we can combat them. The risks are equally of concern.

No intelligence gathered by the *Pueblo* was worth the loss of the *Pueblo* and the capture of her crew. The risks involved in a collision between an American intelligence gathering submarine and a Russian submarine are incalculable. At home, while we wish to know all about how organized crime operates, we do not want the risks of having our phones tapped, our homes burglarized, or our persons made insecure.

We must draw reasonable lines between security and freedom, between "need to know" and "right to know." When any investigation begins we do not know where it will take us.

While the budget seemed a reasonable place to start, we will pursue our investigation where it seems most useful to go.

We will try to travel a difficult road bounded by indifference on the right hand and paranoia on the left.

We will try not to travel well-traveled paths and we will pursue facts rather than headlines.

We are dealing with issues fundamental to all Americans and to America. We are dealing with national security and national honor. We are dealing with individual security and with personal freedom.

Let us never forget that this investigation and the debate which preceded it could not have taken place in most nations on this globe so we should undertake it in pride and not embarrassment. Hopefully, we will so conduct ourselves that we may be a credit to the image of America as a nation among the nations of the world, that the way American Government operates and the way American citizens live will, when we are finished, be envied by those who do not and cannot share them.

Mr. McClory.

Mr. McCLORY. Thank you, Mr. Chairman.

I want to commend you, Mr. Chairman, on your statement and also on your initiative in getting the proceedings of our Select Committee on Intelligence moving. I am confident that you are going to have good support from this side of the committee and I am in full support of the approach which you are recommending insofar as our hearings are concerned.

I am convinced myself that this Nation needs a strong intelligence community and that we want to do everything we can as Members of the Congress and as members of this committee to help assure that we get the best quality, the best coordination, the most efficiency, and the most for our money insofar as the various intelligence activities are concerned.

Insofar as this committee is concerned, I am hopeful that we can operate in a bipartisan and objective way.

DISCLOSURE OF BUDGET INFORMATION ON THE INTELLIGENCE COMMUNITY ([84A], pp. 85–86)

The Pike Committee's Frustrations

An impasse quickly developed on budget disclosure in the congressional hearings on the intelligence community, and this is reflected in the exchange between James Lynn, director of OMB, and Chairman Otis Pike. Reprinted excerpts of Church Committee findings on budget matters follow the exchange.

Chairman PIKE. Mr. Lynn, the other day, in the absence of the President, it was up to you to castigate the Congress when they overrode a veto pertaining to some legislation and you said this: "Today's override of the President's veto of S. 66 indicates that Congress is not yet willing to share the President's resolve to make the hard choices necessary to reform Federal programs and get us back to fiscal responsibility."

Well, that is a good speech.

When Congress wants to choose between national priorities and the amount of money which is spent in area Y is concealed from 90 percent of the Members of Congress, how does Congress make the choice?

Mr. LYNN. We don't conceal anything from the Congress, Mr. Chairman.

Chairman PIKE. Oh; come on.

Mr. LYNN. No; we don't. The Congress has put together its own procedures for review of appropriations in this regard.

Chairman PIKE. Do you prepare the budget of the United States?

Mr. LYNN. Does OMB prepare it for the President?

Chairman PIKE. Yes.

Mr. LYNN. Yes.

Chairman PIKE. You prepare the budget. Does the budget admit that we have a CIA? Is it in the budget?

Mr. LYNN. In the budget presentation?

Chairman PIKE. Is it in the budget?

Mr. LYNN. No. We certainly admit it is in there somewhere.

Chairman PIKE. That's real fine.

Can Members of Congress find the NSA in the document you prepared?

N2

Mr. LYNN. No; it isn't, sir, because 50 U.S.C.——

Chairman PIKE. You don't need to cite the statute to me.

Mr. LYNN. It is not to be put in the budget of the United States.

Chairman PIKE. I say to you Congress is not aware and not being aware they can't make the choice.

Mr. LYNN. What I disagreed with was your word "conceal."

We are not concealing anything. This is in conformance with the law.

Chairman PIKE. When you can't find it in the budget, but you tell us it is there, I submit that it is legitimate to characterize that as being concealed.

Mr. LYNN. Then it is concealed by a statute.

Chairman PIKE. All right.

Mr. LYNN. Not by us.

Chairman PIKE. But it is concealed.

The Church Committee's Report on the Budgetary Process for Intelligence Community Agencies and Its Consequences ([45A], pp. 367–384)

At the present time the aggregate amount spent for the intelligence activities of the United States Government is classified. The individual budgets for the Central Intelligence Agency, the National Security Agency, and certain other units within the Department of Defense which gather national intelligence are likewise classified.

The budgets for these agencies—which spend billions of dollars annually—are kept not only from the American people but also from most Members of Congress. This secrecy prevents the public and most Members of Congress from knowing how much is spent on national

N3

intelligence and from determining whether that amount is consistent with other national needs and priorities. It prevents the public and most Members of Congress from knowing how much is spent by each of the national intelligence agencies and from determining whether that allocation among agencies is appropriate. Because funds for these agencies are concealed in the budgets of other agencies, the public and most Members of Congress cannot be certain that funds in the open appropriations are used for the purposes for which they were appropriated. No item in the overall federal budget is above suspicion as a hiding place for intelligence agency funds.[1] Finally, and most seriously, the present system of secrecy is inconsistent with the constitutional provision which states:

> No Money shall be drawn from the Treasury but in Consequence of Appropriations made by Law; and a regular Statement and Account of the Receipts and Expenditures of all public Money shall be published from time to time.[2]

At present, the Director of Central Intelligence submits to the President recommendations for a consolidated national intelligence program budget. The consolidated national intelligence budget, as well as the budget requests from the various agencies within the intelligence community, are reviewed by the Office of Management and Budget (OMB) in the "same detail that [OMB] reviews the budget requests of any other executive branch agency."[3] As former OMB Director Roy Ash described it:

> The specific amounts of the CIA's approved appropriations request and the identification of the appropriation estimates in the President's annual Budget, within which these amounts are included, are formally provided by the Director of OMB to the chairmen of the Senate and House Appropriations Committees.[4]

In the past, special subcommittees of the House and Senate Appropriations Committees have considered the CIA budget in closed

---

[1] During the recent debate in the House of Representatives on the publication of the CIA's budget Congressman Koch described an encounter with DCI Helms, in which Congressman Koch asked about the size of the CIA budget and the number of CIA employees, questions that DCI Helms told Congressman Koch "we don't answer." As Congressman Koch described it, he then asked Mr. Helms "Are you telling me that I, a Member of Congress, do not have the right to know what the budget is, so that when I vote, I do not know what I am voting on?" DCI Helms said, "Yes . . . The item is placed in some other larger item, and you do not know." Congressman Koch then asked, "Do you mean that it might be included under Social Security?", to which DCI Helms replied, "We have not used that one yet, but that is not a bad idea." Cong. Rec. H9359, daily ed., 10/1/75, remarks of Rep. Koch.)

[2] U.S. Const., Art. I, Sec. 9, Cl. 7. For a fuller discussion of the constitutional and policy issues involved, see "The CIA's Secret Funding and the Constitution," 84 *Yale Law Journal* 608 (1975), "Fiscal Oversight of the Central Intelligence Agency: Can Accountability and Confidentiality Coexist?" 7 *New York University Journal of International Law and Politics* 493 (1974), and "Cloak and Ledger: Is CIA Funding Constitutional?" 2 *Hastings Constitutional Law Quarterly* 717 (1975).

[3] Letter from Roy Ash to Senator Proxmire, 4/29/74, quoted in Cong. Rec. S9604, daily ed., 6/4/74, remarks of Sen. Proxmire. It might be argued that the intelligence budgets should be reviewed in even greater detail by OMB as neither the Congress as a whole nor the public can presently participate in the process of reviewing and debating the budget requests in this area.

[4] Ash letter, 4/29/74.

session; the chairman of the House Appropriations Committee noted that his subcommittee "tried and tried and tried to hold the secrecy of these matters as closely as we could." [5]

These practices have been changing. The entire House Defense Appropriation Subcommittee now scrutinizes the CIA budget. In September of 1975 the Chairman of the House Appropriations Committee invited all the Members of the House of Representatives to review the executive session hearings of the Defense Appropriations Subcommittee on the CIA's budget, although Members had to agree not to remove any documents from the room, not to take notes, and not to reveal the classified information to "unauthorized persons." While the Chairman invited this review by the Members, the full House Appropriations Committee voted not to receive figures on the CIA's budget from the Defense Appropriations Subcommittee.

N4

Neither the Senate Appropriations Committee as a whole nor the Senate as a whole is informed, even in secret session, of the budget figures for the CIA, NSA or certain other intelligence units.

Once the subcommittees of the Appropriations Committee, agree upon the level of funding for the intelligence agencies, these funds are concealed in appropriation requests for other agencies on which the full Appropriations Committees and Senate and House of Representatives vote.

After congressional approval of these appropriations, the chairmen of the Senate and House Appropriations Committees notify the Office of Management and Budget of the size and true location of intelligence agency funds. Funds for the CIA are then transferred to the CIA from these appropriations.[6] Former OMB Director Ash noted:

> The transfer of funds to CIA . . . is accomplished by the issuance of Treasury documents routinely used for the transfer of funds from one government agency to another. The amount and timing of these transfers, . . . are approved by OMB.[7]

This whole process treats the CIA and other intelligence agencies in a manner radically different from other highly sensitive agencies of the United States Government, such as the Atomic Energy Commission and the Department of Defense. While intelligence agency budgets may require somewhat different handling, it is important that any special approach reflect real needs justifying departure from the careful processes which Congress has developed over the years for maintaining its power over the purse.

The Constitutional Requirement

The present budgetary process apparently violates Article 1, Section 9, Clause 7 of the Constitution, which reads:

[5] Cong. Rec. H9363, daily ed., 10/1/75, remarks of Rep. Mahon. Until 1974, even the names of members of these special subcommittees were withheld from the public.

[6] This is done pursuant to 50 U.S.C. 403f which authorizes the CIA to transfer to and receive from other government agencies funds as approved by the OMB.

[7] Ash letter, 4/29/74. Under established procedures, funds approved by OMB for transfer to the CIA are limited to the amounts which the chairmen of the Senate and House Appropriations Committees specified to OMB.

> No Money shall be drawn from the Treasury, but in Conse-
> quence of Appropriations, made by Law; and a regular State-
> ment and Account of the Receipts and Expenditures of all
> public Money shall be published from time to time.

This constitutional provision was intended to insure that Congress
would control the governmental purse and that the public would be
N5   informed of how Congress and the Executive spend public funds.[8]

In keeping with this constitutional mandate, Congress enacted 31
U.S.C. 66b(a), which provides that:

> the Secretary of the Treasury shall prepare such reports for
> the information of the President, the Congress, and the pub-
> lic, as will present the results of the financial operations of
> the Government.

Fulfilling its charge, the Treasury Department publishes a *Combined
Statement of Receipts, Expenditures, and Balances of the United
States Government*, which

> is recognized as the official publication of the details of re-
> ceipt and outlay data with which all other reports containing
> similar data must be in agreement. In addition to serving the
> needs of Congress, [*the report is used by*] *the general public
> in its continuing review of the operations of Government.*
> [Emphasis added.] [9]

The *Combined Statement*, however, contains no entry for the Cen-
tral Intelligence Agency, the National Security Agency or certain
other intelligence units within the Department of Defense. While the
figure for total funds received and expended by the United States
Government is accurate, some funds listed as expended by particular
agencies are, in fact, merely transferred from them to the Central
Intelligence Agency.

William Colby, former Director of the CIA, has argued that the
present practice is constitutional, maintaining that the Constitution
permits concealment of funds for agencies such as the CIA. Not only
does this position ignore the plain text of the Clause, but it is not sup-
ported by the debates, either at the Constitutional Convention or in the
ratifying conventions in the various States.

---

[8] See D. Robertson, *Debates and Other Proceedings of the Convention of Vir-
ginia, 1788* (Richmond, 1805), p. 326. The Chancellor of New York asked if
the public were more anxious about any thing under heaven than the expenditure
of their money?" 2 J. Elliot, *Debates in the Several States' Conventions on the
Adoption of the Federal Constitution*, (Philadelphia:'J. B. Lippencott, 1836),
p. 347.

The clause was implemented during the first Congress. The act creating the
Treasury Department required the Treasurer to annually present each House
of Congress with "fair and accurate copies of all accounts" and a "true and
perfect account of the state of the Treasury." Act of Sept. 2, 1789, Chapter 12,
Section I, I Statute 65.

This Act was replaced by 31 U.S.C. 1029, which provides, "It shall be the
duty of the Secretary of the Treasury annually to lay before Congress . . . an
accurate, combined statement of the receipts and expenditures during the last
preceding fiscal year of all public monies." The receipts, wherever practicable,
were to be divided by ports, districts, and states, and the expenditures by each
separate head of appropriation.

[9] U.S. Dep't of Treasury, Combined Statement of Receipts, Expenditures and
Balance of the United States Government (1973), p. 1.

Mr. Colby's argument relies chiefly on the fact that when the State ment and Account Clause was introduced it provided for annual publication of the account, but it was subsequently amended to allow congressional discretion over timing.[10]

The amendment was intended, however, not to permit concealment of expenditures from the full Congress and the American people, but rather to insure that the information would be made available in a fashion permitting its thorough comprehension.[11] Neither proponents nor opponents of the amendment argued against the assertion that the people had a "right to know" how their funds were being spent.[12]

It should also be noted that the proponents of congressional discretion did not argue that secrecy was needed. Rather they contended that leaving the interval of publication to be fixed by Congress would result in fuller disclosure, since no agency would be forced to publish an incomplete report to meet an inflexible and unrealistic deadline.[13] A fixed schedule would result in statements that would be "incomplete"[14] or "too general to be satisfactory."[15] The proponents of the amendment ridiculed the possibility that granting Congress discretion would mean that information would be concealed forever; Congress would publish the reports at regular, frequent intervals.[16]

It has been implied that the constitutional requirement has been met, at least in the House of Representatives, in that all Members can examine the Defense Appropriations Subcommittee's executive session hearings on the CIA budget.[17] As one Member of the House noted:

> Secrecy in Government is distasteful to a free society, but preservation of our free society demands that we maintain a prudent cloak over vital intelligence operations, so long as the Representatives of the people have the right to examine what is covered—as they do in this situation.[18]

---

[10] William E. Colby testimony, House Select Committee on Intelligence Hearings, 8/4/75, p. 120. Mr. Colby argued as follows:

"The so-called 'Statement and Account' clause . . . was not part of the initial draft [of the Constitution]. The language first suggested by George Mason would have required an annual account of public expenditures. James Madison, however, argued for making a change to require reporting 'from time to time,' Madison explained that the intent of his amendment was to 'leave enough to the discretion of the Legislature.' Patrick Henry opposed the Madison language because it made concealment possible. But when the debate was over, it was the Madison view that prevailed."

Mr. Colby also argued that the provision allowing Congress to keep their proceedings secret demonstrated the intent of the Framers to provide for concealment. That provision, unlike the Statement and Account Clause explicitly provides for secrecy; moreover, the Statement and Account Clause guarantees an accounting for *all* public money. For a fuller treatment of this argument, see "The CIA's Secret Funding and the Constitution," *Yale L.J.* 608 (1975).

It could be argued that the constitutional requirement is not violated as the Combined Statement provides an accurate total for receipts and expenditures. Under this theory all government funds could be appropriated to one government agency and secretly transferred to the other agencies. As long as the total appropriated and expended were published, the constitutional requirement would be fulfilled.

[11] 2 M. Farrand, *Records of the Federal Convention of 1787* New Haven: Yale University Press, 1966), pp. 618–19.

[12] D. Robertson, p. 326. See generally 3 M. Farrand, pp. 149–150.

[13] 2 M. Farrand, pp. 618–619.

[14] *Ibid.*, p. 618.

[15] *Ibid.*

[16] See D. Robertson, p. 326.

[17] As was noted above . . . . . . this is not the case in the Senate.

[18] Cong. Rec., H9360, daily ed., 10/1/75, remarks of Rep. Robinson.

Knowledge on the part of *all* of Congress, would satisfy part of the constitutional requirement. As Justice Story noted, one of the purposes of the constitutional requirements is:

> to secure regularity, punctuality and fidelity in the disbursements of the public money . . . it is highly proper, that Congress should possess the power to decide how and when any money should be applied for these purposes. If it were otherwise, the executive would possess an unbounded power over the public purse of the nation. . . . The power to control and direct the appropriations constitutes a most useful and salutary check upon profusion and extravagance, as well as upon corrupt influence and public speculation. . . . It is wise to interpose in a republic, every restraint, by which the public treasure, the common fund of all, should be applied with unshrinking honesty to such objects as legitimately belong to the common defense and the general welfare.[19]

But even if all of Congress had the information now held by the subcommittees of the Appropriations Committees, the Constitution would still be violated. The Constitution requires that the *public* know how its funds are being spent. The Constitution requires that the statement and account be made public "from time to time." [20] This requirement was imposed to make congressional responsibility "more perfect" [21] by allowing the people to check Congress and the executive through the publication of information on what "money is expended, for what purposes, and by what authority." [22] As Chancellor Livingston pointed out:

> You will give up to your state legislature everything dear and valuable; but you will give no power to Congress, because it may be abused; you will give them no revenue, because the public treasures may be squandered. But do you not see here a capital check? Congress are to publish, from time to time, an account of their receipts and expenditures. These may be compared together; and if the former, year after year, exceed the latter, the corruption will be detected, and the people may use the constitutional mode of redress. [23]

The debates and later commentary indicate that the constitutional requirement was designed to allow citizens to chart the course of policy through an examination of governmental expenditures—to determine, for example, whether too much money is spent on defense and too little on education, or whether funds spent on bombers should be allocated to submarines. Publication of this information would also enable the people, with Congress, to determine whether expenditures by the executive conform to the intent of the appropriation. Publication of appropriations and expenditures would also provide an opportunity for the

---

[19] 2 J. Story, *Commentaries on the Constitution of the United States*, Sec. 1348, pp. 222–223 (5th ed., 1891).
[20] Article I, Section 9, Clause 7 provides for publication in contrast to Article 2, Section 3, which provides that the President "shall from time to time give to the Congress Information on the State of the Union."
[21] 2 J. Story, Sec. 1348, pp. 222–223.
[22] *Ibid.*
[23] 2 J. Elliot, p. 345.

people to ascertain if both appropriations and expenditures were for constitutional purposes.[24]

It is, however, unclear how much information on appropriations and expenditures is required by the Constitution to be published. No one at the Constitutional Convention disagreed with the assertion that it would be impossible to account for "every minute shilling." Even in the present disclosures of appropriations and expenditures of nonsensitive governmental agencies, there is a limit to the amount of detail which can be published.[25]

The Supreme Court in *United States* v. *Robel*,[25a] suggested a standard which might be used to fix the constitutional requirement particularly when claims that publication of the budget would damage national security are raised against the Government's duty to its citizens to publish from time to time a regular statement and account of receipts and expenditures of all public money. The Court held that "when legitimate concerns are expressed in a statute which imposes a substantial burden on First Amendment activities, Congress must achieve its goal by means which have the least drastic impact on the continued vitality of First Amendment freedoms." [26]

Under this test the constitutionality of a level of disclosure of information on expenditures depends on whether there is another system of greater disclosure which, without endangering national security, would have a "less drastic" impact on the public's right to know how its funds are being spent. It is clear, however, that the present secrecy surrounding the appropriations and expenditures for intelligence—particularly the inflation of unspecified appropriations in which funds for intelligence are concealed—vitiates the constitutional guarantee.[27] Under the present system neither the public nor the Congress as a whole knows how much is being spent on national intelligence or by each intelligence agency. In addition, both Congress as a whole and the public are "deceived", as one Senator put it,[28] about the "true" size of other agency budgets. As certain unspecified general appropriations contain funds which are secretly transferred to the CIA, it is impossible for most Members of Congress or the public to know the exact amount of money which actually is destined for

---

[24] Rs David Ramsey, one of the early commentators on the Constitution wrote

If Congress applied any funds for purposes other than those set forth in the Constitution, they would have exceeded their powers. The Clause provides information so that "[t]he people of the United States who pay, are to be judges how far their money is properly applied."

"An address to the Freemen of South Carolina on the subject of the Federal Constitution," in Pamphlets on the Constitution of the United States, p. 374 (P. Ford, ed., 1888). See also *Flast* v. *Cohen*, 392 U.S. 83 (1968).

[25] Of course, a good deal more information, although not published, is available under the Freedom of Information Act.

[25a] 389 U.S. 258 (1967).

[26] 389 U.S. 258, 268. While the public's right to information on governmental expenditures has not been accorded the "preeminent" status of the First Amendment, the test is an appropriate place to begin an analysis.

[27] As Justice Black wrote, "The guarding of military and diplomatic secrets at the expense of informed representative government provides no real security for our republic." *New York Times Co.* v. *United States*, 403 U.S. 713 at 719 (1971). In the same case, Justice Stewart wrote, "In the absence of the governmental checks and balances present in other areas of our national life, the only effective restraint upon executive policy and power in the area of national defense and international affairs may be in an enlightened citizenry." *Id.* at 728. Justice Stewart's remarks apply equally well to the exercises of power by the Congress.

[28] Cong. Rec. S9602, daily ed., 6/4/74, remarks of Sen. Proxmire.

any government agency.[29] Congress is thus unable to set priorities through the allocation of funds,[30] or to determine if expenditures by the executive conform to congressional intent and are being spent wisely and well. Members of the public cannot determine with any confidence whether they agree with Congress' allocation of resources and cannot monitor expenditures by the executive branch.

Alternatives to Concealing Intelligence Budgets from Congress and the Public

Within certain limits, Congress has the power to determine how information about the receipts and expenditures of public moneys is made available to the public.[31]

Congress could choose to publish CIA or NSA budgets and expenditures, for example, in detail equal to those of nonsensitive agencies. This approach, however, might threaten the security of intelligence operations or agents. Congress has available another model for budget disclosure to protect the security of certain activities.

Since 1793, certain agencies, such as the AEC, the FBI, and the Department of State have been appropriated funds specifically for "confidential purposes," which for security reasons, are exempt from normal accounting procedures.[32] In each instance, however, Congress appropriates funds to the agency directly and publicly specifies the small percentage of the appropriation which is for "confidential purposes" and thus exempt from normal accounting procedures. Drawing on this practice, Congress obviously could publish detailed budgets for the intelligence agencies while providing a lump sum to each for "confidential purposes."

Congress could also devise other models. Congress could publish only the total appropriated to each intelligence agency.[33] As the Spe-

---

[29] Cong. Rec., H9361, daily ed., 10/1/75, remarks of Rep. Evans. As Congressman Evans recently noted, the secrecy surrounding these funds for the intelligence community is infectious: "When we are tucking it away in another pocket in the budget, we are also making a secret of something else that should not be a secret."

[30] See e.g., Cong. Rec., H9372, daily ed., 10/1/75, remarks of Rep. Leggett. Congressman Leggett noted, "How can we 'oversee' in any fashion if we have no knowledge of the Agency's command on our resources? How can we set budgetary priorities in a meaningful fashion, if we have no basis for comparing intelligence with unemployment, health, or other competing program areas?"

[31] Cincinnati Soap Co. v. United States, 301 U.S. 308 (1936). In fixing the level of detail revealed, however, a congressional decision cannot override a constitutional requirement such as that of Article 1, Section 9, Clause 7, particularly as one purpose of that requirement was to serve as a check on Congress.

[32] The first such statute authorized special procedures for sums relating to foreign "intercourse or treaty." By the Act of February 9, 1793, Congress provided: "that in all cases, where any sum or sums of money have issued, or shall hereafter issue, from the treasury, for the purposes of intercourse or treaty, the President shall be, and he hereby is authorized to cause the same to be duly settled annually with the accounting officers of the Treasury in the manner following, that is to say; by causing the same to be accounted for, specifically in all instances wherein the expenditures thereof may, in his judgment be made public; and by making a certificate or certificates, or causing the Secretary of State to make a certificate or certificates of the amount of such expenditures as he may think it advisable not to specify; and every such certificate shall be deemed a sufficient voucher for the sum or sums therein expressed to have been expended." [Act of Feb. 9, 1793, ch. 4, sec. 2, 1 Stat. 300, codified as 31 U.S.C. 107 (1970).]

[33] When the AEC was first established only a one line entry in the weapons account was included in the 1947 budget, p. 382.

cial Senate Committee To Study Questions Related to Secret and Confidential Documents [34] suggested in 1973, the publication

> of such funds should provide members with the minimal information they should have about our intelligence operations. Such information would also end the practice of inflating certain budget figures for use to hide intelligence costs and would insure that all Members would know the true cost of each budget item they must vote upon.

The Special Committee recommended that the Appropriations Committee itemize the Defense Department appropriations bill in order that the "total sums proposed to be appropriated for intelligence activities by each of the following agencies: Central Intelligence Agency, Defense Intelligence Agency, National Security Agency, National Reconnaissance Office, and any separate intelligence units within the Army, Navy, and Air Force" could be revealed. [35]

Finally, the Congress could decide that only the total budget figure for national intelligence be published. This would be the aggregate of funds provided to CIA, NSA, DIA, and the national intelligence components in the Departments of Defense, State, and Treasury. Although there may be problems defining what constitutes "national intelligence," the Director of Central Intelligence already prepares a national intelligence budget. The Director could, with the appropriate congressional committees determine what agencies or departments would be included. [36]

N6

The secrecy presently surrounding intelligence expenditures vitiates the constitutional guarantee. Even publishing one figure—the total appropriations and expenses for national intelligence—would have a salutory effect. It would eliminate the inflation of figures presently in the Budget and in the Combined Statement resulting from the concealment of intelligence agency funds in other agency appropriations and expenditures. Congress would be able to establish its priorities by placing the amount appropriated for national intelligence activities against other claims on the public purse; the public could make its own independent judgment about priorities. [37]

As Senator Proxmire noted, publication of the aggregate budget for national intelligence might also have the effect of deterring potential adversaries by showing that the United States Government continues to spend sizeable amounts on intelligence. [38] As former DCI and Secretary of Defense Schlesinger noted, publication of this figure might also

---

[34] S. Res. 93–466, 93rd Cong., 1st Sess., 10/12/73, p. 16.

[35] The Committee specifically did not request that any line items be revealed, although they did recommend the publication of the total number of personnel employed by each agency.

[36] The Senate Select Committee has proposed an oversight committee which would have jurisdiction over authorization for national intelligence activities of the United States Government, S. 93–2893.

[37] Former Director Colby has argued that publication of the CIA budget would not aid the public in any way. As he put it, "Knowledge of the Agency budget would not enable the public to make a judgment on the appropriateness of the amount without the knowledge of the product and the ways it is obtained." (William Colby testimony, House Select Committee on Intelligence, 8/4/75, p. 123.)

[38] Cong. Rec. S9603, daily ed., 6/4/74, Remarks of Senator Proxmire. However, as Senator Pastore noted, if the public figure declined "then the Russians and

decrease speculation about the budget and focus the debate on intelligence on more significant issues.[39]

Finally, the disclosure of any figures on intelligence expenditures might well increase the effectiveness of oversight of the intelligence agencies by both individual members of Congress and by the appropriately charged congressional committees. Members of the House might be encouraged to inspect executive session hearings on intelligence agency budgets; [40] members of the oversight committees of both houses might be spurred to review the proposed budgets more closely, in anticipation of a possible debate on the figures.[41]

The Effect upon National Security of Varying Levels of Budget Disclosure

Even given the constitutional requirement, any disclosure of budgetary information on agencies in the Intelligence Community has been strongly resisted. In responding to a proposal for the publication of the total sum budgeted for the national intelligence community, Senator Stennis noted that:

> [I]f it becomes law and is carried out, [it] would, as its practical effect, virtually destroy 80 to 90 percent of the effectiveness of much of our most important work in the field of intelligence.[42]

And Congressman Burlison told the House that if an amendment which provided for publication of the total figure budgeted for the CIA were adopted, "i[t] will totally paralyze the intelligence community." [43]

An examination of the effect on national security of publication of *any* data on the intelligence community budgets is difficult, in part because the examination itself must not be allowed to jeopardize the national security. Given the constitutional guarantee, however, the burden of proof must fall on those who would deny this information to

---

the Chinese Communists know that we are doing less, and that might let them become more audacious." *Id.* at S9605.

[39] During testimony before the Senate Select Committee, Mr. Schlesinger was asked whether there was a good reason for actually publishing a budget figure, He replied: "Only in that the public debate at the present time covers so wide a range that if you had an official number, the debate would tend to die down and focus on something more significant than whether we're spending $11 billion on intelligence." (James Schlesinger testimony, 2/2/76, p. 54.)

Mr. Schlesinger was later asked whether he thought there was any chance of convincing the American people or the enemy of the truthfulness of any figure that is published, to which Mr. Schlesinger replied: "I do not believe that you could persuade the Soviets that that is a truthful figure, but I am not sure that that is our objective. Whether or not you could persuade the American public, I think there is a large segment of the American public that would be persuaded. . . ." Schlesinger, 2/2/76, p. 56.)

[40] See e.g., Cong. Rec., H9361, daily ed., 10/1/75, remarks of Rep. Obey.

[41] See e.g., Cong. Rec., S9603, daily ed., 6/4/74, remarks of Sen. Proxmire.

[42] Cong. Rec. S9610–11, daily ed., 6/4/74, remarks of Sen. Stennis.

[43] Cong. Rec. H9366, daily ed., 10/1/75, remarks of Rep. Burlison.

the public. The possible effects on the national security of certain levels of budget disclosure are examined below.[44]

1. The Effect on National Security of Publication of the National Intelligence Community Budget

Many individuals familiar with the intelligence community agree that publication of a gross figure for national intelligence would not, in itself, damage the national security.

During his confirmation hearings as Director of Central Intelligence, James Schlesinger, former Secretary of Defense and past head of the OMB, told Senator Harry F. Byrd, Jr., in regard to the publication of the gross figure for national intelligence: "I think that the security concerns are minimal. The component figures, I would be more concerned about but for the gross national intelligence program figures, I think we could live with that on a security basis, yes." [45]

Former DCI Helms told the Senate Select Committee that because it was so large, publication of a single figure for national intelligence might be "satisfactory." [46]

While it has been suggested that the publication of even a total for the national intelligence budget would aid our enemies, Mr. Schlesinger told the Senate Select Committee that our enemies "already know in the first place and it's broadly published. All that you would have is a confirmed official figure for information. That is more or less in the public domain anyhow without public confirmation, without official confirmation." [48]

---

[44] There are many possible variants of budget disclosure running from the full disclosure policy governing such government agencies as the Department of Agriculture, through the budget disclosure utilized by the FBI and AEC which provides for a specific appropriation of funds for "confidential" purposes which are exempted from normal accounting requirements, to the possible disclosure of an aggregate figure for each national intelligence agency or for national intelligence as a whole. The Committee has not attempted to analyze the constitutional implications and effect on national security of each, but has focused on the disclosure of the global sum for national intelligence and the aggregate budgets of each intelligence agency.

[45] Quoted in Cong. Rec., S9603, daily ed., 6/4/74, remarks of Sen. Proxmire.

[46] Richard Helms testimony, 1/30/76, pp. 36, 37. Because the figure is so large, the introduction of expensive collection systems would not result in a "conspicuous bump" in the budget which would alert hostile powers to new activities by the United States....

John Clarke, a former Comptroller of the CIA and an advisor to DCI Colby, was asked about the effects of publication of the total national intelligence budget and specifically whether publication of the figure would disclose the existence of, or the start of, a high-cost technical collection system. Mr. Clarke responded, "I have not run the studies on this, but I would be very hard pressed to find a case that I could support. The budget figures don't reflect that. They are down. Historically, at least they have been down inside of a larger figure and it doesn't really pop out in a big way. And it can be explained away." (John Clarke testimony, 2/5/76, p. 47.)

[48] Schlesinger, 2/2/76, p. 52. Mr. Schlesinger noted that, as the Intelligence Community has "no constituency," it tends to be "blamed for one thing or another," and "if you had an openly published figure . . . there would be pressure within the Congress at budget mark-up time to take a 15 percent or 20 percent whack at it just for good measure and . . . there is no way of having a public debate about the merits of intelligence." Id. at 51–52. Mr. Schlesinger's argument implies that Congress as a whole should not be given information because it should not be allowed to exercise its control over the purse.

Mr. Schlesinger described for the Select Committee the impact of publishing the total national intelligence budget:

> I am not so concerned about that from the security aspect as some people are. I'm not sure I recommend it, but I'm not so concerned about it from the security aspect.
>
> It could do some good in that there are some inflated notions around about how much the United States Government is actually spending on intelligence, and if you had an official statement, I think that would put the total amount of expenditures in better context for the public.

2. The Effect on National Security of Disclosure of the Total Appropriated to or Expended by Each National Intelligence Agency

Publication of the total of the CIA's budget or of the other agencies' budgets has also been opposed. In a Freedom of Information Act suit, DCI Colby argued against publication of the Agency's budget total, as follows:

> Publication of either the CIA budget or the expenditures made by CIA for any given year would show the amounts planned to be expended or in fact expended for objects of a confidential, extraordinary or emergency nature. This information would be of considerable value to a potentially hostile foreign government. For example, if the total expenditures made by the Agency for any particular year were publicized, these disclosures, when taken with other information publicly available . . . would enable such governments to refine their estimates of the activities of a major component of the United States intelligence community, including specifically the personnel strength, technological capabilities, clandestine operational activities, and the extent of the United States Government intelligence analysis and dissemination machinery. . . . The subsequent publication of similar data for other fiscal years . . . would enable a potentially hostile power to refine its estimates of trends in the United States Government intelligence efforts.

He continued:

> The business of intelligence is to a large extent a painstaking collection of data and the formation of conclusions utilizing a multitude of bits and pieces of information. The revelation of one such piece, which might not appear to be of significance to anyone not familiar with the process of intelligence analysis (and which, therefore, might not arguably be said to be damaging to the national security) would, when combined with other similar data, make available . . . information of great use and which would result in significant damage to the national security of the United States.

He provided the following example of the impact on the nation's security of publication of the CIA's budget:

> If it were learned that CIA expenditures have increased significantly in any one given year, but that there has been

no increase in Agency personnel (apparent from traffic, cars in the parking lots, etc.) it would be possible to make some reasonable estimates and conclusions to the effect that, for example, CIA had developed a costly intelligence collection system which is technological rather than manpower intensive; and that such system is operational. Knowledge readily available at the time about reconnaissance aircraft photography, and other technology, can result in a more accurate analysis about a new collection system which would enable a potentially hostile power to take steps to counter its effectiveness . . . the development of the U–2 aircraft as an effective collection device would not have been possible if the CIA budget had been a matter of public knowledge. Our budget increased significantly during the development phase of that aircraft. That fact, if public, would have attracted attention. . . . If it had been supplemented by knowledge (available perhaps from technical magazines, industry rumor, or advanced espionage techniques) that funds were being committed to a major aircraft manufacturer and to a manufacturer of sophisticated mapping cameras, the correct conclusion would have been simple to draw. The U.S. manufacturers in question . . . would have become high priority intelligence targets. . . . And I'm sure that the Soviets would have taken steps earlier to acquire a capability to destroy very-high-altitude aircraft. They did indeed take these steps, with eventual success, but only sometime after the aircraft began operating over their territory—that is, once they had knowledge of a U.S. intelligence project.[49]

A close examination of Mr. Colby's statement raises a number of questions as to the effect of publication of the CIA's aggregate budget. Although Mr. Colby notes that the CIA's total budget figure would allow governments to "refine their estimates of the activities of a major component of the United States intelligence community," he provides no evidence of *how* the publication of this one figure would increase the other government's knowledge of, for example, the clandestine operational activities of the CIA.[50] There would, of course, be some "refinement" if it were known that the CIA's budget was $X millions rather than $X + 1 millions. Such refinement goes on at all times, but the question is whether such a gain by hostile powers is sufficient to justify overriding the constitutional requirement that the American people be told how their funds are spent. Having an officially acknowledged budget total does not signal to a hostile power manpower levels in the Clandestine Service, let alone the number of deep cover

[49] Defendant's Answers to Plaintiff's Interrogatories, *Halperin* v. *Colby*, Civil Action No. 75–0676, United States District Court for the District of Columbia, pp. 3–5. Other knowledgeable figures have reached different conclusions about the effect of publishing the CIA's budget. For example, Elliot Richardson, presently Secretary of Commerce and formerly Secretary of Defense, has stated that publication of the amount of the CIA's expenditures would not be damaging to the national security.

[50] Mr. Colby's statement ignores the fact that figures for the CIA budget are already widely publicized, although not officially confirmed. In this regard, it is interesting to note that the Central Intelligence Agency withdrew its objection to the far more detailed budget disclosure in *The CIA and the Cult of Intelligence* by Victor Marchetti and John D. Marks.

agents. Having an officially acknowledged aggregate figure does not reveal the cost of a reconnaissance vehicle, let alone its technical capability.

Mr. Colby has maintained that one-time publication of the total amount budgeted for the CIA would set a precedent and that information revealed through successive publication would provide hostile powers with insights into United States intelligence activities.

Of particular importance is Mr. Colby's claim that successive disclosures of the CIA's aggregate budget would eliminate the effectiveness of major technical collection systems like the U-2. A change in the CIA's total budget from one year to the next may be due to a number of factors: inflation, cutbacks in activities, a major reorganization, or long term gains in efficiency, for example. Assuming that an increase in the CIA's budget alerted hostile powers to some change in the Agency's activities, it would not in itself reveal what the new activity was—a new covert action project, more material procurement, or an increase in analytical capability through mechanization. For Mr. Colby's argument to be valid not only must the hostile power be able accurately to determine what the activity is—for instance, a new reconnaissance system—but that power would have to gain, covertly, an enormous amount of tightly guarded information, such as the technological capabilities of the vehicle and the surveillance systems which it contained.[51] It would seem that a hostile power able to gain that information would be able to discover the total of the CIA's budget, a much more widely known figure. The possibility that a hostile power may pierce all the barriers designed to limit dissemination of closely held information cannot be used to justify denying the American people information which the Constitution guarantees them, and which is widely published, and which must be assumed to be within the grasp of hostile powers.

It is far from clear, moreover, that the development and introduction of a major new system will be announced by a change in the Agency's total budget.

The CIA budget may be large enough not to change substantially when a new system comes on line. A preliminary analysis of past CIA budgets has indicated that major new activities have not always resulted in "bumps" and that some "bumps" in the budget still are not generally understood.[52] Because of the importance of expensive technical collection systems, however, the Select Committee believes that the "conspicuous bump" argument deserves fuller study by the future oversight committees,[53] particularly in light of the results of the publication of the aggregate figure for national intelligence recommended by the Committee.

---

[51] Beyond that, a hostile power would also have to have both a capability and an inclination to take those steps necessary to counter the system.

[52] One series of activities which did cause a bump in the CIA's budget was the Agency's activities in Laos, which were clearly known to powers hostile to the U.S. but were kept secret from the American people for many years.

[53] If new systems would be revealed by "bumps" in the CIA's budget a solution other than denying all information on CIA expenditures to the American people might be found. James Schlesinger has suggested that the published figure could be based on actual dollars spent by the CIA rather than on the dollars which could be spent; while obligations may fluctuate dramatically over the years, actual outlays "tend to move smoothly over a period of years." (Schlesinger, 2/2/76, p. 55.)

Finally, the claims about damage to the national security resulting from publication of the aggregate figure for each intelligence agency must be viewed in the light of far more detailed, and continuing, exposure of the budgets of other agencies vital to the national security. Enormous amounts of information have been provided to the public, for instance, about the work of the Department of Defense and the Atomic Energy Commission. Yet disclosure of funds appropriated and expended by these agencies did not and does not reveal vital national secrets. As Senator Symington noted, "There's nothing secret about the . . . cost of a nuclear aircraft carrier or the cost of the C–5A." But "knowledge of the cost does not equal knowledge of how the weapons operate or how they would be utilized." Similarly, knowledge "of the overall cost of intelligence does not in any way entail the release of information about how the various intelligence groups function, or plan to function." [54]

The Argument That Publication of Any Information Will Inevitably Result in Demands for Further Information

Some opponents of budget disclosure, while admitting that publishing aggregate figures for the intelligence community or intelligence agencies will not harm national security, have argued that publication of such figures will inevitably lead to demands for ever more detail. As Director Colby told the House Select Committee on Intelligence:

> Moreover, once the budget total is revealed, the demand for details probably would grow. What does it include? What does it exclude? Why did it go up? Why did it go down? Is it worth it? How does it work?
>
> There would be revelations . . . which would gradually reduce the unknown to a smaller and smaller part of the total, permitting foreign intelligence services to concentrate their efforts in the areas where we would least like to attract their attention.
>
> We—and I specifically mean in this instance both intelligence professionals and Members of Congress—would have an acute problem when the matter of our budget arose in the floor of the House or Senate. Those who knew the facts would have two unpleasant choices—to remain silent in the face of all questions and allegations, however inaccurate, or to attempt to keep the debate on accurate grounds by at least hinting at the full story.
>
> My concern that one revelation will lead to another is based on more than a "feeling." The atomic weapons budget was considered very sensitive, and the Manhattan Project was

---

[54] 117 Cong. Rec., p. S42925, remarks of Sen. Symington. As Congressman Leggett of the House Armed Services Committee noted: "We have a book here, the Committee Report of about 4000 secrets of the Department of Defense in which they talk about the money for the SAM–D but yet do we know how the SAM–D works? The answer is: no.

"We have the details of the money for Thailand, and it is spelled out. But do we know what the money is actually used for? No.

"We can go through the FBI budget. Does that tell us what they are doing? The answer is: no." (Cong. Rec., H9371, daily ed., 10/1/75, remarks of Rep. Leggett.)

concealed completely during World War II. With the establishment of the AEC, however, the decision was made to include in the 1947 budget a one-line item for the weapons account. That limitation was short-lived. By 1974, a 15-page breakout and discussion of the Atomic Weapons Program was being published. Were the intelligence budget to undergo a similar experience, major aspects of our intelligence strategy, capabilities and successes would be revealed.[55]

There are several problems with this argument. While there obviously will be pressure, the problem as Mr. Helms agreed "is not insuperable." [56] For many years Congress has refused to reveal the figures for the national intelligence budget and the aggregate budgets of the intelligence agencies. It seems unlikely that given this past history, Congress will suddenly reverse itself and fail to protect information whose disclosure would harm the national security. Much more likely is that Congress will, as Senator Church proposed, "establish very stringent rules when it came to handling the money figures." [57]

More importantly, as Congressman Koch noted:

> The real fear on both sides of the aisle that some have expressed is, "Gee, if we do that, that is the first step."
>
> Maybe it is, but, whatever the second step is, it is what this House wants it to be, and if this House decides that this is the last step, so be it. If the House decides that it wants to have more information it will have to have a vote on it.

---

[55] William Colby testimony, House Select Committee on Intelligence, 8/4/75, p. 122.

Senator McClellan described the consequences of publishing the total budget for national intelligence. "That is when you intend to put the camel's nose under the tent. That is the beginning. That is the wedge. You say you do not want to know all the details and how the money is spent. But, if you get the overall figures of one billion dollars or half-a-billion dollars or five billion, or whatever, then how are you going to know, how can you evaluate, how can you judge or make an intelligent judgment on whether that is too much or too little, whether it is being expended wisely or unwisely, except when you can get the details?

"How? You cannot know. And, if you receive these figures and if you end this ignorance as to the total amount, next you will want to end the ignorance as to the different agencies and how it is spent, and through whom it is spent. Next will want to end the ignorance of what it is spent for. Next you want to end the ignorance of how that intelligence is procured. There is no end to it." (Cong. Rec. S9609, daily ed., 6/4/74, remarks of Sen. McClellan.)

During the same debate Senator Humphrey noted that while he did not oppose the purpose of the disclosure of the total budget for national intelligence, "the problem is it is sort of like loose string or a ball of twine, so to speak, that starts to unravel." (Id. at S9606, remarks of Sen. Humphrey.) During a more recent House debate on the publication of the CIA's budget, Congressman Young described such publication as "the first baby step." (Cong. Rec. H9376, daily ed., 10/1/75, remarks of Rep. Young.)

As James Schlesinger told the Select Committee, "But one of the problems here is the camel's nose under the edge of the tent, and I think that that is the fundamental problem in the area. There are very few people who can articulately argue that the publication of those figures in and of themselves, if it stopped there, would be harmful. The argument is that then the pressure would build up to do something else, that once you have published for example the ... budget, that the pressures would build up to reveal the kinds of systems that are being bought for that money, and it is regarded as the first step down a slippery slope for those who worry about those kinds of things." (Schlesinger, 2/2/76, p. 53.)

[56] Helms, 1/30/76, p. 39.
[57] Ibid.

What is wrong with that? That is what is called the democratic system. We are sent here to be part of that system.[58]

It is instructive to note in this context the amount of budgetary information provided on the Atomic Energy Commission. That information has constantly increased. Yet each step of the way, Congress has had the opportunity to limit disclosure and chose not to. This experience confirms congressional control over the process. More importantly the national security was not harmed by disclosure of a substantial amount of budgetary information about an agency and a weapons program crucial to the defense of the United States.

Finally, the argument is without limits. It could be used to justify much greater secrecy. It could be used to justify the withholding of all information on the Defense Department because information which the Congress wishes to protect would be threatened by pressures caused by the publication of any information on that Department.

The Argument That the United States Should Not Publish Information of Its Intelligence Budget since No Other Government in the World Does

It has also been argued that the United States should not publish its intelligence budget when no other government in the world does.[59] Yet as Congressman Moss noted:

I point out to those Members who do not know the difference between this country and others, and the fact that we become unique in disclosing this that, thank God, we do become unique. We have grown great and maintained our strength as an open society and we should continue to be an open society to the maximum consistent with our true security requirements.

I do not want us to emulate the Russians or the Chinese or even our British brethren in the operation of the various agencies of their governments under their official secrets acts and other areas. I want us to realize the strength that we gain from an alert electorate and informed electorate.[60]

SUMMARY AND CONCLUSION

The budget procedures which presently govern the Central Intelligence Agency and other agencies of the intelligence community prevent most Members of Congress as well as the public from knowing how much money is spent by any of these agencies or even how much is spent on intelligence as a whole. In addition, most Members of Congress and the public are deceived about the appropriations and expenditures of other government agencies whose budgets are inflated to conceal funds for the intelligence community. The failure to provide this information to the public and to the Congress prevents

---

[58] Cong. Rec. H9359, daily ed., 10/1/75, remarks of Rep. Koch.
[59] William Colby testimony, House Select Committee on Intelligence, 8/4/75, p. 120.
[60] Cong. Rec. H9363, daily ed., 10/1/75, remarks of Rep. Moss.

either from effectively ordering priorities and violates Article 1, Section 9, Clause 7, which provides that:

> No Money shall be drawn from the Treasury but in Consequence of Appropriations made by Law; and a regular Statement and Account of the Receipts and Expenditures of all public Money shall be published from time to time.

The Committee finds that publication of the aggregate figure for national intelligence would begin to satisfy the constitutional requirement and would not damage the national security. While substantial questions remain about the relationship between the constitutional requirement and the national security, the Committee recommends the annual publication of the aggregate figure. The Committee also recommends that any successor committees study the effects of publishing more detailed information on the budgets of the intelligence agencies.

A Hypothetical Example ([9], pp. 3–4, 16–17)

Significant testimony on CIA budget practices has been appended to the Church testimony, illustrating the secrecy and lack of accountability regarding the flow of money into the intelligence budget. Floyd Riddick, retired Senate parliamentarian, testified before the Senate Armed Services Committee in 1976 ([9], pp. 3 ff.). He proceeded to educate members of the very committee that had been charged with the responsibility of CIA oversight as to what had been going on within their own committee. His exchange with Chairman John Stennis and Senators Stuart Symington and Robert Taft is reprinted here in substantially abridged form to preserve space.

Mr. RIDDICK. Mr. Chairman, I think we have changed the resolution considerably from what the Government Operations Committee did, as far as protection of information is concerned, and also as far as giving the Appropriations Committee its present status as it had previously. We managed to salvage yesterday a compromise, section 12, which reads as follows:

"Subject to the Standing Rules of the Senate, no funds shall be appropriated for any fiscal year" et cetera, just as Mr. Braswell said. But this clause, "Subject to the Standing Rules of the Senate," retains rule 16 as it exists now. So that the Appropriations Committee can come in with funds not only in a continuing resolution, but in any resolution, or any other committee can make a motion, which after one day's reference to the Appropriations Committee could be brought up on the floor to provide funds for a new item not authorized, or to increase an item above authorization that is in the bill. So you retain to the Appropriations Committee now, if this is retained as is, the existing authority it has now to bring in funds for any purpose not authorized, not subject to a point of order.

I think that is a very significant point. For example, if you wanted to hire a group to do some spy work in Cuba and there was no legislative authorization for it, and you wanted them to go in on a submarine, you could just put an item for an intelligence activity in South America, for $500 million, or whatever you wanted, and no authorization would be necessary under this proviso.

Senator SYMINGTON. But then you bypass the supervisory committee, the regulatory committee.

Mr. RIDDICK. Senator, that is not the intent of this appropriation.

Senator SYMINGTON. I know it is not the intent, but it is what has been going on for 25 years, and it is one of the chief reasons we are in this mess.

Mr. RIDDICK. What the Authorization Committee can do is to come in with legislation that would say, no funds shall be spent, which would give them authority that we now have under this legislative authorizataion authority. The only thing is, as the conference was agreed upon, if this committee acted to take negative action against a certain activity, it certainly would not be expected that the Appropriations Committee would come in unless there was an extreme crisis, and define what the legislative authorization committee had done.

The CHAIRMAN. Let me ask a question right there.

If you had this proposal for this activity in South America, you would have to disclose it right there if you have the authorization, you might say, from the floor in the method that you describe?

Mr. RIDDICK. That is true. But there are other aspects in there, Senator, that are going to be more exposing than this. For example, the proviso which reads here:

On or before March 15 of each year, the select committee shall submit to the Committee on the Budget of the Senate the views and estimates described in section 301(c) of the Congressional Budget Act of 1974, regarding matters within the jurisdiction of the select committee.

So the select committee has to submit its information to the Budget Committee just like any other committee, which, if they want to, can expose the details of what they are proposing.

The CHAIRMAN. Yes. But that increases rather than takes care of the problem as some of us see it at least about unnecessary or undue disclosure.

Mr. RIDDICK. The way this substitute tightens up on the flow of information is that it prohibits any member of the select committee from exposing any of the information submitted to the select committee until the committee votes.

Now, if it is lawfully classified information, then they must, before the information can be released, submit a report to the Senate in closed session, which the Senate will debate in closed session, as opposed to the way this committee decides whether information of that nature is to be exposed. And if the Senate says yes, it will be exposed, and if the Senate says no, it will not be exposed. . . .

Floyd Riddick was subsequently questioned by Senator Robert Taft, who expressed concern at the idea that the CIA can so easily divert funds from amounts specifically appropriated for other purposes.

For my own information, however, I would like to ask Dr. Riddick to describe as he understands it the current situation with regard to the finance backing, whatever the procedure might be, of the CIA.

In other words, I understand there is a code section which permits transfer of funds to the CIA from other areas, it does nothing through authorization committees today, it goes through the Appropriations Committee. And there is some kind of an information procedure. Is that information procedure to various committee chairmen, and so forth, in writing? What is its history, and where do we stand today? What is the current procedure? I don't really understand that. I tried to find out about it at the time of Angola, and I couldn't get any help; I couldn't find anything in writing as to the current procedure.

Mr. RIDDICK. I am in your predicament, too. I know in the appropriations bill they did provide for the transaction not to exceed a certain amount for certain purposes.

Senator TAFT. There is a code authorization for the transfer, I understand that. But as to what checking is done and why the checking is done, is there anything in writing at all?

Mr. RIDDICK. That is kind of a legal question that gets a little out of my field.

Senator TAFT. I don't think it is legal. There isn't anything in the Senate rules that you know of that relates to this consultation process, is there?

Mr. RIDDICK. I don't know of anything that would prohibit it in the rules.

Senator TAFT. Can you tell us what the practice has been? This goes directly to this subcommittee question.

Mr. RIDDICK. The practice has been that when the budget comes up for estimate on the various purposes, even though they might be silent and give it in a lump sum, we refer the whole thing to the Appropriations Committee.

Senator TAFT. If there is a desire to get an appropriation after the bill is passed, and a desire to transfer for a new project of the CIA, some money from another department, what happens?

Mr. RIDDICK. I don't think it is spelled out any more, Senator.

Senator TAFT. Do you know as a matter of practice what happens? Because I got the same kind of answers from where I asked. And I think it does show the need for some institutionalization here.

Mr. RIDDICK. I would assume that it is administrative action pursuant to that transfer of power.

Senator TAFT. Purely the matter of CIA coming to various Members of Congress of their choice or understanding and telling them about it, is that right?

Mr. RIDDICK. After consultation, I assume, with certain Senators who have been doing some oversight in that area.

Senator TAFT. There is nothing in writing that requires in any way that they consult with the chairman of the Armed Services Committee or the chairman of the Foreign Relations Committee or the chairman of the Appropriations Committee, or the ranking membership.

Mr. RIDDICK. Not that I know of.

Senator TAFT. Thank you. That is my understanding, but I am amazed by it. Everything I understood was to the contrary until this came up. Everybody thinks that there is a definite procedure, but there isn't any.

THE ROLE OF THE OFFICE OF MANAGEMENT AND BUDGET ([84A], pp. 51–73)

The Office of Management and Budget plays a significant role as a coordinator of the budgeting process throughout the government, and it is privy to, in part, the secrets of the intelligence community. James Lynn, OMB director, resumed testimony before the Pike Select Committee's hearings on August 1, 1975. He addressed the manner in which OMB and the intelligence agencies work together and the extent to which he, as the president's budget director, is able to exercise a measure of control over their activities. (The Senate Church report also took up OMB's role in the intelligence budget process, concluding that it is important as a means to control abuse, to ensure coherence of policy and action, and that its staff requires expansion in view of its complex task.)

The committee met, pursuant to recess, at 10 a.m., in room 2118, Rayburn House Office Building, the Honorable Otis G. Pike [chairman], presiding.

Present: Representatives Pike, Giaimo, Stanton, Dellums, Murphy, Aspin, Milford, Hayes, Lehman, McClory, Treen, Johnson, and Kasten.

Also present: A. Searle Field, staff director; Aaron B. Donner; general counsel; John L. Boos, counsel; Jeffrey R. Whieldon, counsel; Roger Carroll, Jacqueline Hess, and Charles Mattox, investigators.

Chairman PIKE. The committee will come to order.

I would ask the cameras to remove themselves from this particular spot at this particular time.

This morning our witness is Mr. James T. Lynn, the Director of the Office of Management and Budget.

STATEMENT OF JAMES T. LYNN, DIRECTOR, OFFICE OF MANAGE-MENT AND BUDGET, ACCOMPANIED BY PAUL O'NEILL, DEPUTY DIRECTOR, OMB, AND DONALD OGILVIE, ASSOCIATE DIRECTOR FOR NATIONAL SECURITY AND INTERNATIONAL AFFAIRS

Chairman PIKE. Mr. Lynn, I want to thank you first of all for having provided your statement in advance. I have had an opportunity to look at your statement. It is a relatively lengthy statement.

It seems to me that we might expedite our processes quite a lot if we put your statement, which all of the Members have, in the record and proceed directly to questioning on that statement.

What would you think of that idea?

Mr. LYNN. I have very mixed emotions with regard to it, Mr. Chairman.

Chairman PIKE. I will bet you have.

Mr. LYNN. Because on the one hand I certainly wish to expedite the work of this committee as much as possible and therefore anything we can do to serve your interests best we want to do. On the other hand, I must say that I think that a general understanding of our role and then fitting it into the application to the intelligence community is important.

If I might suggest a reasonable compromise in this regard that should take a very short period of time, why don't I have the statement before me, read in part, skip in part and hold it down to a relatively short period?

Chairman PIKE. Do you suppose if we did that we could finish the reading of your statement in half an hour?

Mr. LYNN. I think so.

Chairman PIKE. Mr. McClory?

Mr. McCLORY. It is true that we have had the statement before us and have had an opportunity to examine it. Our principal interest is with respect to the intelligence community beginning on page 8. It might be that you could omit the preliminaries and begin on that page and even end on page 12 as far as I am concerned.

Chairman PIKE. Mr. McClory, I want to thank you once again for the excellent bipartisan cooperation we are getting in this committee.

Don't you think that is reasonable?

Mr. LYNN. I have a feeling I am getting very strong signals from the dais, Mr. Chairman.

Chairman PIKE. Mr. Lynn, very frankly, we started late with these hearings. We are doing our best to keep them moving. I think that your statement is replete with substance but the substance is of no particular pertinency to the activities of this committee. Therefore, why don't we do it the way Mr. McClory suggested, you start on page 8 of your statement and wind up somewhere around page 12.

If you would like to summarize the beginning of it and then start reading at page 8, that will be all right.

Mr. LYNN. I think that I can say this about the first part: Since our process in budget review is so much the same between any agency and the intelligence community, it was useful to describe our function first as a matter of generality as to how we did it.

I think what we learned from the first eight pages is that it is a rather detailed structure. It is a structure that has been used for some time and there is no magic about it. It is one that is known as far as the procedure is concerned to most people who are interested. With that, and in the same interest that you have expressed with regard to saving time, but with an understanding that this part of the statement will be, the first part will be considered well——

Chairman PIKE. The entire statement without objection will be placed in the record at this point.

STATEMENT OF JAMES T. LYNN, DIRECTOR OF THE OFFICE OF MANAGEMENT AND BUDGET

Mr. Chairman and Members, I am pleased to be with you today to discuss the role of the Office of Management and Budget. I propose to discuss, first, our general role and then focus specifically on our relations with the Intelligence Community.

OMB's general role is comprised of three major functions:

First, we oversee and manage the preparation of the Federal budget.

Second, we work with the agencies to improve the operations of the Executive Branch.

Finally, we coordinate legislative proposals offered by the Administration and the development of Executive Branch views on legislation pending before the Committees of the Congress.

OMB BUDGET ROLE

There are four major phases in the budget process:
(1) Executive formulation.
(2) Congressional enactment.
(3) Budget execution.
(4) Post audit.

OMB's principal role in the budget process is assisting in executive formulation (step 1 above) and budget execution (step 3 above).

Congressional enactment is, of course, the responsibility of the Legislative Branch, although I testify as appropriate. The post audit phase is handled by the General Accounting Office as well as internal audit groups within the various Government departments and agencies.

PREPARATION AND EXECUTION OF THE FEDERAL BUDGET

The President's transmittal of his budget proposals to the Congress in January or February each year climaxes many months of planning and analysis throughout the Executive Branch.

PRELIMINARY STEPS

OMB staff, in cooperation with staff of the Treasury Department and the Council of Economic Advisers, keep under continuous review the relationships between Government finances and the economy generally. This review includes study of recent conditions, as well as the future outlook. Consideration is given to tentative assumptions on the economic environment, projections of revenue expected under these assumptions, and the aggregate range of Government spending levels.

In the late spring, the Office of Management and Budget conducts the Spring Planning Review. Staff prepares estimates indicating a probable range of spending for each of the major programs and agencies for the forthcoming budget. In preparing estimates we draw upon our knowledge of agency programs, agency estimates for particular programs, program evaluation materials and informal discussions with responsible agency budget and planning personnel. We also develop information to relate program objectives to resources requirements.

Paul O'Neill and I then review the fiscal and economic situation, the spending outlook, and the individual program, budget, and management issues posed in the agency presentations. I then discuss our findings with the President, and seek his decisions on planning guidance for each agency and department so that they may reshape their plans and prepare their budgets accordingly. In fact, only a few days ago the planning guidance letters for the FY 1977 budget were sent out.

COMPILATION AND SUBMISSION OF AGENCY BUDGET ESTIMATES

During the next several months agencies revise their program plans in accordance with assigned planning ceilings and program guidance received, and decide upon the budget requests they wish to make for the upcoming budget. They compile schedules and supporting information in accordance with the instructions prescribed by the Office of Management and Budget (Circular No. A–11).

Agency budget submissions are due in the Office of Management and Budget beginning in September. The submission covers all accounts in which money is available for obligation or expenditure, whether or not any action by Congress is required

REVIEW OF AGENCY ESTIMATES IN THE OFFICE OF MANAGEMENT AND BUDGET

When the estimates are received in the Office of Management and Budget, they are referred to the examiners assigned to the programs involved. All the knowledge the examiners possess about the agency—whether based on long-run analyses, field investigations, special studies, or conferences held with agency officials—is brought to bear on the estimates at this time. The examiners must be thoroughly familiar with the President's budget policy and previous Congressional action, as well as with the programs of the agency and their relationship to activities of other agencies.

The examiners give considerable attention to the bases for the individual estimates: the volume of work on hand and forecast; the methods by which the agency proposes to accomplish its objectives; the costs of accomplishments; and the estimates of requirements in terms of supplies, equipment, facilities, and numbers of people required. They review past performance, check the accuracy of factual information presented, and consider the future implications of the program. They identify program, budget and management issues of major importance to be raised for discussion with agency representatives at hearings. The hearings, held in October and November, may last only a few hours for a small agency, but often run into weeks for a large department.

After the hearings are completed, the examiners prepare their summary of the issues and their recommendations for my review. This so-called "Director's Review" provides an opportunity for me and my principal assistants to obtain an understanding of the agency's program and budget requests, an analysis of the significant issues involved, the relationship of the agency requests to the planning ceiling set for the agency as a result of the Spring Planning Review, and recommendations as to budget allowances.

BUDGET DECISIONS BY THE PRESIDENT

Because of the scope and complexity of the budget, I and my principal assistants meet frequently with the President to present major issues for his decision as portions of the Office of Management and Budget reviews are completed during October, November, and December. As soon as the President makes his decisions, OMB notifies each agency head of the amounts which will be recommended to Congress for his agency's programs for the ensuring fiscal year. After any appeals by the agency head to the President have been settled, OMB completes the final preparation and printing of the President's Budget for submission to Congress.

BUDGET EXECUTION

The Anti-Deficiency Act requires that the Director of the Office of Management and Budget apportion, with a few exceptions, appropriations and funds made available to the Executive Branch. This consists of dividing the total available funds into specific amounts available for portions of the fiscal year or for particular projects or activities. It is a violation of law (31 U.S.C. 665) for an agency to incur obligations or make expenditures in excess of the amounts apportioned.

The objective of the apportionment system is to assure the effective and orderly use of available funds and to reduce the need for supplemental appropriations. It is, of course, necessary to insure flexibility if circumstances change.

Changes in laws or other factors may indicate the need for additional funds, and supplemental requests may have to be transmitted to the Congress. On the other hand, reserves may be established under the Anti-Deficiency Act to provide for contingencies or to effect savings made possible by or through changes in requirements or greater efficiency of operations. Amounts may also be withheld for policy or other reasons, but only under specific procedures established by the Congressional Budget and Impoundment Control Act.

Progress on the budget program is reviewed throughout the fiscal year at successive levels, both in the agency and the Office of Management and Budget. Periodic reports on the status of apportionments are supplemented by more specialized reports which relate accomplishments to cost. Shifts in the agency budget plans are frequently required to meet changing conditions—to finance unforeseen circumstances or to provide savings where the workload is less than was estimated or where increased efficiency permits accomplishments at less cost than was anticipated.

PREPARING THE INTELLIGENCE COMMUNITY BUDGET

I have spent some time providing the general backdrop of OMB's process of preparing the President's Budget because the OMB role and process of preparing the intelligence budget is essentially the same as that with respect to the budget of any other Executive Branch department or agency. Let me cite a few examples of this, particularly as it relates to the 1976 budget process for intelligence.

1. The principal U.S. foreign intelligence activities are examined by a single unit in OMB contained within OMB's National Security Division and reporting to OMB's Associate Director, Mr. Donald G. Ogilvie, who is responsible for national security and international affairs. Under Mr. Ogilvie, this unit, consisting of a branch chief and five professional examiners, reviews the budgets of the Central Intelligence Agency, the Defense Intelligence Agency, the National Security Agency, and those intelligence activities of the Army, Navy, and Air Force that bear most directly on U.S. intelligence capabilities.

By way of a footnote, I should state that they do not examine the domestic information gathering of the FBI or other non-foreign intelligence-related activities. They also do not examine most of the military or force-related intelligence activities of the Military Departments that are intended for wartime support to military forces during operations. These activities are the responsibility of other branches of OMB.

2. The intelligence programs are examined in the same context and in the same time frame as are all other Executive Branch activities. The current and projected economic situation is considered; pertinent Presidential guidance on intelligence is taken into account; and the effectiveness of the programs is analyzed.

3. During the 1976 budget formulation process, the Director and Deputy Director held in-depth sessions with the Associate Director and the staff on all these activities. Intelligence activities and programs were evaluated in June of last year, major policy and program issues were identified, and alternative long-range program plans were discussed. Guidance in the form of a planning target for the Intelligence Community's budget submission was provided to the Director of Central Intelligence and the Secretary of Defense in July of last year. We follow the same basic procedure each year.

4. After the budgets were submitted in October and reviewed by the OMB staff, the Director and Deputy Director reviewed the total Intelligence Community budget in December. Then two meetings were held to review the issues with the President who made the final decisions.

5. A final allowance letter was sent by the Director of OMB to the Director of Central Intelligence and the Secretary of Defense informing them of the funds included in the President's budget for the Intelligence Community.

DIFFERENCES IN BUDGET PREPARATION WITH RESPECT TO INTELLIGENCE

The only differences between OMB's role in the preparation of Intelligence Community budgets and those of other agencies result from the sensitive classification of the Intelligence Community budgets and the fact that part of the Intelligence Community budget is subject to joint review by the OMB and the Secretary of Defense.

Because most intelligence budget information is sensitive and classified, it is not specifically identified in the President's Budget. This is a legitimate area for review, but it cannot be clearer that:

1. The Director of Central Intelligence, who by statute is responsible for protecting intelligence sources and methods, has determined that most of the budget information is classified, and

2. The Congress has consistently supported the view this classification of intelligence budget information is appropriate, most recently in a Senate vote of June 1974.

Mr. Colby can provide more detail on this matter.

As a result of the classification of most intelligence budget information, OMB, both in its relationship with the intelligence agencies and in its relationship with the Congress, has taken measures to protect this information, while ensuring that the Congress has the requisite information so that it can perform its constitutional role in reviewing the budgets of the agencies and in authorizing and appropriating funds for these activities. For example, the Director of OMB has by long-standing practice sent letters to the Chairmen of the Appropriations Committees identifying the amount of funds the President is requesting for the Central Intelligence Agency. These Chairmen annually have responded in a classified letter to the Director of OMB indicating Congressional action on this request.

I should emphasize that the classification of intelligence budget information does not mean that Congress is uninformed about the cost, purposes, results, and effectiveness of U.S. intelligence activities. The Director of Central Intelligence testifies annually on the Intelligence Community budget before both the special oversight subcommittees of the Armed Services and Appropriations Committees. The Assistant Secretary of Defense for Intelligence, the Director of the National Security Agency, the Director of the Defense Intelligence Agency, and representatives of the Army, Navy, and Air Force also testify on their budget requests for intelligence.

The second difference in OMB's examination of intelligence activities in comparison to most other nonintelligence activities is related to the OMB joint review with the Department of Defense. For those intelligence activities of the Defense agencies—Defense Intelligence Agency and National Security Agency—and of the Military Departments, OMB participates in a joint review of the budget requests with the Office of the Secretary of Defense.

Let me briefly describe this process. OMB is a formal participant in the joint budget review and plays an informal role throughout the entire Defense program and budget cycle. An outline of the program and budget review calendar is as follows:

January.—The five year Defense plan is updated by the Defense Comptroller staff to reflect decisions made in the just completed budget review.

February.—The Secretary issues Planning and Programming Guidance, including fiscal levels, to the Services for preparation of the next five year plan. These planning levels have historically been higher than those identified in the President's Budget. While OMB has no formal role at this stage, there may be input from the OMB Director to the Secretary regarding appropriate fiscal levels.

March-May.—Based on the Planning and Programming Guidance, each Service submits a Program Objectives Memorandum which proposes a five year force structure and resource plan.

May-August.—The Program Objectives Memoranda are reviewed by the Office of the Secretary of Defense staff, principally the Program Analysis and Evaluation staff with inputs from other components of the Office of the Secretary of Defense. The culmination of the reviews are Program Decision Memoranda issued by the Secretary to the Services which provide both programmatic and fiscal modifications to the Program Objectives Memoranda. The focus of the May-August review is the whole five year period, and the emphasis is on forces, deployments and operating rates. In general, OMB monitors the process and may introduce or critique issues. OMB staff studies may be reviewed by Defense staff at this time and may form a basis for Program Objectives Memorandum issues as well as budget issues at this stage of the process. The historical OMB role has been to maintain an informal presence, reserving a formal role until later when the OMB Director and the President are personally involved.

September.—The Services prepare a budget submission based on Program Decision Memoranda guidance.

October-December (The Joint Budget Review).—The Services submit budgets for "joint" review by the Office of the Secretary of Defense and OMB staff. The joint review is unique to Defense, involving OMB staff working jointly with the DOD staff in reviewing the Service estimates for the Secretary. The function of the joint review is to (a) price out decisions reached during the preceding Program Objectives Memorandum review; (b) allow the Secretary to reconsider decisions made in Program Objectives Memorandum cycle; (c) introduce new program issues. OMB program issues are formally introduced at this stage of the review process. The decisions made by the Secretary of Defense in the joint review form the final budget submission to OMB.

This basic joint review procedure is adhered to with respect to Defense intelligence activities. It culminates, of course, in the final decisions by the President.

DIFFERENCES IN BUDGET EXECUTION WITH RESPECT TO INTELLIGENCE

There are also some differences in the budget execution phase that, while not unique to intelligence activities, I wish to call to your attention.

First, it is normal practice for OMB to apportion funds based on the appropriation structure that is presented and approved by Congress. Since most intelligence activities are included in larger appropriations within the budget, OMB does not take an apportionment action *specifically identifiable* to intelligence activities. Nonetheless, all intelligence funds are reviewed by OMB prior to apportionment of the larger appropriation within which they are included.

One exception to this is the Central Intelligence Agency where OMB apportions all funds for this agency as a separate entity.

Second, reprogramming is handled somewhat differently. For a typical agency or department, reprogramming controls are based on line item identification in appropriations. Such identification is absent from most of the intelligence appropriations because of security considerations. I believe, however, that in spite of this difference, significant changes in the use of funds do not occur without our knowledge. In the various reviews in which OMB staff participates throughout the year, the intelligence agencies do report on significant changes in their activities and the financial changes to the President's budget.

Finally, some transfers are made into certain intelligence activities under provisions of the Economy Act (31 USC 686). This Act permits purchase of supplies and service by one agency for another when it is more economical to do so. These transfers are not formally approved by OMB. Again, there is no lack of OMB or, for that matter, Congressional knowledge of these transfers which are reflected in both budget submissions to OMB and budget justification material provided to the Congress.

These distinctions in OMB practices with respect to execution do not, I believe, materially affect the way OMB approaches its responsibilities or the way the intelligence agencies carry out their responsibilities. I do not believe that the types of problems that are being investigated would have been prevented by changes in the way OMB has approached its responsibilities in execution of the Intelligence Community budget. In the final analysis, abuses of authority can be prevented only by ensuring the integrity and capability of the people in the Intelligence Community.

On the other hand, it is certainly possible that some revisions in Intelligence Community budget execution may be appropriate. For this reason, I have directed that the OMB staff review the present practices, the options available for changes in these practices, and the advantages and disadvantages of these alternative approaches.

OMB MANAGEMENT ROLE

OMB's second major function is to work with Federal agencies in efforts toward better management.

This responsibility is carried out by assisting the Federal departments and agencies in the development of new management systems, such as management by objectives and studies of major policy issues and management problem areas.

OMB monitors the management by objectives program with which you may be familiar. In this program, the objectives of the agencies and departments proposed in discussion with the OMB staff are actively monitored to ensure that important agency and Presidential objectives are being accomplished.

These functions are applied to the Intelligence Community in the same way as the other Federal agencies and departments. OMB staff participate in numerous studies and special reviews of intelligence activities. Director Colby has played an active role in the management-by-objectives process.

OMB LEGISLATIVE COORDINATION

The final role of the Office of Management and Budget is to coordinate the Administration position on legislation. On behalf of the President, OMB works with other elements of the Executive Office of the President and with the agencies to carry out the President's legislative responsibilities, including agency proposals, reports, testimony on pending legislation, and enrolled bills.

The legislative coordination function has several purposes:

It provides a mechanism for staffing out agency legislative proposals which the President may wish to include in his legislative program.

It helps the Executive agencies develop draft bills which are consistent with and which carry out the President's policy objectives.

It is a means of keeping Congress informed (through the "advice" transmitted by the agencies) of the relationship of bills to the President's program.

It provides a mechanism for assuring that Congress gets coordinated and informative agency views on legislation which it has under consideration.

It assures that bills submitted to Congress by one Executive agency properly take into account the interests and concerns of other affected agencies and will therefore have the general support of such agencies.

It provides a means to reconcile divergent agency views.

OMB's legislative coordination function with repect to legislation affecting intelligence activities is no different from that performed in any other area of Federal Government activity. For example, during the last year, OMB in conjunction with other elements of the Executive Office of the President and appropriate agencies has:

1. Coordinated the Executive Branch position on bills affecting the tenure of the Director of Central Intelligence and annuities under CIA's retirement plan.

2. Reviewed draft Department of Defense legislation affecting personnel in the Defense Intelligence Agency and the National Security Agency; and

3. Initiated the legislative clearance process with respect to proposed legislation on the protection of intelligence sources and methods.

CONCLUSIONS

That is a brief overview of our role and the ways in which we work with the Intelligence Community. At this time I will be pleased to answer your questions.

Mr. Lynn. Preparing the intelligence community budget: The OMB role and process in preparing the intelligence budget is essentially the same as that with respect to the budget of any other executive branch department or agency. Let me cite a few examples of this particularly as it relates to the 1976 budget process for intelligence.

1. The principal U.S. foreign intelligence activities are examined by a single unit in OMB contained within OMB's National Security Division and reporting to OMB's Associate Director, Mr. Donald G. Ogilvie, who is responsible for national security and international affairs. Under Mr. Ogilvie, this unit, consisting of a branch chief and five professional examiners, reviews the budgets of the Central Intelligence Agency, the Defense Intelligence Agency, the National Security Agency, and those intelligence activities of the Army, Navy, and Air Force that bear most directly on U.S. intelligence capabilities.

By way of a footnote, I should state that they do not examine the domestic information-gathering of the FBI or other non-foreign intelligence-related activities. They also do not examine most of the military or force-related intellegence activities of the military departments that are intended for wartime support to military forces during operations. These activities are the responsibility of other branches of OMB.

2. The intelligence programs are examined in the same context and in the same time frame as are all other executive branch activities. The current and projected economic situation is considered; pertinent Presidential guidance on intelligence is taken into account; and the effectiveness of the programs is analyzed.

3. During the 1976 budget formulation process, the Director and Deputy Director held in-depth sessions with the Associate Director and the staff on all these activities. The current and projected economic situation is considered; pertinent Presidential guidance on intelligence is taken into account; and the effectiveness of the programs is analyzed.

4. During the 1976 budget formulation process, the Director and Deputy Director held in-depth sessions with the Associate Director and the staff on all these activities. Intelligence activities and programs were evaluated in June of last year, major policy and program issues were identified, and alternative long-range program plans were discussed. Guidance in the form of a planning target for the intelligence community's budget submission was provided to the Director of Central Intelligence and the Secretary of Defense in July of last year. We follow the same basic procedure each year.

5. After the budgets were submitted in October and reviewed by the OMB staff, the Director and Deputy Director reviewed the total intelligence community budget in December. Then two meetings were held to review the issues with the President who made the final decisions.

6. A final allowance letter was sent by the Director of OMB to the Director of Central Intelligence and the Secretary of Defense informing them of the funds included in the President's budget for the intelligence community.

DIFFERENCES IN BUDGET PREPARATION WITH RESPECT TO INTELLIGENCE

The only differences between OMB's role in the preparation of intelligence community budgets and those of other agencies result from the sensitive classification of the intelligence community budgets and the fact that part of the intelligence community budget is subject to joint review by the OMB and the Secretary of Defense.

Because most intelligence budget information is sensitive and classified, it is not specifically identified in the President's budget.

This is a legitimate area for review, but it cannot be clearer that:

1. The Director of Central Intelligence, who by statute is responsible for protecting intelligences sources and methods, has determined that most of the budget information is classified, and

2. The Congress has consistently supported the view that this classification of intelligence budget information is appropriate, most recently in a Senate vote of June 1974.

Mr. Colby can provide more detail on this matter.

As a result of the classification of most intelligence budget information, OMB, both in its relationship with the intelligence agencies and in its relationship with the Congress, has taken measures to protect this information, while insuring that the Congress has the requisite information so that it can perform its constitutional role in reviewing the budgets of the agencies and in authorizing and appropriating funds for these activities.

For example, the Director of OMB has by long-standing practice sent letters to the chairmen of the Appropriations Committees identifying the amount of funds the President is requesting for the Central Intelligence Agency.

These chairmen annually have responded in a classified letter to the Director of OMB indicating congressional action on this request.

I should emphasize that the classification of intelligence budget information does not mean that Congress is uninformed about the cost, purposes, results, and effectiveness of U.S. intelligence activities. The Director of Central Intelligence testifies annually on the Intelligence Community budget before both the special oversight subcommittees of the Armed Services and Appropriations Committees.

The Assistant Secretary of Defense for Intelligence, the Director of the National Security Agency, the Director of the Defense Intelligence Agency, and representatives of the Army, Navy, and Air Force also testify on their budget requests for intelligence.

The second difference in OMB's examination of intelligence activities in comparison to most other nonintelligence activities is related to the OMB joint review with the Department of Defense. For those intelligence activities of the defense agencies—Defense Intelligence Agency and National Security Agency—and of the military departments, OMB participates in a joint review of the Budget requests with the Office of the Secretary of Defense.

Chairman PIKE. Mr. Lynn, I think that would be a very appropriate place to stop because from there on you are once again getting into a rather generalized discussion of the process.

Mr. LYNN. I would say, sir, that I would urge your reading of the difference in the defense process carefully.

I would also say that the last number of pages of this, at least to page 19 where we become more general again, I believe, are specifically related to the intelligence community, but if you do not want it read, we won't read it.

Chairman PIKE. Which particular pages?

Mr. LYNN. I am thinking of page 16 beginning in the middle of the page.

Chairman PIKE. Let's skip over to page 16 in the middle of the page and read 16 and 17.

Mr. LYNN. Up to the top of page 19.

Chairman PIKE. Mr. Lynn, it is not that we don't like to hear you read the statement, it is just that most of us have seen it and are capable of reading it. We would like to get into the questioning.

You start reading at page 16.

Mr. LYNN. Mr. Chairman, if you don't want me to read it, I won't. It is as simple as that.

Chairman PIKE. No, sir. I don't want the Office of Management and Budget to feel they have been precluded from reading something they really wanted to read. Go ahead.

Mr. LYNN. Differences in Budget Execution with Respect to Intelligence.

There are also some differences in the budget execution phase that, while not unique to intelligence activities, I wish to call to your attention.

First, it is normal practice for OMB to apportion funds based on the appropriation structure that is presented and approved by Congress. Since most intelligence activities are included in larger appropriations within the budget, OMB does not take an apportionment action specifically indentifiable to intelligence activities. Nonetheless, all intelligence funds are reviewed by OMB prior to apportionment of the larger appropriation within which they are included.

One exception to this is the Central Intelligence Agency where OMB apportions all funds for this agency as a separate entity.

Second, reprograming is handled somewhat differently. For a typical agency or department, reprograming controls are based on line item identification in appropriations. Such identification is absent from most of the intelligence appropriations because of security considerations. I believe, however, that in spite of this difference, significant changes in the use of funds do not occur without our knowledge.

In the various reviews in which OMB staff participates throughout the year, the intelligence agencies do report on significant changes in their activities and the financial changes to the President's budget.

Finally, some transfers are made into certain intelligence activities under provisions of the Economy Act. This act permits purchase of supplies and service by one agency for another when it is more economical to do so. These transfers are not formally approved by OMB. Again, there is no lack of OMB or, for that matter, congressional knowledge of these transfers which are reflected in both budget submissions to OMB and budget justification material provided to the Congress.

These distinctions in OMB practices with respect to execution do not, I believe, materially affect the way OMB approaches its responsibilities or the way the intelligence agencies carry out their responsibilities.

I do not believe that the types of problems that are being investigated would have been prevented by changes in the way OMB has approached its responsibilities in execution of the intelligence community budget. In the final analysis abuses of authority can be prevented only by insuring the integrity and capability of the people of the intelligence community.

On the other hand, it is certainly possible that some revisions in intelligence community budget execution may be appropriate. For this reason, I have directed that the OMB staff review the present practices, the options available for changes in these practices, and the advantages and disadvantages of these alternative approaches.

I believe that will give the highlights of it, Mr. Chairman. I do not believe we even approached anything near 30 minutes.

Chairman PIKE. You did fine, Mr. Lynn.

Mr. LYNN. Thank you.

Chairman PIKE. Mr. Lynn, in preparing figures on what it costs America for her intelligence-gathering activities, how do you define intelligence-gathering activities?

Mr. LYNN. I am not quite certain I understand your question, Mr. Chairman.

Chairman PIKE. Well, before we can talk about what it costs us to gather intelligence we have to know what we are talking about. There has to be a definition of what is to be included in and what is to be excluded from the cost of intelligence-gathering activities. How do you establish the parameters? How do you define intelligence-gathering activities in order to determine the cost?

Mr. LYNN. I would say that as a matter of overall budget review an effort has been made to identify various functions performed that we believe are in the category of intelligence and then having identified those and their having been brought to us in a systematic way with the coordination of the Director of Central Intelligence, we consider those specific functions.

Now if you want a description of specific functions that are done in the intelligence community and discussion as to whether such functions to be considered in this budget or some other budget——

Chairman PIKE. That is precisely what I am talking about.

Mr. LYNN. I believe that is the kind of thing, Mr. Chairman, I would have to say respectfully would take a closed session. There is no way we can get into specific functions that are performed without being able to classify the material.

Chairman PIKE. I am not asking for a specific function performed. I am asking you how you define that which you include as a cost of getting intelligence. Certainly the definition is not classified.

Mr. OGILVIE. Mr. Chairman, I do not believe that it is possible in open session, without going into specific examples of what we include in the intelligence area of the budget, to fully answer your question.

We can give you some rough general ideas.

Chairman PIKE. Well, give me a rough general idea about a situation where a ship goes off on an intelligence-gathering mission.

I am not asking for specifics but how do you define what part of the cost of that operation will be called intelligence gathering?

Mr. LYNN. I think that what you do is take area by area of activity and look at it and ask logically is its main theme intelligence or is it really so incidental to intelligence that it ought to be categorized something else.

Chairman PIKE. Do you make that determination, Mr. Lynn?

Mr. LYNN. No; we do not make this determination alone.

Chairman PIKE. Who makes that determination?

Mr. LYNN. That determination is made by two different groups essentially, one is the Congress of the United States in its own appropriation and oversight process.

Chairman PIKE. There is no way the Congress of the United States makes that determination because the Congress of the United States by and large does not know.

You talk about a letter which you send to the chairman of the Appropriations Committee. I don't see that letter.

Mr. GIAIMO. I have been on the Appropriations Committee since 1963, and I am on the Defense Subcommittee which deals with the intelligence community. I have never seen the letter. Up until last year, I was never even privy to the briefings of the intelligence community. Your statement that the Appropriations Committee has performed oversight is just not so. Limiting it to certain Members of Congress makes a big difference.

Mr. LYNN. I agree. By your own rules in the Congress, by your own decision in the Congress, it has been decided——

Chairman PIKE. It has been decided that a handful of men will have this authority.

Mr. GIAIMO. It is not Congress who is informed. It is a certain few Members.

Mr. LYNN. I stand corrected. You are absolutely right, Mr. Giaimo.

Chairman PIKE. We have established that it is not Congress that makes this determination. Who is it?

Mr. LYNN. Certainly the Members of the Congress who by its own decisions have been made privy to these budgets are involved in that; because if they had strong objections as to what is included or is not, I am sure that the various heads of the agencies would be told about it and so would we. Now in the executive branch of the Government, of course, we will make recommendations in this regard. I believe that the Director of Central Intelligence will also make recommendations in this regard as will the other agencies involved. Then ultimately, I think, the decision would rest with the President, if there is a disagreement amongst us or if we all agree, but, I think, there is an important decision that should be made at a Presidential level.

Chairman PIKE. I would ask my timekeeper if my time is up. I missed the signal.

Mr. McClory.

Mr. McClory. I want to commend you on your statement, Mr. Lynn, Also, I would observe with respect to this subject that if you did undertake to deliver a letter to all the Members of Congress I am confident that it would be a violation of the trust that we repose in you with respect to the secrecy which surrounds intelligence activities. I would not want to suggest that you have been derelict in not issuing such a letter to all the Members or publicizing it. On the other hand, I would like to ask if it is not possible under executive session or under an assurance of confidentiality that this committee can receive these letters that have been delivered under the rules or practices that have been established by committee of the Congress.

Mr. Lynn. Mr. McClory, let me give you my overall attitude. We want to help this committee in every way we can. Our own concern with respect to this matter is the matter of classification of sensitive material. In answer to your question, I believe that under the appropriate security arrangements, as you suggest in closed session, that this information should be given to you. Now as to who ought to give certain kinds of information as between Director Colby and us, that is a different matter, and is subject to the general way we do business with agencies. Certainly as far as giving information of this kind, you are deeply, by nature of jurisdiction and the things that you have to look into, entitled to information of this kind.

Mr. McClory. Have you supplied similar information to the Rockefeller Commission and to the Church committee?

Mr. Lynn. I will have to ask.

Mr. Ogilvie. The Church committee is being provided with that information, but it is being provided by Director Colby, not by OMB.

Mr. McClory. What about the money left over? The funds that are employed by CIA and other intelligence agencies are sort of secreted or transferred around. They are in various budgets. What happens to the money that is left over? Does that come back to the Treasury or do you get information about that?

Mr. Ogilvie. We do have information about that; yes, sir.

Mr. McClory. You say on page 17 that you apportion the funds of the Central Intelligence Agency and you include that as a separate entity so that CIA funds are different from other intelligence agency funds insofar as your practices are concerned.

Mr. Ogilvie. The difference, Mr. McClory, is in the apportionment process, not in the funds themselves, because intelligence funds are included in larger appropriation categories than the amount of the funds themselves. They are, because of the way OMB apportions funds, apportioned according to the appropriation of which they are a part. In the case of CIA, we specifically identify those funds and apportion them separately.

Mr. McClory. In making up the overall budget are you informed with respect to the specific projects which enter into the overall budget?

Mr. Lynn. I think the answer to that is that on major matters that involve large expenditures, I would say that the intelligence community brings them to our attention and upon our inquiry brings them to our attention. So, I would say we have some knowledge of some projects. We have no knowledge of others. Let me put that in context.

The same thing is true of other departments and agencies. If you take a look at the S. & E. account of HUD, it is a very broad account. It is the one for employees and so on.

I did not have OMB ask me specifically what I was doing with particular people as to what way they were going to approach this, that or the other thing. On major projects, OMB would ask me. From what I have been advised, not having been through this cycle myself from the position of OMB Director except for the spring review, it is much the same with the CIA.

Mr. McCLORY. My time is up.

Chairman PIKE. Mr. Giaimo.

Mr. GIAIMO. Mr. Director, it is a pleasure to see you again and to have this opportunity to talk with you. It is a far cry from the days when you and I sat across the table when you were the Secretary of HUD. This is a whole new ball game insofar as both of us are concerned. Let me say at the outset that I for one, and I am not new to briefings in this area as I stated earlier, I am terribly concerned over the inadequacy of congressional oversight and also equally concerned over what I suspect to be the inadequacy of the executive branch oversight of the intelligence community.

In your statement on page 13 you said, "I should emphasize that the classification of intelligence budget information does not mean that Congress is uninformed"; you then comment on how the various committees of the Congress, the oversight committees and appropriating committees, are apprised.

I think we made clear the distinction that must be made. It is not Congress that gets this information; it is certain Members of Congress. That is one of the problems of the present inquiry, for Congress to change its ways.

Let's consider the executive branch. You are a key area of the executive branch, but do you see in depth all of the budget of the intelligence community?

Mr. LYNN. Do I personally?

Mr. GIAIMO. OMB.

Mr. LYNN. We have a little definitional problem at the outset but in preparation for these hearings I went through some of the materials that are supplied to us. I must admit in the spring review, for example, I was quite surprised at the depth.

Mr. GIAIMO. Is that the first time you went through them?

Mr. LYNN. Yes, because I am a new Director of OMB. In the spring review I went through a number of the materials. It is in substantial depth. When I use that expression, I want to express some caution because as was the case with HUD, you have large items for personnel, for example, and just like with every other agency, OMB does not go into what each and every person or subgroup of people do within the agency.

Mr. GIAIMO. While OMB may not know the particulars of the S. & E. account or some other account at HUD, the difference is that all you have to do is pick up the telephone and ask for the figures. I am sure that OMB, being what it is, will get them.

Mr. LYNN. And Mr. Giaimo, the relationship, as far as I have been able to see is between OMB and the intelligence community, is that OMB can do precisely the same thing with the intelligence community.

Mr. GIAIMO. Would they furnish you with budget items of accounts in areas where admitted wrongdoings have already taken place?

Mr. LYNN. We are talking about human beings.

Mr. GIAIMO. No, we are not. We are talking about governmental agencies.

Mr. LYNN. There is always an opportunity for a person in and out of the Government to fabricate or be less than totally forthcoming. I hope that is not a relationship between these agencies and OMB.

Mr. GIAIMO. If you were to telephone the intelligence community asking for detailed budgets on former paramilitary secret wars, would the information be furnished to you?

Mr. LYNN. Let me make my answer again apart from any particular kind of activity, whether engaged in or not engaged in. That would be that I have no reason to believe that if we asked specific questions we would not get an answer. Let me go on and say that it might be that in some given theoretical instance that the Director of Central Intelligence might feel it is so sensitive that he would want to go to the President of the United States with regard to it or make me do that but I am not aware of any such circumstances ever having happened.

Mr. GIAIMO. Isn't it so that under the law the Director of Central Intelligence has expenditures which are exempt from the usual scrutiny of OMB and that the mere certification of those expenditures by the Secretary of Defense, for example, is sufficient?

Mr. LYNN. I am not aware of any, sir.

Mr. OGILVIE. He does have the authority to obligate funds for which his certificate is sufficient voucher for audit purposes; nonetheless OMB reviews all of the funds in the CIA budget.

Mr. GIAIMO. Would he provide whatever OMB were to request?

Mr. OGILVIE. I can think of no instance where we have not gotten the information.

Mr. GIAIMO. You are not answering the question.

Mr. LYNN. We can only give you what the experience has been.

Mr. Ogilvie, who has been there longer than I have is saying he cannot recall any instance where we have asked for information from the Agency that they have not given us a substantive answer with regard to it.

Chairman PIKE. Mr. Stanton.

Mr. STANTON. Thank you, Mr. Chairman.

Mr. Lynn, I would like to welcome you again as an old friend.

Mr. LYNN. It is good to be here, Mr. Stanton.

Mr. STANTON. Are you satisfied, Mr. Lynn, with the oversight performance of the administration over the intelligence community?

Mr. LYNN. I don't know, Mr. Stanton. We have the President's Commission on the CIA, which has now reported. There also has been, of course, substantial news with regard to the CIA. Your committee and the Senate are looking at it. What I have done within my own area of responsibility has directed my people to take a hard look at this whole area with us and come to our own conclusions because I do believe that in light of the things that have been said and that I have read about and have heard by way of allegations in some cases we all better take a hard look as to whether or not we are carrying out our oversight responsibilities within our own sphere of jurisdiction in the right way.

Mr. STANTON. Do you feel the GAO should play a role as an independent arm of the Government in the accounting and auditing procedures of the intelligence community, particularly the CIA?

Mr. LYNN. I must say I really have not given that a lot of thought. As you know, the GAO is an arm of the Congress. I can say that we do——

Mr. STANTON. It is an independent arm. Go ahead.

Mr. LYNN. As I pointed out in the first 21 pages of my statement, we do not engage in auditing generally in OMB. On the other hand, even GAO does not audit every book and record of every department. They do it on sampling.

Mr. STANTON. We have the testimony of the Comptroller General that as far as the CIA is concerned, since 1962 he has been able to do nothing in terms of any type of auditing. Do you think that that should be allowed to continue?

Mr. LYNN. I just don't know, Mr. Stanton. I will say to you that looking at the statutes that have been passed in this area with respect to trying to give proper respect on the one hand to the need for classification of sensitive documents and on the other hand a natural desire to have outside points of checking, I think we have a balancing act to do. I want to think about it some.

I must admit I have not given that a lot of thought.

Mr. STANTON. I would deeply appreciate your thoughts on it if you want to submit something later on.

You said to Mr. Giaimo you felt there was substantial depth to the procedures by which you examine the records of the intelligence community. Would you be able, to take a hypothetical situation, to assure the American public that they got value for their dollar in the investment of a contract that was executed by the CIA to a particular company without competitive bid, such as the *Glomar Explorer*? In other words, would you know of any procedure that was established to assure that there was not some kind of deal between the company that executed that contract and the people in the CIA or did the CIA submit to OMB procedures by which they showed and justified the value of that contract?

Mr. LYNN. Let me try to answer the question broadly. Whatever the hypothetical situation you referred to, let's take any large project.

Mr. STANTON. That is a large one.

Mr. LYNN. As I said, I would just as soon not get into one way or the other any discussion——

Mr. STANTON. When was the first time you heard of the *Glomar Explorer* contract?

Mr. LYNN. I think to get into the specifics of whether or not there is or is not any such arrangement takes us into a classified area, as to which I will have no comment.

Mr. STANTON. Mr. Colby released testimony on that. So you cannot have it both ways.

I would like you to answer the question in regard to the initial instance. When did you first hear of the *Glomar* contract?

Mr. LYNN. I would prefer to answer your question by alluding to any large project.

Mr. STANTON. Fine.

Mr. LYNN. From what anybody has seen in the newspapers if there were arrangements of this kind it was a large project. But let's talk about large projects of any kind. OMB will look at a large project. It will necessarily come to its attention, particularly if the project involves major items of hardware.

I would assume—and Don Ogilvie can fill in further on this—that one of the things we will look at is whether or not the particular project is being acquired in the most economical way for the benefit of the taxpayer. That is a role that OMB traditionally prepares. Is there a cheaper way of doing something that should be done?

Is that fair, Don?

Mr. OGILVIE. I think that is correct, yes.

Mr. STANTON. How would you make that value?

Chairman PIKE. The time of the gentleman from Ohio has expired.

Mr. Treen.

Mr. TREEN. I have just one question, Mr. Lynn. In the budget process what persons are involved in classifying information?

Mr. LYNN. In classifying material or doing work that involves classified material?

Mr. TREEN. Classifying information as security information—in other words, not to be made public. What person is involved in that process?

In your budget process who attaches the labels to information, documents, et cetera, that come to your attention and that you utilize in the budget process?

Mr. OGILVIE. Mr. Treen, there are within the executive branch some published regulations with regard to who is able to classify information, what individuals and what specific agencies. I simply do not know all of the agencies involved on that list at this point or all the individuals but I can give you some idea of the level of people within the Office of Management and Budget that perform the classification function if that would be useful to you.

Mr. TREEN. I would like to know that, and I would like to know whether OMB simply accepts a classification from an agency.

Mr. OGILVIE. All right. Within OMB the people within the National Security and International Affairs section, of which I am the head, permitted to classify information are myself and the three major division chiefs who directly report to me. Certain other individuals within OMB, in addition to the four of us, also are authorized to classify information under the prescribed criteria if they have work with classified information such as the ERDA and other areas that are classified.

The Director is able to classify it, the Deputy Director is able to classify it and a number of other individuals.

Mr. TREEN. Or to declassify it, presumably. If on your level a decision is made to classify then the Director, or Deputy Director, can declassify, right?

Mr. OGILVIE. Yes.

Mr. LYNN. Except I would like to add that under Executive order a particular agency who has the operational responsibility, and that agency's head—say, Mr. Colby in CIA—has the primary responsibility to put the lines around information that should be classified.

Our function is more or less an interpretive function as to what is within those general guidelines to carry out within our own shop what his overall determination has been. As you know, that authority stems basically from statutes.

So we have to mechanically perform a function on our own material that we are working on within our own shop. The general guidance as to the categories of things that have to be classified comes from the people delegated that authority under the Executive order.

Mr. TREEN. I am trying to determine whether OMB has any impact on the classification process.

If I understand you correctly. If when you receive material it is classified by an agency, you don't reverse that, nor do you take unclassified material and stamp it classified in the OMB, correct?

Mr. Ogilvie. We do originate some classification ourselves.

Mr. Treen. Do you have written criteria for that within OMB?

Mr. Ogilvie. I believe they are written; yes, sir. Let me also point out that whenever we classify a document within OMB if it is not someone else's document, if it is something we originated, the name of the individual who classifies that document is written on a special stamp on the front page which says this document has been classified at a certain level of classification, by Donald Ogilvie in this case, and then sets out the procedures for declassifying it according to a prescribed set of schedules.

Mr. Treen. You have written documents that set forth this classification procedure?

Mr. Ogilvie. Yes.

Mr. Treen. How many levels of classification do you have?

Mr. Ogilvie. Confidential, secret, and top secret are the standard classification levels.

Mr. Treen. Thank you.

Chairman Pike. Mr. Dellums.

Mr. Dellums. Thank you, Mr. Chairman. Mr. Lynn, can you tell me first what security classification you hold?

Secondly, what procedures did you go through and when did you go through those procedures in order to obtain your security clearance?

Mr. Lynn. I know that I hold the classifications through top secret. In connection with the budget activities which, as I say gets into substantial detail, I was asked to sign additional documents that made me aware of the particularly sensitive nature of the materials and what my obligations were under the law with respect to those materials.

I believe I signed four such documents.

Frankly, I think it was a useful procedure. The documents did not say anything more than I would expect to do as a person in my job.

Mr. Dellums. When did you go through those procedures?

Mr. Lynn. Before I had my first briefings with respect to the intelligence community. That was some weeks or a month beforehand, I don't remember which.

Mr. Dellums. Is it a fact that of the six or so employees assigned to the Intelligence Community Branch that three are former CIA agents and at least two have at least 10 years' service?

Mr. Lynn. I believe that is true, sir.

Mr. Dellums. Do you feel that would in any way affect the objectivity of those persons dealing with the CIA and especially other intelligence agencies?

Mr. Lynn. I would certainly hope it would not, sir.

I believe you have to look at each person for his or her own ability, imagination, drive, and ability to do a job. I certainly would think that knowledge acquired over a period of years, assuming it is put to work properly, is extremely useful. I feel that way not only about the intelligence community, but also a number of other economic and social areas. That doesn't mean we should have everybody coming from a given industry or group like the CIA. And there is room for generalists or I would not be sitting here this morning; but on the other hand, to say that a person cannot serve because he has had prior experience with a particular agency, I don't think that is right. I might point out that the man on my right, the Deputy at OMB, had his start in the systems business at the Veterans' Administration. I don't think I would want to disqualify Paul O'Neill from looking at Veterans' Administration matters.

Mr. DELLUMS. I can understand that with respect to Veterans' matters. However, the highly sensitive nature of the information with respect to the function of intelligence community certainly raises some critical and serious questions with respect to objectivity of those persons overseeing the function. As a lay person, representative I am sure of millions of people in this country, my first question would be where are the priorities in terms of loyalty, to OMB or to the agency that trained them for 10 years, recruited them? How do you handle that issue?

I know you are talking about fine persons but what procedures do you use to build in objectivity and at what point do you evaluate whether or not that particular person or those particular persons are being subjective or that their preliminary loyalties are to the company rather than to OMB and to its overall function that you have?

Mr. LYNN. You do as exhaustive a job as you can in the recruitment process and you continuously look at a person's judgment on various matters to see where loyalties are.

I don't limit that to the CIA. When I was in the Commerce Department and had people that came from the business side, I would always look at it the same way. I will say my general experience in the 6½ years that I have been in this town is that although there may be exceptions—and there are always exceptions—the general thing I find is that when people come from a given sector, they are kind of like Caesar's wife, if anything. To show they don't have any bias, they will lean over the other way. That is not always so, but if you count majorities, that is what I have found generally.

Mr. DELLUMS. Mr. Lynn, in your position with OMB, have you had an opportunity to look at the instances of CIA—former CIA employees working in any other agencies, and do you have any particular idea with respect to the numbers?

Mr. LYNN. I have not taken a personal look at any of that, sir.

Mr. OGILVIE. If I could add to that, sir; for all agencies and departments OMB reviews the numbers of people on detail to any one agency, and we treat the CIA no differently in that regard.

Chairman PIKE. The time of the gentleman has expired.

Mr. Murphy.

Mr. MURPHY. Thank you, Mr. Chairman.

Mr. Lynn, under the functions of OMB, one of the official functions includes the following:

To keep the President informed of the progress of activities by agencies of Government with respect to work proposed, work actually initiated, and work completed.

From that general description of the functions of OMB and your duty to inform the President of activities proposed, activities actually initiated, and activities completed, would it be safe to assume then that in intelligence activities of a major undertaking such as the Cuban invasion, the President of the United States would be aware of whatever activity is proposed of that magnitude?

Mr. LYNN. Again, just using this as a base in your question for size of activity, and again drawing on my experience as a layman— because I was not even with the Government at that time and was reading about those descriptions in the paper—whoever organized all of this, I would think the President of the United States would be aware of activities of that kind.

Mr. MURPHY. Would he be informed of a transfer of ownership or control of a number, a large number, of former World War II warplanes to a private domestic corporation for transfer or sale to an outside country or corporation?

Mr. LYNN. I don't know, sir.

Don, can you be of any help on that?

I just don't know.

Mr. OGILVIE. Are you referring to some specific event that occurred?

Mr. MURPHY. I am referring to a sale of aircraft, 25 or 26 World War II bombers.

Mr. LYNN. If there were such a thing, would the President know?

Mr. MURPHY. Would the President know of a transfer of that magnitude?

Mr. OGILVIE. Let me see if I can answer this way, Mr. Murphy. The DOD has an official program to dispose of surplus military hardware. That is a routine function that goes on all the time. Some aircraft and other military vehicles are routinely sold or disposed of within this country. I believe, although I am not sure of this, that foreign countries are also eligible if they receive the proper permission to acquire that type of materials, also. Whether the President would be specifically aware of each and every sale, I don't think it would be fair to say he would be of each and every sale.

Mr. MURPHY. Would he be aware of a transfer from any other department to CIA?

Mr. OGILVIE. It is hard to take a hypothetical example and say he was or was not aware. He certainly could be aware, and there are details, records kept of all transfers and sales.

Mr. MURPHY. One of your functions is to keep him advised of inter-agency activities?

Mr. OGILVIE. That is correct.

Mr. MURPHY. My 5 minutes is fleeting, but what is the total amount spent in all intelligence agencies?

I don't think that should be classified since it would not involve details. I am looking for a lump sum figure.

Mr. LYNN. I wondered how long it was going to take to have that question raised. I would refer to the sections of the law that very carefully provide for a method so that that figure or any figures on these budgets are kept classified and are kept secret. There are statutes passed by the Congress to prevent that kind of thing from becoming a public figure.

While I do believe it is a very legitimate inquiry area for this committee to consider and make recommendations as to how much, if any, of that budget information should be made public, I do not believe that I can in public session give those figures.

Mr. MURPHY. Not even the total?

Mr. LYNN. No, sir. I believe first of all that I would be violating the laws of the United States to do so.

I believe the intent of Congress on the whole is pretty clear from the statutes that have been passed. Now, again in closed session with appropriate security arrangements, we want to be as cooperative as can be. I think with the directions given by these statutes and with the laws that I am even told by counsel may involve criminal violation on my part, I don't believe I can do that in open session.

Chairman PIKE. Mr. Murphy, your time has expired.

I am going to come slightly to your rescue here if I may interject, Mr. Lynn. We do have in the committee certain overall numbers which have been provided to the committee. You are certainly entitled to see them. The reason I started off my own questioning the way I did as to how these things are defined is because I frankly find the numbers, no matter how closely classified, designed as much to conceal as they are to reveal—not out of bad motivation, but just because nobody really knows what is included in and what is included out.

You can include all kinds of things in, and you can include all kinds of things out. We have some numbers. They are available for all the members of the committee.

Mr. LYNN. Mr. Chairman, I don't know what level of figures you have been given.

Chairman PIKE. Since you have the security clearances, I will send it down to you.

Mr. LYNN. Are you sure you do not want to check first?

Chairman PIKE. I presume that a person of your stature in the President's establishment would breeze through a security clearance rather easily.

Mr. LYNN. Thank you, Mr. Chairman.

Mr. Chairman, what I would have to say is I am sure you can get much more detail than that——

Chairman PIKE. You are not only sure we can get much more detail——

Mr. LYNN. We have more detail than that. Mr. Colby has even more detail than that and I would suggest under the appropriate arrangements of the session that you can get into quite a bit of depth.

Chairman PIKE. We are going to get into depth and let there be no question about that.

My point is not whether we can get more detail than that. My point is that those particular numbers do not include huge chunks of dollars which are used in gathering intelligence. That is my only point.

Mr. LYNN. If you have that feeling, Mr. Chairman, again I think in closed session, primarily with Mr. Colby, where we can be of assistance, of course, we would be happy to help.

Chairman PIKE. We will go into that in executive session. I would certainly not expect you to go into this in open session.

Mr. Kasten.

Mr. KASTEN. Thank you, Mr. Chairman.

Mr. Lynn, what happens to intelligence agency funds that are left over at the end of the fiscal year? Are they returned to the Treasury?

Mr. LYNN. Mr. Kasten, respectfully, I think that we ought to leave that for closed session if we might.

As I say, we are perfectly willing to testify on that and I know that Mr. Colby is but I think we should do that in closed session.

Mr. KASTEN. Would it be possible for a given agency to retain unexpended funds and to develop an ongoing slush fund that could be used and the expenditures from that slush fund, if this were possible, would not be reflected in the budget statement of that agency?

Mr. LYNN. I think my answer should be the same.

Mr. KASTEN. Would it be possible for an agency to develop a fund like this and that fund would not be recycled through an appropriate process?

Mr. LYNN. Mr. Kasten, again I will, in closed session with Mr. Colby, be more than willing to get into the whole area of how funds come in, how funds go out, what our role is, what the possibilities are for abuse, if any, and so on, but I don't believe in public session I should do so.

Mr. KASTEN. The Rockefeller Commission Report on pages 74 and 75 states the following: "Although the Director [of the CIA] has statutory authority to spend reserve funds without consulting OMB, administrative practice requires that he first obtain the approval of OMB and the chairmen of the Appropriations Subcommittees of the Congress."

"Administrative practice requires" is the phrase I am concentrating on. What does this really mean, in fact?

I think you can understand the question by—and I don't want to use up the time——

Mr. LYNN. I am trying to find where you were quoting from.

Mr. KASTEN. I haven't the document before me. "Although the Director [of the CIA] has statutory authority to spend reserve funds without consulting OMB, administrative practice requires that he first obtain the approval of OMB and the Chairmen of the Appropriations Subcommittees of the Congress."

What, in fact, does this mean? The question is, does the CIA Director legally have to obtain congressional and/or OMB approval or does he receive such approval merely as a courtesy to the Congress?

Mr. OGILVIE. I think the best way to describe it is that it is an OMB-established requirement. The Director of CIA is not able to use such funds without the approval of the Office of Management and Budget.

Mr. KASTEN. OMB has established this requirement. Does the CIA Director legally have to obtain congressional and/or OMB approval to spend such funds or does he seek such approval merely as a courtesy to OMB and the Congress?

In other words, if the Director of the CIA chose not to seek such approval, would he be in violation of the law?

Mr. OGILVIE. I don't honestly know whether there is a statute prohibiting the Director of CIA from doing that. I do know he would not in fact do it without our approval.

Mr. LYNN. I think, Mr. Kasten, we have many rules at OMB, quite apart from the intelligence community, that go back to our basic function, our basic operation, and the operation is defined very generally in the law dating back to 1920 and 1921, and when we do put out a rule or establish a practice, agencies and departments are supposed to follow it.

Now, I suppose if some person in any agency chose to contest that rule, we would end up, the both of us, with the President of the United States as to whether the rule were appropriate. That would be true in the intelligence community or another department or agency.

Mr. KASTEN. On another subject, it is my understanding—and this is going back to a question of the gentleman from California, Mr. Dellums—that basicaly five individuals at OMB do day to day work on the foreign intelligence budget.

Mr. LYNN. Six.

Mr. KASTEN. One supervisor and five people who are doing the work is the way I interpreted that six.

Mr. LYNN. I would hate to say our supervisor doesn't do any work.

Mr. KASTEN. Is one of these people a Mr. Emory Donaldson who spent 20 years at the CIA and came to OMB directly from CIA in 1969?

Mr. OGILVIE. He works for us.

Mr. KASTEN. Did one William Mitchell spend 10 years with CIA before coming directly to OMB from CIA in 1963?

Mr. OGILVIE. That is correct.

Mr. KASTEN. Is the Director of the group of five people a Mr. Arnold Donahue who spent 5 years with CIA before coming to OMB directly from CIA in 1967?

Mr. OGILVIE. That is correct.

Mr. KASTEN. That is three out of five directly from the CIA. Am I correct that their counterpart at the CIA, Mr. Taylor, who is the Deputy Comptroller of the CIA, is a former CIA budget examiner for you, for OMB?

Mr. OGILVIE. I can't answer the question about Mr. Taylor because I don't know Mr. Taylor, but I can tell you it is three out of six instead of three out of five.

Chairman PIKE. The time of the gentleman has expired. He has used it very well but his time has expired.

ISSUES ON INTELLIGENCE RESOURCE MANAGEMENT ([90], Vol. 7, pp. 52–66)

The Murphy Commission report did not deal with any details on the functions of the intelligence community, but did address the manner in which resources should be managed and allocated. In the following paper, a Murphy Commission consultant, Robert Macy, examines policy recommendation options for the commission. These options were not addressed in any depth in the commission report, but do have relevance to any future review of management alternatives.

INTRODUCTION

This paper is concerned with issues in the management of foreign intelligence collection activities for purposes of supporting U.S. foreign policy, particularly those activities carried on by the Central Intelligence Agency (CIA), the Department of Defense (DOD), and U.S. Embassies. There have been a number of significant changes and improvements in the management of the Intelligence Community in recent years, so that in preparing this paper it was necessary to rely primarily on interviews for background, not on published documents which are usually dated. The Community has a number of minor management problems which could have been identified in this paper, but it was considered more constructive to concentrate on a few major issues. If these important issues can be resolved, most of the others will probably fall into place.

I have also been asked to consider alternative roles for intelligence consumers in determining intelligence expenditures or in funding the acquisition of special intelligence products. This proposal arises from the fact that, for consumers within the U.S. Government, most finished intelligence is essentially a "free good." To illustrate its importance, suppose an Assistant Secretary of State needed certain intelligence that could be obtained by very expensive reconnaissance photography, and that only

an inferior product could be obtained from overt sources. He might be unwilling to pay for the more expensive photography, if the money to pay for it had to come out of his own budget.

The basic idea of making the intelligence consumer more cost conscious through requiring him to pay for the intelligence has merit. However, there appears to be no practical way to achieve such a result. For example, suppose certain finished intelligence were produced from raw data collected by the National Security Agency (NSA) and from certain agents, and partially confirmed by overt sources. 200 persons were involved in its preparation. Dr. Kissinger was then briefed for 30 minutes on this intelligence. How much should he pay for it? He did not know in advance what the intelligence included. He may already have known most of it through personal conversations with foreign diplomats. Or, if Dr. Kissinger received 10 telephone calls last week, each including some intelligence, would he have to pay some pro-rata amount for such information? How much? How would such payments affect the allocation of intelligence resources?

Suppose NSA has tried very hard for 5 years to crack the top codes of three countries, but with no success so far. However, if such codes could be broken, the results would probably be dramatic and five U.S. Departments would be very much affected. Should these five departments share the cost of this part of the NSA operation even though no finished intelligence was produced? If the amounts each agreed to pay did not cover the total cost of the NSA operation, would it be terminated?

How far would you go with the above idea? Would CIA have to pay for all Embassy cables? Would AID have to pay for all foreign agricultural reports of the Department of Agriculture? Imagine just the paperwork involved.

Suppose the State Department was unwilling to pay for reconnaissance photography. Would that mean that State would not be permitted to see any of the results of this photography in the future?

If the payments by consumers were restricted to intelligence consumers within the Department or Agency now producing the intelligence, at least some of the problems mentioned above would be avoided. However, the intelligence collected by DOD, for example, now includes a lot of economic intelligence of use only to other Departments and Agencies. Who within DOD would pay for it? The reconnaissance photography is of vital importance to the Secretary of Defense and the Joint Chiefs of Staff. Does it make sense to give the Air Force the choice of spending a given amount of money on the reconnaissance program or on other Air Force activities? If the Army refuses to pay for reconnaissance photography, does this mean the Army will not be permitted to see the results of this intelligence activity?

I do not think this whole idea will stand close examination, and have not discussed it in this report.

I. BACKGROUND

The following notes are presented as background information for a review of the issues and options presented in this report. It is assumed that the reader has some knowledge of the structure and operation of the Central Intelligence Agency, and the intelligence activities of the Department of Defense.

1. THE SCHLESINGER REPORT

The intelligence situation was reviewed by the Schlesinger Study Group at the Office of Management and Budget (OMB) in 1971. It was found that there was virtually no policy level guidance to the Intelligence Community on substantive intelligence needs. It was also concluded that the review of the quality, scope and timeliness of the Intelligence Community product was neither systematic nor continuing. The President instructed Dr. Kissinger to set up the National Security Council Intelligence Committee (NSCIC) (a) to provide guidance on national substantive intelligence needs, and (b) to provide continuing evaluation of intelligence products.

The NSCIC was established in late 1971, and had one 30 minute meeting a month later. Over two and a half years elapsed before the next meeting, which lasted for a little over an hour. The working group of the Committee met once in April 1973, and was reactivated after the August 23 meeting in anticipation of another Committee meeting which was held in October, 1974.

The President's instruction to provide policy level guidance on intelligence needs through the NSCIC was not met, but the DCI attempted to provide a substitute in the form of Key Intelligence Questions (KIQs), which were developed by collectors and processors, not consumers at the policy level. The KIQs were sent to the various members of the NSCIC for guidance, and useful reactions were obtained, particularly from the DOD.

The President's request for continuing evaluation of intelligence products also has not been met. Several "crises" studies were conducted by the Intelligence Community. No formal evaluations have been completed, and there is no mechanism so far for continuing review. The past crises studies did provide some guidance for refining and strengthening the KIQs.

The President also requested Dr. Kissinger as Assistant to the President for National Security Affairs to establish a Net Assessment Group in the NSC staff for product review and production of net assessments. A small group was established, but no net assessments were produced, and the group was transferred to the Pentagon in the summer of 1973.

The Schlesinger Report included an evaluation of the DCI. He was considered too absorbed in the day-to-day operations of the CIA. The involvement of his personal staff in the management of the Intelligence Community was regarded as minimal and generally ineffective. The limited management of the Community that did take place was handled largely by the U.S. Intelligence Board (USIB) and its many subcommittees that operated largely through consensus and a lot of log-rolling between agencies.

The Intelligence Community Staff

President Nixon directed the DCI in November 1971 to exercise positive leadership in planning, reviewing and evaluating intelligence programs; and to restructure and strengthen his personal staff to accomplish this. Since that time, the DCI's personal staff—the Intelligence Community (IC) Staff —has been very substantially expanded and has become much more involved in Community management and planning.

The IC staff introduced the KIQs program as an annual guide for collection of intelligence. The most recent KIQs are too general and insufficiently selective. They do not clearly define which collection resources should be used for answering the various questions.

The difficulties involved in compiling the KIQs are formidable. If you ask the intelligence processors and consumers what they need from the collectors, they may ask for everything they can think of because it is "free." In theory some arrangement ought to be feasible for having the consumer pay for intelligence and thus restrict his demands to his priority needs, but there appears to be no practical way to introduce this "user charge" principle into the intelligence collection process.

"Crises" studies have been used to analyze the adequacy of intelligence for a past crisis and thus to obtain useful guidance for refining the KIQs. Members of the NSCIC have been asked to review the KIQs, and useful comments were received, particularly from DOD.

The KIQs appear to be one of those management tools that cannot be administered through the routine institutionalized consensus approach. The experienced collectors of intelligence know which collection resources are really worthwhile and which are not, but they are not going to jeopardize their own programs by volunteering the information. In situations like this, and in the absence of helpful guidance from the NSCIC, the DCI must rely on the IC Staff to make the KIQs realistic and useful.

In the Presidential directive of November, 1971, the DCI was also instructed to prepare and submit through OMB a consolidated intelligence program budget, including technical intelligence, and to "allocate all intelligence resources." That assignment is particularly difficult for an official who has only a Presidential directive, whereas DOD, which has 85% of intelligence resources, has a statutory base for allocating them. This whole subject will be discussed later in this report.

The Intelligence Resources Advisory Committee

The Presidential directive included instructions to establish an Intelligence Resources Advisory Committee (IRAC) to advise on the consolidated budget and the allocation of resources. IRAC was designed to advise the DCI on intelligence collection resources in much the same way that USIB advises him on finished intelligence production. IRAC meets regularly and has active working groups, but the DCI, who is Chairman of IRAC, regularly runs into resistance from DOD whenever he tries to use IRAC to look into all of the DOD intelligence programs other than the technical reconnaissance programs, which are jointly managed by DOD and the DCI.

IRAC has been controversial. Its members have certainly benefited by gaining a much deeper understanding of the collection activities and problems of other members of the Community. The Committee has been helpful to the DCI in identifying some of the major collection resource issues. However, each member tends to be so defensive about his own organization's resources that IRAC has great difficulty obtaining a consensus on collection priorities or on shifts of resources between agencies.

On-going Programs

If IRAC has serious shortcomings, just how will the DCI maintain effective surveillance over ongoing programs? There is a natural tendency to concentrate on proposals for new projects. In preparing the annual budget, it is a great temptation to accept 80% to 90% of the budget items uncritically because they are about the same size as last year, or within budget guidelines for increases, and to concentrate nearly all of the budget review on new proposals. The end result is that a substantial part of the various programs of the U.S. Government may be continued for a number of years without critical review. Fifty percent or more of today's product line of a well managed U.S. industrial company may not even have existed 5 years ago. We

need an aggressive policy of keeping the "product line" of the U.S. Intelligence Community up to date.

It is certainly reasonable to expect a heavy turnover of intelligence collection methods and kinds of material collected. There has been a technological revolution in collection techniques during the past 15 years that is still going on. The increased sophistication of local internal security and counterintelligence programs around the world is obviously affecting the collection techniques that will work in a given country, e.g., in cracking codes and recruiting high level agents in many countries. Additionally, it is becoming much easier to collect useful information overtly, as developing countries build highways, remove travel restrictions, introduce greatly improved national statistical systems, expand their technical publications, etc. Last but not least, U.S. intelligence needs for supporting U.S. foreign policy change over time. For example, there is a growing need for economic intelligence, part of which can be obtained by more thorough exploitation of information in U.S. domestic agencies.

One way to force a review of the "base"—of the ongoing programs—is to maintain a very tight budget, or even to cut the budget, as has happened in the Intelligence Community during the past few years. Experience shows, however, that too often a tight budget results in a delay in introducing improvements rather than drastic cuts in low priority items. Alternatively, management may take the easy way out and introduce a horizontal cut. A somewhat more sophisticated approach is to introduce performance budgeting that helps to identify activities that are not measuring up. In any event, it seems clear that a tight or reduced budget by itself does not guarantee a careful review of ongoing projects.

The sharply reduced budget of the Intelligence Community in recent years has undoubtedly forced the elimination of a lot of overstaffing in some ongoing programs and a much harder look at some on-going and proposed new technical collection programs that were formerly examined almost wholly from the standpoint of technical feasibility. We need more sophisticated approaches, however, for continuing future reviews of on-going programs by DCI.

IRAC and the ICS should be able to identify those on-going collection programs that are not working well or are obsolete. For example, a review of scientific journals from around the world is proving to be more rewarding than scientific espionage activities. It is well known that espionage activities in general are becoming less and less effective in many countries. There was not time during this study to investigate how much of a lag may exist in weeding out collection activities that have outlived their usefulness, but the DCI's hand may be too weak to force the termination of low-priority collection programs on a timely basis. Indeed, the DCI apparently must use military officers on active duty to head up the IC staff so that this staff is acceptable to DOD.

Another aspect of updating on-going programs is the need to insure that, when new techniques are accepted, old techniques that they replace are dropped. The IRAC is in a good position to propose such action, particularly because high level research officials of DOD have been tapped for

IRAC meetings. Also, the DCI has the IC staff and the CIA's Office of Research and Development available for such purposes. It has been suggested that the termination of old techniques be a condition for using new techniques after the latter have been thoroughly field-tested.

The really difficult part of the review of on-going collection programs involves the impact of changing U.S. foreign policy on collection requirements. This leads us back to the lack of policy level guidance on substantive intelligence needs discussed earlier in this paper.

In summary, the DCI has been handicapped in keeping a tight rein on on-going collection programs of the Community because of his lack of authority, certain fundamental weaknesses of IRAC for such purposes, an IC staff dominated by military officers (and only one Foreign Service Officer), and an inactive NSCIC. This matter will be discussed further in connection with program guidance by the DCI for the consolidated intelligence budget.

Department of Defense

The Schlesinger Study concluded that the Secretary of Defense did not exercise strong leadership over DOD intelligence resources, that his staff support was diffused, and that programs were not well coordinated. The Presidential Directive provided for (1) a broadening of the DCI's responsibilities to include tactical intelligence (referred to by some on the ICS as "military forces support"), (2) the establishment of a National Cryptological Command for Signals Intelligence (SIGINT), (3) the establishment of a single Office of Defense Investigations, and (4) the estabalishment of a Defense Map Agency.

The Presidential instruction to include tactical intelligence in the coordination responsibilities of the DCI has been implemented. For years there had been a recognition that the historic distinction between tactical intelligence and national intelligence would not stand close scrutiny. For example, the sighting of a submarine may be initially classified as tactical intelligence but a few days later become national intelligence. This broadening of the DCI's collection coordination responsibilities is a significant improvement.

The Presidential instruction to establish a unified National Cryptological Command for SIGINT under the Director of NSA has not been fully implemented. This move was opposed by the OSD staff, the JCS, and CIA, and so very little was done about it. It might be added that the Consolidated Cryptological Program (CCP), operated by the Director of NSA, appears to be more controversial than the other DOD intelligence programs. The collection activities in the field have been cut back sharply as part of the intelligence budget cuts in recent years. The intercept stations overseas have been heavy users of expensive manpower, but are now being more fully automated.

The Presidential instruction to establish a single Office of Defense Investigations out of the investigative agencies of the three military services has been implemented. The investigators handle counterintelligence and security checks on DOD personnel.

Action has also been taken to implement the President's directive to merge the mapping agencies of the three military services into one Defense Mapping Agency. These mappers make important use of reconnaissance photographs and have mapped the entire globe.

In 1972 another promising step was taken: the establishment of the Office of Assistant Secretary of Defense for Intelligence. Its impact has been less than had been expected, but over time it should make an important contribution, particularly in terms of coordinating collection resources.

The largest intelligence program is the technical reconnaissance program. Its output is widely regarded as the most valuable in the Intelligence Community, and it has enjoyed top priority for available intelligence funds. This program is run according to a joint DOD-DCI management plan. Both DOD and the DCI spend large sums for research on this program.

Over the years, the introduction of technical intelligence collection methods by DOD (and to a lesser extent by CIA) has led to the necessity for obtaining rights to install technical collection equipment such as CCP intercept stations in other countries. Some form of "bribery," such as military and economic assistance programs of unusual size or duration, are usually involved. Thus, the true cost of technical intelligence programs may be substantially higher than indicated by their budgets. It is proposed that the DCI seek policy guidance from the NSCIC on this whole matter, and then conduct a joint study with DOD of the true cost of technical intelligence equipment and staff located overseas to determine if we are not paying too high a price for their use in some countries. It is recognized that the analysis will be complicated in some countries by the presence also of military base rights.

2. CONSOLIDATED INTELLIGENCE COMMUNITY BUDGET

As a result of the President's November 1971 directive, the DCI has pulled together Consolidated Community Budgets for two years, and is now working on the third one. This Consolidated Budget is prepared with the help of the IRAC, sent to the President through the OMB, and defended before the Congressional Subcommittees on intelligence matters. (There has never been a leak of information from these Congressional Subcommittees.) The budgets of some of the Intelligence Community members were reduced sharply over a three year period, and the Consolidated Budget is now being held at approximately a stable total dollar amount which is not expected to increase significantly during the next several years. This fiscal policy is forcing further decreases in numbers of personnel and procurement of hardware because of inflation.

Since there can only be one President's budget, the figures in the Consolidated Community Budget must agree exactly with the figures in the individual budgets of Community members. Thus, the preparation of the individual budgets and the consolidated budget must be very closely coordinated. The first year there was not much time for the DCI to prepare the Consolidated Community Budget, and it consisted largely of a summary statistical compilation of the various member budgets plus some thoughtful discussions of considerations involved in such an exercise. The second year the DCI had more time to prepare the Consolidated

Budget, and made a start toward influencing the budget substantively, but the DCI's impact was not very great. Both the OMB and DCI felt that the timing of the DOD budget cycle was such that there was almost no time to consider any major issues that might be raised through the Consolidated Budget process.

Although the DCI may have had less impact than was hoped for in the size and contents of the Consolidated Budget, it is understood that the Congressional Subcommittees of the appropriation committees reviewing this Budget found it very helpful in giving them a better perspective on the activities of the whole Community, and were pleased with the presentations by the DCI. Attention is now focused on next year's budget preparation.

The problems faced by the DCI in preparing a consolidated budget include the following:

a. IRAC may raise budgetary problems, but it is not a suitable committee in which to obtain a consensus on collection priorities or on shifts of resources between agencies, because each member feels defensive about his own budget.

b. The DOD has legislative authority to prepare its budget, but the DCI has only a Presidential directive to prepare the consolidated budget, including the intelligence categories of the DOD budget. In a showdown the DOD would probably win.

c. If the DCI has difficulty in prevailing on a substantive issue in the DOD's intelligence budget, such issues could be taken to the NSCIC for decision, but the NSCIC has not been meeting regularly. The DCI also has the option of sending recommendations to the President with the Consolidated Budget.

d. It is not clear whether the DCI should be concerned only about substantive issues, or also play an active role in determining fiscal policy controlling the preparation of the consolidated budget. The DOD budget has fiscal guidelines which were worked out with the Military Division of OMB that presumably cover all of the DOD budget. The International Affairs Division of OMB is responsible for intelligence programs of the Community. The working relationship between the two divisions of OMB, the DCI, and the Controller in DOD are understandably complex and unique and still appear to leave something to be desired.

e. It was probably assumed when the DCI was asked to prepare a Consolidated Intelligence Budget that it would be sent to the OMB in the Fall at the same time OMB received the individual budget submission from the members of the Intelligence Community. Thus, the OMB could review the intelligence categories in the members' budgets and the DCI's proposals in the latter's Consolidated Budget at the same time. Unfortunately, the DOD budget submission is on a different time schedule. Many years ago, the Military Division of OMB adopted the unorthodox procedure of holding joint hearings with the Controller's office of DOD on the DOD budget, lasting into December each year. Thus, the usual time interval between the submission of a departmental or agency budget to the OMB and the completion of the Presidential budget in late December does not exist, so the DCI has to sit in on the regular budget hearings in order to get his views presented to OMB in time to be considered.

f. Ideally, the DCI would work out substantive program guidelines early in the budget cycle for the guidance of those preparing the various individual budgets included in the consolidated Intelligence Community. At this time it is doubtful if the IC staff has a sufficiently detailed knowledge of all of the intelligence programs in DOD to prepare comprehensive guidelines. Concentration on a few priority issues is one answer.

Experience to date suggests the need to take a hard look at the President's directive of November 1971 regarding a Consolidated Intelligence Budget. The Secretary of Defense, for example, has statutory responsibilities for keeping a close watch on military capabilities and actions around the world. It is difficult to see how you can build a fence around his intelligence activities and assign authority to the DCI to "allocate all intelligence resources" without in effect assigning responsibility to the Secretary of Defense for activities over which he does not have authority.

On the other hand, it is suggested that the basic idea behind the President's November 1971 directive providing for the DCI to send to him through the OMB a consolidated budget with his recommendations is basically sound. The DCI is in much the best position to take a broad look at where the Community has been and where it ought to go, and recommend to the President the key actions that should be taken and incorporated into the consolidated budget. The DCI cannot achieve such an objective, however, by making suggestions in joint OMB/DOD budget hearings in the Pentagon where he has little more than an observer status (except for the technical reconnaissance programs).

It has been suggested that the solution lies in the direction of giving the DCI statutory authority over the Consolidated Intelligence Budget. This would be a mistake, not only because of the position in which it would leave the Secretary of Defense, with his responsibility for activities over which he did not have authority, but also because of the risks involved in exposing the DCI's and CIA's basic authorities to amendment in the Congress. Intelligence activities are unusually controversial at this time, and some very undesirable amendments might be initiated and approved by the Congress.

A more promising approach would appear to be as follows. The DCI would not get involved in budget details. He would not be concerned with "whether they should buy 9 or 12 airplanes, but whether there should be any airplanes in the budget." He would select perhaps not more than six very major issues in the DOD intelligence programs. Careful studies of these issues would be made by the IC staff, and there would be discussion in IRAC. The DCI's recommendations on these six items would be sent to the President for approval via the NSCIC (or perhaps the Council on International Economic Policy where appropriate), fairly early in the budget cycle. Decisions by the President would be forwarded not later than perhaps 1 August by the DCI to DOD for incorporation in its intelligence budget.

In addition to the Presidentially approved decisions, the DCI would also forward to the DOD at about the same time a list of important programs or projects that should be sharply reduced or eliminated. Such a listing would not only help promote a more intensive look at on-going programs during the joint OMB/DOD review but would help to blunt an effort to get the intelligence budget total raised if the Presidential decisions proposed above involved a net increase in expenditures.

DCI representatives should still attend OMB/DOD joint budget reviews, but largely for purposes of background information.

Looking to the future, the staff of the DCI is well aware of the shortcomings of the management information systems of the Intelligence Community which are addressed primarily to accounting and fiscal criteria. These systems are not designed to relate resources allocations to substantive tasks and information, and they are not a good management tool today to measure the effectiveness with which revenues meet requirements. There is a need for a better system for tying the budget and program review together.

3. ECONOMIC INTELLIGENCE

The CIA and most of the rest of the Intelligence Community were designed and staffed for the Cold War period of the 1950s. Since then we have entered a period of détente and lessened tensions overseas. Today we need an Intelligence Community capable of meeting not only the continuing requirement for secret intelligence in the interests of national security, but also the overriding challenges of providing solid intelligence on worldwide inflation, food shortages, energy crises, narcotics control, and so on. Can this challenge be met as additional tasks by the Community? Or does the situation call for a more fundamental reorientation?

This issue is important not just in terms of helping our President to meet his priority concerns. It is also important in terms of continuing Congressional and public support of CIA. Political action programs to fight Communism no longer have unqualified support. Support of military actions seems to be at an all-time low. If, however, the CIA could clearly identify itself as one of those working toward solutions to our domestic and world-wide economic problems, its image might be significantly improved.

Let us consider the environment within which the DCI works today. The basic authority for the DCI and CIA is the National Security Act and a related piece of legislation, enacted in the late 1940s and concerned with the Cold War. The personal staff of the DCI for coordinating the Intelligence Community, known as the IC staff, is directed by military officers on active duty. About 85% of the Community Budget is for the Department of Defense. Policy guidance is supposed to be supplied by the NSCIC, which is chaired by an Assistant to the President who in the past has shown little interest in the field of economics, plus the Deputy Secretary of State, the Deputy Secretary of Defense, and the Chairman of the Joint Chiefs of Staff, the DCI, and the Under Secretary of the Treasury for Monetary Affairs. The CIA chiefs of station overseas are preoccupied with such responsibilities as recruiting agents, and it is reported that few of them have any capabilities or interest in the field of economic intelligence. This does not appear to be an ideal environment for grappling with many, perhaps most, of the crucial intelligence needs of the next decade.

It is true that CIA has the best group of economic intelligence analysts in Washington, that a subcommittee of USIB is concerned with economic intelligence, and that one of the 11 National Intelligence Officers (NIOs) is concerned with economic matters.

However, until the past few years economic intelligence was largely focused on Russia and China, and was often collected for purposes of estimating the war making potential of a given country, not for support of programs to cure the economic ills of the United States and elsewhere.

More recently there have been some very significant developments in the management of U.S. economic policy, both foreign and domestic, which took place well outside the well known "Nixon-Kissinger orbit." At the top was the Committee on International Economic Policy (CIEP), run by senior officials in the White House and the Treasury Department. In addition, several "problem-oriented" committees were established to grapple with such matters as trade, monetary policy, and oil. CIA officials concerned with intelligence on such matters quickly established working relationships with these committees and have been very responsive to their needs for economic intelligence on a worldwide basis. Relationships have been very flexible up to this time with commendable initiative being shown by both consumers and producers of intelligence. A very high percentage of the intelligence provided these committees has been based on specific requests, such as for international negotiations. In some cases this flow of intelligence has been facilitated by "brokers" attached to committees who are knowledgeable about both intelligence production and intelligence needs.

Four Treasury officials, either on loan from or with backgrounds in the Intelligence Community, brief the Secretary of the Treasury and his Deputy on current intelligence early each morning, and then brief the Secretaries and other high officials of domestic departments such as Commerce and Agriculture later each morning. These briefings are done with the full knowledge and support of the DCI. It might be added that, during the past two years, collection agencies have had their priority requirements extended beyond the military area to cover world-wide economic intelligence, through the KIQs, and CIA has recently produced excellent weekly summaries on such topics as trade and energy.

The various ramifications of the world's economic ills are still being sorted out, and Mr. Rush's departure from the White House staff has left the top guidance for our economic policy making temporarily in a fluid state. It seems clear, however, that much progress has been made at high levels in coming to grips with our world-wide economic problems, and that economic intelligence is not an important limiting factor at this time.

Looking to the future, there appear to be several issues that will have to be resolved. Should these problem-oriented committees dealing with world-wide economic problems eventually be drawn into the NSC orbit? Or should CIA's present orientation to the NSC be broadened to encompass a separate complex of high level economic committees as major consumers? Should the KIQs be screened by these new committees? Should the NSCIC's mandate to provide policy level substantive intelligence requirements guidance be shared with the CIEP? If the old Board of Requirements is revived, should it be attached to the NSCIC or to the CIEP? Should the DCI present the Consolidated Intelligence Budget not only to the Armed Services Committee on the Hill but also to appropriate economic-oriented committees? Should CIA publish more unclassified economic intelligence digests? And so on.

4. U.S. EMBASSIES

The DCI and CIA have a large stake today in the operation of U.S. Embassies because they provide cover for most of CIA activities overseas. The DCI in his role as coordinator of collection activities overseas is also intensely interested in "collection" activities of others in the form of Embassy political and economic reports, data collected by agricultural and treasury attaches, military attaches, etc. No matter what this overtly collected information is called, it is raw intelligence to the producers of finished intelligence in Washington.

The DCI has become very interested in the quality of reporting by the various personnel attached to U.S. Embassies, and may initiate a policy of sending U.S. Ambassadors a letter once a year in which the Embassy reporting is evaluated. It is anticipated that such letters will stimulate improvements before the next letters of evaluation are sent out.

Such a letter makes sense if properly coordinated with the Secretary of State, and provides a more formal recognition that the DCI's responsibilities for coordinating collection of intelligence include various reporting activities of U.S. Embassies. If a given Ambassador receives "poor marks" for his reporting, one approach might be to have the Ambassador ask the CIA station chief to prepare a collection plan for all personnel attached to the Embassy which would identify the role to be played by each individual or office, taking into account instructions received by such individuals or offices from their headquarters in Washington. The CIA chief of station would also advise the U.S. Ambassador on a collection program that would identify priority collection requirements and restrict clandestine collection to those items that could not be obtained overtly. The chief of station would also be held responsible for evaluating the effectiveness and efficiency of the implementation of the collection program as a whole. In carrying out these duties, the CIA chief of station would not attempt to exercise line authority over other than CIA personnel, but would act as an advisor to the U.S. Ambassador.

Progress reports on this comprehensive collection program would be sent via the Ambassador to State and to the DCI. Where major conflicts arose between the collection planning and the program desired by the U.S. Ambassador, and instructions received from their Washington headquarters by individuals and offices attached to the Embassy, the DCI would attempt to seek a reconciliation.

The above proposal is considered impractical at this time because CIA station chiefs typically have little proficiency or interest in economic and political reporting. Their training is aimed at such activities as recruiting agents. Nevertheless, the DCI's collection responsibilities would seemingly call for a long term program for maximizing the number of chiefs of station who could serve as the Ambassador's principal advisor on promoting the efficiency of all kinds of reporting. In the meantime, CIA regional specialists on such matters might be used.

II. PRINCIPAL ISSUES

The review of intelligence resource management indicates that there are a number of major issues on which the Commission on the Organization of the Government for the Conduct of Foreign Policy could make an important contribution. All of these issues are well known to senior members of the Intelligence Community, and most of them are under active discussion. In this paper an attempt is made to identify these issues and present several options for consideration.

The *first* issue is concerned with Presidential directives to impose the DCI between the Department of Defense and the President with respect to the programming and budgeting of intelligence resources. Such a move was first attempted back in 1961. It did not work. A second attempt was made in 1971 through President Nixon's directive (reaffirmed by President Ford in October 1974) implementing the recommendations of the Schlesinger study. Although there was considerable enthusiasm for this DCI "leadership" role in allocating intelligence resources during 1972 and 1973, today there is much disillusionment among key officials, and the time is ripe to consider the options.

The *second* issue is concerned with the future cost implications of budget decisions involving intelligence resources. This issue raises questions about multi-year budgets, five year plans, etc. Options on this issue are under current discussion in the Executive Branch and some actions have been taken. The Congressional budget reform legislation included provisions bearing directly on this issue.

The *third* issue is concerned with the rather disorganized, ad hoc situation prevailing today with respect to economic intelligence. Although the major problems involve top management of economic policy and the dispersal around Washington of economic intelligence analysts, there is also an economic intelligence resource aspect worth discussing.

The *fourth* issue is concerned with what action should be taken to provide a better substantive frame of reference for the operation of the intelligence community. More specifically, should there be a more conscious national strategy for the allocation and use of intelligence resources? How will such a strategy be developed?

III. ROLE OF DCI VIS-À-VIS THE DOD

Issue #1: *What steps should be taken to strengthen the hand of the DCI in fulfilling his responsibilities regarding the allocation of intelligence resources?*

Option A. The DCI would support a policy of collecting all of the raw intelligence that was technically feasible with a minimum of budgetary restraints; and would restrict his budgetary activities largely to (1) providing a forum (IRAC) for acquainting each member of the Intelligence Community with the others' programming and budgetary activities and problems, (2) obtaining a consensus when possible on issues brought before IRAC, and (3) preparing a compilation of various members' annual budgets for Congressional presentation.

For:

1. It is rather naive to think that the DCI could have much direct impact on the DOD budget when (a) the DOD budget includes 4/5 of the funds for foreign intelligence activities; (b) the Secretary of Defense has statutory authority for programming and budgeting intelligence activities, whereas the DCI has only a Presidential directive; (c) the strong intelligence policy guidance and support from Dr. Kissinger and his NSCIC, as contemplated in the Presidential Directive of November 1971, has not materialized; and (d) above all, it has always been true that only the OMB stands between the President and Departments and Agencies on budgetary matters.

2. Experience has shown that IRAC has real value for educational purposes, acquainting each member with each other's budgetary and programming problems, airing opposing points of view on various issues, and seeking a consensus where possible.

3. It would make sense to adopt a policy guideline of technical feasibility, with a minimum of fiscal and programming restraints, rather than rely on consumer requests in programming collection activities. It is not realistic to wait for users of intelligence to tell collectors what they need. Sometimes procurement and operational lead times of as much as two years or more are necessary for collecting certain kinds of intelligence. Furthermore, in this highly volatile world situation, it is just not feasible to set detailed priorities for intelligence collection needs.

4. Collectors are in a much better position than consumers to assess trends in collection needs and to make highly technical choices of alternative means for collecting raw intelligence.

Against:

1. Officials favoring this Option (and there are many) are saying in effect, "Just give us the money we need and leave us alone; we are the experts; we know best." The U.S. Government went through an extended period when there was comparatively little in the way of budget restraints or policy guidance, and the result was not only an overextended Intelligence Community but also a number of intelligence activities with excessive funding. The record clearly shows that an option similar to Option A leads to too many wasteful practices to be acceptable.

2. More specifically, periods in the past with conditions approximating those in Option A appeared to lead to (a) excessive preoccupation with technical innovations and technical challenges for collecting raw intelligence almost without regard to cost/benefit consideration, (b) the accumulation of a large amount of "fat" in intelligence expenditures, and (c) an environment which discouraged the DCI from exercising strong leadership in achieving coordinated and efficient operations within the Community.

3. The sharp cuts in intelligence budgets during the past few years, initiated largely by the OMB, do not seem to have resulted in significant shortages of raw intelligence, a clear indication that wasteful practices had been in effect.

4. IRAC, established by the Presidential Directive of November 1971, has been of value as noted above, but each member tends to be very defensive about his own organization's resources, so this Committee is not a good management tool for obtaining a consensus on collection priorities.

Option B: The DCI would make every effort to carry out the Presidential Directive of November 1971 to "allocate all intelligence resources" through making maximum use of IRAC, building up his IC staff, and preparing each year a Consolidated Intelligence Community Budget with his recommendations, for review by the President.

For:

1. Since the needs for foreign intelligence have expanded to many parts of the U.S. Government for an ever-widening number of purposes and since the collection resources are concentrated in DOD, and to a lesser extent in CIA, it stands to reason that there must be some neutral central point, such as the office of the DCI, responsible for allocating these resources in an objective and fair manner. Stated more bluntly, just because over 4/5 of the money is in the DOD budget, the allocation of collection resources should not necessarily be dominated by military-political requirements.

2. Although on the surface the problems faced by the DCI in injecting himself into the DOD budget process appear to be most formidable, in practice it is difficult to recall any major issue on which the DCI and the Secretary of Defense did not reach agreement. As long as there is a will to cooperate among the top officials, administrative difficulties tend to disappear.

3. If the DCI submits his proposed Consolidated Intelligence Community Budget to the President with his recommendations several months in advance of the deadline for completing the President's Budget (end of December of each year), then there will be time to give proper consideration to the DCI's recommendations, and through a channel that does not involve the DCI in a direct confrontation with DOD on a major issue.

Against:

1. Although it may appear on the surface that the DCI is making real progress in asserting his authority over the allocation of collection resources, indicating that Option B is feasible, in fact this Option is *not* working. The DCI has *not* reached agreement with the Secretary of Defense on many major issues as they arose, because the DCI has *not been in a position* to raise the tough questions and take a firm stand. The well known weaknesses of IRAC as a channel for allocating resources were mentioned above. The IC staff, which is the DCI's principal staff resource to turn up the tough questions, is dominated at the top by military officers on active duty. One of them told me that "if the IC staff was not run by a military officer it would not be acceptable to DOD." Finally, the DCI has been waiting for the members of the Community to complete their budgets before he prepared the Consolidated Community Budget. The Consolidated Budget thus arrives at OMB at the end of the budget season when it is too late to consider major revisions. In effect, the DCI is only second guessing members' budgets, not exercising leadership in presenting in advance his views on what should be in the members' budgets.

2. We must find better ways to take advantage of the great potential value of the DCI's office. However, the Secretary of Defense has a fundamental responsibility to keep a constant watch on military and potentially explosive political developments around the world, and, if you attempt to transfer at least some aspects of his authority over such surveillance activities to the DCI, you are putting the Secretary of Defense in the untenable position of being held responsible for activities over which he does not have full authority.

Option C: The management of all of the technical intelligence collection programs financed by the DOD budget would become a shared responsibility, just as the reconnaissance program is today; and the DCI, in carrying out his leadership role in allocating intelligence resources, would not "scatter his shots" but would concentrate each year on perhaps not more than six major issues, studying them in depth, including an analysis of their cost implications for future years.

For:

1. The joint management of the technical reconnaissance program is reported to be working very well and appears to avoid at least most of the difficulties encountered by the DCI in his efforts to influence the program and budgets for the rest of the DOD intelligence activities. It is recognized that the predecessor of the present technical reconnaissance program (the U-2 program) was started by CIA, so that the administrative and jurisdictional problems involved in extending this joint management approach to other DOD activities would probably be more difficult than those encountered in establishing joint management for the technical reconnaissance program.

2. By concentrating on a few major issues, presenting the options to the President for decision, and forwarding the decisions to the DOD several months before the end of the budget cycle, the timing problems faced by the DCI in influencing the present DOD budget process would be reduced, and the issue of the DCI getting between the President and the DOD would not have to arise.

Against:

1. If the DCI jointly managed all of the very expensive technical collection programs, he could lose some of his objectivity in allocating resources, in enforcing the principle of using only clandestine sources when overt sources were not available, and so on. In other words, he might tend to get a vested interest in these technical collection programs.

2. If the DCI concentrated on studies of a few major issues, and decisions on these issues involved a net increase in expenditures, the DOD might thereby have a lever with which to insist on an increase in the planned total expenditures for the year in question.

Discussion: It seems pretty clear that the DCI would be unable to exercise the kind of positive leadership envisioned by the Office of the President unless the joint management role he now has for the reconnaissance program was extended to the other technical collection organizations in DOD. This may appear to be a rather drastic measure, but the alternatives have been tried over the years with very disappointing results.

There is considerable support in the DCI's office and in the OMB for the proposal that the DCI should focus on studies of a few major issues each year. These studies should include analyses of the future cost implications of the various options.

IV. MULTI-YEAR PROGRAMMING AND BUDGETING

Issue #2: What steps should the DCI take in order to insure that adequate recognition is taken of the future cost implications of budget decisions?

Option A. Adopt a 2-year budget for intelligence programs.

For:

1. With today's intelligence budgets dominated by long lead items, it makes sense to prepare budgets for a 2-year period in order to reflect more fully the future costs of budget decisions.

2. Intelligence resources program administrators can proceed in a more orderly, positive way if they know what they can count on for the next 2 years, rather than for just one year.

3. The disclosure of future expenditure implications of proposed major budget decisions is often the most effective way to keep future budgets within prescribed limits. A 2-year budget would disclose a substantial part of such future expenditures.

4. If the future cost implications of budget decisions are not carefully analyzed, the inevitable result would be that over the years a rapidly increasing part of the annual budget would be composed of mandatory expenditures based on past budget decisions. Thus there would be less and less flexibility in the budget to take care of high priority new programs, emergency developments, etc. unless sharp increases were permitted in total expenditures.

5. Budget officials in OMB and the office of the DCI are very much interested in the idea of the two-year budget.

Against:

1. A two year budget would have to be prepared each year.

2. Important budget decisions usually have cost implications extending far beyond two years.

Option B. The DCI would prepare a projection of collection requirements for the next five years, updating it annually, and calculate the budgetary implications for the next five years of major budget decisions currently under consideration.

For:

1. The DCI has already made a start toward this Option by preparing a projection of intelligence needs for the next five years, to be up-dated annually.

2. The Congress already requires the preparation of budgets for the next five years showing the changes in the President's budget for each year if no new programs are introduced. Such a calculation is one way of showing the future cost implications of budget decisions included in next years budget.

3. An annual budget can be quite misleading if the future budgetary implications of its long lead time items are not properly analyzed. For example, approval of a new $50,000 training program

and $100,000 for the site of a new technical collection device might in effect be committing the DOD or CIA to a $50,000,000 expenditure during the next three years. Because of the "technological revolution" in the intelligence collection field during the past two decades, such considerations have become increasingly important.

Against:

1. The five year "perspective" of intelligence needs issued by the DCI is so all inclusive that it is not a good guide to high priority future needs or a restraint on low priority items. On the contrary, it is difficult to think of anything excluded from the list. Thus this five year perspective tends to place a stamp of approval for the next five years on anything the Community wants to collect.

2. The five year projection of the current budget is of limited value because it does not include anticipated budget decisions during the intervening period.

Option C. The DCI would prepare an Intelligence Community Plan for the next five years for major categories of items with long lead time; update it annually; secure approval of the plan by higher authority; and assume responsibility for insuring that the current annual budget proposals are consistent with the approved 5-year plan.

For:

1. This five year projection of budget decisions would include not just the budget decisions proposed in the current budget, but anticipated budget decisions for the intervening years.

2. This five year plan would not include those activities of an administrative nature which do not have any long lead time aspects and would remain about the same during the five year period (e.g. the controller's office).

3. Instead of relying primarily on analyses of a few major ad hoc decisions each year to keep the budget on the track, it would be much better to look ahead a few years, anticipate changes in the priority intelligence needs, and put together a mid-term plan that would anticipate the priority raw intelligence needs, would include necessary budget decisions for the entire period, and would be in line with anticipated limits on future annual budgets. This plan would be approved by higher authority, and the DCI would insure that it is used as an approved guide in preparing annual (or 2-year) budgets.

4. The preparation of this five year plan would provide an opportunity not only to take a look at proposed new projects for collecting intelligence, but also to identify those on-going projects that have outlived their usefulness. It is very difficult to get attention focused on low priority ongoing programs during the annual budget process if increased funding is not requested, attention usually being focused almost entirely on proposed new programs and above-average increases in on-going activities. It is probably much easier to get agreement to eliminate unproductive activities or duplications from a mid-term plan by arguing that "you surely are not going to continue *those* programs for the next five years."

5. Longer term plans are already being prepared for some intelligence programs.

Against:

1. The DOD already has a classified five year plan for its entire DOD budget (including intelligence) which is presented each year. Last year the DCI was officially permitted to see it for the first time. How would a Community-wide five-year plan be reconciled with the DOD plan? Is there any practical way other than a joint DOD-DCI management plan for DOD technical collection programs (Option C of Issue #1 above)?

2. Unless the authority of this five year plan is very clearly spelled out, it would tend to be ignored during the rough and tumble of the annual budget hearings.

3. The existence of an official five year plan would raise important security problems. The plan would have to be highly classified and very closely held.

Discussion: Steps are already being taken in the direction of five year plans and serious consideration is being given in some quarters to a two year budget instead of an annual budget. Congress appears to favor moving in these directions, as indicated by some of the provisions of the recent Congressional budget reform legislation. Moves in these directions are desirable, and the Commission should give serious consideration to giving its blessing to these trends.

V. GROWING IMPORTANCE OF ECONOMIC INTELLIGENCE

Issue #3. *What steps should the DCI take to help overcome the rather ad hoc, disorganized way economic intelligence is being collected and processed today?*

Option A. Continue the present arrangements, CIA responding promptly to whatever requests it receives for economic intelligence from different parts of the U.S. Government, and including economic intelligence requirements in the KIQs.

For:

1. Informed officials indicate that the economic intelligence requirements of the U.S. Government are being met today in spite of rather loose organizational arrangements, and that relationships between CIA and consumers of such intelligence are excellent.

2. Until the "top management" arrangements of the U.S. Government for foreign and domestic economic policy matters are firmly established, and until the probable long-run pattern of economic committees for various major problem areas (food, trade, oil, etc.), and the assignment of economic responsibilities among different departments become clearer, it is not feasible to move toward more permanent, institutionalized arrangements for collecting and processing economic intelligence.

3. Since CIA is prohibited from engaging in intelligence activities within the United States, there appear to be limits on what leadership the DCI can exercise with reference to the many overt sources of economic intelligence in the Executive Branch.

4. Domestic and foreign economic matters are so important at this time, that we can afford to have rather loose arrangements with considerable duplication of effort to encourage initiative and fresh thinking and to provide the President with alternative sources of information for policy guidance during this crucial period.

Against:

1. There is so much at stake, that the collection and processing of economic intelligence should be thoroughly professionalized. Loose arrange-

ments are bound to result in an unacceptable amount of erroneous or misleading economic information floating around Washington, and a lot of "shooting from the hip."

2. More specifically, all processing of economic intelligence should be carried out "under one roof." Those favoring such an arrangement point out that CIA is recognized as having by far the largest and most experienced group of professionals in Washington for analyzing economic intelligence, but unless a firm decision is made soon there will be a rapidly growing duplication of effort in several Departments in the near future.

3. Most of the U.S. intelligence resources and most top officials of the Community are oriented toward military-political intelligence collecting, and there are plans on the drawing board for a lot more investment in resources primarily oriented for such purposes. Even a superficial look at (a) the small percentage of the total intelligence budget earmarked for economic intelligence, (b) the few senior officials of the Community whose primary interest is in economic intelligence, and (c) the presentation of nearly all of the Community Budget only to the Armed Services Committees, suggests that a fresh look at the allocation of intelligence resources is in order, and need not wait for a firming up of the organization of the U.S. Government in the economic field. A point to remember: most military intelligence collected today is for possible future use; but most economic intelligence collected today is used every day for guidance on matters vitally important now.

Option B. Strengthen the DCI's control of economic intelligence collection through (1) more centralization of economic intelligence analysis in CIA; (2) restriction largely to CIA of economic intelligence collection from multinational corporations, on a classified basis; (3) assignment of CIA station chiefs as principal advisors to U.S. Ambassadors on all collection activities performed by persons attached to U.S. Embassies, including economic intelligence; (4) extension of DCI regular budget briefings to other than the Armed Services Committees of the Congress; and (5) creation of a better balance between military-political oriented and economics oriented senior officials in IRAC and the IC staff.

For:

1. For at least most economic intelligence, CIA is in a much better position than anyone else to fit the pieces together and make sophisticated analyses. CIA has the necessary experience, the access to many kinds of highly classified technical programs that collect economic as well as military-political raw intelligence, the extended relationships with corporations for collecting other kinds of intelligence, and the adequate research resources for developing techniques for extracting economic intelligence from reconnaissance photography, etc.

2. Multinational corporations are reluctant to divulge economic information about their companies that might reach their competitors. CIA is in the best position to gain access to such confidential information and protect its sources.

3. The DCI has plans to rate the performance of Embassies in intelligence collection, and many Embassies will need help in improving their effectiveness in collection activities, much of which is concerned with other than military or political matters. The CIA station chiefs could be very helpful to Ambassadors in advising on improved collection methods, focusing more on priority collection needs, limiting clandestine collection only to information not obtainable overtly, etc. Most station chiefs know very little about economics, but their advisory role would be concerned primarily with organization, procedures, and collection techniques, not substance. Future training programs for CIA station chiefs should cover this advisory role.

4. In seeking a better balance between military-political and economic collection resources, it might help for the DCI to offer to brief economic-oriented Congressional committees as well as the Armed Services Committees on the intelligence budget each year.

5. In view of the overriding concern of the Intelligence Community with military-political intelligence during most of the past two decades, it is to be expected that IRAC and the IC staff would be staffed primarily by officials with experience and a primary interest in such intelligence. The comparatively great increase in the importance of economic intelligence in recent years has not been accompanied by an appropriate increase in economic-intelligence-oriented officials at senior levels in IRAC and the IC staff.

Against:

1. There is a danger of over-organizing for economic intelligence collection, and particularly of spending too much money trying to adapt the very expensive techniques for collecting military-political intelligence to collecting economic intelligence. For example, there is much excitement about the use of reconnaissance photography as a source of agricultural intelligence. During the past ten or fifteen years, there has been a tremendous improvement in the domestic statistical programs of developing countries. U.S. agricultural attaches and AID agricultural technicians have learned a lot about interpreting these figures. In practice, of how much value will reconnaissance photography be as a supplement to what we already know? The cost of this photography would pay the salaries of a whole army of agricultural attaches. Or is the reconnaissance photography popular because the users look upon it as "free," i.e. costing them nothing?

2. With reference to using CIA station chiefs as advisors to U.S. Ambassadors, they are trained to recruit agents and seek military-political information. Very few of them have any interest in or knowledge of economic intelligence. At least for the near future, it might be better to think in terms of CIA regional advisors who would specialize in organizational and administrative problems of Embassies in collecting information. These advisors would visit Embassies in their area on a regular schedule, and would assist in laying out collection programs and improving collection techniques—overt as well as covert.

3. There is a danger in linking multinational corporations too closely with CIA.

Discussion: It seems clear that there are further steps the DCI could take to strengthen the collection of economic intelligence without waiting for all of the problems of top management for economic policy to be settled. It is recognized that much has been done during the past few years to broaden the geographic coverage of economic intelligence, and that CIA has done a commendable job during the last two years of meeting many new demands for such intelligence on short notice.

VI. THE ALLOCATION OF COLLECTION RESOURCES

Issue #4: *What steps should be taken to prepare a national strategy for the allocation and use of intelligence resources?*

Option A. Do nothing beyond continuing the preparation of the annual Consolidated Budget for the Intelligence Community, together with recommendations, and continuing to prepare an annual review of the progress of the Community for the President.

For:

1. The Community has been subjected to very sharp budget cuts in recent years, together with a tight budget for the near future in the face of inflation. It takes time to digest these cuts, and the Community should not be kept off balance by the prospect of major reallocations of resources in the near future. It deserves a breathing spell.

2. It is reasonable to assume that these budget cuts resulted in correction of some of the most serious misallocations of resources. Furthermore, there are some built-in corrections that take place over a period of time. If you cannot recruit high level agents in Europe any more, resources for such purposes are reduced. If you can get more good scientific intelligence out of foreign publications than from agents, you spend comparatively more on exploiting published sources. If you find it more and more difficult to crack codes in sophisticated countries, you reduce the number of intercept stations in those areas. Such changes are taking place all of the time behind the scenes.

3. There is no scientific, precise technique for allocating intelligence resources. Judgments by experienced people will always be involved.

4. Some of the evaluation procedures of the DCI are providing important guidance for better allocation of resources. For example, one of the Key Intelligence Questions will be selected for analysis. A study will be made to determine what raw intelligence is being collected and what collection gaps there are in answering this question; and also, to determine if there is proper coordination between the amount of intelligence collected and the amount used. Thus this study provides the "base line" information, against which the situation six months later is evaluated.

Against:

1. The Consolidated Budget for the Community with recommendations has not turned out to be a very dynamic management tool; and the annual progress report to the President is just that, a progress report, not a recommendation as to where we should go from here. The impression is that, to some extent, the DCI is moving along without any firm frame of reference or strategy. There is a good deal of professionalism in the handling of details and specific projects, but some of the major deficiencies seem to be something the Community just has to live with from year to year.

2. Some of those concerned with intelligence resource allocation (especially those who are probably not in full sympathy with the President's view that we should maintain a very strong military posture) believe that, since the DOD budget includes over 4/5 of the total intelligence funds, the DOD budget for intelligence is obviously too high. They think that a careful study of the allocation of resources will result in a recommendation to reduce the proportion of the total intelligence budget allocated to DOD for military-political intelligence. This is not necessarily so, but a study would be useful to help settle the sharp differences of opinion existing within the U.S. Government today on the equitable allocation of intelligence resources.

3. There have been many studies of the Intelligence Community, but nearly all of them seem to have been concerned with "moving the boxes around on the organization chart," and not with the allocation of resources or the general strategy for intelligence.

Option B. Organize a high level study group, composed primarily of individuals from outside the Intelligence Community, to make a detailed study of the allocation of collection resources within the Community, and submit options for taking corrective actions.

For:

1. A study made largely by individuals outside the Community would have more credibility than recommendations developed within the Community.

2. Many new technical collection devices and improved equipment are becoming available, and outside experts could be helpful in determining the best mix of these collection methods for the foreseeable future from a cost/benefit point of view.

3. The study group would require reports and make sample checks to determine what proportion of raw intelligence now collected is processed and used, and would attempt to make some rough checks of the comparative cost/benefit of alternative collection methods.

4. The issue of the proper allocation of collection resources appears to be sufficiently controversial that an outside look would be helpful at this time.

Against:

1. It would be difficult to recruit qualified persons for the outside study group who are not employed by companies selling the complex highly technical equipment used for intelligence purposes or selling research services to DOD. Would such outside experts be more objective than informed personnel employed by CIA or DOD?

2. Could such a study group produce meaningful recommendations in the absence of any approved national strategy for intelligence resources? Could it analyze budget figures for intelligence activities of DOD without reference to the overall budget policies of the Department of Defense? Is it realistic to ask outsiders to analyze budget data?

Option C. The DCI would prepare an annual report whose principal product would be a proposed national strategy for intelligence, with options. The input in preparing this report would be the various Community members' budgets; results of studies of major issues in depth (Option C of Issue #1); results of DCI evaluation studies (see, for example, item #4 under Option A of Issue #4); and near term budget data and longer term issues resulting from 5 year planning (see Option C of Issue #2), the planning being subdivided into three or four functional categories cutting across agency and departmental lines.

For:

1. This annual report would replace the Consolidated Intelligence Community Budget with recommendations prescribed in President Nixon's November 1971 Directive. The Consolidated Budget has not proved to be very successful.

2. This Option would provide a means of making maximum use of the various studies and analyses discussed earlier for purposes of securing Presidential policy guidance for intelligence activities.

3. An overall national strategy for intelligence would replace present intelligence guidelines, which tend to be little more than the summation of ad hoc decisions reached on individual projects. The DCI would have a firmer foundation on which to exercise his leadership role.

4. Certain major issues, such as whether *all* electronic transmissions taking place in a given part of the world should be recorded and analyzed, can only be raised effectively in a broad report structured as proposed in Option C.

Against:

1. Option C assumes there is enough stability in the world to justify making projections several years ahead with some confidence. This assumption is questionable.

2. It is possible to be overorganized, to have too precise policy guidelines that reduce flexibility and stifle initiative.

3. The preparation and clearance of this proposed report would require many hours of the time of very senior officials.

Discussion: The annual Consolidated Budget for the Community, together with recommendations for the President, has not been a success. Various improvements in forward planning, and analysis of stubborn problems, now under discussion or under way, would lay the groundwork for the development of a recommended national strategy for intelligence. A report setting forth such recommendations, with options, should replace the present annual Consolidated Budget.

NOTES AND REFERENCES

1. An examination of the fiscal year 1977 budget ([112]) for the U.S. government reveals no line itemization for the CIA, NSA, or DIA.

2. On the subject of NSA disclosure restrictions, refer to testimony by NSA officials ([10], p. 399).

3. The budgets for NSA and CIA are almost totally obscured by secrecy. Scant information is provided in several documents and it usually pertains to housekeeping functions, retirement, etc. See, for instance, the following sources: [11], p. 39; [47], Part 1, pp. 28, 96, 153, 557, 634; [47], Part 3, pp. 65, 803; [47], Part 5, pp. 1334, 1360; [47], Part 6, p. 79; [50], p. 11239; [52], p. 3388; [54A], p. 2450; [54B], p. 3903.

4. Although the appropriations committees hear testimony on the foreign intelligence budget, almost all such testimony is held in executive (closed) sessions. Note, for instance, [47], Part 1, pp. 1–4, where the DCI is welcomed, exchanges compliments with the chairman, and a unanimous vote is taken to continue in executive session.

5. Further detail on issues regarding congressional control of intelligence expenditures is provided in Chapter 10 under the subject of congressional oversight.

7. Passage of Senate Resolution 400 on May 19, 1976 established an oversight committee in the Senate; see Chapter 10 for review of oversight legislation.

PART II

COMPONENTS
OF THE FOREIGN
INTELLIGENCE COMMUNITY

Chapter 5
Central Intelligence Agency

HISTORY AND ORGANIZATION ([84], pp. 537–544)

The National Security Act of 1947 (reprinted in the Appendix) established the CIA and granted it coordinating functions, and its head, the dual role of director of the CIA and DCI, director of Central Intelligence. It is the principal intelligence agency, both by popular perception and by statute, though it is exceeded in budget and size by the Defense agencies and, in policy impact perhaps, by the National Security Council or any one of the coordinating bodies. But it is still the most significant, the most apparent, and the most crucial intelligence agency of the U.S. government. Its potential as a coordinating body has not been fully realized, and its future was left in question at the conclusion of the several studies conducted during the mid-1970s.

The CIA's failures have been widely reported. Its accomplishments, as several U.S. presidents have noted, remain unheralded*; and it has produced little documentation to reveal its successes. The Church and Pike Committees were created by Congress to examine wrongdoings and their reports focus on these and on methods of improvement. The Executive branch itself was forced by events and revelations also to investigate wrongdoings and issued the Rockefeller Commission Report.

Chapter 5 includes Pike and Church Committee documents that describe the evolution of the CIA since its beginnings with the National Security Act of 1947, its current structure, and its mode of operations. It does not address the CIA budget or manpower levels—since no reliable public documentation could be found beyond those cited in the preceding chapter on the overall intelligence budget question. A summary of the Rockefeller Commission findings is reprinted at the conclusion. The placement of the Rockefeller findings at this point in the book creates an organizational problem, for a number of matters discussed in that report are reviewed in more detail elsewhere in this volume.

*Central Intelligence Agency, *Presidents of the United States on Intelligence* (April 1975).

"CIA Organizational History in Brief"; March 1975

SUMMARY

During the nearly three decades of its existence, the Central Intelligence Agency has continuously adjusted its organizational structure to cope with changing conditions and responsibilities. Within the pattern of constant change, however, there have been four points at which major reorganizations have occurred. In its first two years, CIA took on numerous new activities and shifted responsibilities for those activities frequently. In 1951–52, two separate entities engaged in overseas operations were merged and the rapidly growing intelligence production function was reorganized. Another massive

215

change occurred in 1962. A new Directorate was established to take over the many projects for technical, as opposed to clandestine human source, collection of information that were already underway and to assume the responsibility for conceiving and developing future technical collection systems. Concurrently, the remainder of the Agency was reorganized and important command and control functions were centered in an Executive Director-Comptroller. In 1973 a number of activities were transferred organizationally, with emphasis on grouping together similar functions, and the Executive Director-Comptroller functions were dispersed.

INITIAL ORGANIZATION

A Central Intelligence Group (CIG) headed by a Director of Central Intelligence (DCI) was established in January 1946 by President Truman, and it immediately began assuming intelligence functions carried out by various agencies during World War II. Concurrently, Congress was engaged in a review of the entire national security structure, including intelligence, which resulted in the National Security Act of 1947 directing establishment of a Central Intelligence Agency (CIA). The CIG was accordingly transformed into the CIA, which began with an organizational structure that included a number of administrative functions and four major operating components:

> --The Office of Reports and Estimates, which was initially responsible for all finished intelligence production. The direct forerunner of all the producing offices now in existence, it was subdivided repeatedly as the production function grew in size and diversified in responsibility. It was initially formed in the Central Intelligence Group by personnel transferred from State and the military services.

> --The Office of Special Operations, derived from what remained of the wartime Office of Strategic Services (OSS), which had been attached to the War Department as the Strategic Services Unit in the immediate post-war period. It was responsible for espionage and counterespionage. Following OSS practice, worldwide communications and security support also were assigned to this operating Office.

> --The Office of Operations, responsible for overt and domestic collection of foreign intelligence. It, too, was formed partly out of the remnants of the OSS structure that had been attached to the Pentagon and included a coordinated domestic collection activity which became the Contact Division. It also incorporated the broadcast monitoring assets of the Foreign Broadcast Information Service transferred from the War Department and foreign document centers taken over from the Army and Navy and merged into the Foreign Documents Division.

> --The Office of Collection and Dissemination, responsible for establishing intelligence collection priorities, coordinating the collection efforts of the various agencies, and organizing the dissemination of both raw intelligence and finished reports. It soon assumed control of reference and records centers as well.

As additional activities and assets were transferred to CIA, they were added on to the existing structure. For example, joint military intelligence surveys became a CIA responsibility in October 1947; accordingly, the National intelligence Survey program was organized in a Basic Intelligence Division of the Office of Reports and Estimates.

The National Security Council, established concurrently with the CIA, began issuing a series of directives in December of 1947 which shaped the subsequent structure and missions of CIA. One of the most significant ordered immediate expansion of covert operations and paramilitary activities. In response, on 1 September 1948, the Office of Policy Coordination was established. It had an anomalous relationship with the rest of the Agency, since the NSC ordered it to remain as independent of the remainder of CIA as possible and placed it under the policy direction of the Departments of State and Defense. For OPC's first two years, policy guidance came directly from State and Defense, although the chain of command was through the Director of Central Intelligence.

It was during this period, under OPC, that such activities as Radio Free Europe, the Committee for Free Asia, Radio Liberty, the Asia Foundation, and the youth, student, and labor programs of the Agency began.

Shortly after the establishment of OPC, a Hoover Commission Task Force began making recommendations on national security organization; they were partially endorsed by the Commission itself in February 1949. A separate National Intelligence Survey Group headed by Allen Dulles filed its own report to the NSC in January 1949. The NSC subsequently directed merger of the Office of Special Operations, the Office of Policy Coordination and the Contact Branch. This could not be accomplished under the original charter of OPC, however, and no major change was made until General Walter Bedell Smith took over as DCI in October 1950.

N6

The existence of both OSO and OPC meant that two clandestine organizations were responding to separate chains of command while working within many of the same foreign countries. They had caused continual difficulties--especially by competing for the same potential agents--and General Smith immediately insisted that all orders to OPC be passed through him. He also designated a number of Senior Representatives abroad to coordinate the separate activities. By mid-1951, integration of the two organizations had begun; complete integration was ordered in July 1952, although some overseas stations continued to report directly to the DCI through overseas Senior Representatives until 1954. The new joint organization was renamed the Clandestine Services; whithin it, an International Organizations Division was activated in June 1954 to handle student, youth and labor programs.

General Smith also created two new Deputy Directors, one for Administration and one for Operations; the latter, redesignated the Deputy Director for Plans (DDP) in January 1951, headed what became the Clandestine Services.

Meanwhile reorganization of intelligence production offices was being undertaken. The Office of Research and Estimates was divided into the Office of National Estimates, responsible for national-level policy-related papers that projected analysis into the future, and the Office of Research and Reports (ORR), which handled economic and geographic intelligence and the National Intelligence Survey program. A new Office of Current Intelligence was added in January 1951. A year later, a Deputy Director for Intelligence (DDI) was named, with supervision over the above offices as well as the Office of Scientific Intelligence, the Office of Collection and Dissemination, and the Office of Intelligence Coordination which had been directly under the DCI. In March of 1952, the Office of Operations (engaged in overt functions: domestic contacts, Foreign Broadcast Information Service, and Foreign Documents Division) was placed under the DDI. And that November the Photographic Intelligence Division was established within ORR's Geographic Research Area. A separate Office of Basic Intelligence was formed in 1955.

N7   Between 1950 and 1952 the Agency grew markedly. Administrative support functions increased along with other activities. In February 1955, responsibilities for training, personnel administration and communications were centralized in the Directorate for Administration and the Directorate was renamed the Directorate for Support. By 1955, therefore, the basic structure of the current agency had been established. The Director had three functional deputies, each in charge of a Directorate. Overt collection, analysis, and production of finished intelligence were centralized in the Intelligence Directorate. Other intelligence collection--both espionage and rapidly growing technical forms--was in the Plans Directorate. The Support Directorate provided administrative services of common concern as well as specialized support for the various units.

Much of this structure still exists. Over time, however, functions have been shifted from one Directorate to another, realigned within Directorates or eliminated--usually for one of two reasons:

--Decisions or recommendations have been received from other parts of the governmental structure: the President, the NSC, Congress, and a succession of special commissions and internal study groups.

--Organizational philosophy has changed as personnel have changed.
Various approaches have been taken to organization--grouping
similar functions, grouping organizations by common interest (such
as a geographical region) or forming close organizational links
between the supplier of a service and the principal customer. These
changes have been shifts in emphasis; the organization has always
been a combination of the three approaches.

Changes in the priorities given to particular missions or intelligence
targets have also resulted in changes in the size and authority of organiza-
tional components. Growth in a substantive area has led to occasional divisions
of one unit into smaller ones, providing more reasonable spans of control.

In the half dozen years following establishment of this framework,
most changes were minor. The DCI's Senior Representatives abroad were
eliminated in 1957. A Photo Interpretation Center was established within
the DDI in 1958, combining functions from several components including
the Photo Intelligence Division. It was replaced in 1961 by the National
Photographic Interpretation Center. And the personnel and responsibilities
involved in the development of technical collection devices--primarily
aircraft--were transferred from the office of the DCI to the Plans
Directorate.

1961-1963

Late in 1961, the new DCI, John McCone, established a working group
chaired by the Agency Inspector General, Lyman Kirkpatrick, to study
Agency and Intelligence Community organization and activities. Final
recommendations were submitted in April 1962 and led to the last major
reorganization of the Agency.

Even before the study was completed, one major decision was made.
Technological advances had been numerous and very rapid during the 1950's,
and they had presented new opportunities for intelligence collection by
machines. Reconnaissance aircraft had been developed within the Agency;
collection of electronic intelligence by interception devices was another
fast-growing area. Technology had also made new kinds of information
available for analysis and created a need for more analysis by scientifically
trained people. Mr. McCone designated a Deputy Director for Research, with
initial responsibility for elements drawn from the DDP and additional
responsibilities to await completion of the study, in February 1962. The
Office of Research and Development, the Office of Electronic Intelligence,
and the Office of Special Activities (responsible for overhead reconnaissance
activities) were established immediately. The Office of Scientific Intelli-
gence (from the DDI) and automatic data processing activities (from Support
and the Comptroller) were added in 1963. With the establishment late that
year of the Foreign Missile and Space Analysis Center, the renamed Directorate
of Science and Technology assumed the basic form it still maintains.

The Kirkpatrick study also resulted in a major strengthening of the
Office of the Director. The General Counsel's office, Audit Staff, Comptroller,
Office of Budget, Program Analysis and Manpower and the US Intelligence
Board Secretariat were added to it. By late 1962, the position of an Executive
Director-Comptroller had been established and his role as third in command
of the Agency had been delineated. And the Kirkpatrick study led to centrali-
zation of paramilitary activities, an organization to provide a command mechanism
for future contingencies, and establishment of a Domestic Operations Division,
to develop contacts with foreign nationals in the US.

By the end of 1963, the organization had settled into the pattern it
kept for the next decade. Four directorates existed. They were primarily
differentiated by function, but units performing services frequently were
co-located with their customers. Central direction was strong, with an
Executive Director-Comptroller playing a major role in all Agency activities
and the Board of National Estimates reporting directly to the DCI, although
the supporting Office of National Estimates remained in the Intelligence
Directorate for about another year.

1964-1972

Organizational arrangements remained largely static for the next decade, though growing emphasis on analysis led to further subdivision of analytical offices. The DDI's Office of Operations was organized and renamed the Domestic Contact Service in mid-1965. The Office of Basic Intelligence was enlarged and took over geographic responsibilities from the Office of Research and Reports. The latter was divided in 1967 into the Office of Economic Research and the Office of Strategic Research. In the DDS&T, the Office of Special Projects was established in 1965 to conduct overhead reconnaissance, a duty that had been previously handled by a Staff. Staffs to address special needs were added in the Plans Directorate. Responsibility for proprietary organizations was transferred from the Domestic Operations Division to other DDP components in December 1971, and the Division was renamed the Foreign Resources Division the following month. Some mechanism for coordinating and evaluating national foreign intelligence activities had existed since the establishment of the Agency; in 1972, this took the form of the Intelligence Community Staff in the Office of the DCI.

Activities related to Southeast Asia grew and subsequently contracted during this period. Organizationally, such changes were reflected in the creation of a Special Assistant to the DCI for Vietnam Affairs with a supporting staff and in formation of a number of new low-level components throughout the Agency.

1973-1975

The most recent series of changes began when James Schlesinger was named DCI in early 1973. He put in train a number of organizational studies and directed a number of transfers; some were accomplished during his tenure and some were carried out after William Colby replaced Mr. Schlesinger as DCI in mid-1973.

The organizational moves and personnel reductions of that time led to today's organization:

--The Domestic Contact Service was transferred from the DDI to the DDP; the staff structure was reduced, and the Directorate was redesignated the Directorate of Operations.

--Three technical activities--technical services, communications research and development, and the National Photographic Interpretation Center were transferred to the Science and Technology Directorate. S&T also merged certain functions of the Office of Scientific Intelligence with the Foreign Missile and Space Analysis Center and established the Office of Weapons Intelligence. The Office of Special Projects was transformed into the Office of Development and Engineering, which provides engineering and system development support Agency-wide.

--A new Office of Political Research was established in the DDI.

--Computer services, which has been fragmented but with their largest manifestations in S&T, were transferred to the Support Directorate. And the Support Directorate itself went through two name changes, first to Management and Services and subsequently to the Directorate of Administration.

--The Board and Office of National Estimates were abolished and replaced by a group of senior functional and geographic specialists called National Intelligence Officers drawn partially from outside the Agency. Both the senior NIO and the head of the Intelligence Community Staff were named Deputies to the DCI.

--The position of Executive Director-Comptroller was abolished. Many of its functions were redistributed within the Office of the DCI and the Directorate of Administration. A Management Committee composed of the DCI, his principal Deputy, the four Deputies in charge of

Directorates, the Comptroller, the General Counsel and the Inspector
General was established to advise the DCI on the management policy
questions.

--For budgetary reasons, a decision was made to terminate the
National Intelligence Survey program in the Office of Basic and
Geographic Intelligence; accordingly, the geographic intelligence
unit was redesignated the Office of Geographic and Cartographic
Research.

As of February 1975, therefore, the directorate structure is generally
the same as it was in 1965. However, there is a stricter adherence to
combining similar functions than in earlier periods. Management direction
and control is decentralized. The staff structure has been considerably
reduced and simplified. And the number of full time staff personnel has
been reduced substantially.

The Recent Past, 1971–1975 ([45D], pp. 83–90)

N8
The years 1971 to 1975 were a period of transition and abrupt
change for the CIA. The administrations of DCIs James R.
Schlesinger and William E. Colby both reflected and contributed to
shifts in the CIA's emphases. Spurred on by increased attention from
the Executive branch, intelligence production, the problems of the
community, and internal management changes became the primary
concerns of the DCIs. Essentially, the diminishing scale of covert
action that had begun in the late 1960's and continued in this period
both required and provided the opportunity for a redefinition in
the Agency's priorities.

The decline in covert action was indicative of the broad changes
that had evolved in American foreign policy by the early 1970's.
Détente rather than cold war characterized the U.S. posture toward
the Soviet Union, and retrenchment rather than intervention charac-
terized U.S. foreign policy generally. The cumulative dissension over
Vietnam, the Congress' more assertive role in foreign policy, and
shifts in the international power structure eroded the assumptions on
which U.S. foreign policy had been based. The consensus that had ex-
isted among the press, the informed public, the Congress, and the
Executive branch and that had both supported and protected the CIA
broke down. As conflicting policy preferences emerged and as miscon-
duct in the Executive branch was revealed, the CIA, once exempt from
public examination, became subject to close scrutiny. The Congress and
even the public began to seek a more active role in the activities that
Presidents and the Agency had for so long controlled.

Foreign affairs were a continuing priority in the Nixon Adminis-
tration. Until 1971, Vietnam absorbed most of the time and attention
of the President and his Special Assistant for National Security
Affairs, Henry Kissinger. After 1971, both turned to a redefinition of
United States foreign policy. Sharing a global view of U.S. policy, the
two men sought to restructure relationships with the Soviet Union and
the People's Republic of China. It was Kissinger rather than Nixon
who maintained regular contact with DCIs Helms and Colby, and in
effect, it was Kissinger rather than the DCIs who served as Nixon's
senior intelligence advisor. Under Kissinger's direction the NSC be-
came an intelligence and policy staff, providing analysis on such key

issues as missile programs. The staff's small size and close proximity to policymakers allowed it to calibrate the needs of senior officials in a way that made their information more timely and useful than comparable CIA analyses.

Both Kissinger's and Nixon's preferences for working with (and often independently of) small, tightly managed staffs is well known. However, both were genuinely interested in obtaining more and better quality intelligence from the CIA. In December 1970 Nixon requested a study of the intelligence community. Executed by James Schlesinger, then Assistant Director of the Bureau of the Budget, the study resulted in a Presidential Directive of November 5, 1971, assigning the DCI formal responsibility for review of the intelligence community budget.[1] The intention was that the DCI would advise the President on budgetary allocations by serving in a last review capacity. As a result of the Directive, the Intelligence Resources Advisory Committee (IRAC) was established to advise the DCI in preparing a consolidated intelligence budget for the President.[1a]

The effort faltered for two reasons. First, Nixon chose not to request Congressional enactment of revised legislation on the role of the DCI. This decision inherently limited the DCI's ability to exert control over the intelligence components. The DCI was once again left to arbitrate with no real statutory authority. Second, the implementation of the Directive was less energetic and decisive than it might have been. Helms did not attempt to make recommendations on budgetary allocations and instead, presented the President with the agreed views of the intelligence components. Furthermore, within the Agency the mechanism for assisting the DCI in community matters was weak. Early in 1972 Helms established the Intelligence Community (IC) staff as a replacement for the NIPE staff to assist in community matters. Between the time of the decision to create such a staff and its actual organization, the number of personnel assigned was halved. Moreover, the staff itself was composed only of CIA employees rather than community-wide representatives. This arrangement limited the staff's accessibility to other components of the community, and was a contributing factor to the disappointing results of the Nixon Directive.

1. The Directors of Central Intelligence, 1973–1975

James Schlesinger's tenure as DCI from February to July 1973 was brief but telling. An economist by training, Schlesinger brought an extensive background in national security affairs to his job as DCI. He came to the position with definite ideas on the management of the community and on improving the quality of intelligence.

He began his career as a member of the University of Virginia faculty. From 1963 to 1969 he served as Director of Strategic Studies at the Rand Corporation. He was appointed Assistant Director of the Bureau of the Budget in 1969 and continued as Assistant Director during the transition to the Office of Management and Budget. In 1971 President Nixon named him Chairman of the Atomic Energy Commission. He left that position to become DCI. Schlesinger had a clear sense of the purposes intelligence should serve, and during his six-

---

[1] The directive was addressed to the Secretaries of State, Defense, and Treasury, the Attorney General, the Director, Office of Science and Technology, the Chairman of the Joint Chiefs of Staff, PFIAB, and the Atomic Energy Commission.

[1a] IRAC members included representatives from the Departments of State, Defense, OMB, and CIA.

month term he embarked on a series of changes that promised to alter the Agency's and the DCI's existing priorities.

William E. Colby succeeded Schlesinger. An OSS veteran and career DDP officer, Colby's background made him seem of the traditional operations school in the Agency. His overseas assignments included positions in Rome, Stockholm and Saigon, where he was Chief of Station. Yet Colby brought an Agency and community orientation to his term as DCI that was uncommon for DDP careerists. Colby saw himself first as a manager—for both the Agency and the community—rather than an operator.

His position as Executive Director under Schlesinger exposed him to Schlesinger's ideas of reform and reinforced his own disposition for innovation. Well before public disclosures and allegations regarding CIA activities, Colby was committed to reconciling the Agency's priorities with changing public attitudes and expectations. Soon after his appointment, the Agency became the focus of public and Congressional inquiries, and most of the DCI's time was absorbed in responding to these developments.

II. Attempts at Redirection

A. Internal Changes

It is likely that had Schlesinger remained as DCI, he would have assumed a vigorous role in the community and would have attempted to exercise the DCI's latitude in coordinating the activities of the departmental intelligence services. Schlesinger's overall objectives were to maximize his role as Director of Central Intelligence rather than as head of the Agency and to improve the quality of the intelligence product.

To strengthen efforts at better management Schlesinger altered the composition of the IC Staff by increasing the number of non-Agency personnel. In this way he hoped to facilitate the Staff's contacts with the other components of the community.

Schlesinger felt strongly that the Agency was too large. On the operations side, he believed the DDO [2] was overstaffed in proportion to the needs of existing activities. In the area of intelligence production he identified size as impeding the ability of analysts to interact with policymakers. Within six months he reduced personnel by 7 percent—with most of the cuts occurring in the DDO.

Under Colby attempts at innovation continued. Consistent with his management orientation, Colby attempted to alter existing patterns of decisionmaking within the Agency, specifically in the DDO and the Office of National Estimates. The DDO staff structure had created enormous problems of competing claims on operational areas and had fostered the development of small "duchies."

The counterintelligence function had become a separate entity, administered independently of the divisions and controlled by a small group of officers. Under this arrangement counterintelligence was not an integrated element in the Agency's clandestine capability. By breaking down the exclusive jurisdiction of the staff, Colby attempted to

---

[2] Schlesinger changed the name of the Clandestine Service from the Directorate for Plans to the Directorate for Operations.

incorporate counterintelligence into the day-to-day operations of the geographical divisions.

Colby sought to force the DDO to interact with other elements of the Agency. He supported the transfer of the Technical Services Division (TSD) from the DDO to the DDS&T. At the time of the creation of the DDS&T senior officials in the DDO (then DDP) had opposed the transfer of TSD to the new Directorate. That opposition continued. However, in 1973 Colby ordered the transfer. In addition to achieving management consolidation in the area of technology, Colby was attempting to break down the DDO's insularity.

Colby's enactment of the system of Management by Objectives (MBO) in 1973 tried to alter DDO administrative patterns in another way. The MBO system was instituted throughout the Agency, but it potentially affected the DDO the most by attempting to replace the project-based system with specific program objectives against which projects were to be developed. Under MBO, related projects are aggregated into "programs" aimed at a policy objective. As such, the system is primarily a means of evaluation to measure performance against stated objectives. Although the DDO directive establishing MBO in January 1974 ordered the elimination of the project system for purposes of planning, projects remain the basic units for approval procedures and for budgeting at the station and division levels. Thus, the internal demand created by the project system remains. MBO was not intended to rectify the incentives for the generation of projects, and has not succeeded in replacing the project system administratively. The nature of DDO operations makes it difficult to quantify results and therefore limits the utility of MBO. For example, recruitment of three agents over a given period may result in little worthwhile information, while a single agent may produce valuable results.

The changes that occurred on the intelligence side were at least in part a response to existing dissatisfaction with the intelligence product at the policymaking level. The Board of National Estimates had become increasingly insulated from the policymaking process. In 1950 Langer, Smith and Jackson had established the Board with the assumption that senior experts would serve as reviewers for estimates drafted by the ONE staff. Over time the composition of the Board had changed considerably. Rather than continuing to draw on individuals from outside the Agency, the Board became a source of senior staff positions for DDI careerists themselves. Promotion to the Board became the capstone to a successful DDI analyst's career. This meant that the Office and the Board became insular and lacked the benefit of views independent of the DDI intelligence process.

The Office and the Board had become more narrowly focused in other ways as well. ONE had a staff of specialists in geographic and functional areas. In the process of drafting estimates ONE analysts often failed to interact with other DDI experts in the same fields. As intelligence analysis became more sophisticated and specialized, particularly in the economic and strategic areas, Board members' expertise often did not equal the existing level of analysis. Consequently, the Board could not fulfill its function of providing review and criticism. Overall, the intelligence product itself suffered. With little direct contact between ONE and senior policymakers, there was no continuing link between the NIEs and the specific intelligence needs of United States officials. On occasion, Special NIEs (SNIEs) responded to questions specifically posed by policymakers, e.g., if the United States does such and such in Vietnam will the Chinese intervene. Even these documents, however, were seen by policymakers as seldom meeting their real needs. NIEs were defined and produced by a small group of individuals whose perspective was limited by both their lack of access to consumers and by their inbred drafting process.

After his appointment in 1973, when approximately half the Board positions were vacant, Colby abolished ONE and the Board and established in their place the National Intelligence Officers (NIOs). A group of eleven senior specialists in functional and geographic areas, the NIOs are responsible for intelligence collection and production in their designated fields. The senior NIO reports to the DCI. The NIOs serve two specific functions. First, they are the DCI's senior substantive staff officers in their designated specialties. Second, they are coordinators of the intellgence production machinery and are to make recommendations to the DCI on intelligence priorities and the allocation of resources within the communnty. Their access is community-wide including the DDO. Their job is not to serve as drafters of national intelligence estimates but to force the community's intelligence machinery to make judgments by assigning the drafting of estimates to analysts. They do not collectively review estimates in the way that the Board did. Essentially, they are intended to serve as managers and facilitators of information.

Colby was responsible for another management innovation, the Key Intelligence Questions (KIQs). A major problem in the DCI's fulfillment of his role as nominal leader of the intelligence community has been his inability to establish community-wide priorities for the collection and production of national intelligence. As DCI Colby addressed the problem in managerial terms and defined a set of Key Intelligence Questions (KIQs). By establishing specific categories of information needs and by utilizing the NIOs to activate the community's responses, Colby hoped to encourage better policy-related performance. A year after issuance of the KIQs, the NIOs and the Director evaluated the community's responsiveness to the guidelines. The KIQ system has not altered the agencies' independent determination of intelligence collection and production priorities. This applies to the CIA as well as to DIA and the service intelligence agencies.[3] Although the limitations of the KIQ system are a commentary on the DCI's limited authority with regard to the Departments, the system also represents a larger misconception. The notion that control can be imposed from the top over an organization without some effort to alter internal patterns and incentives is ill-founded.

These changes were accompanied by shifts in emphasis in the DDO and the DDI. In the Clandestine Service the scale of covert operations was reduced, and by 1972 the Agency's paramilitary program in Southeast Asia was dissolved. Yet, the overall reduction did not affect the fundamental assumptions, organization, and incentives governing

---

[3] NSA appears to have integrated its requirements more closely with the KIQ system.

the DDO. The rationale remained the same, and the operational capability was intact—as CIA activities in Chile illustrated. Presidents could and did continue to utilize the Agency's covert action capability. CIA operations in Chile included a wide range of the Agency's clandestine repertoire—political action, propaganda, economic activities, labor operations, and liaison relations. In clandestine collection Soviet strategic capabilities remain the first priority. Responding to recent international developments, the DDO expanded its collection activities in other areas, notably international narcotics traffic—with considerable success.

In the DDI, economic intelligence continued to assume increased importance and to take on new dimensions. In sharp contrast to the British intelligence service, which has for generations emphasized international economics, the DDI only recently has begun developing a capability in such areas as international finance, the gold market, and international economic movements. A major impetus for this change came in August 1971 with the U.S. balance of payments crisis. Since that time, the demands for international economic intelligence have escalated dramatically.

In 1974 the Office of Political Research (OPR) was established to provide in-depth foreign political intelligence analysis. OPR is the smallest of the DDI Offices. For the most part, OPR analysts are insulated from day-to-day requests to allow them to concentrate on larger research projects. The Office's creation represented recognition of the need for long-term political research, which was not being fulfilled in the existing DDI structure.

B. Outside Review

Increased Congressional interest in the CIA's intelligence analysis continued in this period. However, oversight of the CIA did not keep abreast of demands for the intelligence product. In 1971 the CIA subcommittee of the Senate Armed Services Committee did not hold one formal meeting to discuss CIA activity; it met only once in 1972 and 1973. One-to-one briefings between the DCI and the senior members continued to characterize the arrangements for Congressional review.

In 1973 Representative Lucien Nedzi made this comment on CIA-Congressional relations:

> Indeed, it is a bit unsettling that 26 years after the passage of the National Security Act the scope of real Congressional oversight, as opposed to nominal Congressional oversight, remains unformed and uncertain.

Nedzi was reflecting the fact that no formalized reporting requirements existed between the CIA and the Congress, particularly with regard to the initiation of covert action. Judgment and informal arrangements dictated the procedures.

Two changes in this period signalled growing Congressional concern with the oversight function. Yet the changes did not alter the fundamental relationship between the Agency and the Congress, which continued to be one of mutual accommodation. Although both the DCI and the Congressional members who were involved in the process appear to have been satisfied with the frequency of exchange and quality of information provided, in 1973 unrest developed among younger members of the House Armed Services Committee who demanded reform in intelligence oversight. Committee Chairman Edward Hébert responded by appointing Nedzi to chair the CIA subcommittee, thus replacing Hébert himself.

In 1975 the Hughes-Ryan Amendment to the Foreign Assistance Act formalized the reporting requirements on covert action. Fundamentally, it increased the number of committees to be informed of covert operations by requiring that the Senate Foreign Relations Committee and the House International Affairs Committee receive appropriate briefings in addition to the four CIA subcommittees. The Amendment did not provide for prior notification or approval of covert action, and as such, still left Congress in the role of passive recipient of information.

The Hughes-Ryan Amendment also altered procedures in the Executive branch somewhat. The Amendment specified that the President himself must inform the Congress of decisions to implement covert operations and must certify that the program(s) are essential to U.S. policy. Until 1974, 40 Committee decisions on covert action were not always referred to the President. Only if there was a disagreement within the Committee or if a member of the Committee thought the proposed operation was important enough or sensitive enough would the President become involved. Once again, these ambiguous arrangements were intentional, designed to protect the President and to blur accountability. The Amendment forced the President both to be informed himself and to inform the legislative branch of covert activities. Congress' action, though limited, reflected the growing momentum for change in the standards of conduct and procedures governing U.S. foreign intelligence activities.

Public disclosures between 1973 and 1974 of alleged CIA domestic programs had contributed to Congress' demand for broader and more regularized participation in decisions regarding CIA activities. Soon after Schlesinger's appointment the Watergate scandal exposed the Agency to charges of involvement with Howard Hunt, former CIA employee. As a result of repeated allegations concerning Agency acquiescence in White House demands related to Watergate revelations, Schlesinger requested that all Agency employees report any past or existing illegal activities to him or the Agency Inspector General. In response, Agency employees presented their knowledge and recollections of 693 possible CIA violations of internal directives. Known as the "Family Jewels," the file was reviewed by the Office of the Inspector General and by then DCI William Colby.

The review revealed the Agency's extensive involvement in domestic intelligence activities—in violation of its foreign intelligence charter. In response to requests from the Federal Bureau of Investigation and from Presidents Johnson and Nixon the Agency had participated in several programs designed to collect intelligence on domestic political groups. Operation CHAOS, whose purpose was to determine whether or not domestic political dissidents, including students, were receiving foreign support, resulted in the Agency's collection of information on thousands of Americans. The Agency's mail opening program, conducted in partial cooperation with the FBI, was directed against political activists, protest organizations, and subversive and extremist groups in the United States. Although the program had begun in the early 1950's as a means of monitoring foreign intelligence activities in the United States, by the late 1960's it had taken on the additional purpose of domestic surveillance. Following the internal Agency review, the mail opening program and Operation CHAOS were discontinued.

In December 1974 newspaper disclosures made further allegations regarding CIA domestic activities. What had been consensual acceptance of the CIA's right to secrecy in the interests of national security was rejected. The Agency's vulnerability to these revelations was indicative of the degree to which American foreign policy and the institutional framework that supported that policy were undergoing redefinition. The closed system that had defined and controlled U.S. intelligence activities and that had left decisions in the hands of a small group of individuals began to break down. The assumptions, procedures and actions that had previously enjoyed unquestionable acceptance began to be reevaluated.

RELATED CHARTS: CIA FUNCTIONS ([84A], p. 393); CIA ORGANIZATION ([45D], pp. 96–102)

CIA FUNCTIONS

INTELLIGENCE

COLLECTION
- Overt
- Technical
- Clandestine
- Counter Intelligence

PROCESSING
- Photographic
- Electronic
- Data Storage
- Analysis

PRODUCTION
- Political
- Economic
- Military
- Scientific
- Biographic

SUPPORT

MANAGEMENT
SERVICES
COMMUNICATIONS

COVERT ACTION

POLITICAL

PARAMILITARY

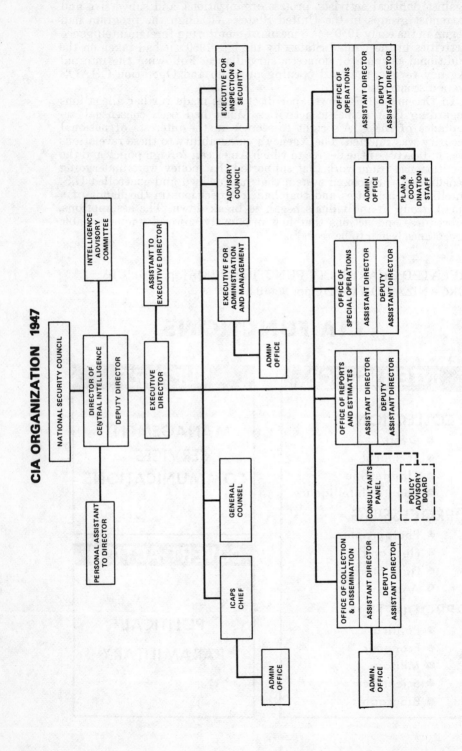

CIA ORGANIZATION 1947

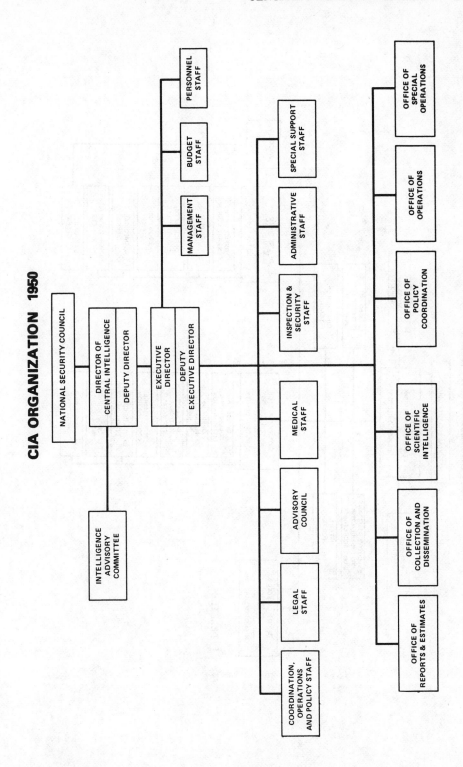

CIA ORGANIZATION 1950

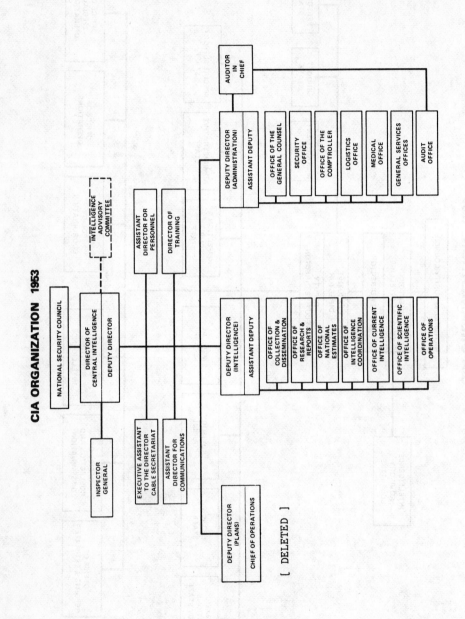

CIA ORGANIZATION 1953

[DELETED]

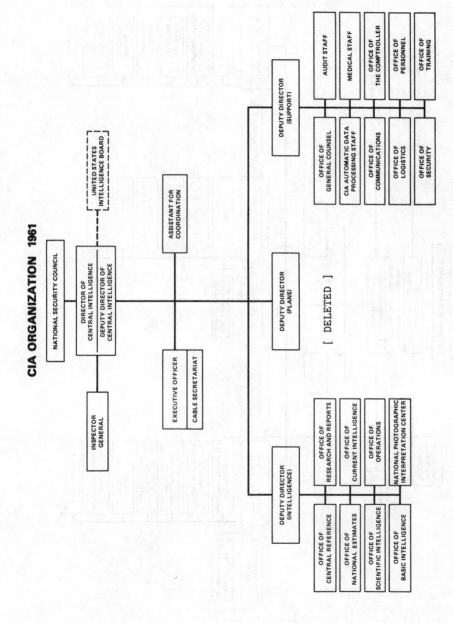

CIA ORGANIZATION 1961

NATIONAL SECURITY COUNCIL

UNITED STATES INTELLIGENCE BOARD

DIRECTOR OF CENTRAL INTELLIGENCE / DEPUTY DIRECTOR OF CENTRAL INTELLIGENCE

INSPECTOR GENERAL

ASSISTANT FOR COORDINATION

EXECUTIVE OFFICER

CABLE SECRETARIAT

DEPUTY DIRECTOR (INTELLIGENCE)

OFFICE OF RESEARCH AND REPORTS

OFFICE OF CURRENT INTELLIGENCE

OFFICE OF OPERATIONS

NATIONAL PHOTOGRAPHIC INTERPRETATION CENTER

OFFICE OF CENTRAL REFERENCE

OFFICE OF NATIONAL ESTIMATES

OFFICE OF SCIENTIFIC INTELLIGENCE

OFFICE OF BASIC INTELLIGENCE

DEPUTY DIRECTOR (PLANS)

[DELETED]

DEPUTY DIRECTOR (SUPPORT)

AUDIT STAFF

MEDICAL STAFF

OFFICE OF THE COMPTROLLER

OFFICE OF PERSONNEL

OFFICE OF TRAINING

OFFICE OF GENERAL COUNSEL

CIA AUTOMATIC DATA PROCESSING STAFF

OFFICE OF COMMUNICATIONS

OFFICE OF LOGISTICS

OFFICE OF SECURITY

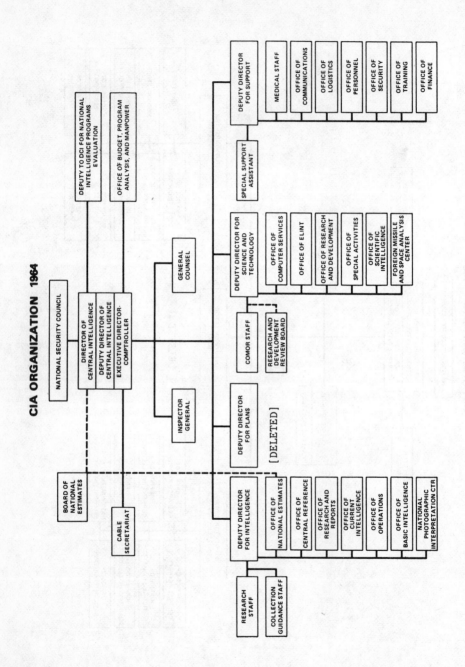

CIA ORGANIZATION 1964

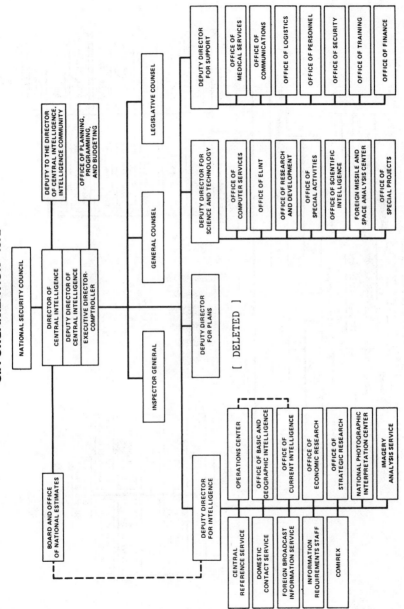

CIA ORGANIZATION 1972

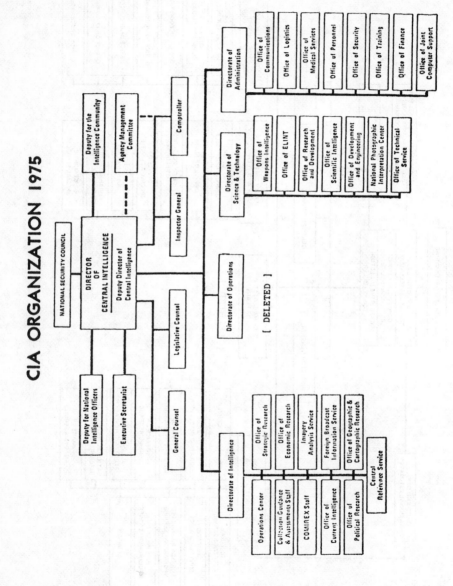

CIA ORGANIZATION 1975

The CIA and the DCI Functions within the Community ([45D], pp. 91–95)

The CIA was conceived and established to provide high-quality intelligence to senior policymakers. Since 1947 the Agency—its structure, its place within the government and its functions—has undergone dramatic change and expansion. Sharing characteristics common to most large, complex organizations, the CIA has responded to rather than anticipated the forces of change; it has accumulated functions rather than redefining them; its internal patterns were established early and have solidified; success has come to those who have made visible contributions in high-priority areas. These general characteristics have affected the specifics of the Agency's development.

The notion that the CIA could serve as a coordinating body for departmental intelligence activities and that the DCI could orchestrate the process did not take into account the inherent institutional obstacles posed by the Departments. From the outset no Department was willing to concede a centralized intelligence function to the CIA. Each insisted on the maintenance of its independent capabilities to support its policy role. With budgetary and management authority vested in the Departments, the Agency was left powerless in the execution of interdepartmental coordination. Even in the area of coordinated national intelligence estimates the Departments did not readily provide the Agency with the data required.

It was not until John McCone's term as DCI that the Agency aggressively sought to assert its position as a coordinating body. That effort demonstrated the complex factors that determined the relative success of community management. One of the principal influences was the support accorded the DCI by the President and the cooperation of the Secretary of Defense. In a situation where the DCI commanded no resources or outright authority, the position of these two individuals was crucial. While Kennedy and McNamara provided McCone with consistent backing in a variety of areas, Nixon and Laird failed to provide Helms with enough support to give him the necessary bureaucratic leverage.

It is clear that the DCIs' own priorities, derived from their backgrounds and interests, influenced the relative success of the Agency's role in interdepartmental coordination. Given the limitations on the DCI's authority, only by making community activities a first order concern and by pursuing the problems assertively, could a DCI begin to make a difference in effecting better management. During Allen Dulles' term interagency coordination went neglected, and the results were expansion of competing capabilities among the Departments. For McCone, community intelligence activities were clearly a priority, and his definition of the DCI's role contributed to whatever advances were made. Helms' fundamental interests and inclinations lay within the Agency, and he did not push his mandate to its possible limits.

The DCI's basic problems have been competing claims on his time and attention and the lack of real authority for the execution of the central intelligence function. As presently defined, the DCI's job is burdensome in the extreme. He is to serve the roles of chief intelligence advisor to the President, manager of community intelligence activities, and senior executive in the CIA. History has demonstrated that the job of the DCI as community manager and as head of the CIA are competing, not complementary roles. In terms of both the demands imposed by each function and the expertise required to fulfill the responsibilities, the two roles differ considerably. In the future separating the functions with precise definitions of authority and responsibilities may prove a plausible alternative.

Although the Agency was established primarily for the purpose of providing intelligence analysis to senior policymakers, within three years clandestine operations became and continued to be the Agency's preeminent activity. The single most important factor in the transformation was policymakers' perception of the Soviet Union as a worldwide threat to United States security. The Agency's large-scale clandestine activities have mirrored American foreign policy priorities. With political operations in Europe in the 1950's, paramilitary operations in Korea, Third World activities, Cuba, Southeast Asia, and currently narcotics control, the CIA's major programs paralleled the international concerns of the United States. For nearly two decades American policymakers considered covert action vital in the struggle against international Communism. The generality of the definition or "threat perception" motivated the continual development and justification of covert activities from the senior policymaking level to the field stations. Apart from the overall anti-Communist motivation, successive Presidential administrations regarded covert action as a quick and convenient means of advancing their particular objectives.

Internal incentives contributed to the expansion in covert action. Within the Agency DDO careerists have traditionally been rewarded more quickly for the visible accomplishments of covert action than for the long-term development of agents required for clandestine collection. Clandestine activities will remain an element of United States foreign policy, and policymakers will directly affect the level of operations. The prominence of the Clandestine Service within the Agency may moderate as money for and high-level Executive interest in covert actions diminish. However, DDO incentives which emphasize operations over collection and which create an internal demand for projects will continue to foster covert action unless an internal conversion process forces a change.

In the past the orientation of DCIs such as Dulles and Helms also contributed to the Agency's emphasis on clandestine activities. It is no coincidence that of those DCIs who have been Agency careerists, all have come from the Clandestine Service. Except for James Schlesinger's brief appointment, the Agency has never been directed by a trained analyst. The qualities demanded of individuals in the DDO—essentially management of people—serve as the basis for bureaucratic skills in the organization. As a result, the Agency's leadership has been dominated by DDO careerists.

Clandestine collection and covert action have had their successes, i.e. individual activities have attained their stated objectives. What the relative contribution of clandestine activities has been—the extent to which they have contributed to or detracted from the implementation of United States foreign policy and whether the results have been worth the risks—cannot be evaluated without wide access to records on covert operations, access the Committee did not have.

Organizational arrangements within the Agency and the decision-making structure outside the Agency have permitted the extremes in

CIA activity. The ethos of secrecy which pervaded the DDO had the effect of setting the Directorate apart within the Agency and allowed the Clandestine Service a measure of autonomy not accorded other Directorates. More importantly, the compartmentation principle allowed units of the DDO freedom in defining operations. In many cases the burden of responsibility fell on individual judgments—a situation in which lapses and deviations are inevitable. Previous excesses of drug testing, assassination planning, and domestic activities were supported by an internal structure that permitted individuals to conduct operations without the consistent necessity or expectation of justifying or revealing their activities.

Ultimately, much of the responsibility for the scale of covert action and for whatever abuses occurred must fall to senior policymakers. The decisionmaking arrangements at the NSC level created an environment of blurred accountability which allowed consideration of actions without the constraints of individual responsibility. Historically the ambiguity and imprecision derived from the initial expectation that covert operations would be limited and therefore could be managed by a small, informal group. Such was the intention in 1948. By 1951 with the impetus of the Korean War, covert action had become a fixed element in the U.S. foreign policy repertoire. The frequency of covert action forced the development of more formalized decisionmaking arrangements. Yet structural changes did not alter ambiguous procedures. In the 1950's the relationship between Secretary of State John Foster Dulles and Allen Dulles allowed informal agreements and personal understandings to prevail over explicit and precise decisions. In addition, as the scale of covert action expanded, policymakers found it useful to maintain the ambiguity of the decisionmaking process to insure secrecy and to allow "plausible deniability" of covert operations.

No one in the Executive—least of all the President—was required to formally sign off on a decision to implement a covert action program. The DCI was responsible for the execution of a project but not for taking the decision to implement it. Within the NSC a group of individuals held joint responsibility for defining policy objectives, but they did not attempt to establish criteria placing moral and constitutional limits on activities undertaken to achieve the objectives. Congress has functioned under similar conditions. Within the Congress a handful of committee members passed on the Agency's budget. Some members were informed of most of the CIA's major activities; others preferred not to be informed. The result was twenty-nine years of acquiescence.

At each level of scrutiny in the National Security Council and in the Congress a small group of individuals controlled the approval processes. The restricted number of individuals involved as well as the assumption that their actions would not be subject to outside scrutiny contributed to the scale of covert action and to the development of questionable practices.

The DDO and the DDI evolved out of separate independent organizations, serving different policy needs. Essentially, the two Directorates have functioned as separate organizations. They maintain totally independent career tracks and once recruited into one, individuals are rarely posted to the other.

In theory the DDO's candestine collection function should have contributed to the DDI's analytic capacity. However, DDO concerns about maintaining the security of its operations and protecting the identity of its agents, and DDI concerns about measuring the reliability of its sources restricted interchange between the two Directorates. Fundamentally, this has deprived the DDI of a major source of information Although DDI–DDO contact has increased during the last five years, it remains limited.

The DDI has traditionally not been informed of sensitive covert operations undertaken by the DDO. This has affected the respective missions of both Directorates. The Clandestine Service has not had the benefit of intelligence support during consideration and implementation of its operations. The Bay of Pigs invasion was an instance in which DDI analysts, even the Deputy Director for Intelligence, were uninformed and represents a situation in which timely analysis of political trends and basic geography might have made a difference— either in the decision to embark on the operation or in the plans for the operation. In the DDI, lack of knowledge about operations has complicated and undermined the analytic effort. Information on a CIA-sponsored political action program would affect judgments about the results of a forthcoming election; information provided by a foreign government official would be invaluable in assessing the motives, policies, and dynamics of that government; information on a CIA-sponsored propaganda campaign might alter analyses of the press or public opinion in that country. Essentially, the potential quality of the finished intelligence product suffers.

The Agency was created in part to rectify the problem of duplication among the departmental intelligence services. Rather than minimizing the problem the Agency has contributed to it by becoming yet another source of intelligence production. Growth in the range of American foreign policy interests and the DDI's response to additional requirements have resulted in an increased scale of collection and analysis. Today, the CIA's intelligence products include: current intelligence in such disparate areas as science, economics, politics, strategic affairs, and technology; quick responses to specific requests from government agencies and officials; basic or long-term research; and national intelligence estimates. With the exception of national intelligence estimates, other intelligence organizations engage in overlapping intelligence analysis.

Rather than fulfilling the limited mission in intelligence analysis and coordination for which it was created, the Agency became a producer of finished intelligence and consistently expanded its areas of responsibility. In political and strategic intelligence the inadequacy of analysis by the State Department and by the military services allowed the Agency to lay claim to the two areas. As the need for specialized research in other subjects developed, the DDI responded—as the only potential source for objective national intelligence. Over time the DDI has addressed itself to a full range of consumers in the broadest number of subject areas. Yet the extent to which the analysis satisfied policymakers' needs and was an integral part of the policy process has been limited.

The size of the DDI and the administrative process involved in the production of finished intelligence—a process which involves numerous stages of drafting and review by large numbers of individuals— precluded close association between policymakers and analysts, between the intelligence product and policy informed by intelligence analysis. Even the National Intelligence Estimates were relegated to briefing papers for second and third level officials rather than the principal intelligence source for senior policymakers that they were intended to be. Recent efforts to improve the interaction include creating the NIO system and assigning two full-time analysts on location at the Treasury Department. Yet these changes cannot compensate for the nature of the intelligence production system itself, which employs hundreds of analysts, most of whom have little sustained contact with their consumers.

At the Presidential level the DCI's position is essential to the utilization of intelligence. The DCI must be constantly informed, must press for access, must vigorously sell his product, and must anticipate future demands. Those DCIs who have been most successful in this dimension have been those whose primary identification was not with the DDO.

Yet the relationship between intelligence analysis and policymaking is a reciprocal one. Senior policymakers must actively utilize the intelligence capabilities at their disposal. Presidents have looked to the Agency more for covert operations than for intelligence analysis. While only the Agency could perform covert operations, decisionmaking methods determined Presidential reliance on the CIA's intelligence capabilities. Preferences for small staffs, individual advisors, the need for specialized information quickly—all of these factors circumscribe a President's channel of information, of which intelligence analysis may be a part. It was John F. Kennedy who largely determined John McCone's relative influence by defining the DCI's role and by including McCone in the policy process; it was Lyndon Johnson and Richard Nixon who limited the roles of Richard Helms and William Colby. Although in the abstract objectivity may be the most desirable quality in intelligence analysis, objective judgments are frequently not what senior officials want to hear about their policies. In most cases, Presidents are inclined to look to the judgments of individuals they know and trust. Whether or not a DCI is included among them is the President's choice.

Over the past thirty years the United States has developed an institution and a corps of individuals who constitute the the the U.S. intelligence profession. The question remains as to how both the institution and the individuals will best be utilized.

THE CIA AS A PRODUCER OF FINISHED INTELLIGENCE ([45A], pp. 257–277)

The main purpose of the intelligence system of the United States is to provide the President, his chief advisers, and the Congress in appropriate ways with the best information about activities abroad that can be obtained. It is not surprising, therefore, that the quality of finished intelligence produced by the intelligence agencies has been a source of continuing concern and controversy. Policymakers are understandably seldom satisfied with the intelligence they receive, for they want and need intelligence which eliminates uncertainties and ensures successful policy decisions. Since such perfection is unattainable, however, the realistic question is how to evaluate and improve the quality

N12

of our finished intelligence. This is an extremely complicated and difficult area. The simple answer is that there are no objective criteria or standards that can be universally applied. In the end, the assessment by policymakers of the value and quality of our finished intelligence is necessarily subjective. There is a record of steadily improved quality over the years, but the need for a higher level of performance is accepted, both at the policy level and among the intelligence agencies of the U.S. Government.

The Committee's examination of the production of finished intelligence focused on the CIA and within it, the Directorate of Intelligence (DDI). This is by no means the whole of national intelligence, but it is the core element in the production of finished national intelligence. The CIA's Directorate of Intelligence is by far the best analytical organization for the production of finished intelligence within the Government, but it does have shortcomings. The CIA for its part has, in the view of the Committee, made creditable efforts to improve the quality of finshed intelligence, although much remains to be done.

Because the provision of the best possible fact and predictive analysis to our policymakers is the most important mission of our intelligence system, the problems of the production of finished intelligence will require the most searching and systematic examination by a future oversight committee. The preliminary work of the Select Committee in this area is based on interviews and hearings, as well as documents from the Intelligence Community Staff concerning their post-mortems of past intelligence failures. Because of the complexity and difficulty of the subject matter, the examination of the Select Committee can only be regarded as a beginning, only broadly indicative of the problems involved, and suggestive of the areas which will require more thorough and comprehensive attention in the future.

Although the provision of intelligence analysis to policymakers is the major purpose of the intelligence mission, the production of intelligence has been referred to as the "stepchild of the community." [1] It is an area which has been overshadowed by the glamour of clandestine activities and the lure of exotic technical collection systems. Yet the basic rationale for intelligence operations is the provision of information to the people who need it in order to do their jobs—the President and other senior officials responsible for the formulation and implementation of foreign policy.

The Pearl Harbor experience, which so heavily influenced the establishment of the Central Intelligence Agency in 1947, pointed to the need for the collection, coordination, and analysis of all national intelligence in a centralized fashion, so that policymakers could be assured of receiving all the information they needed, when they needed it. Finished intelligence represents the "payoff" of investment in the plethora of collection activities.

N13

The CIA and its predecessor body, the Central Intelligence Group, were established to rectify the duplication and biases that existed in the intelligence production of the State Department and the military services. By reviewing and analyzing the data collected by these departments, the CIA was to provide senior government officials with high-quality, objective intelligence. In practice, however, the CIA

---

[1] Office of Management and Budget, "A Review of the Intelligence Community," 3/10/71, (hereinafter cited as the Schlesinger Report), p. 11.

has given precedence to independent collection and production, becoming a competing department in the dissemination of information.

Historically, the departments resisted providing their data to the Agency and thereby prevented the CIA from fulfilling its designated role in the production of "coordinated" intelligence. Moreover, individual Directors of Central Intelligence have not been consistent advocates of the Agency's intelligence production function. For the DCIs, the demands of administering an organization with thousands of employees and in particular, the requirements of supervising clandestine operations encroached on the intended priority of intelligence production. Only three DCIs attempted to address their primary attention to the quality of intelligence production: Walter Bedell Smith, John McCone, and James Schlesinger. In each case, the DCI's attitude was a function of his background, his relative strength as Director, and the particular demands of his time in office.

In recent years, however, and particularly with the introduction of advanced technical collection systems, the requirement for bringing together the vast quantities of information into useable analytic forms has become the primary concern of the intelligence community.

In the course of its investigation, certain problems and issues in the area of the production of finished intelligence in the CIA have come to the attention of the Committee. The Committee believes these problems deserve immediate attention by both the executive branch and future congressional oversight bodies. These problems bear directly on the priority given to finished intelligence by policymakers. Other issues raised here, such as the personnel system of the DDI and the organizational structure of intelligence production, are really functions of the larger issue of priorities.

Briefly defined, the production of intelligence is the process whereby the data collected by the intelligence community is transformed into intelligence reports and studies that are relevant to the concerns of senior policymakers. Intelligence production involves many tasks. It begins with the collation and evaluation of incoming "raw" intelligence reporting—direct from the collectors, whether from open sources, the clandestine service, or signals intercepts and other means of technical collection. The significance of new reporting is analyzed, often in relation to intelligence already available on the subject. The preparation of "finished" intelligence reports—the outcome of the production process—thus entails the evaluation and analysis of the full range of raw reporting from a variety of collection means.

Production of finished intelligence is done within the intelligence community by the Central Intelligence Agency, the Defense Intelligence Agency (DIA), and the State Department's Bureau of Intelligence and Research (INR). Within the CIA (which is responsible for the production of "national intelligence"), both the Intelligence Directorate and the Directorate of Science and Technology (DDS&T) produce finished intelligence. The Select Committee has focused on the DDI, although the issues and problems cited are applicable in varying degrees to the other production elements as well.

A. Evolution of the CIA's Intelligence Directorate

The scope of the DDI mission is global. It covers the affairs of any foreign country from the standpoint of politics, economics, defense, geography, cartography and biography. Scientific reporting is largely the responsibility of the Directorate of Science and Technology.

The Directorate of Intelligence was formally established on January 2, 1952. Specifically, the intelligence activities which the DDI originally administered were:

a. Production of finished intelligence by the Offices of National Estimates (ONE), Current Intelligence (OCI), Research and Reports (ORR), and Scientific Intelligence (OSI).

b. Collection of essentially overt information by the Divisions of the Office of Operations (OO): Foreign Broadcast Information (FBID), Foreign Documents (FDD), and Contacts (CD).

c. Dissemination, storage and retrieval of unevaluated intelligence information and basic reference documentation by the Office of Collection and Dissemination (OCD).

d. Coordination of intelligence collection by the Office of Intelligence Coordination (OIC).

In the twenty-three years since its founding, the Intelligence Directorate has gone through a number of reorganizations stimulated by advice from external panels, changing international circumstances, shifting requirements for finished intelligence production, and reduced resources with which to perform its mission.[2] Changes in the first few years were fairly rare. In 1954, the OIC was abolished, and in 1963 the Office of Scientific Intelligence was transferred to a new Directorate for Science and Technology.

1. Intelligence Production

Estimative Intelligence.—Producing National Intelligence Estimates (NIEs) was the function of the Office of National Estimates which was in the Intelligence Directorate until 1966, when it became a staff under the direction of the Director of Central Intelligence. This move was made, in part, to emphasize that the NIEs were the product of the entire intelligence community rather than a single agency. ONE was abolished in 1973 and its responsibilities were transferred to the newly formed National Intelligence Officers attached to the Office of the DCI. With this move, much of the work of producing draft estimates reverted to the production offices of the Intelligence Directorate.

Current Intelligence.—Primary responsibilities for producing current intelligence remains where it has been since the Directorate was established—in the Office of Current Intelligence. Originally, OCI was responsible for all current intelligence reporting except economic. At present, however, it concentrates on current political reporting, leaving the preparation of reports on economic, military, geographic and scientific developments to the research offices responsible for these matters. OCI coordinates and consolidates this specialized reporting on all subjects for presentation in its daily intelligence publications.

Basic Intelligence.—Production of basic intelligence was stimulated primarily by the realization in World War II that the U.S. Government had too little information about many of the foreign countries

---

[2] The information contained in this section on the evolution of the DDI is derived primarily from a CIA paper prepared for the Select Committee by the Office of the DDI, "The Directorate of Intelligence: A Brief Description". (Hereinafter cited as "The Directorate of Intelligence.") December 1975.

with which it was required to deal. The Basic Intelligence Division (BID) or ORR was charged with responsibility for coordinating the production of "factual intelligence . . . of a fundamental and more or less permanent nature on all foreign countries." Because of the scope of the subject matter, the production of this type of intelligence required a cooperative effort involving the resources and capabilities of several departments and agencies of the Federal Government. The product of this government-wide effort was known as the National Intelligence Surveys (NIS).

In 1955, BID became a separate office, the Office of Basic Intelligence (OBI). This was in line with recommendations made in May 1955 by the Task Force on Intelligence Activities.[3] The elevation of Basic Intelligence to Office status was an acknowledgment of the importance that the Agency and the rest of the national security apparatus attached to the NIS Program.

The early years of OBI were devoted mostly to the coordination of this program. Many of the chapters were written by other elements of CIA or by other government agencies on a contractual basis. In 1961, OBI took over responsibility for the production of the political sections of the NIS from the State Department's Bureau of Intelligence and Research when State claimed that it no longer had the resources to do this work. OBI delegated the task of producing these sections to OCI in 1962. In 1965, the geographic research function was transferred from the Office of Research and Reports, creating the Office of Basic and Geographic Intelligence (OBGI). The NISs continued to be published until 1974 when the program was terminated because of lack of resources. At this time, OBGI became the Office of Geographic and Cartographic Research.

Military Intelligence.—Until the mid 1950's, the production of intelligence on military matters had been considered the primary responsibility of the Department of Defense. But the "bomber gap" and later the "missile gap" controversies gave CIA a role in foreign military research, an involvement which has continued and expanded. In 1960 the DDI created an *ad hoc* Guided Missiles Task Force to foster the collection of information on Soviet guided missiles and to produce intelligence on their manufacture and deployment. The Task Force was abolished in 1961 and a Military Research Area was established in ORR. As a result of increasing demands for CIA analysis of military developments, a new Office of Strategic Research was established in 1967 by consolidating the Military-Economic Research Area of ORR and the Military Division of OCI. The scope and focus of responsibilities of OSR have increased over the years and in 1973 a new component for research in Soviet and Chinese strategic policy and military doctrine was added.

Geographic Intelligence.—The Geographic Research Area (GRA) of the Office of Research and Reports (ORR) originally had the responsibility for geographic intelligence production. The GRA was transferred in 1965 to the Office of Basic Intelligence changing its title to the Office of Basic and Geographic Intelligence (OBGI). In 1974, OBGI became the Office of Geographic and Cartographic Research when the National Intelligence Survey (NIS) Program was abandoned.

---

[3] The Clark Task Force, headed by Gen. Mark Clark, of the Hoover Commission. For members of the task force, see Hearings, Vol. 4, p. 112–13.

Economic Intelligence.—Activity in this area remains the responsibility of the organization that succeeded the Office of Research and Reports in 1967 : the Office of Economic Research. In earlier years, the Agency concentrated its economic research largely on the Communist states. In recent years, however, the Department of State has dropped much of its intelligence production on the non-Communist areas, leaving this job to the Agency. OER has also expanded its research into such subject areas as international energy supplies and international trade. Today it is the largest research office in the Intelligence Directorate.

Biographic Intelligence.—The Hoover Commission Report of 1949 recommended dividing the responsibility for biographic intelligence production within the Community to prevent costly duplicaton. As a result, the foreign political personality files maintained by OCD were transferred to State. In 1961, however, the Bureau of Intelligence and Research claimed it no longer had the resources to provide this service and the responsibility for reporting on foreign political personalities and, subsequently, for all non-military biographic intelligence reporting was transferred to CIA. The task was taken over by OCD's successor organization, now the Central Reference Service.

In-Depth Political Research.—In-depth foreign political intelligence reporting has not been, until recently, represented in the Office structure of the Intelligence Directorate. Originally, whatever efforts were made in this field were concentrated in OCI. In 1962, a modest step toward increased foreign political research was taken with the establishment of a Special Research Staff (SRS) in the Office of the Deputy Director for Intelligence. In recent years, however, the diminished role of State's Bureau of Intelligence and Research in intelligence community affairs, a perceived need for more sophisticated work in this field by CIA, and the appearance of new methods of political research, including computer applications, encouraged the Directorate to invest more resources in this area. Accordingly, an Office of Political Research (OPR) was established in 1974. It incorporated the Special Research Staff, some people from OCI and the then disbanding Office of National Estimates.

Round-the-Clock Watch/Alert.—The Cuban Missile Crisis of the fall of 1962 clearly spotlighted the need for a single Directorate facility for round-the-clock receipt of intelligence information and for a center in which the expertise of all its offices could be rallied in crisis situations. In March 1963, the DDI set up a Special Study Group on DDI Organizational Tasks to study this and other problems. One of the results of its work was the establishment of an operations center under the administrative direction of the Office of Current Intelligence (OCI). Over the next ten years, the Operations Center grew in size and capability, largely as a result of the Vietnam War. In 1974, it was separated from OCI and renamed the CIA Operations Center, a title warranted by the fact that all Directorates of the Agency now maintain permanent duty officers within the Center. Today, the CIA Operations Center provides the mechanism and facilities with which the full information resources of CIA can be mobilized to work in concert with the community in foreign crisis situations.

2. Intelligence Collection

At its founding in 1952, the Intelligence Directorate inherited the Office of Operations (OO) from the then Directorate of Plans—today's Operations Directorate. OO was composed of three main elements : the

Contact Division, the Foreign Broadcast Information Division, and the Foreign Documents Division. The rationale for including these components in the Intelligence Directorate was that their work was essentially overt and thus inappropriately situated within the Clandestine Service.

The Domestic Contact Service originated in the Central Intelligence Group in 1946 as an outgrowth of the World War II effort to insure that all domestic sources of information on foreign activities were contacted by the Government. It was initially placed in OO to keep its essentially overt work separate from the clandestine activity of the other major collection organizations. It maintained this separate status after the founding of CIA, but in 1951 joined the Directorate of Plans. This arrangement lasted for only one year, however, as the OO and its Contact Division (CD) was moved to the Intelligence Directorate in 1952. By 1953, CD was a network of offices in 15 major cities and several smaller residencies established across the U.S. With the abolition of OO in 1965, CD became an independent office known as the Domestic Contact Service (DCS) and continued in that status until the appointment of William Colby as DCI. In 1973, he decided that maintaining the separation of overt and covert collection elements was less important than the goal of consolidation of all human collection capabilities in the Operations Directorate. Accordingly, the DCS was transferred to the Clandestine Service and renamed the Domestic Collection Division.

The Foreign Broadcast Information Division (FBID) had been founded by the Federal Communications Commission in 1940. With the advent of World War II, it was absorbed by the Office of War Information and, shortly thereafter, became one of the original elements of the OSS. At the end of the war, it was briefly administered by the Department of the Army before joining the Central Intelligence Group in 1946. It was formally included in the Agency's Directorate of Plans at its founding in December 1950 and remained there as part of OO until its transfer to the Intelligence Directorate in 1952. By then it had established the worldwide network of broadcast monitoring bureaus which—with some alterations in location—it operates today. FBID received the status of an independent office and was renamed the Foreign Broadcast Information Service with the dissolution of the Office of Operations in 1965.

3. Information Processing

Between the collection and production phases of the intelligence process there is an activity known as "information processing." Information processing involves special skills or equipment to convert certain kinds of raw information into a form usable by intelligence analysts who are producing finished intelligence. It includes things like photointerpretation and translations of foreign documents as well as the receipt, dissemination, indexing, storage, and retrieval of the great volumes of data which must be available to the production offices if they are to do their analytical work.

Information Dissemination, Storage and Retrieval.—One of the original offices of the Central Intelligence Group, the Office of Collection & Dissemination (OCD), began this work in 1948 when it introduced business machines to improve reference, liaison and document security services. Ultimately, this Office became CIA's own departmental library and centralized document service. Its steady growth in size and capabilities was given a boost in 1954, when responsibility for the procurement of foreign documents was transferred to OCD from the Department of State. Other specialized collections also became a part of the holdings of that office, including those of motion picture film and photography. The systems of storage and retrieval developed by OCD were unusually effective for that time and the Office began to gain recognition throughout the intelligence community. In 1955, OCD was renamed the Office of Central Reference to more accurately reflect its Agency-wide responsibilities. In 1967, OCR was renamed the Central Reference Service (CRS). Today, CRS can offer intelligence analysts throughout the community some of the most sophisticated information storage and retrieval systems to be found anywhere in the world.

Photographic Interpretation.—CIA's work with photographic interpretation began in 1952 and was initially centered in the Geographic Research Area, ORR. In 1958, a new Photographic Intelligence Center (PIC) was created by fusing the Photo Intelligence Division of ORR with the Statistical Branch of OCR. The new Center was given office-level status and the responsibility for producing photographic intelligence and providing related services for CIA and the rest of the Intelligence Community. In 1961 PIC was further elevated to become the National Photographic Interpretation Center (NPIC). This Center was staffed by former members of PIC and DIA personnel detailed to NPIC. All personnel were functionally under the Director, NPIC, who continued to report to the DDI.

An interagency study conducted in 1967 concluded that NPIC's national intelligence responsibilities had grown so substantially that departmental imagery analysis requirements were not being adequately served. Accordingly, the DDI established an Imagery Analysis Service (IAS) as a separate office of the Directorate to deal exclusively with the photo intelligence requirements of CIA. In 1973, it was decided that NPIC would be more appropriately placed in the Directorate of Science and Technology with other elements dealing with reconnaissance at the national level.

Translation Services.—The Foreign Documents Division (FDD) of the Office of Operations (OO) had its origin in the Army and Navy's Washington Document Center. Founded in 1944, it was a repository for captured Japanese and German records. It was absorbed by the Central Intelligence Group in 1946 and, during the late forties, evolved from a repository into an exploiter of all foreign language documents coming into the community. It joined the Central Intelligence Agency as part of OO in the Directorate of Plans. With the transfer of OO to the Intelligence Directorate in 1952, FDD continued to expand its work into the field of document exploitation, concentrating increasingly on materials received from the communist countries. In 1964, it was separated from OO to become part of the Office of Central Reference (OCR). This arrangement lasted only three years, however, as FDD was transferred again to become part of FBIS in 1967. The intent of this move was to combine the Directorate's efforts to exploit foreign media—radio and press—in a single service and to concentrate its major assets in terms of foreign language capabilities. FDD remains in FBIS to this day, providing translation services for the Agency, the community, and to a lesser degree, for the Government and the general public.

DIRECTORATE OF INTELLIGENCE

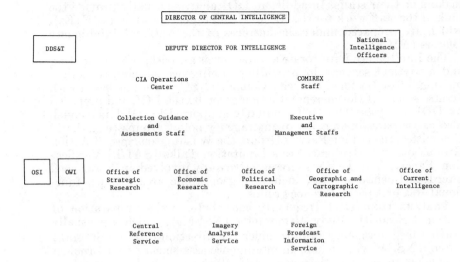

B. The Intelligence Directorate Today

In FY 1976, the DDI had a relatively small share of the Agency's budget and personnel. Resources allocated to intelligence production have represented a relatively steady percentage of the intelligence budget over the years. Intelligence production is a people-intensive activity, requiring relatively little in the way of supplies, equipment, structures, and operational funding. The Intelligence Director spends approximately 75 percent of its budget on salaries. Of the positions in the DDI, 74 percent are classified as professional and 26 percent as clerical. Of the total, 54 percent are directly involved in "intelligence production" (researching data, analyzing information and writing reports), 28 percent are tasked with "intelligence processing" (performing reference and retrieval functions, preparing publications, or providing other support services), and 18% are involved in "intelligence collection" (monitoring overt foreign radio broadcasts and publications).[4]

The most important group of DDI products consists of the daily intelligence publications, designed "to alert the foreign affairs community to significant developments abroad and to analyze specific problems or broadly-based trends in the international arena." [5] These include the *President's Daily Brief;* the *National Intelligence Daily*, prepared for Cabinet and sub-Cabinet level consumers; and the *National Intelligence Bulletin,* distributed more broadly to the defense and foreign affairs communities. The DDI issues a number of weekly periodicals on specialized subjects, prepared in the research offices of the directorate.

---

[4] "The Directorate of Intelligence," p. 4.
[5] *Ibid.,* p. 2.

The DDI also produces in-depth and analytical studies on a periodic or one-time basis. These are monographs on particular problems; some are DDI-initiated, others respond to specific requests of the policy-makers or their staffs. In addition, DDI analysts usually provide the bulk of the staff work for the National Intelligence Estimates (NIEs), which are prepared under the auspices of the National Intelligence Officers (NIOs).[6]

The Intelligence Directorate also performs a variety of coordinating and analytical services in providing intelligence support to policy-making. Most National Security Council (NSC) meetings begin with an assessment of the current situation given by the DCI, and prepared by DDI analysts. The DCI, similarly supported by DDI personnel, also participates in an array of interagency policy groups (e.g., the 40 Committee, the Senior Review Group, the Washington Special Action Group, and the Strategic Arms Limitation Talks [SALT] Verification Panel). The DCI's representatives are involved in lower-level interdepartmental groups, including geographic area groups, functional area groups, and ad hoc groups.

Analysts from DDI frequently contribute to the preparation of National Security Study Memoranda (NSSMs), which are usually drafted by interagency groups under the direction of the NSC staff. Often a NSSM will include an intelligence assessment of the problem at hand as an annex to the memo itself; this might also be summarized in the text.

Three examples illustrate how the DDI contributes such intelligence support. A SALT support staff has been assembled in CIA to coordinate SALT-related activities of production offices in the DDI and DDS&T. The staff serves as the point of contact to respond to intelligence requirements generated by the NSC staff, the Verification Panel, and the U.S. SALT delegation. The staff relies on the analytical offices of the CIA for substantive intelligence.

In another case, after the 1973 Middle East war, the DDI was asked to examine all aspects of possible Sinai withdrawal lines on the basis of political, military, geographic, and ethnic considerations. Eight alternative lines were prepared for the Sinai, a number of which Secretary of State Henry Kissinger used in mediating the negotiations between Egypt and Israel.

Finally, the DDI provided assessments to the policy groups who prepared U.S. positions for the Law of the Sea Conference in 1975, including descriptions of the strategic straits under discussion, analysis of each country's undersea mineral resources, and information about political positions the participating countries would be likely to take.[7]

THE ISSUES

The Select Committee began its examination of intelligence production by considering the relationship between intelligence and policy, and the limits of intelligence. These considerations served to highlight certain problems in production which the Committee feels deserve further attention by both the executive branch and congressional oversight bodies. These problems bear on the key issues of quality, timeliness and relevance of finished intelligence. They derive in large part

---

[6] *Ibid.*, p. 2.
[7] Staff summary of briefing given by Edward Proctor (DDI), 4/24/75.

from the nature of presidential leadership and the particular emphasis and preoccupations of successive Directors of Central Intelligence. In the past, the national leadership has used the CIA more for operational purposes than for its analytic capabilities. Other concerns derive from the structure of the analytical personnel system, the intelligence culture and the nature of the intelligence process, the overload of the system, the preoccupation with current events, and the lack of sufficient quality control and consumer guidance and evaluation.

C. The Relationship Between Intelligence and Policy

The relationship between intelligence and policy is a delicate and carefully balanced one. One witness told the Select Committee that there is a "natural tension" between the two and that

> if the policy-intelligence relationship is to work, there must be mutual respect, trust, civility, and also a certain distance. Intelligence people must provide honest and best judgments and avoid intrusion on decisionmaking or attempts to influence it. Policymakers must assume the integrity of the intelligence provided and avoid attempts to get materials suited to their tastes.[8]

N14

In recent years there has been a tendency on the part of high officials, including Presidents and Secretaries of State, to call for both raw reporting and finished intelligence to flow upwards through separate channels, rather than through a centralized analytical component. This has resulted in many cases in consumers doing the work of intelligence analysts. Presidents and Secretaries of State have all too often relished the role of "crisis managers", moving from one serious issue to another and sacrificing analysis and considered judgment in the pressure of events. In between crises, their attention is turned to other pressing matters, and careful long-range analysis tends to be set aside.

By circumventing the available analytical process, the consumers of intelligence may not only be depriving themselves of the skills of intelligence professionals; they may also be sacrificing necessary time and useful objectivity. In making his own intelligence judgment based on the large volume of often conflicting reports and undigested raw intelligence instead of on a well-considered finished piece of intelligence analysis, a high official may be seeking conclusions more favorable to his policy preferences than the situation may in fact warrant.

The essential questions about the intelligence product concern its usefulness to the policymakers for whom it is intended. Does intelligence address the right questions? Does it deliver the kinds of information and insights policymakers need in order to make foreign policy decisions? Is it timely? Is it presented and disseminated in the manner and format most useful to the consumers? Will they read it in other than crisis situations? The answers to these questions are by no means simple. Still, the Select Committee believes they are deserving of examination—and periodic reexamination—in the interests of maintaining an effective intelligence service.

While intelligence analysts have a very good record in the area of technical assessment (e.g., hard data on foreign military hard-

---

[8] John Huizenga testimony, 1/26/76, p. 14.

ware), the record is weaker in qualitative judgments, trend forecasting, and political estimating. While analysts may be able to furnish fairly complete and reliable reporting on tangible factors such as numbers and make-up of Soviet strategic missile forces, they are not as good at assessing such intangibles as why the Soviets are building such a force. The problem pertains to other issues, too, for example, in analyzing the likely negotiating stance of a particular country in economic negotiations of interest to the United States.

In particular, some policymakers feel that intelligence analysts have not been especially helpful to policymakers on the more subtle questions of political, economic, and military intentions of foreign groups and leaders. The view from the top is, of course, very different from the view held by analysts in the departments and agencies or in the field. Too often analysts are not willing to address such questions directly. Analysts tend to believe that policymakers want answers instead of insights. Some consumers argue that intelligence analysts lack sufficient awareness of the real nature of the national security decisionmaking process—how it really works, where and how intelligence fits in, and what kinds of information are important.[9]

On the other hand, the Select Committee is concerned that analysts are not always kept sufficiently informed, in a timely fashion, of U.S. policies and activities which affect their analyses and estimates. The Committee is concerned that the secrecy and compartmentation surrounding security policy decisionmaking affects the relevance and quality of intelligence analysis. The analysts in the DDI may not always be aware of what a key foreign leader has told high-level American policymakers in private, and so they may be missing crucial information on a particular nation's intentions in a given situation.

The Select Committee's study of covert action has revealed that on a number of occasions in the past intelligence analysts were not told what U.S. covert operators were doing abroad, an omission which could seriously affect the accuracy of intelligence assessments. Likewise, because of security compartmentation, DDI analysts sometimes did not know about particular U.S. strategic weapons R&D programs, and so were not able to assess completely the reasons for countermeasures that were being taken in the development of Soviet strategic forces.

D. The Limits of Intelligence

Clearly what is needed is a realistic understanding by both producers and consumers about the limits of intelligence: what it can and cannot do. As a former senior analyst explained to the Select Committee,[10] what intelligence *can* do is to follow the behavior of foreign leaders and groups over a long period of time in order to get a sense of the parameters within which their policies move. American policymakers are not then likely to be greatly surprised by foreign behavior even though intelligence analysts might not be able to predict precise intentions at any given moment with respect to a given situation. Nor can analysts be expected to predict human events when often the actors themselves do not know in advance what they will do. As the Schlesinger Report said:

---

[9] Staff summary of Andrew Marshall interview, 2/10/76.
[10] Huizenga, 1/26/76, p. 24.

In a world of perfect information, there would be no uncertainties about the present and future intentions, capabilities, and activities of foreign powers. Information, however, is bound to be imperfect for the most part. Consequently, the intelligence community can at best reduce the uncertainties and construct plausible hypotheses about these factors on the basis of what continues to be partial and often conflicting evidence.[11]

To expect more may be to court disappointment. Despite this recognition on the part of many policymakers, if analysis is not correct, there is often the charge of an "intelligence failure." Good intelligence or accurate predictions cannot insure against bad policy, in any case. For example, as the current Deputy Director for Intelligence maintains, the pessimistic CIA estimates on Vietnam had little or no effect on U.S. policy decisions there. Vietnam may have been a policy failure. It was not an intelligence failure.[12] Similarly, the United States had intelligence on the possibility of a Turkish invasion of Cyprus in 1974. The problem of taking effective action to prevent such an invasion was a policy question and not an intelligence failure.

E. The Personnel System

To some extent, problems in the quality of the analytical performance of the intelligence community are simply in the nature of things. The collection function lends itself to technical and managerial approaches, while the analytical job is more dependent on the intangibles of brainpower. In the final analysis, the intelligence product can only be as good as the people who produce it.

The CIA prides itself on the qualifications of its analysts. The Agency's exemption from Civil Service constraints—unlike the DIA, for example—has enabled the DDI to attract the best analysts in the community. Nevertheless, those in the highest positions in the CIA have traditionally come from the operations side of the Agency.

The Agency's promotion system is structured in such a way that the most outstanding lower-level people are singled out for advancement into managerial positions. Such a system works well for the purposes of the Directorate of Operations (DDO), where the skills necessary for good management are essentially the same as those required of a good case officer. But when applied to the DDI, that system encourages the best analysts to assume supervisory positions, reducing the time available to utilize their analytical skills.

Although the CIA has several hundred "supergrade" positions [13]— and very few government agencies are permitted so high a number— there are virtually no "supergrade" slots which involve only, or even primarily, analytic responsibilities. The Agency maintains that DDI supervisors are indeed analysts, since they review and critique the work of junior analysts. In this view, supervisory positions amplify the analytical capabilities of senior personnel. Thus, there is not "supervision" in the usual sense by DDI supervisors; they are viewed as participants in the analytical process.[14]

---

[11] Schlesinger Report, p. 10a.
[12] Staff summary of Edward Proctor interview, 5/16/75.
[13] John Clarke testimony, 2/4/76, p. 37.
[14] Proctor (Staff summary), 3/1/76.

The Office of National Estimates was the only place where a regular arrangement for high-level analysts existed, but that office was abolished in 1973. Today only the DDI's Office of Political Research (OPR) has been able to retain several supergrade staffers who do only analysis (out of a staff of about 40 to 50 analysts.) The OPR, created only in 1974, is treated by the DDI as an elite group. Much of its work is interdisciplinary in nature. The emphasis is placed on keeping OPR analysts out of the everyday routine of requests for current intelligence work which can be performed by other offices in the directorate.[15]

Some analysts complain that the personnel system has fostered too much bureaucratic "layering," and that there are too many people writing reports *about* reports. The effects are predictable. In the words of former DCI and Secretary of Defense James Schlesinger, "If you've got too much specialization and pigeonholing of people, you get the kind of people in the intelligence game who don't mind being pigeonholed, and the entire U.S. intelligence establishment is too much bureaucratized." [16] The Intelligence Community (IC) staff, in its post-mortems of major U.S. intelligence failures, has pointed in all cases to the shortage of talented personnel. As the former deputy head of the IC staff pointed out to the Select Committee in his testimony, "giving people more flexibility in pay scale and so forth doesn't always guarantee that they hire the right people." [17]

F. Recruitment and Training of Analysts

The Agency tends to bring analysts in early in their professional life, emphasizing lifetime careers in intelligence work and the development of institutional commitment. There has traditionally been minimal lateral entry of established analysts and experts into the profession at middle and upper levels (more in DDS&T than in DDI.)[18] This might be characterized as the "craft guild" approach to intelligence, where recruits are brought in to serve their apprenticeships within the ranks of the profession.[19]

Specialized analytical training for intelligence analysts is quite limited. The CIA's Office of Training (OTR) has a program in methodology and research techniques and a variety of mid-career courses and senior seminars. About 25% of the DDI personnel who receive in-house training are in management and executive development courses. Various DDI offices sponsor courses on specific skills such as computers and statistics.[20] For the most part in the past the Agency-run courses available were oriented toward developing skills necessary for clandestine activity. According to Dr. Schlesinger:

> Within the CIA, most of the training effort in the past has gone into training operators rather than training analysts.[21]

The Agency maintains there is now an increased emphasis on the development of sophisticated analytical skills and understanding.

---

[15] *Ibid.*
[16] James Schlesinger testimony, 2/2/76, p. 72.
[17] Clarke, 2/5/76, p. 38.
[18] In FY 1975, 18 analysts out of 105 hired from outside the CIA by the DDI were at GS–12 to 15.
[19] Marshall (Staff summary), 2/10/76.
[20] Proctor (Staff summary), 3/1/76.
[21] Schlesinger, 2/2/76, p. 27.

Most of the substantive training for intelligence analysts takes place outside the Agency, both in academic institutions and in other government departments. Of the total number of DDI personnel participating in such external training in FY 1975, about one quarter were involved in training courses longer than 6 weeks in duration.

G. The Intelligence Culture and Analytical Bias

There is a set of problems stemming from what might be called the intelligence "culture"—a particular outlook sometimes attributed to the analysts which tends to affect the overall quality of judgment reflected in their work. Although the problem of preconceptions is one of the most intractable in intelligence analysis, it clearly is one of the most critical, and has been a focal point of the IC staff post-mortems. As one former senior official told the Select Committee, "By and large, good intelligence production should be as free as possible from ideological biases, and the higher the degree of ideological bias, the greater will be the blind spots." [22]

Among the examples of analytical/intellectual bias and preconceptions are the following: In 1962, some CIA analysts judged that the Soviets would not put missiles into Cuba because such a move would be "aberrational." [23] In 1973 most of the intelligence community was disposed to believe that the Arabs were unlikely to resort to war against Israel because to do so would be "irrational," in light of relative Arab-Israeli military capabilities. [24]

The same mechanism operated—the inability to foresee critical events, in the face of mounting evidence to the contrary—during the Cyprus crisis in the summer of 1974. According to the IC Staff post-mortem of that episode, the CIA analysts were again prey to:

> the perhaps subconscious conviction (and hope) that, ultimately, reason and rationality will prevail, that apparently irrational moves (the Arab attack, the Greek-sponsored coup) will not be made by essentially rational men.

The charge is frequently made that intelligence estimates issued by the Defense Department and the military services are not wholly objective, since those groups have particular departmental interests and programs to advocate. By contrast, the CIA is supposed to be free from such bias. But although the DDI is not in the position of having to defend budgetary items or particular weapons systems, in the view of other parts of the intelligence community, there has been a tendency for a CIA institutional bias to develop over time. The Committee notes that some observers have pointed to a CIA "line" on certain issues.

H. The Nature of the Production Process: Consensus Versus Competition

The nature of the production process can itself undermine the quality of the product. That process is consensus-oriented, varying in degree from the formal United States Intelligence Board (USIB) coordination involved in producing a National Intelligence Estimate to the less structured daily analyst-to-analyst coordination, which

---

[22] *Ibid.*

[23] Huizenga, 1/26/76, p. 25.

[24] IC Staff post-mortem on 1973 Middle East war (January 1974), p. 14.

takes place at the working level. For the monographs produced on an irregular basis by the Intelligence Directorate's research offices, the bulk of the coordination effort is between these offices, although occasionally such coordination will cross directorate lines, and less frequently it will involve going outside the Agency. An analyst from the DDI may meet with his opposite numbers in State or DIA prior to publishing an article in their mutual field.[27] The coordination process, however necessary and desirable, may tend to produce a "reinforcing consensus," whereby divergent views of individual analysts can become "submerged in a sea of conventional collective wisdom," and doubts or disagreements can simply disappear in the face of mutually reinforcing agreements.[28]

Although the purpose of coordination is "to assure that the facts and judgments presented therein are as comprehensive, objective, and accurate as possible," [29] it sometimes has the unfortunate side-effect of blurring both the form and content of the product. The NIEs have been criticized, on occasion, for this. The estimates undergo the most formal coordination process, one which is integral to policy consensus-building. Some consumers complain that finished intelligence frequently lacks clarity, especially clarity of judgment, and that it is often presented in waffly or "delphic" forms, without attribution of views. Opposing views are not always clearly articulated. Judgments on difficult subjects are sometimes hedged, or represent the outcome of compromise, and are couched in fuzzy, imprecise terms. Yet intelligence consumers increasingly maintain that they want a more clearly spelled out distinction between different interpretations, with judgments as to relative probabilities.

In fact, the issue of consensus versus competition in analysis represents a persistent conceptual dilemma for the intelligence community. Policymakers tend to want one "answer" to an intelligence question, but at the same time they do not want anything to be hidden from them. Consumer needs can change drastically in a short period of time, and the same policymakers may need different kinds of intelligence for different kinds of situations.

Some members of the intelligence and foreign policy communities today argue that the consensus approach to intelligence production has improperly come to substitute for competing centers of analysis which could deliver more and different interpretations on the critical questions on which only partial data is available. This conceptual conflict should be closely examined by the successor oversight committee.

I. The "Current Events" Syndrome

The task of producing current intelligence—analyzing day-to-day events for quick dissemination—today occupies much of the resources of the DDI. Responding to the growing demands for information of current concern by policymakers for more coverage of more topics, the DDI has of necessity resorted to a "current events" approach to much of its research. There is less interest in and fewer resources have been devoted to in-depth analysis of problems with long-range importance to policymakers. The Directorate has had to devote considerable resources in order to keep up on a day-to-day basis with events as they

---

[27] "The Directorate of Intelligence," Annex A, p. 2.
[28] IC Staff post-mortem on the 1973 Middle-East War, p. 18.
[29] "The Directorate of Intelligence," Annex A, p. 1.

happen. To some extent, analysts feel they must compete for time-liness with the considerable amount of raw reporting which reaches consumers.

According to some observers, this syndrome has had an unfavorable impact on the quality of crisis warning and the recognition of longer term trends. The "current events" approach has fostered the problem of "incremental analysis," the tendency to focus myopically on the latest piece of information without systematic consideration of an accumulated body of integrated evidence. Analysts in their haste to compile the day's traffic, tend to lose sight of underlying factors and relationships.[30]

For example, the 1966 Cunningham Report points out that the CIA's sinologists were so immersed in the large volume of daily FBIS [31] and other source reports on Communist China in the early 1960s that they failed to consider adequately the broader question of the slowly developing Sino-Soviet dispute.[32]

The Intelligence Directorate is now turning more attention to such increasingly important long-term (and inter-disciplinary) problems as world food balances, raw material supplies, population pressures and pollution of the environment. Nevertheless, the DDI itself feels that an even greater effort should be made in these areas. "Such matters have not been the focus of national security interest in the past, but they clearly will be within the next ten years and this Directorate should be building its capacity to analyze and report in these fields." [33]

J. INNOVATION

The CIA is thought by many observers to be technologically one of the most innovative research centers in the country, and it allocates considerable funds to continue the search for new technology. But despite recent increases, the intelligence community still expends relatively little effort on R&D in the analytical field—in contrast to intensive effort in new and costly collection methods.

The analytic community has suffered from the secrecy that surrounds the work of the intelligence community as a whole. This insulation is recognized to have had a detrimental effect on the quality of analysis. The Agency recognizes the need for conducting a free exchange with academics, contractors, and consultants. For example, in FY 1976, 17 analysts were on leave at private institutions with an additional 14 people in various Government programs (e.g., the State Department senior seminar, or the Congressional Fellows program).[34]

Some DDI offices have panels of consultants (outsiders) to review major papers, and outside speakers are on occasion brought in for special seminars. There have been efforts like the one made by OPR to arrange for one-year sabbaticals for visiting academics during which the visitor could produce both government and public papers. Such efforts have been only partially successful.

---

[30] See IC Staff post-mortems on Middle East war and Cyprus crisis.
[31] The Foreign Broadcast Information Service, run by the Intelligence Directorate, monitors foreign media and open source material and publishes daily surveys by area.
[32] CIA Inspector General, "Foreign Intelligence Collection Requirements," December 1966 (The Cunningham Report). pp. VII–13, 14.
[33] "The Directorate of Intelligence," p. 12.
[34] Proctor (Staff summary), 3/1/76.

The question of CIA relations with academics and private groups like foundations and research organizations is a controversial one. The Committee notes the desirability of a more open attitude on both sides, one which both recognizes the legitimacy of the analytic work of the intelligence community and refrains from the secret use of academics and others for operational purposes.

N16

K. OVERLOAD ON ANALYSTS AND CONSUMERS

Few observers would dispute the fact that as consumer demands have grown and the amount of data collected has burgeoned, the analysts' work load has become a serious problem. But ten years ago the Cunningham Report expressed the concern that:

> In the long run it is not the crude question of work load which matters most, nor even the point that each item uses up customers' time and attention which cannot be given to any other item, so that each of our products must receive steadily less. What matters most is the question whether this quantity of information is degrading the quality of all our work.[36]

And the 1971 Schlesinger Report said that it was "not at all clear that our hypotheses about foreign intentions, capabilities, and activities have improved commensurately in scope and quality as more data comes in from modern collection methods." [37]

Yet today the intelligence establishment remains structured in such a way that collection guides production, rather than vice versa; available data and "the impetus of technology" tend to govern what is produced.[38] To be sure, much of the proliferation in data collected has proven invaluable to the analytic effort. Technical collection systems have provided "hard" data, e.g., on missile silos which have contributed to the generally acknowledged high quality of CIA assessments of Soviet and Chinese strategic forces.

In 1971, the Schlesinger Report said, "It has become commonplace to translate product criticism into demands for enlarged collection efforts. Seldom does anyone ask if a further reduction in uncertainty, however small, is worth its cost." [39] The community's heavy emphasis on collection is itself detrimental to correcting product problems, said the report, for each department or agency sees the maintenance and expansion of collection capabilities as the route to survival and strength within the community. There is a "strong presumption" that additional data collection rather than improved analysis will provide answers to particular intelligence problems.[40]

Analysts naturally attempt to read all the relevant raw data reports on the subjects they are working on, for fear of missing an important piece of information. The Cunningham Report referred to this as the "jigsaw theory" of intelligence—that one little scrap might be the missing piece.[41] The present trend within the DDI is to reduce the amount of raw data coming to analysts by more effective screening processes.

---

[36] Cunningham Report, p. VIII–13.
[37] Schlesinger Report, p. 10a.
[38] Ibid., p. 10a.
[39] Ibid., p. 11.
[40] Ibid., p. 11.
[41] Cunningham Report. p. VII–19.

In the opinion of one intelligence community official, analysts in the future are going to have to rely to a greater extent than heretofore on others' judgments. The collectors themselves may have to present their output in summary form, with some means of highlighting important information,[42] despite the community's sensitivity to the distinction between "raw" and "finished" intelligence reporting.

On the other hand, consumers tend to treat the intelligence product as a free good. Instead of articulating priorities, they demand information about everything, and the demand exceeds the supply. And analysts, perhaps for fear of being accused of an "intelligence failure," feel that they *have* to cover every possible topic, with little regard for its relevance to U.S. foreign policy interests. The community must part with the notion that it has to beat the newspapers in reporting coups in remote areas of the world if what happens in those areas is only of marginal interest to U.S. policymakers. In this regard, there are serious efforts being made by DDI to focus analysis on major areas of importance to the United States.

The community has looked increasingly to the advent of automated information-handling systems to solve the problems of systems overload, but the impact of computerization is not yet clear. In 1966 the Cunningham Report warned that "great technological advances in storage and retrieval" of information can do more harm than good if "drastically higher standards" for what is to be stored and retrieved are not instituted.[43]

It has often been pointed out that not only are analysts swamped with information, but the consumers also are inundated with intelligence reporting, both "finished" and "raw." The volume of paper degrades the overall effectiveness of the product, since there is simply too much to read, from too many sources. In addition to the daily DDI publications and the various DDI Offices' specialized weeklies and other memoranda, a variety of other intelligence publications, regularly cross the desks of senior Government officials. As former DCI Richard Helms has told the Select Committee:

> It seems to me that one of the things that's tended to happen is that almost every agency has got to have its national publication. In other words, it's got to have a publication that arrives in the White House every morning.[44]

Policymakers receive DIA's Defense Intelligence Notices (DINs), produced on particular subjects as the occasion demands—sometimes several per day on a given topic. NSA sends out a daily SIGINT Summary, which is not classed as finished intelligence. And a considerable amount of raw reporting of clandestine human source intelligence is routinely distributed to consumers on the NSC staff, at the Departments of State and Defense, and in the military services.

This glut of paper raises a number of issues which the Select Committee feels deserve further attention. The proliferation of departmental publications tends to undermine the centralized nature of the system for the production of national intelligence. It contributes to confusion rather than clarity in the decisionmaking process, since

---

[42] Staff summary of Richard Shryock interview, 2/10/76.
[43] Cunningham Report, p. VII–12 (footnote).
[44] Richard Helms testimony, 1/30/76, p. 29.

different publications often present different conclusions. Often the reasons for the differences are only clear to a sophisticated intelligence analyst. And direct reporting from the collectors usually arrives before the analytical reporting can, preempting the analysts' work in evaluating the data.

L. QUALITY CONTROL

In 1972 a "Product Review Division" (PRD) was established within the IC Staff. It has the task of regularly appraising intelligence articles and studies, "testing them for objectivity, balance, and responsiveness." [45] The Intelligence Directorate has no formal or independent system for quality control, depending instead upon its regular review and coordination process. [46]

Most of PRD's attention to date has been directed to the conduct of communitywide post-mortems on particular crises—for example, the 1973 Middle East war, the Cyprus crisis in 1974, the Indian nuclear detonation, and the Mayaguez incident. The Division was involved in changing the old daily *Central Intelligence Bulletin* from a CIA publication into a community publication (now called the *National Intelligence Bulletin*). PRD participated in discussions leading to the transformation of the old Watch Committee into the DCI's Special Assistant for Warning, with a Strategic Warning Staff.

PRD has not yet been significantly involved in the development of new analytical methods, in resource allocation for production elements, or in training or recruitment issues. Contact with the consumers of the intelligence product has been on an irregular basis (mostly for post-mortems), although PRD is currently at work, through the NIOs, collecting consumer reactions on particular papers of concern to the USIB.

The Division has no authority to order changes in the management of production which might affect the quality of the product; rather, it has been in the position of making recommendations to the USIB and encouraging their implementation.

M. CONSUMER GUIDANCE AND EVALUATION

The DDI manages its production planning by compiling a Quarterly Production and a Quarterly Research Schedule, outlining those finished intelligence studies slated for publication in the following three months as well as projects which support other intelligence efforts, but which may not be published. The quarterly schedules are prepared by DDI's Executive Staff based on inputs received from each office within the Intelligence Directorate, and the Associate DDI reviews them to ensure that the planned projects are responsive to consumer needs. [47]

While there is no formal or institutionalized review by consumers of the quarterly schedules, there are frequent Directorate-level contacts with policymakers who express an interest in intelligence information and assessments on particular foreign policy issues.

Evaluation of the intelligence product by the consumers themselves is virtually nonexistent. The NSC Intelligence Committee, which was supposed to perform that function, was largely inactive and has now

---

[45] Shryock (staff summary), 2/10/76.
[46] Proctor (staff summary), 3/1/76.
[47] "The Directorate of Intelligence," p. 8.

been abolished in the President's reorganization plan. Rarely, if ever, do high officials take the time to review the product carefully with the analysts and explain to them how the product could be improved and made more useful to policymakers. The intelligence community, then, by default, evaluates its own performance without the benefit of any real feedback. One former senior analyst told the Select Committee:

> I believe there ought to be requirements on the policy side to respond by comment or otherwise to major intelligence products, obviously not the whole flow of stuff, and I think that there ought to be a responsibility at an appropriate level, say at an Assistant Secretary level, to do this, and at the NSC level. This kind of recognition, the sense of participation in a serious process is, I think, the best thing that can be done for analysts.[48]

N. THE CONGRESSIONAL ROLE

Congress does not at present receive National Intelligence Estimates, although some of the estimative material is presented to the Congress in occasional briefings by intelligence officials. In the past, the Senate Foreign Relations and Armed Services Committees received the *National Intelligence Daily*, which could be cut off at executive will, and has been on some occasions, most recently in January 1976.[49] In 1975, the DDI began publishing a daily *Intelligence Checklist* specifically tailored to what it perceived to be the intelligence needs of the Congress.

With the resurgence of an active congressional role in the foreign and national security policymaking process comes the need for members to receive high quality, reliable, and timely information on which to base congressional decisions and actions. Access to the best available intelligence product should be insisted upon by the legislative branch. Precisely what kinds of intelligence the Congress requires to better perform its constitutional responsibilities remains to be worked out between the two branches of government, but the Select Committee believes that the *need* for information and the *right* to it is clear.

THE FORD ADMINISTRATION AND CIA REFORM: SUMMARY OF THE ROCKEFELLER COMMISSION INVESTIGATION ([124], pp. 9–42)

President Gerald R. Ford created the Commission on CIA Activities Within the United States on January 4, 1975, by Executive Order 11828. It was assigned three tasks: (1) Ascertain and evaluate any facts relating to activities conducted within the United States by the Central Intelligence Agency that gave rise to questions of compliance with the provisions of 50 U.S.C. 403 (this statute established the CIA in 1949). (2) Determine whether existing safeguards are adequate to prevent any activities that violate the provisions of 50 U.S.C. 403. (3) Make such recommendations to the president and to the director of Central Intelligence as the commission deems appropriate.

Vice-President Nelson Rockefeller was named chairman. Commission members included former Secretary of Commerce and Allied Chemical Corporation executive, John Connor;

---

[48] Huizenga, 1/26/76, p. 23.
[49] Laurence Stern, "CIA Stops Sending Daily Report to Hill," *Washington Post*, 2/4/76.

former Secretary of Treasury and investment banking firm executive, C. Douglas Dillon; former Solicitor General, Dean of Harvard Law School, and lawyer, Erwin Griswold; AFL-CIO Secretary-Treasurer, Lane Kirkland; former chairman of the Joint Chiefs of Staff, Lyman Lemnitzer; former governor of California, Ronald Reagan; and former president of the University of Virginia, Edgar Shannon, Jr. The president appointed David Belin, a lawyer, as the executive director; a staff of 11 lawyers assisted him.

At its inception, the commission was criticized as a whitewash effort, conducted by members of the "old boy" network. Such criticisms were registered by the *Washington Post* on January 4, 1976 and by the *New York Times* on January 5, 1976. The commission was formed at a time when Watergate revelations on CIA misconduct and investigative reporting in the *Post* and the *Times* suggested a significant pattern of wrongdoing by the CIA. Seymour Hersh, in the *New York Times,* December 22, 1974, charged that the CIA, in violation of its charter, conducted a "massive, illegal, domestic intelligence operation during the Nixon Administration. . . ." This charge, supported by other allegations, both published and rumored, concerning the CIA's role in the destabilization of the Salvador Allende regime in Chile, created a political climate propitious for an official investigation.*

President Gerald R. Ford responded by assigning DCI William Colby to study the matter and report to him by December. Colby did so, and shortly thereafter President Ford created the commission. These same events, combined with a widespread feeling that the Rockefeller group was too close in spirit with the wrongdoers, led to the creation of the Church and Pike Committees.

The final report of the Rockefeller Commission did not provide as much detail as that of the Church and Pike hearings, but the conclusions and recommendations are consistent with the revelations of the congressional committees. Those recommendations are set forth in Chapter 5, along with a summary of the Rockefeller Commission findings.

*An analysis of the public policy issue that faced the commission is provided by CRS analyst Richard Grimmett ([99]). His study also includes a chronology of events and summary of the intelligence community's structure.

As directed by the President, the Commission has investigated the role and authority of the CIA, the adequacy of the internal controls and external supervision of the Agency, and its significant domestic activities that raise questions of compliance with the limits on its statutory authority. This chapter summarizes the findings and conclusions of the Commission and sets forth its recommendations.

A. Summary of Charges and Findings

The initial public charges were that the CIA's domestic activities had involved:

1. Large-scale spying on American citizens in the United States by the CIA, whose responsibility is foreign intelligence.

2. Keeping dossiers on large numbers of American citizens.

3. Aiming these activities at Americans who have expressed their disagreement with various government policies.

These initial charges were subsequently supplemented by others including allegations that the CIA:

—Had intercepted and opened personal mail in the United States for 20 years;

—Had infiltrated domestic dissident groups and otherwise intervened in domestic politics;

—Had engaged in illegal wiretaps and break-ins; and,

—Had improperly assisted other government agencies.

In addition, assertions have been made ostensibly linking the CIA to the assassination of President John F. Kennedy.

It became clear from the public reaction to these charges that the secrecy in which the Agency nesessarily operates, combined with the allegations of wrongdoing, had contributed to widespread public misunderstanding of the Agency's actual practices.

A detailed analysis of the facts has convinced the Commission that the great majority of the CIA's domestic activities comply with its statutory authority.

Nevertheless, over the 28 years of its history, the CIA has engaged in some activities that should be criticized and not permitted to happen again—both in light of the limits imposed on the Agency by law and as a matter of public policy.

Some of these activities were initiated or ordered by Presidents, either directly or indirectly.

Some of them fall within the doubtful area between responsibilities delegated to the CIA by Congress and the National Security Council on the one hand and activities specifically prohibited to the Agency on the other.

Some of them were plainly unlawful and constituted improper invasions upon the rights of Americans.

The Agency's own recent actions, undertaken for the most part in 1973 and 1974, have gone far to terminate the activities upon which this investigation has focused. The recommendations of the Commission are designed to clarify areas of doubt concerning the Agency's authority, to strengthen the Agency's structure, and to guard against recurrences of these improprieties.

B. The CIA's Role and Authority

Findings

The Central Intelligence Agency was established by the National Security Act of 1947 as the nation's first comprehensive peacetime foreign intelligence service. The objective was to provide the President with coordinated intelligence, which the country lacked prior to the attack on Pearl Harbor.

The Director of Central Intelligence reports directly to the President. The CIA receives its policy direction and guidance from the National Security Council, composed of the President, the Vice President, and the Secretaries of State and Defense.

The statute directs the CIA to correlate, evaluate, and disseminate intelligence obtained from United States intelligence agencies, and to perform such other functions related to intelligence as the National Security Council directs. Recognizing that the CIA would be dealing with sensitive, secret materials, Congress made the Director of Central Intelligence responsible for protecting intelligence sources and methods from unauthorized disclosure.

At the same time, Congress sought to assure the American public that it was not establishing a secret police which would threaten the civil liberties of Americans. It specifically forbade the CIA from exercising "police, subpoena, or law-enforcement powers or internal security functions." The CIA was not to replace the Federal Bureau of Investigation in conducting domestic activities to investigate crime or internal subversion.

Although Congress contemplated that the focus of the CIA would be on foreign intelligence, it understood that some of its activities would be conducted within the United States. The CIA necessarily maintains its headquarters here, procures logistical support, recruits and trains employees, tests equipment, and conducts other domestic activities in support of its foreign intelligence mission. It makes necessary investigations in the United States to maintain the security of its facilities and personnel.

Additionally, it has been understood from the beginning that the CIA is permitted to collect foreign intelligence—that is, information concerning foreign capabilities, intentions, and activities—from American citizens within this country by overt means.

Determining the legal propriety of domestic activities of the CIA requires the application of the law to the particular facts involved. This task involves consideration of more than the National Security Act and the directives of the National Security Council; Constitutional and other statutory provisions also circumscribe the domestic activities of the CIA. Among the applicable Constitutional provisions are the First Amendment, protecting freedom of speech, of the press, and of peaceable assembly; and the Fourth Amendment, prohibiting unreasonable searches and seizures. Among the statutory provisions are those which limit such activities as electronic eavesdropping and interception of the mails.

The precise scope of many of these statutory and Constitutional provisions is not easily stated. The National Security Act in particular was drafted in broad terms in order to provide flexibility for the CIA to adapt to changing intelligence needs. Such critical phrases as "internal security functions" are left undefined. The meaning of the Director's responsibility to protect intelligence sources and methods from unauthorized disclosure has also been a subject of uncertainty.

The word "foreign" appears nowhere in the statutory grant of authority, though it has always been understood that the CIA's mission is limited to matters related to foreign intelligence. This apparent statutory ambiguity, although not posing problems in practice, has troubled members of the public who read the statute without having the benefit of the legislative history and the instructions to the CIA from the National Security Council.

Conclusions

The evidence within the scope of this inquiry does not indicate that fundamental rewriting of the National Security Act is either necessary or appropriate.

The evidence does demonstrate the need for some statutory and administrative clarification of the role and function of the Agency.

Ambiguities have been partially responsible for some, though not all, of the Agency's deviations within the United States from its assigned mission. In some cases, reasonable persons will differ as to the lawfulness of the activity; in others, the absence of clear guidelines as to its authority deprived the Agency of a means of resisting pressures to engage in activities which now appear to us improper.

Greater public awareness of the limits of the CIA's domestic authority would do much to reassure the American people.

The requisite clarification can best be accomplished (a) through a specific amendment clarifying the National Security Act provision which delineates the permissible scope of CIA activities, as set forth in Recommendation 1, and (b) through issuance of an Executive Order further limiting domestic activities of the CIA, as set forth in Recommendation 2.

Recommendation (1)

Section 403 of the National Security Act of 1947 should be amended in the form set forth in Appendix VI to this Report. These amendments, in summary, would:

a. Make explicit that the CIA's activities must be related to *foreign* intelligence.

b. Clarify the responsibility of the CIA to protect intelligence sources and methods from unauthorized disclosure. (The Agency would be responsible for protecting against unauthorized disclosures within the CIA, and it would be responsible for providing guidance and technical assistance to other agency and department heads in protecting against unauthorized disclosures within their own agencies and departments.)

c. Confirm publicly the CIA's existing authority to collect foreign intelligence from willing sources within the United States, and, except as specified by the President in a published Executive Order,[1] prohibit the CIA from collection efforts within the United States directed at securing foreign intelligence from unknowing American citizens.

Recommendation (2)

The President should by Executive Order prohibit the CIA from the collection of information about the domestic activities of United States citizens (whether by overt or covert means), the evaluation, correlation, and dissemination of analyses or reports about such activities, and the storage of such information, with exceptions for the following categories of persons or activities:

a. Persons presently or formerly affiliated, or being considered for affiliation, with the CIA, directly or indirectly, or others who require clearance by the CIA to receive classified information;

b. Persons or activities that pose a clear threat to CIA facilities or personnel, provided that proper coordination with the FBI is accomplished;

c. Persons suspected of espionage or other illegal activities relating to foreign intelligence, provided that proper coordination with the FBI is accomplished.

d. Information which is received incidental to appropriate CIA activities may be transmitted to an agency with appropriate jurisdiction, including law enforcement agencies.

Collection of information from normal library sources such as newspapers, books, magazines and other such documents is not to be affected by this order.

Information currently being maintained which is inconsistent with the order should be destroyed at the conclusion of the current congressional investigations or as soon thereafter as permitted by law.

The CIA should periodically screen its files and eliminate all material inconsistent with the order.

The order should be issued after consultation with the National Security Council, the Attorney General, and the Director of Central Intelligence. Any modification of the order would be permitted only through published amendments.

---

[1] The Executive Order authorized by this statute should recognize that when the collection of foreign intelligence from persons who are not United States citizens results in the incidental acquisition of information from unknowing citizens, the Agency should be permitted to make appropriate use or disposition of such information. Such collection activities must be directed at foreign intelligence sources, and the involvement of American citizens must be incidental.

C. Supervision and Control of the CIA

1. External Controls

Findings

The CIA is subject to supervision and control by various executive agencies and by the Congress.

Congress has established special procedures for review of the CIA and its secret budget within four small subcommittees.[2] Historically, these subcommittees have been composed of members of Congress with many other demands on their time. The CIA has not as a general rule received detailed scrutiny by the Congress.

The principal bodies within the Executive Branch performing a supervisory or control function are the National Security Council, which gives the CIA its policy direction and control; the Office of Management and Budget, which reviews the CIA's budget in much the same fashion as it reviews budgets of other government agencies; and the President's Foreign Intelligence Advisory Board, which is composed of distinguished citizens, serving part time in a general advisory function for the President on the quality of the gathering and interpretation of intelligence.

None of these agencies has the specific responsibility of overseeing the CIA to determine whether its activities are proper.

The Department of Justice also exercises an oversight role, through its power to initiate prosecutions for criminal misconduct. For a period of over 20 years, however, an agreement existed between the Department of Justice and the CIA providing that the Agency was to investigate allegations of crimes by CIA employees or agents which involved Government money or property or might involve operational security. If, following the investigation, the Agency determined that there was no reasonable basis to believe a crime had been committed, or that operational security aspects precluded prosecution, the case was not referred to the Department of Justice.

The Commission has found nothing to indicate that the CIA abused the function given it by the agreement. The agreement, however, involved the Agency directly in forbidden law enforcement activities, and represented an abdication by the Department of Justice of its statutory responsibilities.

Conclusions

Some improvement in the congressional oversight system would be helpful. The problem of providing adequate oversight and control while maintaining essential security is not easily resolved. Several

---

[2] Subcommittees of the Appropriations Committees and the Armed Services Committees of the two houses.

knowledgeable witnesses pointed to the Joint Committee on Atomic Energy as an appropriate model for congressional oversight of the Agency. That Committee has had an excellent record of providing effective oversight while avoiding breaches of security in a highly sensitive area.

One of the underlying causes of the problems confronting the CIA arises out of the pervading atmosphere of secrecy in which its activities have been conducted in the past. One aspect of this has been the secrecy of the budget.

A new body is needed to provide oversight of the Agency within the Executive Branch. Because of the need to preserve security, the CIA is not subject to the usual constraints of audit, judicial review, publicity or open congressional budget review and oversight. Consequently, its operations require additional external control. The authority assigned the job of supervising the CIA must be given sufficient power and significance to assure the public of effective supervision.

The situation whereby the Agency determined whether its own employees would be prosecuted must not be permitted to recur.

Recommendation (3)

The President should recommend to Congress the establishment of a Joint Committee on Intelligence to assume the oversight role currently played by the Armed Services Committees.

Recommendation (4)

Congress should give careful consideration to the question whether the budget of the CIA should not, at least to some extent, be made public, particularly in view of the provisions of Article I, Section 9, Clause 7 of the Constitution.[4]

Recommendation (5)

a. The functions of the President's Foreign Intelligence Advisory Board should be expanded to include oversight of the CIA. This expanded oversight board should be composed of distinguished citizens with varying backgrounds and experience. It should be headed by a full-time chairman and should have a full-time staff appropriate to its role. Its functions related to the CIA should include:

1. Assessing compliance by the CIA with its statutory authority.
2. Assessing the quality of foreign intelligence collection.
3. Assessing the quality of foreign intelligence estimates.

---

[4] "No Money shall be drawn from the Treasury, but in Consequence of Appropriations made by Law; and a regular Statement and Account of the Receipts and Expenditures of all public Money shall be published from time to time."

4. **Assessing the quality of the organization of the CIA.**
5. **Assessing the quality of the management of the CIA.**
6. **Making recommendations with respect to the above subjects to the President and the Director of Central Intelligence, and, where appropriate, the Attorney General.**

b. **The Board should have access to all information in the CIA. It should be authorized to audit and investigate CIA expenditures and activities on its own initiative.**

c. **The Inspector General of the CIA should be authorized to report directly to the Board, after having notified the Director of Central Intelligence, in cases he deems appropriate.**

Recommendation (6)

The Department of Justice and the CIA should establish written guidelines for the handling of reports of criminal violations by employees of the Agency or relating to its affairs. These guidelines should require that the criminal investigation and the decision whether to prosecute be made by the Department of Justice, after consideration of Agency views regarding the impact of prosecution on the national security. The Agency should be permitted to conduct such investigations as it requires to determine whether its operations have been jeopardized. The Ageny should scrupulously avoid exercise of the prosecutorial function.

2. Internal Controls

Findings

The Director's duties in administering the intelligence community, handling relations with other components of the government, and passing on broad questions of policy leave him little time for day-to-day supervision of the Agency. Past studies have noted the need for the Director to delegate greater responsibility for the administration of the Agency to the Deputy Director of Central Intelligence.

In recent years, the position of Deputy Director has been occupied by a high-ranking military officer, with responsibilities for maintaining liaison with the Department of Defense, fostering the Agency's relationship with the military services, and providing top CIA management with necessary experience and skill in understanding particular intelligence requirements of the military. Generally speaking, the Deputy Directors of Central Intelligence have not been heavily engaged in administration of the Agency.

Each of the four directorates within the CIA—Operations, Intelligence, Administration, and Science and Technology—is headed by a deputy director who reports to the Director and Deputy Director of Central Intelligence. These four deputies, together with certain other top Agency officials such as the Comptroller, form the Agency Management Committee, which makes many of the administrative and management decisions affecting more than one directorate.

Outside the chain of command, the primary internal mechanism for keeping the Agency within bounds is the Inspector General. The size of this office was recently sharply reduced, and its previous practice of making regular reviews of various Agency departments was terminated. At the present time, the activities of the office are almost entirely concerned with coordinating Agency responses to the various investigating bodies, and with various types of employee grievances.

The Office of General Counsel has on occasion played an important role in preventing or terminating Agency activities in violation of law, but many of the questionable or unlawful activities discussed in this report were not brought to the attention of this office. A certain parochialism may have resulted from the fact that attorneys in the office have little or no legal experience outside the Agency. It is important that the Agency receive the best possible legal advice on the often difficult and unusual situations which confront it.

Conclusions

In the final analysis, the proper functioning of the Agency must depend in large part on the character of the Director of Central Intelligence.

The best assurance against misuse of the Agency lies in the appointment to that position of persons with the judgment, courage, and independence to resist improper pressure and importuning, whether from the White House, within the Agency or elsewhere.

Compartmentation within the Agency, although certainly appropriate for security reasons, has sometimes been carried to extremes which prevent proper supervision and control.

The Agency must rely on the discipline and integrity of the men and women it employs. Many of the activities we have found to be improper or unlawful were in fact questioned by lower-level employees. Bringing such situations to the attention of upper levels of management is one of the purposes of a system of internal controls.

Recommendation (7)

a. Persons appointed to the position of Director of Central Intelligence should be individuals of stature, independence, and integrity. In making this appointment, consideration should be given to individuals from outside the career service of the CIA, although promotion from within should not be barred. Experience in intelligence service is not necessarily a prerequisite for the position; management and administrative skills are at least as important as the technical expertise which can always be found in an able deputy.

b. Although the Director serves at the pleasure of the President, no Director should serve in that position for more than 10 years.

Recommendation (8)

a. The Office of Deputy Director of Central Intelligence should be reconstituted to provide for two such deputies, in addition to the four heads of the Agency's directorates. One deputy would act as the administrative officer, freeing the Director from day-to-day management duties. The other deputy should be a military officer, serving the functions of fostering relations with the military and providing the Agency with technical expertise on military intelligence requirements.

b. The advice and consent of the Senate should be required for the appointment of each Deputy Director of Central Intelligence.

Recommendation (9)

a. The Inspector General should be upgraded to a status equivalent to that of the deputy directors in charge of the four directorates within the CIA.

b. The Office of Inspector General should be staffed by outstanding, experienced officers from both inside and outside the CIA, with ability to understand the various branches of the Agency.

c. The Inspector General's duties with respect to domestic CIA activities should include periodic reviews of all offices within the United States. He should examine each office for compliance with CIA authority and regulations as well as for the effectiveness of their programs in implementing policy objectives.

d. The Inspector General should investigate all reports from employees concerning possible violations of the CIA statute.

e. The Inspector General should be given complete access to all information in the CIA relevant to his reviews.

f. An effective Inspector General's office will require a larger staff, more frequent reviews, and highly qualified personnel.

g. Inspector General reports should be provided to the National Security Council and the recommended executive oversight body. The Inspector General should have the authority, when he deems it appropriate, after notifying the Director of Central Intelligence, to consult with the executive oversight body on any CIA activity (see Recommendation 5).

Recommendation (10)

a. The Director should review the composition and operation of the Office of General Counsel and the degree to which this office is consulted to determine whether the Agency is receiving adequate legal assistance and representation in view of current requirements.

b. Consideration should be given to measures which would strengthen the office's professional capabilities and resources including, among other things, (1) occasionally departing from the existing practice of hiring lawyers from within the Agency to bring in seasoned lawyers from private practice as well as to hire law school graduates without prior CIA experience; (2) occasionally assigning Agency lawyers to serve a tour of duty elsewhere in the government to expand their experience; (3) encouraging lawyers to participate in outside professional activities.

Recommendation (11)

To a degree consistent with the need for security, the CIA should be encouraged to provide for increased lateral movement of personnel among the directorates and to bring persons with outside experience into the Agency at all levels.

Recommendation (12)

a. The Agency should issue detailed guidelines for its employees further specifying those activities within the United States which are permitted and those which are prohibited by statute, Executive Orders, and NSC and DCI directives.

b. These guidelines should also set forth the standards which govern CIA activities and the general types of activities which are permitted and prohibited. They should, among other things, specify that:

—Clandestine collection of intelligence directed against United States citizens is prohibited except as specifically permitted by law or published Executive Order.

—Unlawful methods or activities are prohibited.

—Prior approval of the DCI shall be required for any activities which may raise questions of compliance with the law or with Agency regulations.

c. The guidelines should also provide that employees with information on possibly improper activities are to bring it promptly to the attention of the Director of Central Intelligence or the Inspector General.

D. Significant Areas of Investigation

Introduction

Domestic activities of the CIA raising substantial questions of compliance with the law have been closely examined by the Commission to determine the context in which they were performed, the pressures of the times, the relationship of the activity to the Agency's foreign intelligence assignment and to other CIA activities, the procedures used to authorize and conduct the activity, and the extent and effect of the activity.

In describing and assessing each such activity, it has been necessary to consider both that activity's relationship to the legitimate national security needs of the nation and the threat such activities might pose to individual rights of Americans and to a society founded on the need for government, as well as private citizens, to obey the law.

1. The CIA's Mail Intercepts

Findings

At the time the CIA came into being, one of the highest national intelligence priorities was to gain an understanding of the Soviet Union and its worldwide activities affecting our national security.

In this context, the CIA began in 1952 a program of surveying mail between the United States and the Soviet Union as it passed through a New York postal facility. In 1953 it began opening some of this mail. The program was expanded over the following two decades and ultimately involved the opening of many letters and the analysis of envelopes, or "covers," of a great many more letters.

The New York mail intercept was designed to attempt to identify persons within the United States who were cooperating with the Soviet Union and its intelligence forces to harm the United States. It was also intended to determine technical communications procedures and mail censorship techniques used by the Soviets.

The Director of the Central Intelligence Agency approved commencement of the New York mail intercept in 1952. During the ensuing years, so far as the record shows, Postmasters General Summerfield, Day, and Blount were informed of the program in varying degrees, as was Attorney General Mitchell. Since 1958, the FBI was aware of this program and received 57,000 items from it.

A 1962 CIA memorandum indicates the Agency was aware that the mail openings would be viewed as violating federal criminal laws prohibiting obstruction or delay of the mails.

In the last year before the termination of this program, out of 4,350,000 items of mail sent to and from the Soviet Union, the New York intercept examined the outside of 2,300,000 of these items, photographed 33,000 envelopes, and opened 8,700.

The mail intercept was terminated in 1973 when the Chief Postal Inspector refused to allow its continuation without an up-to-date high-level approval.

The CIA also ran much smaller mail intercepts for brief periods in San Francisco between 1969 and 1971 and in the territory of Hawaii during 1954 and 1955. For a short period in 1957, mail in transit between foreign countries was intercepted in New Orleans.

Conclusions

While in operation, the CIA's domestic mail opening programs were unlawful. United States statutes specifically forbid opening the mail.

The mail openings also raise Constitutional questions under the Fourth Amendment guarantees against unreasonable search, and the scope of the New York project poses possible difficulties with the First Amendment rights of speech and press.

Mail cover operations (examining and copying of envelopes only) are legal when carried out in compliance with postal regulations on a limited and selective basis involving matters of national security. The New York mail intercept did not meet these criteria.

The nature and degree of assistance given by the CIA to the FBI in the New York mail project indicate that the CIA's primary purpose eventually became participation with the FBI in internal security functions. Accordingly, the CIA's participation was prohibited under the National Security Act.

Recommendation (13)

a. **The President should instruct the Director of Central Intelligence that the CIA is not to engage again in domestic *mail openings* except with express statutory authority in time of war. (See also Recommendation 23.)**

b. **The President should instruct the Director of Central Intelligence that *mail cover* examinations are to be in compliance with postal regulations; they are to be undertaken only in furtherance of the CIA's legitimate activities and then only on a limited and selected basis clearly involving matters of national security.**

N18

2. Intelligence Community Coordination

Findings

As a result of growing domestic disorder, the Department of Justice, starting in 1967 at the direction of Attorney General Ramsey Clark, coordinated a series of secret units and interagency groups in an effort to collate and evaluate intelligence relating to these events. These efforts continued until 1973.

The interagency committees were designed for analytic and not operational purposes. They were created as a result of White House pressure which began in 1967, because the FBI performed only limited evaluation and analysis of the information it collected on these events. The stated purpose of CIA's participation was to supply relevant foreign intelligence and to furnish advice on evaluation techniques.

The CIA was reluctant to become unduly involved in these committees, which had problems of domestic unrest as their principal focus. It repeatedly refused to assign full-time personnel to any of them.

The most active of the committees was the Intelligence Evaluation Staff, which met from January 1971 to May 1973. A CIA liaison officer [4] attended over 100 weekly meetings of the Staff, some of which concerned drafts of reports which had no foreign aspects. With the exception of one instance, there is no evidence that he acted in any capacity other than as an adviser on foreign intelligence, and, to some degree, as an editor.

On one occasion the CIA liaison officer appears to have caused a CIA agent to gather domestic information which was reported to the Intelligence Evaluation Staff.

The Commission found no evidence of other activities by the CIA that were conducted on behalf of the Department of Justice groups except for the supplying of appropriate foreign intelligence and advice on evaluation techniques.

Conclusions

The statutory prohibition on internal security functions does not preclude the CIA from providing foreign intelligence or advice on evaluation techniques to interdepartmental intelligence evaluation organizations having some domestic aspects. The statute was intended to promote coordination, not compartmentation of intelligence between governmental departments.

The attendance of the CIA liaison officer at over 100 meetings of the Intelligence Evaluation Staff, some of them concerned wholly with domestic matters, nevertheless created at least the appearance of impropriety. The Director of Central Intelligence was well advised to approach such participation reluctantly.

The liaison officer acted improperly in the one instance in which he directed an agent to gather domestic information within the United States which was reported to the Intelligence Evaluation Staff.

---

[4] The liaison officer was Chief of the CIA's Special Operations Group which ran Operation CHAOS. . . .

Much of the problem stemmed from the absence in government of any organization capable of adequately analyzing intelligence collected by the FBI on matters outside the purview of CIA.

Recommendation (14)

a. A capability should be developed within the FBI, or elsewhere in the Department of Justice, to evaluate, analyze, and coordinate intelligence and counterintelligence collected by the FBI concerning espionage, terrorism, and other related matters of internal security.

b. The CIA should restrict its participation in any joint intelligence committees to foreign intelligence matters.

c. The FBI should be encouraged to continue to look to the CIA for such foreign intelligence and counter-intelligence as is relevant to FBI needs.

3. Special Operations Group—"Operation CHAOS"

Findings

The late 1960's and early 1970's were marked by widespread violence and civil disorders. Demonstrations, marches and protest assemblies were frequent in a number of cities. Many universities and college campuses became places of disruption and unrest. Government facilities were picketed and sometimes invaded. Threats of bombing and bombing incidents occurred frequently. In Washington and other major cities, special security measures had to be instituted to control the access to public buildings.

Responding to Presidential requests made in the face of growing domestic disorder, the Director of Central Intelligence in August 1967 established a Special Operations Group within the CIA to collect, coordinate, evaluate and report on the extent of foreign influence on domestic dissidence.

The Group's activities, which later came to be known as Operation CHAOS, led the CIA to collect information on dissident Americans from CIA field stations overseas and from the FBI.

Although the stated purpose of the Operation was to determine whether there were any foreign contacts with American dissident groups, it resulted in the accumulation of considerable material on domestic dissidents and their activities.

During six years, the Operation compiled some 13,000 different files, including files on 7,200 American citizens. The documents in these files and related materials included the names of more than 300,000 persons and organizations, which were entered into a computerized index.

This information was kept closely guarded within the CIA. Using this information, personnel of the Group prepared 3,500 memoranda for internal use; 3,000 memoranda for dissemination to the FBI; and 37 memoranda for distribution to White House and other top level officials in the government.

The staff assigned to the Operation was steadily enlarged in response to repeated Presidential requests for additional information, ultimately reaching a maximum of 52 in 1971. Because of excessive isolation, the Operation was substantially insulated from meaningful review within the Agency, including review by the Counterintelligence Staff—of which the Operation was technically a part.

Commencing in late 1969, Operation CHAOS used a number of agents to collect intelligence abroad on any foreign connections with American dissident groups. In order to have sufficient "cover" for these agents, the Operation recruited persons from domestic dissident groups or recruited others and instructed them to associate with such groups in this country.

Most of the Operation's recruits were not directed to collect information domestically on American dissidents. On a number of occasions, however, such information was reported by the recruits while they were developing dissident credentials in the United States, and the information was retained in the files of the Operation. On three occasions, an agent of the Operation was specifically directed to collect domestic intelligence.

No evidence was found that any Operation CHAOS agent used or was directed by the Agency to use electronic surveillance, wiretaps or break-ins in the United States against any dissident individual or group.

Activity of the Operation decreased substantially by mid-1972. The Operation was formally terminated in March 1974.

Conclusions

Some domestic activities of Operation CHAOS unlawfully exceeded the CIA's statutory authority, even though the declared mission of gathering intelligence abroad as to foreign influence on domestic dissident activities was proper.

Most significantly, the Operation became a repository for large quantities of information on the domestic activities of American citizens. This information was derived principally from FBI reports or from overt sources and not from clandestine collection by the CIA, and much of it was not directly related to the question of the existence of foreign connections.

It was probably necessary for the CIA to accumulate an information base on domestic dissident activities in order to assess fairly whether the activities had foreign connections. The FBI would collect information but would not evaluate it. But the accumulation of domestic data in the Operation exceeded what was reasonably required to make such an assessment and was thus improper.

The use of agents of the Operation on three occasions to gather information within the United States on strictly domestic matters was beyond the CIA's authority. In addition the intelligence disseminations and those portions of a major study prepared by the Agency which dealt with purely domestic matters were improper.

The isolation of Operation CHAOS within the CIA and its independence from supervision by the regular chain of command within the clandestine service made it possible for the activities of the Operation to stray over the bounds of the Agency's authority without the knowledge of senior officials. The absence of any regular review of these activities prevented timely correction of such missteps as did occur.

Recommendation (15)

a. **Presidents should refrain from directing the CIA to perform what are essentially internal security tasks.**

b. **The CIA should resist any efforts, whatever their origin, to involve it again in such improper activities.**

c. **The Agency should guard against allowing any component (like the Special Operations Group) to become so self-contained and isolated from top leadership that regular supervision and review are lost.**

d. **The files of the CHAOS project which have no foreign intelligence value should be destroyed by the Agency at the conclusion of the current congressional investigations, or as soon thereafter as permitted by law.**

4. Protection of the Agency Against Threats of Violence—Office of Security

Findings

The CIA was not immune from the threats of violence and disruption during the period of domestic unrest between 1967 and 1972. The Office of Security was charged throughout this period with the responsibility of ensuring the continued functioning of the CIA.

The Office therefore, from 1967 to 1970, had its field officers collect information from published materials, law enforcement authorities, other agencies and college officials before recruiters were sent to some campuses. Monitoring and communications support was provided to recruiters when trouble was expected.

The Office was also responsible, with the approval of the Director of Central Intelligence, for a program from February 1967 to December 1968, which at first monitored, but later infiltrated, dissident organizations in the Washington, D.C., area to determine if the groups planned any activities against CIA or other government installations.

At no time were more than 12 persons performing these tasks, and they performed them on a part-time basis. The project was terminated when the Washington Metropolitan Police Department developed its own intelligence capability.

In December, 1967, the Office began a continuing study of dissident activity in the United States, using information from published and other voluntary knowledgeable sources. The Office produced weekly Situation Information Reports analyzing dissident activities and providing calendars of future events. Calendars were given to the Secret Service, but the CIA made no other disseminations outside the Agency. About 500 to 800 files were maintained on dissenting organizations and individuals. Thousands of names in the files were indexed. Report publication was ended in late 1972, and the entire project was ended in 1973.

Conclusions

The program under which the Office of Security rendered assistance to Agency recruiters on college campuses was justified as an exercise of the Agency's responsibility to protect its own personnel and operations. Such support activities were not undertaken for the purpose of protecting the facilities or operations of other governmental agencies, or to maintain public order or enforce laws.

The Agency should not infiltrate a dissident group for security purposes unless there is a clear danger to Agency installations, operations or personnel, and investigative coverage of the threat by the FBI and local law enforcement authorities is inadequate. The Agency's infiltration of dissident groups in the Washington area went far beyond steps necessary to protect the Agency's own facilities, personnel and operations, and therefore exceeded the CIA's statutory authority.

In addition, the Agency undertook to protect other government departments and agencies—a police function prohibited to it by statute.

Intelligence activity directed toward learning from what sources a domestic dissident group receives its financial support within the

United States, and how much income it has, is no part of the authorized security operations of the Agency. Neither is it the function of the Agency to compile records on who attends peaceful meetings of such dissident groups, or what each speaker has to say (unless it relates to disruptive or violent activity which may be directed against the Agency).

The Agency's actions in contributing funds, photographing people, activities and cars, and following people home were unreasonable under the circumstances and therefore exceeded the CIA's authority.

With certain exceptions, the program under which the Office of Security (without infiltration) gathered, organized and analyzed information about dissident groups for purposes of security was within the CIA's authority.

The accumulation of reference files on dissident organizations and their leaders was appropriate both to evaluate the risks posed to the Agency and to develop an understanding of dissident groups and their differences for security clearance purposes. But the accumulation of information on domestic activities went beyond what was required by the Agency's legitimate security needs and therefore exceeded the CIA's authority.

Recommendation (16)

The CIA should not infiltrate dissident groups or other organizations of Americans in the absence of a written determination by the Director of Central Intelligence that such action is necessary to meet a clear danger to Agency facilities, operations, or personnel and that adequate coverage by law enforcement agencies is unavailable.

Recommendation (17)

All files on individuals accumulated by the Office of Security in the program relating to dissidents should be identified, and, except where necessary for a legitimate foreign intelligence activity, be destroyed at the conclusion of the current congressional investigations, or as soon thereafter as permitted by law.

5. Other Investigations by the Office of Security

A. Security Clearance Investigations of Prospective Employees and Operatives

Findings and Conclusions

The Office of Security routinely conducts standard security investigations of persons seeking affiliation with the Agency. In doing so, the

Office is performing the necessary function of screening persons to whom it will make available classified information. Such investigations are necessary, and no improprieties were found in connection with them.

B. Investigations of Possible Breaches of Security

1. Persons Investigated

Findings

The Office of Security has been called upon on a number of occasions to investigate specific allegations that intelligence sources and methods were threatened by unauthorized disclosures. The Commission's inquiry concentrated on those investigations which used investigative means intruding on the privacy of the subjects, including physical and electronic surveillance, unauthorized entry, mail covers and intercepts, and reviews of individual federal tax returns.

The large majority of these investigations were directed at persons affiliated with the Agency—such as employees, former employees, and defectors and other foreign nationals used by the Agency as intelligence sources.

N19

A few investigations involving intrusions on personal privacy were directed at subjects with no relationship to the Agency. The Commission has found no evidence that any such investigations were directed against any congressman, judge, or other public official. Five were directed against newsmen, in an effort to determine their sources of leaked classified information, and nine were directed against other United States citizens.

The CIA's investigations of newsmen to determine their sources of classified information stemmed from pressures from the White House and were partly a result of the FBI's unwillingness to undertake such investigations. The FBI refused to proceed without an advance opinion that the Justice Department would prosecute if a case were developed.

Conclusions

Investigations of allegations against Agency employees and operatives are a reasonable exercise of the Director's statutory duty to protect intelligence sources and methods from unauthorized disclosure if the investigations are lawfully conducted. Such investigations also assist the Director in the exercise of his unreviewable authority to terminate the employment of any Agency employee. They are proper unless their principal purpose becomes law-enforcement or the maintenance of internal security.

The Director's responsibility to protect intelligence sources and methods is not so broad as to permit investigations of persons having no relationship whatever with the Agency. The CIA has no authority to investigate newsmen simply because they have published leaked classified information. Investigations by the CIA should be limited to persons presently or formerly affiliated with the Agency, directly or indirectly.

Recommendation (18)

a. The Director of Central Intelligence should issue clear guidelines setting forth the situations in which the CIA is justified in conducting its own investigation of individuals presently or formerly affiliated with it.

b. The guidelines should permit the CIA to conduct investigations of such persons only when the Director of Central Intelligence first determines that the investigation is necessary to protect intelligence sources and methods the disclosure of which might endanger the national security.

c. Such investigations must be coordinated with the FBI whenever substantial evidence suggesting espionage or violation of a federal criminal statute is discovered.

Recommendation (19)

a. In cases involving serious or continuing security violations, as determined by the Security Committee of the United States Intelligence Board, the Committee should be authorized to recommend in writing to the Director of Central Intelligence (with a copy to the National Security Council) that the case be referred to the FBI for further investigation, under procedures to be developed by the Attorney General.

b. These procedures should include a requirement that the FBI accept such referrals without regard to whether a favorable prosecutive opinion is issued by the Justice Department. The CIA should not engage in such further investigations.

Recommendation (20)

The CIA and other components and agencies of the intelligence community should conduct periodic reviews of all classified material originating within those departments or agencies, with a view to declassifying as much of that material as possible. The purpose of such review would be to assure the public that it has access to all information that should properly be disclosed.

Recommendation (21)

The Commission endorses legislation, drafted with appropriate

safeguards of the constitutional rights of all affected individuals, which would make it a criminal offense for employees or former employees of the CIA wilfully to divulge to any unauthorized person classified information pertaining to foreign intelligence or the collection thereof obtained during the course of their employment.

2. *Investigative Techniques*

Findings

Even an investigation within the CIA's authority must be conducted by lawful means. Some of the past investigations by the Office of Security within the United States were conducted by means which were invalid at the time. Others might have been lawful when conducted, but would be impermissible today.

Some investigations involved physical surveillance of the individuals concerned, possibly in conjunction with other methods of investigation. The last instance of physical surveillance by the Agency within the United States occurred in 1973.

The investigation disclosed the domestic use of 32 wiretaps, the last in 1965; 32 instances of bugging, the last in 1968; and 12 break-ins, the last in 1971. None of these activities was conducted under a judicial warrant, and only one with the written approval of the Attorney General.

Information from the income tax records of 16 persons was obtained from the Internal Revenue Service by the CIA in order to help determine whether the taxpayer was a security risk with possible connections to foreign groups. The CIA did not employ the existing statutory and regulatory procedures for obtaining such records from the IRS.

In 91 instances, mail covers (the photographing of the front and back of an envelope) were employed, and in 12 instances letters were intercepted and opened.

The state of the CIA records on these activities is such that it is often difficult to determine why the investigation occurred in the first place, who authorized the special coverage, and what the results were. Although there was testimony that these activities were frequently known to the Director of Central Intelligence and sometimes to the Attorney General, the files often are insufficient to confirm such information.

Conclusions

The use of physical surveillance is not unlawful unless it reaches the point of harassment. The unauthorized entries described were illegal when conducted and would be illegal if conducted today. Likewise, the review of individuals' federal tax returns and the interception and opening of mail violated specific statutes and regulations prohibiting such conduct.

Since the constitutional and statutory constraints applicable to the use of electronic eavesdropping (bugs and wiretaps) have been evolving over the years, the Commission deems it impractical to apply those changing standards on a case-by-case basis. The Commission does believe that while some of the instances of electronic eavesdropping were proper when conducted, many were not. To be lawful today, such activities would require at least the written approval of the Attorney General on the basis of a finding that the national security is involved and that the case has significant foreign connections.

Recommendation (22)

The CIA should not undertake physical surveillance (defined as systematic observation) of Agency employees, contractors or related personnel within the United States without first obtaining written approval of the Director of Central Intelligence.

Recommendation (23)

In the United States and its possessions, the CIA should not intercept wire or oral communications [6] or otherwise engage in activities that would require a warrant if conducted by a law enforcement agency. Responsibility for such activities belongs with the FBI.

Recommendation (24)

The CIA should strictly adhere to established legal procedures governing access to federal income tax information.

Recommendation (25)

CIA investigation records should show that each investigation was duly authorized, and by whom, and should clearly set forth the factual basis for undertaking the investigation and the results of the investigation.

C. Handling of Defectors

Findings

The Office of Security is charged with providing security for persons who have defected to the United States. Generally a defector

---

[6] As defined in the Omnibus Crime Control and Safe Streets Act, 18 U.S.C. Secs. 2510-20.

can be processed and placed into society in a few months, but one defector was involuntarily confined at a CIA installation for three years. He was held in solitary confinement under spartan living conditions. The CIA maintained the long confinement because of doubts about the bona fides of the defector. This confinement was approved by the Director of Central Intelligence; and the FBI, Attorney General, United States Intelligence Board and selected members of Congress were aware to some extent of the confinement. In one other case a defector was physically abused; the Director of Central Intelligence discharged the employee involved.

Conclusions

Such treatment of individuals by an agency of the United States is unlawful. The Director of Central Intelligence and the Inspector General must be alert to prevent repetitions.

6. Involvement of the CIA in Improper Activities for the White House

Findings

During 1971, at the request of various members of the White House staff, the CIA provided alias documents and disguise material, a tape recorder, camera, film and film processing to E. Howard Hunt. It also prepared a psychological profile of Dr. Daniel Ellsberg.

Some of this equipment was later used without the knowledge of the CIA in connection with various improper activities, including the entry into the office of Dr. Lewis Fielding, Ellsberg's psychiatrist.

Some members of the CIA's medical staff who participated in the preparation of the Ellsberg profile knew that one of its purposes was to support a public attack on Ellsberg. Except for this fact, the investigation has disclosed no evidence that the CIA knew or had reason to know that the assistance it gave would be used for improper purposes.

N20

President Nixon and his staff also insisted in this period that the CIA turn over to the President highly classified files relating to the Lebanon landings, the Bay of Pigs, the Cuban missile crisis, and the Vietnam War. The request was made on the ground that these files were needed by the President in the performance of his duties, but the record shows the purpose, undisclosed to the CIA, was to serve the President's personal political ends.

The Commission has also investigated the response of the CIA to the investigations following the Watergate arrests. Beginning in June 1972, the CIA received various requests for information and assistance in connection with these investigations. In a number of instances, its responses were either incomplete or delayed and some materials that may or may not have contained relevant information were destroyed. The Commission feels that this conduct reflects poor judgment on the part of the CIA, but it has found no evidence that the CIA participated in the Watergate break-in or in the post-Watergate cover-up by the White House.

Conclusions

Providing the assistance requested by the White House, including the alias and disguise materials, the camera and the psychological profile on Ellsberg, was not related to the performance by the Agency of its authorized intelligence functions and was therefore improper.

No evidence has been disclosed, however, except as noted in connection with the Ellsberg profile, that the CIA knew or had reason to know that its assistance would be used in connection with improper activities. Nor has any evidence been disclosed indicating that the CIA participated in the planning or carrying out of either the Fielding or Watergate break-ins. The CIA apparently was unaware of the break-ins until they were reported in the media.

The record does show, however, that individuals in the Agency failed to comply with the normal control procedures in providing assistance to E. Howard Hunt. It also shows that the Agency's failure to cooperate fully with ongoing investigations following Watergate was inconsistent with its obligations.

Finally, the Commission concludes that the requests for assistance by the White House reflect a pattern for actual and attempted misuse of the CIA by the Nixon administration.

Recommendation (26)

a. A single and exclusive high-level channel should be established for transmission of all White House staff requests to the CIA. This channel should run between an officer of the National Security Council staff designated by the President and the office of the Director or his Deputy.

b. All Agency officers and employees should be instructed that any direction or request reaching them directly and out of regularly established channels should be immediately reported to the Director of Central Intelligence.

7. Domestic Activities of the Directorate of Operations

Findings and Conclusions

In support of its responsibility for the collection of foreign intelligence and conduct of covert operations overseas, the CIA's Directorate of Operations engages in a variety of activities within the United States.

A. Overt Collection of Foreign Intelligence within the United States

One division of the Directorate of Operations collects foreign intelligence within the United States from residents, business firms, and other organizations willing to assist the Agency. This activity is conducted openly by officers who identify themselves as CIA employees. Such sources of information are not compensated.

In connection with these collection activities, the CIA maintains approximately 50,000 active files which include details of the CIA's relationships with these voluntary sources and the results of a federal agency name check.

The division's collection efforts have been almost exclusively confined to foreign economic, political, military, and operational topics.

Commencing in 1969, however, some activities of the division resulted in the collection of limited information with respect to American dissidents and dissident groups. Although the focus was on foreign contacts of these groups, background information on domestic dissidents was also collected. Between 1969 and 1974, when this activity was formally terminated, 400 reports were made to Operation CHAOS.

In 1972 and 1973, the division obtained and transmitted, to other parts of the CIA, information about telephone calls between the Western Hemisphere (including the United States) and two other countries. The information was limited to names, telephone numbers, and locations of callers and recipients. It did not include the content of the conversations.

This division also occasionally receives reports concerning criminal activity within the United States. Pursuant to written regulations, the source or a report of the information received is referred to the appropriate law enforcement agency.

The CIA's efforts to collect foreign intelligence from residents of the United States willing to assist the CIA are a valid and necessary element of its responsibility. Not only do these persons provide a large reservoir of foreign intelligence; they are by far the most accessible source of such information.

The division's files on American citizens and firms representing actual or potential sources of information constitute a necessary part of its legitimate intelligence activities. They do not appear to be vehicles for the collection or communication of derogatory, embarrassing, or sensitive information about American citizens.

The division's efforts, with few exceptions, have been confined to legitimate topics.

The collection of information with respect to American dissident groups exceeded legitimate foreign intelligence collection and was beyond the proper scope of CIA activity. This impropriety was recognized in some of the division's own memoranda.

The Commission was unable to discover any specific purpose for the collection of telephone toll call information or any use of that information by the Agency. In the absence of a valid purpose, such collection is improper.

B. Provision and Control of Cover for CIA Personnel

CIA personnel engaged in clandestine foreign intelligence activities cannot travel, live or perform their duties openly as Agency employees. Accordingly, virtually all CIA personnel serving abroad and many in the United States assume a "cover" as employees of another government agency or of a commercial enterprise. CIA involvement in certain activities, such as research and development projects, are also sometimes conducted under cover.

CIA's cover arrangements are essential to the CIA's performance of its foreign intelligence mission. The investigation has disclosed no instances in which domestic aspects of the CIA's cover arrangements involved any violations of law.

By definition, however, cover necessitates an element of deception which must be practiced within the United States as well as within foreign countries. This creates a risk of conflict with various regulatory statutes and other legal requirements. The Agency recognizes this risk. It has installed controls under which cover arrangements are closely supervised to attempt to ensure compliance with applicable laws.

C. Operating Proprietary Companies

The CIA uses proprietary companies to provide cover and perform administrative tasks without attribution to the Agency. Most of the large operating proprietaries—primarily airlines—have been liquidated, and the remainder engage in activities offering little or no competition to private enterprise.

The only remaining large proprietary activity is a complex of financial companies, with assets of approximately $20 million, that enable the Agency to administer certain sensitive trusts, annuities, escrows, insurance arrangements, and other benefits and payments provided to officers or contract employees without attribution to CIA. The remaining small operating proprietaries, generally having fewer than ten employees each, make nonattributable purchases of equipment and supplies.

Except as discussed in connection with the Office of Security......
........................the Commission has found no evidence that any proprietaries have been used for operations against American citizens or investigation of their activities. All of them appear to be subject to close supervision and multiple financial controls within the Agency.

N21

D. Development of Contacts With Foreign Nationals

In connection with the CIA's foreign intelligence responsibilities, it seeks to develop contacts with foreign nationals within the United States. American citizens voluntarily assist in developing these contacts. As far as the Commission can find, these activities have not involved coercive methods.

These activities appear to be directed entirely to the production of foreign intelligence and to be within the authority of the CIA. We found no evidence that any of these activities have been directed against American citizens.

E. Assistance in Narcotics Control

The Directorate of Operations provides foreign intelligence support to the government's efforts to control the flow of narcotics and other dangerous drugs into this country. The CIA coordinates clandestine intelligence collection overseas and provides other government agencies with foreign intelligence on drug traffic.

From the beginning of such efforts in 1969, the CIA Director and other officials have instructed employees to make no attempt to gather information on Americans allegedly trafficking in drugs. If such information is obtained incidentally, it is transmitted to law enforcement agencies.

Concerns that the CIA's narcotics-related intelligence activities may involve the Agency in law enforcement or other actions directed against American citizens thus appear unwarranted.

Beginning in the fall of 1973, the Directorate monitored conversations between the United States and Latin America in an effort to identify narcotics traffickers. Three months after the program began, the General Counsel of the CIA was consulted. He issued an opinion that the program was illegal, and it was immediately terminated.

This monitoring, although a source of valuable information for enforcement officials, was a violation of a statute of the United States. Continuation of the operation for over three months without the knowledge of the Office of the General Counsel demonstrates the need for improved internal consultation. (See Recommendation 10.)

8. Domestic Activities of the Directorate of Science and Technology

Findings and Conclusions

The CIA's Directorate of Science and Technology performs a variety of research and development and operational support functions for the Agency's foreign intelligence mission.

Many of these activities are performed in the United States and involve cooperation with private companies. A few of these activities were improper or questionable.

As part of a program to test the influence of drugs on humans, research included the administration of LSD to persons who were unaware that they were being tested. This was clearly illegal. One person died in 1953, apparently as a result. In 1963, following the Inspector General's discovery of these events, new stringent criteria were issued prohibiting drug testing by the CIA on unknowing persons. All drug testing programs were ended in 1967.

In the process of testing monitoring equipment for use overseas, the CIA has overheard conversations between Americans. The names of the speakers were not identified; the contents of the conversations were not disseminated. All recordings were destroyed when testing was concluded. Such testing should not be directed against unsuspecting persons in the United States. Most of the testing undertaken by the Agency could easily have been performed using only Agency personnel and with the full knowledge of those whose conversations were being recorded. This is the present Agency practice.

Other activities of this Directorate include the manufacture of alias credentials for use by CIA employees and agents. Alias credentials are necessary to facilitate CIA clandestine operations, but the strictest controls and accountability must be maintained over the use of such documents. Recent guidelines established by the Deputy Director for Operations to control the use of alias documentation appear adequate to prevent abuse in the future.

As part of another program, photographs taken by CIA aerial photography equipment are provided to civilian agencies of the government. Such photographs are used to assess natural disasters, conduct route surveys and forest inventories, and detect crop blight. Permitting civilian use of aerial photography systems is proper. The economy of operating but one aerial photography program dictates the use of these photographs for appropriate civilian purposes.

Recommendation (27)

In accordance with its present guidelines, the CIA should not again engage in the testing of drugs on unsuspecting persons.

Recommendation (28)

Testing of equipment for monitoring conversations should not involve unsuspecting persons living within the United States.

Recommendation (29)

A civilian agency committee should be reestablished to oversee the civilian uses of aerial intelligence photography in order to avoid any concerns over the improper domestic use of a CIA-developed system.

9. CIA Relationships With Other Federal, State, and Local Agencies

CIA operations touch the interest of many other agencies. The CIA, like other agencies of the government, frequently has occasion to give or receive assistance from other agencies. This investigation has concentrated on those relationships which raise substantial questions under the CIA's legislative mandate.

Findings and Conclusions

A. Federal Bureau of Investigation

The FBI counterintelligence operations often have positive intelligence ramifications. Likewise, legitimate domestic CIA activities occasionally cross the path of FBI investigations. Daily liaison is therefore necessary between the two agencies.

Much routine information is passed back and forth. Occasionally joint operations are conducted. The relationship between the agencies has, however, not been uniformly satisfactory over the years. Formal liaison was cut off from February 1970 to November 1972, but rela-

N22   tionships have improved in recent years.

The relationship between the CIA and the FBI needs to be clarified and outlined in detail in order to ensure that the needs of national security are met without creating conflicts or gaps of jurisdiction.

Recommendation (30)

The Director of Central Intelligence and the Director of the FBI should prepare and submit for approval by the National Security Council a detailed agreement setting forth the jurisdiction of each agency and providing for effective liaison with respect to all matters of mutual concern. This agreement should be consistent with the provisions of law and with other applicable recommendations of this Report.

Findings and Conclusions

B. Narcotics Law Enforcement Agencies

Beginning in late 1970, the CIA assisted the Bureau of Narcotics and Dangerous Drugs (BNDD) to uncover possible corruption within that organization. The CIA used one of its proprietary companies to recruit agents for BNDD and gave them short instructional courses. Over two and one-half years, the CIA recruited 19 agents for the BNDD. The project was terminated in 1973.

The Director was correct in his written directive terminating the project. The CIA's participation in law enforcement activities in the course of these activties was forbidden by its statute. The Director and the Inspector General should be alert to prevent involvement of the Agency in similar enterprises in the future.

C. The Department of State

For more than 20 years, the CIA through a proprietary conducted a training school for foreign police and security officers in the United States under the auspices of the Agency for International Development of the Department of State. The proprietary also sold small amounts of licensed firearms and police equipment to the foreign officers and their departments.

The CIA's activities in providing educational programs for foreign police were not improper under the Agency's statute. Although the school was conducted within the United States through a CIA proprietary, it had no other significant domestic impact.

Engaging in the firearms business was a questionable activity for a government intelligence agency. It should not be repeated.

D. Funding Requests From Other Federal Agencies

In the spring of 1970, at the request of the White House, the CIA contributed $33,655.68 for payment of stationery and other costs for replies to persons who wrote the President after the invasion of Cambodia.

This use of CIA funds for a purpose unrelated to intelligence is improper. Steps should be taken to ensure against any repetition of such an incident.

E. State and Local Police

The CIA handles a variety of routine security matters through liaison with local police departments. In addition, it offered training courses from 1966 to 1973 to United States police officers on a variety of law enforcement techniques, and has frequently supplied equipment to state and local police.

In general, the coordination and cooperation between state and local law enforcement agencies and the CIA has been exemplary, based upon a desire to facilitate their respective legitimate aims and goals.

Most of the assistance rendered to state and local law enforcement agencies by the CIA has been no more than an effort to share with law enforcement authorities the benefits of new methods, techniques, and equipment developed or used by the Agency.

On a few occasions, however, the Agency has improperly become involved in actual police operations. Thus, despite a general rule against providing manpower to local police forces, the CIA has lent men, along with radio-equipped vehicles, to the Washington Metropolitan Police Department to help monitor anti-war demonstrations. It helped the same Department surveil a police informer. It also provided an interpreter to the Fairfax County (Virginia) Police Department to aid in a criminal investigation.

In compliance with the spirit of a recent Act of Congress, the CIA terminated all but routine assistance to state and local law enforcement agencies in 1973. Such assistance is now being provided state and local agencies by the FBI. There is no impropriety in the CIA's furnishing the FBI with information on new technical developments which may be useful to local law enforcement.

For several years the CIA has given gratuities to local police officers who had been helpful to the Agency. Any such practice should be terminated.

The CIA has also received assistance from local police forces. Aside from routine matters, officers from such forces have occasionally assisted the Office of Security in the conduct of investigations. The CIA has occasionally obtained police badges and other identification for use as cover for its agents.

Except for one occasion when some local police assisted the CIA in an unathorized entry, the assistance received by the CIA from state and local law enforcement authorities was proper. The use of police identification as a means of providing cover, while not strictly speaking a violation of the Agency's statutory authority as long as no police function is performed, is a practice subject to misunderstanding and should be avoided.

10. Indices and Files on American Citizens

Findings

Biographical information is a major resource of an intelligence agency. The CIA maintains a number of files and indices that include biographical information on Americans.

N23

As a part of its normal process of indexing names and information of foreign intelligence interest, the Directorate of Operations has indexed some 7,000,000 names of all nationalities. An estimated 115,000 of these are believed to be American citizens.

Where a person is believed to be of possibly continuing intelligence interest, files to collect information as received are opened. An estimated 57,000 out of a total of 750,000 such files concern American citizens. For the most part, the names of Americans appear in indices and files as actual or potential sources of information or assistance to the CIA. In addition to these files, files on some 7,200 American citizens, relating primarily to their domestic activities, were, as already stated, compiled within the Directorate of Operations as part of Operation CHAOS.

The Directorate of Administration maintains a number of files on persons who have been associated with the CIA. These files are maintained for security, personnel, training, medical and payroll purposes. Very few are maintained on persons unaware that they have a relationship with the CIA. However, the Office of Security maintained files on American citizens associated with dissident groups who were never affiliated with the Agency because they were considered a threat to the physical security of Agency facilities and employees. These files were also maintained, in part, for use in future security clearance determinations. Dissemination of security files is restricted to persons with an operational need for them.

The Office of Legislative Counsel maintains files concerning its relationships with congressmen.

Conclusions

Although maintenance of most of the indices, files, and records of the Agency has been necessary and proper, the standards applied by the Agency at some points during its history have permitted the accumulation and indexing of materials not needed for legitimate intelligence or security purposes. Included in this category are many of the files related to Operation CHAOS and the activities of the Office of Security concerning dissident groups.

Constant vigilance by the Agency is essential to prevent the collection of information on United States citizens which is not needed for proper intelligence activities. The Executive Order recommended by the Commission (Recommendation 2) will ensure purging of nonessential or improper materials from Agency files.

11. Allegations Concerning the Assassination of President Kennedy

Numerous allegations have been made that the CIA participated in the assassination of President John F. Kennedy. The Commission staff investigated these allegations. On the basis of the staff's investigation, the Commission concludes that there is no credible evidence of CIA involvement.

N24

NOTES AND REFERENCES

1. This extract is a digest of the CIA's own history. It was the basis for a more detailed history of the CIA, prepared by staff member Anne Karalekas for the Senate Church Committee ([45D], pp. 1–103). Due to space restraints, it is not included here.

2. In 1947, the Strategic Services Unit of the War Department prepared a "War Report" evaluating the operations of the Office of Strategic Services (OSS) during World War II. The OSS, established in 1942 and liquidated in 1945, was the first U.S. attempt toward the creation of a centralized unit to oversee intelligence gathering. Kermit Roosevelt, chief historian for the War Report and subsequently an intelligence officer, directed the preparation of the report; and Serge Peter Karlow, executive officer for history projects, Strategic Services Unit, was assigned to complete it. This report, which has been declassified, recounts the effectiveness of OSS during World War II and the ongoing need for such an intelligence unit as an integral part of defense operations ([93]).

3. Organizational charts of the CIA, dating from 1947, appear in this chapter.

4. The National Security Act of 1947 and President Harry S. Truman's directive on the "Coordination of Federal Foreign Intelligence Activities" are reprinted in the Appendix.

5. For CIA Director Richard Helms' and Senator Stuart Symington's views on the original intent of the CIA regarding domestic activity, see [17], p. 39.

6. The National Intelligence Survey Group prepared the previously secret 1949 Dulles-Jackson-Correa Survey, whose participants were Allen Dulles, DCI under President Dwight D. Eisenhower; William Jackson, attorney and former Deputy DCI; and Matthias Correa, lawyer and former assistant to Secretary of the Navy Forrestal during World War II. This survey is now available (with deletions of still classified sections) from the NSC under the Freedom of Information Act, which became effective on July 4, 1967, and was amended by PL 93-502 (88 Stat. 1561), effective November 21, 1974. Refer to [109] or order through procedures outlined in [125].

7. During the 1940s and 1950s, intelligence operations underwent continual reevaluation and reorganization with a view toward the entire international political scene. A heretofore top secret document recently released by the NSC summarizes the intelligence community's response to national security threats at that time ([110]).

8. The reprinted history of the CIA from 1971 to 1975 is from the previously cited Karalekas historical study of the CIA prepared for the Church Committee; note Chapter 5, footnote 1.

9. Covert activities and congressional oversight are addressed in Chapters 10 and 11.

10. The CIA's self-policing efforts are reviewed in [45A], p. 288.

11. Operation CHAOS and other domestic activities are dealt with in Chapter 12. The purpose of Operation CHAOS, established in August 1967 and terminated in March 1974, was to determine if American political dissidents were receiving foreign support. Additional information on CHAOS itself is cited in Chapter 12; [25]; [45C], pp. 688–721; and [124], pp. 130–150.

12. An alternative definition of the purpose of intelligence is contained in reprinted material from the Murphy Commission report in Chapter 3.

13. An exposition (from 1948) on the need for coordinated production of finished intelligence (the process by which collected data are established as valid and significant for policymakers) is provided in [107].

14. The role of the intelligence community within the framework of broader U.S. government policy objectives is reviewed more fully in Chapter 3.

15. Consult Chapter 2 for information on the coordinating bodies of the U.S. intelligence establishment.

16. For more details on CIA clandestine relations with academic bodies and voluntary organizations supportive of CIA objectives, see [45A], pp. 179 ff.

17. See [45A], pp. 289 ff. on the role of the inspector general of the CIA.

18. The Church Committee recommended that all mail interception within the United States cease (note recommendation 6, Chapter 12). For an account of mail openings, in New York and elsewhere, see [44D].

19. Federal agencies have experienced breaches of security within their own offices and among their employees. Efforts to investigate this area have resulted in the use of polygraphs and similar devices, including the administration of lie detector tests to CIA employees ([69], pp. 643–663).

20. The Special Subcommittee on Intelligence of the House Armed Services Committee held hearings in 1973 and 1974 to examine the extent to which the CIA was involved in the Watergate scandal and the break-in of Daniel Ellsberg's psychiatrist, Dr. Henry Fielding. See [58], [59], and Chapters 10 and 12. (Ellsberg, a former foreign policy official, was responsible for the disclosure of the Pentagon Papers in 1972. By this act of disclosure, he challenged government policy on secrecy and directed attention to the inadequacy of checks and balances among the branches of government. In his congressional testimony, he raised fundamental moral constitutional questions.)

21. Proprietary companies are government-owned business enterprises and foundations serving a variety of intelligence and covert action purposes. For a more thorough review of the CIA's use of such companies, consult [45A], pp. 205 ff.

22. The director of intelligence, Richard Helms, recalls the events leading up to the rupture of relations with FBI Director J. Edgar Hoover in [17], p. 35.

23. For the Church Committee's recommendations regarding CIA collection of information and maintenance of files on American citizens, see Chapter 12.

24. Although the Rockefeller Commission's conclusion may not be altered by it, the evidence bearing on CIA involvement in the assassination of President John F. Kennedy is still not available to Congress or the public. See hearings in [73].

Chapter 6
Department of Defense

BACKGROUND ([45A], pp. 319–366)

The intelligence agencies of the Defense Department collectively consume about 85 percent of the intelligence community's budget and employ a similar portion of its personnel, if one includes the activities of the National Security Agency and those of the individual armed services. (In this volume NSA is dealt with as a separate agency in Chapter 7.) Defense-related agencies and expenditures amount to approximately $5.8 billion, of which $3.9 billion is consumed by NSA and the Air Force's somewhat related National Reconnaissance Office. This estimate is provided by Victor Marchetti and John Marks in *The CIA and the Cult of Intelligence* ([158]), which continues to be the most reliable unclassified source regarding specific amounts spent by individual intelligence agencies. The sophisticated electronic equipment employed is costly and the transaction and analysis of intercepted communication is labor intensive. Intelligence efforts of DOD have not been subjected to the same level of public and media scrutiny as have those of the CIA, but a number of congressional and in-house panels have sought to evaluate the efficiency of the Defense intelligence effort.

The intelligence units of the military service have been more closely integrated since World War II, primarily because of the transfer of responsibilities for specific functions into newly established bodies that work on behalf of all the services, as well as the civilian portion of the Defense Department. Of particular significance was the formation of the National Security Agency in 1952 and the organization of the Defense Intelligence Agency in 1961. The recommendations of OMB Director James Schlesinger and the Blue Ribbon Defense Panel (Fitzhugh report) in 1971 resulted in the creation of an assistant secretary of defense for intelligence ([104], p. 35). Meanwhile, the House Pike Committee recommended that the DIA be abolished and its functions be transferred to the assistant secretary for intelligence (Pike recommendations are reprinted in Chapter 10).

The Church Committee focused on the national-intelligence-gathering activities of DOD (excluding tactical military intelligence), and in its report provided a description of the workings of Defense intelligence programs. That section of the Church report is reprinted in Chapter 6 in its entirety; supporting charts and tables from other sources are provided at the conclusion. The Church Committee's treatment of DOD reflects a tendency toward criticism. While no DOD rejoinder to the committee's findings was provided in the review of government documents, the testimony of DOD witnesses before the committee offers another perspective. See, for instance, testimony by the secretary of defense and the head of DIA in items [1], [5], [7], [10], [46], [47], [52], and [54] cited in the Bibliography.

The Department of Defense is the nation's primary consumer of intelligence information. It controls nearly 90 percent of the nation's spending on intelligence programs, and most technical collection systems are developed, targeted, and operated by DOD personnel. The sheer size and complexity of the Defense intelligence establishment make it difficult to comprehend the problems and issues which confront policymakers and intelligence managers. Overall security needs and bureaucratic interests, as well as differing intelligence needs, further complicate the quest for solutions to the community's substantive problems and impede efforts aimed at implementing management reform.

This section of the report summarizes the Committee's investigation into the intelligence activities of the Department of Defense. It is limited in content to information that can be released publicly. Although many significant factual details about the national intelligence apparatus are thus not included, the Committee does not believe that such omissions seriously detract from a clear presentation of the central findings of its work.

The Committee focused on national intelligence activities, i.e., those which produce information primarily of interest to national decisionmakers. Tactical intelligence activities, which are organic to or in direct support of operational units, received less attention. This area could not be ignored, however, because new collection and processing technology has significantly affected the relationship between the national intelligence systems and the operational commands.

After an initial review of the entire defense intelligence program, based on documents, briefings, and studies provided by the executive branch, the Committee investigated the following issues of particular interest:

—The resource management and organizational dimensions of the Defense national intelligence community.
—The role of the Defense Intelligence Agency in relation to the CIA and intelligence functions of the military departments.
—The monitoring and reporting activities of the National Security Agency.
—Military counterintelligence and investigative activities of the Department of Defense.
—The chemical and biological research of the Department of Defense as it relates to intelligence missions.

The investigation revealed abuses of authority in all these subject areas, some of which were already known to the intelligence community, Congress, or the public. After a brief review of the relation of intelligence to the major objectives of U.S. military forces, and the history and evolution of intelligence organizations, this report addresses these specific Defense intelligence issues in turn. The concluding section assesses the future requirements for Defense intelligence, particularly as they are affected by technological developments.

OBJECTIVES AND ORGANIZATION OF THE DEFENSE INTELLIGENCE COMMUNITY

The mission of the Department of Defense intelligence apparatus is to provide the defense establishment with accurate and timely information on the military capabilities or political intents of foreign states to assure that U.S. policymakers are forewarned of, and U.S. military forces prepared for, any event which threatens the national security.

There are several important consumers of Defense intelligence. National security policymakers are interested in three areas of national importance: crisis management, which calls for not only advance warning of possible military, economic, or political disruption, but also continued, detailed tracing of developments once they are underway; long-range trends in foreign military, economic, and scientific capabilities, and political attitudes which might warrant a major U.S. response; and the monitoring or verification of specific international agreements which are either in force, such as the SALT agreement or the Middle East ceasefire, or contemplated, such as Mutual and Balanced Force Reductions talks in Europe.

Defense planners, responsible for designing the structure of U.S. military forces, constitute a second important group of intelligence consumers. Although their interests are less far-ranging than those of the policymakers, their demands for insights into the capabilities of opposing military forces are generally phrased in broader terms than other DOD intelligence consumers, if only because the macroscopic analysis which supports major force structure decisions is seldom sensitive to detailed intelligence inputs.

In contrast to the estimative character of the intelligence products most required by policymakers and defense planners, two other consumer groups, the developers of weapon systems and the operating field forces, have greater interest in detailed, factual information. Satisfaction of these demands is generally more a matter of collection and compilation than analysis and inference. The major distinction between the two groups lies in their subject interests. The weapon systems developers emphasize scientific and technical detail regarding the operating characteristics and performance parameters of foreign weapon systems (knowledge of which can be useful in optimizing the design of U.S. systems). The military field commands emphasize "order of battle" data, or the unit identities and the strength, equipage, and disposition of opposing field forces.

The sequence of operations in meeting the intelligence demands of these disparate groups of consumers involves three (or, in the case of signals intelligence, four) basic steps: (1) collection—the gathering of potentially relevant data; (2) production—the translation of these data into finished intelligence products through screening, analysis, and drawing of inferences; and (3) dissemination—delivery of the finished products to the right consumers at the right time. If the collected data are in the form of electronic signals, another step, "processing," between the first and the second, is required to refine the raw signals before they are submitted for human evaluation during the production phase.

A brief review of the major objectives of U.S. military forces may help to place the intelligence contribution in perspective.

1. Objectives of U.S. Military Forces

The paramount objective of U.S. forces is to deter nuclear attacks upon the United States and its allies by maintaining an unambiguous capability to inflict massive damage on the attacker, even after absorbing a first strike by the aggressor's nuclear forces. The defense intelligence community supports this objective by monitoring the technical developments and force deployments of potential enemies, especially those which might attempt to gain the capability for a disarming first strike. U.S. technical collection systems are able to alert leaders to an imminent attack by detecting movement or changes in the status of the Soviet Union's strategic forces. Thus warned, the United States can counter and react to such changes. This so-called strategic warning may be essential to the survival of some components of the U.S. retaliatory force.

Tactical warning, based on indications that a nuclear attack has actually commenced, is the primary responsibility of the alert and warning networks of the operational military commands. Although U.S. intelligence collection systems are not designed specifically to provide such warning, they have some inherent ability to do so. It is generally agreed that no measures would prevent a nuclear exchange from devastating all the participants; thus, relatively little attention has been devoted to developing intelligence systems designed to improve the outcome of an all-out nuclear war for the United States or its allies.

The second purpose of U.S. forces is to deter conventional (i.e., nonnuclear) military attacks on its allies. Although U.S. nuclear forces, both strategic and theater, contribute to this objective by introducing the threat of escalation into a potential aggressor's calculation, the general purpose forces (land combat, naval, and tactical air) of the United States and its allies are considered the prime deterrent to conventional military attack. Planning for the general purpose forces focuses on being able to defend Western Europe, while at the same time being able to conduct a lesser war in the Pacific theater. Again intelligence plays an important role in following the technical and force-level changes of potential enemies, and in predicting future trends. Current intelligence is also relied upon to provide adequate warning of the massive redeployment of men and materiel that would precede a conventional attack.

In the event of war, it will be critical to adapt the missions of the national intelligence-gathering systems to the needs of operational commanders. The planning for such contingencies poses a major challenge for leaders of the defense intelligence community.

The ongoing arms limitations negotiations on strategic and theater forces in Europe are guided by the principle of rough equality between opposing capabilities. Asymmetries in such factors as geography, technology, and manpower must be accommodated so that both sides believe there is an overall balance. Intelligence systems play a critical part in monitoring this balance since they are the only reliable means available for verifying the status of forces of potential adversaries. In fact, advances in technical intelligence collection systems have made the current arms limitation agreements feasible. Establishing compliance with the strategic arms agreements in force, as well as providing assistance in current negotiations, is now among the most vital missions of the national intelligence apparatus.

The technical capabilities of U.S. intelligence systems are probably now adequate to meet the demands of present agreements. Whether they can meet the needs of future agreements is unclear and dependent upon the specific terms negotiated. Some of the proposals advanced in connection with the Vladivostok Agreement and the Mutual and Balanced Force Reduction (MBFR) talks would test the abilities of current or envisioned intelligence systems to detect or verify with high confidence. Three of the most difficult enforcement areas which could arise under future agreements and which pose major problems for the intelligence community are:

—MIRV missiles which are concealed in silos or submarines;
—Cruise missiles whose launchers are easily concealed in bombers and submarines, and which may carry either conventional or nuclear warheads;

—Mobile forces and weapons (particularly nuclear systems) in Europe which can be transferred quickly to and from the theater, and are also readily concealed.

2. Evolution of Defense Intelligence Organizations

The complexities of modern defense have burdened the intelligence community with issues and responsibilities which could hardly have been anticipated when the United States emerged as the world's foremost military power three decades ago. In endeavoring to fill its expanding role in support of the nation's security interests, the defense intelligence apparatus has undergone periodic reorganization, generally leading toward more centralized management control. The desire to make the defense intelligence community more responsive to the needs of policymakers has motivated this trend.

At present, the most likely near-term prognosis is for a continuation of the general peace, interrupted at times by regional conflict and crisis, but not erupting into a major war or likely to involve direct U.S. military participation. The problem has been that in order to avert the big war, the U.S. has had to project a credible appearance of being able to win it, or, at least, not lose it decisively. This means it could not permit its war-fighting capacity, for which the military services hold the final responsibility, to erode unilaterally. Since the defense intelligence apparatus is a major contributor to that capacity, and since most of the important intelligence assets are operated by the armed forces, it is not surprising that the services have resisted efforts to channel these resources in different directions.

The existing organization of the defense intelligence community will be discussed in the following section. It is important to appreciate that it was not designed expressly to serve today's intelligence requirements or to manage today's intelligence functions. Rather, it should be perceived as basically a service to the military, adjusted through several decades of institutional compromise.

3. Early Beginnings

The first traces of U.S. military intelligence activities appeared in the Revolutionary War, when General George Washington, as commander of the colonial Army, recruited and trained a corps of intelligence agents to report on British activities. This effort, which included the use of codes, secret ink, and disguises, was short-lived, and the agents were mustered out of service with the rest of the Continental Army. Following Washington's precedent, commanders of U.S. military forces in later conflicts created *ad hoc* intelligence units on their own authority to serve their individual needs. Andrew Jackson had an intelligence operation in the War of 1812, and Winfield Scott had an intelligence unit in his command in the Mexican War. A number of the military commanders in the Civil War organized their own intelligence networks, and two autonomous organizations, both named the United States Secret Service, engaged in intelligence activities for the Union, although neither had any legal authority to operate.

In 1882, the Secretary of the Navy established an Office of Naval Intelligence to collect and record "such naval information as may be useful to the department in the time of war, as well as in peace." [1]

---

[1] A. P. Niblack, *The History and Aims of the Office of Naval Intelligence*, Division of Operations, United States Navy Department (Washington, D.C.: U.S. Government Printing Office, 1920).

This office developed a naval attache system to overtly collect information on foreign naval activities. It initiated a series of publications summarizing the information it had collected to keep the Navy abreast of foreign naval developments, and specifically provided the Naval War Board with information during the Spanish-American War.

The first comparable Army unit was the Military Intelligence Division of the Office of Adjutant General, established in 1885 to gather information on foreign armies. It, too, was active during the Spanish-American War, but by the outbreak of World War I the entire Division had shrunk to two officers and two clerks.

Both the Army and Navy greatly expanded their intelligence complements during World War I. The Army alone had more than 300 officers and 1,000 civilians engaged in intelligence work. In 1917, a War Department Cipher Bureau was created by administrative directive. This unit, sometimes referred to as the "American Black Chamber," solved more than 45,000 cryptograms (including one from the Sunday Times) and broke the codes of more than twenty nations. It was dissolved at the specific direction of Secretary of State Henry L. Stimson in 1929, who reportedly said: "Gentlemen do not read each other's mail." [2] This and similar measures left the service intelligence arms poorly prepared for World War II.

One of the first steps taken by President Roosevelt in the aftermath of Pearl Harbor was to order the creation of the Office of Strategic Services (OSS) in June 1942 under the direction of General William Donovan. During World War II, OSS, together with the Army and Navy intelligence organizations, was coordinated by the Joint Intelligence Committee of the Joint Chiefs of Staff.

N2

A list of the functions of the principal OSS branches demonstrates the scope of its activity. The Research and Analysis section produced economic, military, social, and political studies, and estimates for strategic areas from Europe to the Far East; the Secret Intelligence group gathered information from within neutral and enemy territory; Special Operations conducted sabotage and worked with the various resistance groups; Counterespionage protected United States and allied intelligence operations; Morale Operations created and spread "black propaganda"; Operational Groups trained, supplied, and sometimes led guerrilla groups in enemy territory; the Maritime Unit conducted marine sabotage; and Schools and Training was in charge of the overall training and assessment of personnel, both in the United States and abroad. In addition, OSS was directed to plan and conduct such "special services as may be directed by the United States Joint Chiefs of Staff." Only Latin America, the FBI's bailiwick, and the Pacific Theater, General MacArthur's, were outside the OSS sphere of operations.

Jurisdiction over subjects of tactical military interest, such as order of battle data and enemy weaponry estimates, was left with the traditional service arms. OSS also did not prevail completely over other intelligence operations of the services, which achieved a number of notable wartime successes. Army Intelligence, for example, captured a high-level Nazi planning group in North Africa, obtained a map of all enemy minefields in Sicily, and captured the entire Japanese secret police force on Okinawa. Naval Intelligence, soon after

---

[2] Herbert O. Yardley, *The American Black Chamber* (Indianapolis: Bobbs-Merrill, 1931), pp. 332, 348.

United States' entry into the war, deduced the impending appearance of German guided missiles, such as the HS 293, the V-bombs, and homing torpedoes.

After World War II, President Truman issued an Executive Order abolishing the OSS on September 20, 1945. The Department of War absorbed some of its functions, such as the work of its Secret Intelligence group and of its Counterespionage program. The State Department assumed others.

The demise of the OSS did not, however, end the concept of a central intelligence organization. On January 22, 1946, President Truman established a National Intelligence Authority to advise him, and created a Central Intelligence Group to assist the NIA in coordinating national intelligence matters. These two organizations evolved, through the National Security Act of 1947, into the National Security Council and Central Intelligence Agency.

The rapid demobilization of the armed forces after the war, the creation of the first peacetime central intelligence organization, and President Truman's conviction that the military must be subordinated to civilian control were all factors which seemed to portend a diminished role for the armed forces within the post-war intelligence community. The National Security Act of 1947, which created the CIA and NSC, also strengthened civilian authority over military services by drawing the War and Navy Departments together under a single Secretary of Defense. The new Secretary was given authority over all facets of the administration of the defense establishment. The identities of the Army and the Navy were preserved, however, under separate civilian secretaries who now reported to the Secretary of Defense rather than directly to the President. At the same time, the air elements of the Army were reformed under a new Department of the Air Force, with the same status as the two older service departments.

The broad powers granted the Secretary of Defense permit him to effect major organizational changes within the Defense Department by the simple expedient of issuing a directive. The Defense Intelligence Agency was created by such a directive in 1961. The Eisenhower administration had concluded in the late 1950s that a consolidation of the services' general (defined rather awkwardly as all non-SIGINT, nonoverhead, nonorganic intelligence activities) was needed, an idea which the Secretary of Defense in the new Kennedy administration, Robert F. McNamara, quickly endorsed.

The Joint Chiefs of Staff and Secretary McNamara disagreed on the form the new agency should take. The JCS were concerned with preserving the responsiveness of the service efforts to the military's tactical intelligence requirements. They therefore wanted a joint Military Intelligence Agency subordinate to them, within which the independence of the several military components, and hence their sensitivity to the needs of the parent service, would be retained.[3] McNamara wanted a much stronger bond. He was determined to utilize better the service assets to support policymakers and force structure planners, and to achieve management economies.

The Defense Intelligence Agency which emerged was a compromise. It reports to the Secretary of Defense, but does so through the JCS. The Joint Staff Director for Intelligence (the J-2) was abolished

N3

---

[3] Memoranda, from Secretary of Defense Robert McNamara to Chief, Joint Chiefs of Staff, Lyman Lemnitzer, 2/8/61; from Lemnitzer to McNamara, 3/2/61; from McNamara to Lemnitzer, 4/3/61; from Lemnitzer to McNamara, 4/13/61.

and replaced by the Director of the new DIA. The functions of the Office of Special Operations—the small intelligence arm of the Office of the Secretary of Defense (OSD)—were absorbed by DIA.[4] There has been continuing controversy among the services due to their reluctance to cede responsibilities to DIA because they feared downgrading wartime combat capabilities. Moreover, the OSD level of the Defense Department has pressed continuously for greater centralization; both of these controversies have hampered DIA throughout its existence.

Unlike the DIA, the National Security Agency (NSA) is a presidential creation. Established in response to a Top Secret directive issued by President Truman in October 1952, NSA assumed the responsibilities of its predecessor, the Armed Forces Security Agency (AFSA), which had been created after World War II to integrate the national cryptologic effort. NSA was established as a separate agency within DOD reporting directly to the Secretary of Defense. In addition, it was granted SIGINT operational control over the three Service Cryptologic (collection) Agencies (SCAs): the Army Security Agency, Naval Security Group Command, and Air Force Security Service. Under this arrangement NSA encountered many of the same jurisdictional difficulties which were to plague DIA. In an effort to strengthen the influence of the Director of the National Security Agency (DIRNSA) over their activities, the SCAs were confederated in 1971 under a Central Security Service (CSS) with the DIRNSA as its chief. The mission of NSA/CSS is to provide centralized coordination, direction, and control for the United States Government's Signals Intelligence (SIGINT) and Communications Security (COMSEC) activities.

N4

4. Current Organization

Describing the management structure of the Defense intelligence community would be a difficult task under the best of circumstances. Authority and influence within any big organization are often determined as much by personalities and working relationships as by formal chains of commands or job descriptions. For the sprawling and complex Defense intelligence network, the task is particularly challenging. Moreover, the community is in the midst of an executive branch-directed transition which may alter second-level management relationships throughout the Department of Defense. The executive branch has not yet revealed exactly what kind of structure it intends, if indeed its full reorganization plan has been decided.

Of necessity, the description which follows applies to the organization of the Defense intelligence community as it existed during most of 1975.[5]

---

[4] Memorandum from Deputy Secretary of Defense Roswell Gilpatric to Secretaries of the Military Departments; Director of Defense Research and Engineering; Chief, Joint Chiefs of Staff; Assistant Secretaries of Defense; General Counsel: Special Assistant; and Assistants to the Secretary, 7/5/61; DOD Directive 5105.21, 8/1/61.

[5] The most significant change apparently now being considered would affect the Office of the Assistant Secretary of Defense for Intelligence (ASD/I). This position is currently (as of April 1976) vacant. Reportedly, the duties of the ASD/I will be assumed by a new Deputy Secretary who will also have executive jurisdiction over the related fields of telecommunications and net threat assessment. In this case, the ASD/I position could be abolished. The possibility cannot

As the Defense intelligence community is presently organized, the Secretary of Defense has three groups of assets: (1) the Defense agencies reporting directly to him, of which the National Security Agency, the Central Security Service, and classified national programs are the most significant (but also including the Defense Mapping Agency and the Defense Investigative Service); (2) the Defense Intelligence Agency, which reports to him through his principal military advisers, the Joint Chiefs of Staff, and is responsible for preparing Defense intelligence reports and estimates drawing upon the data collected by other arms of the intelligence apparatus; and (3) the intelligence arms of the individual military services under the immediate operational control of the service chiefs, which encompass the military's general intelligence collection agencies, their counterintelligence and investigative arms, and activities of tactical interest.

One of the largest organizations in the Defense intelligence community is the National Security Agency. Military personnel, facilities, and equipment play a predominant role in carrying out the mission described by NSA Director, General Lew Allen, Jr., in public session:

> This mission of NSA is directed to foreign intelligence, obtained from foreign electrical communications and also from other foreign signals such as radars. Signals are intercepted by many techniques and processed, sorted and analyzed by procedures which reject inappropriate or unnecessary signals. The foreign intelligence derived from these signals is then reported to various agencies of the government in response to their approved requirements for foreign intelligence.[6]

Other agencies reporting directly to the Secretary of Defense are concerned with more specialized subject areas than the cryptologic group and make smaller demands on resources. The Defense Mapping Agency is responsible for all defense mapping, charting, and geodetic activities. Although a substantial percentage of this Agency's activities are of vital intelligence interest, others are related only marginally to intelligence, and some have no defense connotation at all. Similarly, the Defense Investigative Service, responsible for carrying out background investigations, is generally not considered in the mainstream of the national intelligence effort.

Aside from the Defense Investigative Service, each of the military services retains independent investigative arms responsible for both counterintelligence and criminal matters. These agencies fall within the ordinary military chain of command, and report to the Chief of Staff for each service. Other intelligence activities of national importance conducted under the uniformed services include the reconnaissance operations of Air Force aircraft and drones, and the general intelligence collection and analysis work of the U.S. Army Intelli-

---

be ruled out, however, that the executive envisions the new Deputy Secretary as an additional oversight position, in which case a new ASD/I reporting to him could be appointed. This is along the lines suggested by the Report to the President and the Secretary of Defense by the Blue Ribbon Defense Panel, July 1, 1970, on National Command and Control Capability and Defense Intelligence (hereinafter cited as the Fitzhugh Report, after its chairman, Gilbert W. Fitzhugh).

[6] General Lew Allen, Jr., testimony, 10/29/75, Hearings, Vol. 5, p. 17.

gence Agency, the Naval Intelligence Command, and the Air Force Intelligence Service. The service intelligence agencies are primarily oriented to supporting the tactical missions of the services, but they also collect information used by DIA in producing finished intelligence. The service agencies also continue to engage in activities related to national intelligence, and participate in the national estimates process as observers on the U.S. Intelligence Board.[6a]

A simplified diagram of the DOD-funded intelligence organization is presented.................. As is clear from the diagram, the organizational structure is extremely complicated, with several key individuals serving in more than one capacity, and disparate and diffuse chains of responsibility, both for deciding what is to be done and allocating the resources to do it.

ORGANIZATION* OF THE DOD-FUNDED INTELLIGENCE COMMUNITY

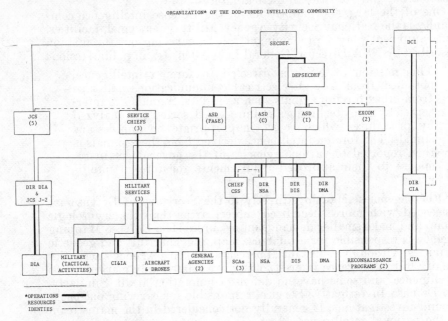

Perhaps the most significant feature of the above chart however, is what it does *not* show: a clear-cut line of authority extending from the highest councils of the executive branch to the operating arms of the intelligence apparatus. This is not surprising since this structure is the product of many years of bureaucratic evolution. Whether one views this arrangement as a crazy-quilt pattern, produced piecemeal over time in response to internal pressures, or as a finely balanced mechanism developed to meet needs as they arose, is largely a matter of perspective. It is hard to avoid observing, however, that if the apparatus has functioned even half as efficiently in allocating intelligence resources as its proponents maintain, it is because its participants have come to understand it well enough to make the system work in spite of itself. On the brighter side, the profusion of checks and balances inherent in the system may serve to reassure those who fear the potential evils of concentrating too much power in the hands of a single intelligence leader.

N5

[6a] USIB was abolished by Executive Order No. 11905, 2/18/76.

THE DEFENSE INTELLIGENCE BUDGET

1. Problems of Definition

N6 The magnitude of national resources devoted to intelligence activities has recently been subject to considerable public speculation. Estimates of U.S. military intelligence spending have ranged from $3–4 billion annually to $15 billion, with most settling around the $6.2 billion figure cited in a recent book.[7]

Much of the controversy stems from definitions. What constitutes an intelligence activity? Which Government entities are intelligence organizations? Unfortunately, the budgeting practices of the intelligence community, and particularly the Department of Defense which controls the overwhelming bulk of intelligence resources, were not designed with much attention to functional clarity. Within DOD, institutional pressures to lower the "fiscal profile" of intelligence activities and rivalries over control of organizational assets have led to such discrepancies as placing the SR–71 program in the strategic forces account (Program I, a totally different section of the Defense budget).[8] Other examples of current budget practices are the exclusion of all communications security, counterintelligence, and mapping and charting activities from the Consolidated Defense Intelligence Budget (CDIB).

Although a case can be made that DOD's narrow definition of intelligence activities offers certain management expediencies in permitting the staff of the Assistant Secretary of Defense for Intelligence (ASD/I) to concentrate its attention on the central elements of the Defense intelligence effort, it produces such functional anomalies as the exclusion of important intelligence activities from the ASD/I's fiscal purview. Certainly, whatever degree of budgeting oversight the Congress elects to assume should address a fiscal presentation assembled on the basis of a more comprehensive definition of national intelligence activities than DOD uses at present.

Furthermore, a congressional oversight committee, in attempting to monitor DOD's counterintelligence budget, may want to group it with the counterintelligence budgets of all other intelligence agencies to provide management visibility to the national counterintelligence effort that is now lacking, even within the executive branch. Practical difficulties in distinguishing counterintelligence activities from ordinary criminal investigations (which, though totally different in purpose, are quite similar in method and often share common assets) should not be permitted to preclude an effort to establish a cross-agency grouping of the counterintelligence budget.[9]

The same problem of distinguishing intelligence and nonintelligence-related functions exists in the budgets for mapping and geodetic activities, most of which are the responsibility of the Defense Mapping Agency. Many of DMA's missions are only marginally

---

[7] Victor Marchetti and John D. Marks, *The CIA and the Cult of Intelligence* (New York: Dell, 1974), p. 95.

[8] The SR–71s were recently transferred from this category to the Strategic Forces (Program I in the Planning, Programing, and Budgeting System).

[9] The investigations for security clearances, previously a hodgepodge of disparate standards for uncoordinated, redundant efforts, were recently consolidated under a newly formed Defense Investigative Service (DIS). Nearly two-thirds of the budget for Counterintelligence and Investigative Activities (CI&IA) remains vested with the service agencies.

related to the intelligence function, but others are of vital importance to all segments of the intelligence community's market. At a tactical military level, what intelligence commodity is of greater importance to a field commander than accurate maps of his area of operations? As with counterintelligence, the difficulties inherent in trying to separate the budgets of those facets of the mapping, charting, and geodetic effort which serve a national intelligence purpose from those which do not should not be solved by the simple expedient of ignoring all such activities.

Still more difficult definitional problems arise when one probes more deeply the budgets of the armed forces in search of "tactical" as opposed to "national" intelligence functions. The difference between these two categories of intelligence lies in the eye of the consumer, not in the intelligence-collection activity itself. Increasingly, intelligence data-collection systems have grown capable of serving both the broad interests of the policymakers and defense planners and the more specific technical interests of the weapons developers and field commanders. In fact, a given set of collected data may often be of interest to all these groups, although the analytical slant with which it is presented is likely to differ markedly in response to consumer preferences.

There is an extensive gray area encountered in attempting to define military intelligence activities at the tactical or field command level. Many components of the military forces make a definite contribution to our intelligence effort during peacetime, but have other important missions as well, particularly during war. A prime example is the Navy's long-range, shore-based patrol planes, which play an important ocean surveillance role in peacetime, but would be an active part of U.S. antisubmarine warfare (ASW) combat forces during war. Although tactical military intelligence and related activities are included in the comprehensive cost estimates presented in the following section, the Committee believes the budgets of such activities should be excluded from the jurisdiction of a congressional intelligence oversight committee, with those committees in which it is currently vested retaining fiscal review authority.

The problem of reflecting costs of activities which are only partly intelligence-related in cost reporting is not confined to DOD. The diplomatic missions of the Department of State are responsible for political, economic, and commercial reporting, as well as normal representational and diplomatic responsibilities. The Department's Bureau of Intelligence and Research, which is both a consumer of intelligence and a producer of finished analyses, was budgeted for $9.5 million in FY 1976, of which 84 percent was spent on salaries. However, much more is spent each year to support State's embassies and consulates which, in addition to other duties, function in their political reporting activities as a human intelligence collection system. As with tactical military intelligence activities, the difficulties of trying to segregate the intelligence portion of the budget costs of these dual-purpose assets appear to outweigh the benefits.

2. The Size of the Defense Intelligence Budget in FY 1976

The Committee's analysis indicated that [deleted] billion [10] constitutes the direct costs to the U.S. for its national intelligence program for FY 1976. This includes the total approved budgets of CIA, DIA, NSA, and national reconnaissance programs.[10a] If the costs of tactical

N7

---

[10] Deleted pending further Committee consideration.

intelligence by the armed services and indirect support costs [10b] which may be attributed to intelligence and intelligence-related activities are added in, the total cost of intelligence activities by the U.S. Government would be twice that amount. This represents about [deleted] percent of the federal budget, and [deleted] percent of controllable federal spending.[10c]

It should be stressed that this larger estimate represents a full cost and includes activities which also fulfill other purposes. Thus the entire amount could not be "saved" if there were no intelligence activities funded by or through the Defense Department.

A breakdown of the DOD intelligence budget divided by activity is shown in the table below. These estimates are based on a broader interpretation of what constitutes an intelligence activity than that used by DOD. The Department manages its national intelligence effort through the Consolidated Defense Intelligence Program (CDIP), and makes no formal effort to attribute indirect support costs. The summary includes only those activities funded through the Defense Appropriation Bill.

The costs of intelligence functions performed by the Departments of State (Bureau of Intelligence and Research), Treasury, Justice (Federal Bureau of Investigation), and the Energy Research and Development Administration (which has assimilated the intelligence division formerly operated by the Atomic Energy Commission) total N8 about $0.2 billion.

Full Costs of Intelligence and Related Activities Within the DOD Budget: Fiscal Year 1976

(*In millions*)

Direct costs:	
Cryptology	-----
Communications security	-----
Reconnaissance programs	-----
Aircraft and drones	-----
Special naval activities	-----
Counterintelligence and investigation	-----
General intelligence	-----
Mapping, charting, and geodesy	-----
Central Intelligence Agency	-----
Subtotal, national intelligence effort	[deleted] [10d]
Strategic warning	-----
Ocean surveillance	-----
Tactical intelligence	-----
Weather reconnaissance	-----
Reserve intelligence components	-----
Subtotal, military intelligence effort	[deleted]
Total, direct costs	[deleted]
Indirect support costs:	
Basic research and exploratory development	-----
Logistics	-----
Training, medical and other personnel activities	-----
Administration	-----
Total, indirect support costs	[deleted]
Total, intelligence costs (budgeted by DOD)	[deleted]

[10a] Direct costs of the intelligence activities of the ERDA, FBI, and State Department are contained in their respective budgets.

[10b] Indirect support costs include costs for personnel, operations and maintenance which support intelligence activities. Examples are the operation of training facilities, supply bases, and commissaries.

[10c] Deleted pending further Committee consideration.

[10d] *Ibid.*

[DELETED]

3. Who Controls the Intelligence Budget?

The nominal head of the intelligence community is the Director of Central Intelligence (DCI), who is also the Director of the Central Intelligence Agency; these two roles, however, are to be viewed as distinct. A cornerstone of President Nixon's 1971 directive, designed to foster the intelligence community's responsiveness to policymakers and promote management efficiency, was "an enhanced leadership role" for the DCI. Yet the DCI was not given direct authority over the community's budget, nor granted the means by which to control the shape of that budget until the announcement of President Ford's Executive Order of February 18, 1976.

As Director of the CIA, the DCI controls less than 10 percent of the combined national and tactical intelligence efforts. His chairmanship of the Executive Committees (ExComs), which oversee the management of certain reconnaissance programs (wherein he serves in what amounts to a partnership with the ASD/I), also affords him some influence over the funds budgeted for these efforts. The remainder spent directly by the Department of Defense on intelligence activities in FY 1976 was outside of his fiscal authority. The DCI's influence over how these funds are allocated was limited, in effect, to that of an interested critic.

By persuasion, he could have some minor influence, but the budgets themselves were prepared entirely within the Department of Defense. The small staff of the DCI may have been consulted in the process, but by the time it sees the defense portion of the national intelligence budget, the budgetary cycle has been well advanced, and hence the budget has been largely fixed. Problems of timing also influence the role of the Office of Management and Budget, which sets broad fiscal guidelines in budget ceilings, but plays an otherwise minor role in shaping the Defense intelligence budget.

The real executive authority over at least four-fifths of the total resources spent on intelligence activities has resided with the Secretary of Defense. Over the past few years, the Deputy Secretary of Defense has shown a particular interest in the intelligence portion of the DOD budget, in effect representing the Secretary on many issues arising in this area. However, the major responsibility for management of intelligence programs will lie with the newly created position of Deputy Secretary of Defense for Intelligence (Mr. Robert Ellsworth).

The Assistant Secretary of Defense for Program Analysis and Evaluation (ASD/PA&E) holds general review authority over the so-called mission forces, the operational forces which include much of the tactical intelligence assets of the military services. A third ASD, the Comptroller, is responsible for reviewing the budgets of the agencies concerned with counterintelligence investigations, and the newly formed Defense Mapping Agency. As explained earlier, DOD considers these activities peripheral to the intelligence effort, and their costs account for only about 5 percent of the overall intelligence budget.

The managers of the various intelligence programs collectively wield the greatest influence on day-to-day intelligence operations. By the budget yardstick, the most influential individual is the Director of NSA (DIRNSA) who, including his dual role as Chief of the Central Security Service, manages the largest single program contained in the national intelligence budget, less than half of which is actually in the NSA budget.

Close behind the DIRNSA, and also directly related to the collection of signals intelligence data, is the United States Air Force in its role of managing certain reconnaissance programs. Decisions made regarding the introduction and development of reconnaissance systems have the greatest impact on the overall size of the intelligence budget, not only because of the direct costs of perfecting and procuring the hardware involved—as expensive as this technically complex equipment has become—but also because of the continuing effect that the choice of a collection system has on processing and other operating costs long after it has been made.

A third grouping of defense intelligence activities is the General Defense Intelligence Program (GDIP). In effect an "all other" category, the GDIP budget is ordinarily one-fourth Defense Intelligence Agency (DIA) costs, and three-fourths service costs (including those of the Air Force Intelligence Service, Naval Intelligence Command, and a part of the U.S. Army Intelligence Agency). The GDIP encompasses all of DOD's non-SIGINT, nonoverhead intelligence collection and production activities deemed by the Department to be of national importance. It does not include activities related to the military field commands.

Although the general intelligence budget managed by the Director of DIA (DIRDIA) has never been more than a fraction the size of the DIRNSA's cryptologic budget, his problems, though similar, are more formidable. Whereas opinion is divided on the DIRNSA's grip over the service agencies that participate in the Consolidated Cryptologic Program (through the Central Security Service), there is little disagreement on the DIRDIA's inability to exert significant influence over the priorities and activities of the service components of the GDIP.

As a consequence, the program management responsibilities for the service general intelligence agencies previously held by the DIRDIA were recently transferred to the ASD/I. The result is that the DIRDIA, who purportedly still speaks for the Secretary of Defense on "substantive" matters within the intelligence community, exerts direct control over only 4 percent of the Secretary's intelligence budget.

The span of authority at each managerial tier—from executive oversight through fiscal review to program management—is summarized in the table . . . .

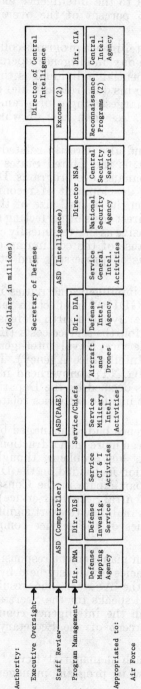

Who controls the Intelligence Budget?
Distribution of the FY1976 Budget
Request by Organization and Recipient of Appropriated Funds
(dollars in millions)

Total

Director of Central Intelligence

Dir. CIA — Central Intel. Agency

Excoms (2) — Reconnaissance Programs (2)

Secretary of Defense

ASD (Intelligence)

Director NSA — Central Security Service — National Security Agency

Dir. DIA — Defense Intel. Agency — Service General Intel. Activities

Aircraft and Drones — Service Military Intel. Activities

ASD(PA&E)

ASD (Comptroller)

Service/Chiefs

Service CI & I Activities

Dir. DIS — Defense Investig. Service

Dir. DMA — Defense Mapping Agency

Authority:

Executive Oversight

Staff Review

Program Management

Appropriated to:

Air Force

Army

Navy & Marine Corps

Defense Agencies

Total for Agency

[Figures deleted.]

Defense agencies each draw on resources funded within the service appropriations in addition to their own agency appropriations. These resources generally take the form of pay and allowances for military personnel who are serving tours outside their parent service with intelligence agencies. DIA's appropriation is supplemented by $39 million in this way; NSA's by $34 million; DIS by $16 million; and the Defense Mapping Agency's by $12 million. The Defense Department makes accounting corrections for these service-incurred costs in its Fiscal Year Defense Plan (FYDP), and the amounts are included in presenting the agency budgets. The important point to be recognized is that the budgets of the Defense intelligence agencies are not fully covered by the funds appropriated to them.

Slightly over a third of the overall DOD-funded intelligence effort is managed directly by the military services. The bulk of these funds support the tactical military requirements of the field commands and include many force components for which the intelligence mission is secondary or of shared importance with other activities. However, activities under service management are of national importance and interest in two areas: peripheral reconnaissance (carried out both by piloted aircraft, such as the SR–71, and unmanned drones), and counterintelligence and investigation (conducted by the Air Force Office of Special Investigations, the Naval Investigative Service, and a number of decentralized Army military intelligence groups).

4. Budget Trends

The preceding section defined a [deleted] billion "package" of DOD-funded activities as a reasonable, comprehensive estimate with the addition of selected non-defense activities of a national intelligence budget subjected to separate congressional authorization. This section focuses on budget trends for this grouping of national activities.

In terms of simple dollar amounts, the FY 1976 DOD budget submission for national intelligence activities is the highest ever—over twice the amount appropriated in FY 1962. During periods of rapid inflation, however, "current dollars" are totally misleading as a measure of time trends in the consumption of real resources. Some allowance must be made for the year-to-year diminution in the purchasing power of a dollar that is brought about by rising prices. The method for doing so employs "price deflators" in an effort to express the worth of a series of heterogeneous "current-year" dollars in terms of the purchasing power of a dollar in some specific "constant" base year. The fact that these adjustments can seldom be achieved with precision does not negate their usefulness.

The chart on............indicates the trends in the DOD-funded national intelligence budget (which includes the CIA as well as Defense agencies and the national activities of the military services) from fiscal year 1962 through fiscal year 1976. The upper, climbing curve plots current dollar amonuts as appropriated by the Congress except for fiscal year 1976, which is the amount requested by DOD. The lower, gradually descending curve shows the equivalent trend in the national intelligence budget after correcting, insofar as possible, for the effects of inflation by expressing each of the historical budgets in terms of the number of FY 1962 dollars it would take to purchase the same level of effort.

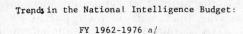

Trends in the National Intelligence Budget:

FY 1962-1976 a/

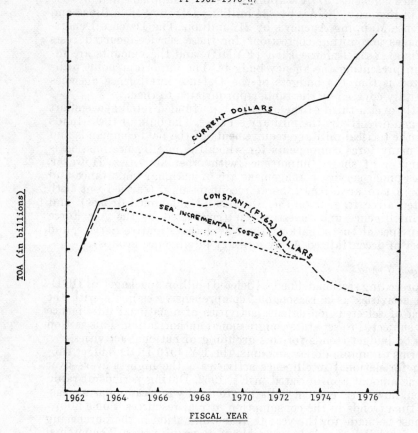

FISCAL YEAR

a/ Includes CIA budget. Does not include costs of tactical military intelligence activities.

After climbing rapidly during the first half of the 1960s, largely as a result of major program initiatives to acquire sophisticated reconnaissance systems (including the $1 billion SR-71 development program), the real "baseline" intelligence budget peaked at mid-decade at about [deleted] billion. Although outlay continued to grow moderately for several more years, the extra cost of supporting activities directly related to the war effort in Southeast Asia grew even more quickly, so that the amount available to support nonwar-related, or baseline, activities began to diminish. Since the mid-1960s, the budget has declined steadily, in terms of the resources that could be bought with the dollars provided, to the FY 1976 level of [deleted] billion, about equal in buying power to the budgets of the late 1950s.

A review of DOD planning documents indicates that every effort will be made by Defense leaders to avoid further erosion in the intelligence effort below the FY 1976 level Conversely, it is not anticipated that significant increases in funding (above those necessary to compensate for continued inflation, now expected to average 5–7 percent annually over the next five years) will be requested. If the Congress accepts these plans, a roughly constant level of real spending with gradually increasing annual appropriations to offset inflation can be expected.

Measured in today's prices, the budget request for Defense intelligence programs is also well below past funding levels: off $0.5 billion, or about 10 percent, from the FY 1962 level, and down nearly 30 percent from the pre-Vietnam peak of [deleted] billion. Compared to FY 1962, the largest reductions have taken place in the resources dedicated to some activities under NSA's management, which declined by 31 percent in real terms; and the development, procurement, and operation of reconnaissance systems, which went down 15 percent. Spending in support of aircraft and drone operations, although far below the peaks associated with the introduction of the SR–71, stands well above the level of 1962. Spending for communications security is also considerably higher today. Reflecting efficiencies achieved through the consolidation of independent service programs within the Defense Mapping Agency, real spending for mapping, charting, and geodetic activities is about $100 million less in FY 1976 than it was in FY 1962. Consolidation has also achieved economies in the field of counterintelligence and investigation, although on a far smaller scale. The $125 million requested for these activities stands about 15 percent below the pre-Vietnam level of effort.[11]

During the Committee's inquiry, informed managers within the Defense intelligence community frequently expressed the judgment that the downward trend in the resources dedicated to their programs has gone as far as it should. While acknowledging that no one has succeeded in devising a sound method by which to relate the value of the community's output to the quantity of resources used, they argue that most of the savings from the elimination of duplication and other forms of nonproductive effort have already been realized, and that further reductions can only be achieved at the risk of curtailing essential intelligence services.

5. *How Much is Enough?*

Because of the difficulties inherent in trying to quantify the intelligence community's output, no one has yet developed a rigorous method by which to relate the amount of intelligence produced to the amount of resources consumed in the intelligence effort. For this reason, it is not possible to state with confidence the effect that changes in the level of resources allocated to the intelligence mission could have on U.S. national security. In other words, no one really knows what comes out of the intelligence apparatus as a function of what goes into it.

The twin peacetime purposes for maintaining a national intelligence organization are to reduce the probability of key decisionmakers

---

[11] An estimated 20–40 percent of this amount will be spent for criminal, as opposed to counterintelligence, investigations.

making a wrong decision, either by taking inappropriate action in some matter important to U.S. interests or by failing to act at all, and to aid in assuring that U.S. Armed Forces are adequately prepared to execute decisions requiring military force. The intelligence apparatus is supposed to promote good policy and military readiness by making the policymakers and generals better informed than they might overwise be. However, the relationship between the quality of the information supplied to a national leader and the quality of the decisions made is obviously extremely complex and ill-defined. Although good intelligence may create a bias in favor of policymakers making good policy, it can offer no guarantees that such will transpire in every instance. All too easily, a bad policy judgment may be attributed to "intelligence failures."

If the level of effort were increased substantially, the quality of intelligence and national security would be enhanced. Conversely, substantial reductions could pose additional security risks. What cannot be ascertained with precision is whether the benefits would be worth the additional costs, or the savings the additional risks. At present, the issue can only be evaluated subjectively, taking into account those few factual statements that are at hand and the judgments of intelligence experts (recognizing, of course, the institutional biases the judgments may reflect).

On the one hand, the way in which the peacetime national intelligence budget has been shrinking has been duly documented. Apparently, these reductions have not significantly detracted from the overall performance of the national intelligence apparatus or seriously jeopardized U.S. security. Community managers interviewed during the Committee's investigation generally felt that present funding was adequate to provide all consuming groups with essential intelligence support. On the other hand, the same individuals were unanimous in their opposition to any further cuts in the budget—a view endorsed by the 1975 report of the Defense Panel on Intelligence, which stated: "We consider that the widely held concern over the inflated size of the intelligence effort is no longer valid." The report maintained that further "substantial" reductions should be contingent on one or more of the following:

—A conscious decision to modify intelligence priorities and coverage.
—The introduction of labor-saving devices (i.e., automation of the intelligence process).
—Reorganization of other management efficiencies.

In making the case against further reductions in the level of the national intelligence effort, it is commonly argued that the intelligence is labor-intensive (meaning that people, not machines, contribute the most to the community's product and account for the greatest share of its costs), and that the number of intelligence workers has declined sharply over the past several years. The community's managers contend that further personnel cuts should be made only as new equipment is introduced which can do more efficiently some of the tasks now performed by people.

The trend in defense intelligence manpower has been sharply downward: the fiscal year-end strength of 89,900 persons (civilian and military, U.S. citizens and foreign nationals) planned for 1976 is one-fifth less than that of fiscal year 1962, and 42 percent below the 1968 peak of 153,800 persons (some of whom were, of course, engaged in support of the Southeast Asia war effort). At the end of fiscal year 1975, 101,500 persons were engaged in defense national intelligence activities.

It is not true that the defense national intelligence effort is labor-intensive. Quite the opposite. Intelligence is highly capital-intensive; the defense intelligence community annually invests more per employee than the DOD-wide average.[12] As shown in Table 5, investment per man-year for the national intelligence sector of the Defense budget will average $16,700, about 11 percent less than was spent in 1962 despite the manpower reductions that have taken place, but still $2,800 more than will be invested by the general purpose forces at large, and only $1,800 less than the highly capital-intensive strategic forces. The downward trend in the investment rate for the intelligence components does not suggest a vigorous effort on the part of community managers to achieve the gains in efficiency through automation that they contend offer the best opportunity to realize further savings.

DEFENSE INVESTMENT RATES: FISCAL YEARS 1962–76

[Thousands of constant fiscal year 1976 dollars per man-year][1]

	1962	1964	1968	1972	1974	1975	1976	Percentage change, fiscal year 1962
Defense national intelligence components	18.7	22.0	15.3	14.8	14.8	16.3	16.7	−10.7
Strategic military forces	37.1	26.2	23.1	25.5	18.0	17.8	18.5	−50.1
General purpose military forces	12.1	12.4	[2] 15.9	[2] 13.1	12.1	10.0	13.9	+14.9

[1] Investment defined as sum of total obligational authority for associated RDT & E procurement and military construction. Average personnel strengths computed to include all military, U.S. civilian, and foreign national employees.
[2] These figures reflect increased investment in support of combat operations in Southeast Asia.

Lacking a sound methodology by which to relate outputs to inputs, management of the intelligence community must remain as subjective as the product in which it deals. The Committee did not receive the impression that the intelligence community was in fact striving to develop such a methodology, if indeed that is possible. The words of former Assistant Secretary of Defense Robert Froehlke sum up the existing situation lucidly: "The intelligence community does not know the minimum level of resources that will satisfy an intelligence requirement. There is no upper boundary set by requirements, only by the resources that are made available."

---

[12] The Department of Defense has requested $37.6 billion for investment (RDT&E, Procurement and Military Construction) in FY 1976 and will consume about 3.1 million man-years of labor for an average investment per man-year of $12,000. This compares favorably with the most capital-intensive sectors of U.S. manufacturing, such as petroleum and chemicals, and is many times greater than the investment spending of such truly labor-intensive industries as textiles.

MANAGEMENT PROBLEMS OF THE DEFENSE INTELLIGENCE COMMUNITY

1. *Previous Studies*

Senate Resolution 21's instructions that the Select Committee undertake a "complete investigation and study" to determine "whether there is unnecessary duplication of expenditure and effort in the collection and processing of intelligence information by United States agencies" strikes a familiar chord. Over the past decade, no fewer than six major studies have been commissioned within the executive branch to probe precisely the same question. Coinciding with the Congress' inquiry, another executive study of the community's organization was conducted, culminating in the actions taken by the President on February 18, 1976.

Earlier studies have not always agreed on details, but all have concluded that the defense intelligence community has performed neither as effectively nor as efficiently as possible, due largely to its fragmented organization. More centralized management control is needed if there is to be improvement in the cost-effectiveness of the community's efforts. Notwithstanding this view, the community's organizational structure has changed little over many years. Since many of the past studies of the community's organization have tapped greater resources than have been available to the Select Committee, the discussion which follows draws heavily upon their findings.

Writing in 1971 from his vantage point in the Office of Management and Budget (OMB), James R. Schlesinger compared the structure and management methods of the intelligence community to those of the Department of Defense prior to the Defense Reorganization Act of 1958. Obviously, this Act did not eradicate all of DOD's management problems. Similarly, reorganization of the intelligence apparatus could not in itself guarantee improved performance nor lowered costs. But reorganization could, in Schlesinger's view, create the conditions for inspired intelligence leadership. In his 1971 paper, Schlesinger concluded: "the main hope for improving cost-effectiveness did in fact lie in a fundamental reform of the intelligence community's decision-making bodies and procedures." [13]

In its letter of transmittal to the President, the 1970 Blue Ribbon Panel on Defense (the Fitzhugh Report), summed up its appraisal of the community's performance with the following criticisms:

N9

    —Intelligence activities are spread throughout the Department of Defense with little or no effective coordination.

    —Redundance in intelligence, within reason, is desirable, and it is particularly important that decision-makers have more than one independent source of intelligence.

    —There is, as has often been charged, evidence of duplication between the various organizations.

    —There is a tendency within the intelligence community to produce intelligence for the intelligence community and to remain remote from and not give sufficient attention to the requirements of others who have valid needs for intelligence.

---

[13] Office of Management and Budget, "A Review of the Intelligence Community" (Schesinger Report), 3/10/71.

—There is a large imbalance in the allocation of resources, which causes more information to be collected than can ever be processed or used.
—Collection efforts are driven by advances in sensor technology, not by requirements filtering down from consumers of the community's products.[15]

The Blue Ribbon panel also cited the following allegations made by "responsible witnesses" during the course of its investigation, noting that there was no way to confirm or disprove any of the charges because there was no existing procedure to evaluate systematically the efficiency of the intelligence process or the substantive value of its output:

—The human collection activities (HUMINT) of the services add little or nothing to the national capability.
—Defense attaches do more harm than good.
—The intelligence production analysts are not competent to produce a sound, useful product.
—Once produced, the product seldom reaches the individuals who need it.

Each of these issues is discussed below.

2. Centralizing Management Controls

On this issue, the views of those who wish to avoid repetitions of past abuses by the community and those stressing the importance of improving the effectiveness and efficiency of the community's operations may not be compatible. Critics of centralization feel that reforms aimed at improving cost-effectiveness by concentrating budget and operational authority within the community might, at the same time, concentrate the power to undertake improper activities in the future. Centralization proponents counter that the diffusion of authority is as apt to encourage improper conduct as its concentration. A streamlined management structure would, they argue, promote the visibility and accountability of controversial programs.

If the Defense intelligence community were reorganized to promote more effective, centralized controls, what form might it take?

The office of the Assistant Secretary of Defense for Intelligence (ASD/I) has been the single most influential office in the preparation of the national intelligence budget under recent organizational arrangements. Although the ASD/I's authority is not absolute, he has more to say about how and where the national intelligence community invests its resources than any other individual by virtue of his fiscal review authority over the Consolidated Defense Intelligence Program (CDIP).

ASD/I was established largely as a result of a recommendation by the 1970 Blue Ribbon Defense (Fitzhugh) Panel, but it was not accorded the full authority the Panel proposed, and certain other complementary reforms were also not adopted. A classified supplement to the Fitzhugh Report called for creation of an ASD/I who would also serve as a new Director of Defense Intelligence (DDI).

---

[15] Fitzhugh Report, 7/1/70.

Under this arrangement, the same individual would have direct line authority over the operations of the DOD intelligence apparatus (via his position as Director of Defense Intelligence) and responsibility for review of resources allocated to it as Assistant Secretary of Defense for Intelligence.

The Blue Ribbon Panel further envisioned a reorganization of the DOD intelligence community along functional lines, separating collection and production activities into two new agencies, the heads of which would report to the ASD/I in his dual role as DDI.

Complementing its objective of creating a clear chain of command from the operating aims of the Defense intelligence establishment to the Department's top policymakers, the Panel also recommended the establishment of a Deputy Secretary of Defense for Operations who would represent the Secretary in all intelligence-related matters, and to whom the ASD/I–DDI would report directly. Although the recommendation to establish a second Deputy Secretary of Defense was not accepted in 1970, it is part of the 1976 executive reorganization plan.

3. Too Much Collection?

Numerous studies since the mid-1960s have concluded that a serious imbalance exists between the amount of data collected by the technical sensor and surveillance systems and the ability of the processors and analysts to digest and translate these data into useful intelligence information. These studies recommend that greater attention be given to producing better insights from the information and less to stockpiling data.

Analyzing the steep rise in the cost of intelligence activities during the 1950s and early 1960s, Schlesinger was among the first to blame the movement to employ ever more sophisticated technical collection systems, which he believed had led to "gross redundancies" within community operations. He concluded that the rapid growth in the collection of raw intelligence data was not a substitute for sorely needed improvements in analysis, inference, and estimation. The scope and quality of intelligence output, he concluded, had not kept pace with increases in its cost.

The Committee did not find any studies suggesting that more collection capacity is needed, although deficiencies in the responsiveness of existing collection systems have been frequently noted. Examples of general observations on overcollection are:

—Like the rest of the intelligence community, it (the CIA) makes up for not collecting enough of the right kind of information on the most important targets by flooding the system with secondary matter.
—The information explosion has already gotten out of hand, yet the CIA and the community are developing ways to intensify it. Its deleterious effects will certainly intensify as well, unless it is brought under control.
—The quantity of information is degrading the quality of finished intelligence.[16]

---

[16] "Foreign Intelligence Collection Requirements: The Inspector General's Survey." (hereinafter cited as the Cunningham Report). December 1966.

—Production resources can make use of only a fraction of the information that is being collected. There exists no effective mechanism for balancing collection, processing and production resources.[17]

The period of rapid growth in intelligence costs that undoubtedly motivated much of the concern about overcollection has passed. Although the level of total real spending has now returned to what it was during the late 1950s, the efficiency with which intelligence resources are being apportioned among the collection, processing, and production functions remains an issue.

An examination of the distribution of the national intelligence budget dollar in FY 1975 indicates that most of the community's resources support collection activities. The community is still spending 72 percent of its funds for collection, 19 percent for processing raw technical data, and less than 9 percent for the production of the finished intelligence products (bulletins, reports, etc.) which the consumer sees as the community's output. There has been no significant change in the allocation over the past several years, nor is any anticipated.

The collection of unused information results in greater inefficiencies than merely the effort wasted on collection. Backlogs in processing and analysis lead to duplicative efforts across the board, since the results of preceding collection missions are not always available to plan and manage current missions. Moreover, the rush to keep pace with the data disgorged by the technical collection systems encourages superficial scanning, increasing the probability that potentially important pieces of information will be overlooked.

4. Alternative Means of Collection

There are major disagreements within the community between proponents of traditional collection methods employing undercover agents (human intelligence, or HUMINT) and advocates and operators of the vast system of technical sensors. Approximately 87 percent of the resources devoted to collection is spent on technical sensors, compared to only 13 percent for HUMINT (overt and clandestine operations).

Most of the intelligence experts interviewed during the Committee's inquiry tended to endorse the existing seven-to-one distribution of resources in favor of technical collection, but the efficacy of the technical sensors was not unanimously acclaimed. Deputy Secretary of Defense William P. Clements, Jr. commissioned the Defense Panel on Intelligence (1975)[18] largely because of his concern with the failure of the analytical community to alert national leadership to the October 1973 Middle East war.

The Defense Panel Report stressed the importance of upgrading HUMINT, noting: "We are not getting [as of 1975] the level or quality of information we need from this source." [18] The Report credited the CIA's Clandestine Service as the most competent U.S. HUMINT collectors, but held this arm was not very responsibe to DOD needs. It

---

[17] Fitzhugh Report, 7/1/70.
[18] Report of the Defense Panel on Intelligence, 1/75.

was concluded that the principal Defense HUMINT collectors, the Defense Attaché System (DAS) managed by DIA, were yielding valuable returns at small cost, but greatly needed a personnel upgrading. Other critics have been less charitable to the attaches.

The problem of measuring intelligence output prevents accurate assessment of the contribution of different collection methods. Shifts in the uses of intelligence systems among peacetime, crisis, and wartime situations further complicate appraisals, as does the divergent interests of the national and tactical consumer groups. Civilian policymakers tend to plan for peacetime situations, whereas military commanders envision quite different wartime demands on the intelligence apparatus. The shifts of importance between peacetime and wartime are illustrated by the fact that much of the economic intelligence collected today would be accorded a much lower priority during a major war. Similarly, the verification of arms control agreements, now a major intelligence task, would be moot after the outbreak of hostilities between the major powers.

Against this backdrop, only an approximate evaluation of the comparative worth of the various methods of intelligence collection has been possible for the Committee. The results of such an evaluation are summarized as follows:

Performance was judged against two criteria: the ability of the method to accomplish specified intelligence objectives, and characteristics deemed desirable in intelligence systems.[19]

The analysis indicated that reconnaissance programs and SIGINT systems rank high in characteristics and performance. Not surprisingly, their costs are also the highest of all the competing systems.

HUMINT did not score as highly as might be expected, based on the emphasis and funds accorded to this activity. Still, overall, the evaluation indicated that a fairly good correlation exists between the benefits achieved by collection activities and their costs.

The priorities for spending among different collection systems appear to be appropriate. This does not mean that there is no need for adjustment in the pattern of resource allocation for collection methods. A major analytic effort on the part of the community offers the only means for achieving such efficiencies.

Although the issue of proper balance between collection, processing, and production is usually phrased in terms of overcollection, it might also be described as a problem of underproduction. Deputy Secretary of Defense Clements stated: "In every instance I know about where there was a horrendous failure of intelligence, the information was in fact available to have averted the problem. But the analysts and the system didn't allow the raw data to surface."[20]

---

[19] The following intelligence objectives are considered: strategic warning; crisis indication; foreign weapons development; foreign military deployments; political and military intent; economic information; political information; tactical military information.

The following characteristics were considered: ability to penetrate denied areas; accuracy and reliability of data; responsiveness; wartime survivability; peacetime risks of incident.

[20] Quoted by William Beecher in Report of the Defense Panel on Intelligence, 1/75.

Similarly, the Defense Intelligence Agency, the arm of the Defense Department charged with the prime responsibility for intelligence analysis and production, concluded in a 1973 report:

> The great disparity in the relative national investment in collection systems versus intelligence processing, exploitation, production and support systems has now reached a platitude [sic] where the anticipated payoff of a high cost collection system is limited by the DIA's capability to exploit them [sic] fully.

If production is the limiting step in the intelligence sequence, improved overall efficiency might be achieved by enhancing this capacity as well as by cutting back on collection. It is not clear, however, that the DIA's suggestion to spend more on production, implied in the above passage, would solve the largely qualitative shortcomings now limiting the performance of some intelligence producers.

5. Setting Intelligence Priorities

Intertwined with the issue of how much should be spent on intelligence activities is the question of how best to spend it. This poses a whole series of complex, interrelated choices ranging from subject matter to "line balance" (i.e., synchronizing the collection, processing, production, and dissemination among methods and means of collection).

The most critical resource allocation choices concern the subjects and geographic areas against which the community should target its energies. Logically this choice would reflect the changing interests of intelligence consumers, weighted according to national importance. Lower-order choices, such as the design and selection of a new technical collection system, would be made in order to meet consumer demands.

Unfortunately, the system does not work this way. Although expressed with varying degrees of forcefulness, almost every previous study of the management problems of the national intelligence community has agreed that the formal mechanism for establishing priorities to guide the community's allocation of resources (i.e., the so-called requirements process) works poorly, if at all. In his 1968 report to the Director of CIA regarding the actions taken in response to the recommendations of the Cunningham Report, Vice Admiral Rufus Taylor put the problem this way:

> After a year's work on intelligence requirements, we have come to realize that they are not the driving force behind the flow of information. Rather, the real push comes from the collectors themselves—particularly the operations of large, indiscriminating technical collection systems—who use national intelligence requirements to justify what they want to undertake for other reasons, e.g., military readiness, redundancy, technical continuity and the like.

The Schlesinger and Fitzhugh reports concluded that the focus of the community's efforts is determined by the program managers and operators of the highly complex technical collection systems that dominate the community's budget, rather than by the priorities of the intelligence consumers. Schlesinger called the formal requirements "aggregated wish lists" that could be interpreted as meaning "all things to all people," thereby creating a vacuum which left the individual intelligence entities free to pursue their own interests. The Blue Ribbon Panel noted that no effective mechanism existed for consumers, either national or tactical, to communicate their most important needs.[21] Requirements, concluded the Panel, "appear to be generated within the intelligence community itself."

In 1960, before major developments in data collection, a joint study group criticized the requirements process and recommended sweeping changes in the system. Six years later, the Cunningham Report described the principal instrument in the requirements process, the Priority National Intelligence Objectives (PNIOs), as a "lamentably defective document which amounts to a ritual justification of every kind of activity anybody believes to be desirable," wryly adding, "We found no evidence that an intelligence failure could be attributed to a lack of requirements."

Poor communication between the producers of intelligence and the consumers continues to be the greatest obstacle to improved efficiency in the use of the community's resources.

6. Resource Allocation

Without judging the appropriateness of the community's subject or geopolitical emphases, a brief description of the way in which resources have been allocated follows.

In FY 1975, more than half the community's effort, about 54 cents of each dollar, was targeted against military subjects such as doctrine, dispositions, force levels, and capabilities. Twelve times more effort went into collecting and processing information of this kind than toward analyzing it. For technical and scientific subjects, the effort was divided in the ratio of six parts collecting and processing to one part analysis. Only about six cents on the dollar was focused on either political or economic subjects. Resource allocation by subject and function is shown in the table below.

N10

NATIONAL INTELLIGENCE PRIORITIES

DISTRIBUTION OF THE FISCAL YEAR 1975 INTELLIGENCE DOLLAR BY SUBJECT [1]

	Collection	Processing	Production	Total
Subject area:				
Military	41.4	8.3	4.1	53.8
Scientific and technical	11.4	1.8	2.3	15.5
Political	2.5	.3	.6	3.4
Economic	2.2	.3	.7	3.2
General	14.9	8.3	.9	24.1
Total, fiscal year 1975	72.4	19.0	8.6	100.0
Total, fiscal year 1974	71.8	19.5	8.7	100.0
Total, fiscal year 1976 (requested)	72.4	19.1	8.5	100.0

[1] Based on the budgets of the Central Intelligence Agency, the State Department's Bureau of Intelligence and Research, and that portion of the Defense Department's budget included within the Consolidated Defense Intelligence Program (CDIP). This does not include mission support costs.

---

[21] Two separate consumer priority polls, one undertaken by the staff of the DCI, the other by the DIA, were explained to the Committee. In neither instance was there evidence that the study had produced a significant or lasting impact on management practices.

A second important way in which the existing priorities of the national intelligence community are revealed is through the distribution of spending across the geopolitical spectrum. There is little doubt that the most formidable potential threat to the United States is posed by the Soviet Union, with the second most dangerous potential military antagonist being the People's Republic of China. Most analysts would also hold that the nation's foremost commitment overseas is to the defense of its NATO allies. Vital interests in Asia include the security and pro-Western orientation of Japan and the defense of the Republic of Korea, to which the United States has had long-standing treaty commitments. Instability in the Middle East, to a lesser degree South America, and for the moment in Africa, would seem to argue for special attention to these areas as well.

The attributable portion of the FY 1975 intelligence effort was distributed among different target areas as follows: nearly two-thirds of the resources consumed, 65 cents of each dollar, were directed toward the Soviet Union and U.S. commitments to NATO; 25 cents of each dollar were spent to support U.S. interests in Asia, with most of this targeted against China; the Arab-Israeli confrontation in the Middle East claimed seven cents; Latin America, less than two cents; and the rest of the world, about a penny.

7. Management Efficiency versus Security

In addition to the issues of balance in meeting the demands of both national and tactical consumers, and in the distribution of resources among the collection, processing, production, and dissemination functions in the intelligence sequence, there is also an issue of balance in the flow of information. Here the opposing considerations are security and management efficiency. There is a legitimate need to protect both what is known about a potential adversary's capabilities and the way in which the knowledge was acquired.

The Committee's investigation surfaced considerable sentiment that the community's preoccupation with compartmented security may have reached a point where communications are so restricted that effective analysis and dissemination of intelligence is impaired. The Cunningham Report observed: "Some [intelligence] tasks require piecing together many bits of information to arrive at an answer. Compartmentalization hinders cross-discipline cooperation."

Supporters of the community's existing security arrangements counter that few analysts with a proven "need to know" are denied the clearances necessary to gain access to the information they require. Yet the problem is more subtle than this. Merely allowing the diligent analyst to acquire information is not enough. Kept in ignorance of certain subject areas by the compartmentalization system, it is difficult to determine which particular security barriers to storm in search of that last, missing fact that could unlock the puzzle with which the analyst is grappling.

The Cunningham Report also noted a "real need to make comparisons and tradeoffs between intelligence activities and programs to select the most efficient systems," a need which the Committee believes to be unmet today, despite organizational changes. The manager constrained to a narrow view by the blinders of compartmentalization is hardly in the best position to make such tradeoffs.

AGENCIES AND ACTIVITIES OF SPECIAL INTEREST

1. The Defense Intelligence Agency

Formally established in August 1961 by Department of Defense Directive 5105.21, the Defense Intelligence Agency (DIA) was envisioned by its civilian proponents as a means of achieving more centralized management control, thereby leading to a "more efficient allocation of critical intelligence resources and the elimination of duplicating facilities and organizations." [23] The Agency was granted full authority for assembling, integrating, and validating all intelligence requirements originating with the Department of Defense, setting the policy and procedures for collecting data, and developing and producing all finished defense intelligence products.

N11

Currently, the Agency is organized into five directorates, each headed by a Deputy Director. The Directorate for Estimates produces all DOD intelligence estimates, including DOD contributions to National Intelligence Estimates (NIEs) for the National Security Council, as well as forecasts in the areas of foreign force structures, weapon systems, deployments, and doctrine. The Deputy Director for Estimates is also responsible for coordinating with CIA, State, and NSA on intelligence estimates, and assisting these agencies with information on military capabilities and strategies.

Intelligence assessments of special interest to military forces in the field are the responsibility of the Directorate for Production. Other directorates specialize in determining foreign technological progress and the performance of foreign weapon systems (the Directorate for Science and Technology); coordinating service requests for intelligence information (the Collection Directorate); and administering the Defense Attache System (the Directorate for Attaches and Human Resources).

The national leaders who established the DIA were alert to the danger that it might evolve into simply another layer in the intelligence bureaucracy, and cautioned against thinking of it as no more than a confederation of service intelligence activities.[24] Nonetheless, a decade later executive branch reviews criticized DIA for perpetuating the very faults it had been designed to avoid—duplication and layering.[25] By 1970, each service actually had a larger general intelligence arm than it had had before DIA was created. At that time, the Blue Ribbon Defense Panel reported:

> Each [military] departmental staff is still engaged in activities clearly assigned to DIA such as intelligence production including the preparation of current intelligence. The Military Departments justify these activities on the basis that DIA does not have the capability to provide intelligence they need. It is interesting that DIA cannot develop a capability to peform its assigned functions, while the Military

---

[23] Press release accompanying the creation of DIA, cited in the Froehlke Report, 7/69.
[24] Gilpatric memorandum to Joint Chiefs of Staff, 7/1/69.
[25] Fitzhugh Report, Appendix: "National Command and Control Capability and Defense Intelligence," 1970, pp. 33–34; William Beecher, Report of the Defense Panel on Intelligence, 1/75.

Departments, which provide a large proportion of DIA personnel, maintain the required capability and continue to perform the functions.[25a]

In trying to integrate massive and disparate defense intelligence requirements, DIA had become increasingly bogged down in management problems, notwithstanding a number of internal reorganizations in search of the right mechanisms of coordination. At the root of the DIA's difficulties lie the opposing pulls from Washington-level civilian policymakers, who demand broad insights of a largely political character, and military planners and field commanders, who require narrower and more specific factual data. DIA has never really known which of these groups of consumers comes first. As the Fitzhugh Report stated: "The principal problems of the DIA can be summarized as too many jobs and too many masters."

In retrospect, a strong case can be made that the DIA has never really had a chance. Strongly resisted by the military services, the Agency has been a creature of compromise from the outset. For example, the Director of the DIA was placed in a position of subordination to the Joint Chiefs of Staff (JCS) by designating him to serve as the JCS director for intelligence (replacing the J–2 on the Joint Staff). Drawing again from the Fitzhugh Report, this arrangement put the Director of DIA in the "impossible position" of providing staff assistance on intelligence matters to both the Secretary of Defense and the JCS, whose respective stances on a given issue "often are diverse."

DIA was also reliant on the military for much of its manpower which was initially drawn almost entirely from the intelligence arms of the various services. The argument for manning the new DIA with these personnel was to minimize the disruptive effects of organizational change on the flow of intelligence information. This same case was made for starting the DIA slowly. As a consequence, the Agency never had the impetus which many other newborn government entities have enjoyed and profited from. Dominated and staffed in large part by the professional military, it is not surprising that DIA has come to concentrate on the tactical intelligence demands of the services and their field commands.

Since DIA has always been heavily staffed with professional military officers on short tours, who are dependent on their parent services for future assignments and promotions, the perspective of Agency analyses has often been biased to reflect the views of the services. When evidence is doubtful, the services have incentives to tilt an intelligence appraisal in a direction to support their own budgetary requests to justify existing operations and proposed new ones.[28] Intelligence issues in the Vietnam war reflected this problem.

On the budget side of the problem, the Agency has been limited in its ability to control the activities of the services by the lack of follow-

[25a] Fitzhugh Report, pp. 23, 31–32.
[28] Harry Howe Ransom, *The Intelligence Establishment* (Cambridge, Mass., Harvard University Press, 1971), p. 103; Department of Defense, *The Senator Gravel Edition: The Pentagon Papers*, Vol. IV (Boston: Beacon Press, 1971); Patrick J. McGarvey, *CIA: The Myth and the Madness*, pp. 149, 134; *Pentagon Papers, passim*; Chester Cooper, "The C.I.A. and Decision Making," *Foreign Affairs*, January 1972.

up authority over intelligence activities: "Once money to support the approved program is allocated to the services, they may or may not use it for its intended purposes." [29] In an effort to remedy this, program management responsibilities over service components of the General Defense Intelligence Program (GDIP) were recently transferred from the Director of DIA to the ASD/I.

The services' concern with autonomy and preservation of wartime capabilities may make the achievement of any appreciable reduction in duplicative effort an impossible goal, at least for general intelligence activities. The problem is not simply one of bureaucratic pettiness; there exist unavoidable trade-offs between tactical and national intelligence interests. The issue of which set of needs should dominate Defense intelligence is a difficult one, with past disagreements on this point having played a major part in the dissatisfaction with DIA that has been expressed by the services, policymakers, and OSD staff.

The jurisdictional dilemma was recognized by Schlesinger in his 1971 report: "If the services retain control over the assets for 'tactical' intelligence, they can probably weaken efforts to improve the efficiency of the community. At the same time there is little question about their need to have access to the output of specified assets in both peace and war." He cited service resistance to the National Security Act of 1947, and to the 1961 DOD Directive establishing the DIA, concluding: "Powerful interests in the military opposed, and continue to oppose, more centralized management of intelligence activities."

A second factor contributing to the dissatisfaction frequently expressed by DIA's customers has been the quality of the Agency's analysis. Most often, this is perceived as a problem of professional competence.

Illustrating the deficiencies in intelligence production as viewed by policymakers, Beecher has quoted former Secretary of Defense Schlesinger: "when you have good analysis, it's more valuable than the facts on a ratio of ten to one. But all decisionmakers get are factual 'snipets.' " Such tidbits, while often interesting in content, are of limited worth if not woven into context. The "analyst" who serves as no more than a conduit for transmitting facts is not providing analysis. Yet, the job of the national intelligence analyst is to sort facts, discarding those which do not appear relevant, and piecing together what remains in a way that yields the broad insights policymakers find most useful.

Besides a thorough understanding of his subject, the competent analyst must possess the qualities of perception, initiative, and imagination. Equally important, the analyst must be kept highly motivated and must be permitted, on occasion, to be wrong. (This is the basis of the argument for maintaining more than one source of key intelligence estimates.)

Critics have often commented harshly on the quality of both civilian and military personnel in DIA.[30] There are two facets to the problem of obtaining first-rate analysts: On the military side, capable and ambitious officers have traditionally avoided intelligence assignments,

---

[29] Fitzhugh Report, p. 23.

[30] e.g., *Ibid.*, p. 29; "Defense Panel on Intelligence," p. 6; McGarvey, *CIA: The Myth and the Madness, passim.*

deeming such positions not conducive to career advancement. Of the officers who have gone into intelligence, many of the best qualified have tended to serve with their individual service agency rather than joining DIA. DIA's leadership maintains, however, that gains have been made in correcting service biases in the intelligence career field. Since 1974, promotion prospects for officers in the service intelligence agencies have become equal to or better than the service-wide averages. This offers scant consolation for DIA, however, since the promotion rates for attachés and Navy and Air Force officers serving with the Agency have not improved proportionately, and remain less favorable than the service averages. There are, in fact, some indications that promotion prospects for officers at DIA may be deteriorating.[31]

On the civilian side of the personnel problem (about 55 percent of the DIA's 2,700 professional-level employees are civilian), it is frequently argued that a predominance of military officers in middle-management positions limits advancement opportunities within the Agency for civilian professionals. In addition, a significant portion of those "civilian" personnel who have reached management ranks are in fact retired military officers.

Many experts who have studied the DIA's personnel problems have concluded that improvement in the competence of the Agency's civilian analysts is contingent upon a relaxation of the constraints imposed by Civil Service regulations. The 1975 Report of the Defense Panel on Intelligence commissioned by Deputy Secretary of Defense Clements, asserted: "The professionalism of the intelligence production process must be improved substantially," and it strongly recommended exempting DIA's analysts from the Civil Service.

Whether exempting civilian professionals from the Civil Service and increasing their management presence would bring about the changes required to transform the DIA into an effective competitor to the CIA in producing national intelligence estimates remains questionable. The DIA has a problem of image. It is a problem that calls for fundamental reform of its management attitudes and orientation, as well as in its professional staffing. In the absence of the complementary reforms,[32] it would seem doubtful that the provision of greater incentives for its civilian analysts, and greater management latitude for the hiring and firing of these analysts by removing Civil Service constraints would in itself suffice to bring about the needed degree of improvement in performance.

Moreover, data on the civilian grade structure of DIA, compared to that of the CIA, suggest that far too much emphasis may be placed on the need to raise the salaries of DIA's civilian analysts. Conventional wisdom holds that the CIA has outperformed the DIA because its superior grade structure permits it to attract and retain more capable analysts. In fact, however, there is no significant difference in the professional grade structure (defined here as GS-9, or equivalent, and above) of the two agencies.

---

[31] Memorandum from Vice Admiral DePoix to Secretary of Defense Schlesinger, 3/4/74. Memorandum from Lt. Gen. Graham to Schlesinger, 11/19/74.

[32] Such as a new headquarters facility—a request that has been repeatedly denied by the Congress, but is an essential first step if a revitalized DIA within the existing organizational structure is decided upon as the preferred course of action.

About one-third of the upper management positions at DIA are filled by military general officers, a much larger proportion than at the CIA, where fewer military personnel serve.

Criticism of the professional standards of DIA's personnel has not been restricted to the Agency's managers and production analysts. The Defense attachés, who serve under the Agency's direction as the Defense Department's human intelligence (HUMINT) collection arm, have also been a topic of considerable concern. One 1970 study of the Defense Attaché System warned that the representational and protocol responsibilities of attachés were assuming precedence over intelligence functions which should constitute the principal purpose of the attachés.[33] This preoccupation with nonintelligence activities remains strong today.

The qualifications of the officers assigned to attaché duty have been questioned. The chances for promotion have usually been low in DAS and the tendency has been to draw a high proportion of attachés from among officers on their last tours before retirement. Former DIA Director Donald Bennett dismissed 38 attachés outright for incompetence when he took over the Agency in 1969.[34]

N12

The arguments cited above suggest two basic alternatives for the Defense general intelligence apparatus: either retain the current centralized arrangement under the Defense Intelligence Agency, giving its Director the authority he needs to fulfill his original mandate to manage all of DOD's intelligence collection and production activities, or disband the Agency, returning its resources to the military services from which they were originally requisitioned, leaving the coordination of the tactical military aspects of these activities to the JCS, and forming a staff close to the Secretary of Defense to produce the national intelligence estimates he requires.[35]

There should either be a major role for DIA, or for the service agencies, but not for both, unless they genuinely serve different functions. Duplication of intelligence analyses can be valuable if it promotes diversity and motivates through competition. This assumes that the separate analysts have different perspectives on the issues. In this sense, competition between CIA analysts and Defense Department analysts for strategic estimates, is very useful. By arguing different points of view in forums in the intelligence community they force disagreements to the surface and expose evaluations to closer scrutiny. DIA now has had little incentive to serve as a CIA-type foil to the services, since DIA has been primarily a military organization.

Specific measures which might improve the performance of DIA within the existing organizational structure include the following:

a. *Enhance professional competence.*—Exempt DIA from Civil Service regulations in the same manner as CIA and NSA. Open more top-level jobs within DIA to civilian staffers. Increase incentives for the military services to send better qualified officers to DIA. Waive seniority requirements for Defense Attachés. Rotate DIA and CIA strategic analysts through each agency on temporary tours.

---

[33] Report of the DIA Defense Attaché System Review Committee, 5/30/70, pp. II–1, II–2.

[34] Staff summary of Lt. Gen. Donald V. Bennett, USA (ret.) interview. 7/23/75.

[35] A nucleus for which already exists in the Office of Net Threat Assessment.

b. Increase the responsiveness of the Agency to the Secretary of Defense and his staff.—Give ASD/I (or the new Deputy Secretary) authority to deal with the substance of intelligence programs as well as the allocation of resources. Have the Director of DIA report directly to the Secretary of Defense, rather than through the JCS, as under the present arrangement. Appoint a civilian as either the Director or Deputy Director and make the Director subject to Senate confirmation.

c. Increase DIA's management authority to match its management responsibility.—Allow DIA to establish more requirements for the service intelligence agencies, and to eliminate intelligence products of the military services which are unnecessarily duplicative.

d. Increase lateral communication between DIA and other components of the defense intelligence apparatus.—To integrate better the work of the operators, analysts, and planners, encourage communication among DIA regional analysts and desk men in CIA, ISA, and other policy staff offices in DOD and State.

2. The National Security Agency

The National Security Agency/Central Security Service (NSA/CSS) provides centralized coordination, direction, and control of the Government's Signals Intelligence (SIGINT) and Communications Security (COMSEC) activities.

The SIGINT or foreign intelligence mission of NSA/CSS involves the interception, processing, analysis, and dissemination of information derived from foreign electrical communications and other signals. SIGINT itself is composed of three elements: Communications Intelligence (COMINT), Electronics Intelligence (ELINT), and Telemetry Intelligence (TELINT). COMINT is intelligence information derived from the interception and analysis of foreign communications. ELINT is technical and intelligence information derived from electromagnetic radiations, such as radars. TELINT is technical and intelligence information derived from the interception, processing, and analysis of foreign telemetry. Most SIGINT is collected by personnel of the Service Cryptologic Agencies located around the world. The Director, NSA/Chief, CSS has authority for SIGINT missions.

The COMSEC mission protects United States telecommunications and certain other communications from exploitation by foreign intelligence services and from unauthorized disclosure. COMSEC systems are provided by NSA to 18 Government departments and agencies, including Defense, State, CIA, and FBI. The predominant user, however, is the Department of Defense. COMSEC is a mission separate from SIGINT, yet the dual SIGINT and COMSEC missions of NSA/CSS do have a symbiotic relationship, and enhance the performance of the other.

A specific National Security Council Intelligence Directive (NSCID) defines NSA's functions. It is augmented by Director of Central Intelligence Directives (DCIDs) and internal Department of Defense and NSA regulations.

NSA responds to requests by other members of the intelligence community, such as CIA, DIA, and FBI, to provide "signals" intelligence on topics of interest. An annual list of SIGINT requirements is given to NSA and is intended to provide the NSA Director and the Secretary of Defense with guidance for the coming year's activities. These requirements are usually stated in terms of general areas of intelligence interest, but are supplemented by "amplifying requirements," which are time-sensitive and are expressed directly to NSA by the requesting agency. NSA exercises discretion in responding to these requirements; it also accepts requests from the executive branch agencies. NSA does not generate its own requirements.

All requirements levied on NSA must be for foreign intelligence. Yet, the precise definition of foreign intelligence is unclear. NSA limits its collection of intelligence to foreign communications and confines its activities to communications links having at least one foreign terminal. Nevertheless, this is based upon an internal regulation and is not supported by law or executive branch directive.

Although NSA limits itself to collecting communications with at least one foreign terminal, it may still pick up communications between two Americans when international communications are involved. Whenever NSA chooses particular circuits or "links" known to carry foreign communications necessary for the production of foreign intelligence, it collects all transmissions that go over those circuits. Given current technology, the only way for NSA to prevent the processing of communications of U.S. citizens would be to control the selection, analysis, or dissemination phases of the process.

Communications intelligence has been an integral element of United States intelligence activities. Foreign communications have been intercepted, analyzed, and decoded by the United States since the Revolutionary War. During the 1930s, elements of the Army and Navy collected and processed foreign intelligence from radio transmissions. Much of their work involved decryption, as well as enciphering United States transmissions. Throughout World War II, their work contributed greatly to the national war effort.

Since President Truman authorized NSA's establishment in 1952 to coordinate United States cryptologic and communications activities, tremendous advances have been made in the technology of communications intelligence. These advances have contributed to an expansion in demands for a wider variety of foreign intelligence and of requirements placed upon NSA/CSS SIGINT personnel and resources. As new priorities arise in the requirements process, greater demands will be placed upon NSA.

It is also necessary to face the problem of integrating intelligence requirements for foreign policy and national security with Constitutional constraints and safeguarding of domestic civil liberties. NSA's intercept programs and possible violation of Fourth Amendment rights are discussed in the section, "National Security Agency Surveillance Affecting Americans," in the Committee's Domestic Intelligence Report.

N13

MILITARY COUNTERINTELLIGENCE AND INVESTIGATIVE ACTIVITIES

1. Background

The Department of Defense defines "military counterintelligence and investigative activity" as all investigative activity apart from foreign intelligence-gathering. Although this nomenclature is relatively recent, the military services have always conducted investigations. None of these investigative activities are expressly authorized by statute; rather, they have been justified as necessary to the military mission. On occasion, investigative activity by the military has exceeded measures necessary to protect or support military operations.

In 1917, for example, Colonel Ralph Van Deman of the Army intelligence bureau recruited civilians in the Army Reserve and used volunteer investigators to report on "unpatriotic" conduct. Van Deman's men were soon dispersed throughout the country, infiltrating such organizations as the Industrial Workers of the World, mingling with enemy aliens in major cities, and reporting on all types of dissenters and radicals. Much of this civilian surveillance continued after World War I, particularly in the area of labor unrest. In the 1920s the Army had "War Plans White" to deal with anticipated uprisings of labor and radicals. In 1932 the Chief of Army Intelligence collected information on the "bonus marchers" arriving in Washington, D.C.

Similarly the activities of the Office of Naval Intelligence (ONI) have not always been restricted to military affairs. Traditionally, ONI has provided security for naval contractors, guarded ships, searched crews, detected illegal radio stations, and investigated naval personnel, enemy sympathizers, and civilians whose activities were "inimicable to the interests of the Navy."

Then, in the late 1960s during a period of considerable civil unrest in the United States, the three services—particularly the Army—were called upon to provide extensive information on the political activities of private individuals and organizations throughout the country.[36]

2. Areas of Investigation

DOD's counterintelligence and investigative activities are conducted for many purposes, both within the United States and abroad.[37]

a. *Violations of the Uniform Code of Military Justice.*—The UCMJ is a code of criminal laws which applies to all military personnel of the Department of Defense. The Secretary of each military department is responsible for enforcement of its provisions within his department. Investigations of UCMJ violations take place within the United States and in foreign locations where military personnel are stationed.

b. *Security Clearances.*—The Department of Defense conducts background investigations to determine whether to award security clearances to its military and civilian personnel or to the personnel of civilian contractors. These investigations are done both in the U.S. and abroad.

---

[36] For a detailed description of this and other improper military investigative activities, see the Select Committee's report entitled "Improper Surveillance of Private Citizens by the Military."

[37] Examples include investigations of security leaks, investigations in support of the Secret Service, investigations of theft at the facilities of Government contractors, and investigations—once military forces have been called in—to suppress domestic violence. None of these activities, however, *currently* represents a significant expenditure of investigative effort.

Military intelligence units also have certain counterintelligence functions to perform which relate to a unit's combat responsibilities.

c. *Counterespionage.*[38]—Under an agreement with the Federal Bureau of Investigation,[39] each of the military departments conducts counterespionage investigations on military and civilian members of their respective military departments, although all such operations are controlled by the FBI. In overseas jurisdictions where military commanders have control over occupying forces, the military departments are given more latitude to conduct counterespionage investigations, but these are coordinated with the Central Intelligence Agency.

Counterespionage investigations may be offensive or defensive in nature. Offensive investigations seek to obtain information on the purposes or activities of a hostile intelligence service. Defensive counterespionage investigations involve the identification of military personnel who are working for agents of a hostile intelligence service. Counterespionage operations are undertaken in both domestic and foreign settings.

d. *Threats to DOD Personnel, Property, and Operations.*—This type of investigation is distinguished from a counterespionage investigation because no hostile intelligence agency is involved. Rather, the "threat" typically arises from civilian groups and individuals whose activities might subvert, disrupt, or endanger the personnel, property, or operations of DOD. While "threat" information is normally obtained from local law enforcement authorities, the military has traditionally reserved the right to conduct its own investigations of such matters both in the U.S. and abroad.

In summary, one should remember that "military counterintelligence and investigative activity" is not a static category. It includes investigations undertaken for any reason apart from foreign intelligence collection. These range from investigations of lost property to investigations of fraud at servicemen's clubs. Moreover, the four general categories cited above expand and contract to meet changing military needs and demands from the Executive.

3. Supervisory Structure

The Secretary of Defense is ultimately responsible for all counterintelligence and investigative activity conducted by the Department of Defense. However, the Secretary has delegated management responsibility for this activity to the Assistant Secretary of Defense (Comptroller).[40] He, in turn, has delegated this responsibility to the Deputy Assistant Secretary of Defense (Comptroller), who was assigned responsibility for the Defense Investigative Program Office (DIPO).

DIPO apportions counterintelligence and investigative resources within the Department of Defense. The Office has budgetary control of funds allocated for these activities, and provides policy guidance. However, although DIPO stays informed of activities of the investigative agencies, it does not exercise formal operational control over them. In fact, no element at the OSD level exerts centralized opera-

---

[38] The counterespionage investigations of the Department of Defense are described in detail in a classified staff report of the Committee.

[39] The Delimitations Agreement of 1949. Each of the military departments has promulgated the agreement as a departmental regulation.

[40] DOD Directive 5118.3.

tional control over counterintelligence and investigative activities.[41] The one Defense Department agency engaged in such activity, the Defense Investigative Service (DIS), and the three military departments largely retain independent operational control of their own activities.

4. The Defense Investigative Service

DIS is the only Defense agency established specifically to carry out counterintelligence and investigative activities.[42] Created in 1972, its chief function is performance of all security clearance investigations for civilian and military members of the Department of Defense as well as for all employees of Defense contractors. DIS also has been assigned responsibility for conducting "such other investigations as the Secretary of Defense may direct," thus making it a special investigative arm of the Secretary.[43]

DIS performs the special function of operating a computer index known as the Defense Central Index of Investigations (DCH). This is a computerized index which contains not only references to previous security clearance investigations, but also references to virtually every DOD investigation conducted in the past.[44] According to recent congressional testimony, the DCII now contains references to DOD files on approximately 15 million Americans.[45] DIS does not maintain the files, but indicates to requesters which DOD counterintelligence and investigative agency holds the file.

DIS has 280 offices across the United States, staffed by 2,620 military and civilian employees. DIS does not have personnel located overseas, but is responsible for security clearance investigations that may require tracking down leads overseas. Normally, an overseas element of one of the services would support DIS in such cases.

5. The Military Departments

In the Navy and Air Force, all counterintelligence and investigative activity, in both domestic and foreign contexts, is centralized in one element. In the Army, such activity is dispersed.

a. Navy.—All foreign and domestic counterintelligence and other investigative activity in the Navy is carried out by the Naval Investigative Service (NIS). The Director of NIS reports to the Director of Naval Intelligence, who has responsibility for foreign intelligence gathering by the Navy. He, in turn, reports to the Chief of Naval Operations. In 1975, 169 military and 744 civilian personnel [46] were assigned to NIS.

---

[41] The Defense Intelligence Agency made an unsuccessful effort to gain control of these activities in the late 1960s.

[42] The National Security Agency and Defense Intelligence Agency also have small elements with counterintelligence and investigative functions. These elements exist solely to protect the activities of the agencies of which they are a part.

[43] DOD Directive 5105.42.

[44] The DCII is routinely purged of references to files which have been destroyed because of their age, files on deceased subjects, or files which DOD directives have stipulated may not be retained.

[45] Testimony of David O. Cooke, Deputy Assistant Secretary of Defense (Comptroller), House Subcommittee on Government Operations, 1975 (unpublished).

[46] NIS agents are all civilian employees.

b. Air Force.—All Air Force investigative activity is carried out by the Air Force Office of Special Investigations (AFOSI). In contrast to NIS, the Director of AFOSI reports to the Air Force Inspector General. In 1975, AFOSI had 1,537 military and 384 civilian personnel assigned to it.

c. Army.—In the Army, criminal investigations are separated from other types of counterintelligence and investigative activity. They are carried out worldwide by the United States Army Criminal Investigation Command, the Director of which reports directly to the Army Chief of Staff.

Remaining counterintelligence and investigative activities are apportioned between the United States Army Intelligence Agency (USAINTA) and the military intelligence units located overseas. USAINTA has responsibility for all activities within the United States and in overseas locations where military intelligence units are not located. Where military intelligence units are part of Army forces stationed overseas (e.g., West Germany and Korea), they ordinarily carry out counterintelligence and investigative activity in their respective locations. Where an investigation proves to be beyond their capacity, USAINTA elements may be called upon.

Both the commanding office of USAINTA and the commanders of military intelligence groups overseas report to the Army Assistant Chief of Staff for Intelligence, who is responsible for the foreign intelligence-gathering activities of the Army. In 1975, the Army had assigned 2,822 military and 1,346 civilian personnel to counterintelligence and other investigative activities.

6. Results of Select Committee Inquiry

The Select Committee carried out an extensive investigation of the counterintelligence and investigative activities of DOD insofar as they have resulted in illegal and unwarranted intrusions into the political affairs of civilians. The results of the investigation are published in detail in the Committee Report entitled "Improper Surveillance of Private Citizens by the Military."

The Committee found that while certain of DOD's past counterintelligence and investigative functions resulted in the collection of information on the political activities of private citizens, DOD has effectively brought its counterintelligence and investigative activities under control since 1971. The Committee found that DOD currently maintains little information on unaffiliated individuals; that which it does maintain arguably falls within the terms of the Department's internal restrictions. Similarly, the Committee found that operations against civilians had been authorized in accordance with departmental directives.

Despite the success of the Department's internal directives to limit intrusions into the civilian community, the Committee nevertheless finds them inadequate protection for the future and recommends that more stringent legislative controls be enacted.

CHEMICAL AND BIOLOGICAL ACTIVITIES

The terrible wounds inflicted by chemical weapons, such as chlorine and mustard gas, in World War I spawned international attempts to ban their use in warfare. The 1925 Geneva Convention succeeded only in banning first use in war of chemical and biological weapons. The United States signed this Convention but Congress failed to ratify it; thus, the United States was not bound by its prohibitions. Nevertheless, there was a widespread belief that the United States would comply with the Convention.

Since the ban applied only to a country's first use of these agents, both the Allied and the Axis powers in World War II researched and stockpiled chemical and biological weapons in order to retaliate against first use by an enemy. Ironically, as the first President publicly to commit the United States to the policy of the Geneva Convention, President Roosevelt announced in June 1943, with the intent of warning Japan against the use of such weapons: "I state categorically that we shall under no circumstances resort to the use of such weapons [poisons or noxious gases] unless they are first used by our enemies." As he spoke, however, he knew the United States had intensified its biological research effort three months earlier with the construction of a facility for drug research at Fort Detrick, Maryland.

The threat of retaliation against a country using such weapons was effective. Although Germany was thought to have a stockpile, it did not touch it, even in the last desperate months of World War II. After the War, the United States program of research and development on such agents continued in order to maintain a weapons capability sufficient to deter first use by hostile powers. The Army's facility at Fort Detrick remained the center of biological weapons research and development.

1. Chemical and Biological Activities

Against this background, the Central Intelligence Agency entered into a special agreement with the Army on a project which the CIA codenamed MKNAOMI. The original purpose of MKNAOMI is difficult to determine. Few written records were prepared during its 18-year existence; most of the documents relating to it have been destroyed; and persons with knowledge of its early years have either died or have been unable to recall much about their association with the project. However, it is fair to conclude from the types of weapons developed for the CIA, and from the extreme security associated with MKNAOMI, that the possibility of first use of biological weapons by the CIA was contemplated.

N14

The Army agreed that the Special Operations Division (SOD) at Fort Detrick would assist the CIA in developing, testing, and maintaining biological agents and delivery systems. By this agreement, CIA acquired the knowledge, skill, and facilities of the Army to develop biological weapons suited for CIA use. In 1967, the CIA summarized MKNAOMI objectives:

a. To provide for a covert support base to meet clandestine operational requirements.

b. To stockpile severely incapacitating and lethal materials for the specific use of TSD [Technical Services Division].

c. To maintain in operational readiness special and unique items for the dissemination of biological and chemical materials.

 d. To provide for the required surveillance, testing, up-grading, and evaluation of materials and items in order to assure absence of defects and complete predictability of results to be expected under operational conditions.[47]

In reviewing the records and testimony of SOD personnel, it is easy, for the most part, to distinguish SOD's work for the Army from its work for the CIA, even though very few SOD scientists knew of the CIA connection. For example, the CIA personnel who worked with SOD were identified as military officers from the fictitious S'aff Support Group, whose interest in SOD was markedly different from the Army's. The CIA was careful to ensure that its moneys were transferred to SOD to cover the cost of CIA projects and the few existing SOD records indicate which projects were to be charged against the funds received from "P–600," the accounting designation for CIA funds.

SOD's work for the Army from 1952 until the early 1960s was primarily to assess the vulnerability of sensitive installations, such as the Pentagon, air bases, and subway systems, to biological sabotage by an enemy. In order to conduct these tests, SOD personnel would develop small, easily disguised devices—such as spray cannisters and spray pens—containing harmless biological agents. SOD personnel would surreptitiously gain access to the installation, leaving the devices to release the biological agent. SOD personnel would then monitor its spread throughout the installation. In this way, SOD could determine how vulnerable the installation was to sabotage of this kind and could advise those charged with security of the installation on counter-measures.

Although the CIA was interested in the kinds of delivery devices which SOD could make for delivery of the biological agents, CIA projects were distinct because they involved the mating of delivery systems to lethal or incapacitating biological agents, instead of harm-less agents used in vulnerability tests. The CIA would ask SOD to produce a delivery system and a compatible biological agent—a request not made by the Army until the early 1960s.

SOD developed pills containing several different biological agents which could remain potent for weeks or months, and dart guns and darts coated with biological agents. SOD also developed a special gun for firing darts coated with a chemical that could incapacitate a guard dog in order to allow CIA agents to knock out the guard dog silently, enter an installation, and return the dog to consciousness when leaving. SOD scientists were unable to develop a similar incapacitant for humans.

SOD on occasion physically transferred biological agents in "bulk" form, various delivery devices, and most importantly, delivery devices containing biological agents, to CIA personnel. Although none of the witnesses before the Select Committee could recall any transfer of such materials for actual use by the CIA, evidence available to the Committee indicates that the CIA attempted to use the material. It is fair to conclude that biological agents and delivery devices prepared at Fort Detrick and transferred to the Staff Support Group were carried

---

[47] Memorandum from Chief, TSD/Biological Branch to Chief, TSD, "MKNAOMI: Funding, Objectives, and Accomplishments," 10/18/67, p. 1.

by CIA agents in attempted assassinations of foreign leaders. However, the Committee found no evidence that such material was ever in fact used against a person by the CIA.

By the early 1960s, the Army also became interested in the type of work SOD was doing for the CIA. The Army apparently decided that this type of surreptitious delivery device might be useful to Special Forces units in guerrilla warfare. SOD developed special bullets containing poison darts which could be fired, with little noise, from standard military weapons and small portable devices capable of spraying biological agents into the air which would form lethal clouds. Ultimately, the Army stockpiled a quantity of these bullets, but never transferred them to field units.

SOD developed another capability according to existing records which, so far as the Committee could determine, was never tapped by Army or by the CIA. Whereas most SOD work was devoted to biological weapons which would kill one individual noiselessly and with almost no trace of which would kill or incapacitate a small group. SOD did research the possibilities of large-scale covert use of biological weapons. SOD scientists prepared memoranda, which were passed to the CIA, detailing what diseases were common in what areas of the world so that covert use of biological weapons containing these diseases could easily go undetected. SOD researched special delivery devices for these biological agents, but it never mated such delivery devices with biological agents.

In addition to CIA interest in biological weapons for use against humans, it also asked SOD to study use of biological agents against crops and animals. In its 1967 memorandum, the CIA stated:

> Three methods and systems for carrying out a covert attack against crops and causing severe crop loss have been developed and evaluated under field conditions. This was accomplished in anticipation of a requirement which was later developed but was subsequently scrubbed just prior to putting into action.

2. Termination

All the biological work ended in 1969. Shortly after taking office, President Nixon ordered the staff of the National Security Council to review the chemical and biological weapons program of the United States. On November 25, 1969, he stated that the United States renounced the use of any form of biological weapons that kill or incapacitate. He further ordered the disposal of existing stocks of bacteriological weapons.

On February 14, 1970, the President clarified the extent of his earlier order and indicated that toxins—chemicals that are not living organisms but are produced by living organisms—were considered biological weapons subject to his previous directive. The Defense Department duly carried out the Presidential directive according to the instructions and supervision of the National Security Council staff. However, a CIA scientist acquired from SOD personnel at Fort Detrick approximately 11 grams of shellfish toxin, a quantity which was approximately one-third of the total world production and which was sufficient to prepare tens of thousands of darts. This toxin, a known danger if inhaled, swallowed, or injected, was then stored in a little-used laboratory at the CIA where its presence went undetected for five years.

The transfer from SOD to the CIA resulted in a major quantity of the toxin being retained by an agency in a manner which clearly violated the President's order. The evidence to the Committee established that the decision to transfer and to retain the shellfish toxin was not made by, or known to, high-level officials of either the Defense Department or the CIA. The Director of the CIA was told of the possibility of retaining the toxin, but he rejected that course of action. The Committee found that the decision to keep the toxin, in direct and unmistakable contradiction of a widely announced Presidential decision, was made by a few individuals in the CIA and SOD.

Nevertheless, the history of MKNAOMI and the atmosphere surrounding it undoubtedly contributed to the mistaken belief of these individuals that they were not directly affected by the President's decision. The MKNAOMI project itself was contrary to United States policy since 1925 and to Presidential announcement since 1943, for it contemplated a first use of biological weapons by the CIA—albeit in the context of small covert operations. Moreover, because of the sensitive nature of MKNAOMI, these scientists gave their superiors little written record of their work and received little or no written guidance. The National Security Council staff, charged by the President with determining what U.S. policy should be, did not discover MKNAOMI in the course of its study and did not, therefore, consider the possibility that the CIA had biological weapons or biological agents. The CIA employee who claims to have made the decision, on his own, to retain the toxin received no written instructions to destroy them. Kept outside the National Security Council's study, the employee had to rely only on the newspaper account of the President's announcement and on his own interpretation of it.

MEETING FUTURE NEEDS IN DEFENSE INTELLIGENCE

The defense intelligence establishment poses two fundamental problems for future national policy. The first is how to improve the quality of intelligence and ensure that intelligence collection and production are responsive to the needs of both the executive and legislative branches; the second is how Congress can exercise responsible oversight of the intelligence agencies. These goals require not only executive-legislative cooperation in control of the intelligence establishment, but also the design of a managerial and consultative system which is conducive to efficiency in routine activities, and adaptive to new priorities.

1. Anticipating New Requirements

It is a truism that generals should not plan for the next war by preparing for the last one; so too the intelligence community should not simply prepare to predict the last crisis. Ideally, allocation of intelligence resources should *precede* crises, not follow them. For example, concentration of a larger proportion of intelligence assets on economic issues should have begun before the 1973 oil embargo and energy crisis, not subsequently. In order to anticipate threats, which is the essential function of peacetime defense intelligence, the agencies must strengthen their ability to anticipate the proper targets for collection and analysis.

The fundamental task of military intelligence will always be to detect the numbers, characteristics, and locations of enemy weapons, personnel, communications, and intelligence systems. As the world changes, however, the identities of enemies and the relative importance of different security threats change. The allocation of intelligence resources which was appropriate in a bipolar world, where the most likely threats were strategic nuclear war or large-scale conventional military engagements in the third world, is less appropriate in a world where power is becoming more diffused. For example, although the energy crisis (which is increasing the spread of nuclear power reactors and eroding the technical and economic barriers to acquiring nuclear weapons) and the growth of regional power rivalries (which increases incentives to acquire such weapons) are combining to make nuclear proliferation an imminent threat, the Air Force unit responsible for nuclear intelligence still directs virtually all of its assigned technical collection resources against the USSR and China.[48]

In the short range, it is obvious that problems such as nuclear proliferation and international terrorism will be given increasingly high priorities in national intelligence. Since DOD has the vast majority of collection assets, it should be increasingly involved in these problem areas. In doing so, a new balance may have to be struck between the national/peacetime intelligence priorities of the Department of Defense and the intelligence community as a whole, and the tactical/wartime requirements of the military. The critical problem for improving intelligence in the long-range, however, is to identify the mechanisms which are conducive to adaptation, re-evaluation of priorities, and flexible distribution of collection and analysis assets. Feedback from consumers of national intelligence—such policy and research agencies as ISA, DDR&E, State, NSC, ERDA, and ACDA—should be regularized, and DOD should also be responsive to the community-wide committees (such as IRAC, NSCIC, USIB, or IC Staff) which consider the interface between issue urgency and collection capabilities.

2. Effects of New Technology

Technological change produces both new capabilities and new barriers in intelligence collection. Unless the U.S. loses its wide lead in capacity for technological innovation, however, scientific advances are likely to be a net benefit.[48a]

In the near future, expanded computer capabilities can be expected to improve the integration and availability of processed information by use of a central bank with data, pictures, and reports digitized for quick retrievability according to title or substance. This would offer the efficiency and thoroughness of a full text search, but it also raises the issue of the proper extent of compartmentation.

Improved technology also offers hedges against vulnerability and political sensitivity. Development of unmanned mobile sensors for dangerous peripheral reconnaissance missions can eliminate most of the risks in current collection programs, or the potential for crises

---

[48] Air Force briefing for Select Committee staff, July 1975.
[48a] See the Committee's detailed report on Intelligence and Technology.

and embarrassments which followed the North Korean seizure of the *Pueblo* and downing of the EC–121. Both a reduction in risk and an increase in cost-effectiveness could be possible if improved technology results in substantial manpower reductions.

Technology is interactive. Availability of new techniques for monitoring or verification may provoke enemy countermeasures, and enemy development of new weapons systems can produce the need for new techniques of verification. (Heavy deployment of cruise missiles or development of mobile land-based ICBMs by either the U.S. or U.S.S.R., given current detection capabilities, would create virtually insoluble problems of verification of strategic arms limitation agreements. Development by either side of certain technical innovations, on the other hand, could be undesirable. A breakthrough in ability to detect and fix the location of submarines, for example, would destabilize mutual nuclear deterrence by increasing the vulnerability of the other side's second-strike capability.) The complex dynamics of these interactions require substantial attention to coordinating R&D for intelligence with policy considerations. The expense which goes with technical sophistication also suggests the need for rigorous cost-benefit analysis in intelligence R&D, to judge the relative utility of new capabilities.

3. Restructuring Defense Intelligence Organizations

The pattern of DOD intelligence organization is obviously important for the division of authority and responsibility within the departments, but it also has ramifications for the control and direction of the intelligence community as a whole. Internally, there are divergent interests and needs, particularly between the civilian leadership in OSD and the military leadership in the JCS and unified commands. Externally, there is an imbalance between the responsibility of the DCI to direct the collection and production of national intelligence, and the predominance of DOD in control of actual assets.

Within the defense establishment there has traditionally been a trade-off in the view of many observers, between the peacetime needs of the Secretary of Defense for "national" intelligence on general politico-military developments and trends, and the wartime needs of the professional military for "tactical" intelligence on enemy forces and operations. This distinction may be eroding since central national sensors can have important tactical applications.

Nevertheless, the Secretary of Defense and JCS have different responsibilities, and thus different intelligence priorities. Dissatisfaction with fragmentation and duplication of service intelligence support to the Secretary led to the formation of the Defense Intelligence Agency 15 years ago. The DIA was supposed to integrate military intelligence activities, and to serve the needs of both OSD and the services. There has been widespread criticism of DIA's performance since it was created.

The new Deputy Secretary of Defense position is designed to assert greater control of DOD intelligence from the OSD level. If OSD staff resources for intelligence are increased, and DIA's role is decreased, the trade-off between service needs and the needs of national leadership may be recognized, accepted, and dealt with, in contrast to the earlier attempt to "cure" the problem by combining managerial functions in DIA. There has been a similar potential problem in NSA, although it has provoked far less concern than DIA since NSA must also serve national and tactical needs. In 1961 the JCS attempted to gain control of that agency,[49] and in recent years some critics at the other extreme have suggested taking NSA out of DOD, since it serves many non-military needs. The entire problem of dealing with the mutual relations of national and tactical intelligence may be clarified as the DCI assumes the additional authority granted to him by the President's Executive Order of February 18, 1976.

N15

While establishment of a Pentagon intelligence czar in the form of the new Deputy Secretary may reduce fragmentation within the department and improve the coherence of military intelligence, it will probably have a major impact on the coordinating role of the DCI. Given that the overwhelming volume of total U.S. intelligence collection and production occurs within DOD, the Deputy Secretary could become, in effect, a second DCI. The definition of the relation between these two officials will be the single most critical factor in top-level organization for management of national intelligence.

N16

4. Requirements for Congressional Oversight

If Congress attempts to exercise more comprehensive and detailed oversight of intelligence agencies, the biggest issue is likely to be what information the executive branch should make available. On defense intelligence there is likely to be less of a problem if Congress concentrates on issues of intelligence process rather than substance. There is, of course, a limit as to how far it is possible to evaluate the former without considering the latter. Therefore, norms will have to be established about what kinds of material (for example, finished intelligence) will be subject to scrutiny by Congress on a routine basis. Provision should also be made to keep basic information on budgets and resource allocation in a clear and available form in the Pentagon, obtainable by the oversight committee on demand. More consistent and thorough documentation of the chain of command could also be required in internal correspondence (thus avoiding the problem of "unattributable" records of controversial decisions turning up in the files, i.e., unsigned directives or cables which cannot clearly be traced to an authoritative source).

N17

If independent ongoing oversight of the substance of defense intelligence is the goal, an oversight committee should have staff expertise in several areas: (1) Political, to weigh the risks and gains of certain programs and targets; (2) Scientific and Technical, to evaluate sensors; (3) Economic, to judge cost-effectiveness; (4) Military, to consider non-national strategic and tactical requirements of DOD intelligence.

---

[49] Memorandum from the Chairman of the Joint Chiefs of Staff Lemnitzer to Secretary of Defense McNamara, 3/2/61.

SELECTED CHARTS ON DEFENSE INTELLIGENCE
([84A], pp. 394–395; [47] Part 1, pp. 544–545)

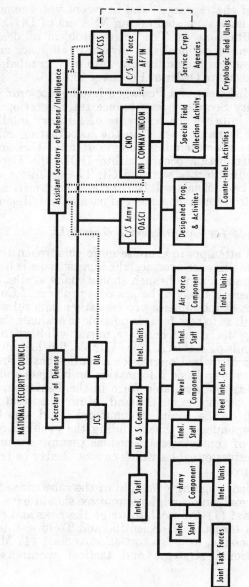

DEFENSE INTELLIGENCE COMMUNITY

DEFENSE INTELLIGENCE AGENCY

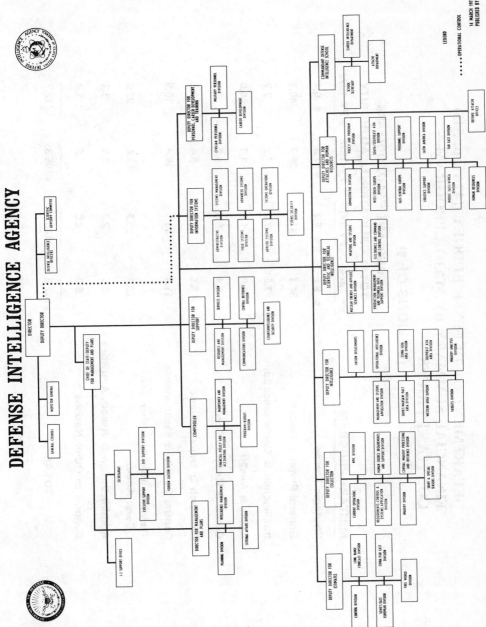

14 MARCH 1975
PUBLISHED BY CC

LEGEND

•••••• OPERATIONAL CONTROL

DEPARTMENT OF DEFENSE BUDGET ([47A], p. 545)
FINANCIAL SUMMARY BY MAJOR PROGRAM—CONSTANT PRICES
(BILLIONS OF $)

CONSTANT FY 1977 DOLLARS
TOTAL OBLIGATIONAL AUTHORITY

MILITARY PROGRAM	FY 1974	FY 1975	FY 1976	FY 1977
Strategic Forces	$ 8.5	$ 8.2	$ 7.8	$ 9.4
General Purpose Forces	34.1	31.9	35.7	40.2
Intelligence & Communications	7.5	7.2	7.2	7.7
Airlift & Sealift	1.0	1.0	1.4	1.6
Guard & Reserve Forces	5.4	5.5	5.8	5.9
Research & Development	8.5	8.8	9.4	10.5
Central Supply & Maintenance	11.1	10.5	10.4	10.9
Training, Medical, other Gen. Pers. Activ.	23.4	23.3	23.4	23.0
Administration & Assoc. Activities	2.3	2.3	2.3	2.1
Support to Other Nations	5.6	2.0	1.9	1.4
TOTAL	$107.3	$100.7	$105.3	$112.7

DEPARTMENT OF DEFENSE BUDGET ([47A], p. 544)
FINANCIAL SUMMARY BY MAJOR PROGRAM
(BILLIONS OF $)

MILITARY PROGRAM	CURRENT DOLLARS TOTAL OBLIGATIONAL AUTHORITY				
	FY 1974	FY 1975	FY 1976	FY 1977	
Strategic Forces	$ 6.8	$ 7.2	$ 7.3	$ 9.4	
General Purpose Forces	27.5	28.1	33.4	40.2	
Intelligence & Communications	6.0	6.3	6.7	7.7	
Airlift & Sealift	0.8	0.9	1.3	1.6	
Guard & Reserve Forces	4.3	4.8	5.5	5.9	
Research & Development	6.8	7.7	8.7	10.5	
Central Supply & Maintenance	8.5	9.1	9.7	10.9	
Training, Medical, other Gen. Pers. Activ.	18.2	20.1	21.8	23.0	
Administration & Assoc. Activities	1.8	2.0	2.2	2.1	
Support of Other Nations	4.3	1.8	1.8	1.4	
TOTAL	$85.1	$87.9	$98.3	$112.7	

NOTES AND REFERENCES

1. A 1968 study of the structure and management of the Defense intelligence community is furnished by the Army War College in [95]. (This college is a training center operated by DOD for staff-level military officers and civilian executives from all the U.S. foreign affairs agencies.)

2. The OSS was created in 1942 and terminated in 1945. It represented the first U.S. effort toward the creation of a centralized agency to oversee intelligence gathering. A previously top secret three-volume report on the operations of OSS during World War II is now available ([93]). This "War Report" was prepared in 1947 by the Strategic Services Unit of the War Department, under the direction of Kermit Roosevelt, chief historian for the War Report.

3. The National Security Act of 1947 and President Harry S. Truman's directive on the "Coordination of Federal Foreign Intelligence Activities" are reprinted in the Appendix.

4. Although NSA is considered part of the Defense Department, it seems to operate with considerable independence. For that reason and because it spends the bulk of intelligence funds, it is addressed separately in Chapter 7.

5. Other DOD organization diagrams on defense intelligence follow at the end of this chapter.

6. The Defense intelligence budget is the only major budget of the intelligence community that receives any degree of public exposure. Material reprinted here provides a look at that budget.

7. For further details on the DIA budget, see the 1972 testimony of DIA director, General Donald Bennett, reprinted in [1], pp. 937 ff.

8. Deletions in this portion of the text were made by the Pike Committee under arrangements with Defense Department security officials.

9. James Schlesinger, the sitting OMB director, prepared "A Report of the Intelligence Community" (the Schlesinger report). This OMB paper was prepared in 1971 and is still classified. For additional information on the Report, see [90], Vol. 7, pp. 53 ff. The 1970 Blue Ribbon Panel on Defense (the Fitzhugh report) investigated the organization, structure, and operations of DOD and issued a report to President Richard M. Nixon and to Secretary of Defense Melvin Laird on July 1, 1970. See [104], p. 35.

10. For a more complete handling of the Defense intelligence community's budget, see Chapter 4.

11. For an inside perspective on DIA operations, see Daniel Graham's article on the "intelligence mythology" ([141]).

12. In 1971, General Donald Bennett, DIA director, commented on DIA reorganization efforts before the Senate Committee on Appropriations ([1], p. 937).

13. See [44E] for Senate hearings on the NSA and a more thorough treatment of intrusion of Fourth Amendment rights. This matter of intrusion into domestic activities and affairs by the intelligence agencies is further discussed in Chapter 12.

14. Project MKNAOMI was the first CIA operation to consider the use of biological weapons. Refer to Chapter 12 for details on this matter and [45A], pp. 385–422. In addition, significant documentary detail on biological weapons and drug experimentation, etc. can be obtained from declassified materials cited in [86] and from the CIA under FOIA procedures.

15. Defense intelligence organizational matters are reviewed in the testimony in Chapter 10.

16. The Pike Committee recommended abolishing the DIA and transferring its functions to the DCI and the assistant secretary of defense for intelligence; see Chapter 10 and [85]. The basis for the Pike Committee's recommendation is probably found in its final report, which has not been made public.

17. The subject of congressional oversight is addressed in Chapter 10, which also includes a reprinted DOD position on the form the oversight should take.

Chapter 7
National Security Agency

TESTIMONY OF LT. GEN. LEW ALLEN, JR.,
BEFORE THE PIKE COMMITTEE ([84A], pp. 367–378)

The National Security Agency is the intelligence community's cryptologic and communications intercept agency. Established in 1952 by NSCID No. 6 (classified), NSA is responsible for the making and breaking of codes, the interception of messages of foreign governments, the development of techniques for clandestine transmission of information, and the use of electronics for all forms of communications related to intelligence. It is a service agency for the entire intelligence community. Its annual budget is estimated at almost double that of the CIA, and it employs approximately 24,000 persons at its headquarters (in Maryland) and even more at its bases across the world. Douglas Watson, in his article of March 2, 1975, in the *Washington Post,* noted that employment at NSA offices throughout the world may reach as high as 100,000.

This "superagency" is relatively unknown to the public and is seldom scrutinized. It receives its billion-plus dollars each year after perfunctory hearings in Congress, is rarely mentioned by the news media, and maintains no public information program beyond that of supplying a four-page leaflet, available upon request.* Rare glimpses of NSA operations are afforded by mishaps, such as the *Pueblo* incident in 1968, the Israeli attack on the U.S. communication vessel *Liberty* during the 1967 Arab-Israeli War (Six-Day War), or the defection of NSA cryptologists Martin and Mitchell in 1960.

In the review of congressional inquiries into the intelligence community between 1970 and 1976, there was no detailed examination of the purpose, structure, or operations of NSA. The Church Committee held open hearings to receive NSA Director Lew Allen's testimony. In welcoming Director Allen to the Senate hearings, Chairman Frank Church observed that no NSA representative had ever appeared before the Senate in a public hearing. The Pike Committee went into executive session shortly after Allen began testifying. Upon opening the House hearings regarding NSA on August 8, 1975, Chairman Otis Pike told his colleagues that the White House had telephoned to caution the committee on the sensitivity of NSA matters. While considerable congressional concern was expressed about possible NSA support of domestic surveillance and intrusion into the personal privacy of Americans, little substantive information was developed that sheds light on this agency.

Chapter 7 brings together the Church and Pike hearings, as well as material from the Church Committee's final report, which discussed the use of technology in intelligence activities.

*The Codebreakers, by David Kahn (London: Weidenfeld and Nicolson, 1967) provides perhaps the most thorough examination of NSA available.

The committee met, pursuant to recess, at 10:05 a.m., in room 2118, Rayburn House Office Building, the Honorable Otis G. Pike [chairman], presiding.

Present: Representatives Pike, Dellums, Murphy, Aspin, Hayes, Lehman, McClory, Johnson, and Kasten.

Also present: A. Searle Field, staff director; Aaron B. Donner, general counsel; John L. Boos, counsel; Jeffrey R. Whieldon, counsel; Roger Carroll, Fred K. Kirschstein, and Charles Mattox, investigators.

Chairman PIKE. The committee will come to order.

I want the members of the committee to know that prior to the meeting this morning I was contacted by representatives of the White House who advised me that the area which we are now addressing involves extremely sensitive information. It is quite possible that we will have to go into executive session fairly early in the meeting.

I am a little hard to convince on this item. I have done my level best to keep our sessions as open as possible as long as possible. We will start in open session. We will go in open session as long as anything useful can be accomplished thereby.

Our witness today is Gen. Lew Allen, the director of the National Security Agency. We are delighted to have you here, General Allen. You can introduce the people who are with you, General Allen, and then you may proceed any way you want.

STATEMENT OF LT. GEN. LEW ALLEN, JR., DIRECTOR, NATIONAL SECURITY AGENCY, ACCOMPANIED BY BENSON BUFFHAM, DEPUTY DIRECTOR; LEONARD MONGEON, DEPUTY CHIEF PROGRAM BUDGET OFFICE; ROBERT ANDREWS, SR., ADVISER TO THE GENERAL COUNSEL, OSD, AND ROY BANNER, GENERAL COUNSEL, NATIONAL SECURITY AGENCY

General ALLEN. First, the people on my right, Mr. Benson Buffham, Deputy Director of the National Security Agency, a professional cryptologist who has been in the field since his service with the Army in World War II.

On my left is Mr. Andrews, who is OSD General Counsel.

On his left is Mr. Banner, who is the National Security Agency General Counsel, and on my far right is Mr. Len Mongeon, who is the budget officer of the National Security Agency, and is, of course, here with details and backup information for your particular interest in matters of the budget.

Chairman PIKE. In fairness to you, before we start, I think it is clear to you—I hope it is clear to you—and I know it is clear to the members of the committee that while we started by pursuing the budget route, we find ourselves this morning not going after the CIA the way most of the people in America are going, but being rather interested in the NSA not because of their budget, but because of allegations which have been made to the effect that the NSA is intercepting the telephone calls of American citizens. That is precisely why we wanted you to be here this morning, General Allen.

Do not spend much time talking about your budget, please, but do tell us what you can tell us in that regard.

Mr. McCLORY. Would the chairman yield?

Chairman PIKE. Of course I yield.

Mr. McCLORY. I just want to add this, Mr. Chairman: That is, while we are interested in the subject matter that you have referred to, the size of the operation, the number of personnel, the amount of money that is expended for these activities, and in what ways, manpower and technological equipment and so on, I think these are all things of interest to us.

Chairman PIKE. Of course they are. It is by following that route that we got to where we are.

Mr. McCLORY. Right.

General ALLEN. Yes, sir. I understand your concern, and, of course, I have not been unaware of some of the concerns that you expressed over the past several days. On the other hand, I did come primarily in response to your letter, which asked me to particularly emphasize those matters of budget polls and procedures as well as proposed and approved budgets themselves, and so it is, of course, in that area, in response to your request, that I am primarily appearing.

Chairman PIKE. Why don't you go right ahead then in open session? Maybe we can get a lot of things in open session.

General ALLEN. All right, sir, fine. I would like to say I have prepared a statement which has been distributed, which is unclassified, and appropriate for open session. However, I would like to point out that as far as I can tell from searching the records, no director of the National Security Agency has ever before been required by Congress to testify in open session.

I will describe some of the statutory bases and concerns which Congress has expressed in the past that has apparently caused them to take those views up until now.

As you anticipate, it is going to be difficult for me to fully respond to many of those matters about which you have concern in open session. I feel it would be a disservice to both you and the American people if I attempted to give inaccurate or incomplete replies which would be inhibited by the statutory provisions on security.

Therefore, on many of these matters it will be necessary, I would prefer that the entire questioning be done in closed session, but knowing your strong feelings about open session, we will certainly do what we can in open session, but it is true we will be severely inhibited in responding.

Chairman PIKE. I feel very strongly, General Allen, that if the telephone communications of American citizens are being intercepted by your agency, the American citizens have a right to know how and why, and the American citizens have a right to make the judgment as to whether they want to spend their money for that purpose. That gets us, by a rather roundabout route, back to the budget. Why don't you go ahead with your statement?

General ALLEN. All right, sir.

Mr. Chairman, members of the committee I appreciate this opportunity to set forth for you the missions and operations of the National Security Agency (NSA). I am here to assist the committee in any way I can, and I shall be forthright and candid in providing whatever information is required.

I shall review the missions of the National Security Agency, the authorities under which it operates, its relationships to other agencies and departments of government and its budget process. Certain aspects of our operations involve the most sensitive intelligence matters.

Consequently, I will be forced to defer discussion of these matters until the committee convenes in closed session. To do otherwise would risk compromise of and possible irreparable damage to cryptologic sources and methods.

Mission

NSA has two missions. One is that of protecting U.S. communications from foreign intelligence exploitation—this is our communications security (COMSEC) mission. Our other mission is to exploit foreign communications in order to provide information to our own Government—this is called our signals intelligence (SIGINT) mission.

Our Comsec mission—that is, the enhancement of the security of our own communications—is a complex undertaking in our modern electronic world. It requires that we know and understand the threats to the security of our communications against which we are trying to protect ourselves. Thus, our two missions—Comsec and Sigint—are mutually enhancing, opposite sides of the same coin, so to speak.

The Secretary of Defense is the executive agent of the Government for communications security. His responsibility in insuring the security of our communications is carried out by the Director, NSA, as the program manager for the national communications security program. This effort includes research and development on modern techniques of encipherment and of communicating the development of prototype equipments and the printing of all of our code material which is used by both the civilian elements of our Government such as embassies and consulates, and by our military forces all over the world.

The Secretary of Defense is the executive agent of the Government for signal intelligence. We respond essentially to information needs expressed by military and civilian authorities of the Government and approved by the U.S. Intelligence Board. Many of our resources are keyed to tasks that support combatant forces.

Information needs are derived from two basic sources. First, there are the very broad intelligence objectives and priorities which are identified as a result of work by bodies like U.S. Intelligence Board, National Security Council, and the President's Foreign Intelligence Advisory Board. These come to us through the U.S. Intelligence Board, in the form of policies which guide our overall resource application. One such objective, for example, is to provide the Nation advance warning of military attack, and we endeavor to collect information which will contribute to an assessment of that possibility. Second, there are specific information needs which are identified directly to us by other governmental or military authorities, and which are satisfied without any reallocation of resources, and within the policy and approval of the USIB. An example might be to contribute to intelligence support to a military exercise or action.

When a need for information is approved, NSA accepts it as a "requirement." A requirement might best be defined as a statement of information need from an authorized source which we believe we are capable of satisfying within the constraints of our authorities and resources, and which we have, therefore, accepted as a task.

When we receive such a statement of information need, we examine our ongoing operation, our authorities, and our data base, and then perform such processing or reporting as may be necessary to satisfy that need. If a requirement or statement of need cannot be satisified without some major adjustment in the collection or processing system, then we would seek DOD or USIB consideration or both before undertaking such an adjustment.

Legal Basis for NSA and Cryptologic Activities

Let me now turn our attention to the legal authorities relating to the National Security Agency.

Our original authority is based on the President's constitutional authority to engage in foreign intelligence gathering operations which he believes necessary to the exercise of his inherent powers as Commander in Chief and as a principal organ of the Nation in the field of foreign affairs.

Prior to and during World War II, signals intelligence was conducted by the military services. In 1951, President Truman commissioned a group of distinguished Americans under the chairmanship of Mr. George Brownell to study the issues involved in conducting the national signals intelligence effort and to make recommendations regarding how this effort should be managed. Pursuant to recommendations contained in the Brownell report, President Truman unified those military efforts under a single program manager; that management concept evolved into our present day National Security Agency. By Presidential memorandum, he designated the Secretary of Defense as the executive agent of the Government for communications intelligence and communications security matters and directed him to establish the National Security Agency.

The Secretary's authority to create the National Security Agency is found in section 133(d) of title 10, United States Code. This law provides that the Secretary may exercise any of his duties through persons or organizations of the Department of Defense. The NSA is the means by which the Secretary discharges his executive agent responsibilities. In 1962, a Special Subcommittee on Defense Agencies of the House Armed Services Committee concluded, after examining the circumstances leading to the creation of defense agencies, that the Secretary of Defense had the legal authority to establish the National Security Agency.

While the legal basis for the gathering of foreign intelligence information is derived from the Constitution itself, the Congress has acted on its own initiative to enable and facilitate the President to acquire foreign intelligence through signals intelligence activities. The Congress has passed a complex of statutes which recognize the legality of signals intelligence activities and provide for the conduct and safeguarding of these activities.

As far back as 1933, the Congress recognized the right of the President to intercept the communications of foreign governments by prohibiting the divulging of the contents of diplomatic messages of foreign countries which have been successfully decoded (18 U.S.C. 952).

The keystone statute is 18 U.S.C. 798, enacted in 1950, which prohibits the unauthorized disclosure or prejudicial use of classified information of the Government concerning communications intelligence activities, cryptologic activities, or the results thereof. This law specifically authorizes the President (1) to designate agencies to engage in communications intelligence activities for the United States, (2) to classify cryptologic documents and information, and (3) to determine those persons who shall be given access to sensitive cryptologic documents and information. Further, this law defines the term "communication intelligence" to mean all procedures and methods used in the interception of communications and the obtaining of information from such communications by other than the intended recipients.

Public Law 86–36, enacted in 1959, provides authority to enable the National Security Agency, as the principal agency of the Government responsible for signals intelligence activities, to function without the disclosure of information which would endanger the accomplishment of its functions. . . .

Public Law 88–290, enacted in 1964, establishes a personnel security system and procedures governing persons employed by the National Security Agency or granted access to its sensitive cryptologic information. Public Law 88–290 also delegates authority to the Secretary of Defense to apply these personnel security procedures to employees and persons granted access to NAS's sensitive information. This law underscores the concern of the Congress regarding the extreme importance of our signals intelligence enterprise. Most personnel security programs of the Government, as you know, are based upon an Executive order and some upon a delegation of authority by the Congress to the head of the Agency. In Public Law 88–290, however, the Congress mandated that the Secretary of Defense, and the Director, National Security Agency, take measures to achieve security for the activities of the National Security Agency.

In 18 U.S.C. 2511 (3) the Congress recognized the constitutional authority of the President to obtain by whatever means, including the interception of oral or wire communications, foreign intelligence information deemed essential to the security of the United States. In this same statute the Congress also recognized the constitutional authority of the President to protect classified information of the United States against foreign intelligence (including foreign communications intelligence) activities. Thus, the Congress acted in title 18, U.S.C. section 2511 (3) to recognize that the President's constitutional powers to conduct signals intelligence and communications security activities were not limited by the statutes prohibiting electronic surveillance.

Finally, for the past 22 years, Congress has annually appropriated funds for the operation of NSA. Following hearings before the Armed Services and Appropriations Committee of both Houses of Congress in which extensive briefings of NSA's signals intelligence mission have been conducted the Congress has provided the funds to permit the National Security Agency to perform this mission. As previously noted, it has also clearly expressed its intent in legislation to ensure maximum protection against unauthorized disclosures of NSA's activities.

The President's constitutional and statutory authorities to obtain foreign intelligence through signals intelligence are implemented through National Security Council and Director of Central Intelligence Directives which govern the conduct of signals intelligence activities by the executive branch of the Government.

I understand that you have been provided a copy of the National Security Council Intelligence Directive (NSCID) No. 6. It describes NSA's authority within the executive branch to conduct the Nation's Signals Intelligence operations, and, as you can see, that authority clearly is limited to foreign intelligence operations.

I might also note that the concern of the Congress regarding NSA's activities has not been limited merely to protecting its mission. As you know, the National Security Agency keeps the Congress informed of its activities through the Subcommittees of the House and Senate Appropriations and Armed Services Committees. We appear before both the House and the Senate Defense Appropriations Subcommittees to discuss and report on the U.S. signals intelligence and communications security programs, and to justify the budgetary requirements associated with these programs. This testimony includes the activities and dollar requirements of both the National Security Agency itself and of the Services cryptologic components working with us on these missions. We do this in formal executive session, in which we forthrightly discuss activities of the most sensitive nature. In considering the fiscal year 1976 total cryptologic budget now before Congress, I appeared before the Defense Subcommittee of the House Appropriations Committee on two separate occasions for approximately seven hours. In addition, I provided follow-up responses to over one hundred questions of the subcommittee members and staff. We also appeared before Armed Services Subcommittees concerned with authorizing research, development, test and evaluation (R.D.T. & E.), construction and housing programs and also before the Appropriations Subcommittees on construction and housing.

In addition to this testimony, congressional oversight is accomplished in other ways. Staff members of these subcommittees have periodically visited the agency for detailed briefings on specific aspects of our operations. Recently we have also had members of the investigations staff of the House Appropriations Committee at the agency for more than a year. The results of this investigation have been provided to that committee in a detailed report.

Another feature of congressional review has been that since 1955, representatives of the General Accounting Office have been assigned at the agency on a permanent basis to perform on-site audits. These resident auditors have generally done administrative compliance audits and report to the Comptroller General. These audits are distinguished from management type reviews which are done on the National Security Agency by resident auditors from the Office of the Assistant Secretary of Defense (Comptroller). In our official regulations governing the General Accounting Office, we have emphasized that the sensitivity of a particular activity should not be an obstacle to properly cleared auditors in their review of any activity affecting their assessment of the agency's efficiency. While two General Accounting Office personnel are generally in residence, a number of other General Accounting Office individuals have been given clearances in preparation for undertaking substantive reviews in selected areas. I understand that Comptroller General Staats has recently commented favorably on our cooperation with his office.

N3   Since 1960, the Congress has conducted no less than 11 different major inquiries into various aspects of NSA activities or into activities in which NSA was a participant. These have included:

1. Security Practices in the National Security Agency—Defection of Bernon F. Mitchell and William H. Martin. House Committee on Un-American Activities. June 1960.

2. Defection of Bernon F. Mitchell and William H. Martin. House Committee on Armed Services. June 1960.

3. Security Practices in the NSA. House Committee on Un-American Activities. July 1961–June 1962.

4. Investigation of Defense Agencies by Special Subcommittee on Defense Agencies of the House Armed Services Committee. July–August 1962.

5. Investigation of the Administration of Internal Security Act and Other Internal Security Laws by the Senate Committee on the Judiciary. November 1963.

6. Use of Polygraphs as Lie Detectors by the Federal Government. House Subcommittee on Foreign Operations and Government Information. August 1964.

7. Gulf of Tonkin—the 1964 Incident. Senate Committee on Foreign Relations. February 1968.

8. Special House Armed Services Subcommittee on National Security Implications Arising from the Loss of the U.S.S. *Pueblo* and the Navy EC 121 Aircraft. July–August 1969.

9. Senate Foreign Relations Subcommittee on U.S. Security Agreements and Commitments Abroad. 1970–71.

10. House Armed Services Special Subcommittee on Defense Communications. September 1970–1971.

11. House Appropriations Committee Investigation Team. March 1975.

As you know, there are also a number of congressional reviews ongoing at this time.

The executive branch also maintains close supervision over the activities of the National Security Agency. Five major investigations of signals intelligence have been conducted by the executive branch. These include:

1. George A. Brownell Committee 1951–52. Recommended organization of the National Security Agency.

2. Hoover Commission Task Force on Intelligence Activities—1955. Survey of Central Intelligence Agency and other foreign intelligence activities.

3. Defense Ad Hoc Committee to inquire into the Use of the Polygraph in the Selection of Military Personnel for Conversion to Civilian Positions at the National Security Agency—1963.

4. Special Study Group on the U.S. Signals Intelligence (Sigint) Effort, 1967—Eaton Committee—Executive Committee.

5. Blue Ribbon Defense Panel—July 1, 1970. Study of the organization, structure and operations of the Department of Defense, and, of course, there are recent investigations.

The Secretary of Defense is the executive agent for the Government for all NSA activities. As an agency functioning within the framework of the Department of Defense, we are fully responsive to applicable directives of that Department, work with the Assistant Secretary of Defense (Intelligence) in developing our programs, and submit our programs and budgets for departmental review. As a member of the Intelligence Community, we adhere to the intelligence policies and priorities established by the Director, Central Intelligence, are responsive to his direction, participate in the activities of the United States Intelligence Board and provide our program recommendations for his consideration and inclusion in his National Foreign Intelligence program.

Other organizations of the executive branch concerned with the review of the National Security Agency programs and the provision of direction or guidance to me as program manager for signals intelligence and communications security include:

President's Foreign Intelligence Advisory Board.

The DCI Intelligence Resources Advisory Committee.

The U.S. Communications Security Board.

The Office of Management and Budget.

The Assistant Secretary of Defense (Intelligence) testimony on Tuesday covered the basic program and budget procedure used in the Department of Defense, and the respective roles of the Office of Management and Budget and Intelligence Community staff of the Director, Central Intelligence in this process. He indicated that as Director, National Security Agency, I am the program manager for the signals intelligence (SIGINT) and communications security (COMESEC) efforts of the U.S. Government. In this capacity, I am responsible for developing a consolidated program involving my agency and other Defense components engaged in both missions. These program plans are developed and reviewed during the spring of the year based on objectives and priorities set forth by the Director of Central Intelligence and the Secretary of Defense and within fiscal constraints established by the latter. The recommended program for signals intelligence is then reviewed for the Secretary of Defense by the Assistant Secretary of Defense (Intelligence) in the early summer. My recommended communications security program is reviewed by the Defense Director of Telecommunications and Control and Command Systems.

This program, when approved by the Secretary of Defense, is the basis against which detailed budget estimates are developed and sub-submitted in the fall to the Assistant Secretary of Defense (Comptroller) and the Office of Management and Budget. NSA and each military department include the funds required for its part of the program in their own request for appropriations. The budget for the National Security Agency is carried in the appropriations of the Defense agencies. The pay for the military personnel assigned to the National Security Agency are budgeted by the parent department.

These budget requests are reviewed in detail by the Assistant Secretary of Defense (Comptroller) and the Office of Management and Budget. Mr. Colby's Intelligence Community Staff and the staff of the Assistant Secretary of Defense (Intelligence) participate in the review of Intelligence budget estimates. The Staff of the Director of Telecommunications and Command and Control Systems is included in the review of the Communications Security budget. Based on these reviews, the approved budget requests for signals intelligence and communications security are included within the Department and Agency budgets for submission to Congress as part of the President's overall Federal Budget.

Thus, our activities now and throughout our existence have had the most thorough and detailed scrutiny of the DCI, the DOD, and the Congress. The participation of both the legislative and executive branches of the Government in the activities of NSA has been most active and most vigorous.

In the closed session I will address the intelligence requirements which are levied on NSA, and which generally are answerable without in any way adjusting out collection activities. I will attempt to explain NSA's role with respect to international communications, describe how the operation is conducted, the manner in which NSA responds to a requirement, and the disposition of requests made by other Government agencies for information that might be generated by those operations.

I hope this statement has been helpful to this committee in understanding the nature of NSA's operations. I would like to emphasize that the signals intelligence and communications security activities of our Government are uniquely vulnerable to compromise, and that the effects of unauthorized or unwise revelations concerning those operations are often very far reaching and prejudicial to our national interests. In May 1974, Mr. McGeorge Bundy in his testimony before the Senate Subcommittee on Government Operations identified the intercept of electronic transmissions as one of six activities which he believed constituted "real secrets." I agree with that assessment. Even small compromises in our interrelated protective and intelligence mechanisms make it possible for foreign governments to institute countermeasures that can dramatically reduce our effectiveness. Such countermeasures could bring to naught our communication security efforts, or deny access to information sorely needed for national security purposes. Indeed, this already has happened in several cases when unfortunate and unauthorized disclosures have been made with damaging effect.

That concludes my prepared statement. I would be pleased to try to answer any questions the committee may wish to put to me.

Chairman PIKE. Thank you very much, General Allen. I think one of the problems that the intelligence agencies have is when you say that your operation is one of six real secrets. I would incline to agree with you, if it were not for the fact that so much of what is happening in America is classified as Top Secret. We just drown in things labeled National Security and Top Secret.

How many different agencies of the Government are authorized sources for requiring the use of your system?

General ALLEN. Our requirements do need to come through the United States Intelligence Board, and the Director of Central Intelligence, as the chairman of that board, has several other agencies of government as advisory to him.

Chairman PIKE. How may different agencies of government can use your collection system?

General ALLEN. I don't know the answer in terms of numbers, but it's essentially all agencies of government who have an established need and who have established appropriate security procedures to receive it.

Chairman PIKE. Does your system intercept the telephone calls of American citizens?

General ALLEN. I would believe that I can give a satisfactory answer to that question which will relieve the committee's concern on that matter in closed session.

Mr. McCLORY. Will the chairman yield?

Chairman PIKE. Yes, I yield.

Mr. McCLORY. Mr. Chairman, here you have asked about three or four questions now. We get into the area where it seems that we are going to get the information only in closed session. I have several questions. I am sure that the General will be unable to answer them.

I think it would be much more productive to our hearing, we would get much more information if we could proceed in a more direct way, if we resolve ourselves now into executive session, and I so move.

Chairman PIKE. I would like to be heard a little bit on the motion before we vote on it. Are you telling us, General Allen, that you can't even tell us in open session yes or no, whether the National Security Agency intercepts the telephone conversations of American citizens in America?

General ALLEN. Sir, I believe that a discussion of our operations is properly held in closed session, and that in closed session I can describe to you the methods of operation and the protection of the fundamental rights of American citizens which are afforded, and that to give you a "yes" or "no" answer or to attempt to describe that in open session would be a disservice to the——

Chairman PIKE. General Allen, recently—in fact two months ago, June of this year—there was a decision by the U.S. Court of Appeals for the District of Columbia Circuit which said that even for national security purposes wiretaps would not be permitted without a court order. Do you feel your operation to be somehow exempt from that decision?

[The case referred to is *Zweibon* v. *Mitchell*, 363 F. Supp. 936 (1975).]

General ALLEN. Mr. Banner, my General Counsel.

Mr. BANNER. Are you referring to what decision, sir?

Chairman PIKE. Sweibon versus Mitchell.

Mr. BANNER. That case holds in essence that before the United States can conduct an interception——

Chairman PIKE. I know what the case holds. I have it here.

Mr. BANNER. The answer to your question, sir, is that we believe that holding does not have any effect upon the conduct of our operations solely for foreign intelligence purposes.

Chairman PIKE. But does it have any bearing on American citizens making phone calls from America?

Mr. BANNER. Yes, the case does where the call, communication, is a domestic communication.

Chairman PIKE. Where it is a domestic communication?

Mr. BANNER. Yes.

Chairman PIKE. Would it affect an American citizen making a phone call overseas?

Mr. BANNER. No, sir, it would not in my judgment.

Chairman PIKE. In other words, you think that although wiretaps are prohibited by that law, intercepting telephone calls by American citizens heading overseas is not prohibited by that decision?

Mr. BANNER. That's correct, sir.

Chairman PIKE. Did the President of the United States say to the Justice Department that they would abide by that decision?

Mr. BANNER. Yes, sir.

Chairman PIKE. And are you telling us that the President of the United States somehow advised the NSA that it need not abide by that decision?

Mr. BANNER. Our view is, Mr. Chairman, that that decision does not affect the communications intelligence operations which are exclusively for foreign intelligence purposes, of foreign communications.

Chairman PIKE. The President as far as was reported in the newspaper said that even if foreign affairs or national security matters are involved, the Department of Justice was to abide by that Federal Court ruling. You are saying that although the Department of Justice must do that, the National Security Agency need not. Is that your position?

Mr. BANNER. No, that is not, Mr. Chairman. I am saying that the decision relates solely to the internal communications inside the United States, and the holding of the case is that before the United States can intercept the communications, internal communications, that it must establish a connection with a foreign power. The activities of the National Security Agency are to obtain foreign intelligence information only, and they are involved with foreign communications only, not internal communications.

Chairman PIKE. Is the committee ready to vote on Mr. McClory's motion?

The clerk will call the roll.
The CLERK. Mr. Dellums.
Mr. DELLUMS. No.
The CLERK. Mr. Murphy.
Mr. MURPHY. Aye.
The CLERK. Mr. Aspin.
Mr. ASPIN. Aye.
The CLERK. Mr. Hayes.
Mr. HAYES. Aye.
The CLERK. Mr. Lehman.
Mr. LEHMAN. No.
The CLERK. Mr. McClory.
Mr. McCLORY. Aye.
The CLERK. Mr. Kasten.
Mr. KASTEN. Aye.
The CLERK. Mr. Johnson.
Mr. JOHNSON. No.
The CLERK. Mr. Pike.
Chairman PIKE. Aye.

By a vote of 6 to 3, the committee will resolve itself into executive. The room will be cleared and swept and whatever else is necessary to satisfy the witnesses.

[Whereupon, at 10:45 a.m., the committee proceeded into executive session.]

TESTIMONY OF LT. GEN. LEW ALLEN, JR., BEFORE THE CHURCH COMMITTEE ([44E], pp. 5–16)

Lt. Gen. Lew Allen, Jr., director of NSA, appeared before the Church Committee on October 29, 1975, in connection with the investigation into violation of U.S. citizens' Fourth Amendment rights by NSA and other intelligence agencies. After five months of preliminary staff-level inquiry, the committee met in open session and acknowledged that it had negotiated ground rules for the open hearing—aimed at narrowing the focus of the investigation to domestic abuses and in no way compromising the secrecy of what Senator John Tower referred to as "the most fragile weapon in our arsenal." Following the Allen testimony, which is reprinted here in part, the committee heard further from NSA's Deputy Director Benson Buffham. On November 6, 1975, Attorney General Edward Levi, and others, testified on the civil rights aspect of NSA's involvement in the Watergate affair and post-Watergate activities; those subjects are reviewed in Chapter 12.

General ALLEN. Mr. Chairman, members of the committee, I recognize the important responsibility this committee has to investigate the intelligence operations of the U.S. Government and to determine the need for improvement by legislative or other means. For several months, involving many thousands of man-hours, the National Security Agency has, I believe, cooperated with this committee to provide a thorough information base, including data whose continued secrecy is most important to our Nation.

We are now here to discuss in open session certain aspects of an important and hitherto secret operation of the U.S. Gvernment. I recognize that the committee is deeply concerned that we protect sensitive and fragile sources of information. I appreciate the care which this committee and staff have exercised to protect the sensitive data we have provided.

I also understand that the committee intends to restrict this open discussion to certain specific activities and to avoid current foreign intelligence operations. It may not be possible to discuss all these activities completely without some risk of damage to continuing foreign intelligence capabilities. Therefore, I may request some aspects of our discussion be conducted in executive session where there can be opportunity to continue our full and frank disclosure to the committee of all the information you require. The committee may then develop an appropriate public statement. We are therefore here, sir, at your request, prepared to cooperate in bringing these matters before your committee.

In the interest of clarity and perspective, I shall first review the purpose of the National Security Agency and the authorities under which it operates. Next, I will describe the process by which requirements for information are levied on NSA by other Government agencies. And finally, I will give a more specific description of an operation conducted in 1967–73 by NSA in response to external requirements, which I will refer to as "the watch list activity." This activity has been subject to an intensive review by this committee and staff in closed session.

Under the authority of the President, the Secretary of Defense has been delegated responsibility for both providing security of U.S. governmental communications and seeking intelligence from foreign electrical communications. Both functions are executed for the Secretary of Defense by the Director, National Security Agency, through a complex national system which includes the NSA as its nucleus. It is appropriate for the Secretary of Defense to have these executive agent responsibilities, since the great majority of the effort to accomplish both of these missions is applied to the support of the military aspects of the national security.

The communications security mission is directed at enhancing the security of U.S. Government communications whenever needed to protect those communications from exploitation by foreign governments—a complex undertaking in today's advanced electronic world.

The United States, as part of its effort to produce foreign intelligence, has intercepted foreign communications, analyzed, and in some cases decoded these communications to produce such foreign intelligence since the Revolutionary War. During the Civil War and World

War I these communications were often telegrams sent by wire. In modern times, with the advent of wireless communications, particular emphasis has been placed by the Government on the specialized field of intercepting and analyzing communications transmitted by radio. Since the 1930's, elements of the military establishment have been assigned tasks to obtain intelligence from foreign radio transmissions.

In the months preceding Pearl Harbor and throughout World War II, highly successful accomplishments were made by groups in the Army and the Navy to intercept and analyze Japanese and German coded radio messages. Admiral Nimitz is reported as rating its value in the Pacific to the equivalent of another whole fleet. According to another official report, in the victory in the Battle of Midway, it would have been impossible to have achieved the concentration of forces and the tactical surprise without communications intelligence. A congressional committee, in its investigation of Pearl Harbor, stated that the success of communications intelligence "contributed enormously to the defeat of the enemy, greatly shortened the war, and saved many thousands of lives." General George C. Marshall commented that they—communications intelligence—had contributed "greatly to the victories and tremendously to the savings of American lives."

Following World War II, the separate military efforts were brought together and the National Security Agency was formed to focus the Government's efforts. The purpose was to maintain and improve this source of intelligence which was considered of vital importance to the national security, to our ability to wage war, and to the conduct of foreign affairs.

This mission of NSA is directed to foreign intelligence, obtained from foreign electrical communications and also from other foreign signals such as radars. Signals are intercepted by many techniques and processed, sorted, and analyzed by procedures which reject inappropriate or unnecessary signals. The foreign intelligence derived from these signals is then reported to various agencies of the Government in response to their approved requirements for foreign intelligence.

The NSA works very hard at this task, and is composed of dedicated, patriotic citizens, civilian and military, most of whom have dedicated their professional careers to this important and rewarding job. They are justifiably proud of their service to their country and fully accept the fact that their continued remarkable efforts can be appreciated only by those few in Government who know of their great importance to the United States.

Congress, in 1933, recognized the importance of communications intelligence activities and acted to protect the sensitive nature of the information derived from those activities by passing legislation that is now 18 U.S.C. 952. This statute prohibits the divulging of the contents of decoded foreign diplomatic messages, or information about them.

Later, in 1950, Congress enacted 18 U.S.C. 798, which prohibits the unauthorized disclosure, prejudicial use, or publication of classified information of the Government concerning communications intelligence activities, cryptologic activities, or the results thereof. It indicates that the President is authorized: (1) to designate agencies to engage in communications intelligence activities for the United States; (2) to classify cryptologic documents and information; and (3) to determine those persons who shall be given access to sensitive cryptologic documents and information. Further, this law defines the term "communication intelligence" to mean all procedures and methods used in the interception of communications and the obtaining of information from such communications by other than the intended recipients.

After an intensive review by a panel of distinguished citizens, President Truman in 1952 acted to reorganize and strengthen communications intelligence activities. He issued in October 1952 a Presidential memorandum outlining in detail how communications intelligence activities were to be conducted, designated the Secretary of Defense to be his executive agent in these matters, directed the establishment of the NSA, and outlined the missions and functions to be performed by the NSA.

The Secretary of Defense, pursuant to the congressional authority delegated to him in section 133(d) of title 10 of the United States Code, acted to establish the National Security Agency. The section of the law cited provides that the Secretary may exercise any of these duties through persons or organizations of the Department of Defense. In 1962 a Special Subcommittee on Defense Agencies of the House Armed Services Committee concluded, after examining the circumstances leading to the creation of defense agencies, that the Secretary of Defense had the legal authority to establish the National Security Agency.

The President's constitutional and statutory authorities to obtain foreign intelligence through signals intelligence are implemented through National Security Council and Director of Central Intelligence Directives which govern the conduct of signals intelligence activities by the executive branch of the Government.

In 1959, the Congress enacted Public Law 86–36 which provides authority to enable the NSA as the principal agency of the Government responsible for signals intelligence activities, to function without the disclosure of information which would endanger the accomplishment of its functions.

In 1964 Public Law 88–290 was enacted by the Congress to establish a personnel security system and procedures governing persons employed by the NSA or granted access to its sensitive cryptologic information. Public Law 88–290 also delegates authority to the Secretary of Defense to apply these personnel security procedures to employees and persons granted access to the National Security Agency's sensitive information. This law underscores the concern of the Congress regarding the extreme importance of our signals intelligence enterprise and mandates that the Secretary of Defense, and the Director, National Security Agency, take measures to achieve security for the activities of the NSA.

Title 18 U.S.C. 2511(3) provides as follows:

Nothing contained in this chapter of in Section 605 of the Communications Act of 1934, 47 U.S.C. 605, shall limit the constitutional power of the President to take such measures as he deems necessary to protect the nation against actual or potential attack or other hostile acts of a foreign power, to obtain foreign intelligence information deemed essential to the security of the United States, or to protect national security information against foreign intelligence activities.

In *United States* v. *Brown*, U.S. Court of Appeals, Fifth Circuit, decided August 22, 1973, the court discussed this provision of the law as follows:

The constitutional power of the President is adverted to, although not conferred, by Congress in Title III of the Omnibus Crime Control and Safe Streets Act of 1968.

Thus, while NSA does not look upon section 2511(3) as authority to conduct communications intelligence, it is our position that nothing in chapter 119 of title 18 affects or governs the conduct of communications intelligence for the purpose of gathering foreign intelligence.

Finally, for the past 22 years, Congress has annually appropriated funds for the operation of the NSA, following hearings before the Armed Services and Appropriations Committees of both Houses of Congress in which extensive briefings of the NSA's signals intelligence mission have been conducted. We appear before both the House and the Senate Defense Appropriations Subcommittees to discuss and report on the U.S. signals intelligence and communications security programs, and to justify the budgetary requirements associated with these programs. We do this in formal executive session, in which we discuss our activities in whatever detail required by the Congress.

In considering the fiscal year 1976 total cryptologic budget now before Congress, I appeared before the Defense Subcommittee of the House Appropriations Committee on two separate occasions for approximately 7 hours. In addition, I provided follow-up response to over 100 questions of the subcommittee members and staff. We also appeared before armed services subcommittees concerned with authorizing research, development, test and evaluation, construction and housing programs and also before the appropriations subcommittees on construction and housing.

In addition to this testimony, congressional oversight is accomplished in other ways. Staff members of these subcommittees have periodically visited the Agency for detailed briefings on specific aspects of our operations. Members of the investigations staff of the House Appropriations Committee recently conducted an extensive investigation of this Agency. The results of this study, which lasted over a year, have been provided to that committee in a detailed report.

Another feature of congressional review is that since 1955 resident auditors of the General Accounting Office have been assigned at the Agency to perform on-site audits. Additional GAO auditors were cleared for access in 1973, and GAO, in addition to this audit, is initiating a classified review of our automatic data processing functions. NSA's cooperative efforts in this area were noted by a Senator in February of this year. In addition, resident auditors of the Office of Secretary of Defense, Comptroller, conduct indepth management reviews of our organization.

A particular aspect of NSA authorities which is pertinent to today's discussion relates to the definition of foreign communications. Neither the Presidential directive of 1952 nor the National Security Council directive No. 6 defines the term foreign communications. The NSA has always confined its activities to communications involving at least one foreign terminal. This interpretation is consistent with the definition of foreign communications in the Communications Act of 1934.

There is also a directive of the Director of Central Intelligence dealing with security regulations which employs a definition which excludes communications between U.S. citizens or entities. While this directive has not been construed as defining the NSA mission in the same sense as has the National Security Council directive, in the past this exclusion has usually been applied and is applied now. However, we will describe a particular activity in the past when that exclusion has not applied.

NSA does not now, and with an exception to be described, has not in the past conducted intercept operations for the purpose of obtaining the communications of U.S. citizens. However, it necessarily occurs that some circuits which are known to carry foreign communications necessary for foreign intelligence will also carry personal communications between U.S. citizens, one of whom is at a foreign location.

The interception of communications, however it may occur, is conducted in such a manner as to minimize the unwanted messages. Nevertheless, many unwanted communications are potentially available for selection. Subsequent processing, sorting, and selecting for analysis is conducted in accordance with strict procedures to insure immediate and, wherever possible, automatic rejection of inappropriate messages. The analysis and reporting is accomplished only for those messages which meet specified conditions and requirements for foreign intelligence. It is certainly believed by NSA that our communications intelligence activities are solely for the purpose of obtaining foreign intelligence in accordance with the authorities delegated by the President stemming from his constitutional power to conduct foreign intelligence.

NSA produces signals intelligence in response to objectives, requirements and priorities as expressed by the Director of Central Intelligence with the advice of the U.S. Intelligence Board. There is a separate committee of the Board which develops the particular requirements against which the NSA is expected to respond.

The principal mechanism used by the Board in formulating requirements for signals intelligence information has been one of listing areas of intelligence interest and specifying in some detail the signals intelligence needed by the various elements of Government. This listing, which was begun in 1966 and fully implemented in 1970, is intended to provide guidance to the Director of the National Security Agency, and to the Secretary of Defense, for programing and operating NSA activities. It is intended as an expression of realistic and essential requirements for signals intelligence information.

This process recognizes that a single listing, updated annually, needs to be supplemented with additional detail and time-sensitive factors, and it establishes a procedure whereby the USIB agencies can express directly to the NSA information needs which reasonably amplify requirements approved by USIB or higher authority.

In addition, there are established procedures for non-Board members, the Secret Service, and the BNDD at the time in question, to ask the NSA for information. The NSA does have operational discretion in responding to requirements, but we do not generate our own requirements for foreign intelligence. The Director, NSA is directed to be responsive to the requirements formulated by the Director of Central Intelligence. However, I clearly must not respond to any requirements which I feel are not proper.

In 1975 the USIB signals intelligence requirements process was revised. Under the new system, all basic requirements for signals intelligence information on U.S. Government agencies will be reviewed and validated by the Signals Intelligence Committee of USIB before being levied on the NSA. An exception is those requirements which are highly time-sensitive; they will continue to be passed simultaneously to us for action and to USIB for information. The new system will also attempt to prioritize signals intelligence requirements. The new requirements process is an improvement in that it creates a formal mechanism to record all requirements for signals intelligence information and to establish their relative priorities.

Watch List Activity

Now to the subject which the committee asked me to address in some detail—the so-called watch list activity of 1967 to 1973.

The use of lists of words, including individual names, subjects, locations, et cetera, has long been one of the methods used to sort out information of foreign intelligence value from that which is not of interest. In the past such lists have been referred to occasionally as watch lists, because the lists were used as an aid to watch for foreign activity of reportable intelligence interest. However, these lists generally did not contain names of U.S. citizens or organizations. The activity in question is one in which U.S. names were used systematically as a basis for selecting messages, including some between U.S. citizens, when one of the communicants was at a foreign location.

The origin of such activity is unclear. During the early sixties, requesting agencies had asked the NSA to look for reflections in international communications of certain U.S. citizens traveling to Cuba. Beginning in 1967, requesting agencies provided names of persons and organizations, some of whom were U.S. citizens, to the NSA in an effort to obtain information which was available in foreign communications as a by-product of our normal foreign intelligence mission.

The purpose of the lists varied, but all possessed a common thread in which the NSA was requested to review information available through our usual intercept sources. The initial purpose was to help determine the existence of foreign influence on specified activities of interest to agencies of the U.S. Government, with emphasis then on Presidential protection and on civil disturbances occurring throughout the Nation.

Later, because of other developments, such as widespread national concern over such criminal activity as drug trafficking and acts of terrorism, both domestic and international, the emphasis came to include these areas. Thus, during this period, 1967–73, requirements for which lists were developed in four basic areas: international drug trafficking; Presidential protection; acts of terrorism; and possible foreign support or influence on civil disturbances.

In the sixties there was Presidential concern voiced over the massive flow of drugs into our country from outside the United States. Early in President Nixon's administration, he instructed the CIA to pursue with vigor intelligence efforts to identify foreign sources of drugs and the foreign organizations and methods used to introduce illicit drugs into the United States. The BNDD, the Bureau of Narcotics and Dangerous Drugs, in 1970 asked the NSA to provide communications intelligence relevant to these foreign aspects, and BNDD provided watch lists with some U.S. names [exhibit 4]. International drug trafficking requirements were formally documented in USIB requirements in August 1971.

N7

As we all know, during this period there was also heightened concern by the country and the Secret Service over Presidential protection because of President Kennedy's assassination. After the

Warren Report, requirements lists containing names of U.S. citizens and organizations were provided to NSA by the Secret Service in support of their efforts to protect the President and other senior officials. Such requirements were later incorporated into USIB documentation. At that time, intelligence derived from foreign communications was regarded as a valuable tool in support of Executive protection.

About the same time as the concern over drugs, or shortly thereafter, there was a committee established by the President to combat international terrorism. This committee was supported by an interdepartmental working group with USIB representatives. Requirements to support this effort with communications intelligence were also incorporated into USIB documentation.

Now let me put the watch list in perspective regarding its size and the numbers of names submitted by the various agencies:

The BNDD submitted a watch list covering their requirements for intelligence on international narcotics trafficking. On September 8, 1972, President Nixon summarized the efforts of his administration against drug abuse. The President stated that he ordered the Central Intelligence Agency, early in his administration, to mobilize its full resources to fight the international drug trade. The key priority, the President noted, was to destroy the trafficking through law enforcement and intelligence efforts. The BNDD list contained the names of suspected drug traffickers. There were about 450 U.S. individuals and over 3,000 foreign individuals.

The Secret Service submitted watch lists covering their requirements for intelligence relating to Presidential and Executive protection. Public Law 90-331 of June 6, 1968, made it mandatory for Federal agencies to assist the Secret Service in the performance of its protective duties. These lists contained names of persons and groups who, in the opinion of the Secret Service, were potentially a threat to Secret Service protectees, as well as the names of the protectees themselves. On these lists were about 180 U.S. individuals and groups and about 525 foreign individuals and groups.

An Army message of October 20, 1967, informed the NSA that Army ACSI, assistant chief of staff for intelligence, had been designated executive agent by DOD for civil disturbance matters and requested any available information on foreign influence over, or control of, civil disturbances in the U.S. [exhibit 1]. The Director, NSA, sent a cable the same day to the DCI and to each USIB member and notified them of the urgent request from the Army and stated that the NSA would attempt to obtain communications intelligence regarding foreign control or influence over certain U.S. individuals and groups [exhibit 2].

The Brownell Committee, whose report led to the creation of NSA, stated that communications intelligence should be provided to the Federal Bureau of Investigation because of the essential role of the Bureau in the national security.

The FBI submitted watch lists covering their requirements on foreign ties and support to certain U.S. persons and groups. These lists contained names of "so-called" extremist persons and groups, individuals and groups active in civil disturbances, and terrorists. The lists contained a maximum of about 1,000 U.S. persons and groups and about 1,700 foreign persons and groups.

The DIA submitted a watch list covering their requirements on possible foreign control of, or influence on, U.S. antiwar activity. The list contained names of individuals traveling to North Vietnam. There were about 20 U.S. individuals on this list. DIA is responsible under DOD directives for satisfying the intelligence requirements of the major components of the DOD and to validate and assign to NSA requirements for intelligence required by DOD components.

Between 1967 and 1973 there was a cumulative total of about 450 U.S. names on the narcotics list, and about 1,200 U.S. names on all other lists combined. What that amounted to was that at the height of the watch list activity, there were about 800 U.S. names on the watch list and about one-third of these 800 were from the narcotics list.

We estimate that over this 6-year period, 1967–1973, about 2,000 reports were issued by the NSA on international narcotics trafficking, and about 1,900 reports were issued covering the three areas of terrorism, Executive protection and foreign influence over U.S. groups. This would average about two reports per day. These reports included some messages between U.S. citizens with one foreign communicant, but over 90 percent had at least one foreign communicant and all messages had at least one foreign terminal. Using agencies did periodically review, and were asked by the NSA to review, their watch lists to insure inappropriate or unnecessary entries were promptly removed.

I am not the proper person to ask concerning the value of the product from these four special efforts. We are aware that a major terrorist act in the United States was prevented. In addition, some large drug shipments were prevented from entering the United States because of our efforts on international narcotics trafficking. We have statements from the requesting agencies in which they have expressed appreciation for the value of the information which they had received from us. Nonetheless, in my own judgment, the controls which were placed on the handling of the intelligence were so restrictive that the value was significantly diminished.

Now let me address the question of the watch list activity as the NSA saw it at the time.

This activity was reviewed by proper authority within NSA and by competent external authority. This included two former Attorneys General and a former Secretary of Defense.

The requirements for information had been approved by officials of the using agencies and subsequently validated by the United States Intelligence Board. For example, the Secret Service and BNDD requirements were formally included in USIB guidance in 1970 and 1971, respectively.

In the areas of narcotics trafficking, terrorism and requirements related to the protection of the lives of senior U.S. officials, the emphasis placed by the President on a strong, coordinated Government effort was clearly understood. There also was no question that there was considerable Presidential concern and interest in determining the existence and extent of foreign support to groups fomenting civil disturbances in the United States.

From 1967 to 1969 the procedure for submitting names was more informal, with written requests following as the usual practice. Starting in 1969 the procedure was formalized and the names for watch lists were submitted through channels in writing [exhibit 3]. The Director and Deputy Director of the NSA approved certain categories of subject matter from customer agencies, and were aware that U.S. individuals and organizations were being included on watch lists. While they did not review and approve each individual name, there were continuing management reviews at levels below the Directorate.

NSA personnel sometimes made analytic amplifications on customer watch list submissions in order to fulfill certain requirements. For example, when information was received that a name on the watch list used an alias, the alias was inserted; or when an address was uncovered of a watch list name, the address was included. This practice by analysts was done to enhance the selection process, not to expand the lists.

The information produced by the watch list activity was, with one exception, entirely a byproduct of our foreign intelligence mission. All collection was conducted against international communications with at least one terminal in a foreign country, and for purposes unrelated to the watch list activity. That is, the communications were obtained, for example, by monitoring communications to and from Hanoi.

All communications had a foreign terminal and the foreign terminal or communicant, with the one exception to be described, was the initial object of the communications collection.

The watch list activity specifically consisted of scanning international communications already intercepted for other purposes to derive information which met watch list requirements. This scanning was accomplished by using the entries provided to NSA as selection criteria. Once selected, the messages were analyzed to determine if the information therein met those requesting agencies' requirements associated with the watch lists. If the message met the requirement, the information therein was reported to the requesting agency in writing.

Now let me discuss for a moment the manner in which intelligence derived from the watch lists was handled.

For the period 1967–69, international messages between U.S. citizens and organizations, selected on the basis of watch list entries and containing foreign intelligence, were issued for background use only and were hand delivered to certain requesting agencies. If the U.S. citizen or organization was only one correspondent of the international communication, it was published as a normal product report but in a special series to limit distribution on a strict need-to-know basis.

Starting in 1969, any messages that fell into the categories of Presidential/executive protection and foreign influence over U.S. citizens and groups were treated in an even more restricted fashion. They were provided for background use only and hand delivered to requesting agencies. When the requirements to supply intelligence regarding international drug trafficking in 1970 and international terrorism in 1971 were received, intelligence on these subjects was handled in a similar manner. This procedure continued until I terminated the activity in 1973.

The one instance in which foreign messages were intercepted for specific watch list purposes was the collection of some telephone calls passed over international communications facilities between the United States and South America. The collection was conducted at the specific request of the BNDD to produce intelligence information on the methods and locations of foreign narcotics trafficking.

In addition to our own intercept, CIA was asked by NSA to assist in this collection. NSA provided to CIA names of individuals from the international narcotics trafficking watch list. This collection by CIA lasted for approximately 6 months, from late 1972 to early 1973, when CIA stopped because of concern that the activity exceeded CIA statutory restrictions.

When the watch list activity began, the NSA and others viewed the effort as an appropriate part of the foreign intelligence mission. The emphasis of the President that a concerted national effort was required to combat these grave problems was clearly expressed.

The activity was known to higher authorities, kept quite secret, and restrictive controls were placed on the use of the intelligence. The agencies receiving the information were clearly instructed that the information could not be used for prosecutive or evidentiary purposes, and to our knowledge, it was not used for such purposes.

It is worth noting that some Government agencies receiving the information had dual functions. For instance, BNDD was concerned on the one hand with domestic drug law enforcement activities and on the other hand with the curtailing of international narcotics trafficking. It would be to the latter area of responsibility that the NSA delivered its intelligence.

However, since the intelligence was being reported to some agencies which did have law enforcement responsibilities, there was growing concern that the intelligence could be used for purposes other than foreign intelligence. To minimize this risk, the material was delivered only to designated offices in those agencies, and the material was marked and protected in a special way to limit the number of people involved and to segregate it from information of broader interest.

In 1973, concern about the NSA's role in these activities was increased, first, by concerns that it might not be possible to distinguish definitely between the purpose for the intelligence gathering which NSA understood was served by these requirements, and the missions and functions of the departments or agencies receiving the information, and, second, that requirements from such agencies were growing, and finally, that new broad discovery procedures in court cases were coming into use which might lead to disclosure of sensitive intelligence sources and methods.

The first action taken was the decision to terminate the activity in support of BNDD in the summer of 1973. This decision was made because of concern that it might not be possible to make a clear separation between the requests for information submitted by BNDD as it pertained to legitimate foreign intelligence requirements and the law-enforcement responsibility of BNDD.

CIA had determined in 1973 that it could not support these requests of BNDD because of statutory restrictions on CIA. The NSA is not subject to the same sort of restrictions as CIA, but a review of the matter led to a decision that certain aspects of our support should be discontinued, and in particular the watch-list activity was stopped.

NSA did not retain any of the BNDD watch lists or product. It was destroyed in the fall of 1973, since there seemed no purpose or requirement to retain it.

With regard to watch lists submitted by FBI, CIA, and Secret Service, these matters were discussed with the National Security Agency Counsel and Counsel for the Department of Defense, and we stopped the distribution of information in the summer of 1973. In September 1973, I sent a letter to each agency head requesting him to recertify the requirement with respect to the appropriateness of the request, including a review of that agency's legal authorities [exhibit 6].

Somewhat later, on October 1, 1973, Attorney General Richardson wrote me, indicating that he was concerned with respect to the propriety of requests for information concerning U.S. citizens which NSA had received from the FBI and Secret Service [exhibit 7]. He wrote the following:

Until I am able more carefully to assess the effect of *Keith* and other Supreme Court decisions concerning electronic surveillance upon your current practice of disseminating to the FBI and Secret Service information acquired by you through electronic devices pursuant to requests from the FBI and Secret Service, it is requested that you immediately curtail the further dissemination of such information to these agencies.

He goes on to say:

Of course, relevant information acquired by you in the routine pursuit of the collection of foreign intelligence may continue to be furnished to appropriate government agencies.

The overall result of these actions was that we stopped accepting watch lists containing names of U.S. citizens and no information is produced or disseminated to other agencies using these methods [exhibit 8]. Thus, the watch list activity which involved U.S. citizens ceased operationally in the summer of 1973 and was terminated officially in the fall of 1973.

As to the future, the Attorney General's direction is that we may not accept any requirement based on the names of U.S. citizens unless he has personally approved such a requirement; and no such approval has been given. Additionally, directives now in effect in various agencies, including NSA, also preclude the resumption of such activity.

INTELLIGENCE AND TECHNOLOGY ([45D], pp. 109–114)

Background

The material reprinted here is not explicitly addressed to NSA, but it touches on some of the technology employed by that agency. For security reasons, NSA restricts disclosure of the nature and application of the technology it utilizes.

The First Amendment right to free speech and the Fourth Amendment right to be secure in one's person, papers, and home have been violated in recent years. Although these rights have been abridged in time-honored ways, in some cases the abridgement has taken place in ways that could not have been foreseen by the framers of the Constitution and the Bill of Rights. A partial list of means employed follows:

Breaking and entering into offices and homes;
Opening of letters in the Postal System;
Bugging or use of hidden microphones with no party to the conversation witting;
Wiretap of telephone communications;
Intercept of telephone communications without actual connection to wires; and
Intercept of facsimile or printer communication.

Although files have existed for many years in all societies, and have sometimes been used to pernicious ends, technology has now made available to the managers of personal files greater speed and efficiency in the retrieval of data, as it has to managers of inventory files, of airline reservations, of the corpus of legal decisions, and of the United States House of Representatives Computer Based Bill Status System. In recent years, too, heightened public sensitivity and legislative activity have begun to introduce legislation, guidelines and standards regarding governmental and private files on individuals, granting the individual in many cases the right to know of the existence and the content of such a file, and to be able to challenge information which may be found in that file (Privacy Act of 1974, 5 U.S.C. 552A). Computer technology may not have been instrumental in the misuse of CIA or IRS files to provide information to the White House on U.S. citizens, but the future impact of such technology must be assessed.

It is a logical possibility that the modern technological tools employed in the exercise of other rights and freedoms for the general and individual good might inadvertently result in such general exposure that the First and Fourth Amendment rights could no longer be preserved, or that their preservation would require severe restriction of other rights and freedoms with major damage to society. For example, such might be the impact of (fanciful and unphysical) spectacles which, while restoring perfect vision to older people, endowed them as well with the ability to look through envelopes and walls.

A second logical possibility is that the general exercise of technology for individual good and the good of society does not in itself imperil the rights under discussion, but that specific targeting of this technology toward individuals can imperil these rights. In this case, the particular threat to these rights could of course be removed by outlawing the subject technology and enforcing such laws. It may be, however, that comparable protection of these rights may be obtainable by legal restrictions on the *use* of such technology, for such invasion, without denying society benefits which would otherwise be obtainable. If similar guarantee of rights may be achieved in this way, the banning of technology (even if politically feasible) would be an exaggerated remedy.

Finally, in some cases new technology may aid in restoring privacy against invasion by people or tools. An old example is the use of locks on doors; newer ones are the use of encryption for written communications and for the privacy of information in files. On the other hand, it would be inappropriate to require the individual to go to great cost to preserve his rights if such preservation could be obtained at lesser social cost. *e.g.* by restrictions of the actions of individuals who would intentionally violate these freedoms or whose activities might inadvertently imperil these rights. Thus, the expectation of privacy for the contents of a post card sent through the mails is quite different from that of a first-class letter in a sealed envelope, and the cost of an envelope is not regarded as an excessive charge for the guarantee of privacy. As the human senses and capabilities of vision, hearing, and memory are expanded by the use of new tools, what is the place for the analog of better envelopes?

Covert Observation and Intercept

Covert hearing (hidden microphones).—It has always been possible for a person to secrete himself, unbeknownst to the participants in a conversation, in such a way as to hear the conversation and so to violate an expectation of privacy ("eavesdropping"). No doubt mechanical aids in the form of tubes were used at times to make eavesdropping easier and less dangerous. Furthermore, rooms equipped with speaking tubes to convey orders to another part of a building were vulnerable to another kind of eavesdropping in which the use of the apparatus was other than that intended.

Microphones were in use in the 19th century for telephone communication and more recently for radio, public address, and recording. The present state of microphone technology is apparent to us all, with microphones a few millimeters across and a millimeter thick common in portable cassette recorders in use for business, education, and pleasure throughout the world. Over the last few years, the development of integrated-circuit technology and its extremely wide use in such recorders, in stereo equipment, and in calculators has provided not only the possibility but also the widespread capability to house amplifiers in a space of a few cubic millimeters and with power consumption of microwatts. Thus, microphones can be hidden in walls or moldings of rooms, in furnishings, or in personal possessions. They can be left behind by visitors or can be introduced as part of the normal resupply or refurbishment process.

Microphones can be accompanied by self-contained recorders or can transmit the signal (usually after amplification) either along near-invisible wires or by radio. In the case of wire or radio transmission, there would normally be a recorder or more powerful relay at some small distance of a few meters to a few hundred meters. The power requirements for microphones and amplifiers can be provided by batteries, by connection to the normal building power supply, from the telephone system, or by silicon or other cells converting sunlight or roomlight into electrical power. Microphones can also be provided with power by the absorption of radio or microwave signals, and can retransmit intelligence on the same carrier waves. In addition to dedicated wires or radio transmission, the microphone signal can also be transmitted on the building power line or on the telephone lines, if any. Under most circumstances, the ability with further advance of technology to make microphones still smaller would not be of great utility. They are already small enough to pose a near-maximum threat.

Not only are apparatus containing microphones available by the tens of millions throughout the world, but the components are also common articles of commerce and can be assembled by any one of millions of people. Many rooms are now permanently equipped (entirely overtly) with microphones for use in recording conferences or in picking up clearly comments made by an audience during question period. Such microphones could easily feed recorders, wires, or transmitters at other times as well. Furthermore, every loudspeaker, whether built-in or part of a portable electronic device, is capable of working as a microphone in just the same way. Individuals with impaired hearing have particularly small microphone-amplifiers, some of them concealed in the frames of eye glasses.

A slightly different kind of covert hearing is said to be possible by detecting with laser beams the vibration of ordinary windows enclosing a room in which the target conversation is taking place. Another approach to overhearing conversations outdoors is to use large directional microphones distant as much as one hundred meters.

Retarding the further development of microphone technology for commercial purposes would be of little help, even if it were feasible, given the already small size of microphones. It seems likely that privacy can be adequately protected against covert hearing in the United

States by proper legislation and enforcement requiring a warrant for the exercise of covert hearing capability. There being no expectation of privacy against a person present, legislation in the future, as now, should not restrict covert recording or retransmission by a person present, whether that person participates in the conversation or not. Of course, covert hearing capability can be banned administratively from designated premises, as it is now, by those in control of the premises—*e.g.*, "no microphones, radios, recorders, etc. at defense installations" (or on premises operated by the XYZ company).

Covert seeing (hidden cameras).—Hidden cameras (whether electronic or film) can imperil Fourth Amendment rights in analogous fashion to hidden microphones. Observation through a crack or peephole; personnel observation via a partially transparent overt mirror; large automatic or remote-control cameras or TV-type sensors behind an overt mirror; small cameras behind a small aperture—this series represents the application of technology to the goal of covert seeing. Vision comparable with that of a person can be obtained through a hole about 3 mm (⅛-inch) in diameter. A 1 mm hole would permit commercial TV-quality picture. Reading the text of papers on a desk across the room will require a larger aperture. Unlike microphones, such cameras are not yet common or cheap. A film camera taking a picture every 5 seconds would need a considerable film supply and would have to be quiet if covert; a TV camera capable of communicating even at such a rate, with human vision quality is feasible, but is at present costly. With time, the technology of fiber-optic signal communication will allow unobtrusive relay from a hidden camera. A command link could direct the view of the camera toward the interesting portion of the room, saving power and communications rate (as could built-in intelligence at a later time).

Clearly, the invasion by covert seeing of privacy would be intentional, not the result of innocent exercise of rights on the part of others. As such, preservation of such privacy can look toward legislation and the enforcement thereof, with such unconsented observation available only under warrant.

Wiretap of telephone lines.—Anywhere on the line running from the telephone instrument through the building to the junction box and on to the local exchange (typically a mile or so from the subscriber's instrument), connection to the line or proximity to that line will allow a high-quality telephone conversation to be provided for listening or recording. For many decades there has been no need for physical contact with the line to allow "wiretap," and no telltale click or change in quality is necessary or likely.

The technology needed for wiretap (whether by contact or noncontact) is primitive compared with that used for covert hearing. There is no way in which this technology can be outlawed without outlawing telephones themselves. However, in this field particularly, there is no necessity to abandon the protection of privacy. The intercept of communications from telephone lines may readily be controlled by legislation and by the requirement of a warrant for such actions by government bodies.[1a]

Intercept of voice from domestic microwave relay.—In the United States, most telephone calls beyond the local area are now transmitted via microwave relay. Towers about 20 miles apart contain receiving

---

[1a] Omnibus Safe Streets and Crime Control Act of 1968 (18 U.S.C. 2510–2520).

antennas, amplifiers, transmitters, and transmitting antennas. The microwave relay system operates near 4000 megahertz and 6000 megahertz. at wavelengths on the order of 6 centimeters.

The transmitted beam from each of these relay towers has an angular width on the order of one degree and so can be picked up well over a wedge some 20 miles long by a third of a mile wide. Leased-line services such as the federal government FTS system, WATS lines, and individual corporate "private-line" networks occupy permanent positions in the frequency spectrum in those relays which are used to carry the signals (not always by the most direct path) over the fixed network. Direct-distance-dialing calls, constituting the bulk of the traffic, cannot be so precisely located. In general, however, these DDD calls are preceded by digital information which serves to direct the call to the receiving telephone number and to indicate the calling telephone number as well.

At present, an individual with an instruction manual and a few thousand dollars worth of equipment can set up a makeshift antenna and listen or record continuously calls on any desired fixed-assigned channel. In principle, even the DDD calls could, at substantially larger investment, be matched with a list of "interesting" telephone numbers so as to record only those calls originating from or directed to a given subscriber number.

These voice messages, having traveled by wire at least some distance may be from the telephone instrument, legally afforded the same protection as calls carried on wire from sendor to receiver.[2] However, questions of extra-territoriality arise. There appears to be no way in which individuals on foreign embassy and consular properties can be forbidden from listening into those microwave links which pass their territories. It must be anticipated that certain powers will use such information not only for affairs of state, but also simply to earn funds by taking advantage of information which is obtained in this way. Communication in regard to commodity markets, stock exchanges, and bidding prices for large contracts all convey information which can have substantial value.

N8

Given this peculiar situation, one might judge that the threat to privacy from all but extra-territorial intercept is adequately controllable by a legislative ban on such intercept (and the requirement of warrants for government "search"), and that the rather limited exposure to personnel controlled by foreign powers and based outside the reach of U.S. law can be controlled by other means. Voice links carrying defense information are all encrypted. Other important information of the federal government can be rerouted to avoid some small number of possible listening posts. Direct-distance-dial calls eventually will be relayed with the destination and origination information going over separate channels. When all-digital transmission is used to carry voice, encryption can be available at negligible cost. It could be implemented with separate keys for each microwave link, or encryption could be done at the point of digitizing each signal, or both.

Intercept of non-voice from domestic microwave relay links.—Many channels on U.S. microwave relay are devoted to the transmission of non-voice information (facsimile machines, teletype, telex service, other printer traffic). The comments above regarding the intercept of

---

[2] 18 U.S.C. 2511.

voice communications from such microwave links apply with equal force to the intercept of non-voice communications. There is, however, a major difference. Existing law protects only communications from which intelligence can be "aurally acquired," [4] so there is at present no legal bar to the intercept of such non-voice communications.

At present, the value of the average non-voice communication relayed over the microwave net is probably greater than that of the average voice communication. Even if non-voice were protected by new legislation, it would still be subject to intercept from extraterritorial sites. Fortunately, the protection of non-voice data transmission by means of encryption is far easier than is the case for voice and is practical now over all telex and printer links. Several machines and electronic devices of varying effectiveness are available to provide end-to-end transmission security. The National Bureau of Standards has begun the promulgation of a national standard for data security via encryption, which apparently satisfies the concerns of the United States Government for maintaining the privacy of non-defense information.

Intercept of voice or non-voice from domestic communication satellite links.—About half the international common-carrier communications originating in the U.S. goes by satellite and half by submarine cable. A rapidly increasing fraction of purely domestic communications is now relayed by satellite. Present satellites may receive communications from any one of a number of ground stations and simply rebroadcast the signal at a different frequency, covering the continental United States with the microwave beam. For some communications with multiple addressees, this large potential receiving area is an advantage; for most communications with a single addressee, the particular ground station to which the message is addressed will recognize the digital address and record or retransmit the message into the local net (or print it and put it into an envelope for delivery, etc.).

Modern relay satellites are in stationary orbit, so that a fixed antenna can be used to receive signals, rather than the tracking antenna initially required for the lower-orbit satellites. Thus, anywhere in the large area illuminated by the satellite microwave beam, a relatively simple antenna and amplifier would allow intercept of messages relayed by satellite. The satellite transmits microwave energy not only onto the land mass of the U.S., but also onto adjacent waters and countries, including Cuba. Non-U.S. citizens on non-U.S. territory are completely free to receive satellite relay of domestic U.S. communications and to do with this information whatever they will.

Although some satellite relay is digital in nature and thus readily protected by encryption at negligible added cost, the voice communication is primarily analog (whereby the intelligence is carried by continuous amplitude or frequency modulation as is the common case for terrestrial multiplex relay). Encrypted voice communication would require a wider channel at present than is needed by analog voice, but the additional cost for privacy via encryption might be small even so, since the satellite resource is a small part of the end-to-end communications cost.

---

[4] 18 U.S.C. 2510(4).

Unfortunately, domestic satellite relay, as presently practiced, is an example of a case in which the indisputable benefits of technology bring with them a threat to privacy. In this case, it is not the application of technology to intercept but the technological nature of satellite transmission which makes intercept as easy outside U.S. territory as within, thus putting protection of privacy outside the reach of U.S. law. Technology in the form of encryption provides an adequate solution. This remedy is available now for non-voice communication and could be used with equal ease for digital voice. Aside from encryption, satellite voice communication could be provided some degree of protection in the near future by avoiding fixed-assignment schemes for users desiring privacy. . . .

NOTES AND REFERENCES

1. The 1959 PL 86-36, authorizing NSA's right to withhold information, is reprinted in [84A], p. 425.
2. See [125] on the availability of NSCIDs relating to foreign policy and national defense that have been released under the FOIA.
3. Refer to the testimony of comptroller general of the United States, Elmer Staats, in Chapter 10 concerning GAO's attempts to audit the activities of the intelligence community.
4. The assistant secretary of defense for intelligence, Albert Hall, testified before the House on the subject of DOD programming and budgeting for intelligence activities ([84A], pp. 176 ff). Additional information on the operations and budget of DOD agencies is found in Chapter 6.
5. Further discussion of the intelligence community's budget, including that of NSA, is provided in Chapters 4 and 6.
6. McGeorge Bundy, president of the Ford Foundation, served as special assistant for National Security to Presidents John F. Kennedy and Lyndon B. Johnson in 1961–1966. In May 1974, he testified on secrecy in government before the Subcommittee on Intergovernmental Relations (of the Senate Government Operations Committee) ([30], pp. 12 ff.). Further testimony by Bundy in January 1976, concerning NSA and CIA operations, appears in [25], pp. 144 ff.
7. The derivation of watch list activity is unclear. All such NSA activity was related to the filtering of information through intercept sources. The initial aim of the watch list was to investigate foreign influence on specific activities of particular significance to U.S. agencies and involving "presidential protection" and U.S. civil disorder. For reprinted correspondence between NSA and other intelligence agencies concerning watch list activity (referred to in this document's citation of exhibits 1–8), see [44E], pp. 145–162.
8. The Commission on CIA Activities Within the United States (Rockefeller Commission) considered the subject of foreign invasion into the privacy of Americans by foreign agents' monitoring telephonic communications in the United States. The commission concluded that Americans subject to such monitoring could be blackmailed or forced into recruitment as espionage agents. Note [124], pp. 7 ff.

Chapter 8
Federal Bureau of Investigation

THE FBI AS A COUNTERINTELLIGENCE AGENCY
([45A], pp. 170–177)

The Federal Bureau of Investigation was established in 1908. It is the main investigative branch of the Department of Justice and is responsible for gathering data, locating witnesses, and collecting evidence in affairs of particular interest to the federal government. The FBI is not a major contributor to the production of foreign intelligence, but its "counterintelligence" activities in the United States are significant and have generated considerable public criticism in the 1970s. Overseas, the bureau maintains agents working as "legal attaches" in U.S. embassies. These attaches operate in liaison with foreign officials on routine police matters, such as extradition and cooperation on investigations related to organized crime. Agents assigned abroad usually pass on intelligence items to CIA officers working within a particular embassy. The domestic intelligence activities of the FBI relating to foreign nationals, foreign policy, and the intelligence community are more complicated.

The primary responsibility of the FBI in national security affairs is the "investigation of espionage, treason, sabotage and other aspects of internal security."* This responsibility involves a "counterintelligence" function, part of which evolved over the years into the CO-INTELPRO effort (Counterintelligence Program), launched officially in 1956.† This was a domestic intelligence and covert action program aimed at investigating, exclusively, U.S. citizens whose "foreign" ties were usually nonexistent or, at most, were based upon ideological viewpoints shared with people in other countries. Among COINTELPRO activities was the harassment of the U.S. Socialist Workers' party; undermining of the stature of civil rights leader, Dr. Martin Luther King, Jr. (who was assassinated in 1968); and the effort to create division and discord among Vietnam War protest groups.

Revelations emerging from congressional and news media inquiries led to the cancellation of COINTELPRO in 1971. (Chapter 12 discusses abuses by the intelligence community concerning the rights of Americans.)

Chapter 8 is devoted to the intelligence activities of the FBI, specifically counterespionage and COINTELPRO, rather than focusing on the entire FBI functions. Included here is the Church Committee examination of the Counterintelligence Branch of the FBI's Intelligence Division (see FBI Intelligence Division chart in this chapter) in connection with the committee's study of counterintelligence generally. The COINTELPRO project is handled separately at the end of Chapter 8 through another Church Committee study, complemented by testimony to the Pike Committee by Attorney General William Saxbe and a statement by FBI Director Clarence Kelley. In conclusion, there is the testimony before the Pike Committee by Justice Department officials on the size and disposition of the FBI's budget for intelligence activities.

*Library of Congress, Congressional Research Service, Richard F. Grimmett, May 28, 1975, p. 5.

†Statement of Attorney General William Saxbe to House Judiciary Committee, Subcommittee on Civil Rights and Constitutional Rights, November 20, 1974, reprinted in this chapter.

The Counterintelligence Branch

FBI counterespionage activities within the United States are supervised by the Counterintelligence Branch of the FBI Intelligence Division. The Branch is made up of four Sections, three of which direct field operations conducted by the Bureau's field offices. The fourth handles liaison with other agencies and supervises the FBI's Legal Attaches assigned to serve in the embassies in several foreign countries.

The formal structure for counterespionage coordination between the FBI and the military intelligence agencies was established in 1939 and embodied most recently in a "charter" for the Interdepartmental Intelligence Conference in 1964.[27a] This formal body, chaired by the FBI Director and including the heads of the military intelligence agencies, has not played a significant decisionmaking role in recent years.

As late as 1974, some FBI officials took the position that the Bureau's counterespionage activities were not under the authority of the Attorney General, since the FBI was accountable in this area directly to the United States Intelligence Board and the National Security Council. A Justice Department committee chaired by Assistant Attorney General Henry Petersen sharply rejected this view and declared:

> There can be no doubt that in the area of foreign counterintelligence, as in all its other functions, the FBI is subject to the power and authority of the Attorney General.

In recent years the FBI has taken steps to upgrade its counterespionage effort, which had been neglected because of the higher priority given to domestic intelligence in the late 60s and early 70s. New career development and mid-career training programs have been instituted. FBI agents specializing in counterespionage begin their careers as criminal investigators and not as analysts; and Bureau officials stress that their role is accurate fact-finding, rather than evaluation. Nevertheless, counterespionage supervisory personnel have recently attended high-level training courses in foreign affairs and area studies outside the Bureau. . . .

The Scope and Basis of FBI Counterintelligence

In the imperfect contemporary world where other nations have interests which conflict with those of the United States, foreign-directed clandestine intelligence activities in this country must be of constant concern to the American people. One of the original reasons for the FBI's domestic intelligence mission was that the United States needed in the late 1930s a coordinated program for investigating "persons engaged in espionage, counter-espionage or sabotage." [34] By mid-1939 the FBI and military intelligence had gathered a "reservoir of information concerning foreign agencies operating in the United States" with efficient "channels for the exchange of information." [35] There is no question that during this prewar period, foreign espionage

---

[27a] Confidential memorandum from President Roosevelt to Department Heads, 6/26/39; memorandum from Attorney General Kennedy to J. Edgar Hoover, Chairman, Interdepartmental Intelligence Conference, 3/5/64.

[34] Memorandum from J. Edgar Hoover to Attorney General Murphy, 3/16/39.

[35] Letter from Attorney General Murphy to President Roosevelt, 6/17/39.

constituted a serious threat to the security of the United States and thus supported the basic decision to conduct investigations of activities which were "not within the specific provisions of prevailing statutes" [36] but which involved "potential" espionage, counterespionage, or sabotage.[37]

One of the major difficulties in any attempt to base investigations of foreign espionage on the criminal statutes has been, from the outset, the restricted and sometimes contradictory scope of the laws. A recent legal analysis has observed that "the legislation is in many ways incomprehensible." [38] Most notably, the espionage statutes do not make it a crime simply to engage in the knowing and unauthorized transfer of classified information to foreign agents.[39] Moreover, the statutes do not extend to a range of privately held information, especially on scientific and technical matters, which would be valuable to a foreign power.

Hostile foreign intelligence activities include more than just looking for classified information or espionage recruits. Information of a highly technical and strategic nature (though unclassified), which is normally restricted or unavailable in other societies, is openly procurable in the United States through academic institutions, trade associations, and government offices. Intelligence officers may seek out persons who have defected to the United States, to induce them to redefect back to their home country.[40] Foreign intelligence targets in this country may include information possessed by third nations and their representatives in the United States.

Moreover, the type of activity which is most easy to detect and which may indicate possible espionage does not always satisfy the normal standard of "reasonable suspicion." As a study prepared by the Fund for the Republic stated twenty years ago:

> The problems of crime detection in combatting espionage are not ordinary ones. Espionage is a crime which succeeds only by secrecy. Moreover, spies work not for themselves or privately organized crime "syndicates," but as agents of national states. Their activities are therefore likely to be carefully planned, highly organized, and carried on by techniques skillfully designed to prevent detection.[41]

Consequently, espionage investigations must be initiated on the basis of fragments of information, especially where there may be only an indication of a suspicious contact with a foreign agent and limited data as to the specific purposes of the contact.

In addition, prosecution is frequently not the objective of an espionage investigation. For one thing, the government may desire "to

---

[36] Memorandum from Hoover to Murphy, 3/16/39.

[37] Directive of President Roosevelt, 6/26/39. While the FBI's responsibilities were also described at times as extending to "subversion," and the lack of outside guidance allowed for overly broad FBI investigations, the problem of spying was always paramount. See the orders of President Roosevelt and Attorney General Biddle regarding warrantless wiretapping, discussed in report on warrantless FBI Electronic Surveillance.

[38] Harold Edgar and Benno C. Schmidt, "The Espionage Statutes and Publication of Defense Information," *Columbia Law Review*, Vol. 53, (May, 1973) pp. 929, 934.

[39] Ibid., p. 1084.

[40] FBI Memorandum, "Intelligence Activities Within the United States by Foreign Governments," 3/20/75.

[41] Fund for the Republic, *Digest of the Public Record of Communism in the United States* (New York, 1955), p. 29.

avoid exposing its own counterespionage practices and information." [42] In addition, the purpose of the investigation may be to find out what a known foreign agent is looking for, both as an indication of the espionage interest of the foreign country and as a means of insuring that the agent is not on the track of vital information. Since foreign agents are replaceable, it may be a better defense not to expel them from the country or otherwise halt their activities, but rather to maintain a constant watch on their operations. This also means investigating in a more limited fashion many of the Americans with whom the foreign agent associates, in order to determine what the agent may be interested in learning from them.

In the 1930s and 1940s, another argument for going beyond the criminal statutes was that there were significant ideological and nationality factors which motivated persons to engage in espionage. As Attorney General Jackson put it in 1940, individuals were a "likely source" of law violation because they were "sympathetic with the systems or designs of foreign dictators." [43] The 1946 Report of the Canadian Royal Commission made similar findings. This was the most persuasive rationale for continuing FBI intelligence investigations of Communists and Fascists, as well as German and other nationality groups, before World War II. It continued to be a substantial basis for such investigations of Communists after the war.[44]

By the mid-fifties, however, the characteristics of foreign espionage had changed substantially. The decline of the Communist Party caused a shrinkage in possible recruits, with the result that Soviet intelligence reverted "more and more . . . to the old type of conventional spy." [45] A report prepared by the Association of the Bar of the City of New York observed that it was "vital" to adjust the government's security programs to "new conditions," one of which was the "decline of the appeal of Communism." The report added:

> In the 1930s and 1940s the Soviet Union could rely on the support of a small but substantial group in this country who were sympathetic with its asserted aims. Now this has largely changed. . . . This has made a radical change in the type and number of persons who might be lured into Communist espionage.[46]

The FBI itself believed that the Community Party had become a "potential" rather than an actual espionage danger.[47] While that

---

[42] *Ibid.*

[43] Proceedings of the Federal-State Conference on Law Enforcement Problems of National Defense, 8/5–6/40.

[44] "A characteristic of most of the cases in which espionage for the Soviet Union has been prosecuted is that the participants seem to have been motivated by ideology. . . ." Fund for the Republic, Digest of the Public Record of Communism in the United States, p. 29.

[45] Alexander Dallin, *Soviet Espionage* (New Haven: Yale University Press, 1955), p. 510. This authoritative study of Communist espionage added that "the traditional type of nonpolitical spy has advantages over a Communist: his past evokes no suspicion."

[46] Report of the Special Committee on the Federal Loyalty-Security Program of the Association of the Bar of the City of New York (New York: Dodd, Mead & Co., 1956), pp. 35–36.

[47] FBI Monograph, "The Communist Menace in the United States Today," (1955), p. (iv–v.)

potential threat was still significant, in view of the Party's subservience to the Soviet Union, the counterespionage justification for sweeping investigations of persons one or two steps removed from the Party (e.g., "sympathizers" or "infiltrated" groups) lost much of its force.

Nevertheless, there continue to be hostile foreign intelligence activities which the FBI characterizes as "efforts to penetrate the American political system" or attempts "to develop an agent of influence in American politics" or efforts "to influence the U.S. policy-making structure." [48]

Therefore, the monitoring of contacts between U.S. government officials and foreign officials who are likely to be carrying out the directions of a hostile foreign intelligence service is a necessary part of the FBI's investigative duties. The subject of investigation is the foreign official, and any inquiry directed towards the American official can be limited to determining the nature of the foreign official's interests. Frequently it is desirable that the American official be informed by the Bureau, especially when the contact is overt rather than furtive or clandestine. (The same is also true with respect to overt contacts with American private citizens.) [49]

There are two areas of special difficulty in prescribing the FBI's proper responsibility. The first involves contacts between Members of Congress or high-level executive officials and equally high-level foreign officials. There have been instances where the FBI has had reason to believe that such contacts might involve the unauthorized disclosure of confidential information to a foreign government. Except in such rare circumstances, however, contacts of this nature need not be the subject of FBI investigation or dissemination. [50]

The second difficulty involves the concept "foreign subversion," used most recently in President Ford's Executive Order defining the counterintelligence duties of the U.S. intelligence community, including the FBI. [51] As noted above, the Bureau characterizes certain hostile foreign intelligence activities as attempts to develop "agents of influence in American politics." The FBI considered one of Dr. Martin Luther King's advisors to be such an "agent of influence." In this case, as with the massive investigations to uncover possible foreign "influence" on domestic protest activities, the concern for "foreign subversion" was distorted so far beyond reasonable definition that the term "subversion" should be abandoned completely. Even with the qualifier "foreign," the concept is so elastic as to be susceptible to future misuse.

Nevertheless, there remains a compelling need to investigate *all* the activities of hostile foreign intelligence services, including their efforts to recruit "agents of influence." This can be accomplished by continuing investigation of the foreign agents themselves. Where a foreign

---

[48] FBI Memorandum, "Intelligence Activities Within the United States by Foreign Governments," 3/20/75.

[49] Contacts made secretly or with the apparent intent to avoid detection justify more extensive investigation.

[50] Where the FBI discovers such contacts as a by-product of its investigations for other purposes, they can be noted without reference to the identity of the U.S. official in order to compile a quantitative measure of foreign activity.

[51] Executive Order 11905, "United States Foreign Intelligence Activities," Sec. 2(a)(2); Sec. 4(b)(4); Sec. 4(g)(1), 2/18/76.

agent makes an overt contact with an American, a limited inquiry regarding the American is appropriate to determine the nature of the foreign agent's interests. This applies whether the agent's interest is information or "influence," and the Bureau can frequently make its inquiry known to the American. But the Bureau's objectives should be confined solely to learning more about the overall mission of the hostile service and the particular assignments of its officers, as opposed to investigating "influence" by foreign officials or agents who do not have intelligence duties and the lawful activities of Americans who are not foreign agents. There is no compelling reason for intensive investigations of U.S. officials (or private citizens) simply because they are targets of foreign "influence." The line must be tightly drawn so that FBI counter-intelligence investigations do not themselves once again intrude into the American political process, with consequences damaging not only to the rights of Americans, but also to public confidence in the Bureau. Citizen cooperation with the FBI is essential to its success in detecting and countering the threat of hostile foreign intelligence operations to the defense of the nation.

To achieve this end, the federal criminal statutes dealing with espionage should be substantially revised to take account of the contemporary counterintelligence responsibilities of the FBI. A realistic definition of foreign-directed clandestine intelligence activity would make it possible for the FBI to base its counterintelligence investigations on the firm foundation of the criminal law, rather than the shifting interpretations of terms like "subversion" in executive orders. The Committee agrees with Attorney General Edward H. Levi that:

> the fact that the FBI has criminal investigative responsibilities, which must be conducted within the confines of constitutional protections strictly enforced by the courts, gives the organization an awareness of the interests of individual liberties that might be missing in an agency devoted solely to intelligence work.[52]

U.S. Counterintelligence Activities ([45A], pp. 163–173)

1. Definition of Counterintelligence

Counterintelligence (CI) is a special form of intelligence activity, separate and distinct from other disciplines. Its purpose is to discover hostile foreign intelligence operations and destroy their effectiveness. This objective involves the protection of the United State Government against infiltration by foreign agents, as well as the control and manipulation of adversary intelligence operations. An effort is made to both discern and decive the plans and intentions of enemy intelligence services. Defined more formally, counterintelligence is an intelligence activity dedicated to undermining the effectiveness of hostile intelligence services. Its purpose is to guard the nation againt espionage, other modern forms of spying, and sabotage directed against the United States, its citizens, information, and installations, at home and abroad, by infiltrating groups engaged in these practices and by

---

[52] Levi testimony, 12/10/75, Hearings, Vol. 6, pp. 314–315.

gathering, storing, and analyzing information on inimical clandestine activity.[1]

In short, counterintelligence specialists wage nothing less than a secret war against antagonistic intelligence services. "In the absence of an effective U.S. counterintelligence program," notes a counterintelligence specialist, "[adversaries of democracy] function in what is largely a benign environment." [2]

2. The Threat

The adversaries of democracy are numerous and widespread. In the United States alone, 1,079 Soviet officials were on permanent assignment in February 1975, according to FBI figures.[3] Among these, over 40 percent have been positively identified as members of the KGB or GRU, the Soviet civilian and military intelligence units. Conservative estimates for the number of unidentified intelligence officers raise the figures to over 60 percent of the Soviet representation; some defector sources have estimated that 70 percent to 80 percent of Soviet officials have some intelligence connection.[4]

Furthermore, the number of Soviets in the United States has triplea since 1960, and is still increasing.[5] The opening of American deep-water ports to Russian ships in 1972 has given Soviet intelligence services "virtually complete geographic access to the United States," observes a counterintelligence specialist.[6] In 1974, for example, over 200 Soviet ships with a total crew complement of 13,000 officers and men called at 40 deep-water ports in this country.

Various exchange groups provide additional opportunities for Soviet intelligence gathering within the United States. Some 4,000 Soviets entered the United States as commercial or exchange visitors in 1974. During the past decade, the FBI identified over 100 intelligence officers among the approximately 400 Soviet students who attended American universities during this period as part of an East-West student exchange program.[7] Also, in the 14-year history of this program, more than 100 American students were the target of Soviet recruitment approaches in the USSR.

Other areas of counterintelligence concern include the sharp increase in the number of Soviet immigrants to the United States (less than 500 in 1972 compared to 4,000 in 1974) ; the rise in East-West commercial exchange visitors (from 641 in 1972 to 1,500 in 1974) ; and the growing number of Soviet bloc officials in this country (from 416 in 1960 to 798 in 1975).[8]

Foreign intelligence agents have attempted to recruit not only executive branch personnel, but also Congressional staff members. The FBI has advised the Committee that there have been instances in the past where hostile foreign intelligence officers have used the opportunity

---

[1] Counterintelligence may also be thought of as the knowledge needed for the protection and preservation of the military, economic, and productive strength of the United States, including the security of the Government in domestic and foreign affairs against or from espionage, sabotage, and all other similar clandestine activities designed to weaken or destroy the United States. (Report of the Commission on Government Security Washington, D.C., 1957, pp. 48–49.)

[2] Staff summary of interview, FBI counterintelligence specialist, 5/8/75.

[3] Staff summary of interview, FBI counterintelligence specialist. 3/10/75.

[4] FBI counterintelligence specialist (staff summary), 3/10/75.

[5] FBI counterintelligence specialist (staff summary), 5/8/75.

[6] Ibid.

[7] Ibid, 3/10/75.

[8] Ibid.

presented by overt contacts to attempt to recruit members of Congressional staffs who might have access to secret information.[8a]

The most serious threat is from "illegal" agents who have no easily detectable contacts with their intelligence service. The problem of "illegals" is summarized by the FBI as follows:

> The illegal is a highly trained specialist in espionage tradecraft. He may be a [foreign] national and/or a professional intelligence officer dispatched to the United States under a false identity. Some illegals [may be] trained in the scientific and technical field to permit easy access to sensitive areas of employment.
>
> The detection of . . . illegals presents a most serious problem to the FBI. Once they enter the United States with either fraudulent or true documentation, their presence is obscured among the thousands of legitimate emigres entering the United States annually. Relatively undetected, they are able to maintain contact with [the foreign control] by means of secret writing, microdots, and open signals in conventional communications which are not susceptible to discovery through conventional investigative measures.[8b]

In several instances the FBI accomplished this most difficult assignment by carefully designed and limited mail opening programs which, if they had ben authorized by a judicial warrant, might have been entirely proper. It is most unfortunate that the FBI did not choose to seek lawful authorization for such methods.[8c]

This brief summary of the threat facing the American counterintelligence corps in this country is troubling enough, yet it does not take into account the worldwide scope of the problem. As an FBI counterintelligence expert states, hostile foreign intelligence services

> are alert for operational opportunities against the United States whether they occur within this country, abroad (in other countries) or in the home country itself. An operation might begin in the home country with recruitment of an American visitor; transfer to the United States with his return; and again, even later, might be transferred to a third country where the American agent may be met outside the normal reach of United States counterintelligence coverage. Regardless of the geographical location, the operation is still directed against the United States and can cause just as much damage from abroad as within our own borders.[9]

The espionage activities of the Soviet Union and other communist nations directed against the United States are extensive and relentless.[9a]

[8a] FBI Memorandum for the Record, 10/30/75. Such recruitment approaches have been reported to the FBI by Congressional staff members. If the FBI otherwise learns of such recruitments, its policy is to report the facts to the appropriate Members of Congress.

[8b] FBI memorandum, "Intelligence Activities Within the United States by Foreign Governments," 3/20/75.

[8c] Testimony of W. R. Wannall, Assistant Director, FBI, 10/21/75, p. 5; see Report on CIA and FBI Mail Opening.

[9] FBI Counterintelligence specialist (staff summary), 3/10/75.

[9a] See Appendix III, Soviet Intelligence Collection and Operations Against the United States.

To combat this threat, American counterintelligence officers have developed various sophisticated investigative techniques to (1) obtain information about foreign intelligence services, (2) protect our intelligence service, and (3) control the outcome of this subterranean struggle for intelligence supremacy. The task is difficult technically, and raises sensitive legal and ethical questions. As the CIA Deputy Director for Operations has testified, the

> U.S. counterintelligence program to be both effective and in line with traditional American freedoms must steer a middle course between blanket, illegal, frivolous and unsubstantiated inquiries into the private lives of U.S. citizens and excessive restrictions which will render the Government's counterintelligence arms impotent to protect the nation from foreign penetration and covert manipulation.[10]

3. CI as Product: Information about "The Enemy"

Counterintelligence is both an activity and its product. The product is reliable information about all the hostile foreign intelligence services who attack the United States by stealth. To guard against hostile intelligence operations aimed at this nation, a vast amount of information is required. It is necessary to know the organizational structure of the enemy service, the key personnel, the methods of recruitment and training, and the specific operations.

This information must be gathered within the United States and in all the foreign areas to which U.S. interests extend. Within the intelligence service, this acquisitive activity is referred to as intelligence collection. The resulting product—pertinent information on the enemy intelligence service—is often called "raw" intelligence data. The efforts of intelligence services through the world to conceal such information from one another, through various security devices and elaborate deceptions, creates the counterintelligence specialist what James Angleton, former Chief of CIA Counterintelligence, calls a kind of "wilderness of mirrors."

4. CI as Activity: Security and Counterespionage

As an activity, CI consists of two matching halves: security and counterespionage. *Security* is the passive or defensive, side of counterintelligence. It consists basically of establishing static defenses against all hostile and concealed acts, regardless of who carries them out.

Counterespionage (CE) is the offensive, or aggressive, side of counterintelligence. It involves the identification of a specific adversary and a knowledge of the specific operation he is conducting. Counterespionage personnel must then attempt to counter these operations by infiltrating the hostile service (called penetration) and through various forms of manipulation. Ideally, the thrust of the hostile operation is turned back against the enemy.

The security side of counterintelligence includes the screening and clearance of personnel and the development of programs to safeguard sensitive intelligence information (that is, the proper administration of security controls). The intelligence services try to defend three things: (1) their personnel, (2) their installations, and (3) their operations.

At the Central Intelligence Agency, the Office of Security is responsible for protection of personnel and installations, while actual oper-

---

[10] William Nelson testimony, 1/28/76, p. 5.

ations are largely the preserve of the CI staff and the operating divisions. Among the defensive devices used for *information control* by intelligence agencies throughout the world are: security clearances, polygraphs, locking containers, security education, document accountability, censorship, camouflage, and codes. Devices for *physical security* include fences, lighting, general systems, alarms, badges and passes, and watchdogs. *Area control* relies on curfews, checkpoints, restricted areas, and border-frontier control.[12] Thus the security side of counterintelligence "is all that concerns perimeter defense, badges, knowing everything you have to know about your own people;" the counterespionage side "involves knowing all about intelligence services—foreign intelligence services—their people, their installations, their methods, and their operations. So that you have a completely different level of interest."[13] However, the Office of Security and the CI staff exchange information to assure adequate security systems.

5. The Penetration and the Double Agent

Several kinds of operations exist within the rubric of counterespionage. One, however, transcends all the others in importance: the penetration. A primary goal of counterintelligence is to contain the intelligence service of the enemy. To do so, it is eminently desirable to know his plans in advance and in detail. This admirable, but difficult, objective may be achieved through a high-level infiltration of the opposition service. As a Director of the CIA has written, "Experience has shown penetration to be the most effective response to Soviet and Bloc [intelligence] services."[14]

Moreover, a well-placed infiltrator in a hostile intelligence service may be better able than anyone else to determine whether one's own service has been penetrated. A former Director of the Defense Intelligence Agency (DIA) has observed that the three principal programs used by the United States to meet, neutralize, and defeat hostile intelligence penetrations are: (1) our own penetrations; (2) security screening and clearance of personnel; and (3) our efforts for safeguarding sensitive intelligence information.[15] The importance of the penetration is emphasized by an experienced CIA counterespionage operative, with mixed but expressive similes: "Conducting counterespionage with penetration can be like shooting fish in a barrel;" in contrast, "conducting counterespionage without the act of penetration is like fighting in the dark."[16]

Methods of infiltrating the opposition service take several forms. Usually the most effective and desirable penetration is the recruitment of an agent-in-place.[17] He is a citizen of an enemy nation and is already in the employ of its intelligence service. Ideally, he will be both highly placed and venal. The individual, say a KGB officer in Bonn, is approached and asked to work for the intelligence service of the United States. Various inducements—including ideology—may be used to recruit him against his own service. If the

---

[12] Staff summary of interview, CIA security specialist, 8/20/75.
[13] Raymond Rocca deposition, 11/25/75, p. 19.
[14] Memorandum from John McCone to Chairman, President's Foreign Intelligence Advisory Board, 10/8/63.
[15] The Carroll Report on the Dunlap Case, 2/12/64.
[16] CIA/CI specialist, staff summary, 11/1/75.
[17] CIA/CI specialist, staff summary, 10/17/75.

recruitment is successful, the operation may be especially worthwhile since the agent is presumably already trusted within his organization and his access to documents may be unquestioned. Jack E. Dunlap, who worked at and spied on the National Security Agency (NSA) in the 1960s, is a well-known example of a Soviet agent-in-place within the U.S. intelligence service. His handler was a Soviet Air Force attaché at the Soviet Embassy in Washington. Of course, a single penetration can be worth an intelligence gold mine, as were Kim Philby for the Soviet Union and Col. Oleg Penkovsky for the United States.

Another method of infiltration is the double agent. Double agents, however, are costly and time-consuming, and they are risky. Human lives are at stake. Double agents also normally involve pure drudgery, with few dramatic results, as new information is checked against existing files. On top of this comes the difficulty of assuring against a doublecross.

Moreover, passing credible documents can be a major problem. The operations must be made interesting to the opposition. To make fake papers plausible, the genuine article must be provided now and again. Classified documents must be cleared, and this process can be painstakingly slow. Also, "this means letting a lot of good stuff go to the enemy without much in return," complains a CI officer with considerable experience.[18]

To accomplish each of these tasks, hard work, careful planning, and considerable manpower are necessary. The extraordinary manpower requirements of the double agent operation restricted the abilities of the British to run cases during the Second World War—approximately 150 double agents for the entire period of the war and no more than about 25 at any one time.[19] Moreover, their mission was eased greatly by the ability of the British to read the German cipher throughout most of the conflict.

6. The Defector

Almost as good as the agent-in-place and less troublesome than the whole range of double agents is the "defector with knowledge." Here the procedure consists of interrogation and validation of bona fides, as usual, but without the worrisome, ongoing requirements for a skillful mix of false and genuine documents and other logistical support. Though an agent-in-place is preferable because of the continuing useful information he can provide, often a man does not want to risk his life by staying in-place, especially where the security is sophisticated; his preference is to defect to safety. In other words, agents-in-place are harder to come by in systems like the Soviet bloc countries; defection is more likely.[20] In contrast, agents-in-place are more easily recruited in so-called Third World areas.

Within the United States, the interrogation of intelligence service defectors who have defected in the U.S. is primarily the responsibility of the FBI, though the CIA may have a follow-up session with the individual. Sometimes the bona fides of a defector remain disputed for many years.

---

[18] Rocca deposition, 11/25/75, pp. 33–34.
[19] Sir John Masterman, *Double Cross System of the War of 1939–45* (New Haven: Yale University Press, 1972).
[20] Bruce Solie, deposition, 11/25/75, pp. 26–27.

CIA-recruited defectors abroad are occasionally brought to the United States and resettled. The FBI is notified and, after the CIA completes its interrogation, FBI may interrogate. CIA does not bring all defectors to the United States; only those expected to make a significant contribution. CIA generally handles resettlement not only of defectors from abroad, but also (at the request of the FBI) of defectors in the United States.

7. The Deception

The penetration or double agent is closely related to another important CE technique: the deception. Simply stated, the deception is an attempt to give the enemy a false impression about something, causing him to take action contrary to his own interests. Fooling the Germans into the belief that D Day landings were to be in the Pas de Calais rather than in Normandy is a classic example of a successful deception operation in World War II.[21]

Deception is related to penetration because our agents operating within foreign intelligence agencies can serve as excellent channels through which misleading information can flow to the enemy. So double agents serve both as collectors of positive intelligence and channels for deception. However, there are opportunities for deception other than our own agents; in fact, "an infinite variety" exists, according to an experienced practitioner.[23] One example: the U.S. can allow penetration of its own intelligence service, and then feed false information through him.

8. Other CI Techniques

Other counterespionage operations include surreptitious surveillance of various kinds (for instance, audio, mail, physical, and "optical"—that is, photography), interrogation (sometimes incommunicado as in the case of one defector), and provocation. Decoding clandestine radio transmission and letters with messages written in secret ink between the visible lines is part and parcel of the CE trade, as is trailing suspected agents, observing "dead drops" (the exchange of material, like documents or instructions, between a spy and his handler), and photographing individuals entering opposition embassies or at other locations. At the recent funeral of CIA agent Richard Welch, two Eastern European diplomats were discovered among the press corps snapping photographs of CIA intelligence officers attending the burial ceremony.[24] Since the focus of offensive counterintelligence is disruption of the enemy service, provocation can be an important element of CE, too. It amounts, in essence, to harassment of the opposition, such as publishing the names of his agents or sending a defector into his midst who is in reality a double agent.

9. CI as Organization

Security at CIA is the responsibility of the Office of Security, a division of the Deputy Director for Administration. Counterespionage policy is guided by the Counterintelligence Staff of the Operations Directorate (Clandestine Service). Besides setting policy, the CI Staff

[21] Masterman, Double Cross System.
[23] CIA counterintelligence specialist (staff summary), 11/1/75.
[24] CIA counterintelligence specialist (staff summary), 1/15/76.

sometimes conducts its own operations, though most CI operations emanate directly from the various geographic divisions as the CI field personnel—through the practice of the counterintelligence discipline—attempt to guard against enemy manipulation of espionage and covert action operations.

Structurally, counterintelligence services are usually composed of two additional sections which support Security and Operations. They are the Research and the Liaison sections. Good research is critical to a good counterintelligence effort, and it may take several forms. It can involve the amassing of encyclopedic intelligence on individuals, including American citizens associated—wittingly or unwitttingly—with hostile intelligence services. Specialists say that the hallmark of a sophisticated CI service is its collection of accurate records.[25] CI research personnel also produce reports on topics of interest to the specialty, including guidelines for the interrogation of defectors and current analyses on such subjects as proprietary companies used by foreign intelligence services and the structure of Soviet bloc intelligence services. CI researchers also analyze defector briefs and, in the case of compromised documents, help ascertain who had access and what damage was inflicted.

Liaison with other counterintelligence services, at home and abroad, is also vital since no effective counterintelligence organization can do its job alone. The various CI units at home are particularly important, as counterintelligence—with all its intricacies and deceptions—requires coordination among agencies and sharing of records. Unlike the totally unified KGB organization, the American intelligence service is fragmented and depends upon liaison to make operations more effective. Coordination between CIA and FBI counterintelligence units is especially critical since, in theory at least, the former has foreign jurisdiction and the latter domestic, yet they must monitor the movements of foreign spies in and out of these two jurisdictions. Sometimes this coordination fails dramatically. In 1970, for example, J. Edgar Hoover of the FBI terminated formal liaison with the CIA and all the other intelligence units in the Government because of a disagreement with the CIA on a question of source disclosure (the Thomas Riha case).[26]

Liaison with foreign intelligence services overseas can undergo strain, too. As one CI specialist has said: "There are no friendly services; there are services of friendly foreign powers." [27] Each service fears the other has been infiltrated by hostile agents and is reluctant to see national secrets go outside its own vaults. Nonetheless, cooperation does take place, since all intelligence services seek information and, with precautions, will take it where they can get it if it is useful.

The CIA will work with friendly services to uncover hostile intelligence operations, including illegals, directed at the government of the friendly service. For example, a CIA-recruited defector may reveal Soviet agents in a friendly foreign government. This information is shared with the friendly government, if there is proper protection of the source. Protection of the CIA source is paramount. . . .

In 1966 an informal agreement was negotiated between the FBI and the CIA to regularize their "coordination." This agreement had as its

---

[25] 6/27/75.

[25] *Ibid.* 6/27/75.

[26] Staff summary of interview, former FBI liaison person with CIA, 8/22/75.

[27] Rocca deposition, 11/25/75, p. 43.

"heart" that the CIA would "seek concurrence and coordination of the FBI" before engaging in clandestine activity in the United States, and that the FBI would "concur and coordinate if the proposed action does not conflict with any operation, current or planned, including active investigation [by] the FBI." Moreover, when an agent recruited by the CIA abroad arrived in the United States, the FBI would "be advised" and the two agencies would "confer regarding the handling of the agent in the United States." The CIA could "continue" its "handling" of the agent for "foreign intelligence" purposes; and the FBI would also become involved where there were "internal security factors," although it was recognized that CIA might continue to "handle" the agent in the United States and provide the Bureau with "information" bearing on "internal security matters." [30a]

Eventually, the much heralded (though actually minor) Riha incident in 1970 became "the straw that broke the camel's back." [31] Hoover ordered the discontinuation of FBI liaison with the Central Intelligence Agency. Though informal means of communication continued between CIA and FBI staff personnel, Hoover's decision was a setback to the coordination of counterintelligence activities in the Government. Not until Hoover was gone from the Bureau did formal liaison relations begin to improve. [32]

Today, most counterintelligence officers in both agencies say that coordination and communication linkages are good, though a recently retired CIA/CI officer points to "a vital need for closer integration of the CI efforts of the CIA and the FBI." [33] The most salient criticisms of FBI counterintelligence voiced at the CIA concern (1) the lack of sufficient CI manpower in the FBI; (2) occasional disputes over the bona fides of defectors: and, (3) differences of opinion on the possibility of hostile penetrations within the Government. Each of these matters also requires immediate review by the executive branch. In particular, the occasional interagency disputes over defector bona fides and differences of opinion on suspected hostile penetrations cry out for a higher level of authority in the executive branch to settle these sometimes divisive disagreements.

THE FBI, DOMESTIC INTELLIGENCE, AND COINTELPRO

The Church and Pike Committees explored the use and the abuse of the intelligence community for political purposes and its effect on the rights of U.S. citizens. The historical sketch reprinted here is followed, in the original document, by a more detailed exposition on the growth of domestic intelligence ([45B], pp. 23–136). Book II ([45B]) and Book III ([45C]), as well as Volume 6 ([44F]), are all Church Committee documents and focus on FBI abuses of citizens' rights. Part 3 of the Pike Committee hearings ([84C]) covers the same issues. See also Chapter 12 of this volume for further FBI domestic operations and pertinent findings and conclusions of the Church Committee. The material in this chapter is presented to elucidate the workings of the FBI's domestic intelligence program and does not include the FBI's accomplishments in this area. Those are best explored through the sources cited above and in the Bibliography at the end of this book.

[30a] Testimony of former FBI liaison person with CIA, 9/22/75, pp. 52–55.
[31] James Angleton testimony, 9/24/75, Hearings, pp. 657–58.
[32] Scott Miller testimony, the Commission on CIA Activities Within the United States, 3/19/75, p. 938.
[33] Statement from Scott Miler to the Senate Select Committee, 1/28/76, pp. 32–33.

The Growth of Domestic Intelligence: 1936 to 1976 ([45B], pp. 21–22)

1. The Lesson: History Repeats Itself

During and after the First World War, intelligence agencies, including the predecessor of the FBI, engaged in repressive activity.[1] A new Attorney General, Harlan Fiske Stone, sought to stop the investigation of "political or other opinions." [2] This restraint was embodied only in an executive pronouncement, however. No statutes were passed to prevent the kind of improper activity which had been exposed. Thereafter, as this narrative will show, the abuses returned in a new form. It is now the responsibility of all three branches of government to ensure that the pattern of abuse of domestic intelligence activity does not recur.

2. The Pattern: Broadening Through Time

Since the re-establishment of federal domestic intelligence programs in 1936, there has been a steady increase in the government's capability and willingness to pry into, and even disrupt, the political activities and personal lives of the people. The last forty years have witnessed a relentless expansion of domestic intelligence activity beyond investigation of criminal conduct toward the collection of political intelligence and the launching of secret offensive actions against Americans.

The initial incursions into the realm of ideas and associations were related to concerns about the influence of foreign totalitarian powers. Ultimately, however, intelligence activity was directed against domestic groups advocating change in America, particularly those who most vigorously opposed the Vietnam war or sought to improve the conditions of racial minorities. Similarly, the targets of intelligence investigations were broadened from groups perceived to be violence prone to include groups of ordinary protesters.

3. Three Periods of Growth for Domestic Intelligence

The expansion of domestic intelligence activity can usefully be divided into three broad periods: (a) the pre-war and World War II

---

[1] Repressive practices during World War I included the formation of a volunteer auxiliary force, known as the American Protective League, which assisted the Justice Department and military intelligence in the investigation of "un-American activities" and in the mass round-up of 50,000 persons to discover draft evaders. These so-called "slacker raids" of 1918 involved warrantless arrests without sufficient probable cause to believe that crime had been or was about to be committed (FBI Intelligence Division memorandum, "An Analysis of FBI Domestic Security Intelligence Investigations," 10/28/75.)

The American Protective League also contributed to the pressures which resulted in nearly 2,000 prosecutions for disloyal utterances and activities during World War I, a policy described by John Lord O'Brien, Attorney General Gregory's Special Assistant, as one of "wholesale repression and restraint of public opinion." (Zechariah Chafee, Free Speech in the United States (Cambridge: Harvard University Press, 1941) p. 69.)

Shortly after the war the Justice Department and the Bureau of Investigation jointly planned the notorious "Palmer Raids", named for Attorney General A. Mitchell Palmer who ordered the overnight round-up and detention of some 10,000 persons who were thought to be "anarchist" or "revolutionary" aliens subject to deportation. (William Preston, Aliens and Dissenters (Cambridge: Harvard University Press, 1963), chs. 7–8; Stanley Coben, A. Mitchell Palmer: Politician (New York: Columbia University Press, 1963), chs. 11–12.)

[2] See Attorney General Stone's full statement, p. 23.

period; (b) the Cold War era; and (c) the period of domestic dissent beginning in the mid-sixties. The main developments in each of these stages in the evolution of domestic intelligence may be summarized as follows:

a. 1936–1945

By presidential directive—rather than statute—the FBI and military intelligence agencies were authorized to conduct domestic intelligence investigations. These investigations included a vaguely defined mission to collect intelligence about "subversive activities" which were sometimes unrelated to law enforcement. Wartime exigencies encouraged the unregulated use of intrusive intelligence techniques; and the FBI began to resist supervision by the Attorney General.

b. 1946–1963

Cold War fears and dangers nurtured the domestic intelligence programs of the FBI and military, and they became permanent features of government. Congress deferred to the executive branch in the oversight of these programs. The FBI became increasingly isolated from effective outside control, even from the Attorneys General. The scope of investigations of "subversion" widened greatly. Under the cloak of secrecy, the FBI instituted its COINTELPRO operations to "disrupt" and "neutralize" "subversives". The National Security Agency, the FBI, and the CIA re-instituted instrusive wartime surveillance techniques in contravention of law.

c. 1964–1976

Intelligence techniques which previously had been concentrated upon foreign threats and domestic groups said to be under Communist influence were applied with increasing intensity to a wide range of domestic activity by American citizens. These techniques were utilized against peaceful civil rights and antiwar protest activity, and thereafter in reaction to civil unrest, often without regard for the consequences to American liberties. The intelligence agencies of the United States—sometimes abetted by public opinion and often in response to pressure from administration officials or the Congress—frequently disregarded the law in their conduct of massive surveillance and aggressive counterintelligence operations against American citizens. In the past few years, some of these activities were curtailed, partly in response to the moderation of the domestic crisis; but all too often improper programs were terminated only in response to exposure, the threat of exposure, or a change in the climate of public opinion, such as that triggered by the Watergate affair.

The Scope of Domestic Intelligence ([45B], pp. 6–20)

In its final report, the Church Committee provided a summary of the scope of domestic intelligence activities, derived from its hearings and staff investigations. The text of the summary is reprinted here in unabridged form. This Church report led to strong recommendations for control of all the intelligence agencies' domestic operations. Footnote references to "hearings" and "testimony" by date can be traced to the pertinent document by referring to the Bibliography under titles issued by the Senate Select Committee on Intelligence.

1. *The Number of People Affected by Domestic Intelligence Activity*

United States intelligence agencies have investigated a vast number of American citizens and domestic organizations. FBI headquarters alone has developed over 500,000 domestic intelligence files,[11] and these have been augmented by additional files at FBI Field Offices. The FBI opened 65,000 of these domestic intelligence files in 1972 alone.[12] In fact, substantially more individuals and groups are subject to intelligence scrutiny than the number of files would appear to indicate, since typically, each domestic intelligence file contains information on more than one individual or group, and this information is readily retrievable through the FBI General Name Index.

The number of Americans and domestic groups caught in the domestic intelligence net is further illustrated by the following statistics:

—Nearly a quarter of a million first class letters were opened and photographed in the United States by the CIA between 1953–1973, producing a CIA computerized index of nearly one and one-half million names.[13]

—At least 130,000 first class letters were opened and photographed by the FBI between 1940–1966 in eight U.S. cities.[14]

—Some 300,000 individuals were indexed in a CIA computer system and separate files were created on approximately 7,200 Americans and over 100 domestic groups during the course of CIA's Operation CHAOS (1967–1973).[15]

—Millions of private telegrams sent from, to, or through the United States were obtained by the National Security Agency from 1947 to 1975 under a secret arrangement with three United States telegraph companies.[16]

—An estimated 100,000 Americans were the subjects of United States Army intelligence files created between the mid-1960's and 1971.[17]

—Intelligence files on more than 11,000 individuals and groups were created by the Internal Revenue Service between 1969 and 1973 and tax investigations were started on the basis of political rather than tax criteria.[18]

—At least 26,000 individuals were at one point catalogued on an FBI list of persons to be rounded up in the event of a "national emergency".[19]

2. *Too Much Information Is Collected For Too Long*

Intelligence agencies have collected vast amounts of information about the intimate details of citizens' lives and about their participa-

---

[11] Memorandum from the FBI to the Senate Select Committee, 10/6/75.

[12] Memorandum from the FBI to the Senate Select Committee, 10/6/75.

[13] James Angleton testimony, 9/17/75, p. 28.

[14] See Mail Opening Report: Section IV, "FBI Mail Openings."

[15] Chief, International Terrorist Group testimony, Commission on CIA Activities Within the United States, 3/10/75, pp. 1485–1489.

[16] Statement by the Chairman, 11/6/75; re: SHAMROCK, Hearings, Vol. 5, pp. 57–60.

[17] See Military Surveillance Report: Section II, "The Collection of Information about the Political Activities of Private Citizens and Private Organizations."

[18] See IRS Report: Section II, "Selective Enforcement for Nontax Purposes."

[19] Memorandum from A. H. Belmont to L. V. Boardman, 12/8/54. Many of the memoranda cited in this report were actually written by FBI personnel other than those whose names were indicated at the foot of the document as the author. Citation in this report of specific memoranda by using the names of FBI personnel which so appear is for documentation purposes only and is not intended to presume authorship or even knowledge in all cases.

tion in legal and peaceful political activities. The targets of intelligence activity have included political adherents of the right and the left, ranging from activitist to casual supporters. Investigations have been directed against proponents of racial causes and women's rights, outspoken apostles of nonviolence and racial harmony; establishment politicians; religious groups; and advocates of new life styles. The widespread targeting of citizens and domestic groups, and the excessive scope of the collection of information, is illustrated by the following examples:

(a) The "Women's Liberation Movement" was infiltrated by informants who collected material about the movement's policies, leaders, and individual members. One report included the name of every woman who attended meetings,[20] and another stated that each woman at a meeting had described "how she felt oppressed, sexually or otherwise".[21] Another report concluded that the movement's purpose was to "free women from the humdrum existence of being only a wife and mother", but still recommended that the intelligence investigation should be continued.[22]

(b) A prominent civil rights leader and advisor to Dr. Martin Luther King, Jr., was investigated on the suspicion that he might be a Communist "sympathizer". The FBI field office concluded he was not.[23] Bureau headquarters directed that the investigation continue—using a theory of "guilty until proven innocent:"

> The Bureau does not agree with the expressed belief of the field office that _____[24] is not sympathetic to the Party cause. While there may not be any evidence that _____ is a Communist neither is there any substantial evidence that he is anti-Communist.[25]

(c) FBI sources reported on the formation of the Conservative American Christian Action Council in 1971.[26] In the 1950's, the Bureau collected information about the John Birch Society and passed it to the White House because of the Society's "scurrilous attack" on President Eisenhower and other high Government officials.[27]

(d) Some investigations of the lawful activities of peaceful groups have continued for decades. For example, the NAACP was investigated to determine whether it "had connections with" the Communist Party. The investigation lasted for over twenty-five years, although nothing was found to rebut a report during the first year of the investigation that the NAACP had a "strong tendency" to "steer clear of Communist activities."[28] Similarly, the FBI has admitted that the Socialist Workers Party has committed no criminal acts. Yet the Bureau has investigated the Socialist Workers Party for more than three decades on the basis of its revolutionary rhetoric—which the FBI concedes falls short of incitement to violence—and its claimed

---

[20] Memorandum from Kansas City Field Office to FBI Headquarters, 10/20/70. (Hearings, Vol. 6, Exhibit 54–3)

[21] Memorandum from New York Field Office to FBI Headquarters, 5/28/69, p. 2. (Hearings, Vol. 6, Exhibit 54–1)

[22] Memorandum from Baltimore Field Office to FBI Headquarters, 5/11/70, p. 2.

[23] Memorandum from New York Field Office to FBI Headquarters, 4/14/64.

[24] Name deleted by Committee to protect privacy.

[25] Memorandum from FBI Headquarters to New York Field Office 4/24/64, re CPUSA, Negro question.

[26] James Adams testimony, 12/2/75, Hearings, Vol. 6, p. 137.

[27] Memorandum from F. J. Baumgardner to William C. Sullivan, 5/29/63.

[28] Memorandum from Oklahoma City Field Office to FBI Headquarters, 9/19/41. See Development of FBI Domestic Intelligence Investigations: Section IV, "FBI Target Lists."

international links. The Bureau is currently using its informants to collect information about SWP members' political views, including those on "U.S. involvement in Angola," "food prices," "racial matters," the "Vietnam War," and about any of their efforts to support non-SWP candidates for political office.[29]

(e) National political leaders fell within the broad reach of intelligence investigations. For example, Army Intelligence maintained files on Senator Adlai Stevenson and Congressman Abner Mikva because of their participation in peaceful political meetings under surveillance by Army agents.[30] A letter to Richard Nixon, while he was a candidate for President in 1968, was intercepted under CIA's mail opening program.[31] In the 1960's President Johnson asked the FBI to compare various Senators' statements on Vietnam with the Communist Party line [32] and to conduct name checks on leading antiwar Senators.[33]

(f) As part of their effort to collect information which "related even remotely" to people or groups "active" in communities which had "the potential" for civil disorder, Army intelligence agencies took such steps as: sending agents to a Halloween party for elementary school children in Washington, D.C., because they suspected a local "dissident" might be present; monitoring protests of welfare mothers' organizations in Milwaukee; infiltrating a coalition of church youth groups in Colorado; and sending agents to a priests' conference in Washington, D.C., held to discuss birth control measures.[34]

(g) In the late 1960's and early 1970's, student groups were subjected to intense scrutiny. In 1970 the FBI ordered investigations of every member of the Students for a Democratic Society and of "every Black Student Union and similar group regardless of their past or present involvement in disorders." [35] Files were opened on thousands of young men and women so that, as the former head of FBI intelligence explained, the information could be used if they ever applied for a government job.[36]

In the 1960's Bureau agents were instructed to increase their efforts to discredit "New Left" student demonstrators by tactics including publishing photographs ("naturally the most obnoxious picture should be used"),[37] using "misinformation" to falsely notify members events had been cancelled,[38] and writing "tell-tale" letters to students' parents.[39]

(h) The FBI Intelligence Division commonly investigated any indication that "subversive" groups already under investigation were seeking to influence or control other groups.[40] One example of the ex-

---

[29] Chief Robert Shackleford testimony, 2/6/76, p. 91.
[30] Senate Judiciary Subcommittee on Constitutional Rights. Report. 1973, p. 57.
[31] Senate Select Committee Staff summary of HTLINGUAL File Review, 9/5/75.
[32] FBI Summary Memorandum, 1/31/75, re: Coverage of T.V. Presentation.
[33] Letter from J. Edgar Hoover to Marvin Watson, 7/15/66.
[34] See Military Report: Sec. II, "The Collection of Information About the Political Activities of Private Citizens and Private Organizations."
[35] Memorandum from FBI headquarters to all SAC's, 11/4/70.
[36] Charles Brennan testimony, 9/25/75, Hearings, vol. 2 p. 117.
[37] Memorandum from FBI Headquarters to all SAC's, 7/5/68.
[38] Abstracts of New Left Documents #161, 115, 43. Memorandum from Washington Field Office to FBI Headquarters, 1/21/69.
[39] Memorandum from FBI Headquarters to Cleveland Field Office, 11/29/68.
[40] FBI Manual of Instructions, Sec. 87, B(2-f).

treme breadth of this "infiltration" theory was an FBI instruction in the mid-1960's to all Field Offices to investigate every "free university" because some of them had come under "subversive influence." [41]

(i) Each administration from Franklin D. Roosevelt's to Richard Nixon's permitted, and sometimes encouraged, government agencies to handle essentially political intelligence. For example:

—President Roosevelt asked the FBI to put in its files the names of citizens sending telegrams to the White House opposing his "national defense" policy and supporting Col. Charles Lindbergh.[42]

—President Truman received inside information on a former Roosevelt aide's efforts to influence his appointments,[43] labor union negotiating plans,[44] and the publishing plans of journalists.[45]

—President Eisenhower received reports on purely political and social contacts with foreign officials by Bernard Baruch,[46] Mrs. Eleanor Roosevelt,[47] and Supreme Court Justice William O. Douglas.[47a]

—The Kennedy Administration had the FBI wiretap a Congressional staff member,[48] three executive officials,[49] a lobbyist,[50] and a Washington law firm.[51] Attorney General Robert F. Kennedy received the fruits of a FBI "tap" on Martin Luther King, Jr.,[52] and a "bug" on a Congressman both of which yielded information of a political N3 nature.[53]

—President Johnson asked the FBI to conduct "name checks" of his critics and of members of the staff of his 1964 opponent, Senator Barry Goldwater.[54] He also requested purely political intelligence on his critics in the Senate, and received extensive intelligence reports on political activity at the 1964 Democratic Convention from FBI electronic surveillance.[55]

—President Nixon authorized a program of wiretaps which produced for the White House purely political or personal information unrelated to national security, including information about a Supreme Court justice.[56]

The Abuse of Domestic Intelligence

(a) *Covert Action*.—Apart from uncovering excesses in the collection of intelligence, our investigation has disclosed covert actions directed against Americans, and the use of illegal and improper surveillance techniques to gather information. For example:

---

[41] Memorandum from FBI Headquarters to San Antonio Field Office, 7/23/69.
[42] Memorandum from Stephen Early to J. Edgar Hoover, 5/21/40; 6/17/40.
[43] Letter from J. Edgar Hoover to George Allen, 12/3/46.
[44] Letter from J. Edgar Hoover to Maj. Gen. Harry Vaughn, 2/15/47.
[45] Letter from J. Edgar Hoover to M. J. Connelly, 1/27/50.
[46] Letter from J. Edgar Hoover to Dillon Anderson, 11/7/55.
[47] Letter from J. Edgar Hoover to Robert Cutler, 2/13/58.
[47a] Letters from J. Edgar Hoover to Robert Cutler, 4/21/53–4/27/53.
[48] Memorandum from J. Edgar Hoover to the Attorney General. 2/16/61.
[49] Memorandum from J. Edgar Hoover to the Attorney General. 2/14/61.
[50] Memorandum from J. Edgar Hoover to the Attorney General, 2/16/61.
[51] Memorandum from J. Edgar Hoover to the Attorney General 6/26/62.
[52] Memorandum from Charles Brennan to William Sullivan, 12/19/66.
[53] Memorandum from J. Edgar Hoover to the Attorney General. 2/18/61.
[54] Memorandum from J. Edgar Hoover to Bill Moyers, 10/27/64.
[55] Memorandum from C. D. DeLoach to John Mohr, 8/29/64.
[56] Letter from J. Edgar Hoover to H.R. Haldeman, 6/25/70.

(i) The FBI's COINTELPRO—counterintelligence program—was designed to "disrupt" groups and "neutralize" individuals deemed to be threats to domestic security. The FBI resorted to counterintelligence tactics in part because its chief officials believed that the existing law could not control the activities of certain dissident groups, and that court decisions had tied the hands of the intelligence community. Whatever opinion one holds about the policies of the targeted groups, many of the tactics employed by the FBI were indisputably degrading to a free society. COINTELPRO tactics included:

N4

—Anonymously attacking the political beliefs of targets in order to induce their employers to fire them;

—Anonymously mailing letters to the spouses of intelligence targets for the purpose of destroying their marriages; [57]

—Obtaining from IRS the tax returns of a target and then attempting to provoke an IRS investigation for the express purpose of deterring a protest leader from attending the Democratic National Convention; [58]

—Falsely and anonymously labeling as Government informants members of groups known to be violent, thereby exposing the falsely labelled member to expulsion or physicial attack; [59]

—Pursuant to instructions to use "misinformation" to disrupt demonstrations, employing such means as broadcasting fake orders on the same citizens band radio frequency used by demonstration marshalls to attempt to control demonstrations,[60] and duplicating and falsely filling out forms soliciting housing for persons coming to a demonstration, thereby causing "long and useless journeys to locate these addresses"; [61]

—Sending an anonymous letter to the leader of a Chicago street gang (described as "violence-prone") stating that the Black Panthers were supposed to have "a hit out for you". The letter was suggested because it "may intensify . . . animosity" and cause the street gang leader to "take retaliatory action".[62]

(ii) From "late 1963" until his death in 1968, Martin Luther King, Jr., was the target of an intensive campaign by the Federal Bureau of Investigation to "neutralize" him as an effective civil rights leader. In the words of the man in charge of the FBI's "war" against Dr. King, "No holds were barred." [63]

The FBI gathered information about Dr. King's plans and activities through an extensive surveillance program, employing nearly every intelligence-gathering technique at the Bureau's disposal in order to obtain information about the "private activities of Dr. King and his advisors" to use to "completely discredit" them.[64]

---

[57] Memorandum from FBI Headquarters, to San Francisco Field Office, 11/26/68.

[58] Memorandum from [Midwest City] Field Office to FBI Headquarters, 8/1/68; memorandum from FBI Headquarters to [Midwest City] Field Office, 8/6/68.

[59] Memorandum from Columbia Field Office to FBI Headquarters, 11/4/70, re: COINTELPRO-New Left.

[60] Memorandum from Charles Brennan to William Sullivan, 8/15/68.

[61] Memorandum from Chicago Field Office to FBI Headquarters, 9/9/68.

[62] Memorandum from FBI Headquarters to Chicago Field Office, 1/30/69 re: COINTELPRO, Black Nationalist-Hate Groups.

[63] William C. Sullivan testimony, 11/1/75, p. 49.

[64] Memorandum from Baumgardner to Sullivan, 2/4/64.

The program to destroy Dr. King as the leader of the civil rights movement included efforts to discredit him with Executive branch officials, Congressional leaders, foreign heads of state, American ambassadors, churches, universities, and the press.[65]

The FBI mailed Dr. King a tape recording made from microphones hidden in his hotel rooms which one agent testified was an attempt to destroy Dr. King's marriage.[66] The tape recording was accompanied by a note which Dr. King and his advisors interpreted as threatening to release the tape recording unless Dr. King committed suicide.[67]

The extraordinary nature of the campaign to discredit Dr. King is evident from two documents:

—At the August 1963 March on Washington, Dr. King told the country of his "dream" that:

> all of God's children, black men and white men, Jews and Gentiles, Protestants and Catholics, will be able to join hands and sing in the words of the old Negro spiritual, "Free at last, free at last, thank God Almightly, I'm free at last."

The Bureau's Domestic Intelligence Division concluded that this "demagogic speech" established Dr. King as the "most dangerous and effective Negro leader in the country." [68] Shortly afterwards, and within days after Dr. King was named "Man of the Year" by *Time* magazine, the FBI decided to "take him off his pedestal," reduce him completely in influence," and select and promote its own candidate to "assume the role of the leadership of the Negro people." [69]

—In early 1968, Bureau headquarters explained to the field that Dr. King must be destroyed because he was seen as a potential "messiah" who could "unify and electrify" the "black nationalist movement". Indeed, to the FBI he was a potential threat because he might "abandon his supposed 'obedience' to white liberal doctrines (non-violence)." [70] In short, a non-violent man was to be secretly attacked and destroyed as insurance against his abandoning non-violence.

(b) *Illegal or Improper Means.*—The surveillance which we investigated was not only vastly excessive in breadth and a basis for degrading counterintelligence actions, but was also often conducted by illegal or improper means. For example:

> (1) For approximately 20 years the CIA carried out a program of indiscriminately opening citizens' first class mail. The Bureau also had a mail opening program, but cancelled it in 1966. The Bureau continued, however, to receive the illegal fruits of CIA's program. In 1970, the heads of both agencies signed a document for President Nixon, which correctly stated that mail opening was illegal, falsely stated that it had been discontinued, and proposed that the illegal open-

---

[65] Memorandum from Chicago Field Office to FBI Headquarters, 12/16/68; memorandum from FBI Headquarters to Chicago Field Office, 1/30/69, re: COINTELPRO, Black Nationalist-Hate Groups.
[66] William C. Sullivan, 11/1/75, pp. 104–105.
[67] Andrew Young testimony, 2/19/76. p. 8.
[68] Memorandum from Sullivan to Belmont, 8/30/63.
[69] Memorandum from Sullivan to Belmont, 1/8/64.
[70] Memorandum from FBI Headquarters to all SACs, 3/4/68.

ing of mail should be resumed because it would provide useful results. The President approved the program, but withdrew his approval five days later. The illegal opening continued nonetheless. Throughout this period CIA officials knew that mail opening was illegal, but expressed concern about the "flap potential" of exposure, not about the illegality of their activity.[71]

(2) From 1947 until May 1975, NSA received from international cable companies millions of cables which had been sent by American citizens in the reasonable expectation that they would be kept private.[72]

(3) Since the early 1930's, intelligence agencies have frequently wiretapped and bugged American citizens without the benefit of judicial warrant. Recent court decisions have curtailed the use of these techniques against domestic targets. But past subjects of these surveillances have included a United States Congressman, a Congressional staff member, journalists and newsmen, and numerous individuals and groups who engaged in no criminal activity and who posed no genuine threat to the national security, such as two White House domestic affairs advisers and an anti-Vietnam War protest group. While the prior written approval of the Attorney General has been required for all warrantless wiretaps since 1940, the record is replete with instances where this requirement was ignored and the Attorney General gave only after-the-fact authorization.

Until 1965, microphone surveillance by intelligence agencies was wholly unregulated in certain classes of cases. Within weeks after a 1954 Supreme Court decision denouncing the FBI's installation of a microphone in a defendant's bedroom, the Attorney General informed the Bureau that he did not believe the decision applied to national security cases and permitted the FBI to continue to install microphones subject only to its own "intelligent restraint".[73]

(4) In several cases, purely political information (such as the reaction of Congress to an Administration's legislative proposal) and purely personal information (such as coverage of the extra-marital social activities of a high-level Executive official under surveillance) was obtained from electronic surveillance and disseminated to the highest levels of the federal government.[74]

(5) Warrantless break-ins have been conducted by intelligence agencies since World War II. During the 1960's alone, the FBI and CIA conducted hundreds of break-ins, many against American citizens and domestic organizations. In some cases, these break-ins were to install microphones; in

---

[71] See Mail Opening Report: Section II, "Legal Considerations and the 'Flap' Potential."

[72] See NSA Report: Section I, "Introduction and Summary."

[73] Memorandum from Attorney General Brownell to J. Edgar Hoover, 5/20/54.

[74] See finding on Political Abuse. To protect the privacy of the targeted individual, the Committee has omitted the citation to the memorandum concerning the example of purely personal information.

other cases, they were to steal such items as membership lists from organizations considered "subversive" by the Bureau.[75]

(6) The most pervasive surveillance technique has been the informant. In a random sample of domestic intelligence cases, 83% involved informants and 5% involved electronic surveillance.[76] Informants have been used against peaceful, law-abiding groups; they have collected information about personal and political views and activities.[77] To maintain their credentials in violence-prone groups, informants have involved themselves in violent activity. This phenomenon is well illustrated by an informant in the Klan. He was present at the murder of a civil rights worker in Mississippi and subsequently helped to solve the crime and convict the perpetrators. Earlier, however, while performing duties paid for by the Government, he had previously "beaten people severely, had boarded buses and kicked people, had [gone] into restaurants and beaten them [blacks] with blackjacks, chains, pistols." [78] Although the FBI requires agents to instruct informants that they cannot be involved in violence, it was understood that in the Klan, "he couldn't be an angel and be a good informant." [79]

Ignoring the Law

Officials of the intelligence agencies occasionally recognized that certain activities were illegal, but expressed concern only for "flap potential." Even more disturbing was the frequent testimony that the law, and the Constitution were simply ignored. For example, the author of the so-called Huston plan testified:

> Question. Was there any person who stated that the activity recommended, which you have previously identified as being illegal opening of the mail and breaking and entry or burglary—was there any single person who stated that such activity should not be done because it was unconstitutional?
> Answer. No.
> Question. Was there any single person who said such activity should not be done because it was illegal?
> Answer. No.[80]

Similarly, the man who for ten years headed FBI's Intelligence Division testifed that:

> ... never once did I hear anybody, including myself, raise the question: "Is this course of action which we have agreed upon lawful, is it legal, is it ethical or moral." We never gave any thought to this line of reasoning, because we were just naturally pragmatic.[81]

---

[75] Memorandum from W. C. Sullivan to C. D. DeLoach, 7/19/66, p. 2.

[76] General Accounting Office Report on Domestic Intelligence Operations of the FBI. 9/75.

[77] Mary Jo Cook testimony. 12/2/75, Hearings, Vol. 6. p. 111.

[78] Gary Rowe deposition, 10/17/75, p. 9.

[79] Special Agent No. 3 deposition, 11/21/75, p. 12.

[80] Huston testimony, 9/23/75. Hearings. Vol. 2, p. 41.

[81] William Sullivan testimony, 11/1/75, pp. 92–93.

Although the statutory law and the Constitution were often not "[given] a thought",[82] there was a general attitude that intelligence needs were responsive to a higher law. Thus, as one witness testified in justifying the FBI's mail opening program:

> It was my assumption that what we were doing was justified by what we had to do . . . the greater good, the national security.[83]

Deficiencies in Accountability and Control

The overwhelming number of excesses continuing over a prolonged period of time were due in large measure to the fact that the system of checks and balances—created in our Constitution to limit abuse of Governmental power—was seldom applied to the intelligence community. Guidance and regulation from outside the intelligence agencies—where it has been imposed at all—has been vague. Presidents and other senior Executive officials, particularly the Attorneys General, have virtually abdicated their Constitutional responsibility to oversee and set standards for intelligence activity. Senior government officials generally gave the agencies broad, general mandates or pressed for immediate results on pressing problems. In neither case did they provide guidance to prevent excesses and their broad mandates and pressures themselves often resulted in excessive or improper intelligence activity.

Congress has often declined to exercise meaningful oversight, and on occasion has passed laws or made statements which were taken by intelligence agencies as supporting overly-broad investigations.

On the other hand, the record reveals instances when intelligence agencies have concealed improper activities from their superiors in the Executive branch and from the Congress, or have elected to disclose only the less questionable aspects of their activities.

There has been, in short, a clear and sustained failure by those responsible to control the intelligence community and to ensure its accountability. There has been an equally clear and sustained failure by intelligence agencies to fully inform the proper authorities of their activities and to comply with directives from those authorities.

The Adverse Impact of Improper Intelligence Activity

Many of the illegal or improper disruptive efforts directed against American citizens and domestic organizations succeeded in injuring their targets. Although it is sometimes difficult to prove that a target's misfortunes were caused by a counter-intelligence program directed against him, the possibility that an arm of the United States Government intended to cause the harm and might have been responsible is itself abhorrent.

---

[82] The quote is from a Bureau official who had supervised for the "Black Nationalist Hate Group" COINTELPRO.

"*Question.* Did anybody at any time that you remember during the course of the programs discuss the Constitutionality or the legal authority, or anything else like that?

"Answer. No, we never gave it a thought. As far as I know, nobody engaged or ever had any idea that they were doing anything other than what was the policy of the Bureau which had been policy for a long time." (George Moore deposition, 11/3/75, p. 83.)

[83] Branigan, 10/9/75, p. 41.

The Committee has observed numerous examples of the impact of intelligence operations. Sometimes the harm was readily apparent—destruction of marriages, loss of friends or jobs. Sometimes the attitudes of the public and of Government officials responsible for formulating policy and resolving vital issues were influenced by distorted intelligence. But the most basic harm was to the values of privacy and freedom which our Constitution seeks to protect and which intelligence activity infringed on a broad scale.

(a) *General Efforts to Discredit.*—Several efforts against individuals and groups appear to have achieved their stated aims. For example:

—A Bureau Field Office reported that the anonymous letter it had sent to an activist's husband accusing his wife of infidelity "contributed very strongly" to the subsequent breakup of the marriage.[84]

—Another Field Office reported that a draft counsellor deliberately, and falsely, accused of being an FBI informant was "ostracized" by his friends and associates.[85]

—Two instructors were reportedly put on probation after the Bureau sent an anonymous letter to a university administrator about their funding of an anti-administration student newspaper.[86]

—The Bureau evaluated its attempts to "put a stop" to a contribution to the Southern Christian Leadership Conference as "quite successful." [87]

—An FBI document boasted that a "pretext" phone call to Stokeley Carmichael's mother telling her that members of the Black Panther Party intended to kill her son left her "shocked". The memorandum intimated that the Bureau believed it had been responsible for Carmichael's flight to Africa the following day.[88]

(b) *Media Manipulation.*—The FBI has attempted covertly to influence the public's perception of persons and organizations by disseminating derogatory information to the press, either anonymously or through "friendly" news contacts. The impact of those articles is generally difficult to measure, although in some cases there are fairly direct connections to injury to the target. The Bureau also attempted to influence media reporting which would have any impact on the public image of the FBI. Examples include:

—Planting a series of derogatory articles about Martin Luther King, Jr., and the Poor People's Campaign.[89]

For example, in anticipation of the 1968 "poor people's march on Washington, D.C.," Bureau Headquarters granted authority to furnish "cooperative news media sources" an article "designed to curtail success of Martin Luther King's fund raising." [90] Another memorandum illustrated how "photographs of demonstrators" could be used in discrediting the civil rights movement. Six photographs of participants in the poor people's campaign in Cleveland accompanied the memorandum with the following note attached: "These [photographs] show the militant aggressive appearance of the participants

[84] Memorandum from St. Louis Field Office to FBI Headquarters, 6/19/70.
[85] Memorandum from San Diego Field Office to FBI Headquarters, 4/30/69.
[86] Memorandum from Mobile Field Office to FBI Headquarters, 12/9/70.
[87] Memorandum from Wick to DeLoach, 11/9/66.
[88] Memorandum from New York Field Office to FBI Headquarters, 9/9/68.
[89] See King Report: Sections V and VII.
[90] Memorandum from G. C. Moore to W. C. Sullivan, 10/26/68.

and might be of interest to a cooperative news source." [91] Information on the Poor People's Campaign was provided by the FBI to friendly reporters on the condition that "the Bureau must not be revealed as the source." [92]

—Soliciting information from Field Offices "on a continuing basis" for "prompt . . . dissemination to the news media . . . to discredit the New Left movement and its adherents." The Headquarters directive requested, among other things, that:

> specific data should be furnished depicting the scurrilous and depraved nature of many of the characters, activities, habits and living conditions representative of New Left adherents.

Field Offices were to be exhorted that: "Every avenue of possible embarrassment must be vigorously and enthusiastically explored." [93]

—Ordering Field Offices to gather information which would disprove allegations by the "liberal press, the bleeding hearts, and the forces on the left" that the Chicago police used undue force in dealing with demonstrators at the 1968 Democratic Convention.[95]

—Taking advantage of a close relationship with the Chairman of the Board—described in an FBI memorandum as "our good friend"— of a magazine with national circulation to influence articles which related to the FBI. For example, through this relationship the Bureau: "squelched" an "unfavorable article against the Bureau" written by a free-lance writer about an FBI investigation; "postponed publication" of an article on another FBI case; "forestalled publication" of an article by Dr. Martin Luther King, Jr.; and received information about proposed editing of King's articles.[96]

(c) Distorting Data to Influence Government Policy and Public Perceptions

Accurate intelligence is a prerequisite to sound government policy. However, as the past head of the FBI's Domestic Intelligence Division reminded the Committee:

> The facts by themselves are not too meaningful. They are something like stones cast into a heap.[97]

On certain crucial subjects the domestic intelligence agencies reported the "facts" in ways that gave rise to misleading impressions.

For example, the FBI's Domestic Intelligence Division initially discounted as an "obvious failure" the alleged attempts of Communists to influence the civil rights movement.[98] Without any significant change in the factual situation, the Bureau moved from the Division's conclusion to Director Hoover's public congressional testimony characterizing Communist influence on the civil rights movement as "vitally important." [98a]

---

[91] Memorandum from G. C. Moore to W. C. Sullivan, 5/17/68.
[92] Memorandum from FBI Headquarters to Miami Field Office, 7/9/68.
[93] Memorandum from C. D. Brennan to W. C. Sullivan, 5/22/68.
[95] Memorandum from FBI Headquarters to Chicago Field Office, 8/28/68.
[96] Memorandum from W. H. Stapleton to DeLoach, 11/3/64.
[97] Sullivan, 11/1/75, p. 48.
[98] Memorandum from Baumgardner to Sullivan, 8/26/63 p. 1. Hoover himself construed the initial Division estimate to mean that Communist influence was "infinitesimal."
[98a] See Fniding on Political Abuse, p. 225.

FBI reporting on protests against the Vietnam War provides another example of the manner in which the information provided to decision-makers can be skewed. In acquiescence with a judgment already expressed by President Johnson, the Bureau's reports on demonstrations against the War in Vietnam emphasized Communist efforts to influence the anti-war movement and underplayed the fact that the vast majority of demonstrators were not Communist controlled.[99]

(d) *"Chilling" First Amendment Rights.*—The First Amendment protects the Rights of American citizens to engage in free and open discussions, and to associate with persons of their choosing. Intelligence agencies have, on occasion, expressly attempted to interfere with those rights. For example, one internal FBI memorandum called for "more interviews" with New Left subjects "to enhance the paranoia endemic in these circles" and "get the point across there is an FBI agent behind every mailbox." [100]

More importantly, the government's surveillance activities in the aggregate—whether or not expressly intended to do so—tends, as the Committee concludes at p. 290 to deter the exercise of First Amended rights by American citizens who become aware of the government's domestic intelligence program.

(e) *Preventing the Free Exchange of Ideas.* Speakers, teachers, writers, and publications themselves were targets of the FBI's counterintelligence program. The FBI's efforts to interfere with the free exchange of ideas included:

—Anonymously attempting to prevent an alleged "Communist-front" group from holding a forum on a midwest campus, and then investigating the judge who ordered that the meeting be allowed to proceed.[101]

—Using another "confidential source" in a foundation which contributed to a local college to apply pressure on the school to fire an activist professor.

—Anonymously contacting a university official to urge him to "persuade" two professors to stop funding a student newspaper, in order to "eliminate what voice the New Left has" in the area.

—Targeting the New Mexico Free University for teaching "confrontation politics" and "draft counseling training".[102]

Cost and Value

Domestic intelligence is expensive. We have already indicated the cost of illegal and improper intelligence activities in terms of the harm to victims, the injury to constitutional values, and the damage to the democratic process itself. The cost in dollars is also significant. For example, the FBI has budgeted for fiscal year 1976 over $7 million for its domestic security informant program, more than twice the amount it spends on informants against organized crime.[103] The

---

[99] See Finding on Political Abuse. p. 225.

[100] "New Left Notes—Philadelphia." 9/16/70, Edition #1.

[101] Memorandum from Detroit Field Office to FBI Headquarters 10/26/60; Memorandum from FBI Headquarters to Detroit Field Office 10/27, 28, 31/60; Memorandum from Baumgardner to Belmont, 10/26/60.

[102] See COINTELPRO Report: Section III. "The Goals of COINTELPRO: Preventing or disrupting the exercise of First Amendment Rights."

[103] The budget for FBI informant programs includes not only the payments to informants for their services and expenses, but also the expenses of FBI personnel who supervise informants, their support costs, and administrative overhead. (Justice Department letter to Senate Select Committee, 3/2/76).

aggregate budget for FBI domestic security intelligence and foreign counterintelligence is at least $80 million.[104] In the late 1960s and early 1970s, when the Bureau was joined by the CIA, the military, and NSA in collecting information about the anti-war movement and black activists, the cost was substantially greater.

Apart from the excesses described above, the usefulness of many domestic intelligence activities in serving the legitimate goal of protecting society has been questionable. Properly directed intelligence investigations concentrating upon hostile foreign agents and violent terrorists can produce valuable results. The Committee has examined cases where the FBI uncovered "illegal" agents of a foreign power engaged in clandestine intelligence activities in violation of federal law. Information leading to the prevention of serious violence has been acquired by the FBI through its informant penetration of terrorist groups and through the inclusion in Bureau files of the names of persons actively involved with such groups.[105] Nevertheless, the most sweeping domestic intelligence surveillance programs have produced surprisingly few useful returns in view of their extent. For example:

—Between 1960 and 1974, the FBI conducted over 500,000 separate investigations of persons and groups under the "subversive" category, predicated on the possibility that they might be likely to overthrow the government of the United States.[106] Yet not a single individual or group has been prosecuted since 1957 under the laws which prohibit planning or advocating action to overthrow the government and which are the main alleged statutory basis for such FBI investigations.[107]

—A recent study by the General Accounting Office has estimated that of some 17,528 FBI domestic intelligence investigations of individuals in 1974, only 1.3 percent resulted in prosecution and con-

---

[104] The Committee is withholding the portion of this figure spent on domestic security intelligence (informants and other investigations combined) to prevent hostile foreign intelligence services from deducing the amount spent on counterespionage. The $80 million figure does not include all costs of separate FBI activities which may be drawn upon for domestic security intelligence purposes. Among these are the Identification Division (maintaining fingerprint records), the Files and Communications Division (managing the storage and retrieval of investigative and intelligence files), and the FBI Laboratory.

[105] Examples of valuable informant reports include the following: one informant reported a plan to ambush police officers and the location of a cache of weapons and dynamite; another informant reported plans to transport illegally obtained weapons to Washington, D.C.; two informants at one meeting discovered plans to dynamite two city blocks. All of these plans were frustrated by further investigation and protective measures or arrest. (FBI memorandum to Select Committee, 12/10/75; Senate Select Committee Staff memorandum: Intelligence Cases in Which the FBI Prevented Violence, undated.)

One example of the use of information in Bureau files involved a "name check" at Secret Service request on certain persons applying for press credentials to cover the visit of a foreign head of state. The discovery of data in FBI files indicating that one such person had been actively involved with violent groups led to further investigation and ultimately the issuance of a search warrant. The search produced evidence, including weapons, of a plot to assassinate the foreign head of state. (FBI memorandum to Senate Select Committee, 2/23/76)

[106] This figure is the number of "investigative matters" handled by the FBI in this area, including as separate items the investigative leads in particular cases which are followed up by various field offices. (FBI memorandum to Select Committee, 10/6/75.)

[107] Schackelford 2/13/76, p. 32. This official does not recall any targets of "subversive" investigations having been even referred to a Grand Jury under these statutes since the 1950s.

viction, and in only "about 2 percent" of the cases was advance knowledge of any activity—legal or illegal—obtained.[108]

—One of the main reasons advanced for expanded collection of intelligence about urban unrest and anti-war protest was to help responsible officials cope with possible violence. However, a former White House official with major duties in this area under the Johnson administration has concluded, in retrospect, that "in none of these situations . . . would advance intelligence about dissident groups [have] been of much help," that what was needed was "physical intelligence" about the geography of major cities, and that the attempt to "predict violence" was not a "successful undertaking." [109]

—Domestic intelligence reports have sometimes even been counterproductive. A local police chief, for example, described FBI reports which led to the positioning of federal troops near his city as:

> . . . almost completely composed of unsorted and unevaluated stories, threats, and rumors that had crossed my desk in New Haven. Many of these had long before been discounted by our Intelligence Division. But they had made their way from New Haven to Washington, had gained completely unwarranted credibility, and had been submitted by the Director of the FBI to the President of the United States. They seemed to present a convincing picture of impending holocaust.[110]

In considering its recommendations, the Committee undertook an evaluation of the FBI's claims that domestic intelligence was necessary to combat terrorism, civil disorders, "subversion," and hostile foreign intelligence activity. The Committee reviewed voluminous materials bearing on this issue and questioned Bureau officials, local police officials, and present and former federal executive officials.

We have found that we are in fundamental agreement with the wisdom of Attorney General Stone's initial warning that intelligence agencies must not be "concerned with political or other opinions of individuals" and must be limited to investigating essentially only "such conduct as is forbidden by the laws of the United States." The Committee's record demonstrates that domestic intelligence which departs from this standard raises grave risks of undermining the democratic process and harming the interests of individual citizens. This danger weighs heavily against the speculative or negligible benefits of the ill-defined and overbroad investigations authorized in the past. Thus, the basic purpose of the recommendations contained in Part IV of this report is to limit the FBI to investigating conduct rather than ideas or associations.

---

[108] "FBI Domestic Intelligence Operations—Their Purpose and Scope: Issues That Need To Be Resolved." Report by the Comptroller General to the House Judiciary Committee, 2/24/76, pp. 138–147. The FBI contends that these statistics may be unfair in that they concentrate on investigations of individuals rather than groups. (Ibid., Appendix V) In response, GAO states that its "sample of organization and control files was sufficient to determine that generally the FBI did not report advance knowledge of planned violence." In most of the fourteen instances where such advance knowledge was obtained, it related to "such activities as speeches, demonstrations or meetings—all essentially nonviolent." (Ibid., p. 144)

[109] Joseph Califano testimony. 1/27/76, pp. 7–8.

[110] James Ahern testimony, 1/20/76, pp. 16, 17.

The excesses of the past do not, however, justify depriving the United States of a clearly defined and effectively controlled domestic intelligence capability. The intelligence services of this nation's international adversaries continue to attempt to conduct clandestine espionage operations within the United States.[111] Our recommendations provide for intelligence investigations of hostile foreign intelligence activity.

Moreover, terrorists have engaged in serious acts of violence which have brought death and injury to Americans and threaten further such acts. These acts, not the politics or beliefs of those who would commit them, are the proper focus for investigations to anticipate terrorist violence. Accordingly, the Committee would permit properly controlled intelligence investigations in those narrow circumstances.[112]

Concentration on imminent violence can avoid the wasteful dispersion of resources which has characterized the sweeping (and fruitless) domestic intelligence investigations of the past. But the most important reason for the fundamental change in the domestic intelligence operations which our Recommendations propose is the need to protect the constitutional rights of Americans.

In light of the record of abuse revealed by our inquiry, the Committee is not satisfied with the position that mere exposure of what has occurred in the past will prevent its recurrence. Clear legal standards and effective oversight and controls are necessary to en ure that domestic intelligence activity does not itself undermine the democratic system it is intended to protect.

---

[111] An indication of the scope of the problem is the increasing number of official representatives of communist governments in the United States. For example, the number of Soviet officials in this country has increased from 333 in 1961 to 1,079 by early 1975. There were 2,683 East-West exchange visitors and 1,500 commercial visitors in 1974. (FBI Memorandum, "Intelligence Activities Within the United States by Foreign Governments," 3/20/75.)

[112] According to the FBI, there were 89 bombings attributable to terrorist activity in 1975, as compared with 45 in 1974 and 24 in 1973. Six persons died in terrorist-claimed bombings and 76 persons were injured in 1975. Five other deaths were reported in other types of terrorist incidents. Monetary damage reported in terrorist bombings exceeded 2.7 million dollars. It should be noted, however, that terrorist bombings are only a fraction of the total number of bombings in this country. Thus, the 89 terrorist bombings in 1975 were among a total of over 1,900 bombings, most of which were not, according to the FBI, attributable clearly to terrorist activity. (FBI memorandum to Senate Select Committee, 2/23/76.)

HEARINGS EXHIBITS [1]

EXHIBIT 1

FBI Organizational Charts ([44F], pp. 347–348)

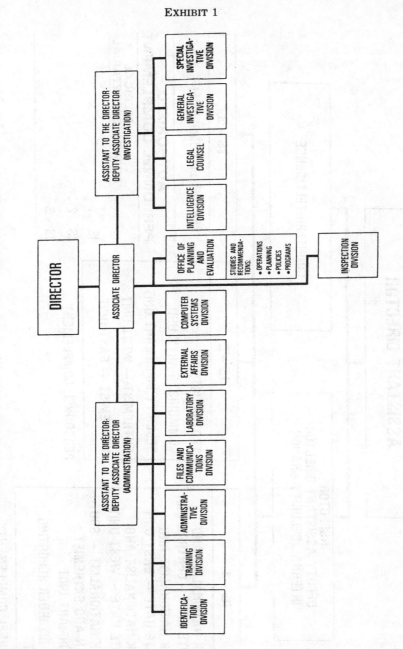

[1] Under criteria determined by the Committee, in consultation with the Federal Bureau of Investigation, certain materials have been deleted from these exhibits, some of which were previously classified, to maintain the integrity of the internal operating procedures of the FBI. Further deletions were made with respect to protecting the privacy of certain individuals and groups. These deletions do not change the material content of these exhibits.

EXHIBIT 2

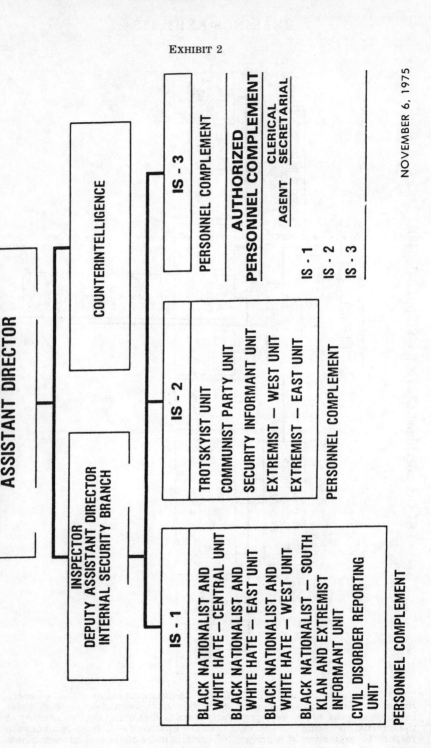

NOVEMBER 6, 1975

INTELLIGENCE DIVISION
ASSISTANT DIRECTOR

COUNTERINTELLIGENCE

INSPECTOR
DEPUTY ASSISTANT DIRECTOR
INTERNAL SECURITY BRANCH

IS - 1

BLACK NATIONALIST AND
WHITE HATE — CENTRAL UNIT

BLACK NATIONALIST AND
WHITE HATE — EAST UNIT

BLACK NATIONALIST AND
WHITE HATE — WEST UNIT

BLACK NATIONALIST — SOUTH

KLAN AND EXTREMIST
INFORMANT UNIT

CIVIL DISORDER REPORTING
UNIT

PERSONNEL COMPLEMENT

IS - 2

TROTSKYIST UNIT

COMMUNIST PARTY UNIT

SECURITY INFORMANT UNIT

EXTREMIST — WEST UNIT

EXTREMIST — EAST UNIT

PERSONNEL COMPLEMENT

IS - 3

PERSONNEL COMPLEMENT

AUTHORIZED
PERSONNEL COMPLEMENT

	AGENT	CLERICAL SECRETARIAL
IS - 1		
IS - 2		
IS - 3		

Justice Department Report on COINTELPRO ([80], pp. 9–15)

Details of the COINTELPRO activities began circulating shortly after a group of antiwar protesters broke into the FBI office in Media, Pennsylvania, in 1971. This incident prompted NBC television newsman Carl Stern to file suit, under the Freedom of Information Act, against the Justice Department in order to obtain release of FBI documents bearing on its questionable activities. After almost two years of litigation, the FBI released some documentation, which brought the term "COINTELPRO" before the public. (The emergence of the COINTELPRO scandal is discussed further in [80].)

By November 1974, when the House Judiciary Committee began a probe into FBI counterintelligence operations, the Justice Department was disposed to issue a public report admitting the existence of the program, describing some of its activities, and stating that it had been terminated in 1971.* The Justice Department report, preceded by a statement from Attorney General William Saxbe, was submitted to the House committee and is reprinted here.

*For information on similar intelligence activities since 1971, see [45B], pp. 131 ff.

STATEMENT OF HON. WILLIAM B. SAXBE, ATTORNEY GENERAL OF THE UNITED STATES

In January of this year during the course of my initial briefing on current issues facing the Department of Justice, I was informed of the existence of an FBI "Counterintelligence Program".

After ascertaining the general thrust of the counterintelligence programs, I directed Assistant Attorney General Henry Petersen to form a committee charged with the responsibility of conducting a complete study and preparing a report for me which would document the Bureau's activities in each of the separate counterintelligence programs. That study committee consisted of four Criminal Division representatives and three representatives from the Federal Bureau of Investigation, selected by Director Kelley.

The Committee's report to me stated that there were seven separate programs—five directed at domestic organizations and individuals, and two programs directed at foreign intelligence services, foreign organizations and individuals connected with them. These programs were implemented at various times during the period from 1956 to 1971 when all programs were discontinued. The Committee further found that 3247 counterintelligence proposals were submitted of which 2370 were approved. In 527 instances, known results were ascertained.

It is not my intention at this time to detail for you the particulars of the seven programs inasmuch as you have been provided with a copy of the Committee's report which has been edited to delete national security information. That document describes fully the activities involved in each of the programs.

The materials released today disclose that, in a small number of instances, some of these programs involved what we consider today to be improper activities. I am disturbed about those improper activities. However, I want to stress two things: first, most of the activities conducted under these counterintelligence programs were legitimate—indeed, the programs were in response to numerous public and even Congressional demands for stronger action by the Federal Government. Second, to the extent that there were, nevertheless, isolated excesses, we have taken steps to prevent them from ever happening again. In this connection, Director Kelley last December sent a memorandum to FBI personnel strongly reaffirming the Bureau policy that: "FBI employees must not engage in any investigative activity which could abride in any way the rights guaranteed to a citizen of the United States by the Constitution and under no circumstances shall employees of the FBI engage in any conduct which may result in defaming the character, reputation, integrity, or dignity of any citizen or organization of citizens of the United States."

Attorney General William B. Saxbe and Federal Bureau of Investigation Director Clarence M. Kelley released today the details of certain counterintelligence programs conducted by the FBI from 1956 to 1971 against several domestic and foreign-based subversive or disruptive groups, organizations, and individuals.

These efforts, which carried the designation "COINTELPRO," were targeted against the Communist Party U.S.A., the Socialist Workers Party, the New Left, White Hate groups, and Black Extremist organizations, as well as certain espionage operations and hostile foreign-based intelligence services.

The materials released today significantly expand upon material released in December, 1973, by Director Kelley concerning the counterintelligence program conducted against radical and violent elements as part of the COINTELPRO—New Left.

FBI COINTELPRO ACTIVITIES

I. INTRODUCTION

In Fall, 1973, the Department of Justice disclosed certain documents relating to a "counterintelligence" program of the Federal Bureau of Investigation entitled "COINTELPRO—New Left." Among the documents disclosed was a directive indicating that the FBI had also instituted six other counterintelligence programs ("COINTELPRO"), to wit: Espionage; White Hate Groups; Communist Party, U.S.A.; Special Operations; Black Extremists and the Socialist Workers Party. Based on these disclosures, additional requests have been made for numerous other documents relating to these FBI COINTELPRO activities. This paper is in response to those requests.

In January, 1974 Attorney General William Saxbe requested Assistant Attorney General Henry Petersen to form a committee to review these FBI COINTELPRO activities. The Committee was chaired by Assistant Attorney General Petersen, and consisted of four Criminal Division representatives and three FBI representatives selected by FBI Director Clarence Kelley.

In June, 1974 the various COINTELPRO programs were discussed at length by Attorney General Saxbe and FBI Director Kelley with the FBI Oversight Subcommittee of the Senate Judiciary Committee. More recently, the COINTELPRO activities of the FBI were discussed by Attorney General Saxbe and Director Kelley with Chairman Rodino and Ranking Minority Member Hutchinson of the House Judiciary Committee.

II. THE COINTELPRO PROGRAMS

A. Origin, scope, and objectives of COINTELPRO activities

The term "COINTELPRO" is a generic term used by the FBI to describe seven separate "counterintelligence" programs which the Bureau implemented at different times during the period from 1956 to 1971, when all were discontinued. Five of these programs were directed at domestic-based groups and individuals—Communist Party, U.S.A., the forerunner of all other COINTELPROS (1956–1971); Socialist Workers Party (1961–1970); White Hate Groups (1964–1971); Black Extremists (1967–1971); and New Left (1968–1971). The documents authorizing these five programs define their objective as being either simply the disruption of the group's activities; or the disruption, exposure and neutralization thereof.

The other two COINTELPRO programs were in the area of foreign counterintelligence—Espionage or Soviet-Satellite Intelligence, which was in effect from 1964 to 1971; and Special Operations, which was in effect from 1967 to 1971. According to Bureau documents, the overall objectives of these two programs were to encourage and stimulate a variety of counterintelligence efforts against hostile foreign intelligence sources, foreign Communist organizations and individuals connected with them.

B. The background and context of COINTELPRO activities

A fair, accurate and comprehensive understanding of the various COINTELPRO activities undertaken by the FBI is possible only in light of the context and climate in which the programs were established.

As indicated above, COINTELPRO—Communist Party, USA was the predecessor—and in some respects the model—of subsequent FBI COINTELPRO activities. The Communist Party, USA program grew out of the "Red Scare" of the early and middle 1950's. This era of American political history was characterized by the growth and decline of "McCarthyism;" numerous and well-publicized "spy trials;" and, in general, a prevailing view in Congress and the American people that the Federal Government should take appropriate steps against domestic subversion. The period was also characterized by a widespread concern that subversive elements, spearheaded by the Communist Party, were not only pervasive, but were also in varying degrees *effective* in such areas as sabotage and espionage. Moreover, although domestically based, it was clear that the operations and activities of the Communist Party USA were in fact directed by foreign countries. Indeed, the fact of foreign (Soviet) direction and control of the Communist Party USA was recognized by the Supreme Court in *Communist Party USA* v. *United States*, 368 U.S. 871.

The original COINTELPRO was, then, conceived as a "counterintelligence" effort in the purest sense. Moreover, the overwhelming bulk of the activities carried out under the program were legitimate and proper intelligence and investigative practices and techniques. What was new in the *COINTELPRO* effort was primarily the *targeting* of these activities against one specified group or category of organizations. Although, as discussed in more detail below, some COINTELPRO activities involved isolated instances of practices that can only be considered abhorrent in a free society, it is important to understand that these improper activities were not the purpose or indeed even the major characteristic of the FBI's COINTELPRO efforts.

COINTELPRO—Socialist Workers Party, undertaken in 1961, appears to have been a direct outgrowth of the earlier effort targeted against the activities of the Communist Party, USA. Later COINTELPRO activities were based on the Communist Party, USA model, but reflected the changing threats to domestic order that emerged in the decade of the 1960's.

The next COINTELPRO undertaken was against White Hate Groups. This program, which began in 1964, grew out of the disruptive and harrassing activities of these groups in their attempt to subvert the civil rights movement. The activities of these groups were characterized by lynchings, burnings, bombings, and the like—a climate of violence and lawlessness which society and its law enforcement mechanisms seemed incapable of countering.

The next COINTELPRO undertaken was against Black Extremists in 1967. As in the case of the White Hate Groups, the activities of these extremist groups were marked by violence, arson and bombings. In addition, the activities of many of these extremist groups included police shootings and, as is well known, the fostering and fomenting of riots and other civil disturbances in cities all across the land.

Finally, many of these activities were led by or included individuals who publicly proclaimed their association with the political doctrines or leadership of hostile countries, including Communist nations.

The last domestic COINTELPRO was instituted in 1968 against the "New Left." The origin and purposes of this effort were best described by FBI Director Kelley in a press release on December 7, 1973:

"In the late 1960's, a hard-core revolutionary movement which came to be known as the 'New Left' set out, in its own words, to bring the Government to its knees through the use of force and violence.

"What started as New Left movement chanting of Marxist-Leninist slogans in the early years of their 'revolution' developed into violent contempt, not only for Government and Government officials, but for every responsible American citizen.

"During these years, there were over 300 arsons or attempted arsons, 14 destructive bombings, 9 persons killed, and almost 600 injured on our college campuses alone. In the school year 1968–69, damage on college campuses exceeded 3 million dollars and in the next year mounted to an excess of 9.5 million.

"In this atmosphere of lawlessness in the cities mobs overturned vehicles, set fires, and damaged public and private property. There were threats to sabotage power plants, to disrupt transportation and communications facilities. Intelligence sources informed the FBI of plans that were discussed to poison public water supplies.

"At this time of national crisis, the Government would have been derelict in its duty had it not taken measures to protect the fabric of our society. The FBI has the responsibility of investigating allegations of criminal violations and gathering intelligence regarding threats to the country's security. Because of the violent actions of the leadership of the New Left, FBI officials concluded that some additional effort must be made to neutralize and disrupt this revolutionary movement. This effort was called the 'Counterintelligence Program—New Left' or 'COINTELPRO-New Left.'

"While there is no way to measure the effect of the FBI's attempt at countersubversion, I believe that it did have some impact on the crisis at that time.

"Now, in the context of a different era where peace has returned to the college campuses and revolutionary forces no longer pose a major threat to peace and tranquality of our cities, some may deplore and condemn the FBI's use of a counterintelligence program—even against hostile and arrogant forces which openly sought to destroy this nation.

"I share the public's deep concern about the citizen's right to privacy and the preservation of all rights guaranteed under the Constitution and Bill of Rights."

As indicated in Director Kelley's statement—and as is apparent in the case of all COINTELPRO activities—"there is no way to measure the effect of the FBI's attempt at countersubversion." Unfortunately, no empirical data exist with respect to the effectiveness of the various COINTELPRO efforts undertaken in countering the threats perceived to the domestic order. Perhaps the nature of intelligence work is such that no such objective measure exists.

C. Authorization and implementation of COINTELPRO activities

According to FBI documents, all seven programs implemented under COINTELPRO were specifically authorized by former FBI Director J. Edgar Hoover. COINTELPRO programs were apparently not reported to any of the Attorneys General in office during the periods in which they were implemented. Only certain aspects of the Bureau's efforts to penetrate and disrupt the Communist Party USA and White Hate Groups—apparently conducted under COINTELPRO although not specifically stated as such (the term "COINTELPRO" was used only inside the Bureau), were reported to at least three Attorneys General and key White House staff of two Presidents between 1958 and 1969. It must be emphasized that none of the activities so reported involved any improper conduct. One additional Attorney General during this period was briefed on the Bureau's "counterattack" against the Communist Party USA.

Finally, Bureau documents disclosed that the House Appropriations Subcommittee was briefed on the Bureau's counterintelligence programs including the character of COINTELPRO and examples of specific activities undertaken in connection with this program, as early as 1958. Under the directives establishing the programs, no counterintelligence action could be initiated by the field without specific prior Bureau authorization. Except in a very small number of instances this policy was strictly adhered to. The great majority of actions were either approved or disapproved at the Assistant Director level or above, while a very small number were acted on at a lower level.

D. Statistical analysis of COINTELPRO activities

As indicated above, the maximum time span of all seven COINTELPRO programs covered the period 1956 to 1971. All programs, however, were not in effect during this entire period.

With respect to the five programs directed at domestic-based organizations and individuals, a total of some 3,247 proposals for counterintelligence activity were submitted by the various FBI field offices for consideration from the inception of the programs in 1956 to their termination in 1971—more than half of them arising under the Communist Party USA program. Some 2,370 of these proposals, or approximately 73%, were approved and implemented. Of those proposals which were approved and implemented, known results were obtained in only some 527, or approximately 22%.

The individual statistics on each of these five programs are as follows:

Organization	Proposals	Approved and implemented	Known results
Communist party U.S.A.	1,850	1,388	222
Socialist Workers Party	72	46	13
White Hate Groups	404	289	139
New Left	381	285	77
Black Extremists	540	362	76
Total	3,247	2,370	527

With respect to the two other "COINTELPRO" programs, Special Operations and Espionage or Soviet-Satellite Intelligence—both of which related to operations primarily targeted against hostile foreign intelligence services, foreign organizations and individuals connected with them—no statistics are set forth in this report. Because of the nature of these activities, all documents relating to "Espionage or Soviet-Satellite Intelligence" are classified Secret, and a very substantial part of the documents relating to "Special Operations" are likewise classified Secret. Publication of these statistics would be inappropriate in terms of the national security.

E. *Analysis of types of activity conducted under COINTELPRO domestic-based programs*

Reports with respect to the five domestic based COINTELPRO programs disclosed a close similarity in the types of activities conducted under each program. In general, the activities common to all programs may be grouped into approximately a dozen categories. As indicated above, the overwhelming bulk of these activities were clearly legitimate and proper undertakings, within the scope of the FBI's ongoing responsibilities, and are listed as "COINTELPRO" activities only because they were reported as such. They may be characterized as follows:

(1) *Sending anonymous or fictitious materials to members or groups.*—The vast majority of these actions consisted of items of information designed to create dissention and cause disruption within the various groups. Of the total number of actions implemented under all five domestic based programs, approximately, 40% fell under this category.

(2) *Dissemination of public record information to media sources.*—Actions implemented under this category consistetd primarily of making public source material available to friendly media representatives for the purpose of using such material in a newspaper, magazine, or radio or television program in order to expose the aims and activities of the various groups. This type of activity represented approximately 20% of all actions implemented under domestic COINTELPRO efforts. It was implemented in some 360 instances in connection with the Communist Party USA program; in six instances in connection with the Socialist Workers Party; in 26 instances in connection with Black Extremists; in 15 instances in connection with White Hate Groups; and in 25 instances in connection with the New Left.

(3) *Leaking informant based on non-public information to media sources.*—Most of the actions implemented in this category related to the leaking of investigative material to friendly media sources for the purpose of exposing the nature, aims and membership of the various groups. There were no instances of this type of activity in connection with the Socialist Workers Party program, and relatively few in connection with the Communist Party USA and New Left programs. Approximately one-seventh of the actions implemented under the Black Extremists program, and one-sixth of the actions implemented under the White Hate Groups program fell under this category.

(4) *Advising local, State and Federal authorities of civil and criminal violations by group members.*—This activity—totally legal—represented approximately 8% of the total number of actions implemented under all five domestic based programs.

(5) *Use of informants to disrupt a group's activities.*—Most of the actions implemented under this category were for the purpose of using informants to disrupt the activities of various groups by sowing dissention and exploiting disputes. No statistics are available as to the number of instances of this type of activity in connection with the Communist Party USA program, but it seems that informants were used in this program to cause disruption but not as agents provocateurs. This type of activity represented less than two percent of the activities undertaken in connection with the four other domestic based COINTELPRO programs.

(6) *Informing employers, credit bureaus and creditors of members' activities.*—The majority of actions implemented under this category consisted of notifying credit bureaus, creditors, employers and prospective employers of members' illegal, immoral, radical and Communist Party activities in order to affect adversely their credit standing or employment status. No statistics are available as to the number of instances in which this type of activity was used in connection with the Communist Party USA program, although the Bureau has reported that it was used in a number of instances. It was used in only a small number of instances in connection with the four other domestic based COINTELPRO programs, namely in one instance in connection with the Socialist Workers Party, seven instances in connection with Black Extremists, 15 instances in connection with White Hate Groups, and 20 instances in connection with the New Left, or a total of some 43 instances in all domestic based COINTELPRO programs other than the Communist Party USA.

(7) *Informing or contacting businesses and persons with whom members had economic dealings of members' actviities.*—The majority of actions implemented under this category consisted of notifying persons or businesses with whom members had economic dealings of the members' association with the various groups involved for the purpose of adversely affecting their economic interests.

No instances of this type of activity were reported in connection with the Communist Party USA program. It was implemented in only one instance in connection with the Socialist Workers Party program, in 62 instances in connection with the Black Extremists, 14 instances in connection with the White Hate Groups, and eight instances in connection with the New Left, or a total of some 85 instances in all domestic based programs.

(8) *Interviewing or contacting members.*—This type of activity—again, totally legal—was implemented in only a small number of instances for the purpose of letting members know that the FBI was aware of their activity and also in an attempt to develop them as informants. No instances of this type of activity were reported in connection with the Communist Party USA, Socialists Workers Party and Black Extremists programs, and in only eleven instances in connection with White Hate Groups and in one instance in connection with the New Left. It should be noted that many FBI field offices carried on this activity routinely but did not attribute it to a counterintelligence function but rather to the routine investigation of individuals or organizations.

(9) *Attempting to use religious and civil leaders and organizations in disruptive activities.*—The majority of actions implemented under this category involved furnishing information to civic and religious leaders and organizations in order to gain their support and to persuade them to exert pressure on state and local governments, employers and landlords to the detriment of the various groups. No instances of this type of activity were reported in connection with the Communist Party USA program. It was used in only 2 instances in connection with the Socialist Workers Party program, in 36 instances in connection with Black Extremists, in 13 instances in connection with White Hate Groups and in 10 instances in connection with the New Left, or a total of some 61 instances in connection with all domestic based programs.

(10) *Activity related to political or judicial processes.*—This type of activity represents less than one half of one percent of all COINTELPRO activities—a total of only 12 instances in connection with all five domestic based programs.

Although small in number, these 12 instances are among the most troubling in all of the COINTELPRO efforts. Consequently, in the interest of full disclosure, they are described in detail as follows: tipping off the press that a write-in candidate for Congress would be attending a group's meeting at a specific time and place; leaking information to the press that a group official was actively campaigning for a person running for public office; furnishing the arrest and conviction record of a member of a group who was a candidate for a local public office to a friendly newspaper which published the information; sending an anonymous letter to a political candidate alerting him that a group's members were active in his campaign and asking that he not be a tool of the group; sending an anonymous letter to a local school board official, purporting to be from a concerned parent, alerting him that candidates for the school board were members of a group; mailing an anonymous letter to a member of a group who was a mayoralty candidate in order to create distrust toward his comrades; furnishing background of a group who was a candidate for public office, including arrests and questionable marital status, to news media contacts; furnishing public source data on a group to a local grand jury chairman who had requested it in connection with the grand jury's probe of the shooting of police by group members; furnishing information concerning arrests of an individual to a court that had earlier given this individual a suspended sentence and also furnishing this same information to his employer who later discharged the individual; making an anonymous telephone call to a defense attorney, after a Federal prosecution had resulted in a mistrial, advising him (apparently falsely) that one of the defendants and another well known group individual were FBI informants.

(11) *Establishing sham organizations for disruptive purposes.*—This type of activity was utilized only in connection with the White Hate Groups program and was implemented in only five instances primarily for the purpose of using the organizations to send out material intended to disrupt various such groups.

(12) *Informing family or others of radical or immoral activity*—The majority of actions implemented under this category involved the sending of anonymous communications to family members or groups to which individuals belonged advising them of immoral or radical activities on the part of various individuals. These activities represent a little more than one percent of all COINTELPRO activities—a total of some thirty instances in all domestic-based programs. This type of activity was reported to have been used infrequently in connection with

the Communist Party USA program, and was not used in connection with the Socialist Workers Party program. It was reported to have been used in twelve instances in connection with the Black Extremists program, in two instances in connection with White Hate Groups, and in 16 instances in connection with the New Left.

In addition to the above twelve categories, it was found that a small number of miscellaneous actions, approximately 20 instances in all the domestic-based programs, were implemented which did not fit in any specific category. Again, it is appropriate in the interests of full disclosure that these activities be set forth in detail. The most egregious examples of these miscellaneous types of activity are as follows: making arrangements for local authorities to stop two group members on a narcotics pretext and by prearrangement having a police radio operator indicate that another individual wanted them to call her with purpose of having this individual come under suspicion as a police informer; use of "citizen band" radio, using the same frequency being used by demonstrators, to provide disinformation; making telephone calls to parents of members of a group advising them of the connection of their son with the group; or advising the mother of a group leader that his actions would put him in danger; forging of a group's business card for informant purposes; reproducing a group leader's signature stamp; obtaining tax returns of members of a group; reproducing a group's recruiting card; and investigating the love life of a group leader for dissemination to the press.

F. *Foreign intelligence activities*

Two programs in the area of foreign counterintelligence—"Special Operations" and "Espionage" or "Soviet-Satellite Intelligence"—were implemented by the FBI under "COINTELPRO." The overall objective of each was to encourage and stimulate a variety of counterintelligence efforts against hostile foreign intelligence services, and, in the case of "Special Operations," also against foreign Communist organizations and individuals connected with them.

(1) *Special operations.*—The title "Special Operations" does not designate a program directed against a specific target. Rather, the title and the file on it are of a *control* character, and the file contains copies of correspondence of an informative or coordinating nature relating to ongoing intelligence operations and/or investigations primarily targeted against hostile foreign intelligence services, foreign Communist organizations and individuals connected with them. A very substantial part of this file is classified "Secret." Although it is not appropriate to provide statistics as to the precise number of actions implemented under this program, it can generally be stated to include approximately ten general types of activity, such as operations involving travel of confidential informants abroad; extended utilization of cooperative individuals and informants abroad; anonymous mailings for the purpose of disrupting activities of a suspected agent of a foreign intelligence service; etc.

(2) *Espionage or Soviet-satellite intelligence.*—This program, although officially designated a COINTELPRO program, emphasized intelligence gathering and counterintelligence efforts already being pursued in connection with the Bureau's ongoing foreign intelligence responsibilities. It did not curtail any activity or in any way change the scope of counterintelligence efforts already in effect and continuing today. It was primarily intended to inspire initiative and to encourage ingenuity in the Bureau's continuing counterintelligence efforts against hostile foreign intelligence services.

In the interest of the national security, no statistics or examples of the types of actions implemented under this program may appropriately be disclosed.

Director Clarence Kelley Defends the FBI ([80], pp. 44–47)

Clarence Kelley, director of the FBI, was faced with morale problems within the bureau and a growing public outcry for reform of the FBI's approach to the civil liberties of citizens. In response to these concerns, he released a "defense" of FBI personnel and submitted it to the House Judiciary Subcommittee, which held hearings on COINTELPRO.

STATEMENT OF HON. CLARENCE M. KELLEY, DIRECTOR, FEDERAL BUREAU OF
INVESTIGATION

Attorney General William B. Saxbe today has released a report regarding FBI
counterintelligence programs. The report was prepared by a Justice Department
committee which included FBI representatives that was specially appointed early
this year to study and report on those programs.

Since taking the oath of office as Director on July 9, 1973, I also have made a
detailed study of these same FBI counterintelligence programs.

The first of them—one directed at the Communist Party, USA—was instituted
in September, 1956. None of the programs was continued beyond April, 1971.

The purpose of these counterintelligence programs was to prevent dangerous,
and even potentially deadly, acts against individuals, organizations, and institu-
tions—both public and private—across the United States.

They were designed to counter the conspiratorial efforts of revolutionary ele-
ments in this country, as well as to neutralize extremists of both the Left and the
Right who were threatening, and in many instances fomenting, acts of violence.

The study which I have made convinces me that the FBI employees involved in
these programs acted entirely in good faith and within the bounds of what was
expected of them by the President, the Attorney General, the Congress, and the
American people.

Each of these counterintelligence programs bore the approval of the then-
Director J. Edgar Hoover.

Proposals for courses of action to be taken under these programs were subject
to approval in advance, as well as to constant review, by FBI Field Office and
Headquarters officials.

Throughout the tenure of these programs, efforts admittedly were made to dis-
rupt the anarchistic plans and activities of violence-prone groups whose publicly
announced goal was to bring America to its knees. For the FBI to have done less
under the circumstances would have been an abdication of its responsibilities
to the American people.

Let me remind those who would now criticize the FBI's actions that the
United States Capitol *was* bombed; that other explosions rocked public and
private offices and buildings; that rioters led by revolutionary extremists laid
siege to military, industrial, and educational facilities; and that killings, maim-
ings, and other atrocities accompanied such acts of violence from New England
to California.

The victims of these acts of violence were human beings—men, women, and
children who looked to the FBI and other law enforcement agencies to protect
their lives, rights, and property. An important part of the FBI's response was
to devise counterintelligence programs to minimize the threats and the fears
confronting these citizens.

In carrying out its counterintelliegnce programs, the FBI received the per-
sonal encouragement of myriad citizens both within and without the Govern-
ment. Many Americans feared for their own safety and for the safety of their
Government. Others were revolted by the rhetoric of violence and the acts of
violence that were being preached and practiced across our country by hard-core
extremists.

I invite your attention to the gravity of the problem as it then existed, as
well as the need for decisive and effective counteraction by the criminal justice
and intelligence communities.

I want to assure you that Director Hoover did not conceal from superior
authorities the fact that the FBI was engaging in neutralizing and disruptive
tactics against revolutionary and violence-prone groups. For example, in a com-
munication concerning a revolutionary organization that he sent to the then-
Attorney General and the White House on May 8, 1958, Mr. Hoover furnished
details of techniques utilized by the FBI to promote disruption of that
organization.

A second communication calling attention to measures being employed as an
adjunct to the FBI's regular investigative operations concerning this same rev-
olutionary organization was sent to the Attorney General-designate and the
Deputy Attorney General-designate by Mr. Hoover on January 10, 1961.

Mr. Hoover also sent communications to the then-Attorneys General in 1965,
1967, and 1969 furnishing them information regarding disruptive actions the
FBI was employing to neutralize activities of certain Rightist hate groups.

I have previously expressed my feeling that the FBI's counterintelligence
programs had an impact on the crises of the time and, therefore, that they
helped to bring about a favorable change in this country.

As I said in December, 1973 :

"Now, in the context of a different era where peace has returned to the college campuses and revolutionary forces no longer pose a major threat to peace and tranquility of our cities, some may deplore and condemn the FBI's use of a counterintelligence program—even against hostile and arrogant forces which openly sought to destroy this nation.

"I share the public's deep concern about the citizen's right to privacy and the preservation of all rights guaranteed under the Constitution and Bill of Rights."

My position remains unchanged.

COUNTERINTELLIGENCE PROGRAM—BACKGROUND MATERIAL

I. INTRODUCTION

The FBI's counterintelligence program was developed in response to needs at the time to quickly neutralize organizations and individuals who were advocating and fomenting urban violence and campus disorder. The riots which swept America's urban centers, beginning in 1965, were quickly followed by violent disorders which paralyzed college campuses. Both situations led to calls for action by alarmed Government leaders and a frightened citizenry.

II. TENOR OF THE TIMES

An Associated Press survey noted that, during the first nine months of 1967, racial violence in 67 cities resulted in 85 deaths, injuries to 3,200 people and property damage of over $100,000,000. The February, 1970, issue of "Security World" stated that during the period January 1 to August 31, 1969, losses specifically traced to campus disorders amounted to $8,946,972.

In March, 1965, then Senator Robert F. Kennedy predicted more violence in the South and North after Congress passed voting rights legislation. Kennedy said, "I don't care what legislation is passed—we are going to have problems . . . violence."

A United Press International release on December 5, 1967, quoted Pennsylvania's Governor Raymond P. Shafer as warning that "urban disaster" in the form of "total urban warfare" is waiting in the wings to strike if the race problem is not solved in the Nation's cities.

Attorney General Ramsey Clark reported to President Johnson on January 12, 1968, according to the "Washington Star," that extremist activity to foment "rebellion in urban ghettos" has put a severe strain on the FBI and other Justice Department resources. Clark called this "the most difficult intelligence problem" in the Justice Department.

A United Press International release on February 13, 1968, stated that President Johnson expected further turmoil in the cities and "several bad summers" before the Nation's urban problems are solved.

III. CALLS TO ACTION

President Lyndon Johnson said in a television address to the Nation on July 24, 1967, in describing events that led to sending troops to Detroit during that city's riot, "We will not tolerate lawlessness. We will not endure violence. It matters not by whom it is done, or under what slogan or banner. It will not be tolerated." He called upon "all of our people in all of our cities" to "show by word and by deed that rioting, looting and public disorder will just not be tolerated."

In a second address to the Nation in just three days, President Johnson announced the appointment of a special Advisory Commission on Civil Disorder to investigate origins of urban riots. The President said that this country had "endured a week such that no Nation should live through; a time of violence and tragedy." He declared that "the looting and arson and plunder and pillage which have occurred are not part of a civil rights protest." "It is no American right," said the President, to loot or burn or "fire rifles from the rooftops." Those in public responsibility have "an immediate" obligation "to end disorder," the President told the American people, by using "every means at our command. . . ."

The President warned public officials that "if your response to these tragic events is only business-as-usual, you invite not only disaster but dishonor." President Johnson declared that "violence must be stopped—quickly, finally and permanently" and he pledged "we will stop it."

House Speaker John W. McCormick said on July 24, 1967, after conferring with President Johnson that the President had told party leaders that "public order is the first business of Government." The next day, Senator Robert C. Byrd advocated "brutal force" to contain urban rioting and said adult looters should be "shot on the spot."

On April 12, 1968, Representative Clarence D. Long of Maryland urged J. Edgar Hoover in a letter and in a public statement to infiltrate extremist groups to head off future riots and said FBI Agents "could take people like Negro militants Stokely Carmichael and H. Rap Brown out of circulation."

The "St. Louis Globe—Democrat" in a February 14, 1969, editorial entitled, "Throw the Book at Campus Rioters," described campus disorders then sweeping the Nation as "a threat to the entire university educational system. This newspaper called on the Attorney General to "move now to stop these anti-American anarchists and communist stooges in their tracks. He should hit them with every weapon at his command. The American people are fed up with such bearded, anarchist creeps and would applaud a strong drive against them. They have been coodled and given license to run roughshod over the rights of the majority of college students far too long. It is time to hit them hard with everything in the book."

On October 2, 1969, Senator Byrd said that "events in the news in the past few days concerning activities by militant radical groups should alert us to the new trouble that is brewing on the Nation's college campuses and elsewhere." Senator Byrd said that "all of us would do well to pay heed now, and law enforcement authorities should plan a course of action before the situation gets completely out of hand."

After the August 24, 1970, bombing at the University of Wisconsin, Madison, a group of faculty members called for disciplinary action aaginst students involved in disruption and violence. In a statement delivered to the Chancellor, 867 faculty members said "the rising tide of intimidation and violence on the campuses in the last few years has made normal educational and scholarly activities increasingly difficult. There has been a steady escalation of destructiveness that has culminated in an act of homicide. Academic freedom, meaning freedom of expression for all ideas and viewpoints, has been steadily eroded until now many are questioning whether it exists on the Madison campus." The faculty members said that "the acts of a few must not be allowed to endanger the rights and privileges of all members of the academic community."

"The New York Times" reported on October 11, 1970, on "The Urban Guerrillas—A New Phenomenon in the United States" and noted that the Senate Subcommittee on Internal Security recently heard four days of testimony on four bills aimed at "crushing the urban guerrillas," including one "that would make it a crime to belong to or aid organizations advocating terrorism, and would prohibit the publication of periodicals that advocate violence against police and the overthrow of the Government."

The President's Commission on Campus Unrest in detailing "the law enforcement response" noted that "it is an undoubted fact that on some campuses there are men and women who plot, all too often successfully, to burn and bomb, and sometimes to maim and kill. The police must attempt to determine whether or not such a plot is in progress, and, if it is, they must attempt to thwart it."

Finally, Allan C. Brownfeld, a faculty member at the University of Maryland, writing in "Christian Economics," February 11, 1970, on "The New Left and the Politics of Confrontation" noted that "in many instances, those extremists who have fomented disorder have been in violation of state and Federal statutes." But, Mr. Brownfeld noted. "What is often missing is the will to prosecute and to bring such individuals before the bar of justice." Mr. Brownfeld's article was subcaptioned "A Society Which Will Not Defend Itself Against Anachists Cannot Long Survive."

IV. APPROPRIATIONS TESTIMONY

On February 10, 1966, FBI Director J. Edgar Hoover testified regarding the Ku Klux Klan, saying that "the Bureau continues its program of penetrating the Klan at all levels and, I may say, has been quite successful in doing so. The Bureau's role in penetrating the Klan has received public attention due to the solution of the brutal murders of Viola Luizzo in Alabama, Lieutenant Colonel Lemuel A. Penn in Georgia and the three civil rights workers in Mississippi. We have achieved a number of other tangible accomplishments in this field, most of which are not publicly known but are most significant." Discussion off the record followed.

v. PUBLIC SUPPORT OF THE COUNTERINTELLIGENCE PROGRAM

Following acknowledgement that the FBI had a counterintelligence program, syndicated columnist Victor Riesel wrote on June 15, 1973, "no apologies are due from those in the highest authority for secretly developing a domestic counter-revolutionary intelligence stratagem in early 1970." Mr. Riesel detailed the record of "dead students," "university libraries in flames," and "insensate murdering of cops," and concluded "it would have been wrong not to have attempted to counter the sheer off-the-wall terrorism of the 1969–70 bomb seasons. And it would be wrong today. No one need apologize for counterrevolutionary action."

"Our reaction is that we are exceedingly glad he ordered it," wrote the "St. Louis Globe—Democrat" in a December 11, 1973, editorial on the counterintelligence program. This newspaper noted that "the Federal Bureau of Investigation under the late J. Edgar Hoover conducted a three-year campaign of counter-intelligence 'to expose, disrupt, and neutralize' the New Left movement . . ." and that "many of these New Left groups were doing everything they could to undermine the Government and some of them resorted to bombings, street riots, and other gangster tactics. Others waged war on police across the Nation and on our system of justice. Still others disrupted the Nation's campuses. The Nation can be thankful it has a courageous and strong leader of the FBI to deal with the serious threats posed by New Left groups during this period."

On June 18, 1974, Eugene H. Methvin, Senior Editor, "The Reader's Digest," testified before the House Committee on Foreign Affairs regarding terrorism and noted, ". . . the FBI's counterintelligence program against the extremist core of the New Left was a model of sophisticated, effective counter-terrorist law enforcement action first developed and applied with devastating effect against the Ku Klux Klan in the mid-1960's. In that context the strategy won great publicity and praise; yet now we have the Attorney General condemning it. In the current climate of justifiable revulsion over Watergate, we are in danger of crippling law enforcement intelligence in a hysteria of reverse McCarthyism in which we close our eyes to evidence and some compelling necessities of domestic and international security."

THE FBI'S INTELLIGENCE BUDGET

The FBI, like other members of the intelligence community, is reluctant to report either the amount or the application of the funds it spends each year for intelligence activities. The Pike Committee set as its goal the revelation and analysis of the intelligence budget for all the intelligence agencies and, in so doing, encountered resistance from its witnesses. The FBI testimony provided little more than that offered by the other agencies. A specific figure of $82 million was presented to the committee as the FBI "intelligence" budget, but under scrutiny could not be broken down into components that would separate money spent for work on organized crime from amounts spent for counterespionage. (Victor Marchetti lists FBI foreign intelligence costs alone at $40 million [158], p. 95.) Appearing before the Pike Committee on August 7, 1975, Assistant Attorney General Glen Pommerening offered the following testimony, reprinted here in abridged form.

Testimony of Glen Pommerening, Assistant Attorney General for Administration ([84A], pp. 278–285)

Mr. POMMERENING. Thank you, Mr. Chairman.

I appreciate the chance to appear before you today to talk about the Department of Justice budget as it relates to intelligence activities and the process by which these activities are reviewed.

My comments, of course, will be based upon my firsthand knowledge of the process, a review of the records of my organization and its predecessor, and such elements of historical knowledge of the Department as may be within my knowledge.

Part 28, subpart O, of the Code of Federal Regulations, vested in the Assistant Attorney General for Administration the responsibility to supervise, direct, and review the preparation, justification, and execution of the Justice budget. This responsibility encompasses the setting of general policies and procedures for the formulation of the overall budget requests for the Department and for each subordinate organization for a given fiscal year.

Our budget, like that of most other agencies, has traditionally reflected a "categorical" approach, organized by appropriation and organization, so that the programs of a given organization have fallen under one or more generalized budget "activities." In the past, these broad categories have not, by themselves, provided much detail on the scope of particular programs.

Beginning with the fiscal year 1975 budget cycle, however, the Department took steps to initiate a more thorough form of budget review when it initiated its management-by-objectives (MBO) program. Under this program, all organizations provided specific objectives for all of their programs for that year.

In the fiscal year 1976 cycle, the Department integrated the management-by-objectives program with the traditional budget process. This step required all organizations to provide specific program objectives in support of their fiscal year 1976 funding request. For the first time, the Department received financial data at the program level of detail, and all major organizations participated in an indepth internal hearing process with senior department officials.

The purpose of these internal departmental hearings was to explore significant policy, program, and resource issues, including those matters relating to the intelligence activities of the Federal Bureau of Investigation.

In carrying out this new program, the Federal Bureau of Investigation made the most extensive submission of data that had ever been given the Department.

While the Department's fiscal year 1976 management-by-objectives budget formulation and internal review process did provide a more comprehensive level of information to the Department's leadership, it was evident that a more structured, programmatic perspective was required to provide greater detail and to facilitate cross-organizational analysis of Department programs.

Consequently, for fiscal year 1977, the Department has developed and implemented an MBO/budget planning system with a detailed program budget structure which highlights over 350 specific programs, including those dealing with intelligence gathering.

This structure enables, and indeed requires, each organization to describe to the Department its fiscal year 1977 plans and the level of resources required. This system is still developmental in the sense that this is the first year it has been tried, but we expect to refine and follow th's basic programmatic approach in future years, at least for internal review purposes.

In the fiscal year 1977 cycle, the FBI submitted detailed data on 42 separate programs, some of which are linked directly to its intelligence and counterintelligence programs. Much of this material is classified "Secret," but the submission is the most comprehensive the FBI has ever submitted as part of the Department's budget review process.

The Drug Enforcement Administration reported 38 program areas for fiscal year 1977, of which 6 related to intelligence, it noted that DEA has a budget activity for intelligence activities. The Immigration and Naturalization Service reported 34 program areas for fiscal year

1977, of which two were related to intelligence. Other organizations reporting programs related to intelligence activities in fiscal year 1977 are the Criminal Division and the Office of the Deputy Attorney General, which reported one intelligence program area respectively.

The internal review process for fiscal year 1977 continued the practice of extensive internal hearings oriented toward policy and program issues.

In summary, the Department had a basic but limited capacity to evaluate program and budget requests prior to 1974. Since then the amount of program information and analytical expertise available to the Department has increased markedly. These changes have improved the Department's ability to review programs. Although the formal submission to the OMB and the Congress does not reflect a comparable level of detail, we believe that our new MBO/budget planning system, and any subsequent refinements, will continue to insure Department awareness of intelligence programs and facilitate our ability to evaluate these programs and supporting budget requests.

This concludes my prepared statement, Mr. Chairman. Accompanying me today are Mr. Eugene W. Walsh, Assistant Director for the Administrative Division of the FBI and Mr. James F. Hoobler, Director, Management Programs and Budget Staff for the Department. We will be happy to answer any questions we can in this session and if you have questions related to classified material, we would be happy to respond to them at the appropriate time. Mr. Walsh also has a prepared statement.

[Mr. Walsh's prepared statement follows:]

STATEMENT OF MR. EUGENE W. WALSH, ASSISTANT DIRECTOR, ADMINISTRATIVE DIVISION, FEDERAL BUREAU OF INVESTIGATION

Mr. Chairman and members of the committee, the opportunity to appear before this committee is appreciated and I will do my best to respond fully and accurately to questions regarding the FBI's budget and programs.

While the FBI has submitted its budget request to the Department in a programmatic form only since the fiscal year 1975, it has always submitted its requests in strict conformance with Office of Management and Budget circular A–11 as do other agencies. This circular sets forth very detailed instructions concerning the preparation and submission of budget estimates.

However, extensive detail was provided in testimony before the Office of Management and Budget and congressional Appropriations Subcommittees with regard to the various FBI programs. Prior to the hearings for fiscal year 1975, the congressional appropriations hearings were held in executive session. Former Director Hoover customarily gave a portion of his testimony off-the-record when counterintelligence or other highly sensitive matters were discussed. At the conclusion of the open hearings held by the House Appropriations Subcommittee in connection with the fiscal year 1976 request, an executive session was called by the chairman to permit a discussion of counterintelligence and other similarly sensitive matters.

The FBI has always been willing to answer any inquiries by the Appropriations Committees or any other congressional committees concerning its programs or its use of funds. During the course of this present hearing, Mr. Chairman, should sensitive questions of a classified nature involving national security be brought up for response or discussion, I would request that this be done in executive session.

Chairman PIKE. Let us start with the basic question as to classified material. Who classifies it?

Mr. POMMERENING. Materials we receive are classified by the Federal Bureau of Investigation.

Chairman PIKE. Are they classified by the Director of the Federal Bureau of Investigation or are they classified at some lower level?

Mr. POMMERENING. I believe they are classified at a lower level but Mr. Walsh could better respond to the question.

Chairman PIKE. Who classifies the budget "secret?"

Mr. WALSH. In this particular response, Mr. Chairman, I acted as the classification officer, and it bears my number, No. 9.

Chairman PIKE. Now, what is there about the budget of the FBI that requires it to be secret?

Mr. WALSH. Mr. Chairman, there is nothing about the total budget that requires it to be secret. The only classification——

Chairman PIKE. All right, then what is the total budget of the FBI?

Mr. WALSH. The total budget of the FBI, Mr. Chairman, for fiscal year 1975, amounts to $449,546,000.

Chairman PIKE. Roughly $450 million?

Mr. WALSH. That is right, sir.

Chairman PIKE. Now, of that total amount, can you tell us how much is classified "secret?"

Mr. WALSH. I can't tell you exactly, Mr. Chairman, but the idea of the classification is——

Chairman PIKE. You mean you can't tell us because you don't know or you decline to tell us in open session?

Mr. WALSH. No, sir. What I mean is, if I may have an opportunity to explain in my own way, what we are seeking to do is not to reveal the specific resources and manpower committed to counterintelligence——

Chairman PIKE. I understand that, but I am not asking you specifically about resources and manpower. I am asking you for the number of dollars as to which you can't give us any details. How much of that $450 million FBI budget is secret?

Mr. POMMERENING. Mr. Chairman, in our interpretation of the budget submission we have received from the FBI and the classifications that have been applied to them, the amount that we consider in one way or another constrained by classification is $82,488,000, which is for fiscal year 1975.

Chairman PIKE. Of the amount which is not classified, how much is dedicated to gathering intelligence?

Mr. POMMERENING. None.

Chairman PIKE. So all of the money which is dedicated to gathering intelligence falls within the secret budget?

Mr. POMMERENING. That is correct.

Chairman PIKE. Is all of the money within the secret budget dedicated to gathering intelligence?

Mr. POMMERENING. My interpretation of the budget submission is that the answer is yes.

Chairman PIKE. Now, tell us why the amount of money—well, I guess it isn't secret any more because you have now told us how much of it is secret, so that is no longer a secret.

We have got $82 million worth of "un-line-itemed" expenditures for the gathering of intelligence.

Does the GAO audit these expenditures?

Mr. POMMERENING. Yes; they do.

Chairman PIKE. On a complete line item basis whenever they want to without any restrictions?

Mr. WALSH. May I respond to that, Mr. Chairman?

Chairman PIKE. Certainly.

Mr. WALSH. Before I do, I would ask your leave to clarify one statement. I am not positive that the $82 million figure mentioned by Mr. Pommerening includes intelligence gathered in the field of organized crime.

I would have to check that to make absolutely certain but I feel that type of intelligence is not included in the figure that Mr. Pommerening mentioned.

Chairman PIKE. Are you saying what we spend for intelligence against organized crime is not secret?

Mr. WALSH. It isn't secret in the category of the national defense or security category, but it would certainly be harmful to our effort I would say, Mr. Chairman, if organized crime were aware in specific detail——

Chairman PIKE. I don't have any trouble agreeing with you; all I am trying to find out is, is the $82 million figure secret intelligence-gathering activities of the FBI which have nothing to do with organized crime?

Mr. WALSH. Mr. Pommerening has advised me that the entire intelligence effort is included in the $82 million and I stand corrected on that.

Chairman PIKE. Mr. McClory?

Mr. McCLORY. You say that the GAO has reviewed the budget of the Department of Justice and the FBI, and if so, where is the GAO report? Is that available to us? May we have a copy of that?

Mr. WALSH. If I may explain, Congressman McClory, I have some exact data here on the extent of their audit and it is as follows:

During the past 15 years the General Accounting Office has conducted two separate site audits relating to an examination of the Bureau's payroll records.

On January 18, 1964, an audit of payroll records covering the period June 1, 1961, through January 18, 1964, was completed.

On August 3, 1972, GAO completed an audit of payroll records covering the period January 19, 1964, through January 8, 1972.

Mr. McCLORY. They have really never audited the expenditures of the FBI, have they?

Mr. WALSH. For the record, if I could add one additional thing, with regard to the GAO audit of voucher records, three separate site audits have been made during the past 15 years.

In January, 1965, GAO completed an audit of all voucher and related records for the fiscal years 1961 through 1964.

In May 1969 their audit covered the fiscal years 1965 through 1968 period and in April 1972, GAO audited these records covering fiscal years 1969 through 1971. That is the extent of their audit except for what is going on at the present time.

Mr. McCLORY. The FBI refused access to GAO for auditing their expenditures. How about the secret funds, the intelligence funds? They haven't been audited by the GAO, have they?

Mr. WALSH. No; Mr. Congressman, they have not specifically audited funds for intelligence.

Mr. McCLORY. How many people worked on the FBI budget?

Mr. POMMERENING. Mr. Chairman, I think that is a question for me. Mr. Walsh, of course, has an extensive staff assisting him in the preparation of the budget submissions of the FBI.

The staff which is available to me in budget preparation for the entire Department is 53 in number.

Mr. McCLORY. How many do the FBI?

Mr. POMMERENING. There are a total of five analysts assigned to the Federal Bureau of Investigation.

Mr. McCLORY. How many OMB personnel really go into the FBI budget?

Mr. POMMERENING. The Office of Management and Budget, I understand, has seven people whose responsibility includes the entire Department of Justice and the entire Department of the Treasury. They only have one person that I know of with the FBI.

Mr. McCLORY. Now, did the former Director, J. Edgar Hoover, defend funds that were available to him separately for his personal investigations, or his personal files that he maintained?

Mr. WALSH. To my knowledge, sir, he did not.

Mr. McCLORY. Would that be covered in any fiscal report, any budgetary report?

Mr. WALSH. I don't know that it would be covered anywhere, Mr. McClory. I just have never heard this situation raised.

Mr. McCLORY. How about the program of Cointelpro? Are you familiar with that?

Mr. WALSH. I am familiar with that, sir, in a very general way. It was never under my supervision——

Mr. McCLORY. Was that program presented to the Appropriations Committees of the House and the Senate, and appropriations specifically designated for that program?

Mr. WALSH. The Cointel program, as I understand it, was discussed off the record by Mr. Hoover before the House Appropriations Committee, on at least six occasions.

Mr. McCLORY. That would be a program that would go into the secret, unaudited funds, would it not?

Mr. WALSH. That program, sir, was not separately funded. There is no fund specifically assigned to what you are referring to as the Cointelpro.

Mr. McCLORY. Are the funds for those purposes discontinued, at the present time, do you know?

Mr. WALSH. That program has been discontinued.

Mr. McCLORY. My time is already up. Thank you.

Chairman PIKE. Mr. Dellums?

Mr. DELLUMS. Mr. Chairman, I request unanimous consent to reserve my time.

Chairman PIKE. Mr. Murphy?

Mr. MURPHY. How are the covert programs in the FBI currently reflected in the budget?

Mr. POMMERENING. Mr. Murphy, the way the budget is submitted through the Office of Management and Budget and to the Congress, the funds which are used for intelligence purposes are included under the category Security and Criminal Investigations and Field Investigations.

Mr. MURPHY. Is any of this money ever transferred to other agencies?

Mr. WALSH. No, sir.

Mr. MURPHY. Could you tell us how much money was spent last year on electronic surveillance?

Mr. WALSH. I do not have that information, Mr. Murphy. I would regard it as being confidential in the interests of national security. I would say if this committee required that information, we could obtain it and submit it but I do not have that information.

Mr. MURPHY. I wish you would submit it. We do require it. Would you please submit it to the committee?

[The information requested by Congressman Murphy will be printed in the appendixes of the November 18, 1975, hearing.]

Mr. MURPHY. Let me know if you use any other intelligence, garnered through electronic surveillance, from any other agency. In other words, does the NSA or the Central Intelligence Agency, do they let you share information they receive through electronic surveillance, or any other method in which they get it?

Mr. WALSH. If I may preface my response, Mr. Murphy, I am not an expert in this field.

Mr. MURPHY. To whom should we address these questions?

Mr. WALSH. That particular question would be within the realm of the responsibility and knowledge of Assistant Director Wannall. I know in a general way, Mr. Murphy, that all agencies in the intelligence community share intelligence information.

Mr. MURPHY. Did our staff indicate to you that we might get into these areas before your appearance here today?

Mr. WALSH. Not this particular area; no.

Mr. MURPHY. Any of you gentlemen? Your answer is no?

Mr. POMMERENING. No.

Mr. MURPHY. Do you maintain a central registry of informants' names?

Mr. WALSH. Yes, we do, Mr. Murphy.

Mr. MURPHY. Mr. Chairman, I am going to reserve what time I have left and pass at this moment.

Chairman PIKE. Mr. Aspin?

Mr. ASPIN. Thank you, Mr. Chairman.

Are any of you gentlemen the kind of person who could give us some opinions about the current status of wiretapping and what is legal and what is not legal? Is that in your purview?

Mr. WALSH. It is not in mine, Mr. Aspin.

Mr. ASPIN. Do you know, for example, does the FBI or the Justice Department provide information to the NSA and ask the NSA to help in conducting surveillance? I am thinking particularly of the NSA's wiretap operations. Do you provide input for them on those?

Mr. WALSH. I honestly can't respond to that because of lack of knowledge, Mr. Aspin. It is not in my field and I really don't have that information.

Mr. ASPIN. Could you tell us about the $82 million in the budget? Give us broad categories as to what that goes to. What are the different things for which that money is spent?

Mr. POMMERENING. Mr. Aspin, the subcategories of that item—and I hasten to add that these are not all secret funds—the security classification is applied to the total, to eliminate the possibility, by subtraction, of isolating the figure which is the figure sought to be protected.

The program activities which are included in that category are, internal security, counterintelligence, and intelligence—broken down into general criminal, organized crime, internal security intelligence, and counterintelligence.

Mr. ASPIN. Can you tell us broadly within that—are there any numbers that can be released about how much is spent on those things?

Mr. POMMERENING. That is the problem we have, Mr. Aspin. If we release some, by the process of elimination——

Mr. ASPIN. Which is the biggest? Can you give me an order of magnitude of how much is spent?

Mr. POMMERENING. There are three of them that are at about the same level.

Mr. ASPIN. Can you tell us which three those are? Are those the three largest?

Mr. POMMERENING. Internal security, counterintelligence, and intelligence with its subcategories, are all——

Mr. ASPIN. Are all three about the same?

Mr. POMMERENING. That is correct.

Mr. ASPIN. What is the difference between internal security and counterespionage?

Mr. POMMERENING. In general terms—and, of course, the interpretation of these definitions, in large part, must rest with the operating agency which must assign costs and man-years between them. Under the internal security category—general guidelines—we have violation of constitutional rights, including civil rights; problems of terrorism, and problems of anti-Government activity.

Mr. ASPIN. Counterespionage would be what?

Mr. POMMERENING. In counterintelligence, we have the general problems of reviewing and being aware of intelligence activities of other nations, and attempts to assess the extent of them and to take appropriate measures to deal with them.

Mr. ASPIN. If you did wiretaps, for example, they might be under any of those?

Mr. POMMERENING. Yes.

Mr. ASPIN. As the cost of a particular wiretap connected with it, it would fall under the category of whatever it was, espionage, or there might be an internal security wiretap; is that right?

Mr. POMMERENING. Yes.

Mr. ASPIN. Mr. Chairman, my time is up.

Chairman PIKE. Mr. Kasten?

Mr. KASTEN. I want to go back to a question Mr. McClory raised. How was Cointelpro reflected in the FBI budget?

Mr. WALSH. Mr. Kasten, there is no such program at the present time.

Mr. KASTEN. How was it reflected in the FBI budget? It is my understanding it was not reflected in the FBI budget. Is that your understanding?

Mr. WALSH. Yes, sir. It was part of a general category of field investigations.

Mr. KASTEN. If another program like that were instituted today or tomorrow, would it be reflected in the budget under the new procedure, under the new format, or would it still be not listed? Would it still be completely hidden?

Mr. WALSH. It would have to be reflected in the material that we submit to the Department of Justice, specifically to Mr. Pommerening's organization, but I don't believe the formal budget submission has been adjusted by Congress to require, or reflect, that type of information.

Am I correct on that?

Mr. POMMERENING. Yes.

Mr. KASTEN. In fiscal year 1976 how many FBI personnel were stationed abroad?

Mr. WALSH. From recollection, sir, I would say 83, subject to correction of one or two employees.

Mr. KASTEN. It could be there were 77—54 legal attachés and 43 support people?

Mr. WALSH. That would be approximately correct.

Mr. KASTEN. About how much money do you think these people cost?

Mr. WALSH. I don't have that, sir, but I can easily obtain it.

Mr. KASTEN. Would $4.2 billion be it?

Mr. WALSH. That does sound reasonable, sir; yes.

Mr. KASTEN. I want to ask some questions about the activities of the FBI abroad. Would you characterize a program to insure—I am quoting from a report that you prepared—"a program to insure a constant and prompt exchange of information" a form of intelligence gathering?

Mr. WALSH. I think it could be so characterized.

NOTES AND REFERENCES

1. "Counterespionage" and "counterintelligence" are at times used interchangeably. "Counterespionage" may be used to refer to the means by which the disruptive objectives of counterintelligence are attained.

2. There is within the FBI organizational structure the Intelligence Division, which is separated into an Internal Security Branch and a Counterintelligence Branch. Section one (CI-1) of the Counterintelligence Branch concentrates on the U.S.S.R.; C-2 handles other countries; C1-3 is organized along nongeographic lines and focuses on such matters as flow of foreign currency, Atomic Energy Act violations, bombings, etc. An organization chart of the FBI appears in this chapter; a more detailed chart on the FBI is available in [84A], p. 396.

3. Specific citizens and domestic groups have been targets of FBI domestic intelligence investigations. Such examples of FBI inquiry included in this portion of the text were drawn, in large part, from committee hearings in November and December 1975, published as Volume 6 ([44F]) by the Church Committee. The exhibits reprinted are among those in over 600 pages of letters and memoranda, providing a rich documentary resource for study of the FBI's inner workings in the J. Edgar Hoover period.

4. The FBI Counterintelligence Program (COINTELPRO), established in 1956, was a domestic intelligence and covert action program aimed at investigating U.S. citizens believed to have questionable "foreign" ties. This program is described and analyzed in detail in Book III of the Church Committee ([45C], pp. 3 ff.).

Chapter 9
Department of State

INTELLIGENCE FUNCTIONS OF THE DEPARTMENT OF STATE ([45A], pp. 305–315)

The Department of State is charged with developing and implementing U.S. foreign policy. It is a participant, a client, and, at times, a victim of the U.S. intelligence community. Through the Foreign Service establishment operating in most countries of the world, the State Department itself generates a massive amount of intelligence-related information; this information is fed to its analysis unit (the Bureau of Intelligence and Research), as well as to other intelligence agencies. The department, in effect, consumes the finished intelligence product of the CIA, DIA, and others. When the intelligence product is wrong or an operation goes awry, it is usually the State Department and the embassy that must deal with its effect on U.S. relations.

The overall organization of the State Department and the Foreign Service has been subjected to critical scrutiny by the Commission on the organization of Government for the Conduct of Foreign Policy (Murphy Commission [90]). The Murphy Commission material provides a well-documented study resource of the State Department, its role in the intelligence community, and the function of intelligence in U.S. foreign policy. But the Church Committee's final report provides a more concise description of this department's intelligence operations and the manner in which they relate to the rest of the intelligence community. A portion of the Church Committee's 1976 report dealing with the State Department is reprinted here.

In addition to strengthening our defense, the purpose of U.S. intelligence activities is more effective foreign policy. Intelligence informs foreign policy decisions and in the role of covert action seeks to attain foreign policy objectives. In sum, intelligence is a service, a support function, indeed it is so designated and structured by the military services. However, in the field of foreign policy, intelligence activities have sometimes become an end in themselves, dominating or divorced from policy considerations and insulated in important respects from effective policy oversight.

The Department of State is responsible for the formulation and execution of foreign policy. Yet unlike the Department of Defense, the State Department has no command over intelligence activities essential to its mission except the Foreign Service.

The Department of State and the American Foreign Service are the chief producers and consumers of political and economic intelligence in the United States Government. The Department participates actively in the interagency mechanisms concerned with collection and production of intelligence. However, it has been unable or unwilling to assume responsibility over clandestine intelligence activities.

The Foreign Service competes with the Clandestine Service in the production of human source intelligence, but operates openly and does not pay its sources. The State Department, as well as American ambassadors abroad, is called upon, at least in theory, to exert a measure of control over certain aspects of CIA's secret overseas activities. Indeed, the State Department through U.S. embassies and consulates offers the only external check upon CIA's overseas activities; they are the only means abroad that can help assure that America's clandestine activities are being carried out in accord with the decisions made at the highest level in Washington.

The primary purpose of the Select Committee's inquiry was to examine the effectiveness of the Department of State and the Foreign Service in this role. The Committee also examined the Foreign Service intelligence collection efforts.

To this end, the Select Committee visited several overseas missions, embassies and consulates and conducted extensive interviews with ambassadors, Foreign Service officers and State Department personnel as well as taking sworn testimony. From this investigation it is evident that the role of the Department of State is central to fundamental reform and improvement in America's intelligence operations overseas.

Origins of the State Department Intelligence Function

It has been the traditional function of the Department of State and the Foreign Service to gather, report and analyze information on foreign political, military, economic and cultural developments. That intelligence function, like most of the responsibilities of the Department, is not established by statute. The basic statement of the duties and responsibilities of the Secretary of State is contained in an Act of Congress of July 27, 1789, as follows:

The Secretary of State shall perform such duties as shall from time to time be enjoined on or intrusted to him by the President relative to correspondences, commissions, or instructions with public ministers from foreign states or princes, or to memorials or other applications from foreign public ministers or other foreigners, or to such other matter respecting foreign affairs as the President of the United States shall assign to the department and he shall conduct the business of the department in such manner as the President shall direct.[1]

The statutes are no more precise about the functions of the Foreign Service, and the members which

shall under the direction of the Secretary [of State], represent abroad the interests of the United States and shall perform the duties and comply with the obligations resulting from the nature of their appointments or assignments or imposed on them by the terms of any law or by any order or regulation issued pursuant to law or by any international agreement in which the United States is a party.[2]

Most Presidents have chosen to use the Secretary of State as their principal advisor and agent in foreign affairs; foreign intelligence activities of the Department and Foreign Service have developed in a logical pattern from that practice.

[1] R.S. § 202, 22 U.S. 2556.
[2] 22 U.S. 841.

Today the President's Executive Order assigns to State responsibility for collecting overtly "foreign political, political-military, sociological, economic, scientific, technical and associated biographic information."   The reporting of the Foreign Service, together with that of the military attaché system, based on firsthand observation and especially on official dealings with governments, makes up the most useful element of our foreign intelligence information. Clandestine and technical sources provide supplementary information, the relative importance of which varies with the nature and accessibility of the information sought.

While clandestine and technical sources of information are today the responsibility of the CIA and other agencies, State is not without past experience in such matters. The Department operated one or more clandestine intelligence networks during and after World War II and closed them down, at CIA insistence, only in the 1950s. The Department engaged in such activities in earlier times. On the technical side, the State Department operated a cryptanalytic unit called the Black Chamber during the inter-war years. It was abolished by Secretary Stimson in 1929 on the ground that "gentlemen do not read each other's mail."

Although foreign intelligence has always been a major function of the State Department, the Department had no separate—and acknowledged—intelligence unit prior to World War II. At the end of the war, the research and analysis branch of the Office of Strategic Services (OSS), numbering over 1,500, was transferred to the Department, and the position of Special Assistant to the Secretary for Research and Intelligence was established to head the new organization into which was incorporated as well certain existing State units.

President Truman initially contemplated a much more significant intelligence role for State and directed Secretary Byrnes to

> take the lead in developing a comprehensive and coordinated foreign intelligence program for all Federal agencies concerned with that type of activity. This should be done through the creation of an inter-departmental group, heading up under the State Department, which should formulate plans for my approval.[2b]

Although Dean Acheson, as Under Secretary, moved promptly in the fall of 1945 to develop such plans, he soon

> encountered heavy flak. It came from three sources: congressional opposition to professional intelligence work, civil disobedience in the State Department [i.e. the geographic divisions opposed "intelligence work not in their organizations and under their control"] and indecision in high places brought on by military opposition to both unification of the services and civilian control of intelligence.[3]

In the end Secretary Byrnes bowed to this opposition and joined in recommending to the President what Acheson calls "an odd plan for a National Intelligence Authority and a Central Intelligence Group,

---

[2b] Dean Acheson, *Present at the Creation* (New York: W. W. Norton and Co., 1969), p. 158.

[3] *Ibid.*, p. 159.

. . . thus moving primacy in intelligence from the State Department to the Executive Office of the President." [4]

Byrnes also adopted the recommendations of the Department's geographic divisions and broke up the OSS research and analysis unit which State had inherited, dispersing its personnel to those divisions. However, this decision was reversed by General Marshall shortly after he became Secretary of State in January 1947 and State has since then had a central intelligence unit, now generally known as INR (Bureau of Intelligence and Research). INR's stature and influence in the Department have gradually increased, though its size has been greatly reduced, numbering today some 325 with a budget of less than $10 million. The reduction has resulted in part from budgetary pressures, in part from the transfer of certain functions (e.g., contributions to the now-defunct National Intelligence Survey, biographic reporting) to the CIA.

The organization is made up of two directorates reflecting the two basic responsibilities of the organization. The Directorate for Research produces finished intelligence (reports and estimates) to meet the operating and planning requirements of the Department. The Directorate also participates in the production of National Intelligence Estimates. The Directorate for Coordination is concerned with the Department's relations with the other intelligence agencies on matters other than the production of substantive intelligence. This includes (a) the provision of Departmental guidance on operational intelligence questions, including staff support for State participation on the 40 Committee; (b) management of assignment of Defense Attaché personnel; and (c) development of positions on intelligence requirements and the allocation of intelligence resources.

However, INR has no personnel abroad and is not responsible for the collection of intelligence overseas. The substantive direction of the U.S. embassies and consulates, which are the intelligence collectors, is the responsibility of the geographic bureaus.

Command and Control

In viewing the role of the Department of State in command and control of intelligence operations, it is necessary to distinguish between Washington and the embassies abroad. The authority and responsibility of the Secretary of State in this area differs markedly from that of the Ambassador. Secondly, a distinction must be made between covert operations, where the influence of the Department and the Ambassador is normally substantial, and clandestine intelligence and counterintelligence operations (espionage and counterespionage), where the role of the Department, and sometimes but not always that of the Ambassador, is minimal.

ROLE OF THE STATE DEPARTMENT IN WASHINGTON

The duties and responsibilities of the Secretary of State, in general, and for the direction and supervision of U.S. foreign intelligence operations in particular, have not been defined by statute. Proposals after World War II to put the Secretary of State in overall control of U.S. foreign intelligence activities were rejected. The role of the Secretary appears to be further downgraded in the President's Executive Order

---

[4] *Ibid.*, pp. 160–161.

of February 1976. The State Department is not represented on the new Committee on Foreign Intelligence and the Secretary is only authorized to "coordinate with" the DCI to ensure that United States intelligence activities and programs are useful for and consistent with United States foreign policy.

Nevertheless, the Secretary is the senior Cabinet member, his primacy within the executive branch in foreign relations has usually been accepted, and his Department is the only one with knowledge, personnel and facilities abroad to exercise effective control over foreign operations. A Secretary who is disposed to assert his potential influence and who has the support of the President can exercise considerable control over CIA activities. This is clearly the situation today. It is equally clear that it was not the situation under the previous Secretary of State, William Rogers, who not only did not play an active role in the intelligence area but on at least one occasion, the Committee found, was systematically and deliberately kept in the dark regarding important CIA operations.[5]

N2

Apart from his relationship with the President, however, the Secretary of State has had only limited influence upon the CIA. The Secretary of State does not have access to CIA communications, except as prescribed by the DCI. This privileged position, it is contended, is sanctioned by the provision of the National Security Act of 1947 making the DCI responsible for protecting intelligence sources and methods from unauthorized disclosure. The Secretary of State knows only as much about CIA operations as CIA elects to tell him. Secondly, except for covert action operations considered by the 40 Committee, he has had no voice in the expenditure of CIA funds abroad. This is in contrast to the role the Secretary of State has with regard to expenditure of Military Assistance Program funds.

The Secretary of State's influence or control over CIA operations varies greatly, depending upon the nature of the activity. It has been greatest in the area of covert action, least in the area of espionage. In the setting of intelligence requirements and the allocation of intelligence resources, the Secretary of State has a voice but it is only one voice out of many.

N3

Authority for State influence over covert operations derives from NSC directives and is exercised through membership on the 40 Committee (now the Operations Advisory Group—OAG), which reviews and recommends approval of such operations and certain sensitive reconnaissance programs. Until the Kennedy administration, State chaired the Committee. During the Kennedy and Johnson administrations, even without the chairmanship, State often had a virtually controlling voice, through its veto power. Covert action and sensitive reconnaissance operations are normally not presented to the Committee unless cleared in advance with (or originated by) State and, where this is not the case, a negative State position has rarely been overridden. There have, however, been important exceptions, notably during the first Nixon term when State influence declined markedly. On one occasion the 40 Committee itself was bypassed.[6]

The leading role which State has normally played in the 40 Committee stems from the fact that covert actions are designed to further foreign policy objectives. But operations clearly have driven policy in many instances. It is the CIA, not State, which is called on, in the

---

[5] Senate Select Committee, "Alleged Assassination Plots Involving Foreign Leaders," p. 231.

[6] *Ibid.*, p. 225.

first instance, to explain and justify these programs to Congress. In part this has been due to a desire to preserve State's "deniability." However, that has apparently ended with President Ford's Executive Order which formally requires Secretary of State attendance at OAG meetings.

In contrast to the 40 Committee mechanism for covert action operations, there is no systematic procedure for Washington review and approval of clandestine intelligence and counterintelligence (espionage and counterespionage) operations outside CIA. The distinction was made by former DCI Richard Helms in this way:

> Mr. HELMS. Exactly. Now this was one kind of approval for the so-called political action projects. They had to be approved not only once a year, but as they came forward each time. And thus they had to be sent to the Approval Committee, you know, it has been variously known as 303 and Forty and Special Group and so forth. So there was a special mechanism to have those projects cleared in the Special Group.
>
> The intelligence projects had a different kind of clearance mechanism, because they could be done under the Director's own authority. As you recall, NSCID Number 5 gives the Director the authority to do foreign intelligence [checks?] and counterespionage on his own recognizance, he doesn't have to check it out with anybody as to whether he did this or that or something else.
>
> Q. Is that a good system? When you were Director you had a sensitive collection program or counterintelligence program. Did you often or sometimes check with the President or somebody in the White House or the Secretary of State about the advisability or risks? Did you regard that as really basic to your job?
>
> Mr. HELMS. It was left to my judgment when I was Director as to whether I cleared it with anybody or not.
>
> Q. Did you very often?
>
> Mr. HELMS. From time to time I did. I was involved with that Berlin Tunnel, for example, and I remember, we did check that out before we went ahead with it.
>
> Q. You did or did not?
>
> Mr. HELMS. We did. And there were certain others that we checked out before we went ahead with them. I don't remember what they all were now. But there was a rule of reason that was permitted to prevail here. And I think most directors were sensitive enough fellows that if you were really going to run a serious risk to our diplomatic life or our foreign policy life, you might want to go to see the Secretary of State or somebody to hold hands on those things.[7]

N4

Thus State is effectively excluded from the decision to carry out espionage operations unless CIA elects to consult. Because in practice State is rarely consulted,[8] it does not have institutional arrangements to develop advice and guidance in this area—as it does for covert action operations.

---

[7] Staff summary of Richard Helms interview, 9/11/75, p. 62.
[8] Out of hundreds of agent recruitment efforts last year the Secretary of State was consulted on less than five.

The Committee is strongly of the view that these informal arrangements, which leave consultation to the discretion of the DCI and which do not fix any responsibility on the Secretary of State, have proved to be harmful. Two areas of concern can be cited : First, some espionage operations, e.g., the attempted recruitment as an agent or an official of a friendly government, can have major adverse foreign policy repercussions. Second, certain types of espionage operations have had the effect of covert political action. For example, a subsidy to the leader of a dissident group to facilitate the collection of information about the group, has been taken by the leader (and the government in power) as support for his dissidence. Thus a DCI cannot be subject to 40 Committee or other controls by defining an operation with significant political impact as espionage. State Department review of espionage operations is needed to provide support and advice to ambassadors in field supervision of CIA activities.

COMMAND AND CONTROL IN THE FIELD

The Chancery of a U.S. embassy abroad provides offices and a measure of cover for a number of intelligence community people who appear on the staff roster with such titles as "attache," "political research officer," or "special assistant"—the same titles used by other personnel. In most embassies it is common knowledge as to who is a "spook," slang designation for a CIA person; they are often listed as "political officers," but occupy offices separate from the embassy political section. The head of the CIA group within the embassy, or "station chief," is usually a high ranking person who deals directly with the ambassador and the "country team" (composed of the local heads of all U.S. agencies operating within a given country). The Defense (Department) Attache system is more overt than that of the CIA and the operatives are simply listed as "defense attaches." The staff of NSA, assigned to embassies or consulates, tends to operate within the communications unit of the embassies, isolated in a highly secure space and often assumes clerical titles. The "clandestine" agents working in a country operate on the "other side of the house"—jargon for those who do not use an official U.S. position as cover or, if they do, do not acknowledge any CIA association to peers within the embassy. The clandestine agents usually work under the supervision of, and maintain some form of contact with, the station chief or his aides. They appear to have more ordinary jobs as business executives, scholars, writers, etc. The ability of an ambassador to maintain a measure of awareness and control over the size and activity of the intelligence group assigned to his embassy is usually limited. It raises serious questions regarding the coordination of foreign policy objectives in the field and was a subject addressed by the Church Committee.

In contrast to the uncertain authority of the Secretary of State, the authority of the Ambassador with respect to U.S. intelligence activities in his country of assignment is clear, and, since 1974, has had a statutory basis.

In 1961, President Kennedy addressed a letter to each Ambassador stating that he expected him "to oversee and coordinate all activities of
N5   the United States Government" in his country of assignment.[9]

---

[9] "The Ambassador and the Problem of Coordination, A Study Submitted by the Subcommittee on National Security Staffing and Operations (Pursuant to S. Res. 13, 88th Cong.) to the Committee on Government Operations, United States Senate."

That letter appears to have remained in force until it was superseded, in December 1969, by a similar letter from President Nixon which included the following:

> As Chief of the United States Diplomatic Mission, you have full responsibility to direct and coordinate the activities and operations of all of its elements. You will exercise this mandate not only by providing policy leadership and guidance, but also by assuring positive program direction to the end that all United States activities in (the host country) are relevant to current realities, are efficiently and economically administered, and are effectively interrelated so that they will make a maximum contribution to United States interests in that country as well as to our regional and international objectives.[10]

This letter was supplemented by a classified State Department instruction,[11] concurred in by the Director of Central Intelligence, which advised the Ambassador how the President's letter should be interpreted with regard to CIA. The effect of this instruction is to make the Ambassador's access to information on intelligence sources and methods and his authority to approve or disapprove CIA operations subject to the agreement of the Chief of Station and, in the event of disagreement, to Washington for decision. It may well also have had the effect of inhibiting ambassadors in seeking to inform themselves fully in this area.

In 1974, the authority of the Ambassador was given a statutory basis. The following new section was added to "An Act to provide certain basic authority for the Department of State," approved August 1, 1956, as amended: [12]

> *Authority and Responsibility of Ambassadors.* Under the Direction of the President—
>
> (1) the United States Ambassador to a foreign country shall have full responsibility for the direction, coordination, and supervision of all United States Government officers and employees in that country, except for personnel under the command of a United States area military commander;
>
> (2) the Ambassador shall keep himself fully and currently informed with respect to all activities and operations of the United States Government within that country, and shall insure that all government officers and employees in that country, except for personnel under the command of a United States area military commander, comply fully with his directives; and
>
> (3) any department or agency having officers or employees in a country shall keep the United States Ambassador to that country fully and currently informed with respect to all activities and operations of its officers and employees in that country, and shall insure that all of its officers and employees, except for personnel under the command of a United States

---

[10] State Department Foreign Affairs Manual, 1 FAM 011.2, 1/27/70.
[11] CA–6693, 12/17/69.
[12] 22 U.S. 2680a.

area military commander, comply fully with all applicable directives of the Ambassador.

The legislative history indicates that this statute was intended to give statutory force to existing directives. However, under any reasonable construction, it goes well beyond the Nixon letter, particularly as interpreted by the State Department instruction cited above. Nevertheless, more than a year after its enactment, no new regulation or directives have been issued by the executive branch in implementation of the statute, nor does it appear that it necessarily plans to take any action to modify present guidelines. In response to the Committee's inquiry, the White House has advised the Chairman as follows:

> As you know, the issues addressed by this legislation were encompassed in President Kennedy's letter of May 29, 1961, President Nixon's similar letter of December 9, 1969, and the Department of State Circular Airgram 6693 of December 17, 1969. In addition, the Department of State in July 1975 sent the relevant section of Public Law 93–475 [13] to all major embassies in confirmation and reinforcement of existing guidelines. The President is considering further steps and we will keep you informed of any additional action that is taken.[14]

So far as the Committee knows, no Ambassador has sought to invoke the statute in seeking information on CIA operations. One senior Ambassador testified that the statute is not really in effect without implementing regulations in the executive branch:

> Ambassador PORTER. Yes, but when you get the legislation but you don't get the regulation based on it, you're not much better off. That '74, yes, sir, that '74 addition to the basic State Department Authorization Act, that really isn't in force because the implementing regulations have not been issued.
>
> Senator MONDALE. Well, Mr. Ambassador, when a law is passed, that is the law, is it not?
>
> Ambassador PORTER. Yes, sir.
>
> Senator MONDALE. Can a law be repealed by failing to issue regulations?
>
> Ambassador PORTER. Repealed?
>
> Senator MONDALE. Suspended.
>
> Ambassador PORTER. Suspended? I would say yes.
>
> Senator MONDALE. I think the word is "inoperative." [15]

The statute is apparently also "inoperative" so far as the CIA is concerned, as indicated by the following CIA written responses to Committee questions:

> —*If the Ambassador asked to see every operational report (as opposed to intelligence report) what would the Chief of Station say?*
>
> The Chief of Station would inform the Ambassador that he is referring the Ambassador's request immediately to his headquarters for guidance.

---

[13] *Ibid.*

[14] Letter from Philip Buchen, Counsel to the President, to Senator Church, 12/22/75.

[15] William J. Porter testimony, 11/11/75, pp. 45–46.

—Is there any place where agent recruitments are cleared by the Ambassador or the Secretary of State, including real names?

Individual agent recruitments are not cleared with either the Ambassadors or the Secretary of State.[16]

The Committee staff has learned that there are divergent views within the executive branch regarding implementation of the new statute. It is clear from the testimony that CIA opposes giving the Ambassador the unrestricted access to its communications and other operational information that the law would appear to authorize. In the past, the Agency has argued that this would conflict with the provision of the National Security Act making the Director of Central Intelligence responsible "for protecting intelligence sources and methods from unauthorized disclosure." However, the statute resolves any doubts as to whether disclosure to the Ambassador is authorized.

There are also other problems, of a practical nature, in implementing the statute. Can an Ambassador, without additional support from Washington, effectively direct and supervise the work of CIA personnel? The basic responsibility of the Ambassador is for United States relations with the country to which he is accredited. The Ambassador is expected to be highly knowledgeable about the country to which he is assigned. For CIA operations conducted within his country of assignment, the Ambassador should be a good judge of the risks of such operations, and of their possible usefulness to the U.S. It is often the case, however, that CIA espionage operations mounted from his embassy are directed against a *third* country, more often than not a denied area country.[17] There is no assurance that the Ambassador is qualified to assess fully the risks or benefits of such operations. Nor, if he perceives that an operation directed from his embassy in Country X against the denied area country poses a risk to U.S. relations with Country X, is he able to weigh that risk against the potential benefits of the intelligence to be gained. Such judgments often can only be made in Washington. Washington is where the problem arises. No one outside the CIA, unless it be the President himself, is responsible for directing and supervising CIA clandestine intelligence operations or is authorized access to the information necessary to do so.

A logical corollary to 22 U.S. 2680a would, thus, be to assign to a Washington authority responsibility for control and supervision of clandestine intelligence collection paralleling that assigned to the ambassadors. The responsibility might be assigned to the Secretary of State or to the 40 Committee. Either way, the Department of State would have to have access to operational and source information to which it is not privy today, if meaningful supervision and control is to be exercised.

Ambassadors interviewed by the Committee all recognize some degree of responsibility for supervision of CIA activities and cite President Nixon's letter of 1969 as the governing document. Most express misgivings about their ability to do so with confidence of support from Washington. The lack of access to CIA communications leaves a residue of doubt that the Ambassador really knows what is going on. Vigor and initiative on the part of Ambassadors seems lack-

---

[16] William Nelson testimony, 12/10/75, Attachment B.
[17] Essentially the communist countries.

ing. Most Ambassadors the Committee has talked with have not appeared inclined to request detailed information, particularly regarding espionage operations.

Supervision of intelligence activities by Ambassadors is in fact uneven and, when exercised, the methods used differ widely. Much depends on the knowledge and experience of the Ambassador, and the support he has or believes he has in Washington. Further, the Committee's inquiries have turned up no evidence that the State Department today attaches more than routine importance to this ambassadorial function.

In the absence of detailed guidance or indication of support from Washington, ambassadorial performance varies widely. One Ambassador, who generally is known to "run a tight ship," exercises detailed supervision and control over the CIA Station. For example, he insists on knowing source identities and on approving any sensitive espionage operation in advance and CIA, or at least the Station Chief, has accepted such control. This Ambassador, a career Foreign Service Officer, tends to attribute his good working relationship with the CIA Station in large measure to the fact that he has had a great deal of prior experience with CIA in Washington and in the field. Such experience is clearly required by Ambassadors assigned to important countries, though in practice, the assignment of Ambassadors has not considerably reflected this requirement.

For whatever reason, this degree of detailed supervision appears to be unusual, if not unique. Our inquiries suggest that Ambassadors rarely seek to learn source identities. In this area they seem to be affected by what one Ambassador has called "self-inflicted intimidation." In one post—where there is a serious terrorist problem—the Ambassador explained that he preferred not to know source identities because of the possibility of being kidnapped. However, the same Ambassador has taken a very strong stand that control of communications is essential if the Ambassador is to exercise effective supervision over CIA. Still another senior Ambassador does not consider that control of communications would really ensure that the Ambassador knows everything that is going on. This Ambassador controls by what amounts to a threat; he informs each Chief of Station that he expects to be consulted in advance about any operation which could cause embarrassment. If any CIA operation about which he has not been consulted causes difficulties, the Station Chief can expect no support from the Ambassador. This would appear to be a more typical procedure.

It should be noted that these are techniques designed to forestall surprise and embarrassment. There is no body of doctrine or standards against which judgments can be made on whether to approve a given operation, nor are Ambassadors given any basic instruction on espionage techniques and risks. It is hardly surprising, therefore, if there is a wide variation in practice and that judgments tend to be *ad hoc* and subjective. This is not likely to change so long as the matter is left to individual Ambassadors.[17a]

[17a] At the request of the CIA, the Committee has deleted a section of this report entitled "Support : Cover" to protect sensitive intelligence sources and methods. A classified version of this section is available to Members of the Senate under the provisions of S. Res. 21 and the Rules of the Senate.

Chart: Bureau of Intelligence and Research—INR ([91], p. 12)

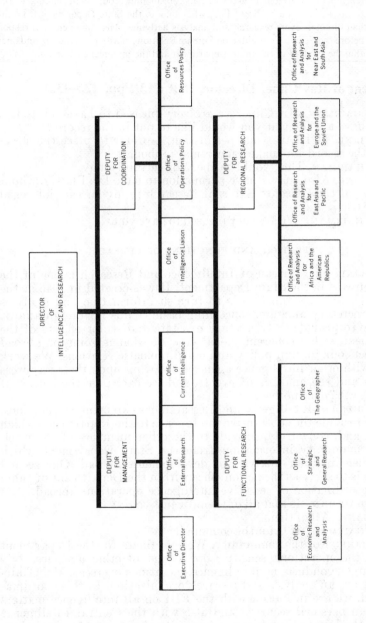

OPERATIONS OF THE BUREAU OF INTELLIGENCE AND RESEARCH

The Bureau of Intelligence and Research (INR) is the State Department's principal producer of finished intelligence and an element in the various coordinating groups of the intelligence community. In 1973, it was headed by Ray Cline, who came to the State Department from the CIA, where he had directed overt research and analysis activities. His statement and responses to questions before the Senate Committee on Foreign Relations clarify the structure and operations of INR within the context of the State Department and the intelligence community.

Statement of Ray Cline, Director, INR ([13], pp. 422–432)

The CHAIRMAN. Mr. Cline, we are very pleased to have you today. Do you have a statement you would like to put in the record?

Mr. CLINE. If I have your permission, I prefer to place the statement in the record and make a few remarks about it.

The CHAIRMAN. That would be fine. You certainly may.

Mr. CLINE. Also, may I have permission to have Dr. Plattig, who is in charge of the Office of External Research in my bureau, join us at the table?

The CHAIRMAN. We are very pleased to have you.

CREATION AND FUNCTIONS OF BUREAU

Mr. CLINE. The Bureau of Intelligence and Research is one of the newer bureaus in the State Department. It was created in 1946 at the end of the war. Its function is to furnish information and analyses for the Secretary of State, concerning basic trends in foreign affairs. It is also to provide the Secretary of State and senior officers of the Department with a coherent global view of what is going on abroad that affects our foreign policy and our diplomatic relations. We work closely with other intelligence agencies, drawing upon their resources for data and the analysis of events, and we exchange the output of our staffs with one another.

The Bureau of Intelligence and Research has two primary functions. First we provide the substantive intelligence to the Department which it needs, and, conversely, provide to the other members of the intelligence community information from the State Department which assists them in their analysis of developments abroad. Our second function is to serve as the action office within the Department of State for the coordination of sensitive intelligence operations abroad.

The CHAIRMAN. Is that all of them, or just yours?

Mr. CLINE. All of them.

The CHAIRMAN. It is for the community?

Mr. CLINE. For the community. We coordinate for the Department of State the operations, sensitive operations, of other agencies.

My bureau conducts no intelligence operations overseas, Mr. Chairman. We are an analysis and research organization. In this coordination field, we are in liaison with the FBI on all intelligence matters other than personal security, and also with the Central Intelligence Agency, the Defense Intelligence Agency, and the rest of the members of the intelligence community. I represent the Department on the United States Intelligence Board, which is chaired by the Director of Central Intelligence, Mr. Helms. Members of my staff represent the

Department on all of the committees and subcommittees of this board, which work on programs and priorities in the many fields of collection and analysis of intelligence.

I wanted to mention specifically that our bureau conducts for the Department of State, an external research program. We have a staff which monitors, coordinates and supports the nongovernmental research on foreign areas and foreign policy problems funded by the Federal Government. The thrust of our effort in this field is to seek out private research in the social and behavioral sciences which can bring useful information to bear on our foreign policy, including social, political, economic, and psychological studies of contemporary developments in foreign countries. And, of course, we bring these studies to the appropriate government officers' attention.

In this way, we supplement our basic in-house staff capacity to give the Department of State a solid data base on which to build its policies and to guide conduct of its diplomatic operations.

I think that is a summary of our task, Mr. Chairman.

(Mr. Cline's prepared statement follows:)

Mr. Chairman and Members of the Committee: INR was created in 1946 to furnish information and analysis for the Secretary of State on basic trends in foreign affairs that would parallel the traditional work of the policy bureaus of the Department and to do so independently of bureaus whose central focus is formulation of policy rather than a coherent global view of what is happening abroad. INR works closely with other intelligence agencies, draws upon their resources for data and analysis of events, and exchanges output with them. Primarily, however, INR gears its output to the specific needs and responsibilities of the Secretary of State and his principal assistants.

We have two primary responsibilities:

(1) To provide substantive intelligence to the Department and to the intelligence community.

(2) To serve as the action office, within the Department, for the coordination of sensitive intelligence operations here and abroad.

In the substantive intelligence field, our principal focus is on the production of "policy oriented" research. Thus, the work is timely and focused on current problems. We believe that intelligence officers should be sensitive to issues of policy and need not necessarily sacrifice objectivity if their work meshes closely with officials dealing with real foreign policy issues. Through a close working relationship between INR and other officials in the Department—beginning with my regular contacts with the Secretary and expanding it all levels throughout the Department—we maintain a consistent awareness of the key problems facing the policy officials and adjust our priorities accordingly.

In the coordination field, we are in liaison with the FBI on all intelligence matters other than personnel security, with the CIA, the DIA and other agencies in the intelligence community. Secondly, we represent the Department on the United States Intelligence Board and on all of its committees which work on programs and priorities in the many fields of collection.

The Bureau of Intelligence and Research is organized into segments reflecting its two principal responsibilities. Offices of research and analysis concentrate on regional problems of concern to the Department's regional policy bureaus a swell as politico-military, scientific, and other functional matters. The coordination activities are carried out by a small staff under the direction of the Deputy Director for Coordination (DDC).

As the Director of INR, I rank with the Assistant Secretaries who head other bureaus. I regularly participate with the Assistant Secretaries in staff meetings conducted by the Secretary and the Under Secretary, and have further a direct personal responsibility to the Secretary as his senior adviser on intelligence matters. I represent the Department of State on the United States Intelligence Board, thereby providing a close link between the Department and the work of the rest of the intelligence community. As a substantive aspect of this responsibility, I make available to the Secretary the most essential current intelligence from all segments of the community; and we provide for the Secretary at least weekly a private, all-source global intelligence briefing that can be tailored to the primary needs and problems of the Secretary for that particular period of time.

For the production and presentation of intelligence, INR has no overseas arm and no independent collection capability. Rather, for its briefings, analyses, and research it draws upon the same body of intelligence information available to all other segments of the community : Foreign Service reporting : information collected by CIA, the Defense Intelligence agencies, and the FBI, FBIS ; and the press. INR's Communications Center has a dual function. Aside from serving the information needs of INR's own personnel, it is the distribution center for the entire department for intelligence reports received from other agencies.

In addition to all-source briefing of the Secretary, INR provides similar individualized briefings each day for the Under Secretary, the Under Secretary for Political Affairs, and the Deputy Under Secretary for Economic Affairs. Each of these briefings comprises a distillate of worldwide current intelligence from the entire community and from open sources, along with interpretive comment, and each is tailored to the immediate needs of the officer being briefed. Comparable, but more narrowly focused intelligence briefings are also conducted at other levels in the Department throughout the day.

The Office of Current Intelligence (INR/RCI) maintains a 24-hour watch center for the receipt of sensitive intelligence information, provides facilities for screening, processing and disseminating it under requisite security safeguards Within this center are electrical communication facilities, including the Department's primary CRITICOM terminal. This watch service, backed up by other appropriate officers of INR when necessary, assures timely alerting of Department Officers on urgent intelligence items and gives them speedy access to the items and to INR's own comments and studies on the subject.

We also are the action office within the Department on all questions dealing with sensitive intelligence activities conducted by the Department of Defense, the Central Intelligence Agency, and the Federal Bureau of Investigation (other than personnel and physical security). In meeting this responsibility, INR works closely with each of the policy bureaus, the Deputy Under Secretary for Political Affairs, and the White House. The matters dealt with are diversified, highly sensitive, and potentially of great significance to the conduct of foreign affairs.

INR serves also as action office for slightly less esoteric interdepartmental relationships. Included in the non-clandestine field are such matters as the Defense Attache system and staffing ; enforcement by the Justice Department of the Foreign Agents Registration Act ; overseas procedurement of maps and publications ; participation in intelligence coordinating committees that guide and set priorities in fields like aerial reconnaissance and defectors.

We do all of our activities with 324 personnel funded from the Salaries and Expenses Appropriation but this position total does not reflect the imminent reductions we must take prior to June 30 in keeping with the President's request for a reduction in federal employment.

INR through its Office of External Research (XR) has a number of distinctive supportive, liaison, coordinating, and monitoring functions relating to non-governmental research on foreign areas and foreign policy problems. One central function is to make available to INR and the Department the relevant research capabilities and findings of personnel and programs located outside the Government. It does this by collecting and disseminating research papers and reports ; by arranging for outside experts to work with the Department as consultants, discussants, conferees, and seminar leaders ; and by a small program of our own contract research.

In its major coordinating role, XR provides the staff to support the Interagency Subcommittee on Foreign Affairs Research (USC/FAR) which is comprised of thirteen (Member and Observer) agencies chaired by the Director of INR. The following functions have been assigned to the USC/FAR : (a) to develop a Foreign Affairs Consolidated Research Plan ; (b) to recommend joint funding of projects and programs ; (c) to collect and disseminate information on research and improve utilization of research results ; and (d) to arrange interagency working group consultations. Finally, in its major monitoring role, XR provides the staff for the Department of State's Research Council (DSRC) chaired by the Director of INR. Guided by a Presidential directive to the Secretary and by the agreed procedures of the DSRC, XR officers review a large number of research projects and related activities of other agencies and prepare for Research Council approval the Department's clearance or make suggestions which will minimize any adverse effect of the proposed research on our foreign relations.

Let me now speak specifically and in more detail about the work of the Office of External Research within INR.

The Office of External Research works to develop and maintain a steady exchange of information and ideas between Government officials, both researchers and policy-makers, and private scholars engaged in research on foreign affairs. It identifies the State Department's external research needs and seeks to meet them through the use of contractors and consultants, encouragement of private research, and various information and documentation services. It develops cooperative effort in the contract research activities related to foreign affairs of other Government agencies and provides leadership in the coordination and improvement of such research. Serving the external research needs of the Department, the Office works closely with AID, USIA, ACDA, DoD and other agencies to promote fruitful government-academic relations in the research area.

The main thrust of our whole effort is to seek out private research in the social and behavioral sciences which can bring useful information to bear on the conduct of American foreign policy, including social, political, economic and psychological studies of contemporary developments in foreign countries, and to bring these studies to the attention of appropriate government officers.

Other Bureaus in the Department of State and other agencies concerned with foreign affairs have used the INR Office of External Research services to maintain contact with the academic world.

Among other things, INR maintains, on behalf of the USC/FAR, a project reporting service and information clearinghouse for government research contracts on foreign areas and international affairs. It provides the only central catalog of all government contracts in these fields and publishes annotated inventories of Government-sponsored research on foreign areas.

Additionally it maintains the Foreign Affairs Research Documentation Center to identify, collect and disseminate both the reports produced under Government-sponsored research contracts and papers related to foreign policy produced by private research. It lists newly acquired documents in a monthly compilation that is circulated widely throughout the government and to selected scholars, research centers and libraries. Each month the Center fills over 1,400 requests for papers from the Department, other agencies, and Foreign Service posts.

And finally the office participates in, and reports on, the proceedings of professional associations relating to foreign affairs. It maintains liaison with universities and foundations, research organizations and private scholars in order to identify and utilize private research resources in support of the research program of the Department and other agencies with foreign policy interests.

INR is requesting $7,309,900.00 for FY 1973 for the Administration of Foreign Affairs and under the Salaries and Expenses Appropriation. Of this total, $6,204,800.00 will be applied to salary costs for our 324 personnel, $905,100.00 will cover our miscellaneous operating expenses, which includes our present Foreign Affairs External Research Program. The remaining $200,000.00 will be for a modest expansion of our Foreign Affairs External Research Program.

Mr. Chairman, this completes my presentation but I would be pleased to answer any questions or clarify any points you or the members of the Committee might have. . . .

RESEARCH PROGRAMS IN SOCIAL AND BEHAVIORAL SCIENCES

The Chairman. That last item you mentioned reminded me of quite a discussion I had once about the Defense Department's research programs in the social and behavioral sciences all scattered around the world. They seemed to have many more of those projects than you have.

Mr. Cline. Mr. Chairman, I am doing my best to change that. It is a slow process. We have increased our efforts in this field materially in the past two years since I have been director of the bureau.

The Chairman. It strikes me those studies are much more relevant to your responsibilities than they are to those of the Department of Defense. Anyway, that is neither here nor there. You are familiar, I guess, with those discussions?

Mr. Cline. Yes.

INFORMATION PROVIDED BY BUREAU

The CHAIRMAN. I understand you are an analysis operation. You do not gather information. You do not have any sleuths around eves-dropping around the world on everybody; do you?

Mr. CLINE. That is correct. The information which we provide is that which comes from our political and economic officers abroad.

INFORMATION GATHERED BY OTHER AGENCIES

The CHAIRMAN. Does the information gathered by the other agencies, such as NSA and CIA and the DOD and so on come through your office and you are supposed to subject that to your analytic powers? Is that what happens?

Mr. CLINE. In most cases. In many cases, of course, the information is of such a directly useful nature that it requires no analysis, in which case we simply distribute it to the proper levels of officials in the Department to use it.

BASIC TRENDS IN FOREIGN AFFAIRS

The CHAIRMAN. You said "information and analyses of basic trends in foreign affairs." What do you mean by "basic trends in foreign affairs"?

Mr. CLINE. I mean those which are of more than day-to-day concern to our diplomatic operations. Naturally, if we are conducting a negotiation abroad, the officers in the Department who are dealing with the problem would be very alert to the day-to-day conduct of those negotiations. But on the background thinking of the people with whom we are negotiating, the situations in the countries which we are negotiating about, we would attempt to keep a historical continuity and interest in them and project what we know into the future, so as to make a reasonable estimate of what the United States is up against.

BUREAU'S RELATION TO POLICY PLANNING STAFF

The CHAIRMAN. You sound very much as if you are describing the work of the Policy Planning Staff. What is your relation to that Policy Planning Staff?

Mr. CLINE. I think we are a parallel organization, in that our responsibility is not to recommend or to make policy. Our responsibility is to give an objective, very carefully considered description of the present situation and analysis of the trends which are likely to be present in the future. The decision as to what to do about those trends, how to conduct the U.S. foreign policy, is the work of the operational bureaus and the Policy Planning staff.

BACKGROUND INFORMATION SUPPLIED FOR PRESIDENT'S TRIP TO CHINA

The CHAIRMAN. I wonder, in the recent trip of the President and his associates to China, did you supply him with a thorough going analysis of the attitude, background, and everything else you could, of Mr. Chou En-Lai, and Mr. Mao Tse-Tung, and the history of that situation? Did you do that?

Mr. CLINE. My staff made a substantial contribution to this kind of background information on the trip. Yes, sir. We supplied it to our representatives on the team, of course. . . .

The Chairman. In that connection, have you ever read Colonel Barrett's book on the Dixie Mission?

Mr. Cline. I have. I am afraid it is a long time ago. I do not remember it very well.

The Chairman. It was only published last year.

Mr. Cline. I don't remember the thrust of it.

The Chairman. I wondered if you had. It was a rather interesting one. Do you know who Colonel Barrett was?

Mr. Cline. I don't know him.

The Chairman. Are you familiar with that mission in 1944?

Mr. Cline. You will have to refresh my memory.

The Chairman. Colonel Barrett was on General Stilwell's staff and was the head of the mission that was sent to Yenen to be with and to study and to obtain information from the communist headquarters. It is a fascinating little booklet. It is only about 100 pages, I think. I thought maybe it came within your purview in the study of the background of the Chinese.

Mr. Cline. I think it is one of many books on my bedside table.

The Chairman. I recommend it if you are interested in that area.

OTHER AGENCIES ENGAGED IN BUREAU'S KIND OF ANALYSIS

As I said, the way you described it reminds me of the Policy Planning Staff. You explained that, I think. Do you think there are many other agencies engaging in this same kind of analysis?

Mr. Cline. Not many, but there are comparable staffs in other agencies. The main analytical work in the intelligence field which is comparable to ours is done by the Central Intelligence Agency. However, our point of view, our concern to develop that information and those ideas which are useful to foreign policy and to the Secretary of State in particular, differentiates our work. We are a specialized part of the intelligence community, an analytical staff concentrating on political and foreign policy areas.

GOVERNMENT SPENDING ON GATHERING AND ANALYZING INTELLIGENCE

The Chairman. Mr. Cline, could you estimate for the committee how much is spent throughout the Government in gathering and analyzing for intelligence?

Mr. Cline. Yes, sir. There are a number of ways of keeping the books on this, as you might imagine, but I would be willing to hazard a horseback estimate that it is on the order of $3 million.

The Chairman. $3 million.

Mr. Cline. Billion.

The Chairman. That is a very low estimate, the lowest I have heard. Did you understand the question? When we attempted to put a ceiling of $4 billion on it on the floor, the Chairman of the Appropriations Committee and his colleagues raised cain. I could not imagine why they would if they were only spending $3 billion.

Mr. Cline. It has been a little higher than that, and there are activities which could be included which are not in my view properly part of the intelligence budget, which would make the figure higher. Obviously, this is a subject the Director of Central Intelligence is primarily responsible for.

The Chairman. Under the direction of the Director of the Office of Management and Budget, we are told to look to you and not CIA about these matters. We have to ask you about these matters. We no longer can ask those people anything. At least, we cannot ask them and expect to get an answer. I appreciate it and after you have thought about it, if you would care to, I would like to have a memo on that subject because it is one that eluded us.

(The information referred to follows:)

GOVERNMENT SPENDING ON GATHERING AND ANALYZING INTELLIGENCE (SUPPLIED BY DEPARTMENT OF STATE)

I have carefully considered my response and the $3 billion order of magnitude figure given, and after consultation with appropriate sources, my information and testimony, as indicated, is appropriate.

COMMITTEE ACCESS TO ANALYSES OF FOREIGN INTELLIGENCE

Do you think this committee should have access to the analyses of foreign intelligence?

Mr. CLINE. Insofar as this would not, in the judgment of people responsible for protecting sources and methods of intelligence gathering, jeopardize those sources, I think it should.

PUBLISHED LISTS OF RESEARCH AND ANALYTIC PRODUCT

The CHAIRMAN. Does the bureau publish a list of its research and analytic product?

Mr. CLINE. Yes. We publish several different lists. Of course, as you are aware, sir, intelligence is distributed under a variety of classifications, according to the sensitivity of the data described in them. But we do keep a list of what we produce, and I believe a certain number of our reports are made available to the Congress.

The CHAIRMAN. I was going to ask you if you could furnish these to this committee, so we can see the type of research and analytical products you have. If you could furnish these to the committee at a later date, not right now.

Mr. CLINE. We have presented the unclassified material. We do that regularly. The classified material, of course, we would present in a separate communication.

The CHAIRMAN. We will get together with the staff. I would think that this would be the type of thing we would probably like on a regular basis, whenever it is available. It would be very useful to us.

(The information referred to follows:)

RESEARCHED AND ANALYTICAL REPORTS PRODUCED BY INR (SUPPLIED BY DEPARTMENT OF STATE)

INR regularly produces four categories of research and analytical reports. They are: (1) Research Studies, which usually involve extensive research and sometimes present complicated material and analysis; (2) External Research Studies, which are similar to the RS's described above, but are produced by INR consultants and contractors for the Department of State under its External Research Program; (3) Intelligence Notes, which are short—sometimes tentative—assessments of significant current and developing situations, and (4) Miscellaneous Special Reports, which are usually long studies printed and distributed directly by the Government Printing Office. In this category is included the annual publication *World Strength of Communist Party Organizations*.

Aside from this periodical, titles chosen for INR reports and the total number of releasable papers produced in each category follow no set pattern from year to year, but vary to reflect changes in international developments and the needs of Department officers who participate in the decision-making process. Attached is a list of unclassified INR reports produced in 1971. Titles of other reports that were forwarded to the Committee during the year cannot be furnished on an unclassified basis.

INR STUDIES

JANUARY 1971–DECEMBER 1971

The Multinational Corporation and National Sovereignty. January 22, 1971.

Implications for the United States of Possible EC Monetary Developments. March 5, 1971.

Economic Growth of OECD Countries, 1960–1970. May 28, 1971.

NATO Countries Trade With Warsaw Pact Countries, 1966–1970. June 14, 1971.

Controlling Private Short-Term Capital Outflows From the United States. June 15, 1971.

The Future of the Asian Development Bank. June 29, 1971.

The Preferential Agreements Between the European Economic Community and Tunisia, Morocco, Spain, and Israel: Implications for US Commodity Exports. July 19, 1971.

Trade Patterns of the West, 1970. July 27, 1971.

Multinational Production Consortia: Lessons from NATO Experience. August 1971.

Diplomatic Relations of the Republic of China and the People's Republic of China. August 27, 1971.

Educational and Cultural Exchanges Between Communist and Non-Communist Countries in 1970. August 30, 1971.

Communist States and Developing Countries: Aid and Trade in 1970. September 22, 1971.

The Planetary Product in 1970: Preliminary Tables. October 1, 1971.

National Academy of Sciences' Study *Rapid Population Growth* Provides Guides for Policymakers. October 6, 1971.

A Reconnaissance of the Foreign Trade Adjustment Assistance Problem for the United States. October 12, 1971.

Soviet Diplomatic Relations and Representation. November 8, 1971.

Nationalization, Expropriation, and Other Takings of United States and Certain Foreign Property Since 1960. November 30, 1971.

Diplomatic Relations of the Republic of China and the People's Republic of China. December 1, 1971.

Impact of Economic Nationalism on Key Mineral Resource Industries. December 17, 1971.

All Geographic Notes and papers in the International Boundary Study series.

DEPARTMENT'S MAINTENANCE OF POLICY GUIDELINES TO INTELLIGENCE COMMUNITY

Is the State Department able to maintain normal policy guidelines to the intelligence community, especially in the area of clandestine operations?

Mr. CLINE. Yes, sir.

IS DEPARTMENT ALWAYS INFORMED OF CLANDESTINE OPERATIONS?

The CHAIRMAN. Is the State Department always informed of clandestine operations?

Mr. CLINE. When they are of a nature to create any political risk to the successful mission of the diplomatic establishment abroad. That does not mean we follow every intelligence operation. But whenever there is any threat of its being a matter which might endanger or compromise our general foreign policy objectives, we would expect to be informed.

The CHAIRMAN. I was of the impression that at the time of the Bay of Pigs the State Department exercised little if any influence and that it was wholly CIA's operation.

Mr. Cline. Mr. Chairman, I had the good fortune to be overseas during that episode.

The Chairman. I did not mean to be personal. It was an institutional observation.

Mr. Cline. I think you are correct.

The Chairman. That was certainly my impression about it.

Mr. Cline. Except at the very senior level. The Secretary of State knew about it.

The Chairman. Are you kept apprised of the operations in which the military intelligence engages and knows about? Do they inform you, do you think, about all of those operations?

Mr. Cline. In a general way. We have a close liaison with the agencies conducting those operations. They explain to us what their programs are as in the case of Central Intelligence Agency's operations. We do not try to pass on each one.

The Chairman. This is going back into history, but that is all I can do. I was under the impression that the State Department was probably not aware of the rather involved intelligence gathering operations at the time of the Gulf of Tonkin incident. That was entirely within the Defense Department. If the State Department knew about it, it did not appear in the record. It appeared to be wholly a Naval and Defense Department activity.

Mr. Cline. I think it is a little more complicated than that.

The Chairman. It was complicated all right. In fact, the Secretary of Defense denied that they knew anything about what is called Operation 34A, if you read the books on it, which later became a very questionable statement.

Response to Written Committee Questions ([13], pp. 450–455)

Director Ray Cline's testimony before the Senate Committee on Foreign Relations continued, dealing with a number of housekeeping items that have here been deleted. Subsequently, he submitted to the committee written answers to several questions.

ANSWERS TO QUESTIONS SUBMITTED TO RAY CLINE, DIRECTOR, INR

Question 1. Would you describe the mechanism by which other elements in the intelligence community are made aware of your analyses and research products and you of theirs?

Answer. Under existing procedures INR analyses and research products, that is, research studies, intelligence notes, geographic and boundary notes and studies, and external research studies are automatically transmitted to other agencies of the intelligence community, represented on the U.S. Intelligence Board (USIB). Reciprocally, State/INR automatically receives from other intelligence agencies a regular and substantial flow of their analyses and research products, as presented both in periodicals and in special reports. State/INR participates in scheduled studies jointly undertaken by members of the intelligence community, particularly in the National Intelligence Estimates authorized by USIB. Finally, information as to studies and analyses planned or in process is additionally conveyed informally, in the manifold informal contacts among agency staff. Arrangements are also made, through both formal and informal channels, for studies to be undertaken by a single agency or cooperatively.

Question 2. How does your rank compare with that of other members of the United States Intelligence Board?

Answer. The Director of the State Department Bureau of Intelligence and Research is equal or superior in rank to all of the other full members of the U.S. Intelligence Board. As the representative of the senior agency on the board, he sits next to the Director of Central Intelligence at the Board meetings.

Question 3. Your office works with the Justice Department in the enforcement of the Foreign Agents Registration Act. What use does the Department make of the information it obtains from filings by foreign agents? Do you think the Act is effective in providing sufficient information about the activities of foreign agents or visitors who are here to raise money for use for political purposes in foreign countries?

Answer. The filings by foreign agents are used by the Department both for information and as an aid to the Justice Department in the enforcement of the Act. Each such statement is forwarded to the office of the appropriate Geographic Bureau for examination and comment. Any comments or observations are then transmitted to the Justice Department for its information or action. Items of political propaganda transmitted to the Department are circulated to INR research divisions for information. While I cannot report that much of this material has proved to be useful, there have been several individual items that have been quite helpful to us.

As for effectiveness of the Act itself, I feel I must refer you to the Justice Department, for we defer to Justice on questions as to general effectiveness, interpretation, and the like. From our standpoint, however, the Act appears to be effective.

Question 4(a). How many people in your office work on matters relating to coordination of foreign research?

Answer 4(a). The number of people involved depends on what is meant by coordination. Two people are concerned with the review of other agencies' proposed contract research projects in the social and behavioral sciences for the purpose of avoiding damage to U.S. foreign relations. The equivalent of two more man years is devoted to the work of the Under Secretaries Subcommittee on Foreign Affairs Research (USC/FAR), which is charged with the coordination of contract research programs. And three people maintain an information bank of Government-supported research projects on foreign areas and international affairs.

Question 4(b). Does the State Department have a veto power over proposed research projects by other agencies? Are proposed projects actually approved or rejected by the inter-agency committee or is it only an information gathering mechanism? Describe the clearance process.

Answer 4(b). The Department of State does have a veto power over foreign area contract research projects in the social and behavioral sciences of other agencies. In 1965 the President directed the Secretary of State to assure that no Government-supported research be undertaken which in his judgment could adversely affect United States foreign relations. Since that time the Department of State Research Council, chaired by the Director of Intelligence and Research, has reviewed proposed contract research projects. The Council is not an inter-agency committee, but is a Department group in which all bureaus are represented. It also plans the Department's own contract research program. The inter-agency committee referred to is probably the Under Secretaries Subcommittee on Foreign Affairs Research of the National Security Council (USC/FAR), which coordinates contract research programs. USC/FAR does not approve or reject projects.

The clearance process centers on proposed research projects involving foreign travel or contacts with foreign nationals which are sponsored by the military and foreign affairs agencies. The Department receives information on other projects (domestic agency studies) and may take action in regard to them should the need arise. Certain categories of research support have been exempted from review—National Science Foundation, Humanities Endowment, National Institutes of Health, Fulbright Program, and National Defense Education Act grants—on the ground that such support is different in kind and therefore substantially less sensitive than research contracts designed to meet Government policy needs. Department review is limited to the risk a project may pose for U.S. foreign relations and is not concerned with the cost, need or design of a project, except insofar as these may affect foreign relations sensitivity. Projects are discussed with the appropriate Departmental policy units and in many cases the advice of one or more American embassies is obtained before clearance is granted. Since 1965 more than 750 projects have been reviewed.

Question 4(c). Have any inter-agency criteria been established for research abroad or involving foreign areas? Would you provide a copy of the criteria to the Committee as well as a copy of the general directive for operation of USC/FAR?

Answer 4(c). In the review of proposed foreign area contract research projects, the Department of State Research Council operates on the basis of its Procedures for Department of State Review of Government-Supported Foreign Affairs Research. The Council also has issued Guidelines for the Review of Domestic Agency Research by the Department of State Research Council. Both documents include criteria for determining whether or not a project may have adverse effects on U.S. foreign relations. There are also Government Guidelines for Foreign Area Research, issued by the Foreign Area Research Coordination Group, the predecessor organization of the present Under Secretaries Subcommittee on Foreign Affairs Research (USC/FAR). These Guidelines establish certain general principles applicable to the relationship between Government and the academic community in the use of contract research in foreign affairs. The general directives for the operation of the USC/FAR are the Terms of Reference of the Under Secretaries Subcommittee on Foreign Affairs Research. All documents mentioned are attached.

FEBRUARY 1972.

GUIDELINES FOR THE REVIEW OF DOMESTIC AGENCY RESEARCH BY THE DEPARTMENT OF STATE RESEARCH COUNCIL

A. PURPOSE

These guidelines are designed to assist Federal agencies decide whether or not to submit their proposed research projects to the Department of State Research Council for review in accordance with the Procedures for Department of State Review of Government-Sponsored Foreign Affairs Research, dated November 18, 1965 (hereinafter called the Procedures). The guidelines apply to all Federal departments and agencies, with the exception of (1) those specifically defined in the Procedures as being military and foreign affairs agencies, and (2) those whose research programs have been specifically exempted from review by the Chairman of the Department of State Research Council.

B. APPLICABILITY

The Department of State Research Council is concerned with foreign affairs research, defined as studies dealing in whole or in part with international relations, or with foreign areas and peoples, whether conducted in the United States or abroad, which are supported by contracts or grants awarded by agencies of the United States Government. In-house research is not included.

For the most part, such studies involve one or more of the social, behavioral or humanistic disciplines or fields and include those concerned with the implications for man and society of developments in the life, physical and environmental sciences and technologies and in mathematics. The full range of human, social and behavioral problems, disciplines and fields are included, as is both basic and applied research.

C. DOMESTIC AGENCY RESPONSIBILITY

1. *Appointment of Clearance Point.*—Each agency supporting foreign affairs research will designate an officer as clearance point with the Department of State Research Council. The clearance point will be responsible within his agency for reviewing foreign affairs research projects for potential foreign relations sensitivity, supplying information about all projects to the Department of State, deciding which projects need State Department clearance, and submitting the latter for review in conformity with the Procedures. Projects will be submitted before the contract is signed or the grant awarded.

2. *Review of Projects.*—The clearance point within agencies will submit to the Department of State Research Council for review those projects he decides

might have potential adverse effects on U.S. foreign relations. Potentially sensitive projects are defined below in section D. Projects thus submitted will be considered cleared unless the Department of State otherwise notifies the clearance point within 15 working days after the project has been received by the Department for review. When projects are submitted for review the clearance point should submit the information specified in Section I of the Procedures.

3. *Information on Projects.*—When the clearance point determines that a project does not need Department of State review, he will submit summary information to the Department before a contract is signed or a grant awarded. The summary information will include:

(*a*) Title of project and brief description.

(*b*) Sponsoring agency or agencies (including information of any funding by other agencies).

(*c*) Contractor, estimated cost, and principal researchers.

(*d*) Extent to which discussion with a U.S. diplomatic mission has already been held in the formulation of the project proposal.

(*e*) Classification of project and proposed disposition of reports.

4. *USC/FAR Reporting System.*—All projects begun should be reported on the Foreign Affairs Research Project Information Form for inclusion in the research reporting system of the Under Secretaries Subcommittee on Foreign Affairs Research (USC/FAR). Projects are to be reported within 10 working days after a contract is signed or a grant awarded.

5. *Liaison with Ambassador.*—The clearance point will insure that in cases of projects not submitted in accordance with paragraph 2 above, but involving foreign travel, the American Ambassador in the country concerned is notified through Department of State channels of the travel involved. The notification should be given sufficiently in advance of the arrival of contractor or grantee so that the Ambassador may transmit timely advice to Washington.

D. POTENTIALITY SENSITIVE PROJECTS

Potentially sensitive projects are those which:

1. Deal with the authority of a foreign government or with the attitude of the people toward the government, especially if the government is characterized by instability) ; or

2. Involve large-scale or formalized surveys or interviews; or

3. Are conducted by large teams, or cover extensive or remote areas of a foreign country.

E. PROJECTS OF LESSER SENSITIVITY

In general the more of the following points that characterize a proposed project, the less it is likely to have high sensitivity:

1. Is conducted entirely in the United States;

2. Deals with historical rather than contemporary subjects;

3. Gathers information in the host country through documentary investigation rather than interviews or questionnaires;

4. Has the approval of interested agencies of the host country government;

5. Involves professional participation by host country nationals as researchers;

6. Is not designed to contribute specifically to the operating mission of an agency of the United States Government.

F. AVAILABILITY OF RESEARCH COUNCIL STAFF ASSISTANCE

The staff of the Department of State Research Council is available for consultation on the possible sensitivity of projects. It is sometimes the case that topics of no apparent sensitivity on general principle may prove to be quite sensitive in a particular time or place. Advance consultation often serves to expedite projects and assure that a proposed study can in fact be carried out. Clearance points having any doubts about the potential sensitivity of projects should resolve them *in favor of* Department State Research Council review, i.e.. in favor of submitting in accordance with paragraph 2 above.

(Additional material is in the Committee files.)

Question 5. According to the information provided the Committee, the Department of the Army spends $1 million per year on "area handbooks." In 1971 nineteen of these books were published, for such countries as Iraq, Ceylon, Albania, and Honduras. Did the FAR Committee approve this project? If so, what is the justification? Is this project being continued? If so, how much is being spent in FY 1972 and how much is budgeted for FY 1973?

Answer. The Foreign Area Research Coordination Group (FAR) neither approved for disapproved the U.S. Army Area Handbook Program because it had no authority to approve or disapprove research programs or projects. The same is true of the FAR's successor group, the Under Secretaries Subcommittee on Foreign Area Research (USC/FAR). The Army Handbook Program was already in existence when the Department of State Research Council was established in 1965 and the Council has never reviewed the program as a whole. Individual handbooks are-reviewed by policy officers in the Department's regional bureaus. The Department of the Army has informed us that the program is being continued. In FY 1972 $1,000,000 was budgeted for the program and the same amount has been requested for FY 1973. A Department of the Army justification for the program is attached.

U.S. Army Area Handbook Series (DA Pamphlets 550-xx Series)

The US Army Area Handbook Program, solidly based upon an indicated need by military schools, operational planners, intelligence staffs, military assistance personnel, military libraries, contingency and deployed troop units provides pesonnel with tools for understanding foreign countries and peoples. This program has been in operation since 1955 and since 1966 has been administered under US Government Contract DAHC 15 67 C 0015, with annual amendments. Major General Clarke T. Baldwin, Jr., Director, DAMO–IA, is the approving officer. Area Handbooks are studies of a country's social, economic, political and military organization. Each handbook provides in a useful, single-volume format a description of a country or area with its peoples, depicting cultural and historical origins and the role these play in the present institutional organization and functioning. Compiled from unclassified sources by an interdisciplinary team, the objective of any handbook is to describe a whole society as a coherent dynamic system of relationships and interactions. While the emphasis is on the contemporary society, the handbooks try to make possible an understanding of past trends and future probabilities. The Area Handbooks are intended to provide insights into general patterns rather than a wealth of encyclopedic knowledge.

The Army requires accurate, factual information in a convenient, usable form for field commanders with mission assignments in or related to various countries and areas of the world. The Area Handbooks provide background and orientation material for persons assigned as attaches or as members of MAAGS, Millions and MilGroups. Army schools make extensive use of these materials in country and area-oriented instruction, and staff contingency planning requires solid grounding in the facts of life and conditions in many key areas. The Area Handbooks are designed to meet all of these Army requirements. In addition, other government agencies receive distribution to meet their needs in the conduct of international affairs responsibilities. In recent years many thousands of copies have been sold by the Superintendent of Documents to meet various needs of the public.

An Army-wide and nation-wide evaluation survey of Area Handbook users was completed in early 1972. It shows that for field commanders, staff officers and schools the handbooks contribute substantially to saving time and effort, are excellent in providing background data, and give valuable assistance in accomplishing assigned missions. Responses were unanimous in attesting to the accuracy and factual nature of the handbooks and the great preponderance of replies indicated that this information was not readily available from other sources. As a secondary benefit, analysis of responses from other governmental agencies, Federal Depository Libraries, educators, corporations and individuals in the civilian community shows the great public relations value of this program to the Army and gives added testimony to the high calibre of the product.

The survey analysis showed that users require more frequent revision of existing handbooks (81% want handbooks revised every 2 or 3 years) and preparation of additional handbooks for areas/countries not yet covered. Of 233 countries, dependencies, and areas of special sovereignty listed in the Federal General Standard Catalogue (9/30/69), 125 are candidates for Area Handbook preparation. Eliminating both the highly developed countries of Western Europe and the British Commonwealth on which information is readily available and also those newly established, sparsely settled and little developed non-strategic areas of Africa, Asia and Latin America leaves a requirement for handbooks on 115 areas/countries. Only 74 handbooks are now available. Generally, it has been established that each handbook should be fully revised on the average of every five years. On that basis 11 of the 74 current handbooks are out of date and 17 more will become so during the next two years.

The program currently underway is based upon $1,000,000 annual funding. In FY 69 this program was based on $1,335,000 which provided for the publication of about 20 to 21 handbooks annually. This rate would have provided for revisions of all handbooks about every five to seven years and still permit research and writing of handbooks on countries not yet covered. Because of the budget reductions in FY 70 and FY 71 amounting to $335,000 and increased costs of research due to inflation and cost of living rises, FY 72 and FY 73 production has been reduced to 14–15 handbooks per year. This is the output capacity of five research teams—one each in the major areas of Asia, Europe, Middle East and North Africa, Africa South of the Sahara, and Latin America.

Question 6. How much is being requested in FY 1973 for the State Department's external research program compared with the budget requests for other agencies for research involving foreign areas or foreign affairs?

Answer. In FY 1973 $641,000 has been requested for Department of State contract studies as part of the Department's external research program. An additional $150,000 has been requested for other parts of the program, including employment of outside consultants, consultant travel and travel by Department officers to research centers and academic meetings, publication of contract and consultant studies, typing and editing support, and related activities connected with the use of outside research. The approximate budget requests for foreign affairs (contract) research in FY 1973 by the member agencies of the Under Secretaries Subcommittee on Foreign Affairs Research are given below:

Agency for International Development	$7, 000, 000
Arms Control and Disarmament Agency	250, 000
Department of Defense	4, 000, 000
National Security Council Staff	300, 000
Department of State	641, 000
United States Information Agency	620, 000

Question 7. Would you provide a list, by agency, of all research projects currently underway abroad, the cost of each project, and an estimate of the amount of each agency's request for foreign-based research in FY 1973?

Answer. It is impossible for us within the time available to categorize projects in the general contract research program and plan so as to identify those involving research abroad as distinct from simply requiring research on foreign affairs trends and topics. Government Financed Research Projects Concerning Foreign Policy or Foreign Areas Reported as Currently Underway.[1]

N8

---

[1] Many of these projects are believed to involve research abroad.

BUDGET OF THE BUREAU OF INTELLIGENCE AND RESEARCH

Summary: Domestic ([48], pp. 55–56)

	1975 Actual		1976 Estimate		1977 Estimate		Increase or Decrease	
	No.	Amount	No.	Amount	No.	Amount	No.	Amount
Estimated Net Cost of Permanent American Employment (Central American Salary Account)*..	317	$7,182,900	317	$7,970,600	317	$8,084,300	-	+$113,700
Operating Expense Funds Managed by This Office..		1,186,871	-	1,517,600		1,528,200	-	+ 10,600
Total.........	317	8,369,771	317	9,488,200	317	9,612,500	-	+ 124,300

EXPLANATION OF DECREASES AND INCREASES:

	Centrally Managed American Salary Account			Operating Expenses of This Office		
	No.	Amount	Page	No.	Amount	Page
DECREASES:						
Non-Recurring Costs:						
Extra Day's Pay.......	-	-$29,700	14	-	-	
Total Decreases........	-	- 29,700		-	-	
INCREASES:						
Annualization:						
1976 Federal Salary Increase...........	-	+109,700	14	-	+$2,500	22
Within-Grade Salary Increases.........	-	+ 33,700	15	-	-	
Price Increases............	-	-		-	+ 8,100	23,24
Total Increases...........	-	+143,400		-	+10,600	
NET INCREASE/DECREASE.........	-	+113,700		-	+10,600	

*In addition to salary costs includes Retirement, Health Benefits, and Life Insurance Contributions; Terminal Leave; and similar costs.

Permanent Staff by Organizational Unit

	1975 Actual		1976 Estimate		1977 Estimate	
	No.	Net Cost	No.	Net Cost	No.	Net Cost
Office of the Director	4	$97,860	4	$108,625	4	$110,167
Office of the Deputy Director	2	55,861	2	62,006	2	62,874
Staff Offices:						
Current Intelligence Staff	15	338,717	15	375,976	15	381,240
Reports Coordination Staff	7	134,737	7	149,558	7	151,652
Office of the Executive Director	11	221,424	11	245,781	11	249,222
Office of Comm. and Infor. Handling	30	514,093	30	566,243	30	573,610
Office of External Research	28	647,389	28	716,402	28	726,152
Deputy Director for Research	2	56,348	2	62,546	2	63,422
Office of Economic Research	27	624,930	27	689,272	27	698,362
Office of Strategic Research	12	285,694	12	312,189	12	313,258
Office of the Geographer	9	209,311	9	232,355	9	235,608
Office of Political/Military Affairs	13	324,682	13	355,997	13	360,421
Office of R&A for Africa	15	312,161	15	346,499	15	351,350
Office of R&A for American Republics	19	432,059	19	479,585	19	486,299
Office of R&A for East Asia and the Pacific	28	533,002	28	591,632	28	599,915
Office of R&A for Western Europe	16	431,929	16	479,441	16	486,153
Office of R&A for the Soviet Union and Eastern Europe	32	814,942	32	918,148	32	937,864
Office of R&A for Near East and South Asia	23	478,807	23	531,955	23	539,402
Deputy Director for Coordination	6	210,388	6	233,531	6	236,800
Office of Intelligence Liaison	9	189,827	9	210,708	9	213,658
Office of Operations Policy	4	88,078	4	97,767	4	99,136
Office of Resources Policy	5	180,661	5	204,384	5	207,735
Total, Bureau of Intelligence and Research	317	7,182,900	317	7,970,600	317	8,084,300

NOTES AND REFERENCES

1. President Gerald R. Ford's message on Executive Order 11905 is reprinted in the Appendix.
2. On February 7, 1969, Secretary of State William Rogers sent a message to all State Department employees outlining plans for an expanded State Department role in the NSC. Rogers' announcement came as a result of President Richard M. Nixon's decision (also dated February 7, 1969) to restructure the NSC and to provide more coordination among intelligence agencies in order to meet U.S. foreign policy objectives. No documentary evidence has been found indicating that Nixon's and Rogers' plans were realized. See [13], pp. 657–661, for copies of these announcements.
3. Dean Rusk, University of Georgia professor and former secretary of state under Presidents John F. Kennedy and Lyndon B. Johnson, recalled his experience as secretary of state and described the department's coordination with the other intelligence bodies, particularly the CIA, for covert action operations. His testimony before the Senate Committee on Government Operations, chaired by Senator Abraham Ribicoff, appears in [25], pp. 73 ff.
4. National Security Council Intelligence directives (NSCIDs) are NSC directives sent to the intelligence agencies; they are often supplemented by more detailed Director of Central Intelligence directives (DCIDs). Senator William Proxmire has charged that NSCIDs are used to provide a "secret charter" outside the legal processes (*Congressional Record,* June 4, 1973, p. 10222). NSCIDs are generally classified, but some are now available under the FOIA ([125], p. 6).
5. In 1961, President John F. Kennedy sent a letter to American ambassadors assuring ambassadorial authority and oversight in CIA activities; the text of the letter is reprinted in [44G], p. 137. In 1969, President Richard M. Nixon reiterated that authority in a similar letter to ambassadors, the text of which is reprinted in [13], pp. 89–96. Further efforts in this area are described by ambassador to Iran and former DCI, Richard Helms, before the Senate Fulbright Committee on Foreign Relations ([18], p. 4).
6. A 19-page outline of INR activities, prepared by the State Department, is available ([91]).
7. Consult Chapter 4 for an examination of the overall intelligence community budget. Director of INR Ray Cline's estimate of a $3 billion total expenditure for governmentwide intelligence activities is significantly lower than others found in both government and nongovernment literature.
8. The director of INR, Ray Cline, supplied a list of research projects, financed by INR and other agencies, to the Fulbright Committee ([13], pp. 455 ff.). The "Additional List of Research Projects" has been deleted from this portion of the text.

PART III

THE PUBLIC ISSUES

Chapter 10
Accountability and Oversight

SECRECY ([20B], pp. 2430–2431)

Secrecy is essential to the success of intelligence activities. However, once the practice of strict secrecy becomes a morally legitimatized administrative practice, it can be used to mask all manner of mistakes and wrongdoing. The Church Committee's final report inquires rhetorically: "What is a valid national secret? What can properly be concealed from the scrutiny of the American people, from various segments of the executive branch or from a duly constituted oversight body of their elected representatives? Assassination plots? The overthrow of an elected democratic government? Drug testing on unwitting American citizens? Obtaining millions of private cables? Massive domestic spying by the CIA and the military? The illegal opening of mail? Attempts by an agency of the government to blackmail a civil rights leader? These have occurred and each has been withheld from scrutiny by the public and the Congress by the label 'secret intelligence.' " ([45A], p. 12).

The first part of Chapter 10 deals with secrecy as an issue in government information policy. Some of the material reprinted concerns general concepts, such as freedom of information and Executive privilege, and was drawn from documents related to matters other than intelligence. The system of security classification, a vehicle for secrecy, its dimensions, and its abuses, are examined first. Then several prominent legal scholars address the subject of Executive privilege, a right sometimes invoked by presidents (and others on their behalf) to thwart inquiry into the activities of the Executive branch by the courts and/or the Legislative branch. In addition, there is the testimony of former foreign policy official Daniel Ellsberg, who disclosed the classified "Pentagon Papers" in 1972. He relates his experiences and his views on the implications of the security classification system and the intelligence community's emphasis on secrecy in what is a democratic government. The problems faced in conducting historical research under the prevailing practices (in national security information policies) are also addressed and appear in a concluding study extracted from a 1973 House Government Operations Committee report on secrecy.

All of the documents presented illuminate the public policy issues created by the "necessity" to maintain secrecy in the conduct of foreign intelligence, but no clear-cut procedure is set forth for preventing abuses. "What should be regarded as a national secret? Who determines what is to be kept secret? How can decisions made in secret or programs secretly approved be reviewed?" These were the fundamental questions on information policy addressed by the Church Committee report ([45A], p. 13). They remain to be considered and to be answered.

The Executive Branch consistently over-classified information relating to foreign policy that should be a matter of public record.

This is partly the result of bureaucratic timidity, especially at middle and lower levels, where the prevailing approach is to look for some reason either to cover up or to withhold facts.

At least as important, this tendency to over-classification is but part of the process of "creeping commitments," frequently done at the request of a foreign government because the latter desires to keep a particular agreement or program secret from its own people.

More often than not, these governments are found in countries which have neither a free press, nor a responsible political opposition.

Examples: The Government of Thailand did not want it known that the United States was using air bases in that country. The Government of Laos did not want it known that the United States was fighting in major fashion in that country. Even in the Philippines where there is a free press and a highly articulate political opposition, the Government of the Philippines did not want it known that the United States was paying heavy allowances to the Philippine non-combat contingent that went to Vietnam.

Yet in each of these instances—and others could be cited—one secret agreement or activity led to another, until the involvement of the United States was raised to a level of magnitude far greater than that originally intended.

All of this occurred, not only without the knowledge of the American people, but even without the full knowledge of their representatives N1   on the proper Committees of the Congress.

Whether or not each of these expensive and at times clearly unnecessary adventures would have run its course if the Congress and/or the people had been informed, there would have been greater subsequent national unity, often a vital prerequisite to any truly successful outcome.

The dissembling to which the Congress and the American people have been subjected, however, cannot be attributed entirely to foreign governments. In the beginning, the Executive Branch of the United States, as much as the Governments of the Philippines and Thailand desired to keep secret the arrangements under which Filipino and Thai troops were sent to Vietnam. This secrecy made it appear that United States policy in Vietnam had far greater support from other countries than was the case.

This was pure deception, and it is one of the worst offenses a supposedly free and democratic government can commit against its own people, because it tends to destroy that trust which is an indispensable element of self-government.

Classification often permits an ambiguity about various commitments to be purposely developed by the Executive Branch.

The practice often is to:

Maximize commitment in secret discussions with foreign governments; then minimize the risk of commitment in statements made to the American public.

Maximize in public the importance of our friendly relationship and cooperation with a foreign government; then minimize, and often classify, that government's obstructiveness, failures and non-cooperation.

These actions make policy change and review both unlikely and politically difficult.

Americans pride themselves on having an open society. Nevertheless it is becoming an increasingly closed government. Yet neither the Congress nor the people can make intelligent judgments without questions which may literally involve our survival unless they have free access to all pertinent information which would not aid a possible enemy.

There is no merit to the argument that certain activities must be kept secret because a foreign government demanded they would be kept secret. Such a policy involves the Government of the United States in a web of intrigue which is alien to American traditions.

None of this is to say that there is no room for confidential discussions between governmental representatives. When agreements result from these discussions, however, particularly agreements which lead to large expenditures or even the commitment of Americans to combat, those agreements should be subjected to what Woodrow Wilson called "the broad daylight of public discussion."

Developments incident to our relationship with Laos provide basic examples of the problems incident to classification.

Without knowledge of the range of United States commitments and activities in and over Laos, neither the American people nor the Congress could understand, and thus either approve or disapprove, our policies toward that country.

Everyone recognizes that national security imposes limits on the disclosure of information. Knowledge of much intelligence information deserves to be held, even within the government, by a relatively small number of people. But the multimillion dollar support of a 30,000 man army can in no way be considered an intelligence operation; and to try to keep it classified is to deny information to those who also have responsibility and authority for our defense structure and its functioning.

Another example: by classifying the number of daily missions flown by United States aircraft over northern Laos since 1964—as distinguished from those missions flown over the Ho Chi Minh Trail and thus directly connected to the Vietnam war—the Executive Branch hid from the Congress as well as the people that additional major commitment, in men and dollars, undertaken to support the Royal Government of Laos.

A wide assortment of reasons for this type of classification have been given to the Subcommittee, to individual Senators, to newsmen on the scene, even to high officials of our government. The result of such effort to classify over here information that is available to the public overseas has contributed to a growing discontent among the American people as to the credibility of their own government.

Dimensions of the Classification Problem ([64], pp. 32–49)

The House Government Operations Committee considered and reported on amendments to the Freedom of Information Act during 1973 in an effort to broaden its application and strengthen its enforcement. The revised act was passed by Congress and became law on November 21, 1974, excepting from coverage certain documents held to be "classified" under the terms of various Executive orders and national security statutes. In its report on those exceptions to the law, the committee examined the dimensions of security classification practices in the federal government and the abuses that occur. That portion of the committee report is reprinted here and provides a background on the subject of secrecy.

The broad scope of the increasingly difficult problem in dealing with the many facets of the security classification system came into sharper focus during the summer of 1971. The publication of the Pentagon Papers, and the subsequent attempts by the administration to invoke prior restraint against the printing of additional articles in the press based on these controversial top secret documents made millions of Americans more aware of the operation of the classification system. The 6 to 3 Supreme Court decision against the Government in the New York Times and Washington Post cases and the depositions presented in those cases by both Government and outside classification experts revealed operational details of the system. Expert witnesses who testified at hearings by the House Foreign Operations and Government Information Subcommittee during the controversy uncovered other salient details as well as focusing attention on the growing Constitutional crisis affecting the right of Congress to obtain information from the executive branch.

Later leaks of Government documents during the India-Pakistan conflict in December 1971, the leak of a National Security Council memorandum early in 1972, revealing administration policy conflicts on Vietnam war strategy, and the continuing public attention on the Ellsberg-Russo trial in connection with the Pentagon Papers have all contributed to a broader understanding of the dimensions of the security classification problem.

The dimensions of the public policy and constitutional issues involved in the security classification problem were stated by President Nixon in his statement when he issued Executive Order 11652 on N2   March 8, 1972:

> The many abuses of the security system can no longer be tolerated. Fundamental to our way of life is the belief that when information which properly belongs to the public is systematically withheld by those in power, the people soon become ignorant of their own affairs, distrustful of those who manage them, and—eventually—incapable of determining their own destinies.
>
> Yet since the early days of the Republic, Americans have also recognized that the Federal Government is obliged to protect certain information which might otherwise jeopardize the security of the country. That need has become particularly acute in recent years as the United States has assumed a powerful position in world affairs, and as world peace has come to depend in large part on how that position is safeguarded. We are also moving into an era of delicate negotiations in which it will be especially important that governments be able to communicate in confidence.
>
> Clearly, the two principles of an informed public and of confidentiality within the Government are irreconcilable in their purest forms, and a balance must be struck between them.

Hearings were held by the House Foreign Operations and Government Information Subcommittee in May 1972 on security classification problems involving section 552(b)(1) of the Freedom of Information Act. They supplemented the subcommittee's June 1971 hearings on the "Pentagon Papers" and their relationship to the security classification system.

When the subcommittee subsequently resumed its hearings on various aspects of the security classification system as part of its overall review of the operation of the Freedom of Information Act, Chairman Moorhead described the dimension of the problem in his May 1, 1972 opening statement:

There are 55,000 arms pumping up and down in Government offices stamping "confidential" on stacks of Government documents; more than 18,000 Government employees are wielding "secret" stamps, and a censorship elite of nearly 3,000 bureaucrats have authority to stamp "top secret" on public records.

These are not wild estimates. These numbers were provided by the Government agencies, themselves. But even this huge number of Government censors is just the top of the secrecy iceberg.

These Government officials are the ones who have been granted authority, under a Presidential order, to put "top secret," "secret," and "confidential" on Government records which are to be hidden from the public in the interests of national defense. It seems to me that this sort of national defense effort creates little more than a Maginot line made of paper—and it is even more dangerous than France's concrete and steel Maginot line which gave that country false confidence in its safety just before it was overrun by the German Army in World War II. * * *

In an article on "The Public's Right To Know," published in the January–February 1972, issue of Case & Comment, Representative Horton likewise pointed out that, "on balance, more emphasis is given in Executive Order 10501 to protection of classified material than to declassification of information that is no longer sensitive." He added:

This has resulted in much overclassification of information and a tremendous backlog, numbering in the millions of documents, of material which, while properly kept secret initially, should have been declassified years ago.

Many of the witnesses testifying at both the 1971 and 1972 hearings—from Government as well as outside experts—presented examples of specific abuses of the classification system as well as broadgage criticism of its overall operational shortcomings. Many of these specific cases are described in other sections of this report.

But perhaps the most telling case against the security classification system as it operated under Executive Order 10501 for almost 20 years was made by President Nixon himself in this further quotation from his statement upon issuing Executive Order 11652:

Unfortunately, the system of classification which has evolved in the United States has failed to meet the standards of an open and democratic society, allowing too many papers to be classified for too long a time. The controls which have been imposed on classification authority have proved unworkable, and classification has frequently served to conceal bureaucratic mistakes or to prevent embarrassment to officials and administrations. * * *

N3

Volume of Classified Material

The precise volume of classified documents that has accumulated in Government files was the subject of considerable inquiry during the subcommittee's hearings because of its important relationship to the overall scope of the classification problem. Various estimates were provided by governmental and outside witnesses.

Mr. William G. Florence, a retired Air Force security classification expert, with 43 years' Federal service, estimated that the Department of Defense had "at least 20 million classified documents, including reproduced copies."

Later in the 1971 hearings, Mr. David O. Cooke, Principal Deputy Assistant Secretary (Administration), Department of Defense, was questioned by Congressman Horton on the 20 million figure:

Mr. Horton. Mr. Cooke, I wanted to ask you, have you had an opportunity to read the statement of Mr. William Florence who testified before this committee last week?

Mr. Cooke. Yes, I have read it once, sir.

Mr. Horton. In his statement on page 5 he makes this statement:

* * * the practice (overclassification) has become so widespread that the defense classification system is literally clogged with material bearing classification markings. I would guess that there are at least 20 million classified documents, including reproduced copies. I sincerely believe that less than one-half of 1 percent of the different documents which bear currently assigned classification markings actually contain information qualifying even for the lowest defense classification under Executive Order 10501. In other words, the disclosure of information in at least 99½ percent of those classified documents could not be prejudicial to the defense interests of the United States.

Mr. Horton. How do you react to that statement?

Mr. Cooke. Mr. Horton, I am not a—Mr. Florence spent a long and distinguished career with the military in the Department of the Air Force, and I am not aware of the factual basis or data which he used to express this purely personal judgment. We do not have any available figures on a defensewide basis. Classified documentation is used or is stored in active files and in DOD record-holding areas around the world. No reports are required at this time of the number of classified documents maintained by every DOD activity.

The closest we can come to it, sir, is biennial record reports indicating DOD holdings in total, classified and unclassified, of approximately 6 million cubic feet in active files. It was the estimate of one military department several years ago that 17 percent of the documents in their files were classified. If that figure is a valid estimate across the board, and we do not know whether it is, but assuming it is, I would say of our active record holdings, approximately 17 percent represent classified documents of all levels of classification. But I do not know the basis upon which the witness who appeared before you last week expressed that judgment. We have no data that we have been able to uncover which would support his assertion.

Mr. HORTON. Based on your knowledge of classified documents, from your position, how many would you estimate are classified?

Mr. COOKE. Based upon the collective judgment here, I would think, including reproduced copies, there could be more than 20 million classified documents. There is just no basis for reaching a judgment which could offer you any degree of reliable validity as to the precise number of documents.

Mr. HORTON. If you use the figure of 20 million, you would say there would be more than that?

Mr. COOKE. I would say there could quite possibly be more than 20 million classified documents, but I do not know. It could be less. As I said, the only approach we have to it was not by documents but by percentage of cubic feet of records and that was an estimated figure from one military department several years ago.

Mr. REID. What departments does that estimate you just made include?

Mr. COOKE. I believe the estimate of 17 percent was an estimate of the Department of Air Force.

The Defense Department supplied additional information on the magnitude of top secret documents:

Centralized records are not maintained in the Department of Defense on the number of top secret documents which are declassified, or on the subject matter contained in such documents. The following general items of information, however, may be of interest:

1. In 1965, all elements of the Office of the Secretary of Defense reviewed all top secret documents in current files with a view to the elimination of the maximum possible number. There was an overall reduction of about 33 percent. The eliminated documents comprised 7,200 nonrecord documents destroyed, 1,700 retired to record centers, 49 downgraded, and nine declassified. In 1966, other elements of the Department of Defense made a similar review. Eight major elements reported. Of a starting total of over 1 million, 344,-300 nonrecord documents were destroyed, 11,350 were retired to record centers, 9,000 were downgraded, and 710 were declassified, a reduction total of over 33 percent.

2. One major military command supplied the following figures derived from the annual classified document review of current file holdings. The figures are in linear feet. One linear foot represents 2,000 pages. A document may be one page or a thousand pages. A linear foot represents an average of 32 documents.

Top secret documents	1967	1968	1969
Destroyed (linear feet)	590	2,093	2,207
Downgraded (linear feet)	8	31	54
Declassified (linear feet)	1	0	210
Retired (linear feet)	0	0	0
Remaining (linear feet)	3,547	2,622	2,286

A conceptual idea of the volume of documents involved in the Defense Department's estimate of 6 million cubic feet was discussed during the hearings by Congressman Reid:

> We have some expert mathematicians here on the committee, and they have taken your figures at face value, 6 million cubic feet of active files, and based on your possible estimate of 17 percent of these being classified are most favorable.
>
> The staff says that is about one-sixth or a million cubic feet, and it equals 18 stacks of documents 555 feet high, each as high as the Washington Monument.

The volume of classified documents in the State Department was discussed by two Department witnesses, who gave widely varying estimates. Deputy Assistant Secretary of State William D. Blair gave one figure in a colloquy with Congressman Moss:

> Mr. Moss. Then this massive material, and you indicate in your statement that there are about 150 million documents in State. Mr. Blair——
>
> Mr. BLAIR. Yes, sir.
>
> Mr. Moss. One hundred fifty million previously classified.
>
> Mr. BLAIR. These are not all classified. This is classified and unclassified. But perhaps roughly one-quarter of them are classified.
>
> Mr. Moss. Thirty-five million documents classified under 10501 or prior to 10501?
>
> Mr. BLAIR. Well, not prior to 1945, Congressman Moss, because we have retired to the National Archives—that may not be quite completed, but we are in the process of retiring to the National Archives and opening up our files behind 1946. That is, through 1945. * * *

But testimony from Mr. William B. Macomber, Jr., Deputy Under Secretary of State for Administration, presented to the subcommittee in July 1971, gave a much lower estimate:

> Mr. REID. How many documents are classified in the Department now; do you have any idea?
>
> Mr. MACOMBER. Well, yes, I can give you a rough idea. We have accumulated in our central files about 400,000 documents a year, of which about 200,000 are classified. So you can assume that we are accumulating classified documents at least at a 200,000-a-year rate.
>
> I looked historically to see, the other day, and the last 20 years we have accumulated at a rate, averaged about 100,-000 classified documents a year over a 20-year period.
>
> Mr. REID. So we are talking of 2 million, roughly?
>
> Mr. MACOMBER. Yes, about 2 million, although the annual accumulation is greater now.

The most definitive estimates of the vast amount of classified documents in existence were presented by Dr. James B. Rhoads, Archivist of the United States.

> In the last generation we have grown a great deal. We have become the National Archives and Records Service. We conduct an ongoing records management program working with agency officials and their files. We operate 15 Federal

Records Centers and six Presidential Libraries, in addition to the National Archives itself. We have in our custody approximately 30 billion pages of Federal records, something more than 40 percent of the total volume of the Government's records. But while both our activities and our holdings have expanded, our goals remain the same: to serve the rest of the Government by caring for its non-current records and to serve the public in general by making available the documents of enduring value. * * *

Perhaps, Mr. Chairman, a few statistics will demonstrate the dimension of this problem. We estimate that for the period 1939 through 1945 the National Archives and the several relevant Presidential Libraries possess approximately 172 million pages of classified material, including a small amount of material of permanent value in our Federal Records Centers. For the period 1946–1950 we estimate our classified holdings at approximately 150 million pages, and for the period 1950–1954 we estimate an additional 148 million pages. These estimates indicate that for the period from the beginning of the Second World War through the end of the Korean War we possess some 470 million pages of classified documents.

President Nixon, in his statement upon issuing Executive Order 11652, used similar figures in estimating the volume of classified documents for the World War II period through 1954:

Once locked away in Government files, these papers have accumulated in enormous quantities and have become hidden from public exposure for years, for decades—even for generations. It is estimated that the National Archives now has 160 million pages of classified documents from World War II and over 300 million pages of classified documents for the years 1946 through 1954.

Of course, relatively few classified documents originated later than 1954 have made their way into the National Archives, so that the almost half billion pages represents but a fractional part of the total volume of classified material presently in existence. It is virtually impossible for Government officials to make even a rough estimate of the total magnitude of even the original copies of such documents. And the problem is compounded when unknown numbers of reproduced copies are added to the total.

Authority To Classify

The volume of classified documents is directly related to the number of Government agencies and individuals within such agencies who are authorized to apply classification stamps. As noted earlier, Executive Order 10290, issued by President Truman in 1951, extended classification authority to all Federal departments and agencies. Agency regulations implementing the order extended uniform original classification authority to their employees. The proliferation of classification authority and the growth of the volume of classified material were taken into account by President Eisenhower when he superseded the Truman order in 1953 with Executive Order 10501. He denied original classification authority to 28 agencies and limited the authority in 17 others, including a number of Cabinet departments. Amend-

N5

ments to this order in subsequent years removed the authority to classify from several other agencies, as had been recommended by this committee.[108]

Under Executive Order 10501, as amended, 47 executive departments, agencies, boards, commissions, and offices eventually had authority to classify documents as top secret, secret, or confidential, including 10 units connected with the White House office. In 34 of these, where security classification was essentially linked to matters pertaining to the national defense, such authority could be delegated by the departmental or agency head. The authority was limited to the head of the other 13 departments and agencies which were not so closely related to the national defense.[109]

The Foreign Operations and Government Information Subcommittee's August 1971 questionnaire to executive departments and agencies solicited statistical data on the operation of the Freedom of Information Act. It also requested data on the numbers of employees authorized to classify under Executive Order 10501. The results of this study and a supplemental series of inquiries in January 1972 to 12 selected agencies having primary responsibility in the defense and foreign policy areas show that about 55,000 Government officials were authorized to classify documents or other material as top secret, secret, or confidential.

The 55,000 total figure included 2,849 persons authorized to classify top secret, secret, and confidential and 18,029 persons authorized to classify secret and confidential. The remainder had confidential classification authority only. All of these figures refer to original classification authority.[111] The Department of Defense, including the Army, Navy, and Air Force, authorized 29,837 persons to classify under Executive Order 10501—783 top secret and 7,677 secret. The State Department, including the Agency for International Development, authorized 5,964 persons to classify—929 top secret and 2,155 secret. The Atomic Energy Commission authorized 6,173 persons to classify under the Executive order—310 top secret and 6,173 secret and confidential. None of these statistics, however, takes into account the extent of "derivative classification," the clerical reassignment or transfer of an existing classification of information contained in a document when portions of such classified documents are used in another document, report, or memorandum.

During the hearings, witness Florence provided the subcommittee insights into the extent to which "derivative classification" is a proliferating factor:

> * * * (DOD Instruction 5210.47) delegates something called derivative classification authority to any individual who can sign a document or who is in charge of doing something.
>
> Such individual may assign a classification to the information involved if he believes it to be so much as closely related

---

[108] Report of the Commission on Government Security, pp. 160–161.

[109] Analysis of listing in section 2 of Executive Order 10501.

[111] "Original Classification" is defined in Department of Defense Instruction No. 5210.47 (Dec. 31, 1964) as follows:

> Original Classification is involved when—
>
> a. An item of information is developed which intrinsically requires classification and such classification cannot reasonably be derived from a previous classification still in force involving in substance the same or closely related information; or
>
> b. An accumulation or aggregation of items of information, regardless of the classification (or lack of classification) of the individual items, collectively requires a separate and distinct classification determination.

to some other information that bears a classification. This is called derivative classification authority.

In the past several years I have not heard one person in the Defense Department say that he had no authority to classify information. The restrictions in Executive Order 10501 on delegating authority to classify have virtually no effect. * * *

* * * The derivative classification practice is the serious problem in the Government today. Under this concept of derivative authority to classify, anyone can assign classifications, sir. Anyone. I used the statement, I believe, "hundreds of thousands" in my comments. * * *

One of the most salutary results of the new Executive Order 11652 thus far observed is the reduction in both the number of agencies and the number of persons now authorized to exercise original classification authority. An August 3, 1972, statement from the White House Press Secretary's office, cited an oral report to the President by Ambassador John Eisenhower, Chairman of the Interagency Classification Review Committee, created by the new Executive order. The report indicates that the number of departments and agencies authorized to originally classify had been reduced to 25, excluding White House office agencies and that the number of persons having authority to originally classify information had been reduced by 63 percent—from 43,586 to 16,238.[113]

He indicated that top secret original classification authority had been reduced by 53 percent—from 2,275 to 1,076; secret by 39 percent—from 14,316 to 8,671; and confidential by 76 percent—from 26,995 to 6,491. These figures do not include the Central Intelligence Agency, which, according to the report made an overall reduction of 26 percent and a reduction in top secret of 84 percent. The April 1973 ICRC progress report, however, states that the number of top secret classifiers was reduced from 3,634 to 1,056 and that CIA top secret classifiers was reduced by 81 percent.

Overclassification Under Executive Order 10501

There has been virtually unanimous agreement—from the President on down—that serious abuses of overclassification had marked the operation of the security classification system under Executive Order 10501.

N6

Defense Secretary Laird, speaking at the April 20, 1970, Associated Press luncheon in New York, said: "Let me emphasize my convictions that the American people have a right to know even more than has been available in the past about matters which affect their safety and security. There has been too much classification in this country."

---

[113]
Note the discrepancy between this figure and the total number of persons authorized to classify under Executive Order 10501, as reported the previous year by the agencies themselves in response to the subcommittee's questionnaire; that total was 55,000. An April 17, 1973, progress report of the Interagency Classification Review Committee used the figures 48,814 to 17,883.

Ambassador Eisenhower was appointed as Chairman of the newly established Interagency Classification Review Committee, authorized in sec. 7 of Executive Order 11652, on May 17, 1972. Other members of the Committee are the General Counsels of the State Department (John R. Stevenson), the Defense Department (J. Fred Buzhardt), the CIA (Lawrence R. Houston), the Justice Department (Ralph E. Erickson), and representatives of the Atomic Energy Commission (John V. Vinciguerra), and the National Security Council staff (David R. Young), who served as the Committee's Executive Director. Ambassador Eisenhower resigned as Chairman in April 1973; Executive Director Young of the NSC staff likewise departed that same month. By Executive Order 11714, issued by President Nixon on April 24, 1973, the Archivist of the United States was added to the Committee. Dr. James B. Rhoads, who currently holds that position, was named as Acting Chairman of the Committee.

Former United Nations Ambassador and Supreme Court Justice Arthur Goldberg told the subcommittee:

> Anyone who has ever served our Government has struggled with the problem of classifying documents to protect national security and delicate diplomatic confidences. I would be less than candid if I did not say that our present classification system does not deal adequately with this problem despite the significant advances made under the leadership of this committee and Congress in the Freedom of Information Act of 1966. I have read and prepared countless thousands of classified documents. In my experience, 75 percent of these documents should never have been classified in the first place; another 15 percent quickly outlived the need for secrecy; and only about 10 percent genuinely required restricted access over any significant period of time.
>
> Moreover, whatever precautions are taken, leaks occur in a government of fallible men.
>
> In short, the classified label in our experience has never been 100 percent respected.

William B. Macomber, Jr., Deputy Under Secretary of State for Administration, candidly stated: "We all know, I think, that there is a tendency in the executive branch to overclassify."

Mr. Ralph E. Erickson, then Assistant Attorney General, Office of Legal Counsel testified:

> There is nearly universal agreement among those familiar with the operation of Executive Order 10501 that the existing system of classification has failed to strike the right balance between the public's need to know and the necessity to maintain certain information in confidence. The President put it well when he announced the issuance of the new order:
>
>> Unfortunately, the system of classification which has evolved in the United States has failed to meet the standards of an open and democratic society, allowing too many papers to be classified for too long a time. The controls which have been imposed on classification authority have proved unworkable, and classification has frequently served to conceal bureaucratic mistakes or to prevent embarrassment to officials and administrations.
>
> Material classified under Executive Order 10501 and under preceding authorities has accumulated in vast quantities in Government files and storehouses. Only with the commitment of extensive Government resources can this mountain of classified material be reviewed or declassified within a reasonable period of time. Perhaps the chief deficiency of Executive Order 10501 was the failure of that order to provide an effective administrative system. Without an effective administrative system, its well-intended provisions turned out to be empty exhortations for the most part.

Classification expert William G. Florence, a retired Air Force security classification official with some 43 years of Federal service, testified:

> I sincerely believe that less than one-half of 1 percent of the different documents which bear currently assigned classifi-

cation markings actually contain information qualifying even for the lowest defense classification under Executive Order 10501. In other words, the disclosure of information in at least 99½ percent of those classified documents could not be prejudicial to the defense interests of the Nation.

In subsequent testimony, during the May 1972, hearings, Mr. Florence asserted that "the administrative security classification system currently in Executive Order 10501 is the source of most of the secrecy evils in the executive branch." He blamed loose implementation at the outset, and incredibly inept administration of the policy in recent years, (that) have invited and promoted widespread use of the three security classifications, "Top Secret," "Secret," and "Confidential."

He went on to point out:

> The contagion of the classification philosophy long ago reached the point where the security system in Executive Order 10501 represents the greatest hoax of this century. Officials occupying even the highest positions in our Government have been conditioned to promote the belief that the words "top secret," "secret," and "confidential" on a paper automatically give it a substantive value of extraordinary importance, and beyond the ken of most people. * * *

Columnist Jack Anderson testified:

> Not only does the executive branch sweep its bungles and blunders, its miscalculations and embarrassments under the secrecy labels, but our entire foreign policy and defense posture remains secret except for what the executive branch thinks is in its own interest to make available to the public. * * *

> It isn't just hush-hush Government activity that is classified. Newspaper clipping, public speeches and a wide variety of other public information have wound up with secrecy labels. When the Government went to court in its desperate bid to stop publication of the Pentagon papers by the Washington Post, the information cited as most sacrosanct repeatedly was shown by the Post to have already appeared in print. Ultimately, the Government itself acknowledged that there was "massive overclassification" of public papers.

> Does this mean there should be no Government secrets? Of course not. Our weapons technology, intelligence sources, and diplomatic contacts must be kept confidential. But the executive branch has used the classification system to censor the facts, to manage the news, to control the flow of information to the people.

Mr. William D. Blair, Jr., Deputy Assistant Secretary of State for Public Affairs, testified on the causes of the weaknesses of the security classification system established by Executive Order 10501:

> As you know, Executive Order 11652 was the result of a year-long study of our system of handling national security information a study set in motion by President Nixon in January 1971, with a view to reform of that system. In these opening remarks I would like to summarize very briefly the principal conclusions which we, in the Department of State,

drew from that year-long study—conclusions which I believe were broadly shared by our colleagues in the other agencies concerned—and which the new Executive order now reflects.

The first of these basic conclusions was simply this, that our existing system of classification and declassification, governed by Executive Order 10501, was not working as it should. Too much information, probably far too much, was being classified to begin with, and too much of that was being overclassified. In addition, the automatic declassification provision of Executive Order 10501 was virtually inoperative, since the language of the exceptions to it—particularly the definition of group 3—was so broad as to allow almost any classified document to be excluded from automatic declassification, and this privilege was being widely used or abused. * * *

He listed the following specific causes for the failure:

1. The system established under Executive Order 10501 was too complicated. The establishment of four groups for classification purposes, superimposed on three categories of classifications, required a list of definitions and rules which was hard to teach, hard to learn, and hard to remember. As a result, the terms of the order were widely misunderstood and even ignored.

2. This system as implemented gave too much authority to classify, and to exclude from automatic declassification, to too many people. This tended to insure a maximum flow of classified paper into the files, and a minimum return flow of automatically declassified paper out of the files.

3. The sheer volume of national security information, multiplying rapidly in the post-World War II period with the enormous expansion of our defense and foreign policy interests and programs has become so great that it simply overwhelms any declassification effort which is not largely and effectively automatic. * * *

4. Executive Order 10501 failed to provide an effective means of monitoring its implementation. And the handling of national security information, like any other large and complex undertaking, clearly requires leadership and management on a continuing basis if it is to be made to work.

These in my opinion were the essential conclusions to emerge from the interagency study which the President launched. I might add one more: the obvious fact that the conditions here suggested were contributing to a growing lack of respect, in and out of Government, for the classification system, with resulting damage both to the public's right to be informed and to its right to effective protection of its security interests.

The implications of security classification abuses were clearly stated by David Wise, coauthor of "The Invisible Government," a critical study of the U.S. intelligence community:

Mr. Chairman, I believe that the central fact about the American political system today is that large numbers of people no longer believe the Government or the President, and I am speaking of any President. They no longer believe the Government because they have come to understand that the Government does not always tell the truth; that indeed it very often tells just the opposite.

This erosion of confidence between the people and the Government is perhaps the single most important political development in America in the past decade. * * *

President Nixon has recognized Government credibility as a continuing problem, and it is certainly not a problem associated only with the one administration or one political party. The American people have not been told the truth. If the people aren't told the truth, if they are misled, then I don't believe we can continue for very long to have a properly functioning democratic system. I think that there is obviously a very close relationship between public mistrust of Government, and of Government information, and the question of secrecy and document classification. I think that is very clear from the Pentagon study of the Vietnam war which led to the historic constitutional confrontation between the Federal Government, the New York Times and several other newspapers in recent days. Those materials make it clear that it is very simple for Government officials, by using the security classification system, to keep from public view policies, programs, plans, decisions and actions that are just the opposite of what the public is being told. In other words, we now have a system of institutionalized lying. Fortunately, no one has yet invented a rubberstamp or security classification that can keep the truth from eventually becoming known. But all too often, it does not become known quickly enough to inform the voters.

A similar theme was expressed by Senator Mike Gravel of Alaska in his testimony:

I think the cocoon of secrecy that we have woven over the years, particularly since the Second World War, is what has permitted us to go into Vietnam, permitted us to waste not only our blood, our young people, but also to waste our economic fiber. To what degree I don't think we will ever know. I think only history can judge that.

I personally feel that our democracy is under assault, assault in a very unique way and in a very evolutionary way, and unless we can turn the tide we will lose the system of government we presently enjoy. And the single item that will be responsible for this loss of government, this great experiment at self-government here in the United States, will be secrecy itself and nothing more, nothing more complex than that, because secrecy is anathema to democracy. It is that fundamental.

You can't ask people to go vote—and in our society the person who votes is supposed to be the final word—when secrecy prevails. It is a government of the people, by the people, for the people, so they have to give the final word. Quite obviously they can't vote intelligently or exercise their franchise with any efficiency if they don't know what they are voting about, and that depends upon the amount of knowledge they have.

Now, if that knowledge is spoon fed to them so they will arrive at preconceived conclusions, then obviously you develop a type of government that becomes first an autocracy and from there a dictatorship.

Congressman Otis Pike of New York, a member of the House Armed Services Committee testified:[124]

The record of the Department of Defense in this area is uniformly on the side of secrecy. They have, in the past, been completely successful in getting Congress to approve weapons systems for which neither Congress nor the American public is told the ultimate cost, so why should they change.

Far beyond classifying for purposes of national defense, they classify to change their testimony, to avoid embarrassment, and I expect most frequently through sheer stupidity and because no one ever tells them not to.

We have all seen page after page after page of testimony stamped "secret," and then seen the Department of Defense release the same testimony with no change whatsoever. We have seen the biographies of generals and admirals stamped "secret." * * *

In conclusion, it is my own judgment that 90 percent of what is classified should not be. Physically, there should be just as many people employed by the Pentagon declassifying material as there are classifying it. Their attitude has always been, "If in doubt—mark it secret." In a free society our attitude should always be, "If in doubt—tell the people the truth."

Historian Lloyd C. Gardner of Rutgers University observed:

One can trace the growth of official secrets, both in volume and length of classification, with America's rise to "a powerful position in world affairs." As interest multiplied, so did secrecy. There is something uncomfortable in a democracy about that fact alone, something that bears close watching.

He went on to point out:

Nations, like individuals, depend in part upon memory in order to be able to function rationally in the present. Historians are to a degree responsible for what stands out in a nation's memory; they supply experience longer than one generation's lifespan, and broader than that of any group of individuals.

As one approaches the present, the historian's most valuable asset, perspective, is diminished chronologically, and in a secrecy-conscious nation, by the lack of available evidence as well.

The Nation's memory is thus weakest for the years of the recent past, a serious defect, unless one is prepared to concede that the public should reach its conclusions on the

---

[124] . . . . .an example illustrating unnecessary classification by the Navy of a 1969 letter to Congressman Pike, classified "Secret," by then Navy Secretary Chafee came out during the hearings. The letter, involving CTF 96 Op-Order 301–68 connected with the North Korean capture of the U.S. vessel *Pueblo*, had been included in the prepared text of Mr. Pike's May 1972 statement to the subcommittee. Subcommittee efforts to have it declassified by the Navy immediately prior to the hearings failed, but it was subsequently reviewed and declassified by Secretary Chafee during the course of Mr. Pike's testimony before the subcommittee.

basis of little or no information, or that the policymaker is the only one who needs the memory.

Other witnesses were more specific in their discussion of abuses in the security classification system, providing detailed information on cases of overclassification or needless classification that illustrates many of the basic shortcomings of Executive Order 10501.

Classification expert William G. Florence gave a number of examples in his testimony:

> Some time ago, one of the service Chiefs of Staff wrote a note to the other Chiefs of Staff stating briefly that too many papers were being circulated with the top secret classification. He suggested that use of the classification should be reduced. Believe it or not, Mr. Chairman, that note itself was marked "top secret."
>
> The Air Force Electronics Systems Division at Hanscom Field, Mass., adopted the following statement for use on selected documents: "Although the material in this publication is unclassified, it is assigned an overall classification of confidential." We attempted some extra orientation in the Air Force regarding the definition of "confidential" at that time. I would not say our immediate success lasted very long. I still see practices of this sort.
>
> Not so very long ago, someone in the Navy Department placed the "secret" marking on some newspaper items of particular interest to the Navy. Subsequently, that action caused some embarrassment to the Department of Defense. As a result, a special directive had to be published to tell people not to classify newspapers. I see recently that practice within the Department of Defense is continuing anyway, the best I can tell from reading the newspapers today about the disclosures in the New York Times, the Washington Post, and the Boston Globe.
>
> A great many individuals in the Department of Defense, including highly placed officials, classify or strongly support the imposition of defense classifications on privately owned information, including privately generated applications for patents, regardless of the fact that Executive Order 10501 is clearly limited to official Government information. This really spreads classification beyond any possible control. And we can be certain that the tremendous costs which stem from this type of unnecessary classification, as well as all other unnecessary classifications, are charged to all of us as taxpayers.

Mr. Forrest M. Mims III, a former security officer at the Air Force Weapons Laboratory, Kirtland Air Force Base, N. Mex., also cited what he considered to be abuses of classification authority and procedures:

> Some examples of overclassification I observed at the Air Force Weapons Laboratory include the following:
>
> 1. In 1967, the Department of Defense classified a project to develop a personnel sensing system based on a principle of nature familiar to any school boy. Both the project and the principle were classified Top Secret (Special Access Re-

quired). The project was downgraded to a more reasonable classification level in 1970.

2. The Air Force classified as Secret (Special Access Required) a certain laser weaponry program because revelation of the weapon's target would result in revulsion and disapproval on the part of the general public. The project, though compromised on several occasions as a result of unclassified supporting experiments and studies, is still classified as Secret. An identical Army program, since discontinued as being impractical, was classified only Confidential.

3. An Air Force scientist invoked the classification system to prevent a research project from being transferred to an Air Force research laboratory with the assigned task of performing identical work but without the required security access. The classification system was invoked even though nearly all aspects of the project were treated as unclassified at the scientist's own laboratory.

While these examples of overclassification may seem inconsequential, they seriously impede the efficiency and communication necessary for high quality research.

Overclassification is by no means limited to Air Force research laboratories. I witnessed many examples of the practice elsewhere. For example:

1. In 1966, a brief lesson block on the history of the Bolshevik revolution taught at the Armed Forces Air Intelligence Training Center was classified Secret.

2. In 1967, a large selection of photographs showing atrocities wrought by communist troops against Vietnamese civilians was classified Confidential.

3. Also in 1967, aerial reconnaissance photographs taken by Air Force planes which revealed bombing of civilian structures in North Viet-Nam were classified Secret.

Congressman Michael J. Harrington of Massachusetts, a member of the House Armed Services Committee, said in his statement to the subcommittee:

But the military, by its constant penchant for secrecy, erodes whatever public confidence it may ever hope to have. The military has been sharply criticized lately, but instead of offering candid explanations for its policies, it hides behind the cloak of "Top Secret." I asked Secretary of the Navy Chafee why dumping at sea or the problems of race relations in the service were stamped "Confidential." While he agreed that the Navy should make every effort to bring dialog before the public, he explained that parts of the document were classified so all of it was classified.

Still other examples were provided by Mr. William G. Florence in his May 1972, testimony:

This subcommittee has an abundance of examples of unnecessary classification assignments showing that classification markings on a document usually are clearly unwarranted. I will describe only one at this time to emphasize how utterly ludicrous the classification system is in practice.

Compilations of unclassified information are still being classified frequently by individuals who seem to believe that multiplicity or complexity itself should be protected. The Department of Defense affidavit given the court last summer in the Washington Post case involving the Vietnam study included the following: "It is sometimes necessary to classify a document in which no single piece or part is itself classified." This falsification of policy in Executive Order 10501 has led to unnecessary classification of millions of documents of the Department of Defense. * * *

Another example of the classification of unclassified information is a document prepared by the Massachusetts Institute of Technology for the Air Force Space and Missile Systems Office, with the title, "Assembly Manual—Gyro Float." It was issued in February 1971 with the classification of confidential, which was the responsibility of the Air Force. Here is a copy of the document with the marking "confidential" on the cover. This document, with its confidential classification marking, contains the following statement:

> Each section of this volume is in itself unclassified. to protect the compilation of information contained in the complete volume, the complete volume is confidential.

Also in the foreword of the document is the following statement, which is required by Executive Order 10501 on all classified documents held by contractors and others outside the executive branch:

> This document contains information affecting the national defense of the United States within the meaning of the Espionage Laws, title 18, United States Code, sections 793 and 794, the transmission or revelation of which in any manner to an unauthorized person is prohibited by law.

This nonsensical practice of the Department of Defense not only is outrageously expensive in terms of wasted money but it is atrocious in its application to individuals who happen to become involved in an allegation of mishandling the unclassified information. I have seen people in responsible positions blindly take punitive action against employees in the Government and in industry for handling such unclassified information as being unclassified.

One opinion showing the widespread extent of abuse in the security classification system was presented by Gene R. LaRocque, rear admiral (retired), U.S. Navy, a much-decorated veteran of 31 years of naval service. He testified:

> In the military the best way to prevent disclosure of information is to classify it. Classification is made for a variety of reasons. First, to prevent it from falling into the hands of a potential enemy; this is legitimate but accounts for only a small portion of the material classified. Other reasons for classifying material are: to keep it from the other military services, from civilians in their own service, from civilians in the Defense Department, from the State Department, and of course, from the Congress. Sometimes, information is classified to withhold it for later release to maximize the effect on the public or the Congress.

Frequently, information is classified so that only portions of it can be released selectively to the press to influence the public or the Congress. These time released capsules have a lasting effect.* * *

Admiral La Rocque also stated:

Regrettably, far too much material is classified, much of it just because it is easier to classify than not. You cannot get into trouble by overclassifying, only by failing to classify. And, it is easier to maintain secure files if all material is classified. In that way, only one set of files need be maintained.

Classification is also very simple; all one needs is a typewriter or a Secret stamp. In most offices, the secretaries or the yeomen establish the classification. And since most typed matter is not signed, no one ever knows who classified the material or for what reason. There is no central record of what was classified by whom, when, or for what purpose.

The Legal Foundations of Executive Secrecy

The legal basis for security classification practices and the use of Executive privilege by a president and his aides are examined here by three authorities. Robert Dixon, Jr., assistant attorney general during President Gerald R. Ford's administration, testified before the Senate Government Operations Committee's Subcommittee on Intergovernmental Relations in May 1974. The transcript of those hearings covers more than 800 pages and represents an extensive study of secrecy in government. The Dixon testimony provides a brief historical background of security classification and the constitutional authority for the use of security classification to control the flow of information. Dixon's statement has been abridged to delete references to legislation then pending (and not passed) concerning limitations of classification authority.

Following the Dixon text is an exposition on Executive privilege by Raoul Berger, then a senior fellow of the Harvard Law School. He appeared before the Senate in May 1973 during the hearings on Executive privilege, secrecy in government, and freedom of information. Finally, there is the statement of Norman Dorsen, general counsel of the American Civil Liberties Union and professor of law at New York University. He testified after the appearance of Raoul Berger, and his statement addresses the relationship among the Executive, Legislative, and Judicial branches of government in treating the matter of Executive privilege and the legal limits of secrecy and classification practices.

ROBERT DIXON ON SECURITY CLASSIFICATION
([30], pp. 143–153)

HISTORICAL BACKGROUND

The practice in the United States of designating official information with markings such as "Secret", "Confidential", or "Private" can be traced to the early nineteenth century, although no formal system then existed. During periods of military conflict, however, more formal controls developed. For example, during the Civil War some broad guidelines relating to the dissemination of war information were agreed upon by Union military leaders and the press. The Congress enacted a criminal espionage statute in 1911, and refined and strengthened it in 1917 after the outbreak of World War I. The military then administratively established a classification system requiring certain information to be marked "Secret", "Confidential", or "For Official Circulation Only". Early in 1917, the Departments of State, War and Navy specified by regulation types of nonpublishable information, and sought the voluntary cooperation of the press. For example, "no information, reports, or rumors, attributing a policy to the government in any international situation, not authorized by the President or a member of the cabinet [were to] be published without first consulting with the Department of State". To further formalize the system, President Wilson issued Executive Order 2954, creating the Committee on Public Information. Despite the fact that press cooperation was generally good, much of the information sought to be protected was disseminated through other sources. This experience led to the belief that the only effective means of control was "secrecy at the source," without the necessity of relying upon independent judgment thereafter.

Following the war, the military departments maintained their internal classification systems with only minor changes. For example, in 1935, the Army amended its document security regulations to provide that all classified documents be stamped with a notice that they contained defense information within the meaning of the Espionage Act of 1917. A new espionage statute enacted in 1938 gave the President authority to designate sensitive military installations and equipment, and by doing so to make it a crime to photograph, sketch or produce representations of them. Pursuant to this authority, President Roosevelt also designated, as sensitive, and subject to criminal sanctions if disclosed, all documents and other material classified under the authority of the Secretaries of War and Navy.

World War II led to further refinements in the information security system, but no comprehensive program survived the end of the War.

In 1948, the unresolved problem of a permanent information security system was referred by the National Security Council to the Interdepartmental Committee on Internal Security (ICIS). The committee then drafted new regulations establishing minimum standards for the handling and transmission of classified information in executive departments and agencies. Noting a Yale University study which indicated that 95% of all secret government information was at that time being published in the press, President Truman, on September 24, 1951, issued Executive Order 10290, adopting these minimum standards.

PRESENT EXECUTIVE ORDER SYSTEM

A. Orders of Presidents Truman, Eisenhower, and Kennedy

The Truman Order incorporated the then existing four-tiered classification system—Top Secret, Secret, Confidential, and Restricted. The definitions of the classification categories indicate the extreme difficulty of reducing discretion in this area. The "Top Secret" designation was assigned to information the disclosure of which "would or could cause exceptionally grave danger to the national security". "Secret" information was defined as that which required "extraordinary protection." The "Confidential" designation was used to indicate information which required "careful protection." "Restricted" information was that which required "protection against unauthorized use or disclosure".

The Order contained no limitation on the number of persons authorized to classify. It did require "wherever practicable," that the classifier mark the document to indicate a date or event after which the document could be downgraded or declassified. If the document was not so marked, it was subject to downgrading or declassification only when circumstances no longer warranted the original classification. Primarily because of the vagueness of the "wherever practicable" standard, most documents were not marked for automatic downgrading or declassification and the Order contained no procedures for conducting classification review.

The Truman Order was criticized severely in the press. For instance, a New York Times editorial charged that:

"A striking weakness is the failure to make any provision for systematic and periodic review of how it is being put into use. Vast discretion is placed in the hands of a large number of officials with no adequate check upon how that discretion is exercised."

Upon taking office in January 1953, President Eisenhower referred the Order to the Attorney General for revision or recission as deemed necessary, and on November 6, 1953, President Eisenhower issued Executive Order 10501. The new Order eliminated the "Restricted" classification category, decreased the number of agencies authorized to classify, and established general procedures for declassification of documents no longer warranting protection. Its major features may be summarized as follows:

"Top Secret" classification was to be used only for "defense information or material which required the highest degree of protection . . . the unauthorized disclosure of which could result in exceptionally grave damage to the "Nation." "Secret" classification was to be applied to information the unauthorized disclosure of which could result in serious damage to the Nation. "Confidential" classification was to be applied to information the unauthorized disclosure of which could be prejudicial to the defense interests of the Nation.

"The Order withdrew authority to classify from 28 agencies. As to 17 other agencies it limited authority to classify to the agency head without power to delegate. Ultimately, 34 departments and agencies were given full power to classify and delegate classifying authority, while 12 were given limited power. Even within departments and agencies possessing delegable authority the Order required that delegation be limited "as severely as is consistent with the orderly and expeditious transaction of governmental business."

The Eisenhower Order sought also to improve downgrading and declassification procedures. Heads of departments and agencies having authority to classify were required to designate subordinate officials to conduct continual classification reviews. While automatic downgrading and declassification were not made mandatory, the Order required their utilization to the "fullest extent practicable."

In 1961, President Kennedy, through the issuance of Executive Order 10964, amended the Eisenhower Order to establish more specific standards for downgrading and declassification.[1]

The Kennedy approach yielded further improvement in reducing the volume of classified information which unnecessarily burdened the information security system. Nevertheless, the system continued to function in a manner viewed by some critics as failing to balance properly the interests of an informed citizenry with the need for protecting national security information.

B. The Order of President Nixon (Executive Order 11652)

In recognition of the continuing problem, President Nixon directed, on January 15, 1971, the establishment of an interagency committee to review the security classification system and to make recommendations for its improvement.

This committee was chaired by then Assistant Attorney General in charge of the Office of Legal Counsel, now Justice William H. Rehnquist, and was composed of representatives from the Departments of Defense, State and Justice, the Atomic Energy Commission, the Central Intelligence Agency and the National Security Council. The principal focus was the long-needed revision of Executive Order 10501. After Mr. Rehnquist left the Department in mid-December, the cooperative effort was coordinated by the National Security Council staff.

On March 8, 1972, President Nixon signed Executive Order 11652, embodying the recommendations of the interagency committee. Upon issuing the Order the President summarized the reasons which prompted him to take this far-reaching action:

"Fundamental to our way of life is the belief that when information which properly belongs to the public is systematically withheld by those in power, the people soon become ignorant of their own affairs, distrustful of those who manage them, and—eventually—incapable of determining their own destinies.

*   *   *   *   *   *   *

"Yet since the early days of the Republic, Americans have also recognized that the Federal Government is obliged to protect certain information which might otherwise jeopardize the security of the country.

*   *   *   *   *   *   *

---

[1] This Order required information classified by one of the three protection-level designations to be further categorized into four groups, two of which exempted the information so categorized from automatic downgrading and declassification, one of which subjected it to automatic downgrading and one of which subjected it to automatic downgrading *and* declassification.

"Clearly, the two principles of an informed public and of confidentiality within the Government are irreconcilable in their purest forms, and a balance must be struck between them."

Executive Order No. 11652 of March 8, 1972, established the current Executive branch procedures for classifying and declassifying official information or material relating to the national defense or foreign relations of the United States, referred to collectively as "national security" information. Section 1 of F.O. 11652 provides that:

"Official information or material which requires protecton against unauthorized disclosure in the interest of the national defense or foreign relations of the United States (hereinafter collectively termed 'national security') shall be classified in one of three categories, namely 'Top Secret,' 'Secret,' or 'Confidential,' depending upon the degree of its significance to national security * * *."

Material may be classified "Top Secret" only if its "unauthorized disclosure could reasonably be expected to cause exceptionally grave damage to the national security." Examples of "exceptionally grave damage" are described as "* * * armed hostilities against the United States or its allies; disruption of foreign relations vitally affecting the national security; the compromise of vital national defense plans or complex cryptologic and communications intelligence systems; the revelation of sensitive intelligence operations; and the disclosure of scientific or technological developments vital to national security."

Material may be classified "Secret" only if its "unauthorized disclosure would reasonably be expected to cause serious damage to the national security." Examples of "serious damage" are described as "* * * disruption of foreign relations significantly affecting the national security; significant impairment of a program or policy directly related to the national security; revelation of significant military plans or intelligence operations; and compromise of significant scientific or technological developments relating to national security."

Material may be classified "Confidential" only if its "unauthorized disclosure could reasonably be expected to cause damage to the national security."

Section 2 authorizes a limited number of high executive officials to classify information. Section 3 is less restrictive in providing authorization to downgrade and declassify information.

Section 4 provides that persons shall be held accountable for the propriety of classifications attributed to them. Additionally, that section unequivocally instructs that no information shall "* * * be classified in order to conceal inefficiency or administrative error, to prevent embarrassment to a person or Department, to restrain competition or independent initiative, or to prevent for any other reason the release of information which does not require protection in the interest of national security."

Section 5 provides rules for downgrading and declassifying material.

Section 6(A) provides that: [n]o person shall be given access to classified information or material unless such person has been determined to be trustworthy and unless access to such information is necessary for the performance of his duties.

It is important to stress that Executive Order 11652 applies only to material related to national security and that a decision to classify a document is not necessarily a decision to withhold it from Congress in a particular case.

CONSTITUTIONAL AUTHORITY FOR EXECUTIVE ORDER NO. 11652

The authority for Executive Order No. 11652, like its predecessors, stems from the President's power under Article II of the Constitution to conduct foreign relations and to maintain the national defense as Commander-in-Chief of the Armed Forces. In *New York Times* v. *United States*, 403 U.S. 713, 729–30 (1971), Justice Stewart, in a concurring opinion joined by Justice White, stated that the President's constitutional power in these areas implied a corresponding duty and authority to establish a system of classifying documents. Justice Stewart wrote:

"It is clear to me that it is the constitutional duty of the Executive—as a matter of sovereign prerogative and not as a matter of law as the courts know law—through the promulgation and enforcement of executive regulations, to protect the confidentiality necessary to carry out its responsibilities in the fields of international relations and defense."

It is worth noting that Justice Marshall, in a concurring opinion, also recognized the Executive's authority to classify information. 403 U.S. at 741. The views expressed by Justice Stewart, White, and Marshall are supported by other Supreme Court cases, by congressional statutes, and we think by the intent of the Framers of the Constitution. In the area of international relations and defense the powers of the Executive traditionally have been treated as very broad, although not limitless.

In *C & S Air Lines* v. *Waterman Corp.*, 333 U.S. 103, 109 (1948),[2] the Supreme Court stated that the "President * * * possesses in his own right certain powers conferred by the Constitution on him as Commander-in-Chief and as the Nation's organ in foreign affairs." Acting in these capacities, the Court added, the President "has available intelligence services whose reports are not and ought not to be published to the world." Id. at 111.

In *United States* v. *Curtiss-Wright Corp.*, 299 U.S. 304, 319 (1936), the Court stated that in the area of foreign affairs, "with its important, complicated, delicate and manifold problems, the President alone has the power to speak or listen as a representative of the nation." The Court quoted with approval John Marshall's statement made as a Congressman that "[t]he President is the sole organ of the nation in its external relations, and its sole representative with foreign nations." An 1816 Senate Foreign Relations Committee Report, quoted with approval by the Court in the *Curtiss-Wright* case, also recognized the President's constitutional power with respect to foreign affairs and the national safety and observed: The nature of transactions with foreign nations, more-over, requires caution and unity of design, and their success frequently depends on secrecy and dispatch.

Article II of the Constitution interpreted in the light of the President's constitutional responsibilities as Commander-in-Chief and conductor of our international relations, properly implies a Presidential power to establish a system of classifying national security information. See *McCulloch* v. *Maryland*, 4 Wheat. (17 U.S.) 316 (1819). By instructing executive branch members how to handle national security information Executive Order 11652 is clearly a necessary and proper aid to the fulfillment of the President's constitutional responsibilities.

That the President would have authority to establish a classification system to secure the secrecy and confidentiality necessary to the successful conduct of foreign affairs in a militarily unfriendly world was intended by the Framers of the Constitution. Writing in *Federalist*, No. 64, John Jay stated:

"It seldom happens in the negotiation of treaties, of whatever nature, but that perfect secrecy and immediate despatch are sometimes requisite. There are cases where the most useful intelligence may be obtained if the persons possessing it can be relieved from apprehensions of discovery. Those apprehensions will operate on those persons whether they are actuated by mercenary or friendly motives; and there doubtless are many of both descriptions who would rely on the secrecy of the President, but who would not confide in that of the Senate, and still less in that of a large popular Assembly. The convention have done well, therefore, in so disposing of the power of making treaties, that although the President must, in forming them, act by the advice and consent of the Senate, yet he will be able to manage the business of intelligence in such a manner as prudence may suggest."

Jay then elaborated in some detail on why the President needed authority to provide for secrecy in the conduct of international relations, noting that the rapidly changing tides of foreign affairs could be best handled by the executive branch which has the most experience and knowledge in this area.

It may be observed that most of the judicial decisions discussed above and the quotation taken from *Federalist* No. 64 concerned the President's powers over foreign relations and did not address the question of Presidential powers in the national defense information area. Of course, Executive Order 11652 provides for classification of both national defense and foreign relations information. However, the national security principles underlying the statements made regarding Presidential power in the foreign relations area justify also his power to classify national defense information.

Moreover, it may properly be said that all national defense information is necessarily related to foreign relations. Defense planning and appropriations,

---

[2] There the Court held that a Presidential decision approving or disapproving a Civil Aeronautics Board order granting or denying an application to engage in foreign air transportation was not subject to judicial review.

military base closings, procurement practices, allocation of manpower, location of missile sites, and similar information is generally referred to as national defense information. But clearly all such information has a close relationship to our foreign relations. For example, negotiations over a SALT II agreement, mutual and balanced force reductions with the Warsaw Pact countries, and the East-West security conference all are affected by what is commonly called national defense information. Accordingly the precedents establishing the President's foreign relations power to classify information also establish his power to classify national defense information.

The firm constitutional basis for Presidential authority to classify both types of national security information is recognized also by a number of congressional enactments. The espionage laws, 18 U.S.C. §§ 792–798, alternately refer to classified information or make it imperative to establish a classification system in order to enforce them fairly and effectively. Subsection (b) of the Internal Security Act of 1950, 50 U.S.C. § 783, makes it a crime "for any officer or employee of the United States" to communicate to a foreign agent "any information of a kind *which shall have been* classified by the President as affecting the security of the United States * * *." [Emphasis supplied.] See also 50 U.S.C. § 783(c). The Freedom of Information Act protects from disclosure matters "specifically required by Executive Order to be kept secret in the interest of national defense or foreign policy." 5 U.S.C. § 552(b)(1).

The constitutional basis for Executive Order 11652 is thus manifest. It should be added, moreover, that the Executive, as a matter of policy, is best equipped to establish an appropriate classification scheme. Events in the area of foreign relations unfold rapidly. The Executive is in possession of the most timely and complete information that is necessary to determine whether information needs classified status to protect the Nation from harm. A military coup and the elevation of persons to prominent government positions often transform an innocuous document into one of a highly sensitive nature. The President possesses the flexibility and authority in the area of classification to respond quickly to such unforeseen changes in a manner that prevents unwarranted disclosure of information. A statutory classification scheme, in contrast, would lack the flexibility and speed needed to respond to the manifold contingencies of foreign affairs. . . .

CONGRESSIONAL AND EXECUTIVE ROLES

A. Shared Concern—Distinguished from Shared Administration

Our governmental system does not apex in the President, or the Congress, or the Courts, but in the shared concern and checked and balanced functions and powers of all three. It lacks the simple symmetry of a dictatorship but achieves the higher virtue of perpetual consensus.

National security is an intrinsically amorphous concept, which detracts not one whit from its necessity in the interest of national survival. As an amorphous concept it can be abused and employed to conceal a mere error. Congressional and popular concern therefore is natural. More effective review and oversight in the interest of exposing abuses and maintaining public confidence is a goal on which all can agree.

Shared administration, however, is a quite different thing, and we are troubled by those aspects of the proposed bills which seem to contemplate a transfer of final decisional power on particular security matters from executive to legislative hands, congressionally-controlled agencies, or independent agencies. Our concern is practical and also constitutional. Practically speaking in regard to shared administration a law-making body does not have the time to immerse itself in the details of national security considerations on particular matters. At the same time, the congressional apparatus is a sound and effective instrument to evoke and distill a national political consensus, which is a major objective of a legislative body.

Constitutionally speaking our Founding Fathers consciously chose a separation of powers system, and provided the executive with a separate base, rather than a parliamentary system in which the legislature controls the executive. The Founding Fathers thus rejected shared administration. It follows that we have serious doubts about those aspects of the present bills which would confer on a joint congressional committee the power to declassify national security documents, or confer similar power on any agency outside the control of the executive where does rest the front-line constitutional and practical responsibility for foreign negotiations and military defense.

Legislation that would specify classification standards, as distinct from the administration of the standards, is a more complicated matter. Legislation in that area must be distinguished from conventional areas of legislative policy-making such as commerce or welfare. A national security classification system touches foreign policy and military defense information. Congress provides the funds and basic structure, and has a natural concern for oversight in respect to the monitoring of the system and in being assured of its credibility.

This concern, I think, properly centers more on oversight than on shared administration, or detailed control of the specification of standards. In this field, and I am no expert but the thought has come to me, the so-called "standards" must necessarily be so broad that they will be about the same whether promulgated by statute or by executive order: Whether called Top Secret, or Restricted, the classification standard can do little more than specify that documents should not be disclosed if disclosure would have a significant adverse effect on our interrelated foreign policy-military security interests, but jurisprudentially what is significant? What is adverse? These are ineluctably matters of judgment which are best tested by repetitive and I stress the word "repetitive" expert review by those on the firing line, rather than by spasmodic guess-work by a court or legislative body.

In the background, of course, as the Supreme Court recognized in the *Mink* case, lies executive privilege, which surprisingly in the era of Watergate has received more explicit judicial recognition in sharper areas of conflict than at any prior time in our history. It behooves us here to strain for accommodation, and to try to avoid confrontation.

I do not think we have begun to exhaust the possibilities for reporting, analysis, self-triggering mechanisms compelling declassification of documents unless a new judgment of security need is made, and for informing the Congress. We should work more in this direction. A running battle between the Executive and the Congress over particular classification decisions may provide heat and excitement, but will not serve the cause of developing a mature, experienced, professionally operating security system.

B. Enforcement of Federal law, including the administration of a national security information classification system, is an executive function

Article II, § 1 of the Constitution vests the executive power of the United States in the President. Article II, § 3 commands the President to "take care that the laws be faithfully executed." The plain language of the Constitution, the history of these sections, and the case law compel the conclusion that: First, the enforcement of the laws is an executive function; and second, the executive branch has the exclusive constitutional authority to enforce the laws, except in those rare circumstances where Congress has authorized an independent establishment to exercise limited enforcement power as "incidental" to its primary delegated quasi-legislative or quasi-judicial power.

Every proposal at the Constitutional Convention placed the power to execute the national laws in the Chief Executive.[5] James Madison stated in the First Congress "that if any power whatsoever is in its nature executive, it is the power of appointing, overseeing, and controlling those who execute the laws."[6]

In *The Federalist* No. 77, Hamilton wrote that no objection had been made to the provision giving the President the duty to faithfully execute the laws.

The reason for separating the power to enact laws from the power to execute them was explained by Montesquieu, and quoted with approval by Madison in *The Federalist* No. 47: When the legislative and executive powers are united in the same person or body there can be no liberty, because apprehensions may arise lest *the same* monarch or senate should *enact* tyrannical laws to *execute* them in a tyrannical manner.

Thus, the Founding Fathers clearly intended that the execution of the laws be constitutionally entrusted solely to the President.

---

[5] See, 1 M. Farrand, *The Records of the Federal Convention of 1787* (1937 Ed.), 21, 63, 65–66, 226, 244, 292 (hereinafter "Farrand") ; 2 *id.* at 23, 116, 185, 404–405, 597.

[6] 1 Annals of Congress 481–482 (1789). Madison also stated during the Constitutional Convention that "certain powers were in their nature executive, and must be given to that department * * *." Madison then urged that the Convention enumerate these inherently executive powers in the Constitution. Madison himself proposed as one of these enumerated executive powers the "power to carry into effect the national laws * * *." (2 Farrand 66–67).

In accord with that constitutional intent, the courts have consistently reaffirmed the proposition that the authority to enforce the laws is an executive function.

In *Springer* v. *Philippine Islands*, 277 U.S. 189, 202 (1922), the Supreme Court, in a general discussion of the separation of powers principle, observed, "[l]egislative power, as distinguished from executive power, is the authority to make laws, but not to enforce them or appoint the agents charged with the duty of such enforcement. The latter are executive functions."

Applying this principle I have just mentioned, the courts have consistently reiterated that the enforcement of the criminal laws is within the exclusive domain of the executive.[7] It would seem to follow in light of the President's special powers over foreign relations and national defense that the power and duty to classify national security information is equally within the executive domain. Moreover, because we are dealing with national security information, the executive claim to control the declassification decision may be even stronger. Could any institution other than the Executive be entrusted with classification decisions in wartime? If not, how can there feasibly be a different rule for peacetime versus wartime eventualities? . . .

C. Through an ultimate power of removal, the President is constitutionally entitled to control officials given the power to classify or declassify national security information

. . .

In *Myers* v. *United States*, 272 U.S. 52 (1926), a landmark case, the Supreme Court held that the President had the constitutional power to remove a postmaster of the first class, without the advice and consent of the Senate as was required by statute. Concluding that the President has the constitutional right to remove executive officers of the United States whom he has appointed with the advice and consent of the Senate, the Court reasoned that any other rule "would make it impossible for the President * * * to take care that the laws be faithfully executed."

Some of the broad language in *Myers* was limited by the Supreme Court's subsequent decision in *Humphrey's Executor* v. *United States*, 295 U.S. 602 (1935). There a statute limiting the power of the President to remove members of the Federal Trade Commission for "cause" was challenged as unconstitutionally interfering with the executive power of the President. Upholding the constitutionality of the challenged restriction on the President's removal power, the Court drew a distinction between "purely executive officers" and other officers for purposes of analyzing the President's constitutional removal power. Regarding "purely executive officers," including postmasters, the Court stated that the *Myers* decision established the constitutionality of the President's illimitable power of removal. However, the Court reasoned that F.T.C. Commissioners exercised mainly quasi-legislative and quasi-judicial powers and that their executive powers were only incidental and necessary to the effectuation of their main powers. Accordingly, the Court concluded that those Commissioners were not "purely executive" and thus Congress could constitutionally place restrictions upon the President's power to remove them.

The *Myers* and *Humphrey's Executor* cases therefore establish the proposition that the President's constitutional power to remove purely executive officers is absolute, at least when those officers are appointed by the President with the advice and consent of the Senate. As discussed above, officials who determine whether or not to classify national security information are performing purely executive duties. Thus, whatever the reach of *Humphrey's Executor*, in our view it does not authorize Congress to place the administration of a national security classification system in an independent agency removed from responsibility to popularly elected officials and from the restraints of public opinion. Entrusting the security of the Nation to such a politically irresponsible body would violate basic precepts of democracy.

---

[7] See, *e.g.*, *Ponzi* v. *Fessenden*, 258 U.S. 254, 262 (1922); *Weisberg* v. *Department of Justice, No.* 71–1026, decided on rehearing en banc October 24, 1973 ("Functions in this area [prosecutorial discretion] belong to the Executive under the Constitution, Article II, Sections 1 and 3 * * *."); *United States* v. *Cox*, 342 F. 2d 167, cert. den., 381 U.S. 935 (1965); *Parker* v. *Kennedy*, 212 F. Supp. 594, 595 (D.D.C. 1963) (Determinations whether prosecutions should be commenced are within the ambit of the Attorney General's executive discretionary power); *Pugach* v. *Klein*, 193 F. Supp. 630 (D.D.C. 1961) ("The prerogative of enforcing the criminal law was vested by the Constitution, not in the Courts, nor in private citizens, but squarely in the executive arm of the government."). See also *Nader* v. *Kleindienst*, Civ. No. 243–72 (D.D.C. 1973); and *Moses* v. *Kennedy*, 219 F. Supp. 762 (D.D.C. 1963).

D. *Disclosure and Judicial Review*

Any legislation that would compel the disclosure of particular items of national security information, or provide for judicial review of whether information is properly classified, would be limited by separation of powers precepts including the doctrine of executive privilege mentioned by the Courts recently.

In *EPA* v. *Mink*, 410 U.S. 73 (1973), the Supreme Court held that under the Freedom of Information Act all documents classified under executive order were automatically exempt from disclosure under 5 U.S.C. 552(b)(1). Although indicating that Congress might modify some procedural aspects of the existing classification scheme by legislation, the Court concluded that any such changes would be subject "to whatever limitations the Executive privilege may be held to impose upon such congressional ordering." (410 U.S. at 83).

The recent decision in *Senate Select Committee on Presidential Campaign Activities* v. *Nixon*, — F. 2d —— (D.C. Cir. May 23, 1974), suggests that circumstances which justify compelled disclosure of classified national security information will be exceedingly rare. There the Court of Appeals dismissed the Senate Watergate Committee's request for five Presidential tapes on the ground that the Committee's need was not sufficient to outweigh the presumptive privilege of confidentiality accorded presidential conversations. National security information is entitled to even a stronger claim of privilege than presidential conversations. See *Nixon* v. *Sirica*, 487 F. 2d 700, 721 (D.C. Cir. 1973). Accordingly, only the most compelling showing of need will justify compelled disclosure of national security information. *United States* v. *Butenko*, — F. 2d —— (C.A. 3 en banc, March 4, 1974) (sl. op. p. 34).[8]

Whether Congress constitutionally could provide for a system of judicial review to determine whether the executive had properly classified national security information is a gray area of law. In *Nixon* v. *Sirica* the Court of Appeals indicated that on the facts of that case the District Court could review an Executive determination that certain information related to the national security. We do not know where the *Nixon* v. *Sirica* precedent may lead. Without further experience under Executive Order 11652, I think it would be premature for Congress to establish any provisions for judicial review of such classification decisions. Perhaps judicial review would be proper to guard against extreme arbitrariness, *United States* v. *Butenko, supra* (sl. op. at 36), but certainly not to substitute the judgment of the court for the judgment of the executive. See *C & S Air Lines* v. *Waterman Corp., supra.* at 111; *United States* v. *Belmont*, 301 U.S. 324, 328 (1937). Courts lack the range of experience and expertise to determine whether information may cause damage to the national security. That fact is one of the reasons why courts have applied the political questions doctrine frequently in the area of foreign relations. See discussion in *Baker* v. *Carr*, 369 U.S. 186, 211 (1962).

POSSIBILITIES FOR MUTUAL ACTION

In instances such as the enactment of criminal laws relating to unauthorized disclosure Congress has a necessary role in legislating with respect to the classification of documents. Equally clear is the responsibility of the President to safeguard information relating to his unique roles as Chief Executive, Commander-in-Chief, and organ of foreign relations. Here, perhaps, the obvious example is the safeguarding of diplomatic secrets. What is not as clear is where the exclusive jurisdiction of each Branch ends and the concurrent jurisdiction of both begins. In marking this line, not only constitutional theory but also historic practice and practical administrative and political judgment come into play.

While only Congress can set criminal penalties for disclosure of diplomatic secrets, it would not seem to be the province of Congress to decide what specific items of diplomatic information may merit classification in any given set of circumstances. For example, Congress may see no need to classify information relating to the health of foreign officials as a general rule but it should not write standards so narrowly that a report on the health of a particular official who is crucial to certain negotiations cannot be classified. This is a decision that only the Executive can make based on each distinct and unique fact situation.

---

[8] There the Court held that the President possesses the constitutional right to order warrantless electronic surveillance for the purpose of gathering foreign intelligence information and to use such information in a criminal prosecution.

What we must explore here is the integration of the congressional and executive areas of jurisdiction with respect to classification in order to produce a constitutionally proper and workable accommodation.

In my view, Congress could properly outline the general areas of classification, indeed it has done so in the atomic sun, but only if it leaves sufficient flexibility to the Executive to deal with specific circumstances and unforeseen events. Standards which would have barred classification of information relating to a Manhattan Project, a defection of an important national of another country, or tactical instructions for diplomatic negotiations cannot be tolerated. The difficulty, of course, is in drafting standards that express congressional intent without destroying the necessary authority of the Executive to cope with unique situations.

Congress could establish and fund an executive structure to superintend the execution of a classification system but it cannot execute the laws or direct the day-to-day operations of an executive agency. This responsibility is vested constitutionally in the Executive. What may accommodate the respective interests of the Congress and the President is a statutorily created Executive entity which remains subject to the direction of the Chief Executive in carrying out the duties imposed by Congress.

We recognize that the drafting of such legislation will not be easy. Nevertheless, it is necessary that we attempt to reconcile the jurisdictional lines established by the Constitution while attempting to structure a classification system that will reflect both your concerns and the necessary executive control of the day-to-day operations of the classification of executive documents.

PROFESSOR RAOUL BERGER ON EXECUTIVE PRIVILEGE
([28A], pp. 243–253)

It is a privilege to respond to your invitation to speak to the issue of executive privilege. That issue does not constitute a mere jurisdictional squabble between Congress and the President; it goes to the very heart of our democratic system. As Justice Potter Stewart said about the withholding of agency and departmental reports respecting the contemplated underground atomic explosion in Alaska,

"With the people and their representatives reduced to a state of ignorance. the democratic process is paralyzed."

He who controls the flow of information controls our destinies; so much the mounting escalation in Vietnam alone should teach.

In the twenty-odd months that have elapsed since I testified on the subject before the Subcommittee on Separation of Powers, the atmosphere has changed very considerably. Mounting frustration has brought your leadership to realize that the steady drain on your energy and time caused by executive withholding of needed information must not be endlessly protracted. Some of you are prepared to resort to enforcement via a contempt proceeding. As you know the contempt power of Congress has been sustained in suits against private individuals, to mention only *McGrain* v. *Daugherty*. In June 1971, Assistant Attorney General William H. Rehnquist acknowledged that Congress can cite an officer of the government who refuses to appear or to supply information for contempt, and that an executive officer who has custody of desired documents must [1] respond to a Congressional subpoena. Thus the contempt procedure has judicial sanction, and according to now Justice Rehnquist, it extends to recalcitrant officials.

The issuance of a citation for contempt need not be regarded as a punitive measure but rather as a means of opening the door to judicial review. Arrest of a recalcitrant by your Sergeant at Arms enables him to obtain a writ of *habeas corpus* whereby the constitutional issue may be judicially resolved. Happily President Nixon has stated that he would welcome submission of the issue to the courts, and a contempt citation offers a proven and direct route. To proceed in this manner obviates the "political question" issue. When a court is asked to free a man who contends that his detention is unconstitutional, it cannot very well evade the issue and leave him to rot in jail. That course becomes even more dubious when both Congress and the President desire the Court to adjudicate the controversy. Indeed, Madison stated that neither branch can decide a boundary dispute between them. Professor Alexander Bickel expressed a similar view in

---

[1] Hearings before a Subcommittee on Foreign Operations and Government Information of the House Committee on Government Operations on the Pentagon Papers, pt. 2, pp. 379, 385 (June 1971) hereafter cited as Moorhead Hearings.

his testimony during the Hearings on Executive Agreements before the Senate Committee on Foreign Relations, p. 31 (October 1971).

President Nixon's confidence that the Court will sustain his position needs to be measured against the historical facts. With George Ball, former Under Secretary of State, I consider that executive privilege is a "myth", without "constitutional foundation." We need to recur to the facts which riddle the myth because estimable members of your body as well as important molders of public opinion have been influenced by executive propaganda to believe that there is such a constitutional attribute as executive privilege, that Washington, for example, was the first to invoke the doctrine.

In 1965 I published an extensive critique of the view, expressed by then Deputy Attorney General William P. Rogers in a 1958 Memorandum submitted to the Senate, that the President had "uncontrolled discretion" to withhold information from Congress. So far as I can find, no member of the executive branch, past or present, or for that matter, no academician, has attacked my critique in a published writing. For the purpose of expanding my study into a book, I have engaged for the last 20 months in restudying and rethinking the problem, and in considerable additional research, particularly in the English sources and our own constitutional history. I found that Parliament enjoyed an untrammeled power of inquiry into executive conduct, that no Minister or subordinate interposed any objection to the right of Parliament to inquire, and substantial evidence that the Founders meant to adopt this power of the "Grand Inquest of the Nation," without the slightest indication that they intended in any way to cut it down. Against this history, the pseudo-precedents after 1787 carry an all but impossible burden. Permit me to spread some of this history before you.

I

McGrain v. *Daugherty* offers a good starting point. Decided in 1927, it declared that the investigatory power was "regarded as an *attribute* of the power to legislate in the British Parliament . . . before the American Revolution"; and that "the constitutional provisions which commit the legislative functions to the two houses are intended to include this attribute." To obtain light as to the *scope* of this attribute we may, therefore, turn to parliamentary history.

There I found that the power of inquiry had its inception as an *auxiliary to the power of impeachment*, on the sensible ground that one does not indict before inquiring whether there is cause. This fact is of immense importance because, as you recall, "The President, Vice President and all civil officers" are subject to impeachment, and it follows that they are all subject to preliminary inquiry. Of this, I shall have more to say later.

In performing this inquiry function, the House of Commons acted as the "Grand Inquest of the nation"; and we need to bear in mind, as Chief Justice Lord Denman stated in 1839, that:

"The Commons . . . are not invested with more of power and dignity by their legislative character than by that which they bear as grand inquest of the nation."

In a random sampling of parliamentary debates at different periods, stretching from 1621 to 1742, I found legislative oversight of administration across the board: inquiries to lay a foundation for legislation, into corruption, the conduct of war, execution of the laws, disbursement of appropriations, in short, into every aspect of executive conduct. Foreign affairs, about which American Presidents have drawn a curtain of secrecy, were not excepted. The great English historian, Henry Hallam, after adverting to the investigations of 1691 and 1694, concluded:

"* * * it is hardly worth while to enumerate later instances of exercising a right which had become indisputable, and, even before it rested on the basis of precedent, could not reasonably be denied to those, who might advise (*i.e.*, legislate), remonstrate and impeach."

The highest officers of the land responded to such inquiries without demur. No hint turned up in my search of the parliamentary records of a challenge by a Minister or subordinate to the right of Parliament to inquire or to the scope of inquiry into executive conduct. Speaking of inquiries instituted in 1689 with respect to miscarriages in the conduct of war in North Ireland, Hallam stated, "No courtier (*i.e.*, Minister) has ever since ventured to deny this general right of inquiry." Colonial recognition of these facts is to be found in 1774 by James Wilson, with Madison the leading architect of the Constitution. The House of Commons, he wrote:

"Have checked the progress of arbitrary power, and have supported with honor to themselves, and with advantage to the nation, the character of the grand inquisitors of the realm. The proudest ministers of the proudest monarchs have trembled at their censure; and have appeared at the bar of the house, to give an account of their conduct, and ask pardon for their faults."

From this, two complementary conclusions may be drawn: (1) Parliament enjoyed a plenary power of inquiry into executive conduct; and (2) no Minister or subordinate, no subject of inquiry was immune from investigation into any aspect of administration. It is a striking fact that neither the Eisenhower nor Nixon Administration, where "executive privilege" has been most extravagantly claimed, has advanced a single pre-1787 precedent for executive refusal to turn over information to the legislature. Thus, whereas Congressional inquiry, rested by the Supreme Court on the example of Parliament—which had plenary power, has a solid foundation, there is *no pre-Convention historical basis* for the claim that the power to withhold information from the legislature was an *attribute of the executive*. All inferences are to the contrary. This, as I shall show, has important implication for the executive appeal to the separation of powers.

That the Founders were aware of this legislative-inquiry attribute is demonstrated by four or five references in the Convention and the several Ratifying Conventions to the function of the House as the "grand inquest of the nation." Wilson's 1774 publication, earlier quoted, exhibits a thorough appreciation of what that function embraced, above all that "the proudest Ministers * * * appeared." It calls for solid evidence that Wilson abandoned his admiration for this practice of the Commons, particularly since he viewed the executive power merely as a power to execute the laws. In fact, there is not the slightest intimation in the records of the several Conventions that the Founders intended to curb the functions of the Grand Inquest in any way.

The executive branch builds its case on the separation of powers. But resort to the separation of powers assumes the answer; it assumes that the executive had a withholding power upon which legislative inquiry encroaches. John Adams spelled out in the 1780 Massachusetts Constitution that the separation of powers was designed to prevent one department from exercising the powers of another. Since *it was not an attribute of executive power* at the adoption of the Constitution to refuse information to the legislature, a congressional requirement of information from the executive does not encroach on powers confided to the President; it does not violate the separation of powers. This is confirmed by a statement of Montesquieu, who was repeatedly cited by the Founders as the oracle of the separation of powers. The legislature, he said—exhibiting his familiarity with the English practice—should "have the means of examining in what matter its laws have been executed by the public officials." Given repeated recognition of the function of the House as Grand Inquest, something more than appeals to an abstract separation of powers is required to curtail the function. Unless evidence is inherently incredible, the courts hold, it is not to be defeated by speculation based on no evidence.

The fact that the separation of powers was not designed to reduce the "Grand Inquest" function is again confirmed by the Act of 1789, which made it—

"The duty of the Secretary of the Treasury * * * to make report, and give information to either branch of the legislature in person or in writing (as he may be required). respecting all matters referred to him by the Senate or the House of Representatives, or which shall appertain to his office."

The Act contains no provision for executive discretion to withhold information, and there is no reference whatsoever to such discretion in the legislative history of the Act. This provision was drafted by Alexander Hamilton who, as a member of the Convention and coauthor of The Federalist, knew well enough whether a duty could be imposed on the executive branch to furnish information to Congress. Adopted by the First Congress, whose construction of the Constitution is given great weight, and signed by President Washington, who had been presiding officer of the Convention, this Act can hardly be deemed in violation of the separation of powers.

Were the issue in doubt, President Nixon has just supplied the clincher by his instruction to members of his staff to appear before the grand jury that is investigating the Watergate conspiracy. He is scarcely consistent: the separation of powers does not bar inquiry by the judiciary, one coordinate branch, while it does bar inquiry by another, the Congress. Yet it is the legislature, acting as the Grand Inquest, which is the highest grand jury in the land. And why does disclosure to the grand jury of confidential communications between members of the White House staff not "inhibit" the candor allegedly essential to performance of executive functions, whereas disclosure to Congress, according to President Nixon, would "weaken and compromise" the "candor with which such advice is rendered?"

Lest it be thought that the President's instruction to appear before the grand jury was a matter of grace, I submit that no man is immune from testifying before the grand jury as to the commission of a crime. If a member of the White House staff, for example, were the sole witness to a murder, he could scarcely refuse to testify on the ground of executive privilege. That the separation of powers interposes no obstacle to the judiciary is immediately apparent from two cases. In 1953, the Supreme Court held in *United States* v. *Reynolds* that the decision whether military secrets may be withheld from a party in litigation cannot be left to the caprice of an administrator but is for the determination of the courts. Much earlier Chief Justice Marshall held on the *Trial of Aaron Burr* that President Jefferson could be required to furnish to a defendant in a criminal trial a letter to Jefferson from General James Wilkinson. Marshall, who had been a vigorous advocate of the Constitution in the Virginia Ratification Convention was hardly unaware that his ruling was not barred by the separation of powers; nor can it be presumed that in 1953 the Supreme Court was oblivious to that problem. If judicial insistence on executive disclosure does not offend against the separation of powers, Congress, too, is not barred.

Let us now return to inquiry as a prelude to impeachment, bearing in mind that the Constitution makes express provision for impeachment of "The President, Vice President and all civil officers." James Iredell, later a Justice of the Supreme Court, adverted in the North Carolina Convention to the maxim that the King can do no wrong, and exulted in the "happier" provision which made the President himself triable. The President, it should not be forgotten, was not looked at with awe but with apprehension. Of this power of impeachment, a Committee of the House, faithfully reflecting parliamentary history, stated in 1843 that:

"The President himself, in the discharge of his most independent functions, is subject to the exercise of this power—a power which implies the right of inquiry on the part of the House to the fullest and most unlimited extent."

Since the Constitution expressly provides for impeachment of the President, since historically inquiry may precede impeachment, President Nixon errs in asserting that "the manner in which the President exercises his assigned executive powers is not subject to questioning by another branch of the Government." Even the headstrong Andrew Jackson acknowledged that:

"Cases may occur in the course of (Congress) proceedings in which it may be indispensable to the proper exercise of its power that it should inquire or decide upon the conduct of the President or other public officers, and in every case its constitutional right to do so is cheerfully conceded."

Consequently, Mr. Nixon's argument that "If the President is not subject to such questioning, it is equally appropriate that members of his staff not be so questioned for their roles are in effect an extension of the President" falls to the ground. Moreover, since "all civil officers" are impeachable by the terms of the Constitution, they are subject to inquiry without the leave of the President. Impeachment, said Elias Boudinot in the First Congress—that almost "adjourned session" of the Constitutional Convention, enables the House "to pull down an improper officer, although he should be supported by all the power of the Executive." The point was made again and again, among others, by Abraham Baldwin, a Framer. English history affords no instance where Parliament was required to seek leave of a Minister for the appearance of a subordinate; and the imposition of such a condition by the President has no historical warrant.

My search of the several Convention records, let me repeat, turned up not a shred of evidence that the President was empowered to withhold *any* information from the Congress. One constitutional provision, in fact, speaks against it. The Framers authorized secrecy in only one case, and then by Congress, not the President. Congress is required to keep and publish Journals except "such part as may in their (each House's) judgment require secrecy." This provision encountered rough going, being harshly criticized by James Wilson, George Mason, Elbridge Gerry, Patrick Henry and also by Jefferson. To allay fears of this secrecy provision, proponents explained that it had very restricted scope. So, John Marshall stated in Virginia that the debates "on the propriety of declaring war" and the like, could not be conducted "in the open fields," and said, "In this plan, secrecy *is only to be used* when it would be fatal and pernicious to publish the schemes of government."

In light of the denial of limitless power to conceal to the "legislative authority"—which Madison said "necessarily predominates" in "republican government"—how can an intention be derived of an *implied* grant to the executive of power to keep anything and everything secret? Rather, as the Supreme Court held in analogous circumstances, the express authorization for limited discretionary secrecy by Congress and the omission to make similar provision for the President indicates an intention to withhold such authority from him. What might momentarily be concealed from the public by Congress had to be divulged by the President to Congress, if that senior partner in government was to participate in making the momentous decisions which alone were to be kept secret. Marshall's limitation of the express secrecy provision to "fatal and pernicious" publications renders laughable the wholesale executive claim to secrecy for communications between several million subordinates in the executive department.

II

Before I examine the pseudo-"precedents" on which administration spokesmen base their claim of executive privilege, it should be noted that there is a long line of Congressional precedents, solidly based on the investigatory power of Parliament and unequivocally asserted in plenary terms.

President Nixon tells us that executive privilege "was first invoked by Washington." Preliminarily, the first use of the phrase, so far as I could find, occurred in a private litigation in 1958. An independent search by Professor Arthur Schlesinger likewise turned up no use of the phrase prior to the Eisenhower Administration, scarcely testimony of a well-established doctrine. There were two incidents. First, there was the 1792 inquiry into the disastrous St. Clair expedition against the Indians; Washington turned over all the documents; "not even the ugliest line in the flight of the beaten troops was eliminated," states his biographer, Douglas Freeman.

Executive reliance on St. Clair is based, *not on refusal*, of the documents, but on Jefferson's notes of a Cabinet meeting at which it was agreed that the "house was a grand inquest, therefore might institute inquiries," but that the President had discretion to refuse papers "the disclosure of which would injure the public." These notes are not reconcilable with the 1789 Act which Washington had earlier signed, and which permitted unqualified inquiry. What little precedential value may attach to the notes vanishes when it is considered that only four years later Washington himself did not think to invoke the St. Clair "precedent" in the Jay Treaty case upon which the Executive next relies, and instead stated his readiness to supply information to which ever House had a "right", such as the Senate had to treaty documents.

Jefferson's notes did not find their way into the government files; there is no evidence that the meditations of the Cabinet were ever disclosed to Congress. Indeed, it would have been most impolitic and unsettling to excite the House by a claim of discretion to withhold when all the required information was, in fact, turned over. The notes were found among Jefferson's papers after his death and published many years later, under his "Anas," what he described as "loose scraps" and "unofficial notes." There this "precedent" slumbered until it was exhumed by Mr. Rogers in 1957. Some precedent!

Time does not permit me to show that Jefferson, who unlike Rogers, turned to English precedents for the scope of the executive power, was mistaken in his reading of some remarks in the Walpole proceedings of 1742. It must suffice to say that William Pitt more accurately reflected the state of English law in those proceedings:

"We are called the Grand Inquest of the nation, and as such it is our duty to inquire into every step of public management, either abroad or at home, in order to see that nothing is done amiss."

And so it remained, as Justice Coleridge stated in 1845:

"That the Commons are, in the words of Lord Coke, the general inquisitors of the realm, I fully admit * * * it would be difficult to define any limits by which the subject matter of their inquiry may be bounded * * * they may inquire into everything which concerns the public weal for them to know; and themselves, I think, are entrusted with the determination of what falls within that category."

The second Washington "precedent" is his refusal to turn over the Jay Treaty papers to the House. He had *delivered* them to the Senate but refused them to the House because, he said, the House had no part in treaty-making and hence no "right" to the papers. He emphasized, however, that he had no disposition to withhold "any information * * * which could be requested of him as a right," a repudiation of Jefferson's "discretion to withhold."

And as an example of a "right" to require documents (which explains his delivery to his partner in treaty-making, the Senate) he instanced impeachment;

but stated that "It does not occur that the inspection of the papers asked for can be relative to any purpose under the cognizance of the House of Representatives except that of impeachment; which the resolution has not expressed." This put the cart before the horse; it required the House to prejudge the case, to "purpose" impeachment before it inquired whether there was just cause. Then, too, the procedure required for impeachment was left to the House, for to it was given "the sole power of impeachment," so that Washington invaded the House's prerogative in suggesting a decision to impeach must precede inquiry. Nonetheless, here Washington recognized what parliamentary practice teaches, that inquiry was auxiliary to impeachment and could even reach an ambassador plenipotentiary, Chief Justice Jay.

A Washington precedent that sheds more light on President Nixon's invocation of executive privilege to shield his counsel, John Dean, from inquiry as to his knowledge of, or participation in the "Watergate" conspiracy, is the Hamilton incident. When Washington learned that an investigation into the conduct of his "intimate adviser," Alexander Hamilton, his Secretary of the Treasury, was rumored, Washington stated:

"No one . . . wishes more devoutly than I do that (the allegations) may be probed to the bottom, be the result what it may."

Washington would have welcomed, not thwarted, the interrogation of Mr. Dean.

Following Washington's example, President Polk stated in 1846:

"If the House of Representatives, as the grand inquest of the nation, should at any time have reason to believe that there has been malversation in office * * * and should think proper to institute an inquiry into the matter, all the archives and papers of the Executive Department, public or private, would be subject to the inspection and control of a committee of their body, and every facility in the power of the Executive be afforded them to prosecute the investigation."

This, it will be recalled, was also the view of President Jackson.

It would be stale and unprofitable to rehearse subsequent presidential assertions of a right to withhold information from Congress, for the last precedent stands no better than the first. Bare assertion, even if oft-repeated, can no more create power than the President can lift himself by his bootstraps. As the Supreme Court stated in the *Steel Seizure Case*, "That an unconstitutional action has been taken before surely does not render the same action any less unconstitutional at a later date."

Let us rather focus on that branch of executive privilege which, according to President Nixon, was "designed to protect communications within the executive branch" and is allegedly "rooted in the Constitution." When Assistant Attorney General William H. Rehnquist appeared before Congress in 1971, the instances he cited for the refusal of the President's "intimate advisers to appear" went back no farther than the Truman Administration. These refusals, said he, were based tions * * * with the President." Be it assumed that communications between the President and members of his Cabinet enjoy constitutional shelter—by no means an incontrovertible assumption—and that still does not stretch to communications between several million subordinate employees.

What the President conceives to be "rooted in the Constitution" is in fact *first met in 1954*, when President Eisenhower sought to ward off Senator Mc-Carthy's savage attacks on Army personnel by a directive that communications between employees of the Executive branch must be withheld from Congress so that they may "be completely candid in advising with each other." Overnight this "doctrine" was expanded to shelter mismanagement, conflicts of interest such as led the Supreme Court to set aside the Dixon-Yates contract, inexplicable selection of low bidders, etc., etc. A detailed account of the rank, jungle-like growth of the "candid interchange" doctrine in the Eisenhower years is to be found in Clark Mollenhof, *Washington Cover-Up*.

It is strange doctrine that the acknowledged power to probe "corruption, inefficiency and waste" does not extend to "candid communications" which are often at the core of such misconduct. Had that doctrine prevailed, many an investigation of corruption and maladministration, *e.g.*, Teapot Dome, would have been stopped in its tracks. Congress, declared the Supreme Court in *McGrain* v. *Daugherty*, may investigate "the administration of the Department of Justice * * * and particularly the Attorney General and his assistants." To shield communications between suspected malefactors from such inquiry would go far to abort investigation.

As a Congressman in 1954, President Nixon protested against Truman's instruction to withhold an FBI letter, saying, "That would mean that the President could have arbitrarily issued an Executive order in the (Bennet) Myers case, the

Teapot Dome case * * * denying the Congress * * * information it needed to conduct an investigation of the executive department."

Eisenhower's claim that "candid interchange" among subordinates is an indispensable condition of good government is an unproven assumption. It is disproved by the fact that his withholding on that ground of information respecting alleged maladministration or foreign aid in Peru was immediately countermanded by President Kennedy, with the salutary result that exposure led to correction, not to the toppling of administrative towers. Both the Kennedy and Johnson Administrations sharply whittled down claims of executive privilege with no noticeable ill effects on administration.

In England, "candid interchange" was laughed out of court by the House of Lords in *Conway* v. *Brimmer* (1968). Against the debatable assumption that fear of disclosure may inhibit "candid interchange," there is the proven fact that such interchanges have time and again served as a vehicle of corruption and malversation, so that, to borrow from Lord Morris, "a greater measure of prejudice to the public interest would result from their non-production." Can the costs of suppressing the Pentagon Papers be weighed in the scales with preservation of confidences between subordinates? Disclosure to Congress and the people of reports about the untrustworthiness of and lack of internal support for a succession of Saigon satraps, of bleak intelligence estimates, of growing pessimism in the inner circle about the outcome of the Vietnam involvement, might have enabled Congress to weigh the mountainous costs against the increasingly doubtful benefits of the accelerating escalation.

The issue posed by President Nixon's claim for immunity for Messrs. Henry Kissinger, Peter Flanigan, and John Dean on the basis of mere membership in the White House staff calls for comment.

You will recall that Assistant Attorney General Rehnquist went no further than to say that the "intimate advisers" of the President "ought not to be interrogated as to conversations . . . with the President." On practical grounds, it may be desirable to shield such conversations from Congressional inquiry, and Congress itself generally has not insisted on their disclosure. But it does not follow that there is a constitutional basis for the withholding claim. Indeed, Mr. Dean himself wrote on April 20, 1972, that:

"The precedents indicate that no recent President has ever claimed a 'blanket immunity' that would prevent his assistants from testifying before the Congress on any subject."

Such a claim would be without historical foundation.

"Pernicious advice" to the King by his Ministers was a repeated cause for impeachment; and Francis Corbin in the Virginia Convention, Henry Pendleton in the South Carolina Convention, and James Iredell in the North Carolina Convention, alluded to such "advice" as within the scope of impeachment. Given impeachable "advice", inquiry whether it was communicated cannot be barred on constitutional grounds, whatever may be the merits of the practical arguments for confidentiality. Practical desiderata cannot be converted into constitutional dogma.

In a dictum in *Marbury* v. *Madison*, Chief Justice Marshall stated that if anything was communicated to the Attorney General in confidence by the President, "he was not bound to disclose it." Sitting on the *Trial of Aaron Burr*, Marshall confined that dictum, as deputy Attorney General Rogers stated, to non-disclosure of "communications from the President," and held that Burr was entitled to have a letter to President Jefferson from General James Wilkinson, obliquely confirming the right of inquiry into "advice".

It needs to be emphasized that the *Marbury* dictum is altogether irrelevant to Congressional inquiry. That was a suit by a private individual, and Marshall stated that the "province of the court . . . is not to inquire how the executive or executive officers perform their duties." Precisely that function, however, does lie within the province of the legislature, as parliamentary history makes clear, as Montesquieu and James Wilson perceived, and as the Supreme Court has repeatedly recognized. In sum, there is no historical warrant for the claim that confidential advice to the President is shielded from Congressional inquiry by the Constitution, though Congress may choose, as a matter of comity, not to probe into such advice.

Information is the blood stream of democracy; he who controls it controls our destinies, as the progressive escalation in Vietnam alone should teach. I cannot improve on President Nixon's 1972 statement:

"When information which properly belongs to the people is systematically withheld by those in power (*e.g.*, the facts behind the Vietnam escalation), the people soon become ignorant of their own affairs, distrustful of those who manage them and eventually incapable of determining their own destinies."

The people, therefore, have an immediate stake in opening all channels of information to Congress, the great American forum of national debate. . . .

Mr. BERGER. Now, I hold myself open for your questions, because that always illuminates things.

Senator KENNEDY. On this point that you are talking about, the balance between reserving technical things and things that the Congress has a right to know, what are the safeguards that you are putting in there?

Is it just the restraint of the Congress concerning the type of information that is required?

Mr. BERGER. I would suggest to you, Mr. Chairman, that that should be codified, because it will win you a great deal of respect, and not as a question of lack of constitutional power to go that far, but just as a matter of decency and good judgment. And I may say, where somebody is vilified, today the courts are also opened under the right to privacy. But if you blast a man to perdition and then he goes into a court and gets vindication 2 years later——

Senator KENNEDY. Have you published anything along those lines, Professor?

Mr. BERGER. I haven't really worked on that in detail, but I would be pleased to——

Senator KENNEDY. Would you work with this group here in attempting to develop some legislation?

Mr. BERGER. I could mention for the record three things. I think one is respecting, as you have respected in the past, the conversations between the President and General Bradley, for instance.

I would also seek to avoid the dissemination of raw files. You should have a mechanism within the Senate so that nothing is disseminated that contains that sort of material.

And I would say that you ought to employ your senatorial powers to censure a Senator who breaks your rules. You only will gain respect for your function if you conduct it in a respectable fashion.

I want to say one thing before I close.

This whole pernicious doctrine of candid interchange—and I have to differ with my esteemed colleagues—the notion that disclosure will inhibit advice on all the tiers, I don't mind the close confidence of the highest levels, but when you extend it to the portions that are being filtered up between three or four or five levels, that troubles me. I want to say first, it is a nonproven assumption disproved by the fact that a great deal of information is in fact turned over; the bulk of it Kleindienst claims is turned over. A lot of that contains confidential communications so the communicators are not inhibited. Kennedy, the moment he took office, turned over the very "candid interchange" that Eisenhower had refused under the opinion of Attorney General Rogers.

And the House of Lords in 1968 laughed the whole doctrine out of court—they said anybody of ordinary fortitude must be expected to render an opinion without fear of future disclosure—doctors, lawyers, others do it all the time. In antitrust files there are lawyer's opinions, which may prove embarassing when disclosed. And this candid interchange, by the way, is of very recent vintage, 1954; it hasn't got a single precedent in American history for it, let alone English history. And don't sanctify it.

Senator KENNEDY. Senator Muskie?

Senator MUSKIE. Professor Berger, I think that one point that is implicit in what you said to us is that although we have a tripartite government of three branches, that the most fundamental of the powers involved is the power to make the laws. It is that power that the people began to carve out from the powers of the king going back to King John. The most fundamental of these powers is the power to make the law. The courts have the power to apply them, the executive has the power to execute them, but only the Congress has the power to make them. And surely, as an attribute of this most fundamental of the powers, there must be the power to inquire, and that is what Mr. Kleindienst simply doesn't understand.

Mr. BERGER. May I elaborate on what you have just said.

The constitutional distribution of powers tells that in most eloquent terms. For example, all the war powers that the Founders gave to the President are given by three little words: Commander-in-Chief. And that merely means the power of a "first general," as Hamilton said. All the rest were given to the Congress. Time and again you see the tremendous galaxy of powers conferred in Congress, not the President. The power of the President was deemed largely a power to execute the laws. And then the Framers stepped outside the President's powers and gave him the Commander in Chief power, plus the right to receive ambassadors, and to appoint ambassadors with the consent of the Senate, the very smallest powers. And finally, Madison said, in a republican form of government the legislature necessarily predominates. You are the senior partner. Yet time and again you have a fellow like Secretary Laird telling you, "I don't think it is in the national interest for you to have the Pentagon papers." He treats you like an office boy. And you will be treated that way until you get up on your hind legs and kick him in the slats.

NORMAN DORSEN ON EXECUTIVE PRIVILEGE, THE CONGRESS, AND THE COURTS ([28A], pp. 414–420)

I. Introduction

N8
The doctrine of executive privilege has proliferated over the decades very much as executive power itself has grown. The origins of the doctrine were modest, asserted by early Presidents rarely, in narrow circumstances, and often under a formulation which implied that the Executive could withhold information only with the express consent of Congress.

Modern presidential government, on the other hand, is symbolized by the frequency with which information is withheld from Congress at the sole discretion of the Executive. The Library of Congress reported this year that executive privilege has been asserted 49 times since 1952, including 19 times by the Nixon Administration alone.

Executive privilege is a vital pressure point in the struggle between Congress and the President because it is often used to cut off congressional inquiry into the very issues over which Congress and the President are most sharply divided. By withholding crucial information or witnesses, modern Presidents have discovered that they can exercise an informal veto over attempts by Congress to act in certain areas, particularly foreign affairs.

II. The claim of a discretionary executive privilege to withhold information from Congress

Former Attorney General Richard Kleindienst, speaking for the Nixon administration, recently asserted that Congress had no power to order an employee of the executive branch to appear and testify without the President's express consent. It is important to distinguish several strands in his testimony. First, its breadth: the Attorney General claimed that *all* employees of the federal government could be totally insulated from Congress at the order of the President. Second, he did not spell out in any detail the constitutional or other legal basis for this power, but merely stated that it was inherent in the executive branch. Third, the Attorney General asserted that the President's judgment on whether to produce documents or witnesses for Congress was final, and that neither the Congress nor the courts had the constitutional authority to interfere.

The subject matters that have been included in the executive privilege as it has been broadly asserted during the last two decades have not varied much since the Eisenhower Administration. Speaking on behalf of that administration in 1957, Attorney General William Rogers identified at least five categories of information privileged from disclosure to Congress :

1. military and diplomatic secrets and foreign affairs :
2. information made confidential by statute ;
3. investigations relating to pending legislation, and investigative files and reports ;
4. information relating to internal government affairs privileged from disclosure in the public interest ; and
5. records incidental to the making of policy, including interdepartmental memoranda, advisory opinions, recommendations of subordinates and informal working papers.

Dean Roger Cramton, former Assistant Attorney General in the Nixon Administration, recently consolidated these sweeping claims by asserting that executive privilege is most frequently and justifiably exercised in three of these areas: (1) military and foreign affairs; (2) investigatory files of law enforcement agencies; and (3) testimony of presidential advisors. Mr. Cramton's one deviation from the formulation of Attorney General Rogers is his limitation of the privilege to advisors *to the President* and not to all members of the executive branch. On the other hand, Mr. Kleindienst's recent claims exceed even those of the Eisenhower Administration because the latter sought to insulate not all executive branch employees, but only those who were engaged in the "making of policy."

A discretionary executive privilege has no historical or judicial precedent, and is not supported by the doctrine of the separation of powers. Two of the three basic categories of asserted privilege—national security information and investigatory files—while raising issues about executive secrecy, can be explained and defined wholly apart from "executive privilege." The third category—internal advice within the executive branch—raises more difficult problems. While there may be a necessity for executive secrecy in this area, it is based on the same limited constitutional premise that justifies some secrecy among members of Congress and judges as well as executive officials : each branch of government has an implied power to protect its legitimate decision-making processes from scrutiny by the other branches. This does not mean, however, that *any* branch, including the Executive, can keep secret its decisions, or the facts underlying them, or shield wrong-doing by its officials or employees.

III. The untenability of a discretionary executive privilege

History lends little support to the claims now being advanced by the Executive. It was not until 1835, during the presidency of Jackson—a full 46 years after the formation of the Republic and the enactment of the initial statute authorizing congressional inquiries into the workings of the Executive branch—that there was an unequivocal assertion of discretionary power to withhold information from Congress. The earlier incidents of executive questioning of Congressional authority during Washington's administration were cases which the Executive eventually acceded to the requests of Congress and did not confront the legislature with a refusal to disclose.

During this same period, a congressional practice developed of extending to the President a qualified "privilege" to withhold certain investigative reports and state secrets from public disclosure. In the instances where the offer by Congress was actually accepted by the President and documents were withheld, the congressional power to compel their release was explicitly recognized by both parties.

The judicial record is equally barren of authority sustaining the broad claims of the Executive. Although no Supreme Court decision explicitly rejects such a privilege, there are no cases in this country or in England that recognize it.

The most comprehensive attempt to muster judicial authority on behalf of an executive privilege was made by Attorney General Robert Jackson in a 1941 memorandum, declining to make available to the House Committee on Naval Affairs certain investigative reports of the Department of Justice concerning labor disturbances in industries with naval contracts. While some of the cases cited by Mr. Jackson support a limited power to withhold security data and confidential informers' communications from the courts, none lends credence to a discretionary privilege.

In the absence of historical and judicial precedents, we turn to even more fundamental sources of potential power, in particular, the constitutional doctrine of separation of powers. In our judgment, three distinct facets are involved, none of which supports an unreviewable executive discretion to withhold information from Congress.

1. The first is the Article I power of the Congress to conduct investigations. Long before 1789 the English Parliament, in the words of Pitt the elder, was inquiring "into every step of public management, either abroad or at Home, in order to see that nothing has been done amiss." Legislative practices in the American colonies followed the parliamentary model.

While there is no express mention in the federal Constitution of a congressional power to investigate and gain access to the documents of executive departments, such a power was assumed from the outset to be a fundamental attribute of Congress. In one of its first legislative acts, for example, Congress provided in the Treasury Reporting Act of 1789 that "[i]t shall be the duty of the Secretary of the Treasury . . . to give information to either branch of the legislature in person or in writing (as may be required) respecting all matters . . . which shall appertain to his office." The statute was drafted by Alexander Hamilton, hardly an advocate of limited power.

An instructive definition of the scope of the congressional investigating power is found in *Watkins* v. *United States:*

> The power of the Congress to conduct investigations is inherent in the legislative process. That power is broad. It encompasses inquiries concerning the administration of existing laws as well as proposed or possible needed statutes . . . It comprehends probes into departments of the Federal Government to expose corruption, inefficiency or waste.

> In *Watkins* Chief Justice Warren explicitly stated that "broad as is this power of [congressional] inquiry, it is not unlimited."

> There is no general authority to expose the private affairs of individuals without justification in terms of the functions of the Congress. . . . Nor is the Congress a law enforcement or trial agency. . . . No inquiry is an end in itself; it must be related to, and in furtherance of, a legitimate task of the Congress. Investigations conducted solely for the personal aggrandizement of the investigators or to "punish" those investigated are indefensible.

These limitations, however, are designed to protect the rights of witnesses, and do not support a discretionary executive privilege. It is of course true that *Watkins* dealt with the power of Congress to obtain information from a private individual, but its broad appraisal of congressional power is consistent with history and with earlier judicial pronouncements.

2. The second aspect of separation of powers concerns the implications of the President's Article II power to "take care that the laws be faithfully executed." It is this general constitutional provision on which the Executive has chiefly relied to buttress its claim of a discretionary privilege.

Taken to its essentials it is a claim of inherent or implied power, because the general constitutional language surely does not authorize a broad discretionary withholding of executive information. The Supreme Court has reviewed a similarly broad claim of inherent executive power. In the *Steel Seizure* Case, Justice Black, speaking for the Court, rejected in comprehensive terms the claim of an inherent presidential power to override the will of Congress.

It is unnecessary to accept Justice Black's broad assertions about the lack of presidential power to reach his conclusion. In a more discriminating analysis in the same case, Justice Jackson distinguished three situations—those in which the President acts pursuant to an express or implied authorization of Congress, where his authority is at a maximum; those in which Congress is silent, where the President can rely only on his own powers and frequently the result is uncertain; and those in which the President takes measures "incompatible with the expressed or implied will" of Congress. In the latter situation, according to Justice Jackson, the President's power "is at its lowest ebb."

The case of executive privilege is plainly of the third type. While Congress has not legislated explicitly on the privilege, it has expressed its intention unmistakably to obtain all necessary information from the executive branch in statutes going back to the Hamilton Treasury Reporting Act.

Two other considerations, one textural and one rooted in history, support this conclusion. Concerning text, the only reference to secrecy in the Constitution is the power given to Congress to keep and publish Journals, except "such parts as may in their judgment require secrecy," and the only reference in the text to making information available to another branch of government is the duty imposed on the *President* "from time to time to the *Congress* information of the State of the Union." While nothing definitive can be read into these clauses, their presence in the Constitution cuts in the direction of legislative access to executive documents and away from executive discretionary authority.

Even more important than the powers explicitly found in the Constitution or those fairly implied are the numerous examples, multiplying in recent years, of executive action that seems to go beyond traditional bounds. For instance, Professor Kurland has recently prophesied, without enthusiasm, that we will continue . . . to see the President wage war without Congressional declaration, to see executive orders substitute for legislation, to see secret executive agreements substitute for treaties, and to see Presidential decisions not to carry out Congressional programs under the label of "impoundment of funds."

Other examples are available. The President has expanded the use of the Pocket Veto, has tightened White House budgetary controls over what used to be known as the "independent" regulatory agencies, and has twice devalued the dollar by executive action although a 1945 statute provides that only Congress can set the price of gold. Taken as a whole, these represent a significant change in the balance of power between the executive and legislative branches.

All this suggests that we should be slow indeed to permit the executive branch to accrete further power by uncontrolled discretion over the information it provides a coordinate branch. To acknowledge such power would increase the constitutional imbalance at a time when counter measures seem called for.

There are further aspects of the problem which underscore the danger of uncontrolled executive discretion: the vast expansion in the size and role of the White House staff, and the recent practice of assigning one person the dual role of cabinet officer and presidential advisor on the White House staff.

These modern developments emphasize the difficulty of accepting the President as final arbiter of the issue. For it is the President who decides the size of the White House staff, the allocation of responsibilities between it and the cabinet departments, and whether or not to fuse in one individual both line and staff assignments that formerly were kept distinct. To permit the President also to determine, finally, when an individual may be immunized from legislative questions or a document sequestered is surely to defeat the goal of a balanced federal government.

3. Closely related to the President's power faithfully to execute the laws is the question, also an aspect of separation of powers, of the role of the courts in resolving the problem of executive privilege. In our judgment, if an issue concerning the privilege cannot be negotiated, it should be for the Supreme Court to decide. Neither the President nor the Congress should be the judge in its own cause. Accordingly, just as we deny the right of the President to determine the issue finally, we also reject the suggestion that a Senate committee should be "the final judge on whether a White House aide could refuse to answer any of the committee's questions."

Of course there will be difficulties concerning a judicial resolution of a claim of executive privilege, assuming a proper controversy reaches the courts. But these difficulties pale in comparison with the present position, in which two unacceptable solutions are possible. The President may continue to be the final arbiter, in flat conflict with elementary notions of justice as well as the precept embodied in the Federalist Papers that "neither the executive nor the legislative branch can pretend to an exclusive or superior right of settling the boundaries between their respective powers."

It is sometimes suggested that executive privilege controversies can be settled, ad hoc, by what has been called "the accommodations and realities of the political process." We are not unmindful that this process of "accommodation" permits judicious leaks of information from the Executive to the Congress that could not be provided on the record, as well as the familiar informal meetings between congressmen and presidential advisors at which, presumably, valuable data is provided—in short permits a flexibility in the deliverance of information that many will regard as satisfactory. We reject this modus operandi, however, and we are pleased that many congressional leaders likewise reject it. A surreptitious and informal means of communication demeans the Congress and indeed the entire governmental process.

Finally, the problem of enforcement, while complicated, cannot serve to bring the political question doctrine into operation when all other indices point toward a judicial resolution of the issue. The enforcement of a legislative contempt citation against an executive officer would not appear to present the courts with more than an ordinary contempt case, although admittedly in an unusual context. The real problem would lie in compelling the contested disclosure. Since a court would not find it difficult to frame the appropriate relief, speculation about the executive's willingness to comply with a judicial order should not enter into consideration of whether the order should issue in the first instance. As the Supreme Court said in the *Adam Clayton Powell* case, in which it ruled on what the Congress maintained was an "internal matter," "it is an inadmissible suggestion that action might be taken in disregard of a judicial determination." We do not maintain that an absolute congressional power to compel information should be substituted for an absolute executive power to withhold it. All "unlimited power" is inherently dangerous, and it is the salutary function of the courts to circumscribe the boundaries of the executive and legislative powers so that neither branch is exalted at the expense of the other. The so-called executive privilege seems pre-eminently an issue to be resolved in this manner.

V. *The proper scope of the privilege assertable by the Executive branch*

If our conclusion is correct that a discretionary executive privilege is untenable, this does not foreclose the question whether secrecy can properly be maintained by the President and his assistants in the three types of cases where a privilege has been asserted: foreign or military affairs, investigatory files and litigation materials, and advice within the executive branch. We shall now explore each of these areas of interest.

A. *Foreign or Military Affairs*. A degree of executive secrecy is probably necessary in foreign or military affairs. Nevertheless, the Congress must have access to foreign and military information in order to effectively exercise its express constitutional powers under Article I to advise the President in making treaties, to declare war, and to appropriate funds for raising and supporting armies.

Congress can, should and has delegated authority to the President to shield certain foreign and military activities from the public. It has authorized him to enforce administrative secrecy through classification. The classification system administered pursuant to Executive Order specifically derives its authority from provisions of the Espionage Act, the National Security Act of 1947, and the Atomic Energy Act of 1954. In the Freedom of Information Act, moreover, Congress has incorporated by reference the provisions of the Executive Order, and President Nixon, in March 1972, cited the Information Act as statutory authority for instituting reforms in the classification system through a new Executive Order. On the other hand, as the Supreme Court pointed out in its decision earlier this year in *Environmental Protection Agency* v. *Mink*, "Congress could . . . establish its own procedures for classification."

Information properly classified, therefore, may be withheld in certain circumstances from the general public and provided to reliable persons within the executive branch only on a need to know basis. But this conclusion provides no justification for denying Congress the foreign and military information it requires in order to fulfill its constitutional responsibilities. Accordingly, Congress has the power to compel production of such information by statute or Congressional resolution.

B. *Investigatory Files and Litigation Materials*. The second major category of information frequently included under the umbrella of executive privilege is information which the government may have to produce in court—principally investigatory files and other litigation materials. Roger Cramton recently described this as a "widely accepted legitimate area of executive privilege," agreeing with Attorney General Jackson that disclosure of investigatory files would prejudice law enforcement, impede the development of confidential sources, and result in injustice to innocent individuals.

It is unnecessary to dispute the validity of these conclusions to demonstrate that investigatory and litigation files need not be protected from unwarranted disclosure to Congress by anything so grand as an executive privilege. The government's law enforcement interest, as well as the privacy of individuals under investigation, are amply safeguarded by common law evidentiary privileges, by the statutory exemptions from the Freedom of Information Act, and by the constitutional protections against self-incrimination and denials of free speech and due process which apply in legislative as well as judicial settings.

Unlike the blunderbuss of an unreviewable executive privilege, these doctrines assimilate and attempt to balance competing interests in disclosure which are frequently advanced by private litigants, by Congress and by the public. Furthermore, it would be difficult to imagine a greater inconsistency in the law than that a private litigant could compel the disclosure of information from the Executive not accessible to Congress. But this is precisely the effect of extending executive privilege into the area of investigatory files and litigation materials.

C. *Advice Within the Executive Branch*. This brings us to the only aspect of the so-called executive privilege that deserves scrutiny as a possible constitutional privilege based on the separation of powers. That is, in the words of President Eisenhower, the power to withhold "conversations or communications, or any documents or reproductions" that relate solely to internal advice within the Executive Branch.

This "advice" privilege, as we think it should be called, has been the subject of unconscionably broad interpretation by the Executive. In our view, the privilege is not one that is exclusively "executive." Insofar as there is such a privilege, it would apply to attempts to extract data concerning the advice that judicial law clerks or legislative assistants render to their superiors. The principle involved is the necessity to protect the delicate internal decisionmaking process of *each* branch of government. Freewheeling debate among colleagues and the presentation of iconoclastic ideas are inhibited if the prospect looms of later cross-examination. To require all advice to be subject to often unfriendly scrutiny would surely dry up many sources of innovation and truth.

There is a second reason for protecting the "advice" that flows from one official to another. It is essentially a recognition of the realities of power and personal vulnerability. Protecting the lower ranking individuals is especially needed because members of Congress, in their desire to score a point for the folks back home, may run roughshod over the reputation and sensibilities, if not the legal rights, of an honest but uninspired bureaucrat. If this can be avoided, it should be. This is why we conclude that if an implied constitutional privilege is admitted on practical grounds to allow executive officers to decline to testify, at the direction of the President, it should apply down the line to the lesser and weaker members of the bureaucracy.

The practical necessities of the case, however, may not be thought to justify a constitutional privilege, particularly since there is no express language in the Constitution to support one. In this view the courts would have a more limited, although still important reviewing role. An unsuccessful attempt by the Congress to obtain information from the Executive would not precipitate a constitutional question as to the scope of an "advice privilege," but it could lead to a law suit in which the critical question was whether the information sought was germane to a proper congressional inquiry. Courts might tend to shy from limiting Congress under such a vague standard. But because there would be situations in which the Congress reasonably needed to know what action or decisions the Executive took, but not what advice it acted on, there would still be a live question for judicial determination.

Under either formulation, the issue would remain, what sort of protection does the Executive require? Whom shall it cover, and what types of information? Who can invoke it, and by what procedures?

We shall now attempt, not without apprehension, to block out a workable and coherent set of principles answering these questions.

1. No witness summoned by a congressional committee may refuse to appear on the ground that he intends to invoke the "privilege" as to all or some of the questions that may be asked.

If an employee of the executive branch is directed by a superior not to testify, he should make himself available to explain the reasons for the refusal. Congress is entitled at least to this. Any other rule—and we fear that it is the rule by which we now live—opens the door wide to unjustified and even arbitrary assertions of privilege, and to the denial to the legislative branch of information it rightfully seeks in order to carry out its constitutional responsibilities.

2. a. A witness summoned by a congressional committee could claim advice privilege only when accompanied by, and at the direction of, the Attorney General, Deputy Attorney General or Counsel to the President, who would assert that they were acting at the direction of the President personally.

b. A witness could decline to answer questions about recommendations, advice and suggestions passed on to superiors or associates for consideration in the formulation of policy. (Nor could Congress question others, including the superiors or associates of an employee, about such advice.)

c. An individual summoned could not decline to answer questions about policy decisions that he personally made or personally implemented. Whatever the title of an individual, and whether or not he is called an "advisor," he should be accountable for actions that he took in the name of the government and decisions that he made leading to action on the parts of others.

d. An individual summoned could not decline to answer questions about facts that he acquired personally while acting in an official capacity.

The separation of "fact" from "advice," while sometimes difficult, is not impossible. Indeed, executive departments are often required by the courts to make this separation in order to comply with requests for documents under the Freedom of Information Act and other litigation. Without the separation an advice privilege invites abuse.

e. Congress could require answers to questions about actions or advice by executive officials which it has probable cause to believe constitute criminal wrongdoing or official misconduct, such as the anti-trust settlement with ITT, as well as the Watergate events. In such situations, of course, individuals summoned before Congress would be entitled to exercise their constitutional rights, including, for example, the privilege against self-incrimination.

f. Past employees of the executive branch should also be able to exercise the privilege, since the possibility that advice given in confidence might be revealed after an employee left the government could also have an inhibiting effect on free interchange. If called upon to review the exercise of a privilege over advice given by a former employee, a court in accommodating the respective interests of the legislative and executive branches might well conclude that the privilege is not permanent but expires after a given period of time—for example, a set number of years after a change in administrations, or the death of the former advisor.

3. a. Documents could be withheld from Congress or a committee of Congress only on the personal signature of the President.

b. The privilege should extend not to entire documents but only to those portions of documents that embody the criteria we have set out to justify an exercise of privilege. It would have been proper, for example, for the President to have ordered purely advisory parts of communications among the Pentagon papers to be withheld from Congress if he had complied, as he should have, with the Senate Foreign Relations Committee's request for the documents in December 1969.

Executive privilege is inconsistent with constitutional principles underlying the investigative power of Congress and the judicial reviewing function of the Supreme Court. The executive branch is therefore on weak ground in asserting that an entire document may be withheld solely because a portion of a document contains "advice." Of course, if facts within the personal knowledge of a witness, or information relating to decisions that a witness personally made or implemented, are "inextricably intertwined with policy-making processes," secrecy should prevail. But if the separation can be made, Congress is entitled to the information not protected by executive privilege.

[Whereupon, at 12:45 p.m., the committee recessed.]

Daniel Ellsberg on Secrecy and Dissent ([28A], pp. 423–436)

Daniel Ellsberg, responsible for the disclosure of the classified "Pentagon Papers" in 1972, was a high foreign policy official and one who publicly challenged government policy on secrecy. He testified before the joint Senate hearings held on May 17, 1973 by the Committees on the Judiciary and Government Operations. His remarks covered a variety of subjects concerning secrecy and foreign policy. The Ellsberg testimony is important to an understanding of both the procedures and the potential consequences of government secrecy. As a former insider, privy to some of the most closely guarded foreign intelligence, Ellsberg spoke of the manner in which the classification system is used, the hierarchy of security clearances, and the effect that "privileged" information has upon the minds of those who share in its access. Although he presents a moral case for breaking the secrecy system in defense of human values that are threatened by the misuse of security classification, his priority appears to lie in the application of checks and balances among the branches of government. Indeed, he addresses fundamental moral and constitutional questions in American political life. Space limitations and digressions in the course of the hearing required abridgement of his testimony. The complete text is informative in its detail of Ellsberg's experience and his place within the controversies associated with the Watergate period of the Nixon administration.

Mr. ELLSBERG. Thank you, Senator Muskie.

As you can understand, over the last week and last 5 months, I have not been drafting statements, but it was suggested I speak for about 20 minutes and then have questions, though I will be glad to be interrupted at any time.

I do feel my being here this week and in these halls represents a celebration not only for me, just as I think the hearings about to start tomorrow are a celebration not for one party, not for one branch of government.

What I mean by that is that nothing could better exemplify the spirit of this country and this Constitution than the existence of these hearings and the facts they are bringing out to the American people.

The facts themselves are painful to us and startling to everyone in the world, yet I suspect in most countries in the world, including those countries Mr. Nixon recently visited, the strongest impression of this kind of disclosure and governmental check and balance taking place is that we live in a world so different from theirs.

In fact, I literally was just reminded as you spoke to me here, you asked me if I had been under similar circumstances before, and it reminded me when I had been:

On May 13, 1970, I spoke before the Senate Foreign Relations Committee, among the chaos in Washington, during the Cambodian invasion. We are reminded that invasion was a little more than 3 years ago.

It was a country almost untouched by war.

Since that time not as many bombs have fallen on Cambodia as on South Vietnam, and yet, as you know, half of the population of Cambodia has been made into refugees, 3 million out of 6.7 million in the 3 years since I spoke here.

That makes me feel not a fool——

Senator THURMOND. Mr. Chairman, if you would have him speak up. We can't hear him.

Mr. ELLSBERG. I was saying that this is almost an anniversary for me of 3 years since having addressed previously a committee of Congress, the Senate Foreign Relations Committee, and I spoke in the midst of clouds of tear gas in Washington.

As a matter of fact, the famous Senator on your right, Senator Mathias, and I flew back from a speaking engagement in St. Louis, came down to the city of Washington, and on that day Senator Mathias got me in a car and we drove by a city that was already beginning to smell of tear gas and hundreds of thousands of people had come to protest. They were exercising their rights in the only way they knew how to exercise their rights at that time.

Congress was investigating what was going on in Cambodia. What is still going on.

Despite the will of Congress, since as we all know in the few months since the alleged cease fire in Indochina, we have dropped as many bombs on Cambodia and Laos as the United States dropped on Japan in World War II, all of World War II. That is 145,000 tons of bombs, almost exactly what we dropped in Japan.

But I am here not to speak of the impact on all these countries but on our own country.

As you reminded me of that today, I have my opening statement of which I would like to read one paragraph, which was very much off the top of my head because of what was happening 3 years ago, May of 1970, when I said to Senator Fulbright who was chairman of the session,

Personally, I thought during the last couple of years of protest in this country it was still possible to exaggerate the threat to our society that this conflict posed for us. I feared that we might come to a pass in which there would be a major threat to our society but we were not there yet. . . . But I am afraid we cannot go on like this, as it seems likely we will unless Congress soon commits us to total withdrawal—and survive as Americans. There would still be a country here and it might have the same name but it would not be the same country.

I said 3 years ago,

I think that what might be at stake if this involvement goes on is a change in our society as radical and as ominous as could be brought about by our occupation by a foreign power.

I would hate to see that and I hope very much that deliberations such as the Senate is undertaking right now would prevent that.

Unfortunately, those deliberations did not end what was happening in Vietnam or in this country.

How shall we call what was happening in this country, as we prepared in the last year or two to celebrate in a superficial manner the 200th anniversary of our Republic, the year of 1976.

I sometimes ask myself whether we faced the betrayal of our Revolution by or before 1976. I am assured by this hearing and my being here and by the end of my case that the American Revolution does live and we are here because we all realize that it does need a renewal at this time, in substance.

How could these bombs have been dropped despite the will of Congress?

I believe that secrecy, executive secrecy has had a major role to play—and that is the subject of these hearings—in the path that has led us to the Watergate and to the war that continues in Indochina.

Over the last year when I have been questioned by newspapermen I have really been dismayed to discover how quickly to the minds of Americans come questions that reveal their fear of openness. Even newspapermen. the people who printed the Pentagon Papers—some of them got a Pulitzer Prize for it—think very quickly: But don't there have to be secrets?

What if everyone did what you did? All of which of course are fair questions, that you are addressing and you have addressed.

What dismayed me is that it seems they are much more aware of the risks of no secrecy than of the risks of secrecy. The risks of no secrecy are the risks of democracy. That is a gamble that the Founders of our Constitution made for us 200 years ago.

The question is: Are the Bill of Rights, and the constitutional checks checks and balances obsolete in the 20th century?

Have nuclear bombs made it impossible for an American Government to be open to its own people, as so few governments in the world are today?

Isn't it impractical and naive and idealistic to imagine that government can be transparent to its people or that the homes of citizens can be allowed to be opaque and impenetrable to the police and to Congressmen?

I am saying these are attitudes shared not only by executive officials and not only by police, but really by every class of people including Congressmen and newsmen.

I expect questions and I welcome questions along those lines today because they are part of the problem.

I would use my opening statement to answer the unasked questions. What are the costs and risks of executive secrecy, however beneficial it might be?

Very specifically, I believe that the price of executive secrecy of the sort we have practiced over the last generation has been Vietnam in foreign affairs and Watergate in our domestic affairs.

The two together spell the subversion of our form of government and spell death not only for Americans but for more victims who are not American.

In fact, I heard Senator Mathias speak of a mood today of cynicism, suspicion, distrust.

Is that a symptom of sickness or of health?

The fact is that our Constitution was written in a spirit of cynicism, suspicion, and distrust, and every clause reflects those attitudes, every clause reflects the attitude that humans in authority and power cannot be trusted to become angels by virtue of their office; cannot be trusted at all, as a matter of fact, and need to be set watching each other.

Branches of government must be given special rights to investigate: the press must be given protection from government so that it can expose the government and monitor the public servants and keep them from abusing the power they inevitably hold, the power to kill, make laws, repress, the power to wield the police authority.

So the spirit in our citizenry at large of cynicism and skepticism is healthy.

Democracy may not be the most pleasant form of government. So I say we are alive now and we have the responsibility, and the issue was not what was chosen 200 years ago, but what we should choose today.

I want to argue why we should make the same constitutional checks and Bill of Rights as 200 years ago and why they are not, in my opinion, obsolete.

In particular, I speak not as a lawyer, let alone a constitutional lawyer, but as someone who has had a very expensive education in the law of secrecy over the last 5 months and before that as someone who had an expensive education in the practice and attitudes of secrecy, who lived in the world of secrets for 12 years before that, a period when I certainly did not know much of the law of the Constitution because I worked for the executive branch. I worked for the President and thus I thought I was beyond the law, like all other executive servants.

The attitudes that we are seeing in the White House today did not start with the Republicans or this administration. Their attitudes are absolutely familiar to me in every respect from my own time even if the actions have gone further.

But the first thing I want to suggest is the attitudes which have been growing for 30 years now in the executive branch, even if they never led to actions of the sort we have heard about in the last months.

It started, I think, first in the New Deal answer to the Depression, where it was thought that central government and the executive branch was the only solution to our problems; next, in a world war in which it was obvious that was the case: where we needed a kind of military leadership exemplified by a commander in chief.

That President Nixon likes to use that title today, 30 years after World War II, is a sign of sickness in our society, but I think an inevitable kind.

The Pentagon Papers—which I felt Congress needed to know 4 years ago when I first came to Senator Fulbright—revealed to me, above all, a conspiratorial style in executive decisionmaking, a style that I was part of in the 12 years that I have worked with it.

I think that doesn't answer the question but rather poses the question: Why have our executive officials been led to act as if they are members of a conspiracy? Because I think that does describe it.

I repeat and I will repeat it again, I am sure, what we are seeing in Watergate is the same attitudes, the same style, the same conspiratorial attitude we have used for generations to subvert self-determination in other countries in the world.

I am including in that process South Vietnam, something that I witnessed at close hand in the time I spent there.

We are seeing the same attitudes and, indeed, the same personnel brought home, people we have sent abroad to subvert Cuba or South Vietnam or North Vietnam; we brought them home and they are doing their thing here and their thing is subverting democracy, their thing is working for the President and the executive branch. And executives in every country of the world understand each other better than they understand their own citizens.

To get relatively specific here, I want to describe a little bit of the feeling that is imparted to these people when they enter, as though a priesthood, when they enter the executive branch, as I did in effect 12 years ago, although I was working for the Rand Corp. which was a consultant to the executive branch, but had a special relationship privy to many of the secrets.

I could sum it up by saying that secrecy corrupts just as power corrupts. The secrecy now is corrupting. Perhaps I could cut through it best by just relating to you some advice that I gave to a man who entered Government 4 years ago, and I might as well name him— Henry Kissinger—someone I had known academically or professionally for 10 years.

By that time, I had been in the system for more than a decade. It seemed to me it was appropriate to pass on some thoughts to him in advance and perhaps inoculate him against the transformation that I feared was going to come over this person.

It was appropriate to do it to this person because I felt he was going to be initiated into the most esoteric and sinister parts of this system.

He was not only going to have a top secret but perhaps a score or two score, for all I know, of the clearances higher than top secret of which I had held an even dozen when I worked as special assistant to the Assistant Secretary of Defense.

I told him at that time, and he may well not remember this conversation, or deny it, but I am sure you will give him equal time if he finds I am saying anything inaccurate and will be glad of the opportunity to do it, I am sure.

But in December of 1968 in the Hotel Pierre, before he took up residence in the Executive Office Building, I said to him, "You are about to get 10, 15, or 20 clearances of a sort that you never knew existed. Their very names are classified." I am elaborating here a little for your benefit on the assumption it might be necessary for some of you.

Their names are classified, unlike the words "top secret."

Code words that identify them on pieces of paper are classified.

They are referred to by the first letters of their codewords; they are never to be photographed. In fact, when one special assistant to the President—I am adding now—was once photographed with one of those code words on a piece of paper in addition to the words "top secret," a quarter of a million dollars had to be spent changing that word wherever it existed.

Why a quarter of a million dollars? Because it existed on hundreds of thousands of pieces of paper not one of which is available to your staff and which you yourselves would have considerable trouble getting.

That applies only to the lowest of these clearances to which I refer.

As I say, I had a dozen.

Secretary McNamara had at least a few more. I wouldn't suggest how many each person had in the Defense Department. Persons in the White House could have many more in the NSA and CIA and many places I didn't deal with.

Coming back to Mr. Kissinger, "The first impact," I said, "will be upon you when you feel like a fool, because you have written books on subjects of defense and foreign policy."

His first book was "Nuclear Weapons and Foreign Policy."

You have written articles and rubbed shoulders for a decade with people who had these clearances and access to information that you didn't know existed, and you will feel like a fool because you didn't know it. You will feel like a fool for having written all that without having this special information on which to judge. You will realize that the people that you talked to had it and you didn't.

But that feeling will only last for a week or two, because after a week or so of having four-star generals, or at that time one-star generals, like General Haig bring you in special brief cases, special pouches, books that are available only to you and your boss and a few other people—and I will get back to that—that are not available to Senators or James Reston or Arthur Krock, unless occasionally, and certainly not to members of the public, you will forget that you were once a fool and remember only that everyone else is a fool who does not have this information.

Moreover, in signing agreements to have this information, you will come to understand that the only way of keeping secrets this well is to lie.

A contract to observe those clearances, and these are essentially contractual arrangements in the executive branch, conditions of employment, is a contract to lie; in a good cause, it would appear to protect intelligence secrets.

When I say lie, on the first hand, if you are asked if you have this clearance, you are not allowed to say, no comment. That would confirm it. Your duty is to lie and say you do not have it.

If you are asked about the contents, you are to lie and say you know nothing about the contents.

If you are asked whether you have a particular piece of information, you must lie and say you do not.

These go back to the practices of World War II, when thousands of civilians were introduced to the need to lie to their fellow scientists despite the supposed sharing of scientific information. Lying is legitimatized with an enemy like Hitler or Stalin. Thus, some people learn these practices in a context that seems thoroughly legitimate to them and inevitable.

But I went on to say to Kissinger:

The effect of that is that you will have to lie and you will succeed in lying and you will fool your former academic colleagues. You will discover, in collaboration with thousands of other executive officials all telling the same cover story, that it's easy to fool people.

And that is what the President learns.

I suspect that those of you at this table in your life have fooled this person or that, but you also know you are subject to reelection, whether it is every 2 years or 6 years, and that there is a limit to how many people you can fool and how much.

In fact, if I have learned one thing in 5 months in court, it is to respect the wisdom of allowing 12 ordinary citizens to be the judges of truth or honesty on the witness stand. I believe they are shrewd and extremely effective weighers of lying on that stand and those are the people you deal with.

But you will find if any of you go into the executive branch, you will discover that given the benefit of the doubt that accrues to the President or anyone who works for him, it is easy to fool people. There really are secrets and they are very well kept.

The notion that everything comes out in the New York Times is untrue. It is a cover story meant to keep people from prying too closely because they will supposedly read it next month anyway in the New York Times. That is untrue.

You will learn as Kissinger would, as I told him, you will learn there are secrets that are very well kept, that people can, in effect, be easily fooled if you work for the President; and it is a short step which is hard to avoid making from that perception to the belief that they are fools, and that they have no legitimate role in decision-making.

You have the information, they don't; they don't even have the wisdom to know what they don't know; therefore they have no legitimate role.

And that applies not only to my jury, but to you gentlemen sitting right there, the Senate of the United States.

So from that time on, and that could be a matter of weeks from entering office, and it could happen to anyone of you, Senator Muskie, with all respect, you have been a candidate and may be again a candidate for the highest office and in effect I am talking to vou with full respect.

What I would like to say to you, since I have the chance, to anyone who might enter the White House or any part of the executive branch: The security system is an education in contempt for law, because you cannot be held accountable to law, at least we used to think we could not if we worked for the President, whose Justice Department controls the Federal indictment process.

You are then beyond the law if you do the President's wishes, and the President is thought to be beyond the law.

Moreover, you cannot be accountable to Justice or even the public if the secrets of your advice and your actions are bound to be well kept.

You are safe from accountability. Contempt follows for the public that is so easily fooled, and that contempt is the death in that individual for the democratic spirit.

Indeed, we cannot, our democracy cannot be served or guarded by people whose basic core of belief is contempt for the democratic process and for the citizens who elect them and to whom they supposedly are responsible.

So, finally, I went on to say to Dr. Kissinger a little colorfully:

You will become, if you yield to this process, you will become unable to learn from anyone who does not have these clearances.

Someone will stand before you, whether Walter Lippman or a past former official—a former official is different because he knows what you know and perhaps you can talk to him—but someone who has never had those clearances, you won't listen to. You would have to ask yourself, "What would he be telling me if he knew what I know?" and that is just too much work and you will stop listening and from then on, conversations will not be conversations. They will be situations in which you listen to someone while you ask yourself, what do I want from this man; what do I want him to believe? Not, what can I learn from him? Because most knowledge resides outside the executive branch, you will be cut off from that and you will become something like a moron.

I knew him at that time, not well, but just well enough to say that, considering it was important enough.

This was the image in my mind on the effect of secrets on a high-level official; not the low level because mere top secrets don't have this effect, they are so low, so close to what you read in the New York Times; but the other information, much of which is wrong, much of which is contradictory, much of which is incomplete, but which nevertheless is different from what you read in the New York Times.

So you live in a different world of information. You come to think of yourself as a resident of a different world with different powers and responsibilities.

As I say, I thought of that access like the potion that Circe gave Ulysses' men that turned men into swine, and made fools of them.

I have talked long enough to establish that point I think. I should say this doesn't come just from reading the particular information. The secrets are kept not only by this conspiratorial type of honor among thieves, but by the entire apparatus of conspiracy and that is the last point I want to touch on here.

I am saying, I have to reiterate, the secrets are better kept than you know, and I am well aware I am talking to you as Senators, and I am talking to the press and public.

I am saying I have never met in 12 years working for the executive branch a newspaperman, no matter how canny, how experienced, who could imagine how often and how easily he was lied to by my bosses.

That is one thing I hope to suggest by the Pentagon Papers; people should be more skeptical and probing.

In the field of foreign affairs we have come to expect this from the President; it is his job and we don't need to know.

The President shares that belief: That the public does not need to know and cannot be trusted with the information—the two requirements of sharing information with him, in the regulations.

But the need for this conspiratorial style, as I say, starts with the notion that you are fighting a subversive enemy, like Hitler or Stalin, and must imitate his methods.

To do that you must build a physical capacity to keep secrets. That begins, of course, with a dedicated corps, a bureaucracy that can be relied upon to keep their mouths shut.

But that is not hard for a President. The prestige and the power he offers them and the threat of taking that away is more than enough to keep their lips sealed most of the time.

But next they have to have an apparatus to keep these secrets even from their own secretaries—and you will recognize that is a very unusual state of affairs—or their own deputies or wives, people who work closely with them.

If you are interested, I will go into that more later, but let me give you a slight feel for it. If you had worked all your life with top secret material in the Pentagon for Assistant Secretaries, unless you were one of the elect, you would not be aware that there are entire rooms in the Pentagon with safe doors outside, with a guardian, with a computer list up to date hourly and daily as to who is admitted in that room, and unless you know the codeword and are on that list, you cannot enter that room or know of its existence.

It will have a very nondescript door in the hall that will not suggest what is inside. You can go in that room and discover yourself in something like the reading room of the New York Public Library, not a closet, not a safe, but a room with charts, with library shelves of material, no word of which you were previously aware existed.

You did not know how it was gotten. You did not know the President had this kind of information at all. Of course, the effect of that is very euphoric at first. You go around and take things off the shelves and begin reading it and imagine you are about to learn all the answers, that Godlike knowledge is now available to you.

Now, you can be introduced into one of those rooms and still have no idea that there exist still other rooms with other sources of information, other access lists just as large and just as secret.

I would say it is not until you have four or five such clearances, that the next level of mystery is revealed to you. Then you become aware that there is no limit to this; that these clearances can be generated very quickly in a day or two; and such types of information can be segregated—I am not saying only from the public or Congress, but even from other people who have two or three other clearances—very effectively.

Once you have a dozen, from then on, you live in the knowledge there must be others you don't have.

I still keep finding out about new ones.

Could there be clearances the President doesn't know about? Of course, certainly, without any doubt, because the physical nature of generating these things is such that they can multiply and proliferate in a way that no individual has any way of knowing about.

I am not saying that is the case in Watergate. I do not believe it is. My suspicion—for other reasons than I can go into, for substantive reasons—is that the President—and I am not convicting him; I am stating my experience and belief—the President likely knows all those details.

Could it, however, be withheld from him? The answer is "Yes," and even by close associates.

The reason I am going into this is that this committee, if you are interested in secrecy, should explore the world of secrecy, to restrict and change it and bring it under control.

Unless you have a sense of the variety of that world and its dimensions, you really won't be able to do it.

I will close with the fact that 1 year later, I saw Henry Kissinger, then in San Clemente, the Western White House. I had gone there in part to give him my sense that the Cambodian operation and what I knew of his Vietnam policy was a replay of the experience that I regrettably lived through in the Defense Department in 1964–65. Not only the smell of conspiracy was in the air, but the very details, every aspect was recapitulating every aspect I went through and kept my mouth shut about in 1964 and 1965, when two Cabinet Secretaries and the President, two Secretaries were lying to Senate committees in executive session, lying not because they were different from current ones but because they had little chance of being found out by U.S. Senators.

You might remember just parenthetically that at one point Secretary McNamara, testifying about the Tonkin Gulf incidents, forced every staff member to leave the room because they were not cleared for this information.

That was the lowest level of clearance above top secret, what we have read in the newspapers the last 2 days, by official release, described as "Comint," communications intelligence, which has special code words.

The Senators at that moment were allowed to see it but not really examine it and in fact, knowingly or not, Secretary McNamara deceived them as to the meaning of those cables.

That is what Anthony Austin, the New York Times newspaperman, in his book, "The President's War," stated.

What I want to state here is that the super-secret material which the Senate staff was not able to see, as I say, was "Comint."

"Comint" is the lowest of these clearances that I have described, the next highest above top secret.

Top secret, you have heard in testimony, top secret is accessible to 400,000 to 500,000 people, a large number of people, though a small part of our electorate.

Comint clearance, of course, is far more secret, far more sensitive. That is why your staff couldn't see it, and that is why you don't see it routinely the way the President does.

It is accessible to only about 120,000 people. Not to the 535 Members of Congress or their staffs; they can't be trusted, but to 120,000 sergeants, warrant officers, generals, and Cabinet Secretaries.

The next clearance above that cuts way down to about 14,000 to 20,000. What I am saying is that the world of secrets is lived in by a very large number of people, though a very small part of our electorate and only one branch of our Government.

Henry Kissinger lives in a much smaller world, a world that for some pieces of information might be inhabited only by a couple of people.

Although one White House staffer told me about Henry's relations with General Haig at that time, "I wonder if Henry realizes there were certain things known only to him, the President, and the Army General Staff," thanks to that particular liaison, so it wasn't quite as discrete as I thought.

But I am saying, as many as 100,000, or 400,000, nevertheless keep secrets very well because of this apparatus of conspiracy, special channels, special couriers for each clearance.

The couriers for one clearance do not know the existence of the other ones. Special briefings, special access lists, special libraries, each separate, the apparatus of an espionage ring; a Government that consists of cells but with the President at the top.

Certainly, when I say there are clearances that the President may not know of, I say that only to make a point. The more important point is, the President does know virtually all of this and spends too much of his time in a James Bond role in running a mere apparatus.

After a year of his indoctrination, I came upon Henry Kissinger living on Circe's Isle. I could see the effects pretty clearly. I wanted to tell him first that his Vietnam policy was not necessarily a secret. It was a policy of escalation in my opinion, although too many people thought it was a policy of withdrawal.

I wanted him to be aware that was visible.

Basically, they were fooled for 4 years. A mass hoax was played on the American public. A preplanned policy of escalation likely to bring us into Laos and Cambodia and North Vietnam, into the bombing of North Vietnam: All that was likely in the spring of 1969 when these White House phones began to be tapped, and that is why they were tapped, because that had to be kept super-secret. And it was carried out to the tune of 4 million tons of bombs by a President supposedly ending the war.

But I wanted to tell him to read the Pentagon Papers to learn from them, to learn as I had, to make known the same mistakes to him.

When I asked him if he had the Pentagon Papers, his answer was. "Yes," which I knew. I knew they were in the White House.

Some years later, when they were revealed, he was asked when he heard of them, and his answer was, "When they came out in the New York Times."

That was a lie. But as I say, President's men think they have a right to lie, always.

I asked him if he had read them. He said: "No." I said he should at least read the summaries or members of his staff, like Winston Lord, should read these and learn lessons from them.

His answer was: "But do we really have anything to learn from these studies?" At which point I recognized a man who had been eating honeydew for a year, and that the Republicans couldn't learn from Democrats any more than the Democrats could learn from the French.

I said: "Yes, this is 20 years of history; yes; I do think you have a lot to learn from it."

He said: "But we make decisions very differently now."

I said: "Cambodia did not look so different."

He said: "Cambodia, you must understand, was made for very complicated reasons." Secret reasons which could not be exposed to the Senate or the Congress, and therefore couldn't be discussed or argued with, reasons so foolish, and yet their foolishness could not be exposed by democratic give and take because they couldn't be discussed.

That is why men can live with moronic policies for years, because they are secret.

I said,

Henry, there hasn't been a miserable policy in Vietnam in the last 20 years that was not made for very complicated reasons.

When I mentioned honeydew, I am thinking of Samuel Coleridge's Kubla Khan:

Beware! Beware! His flashing eyes, his floating hair! Weave a circle round him thrice. And close your eyes with holy dread. For he on honeydew hath fed, And drunk the milk of Paradise.

I recognized the man who had been eating secret honeydew for a year and there was no talking to him, keeping him from the course that led us to 4 million tons of bombs and to making half the population of Cambodia refugees.

That is the task which is up to you: To decompress, to deintoxicate these officials. Don't ask them to do it themselves.

Only you can take charge of the secrecy process. Learn about it first—expose it, collapse it down to where it is in your control and where it is no longer a threat to the democratic process.

Only that can keep us alive as Americans.

Thank you.

Senator MUSKIE. Thank you, Dr. Ellsberg, for what I think is one of the most perceptive exposures of the corrupting ability of secrecy this committee has heard.

I think it is a terribly important contribution to the record.

I assume you have heard of, if not read, David Wise's book?

Mr. ELLSBERG. I have received an advance copy, but I haven't had the chance to read it.

Senator MUSKIE. "The Politics of Lying."

Well, I haven't had a chance to read it altogether, but I have read two or three chapters that touch the same points, some of the same points that you did, this morning.

I think because there are several Senators who are present who would like to ask questions, we will begin by observing the 10-minute rule on questions and then take it from there.

Mr. ELLSBERG. I apologize for taking longer.

Senator MUSKIE. No apologies necessary.

I would like to ask you two or three fundamental questions to begin with to emphasize some points about our policies of secrecy.

First of all, the classification system has no basis in statutory law?

Mr. ELLSBERG. Yes.

Senator MUSKIE. It is entirely a Presidential system?

Mr. ELLSBERG. That is correct.

Senator MUSKIE. It did not exist at all prior to World War I and was only military prior to World War II; is that correct?

Mr. ELLSBERG. That is correct.

Of course, there had been military restrictions on military history that go back through our system. But as a formal administrative system, that has blossomed from the Second World War on.

Senator MUSKIE. It wasn't until President Truman's action following World War II, that the system was expanded from the military departments and spread out to cover other agencies of the Government?

Mr. ELLSBERG. That is correct.

Senator MUSKIE. Now the conspiracy count against you charged that you conspired to defraud the United States by impairing, obstructing, and defeating its lawful governmental function of controlling the dissemination of classified Government studies, reports, memoranda, and communications, and your defense argued that no statute or combination of statutes could be read as creating such a sweeping governmental function. The question before Congress is whether or not there should be a law controlling the dissemination of classified information.

Do you think a sound law is possible and where is it needed?

Mr. ELLSBERG. I do think that whatever the process of keeping secrets, it should be brought under congressional scrutiny and that can only be done, I believe, first by, as I say, investigation and exposure as is happening here and in the Watergate and Ervin committees.

I have learned a tremendous amount from the large volume of the Moorhead hearings and Ervin hearings which I read in court in dull periods and with great benefit.

The first process is to expose it to the public and the second is to take control of it by statute.

Senator MUSKIE. So you agree, notwithstanding your deep feeling about the corrupting ability of secrecy, you still believe there are secrets that the Government needs to protect?

Mr. ELLSBERG. Yes, of course, but the question is where do you draw the line, and even more fundamentally, who draws it?

If I have come to one clear conclusion after, as I say, 12 years working in the executive system of secrecy and several years of thinking critically about it, it is that democracy cannot let that line be drawn by any one man, the line between inside dope and outside ignorance or fools.

There is room for some suggestive puns there. I believe this is a dope; that it is addictive to the executive officials and it makes them into dopes.

It is a class of inside dopes, as a matter of fact, but as I say, it makes them moronic.

But the line must not be drawn between the executive branch or the legislative branch or the courts.

The question of who draws the line is, as I say, very fundamental.

Congress must have a role in both setting the guidelines for the system and keeping the amount of secrets down to a reasonable level which has no relation to the current status.

The word "reduction" of secrets hardly describes the process that means that there should be one-ten-thousandth of the number of secret pages.

There are right now a billion pages of classified information. The administration is very proud of having declassified recently some 29,000 or 30,000 pages, if that is what it is.

Senator MUSKIE. Thirty-five-million, I think.

Mr. ELLSBERG. Million, fine. I am off by a very large factor.

Thirty-five million is still—by the way, I think you are wrong as a matter of fact.

Senator MUSKIE. Well, it is the administration's claim.

Mr. ELLSBERG. Let's see what my concentration during the trial—my memory is—you are correct. There are 160 million papers from World War II. Thirty-five million. It is hard to believe. I can't sit here talking to you and believe they have declassified 35 million pages, leaving only some 125 million left from World War II, plus about 350 million from the end of World War II to the end of Korea, and another half billion pages since Korea.

That is a billion pages of classified information.

So if you cut that down by let's say of a factor, not of a thousand, but of 10,000 or 100,000, you would still be left with too many secrets.

That is the task before you and as I say, that is a task that is not a task for a handful of librarians crossing through "top secret" on a bunch of pages. It calls for wholesale declassification by period and subject, wholesale and by legislation that keeps that from happening again.

Senator MUSKIE. What standards should be devised for defining the need for secrecy?

Mr. ELLSBERG. I put first emphasis on standards that would keep the system within the bounds of democratic government.

You could approach this from two directions, of course.

Congress has passed separate statutes that involved nuclear weapons data and communications intelligence and for them one could say that an official secret sense does exist despite the first amendment.

I might say, by the way, that I was frequently and ruthlessly accused 2 years ago, when the Pentagon Papers came out, of threatening communications data or codes, threatening codes.

I knew that not a page of those documents compromised codes for the simple reason they didn't have the right words. Had they in fact threatened codes I knew very well they would have had one to a dozen other words on that cover that would have warned me very effectively, and I had no desire to compromise codes.

I think Congress does have that power to devise the same kind of narrow standards, then. In fact, I am not sure law should go beyond that except to establish a category of secret as William Florence, my consultant—I learned much from him—has suggested, that the notion of a single category of classified defense information might be worth while. But the key points there are that, in principle, any secrecy about Government operations is to some extent an abridgment of our First Amendment.

Freedom of speech, freedom of the press, and implicitly behind it the freedom to know and gather information is, above all, given to us in hopes of maintaining this a republic, so that citizens shall know how their officials are working.

It is the absolute core of our Government. So any abridgement, of course, has to be regarded with the utmost skepticism and worry.

But as I say, Congress has to make some allowance for some abridgement and so does the Supreme Court.

The key characteristics that make that viable in a democracy are: the number of secrets must be very small; so the guidelines have to be set to keep them small; but above all, the system must be monitored as it goes on to see that the guidelines are being met.

Third, there must be a form of appeal both in the executive branch, in Congress, and in the courts.

Not one of these three characteristics is currently possessed by our classification system.

Everything is routinely classified. That is why there are a billion pages of classified material.

There is essentially no monitoring of the process by anybody, or anything leading to the same result, and almost nothing gets declassified.

In fact, you can't challenge that classification in the courts. Most judges have refused to question the validity of the classification.

Our Judge Matthew Byrne, in fact, did allow us to challenge that not formally, but implicitly.

Certainly Congress has not thought itself to have the power to challenge that classification, although in fact since there was no law, since it was executive regulation, of course, it did.

In short, there must be the possibility of questioning the validity of any mark and the motives of it. We haven't discussed that, but I could go into it.

You know, having one last footnote on my case, at this moment, the State Department has refused to assert that four volumes of the Pentagon Papers which I had released only to Congress, the negotiations contacts, must still be regarded classified, along with half a dozen other volumes that were in my case.

The fact is that the Government, by putting those volumes in the indictment, made it part of a process which I am glad to say is still a public process, so those documents in the courtroom became available to every newspaperman who wanted to look at them and make stories on them and copy them exactly, and yet they are still regarded as top secret. They cannot be published without saying they are violating the classification statute.

Nothing could exhibit better that classification is forever.

The Classification System and Historical Research Problems ([64], pp. 88–92)

The reprinted excerpts from the May 22, 1973 House Committee on Government Operations report on classification and freedom of information highlight the problems faced by scholars and researchers working with classified foreign affairs documents. The declassification project referred to in the text progressed under the stimulus of President Richard M. Nixon's Executive Order 11652 (reprinted in the Appendix), as well as continuing pressure from Congress and individuals. Hearings held by the Senate Government Operations Committee in May and June 1974 comment on the progress made and the procedures followed by various intelligence agencies in declassifying information. However, Representative Bella Abzug reported considerable frustration in attempting to obtain declassification of certain documents pertaining to the Warren Commission (President's Commission on the Assassination of President Kennedy) probes of President John F. Kennedy's assassination ([73], pp. 86 ff.). The provisions of Executive Order 11652 and the Freedom of Information Act permit the agencies that supply documents upon request, classified or not, to charge fees for both searching and copying. When the material requested is voluminous, the charges of 5¢ to 20¢ per page copied and $3 to $6 an hour for "search time" can price government out of the reach of many.*

*For information on ordering documents from intelligence agencies under FOIA procedures, see "Abstracts of Documents Released under the Freedom of Information Act Relating to Foreign Policy and National Defense" in the Appendix. *The Federal Register* also publishes rules and procedures for FOIA requests, including a schedule of copying charges. The intelligence agencies are covered in the following editions of the *Register:* NSA, vol. 40, no. 34, p. 7316; vol. 40, no. 16, p. 3612; CIA, vol. 40, no. 34, p. 7294; vol. 40, no. 12, p. 3010; vol. 40, no. 168, p. 39778; vol. 40, no. 113, p. 24897; DOD, vol. 40, no. 39, p. 8190; DIA, vol. 40, no. 34, p. 7303; DMA, vol. 40, no. 29, p. 6336; State Department, vol. 40, no. 34, p. 7256.

The unique problems of scholars and historians seeking access to classified Government documents and records of events are a highly specialized part of the total security classification dilemma. Over the years the subcommittee has received many complaints of governmental abuses and many requests for assistance from researchers who are endeavoring to cope with the vast and complex maze of security restrictions in order to obtain access to various departmental or Archives records for scholarly purposes.

Few would argue with the general premise concerning the overall need of Government to avoid carrying out its certain sensitive operations in a "goldfish bowl," particularly in these days of international tension. Certainly, there can be overwhelming public support for the following broad policy statement contained in the preamble to

N9 Executive Order 11652:

> Within the Federal Government there is some official information and material which, because it bears directly on the effectiveness of our national defense and the conduct of our foreign relations, must be subject to some constraints for the security of our Nation and the safety of our people and our allies. To protect against actions hostile to the United States, of both overt and covert nature, it is essential that such official information and material be given only limited dissemination.

Such a statement is even more readily acceptable when it is placed within the context of the first paragraph of Executive Order 11652:

> The interests of the United States and its citizens are best served by making information regarding the affairs of Government readily available to the public. This concept of an informed citizenry is reflected in the Freedom of Information Act and in the current public information policies of the executive branch.

Noted historian Arthur Schlesinger, Jr., pointed out in a recent article that "the functioning of democracy requires some rough but rational balance between secrecy and disclosure, between official control of information and public need for it."

During the past several years, the secrecy policies of Government have become more and more a matter of public attention and concern. Historians, political scientists, journalists, and others have become more interested in the study and analysis of contemporary foreign policy and recent diplomatic history and have protested governmental restrictions on study and research of official records. A report on scholar's access to Government documents, prepared by the 20th Century Fund earlier this year, describes the broad scope of the problem: [219]

> In essence, the security classification system and other restrictions on access to records permit government officials to control the flow of information to the public. The executive departments, particularly the presidency, can dominate the headlines with official pronouncements, news releases, press conferences, and publication of documents. An administration can even "blow the lid" on its own secrecy, as shown by

---

[219] Carol M. Barker and Matthew H. Fox, "Classified Files: The Yellowing Pages." A report on scholars' access to Government documents. New York: The Twentieth Century Fund: 1972. pp. 4-5.

President Nixon's recent disclosure of the secret negotiations with the North Vietnamese. Off-the-record briefings and leaks to the press permit officials to discuss policy and events—often without taking responsibility for what they reveal. Former officials publish memoirs of their years in office; government departments issue their own histories of significant events; favored scholars and journalists are sometimes given access to official records that remain off limits to others.

In each case, officials or former officials exercise discretion in choosing what to reveal and what to conceal. As a consequence, the public must rely on sources that have some vested interest in the information that is given out.

What the public has not received—or has waited decades for—are accounts of government operations based on firsthand records and commentaries by detached observers. The State Department, which has maintained a thirty-year limit on classification of its files, did not make the official record of American diplomacy in World War II available to the general public until January 1972. The documents on most of our Cold-War diplomacy remain in closed files. The Joint Chiefs of Staff have only recently opened segments of their World War II records, and their postwar files are unavailable for any nonofficial purpose. Few Army records from the post-1945 period are available to unofficial researchers even on a restricted basis. Researchers at the Truman Library in Independence, Missouri, still cannot use some of the secret documents on which Mr. Truman based his memoirs, published in 1958.

The importance of scholarly research access to historical documents in our free society cannot be overemphasized. As one witness, Lloyd C. Gardner, chairman of the history department at Rutgers University, pointed out:

Historians and other scholars concerned with the reconstruction of the past perform, or should perform, an important service in a democratic society.

Traditionally, historians provide a nation with its memory, but in an open representative society, they are also obligated to sustain a dialog with the government and its policymakers. It is not too much to say that this second aspect of the citizen-scholar's responsibility is an essential part of the definition of an open society.

Without access to Government documents, however, he cannot function effectively in either capacity. In 1959, as a graduate student researching a book on New Deal diplomacy, I was able, with much difficulty, to see certain files for the years 1940-41. Thirteen years later the latest date open to scholars is only 1945, with certain classified documents still exempted. In those 13 years, scholars have thus lost eight or nine in terms of access.

Mr. Paul L. Ward, executive secretary of the American Historical Association, said:

Historians and their fellow scholars who have dealt with official documents are fully aware, at the same time, of the human and practical realities surrounding the generation and preservation of records, both official and personal. We recognize the importance for rational decisionmaking and for responsible administration of both putting on paper communications and proposals and of keeping these pieces of paper as records for consultation when related problems thereafter arise. We recognize the threat to these necessary practices when confidentiality for an appropriate time cannot be assured. We would argue, indeed, that the confidence of working administrators in this necessary confidentiality, a confidence so shaken in recent months by a whole series of leaks to the press, cannot be reestablished without a better structure of classification and declassification of documents, a structure that both protects confidentiality while needed and also assures public scrutiny in time enough so that government mistakes do not snowball into self-perpetuating burdens upon our country's minds and energies.

N10

Dr. James B. Rhoads, Archivist of the United States, described the dimensions of the problem that the 38-year-old National Archives faces in this regard in the following terms:

In the last generation we have grown a great deal. We have become the National Archives and Records Service. We conduct an on-going records management program working with agency officials and their files. We operate 15 Federal Records Centers and six Presidential libraries, in addition to the National Archives itself. We have in our custody approximately 30 billion pages of Federal records, something more than 40 percent of the total volume of the Government's records. But while both our activities and our holdings have expanded, our goals remain the same: to serve the rest of the Government by caring for its non-current records and to serve the public in general by making available the documents of enduring value.

Because of our double mission—serving both the rest of Government and the public—we are particularly sensitive to the problem of restrictions on access to records and other historical materials. We are well aware of the conviction within Government that a degree of confidentiality is essential for the national security and for the proper operation of Government. We are also aware of the equally widespread insistence on the part of historians and other researchers that they receive access to records, for we are most often the first to receive their requests and their complaints.

As we have grown in recent years and as agencies have retired their more recent, 20th century, records, we have increasingly had to face the problem of handling classified documents. This is a difficult problem. Indeed, it is one of the most difficult problems that we in the National Archives and Records Service face.

Dr. Rhoads went on to describe the relationship between researchers, the National Archives, and the handling of classified documents:

* * * There are now six Presidential libraries. All are open for research, and all but one, the Herbert Hoover Library, contain significant quantities of classified material originated by the White House. In the absence of any explicit means in

the earlier Executive order for declassification of this material, this has created a very serious and obvious problem. Section 11 of the new Executive order provides an explicit means for the declassification of such documents, most of which have come to rest—and hopefully, will continue to come to rest— in one of our Presidential libraries. This section provides that we can now declassify Presidential and White House classified documents. In doing so, we must observe the guidelines provided by the new Executive order itself in section 5, consult with departments having primary subject matter interest before making a final decision, and observe the terms of the donor's deed of gift. Section 11, contrary to certain comments, does not add new or extra restrictions. In fact, it liberalizes access by providing an explicit, and we believe, effective means of declassifying the all important Presidential and White House documents which hitherto have existed in a kind of classification limbo.

He cited a provision of the new Executive order that he felt would greatly expedite the declassification process by the Archives:

I am aware, Mr. Chairman, that the new Executive order has been described by some as not going far enough. However, there are a number of new elements in the order which would materially hasten the process of declassification.
Section 3(E) of the new order provides that:

Classified information or material transferred to the General Services Administration for accession into the Archives of the United States shall be downgraded and declassified by the Archivist of the United States in accordance with this order, directives of the President issued through the National Security Council and pertinent regulations of the departments.

N11

This is new. For the first time the staff of the National Archives and Records Service will have the authority to declassify classified documents. In the past, much time and much paper has been expended in our obtaining authorization from individual agencies to declassify particular records of those agencies. Now, equipped with nothing more than the guidelines that will be provided to us by the agencies and the National Security Council, along with those already spelled out in the new Executive order itself, we can take the action of declassification on our own. This will eliminate the time-consuming delays which so annoy researchers and the paper-producing memos which annoy both those who must write them and those who receive them. * * *

CONGRESSIONAL OVERSIGHT

As secrecy is an imperative in intelligence activities, accountability is an imperative in a democratic society. And while there is an elaborate system designed to protect matters of secrecy within the intelligence community, accountability has proven ineffective, especially in the area of covert action. An efficient system for public accountability can only be realized through the oversight of the elected representatives of the people—the Congress. This has been recognized in the past in varying degrees, but only reached the level of broad national concern in the 1970s, when revelations about CIA involvement in various covert enterprises, including assassination attempts, became public.*

The 94th Congress narrowed the oversight issue to that of committee structures and operating orders that would "facilitate the process of: (a) restoring the confidence of the Congress and the public in U.S. intelligence agencies and in Congressional oversight thereof; (b) considering proposals by the Select Committees on Intelligence and the Administration regarding reform of the intelligence community; (c) reviewing and, if necessary, revising the basic legislation governing the intelligence agencies, and monitoring compliance therewith; (d) monitoring the activities of the intelligence agencies; (e) providing the intelligence agencies with the necessary funds and support for their missions."†

Of paramount concern in the hearings and debate on congressional oversight was the sharing of intelligence information with the committees and procedures to be followed for congressional oversight and/or approval of covert action. By the conclusion of the 94th Congress, committee jurisdictions had been established and a record of congressional concern and oversight interest had been established to guide the House and Senate committees.

In the documents that follow, the views of various experts on intelligence oversight matters are presented, including those of the Pike Committee and the Murphy Commission. Chapter 10 concludes with excerpts from the Senate debate on the passage of Senate Resolution 400, which established the Senate Select Committee on Intelligence and named as its chairman (during the 95th Congress) Senator Daniel Inouye.

*William N. Raiford, a senior analyst in the Foreign Affairs and National Defense Division of the Congressional Research Service, prepared an "Issue Brief" on congressional oversight of intelligence that contains a detailed chronology of past congressional interest in oversight. Another Congressional Research Service study by Raiford, Mark Lowenthal, and Gene Resnick provides annotated listings of published congressional hearings and reports concerning the intelligence community ([97], [102]). Their index was compiled from *Congressional Information Service Annuals* for 1970–1975.

†[97], p. 1.

Congress and the Growth of the Intelligence Community ([90], pp. 89–94)

Harry Howe Ransom, a member of the Vanderbilt University and University of Texas faculties, served as a consultant to the Commission for the Study of the Conduct of Foreign Policy (Murphy Commission). Prior to the formation of the Pike and Church Committees, he prepared a critique of congressional oversight procedures and past practices (vol. 7 of the Murphy report appendices). This study provides an insight into the issues that confronted the Murphy Commission.

When Congress established the CIA in 1947 and expanded the authority of its Director in 1949, other existing government intelligence units were by no means eliminated. These included Army, Navy and Air Force intelligence with many specialized sub-units (such as the Army Mapping Service). Also included are the State Department, the Atomic Energy Commission, and the Federal Bureau of Investigation (F.B.I.). During World War II the F.B.I. had extensive intelligence operations in Latin America, but, after 1947, its activities were confined to counter-intelligence within the United States.

In the quarter century of Cold War, existing intelligence agencies grew in size and several new ones were created. Notable among the new ones were the National Security Agency (NSA), created by Executive Order in 1952, and the Defense Intelligence Agency (DIA), created by Department of Defense Directive in 1961. Note that these two enormous institutions, NSA and DIA, were created by executive fiat rather than congressional statute. Meanwhile, technology constantly offered new tools for each step in the intelligence process, from collection through evaluation and interpretation to dissemination. And so additional giant bureaucracies arose, such as the Air Force-affiliated program for overhead reconnaissance and the National Photo Interpretation Center (NPIC). A proliferation of organizations, bureaus, mechanical apparatus, and personnel boosted the annual cost of foreign intelligence to the United States to a peak estimated at $6 billion.

The control which Congress has over this elaborate and extensive system will be discussed below. As a preview of the situation, the recent (Oct. 1974) comment of one U. S. Senator, Howard Baker (R., Tenn.), can be cited. He said: "I do not think there is a man in the legislative part of government who really knows what is going on in the intelligence community. . . ."

CONTROLS WITHIN CONGRESS

To the extent that Congress formally monitors the various intelligence agencies of the Executive Branch, such surveillance emanates from four separate units on Capitol Hill. In the Senate, the Armed Services and Appropriations Committees have designated specific members as intelligence "watchdogs." In both the House and Senate, there are separate subcommittees on intelligence of the Appropriations and Armed Services Committees. A total of nine members in the Senate and twelve in the House has the formal responsibility for monitoring intelligence. The basic question is whether the work of these groups constitutes a thorough detailed monitoring of a multi-billion dollar intelligence system.

At the outset it should be made clear that adequate research has not been done to determine the complete facts about the processes for, and degree of, scrutiny given to the intelligence system by various units of Congress. One reason for this is that members of those units in Congress with this jurisdiction have been very reticent in revealing how they operate, and no systematic survey has been conducted on Capitol Hill.

From the evidence available, the impression is that formal congressional surveillance of the CIA and intelligence system over the years has been sporadic, spotty, and essentially uncritical. Furthermore, it is probably true that most members of Congress know very little about the intelligence community or about the Congressional structure for overseeing that community. At least a number of members in both houses have stated this to be so.

In their more active years the House subcommittees may have met around a half a dozen times annually. In other words, the House subcommittees may have spent as much as 15–20 hours per year on their surveillance assignment. And this would be in an active year. Also, the absence of a staff or of a record of the committees' hearings or reports may make even this amount of time less significant than it would seem to be. Exceptions would be special ad hoc investigations, including Watergate-related matters.

The Armed Services and the Appropriations intelligence subcommittees in the Senate have been similarly inactive. For a number of years they met separately. In the 1960s, however, because of overlapping membership, the two groups began to meet jointly. In fact, the late Senator Richard Russell was chairman of both subcommittees for several years; during this period there was in effect only one Senate Committee. Has it become more active in recent years? The subcommittee did not meet in 1971! One part-time staff member has served the Senate subcommittees. Three "visiting members" were added in 1966 from the Foreign Relations Committee, after a bitter controversy. Without adequate professional staff assistance, busy legislators are not likely to be prepared often to ask the right questions.

The basic criticism of the activities of the House and Senate intelligence subcommittees are these, in order of importance: first, they tend not so much to control or criticize the system as to protect it from its critics; they meet infrequently; they have little or no staff, and with rare exceptions publish no hearings or reports, do not communicate their findings to their colleagues in the House or Senate, or to the public; and they are inhibited in conversations with colleagues by being privy to some state secrets. In a word, they appear to have been co-opted by the intelligence system. Put another way, they do not seem to function as independent critics.

Members of the House and Senate subcommittees are selected by Armed Services and Appropriations Committee chairmen with apparent great care, guided normally by the seniority system. The Armed Services subcommittees review structure and some operations, but not the budgets, which come under Appropriations subcommittee jurisdiction.

Who are these watchdogs? *Congressional Quarterly* has reported the view that the oversight subcommittees are biased in favor of the agencies they monitor. The American Security Council, a private interest group that keeps score on members of Congress in terms of their support for a large defense establishment, "graded" these subcommittee members. In the House, 10 of the 12 oversight committee members were given 100 per cent favorable ratings on the ASC survey; one received 90 per cent; and one received zero (Lucien Nedzi). In the Senate group, of the nine Senators, three received 100 per cent ratings; four recieved ratings of 80 per cent or better; the remaining two received ratings of 33 and 10 (Pastore and Symington).

Defenders of the adequacy of present Congressional supervision of intelligence activities point to the existence of the previously mentioned four subcommittees created to review the activities of the CIA and other intelligence agencies.

The official stand of the CIA is that the Agency keeps the House and Senate subcommittees informed on every aspect of its operations, programs, budget, and personnel strength and that it provides periodic briefings on world events. The Agency also claims to be in continuing contact on virtually a daily basis with the chairman and staff members of the four subcommittees. The Agency also briefs a number of other Congressional committees on substantive issues on request. For the period 1967-72, the Agency says it averaged some 23 briefings of this type per year. Briefings for individual Congressmen are also given; in the same period, these averaged some 80 per year. Additionally, in the same period there were more than one thousand written communications, and 1,500 personal contacts per year between agency officials and individual Congressmen. As of September, 1974, CIA Director Colby reported that "the CIA has appeared before 13 committees on 28 occasions this year (Armed Services, Appropriations, Foreign Affairs, Atomic Energy, and Economics) testifying on a variety of subjects."

A strong move was made in the Senate in 1956, under the leadership of Mike Mansfield, to create a Joint Congressional Committee on Intelligence Activities. After a substantial debate on the floor, the Mansfield resolution was defeated by a vote of 59 to 27. Among those voting for the Joint Committee was Senator John F. Kennedy; among those opposing was Senator Lyndon B. Johnson. In general, the Senate's "inner Club" killed the measure, feeling that the Senate's leaders could know all they needed to know at any time about the intelligence system. One well informed observer, plausibly explained Senate behavior as follows: "To be blunt about it, and perhaps to overstate it, neither the

CIA nor the people who now watch over it [in the Senate] fully trust the people who want to watch over it; and the people who want to watch over it do not fully trust either the agency or its present watchers." At any rate, some of those with access to secrets felt that they had little "need to know" of details of the dirty business of espionage and underground political action overseas.

The issue was debated again in 1966 when Senator Eugene McCarthy, a member of the Senate Foreign Relations Committee, attempted to have that committee investigate United States Intelligence activities abroad. Failing that, McCarthy pushed for a watered-down compromise which no more than included several members of the Foreign Relations Committee on the Senate's intelligence surveillance committee (Armed Services). This mild measure failed in a Senate vote of 61 to 28.

In debates over such proposals the basic question has been: how thorough is congressional surveillance? Because the existing watchdog committees have no full-time staff, as such, and because they keep no records or minutes and because their membership tends to be reticent in discussing activities, it is difficult to judge precisely the extent to which these groups pay careful attention to details of the intelligence system. One gains the impression, however, that surveillance is very sporadic and timid. It would appear that the surveillance committees are particularly manipulable by the intelligence establishment.

A former Secretary of the Air Force and veteran member of the Armed Services Committee, Senator Stuart Symington, observed: "There is no federal agency in our government whose activities receive less scrutiny and control than the CIA." To supplement Symington's point, it should be noted that the House Armed Services Subcommittee for the CIA met only twice in 1970 and 1969. The Senate Armed Services CIA subcommittee held no sessions in 1973 prior to confirmation hearings for Colby; it met once in 1969 and twice in 1970. And recall that, with the exception of Watergate-related matters, in neither House has any of the four subcommittees on intelligence ever issued a report on its supervisory work. In November, 1971, Symington got only 30 votes when he proposed to create a Select Committee to oversee activities of the CIA. And so in 1956, 27 votes; 1966, 28 votes; and 1971, 30 votes. Until Watergate, the persuasive case could not be made in Congress that a more institutionalized and active surveillance of intelligence activities is a Congressional responsibility. Whether Watergate will effect permanent changes remains to be seen.

To summarize, Congress has a committee structure for monitoring the intelligence community. Knowledge of the workings of this structure is incomplete. It would appear that certain types of intelligence information are in fact given only to the chairman and ranking minority member of these committees; the other members appear to be both somewhat complacent and decidedly reticent. A sharp view of this situation has been expressed by Congressman Drinan, who asserted in 1973: "The senior members of the House and of the Senate have conspired to prevent the younger members of the House and of the Senate [from] knowing anything about the CIA." And the Director of Central Intelligence testified in 1973 that "the appropriations arrangements [for the intelligence budget] are in accordance with the wishes of the Appropriations Committees."

Over the years since 1947, the Congressional structure has been inactive, except on occasions of publicity about intelligence operations that have failed or covert operations that have been exposed. Since 1947, more than 200 bills have been introduced in Congress to expand the system for Congressional surveillance of the intelligence community. To date, none has been enacted. The responsibility for this inaction rests with Congress rather than the leaders of the Executive Branch or the intelligence community. However, Presidents and Directors of Central Intelligence have no doubt manipulated this issue to some extent over the years. The Director in 1974 publicly stated his position that "the method by which Congress exercises its oversight of intelligence activity is a matter for Congress to decide." In making this decision, Congressional leaders no doubt are influenced by the judgments of intelligence professionals as to what should be disclosed. The adequacy of Congressional oversight will be discussed in the conclusions below.

THE "CONGRESSIONAL BACKDROP"

Those who focus on the formal structure of Congressional controls—and usually find them, as I do, inadequate—often overlook the "Congressional backdrop" role. Congress is a formidable presence in the minds of leaders of the Executive agencies. They know that no penny can be disbursed from the Federal Treasury until authorized and appropriated on Capitol Hill. They know of the potent investigative and publicity power of Congress. And they know that what Congress gave in the way of discretionary authority to, for example, the Director of CIA in 1947 and 1949, Congress can take back. They know, too, that the temper of the times can change, so that Congress may increasingly question the value or necessity of world-wide intelligence activities by the U.S. government. They know that Congress can demand information about secret operations that it has not sought in the past. And they now know that by leaks or by the acts of disaffected former employees, facts will come to light that may reveal that Congress and the public have been duped. The "Top Secret" or other higher secret classification labels are no longer guarantees of controlled secrecy. In various ways, then, the existence of Congress with its several roles and ultimate authority provides real pressures and constraints on the Executive. The ultimate constraint is an aroused public opinion demanding that Congress exert itself in a given realm.

In spite of a weak formal structure for systematic surveillance of intelligence activities, Congress has, over the years, probed the intelligence system from time to time in such a way that the Congressional presence is not likely ever to have been fully ignored by intelligence leaders in the Executive Branch. In the process, Congress, and its units, can of course be used as weapons in the internecine struggles from time to time among various parts of the intelligence establishment within the Executive Branch.

Without going into detail, examples of Congressional activity can be listed:

Hoover Commission Reports, 1949, 1955, in each case issuing reports critical of the intelligence system and proposing reforms.

Cuban Missile Crisis, 1962 in which the Senate Preparedness Investigating Subcommittee found that intelligence agencies had performed poorly in some areas and committed substantial errors.

The Pueblo Incident, 1968 in which a House Armed Services subcommittee found serious deficiencies in intelligence policy, organization and control.

Symington Investigation of the Secret War in Laos, 1970–71, in which a foreign relations subcommittee disclosed that the U. S. was fighting a CIA-managed "secret war" in Laos, (without Congressional authorization or knowledge).

Secret Funding of Radio Free Europe (RFE), in which the Senate, under the initiative of Senator Clifford Case and others, forced the end of the subsidy to RFE, and Radio Liberty, which had begun in secret in 1950.

Restraints on Foreign Aid Bill, in which Congress, in early 1972, passed a foreign aid authorization bill placing new and unprecedented controls on the cost, operations, and personnel of the CIA, prohibiting transfer of funds from the Pentagon. The purpose was to prevent the development of secret warfare in Cambodia, as had happened in Laos.

Investigation of CIA Role in Watergate-related matters, in which the House Armed Services Subcommittee on Intelligence under its Chairman, Lucien Nedzi, investigated, in 1973, how the CIA allowed itself to be used improperly by the White House in domestic political action. Revision of the National Security Act of 1947 to prevent future abuses was recommended.

A number of other examples of this sort could be cited, such as Congressional investigations and public reports on the U-2 incident in 1960; the Bay of Pigs in 1961; Senator Howard Baker's special investigation, as part of the Ervin Committee probe, of CIA's involvement in Watergate; and other intelligence flaps, including still-unfolding Watergate-related scandals.

Suffice it to say that all such events are part of an "interactive" process in which Congress and the Executive joust with each other in a dynamic political process. Meanwhile, one may be certain that leaders of the Intelligence Community from time to time see their opportunities and take advantage of them. Presumably CIA: (a) discreetly does favors for individual legislators from time to time, such as providing material for speeches or special favors overseas; (b) offers special confidential briefings; and (c) any CIA leadership worth its salt knows how to "lobby" privately and at the appropriate time with legislators behind closed doors. About these assumed "interactions" we have too little evidence. But surely they are part of the system, with substantial impact on policy outcomes.

As a generalization it is probably true that, the greater the perceived external threat to national security, the fewer the questions that Congress will ask about secret intelligence. As perceptions of external dangers change, Congress may be expected to reassert itself and demand to be more fully informed, and may be somewhat less susceptible to executive manipulation.

CONCLUSIONS

Let us in conclusion return to the basic questions earlier posed. *First,* what did Congress intend when it created a Central Intelligence Agency in 1947 and revised the legislation in 1949? The record clearly suggests that the legislative intent in 1947 was to create an agency for the collection, evaluation, analysis, interpretation, and communication of information on foreign affairs to decision makers. Congress did not intend in 1947 to create an agency for covert political operations. The 1949 amendments are somewhat ambiguous in this regard, for they gave to the Director of Central Intelligence a great deal of discretionary authority for the secret expenditure of funds and Congress, in effect, removing the CIA from the usual requirements for disclosure of personnel, methods, and expenditures. It is not clear that Congress as a whole realized what was being given up in 1949 and for what purpose. It would seem that the purpose was in part covert operations; similarly it would seem that Congress was deceived in this regard. Congress should now take another close, hard look at the statutory base for the Central Intelligence Agency and related intelligence activities.

A *second* question posed was whether the Congressional "watchdog" system has either a bark or a bite. On the most secret matters the Congressional watchdog function is in the hands of four or five senior legislators—as chairmen of Armed Services and Appropriations Committees or subcommittees in the House and Senate. Each member of Congress may technically have access to some of the deep secrets about covert operations and intelligence that come to Capitol Hill. But few avail themselves of this opportunity. Indeed, the senior watchdogs appear to have maintained only a casual interest in these matters over the years. For example, when Director of Central Intelligence Colby testified on covert operations in Chile (April, 1974), only the House Armed Services Intelligence Subcommittee Chairman, Lucien Nedzi, and one staff member, were in attendance. The record indicates that Congress has supervised the intelligence system in sporadic and haphazard form over the years, with jurisdictions split between armed services and appropriations and with foreign relations frozen out by these jurisdictional boundaries.

Nearly twenty years ago a Hoover Commission Task Force on Intelligence Activities (Gen. Mark Clark, chairman) recommended the creation of a Joint Congressional Committee on Foreign Intelligence Activities. The group feared "the possibility of the growth of license and abuses of power where disclosures of costs, organization, personnel, and functions are precluded by law." Aware of the pros and cons of the debate over the desirability of creating a Joint Committee, I have believed for many years that this would be not only desirable but is an urgent need to counter a sometimes overwhelming Executive power. Such a committee would be no panacea, but on balance it would be valuable to the preservation of the democratic idea. Such a committee would have a professional staff and would have access to full information about budgets, organization, personnel, programs, and operations. Some of such material obviously would have to be handled as classified information and not disclosed publicly.

A *third* and related question is whether relevant committees of Congress, especially Appropriations, Armed Services and Foreign Relations-Affairs, should have legally full access to all intelligence reports, estimates and special studies that are available to Executive Branch decision makers. Here again, in principle, it seems clear and logical, that Congress cannot perform a meaningful role in the formulation of foreign policy if it does not have equal access to all intelligence information available to the President and his foreign policy advisers. Senators John Sherman Cooper and Clifford Case proposed to amend the National Security Act in 1972 (S. 2224) to give Congress legal access to intelligence, but Congress has not adopted the proposal. The rationale for it is best stated by Senator Cooper: ". . . Congress, which must make decisions upon foreign policy and national security, which is called upon to commit the material and human resources of the nation, should have access to all available information and foreign intelligence to discharge properly and morally its responsibility to our government and its people." Who can quarrel with that? Well, Executive Branch representatives did quarrel on the basis of the problem of selectivity, of security and Executive privilege, and the proposal was defeated. Without full intelligence information, the Congressional participation in national security policy will be a sham. Congress, to be sure, will continue to play its "deterrent" or "backdrop" role, but this will remain limited and ad hoc. Suffice it to say that adequate information is a key to a meaningful role in foreign policy decision making. Indeed, an uninformed Congress is as much a danger to the Republic as a Congress manipulated by a President.

Fourth, and finally, is the most difficult question of whether Congress should participate in the authorization of covert operations. This issue will be determined ultimately by how one conceptualizes covert political operations overseas. If one sees them simply as another instrument in the arsenal of foreign policy tools, one may allow wide Presidential discretion in determining the use of such operations. Perhaps some minimal Congressional guidelines and general Congressional approval might be expected. On the other hand, if covert operations are seen as acts just short of war, violating international law and the United Nations Charter, one might stipulate that Congress ought to approve any covert operation in much the same manner as a declaration of war. Otherwise, a danger exists that the nation would lapse into Presidential dictatorship in the realm of foreign policy. I believe that a major covert intervention in the political affairs of a sovereign nation constitutes an act of extreme

coercion, just short of war. I believe it would be wise for Congress to be involved, through a generally representative committee in such decisions. I believe further, as earlier indicated, that present statutory authority with regard to the CIA is insufficiently explicit to authorize most kinds of covert political operations. Congress should clarify its legislation for the intelligence system. In the process of reconsidering the CIA statute, the whole issue of intelligence policy, organization, and controls could be thoroughly studied and debated. To assist in such a debate, it would be useful for President and Congress to create a "Hoover Commission" type study of the intelligence establishment for a thorough study of the whole system for secret foreign intelligence and covert operations. It has been twenty years since a study of this kind has been made. Perhaps the Murphy Commission will want to recommend such further study of the problem. It would be a great mistake not to give this matter a most careful study for it may be that our democratic form of government hangs in the balance among security, secrecy, and representative government. It may be, as some have argued, that there is no democratic way to manage or conduct secret foreign operations. If so, this should be an acknowledged cost in any calculation of the benefits versus the costs of such activities. To date, I believe that the costs have exceeded the benefits of covert operations. It is somewhat encouraging to note what the current CIA Director said in his Senate confirmation hearings (1973). Said William E. Colby: "We are not going to run the kind of intelligence service that other countries run. We are going to run one in the American society, and the American constitutional structure, and I can see that there may be a requirement to expose to the American people a great deal more than might be convenient from the narrow intelligence point of view."

Finally, let me say that perhaps now is the time to seek detente with our major adversaries in the nether world of covert operations. For secret operations and secret operators can threaten any form of government. What we don't know can harm us.

Congress and Oversight Issues

SENATOR SAM ERVIN ON EXECUTIVE PRIVILEGE
([28A], pp. 4–7)

While security classification conceals intelligence secrets from public scrutiny, Executive privilege is invoked by the Executive branch to shield secrets from the Legislative and Judicial branches, whose members can and do claim legitimate access to state secrets. The notion that the president has Executive authority to withhold "privileged" information from the Congress and the courts has been examined earlier in this chapter by prominent legal scholars.

Sam Ervin, chairman of the Senate Select Committee on Presidential Campaign Activities, and himself a constitutional authority, was charged with the investigation of the Watergate affair. In the following document, Ervin attacks both the legal validity of Executive privilege and the use to which it had been put by the administration of President Richard M. Nixon. His statement, partially reprinted here, was presented as an "expert witness" during the joint hearings of the Senate Committees on the Judiciary and Government Operations in the course of their hearings on Executive privilege, secrecy in government, and freedom of information. It provides an insight into the effect of Executive privilege upon congressional oversight activities generally, as well as those regarding the intelligence community.

The use of so-called executive privilege as a device by which the Executive withholds information from the Congress has given rise to increasing concern voiced by many Members of the Congress, especially in light of the recent hearings on the nomination of L. Patrick Gray as Director of the FBI and the impending investigation by the Select Committee on Presidential Campaign Activities.

As we are all aware, the failure or outright refusal of Federal officers and employees to produce information requested by the Congress for its use in carrying out its constitutional obligation to legislate has resulted in a serious erosion in the separation of powers principle embodied in the Constitution.

In an attempt to determine the extent to which departments and agencies of the Federal Government have refused to furnish to the Congress information requested in the form of written documents or oral testimony, the Subcommittee on Separation of Powers several weeks ago embarked on an ambitious project: It made a detailed survey of every joint committee, committee, subcommittee of the Congress and the General Accounting Office. While the survey is not completed, *the subcommittee has received sufficient results to show that over one hundred and thirty specific instances of refusals to provide written information or testimony to the Committees of the Senate and House have occurred since January 1964.* These preliminary results of the survey show beyond peradventure that the executive branch has failed to furnish a substantial amount of the information the Congress has requested from executive departments and agencies. When the survey is completed I believe the evidence compiled will leave no doubt that Congress must devise some means to require executive departments and agencies to adhere to the Constitutional duty to furnish to the Congress the information it seeks.

For almost 6 years, the Senate Judiciary Subcommittee on Separation of Powers, which I am honored to serve as chairman, has studied the problems raised by so-called executive privilege, and in July 1971, the subcommittee conducted 5 days of hearings on the subject. At that time the subcommittee considered S. 1125, a bill introduced by Senator Fulbright, designed to limit the assertion of executive privilege. During those hearings, the subcommittee explored the conflict between the alleged power of the President to withhold information when he feels its disclosure would impede him in the conduct of his office, and the power of the legislative branch to obtain information needed to legislate wisely and effectively. The basic right of the tax-paying public to know what its Government is doing and the underlying facts upon which it bases its actions also were considered.

These basic interests have clashed repeatedly since President Washington's first term, when the Congress undertook to investigate the St. Clair expedition. Without objecting to the propriety of the investigation, President Washington's advisors concluded that, while the Congress might institute inquiries, and call for papers generally, and while the Executive ought to provide those that the public good would permit, the Executive nonetheless had the discretionary power to refuse *to communicate any information the disclosure of which would injure the public.* Despite this contention of his advisory, President Washington did turn over all of the requested papers to the Congress. Thus, the often-cited St. Clair incident by no means constitutes precedent for withholding of information from the Congress by the President or departments or agencies of the Federal Government.

There is little disagreement that the power to institute inquiries and exact information is integral to the congressional power to legislate—*McGrain* v. *Daugherty*, 273 U.S. 135 (1927). However, several Presidents have urged that the Chief Executive has the power to withhold information from the Congress and from the public, based upon Article II Section 3 of the Constitution, which requires the President to see that the "laws are faithfully executed". Chief Executives have argued that a certain amount of secrecy is mandatory to give the President the necessary autonomy to discharge his duties. Since he cannot exercise all of his powers alone, it is urged that there is a derivative power applicable to all the members of the executive branch, an assertion that is even more devastating to the checks-and-balances principle.

In 1962, President Kennedy attempted to end the practice of delegating to employees the authority to claim executive privilege. In his March 7, 1962, letter to the House Special Government Information Subcommittee of the Government Operations Committee, President Kennedy stated that the basic policy of his administration on the question of executive privilege would be that only the President could invoke executive privilege, and that the privilege would not be used "without specific Presidential approval." Presidents Johnson and Nixon reaffirmed in writing this policy of limited exercise of executive privilege. Nevertheless, this theoretical control over the withholding of information does not operate satisfactorily in practice, and over the years Congress has encountered numerous instances of withholding of information essential in carrying out its constitutional powers.

Even if these Presidential policy statements were to operate as well in practice as in theory, it still would be notable that the practice of executive privilege has developed subject to the will or whim of each succeeding President, and that there has been no legislative enactment relating to its existence or exercise, nor have there been any definitive judicial decisions. The result has been that the formal or informal withholding of information from the Congress has become part and parcel of the growing power of the executive branch vis-a-vis the Congress.

This shifting of power away from the legislative branch and into the hands of the Executive has come about primarily from the failure of the Congress to assert and exercise its constitutional powers. This, in conjunction with the almost unlimited delegation of authority to the bureaucracy, has placed the Congress in the position of being the chief aggrandizer of the Executive. The resulting increase in executive power has come close to creating "a government of men, not of laws."

Aside from the enormous problems that refusals to provide information pose in terms of the separation of powers principle, the practice contravenes an underlying assumption of the Constitution; namely, that the free flow of ideas and information and the open and full disclosure of the governing process is essential to the operation of our democratic form of government. Any lessening in available information results in lessened citizen participation, and in a virtual absence of accountability on the part of those who govern. Thus, it is plain that the exercise of the assumed power of executive privilege undergirds the growing policy of governmental secrecy that is so inimical to our freedoms.

Despite growing objections to this unwarranted use of executive power, the past months have seen no letup; indeed, in February, during the hearings which the Subcommittee on Separation of Powers conducted in conjunction with an ad hoc subcommittee of the Government Operations Committee, it appeared that Secretary of Agriculture Butz and Administrator William Ruckelshaus of the Environmental Protection Agency, under the direction of the Administration, would refuse to come and testify on the subject of executive impoundment of funds appropriated for programs to be carried out by their respective departments. Only after the subcommittees made it plain that the testimony of the two government witnesses was essential to the inquiry and that they were prepared to issue subpoenas, if necessary, did the administration decide that it would be appropriate for these two officials to appear and present the testimony requested.

Moreover, during the hearings held in the last Congress by my Subcommittee on Constitutional Rights on the reprehensible practice of Army surveillance over civilians, the subcommittee repeatedly requested information, documents, and the testimony of certain military officers. However, the subcommittee was refused consistently on the ground, inter alia, that it had no need for the information or testimony requested, but at no time was the doctrine of executive privilege formally invoked by the President. There are numerous similar instances involving the heads of Federal departments and agencies.

Even the hearings today have not been spared of administration refusals to offer pertinent testimony. In a letter dated March 23, 1973, Mr. Roy L. Ash, Director of the Office of Management and Budget, refused a request to appear before these subcommittees on the grounds that ". . . the questions raised by the subjects of executive privilege and freedom of information are essentially legal in nature . . . therefore, there is nothing of real substance which I could add to the testimony you will receive from the Department of Justice."

In light of the position Mr. Ash occupies, at the very pinnacle of power over budgetary information, and his astonishing statements before the hearing in February, concerning the withholding of budgetary information, Senator Muskie and I thought his testimony would be most germane and beneficial to our exploration of the areas of policy concerning the handling, protection, and disclosure of information controlled by government officials. So, here, we witness, first hand, a refusal by an administration official to testify. Such a refusal puts a congressional committee in the untenable and frustrating position of being unable to fully explore and analyze an administration practice which, I believe, goes counter to the intent of the Congress.

Thus, it is not the formal invocation of executive privilege alone that causes difficulty, but also the multitude of specious reasons given by the department and agency heads and other officers and employees of the Federal Government for their refusals to provide the information sought by Congress.

According to a story in the Washington Post, of March 3, 1973, the President stated at a press conference that he would invoke executive privilege if the Senate Judiciary Committee requested the appearance of his counsel, John W. Dean III, in regard to the nomination of L. Patrick Gray III to be the Director of the Federal Bureau of Investigation. Mr. Nixon reportedly stated, "No President could ever agree to allow the counsel to the President to go down and testify before a committee," making no distinction whatever between the various types of information that might be sought from such a person. While I recognize that there is a need for a President to seek counsel and advice from his closest staff members, and that such conversations on certain occasions necessarily must be kept confidential, it appears to me that the President's broadside statement that no President could ever agree to allow his counsel to testify, goes well beyond any past precedent and usage of so-called executive privilege, and is in total contradiction with the opinion of his Counsel, Mr. Dean, as indicated in a letter to Dr. Jeremy Stone of the Federation of American Scientists on April 20, 1972, when he stated that the "precedents indicate that no recent President has ever claimed a 'blanket immunity' that would prevent his assistants from testifying before the Congress on any subject". And then we learned that he had expanded this prohibition to include even former aides who are no longer connected with the White House.

The President's recent interpretation of executive privilege appears to be based on the assumption that White House aides constitute a new nobility, immune from publicly testifying under oath as all other citizens are required to do. It has always been my belief that in our country divine right went out with the American revolution; and that clearly it does not belong to White House **N12** aides.

It is clear that the President, and agency and department heads and employees, are making unilateral decisions regarding the information that the Congress is allowed to obtain in carrying out its constitutional duty to legislate and to approve Presidential appointments. Further, these unilateral determinations appear to be made with no reasonable discriminatory ground rules. I believe that the Congress and the President must cooperate in seeing that the American people receive the informed governance that they deserve and the fullest possible information regarding the operations of their Government, and that those who govern must, in turn, be accountable to the taxpayers.

In view of the continued reluctance of the President and employees and officials of Federal departments and agencies to provide the Congress with the information which it must have in order to legislate intelligently, I believe it is essential that the Congress adopt some means of determining whether such refusals are justified, and, if they are not, that the information will be forthcoming.

S.J. Res. 72, which I introduced on March 8, 1973, is an attempt to permit the Congress to determine whether it requires information or testimony from the executive branch of the Government. If the President decrees that an agency or department head shall not come forward and testify or produce the documents sought, then he has the burden of showing the Congress that his refusal is well taken. Under the provisions of this resolution, the Congress will not again find itself in the belittling role of having to beg and lobby executive departments and agencies for information which it needs to legislate wisely under its constitutional mandate.

The measures introduced by my colleagues, Senator Muskie and Senator Fulbright, also are steps toward restoring to the Congress its rightful role under the Constitution and the separation of powers doctrine.

With the present inquiry of the Select Committee on Presidential Campaign Activities, it is, in my judgment, of the utmost necessity for the executive branch to cooperate with Congress in all honesty and candor. Presently, the President's refusal to cooperate presents his office in such a way as to reasonably engender in the minds of the American people the suspicion that he is afraid of the truth.

At issue in these hearings, then, are three conflicting principles: the alleged power of the President to withhold information the disclosure of which he feels would impede the performance of his office; the power of the legislative branch to obtain information in order to legislate wisely and effectively; and the basic **N13** right of the taxpaying public to know what its Government is doing.

These opposing principles have clashed for many years while the executive branch has been developing so-called "precedents" justifying its practice of the doctrine. To my mind, precedents do not legitimize practices which are without legal or constitutional basis. In the words of a colleague, "usurpation is not legitimized simply by repetition, nor is a valid power nullified by failure to exercise it".

The Congress has inflicted upon itself a condition of "institutional anemia", draining itself of obligations prescribed by the Constitution. It is high time that we, in Congress. accept our responsibilities and reclaim those which we have parceled away, so that we may become a more vital force in the determination of the national priorities and so that we may once again be heralded by the people as "the most glorious gem in the crown of democracy."

It is mandatory for the survival of our system of government that we take all reasonable measures to ensure that the separation of powers principle survives, for if it does not, the basis of our freedoms will have retreated into history.

BUDGET OVERSIGHT—STATEMENT OF ELMER STAATS, COMPTROLLER GENERAL OF THE UNITED STATES
([84A], pp. 3–29)

Congressional oversight of the intelligence community should be most effective through the appropriations process, for it is through control of appropriated funds that the constituted authority of Congress to oversee the Executive is explicit. Representative Otis Pike recognized that point and based much of his committee's inquiry upon the legitimate concern of Congress as to the use of funds it appropriates. Although the Pike Committee did not succeed in bringing many details of the national intelligence budget before the public, it did document the failure of Congress to oversee. The frustrations over the lack of Executive cooperation expressed by Chairman Pike in the hearings reprinted here are elaborated upon further in the first section of the committee's final report. That section, never released by Congress, was leaked to CBS News reporter Daniel Schorr, who, in turn, passed it to *The Village Voice* newspaper, where it appeared on February 23, 1976.

The following testimony by comptroller general of the United States, Elmer Staats, was given before the Pike Committee in July 1975. Staats, as head of the General Accounting Office, the permanent investigatory unit of the Congress, testified on the restraints (some congressional) imposed on his agency's inquiries into intelligence matters. The extent to which Congress has constructed its oversight powers is reflected throughout his testimony, where at times Staats, an employee of the Congress, is unable to provide information to the committee because of earlier agreements on preserving secrecy.

STATEMENT OF ELMER B. STAATS, COMPTROLLER GENERAL OF THE UNITED STATES, ACCOMPANIED BY ROBERT F. KELLER, DEPUTY COMPTROLLER GENERAL, MARTIN J. FITZERALD, LEGISLATIVE ATTORNEY, GAO, AND FRED SHAFER, DIRECTOR, LOGISTICS AND COMMUNICATIONS DIVISION, GAO

Mr. STAATS. Thank you very much, Mr. Chairman.

We are pleased to accept your invitation to discuss the relationship of the General Accounting Office and executive branch agencies composing the so-called intelligence community. The agencies generally included under this umbrella term are: The Central Intelligence Agency; the Defense Intelligence Agency; the National Security Agency; the intelligence components of the Army, Navy and Air Force; the Federal Bureau of Investigation; the Department of the Treasury; the Energy Research and Development Administration (formerly the Atomic Energy Commission) and the Bureau of Intelligence and Research in the Department of State.

The intelligence community is also usually defined to include, in addition, entities whose functions are to review and evaluate the product of the intelligence agencies, to advise the President, and to prescribe policies governing activities of the intelligence agencies. These other units include: The National Security Council; the Intelligence

Resources Advisory Committee; the U.S. Intelligence Board; and the Foreign Intelligence Advisory Board.

Our experience in reviewing intelligence activities has been quite limited and, to a large extent, has arisen from matters not directly related to intelligence collection, analysis or dissemination but having instead to do with such matters as a comparative analysis of Soviet and United States research and development efforts, defense procurement, international narcotics control, foreign language training programs, and certain matters in international trade and economics. The other main source of experience in this area is a series of recent reviews we have conducted in response to congressional requests.

In general, we have not pressed for reviews of intelligence operations on our own initiative for the simple reason that our legal authority is quite limited and the problems of access to information have been such as to cause us to conclude that efforts to review these activities would have little practical result.

GAO's basic audit authority is contained in the Budget and Accounting Act of 1921, the Accounting and Auditing Act of 1950, the Legislative Reorganization Act of 1970, and the Congressional Budget and Impoundment Control Act of 1974. As an independent, nonpolitical agency in the legislative branch of the Federal Government, its authority is extensive, encompassing not only financial auditing, but also management reviews and evaluations of the effectiveness of programs. These statutes authorize GAO to audit the activities of most executive branch agencies, and grant it access to the records of the agencies necessary to the discharge of this responsibility.

However, certain restrictions on our audit authority are also provided for by law, including instances where moneys are accounted for solely on certification by the head of a department or establishment. For example, expenditures of a confidential, extraordinary or emergency nature by the CIA are to be accounted for solely on the certificate of the Director. Sometimes such restrictions are contained in appropriation acts. For example, annual appropriations for the FBI have included funds to meet unforeseen emergencies of a confidential character to be expanded under the direction of the Attorney General and accounted for solely on his certificate.

In addition to legal restrictions on our audit and access to information authority, there are serious practical considerations which further inhibit our ability to perform meaningful reviews. These factors stem from an innate characteristic of all agencies involved in intelligence gathering or analysis, namely, the need and desire to maintain close security so as to reduce the risk of leakage by minimizing the number of people having access to such matters.

First is the problem of obtaining the necessary special security clearances and satisfying multitudinous need-to-know requirements. A "Top Secret" Defense clearance or Atomic Energy "Q" clearance is in most cases insufficient for access to intelligence data. Because of this requirement, the limited work conducted by GAO requiring such clearances, and the time and expense involved, only a limited number of our staff have these clearances at present. A closely related problem is the difficulty of developing acceptable arrangements for the reporting of our findings and conclusions to the Congress.

Second is the restrictive policy established to maintain security by the intelligence agencies. Access to basic information is, at best, very limited. On occasion, the community cooperates to the extent of giving us certain requested information, but even then we are usually afforded insufficiently broad access to agency records to verify independently the accuracy and completeness of the material supplied to us.

We recently commented in some detail with regard to security clearances and our limited access to information in a May 10, 1974, letter to Senator William Proxmire, which was supplemented and updated in a July 10, 1975, letter to Senator Frank Church, chairman of the Senate Select Committee on Intelligence Activities and by a more recent letter to this committee. We would like to offer these letters to the committee so that, if you desire, they may be included in the record of these hearings.

Mr. PIKE. Without objection, the letters will be included in the record. . . .

Mr. STAATS. We know of this committee's deep interest in information regarding the size of the Government's commitment of resources, both in personnel and financial terms, to the intelligence function. We understand that the committee will be inquiring into the potential for achieving fiscal savings and increased management efficiencies in the execution of the intelligence activities of the Government. The magnitude of the financial resources devoted to intelligence work has been a subject of particular public concern and speculation.

Chairman PIKE. May I interrupt you just for a moment. I would like to announce to the members of the committee as a matter of policy that I am not going to stop the hearing for the purposes of this quorum call. If any member of the committee wishes to go to the quorum call, please feel free to go when you are obliged to do so. It is my personal judgment that what we are doing here is more significant than going over there and marking ourselves present and returning.

Go ahead, Mr. Staats.

Mr. STAATS. I should emphasize at this point that we cannot independently verify the accuracy of any estimates which may have been made as to the size of the intelligence community budgets. And, in any attempt to calculate an overal intelligence budget, there will always be judgmental issues over how to account for the cost of such things as submarines, reconnaissance aircraft, and satellites, where both intelligence and nonintelligence purposes may be involved concurrently. Furthermore, we understand that large segments of the total intelligence budget are concealed within the budgets of various Government departments and agencies, which would further complicate an attempt at verification of data.

As I have indicated, we have recently been engaged in several intelligence-related assignments which were prompted by specific congressional requests. One of these, undertaken at the request of Senator Charles Percy in July of 1974, and later endorsed by the chairman of the Senate Government Operations Committee, involved an attempt to obtain budgetary, organizational, and personnel information for all units, departments, and agencies of the Federal Government that perform police, investigative, or intelligence activities. A questionnaire was used to solicit the information from 173 units, departments, and agencies. Some data was gathered from responses to the questionnaire, while certain other agencies, apparently due to the sensitivity of the information, provided it to us during onsite visits.

A limited verification of data furnished by civil agencies was conducted by means of followup interviews with agency officials and through review of documents and reports. The extent of verification was limited because of time and volume constraints; we were not able to verify any of the Defense Department intelligence information which was provided to us. We also had to rely on each agency's interpretation regarding the extent to which it performed police or investigative, or intelligence activities. In some cases, existing accounting records did not readily identify the requested information, and we had to depend upon estimates made by the agencies as to their funding and personnel levels. Also, while we attempted to obtain the data in a uniform manner, some agencies did not furnish data in the requested format.

We issued two reports to Senator Percy on June 9, 1975, one dealing with police and investigative funding and personnel, and the other covering intelligence funding and personnel. The latter report, which is classified "Secret," contains data on six departments and agencies which volunteered information to us, including some data on the Defense Department. However, we were formally refused data on the Central Intelligence Agency, the National Security Agency, and certain other sensitive Defense Department intelligence activities. In some cases, statutory authority was cited as the basis for the refusal; while in most cases, we were directed to the congressional intelligence oversight committees for the data. We decided, after discussion with representatives of Senator Percy's office and the Government Operations Committee, and because select congressional committees had been created to investigate intelligence operations, that we would not make further attempts to obtain such data from the agencies which had refused it to us.

We are currently conducting, at the request of the House Judiciary Committee, a review of the domestic intelligence operations of the FBI. We are examining relevant policies and procedures, and the application of resources to these operations.

In order to determine how the Bureau carries out its domestic intelligence activity, it is necessary for us to review investigative cases. The Bureau was and is concerned that if we had access to its domestic intelligence files, the FBI's capability to develop informants and to conduct intelligence investigations would be negatively affected. In response to this concern, we worked out with the Bureau a procedure whereby the Bureau prepared special summaries of the case files which we had randomly selected for review. Through these summaries and followup interviews with FBI personnel associated with the cases, we are obtaining information on how the Bureau's policies and procedures are carried out in domestic intelligence investigations.

To insure the accuracy of the summaries, we need to verify the information contained in them. We therefore proposed a verification procedure under which we would randomly select documents from the case files to assure ourselves that the documents were accurately reflected in the summaries; the Bureau would block out informants' names before allowing us to read the documents. However, the FBI Director and the Attorney General have not been willing to agree to this procedure and have so notified the chairman of the Judiciary Committee. An alternative procedure was suggested by the Attorney General, but the chairman has advised the Attorney General that the alternative procedure would not be acceptable and has asked him to reconsider his position. Unless the verification problem is resolved, our report to the Judiciary Committee will have to be qualified because of our inability to fully verify the information on which it is based.

In the fall of 1974, we received two requests which would have necessitated that certain information be provided to us by the Central Intelligence Agency. One request was made by the chairman of the Subcommittee on Europe, House Committee on International Relations, concerning the cutoff of funds for Turkey. The second was made by Senator James Abourezk, and it concerned former oil company officials currently employed by several Government agencies, including the CIA. In both cases, we did not receive the information we requested; and in one case, this precluded us from making the requested review. In the other case, our review was limited but not completely frustrated by our lack of access to CIA information.

On the other hand, we have recently performed, at the request of the Special Subcommittee on Intelligence of the House Armed Services Committee, two reviews of the reasonableness of the procedures followed by the CIA in the divestiture of certain proprietary interests. The reviews were performed by GAO staff members holding security clearances, but no special intelligence clearances, and we were given excellent cooperation by the CIA personnel with whom we worked. Our reviews were completed in an expeditious manner, and we have issued our reports to the Special Subcommittee.

Perhaps at this point I should describe to this committee the sequence of events leading up to our termination, in 1962, of all GAO-initiated audit work at the CIA. The history begins with the enactment of the Central Intelligence Agency Act, after which the Director of the Agency requested that, in spite of the provisions of the law granting him broad and unusual powers, we continue to make a site audit of expenditures. We agreed to do so under the same arrangements as existed when we made audits at the predecessor Central Intelligence Group. However, in view of the provisions of the act, we referred any apparently questionable payments to the CIA comptroller's office for corrective action. No audit whatsoever of unvouchered funds was made; these are the funds expended on the certificate of the Director. Furthermore, this work did not include substantive reviews of CIA policies, practices, and procedures.

About this point in time, GAO began to expand the scope of its audits to review not only agency financial transactions but also to determine whether authorized agency programs and activities were being conducted in an efficient, economical, and effective manner. In light of this development, a senior GAO official attended an executive session of the special subcommittee, Central Intelligence Agency, of the House Armed Services Committee, to discuss our work at CIA. During this meeting, the subcommittee suggested that we submit our recommendations regarding future GAO activity at CIA. On May 29, 1959, the former Comptroller General wrote to the chairman of the subcommittee to the following effect:

He believed that the broader type of audit was appropriate for GAO work at CIA and would be more likely to produce evaluations helpful to the Congress and the Agency;
The type of limited audit effort therefore conducted should no longer be continued;
He would not attempt to evaluate the intelligence activities of the Agency; and
The Subcommittee could be helpful in effecting a change in the scope of GAO work by advising the Agency of the Subcommittee's interest on behalf of a broadened GAO audit.

In July 1959, the former Comptroller General was briefed by CIA concerning activities and functions of the Agency. Thereafter, a series of staff level discussions were held on the subject of improving our audit of the CIA. The culmination occurred in October 1959, with an exchange of correspondence among the CIA, GAO, and the subcommittee. On October 16, the CIA Director wrote to the Comptroller General and, in substance, made these points:

He believed GAO could expand its audit activities with respect to a considerable portion of CIA;

Expenditures made on the certificate of the Director for confidential, extraordinary, or emergency purposes would not be subject to review;

The policy of the Agency was to limit as much as possible this authority of the Director;

Consequently, many vouchered expenditures were made which were related to activities which were not sensitive in themselves but which were conducted in support of highly confidential operations;

The Director's special authority extends protection to this category of vouchered expenditures, which would therefore also have to be excluded from any expanded audit coverage; and

He solicited agreement on these principles and, if agreement were achieved, suggested continuance of discussions toward broadening the scope of GAO audits.

In a letter dated October 21, 1959, to the CIA Director, with a copy to the subcommittee chairman, the Comptroller General—

Agreed that expenditures made on the certificate of the Director were not subject to GAO audit without his concurrence;

Said that it seemed possible to expand GAO audits considerably, even though these reviews would be outside the area of sensitive security operations;

Expressed a willingness to attempt to broaden GAO activities, within the principles expressed in the Director's October 16 letter, for a trial period; and

Said that if the trial period showed that GAO reviews were so limited that it could not accomplish any worthwhile objectives, he would have to consider whether the effort should be continued.

On May 16, 1961, the Comptroller General wrote to the subcommittee chairman and the CIA Director to express the view that, under existing security restrictions, GAO did not have sufficient access to information to make comprehensive reviews on a continuing basis that would be productive of evaluations helpful to the Congress and that, as a result, it planned to discontinue audits of CIA activities. The GAO specifically related that, while access to overt activities of the intelligence component was reasonably good, its activities were not such as would be generally susceptible to productive audits. There was no access at all to the plans component. The overt and confidential activities of the support component were so integrated that a reasonably comprehensive audit could not be made. That same day, the subcommittee chairman discussed the contents of the May 16 letter with GAO staff; he expressed concern over plans to terminate audit activities at CIA.

On May 17, 1961, the CIA Director wrote the Comptroller General to express his opinion that GAO's reviews had been helpful in bringing certain matters to the attention of Agency officials and had formed the basis for taking corrective action. He further expressed regret over the plan to discontinue completely GAO's work at CIA and asked that, before final action was taken, he have an opportunity to discuss the possibility of continuing an audit on some scale. On May 18, 1961, the chairman of the House Armed Services Committee wrote to the Comptroller General, recommending strongly against the discontinuance of GAO efforts at CIA pending further discussion between CIA, GAO, and the committee. He further stated that, despite the "inherent" restrictions on the scope of a GAO audit at CIA, even a limited audit of overt accounting actions would serve a worthwhile purpose and that precipitous action was not required. He also mentioned that there were other overriding considerations which could not be divorced, under the prevailing circumstances, from any change in the existing relationship between GAO and the CIA.

On May 23, 1961, the Comptroller General wrote to the chairman of the Armed Services Committee and the Director of CIA to restate the restrictions GAO experienced on the scope of its audit; he also restated the conclusion that no worthwhile audit activity could be conducted under the circumstances. However, because of the views of the committee, he said he would continue a limited audit program at CIA pending further discussion of the matter.

In June of 1962, meetings were held between GAO staff and the CIA, and between GAO and the staff of the committee, to further discuss the matter. The GAO again restated the problems stemming from lack of adequate access to information, again proposing to terminate all effort at the CIA. As a result of these discussions and at the request of the committee staff, the Comptroller General recited the history of the matter in a letter dated June 21, 1962; he said that since May of 1961 nothing had caused him to change his views and that a conclusion had been reached only after having fully considered all the factors. He again specified the type of access he would need to make reasonably comprehensive reviews. He requested an expression of the committee's views on these matters. On July 18, 1962, the committee chairman wrote to the Comptroller General as follows:

The restrictions imposed by CIA were necessary;
The comptroller and internal audit functions at CIA had been strengthened; and,
For these reasons and because of the Comptroller General's belief that further effort at CIA was not worthwhile, the conclusion to withdraw from further audit activities would be accepted.

Therefore, since 1962, GAO has not conducted any reviews at the CIA nor any reviews which focus specifically on CIA activities, except for the two recent reviews noted earlier, which were done at the request of the Special Subcommittee on Intelligence of the House Armed Services Committee....

A somewhat different situation is presented in the case of the National Security Agency. In 1955, in response to a request by the Director of NSA, the Comptroller General assigned a GAO staff member to NSA on a permanent basis to perform limited onsite audits of NSA's vouchers and accounts. Under the present onsite audit procedures, all accounting and supporting documents are maintained at NSA or designated records storage sites for audit purposes; these security measures are necessary because the majority of the documentation is of a classified nature. The mutual accessibility of the GAO staff members and NSA officials permits prompt and informal resolution of questionable expenditures. To the present, our audit effort has been primarily of a financial accounting nature, plus a very limited effort in the area of procurement. No formal report has been published on the results of our continuing examinations at NSA. Section 6 of Public Law 86–36 provides that no law shall be construed to require the disclosure of the organization or any function of NSA, of any information with respect to the activities thereof, or of the names, titles, salaries, or number of persons employed by NSA. We do not construe this section as precluding our access on a confidential basis; we view section 6 as a prohibition on any disclosure of our findings to the public at large.

The onsite GAO representative is required to obtain a special security clearance. From 1955 to 1973, only two or three of our staff had this special clearance at any one time. However, we have recently obtained clearances for a few additional members of our staff. We have informally discussed with NSA officials the potential for GAO conducting management-type reviews of certain aspects of NSA's operations. The preliminary conclusion we reached is that these are feasible, although we recognize that there are legal and practical limitations. One area in which we preliminarily believe some constructive, broader GAO reviews could be conducted is NSA's automatic data processing and communications activities.

There are several general considerations which bear upon the question of how we can most properly relate our audit responsibilities to the special characteristics of the intelligence community. On the one hand we must keep in mind:

Legal limitations placed on the scope of the audits we could perform and the lack of explicit legislative authority to audit intelligence agencies;
The probability of continued restricted access to information;
Probable requirements for additional staff; and
The fact that any substantive reports would probably be available only for very limited distribution.

There are other factors, however, and they are also entitled to be given due weight. These would include:

The certainty that, whatever the exact amount, large expenditures are made in the execution of the intelligence function;
Growing recognition of the need for improved oversight machinery in the Congress and the support role which GAO might play; and
The indications of a potential for significant contributions toward more efficient and effective management of certain of the activities pursued by intelligence agencies.

Given the necessary charter, some of the areas where we believe that GAO studies might be conducive to improved management would be, for example, examinations into intelligence requirements and analysis capability compared with data-collection capability. In addition, procurement, property management, and personnel management usually present opportunities for economies and improved management. Furthermore, exploration should be undertaken of the potential, within and among the agencies, for a duplication or a lack of coordination of collection, analysis, and research activities.

We perceive several available options:

(1) Undertake reviews only in response to specific congressional requests.

(2) Perform audits and reviews on behalf of oversight committees.

(3) Initiate, renew, or continue discussions with agency officials with a view toward obtaining, independently of the interest of a specific committee, sufficient access to information to permit useful self-initiated management reviews.

(4) Assign professional staff members to the oversight committees.

(5) Seek explicit legislative authority for our audit of the intelligence agencies and access to the requisite information.

(6) Pursue any combination of the first five options.

While we certainly do not rule out any of these courses of action, our view is that, for the present, we want to assist the oversight committees to the extent possible. Of course, other current activities, such as our work at the FBI and further discussions with NSA, will be continued.

The role of the GAO in the oversight of the intelligence community cannot be fully determined, in my view, until the oversight role of the Congress is agreed upon and machinery established to exercise this role.

The GAO shares a common problem with the Congress in balancing the need for adequate review of the operations and finances of the intelligence community, the need for public confidence in intelligence operations, and the need for confidentiality essential to the successful execution of many intelligence programs.

This concludes my statement but with your permission, I would like to read some parts from my letter to this committee which spell out some thoughts we have.

We say:

We believe the Congress should once again, as it has in the past, consider the manner in which oversight of the intelligence community is managed in the light of the constitutional provision that no moneys be spent from the public treasury unless appropriated by the Congress. In this regard, the Congress should consider the role GAO is to play in what the Congress ultimately decides should be the requisite Congressional approval of intelligence community funding and activities. GAO's role should be sufficiently clarified so that it can determine its reporting responsibilities.

Then, as the second point, we say:

We believe the Congress should address the questions of whether some broad policy guidelines and criteria for certain types of covert national security activities should be established by legislation; whether any agency responsible for intelligence collection should also be responsible for carrying out actions; and whether the existing Congressional system for identifying, approving, or disapproving significant individual covert projects is adequate.

Then we conclude by saying that:

Given this situation, the question arises as to the adequacy of the available management review function within the CIA particularly. Are the agencies within the intelligence community so organized and structured as to permit such a management review function as an internal matter? If not, can they be made so to enhance the possibility of effective congressional oversight management review, either by the oversight committees themselves or with the assistance of GAO or others?

This concludes my prepared statement, Mr. Chairman. I will be happy to respond to questions.

Mr. Keller, to my left, the Deputy Comptroller General, and Mr. Fitzgerald of our General Counsel's office are here to assist me.

Chairman PIKE. Thank you very much. Before starting I would simply like to advise the members of the committee that we will proceed under the 5-minute rule.

It applies to all members. It will hurt me just as much as it does you.

Mr. Staats, you have been most constructive and most specific.

I would like to paint with a rather larger brush. Does the General Accounting Office, which has the responsibility for representing the legislative branch of our Government in overseeing the expenditures of the public moneys, know how much we spend on intelligence?

Mr. STAATS. No, sir, we do not. As I have indicated in my statement, in preparing the report for the Senate Government Operations Committee, we were not able to obtain that information specifically.

Chairman PIKE. Because of the restrictions which have been placed on your access to information, does the GAO know whether there is duplication in the realm of our intelligence-gathering activities?

Mr. STAATS. We would have no way of finding out, Mr. Chairman. This information is not available to us and, unless we know where the money is and where the people are, we would have no basis for making a judgment that there is duplication or lack of coordination or poor management.

Chairman PIKE. In your letter to this committee, Mr. Staats, you referred to the first part of the seventh clause, article I, section 9 of the Constitution. That is the provision which states that no money shall be drawn from the Treasury but in consequence of appropriations made by law. It is my feeling that the Congress does in fact make the appropriations but they do not in fact know what they are appropriating when they make the appropriations. I am more interested in the second part of that clause which says, "and a regular statement and account of the receipts and expenditures of all public money shall be published from time to time."

In your judgment, is a regular statement and account of all public money published?

Mr. STAATS. This provision is susceptible to interpretation as to whether or not it refers to the totals of the Government or whether it relates to departments or to activities or to functions. It has never been fully litigated.

Chairman PIKE. If there has been an attempt to litigate it, it was in the case of *United States* v. *Richardson.*

Mr. STAATS. Yes, but it was eventually thrown out by the Supreme Court on lack of standing, if my understanding is correct.

There is, of course, disclosure by the Treasury and through the budget of overall expenditures.

Chairman PIKE. You are really an expert in this field. Do you consider the kind of disclosure which we get to be that which the Founding Fathers had in mind when they referred to a statement and account of all public moneys?

Mr. STAATS. I would certainly agree that it does not represent full disclosure. But at the same time, I would have to say, Mr. Chairman, that from the early days of our history there have been provisions written into law which authorize agency heads to maintain certain expenditures in secret.

Chairman PIKE. Yes, but we cannot write into the law anything which overrides the Constitution.

Mr. STAATS. But I think it is the other way around. The Congress has written into law provisions which authorize agency heads to maintain expenditures confidential in spite of this provision. That practice has not really been challenged in our long history for reasons of which I am unaware.

Chairman PIKE. The time of the chairman is up.

I yield to Mr. McClory.

Mr. McCLORY. Thank you, Mr. Chairman. Do we have any estimates as to the overall costs of the entire intelligence community? It seems to me I recall some statement about $5 or $6 billion or something like that.

Mr. STAATS. We have seen those figures, too, Congressman McClory. But we would have to simply——

Mr. McCLORY. That is just a guess?

Mr. STAATS [continuing]. Regard those as guesses unless they can be verified.

Mr. McCLORY. You have prepared two reports for Senator Percy. They are fairly recent, last year, I believe. Those are considered as secret, but you have received extensive information, I gather, from the intelligence agencies other than the CIA and the NSA.

Now have those been made available to other persons than Senator Percy?

Mr. STAATS. I believe they have been made available to this committee. There is no restriction on information which is classified as secret except for individuals receiving it being qualified to receive it. We make many reports which are of a classified nature.

Mr. McCLORY. So you either could or have released that to this committee with the understanding that it is a secret document.

Mr. STAATS. That is right. Any person who is willing to receive the information under the rules that apply to classified information is eligible to receive this kind of report.

Mr. McCLORY. Now if you were authorized to conduct investigations such as you perform for the Congress with respect to other agencies of CIA and other intelligence agencies on a confidential basis that would be legislative authority which would give you the prerogatives which you don't seem now to have.

Mr. STAATS. That is correct.

We may have to have more explicit authority than we have today.

Mr. McCLORY. Would you encounter any difficulty, do you think, if ultimately we should recommend the establishment of a joint congressional committee on intelligence to overview the intelligence community with respect to the subject of the secrecy of the reports you might prepare for the benefit of such committee.

Mr. STAATS. I would like to say two or three things with respect to your question. This is to some degree a personal judgment and based on my own background . . . I would favor a joint committee. I would favor it partly growing out of the experience of the Joint Committee on Atomic Energy which has in my opinion been quite successful in receiving highly sensitive information. To the best of my knowledge there has never been any problem concerning disclosure of unclear information from the committee. It has been an effective method by which the House and Senate could exercise oversight of that program.

The other thing I would like to say is more related to our role. Without some committee of this type to which we could relate, with which we could agree regarding areas in which we would investigate and study and develop recommendations, so that we had someplace in the Congress where we could have an audience and a body to report to, we would be, I think, relatively ineffective. So I would favor for both those reasons a committee of the type you are suggesting.

Mr. McCLORY. There is an existing rule of the House which permits any Member of the House to see and examine secret information with the same limitations as other Members who originally receive such information. Do you have an opinion as to that rule or whether you think it might be susceptible to some modification in order to retain greater secrecy of such reports.

[The rule referred to is House Rule XI(2)(e)(2). Derived from section 202(d) of the Legislative Reorganization Act of 1946, it was made a part of the rules on January 3, 1953.]

Mr. STAATS. Speaking for GAO, we certainly would not want to be in a situation where there was any concern that we would be supplying information to other than a body authorized by the Congress to obtain that type of information, and we would not do so. By the same token, because of the sensitivity of the information we are dealing with, we need some part of the Congress to which we can relate and with which we could have agreement on the areas on which we would undertake reviews.

Mr. McCLORY. Thank you very much.

Chairman PIKE. Mr. Giaimo.

Mr. GIAIMO. In reading and listening to your testimony, you state on page 13 that since 1962 GAO has not conducted any reviews of the CIA nor any reviews which focused specifically on CIA activities. On the bottom of page 16, you say that the role of the GAO in the oversight of the intelligence community cannot be determined fully until the oversight role of the Congress is agreed upon and machinery established to exercise this role.

Then you go on to say how there has to be a balance between adequate review by the Congress and the needs of confidentiality. Is it a fair inference then that the General Accounting Office has very little if any information on the activities and expenditures of public funds by the intelligence community and the members of the intelligence community of the U.S. Government?

Mr. STAATS. That is correct.

Mr. GIAIMO. Is it also correct that you are not, nor is the General Accounting Office, in a position to know whether or not the CIA or other members of the intelligence family are acting within the parameters of the statutes which established their existence and their missions?

Mr. STAATS. That is correct. I should add here that we are also not able to give the Congress any appraisal as to the adequacy of the agencies' own internal control machinery. This includes internal review of their financial requirements, accounting to the Director, accounting to the National Security Council or to anyone else. So we are in no position to make any judgment as to whether they are running a good internal management shop.

Mr. GIAIMO. Would you care to give us your opinion as to whether or not you think this is a healthy balance between the public's need to know and the Congress' need to conduct watchdog or oversight operations. Do you think we now have a healthy balance between the intelligence community and the oversight community?

Mr. STAATS. Absolutely not. I would emphasize that it is important that the Congress know. Many things the Congress is aware of cannot be made public, and people understand that, I am sure. But I think there is a public confidence element here as to whether or not there is an oversight agency conducting reviews in the intelligence community, even though the results cannot be fully divulged. I think the public needs to be assured in this area as in any other area that there is an oversight agency with adequate authority to get the information and make that information available to the Congress of the United States.

Mr. GIAIMO. Did I understand you to say that you favor the establishment of a Joint Congressional Committee on Intelligence to oversee the activities of the intelligence community?

Mr. STAATS. That is correct.

Mr. GIAIMO. You made reference in your statements to earlier meetings with GAO and conversations going back to the early 1960's, particularly with the Armed Services Committee. Would you characterize earlier oversight activities by congressional committees as having been done by very few individuals in the Congress? Do you know of your own knowledge whether that was so?

Mr. STAATS. That is correct.

Mr. GIAIMO. For example, you speak of the Armed Services Committee in 1959 and 1961 and 1962, and you mentioned the subcommittee chairman and the chairman. In those days, if I recall correctly, the chairman was Mr. Vinson of Georgia. Can you tell us who was then the subcommittee chairman of that Subcommittee on Intelligence?

Mr. STAATS. Mr. Keller was present at that time. I think it would be better if he answered the question.

Mr. KELLER. Congressman Paul Kilday was chairman of the subcommittee at that time.

Mr. GIAIMO. Do you know whether those conversations involved all of the members of the Armed Services Committee?

Mr. KELLER. I would have no way of knowing that.

Mr. GIAIMO. Do you know whether there were many people in the Congress in the early 1960's who were privy to the information, which you have told us here today, as a result of the communications between the GAO and the congressional committee involved?

Mr. KELLER. My judgment would be that there were probably very few.

Mr. GIAIMO. Would you care to give us your opinion as to whether or not part of the problem with the inadequacy of congressional oversight over the many years, particularly in the early 1960's, has been the fact that there have been too few Members of the Congress who were privy to this information?

Mr. STAATS. That would be my view although again we would have no way of knowing with how many members of the committee the information was shared. I think only the individuals themselves could tell you that.

But part of the value of a joint committee would be that the membership of that committee would represent a judgment by the Congress of those who would have a legitimate interest in the subject. It would not be uncertain. It would not be a vague understanding about who was going to get the information or who was not. I think that there is great value in that kind of situation.

Chairman PIKE. Mr. Stanton?

Mr. STANTON. Thank you, Mr. Chairman. Mr. Staats, first of all let me thank you for your candor and your testimony which I consider excellent in terms of its presentation. Could you tell me, you have stated in your testimony that you do not know the amount of money expended by the intelligence community because there is no way that you can audit it; is that correct?

Mr. STAATS. That is correct.

Mr. STANTON. Then you would have no way of knowing in a time frame, say, from 1955 to 1975 what the increase in fiscal outlay has been to any particular agency; is that correct?

Mr. STAATS. That is correct.

Mr. STANTON. Is it true that the reason that you cannot tell is because such funds are hidden in other parts of the Federal budget and that there are only specific Members of Congress who know, on the Appropriations Committee, in what particular agency budget that money is contained; is that correct?

Mr. STAATS. Both for that reason and for reasons of secrecy and confidentiality.

Mr. STANTON. As to your experience with the NSA, where you did institute audit procedures, is it your belief that the same procedures could be instituted with respect to the CIA?

Mr. STAATS. I would be inclined to say "yes" if you assume that we will be able to make meaningful reviews of the managerial side of NSA. We think we can, and we have no contrary indications to date from NSA that they would not be agreeable to managerial type reviews. I mentioned two potential areas where we feel that GAO audits could be made: automatic data processing and communications. But we recognize again that even there we need to have someone to whom we can report because I would be willing to venture today that those could not be public reports.

Mr. STANTON. Would you say that, when you need somebody to report to, you are talking about the Congress and, specifically, I assume, the joint congressional committee concept that has been advocated for about 20 years.

Mr. STAATS. That is correct.

Mr. STANTON. Do we not run the risk of a joint congressional committee becaming part of the establishment of the agency over which it performs oversight? For example, it has been said that certain committees of this House who have oversight responsibility have been so involved with the object agency that they have failed in terms of performing oversight. Is that danger not possible through a joint congressional committee performing that function?

Mr. STAATS. Not inherently so, as I see it. I suppose there is a danger of any committee, whether we are talking about an oversight committee of this type or any other committee, becoming, you might say, advocates of the program. This is a matter, I think, of broader concern than just the field that we are talking about here.

But there are ways that you can protect against that, also.

Mr. STANTON. That is correct.

For that purpose would you think that one of the ways might be a limitation on the amount of time that a Member serves on that committee, as we do on the Budget Committee of the House presently, with a limitation of serving on the joint congressional committee for 2 to 6 years, or for a specific period of time?

Mr. STAATS. I think that might be one way to deal with it. If that were done, I would hope it would not be such a short period of time that individuals would not be able to become fully knowledgeable about the area they are working in. I have a feeling that, concerning the arrangement of the House Budget Committee, the period of time is too short; but that is another matter.

Mr. STANTON. Would it be possible and practical in your judgment to institute, for the protection of the public and the building of confidence of the public in Government the activities in this sensitive area, explicit expressed authority for the GAO for audit review through enactment of legislation as recommended by our committees to other committees in the House?

Mr. STAATS. Yes, indeed. I referred to several avenues of approach in my statement. I would want to emphasize that I doubt that we could be fully effective, even with a joint committee, unless we specifically had access authority to information. I do not believe we would be able to get that information as readily without such explicit authority.

Mr. STANTON. I concur. I thank you very much for your testimony.
Chairman PIKE. Mr. Treen.

Mr. TREEN. Thank you, Mr. Chairman. I appreciate, Mr. Staats.
your being here today. I would like to ask you if you know, either as
a result of review of the experience during Project Manhattan or
because you were with the U.S. Bureau of the Budget from 1939 to
1953, how the Congress appropriated funds for the Manhattan project,
how they were accounted for when expended, and who had access to
that information?

Mr. STAATS. I do not know specifically the names of the individuals
who had access to that information, but I believe that there were
only two individuals who had access to that information.

Mr. TREEN. Do you know how the money was appropriated, under
what heading, under what category did we appropriate the money for
the research to develop the atomic bomb in the early 1940's?

Mr. STAATS. That information is now available and we would be
glad to supply it for the record. My recollection was that it was made
available largely through the Corps of Engineers construction
appropriation.

Mr. TREEN. I would appreciate, Mr. Chairman, if that is satisfactory
with you, getting the details of that for the record.

Chairman PIKE. Yes; we would appreciate your providing that for
the record, Mr. Staats.

Mr. STAATS. We will be glad to.

[The information follows:]

The history of the Manhattan Project is the subject of "Now It Can Be
Told," by Lt. Gen. Leslie R. Groves, who was director for the Manhattan Project
from September 17, 1942, to December 31, 1946. Chapter 26 specifically concerns
the extent to which the nature of the project and the sources of its funding
were made known to Members of Congress. Involvement of the General Account-
ing Office in auditing the expenditures of the Manhattan Project was discussed
in hearings before the Senate Select Committee on Atomic Energy on April 4
and 8, 1946. The audit conducted during that period was essentially a voucher-
type audit.

See also, "On Active Service in Peace and War," by Henry L. Stimson and
McGeorge Bundy, particularly page 614. Volume I of "A History of the United
States Atomic Energy Commission," by Richard G. Hewlett and Oscar E. Ander-
son, Jr., contains in Chapter 9 a discussion of Congress and appropriations for
the Manhattan Project.

Mr. TREEN. I would like to get into the question now of your au-
thority to examine accounts. Basically you have authority under 31
U.S.C., sections 54 and 60 which seem to me to contain a rather broad
charter. Section 54, title 31 states that all departments of the Govern-
ment shall furnish to you "such information regarding the powers,
duties, activities, organization, financial transactions, and methods of
business of their respective offices as he may from time to time require
of them."

You are given the authority to secure and "have access to and the
right to examine any books, documents, papers, or records of any such
department or establishment." Under section 60 you are "authorized
and directed to make an expenditure analysis of each agency in the
executive branch of the Government * * * which, in the opinion of
the Comptroller General, will enable Congress to determine whether
public funds have been economically and efficiently administered and
expended."

Before getting your response thereto, I assume that you feel that the appropriations acts that contain provisos about expenditures on the certificate or warrant of the head of an agency cut across these statutes, is that correct?

Mr. STAATS. Yes, that is correct, and in the case of CIA there is a specific provision in its organic act, as you know, which authorizes the Director to make expenditures on his own certificate, which means we do not have any authority to go behind——

Mr. TREEN. I would like to examine that a little bit legally. I have never examined into this area before, but when Congress says that the head of an agency may expend money on his own certificate, of course that means that he then is given a great deal of discretion in how that money is spent, but do you interpret that to mean that you cannot then look at how it was spent?

Mr. STAATS. That is correct.

Mr. TREEN. He is given the authority to spend it?

Mr. STAATS. That is correct. Legislation has been introduced in the House by Congressman Eckhardt on January 16 of this year for himself and a number of other Members, which would at least authorize us to go behind the certification to the extent of making a judgment as to whether it was in fact a justifiable certificate in the sense of being secret or confidential.

[The bill referred to is H.R. 1513.]

Mr. TREEN. You don't think you have that authority now? Are there any court decisions upon which you base that opinion?

Mr. STAATS. No, sir.

Mr. TREEN. It seems to me the discretion to spend on the certificate of a head of an agency doesn't mean that you can't examine that expenditure; at a very minimum you can—you can total up the amounts he has spent on his own certificate, can't you?

Mr. STAATS. We may not even be permitted to know the amount.

Chairman PIKE. The time of the gentleman from Louisiana has expired.

Mr. Dellums.

Mr. DELLUMS. Thank you very much, Mr. Chairman.

Mr. Staats, I am appreciative of your being here this morning.

On page 8 of your testimony you allude to divestiture of certain proprietary interests on the part of the CIA.

Now, my first question may elicit from you classified information. Maybe the question that would elicit classified information could be answered for the record.

First of all, did you do an audit on the CIA's sale of both Southern Air Transportation and Air Asia?

Mr. STAATS. I am advised, Congressman Dellums, this would be classified information and we would have to supply that answer to you in a classified manner.

Mr. DELLUMS. I would request unanimous consent that material be given to this committee, Mr. Chairman.

Chairman PIKE. Just a moment. Before we do that, are you telling us that whether or not you performed an audit is, itself, classified information?

Mr. STAATS. That is my advice at the moment, Mr. Chairman; that would be the case with respect to any specific operation.

Chairman PIKE. The matter will be either provided for the record or heard in executive session at some subsequent time.

Mr. DELLUMS. Thank you, Mr. Chairman.

Is it correct you did do an audit on the divestiture of two proprietary companies?

Mr. STAATS. Yes. We were asked to look at whether or not the procedures that they went through to divest themselves of these interests were adequate, and we did get the necessary information, and we rendered opinion on the questions in each case.

Mr. DELLUMS. Did you look at or audit the profit and loss statement of either or both of these proprietary companies?

Mr. STAATS. I am sorry, I didn't get the first part of your question.

Mr. DELLUMS. Did you look at or audit the profit and loss statement of either one or both of these proprietary companies?

Mr. STAATS. I am advised that we did not make an audit of any profit and loss statement.

Mr. DELLUMS. So you have no way of answering the question of whether or not these companies made a profit?

Mr. STAATS. No, sir.

Mr. DELLUMS. What happened to the money from the sale of these two proprietary companies?

Mr. STAATS. I believe our reports would be available to this committee, Mr. Chairman.

Chairman PIKE. Will the gentleman from California yield?

Mr. McClory.

Mr. McCLORY. I have a point of order.

The point is that the witness stated this is classified information and you have stated that you would receive the information in executive session.

Chairman PIKE. That is not my understanding. The witness, who is a very experienced, old hand in these things, has said that naming the specific corporations involved did constitute a classified statement.

Mr. Dellums thereafter rephrased his question to cover unnamed corporations. If at any time Mr. Staats feels the matter is or should be classified, he has an absolute right to say so.

The Chair overrules the point of order.

Mr. McCLORY. I think he was referring to the specific cases to which the witness had already stated——

Chairman PIKE. As I said, I am not going to raise the question of secrecy if Mr. Staats does not opt to do so.

Mr. DELLUMS. Mr. Chairman, I would restate my question: What happened to the money from the sale of these two unnamed proprietary companies?

Mr. McCLORY. Mr. Chairman, I think the witness—I think that our colleague——

Chairman PIKE. Does the gentleman make a point of order?

Mr. DELLUMS. I am not yielding time to the gentleman.

Mr. GIAIMO. Will the gentleman yield to me for a moment?

Mr. DELLUMS. I yield to my distinguished colleague.

Mr. GIAIMO. For many years, one of the problems has been that even before we have objections from the executive branch or the agencies themselves, there is all too often a predisposition on the part of certain people in the Congress to impose our own cloak of secrecy—

in addition to executive branch cloaks of secrecy—over the activities of agencies. That has been part of the problem with congressional oversight.

Chairman PIKE. The Chair will simply state that any man can make a point of order at any time.

Mr. McClory made a point of order and was overruled.

Mr. Dellums.

Mr. DELLUMS. Thank you.

Mr. Staats, on the question——

Mr. STAATS. I am sorry, Congressman Dellums, we are not able to respond to that question for the reasons I have indicated.

I hope the members will appreciate the fact we are bound by the same laws that bind everyone else with respect to the classification of information.

Mr. DELLUMS. I respect that. I am simply raising questions; if it it classified I would simply request that the information be given to the committee or heard in executive session. I am simply raising the question.

Mr. STAATS. I believe that can be done.

Mr. DELLUMS. Thank you.

My next question is, was the company or companies sold at true market value?

Mr. STAATS. We are not able to respond to that.

Mr. McCLORY. I think the witness is entitled to be protected by the confidentiality under which he guards this information——

Chairman PIKE. Mr. McClory, I am just going to say flatly the witness is wholly capable of taking care of himself.

Mr. McCLORY. And the——

Chairman PIKE. This witness has been around longer than you and I have been around. What has happened here is that by your raising points of order and interrupting Mr. Dellums, Mr. Dellums' time has expired and accordingly the Chair now is obliged to recognize Mr. Murphy.

Mr. McCLORY. A further point of order. I want to make it perfectly emphatic here that I intend, when a witness is pursued after he has made the point, to provide the information, would violate the confidentiality under which the information is held, I am going to persist in objecting to questions which would endeavor to elicit information which the witness has indicated he is not at liberty to provide and to persist in the questioning after that point has been made.

It seems to me quite improper as far as the members of this committee are concerned.

I am not raising any question with regard to secrecy which is not already inherent in the law, but I am going to be certain that whatever is inherent in the law is going to be preserved and protected in this hearing.

Chairman PIKE. The gentleman from Illinois did not state a point of order. Any time that the gentleman from Illinois does state a point of order, the Chair will rule on the point of order, but the Chair is not going to let the time of any member of the committee be used up in that fashion and from now on the Chair will exercise his discretion in granting additional time, if we run into that situation again.

The Chair recognizes the gentleman from Illinois, Mr. Murphy.

Mr. MURPHY. Mr. Chairman, I will yield 1 minute of my 5 minutes to Mr. Dellums.

Mr. DELLUMS. Thank you very much.

Mr. Staats, with a view toward understanding that the questions I am raising with you are in no way an effort to compromise you, but simply to raise the questions: If in fact in your judgment the matters are security matters that should be given to this committee in executive session, I accept that as a member of committee.

I simply raised the question in order to elicit the response today or at some future date.

My next question in the remaining seconds I have is, were the companies sold strictly to the highest bidder? If not, why not?

My next question, who bought these companies? Were any of the buyers previously associated with the CIA and, finally, what kind of CIA audits have been made on company ledgers? If you could supply us with answers to all of the questions that I have raised with you that are of a classified nature, I will deeply appreciate it and with that I yield back my time to my distinguished colleague.

[The information may be found in the committee files.]

Mr. MURPHY. Thank you.

I too would like to thank you for your forthright testimony here today, Mr. Staats.

In your testimony you pointed out legal restrictions on your auditing and your access to information authority, and later on page 3 you say a closely related problem is the difficulty of developing acceptable arrangements for the reporting of GAO findings and conclusions to Congress.

My question, Mr. Staats, is whether we could have your recommendation in developing acceptable arrangements for the reporting of your findings and your auditing to the Congress?

Mr. STAATS. Yes. This very definitely relates to the discussion we had a few minutes ago with respect to a joint committee, or some alternative arrangement——

Mr. MURPHY. I understand you agree with the theory of the joint committee as I do.

I would like, at your leisure, for you to supply us with acceptable reporting arrangements to the Congress, taking into consideration the confidence you must preserve and the Congress has to preserve.

Mr. STAATS. We will be happy to elaborate and develop that point further.

Mr. MURPHY. Thank you, Mr. Staats.

Thank you, Mr. Chairman.

Mr. MURPHY. I yield to Mr. Dellums if I have time.

Mr. DELLUMS. Mr. Staats, what is your opinion of the legality of an agency investing appropriated funds in the stock market?

Mr. STAATS. I don't really know what your question alludes to, but I would say that the freedom which CIA has been given in the statute does not preclude any investment or any expenditure which in the judgment of the Director would carry forward his own program and there is no way that you can really go behind that. That is really the substance of what I have been saying here.

Mr. DELLUMS. So you are suggesting that the authority for the CIA or any other agency of the so-called intelligence community to establish proprietaries and spend appropriated funds for that purpose is within their authority, given the present law?

Mr. STAATS. If the Director makes that determination, yes.

Mr. KELLER. The CIA Act specifically provides that the moneys available to the Agency can be spent without regard to any other provisions of law and regulations relating to the expenditure of Government funds. It is a very broad provision.

Mr. DELLUMS. One other question: What is the legality of covert Government proprieties competing for Government contracts with public companies? Do you have any opinion on that?

Mr. STAATS. Our response would have to be the same as the one we have given to your previous question.

Mr. DELLUMS. I appreciate that.

Chairman PIKE. Mr. Kasten.

Mr. KASTEN. Title 31, section 60 of the United States Code directs the Comptroller General to report directly to the Government Operations Committees, et cetera, on a number of different expenditures and evaluation of expenditures of executive branch agencies.

On page 6 of your letter of July 31 to the chairman you state that in general GAO has not taken the initiative in pressing for oversight of intelligence operations, but has made serious efforts to assist the committees on a request basis.

Does the GAO make a distinction between the congressional and self-initiated audits relative to the methodology and also relative to the legal authority? Do you draw a line between the statute here and what you are supposed to be doing, and also the initiated studies?

Mr. STAATS. The legal problem is there in either event. What is different is that if there is a strong interest on the part of a committee such as the Armed Services Committee or the Foreign Relations Committee in a particular matter, then our chances of getting the necessary information on a voluntary basis are better.

Mr. KASTEN. Under the normal procedure of reporting periodically, what reports have been submitted to the committees in accord with this statute? What reports having to do with intelligence and what reporting arrangements and procedures now exist between the GAO and the various committees that have oversight responsibilities at the present time?

Mr. STAATS. Let me respond to your question in the general framework in which we operate with respect to all the committees of the Congress.

The statutes, beginning with the Legislative Reorganization Act of 1970, and reincorporated in the Congressional Budget Act of 1974, require that we respond to requests that come from committees of the Congress to the best of our ability and we have worked with virtually all the committees in the Congress in that manner. These would be reviews that are undertaken specifically on request of committees, and the reports are made to the requesting committees. The availability of those reports to other elements in the Congress is a matter that is handled on a case by case basis. In some cases they are made widely available. In other cases they are held for hearings and for other reasons.

Now, regarding reports that we make on our own initiative under the broad charter that we have, these are made available to the public unless classified, the day after they are forwarded to the Speaker of the House and the President of the Senate. All of these reports are referred to the interested committees and in all instances, to the Government Operations and Appropriations Committees. The Government Operations and Appropriations Committees have a specific responsibility under the Legislative Reorganization Act for following up on our reports and the recommendations we make in those reports, including, for example, receiving agencies' responses to those recommendations. Each agency is required within 60 days to tell the committees whether they intend to accept our recommendations or not. So the Government Operations Committee does have a special responsibility concerning our self-initiated reports.

Mr. KASTEN. The point of my questioning is, I think there may be as many problems on our side—on our side as the Congress—as there may be on the other side, the CIA or you.

Have, since 1962, any congressional committees requested the GAO to resume its financial audits of the CIA?

Mr. KELLER. Not since 1962.

Mr. KASTEN. There has not been that request?

Mr. KELLER. No, sir.

Mr. STAATS. The only requests we have had, Congressman Kasten, relate to those which we cite in our testimony here this morning.

Mr. KASTEN. In the letter you provided to us and also the letter to Senator Proxmire, you said that the GAO terminated all audits of the CIA because of disinvolving access to records.

Specifically, what difficulties have been encountered by the GAO in its attempt to conduct meaningful audits of the CIA?

Mr. KELLER. Perhaps I could answer that, sir. In the first instance there is the provision in the CIA Act which allows the Director to make expenditures on his own certificate. The law goes on further to say that the certificate "shall be considered a sufficient voucher for the expenditure"; to accountants that means that is all the data which is to be available.

Second, the position taken in the early sixties by the Director of CIA was that not only were unvouchered, certificated expenditures exempt from review by our office, but that also vouchered expenditures, if they were made in support of the covert activities, would not be subject to GAO review. And then you begin to get the whole thing mixed up.

Also, it is my understanding that our people who were out there were given limited access to certain things they wanted to look at, were never allowed to see very much of the whole picture and after a 2- or 3-year trial period of trying to expand our audits we came to the conclusion it was not a worthwhile effort.

Mr. STAATS. When the definition includes those activities which support covert operations, then it includes literally almost everything the Agency does, because nearly everything can be regarded as being in support of confidential operations. It was a hopeless situation as the GAO saw it, and we properly withdrew.

Chairman PIKE. Mr. Aspin?

Mr. ASPIN. Thank you, Mr. Chairman.

Mr. Staats, you have already said that you don't know the total amount of money that we are spending here. That would be one of the questions in which I am interested.

I don't know to what extent you can help, but I am trying to find out something about where does the money come from and who has control over it.

Now, where the money comes from apparently is scattered—mostly we talk about it being scattered throughout various other budgets, in the federal budget system and then shifted to the intelligence community after the appropriations process.

You are an expert. You have been around a long time. How else could the CIA or any other intelligence organization get money other than through that process? Is there any way other than through that process they might get money?

Mr. STAATS. I don't personally have too much difficulty with the process, provided that there is a policy——

Mr. ASPIN. I am just trying to determine if you can think of any other way they might get money. For example, what is the legal status over any profits made from proprietary companies? Have they complete discretionary control over that?

Mr. STAATS. It is all considered during the appropriations process.

Mr. ASPIN. Is that recycled through the appropriations process? Do they have to return that money to the Treasury?

Mr. STAATS. Let me answer your question this way: There is disclosure of these operations within the framework of the existing arrangements for review——

Mr. ASPIN. What happens to the money? If they make a profit at the end of the year, what happens to that profit? Does that go back into the Treasury and they have to get appropriations from it or can they use that money as they see fit?

Mr. STAATS. No; they cannot use it as they see fit but it is subject to the same monitorship by the OMB that all of their funds are subject to.

Mr. ASPIN. Do you know how that works? I mean, do you know what happens to that money?

Mr. STAATS. I do not believe that I am the best person to answer your question. Mr. Lynn probably can answer your question.

Mr. ASPIN. Who can we ask?

Mr. STAATS. Mr. Lynn.

Mr. ASPIN. Where else could they get money? Could they be, for example, printing the stuff? Is that possible? Can you think of any other place? I am trying to find out where all the possible sources of funds for the intelligence community come from. Where do they come from?

Mr. STAATS. The only basic source is appropriations.

Mr. ASPIN. You can't think of anything else? Appropriations, proprietary companies, selling such companies, profits from such companies?

Mr. STAATS. Those would not be significant in relationship to the total operation, no, sir.

Mr. ASPIN. Let me speak to the question of who has control over it. Do you have any feel for—the head of the Central Intelligence Agency is also head of the entire intelligence community. Do you have any feel for how much control he has over that total intelligence budget of other intelligence agencies other than the CIA?

Mr. STAATS. I can only refer you to the statute under which he wears two hats; he is Director of Central Intelligence——

Mr. ASPIN. Does he help set the budgets for other agencies? Does he help set the budget for the NSA?

Mr. STAATS. He helps.

Mr. ASPIN. How much authority does he have, like the Secretary of Defense helps to set the budget for the Army, Navy, and Air Force? Has he that kind of authority, to set the budget for DIA, NSA, and other intelligence agencies?

Mr. STAATS. Legally he does participate in that.

Mr. ASPIN. Never mind what happens legally. What happens in fact? Does he really control the budgets of all those agencies?

Mr. STAATS. The word "control" is too strong a term. Legally he has the responsibility for advising the President with respect to that function. If there were an issue involved, undoubtedly he would have to get the President's decision, but his charter to advise the President is very broad. His concern relates to the total community, that is quite correct.

Mr. ASPIN. Do the other intelligence agencies present their budgets to him for their approval? Where do they present their budgets, do you know?

Mr. STAATS. I think you should direct this question to Mr. Lynn, who will be with you tomorrow. He is much more recently involved in this than I.

Chairman PIKE. The time of the gentleman has expired.

Mr. Milford.

Mr. MILFORD. Thank you, Mr. Chairman.

Mr. Staats, effective intelligence work, by its very nature, is highly secret and strict—and requires strict "need to know" rules.

The standard operating procedures within intelligence organizations are carried on in such a way that even their own employees have very limited knowledge of the overall mission and activities. And, as you know, the CIA and others use a so-called compartment system where even high level department officials will not be aware of special missions and operations. This, of course, is a very necessary procedure.

Now, in your opinion, can professional auditing procedures be devised wherein your own employees could audit these agencies and yet maintain this compartmental concept?

In other words, can you keep your auditors departmentalized and yet come up with a reasonable appraisal or audit wherein a very limited number of your key people would be aware of the overall audit results?

Mr. STAATS. Our staff has had experience with many highly secret, highly sensitive operations, and I think our record is very good in that we have not been the source of any disclosures of that type of information. We have been involved in reviews of military readiness, the performance of highly sensitive weapons systems and matters of this type. So I have no concern about our ability to deal with secret, classified, confidential information.

Now, referring to the compartmentation which exists within certain intelligence operations, I have to be very frank that there will probably have to be clear legal authority to have access to the necessary information on a sufficiently broad basis. That may present a problem to the intelligence agencies, but I think that there must be some recognition here that without the ability to get information in that manner, there is not going to be adequate oversight, whether done by us or by anybody else. You are not going to have it.

Mr. MILFORD. I agree with you.

My question, primarily, goes not toward the executive agency so much as, can you devise auditing procedures that would maintain this compartmental concept?

Mr. STAATS. I think we can. 1 think we would have to be guided by and would take into account the agency's own problems in this regard. We do that today in similar situations.

Mr. MILFORD. Obviously, at some point there must be interdepartmental correlation, but my question is, can it be assumed that only a very limited number of people, such as the intelligence agency itself, have access to it? It is very limited?

Mr. STAATS. We would have to recognize that problem, and in fact today all of our classified reports are reviewed by the agency before we release them to the Congress from the standpoint of what specific information in them has to be classified.

On any of these subjects, we send the report in draft form to the agency and many times, as you may know, we send classified reports up to Congress. Often part will be classified, part will be unclassified. Or there may be even pages where certain parts of the information are classified, the remainder unclassified. This judgment is not made by us; it is made by the agency when it gives the draft its security review, and I think that would have to apply in this case.

Mr. MILFORD. You mentioned briefly in your statement that audits of the intelligence agencies might require more personnel. Do you have any idea of how many or what percentage of an increase would be required if you get into this?

Mr. STAATS. We couldn't really venture any guess at this point. It would depend a great deal on the wording of the statute giving us authority, and I think it would depend a great deal on the interests of the oversight committee itself as to how much it would like us to do. But I couldn't venture a guess at the moment.

Mr. MILFORD. It would follow this compartmental concept in your auditing. Would this proportionately require more people to carry out than your routine types of investigations and audits?

Mr. STAATS. I would say yes. Generally, yes.

Mr. MILFORD. Thank you, Mr. Chairman.

Chairman PIKE. Mr. Johnson.

Mr. JOHNSON. Mr. Staats, you have mentioned the figure $6 billion in your letter to the committee as being the probable amount or at least the figure that is bandied about as being spent on the intelligence.

Mr. STAATS. That was not GAO's figure; no, sir.

Mr. JOHNSON. I think it is in your letter to the Congress.

Mr. STAATS. We are attributing that figure to other sources.

Mr. JOHNSON. You say it comes from other sources, but that is the figure that you use. You didn't say that you had determined that. Obviously it is a large figure. We all recognize it is in the billions.

Mr. STAATS. Yes.

Mr. JOHNSON. It is also my understanding it is hidden throughout the budget in the budgets of many different agencies and departments of the Government; is that correct?

Mr. STAATS. That is right.

Mr. JOHNSON. When you are making audits of these other agencies and departments of the Government, do you ever run across these blocs of funds which are somehow squirreled away for the intelligence activities of the Government?

Mr. STAATS. We do run into situations on other reviews that we make, reviews of the type I referred to on page 2 of my statement, where we are simply told that that is information not available to us.

Mr. JOHNSON. Then you do not pursue that further?

Mr. STAATS. We have no way to pursue it.

Mr. JOHNSON. I hesitate to use the word "stonewalled" but when you run into that stone wall attitude, do you take it for granted you haven't authority to pursue it? How do you know it doesn't go beyond intelligence activities?

Mr. STAATS. With our present authority, we are not able to go beyond that point, although we make an effort to get them to give us information on a voluntary basis.

N14

Mr. JOHNSON. I understand that the CIA has statutory authority to do as it pleases with the money and I agree with your interpretation of that.

You have mentioned in your testimony or in your letter, I have forgotten which, that in response to a letter concerning Senator Percy's request, that you did not get responses from the CIA, the Defense Department, and the NSA, I believe. You mention that they cited statutory authority. What statutory authority does NSA and the Department of Defense have to refuse to give you information legitimately requested?

Mr. STAATS. We have that information here. If you like, we can specify it now or give it to you.

Mr. JOHNSON. If you can submit that to the committee, I would like to see if the legislation we are talking about needs to be expanded beyond CIA. . . .

Mr. JOHNSON. The Defense Department evidently, if they tell you it is secret, you won't pursue it, or if NSA tells you, you won't pursue it.

Mr. STAATS. We might pursue it to see whether or not they would be agreeable to declassifying enough of it to meet our requirements. For example, if we are dealing with something like narcotics control, or if we are dealing with some other matter then we do pursue it in that sense, but the ultimate decision is theirs, not ours.

Mr. JOHNSON. In your letter you indicated you wrote a letter to CIA January 17 of this year and never received a response and made attempts to get a response and could not.

What attempts do you make when they refuse to talk to you?

Mr. STAATS. These are handled by telephone or visitation.

Mr. JOHNSON. And if they flatly refuse, there is nothing you can do about it?

Mr. STAATS. That is correct.

Mr. JOHNSON. Well, we have this amendment to the Foreign Assistance Act of 1974 which was passed last year, which prohibits CIA expenditure of funds "for operations in foreign countries other than intelligence activities, intended solely for obtaining necessary intelligence" unless the President determines it is important to the national security.

Presently then there would be no way of determining, no way that anybody in the U.S. Government, unless the President himself went into an investigative posture, could determine whether or not that provision of the law is being honored; is that correct?

[The reference is to the Hughes-Ryan amendment—section 32 of the Foreign Assistance Act of 1974, P.L. 93–559, "Intelligence Activities and Exchange of Materials"—which amended section 662 of the Foreign Assistance Act of 1961; 22 U.S.C. 2422. . . .

N15

Mr. STAATS. That is correct.

We do find that in some cases the agency will let us have information. For example, in connection with the report we made to the Congress on the legislative ceiling on expenditures in Laos, we were able to get the information because they were willing to supply it.

Mr. JOHNSON. They gave you the information, but did you have any way of verifying if the information they gave you was correct?

Mr. KELLER. Probably not.

I would like to follow up a little bit on your earlier question for a minute. The law is quite clear in that it says we shall have access to all information and papers and records of agencies. At the same time, there is no enforcement power in the Comptroller General. In other words, if we do get a refusal, we have no subpena power, we have no way of going to a court and trying to enforce our right. We have presented testimony on this problem to Congress, not primarily with regard to security agencies, but concerning many agencies; we have asked for subpena power in order to get a resolution of whether we have a right to these records or not.

It is just as simple as this—that we can have all the rights in the world and the agency has the papers and doesn't give them to us.

Chairman PIKE. Mr. Hayes?

Mr. HAYES. Mr. Staats, do you know the mechanical method by which moneys allocated in one budget—for example, in the Air Force budget for intelligence purposes—are then transferred to another intelligence agency—for example, to the CIA?

Mr. STAATS. Mr. Lynn, again, can outline this. I am sure he will tomorrow, but, in general, this is handled through the OMB with the advice of the DCI and it becomes a Presidential decision.

Mr. HAYES. So that the physical method then is determined by OMB?

Mr. STAATS. At the beginning of the fiscal year or as soon as the funds are available, there would be a transfer that would take place.

Mr. HAYES. Do you have information concerning how employees are detailed between the various intelligence agencies and other executive branch departments?

Mr. STAATS. No, sir, I do not.

AGENCY ABUSES—CONFIRMATION TESTIMONY OF GEORGE BUSH ([8], pp. 26–40)

George Bush, former ambassador to China, was appointed by President Gerald R. Ford to succeed William Colby as DCI and head of the CIA. Bush testified at his confirmation hearings before the Senate Armed Services Committee in December 1975, when Congress was still considering the form and substance of its oversight responsibilities in the intelligence field. Senator Phillip Hart questioned Bush on covert operations and the need for accountability. His responses, qualified as they were regarding public disclosure of security information, signaled a willingness of the Ford administration to inform responsible parties in the Congress of covert operations. Bush acknowledged a potential for moral abuse by the CIA and appeared to accept the notion that an independent "check" on Executive branch authority could curtail abuses.

Senator HART. Thank you, Mr. Chairman.

Mr. Ambassador, along with Senators Tower and Goldwater, I have worked for the last 10½ months on the select committee looking into the intelligence community. Those of us who have been involved in that experience feel strongly not just about this confirmation but about the future of the intelligence structure of this country.

You have said, and I think it is admirable, that "things were done that were outrageous and morally offensive. These must not be repeated and I will take every step possible to see that they are not."

I would like to probe a little about what steps you would take to see that they are not.

You have talked, and I think rightly so, about political insulation but primarily along the lines of insulating the agency from your own political background. I am more concerned about insulating you from the rest of the political process, particularly in the White House. What those of us on the committee have found out is that sometimes the agency was off on its own, but just as often it was operating under the direction of political figures of various administrations in both parties.

What steps would you take to insulate yourself from the desires of a President to promote his own political purposes or to conduct some operation abroad that in your judgment was not in this country's interests?

Mr. BUSH. Senator, I do not know how one insulates oneself from the wishes of somebody else. I mean I do not—if one has access he is—this is going to be nitpicking here but it is hard to insulate oneself from the wishes.

In terms of the execution of something I think is wrong I would clearly—and it gets tough because the President has certain rights and certain responsibilities over the intelligence community and certainly over the Defense Intelligence Agency where he is Commander-in-Chief of the Armed Forces, but again I would not try to insulate myself from the President per se as an answer to the question. I would insist that to the degree it was possible, given the timeliness of whatever the situation was, that the proper bodies of the National Security Council, have the right to act on these matters.

I think we need to study it. There is a wide range of committees in the intelligence community, some of which I am familiar with, many of which I am not, and I think there are all kinds of ways to be sure that what you do in the final analysis is properly recommended. But once it was recommended and you get down to a moral question that you disagree with, you in the final analysis after urging reconsideration or saying I want 24 hours to present the views of the intelligence community or the CIA or whatever it is, in the final analysis you have only one remedy. I think we both know what that is. That is to get out.

Senator HART. There is another one. That is to let the President know where you stand on some of these things before you go into office. There is no doubt in his mind how far you are willing to let the CIA go.

Mr. BUSH. I accept that, sir; yes, sir.

Senator HART. Let us probe what you feel to be morally offensive and outrageous. How do you feel about assassinations?

Mr. BUSH. I find them morally offensive and I am pleased the President has made that position very, very clear to the Intelligence Committee and I think also Director Colby who I think knows about this, I know he feels——

The CHAIRMAN. Excuse me. What was your question?

Senator HART. The question was whether a Director of the CIA can insulate himself from wrong political pressures by letting the President know the bounds beyond which he will not go as director— before he takes office.

The CHAIRMAN. Yes.

Mr. BUSH. I accept that. I think it is an excellent suggestion and I would be prepared to do it. I think in matters that did come up violating the rights of citizens in this country, I think if I continue to emphasize we are talking about foreign intelligence, that will help. There are some legitimate things that must be done domestically by the CIA, in its own security, for example, but emphasizing foreign intelligence could help with the problem that understandably troubles the citizens in this country.

Senator HART. I want to get to that, but let me pursue some of the foreign techniques. What about supporting and promoting military coups d'etat in various countries around the world?

Mr. BUSH. You mean in the covert field?

Senator HART. Yes.

Mr. BUSH. I would want to have full benefit of all the intelligence. I would want to have full benefit of how these matters were taking place but I cannot tell you, and I do not think I should, that there would never by any support for a coup d'etat; in other words, I cannot tell you I cannot conceive of a situation where I would not support such action.

Senator HART. What about supporting the overthrow of a government that was constitutionally elected?

Mr. BUSH. I think we should tread very carefully on governments that are constitutionally elected. That is what we are trying to encourage around the world and I feel strongly about that.

Senator HART. What about paramilitary operations, providing funds and arms to establish a government that we wanted?

Mr. BUSH. I can see certain circumstances where that would be in the best interests of the United States, the best interests of our allies, the best interests of the free world.

Senator HART. How about providing money for political parties and candidates in various countries?

Mr. BUSH. I have a little more difficulty with that one but, again, without having the benefit of the facts and what the situation is surrounding it, I would not make a clear and definitive statement whether that ever or never should be done.

Senator HART. You raised the question of getting the CIA out of domestic areas totally. Let us hypothesize a situation where a President has stepped over the bounds. Let us say the FBI is investigating some people who are involved, and they go right to the White House. There is some possible CIA interest. The President calls you and says, I want you as Director of the CIA to call the Director of the FBI to tell him to call off this operation because it may jeopardize some CIA activities.

Mr. BUSH. Well, generally speaking, and I think you are hypothecating a case without spelling it out in enough detail to know if there is any real legitimate foreign intelligence aspect, but generally speaking the CIA should butt out of the domestic business and it certainly ought not to be a domestic police force and it certainly ought not to be involved in investigations domestically of this kind of thing.

Senator HART. That is the easy side.

Mr. BUSH. Well, it is not——

Senator HART. I am hypothesizing a case that actually happened in June 1972. There might have been some tangential CIA interest in something in Mexico. Funds were laundered and so forth.

Mr. BUSH. Using a 50–50 hindsight on that case, I hope I would have said the CIA is not going to get involved in that if we are talking about the same one.

Senator HART. We are.

Senator LEAHY. Are there others?

Senator HART. There has been a doctrine operating between the political structure and the intelligence community for many years called plausible deniability. It is letting the President know just enough about what is going on, but not enough so that when the question is asked, "Did you know this was going on?" he has some grounds for denying that he knew.

How do you feel about that, particularly where major covert operations were involved?

Mr. BUSH. I think the President should be fully involved and though I understand the need for plausible deniability, I think it is extremely difficult. I just do not think a President should be shielded when you are dealing with something this important, from the totality of the information. That is my own view on it.

Senator HART. Now, Senator Symington pointed out that too few people in this country are aware that the Director of Central Intelligence controls only about 15 or 20 percent of the intelligence budget. Eighty percent of that is under the control of the Secretary of Defense.

Do you have any recommendations or thoughts on how one operates as the Director of the entire intelligence community and yet does not control the vast bulk of their budget?

Mr. BUSH. No. I will welcome the recommendations from your committee or welcome the recommendations of the Pike committee. I will welcome the recommendations that are being prepared as I understand it in the White House now. I have been here a week and I have no firm judgment on how that should be done. I would make a general statement, though, that if it is determined by these recommendations that the Director should have the authority, it seems to me that the best way to have the responsibility is to have something to say about the funds; and so I think in that area you might find the answer. But, again look at and study, before I took a personal position, the views of the various committees that are studying these matters. They have been on it for several months and I have been back here 1 week, and I would be presumptuous, I think, to say these are my final views.

On separating the Director of Central Intelligence from his CIA responsibilities, I have some general feelings on it. One is the Director of Central Intelligence needs some kind of a base. He has one now in CIA and I am not enthralled with the concept that everybody has his empire and you are just floating around EOB someplace. That is a generalized concept, but if you are going to have the responsibility, you ought to have some muscle, some authority, to do something about it with.

So I would hope whatever your committee recommends and whatever others recommend they do not set up some Director of Central Intelligence and then not give him the tools to enforce these coordinated activities through budgetary control.

That is very general, Senator Hart, but I do not——

Senator HART. But I think what you are saying——

Mr. BUSH. I have no recommendations yet.

Senator HART. You would be willing to go to the mat with the Secretary of Defense to get a little more authority over how that 80 percent of the intelligence budget is spent.

Mr. BUSH. The answer is yes, sir, but particularly if you are supposed to have the responsibility for it, I think you must do that, and I think I would be in a position to—I would not say have equal standing because those are Cabinet positions, both State and Defense, with policymaking functions. This is not, as I conceive it, and I think it is properly conceived as defined in the statute, a policy job; but I can see situations where I would want to forcefully present the views of the intelligence community even though they might be on a different direction from existing policy, and let somebody else make the policy, but get those views in there.

Senator HART. How is my time, Mr. Chairman?

The CHAIRMAN. You have run over.

Senator HART. I had some other questions, but let me just make one observation that I made to you when we visited in my office briefly, and that is—leaving aside your qualifications, background, integrity, and ability to convince us you will not politicize nor permit the CIA to be politicized despite your political background—there is still a separate question all of us have to acknowledge. This is the precedent established by this kind of appointment. Despite your qualifications, it is a step in the direction that troubles many of us, but it does not reflect on your personally one iota.

Mr. BUSH. May I respond to that, Mr. Chairman?

The CHAIRMAN. Yes; but make it as brief as you reasonably can. Mr. Leahy has been waiting.

Mr. BUSH. Senator Hart, I would simply appeal that you not make judgments on your vote based on outside appearances, editorials, fear of whether somebody is going to say a "politician," which I do not think is a bad word there. I think it should be made on the basis of qualifications and integrity and how it is going to be viewed a year from now, 2 years from now, 3 years from now, and that is what I appeal to you to do in determining whether I am fit to take this job.

Senator HART. Mr. Bush, I do not make my judgments based on editorials.

Mr. BUSH. Yes.

The CHAIRMAN. Senator Leahy.

Senator LEAHY. Thank you, Mr. Chairman.

Mr. Ambassador, earlier in a statement made by Senator Stennis as chairman of this committee, he said that he would question your judgment if you were using the CIA as a steppingstone to the Vice-Presidency. I might add that I would question your sanity if you were going to use the CIA as a steppingstone to the Vice-Presidency. I cannot imagine any worse way today to get into that. But I would like to go into a couple of areas.

Mr. BUSH. Yes, sir.

Senator LEAHY. Senator Hart has asked you about political assassinations and absent, I would assume—we will not get the question too muddy—absent a declaration of war in a particular area, do I understand your answer to be that you are totally opposed?

Mr. BUSH. Yes, sir.

Senator LEAHY. To political assassinations?

Mr. BUSH. I understand a directive has gone out on that. We would not need it as far as I am concerned. I do indeed. It is appalling to me.

The CHAIRMAN. Mr. Bush, excuse me a minute. Use your microphone please.

Mr. BUSH. I am opposed to political assassinations and——

Senator LEAHY. I understand there is a directive from President Ford on that. Suppose you were serving under another President and such a request was made of you as CIA Director. What would you do?

Mr. BUSH. I would—I feel strongly enough about that one—you have precluded wartime—to say that would be the place where I got off or he changed his mind, one.

Senator LEAHY. Let me follow up on a question asked by Senator McIntyre. Besides resigning, would you feel strongly enough about that to report it to the proper oversight committees? For example, in the Senate, the Armed Services Committee?

Mr. BUSH. On that matter, yes, sir.

Senator LEAHY. Then let me ask you——

Mr. BUSH. Can I elaborate once more? I can see situations where I might resign.

Senator LEAHY. Certainly.

Mr. BUSH. Over something that I conceived to be a real moral problem but where the Chief—where the President had the legal right to go through with it where I would not do that or I might quietly fade away without calling a press conference or without making a scene—but I would always faithfully try to testify before the appropriate oversight committees of the U.S. Congress.

Senator LEAHY. I am concerned over what is the best way for Congress to carry on this oversight function. For example, can the Congress carry on its oversight function if it has full control and debate over the CIA budget or should they——

Mr. BUSH. I think the proper investigative bodies of Congress, I mean the proper oversight committees, should be informed on the budget but I would oppose making the CIA budget public.

Senator LEAHY. I am concerned—I recall once in a debate in this committee, and without giving out any secrets, having a whole series of little items, $5 million and $10 million, and so forth, until we got down to the bottom item of several hundred million dollars put in there for miscellaneous use. Coming from a small state, that seemed to be a lot of money, and I wondered exactly what it was. I am wondering how we can carry out this oversight.

Mr. Ambassador, do you feel the Congress has done an adequate job of carrying out its oversight function of the CIA during, say, the past 4 or 5 years?

Mr. BUSH. I think many individuals in the Senate that I have talked to feel that it has not and I would be inclined to go along with that. But I again do not have all the evidence on that that has come to your committee.

Senator LEAHY. Has this committee itself, the Armed Services Committee, done an adequate job?

Mr. BUSH. I am not about to sit here criticizing the Senate Armed Services Committee, given the limited amount of information I have. Your committee has had access to a tremendous amount of information. I have had access to none of it, and I do not know how many meetings they have had and I just simply am not going to criticize this committee because I do not know how many times you have met on this. I have not been briefed.

Senator TOWER. Would the Senator from Vermont yield for a comment from a member of the select committee on that point? Senators Hart, Goldwater, and I serve on the Senate Select Committee on Intelligence. I think it would be useful for the committee to know, at this point, that the select committee is at the moment considering various oversight options to recommend to the Senate. That is currently ongoing in the select committee and on the 20th of December the chairman of the committee, the vice chairman, and myself, will testify before the Government Operations Committee on this very matter. So it is a matter currently under consideration.

The CHAIRMAN. All right, Senator Leahy.

Senator LEAHY. The Congress has this year carried out two fairly substantial investigations of the CIA, both in the House and in the Senate. Has that hurt the CIA in your estimation?

Mr. BUSH. I have not been out there. I do not know what effect it has had on the morale of the CIA. I simply cannot answer that question. Around the world I think some do not seem to understand our constitutional process, and so perhaps it has raised some eyebrows. I know it has in some other countries, but whether it has hurt it here, I simply cannot say. To the degree it has encouraged the outside and wanton disclosure, and my understanding since I have been back here for 6 days is that these committees have both been very responsible with classified information and I do not see how the charge can be made that in doing its constitutional duty that it has hurt.

Senator LEAHY. If the Congress had done a thorough, continuing, ongoing oversight of the CIA during the past 5 years, would these committees have been necessary?

Mr. BUSH. Probably it would not have been necessary.

Senator LEAHY. Thank you.

Mr. BUSH. On the other hand, perhaps it is timely to have a review that will make some substantive suggestions. It is my understanding that both committees are empaneled in order to suggest legislative change and it is those suggestions that I would like to see and I would certainly believe to the degree they are left for administrative decision, I would consider them very, very thoroughly because I know people have put in an awful lot of hard work on those committees.

Senator LEAHY. How would you feel about taking the oversight away from the present committees that have it and putting it into a special joint committee?

Mr. BUSH. My 4 years in the Congress taught me one thing and that is to let the Congress determine its own procedures, and I would simply bow to the will of the Congress and cooperate fully with whatever is decided by the Congress. I would cooperate.

Senator LEAHY. I am not on the Select Committee. Senator Hart, Senator Tower and Senator Goldwater are but could that be an effective way of carrying out the oversight of the CIA?

I am not lobbying for any particular method of doing it, Mr. Ambassador.

Mr. BUSH. I think it could and it is a recommendation of the Rockefeller Commission. I support that recommendation, but having said so I would, if there is some new situation that comes forward, I would be glad to consider that—I will offer my full cooperation if I am confirmed to whatever vehicle Congress decides upon.

Senator LEAHY. Mr. Ambassador, you mentioned the Rockefeller Committee which has spoken of having a Presidential Advisory Committee on Oversight. Do you support that?

Mr. BUSH. There already is a Presidential Advisory Committee—the Foreign Intelligence Advisory Board—and it would have my full cooperation, sir.

Senator LEAHY. Well, that was going to be my next question.

The Foreign Intelligence Advisory Board was first established back in the mid–50's by President Eisenhower. It was the President's board of consultants on foreign intelligence activities. I understand the name was changed in 1961 by President Kennedy to the President's Foreign Intelligence Advisory Board (PFIAB).

There have been three different charters—1956, 1961 and 1969. The contents were about the same.

This summer I had my staff look at the President's Foreign Intelligence Advisory Board. I cannot really see where it can carry out much in the way of oversight functions. They have had a relatively small budget. They get almost all their information from the CIA, according to their staff director on foreign intelligence matters.

According to their staff people down there, they point out that their job did not include oversight and review of the CIA but rather is confined to coming up with ideas which would improve our intelligence efforts and they brought out one of them, the U–2. The Commission report on the Board said it does not exert control over the CIA. In fact, the CIA is the Board's only source of information about CIA activities.

Do you think that is really going to do an awful lot for us?

Mr. BUSH. I think that depends on what these committees come up with. If your implication is, and maybe I missed it in the question, Senator Leahy, you said they rely on the Director of Central Intelligence or the CIA for intelligence. I would oppose yet another intelligence-gathering organization. So maybe I misread that. But I feel that the Board has a useful function.

I notice one of the recommendations in the Rockefeller Commission is that the Inspector General should report any irregularities that he finds to the President's Board and I think in those areas and perhaps others that your committee can suggest it would be good. The fact that they get their information from the existing intelligence community does not trouble me because I do not think we need another intelligence agency.

Senator LEAHY. I agree with you on the inspector general, but the Commission also found that because of the CIA's compartment—the way they have set up their compartments in there, their compartments' secrecy and all, that the inspector general never even knew of the illegal and improper activities which recently have come to light.

Would you, if you were the Director of the CIA, upgrade the staff and responsibility of the Inspector General? Would you give him access to all CIA files?

Mr. BUSH. I think I read enough on that, sir, to answer affirmatively, yes, I would.

Senator LEAHY. Would he be allowed to report directly to the appropriate congressional oversight committee if one is set up?

Mr. BUSH. I sure would want to be sitting next to him——

I do not think that you need to be able to have absolutely everybody go off freewheeling but certainly the inspector general should be made available to these committees, but I would like to know what was going on, and it is my intention if confirmed for this job to know what is going on as much as possible.

If you suggest, and I may be misreading it, that I would not know what the testimony was or I would not know what he was doing, just testifying——

Senator LEAHY. I am not suggesting that at all.

Mr. BUSH. So I would simply think, yes, he should be available. I would like to know about it.

Senator LEAHY. I am not suggesting you not know what he was talking about at all, Mr. Ambassador. I would not suggest that of any agency head of their own inspector general.

What I was concerned about is that the inspector general in many ways has far more time to look for these things than the Director does, and I want to be sure that he has such access because in the past apparently he has not had such access and that is probably one of the reasons we are facing this problem today.

Mr. BUSH. Let me tell you why I respond that way.

In the Rockefeller report there was a suggestion that he go directly to the PFIAB. I have no problems with that. But I want to be informed. I want to know about it. And if he was saying what his suggestions were, I would like as the Director, to know about it and then also have the right to say whether I agreed or disagreed.

You have got to have a disciplined organization.

The CHAIRMAN. I am sorry Senator but your time has run over. You may ask one more question.

Senator LEAHY. I will wait until the next go-around.

The CHAIRMAN. All right.

Mr. Bush, some minutes ago on the proposition of having a request from the executive department, be it the President or someone under the President, you gave a response as to what your action would be. Would you direct your first deputy, we will say, to report directly to you any request of that nature that he might receive?

Mr. BUSH. Yes, sir; I would.

I think it is essential that the Director be informed of White House requests.

The CHAIRMAN. Yes.

Mr. BUSH. And I do not know how many they get over there. Some of them I am sure are strictly routine, but certainly as a matter of principle I think whether they come into the Counsel's office, the inspector general's office, the deputy's office, I would insist on being informed.

The CHAIRMAN. I was directing the question mainly at matters of serious importance and consequence. Would you apply that same rule, then, to your chiefs of divisions? I do not know just what term you may use in the CIA but I am thinking in terms of those who have charge of various major operations. Would you instruct them, too?

Mr. BUSH. Yes, sir.

The CHAIRMAN. It seems to me that is getting at the thing in such a way as to make the total responsibility and authority yours.

Mr. BUSH. Yes, sir. I would.

There are four deputies in addition to the—and I would do that, the same for the inspector general, the same for the General Counsel's office.

The CHAIRMAN. And to ensure that you are directing the policy on those kinds of questions—I am not hitting at any President—but to ensure that you did have that responsibility and power you would also direct any others who are in key positions to give the same reports to you.

Mr. BUSH. I would, Mr. Chairman.

The CHAIRMAN. A matter that I have been concerned with for years is the fact that you are not only Director of the CIA but you are Director of all the central intelligence community which includes operations of the DIA and others, but still you do not have the authority over them. You just have the authority over what I call the CIA proper or hard core. That money is put in another budget. It is a separate matter.

Now, if you are confirmed, I want to strongly suggest that you take the lead in trying to get a workable, practical plan, because if you are going to have the responsibilities, you must have the authority. Did I make that clear to you?

Mr. BUSH. Yes, sir.

The CHAIRMAN. What is your response to that?

Mr. BUSH. My response, Mr. Chairman, is I hope I can find ways to implement that suggestion.

The CHAIRMAN. Yes. Some very able men have tried and have undertaken such a mission but due to the pressure of various other matters have not come up with anything very practical. You already see that problem facing you, do you not?

Mr. BUSH. I see the problem, Mr. Chairman, but I cannot in conscience tell you I see the clear answer.

The CHAIRMAN. No.

Mr. BUSH. Because I see between the Defense Intelligence Agency and CIA and others in the community, an enormous problem of coordination, but I can pledge to this committee I will address myself to it as best I can.

The CHAIRMAN. Yes.

It is a very delicate and sensitive matter by nature and then it is a very practical problem, too, but I think it can be handled. It just takes some cooperation between the executive branch and the legislative branch.

I have been impressed with your answers to Senator Leahy's questions, all of which were good, regarding the Inspector General. You said you would want to be with your Inspector General, or be informed. I judge that it is by no means that you would try to control what he said, or anything of that kind, but feel that since the responsibility rests on you, you would want to know and would be entitled to know, I think, what his testimony was or what he was saying. Is that correct?

Mr. BUSH. That was my point, Senator.

The CHAIRMAN. Well, I have always advocated keeping the power where the responsibility is and keeping the responsibility where the power is. I said earlier in a brief opening statement that through these hearings we can emphasize the absolute necessity of a clear consciousness on the part of the Chief Executive of the Nation of this special power that is vested in him under the act and of the care and personal attention the President must give through this exceptional power and also to the individual that he selects to act for him.

Quoting further I said "I hope these hearings will emphasize that point." I think the hearings have emphasized that point to you, to the public, and to the President, in the questions that came from Members other than me, and my time has expired. As I see it, it is an obligation that you owe to the President especially, to keep him directly advised of the enormous duties.

I believe it is almost beyond human comprehension, the ability the President must have to reach his obligations. But this is a special law and operates in a special way. It is not within the pattern of other agencies as I see it, and the President is going to need your help as well as you need him. So you are conscious of your obligation in that way.

Mr. BUSH. Yes, sir; I am, Mr. Chairman.

The CHAIRMAN. Not trying to protect him from things but to protect the country, your position, and the obligation that you assume. Is that the way you see it?

Mr. BUSH. Yes, sir. I see it—I see that relationship clearly.

The CHAIRMAN. Yes.

Mr. BUSH. Some have charged that because I know the President personally, that would be bad for some reasons. I think it is good. If I have the proper integrity for this job I think the intelligence community is entitled to have its views forcefully, firmly presented to the President and then have the policymakers take over. That is my concept of this relationship, and certainly if there was wrongdoing or I detected improper pressures from the White House, I think, because of access, I would be in a reasonable position to do something about it.

I am not saying I am omniscient and would see right away that it was good or bad. I think there are some gray areas. But I would have the access and I think I would use it not to do bad things suggested by the White House but to see that the CIA views are fairly presented.

The CHAIRMAN. You would either correct those matters of any greatness at all yourself or take it up with him.

Mr. BUSH. Yes, sir.

The CHAIRMAN. All right.

I thank you very much.

Senator Symington?

Senator SYMINGTON. Mr. Ambassador, several points you made this morning worried me a bit. I do not think you really meant it that way when you said; maybe you were old fashioned, but you still believed in patriotism.

I have watched my four grandsons, children of today—and believe the youth of today are equally patriotic. I think leadership in the executive branch—and I am not talking about any one administration—and leadership in the Congress is more responsible for the recent lack of desire to join the armed services than anything, these "no-win" war concepts, for example.

I would hope you would not think most of the youth of today are not patriotic.

Mr. BUSH. I have four sons, one daughter. I have just as much confidence. I do get concerned about what sometimes seems to be—well, take the word "politician." The connotation of the politician has changed, some of it with reason, some of it in my view without. I stand here and say I think it is honorable. I know a lot of people do not. So it is this kind of general feeling I have rather than any lack of confidence in my four sons and I am sure yours, sir.

Senator SYMINGTON. I wanted you to expand on that because I felt I knew how you really felt about it. The basic problem, in my opinion, in the United States today is "greed." As I watch many operations around this country I am saddened. The efforts for authority, the efforts for votes. Often it has little to do with money, although there are a lot of people interested in getting as much money out of the Government as they can. The record so proves. Most are not in Government. Some are.

So I think that is perhaps our great problem today, and the only way we are going to solve it is through sacrifice. I do not know anybody who is asking me to sacrifice anything. 1 watch people go by 20, 30 miles above the speed limit, one person per car. We could go into more detail about that, but I think you know what I am getting at.

Mr. BUSH. I do, sir.

Senator SYMINGTON. This country has to have leadership that shows the way. I will take my full responsibility, inability to handle in the legislative branch. I honestly do not think in recent years proper leadership has been characteristic of the executive branch either.

Another matter: We are getting very open, you might say. I hope that does not impinge too heavily on your intelligence job. It is my understanding the man who runs the system of the country considered generally to be probably our leading opponent, has the title at least among his colleagues, of director of misinformation. So I hope you do not feel over obligated by what has happened in the past. Otherwise you, in effect, defeat the basic concept of your job which has vitally important covert operations so as to obtain vital intelligence information.

This is said with the premise that such information is important to the security of the United States. I would hope you agree there is information you only have to give the President, not necessarily the Congress at the time.

Mr. BUSH. I agree. I do feel that one of the things that troubles me is the tendency to wantonly disclose secret information. I understand it, the employees of the CIA, and I think properly, take a pledge of secrecy, not to disclose classified information when they are there and not to disclose it after they leave, and I am appalled at indications that some do not take that pledge seriously. It is not fair to those who are working faithfully for their country in this important place.

I think it is wanton and I do not think it is right and I will certainly do what I can—this is a side area but I will certainly do what I can to see that the families and the individuals who do abide by the rules of that game are not endangered by the wanton disclosure on the part of others. That clearly moves over into some of the more sensitive areas, I think, but I have a general feeling that Congress must be kept closely informed, and yet I am confident when I get in there I will find things that are between the Director and the President just as there are between the President and other appointees.

Senator SYMINGTON. I agree with you.

Mr. BUSH. That should be kept confidential.

Senator SYMINGTON. We are talking about covert operations.

One other point that worried me in your testimony is when you said something about not being a Cabinet member, did not have Cabinet rank, were an operating man primarily. I agree only partly with that. Based on my experience, it is difficult to separate policy and operations—very hard. I would hope the fact you were not a member of the Cabinet would not give you hesitation in giving the President the situation as you saw it regardless of whether or not you were formally a Cabinet member.

Mr. BUSH. That would be my intention, sir, and I was simply referring to the essentialities of presenting to the policymakers the most objective possible analysis, whether it agreed with existing policy or not, but I do recognize the Director of Central Intelligence and the CIA function as well does not make foreign policy. That is the point I was trying to make.

Senator SYMINGTON. You have cleared that up. Thank you for your courtesy.

The CHAIRMAN. Gentlemen of the committee, turning to this matter of the so-called conflict of interest that we always go into, Mr. Bush has conferred with Mr. Braswell, our valuable chief counsel and staff director, and has written a letter, dated December 14, addressed to me as chairman, and I consider that to be to the committee regarding these matters and I have it here for the inspection of any member of the committee that might want to review it.

Let me ask Mr. Braswell one question. Mr. Braswell, you heard my statement made here. You have handed me this letter dated December 14, 1975, and in your conferences with Mr. Bush and those representing him, does he meet all the requirements of the committee that we customarily apply with reference to reported nominees?

Mr. BRASWELL. Mr. Chairman, Mr. Bush does meet these requirements. The letter indicates that he will sell any holdings which pose any conflict of interest with the Central Intelligence Agency. There are a limited number of securities which have certain relationships and it is indicated that he will dispose of those within 30 days after confirmation.

The CHAIRMAN. All right. Members of the committee, we will put this letter with its exhibit in the office file. It is available to any committee member who might want to examine it. We do not customarily put these matters in the public record, but keep a special file on it.

[The document referred to will be found in the files of the committee.]

The CHAIRMAN. Senator Hart, that brings us now to you.

Senator HART. Thank you, Mr. Chairman.

Mr. Ambassador, back in 1952 at the request of President Eisenhower, the committee or Commission looked into the state of the intelligence community at that time. Under the chairmanship of General Doolittle they reported back some recommendations for changes, but most importantly in the preamble of their report there is a statement that I think many of us have found rather shocking. It is to the effect that during the period of the cold war this country was faced with a ruthless enemy and that to survive in the world, a world populated by enemies of this sort, we had to become at least as ruthless as our enemies and in effect discard or shelve what the report called the "traditional American values."

In the judgment of some of us who have been looking into this area for many months, it is that kind of an attitude or mentality which has led to some of the conduct which you described as outrageous. What is your feeling generally about the activities of this country in relation to the activities of other countries? Do we in your judgment have to adopt the same techniques to survive in this world?

Mr. Bush. Senator, I made my public position on assassination. Having said that, I am somewhat aware, not perhaps as aware as the committee, having not had access to the information, that we are up against some pretty ruthless people. They are today ruthless and they are tough and today they will resort to schemes that are not overly pleasant.

I am not going to sit here and say we need to match ruthlessness with ruthlessness. I do feel we need a covert capability and I hope that it can minimize these problems that offend our Americans. We are living in a very complicated, difficult world.

Senator Hart. But you would not go so far as to say we have to abandon our traditional values or sense of fair play.

Mr. Bush. I would not abandon my own traditional values or sense of fair play, certainly, and I do not think we should as a Nation.

Senator Hart. The principal intelligence judgments are products of the intelligence community, national intelligence estimates. They are not presently or have not been traditionally given to the Congress or congressional committees. Rather, the judgment of the intelligence community is summarized when it is given.

What would be your view on having the CIA's national intelligence estimates made available to the appropriate committee of Congress, particularly Foreign Relations and Armed Services?

Mr. Bush. I would want to take a close look at that. I would—I am not too familiar with the totality of the national intelligence estimates, what that involves, so I am not going to commit ahead of time to what would be delivered, but certainly in terms of keeping these committees involved, keeping them involved on important matters, I would be inclined to say at this point, yes, but I would reserve the right, if I could, to at least understand the totality of what we are talking about.

I think, getting back to Senator Symington, I think there are some things that must be between the intelligence and the President and must be determined by the President, and that I would have to stand with.

Senator Hart. Under present procedures, when the Congress is informed about covert operations, it is informed after the executive branch has already approved those operations. It seems to me that an alternative would be for the Director of Central Intelligence to present the proposed action to the Congress, or the appropriate committees, at the same time, simultaneously with proposing that action to the executive branch. What would your feeling be about that?

N17

Mr. Bush. I would oppose that.

Senator Hart. On what grounds?

Mr. Bush. On the grounds I think it is the obligation of the President to determine the covert activities and I would say after plenty of adequate consultation with the NSC and representatives of the intelligence community, but I think he must make that decision and I do not think it ought to be a joint decision and I think it might be a joint decision if it were done in the manner you suggest.

Senator Hart. So the only way to prevent the Congress from vetoing a decision is to just not let them know.

Mr. Bush. There are things in intelligence, Senator Hart, that I think have to be kept confidential, but that is not to say they should not be disclosed to Congress and that is not to say Congress should not be fully informed at the appropriate time. The law specifically, as I understand it—the amendment specifies they shall be informed and I will do my best to inform them but before a foreign policy decision is made, I do not think that there has to be a group decision on that. I think that is what the Presidents are elected to do.

Senator HART. Well, one, information does not presume decision. Nor does it presume disclosure.

Mr. BUSH. I did not suggest, sir, that it meant disclosure.

Senator HART. You certainly did. Your response was you do not think there should be disclosure.

Mr. BUSH. I mean public disclosure. I was not suggesting a leak if that is what you meant.

Senator HART. Well, that takes us to a current case and that is Angola. It has been suggested in situations such as Angola that rather than have assistance provided, if you will, under the table, why do we not just openly acknowledge the fact that we are assisting certain governments and certain political groups around the world, that we feel that they stand for democracy and the kinds of things we represent. We are assisting them openly, rather than have it sort of come out piecemeal as it always is done.

Mr. BUSH. I think in some instances we should do that. Angola I have not been briefed on. I do not know the facts. I do not know the problems with neighboring countries—I do not know what the extent of the Soviet aid is to the MPLA. I just simply do not know, so I would have to defer but I think in this instance that is correct, and in some instances we do this with arms programs.

Senator HART. So you would not preclude the possibility that there might be situations in the world where we would want, in a political conflict, to take sides with one party or another and openly provide them financial assistance or arms in the struggle. Do you think that would be a possibility?

Mr. BUSH. This gets close to the responsibilities of the Congress during war and things of that nature, you see.

Senator HART. That is right.

Mr. BUSH. And I think each case has to be looked at on its own merits.

Senator HART. But you do not preclude that possibility?

Mr. BUSH. Would you repeat what I am not precluding once more?

Senator HART. That we would openly assist financially and with arms where a dispute is going on as to what kind of government should emerge in a country, but not after a government has emerged and been recognized, and then provide arms. When there is conflict, when there is hostility, when the nature of that government is not determined we would become involved.

Mr. BUSH. I would not preclude that in some cases this might be done, but I am not arguing the merits of how Angola is being handled at this time because very candidly I am not briefed on that.

OVERSIGHT OF DEFENSE INTELLIGENCE ([25], pp. 236–242)

Several months after DCI Director designate George Bush had expressed a willingness to cooperate on stricter congressional oversight of the intelligence community, the Senate Committee on Government Operations began hearings on bills to establish intelligence oversight committees. The bills under review by this committee were S. 317, S. 189, Senate Concurrent Resolution

4, S. 2893, and S. 2865, none of which was enacted. A compromise bill, Senate Resolution 400, was passed in May 1976 and resulted in the establishment of the Senate Select Committee on Intelligence.

As it became apparent that the Senate would begin to enforce stronger oversight, administration witnesses seemed to welcome the new congressional role, but they also were concerned with the form the congressional oversight mechanism might take. In his testimony, Deputy Secretary of Defense Robert Ellsworth showed a preference for keeping defense intelligence appropriations within the jurisdiction of the House Appropriations Committee, arguing that this committee had the necessary staff expertise and that intelligence functions were not easily separated from the overall defense budget.

TESTIMONY OF ROBERT F. ELLSWORTH, DEPUTY SECRETARY OF DEFENSE

Mr. ELLSWORTH. Thank you very much, Mr. Chairman.

Mr. Chairman and members of the Senate Government Operations Committee, I appreciate the opportunity you have afforded me today to present the views of the Department of Defense on the issue of congressional oversight of the Nation's intelligence organizations.

At the outset, let me emphasize that Secretary Rumsfeld and I both believe strongly in the need for effective congressional monitoring of the intelligence community. Precisely how the Congress organizes itself to accomplish its oversight role is, of course, for the Congress to decide. Since this committee has asked for our comments, however, I will offer some observations.

First, I would like to observe that the existence of so many committees of Congress engaged in oversight of the intelligence community suggests some degree of uncertainty on the part of Congress about how to handle the oversight function.

Last year in addition to the normal oversight committees—the Senate and House Armed Services Committees and the Senate and House Appropriations Committees—a number of other committees and subcommittees undertook to exercise some degree of oversight over various aspects of the intelligence community.

Last year there were some 24 appearances before House committees by 15 key Defense intelligence personnel, and 15 appearances before Senate committees by 11 key Defense intelligence personnel. Now this year, both the Senate and House Select Committees on Intelligence are proposing the creation of follow-on permanent intelligence oversight committees.

The proliferation of competing intelligence oversight committees poses two major problems. One problem is the number of man-hours consumed in duplicative efforts. The other problem concerns the danger to secrecy which inevitably occurs when more and more people know about and talk about intelligence activities.

If the Congress can help resolve these two problems by creating one strong oversight committee, which the rest of the Congress will trust to monitor the intelligence community, the Department of Defense would welcome that committee.

On the other hand, if another committee is created to exercise intelligence oversight, in addition to those which already serve that function, we would have some reservations.

We assume that the driving force behind the creation of the Senate Select Committee on Intelligence—and indeed the House Select Committee—was the perceived need to insure that the abuses which had surfaced are corrected and that measures are taken to guard against abuses in the future.

For our part in the Department of Defense, we moved quickly to correct the abuses which had occurred and to create mechanisms to continually review our intelligence and investigative organizations.

In 1971, for example, the DOD created the Defense Investigative Review Committee—DIRC—to oversee all DOD investigative and counterintelligence operations. I believe the Senate Select Committee has expressed satisfaction with the way the DIRC operates.

In the area of foreign intelligence collection, including collection by Defense agencies, I would like to suggest that the committee give consideration to the idea of creating a communitywide Inspector General—IG—for intelligence who would be appointed by the President and confirmed by the Senate for a fixed term which is out of phase with the term of the President, that is, for 3, or 5, or 9 years.

This would provide both the President and the Congress with an IG possessing some of the independent quality of a member of the Federal Reserve Board, for example.

This independent status should give Congress confidence in the ability of the Inspector General to withstand ad hoc political pressures from any future White House staff.

Of the bills now before this committee, the bill prepared by the Senate Select Committee to Study Governmental Operations with Respect to Intelligence Activities represents the latest and most comprehensive effort to assert congressional prerogatives in the areas of national and foreign intelligence.

However, in translating those propositions into legislative form, the executive branch and the legislative branch have understandable differences as to how to proceed.

In the succeeding pages, I will address the language of the Senate Select Committee bill and the extent to which its provisions warrant rewriting.

First, the requirement to be kept informed. The requirement that the Committee on Intelligence Activities be kept fully and currently informed about all intelligence activities, and that documents and witnesses be produced whenever requested, poses a fundamental issue as to the supremacy of each branch within its own assigned area of constitutional responsibilities.

The failure of the proposal to respect occasional claims of constitutional privilege—claims which are expressly recognized in *United States* v. *Nixon*—and the unqualified obligation to inform the committee about intelligence matters, whether or not requested, has already been addressed by other witnesses.

During the year long investigation conducted by this Senate Select Committee on Intelligence, pursuant to Senate Resolution 21, the Defense Department furnished literally thousands upon thousands of pages to the committee. It also made available for interviews and hearings large numbers of DOD personnel concerned with intelligence operations.

However, these responses were made to specific requests from the committee rather than to any generalized charge to disclose information. Further, on those occasions when the release of specific information would not be in the public interest—because it involved communications to or from the President or because its release would jeopardize sensitive national security activities—means were found to meet the needs of the committee without violating the historic and well-recognized separation of powers doctrine.

This recognition by both sides that the Congress does not have the power to subject the executive branch to its will, any more than the executive branch may impose its unrestrained will upon the Congress, avoided unnecessary confrontations. To avoid these difficulties in the provision calling for the furnishing of information to the committtee, it is recommended that the proposal be modified so as to require the Intelligence Community to supply "information and timely intelligence necessary for sound decisions affecting the security of the Nation," as used in section 1 of the Senate Select Committee bill.

There are those who contend that the disclosures about past activities of certain foreign intelligence organizations necessitate daily oversight. When it is suggested to them that a general reporting requirement is sufficient, they reply that the only way they can determine whether the reports are accurate is to keep a constant, almost micrometric track of what is going on.

As Attorney General Levi stated in his remarks to the Administrative Conference of the United States on December 12, 1975, "The line between that and their management of what is going on is a very slight one."

Given the kinds of oversight proposed by some, it is clear that they have forgotten or choose to ignore the fundamental principle of our system that persons entrusted with power in each of the three branches of Government must not encroach upon the authority confided to the others. Execution of the laws and the conduct of the executive branch rests, not with an oversight committee, but with the Chief Executive.

Next, the prior notification requirement. The provision requiring advance Senate notice before a designated "intelligence activity" may be initiated, represents an unacceptable infringement on the authority of the Department of Defense to conduct intelligence operations essential to the conduct of its national defense mission.

Under our constitutional system, this Department and other departments and agencies of the intelligence community are answerable to the Chief Executive. We cannot be fettered in actions of this nature by a requirement that presumes there will be no obedience to Presidential instructions until after a Senate committee has been "fully informed of the proposed activity."

It is assumed that the genesis of this provision arises from allegations that certain members of the intelligence community actively engaged in clandestine activities to overthrow an unfriendly foreign government, or to the effect the assassination of their leaders.

In any sense which we in DOD understand, this kind of operation is not an "intelligence activity," that is, it is not concerned with the "collection, analysis, dissemination, and use" of information.

Yet, since the committee can designate anything it pleases as an "intelligence activity" requiring advance notice, even the most modest and noncontroversial intelligence operation could be subject to advance Senate committee notification.

For example, the committee could insist that no sensor devices be placed in country x, no intelligence agents be transferred to country y, and no intelligence-gathering operations even overt ones, be conducted in country z without first consulting the committee.

Should the executive branch ignore the advice of the committee, the latter could vote to disclose publicly the full operation—thus effectively negating the entire exercise. Only if the President himself certifies that "the probability of grave harm to the national security" outweighs the "national interest" in disclosing it, would the committee withhold publication. But even then, the bill reserves the right of the committee to refer the issue to the Senate, which presumably could then override the Presidential certification.

The foregoing presumes that a committee, and its individual members, will scrupulously adhere to these procedures. Experience over the past year has shown that this would not necessarily be the case.

Both the Senate and the House select committees have conceded that despite formalized security control procedures, there are few effective brakes on an individual Senate or House Member from disclosing what he alone decides is in the public interest.

The practical effect is that any single Member of Congress can prevent, or bring to a grinding halt, an extremely sensitive ongoing operation simply by issing a public statement.

Next, the authorization question. In support of the general intent to increase congressional oversight of the intelligence community, it has been suggested that congressional authorization of the intelligence N18 activity be separated from the major Defense authorization bills.

This proposal may seem simple in concept. In practice, however, an effort to distill mission-oriented information from the functional construction of the congressional authorization/appropriations process would be extremely difficult and confusing to both the Congress and the Defense Department.

Congress authorizes and appropriates funds, and at times sets ceilings, for such budget categories as military personnel, investment, operations, and research and development. In DOD, accounting systems develop these figures in the aggregate to support functional budgetary request.

In the Defense Department, intelligence is a support function integral to our combat elements. To a considerable degree, it lives off other integral support functions such as logistics, research and development, procurement, and construction.

It would be extremely difficult to break out of those categories the precise amounts of money which support intelligence and therefore should be authorized and appropriated for intelligence alone.

In addition, the line between so-called national and tactical intelligence is not that easily defined. Many intelligence functions, even at the national level, have tactical output and orientation. Many tactical organizations provide both collection and analysis to the national level.

How does one separate these tasks on a reasonable basis? In the research and development area, many tactical efforts, such as avionics, have major, inherent intelligence uses and provide spinoff possibilities for further intelligence-related development.

How does one approach this problem on a basis that will lead to proper information, decisionmaking, and resource allocation?

Finally, Mr. Chairman, I believe that we should all recognize that the Congress and the executive branch have cooperated in the most extensive investigation ever of this Nation's intelligence community. Shortcomings have been revealed and excesses disclosed. I am pleased to note that while the record of the Department of Defense has not been perfect, it is generally recognized to have served the Nation well.

It is now a question of where we go from here. Do we need a continuing investigation of intelligence activities?

Certainly, the Congress has the right to oversight: that is not in question. But how should that oversight be conducted? Should it be through an extension of an investigative type committee or should it be through the established committees of the Congress?

This is the judgment which the members of this committee and the Senate must make.

In fact, there has already occurred a change in how oversight is being conducted. For example, in a letter to the Secretary of Defense, dated September 25, 1975, the chairman of the House Appropriations Committee made it very clear how intelligence funding would be addressed by his committee in 1976.

I offer these extracts from Mr. Mahon's letter:

> The committee is concerned about apparent attempts to lessen the visibility of intelligence funding. Therefore, the committee directs that the 1977 budget presentations include manpower and dollar amounts for intelligence, direct support, and intelligence-related activities.
>
> The committee insists that the total cost of intelligence be presented to the Congress, and by requiring submission of justifications for these programs the committee hopes to assure the accomplishment of this goal.

The Defense Department and agencies are following this directive and are supplying to the committee a thorough justification of intelligence and intelligence-related activities in the fiscal year 1977 budget.

Thank you, Mr. Chairman.

Chairman RIBICOFF. Thank you, Mr. Ellsworth.

I think the committee will confine ourselves on the first go-around to a 10-minute time limitation. If there are further questions, I will give the members an opportunity to question further.

Mr. Ellsworth, the House Intelligence Committee's final report called for the abolition of the Defense Intelligence Agency.

What is your reaction to this?

Mr. ELLSWORTH. I have not read that report, Mr. Chairman.

Chairman RIBICOFF. What about the concept?

Mr. ELLSWORTH. It is not the first time that someone has suggested the abolition of the Defense Intelligence Agency. I think that it is too soon to make a judgment on that subject.

N19   The Defense Intelligence Agency was created in 1961 for two or three reasons, which still have validity. In the first place, it was created so that the Secretary of Defense might have his own analysis of information on foreign military developments, from an intelligence point of view, in order that he might have an independent way of doing his own planning, that is, independent of the military services.

I think that is still a valid objective and a valid reason for the existence of a Defense Intelligence Agency.

Another reason for the creation of the DIA in 1961, was to eliminate unnecessary duplication of intelligence work that was being done by the military services. I think that is still a valid reason for the existence of a centralized Defense intelligence organization—separate from the Central Intelligence Agency—within the Department of Defense. DIA has served that legitimate purpose.

The problem that we have had with the Defense Intelligence Agency, as I see it the same problem that we have generally with all intelligence in this Nation. That is, there are weaknesses in the quality of analysis and estimates that our intelligence community provides to us.

I do not think that there is anyone in the intelligence community that would take issue with that.

Our objective is, as far as the DIA is concerned, to very substantially improve the quality of the analysis and estimates that the DIA produces for the Secretary of Defense and the Joint Chiefs of Staff.

If we cannot achieve that objective, then we have got to think of some other way of structuring defense intelligence activity so that we can improve the quality of the finished intelligence product.

Chairman RIBICOFF. As I understand your testimony, you feel that the executive branch should not be required to inform an appropriate committee of the Congress concerning plans for covert operations.

Suppose you had a plan involving many, many millions of dollars which would entail a serious international risk.

Do you think that under those circumstances Congress should not be brought in?

Let us take the current problem of Angola. Here is a covert operation involving a lot of money and serious foreign policy considerations. Now the Secretary of State and President find themselves embarrassed because they fail to have congressional support. Yet if there were discussion before this were undertaken, the Secretary of State and the President might have had a different point of view.

When, in your opinion, should that committee be informed of covert operations?

Mr. ELLSWORTH. Senator, it is not my belief that the Congress should not be informed of a covert operation. I attempted, in my testimony, to draw a sharp distinction between covert operations on the one hand and what we, in the Defense Department, regard as intelligence on the other hand, which is the collection, analysis and dissemination of information. My comments on the select committee's proposed bill about information related to the question of being required to provide information on all intelligence activities, by its terms, the bill would require that the Congress become involved in the management of day to day intelligence activities, as far as the Defense Department is concerned.

Chairman RIBICOFF. Do I understand the difference is that you object to the day-to-day operations, but when it comes to basic policy considerations of the covert operation there would be no objection on your part to bring in the oversight committee?

Mr. ELLSWORTH. I have no problem, for example, with the testimony of Ambassador Helms a few minutes ago that it would be desirable if the executive branch contemplated a covert operation of the Angolan type for the executive branch to inform the Congress in some appropriate way. I have no problem with that measure of congressional oversight.

I would hope that the committee and that the Senate would in its work, draw a very sharp distinction between covert operations on the one hand, and intelligence collection, analysis, and dissemination on the other hand. They are two entirely unrelated functions of the executive branch, and I think that it is difficult to overstress the importance of keeping those activities separate.

Now, then, as far as Angola is concerned, or that kind of operation, yes, I certainly agree that it would be desirable for the Congress to be onboard at the takeoff of an operation of that kind, and if the indications are, upon consultation with the Congress, that that is not the kind of an operation that would be supported down the line, then I think the executive branch would be well-advised not to initiate the operation.

If I might just say as a footnote, I was not involved in the beginnings of that or in the consultations, but it was my understanding that the Congress was consulted with regard to Angola, in accordance with procedures that had been worked out between the Congress and the executive branch. I do not know that for a fact, but I had thought that that had been the case.

Chairman RIBICOFF. Mr. Ellsworth, we are going to start marking up our legislation on the 18th. We do not have the Church bill before us. We have no suggested draft of legislation from the administration.

I do not know what the administration's intentions are. I was going to suggest to my colleague Senator Percy, the ranking minority member of the committee, with whom I work very closely, that during the period of the congressional recess our staffs get together to try to work out many of these problems so that suggestions may be presented to the members of the full committee before the markup.

I agree with Senator Weicker that this is something that should be achieved and accomplished as soon as possible. I would hope that the administration, because they are concerned, and rightfully so, would present to the Congress, the thinking of the executive branch before the 6th of February.

Mr. ELLSWORTH. The 6th of February.

Senator PERCY. I will have underway an endeavor to learn from the administration whether they will have that or not. I will call directly to the White House and convey to them your invitation for them to do so. I think it would be to the advantage of the administration to give us guidelines.

Certain areas are our prerogative, obviously, but it is always helpful to have the best thinking the administration can put into it.

Mr. ELLSWORTH. We, on our part, will be glad to cooperate, Mr. Chairman and Senator Percy.

Chairman RIBICOFF. One final question.

I assume that your testimony was cleared with the Secretary of Defense and the Office of Budget and Management?

Mr. ELLSWORTH. I do not know about OMB; it was cleared with the Secretary.

Chairman RIBICOFF. Is it the policy of the administration to recommend a new office of Inspector General or Director-General of Intelligence?

Mr. ELLSWORTH. No, that particular part of my testimony I was permitted to give without objection, but that is not a policy.

Chairman RIBICOFF. You do not think it will be a policy?

Mr. ELLSWORTH. I do not know.

Chairman RIBICOFF. You do not know.

I think that we need oversight, yet not only on the congressional side. My feeling is, as I follow these hearings and follow the controversy, that the executive branch is deeply in need of a better oversight arrangement, and I would hope in discussions within the executive branch that you would urge the Inspector General concept.

I think it would be most helpful to both the executive branch and to the Congress, not only today, but in the years ahead.

EXECUTIVE-LEGISLATIVE RELATIONS ([25], pp. 415–424)

Secretary of State Henry Kissinger, testifying before the Senate Committee on Government Operations on the subject of oversight legislation, acknowledged the need for a "sounder" relationship between the Executive branch and Congress. Once he articulated the necessity for mutual understanding and agreement on objectives for a "coherent" and "coordinated" U.S. foreign policy, Kissinger turned to two abiding concerns of administration spokesmen: leaks of information and the independence of the Executive branch. He recommended a joint oversight committee be established to diminish the exposure of breaches of security. Kissinger also perceived a move afoot to have some form of congressional approval, in advance, of covert operations; he viewed that as impractical and inconsistent with the constitutional division of powers. A portion of his testimony is reprinted here.

TESTIMONY OF HENRY A. KISSINGER, SECRETARY OF STATE

Secretary KISSINGER. Mr. Chairman, I welcome this opportunity to appear before this committee to give you my views on the relationship I hope will develop between the Congress and the U.S. intelligence community.

The executive-legislative relationship and foreign policy first.

It is essential that a sounder relationship between the executive and the legislative evolve. The present relationship has reached a point where the ability of the United States to conduct a coherent foreign policy is being eroded.

This is certainly true in the intelligence field. One has only to look at the recent leakage—indeed, official publication—of highly classified material and the levying of unsubstantiated charges and personal attacks against the executive to see the point the relationship has reached and the harm we are doing to ourselves.

This situation must be unacceptable to us in both branches of the Government, and it must be unacceptable to the American people. Fundamental changes are taking place in the world at an unprecedented rate. New centers of power are emerging, altering relations among older power centers. Growing economic interdependence makes each of us vulnerable to financial and industrial troubles in countries formerly quite remote from us. And, most important, we are working hard to establish more rational and reliable relationships with powers whose values and interests are alien and inimical to us and who, in some cases, have the power to destroy us.

The conduct of foreign policy in this complex and fast-changing situation requires that there be close coordination and mutual trust between Congress and the executive branch and a large measure of trust in both branches by the American people.

I am aware of the benefits of a certain amount of dynamic tension between the branches of our Government. Indeed, the Founding Fathers designed this into the Constitution with the principle of the separation of powers. But there is an adverse impact on the public mind in this country and on our national image abroad when this beneficial tension deteriorates into confrontation. We have recently seen this happen. This is why I hope this committee and the Congress as a whole, with the help and suggestions from the Executive, can construct an oversight mechanism for U.S. intelligence that can bring an end to the strife, distrust, and confusion that have accompanied the investigations of the past year.

I look to the development of means by which Congress can participate more fully in the guidance and review of the intelligence activities of this Government and by which the Executive can direct and conduct those activities with the confidence of being in step with Congress in this vital area of our foreign affairs.

THE NEED FOR INTELLIGENCE

Our foreign policy must cope with complex problems of nuclear and conventional arms races; traditional and ideological disputes which can trigger wider wars and sweeping economic dislocations; emerging new nations which can become the arena for great-power contests; environmental pollution, food shortages, energy maldistributions which affect the lives of hundreds of millions; and financial shifts which can threaten the global economic order. In the face of these great challenges our goals are to foster the growth of a rationally ordered world in which states of diverse views and objectives can cooperate for the common benefit. We seek a world based on justice and the promotion of human dignity.

We cannot pursue these goals in this hazardous world unless we are secure, and we cannot be secure unless we are strong and alert. Our ability to be both strong and alert depends in part on good intelligence.

To be strong, we must know as precisely as possible how we are threatened. In this age of highly sophisticated and expensive weapons systems, we cannot afford to arm ourselves against all possible threats; we must concentrate on those that are most likely in order to save our resources for other purposes that make our country economically, socially, and morally strong.

To be alert is not just a matter of knowing where the dangers of war and change are increasing, basic as that knowledge is. We must have the knowledge essential to our ability to try to help reduce the dangers to peace. Intelligence is crucial to the future of this Nation.

To help construct a more cooperative world we must understand trends and possibilities. Intelligence is an indispensable tool in this effort.

The intelligence on which such judgments must be based can come only from a highly professional intelligence service supported by Congress and the people of this country. President Ford expressed it very well in the State of the Union address when he said:

As conflict and rivalries persist in the world, our United States intelligence capabilities must be the best in the world.

The crippling of our foreign intelligence services increases the danger of American involvement in direct armed conflict. Our adversaries are encouraged to attempt new adventures, while our own ability to monitor events, and to influence events short of military action—is undermined.

Without effective intelligence capability, the United States stands blindfolded and hobbled.

Let me give you just two examples:

Our policy to establish a more rational and reliable relationship with the Soviet Union—commonly referred to as détente—would be impossible without good intelligence. Indeed, our confidence in the SALT agreements is based in large measure on the specific provisions which permit each side to check on the compliance of the other through national technical means of verification.

Similarly, without excellent intelligence the United States would not have been able to play the leading role in seeking to bring about a

negotiated settlement of the conflict in the Middle East. All agree that
a new conflict there could bring the United States and the Soviet Union
to the brink of war.

Let me turn to the principles involved in the congressional over-
sight. As I have repeatedly said, this Nation's foreign policy must
reflect the values, aspirations, and perceptions of its people; it must
have broad public support. The American people must have confidence
not only in our policies but also in the institutions which formulate
and carry out those policies. This means that our foreign policy must
reflect consultation and accommodation between the executive and
legislative branches. But each branch has its special responsibilities
as well. The Executive must provide strong central direction of foreign
policy and must consult with the Congress. Congress must provide
mature counsel and must protect the confidentiality of its consultations
with the Executive.

That brings me to the question this committee is addressing: How
should a democracy provide for control of its intelligence activities
which, if they are to be effective, must operate in secret?

It is not my place as Secretary of State to recommend how the
Congress should organize its oversight effort, but for oversight to be
effective and constructive, conditions must be created which will pro-
mote mutual trust in dealing with the necessarily sensitive aspects of
intelligence information and operations. Both overseers and those
overseen must be able to feel sure that information given in confidence
will remain in confidence. No other single condition for success is as
important as this. The system cannot function in the atmosphere of
distrust that has prevailed in recent months.

Rather than make specific proposals for oversight, I would prefer
to set forth some general principles which I believe are important and
should be given serious consideration.

First: I believe that the goal of congressional oversight should be
to insure that the intelligence activities of the United States are
grounded in the basic values, perceptions and aspirations of the people
of this country as well as in a clear view of the national interest. Con-
gress has a particular responsibility in insuring that this is so because
N20   intelligence does not lend itself to extensive public or media debate.
This requires that the public have great confidence in the congressional
oversight mechanism. Americans must be assured that their constitu-
tional rights will not be abridged by intelligence operations.

I welcome congressional oversight because I believe it will build
public confidence in our intelligence system, and we in the executive
branch can benefit from the wise counsel oversight can provide. But
correction of the errors of the past must not take the form of controls
in the future that would stifle intelligence.

Second: I believe we must maintain the proper constitutional per-
spective. Under the Constitution, the conduct of foreign relations is
the responsibility of the President as the Nation's Chief Executive
officer. Congressional oversight must not infringe on the President's
responsibility for intelligence in a way which would violate the prin-
ciple of the separation of powers. The Constitution is written as it is
for practical as well as for political reasons. Congress is a deliberative
and lawmaking body, not an executive organ, and it is not organized
to provide day-to-day operational direction to ongoing intelligence
programs. Any proposal based on the idea of executive management by

Congress is, in my judgment, a mistake. Existing legislation requires the President to determine that covert action operations are important to national security and to give timely notice of those operations to appropriate bodies of the Congress. I believe this is adequate for oversight. I recommend that this or a similar arrangement be continued but that it be concentrated in the oversight committee.

Third: Is the crucial matter that the information provided to the congressional oversight body must in many cases remain secret. Much of this information is highly classified and is gathered from intelligence sources and methods whose cooperation could be lost by public exposure. Some of it also bears on U.S. plans or policies whose effectiveness depends on continued protection from disclosure. Unauthorized release of such information could do great damage to national security and our foreign policy. Protection of it is a responsibility both the Congress and the Executive must share. I strongly believe that any legislation to establish an oversight committee must include safeguards for the protection of this sensitive and important information. Classified information given to the Congress should not be made public without the concurrence of the President or his representative.

N21

As a related point, I would like to state my agreement with Mr. Colby that it is essential to establish procedures and sanctions to prevent unauthorized disclosure of classified material. Legislation for this purpose is currently under consideration in the executive branch. It would provide for the prosecution of Government employees who disclose such information without authority.

Fourth, and last: I believe the best oversight is concentrated oversight—ideally by a joint committee. The benefits of such an arrangement are numerous: It would permit rapid responses both ways between the Congress and the intelligence community when time was crucial; it would reduce the chance of leaks by limiting the number of people with access to sensitive information; it would encourage maximum sharing of information; and it would permit a rapid development of expertise to facilitate penetrating and effective oversight.

If a joint committee is not possible, I ask that you keep the principle and benefits of concentration in mind and limit oversight to the minimum number of committees required to conduct oversight effectively.

In concluding, I would like to express again my fervent hope that we can rapidly end the divisive debate over the intelligence community which has been so harmful over the past year. I hope this committee will quickly complete its task of establishing effective oversight so that we can all turn to the real challenges that face us in this dangerous world.

I stand ready to help in any way I can, and I am ready to answer any questions you may have.

Chairman RIBICOFF. Thank you very much, Mr. Secretary.

If there is no objection, each member will confine himself to 10 minutes of questioning on the first round.

Mr. Secretary, does the administration support the creation this year of a new congressional committee on intelligence oversight?

Secretary KISSINGER. Yes.

Chairman RIBICOFF. Chairman Church and several other members of the Select Committee introduced a bill creating a new Senate Committee on Intelligence.

Does the administration have any position on the Church bill?

Secretary KISSINGER. Our preferred position is a joint committee. The next best thing would be one committee in each House that concentrates the intelligence oversight, so we support this part of the Church bill.

There are other provisions in the Church bill which we cannot support, such as the prior approval by the committee of covert operations.

Chairman RIBICOFF. We complete our hearings tomorrow. Congress takes a recess until the 16th. On the 18th, this committee will start marking up an intelligence oversight bill.

Could we expect from the administration its point of view on the bills, including the Church bill, and suggestions from the administration before the 18th indicating what its position may be?

Secretary KISSINGER. I would hope so. I would like to make clear that I do not have principal responsibility for developing the administration's position on these bills.

The President has before him various approaches to the organization of intelligence which include also his final position on the attitude to take toward congressional oversight.

I hope that they can be completed before the 18th.

Chairman RIBICOFF. According to Senator Church, you told his committee that an oversight committee should be briefed in advance before any significant covert operation.

Your statement this morning suggests a committee of Congress—I read from page 8—should have timely notice of covert operations.

Does your reference today to timely notice mean advance notice?

Secretary KISSINGER. Excuse me.

Chairman RIBICOFF. Does your reference today to timely notice mean advance notice, as you indicated to Senator Church when you briefed his committee?

Secretary KISSINGER. Let me separate two things, Mr. Chairman.

I would think that a wise administration would consult with an oversight committee prior to conducting a covert operation. This is a different matter from writing in the law a requirement that would preclude an administration under conditions of emergency or under conditions that have some special now unforeseeable conditions that would preclude the administration from conducting such operations.

So I would think that on the whole, the notice should be timely, which means literally—and which in fact would probably mean—some consultation ahead of time.

Chairman RIBICOFF. What do you think should happen in the event that a majority of an oversight committee disagrees with the proposed operation?

Should the President go ahead with the operation in spite of congressional opposition as conveyed to the President before the operation starts, or while it is being contemplated?

Secretary KISSINGER. Again, I would separate the practice from what the law should be.

I would think that as a practical matter the President would have to weigh very seriously, take very serious account of an opposition of a congressional oversight, just as we would take very seriously, say, the opposition of the Senate Foreign Relations Committee to a major departure in policy.

If, however, the President believes that the overwhelming national interest requires him to proceed even when the oversight committee disagrees, then he should have the right to do so, recognizing that this may lead to a constitutional confrontation, and that it cannot be either in his interests or in the interests of the country to provoke that.

Chairman RIBICOFF. I have been following your speeches in the last few days, in your western trip, and you talked about the need for close cooperation between the executive and Congress if we are going to have an effective foreign policy.

I think all of us agree with you. Yet, if the President or the Secretary of State proceeds with an operation in spite of congressional opposition, how can you have cooperation?

Let us take Angola. Here is a typical example of where the President and yourself are in serious trouble, because there is an overwhelming sentiment in the Congress against our involvement in the Angolan situation—and this has been indicated by heavy votes against covert aid to Angola, both by the Senate and the House.

Now, could not this have been obviated if you had told the oversight committee in advance of your intentions in a place like Angola and immediately could have received the warning bells from a representative group of Senators that this is just not going to fly in the Congress and in the country?

What would you have done under those circumstances?

Secretary KISSINGER. Mr. Chairman, first of all, the administration followed the existing procedures with great care. There was no oversight committee. There were three oversight committees in each House, plus the two intelligence committees.

Each of these committees was briefed not once but several times. Every time a new decision was made with respect to Angola, these committees were briefed. Altogether, 8 congressional committees were briefed 24 different times. Over 20 Senators, over 100 Congressmen and over 150 staff members were briefed about what we were doing in Angola.

We did not get the warning bells that you mentioned.

It does not mean that everybody agreed with it, but I think you will agree, Mr. Chairman, there is a difference between some quibble or with some disagreement about policy and a clear indication that the Congress would absolutely or strongly oppose this.

Maybe there was a breakdown in communication, but the fact of the matter is that we not only complied with the letter, we complied with the spirit in the sense that every time something new was done in Angola, we either briefed the committees just before or just after the decision was made and well before it was underway to full implementation.

We did not receive the warning bells.

The second question is whether something flies in the Congress or in the public depends very importantly on how the issues are presented and therefore the nature of the Angola debate has taken a turn that was not foreseeable on the basis of the congressional consultations that we engaged in before that.

I would hope, however, that an oversight committee with a regular procedure, with a clearer understanding of the mutual responsibilities could avoid the problems that we have faced with respect to Angola.

But I would like to say one final thing about Angola, Mr. Chairman.

We know the congressional sentiment and we are going to abide by it, but we also have an obligation to put before the country our concerns as to the impact on future policy, even if it does not affect the immediate decision.

We have to prevent similar things from happening again, and therefore we have an obligation to state what we think the foreign policy implications are. And that does not indicate a disrespect for the Congress, it indicates a necessity of shaping the public debate if a similar circumstance should arise again.

Chairman RIBICOFF. Secretary Kissinger, I owe you a personal apology. I understand that Mrs. Kissinger went to the hospital this morning for surgery and that this was the reason you were late for the committee. I want to state that I was not aware of that.

Secretary KISSINGER. She is going tomorrow, but we had to wait for the medical report.

Chairman RIBICOFF. One final question.

In view of what you have said, may I say that speaking for myself and, I believe I have talked personally and privately with practically every member of this committee, we in this committee are not committed to any specific oversight method, the Church bill or any other bill. We approach this problem with a deep desire to come up with an oversight committee so established as to do a responsible job to achieve what you seek, good cooperation and effective cooperation between the Executive and Congress.

So the question of prior notice is going to be very important for us, including the problem of what is done in the event that there is a basic disagreement between the majority of the committee and the Executive? How do we make this known to the Congress as a whole?

That is why I am anxious to have the point of view of the executive branch.

That view will be considered very carefully and respectfully, and I would hope that you would make this known to the President and to whoever is working on it that we are under direction by the Senate to report a bill by March 1. As far as the chairman is concerned, we will do everything possible in this committee to get the bill out by March 1, and I would hope that we do not wait until February 28 to receive the recommendations from the executive branch.

Secretary KISSINGER. I will transmit this to the President. I know he is working very hard on developing his own recommendations. I just do not know what deadline he is working against, but we will certainly communicate this, and hope that we can cooperate with this committee.

Chairman RIBICOFF. Senator Percy?

Senator PERCY. Secretary Kissinger, is there any question in your mind that Congress has failed in the past to exercise the proper, legitimate oversight responsibility with respect to our intelligence operations?

Secretary KISSINGER. It is difficult to know what the definition of effective oversight is. I believe, in light of events, that a more coherent oversight procedure, one in which the public can have a greater degree of confidence, is in the national interest.

Senator PERCY. Is it essential that we carry on an effective intelligence operation, including possibly covert activities and is it essential that we do organize ourselves so that we can work effectively, harmoniously, and cooperatively with the executive branch?

Secretary KISSINGER. I think that it is vital for the United States to have an effective intelligence service that is independent of really both the Executive and congressional direction but is subject to Executive direction and congressional oversight.

Senator PERCY. Because of your recent comments about Congress, I would just like to personally assure you that this committee, the membership that you see here, and others that are unable to be present, has conducted, I think, the finest set of hearings that I have ever participated in, in 9 years.

The chairman has said that within his power he is going to report a bill out, the best bill we possibly can on the deadline schedule of March 1. I can assure the chairman, from the minority standpoint there is no partisanship in this matter whatsoever. We will diligently work toward that deadline. We have had a body of evidence to date that has been extraordinarily helpful in enabling us to put together something we think is essential and in the national interest.

Secretary KISSINGER. Let me make clear what my concern is, Senator. It is not a question that individuals are behaving unpatriotically, arbitrarily, or with anything but the best intentions.

My concern is not what will happen this year. My concern is that as we look ahead, 2, 3, 4 years, how the United States can conduct an effective foreign policy, and it can do so only if it appears to other nations as representing essentially one voice when it acts in the field of foreign policy, and the tragedies that can occur in the conduct of foreign policy are precisely those when men of good intentions, pursuing the best motives on each side, are producing paralysis with the best of intentions.

And I am trying in my public speeches not to win an argument between the Executive and the Congress, because I recognize that the Executive also has to change some of the procedures that have developed in recent decades, but to find a basis by which a coherent, long-term national policy is possible, in which the Executive does those things that really the Executive is designed to do, and the Congress in turn exercises the oversight and the guidance over basic policies which have been assigned to it.

It is not criticizing this or that decision which is always taken in the best of ways.

Senator PERCY. Again, I would like to assure you, there are two of us here who sit on both the Foreign Relations Committee and Government Operations Committee. The climate in which we are working is extraordinarily difficult. We cannot overlook 10 years of Vietnam. We have had a divisiveness between us.

We were misled. We were lied to. There was policy adopted that later proved to be disastrous. It was out of control in a sense, and that is the climate in which we began to work. And then the Watergate climate did not contribute to your work or our work as well. In respect to the intelligence operations, we did not handle ourselves well. We did not exercise and fulfill our responsibility.

But also, there is fairly solid evidence that the Congress was misled, was lied to on occasion, so it is in that climate that we are now trying to reconstruct a relationship.

I can assure you of that even though the statement you made on the West Coast that our domestic divisions are more dangerous to this country than our overseas adversaries is a pretty strong statement.

Secretary KISSINGER. I did not make that statement.

The statement I made is that the foreign policy design is in relatively good shape and that our domestic divisions at this moment are impeding the conduct of foreign policy. That is not the same thing as saying that our domestic divisions are more dangerous to us than our foreign adversaries.

The basic problem that we face is that when the scope of national action is the greatest, the knowledge to base such action on is inherently ambiguous. Therefore, it is essential that there is a minimum of trust and confidence, not only the relation between the executive and the legislature, but also in the relations between the public and the whole Government, and without a degree of faith in the future, without some confidence that responsible people are trying to do a serious job, we will paralyze ourselves, and if we turn the governmental process into one gigantic permanent investigation into motives, than we may achieve purity but we will also achieve paralysis.

Therefore, what I said—and I think if you read the text, I do not know what newspaper account you refer to——

Senator PERCY. This is from the New York Times this morning.

Secretary KISSINGER. If you read the text of what I said it did not say foreign adversaries are less dangerous to us than our domestic division. I said that our domestic divisions are inhibiting the conduct of our foreign policy, and I grant you, that Vietnam, Watergate and its aftermath, and many of the mistakes on the part of the Executive have contributed to this situation, but the problem we face is when are we going to turn to the future.

Senator PERCY. The subheadline on this story is, "He sees a greater threat at home than abroad," and the first paragraph indicated, "He said today the United States is more endangered by its domestic divisions than by overseas adversaries."

I know the point you are trying to make. I think it is a good point. I think these talks around the country have been immensely valuable and very important.

I think it would be helpful rather than just emphasizing our divisions to say in some areas that we are really working together. On the Middle East, I think we have had marvelous cooperation between Congress and the executive branch on the whole. I think our relationships on China and the Soviet Union on SALT have been extraordinarily good.

I think you are going to get a lot of backup on the Concorde decision now. It was a very important foreign policy decision as well as a domestic one, I think, on Cuba.

You are getting support on the military assistance bill now on the floor.

I would just hope that we would put balance into our relations. It is not all bad. it is not all good. We are trying to reach out.

Secretary KISSINGER. When you give a 45-minute speech and three paragraphs are reported, it is difficult for both the newspapers and the readers to judge what the balance of the speech was.

Senator PERCY. In our session on this legislation we are dealing with today, I understand from your testimony that you prefer a joint committee.

Secretary KISSINGER. I prefer a joint committee.

Senator PERCY. That can only be done if the House concurs.

Secretary KISSINGER. Yes.

Senator PERCY. If they do not concur, then we have to go ahead. If we feel ahead of time that they are not going to, it would be futile for us to send a bill over there and delay it a year if they are going to hold it up. Then we have to go ahead.

Do you see any possibility that we can combine in that same committee, if there is a House and a Senate committee, the authorization and appropriation authority, so you only have to really reveal everything to one committee in the Senate and one in the House and not proliferate it by four or eight, as it is now?

Secretary KISSINGER. I cannot really tell the Senate how to organize itself. As far as the executive is concerned, the more concentrated the oversight procedure, the easier it will be to share the maximum of information.

Senator PERCY. I personally feel it would be disastrous for the Congress to be in a position to veto covert actions ahead of time. I do think, however, that more control and oversight is needed.

CIA CONCERNS ([25], pp. 117–125, 132–143)

Director of Central Intelligence William Colby testified before the Senate Government Operations Committee on pending oversight legislation before his departure and replacement by George Bush. He had served as director of the CIA for over two and a half years, during a time when congressional inquiry into intelligence activities was at its most intense. The number of public congressional hearings and reports published in Colby's first full year as DCI (1974) was double that of 1970 (36 versus 18) ([102], p. 34). Colby testified frequently and was involved in most of the inquiries. His concern over the security of information provided to oversight committees was common to most intelligence community spokesmen; and his views on preserving independence of decision making in the Executive branch were similar to those expressed earlier by Henry Kissinger on behalf of the Ford administration.

Frequent mention of U.S. intervention in Angola appears in the dialogue between Colby and individual senators. Cuban troops were fighting in support of a faction in Angola, and it appeared their cause was about to prevail. The situation seemed analogous to prior ones, such as the Dominican Republic and Chile, where the United States employed covert action to support the faction it preferred. (Meanwhile, no evidence of U.S. covert involvement in Angola has emerged.) The following testimony is taken from January 1976 and appears here in abridged form.

TESTIMONY OF W. E. COLBY, DIRECTOR OF CENTRAL INTELLIGENCE, ACCOMPANIED BY MITCHELL ROGOVIN, SPECIAL COUNSEL TO THE DIRECTOR OF CENTRAL INTELLIGENCE; GEORGE L. CORY, LEGISLATIVE COUNSEL, AND DONALD F. MASSEY, ASSISTANT LEGISLATIVE COUNSEL

Mr. COLBY. Thank you, Mr. Chairman.

Thank you for this opportunity to discuss congressional oversight of our intelligence activities. Despite all the excitement in recent months over CIA and other intelligence activities, this is one of the most critical issues which must be faced in any serious investigation into our Government's intelligence activities.

Traditionally, intelligence is assumed to operate in total secrecy and outside the law. This is impossible under our Constitution and in our society. As a result, when CIA was established in 1947, a compromise was made under which broad, general statutes were drawn, and carefully limited arrangements for congressional review were developed. It was then believed necessary to limit oversight in the interest of secrecy.

Our society has changed, however, and a greater degree of oversight is now considered necessary. U.S. intelligence has already moved out of the atmosphere of total secrecy which previously characterized it. We who are in intelligence are well aware of the need to retain public confidence and congressional support if we are to continue to make our contribution to the safety of our country.

Thus, from the earliest days of the current investigations, I have stressed my hope that they will develop better guidelines for our operations and stronger oversight, to insure that our activities do remain within the Constitution and the laws of our country.

But I have not swung all the way to the other extreme of the pendulum to the position that there can be no secrecy. General Washington once said: "Upon secrecy, success depends in most enterprises of [intelligence]." We have many secrets in America which are necessary to the functioning of our democracy—the ballot box, the grand jury, and our attorney-client relationships. The secrecy of our sources of intelligence is equally important to the preservation of our democracy, and even our Nation in the turbulent world in which we live.

In 1947 we took a small step away from total secrecy by enacting general statutes and constructing careful oversight arrangements in the Congress. Proposals now under consideration would alter these arrangements to assure more detailed oversight. But it is essential that the pendulum not swing so far as to destroy the necessary secrecy of intelligence, or destroy intelligence itself in the process.

In former comments on this subject, I many times said that it was up to Congress to organize itself to exercise the necessary oversight of our intelligence activities. This is still true, but I believe that recent experience permits me to draw some conclusions on this topic which this committee has graciously invited.

The matter has been extensively studied within the administration during the past year, as President Ford shares many of the concerns of the Congress on this subject. The Rockefeller Commission, the Murphy Commission, our discussions with the select committees and other committees reflect this interest. A number of detailed studies were also made within the executive branch, reaching the level of two extended meetings President Ford had with National Security Council members.

The views of the administration are not yet formally fixed, so the comments I will make will be personal and based on my experience. My participation in the studies above, however, assures me that my views are in general compatible with the thrust of what President Ford will probably decide, although there may be some variation in the details.

Too great a stress on secrecy has led to situations in which Members of Congress who were fully briefed on intelligence activities pleaded later that they had never heard of them when they came to public attention. One of the chairmen of our committees once indicated, on the floor of the Senate, that he had no inkling of one of our operations, although he had approved the specific appropriation necessary to continue it. His statement certainly kept the secrecy of his participation in our operation, but at the sacrifice of implying that our intelligence activities were operating without oversight and control. Indeed, he added to public concern that we constituted some independent "invisible government."

On a number of occasions, especially since 1956, proposals have
N22 been made to establish a Joint Committee on Intelligence, but the
Congress has never seen fit to adopt them. During this past year
jurisdictional problems have been highlighted in the Congress as
a result of two things.

First, foreign intelligence today is not primarily limited to military
intelligence, as it may have been in earlier years. It is also now of
interest to those committees concerned with our economy, our foreign
relations, our agriculture, space, and a wide variety of other activities.
As a result, we have had a proliferation of demands for congressional
review of sensitive foreign intelligence matters in these fields by
other committees, to the degree that 59 Senators and 149 Representa-
tives have been briefed on some aspect of our activities this past year
alone.

Second, during 1974, there was much congressional interest in our
covert action activities, sparked by exposure of testimony I gave to
one of our oversight committees on the subject. Both the House and
the Senate, by 3 to 1 majorities, turned down proposals that CIA be
barred from such activities. But in December 1974, a provision was
added to the Foreign Assistance Act which required that any CIA
activity abroad other than intelligence gathering could only be con-
ducted if it were found by the President to be important to the na-
tional security and reported in a timely fashion to the appropriate
committees of the Congress. Together with the two select committees,
these appropriate committees now number eight.

I might quote, Mr. Chairman, from the conference report which
led to the adoption of that new act. It says that: "The Committee
of Conference agrees that strict measures should be taken to insure
maximum security of the information submitted to the Congress pur-
N23 suant to this provision."

The executive branch is fully complying with the provisions of
the new law. The President made the appropriate findings, and brief-
ings were given to the committees according to whatever arrange-
ments the committees made. It was stressed and understood on all
sides that these matters were sensitive, secret operations, whose ex-
posure would cause political damage to our foreign policy as well as
frustration to the operations concerned. The result of the year's
experience, in my mind, is clear. The system won't work. Every one
of the new projects that were subjected to this process has leaked
into the public domain. I am prepared to argue the value of each of
these projects, but that is not my current point. The fact is that a
secret operation conducted precisely according to the procedure set
up by the Congress cannot be kept secret. I believe it essential to
repeal that procedure and replace it by another which will include
provisions for adequate secrecy.

In this Bicentennial year, it is appropriate to note an earlier Amer-
ican experience with this problem. On November 9, 1775, the Con-
tinental Congress adopted a resolution of secrecy under which any
Member who disclosed a matter which the majority had determined
should be kept secret, was to be expelled "and deemed an enemy to the
liberties of America." On November 29, 1775, the Congress established
the Committee on Secret Correspondence and gave it foreign intelli-
gence responsibilities, managing a network of secret agents in Europe.
The committee took steps to protect the secrecy of its intelligence ac-

tivities by sharply restricting access to operational matters. On one occasion, the committee justified the secrecy of its information as follows:

Considering the nature and importance of it, we * * * agree that it is our indispensable duty to keep it secret, even from Congress * * *. We find, by fatal experience, that Congress consists of too many Members to keep secrets.

Mr. Chairman, at that time there were 56 Representatives in the Congress, compared to the 208 that I reported briefing during 1975.

If the Congress should decide to adopt new oversight arrangements, I believe it should establish a representative group to oversee intelligence activities on Congress' behalf. This representative group could be a joint committee or another arrangement. In any event, a representative group should consist of a restricted number of Members so that we do not involve the large numbers of Congressmen currently briefed on our sensitive activities.

The representative character of such an oversight body must be respected by us in the intelligence community, so that we make available the information it needs to do its job.

At the same time, arrangements can and should be developed between such a representative body and the intelligence community by which reasonable limits are established as to the matters made available even to it. In my present post as Director of Central Intelligence, I do not insist, for example, upon knowing the name of a foreign agent in some dangerous situation. It is not necessary to my duties that I know his specific identity. It is essential that we be able to assure our foreign agents abroad, a number of whom have already expressed their alarm and limited what they tell us, that their names will be totally protected, since their lives or livelihoods are at peril. I would expect that a responsible representative committee of Congress would similarly not request such specific identification, as our current oversight and select committees have not requested such sensitive information. Understanding of this nature between a responsible oversight body and the intelligence community would be more productive than adversary debates over either branch's "right" to have or to withhold such information.

A responsible oversight body must not discourage the intelligence community from conducting its own investigations and correcting its activities. A great portion of this year's investigations has consisted only of public repetition of the private reviews by the intelligence community of its own activities. Since the full story of American intelligence remains secret, the impression is left with our public that what was revealed is characteristic of the whole. The experience has done little to encourage objective and hard-hitting self-examination in the future. CIA's collation of a list of some questionable activities in the domestic field was used as the basis for sensational charges of a massive illegal domestic intelligence operation. In truth, our misdeeds were few and far between, as the final Rockefeller Commission report reveals. CIA's investigations into possible assassination activity, which led to specific directives in 1972 and 1973 against such activity, have been the basis for sweeping allegations that assassinations are part of our function. We never assassinated anyone, as the Senate report on intelligence reveals. And our own post mortems of our performance in various intelligence situations have been selectively exposed to give a totally erroneous impression of continued failures of American intelligence. In fact, we have the best intelligence service in the world. But we cannot keep it that way if every one of its corrective efforts is trumpeted to its enemies.

In the consideration of any altered oversight arrangements, the Congress should, I believe, deal with the problem of proliferation of congressional review of intelligence activities. I strongly urge that oversight be concentrated exclusively in the minimum number of committees necessary to effectively conduct it, which to me means one. Otherwise, we are in danger of reverting to the situation of reporting to a myriad of committees and exposing parts of our activities in all directions. It should be possible to concentrate congressional oversight, perhaps arranging that the oversight committee have representation from the other standing committees with interest in this subject.

The issue of giving prior notice to Congress of sensitive intelligence oprations has been raised, Mr. Chairman. I believe this is a thoroughly false issue. The present statute calls for the appropriate committees to be informed "in a timely fashion" with respect to activities abroad other than intelligence gathering. Our regular oversight committees are kept currently informed of major developments, and each year they review our appropriation request in great detail.

A requirement of prior notice before any intelligence activity could be undertaken would, in my view, conflict with the President's constitutional rights, would be totally impractical during times of congressional recess when crises can arise, and would add nothing to the ability of the Congress to express its views about any of our activities. We currently inform the Congress on any decision immediately, although the actual hearing may be delayed by the committee in question for several weeks. Almost none of our activities are single-step operations which take place on only one occasion. An intelligence or covert action operation is generally a continuing effort running over some time. Informed of such an activity, a committee has every ability to express the concern of its individual members, to vote in committee its opinion with respect to the activity, to appeal to the congressional leadership, and even to seek an appointment with the President himself. The committee also retains the ultimate legislative or appropriation sanction, if its views are not given due weight.

The unilateral exposure of an operation to public notice is not the solution. In essence, the theory adopted by some is that the right to expose such operations constitutes a superconstitutional individual veto of any secret activity. We cannot run such secret operations, Mr. Chairman, if Congressmen confirm to inquiring newsmen operating on a lead that indeed they were given a secret briefing on a covert operation in a certain country, instead of refusing to comment. Neither can we run secret operations if individual Congressmen announce that there are three other operations which have not yet been disclosed, thereby stimulating every investigative reporter in Washington to determine the specifics thereof by some hypothetical questions. And we cannot conduct covert operations if a committee puts out a report which refers to an activity, leave out the name of the country or individual concerned, but giving enough evidence for any amateur sleuth to identify it beyond a shadow of a doubt in time for its identification to be carried with the newsstory of the report.

An essential element of new congressional oversight arrangements is better procedures for protecting sensitive information. Senate rule 36 (3) and (5) states that confidential communications from the President or head of any department are to be kept secret unless the Senate votes. But the Senate, on November 20 last year, failed to vote on the release by the select committee of information which the President specifically requested be kept secret and in the face of my request that certain names of CIA personnel therein be deleted.

In the House of Representatives, rule XI.2.(e)(2) provides that the records of any committee are open to any Member, which on at least one occasion has let to the exposure of certain CIA operations despite the written promise of a Member to keep them secret.

The arrangements for Congress to receive and protect sensitive information are most imperfect. A prior security clearance of staff members and termination of employment for disclosure are hardly adequate sanctions to insure the protection of sensitive intelligence sources whose disclosure can produce substantial royalties. The extensive briefings and indoctrination, and the secrecy agreements employed in the executive branch, have even proved inadequate in the state of our present legislation. With respect to staff members, therefore, I believe it essential that a regular procedure of security protection be established. This must be enforceable not only by indoctrination and discipline but also by sanctions. These are contained in legislation which I have proposed and which is about to be recommended in the executive branch to cover those who voluntarily undertake the obligation of secrecy as an aspect of their employment. This proposal should apply equally to executive branch employees and congressional staff members who obtain privileged access to our intelligence secrets. With respect to Members of Congress themselves, we must, of course, look to the self-discipline of the two Houses with respect to their membership.

Mr. Chairman, we also need a procedure to determine the declassification and public release of those secrets that no longer need to be protected. This cannot be left to the individual staff member in the executive or the legislative branch. Under the Constitution, it cannot be assumed by the legislative branch alone, and any such contention would inevitably restrict the flow of sensitive information from the Executive. This could consist of an agreement that if the committee decides on release, the President has reasonable opportunity to certify that the release would be detrimental to the national security, and his determination then would govern in the absence of further resolution of the constitutional questions involved. And this must apply to any release of the information, so as not to lead to an absurd situation in which a committee agrees not to release individual reports of secret activities but then proposes to publish them in its final report.

In conclusion, Mr. Chairman, I believe that congressional oversight of our intelligence activities can be strengthened. The degree of oversight can be increased relative to that in the years in which there was a general consensus that these matters were better not known by outsiders. The structure can be improved by focusing responsibility so that a depth of knowledge and expertise about our intelligence operations can be developed. The structure can also be improved by clear assignment of responsibility for exclusive supervision of our intelligence activities to a limited number of Members of the Congress, representing the Congress as a whole, who would have full access to all information appropriate to exercise their responsibilities. And congressional oversight can be improved by making arrangements with Congress to protect the sensitive intelligence activities of our Government in the same way as we protect other secrets essential to the survival of American democracy. Executive branch supervision can also be improved by insuring the discipline of those in the intelligence profession and of their supervisors as to their respect for those important national secrets, and by giving us the ability to enforce such protection against those who would wantonly destroy them. These improvements, Mr. Chairman, in supervision of our intelligence activities, would have truly more long-lasting value as a result of this year of investigation than any other single action taken by the Congress. They would be a fitting conclusion to this year of investigation of intelligence, so that our intelligence service will be responsible to our Constitution, its legislative oversight will be equally responsible, and we will continue to have the best intelligence in the world.

It will give, Mr. Chairman, new meaning to the initials "CIA," Constitutional Intelligence for America, with equal stress on the needs of all three; the Constitution, intelligence, and especially America.

Thank you, Mr. Chairman.

Chairman RIBICOFF. Thank you very much, Mr. Colby.

Mr. Colby, you are for the establishment of an oversight committee on intelligence?

Mr. COLBY. A committee with exclusive jurisdiction for the oversight of foreign intelligence, Mr. Chairman.

Chairman RIBICOFF. Senator Mansfield, in his testimony, states that that committee should be established in this session of Congress.

Senator Weicker states that if this session of Congress does not establish such a committee, it will not be established.

Senator Tower says that we should not establish it in this session of Congress, but put it over to the next session of Congress.

Do you agree that Congress should establish that oversight committee in this session of Congress?

Mr. COLBY. I think the sooner the better, Mr. Chairman.

Chairman RIBICOFF. On page 6, you state that the CIA has never assassinated anyone.

Would you support a prohibition against the assassination of anyone in the absence of war?

Mr. COLBY. I have issued directives to that effect in the CIA, Mr. Chairman. I would have no reservation against such a prohibition.

Chairman RIBICOFF. What do you think, Mr. Colby, that a congressional committee should do if it opposes a decision to conduct a covert operation and Congress has only a few days in which to act before an operation goes into effect?

Mr. COLBY. I believe the committee might vote, the committee might express their views to the President specifically. The committee can obviously indicate that it has an ultimate authority to pass new legislation in the future, or affect appropriations in the future of the agency involved in such activity. I think the normal workings of the constitutional tension between the two branches will bring about some resolution, perhaps not of that particular action, if the President felt it to be terribly important, but a relationship would develop between the executive branch and the legislative which would give full consideration to the views of the legislative as well as the excutive side.

Chairman RIBICOFF. May I say, for the benefit of the members of the committee, we will confine ourselves to 5 minutes each for questioning because Mr. Colby must leave by 12 :15.

Suppose there was such a committee and you came before it with an operation such as Angola and you found that the committee was overwhelmingly against the United States getting involved in Angola because they sensed the congressional feeling, as it has now been expressed, by votes in the U.S. Senate.

What do you see an intelligence agency doing under those circumstances?

Mr. COLBY. I would certainly report that reaction to the President. We would discuss what we should do in that situation. The situation has not arisen, Mr. Chairman. I have had situations where individual members have indicated opposition, but my sense of the feeling of the committee in question has been that other members were equally positive about it.

There are certain situations in which I have had formal documents from committees urging action in certain areas and we have taken that action and then been met with substantial opposition from other members, individual members.

I think that is the kind of thing that could be worked out. If it were organized in a fashion so that the committee could vote, we could have a decision as to what the committee's real thought was.

There was one committee that I briefed in great detail on one project and at the end of it, I was asked to summarize the result of the committee's attitude. I said that I gathered from my extensive briefing that the committee was not very strongly for it, and it was not very strongly against it. That met with general approval as a statement of the committee's view.

I think that there is a further question, Mr. Chairman, which is whether the individual members wish to be put in a position of a formal vote on these kinds of operations or whether they would rather be in a situation where they have not been committed to responsibility for the operation, freeing themselves to make congressional criticism of them afterwards if they do not work out.

Chairman RIBICOFF. We have been talking here about congressional oversight, but there is a problem of oversight in the executive branch.

You testified before the Senate Appropriations Committee in January 1975, "The arrangements for administrative supervision of the CIA and the intelligence community by the executive branch appears sufficient at this time."

Yet Secretary Rusk appeared before us yesterday and stated that while he was Secretary of State, operations were conducted by the CIA which he did not know about at that time, but only has discovered in recent days. And Mr. Katzenbach, who was Under Secretary of State at that time, when I asked him the question, he said he did not know about it, but he assumed that the Secretary of State knew about it.

How do you go about assuring that the National Security Council and the President are aware of basic and important operations by the intelligence agencies?

Mr. COLBY. Our normal procedure is to submit a proposal for a certain operation. This goes to a subcommittee of the National Security Council, the so-called 40 Committee. It is debated and discussed there. The consensus or the different positions are recorded, the matter is then taken to the President for final decision.

The National Security Council is advisory to the Presilent. It is not an independent body of its own. It is advisory to the President.

There have been a very few occasions, Mr. Chairman, in which the President has given direct instructions to the CIA to conduct operations without informing certain other members of the National Security Council, the State Department, or the Defense Department.

There are many situations in which we conduct operations which are not known to the bureaucracy of any one of the other departments because we have the same problem of retaining secrecy, if the information spreads too far in the executive branch, as I referred to with respect to its spreading too far in the legislative branch.

The President's arrangement for the working of this kind of activity call upon us normally to go through a consultative procedure before he makes his decision, but since we are essentially using his authority in this kind of operation, I think that we have to be responsive to him directly if he so decides.

However, under present law, the point has clearly been made several times that even if the President gave a personal and direct order about a particular operation, it would still, under the law, have to be reported to the six committees of the Congress.

Chairman RIBICOFF. In other words, the committees of Congress would know, and the Secretary of State and the Secretary of Defense would not know?

Mr. COLBY. Potentially, but very hypothetically; I think that more or less will compel consultation with the other departments. . . .

Senator BROCK. I think I might preface this question by admitting an enormous degree of frustration, and frankly anger and disgust, over the recent leaks from the Congress of the United States, and I have particular reference to the actions of the House committee and its printing of a report which I thought there was an agreement—and I think everybody else thought there was an agreement—including the members of the committee with the President with regard to the release of national security information.

I gather that that information has now been leaked in the form of a final report, distinct from the documents.

Mr. COLBY. I do not think they have voted.

Senator BROCK. I do not think they have voted, but the information was in the Washington Post this morning, so it does not really matter, does it?

I wonder how we can guard against that, no matter what our format is. I wonder what we can do.

I think that we can apply rather specific sanctions to staff. I think that is essential. But I do not think this is a staff problem. I may be wrong.

The Constitution very clearly limits the law and its application to the Congress or a Member of Congress. He cannot be held accountable in any other place for words he uses in his official duties.

That is where I see a problem.

I wonder if you would comment in this particular context on the choice, for example, between having a House committee and a Senate committee separately, or a joint committee or the choice Senator Percy mentioned on having both in the appropriations and authorization process.

Mr. COLBY. I go at it with a mathematical approach, Senator Brock. A secret becomes half a secret when two people become aware of it. You can carry on that arithmetical progression from there on.

The fewer members that are on the appropriate oversight, the better. Obviously there has to be a substantial enough body to be representative of the House or the Senate as a whole. I think the idea of limiting the number to a rather smaller number increases a sense of self-discipline about the secrets.

Second, I think that there are some improvements that could be made in the rules of the Houses to stress the importance of secrecy. Then it is up to the Houses to discipline their own Members and there are ways in which that has been done, both in the formal ultimate sense and the informal sense of the relationship among the Members.

I believe there are many countries in the world where the Parliament has members, not just of the loyal opposition, but of a disloyal opposition, and those Parliaments have worked out systems whereby they continue to do the business of the majority of the Parliament and the majority of the nation, even though there are some disloyal opposition members in those Parliaments.

I do not think we have any disloyal Members of our Congress and the Senate, but I think that the techniques of controlling secrets and controlling a responsible management of the Government are somewhat similar and could be adaptable.

Senator BROCK. In essence then, and probably, if I could put words into your mouth, you would prefer—I think you said this in your statement—a joint committee, No. 1, and No. 2, that that committee have both authorization and appropriation responsibilities.

Mr. COLBY. Yes.

Senator BROCK. Can I ask you, for my own personal information, to comment or describe for me the understanding that you did have in that particular instance in regard to the committee's final report?

Mr. COLBY. We had a dispute over the publication of certain words in some documents that we had provided to the House committee. I said that those words did have some significance which a careful study by another foreign intelligence service could track back to some specific actions that they had taken.

The committee has cited a reference to this general subject in a published book. That was not my concern. What was in the book was not a matter of concern to me. It was appropriate for that to be in the book. What I was concerned about was a further study of some of the leads that those words gave. Then, by direction of the President, we said we would no longer provide the kind of classified information to the committee that we had been in the process of providing. This led to an impasse between the committee and the Executive. It led finally to a conference between the committee chairman, the House leadership, the President and myself, and in the course of that discussion agreement was reached on procedures whereby if the committee believed that something should be released, and I believed that it should not, the matter would be referred to the President. If he found release to be detrimental to the national security in a formal sense, then the material would not be released, pending further resolution of the constitutional and legal issues involved.

We went through that process with respect to the specific reports a couple of weeks ago. and until this day, the President's certification has been respected by the committee. There have been a few leaks, but nonetheless in a formal sense the committee has respected it.

The committee now contends that that agreement does not apply to the committee's final report. This is just impossible, Senator.

We are not talking about individual documents; we are talking about the information which is contained on the documents, and we are talking about names, and we are talking about groups, and we are talking about funds, we are talking about numbers. Those numbers do not become unclassified by being taken off of one piece of paper and put on another. They are still classified information.

We are at present having a discussion about how to handle that. Our staff has been in consultation with the committee staff in an attempt to narrow the area of disagreement and they are discussing how this is going to work out.

Mr. ROGOVIN. Senator, the issue is one of access. It is a good example of what an oversight committee is going to have to face. The committee obtained complete access with the understanding that when they were going to make any kind of public disclosure there would be this system of consultation. The access took place, then at the end of the line when no more information was sought, the committee concluded that it would be a censorship of its report if they allowed the President to determine that any particular piece of information was detrimental to the national security.

Any future oversight, using this as an example, has to meet this problem, because committees will make reports. It is a constitutional responsibility to inform, and that is where the issue has to be resolved as to how particular material can be made public. Any process that should reflect the coequal nature of the branches of the Government. You should not set up a situation where a slim majority of one committee of one house will declassify a piece of information where the President has said that it will be detrimental to the national interest.

I think it is extremely important that this issue be faced in any oversight legislation.

Mr. COLBY. This is not in any sense an attempt to censor, Senator Brock. We have worked with committees to try to work out phrasings by which things can be said, even critical things can be said, without revealing the details of the specific country, the specific group that is helped, the specific individuals involved.

The overall line we can handle without any trouble. We have done that in our discussions with our ex-employees who wish to write books. We negotiate with them as to, well, if you can refer to this in somewhat more of a general term, please go ahead, but do not reveal this particular detail.

It is that exact technique that we think can be applicable in a relationship with the Congress.

Senator BROCK. The situation would require that if you could not get an agreement, you would go to court and you would get a decision of the constitutional requirement?

Mr. ROGOVIN. We reached an impasse with both the executive and legislative branch. We are talking about absolute positions. In order to be able to move this forward, we have this ultimate resolution that through the subpena power of the committee, we then see the document and the court would ultimately resolve the question of whether it was classified or not. It was really a recognition that we had gone about as far as we could go without resolving questions of absolute privilege.

Senator BROCK. I think you and the President have been had. Thank you.

Chairman RIBICOFF. Senator Glenn?

Senator GLENN. Thank you, Mr. Chairman.

Mr. Colby, you have been in a most difficult job. I would like to associate myself with the remarks of my colleagues in complimenting you on the way that you have handled this.

Mr. COLBY. Thank you, Senator.

Senator GLENN. I think that we absolutely must have a strong, and if it is found necessary, even an expanded intelligence activity in these times in which we live. Having said that, we all agree, I am sure, that we want to prevent the mishandling of some intelligence operations and the covert activities.

I think most of the American people and probably all of us in this room agree that we would not condone some of the past operations.

I am concerned that maybe we are putting too much attention on whether we have a joint or a single committee or whatever. We are concerned with organization of an oversight committee here, but I think perhaps that there is a much more basic problem.

We could set up a committee which seemed to be organizationally perfect, and still not be getting to the center of the problem, touching the spot where these decisions are being made. I am concerned that in whatever oversight we set up that really we are overseeing what is important, that decisions are not being made at some different level that involve this Nation internationally and can influence the whole foreign policy.

I am very concerned that we know what we are dealing with, and we are getting to the real sources of the decisions, that we are getting to where they are made. I am not sure that we have approached that yet.

You indicated in your testimony that your authority came only from using Presidential authority, I believe was the word, that he must be kept fully informed.

Just to make a point here of where that decision is made, did every President know of these assassination plans?

Mr. COLBY. The record on that, Senator Glenn, is very murky. One can put up a contention that the President did not know or was protected from the details of the information.

One can also put up a contention that there was a general climate of discussion where he probably did know of it and should have known of it. You cannot prove either case by examining the available evidence.

Senator GLENN. The Committee of 40, did they know?

Mr. COLBY. I believe they did not know of the specific cases we are talking about. Again, it is the difference between a specific, detailed activity and a general grant of authority to go into a general category of activity. Again, that did not get specific enough so that you have records that clearly indicate it.

Senator GLENN. Perhaps those kinds are of a specialized case, maybe they are not as typical as some others.

Let us say Angola, plans to go there: were they approved specifically by the President?

Mr. COLBY. I cannot confirm or deny specifically any present covert activity, Senator Glenn. I will say that any activity that we are conducting at this time or have conducted under my directorship has been discussed with the 40 Committee and has been the result of a Presidential approval.

Senator GLENN. What concerns me here, obviously, is that we could set up an oversight committee, but which turns out to be a facade, a papier mache type approach to this thing, because the American people think, now we are protected, our checks and balances are now working between our executive and legislative branches of Government, but they really will not be, it will be a charade unless we really get to where these decisions are being made.

I am not sure the Church committee—and I am certain that I am still at sea a little bit about where these decisions are made and what kind of organization or committee structure we should set up to oversee this.

Would you care to comment on that and what, from out of your experience you would advise, what should be our touchstones in the executive branch to make sure we are overseeing what we think we are going to oversee or hope that we will.

Mr. COLBY. The present legislation has one positive feature that requires that the Agency report any activity other than intelligence gathering in a timely fashion. That is a matter of law, and the Agency must do it. My successor must do it.

It has some weaknesses in that it requires us to report to too many committees, but the concept of a responsiveness by the CIA or by anyone else who is engaged in this particular kind of activity is proper. The law requires officials of the Government to respond to the appropriate committees. I would hope that would be a minimum number of committees, because our experience has shown that too many of them means that there are no secrets.

Senator GLENN. I would agree with your statements on the need for secrecy. I think that what has happened in some of these areas has just been abominable. That is one reason that I tend to favor the joint committee approach rather than the single because of the proliferation of people who would know things.

Obviously, from our setup here an oversight function would be much simpler if we could deal with one spot, the Director of Central Intelligence and have full confidence that he in turn, is fully informed about all DOD operations and NSA and all of the other functions of Government, intelligencewise.

Do you favor that type, one central location for all of this, coming to the peak of the pyramid here, or do you think it should be kept a little more diversified?

Questions were asked earlier about the FBI and the interrelatedness there, and DOD and the military intelligence area that comes somewhat under you, somewhat under them.

Do you think that we should have one man with that Czar-type responsibility and should there be that deliberation, and should we in our oversight deal with several different areas to see what is going on?

Mr. COLBY. I think there is a clear distinction, as I indicated, between the responsibilities for domestic counterintelligence and internal security in the hands of the FBI and the problems of foreign intelligence. I think it is quite different.

With respect to the relationship with the military, I believe it is very useful to our country that you be able to look to one individual to get an overall look at what I call national intelligence. I think there should be a distinction between national intelligence and what can be called tactical intelligence. For the tactical or departmental intelligence activities, you should look to that particular force or that particular department or to the details of intelligence activities at the local level.

You cannot have a single intelligence Czar responsible for every radar and every destroyer in the Nation. If you have a destroyer, you are going to have a radar. It is properly looked at as a part of the Navy, not as a part of intelligence.

On the other hand, there are military activities that do relate very directly to the national intelligence problems. There the Director should have a view, and does have a view, of those activities. There is full disclosure to the Director and I have, on many occasions, reported on the budgets of these national intelligence activities in great detail.

Senator GLENN. Do you think that throughout the executive branch and throughout all of the different intelligence activities, there is adequate definition of the level that appropriate decisions should be made?

Let us go back to the assassinations. Is it possible for one of your agents someplace—I suppose it would be possible, of course, for someone to make the decision, "yes, it is in the national interest, the best interest," and this has not been run uphill through the NSC and the appropriate people, and has not been checked with the President— do we have adequate checks to make sure that these decisions are not being made by someone who might be quite misguided at his level as to what is in the national interest?

I am just trying to get this whole picture.

Mr. COLBY. We have some very specific directives and instructions. We have a law that requires that anything other than intelligence-gathering only be done if the President certifies it as important to the national security and it is reported to the committees of the Congress. This is known throughout our structure, that no such activity can be undertaken without that kind of approval.

We have an excellent communications system that keeps us in very close contact with our people everywhere in the world, and we have the discipline of the organization itself, a control through the organization. There have been occasions in the past in which it broke down. The Senate select committee looked into the fact that there was a small amount of toxin that was left over and not found and was in an old storeroom. It is possible for that sort of thing to happen in any large institution. But I believe our control structure will stand up to any other terms of its effectiveness.

Senator GLENN. Mr. Chairman, my time is up. I would just like to make one short statement here.

I think that before we make any decision of whether we have a joint or single committee or whatever, we really have to pin down what it is we are going to oversee first, so we know what the organization is and what contacts the oversight committee would develop and what the committee staff would be set up to do and so on.

I think that really has to be closely defined. Without knowing some of these things, I do not know whether I could, in good conscience, vote for a single or a joint committee now.

We have to define the jobs they are going to do. To really define that, we are going to have to home in on who their contacts are going to be, and what levels they are going to oversee. Is it just one spot, just the President or the CIA, or are we going to be required to do a dozen agency checks to perform our oversight function.

Unless we define that, and define it very closely, it seems to me that any committee structure whatever, one, two, three or half a dozen committees, are going to do nothing but be a window-dressing that will mislead the American people more than lead them.

Chairman RIBICOFF. My response to that as chairman, Senator Glenn, is that we will have some 25 witnesses. This is exactly what we are exploring in these hearings.

As chairman, I entered these meetings with an open mind, without any preconceived ideas seeking guidance from my fellow members on this commitee, the executive branch, and all of those in this country who have something to offer.

The Church committee will not have a bill before us for the next week. We will have their point of view.

You, Mr. Colby, made the statement that the sooner this committee is established, the better. We will welcome, of course, as soon as possible, the input from the executive branch.

This committee will give complete consideration and respect to the views of the President of the United States as well as the Church committee. The sooner we have your input. and the Church committee's, the better for us. We agree, the sooner the better. And, by having the cooperation of the membership of this committee, these hearings are going forward day after day.

Once we complete the hearing, we will immediately go toward markup. Senator Glenn, you are a very valuable and thoughtful member of this committee. Any ideas you have will certainly be given the most careful consideration.

Senator GLENN. Maybe what I just outlined is the first job of the new committee. We have to determine where to go. Maybe that is the job of the oversight committee which we will set up.

Senator NUNN. One observation, Mr. Chairman. if you will permit it.

I would like to solve all of these organizational problems of intelligence while we go. I believe it is one of the very purposes of the oversight committee.

Someone is going to have to spend hours and hours to get all of the pegs in the right hole, or to find out where they are. I do not know if we can take that on. I certainly think we ought to learn as much about it as we can.

I believe our hope is this oversight committee can undertake a lot of that themselves in their deliberations with the intelligence community and with the executive branch. I believe that if we are looking for a simple solution, we are going to be very disappointed.

Chairman RIBICOFF. Senator Weicker?

Senator WEICKER. Thank you, Mr. Chairman.

Would you agree with me that really the CIA will not be able to operate efficiently until we have an oversight committee in place? I think it is essential, in other words, in restoring confidence and allow you fellows to operate.

Mr. COLBY. I think it would be a substantial step ahead, Senator Weicker.

Senator WEICKER. Let me say this.

I think that both of us appreciate the necessity to go ahead and stop the pendulum in mid-swing. If indeed you are spending 122 percent of your time on the Hill——

Mr. COLBY. That was my associate's number.

Senator WEICKER. It is probably a good figure. It illustrates the problem as a reaction to the zero percent that used to be spent on the Hill. That is the problem, to try to bring this thing back into some sort of perspective.

I am troubled as to where we go from here, having wrestled with the concept of oversight and having wanted it for 3 years. Other Members of this body, the Majority Leader stated yesterday, have wanted it for longer than that.

I think, if Senator Mansfield's proposals had been put into effect many years ago, we would not have gone through this mess we are going through now.

There is a great deal of difference between the rhetoric on the Hill and the deeds.

This is probably going to be measured rather carefully by the American people in the weeks ahead.

I will present to you one of the areas that I am truly troubled about and I want your reaction. I have a vote coming up next week on the confirmation of the CIA Director. Both of us know George Bush to be a fine man; there is no argument, both in the sense of his qualities of mind and heart. So let us leave George Bush out of this, it has nothing to do with him as an individual.

My question, the question I have to ask myself, and I would like to have your reaction, while we are trying to reestablish confidence in this Agency, which not only holds for the present, but obviously for the future—should anyone so closely identified with politics, Democrat or Republican, be the head of that Agency?

And I want you to eliminate the individual, George Bush, from your mind. I knew his dad, I have a great affection for his family and I respect him.

There is a problem. This body is going around alerting the American people. We want good intelligence and we want to reestablish confidence, and right out of the box we are going to do something that is going to come under question.

I would just like to have your professional opinion as to whether anyone closely identified with politics should head up this Agency.

Mr. COLBY. I started from a slightly different starting point, Senator Weicker. Although I am a professional and grew out of the profession, I have many times expressed my belief that I think it is somewhat better that a nonprofessional be the head of the Agency and be supported by the professionals in it, somewhat in the same fashion that the head of the Army, Defense Department, Navy and so forth are appointees, civilian appointees, outside of the profession itself and the profession supports and performs under that kind of disinterested guidance that an outsider poses.

Once you say that, then the question is, obviously you do not want a partisan political figure in the post.

I think that Mr. Bush has given every indication and every assurance that he intends to avoid any such situation. I am sure there will be a lot of attention addressed to this by critics of the CIA in the future, and any step in that direction would be immediately highlighted. Consequently, Ambassador Bush would make every effort to keep himself independent of politics.

There has been a major letter by the President withdrawing his name from one particular political potential. I think he has given every indication that he intends to perform in an independent manner, befitting this particular Agency.

Senator WEICKER. Again, I want to make clear that George Bush is not the subject matter of my question. It is the fact that we are trying to restore confidence in this Agency.

I have to confess to you, do you feel that the former chairman of one of the major political parties, either one, Democratic or Republican, is going to be viewed by the American public as bringing the right degree of objectivity to a job that I think everybody realizes is one in which they want to have objectivity.

Mr. COLBY. Of course, I do not believe that it is possible to answer that question without referring to the individuals who have held that post. There are very few of those posts, and very few of those individuals. I repeat what I said before. I do not believe that a partisan political figure should manage the Agency. In other words, it should not be managed as a partisan political tool of any administration. I have expressed my confidence in Ambassador Bush and he has given every assurance that he will avoid that. Therefore, I think the background of whether someone did something once is not the touchstone and determinant of the matter.

Senator WEICKER. We have had testimony by others, not only on this committee, but in other committees, that the Attorney General of the United States should not be a partisan political figure, even though that has been the case. The Democrats are the ones that come to mind on this score.

I wonder, if in this day and age, the American public is not looking for something, or for someone, quite frankly, very extraordinary to head the Justice systems, the FBI, CIA, or the Department of Justice.

I am not so sure that you answered my question.

Mr. COLBY. I am not so sure that I could.

Senator WEICKER. I understand your position. You are probably having difficulty dividing the man, in this case George Bush, from the position, but we are dealing—the problem is, Mr. Colby, that both you and I understand that we have to have intelligence, we have to have the American people believing in their intelligence agency. That is what is at stake right here, whether this thing is going to survive or be washed out at sea. That is why it requires the most extraordinary measure.

Mr. COLBY. I do not think that it is appropriate for me to discuss my successor, Senator Weicker. I stated my position, as accurately as I can.

Senator WEICKER. One last question. I wish I had greater time to get into it, but this great chart that we have up here, next to the wall indicates a chain of command. I would like, if I could, put names to this.

Director Colby, when did you take over as the head of CIA?

Mr. COLBY. I was sworn in in September 1973. Mr. Schlesinger left in May, and I essentially ran it in between.

Senator WEICKER. Point No. 2, the head of the National Security Council, am I correct in assuming that that has been Dr. Kissinger?

Mr. COLBY. The Chairman is the President but the Executive Secretary of it and the manager of the staff as distinct from the Council is the Assistant to the President for National Security Affairs, which up to a few months ago was Dr. Kissinger.

Senator WEICKER. Do you think it is advisable, as a practical matter, that a line run from the Secretary of State up to the National Security Council that way? Do you think that is a particularly good situation to have, the Secretary of State being, for all practical intents and purposes, the head of the National Security Council?

Mr. COLBY. We are talking about the President and the way he runs his particular office with the people that he has around him. I think organizations should reflect the people and the demands and the political situations. I do not think they are immutable. I think they are subject to change with new personalities and new relationships that come up between people.

Senator WEICKER. Aside from whatever oversight the Congress can give, however, the National Security Council, in effect, is the executive oversight relative to the CIA activities, is it not?

Mr. COLBY. Under the National Security Act, the CIA reports to the National Security Council. The NSC consists of the President, Vice President, Secretary of State, Secretary of Defense——

Senator WEICKER. May I have 1 more minute, Mr. Chairman?

Chairman RIBICOFF. There is a vote, and we still have Senator Javits. Go ahead.

Senator JAVITS. I yield.

Senator WEICKER. Thank you, Mr. Chairman.

The only thing that concerns me is the testimony of James Gardner from the State Department was that between 1973 and 1974, the 40 covert operations by the CIA were approved by the special Forty Committee but apparently the committee never met. It was strictly a telephone type of operation, with Secretary of State Kissinger not actually having face to face dialogue.

Mr. COLBY. At that time Senator Weicker, we were very sharply reducing the numbers of those operations. By 1973 only about 5 percent of our budget was involved in that kind of operation. Most of those 40 Committee decisions were 6-month or yearly status reports on ongoing activities. They required no great consideration, no great policy questions were involved. There were some meetings of the 40 Committee on one very important program which was not actually a covert action program. It was an intelligence collection program, but it was a very significant and delicate one. We did meet and discuss that and argued about it, but most of it was not of the level of importance, the individual actions were not of the level of importance that required actual debate and discussion.

Senator WEICKER. Thank you, Mr. Chairman.

Mr. COLBY. I might add that the more important decisions that have been made this year have been the subject of a considerable number of 40 Committee discussions.

Senator JAVITS. Mr. Colby, I would like to join my colleagues in my expression of confidence in you and my appreciation as a U.S. Senator from New York for the job that you have done.

I have had a lot of experience with you beginning with the job in Vietnam.

Mr. COLBY. Thank you very much.

Senator JAVITS. I take great pleasure in being able to say that.

One of my colleagues has asked me to raise an issue with you which I would like to raise.

Senator Case yesterday in a statement said, with respect to news leaks—I think he was talking particularly about the leak relating to Italian political parties—he said, "it is a hard thing to prove, but I have a powerful suspicion that they"—meaning the CIA—"are leaking these things themselves, then they can blame it on Congress you see and discredit our disclosure requirements."

Then he went on to say, the agencies have not been happy with our requirements that they brief us, and so on.

A two-part question, one : is there any truth to that as far as the CIA is concerned, or to your knowledge, as to any other executive department agency; and second, what precautions do you take in the agencies against such duplicity.

Mr. COLBY. Senator Javits, I flatly deny that the CIA leaked information for that kind of a purpose. The CIA was trying to conduct covert actions. We have held these secrets for a number of months. Most of these exposures came out of some combination of testimony, an event abroad which brought the matter to public attention, and the energetic efforts of our news colleagues and journalists in the country who pick up little bits and pieces and add them up to a total picture.

There was certainly no conscious effort by CIA.

I must state again, however, that our controls, our legal controls over our own employees are not those they should be to give us proper control.

We conduct a number of activities within the Agency limiting the number of people who know about these matters. Large numbers of people in the Agency know nothing about these matters and are deliberately kept ignorant of them for security purposes, but a certain number do have to know about them. We have no indication of dissatisfaction in the Agency with the programs we are undertaking. As a matter of fact, I believe that the Agency has done a splendid job of maintaining its ability to carry out intelligence operations, and also to carry out a very energetic and imaginative program in the covert action field when this has been properly approved.

Senator JAVITS. I therefore take it that that flat denial means that as far as you know, the CIA has not leaked anything for any purpose?

Mr. COLBY. The CIA itself has not leaked. I absolutely and flatly deny that the Agency has ever leaked information so that Congress' ability to keep secrets, or that the reporting requirements of section 662 of the Foreign Assistance Act, would be discredited. Unfortunately, I cannot say that no individual CIA employee has ever leaked information. As I have mentioned, a stronger law against disclosures is needed.

Senator JAVITS. Have you already given us, or can you give us, your suggestions for the legal tightening up that you feel is desirable for the CIA?

Mr. COLBY. I have submitted some recommendations for legislation and we have worked these through the Justice Department, and they are about to be sent by the Office of Management and Budget to the Congress. The legislation will give us criminal sanctions over the disclosure of sources and methods by those who have voluntarily undertaken the obligation to keep those secret.

I believe that the specifics of the recommendation are fully compatible with the first amendment of our Constitution and are also necessary to protect the liberties of Americans.

Senator JAVITS. Thank you, I am very pleased with the latter assertion, and we shall await that .

One other question, since we all have to vote.

There has been a lot of attention to what the CIA has done covertly and who it tells about it and why; what responsibility there is in the President and the National Security Council, et cetera.

I have a totally different question. What about the right of the Congress to know, in order to legislate? What is your appraisal, as now our retiring Director of the CIA of what we have to know to legislate intelligently?

I am now a member of all kinds of committees that need to know what you are discovering covertly or overtly in order to deal intelligently with a wide range of issues, whether it is Angola or U.S. trade policy or the Panama Canal.

Do you have any recommendations for us on that?

Mr. COLBY. We have a procedure, Senator Javits, by which an Agency spokesman briefs on request on any subject in the world, using the most sensitive information available to us.

I spent yesterday with a House committee discussing some of the most sensitive details of our knowledge of one particular foreign situation. I also developed a special current intelligence publication for the Congress some months ago. This was made available to relevant committees of the Congress in the hope that the individual Members will find it convenient to look through the publication quickly and profit from the kind of intelligence we collect.

Senator JAVITS. There is nothing you recommend which would strike out that requirement of having the Director or authorized representatives coming to brief committees or individuals as to what they ought to know from the legislative point of view?

Mr. COLBY. Absolutely not, Senator. I believe we Americans share our decisionmaking. Part of it is made in the executive branch; part of it also involves the Congress. In order for those decisions, those national decisions, to be the best possible, we have to provide the substance of the intelligence information to the Congress to the extent that we possibly can.

Senator JAVITS. Nothing we do in oversight committee legislation or anything else ought to strike out that responsibility and that right on our part in the Congress?

Mr. COLBY. No.

I would only ask again that the self-discipline in the Congress itself and the control of its staff members be such that sensitive information can be protected. In addition to operational information, substantive assessments may also require protection.

Oversight Recommendations

In addition to hearings held on specific oversight bills by the House and Senate committees, four separate investigative bodies addressed the general problem of congressional oversight in the 1970s (see Bibliography in the Appendix). The 1976 recommendations of the House Select Committee on Intelligence and the Commission on the Organization of the U.S. Government for the Conduct of Foreign Policy (Murphy Commission) are reprinted here. The Commission on CIA Activities Within the U.S. (Rockefeller Commission) published its report in June 1975 and made two recommendations on congressional oversight ([124], p. 81): (1) The president should recommend to Congress the establishment of a Joint Committee on Intelligence to assume the oversight role currently played by the Armed Services Committees: (2) Congress should give careful consideration to the question of whether the budget of the CIA should not, at least to some extent, be made public, particularly in view of the provisions of Article I, Section 9, Clause 7, of the Constitution. This clause states that "no money shall be drawn from the Treasury, but in Consequence of Appropriations made by Law; and a regular Statement and Account of the Receipts and Expenditures of all public Money shall be published from time to time."

The Church Committee findings and recommendations on foreign and military intelligence are reprinted in Chapter 3; additional views and recommendations of the committee appear in [45A], pp. 563 ff. Among the more significant recommendations dealing explicitly with oversight by Congress are the following:

"No. 38. By statute, the intelligence oversight committee(s) of Congress should require that the annual budget submission for covert action programs be specified and detailed as to the activity recommended. Unforeseen covert action projects should be funded from the Contingency Reserve Fund which could be replenished only after the concurrence of the oversight and any other appropriate congressional committees. The congressional intelligence oversight committees should be notified prior to any withdrawal from the Contingency Reserve Fund.

"No. 39. By statute, any covert use by the U.S. Government of American citizens as combatants should be preceded by the notification required for all covert actions. The statute should provide that within 60 days of such notification such use shall be terminated unless the Congress has specifically authorized such use. The Congress should be empowered to terminate such use at any time.

"No. 40. By statute, the executive branch should be prevented from conducting any covert military assistance program (including the indirect or direct provision of military material, military or logistics advice and training, and funds for mercenaries) without the explicit prior consent of the intelligence oversight committee(s) of Congress.

"No. 77. The intelligence oversight committee(s) of Congress should authorize on an annual basis a 'National Intelligence Budget,' the total amount of which would be made public. The Committee recommends that the oversight committee consider whether it is necessary, given the Constitutional requirement and the national security demands, to publish more detailed budgets.

"No. 78. The intelligence oversight committee(s) of Congress should monitor the tactical and indirect support accounts as well as the national activities of intelligence agencies in order to assure that they are kept in proper perspective and balance.

"No. 79. At the request of the intelligence oversight committee(s) of Congress and as its agent, staff members of the General Accounting Office should conduct full audits, both for compliance and for management of all components of the intelligence community. The GAO should establish such procedures, compartmentation and clearances as are necessary in order to conduct these audits on a secure basis. In conducting such audits, the GAO should be authorized to have full access to all necessary intelligence community files and records."

HOUSE SELECT COMMITTEE ON INTELLIGENCE RECOMMENDATIONS ([85], pp. 1–7)

The Pike Committee recommendations on intelligence community oversight were interspersed with others bearing on the internal functioning of the intelligence community. The full set of recommendations is reprinted here.

1. The select committee recommends that there be formed a standing Committee on Intelligence of the House of Representatives.

a. The committee membership should reflect a broad representation of political and philosophical views.

b. The committee should consist of not more than 13 or less than nine members, designated by the Speaker in consultation with the minority leader, representing approximately the same political ratio as the House of Representatives.

c. No member of the committee may serve more than 3 consecutive terms on the committee, and no member of the staff may serve more than 6 years.

d. Any past or current member of the committee staff who shall release, without authorization of the committee, materials or information obtained by the committee shall be immediately terminated from employment and shall be fully subject to criminal and civil action, notwithstanding legislative immunity.

e. The committee shall be vested with subpoena power and shall have the right to enforce by a proceeding for civil contempt its subpoenas in the U.S. District Court for the District of Columbia or any other court of competent jurisdiction, without authorization from the House, provided the committee has so designated by resolution. The committee staff shall be given statutory standing to represent the committee in any proceeding arising from the issuance of a subpoena.

f. The committee's jurisdiction shall include all legislative and oversight functions relating to all U.S. agencies and departments engaged in foreign or domestic intelligence. The committee shall have exclusive jurisdiction for budget authorization for all intelligence activities and exclusive jurisdiction for all covert action operations. All remaining oversight functions may be concurrent with other committees of the House.

B. RELEASE OF INFORMATION

1. The select committee recommends that rule XI.2 (e) (2) of the House Rules is amended to read as follows:

"Each committee shall keep a complete record of all committee action which shall include a copy of all reports, statements, and testimony of witnesses whether received in open or in executive session."

2. The committee shall have the right to release any information or documents in its possession or control by a vote of a majority of the members of the committee under such terms and conditions as the committee shall deem advisable. The committee, in making the decision whether or not to release such information, shall have the right, but not the duty, to consult with other agencies of the Government within the intelligence community or executive branch with regard to any decision relating to the release of such heretofore secret information.

3. In the event of a negative vote by the committee on the release of certain classified information, a member of the committee may apprise the other Members of the House that the committee possesses information which he believes ought to be made public. Other Members of the House would then be authorized to have access to that information, provided they sign an agreement not to divulge the information. If these other Members agree that this information ought to be made public, they will sign a petition attesting to that. Upon obtaining the signatures of one-fifth of the House, the House shall convene in

secret session for the purpose of advising the entire membership of the House of that information. The House may then vote to release the information to the public.

4. The select committee recommends that the rules of the House be revised to provide that any Member who reveals any classified information which jeopardizes the national security of the United States may be censured or expelled by a two-thirds vote of the House.

C. COVERT ACTION

1. The select committee recommends that all activities involving direct or indirect attempts to assassinate any individual and all paramilitary activities shall be prohibited except in time of war.

2. The select committee recommends that as to other covert action by any U.S. intelligence component, the following shall be required within 48 hours of initial approval.

a. The Director of Central Intelligence shall notify the committee in writing, stating in detail the nature, extent, purpose, risks, likelihood of success, and costs of the operation.

b. The President shall certify in writing to the committee that such covert action operation is required to protect the national security of the United States.

c. The committee shall be provided with duplicate originals of the written recommendations of each member of the 40 committee or its successor.

3. All covert action operations shall be terminated no later than 12 months from the date of affirmative recommendation by the 40 committee or its successor.

D. NSA AS AN INDEPENDENT AGENCY

1. The select committee recommends that the existence of the National Security Agency should be recognized by specific legislation and that such legislation provide for civilian control of NSA. Further, it is recommended that such legislation specifically define the role of NSA with reference to the monitoring of communications of Americans.

E. DISCLOSURE OF BUDGET TOTALS

1. The select committee recommends that all intelligence related items be included as intelligence expenditures in the President's budget, and that there be disclosure of the total single sum budgeted for each agency involved in intelligence, or if such an item is a part or portion of the budget of another agency or department that it be separately identified as a single item.

F. PROHIBITION OF FUND TRANSFERS

1. The select committee recommends there be appropriate legislation to prohibit any significant transfer of funds between agencies or departments in connection with intelligence activities.

2. The select committee recommends there be appropriate legislation to prohibit any significant reprograming of funds within agencies or departments in connection with intelligence activities without the specific approval of the Intelligence Committee and appropriate committees of Congress.

3. The select committee recommends there be appropriate legislation to prohibit any significant expenditures of reserve or contingency funds in connection with intelligence activities without specific approval of the Intelligence Committee and appropriate committees of Congress.

G. DIRECTOR OF CENTRAL INTELLIGENCE

1. The select committee recommends that a Director of Central Intelligence shall be created, separate, from any of the operating or analytic intelligence agencies for the purpose of coordinating and overseeing the entire foreign intelligence community with a view to eliminating duplication in collection and promoting competition in analysis. The DCI shall be nominated by the President with the advice and consent of the Senate. This office shall have the following powers and duties:

(*a*) The DCI shall be the chief foreign intelligence officer of the United States, and shall be responsible for the supervision and control of all agencies of the United States engaged in foreign intelligence.

(*b*) The DCI shall be a Member of the National Security Council.

(*c*) the DCI may not hold a position or title with respect to any other agencies of Government.

(*d*) The DCI shall, along with such other duties, constitute an Office of Inspector General for all of the foreign intelligence agencies, including other agencies of government or branches of the military which have foreign intelligence functions. Such agencies shall have the obligation to report all instances of misconduct or allegations of misconduct to the DCI. This shall not constitute a limitation upon the respective agencies reporting to the DCI from maintaining their own Inspector General staff or similar body.

(*e*) The DCI shall have an adequate staff for the purposes expressed herein and be responsible for the national intelligence estimates and daily briefings of the President.

(*f*) The DCI shall be responsible for the preparation of the national intelligence estimates and such reports shall be immediately supplied to the appropriate committees of Congress on request.

(*g*) All budget requests shall be prepared by the agencies under the jurisdiction of the DCI. As those parts of budget of the military services or components of Department of Defense, they shall be submitted as an independent part of such budgets to the DCI.

(*h*) The DCI shall be charged with the functions of coordinating foreign intelligence agencies under its jurisdiction, the elimination of duplication, the periodic evaluation of the performance and efficiency of the agencies in question, and shall report to Congress on the foregoing at least annually.

(*i*) The DCI shall conduct a comprehensive inquiry into the causes of intelligence failures, including: inadequate collection tasking; analytical bias; duplication; unusable technical output; excessive compartmentation; and withholding of information by senior officials, and report to the Committee on Intelligence within 1 year.

H. FULL GAO AUDIT AUTHORITY

1. The select committee recommends that the General Accounting Office be empowered to conduct a full and complete management as well as financial audit of all intelligence agencies. There shall be no limitation on the GAO in the performance of these functions by any executive classification system, and the audit function of GAO shall specifically apply to those funds which presently may be expended on certification of a Director of an Agency alone.

I. INTERNAL FINANCIAL MANAGEMENT

1. The select committee recommends that the CIA internal audit staff be increased and given complete access to CIA financial records, and that overseas stations be audited at least annually. It is further recommended that all proprietary and procurement mechanisms be subjected to annual comprehensive review, by the CIA's internal audit staff.

J. FULL DISCLOSURE TO CONGRESS

1. The select committee recommends that existing legislation (National Security Act of 1947, Sec. 102 (d) (3)) restricting the Directors and heads of foreign intelligence agencies from providing full information to Congress should be amended to exclude committees of Congress having appropriate jurisdiction.

K. NEW FOREIGN OPERATIONS SUBCOMMITTEE OF NSC

1. The select committee recommends that the National Security Act of 1947 be amended to provide for the establishment of a permanent Foreign Operations Subcommittee of the National Security Council. The subcommittee's jurisdiction, function and composition shall be as follows:

(*a*) The subcommittee shall have jurisdiction over all authorized activities of U.S. foreign intelligence agencies except those solely related to the gathering of intelligence.

(*b*) The subcommittee shall advise the President on all proposed covert or clandestine activities and on hazardous collecting activities.

(*c*) Each member of the subcommittee shall be required by law to submit his individual assessments of each proposal to the President in writing. The assessment should cover such matters as the likelihood of success, the benefits of success, the damage resulting from failure or exposure, the risks against the potential benefits and alternate ways of accomplishing the goal.

(*d*) The subcommittee shall be chaired by the Assistant to the President for National Security Affairs and shall be composed of:

Assistant to the President for National Security Affairs;
Director of Central Intelligence;
Secretary of State;
Secretary of Defense;
Deputy Director for Intelligence of CIA;
Chairman of the Joint Chiefs of Staff;
The ambassador(s), if there is one, and assistant secretaries of state for the affected countries and areas.

L. DEFENSE INTELLIGENCE AGENCY

1. The select committee recommends that the Defense Intelligence Agency be abolished and that its functions be transferred to the Assistant Secretary of Defense for Intelligence and the CIA.

M. DETAILEES

1. The select committee recommends that intelligence agencies disclose the affiliation of employees on detail to other Government agencies or departments to all immediate colleagues and superiors.

N. ASSISTANT FOR NATIONAL SECURITY AFFAIRS

1. The select committee recommends that the Assistant to the President for National Security Affairs be prohibited from holding any cabinet-level position.

O. RESTRICTIONS ON POLICE TRAINING AND RELATIONSHIPS

1. The select committee recommends that no agency of the United States engaged principally in foreign or military intelligence, directly or indirectly engage in the training or the supplying of domestic police agencies of the United States, and that contacts between police agencies of the United States and U.S. foreign or military intelligence agencies be limited to those circumstances which shall be required on account of internal security or the normal requirements and functions of such police agencies.

P. MEDIA, RELIGION, AND EDUCATION

1. The select committee recommends that U.S. intelligence agencies not covertly provide money or other valuable consideration to persons associated with religious or educational institutions, or to employees or representatives of any journal or electronic media with general circulation in the United States or use such institutions or individuals for purposes of cover. The foregoing prohibitions are intended to apply to American citizens and institutions.

2. The select committee further recommends that U.S. intelligence agencies not covertly publish books, or plant or suppress stories in any journals or electronic media with general circulation in the United States.

Q. RESTRICTIONS ON MILITARY INTELLIGENCE

1. The select committee recommends that the intelligence components of the armed services of the United States be prohibited from engaging in covert action within the United States. It is further recommended that clandestine activities against nonmilitary U.S. citizens abroad be proscribed.

R. CLASSIFICATION

1. The select committee recommends that the classification of information be the subject of the enactment of specific legislation; and further, as an adjunct to such legislation there be provided a method of regular declassification.

S. INSPECTOR GENERAL FOR INTELLIGENCE

1. The select committee recommends the establishment of an independent Office of the Inspector General for Intelligence, who shall have full authority to investigate any possible or potential misconduct

on the part of the various intelligence agencies or the personnel therein. The IGI shall be appointed by the President, with the approval of the Senate, for a term of 10 years and shall not be permitted to succeed himself. The IGI shall have full access on demand to all records and personnel of the intelligence agencies for the purpose of pursuing his investigations. He shall make an annual report to the Congress of his activities and make such additional reports to the intelligence committees or other appropriate oversight committees as he may choose or the committees may direct.

T. DOMESTIC

1. The select committee recommends that judicial warrant must issue, on probable cause, before an informant or any other agent of the FBI may infiltrate any domestic group or association, when investigation of such group or association or its members is based solely on title 18 U.S.C. §§ 2383, 2384, 2385.

2. The select committee recommends that the Director of the FBI have a term of office no longer than 2 presidential terms.

3. The select committee recommends that the Internal Security Branch of the Intelligence Division be abolished and that the counter-intelligence branch be reorganized to constitute a full division named the Counter-Intelligence Division; that the mission of this Division be limited to investigating and countering the efforts of foreign directed groups and individuals against the United States.

4. The select committee recommends the transfer of all investigations of alleged criminal activity by domestic groups or individual members thereof to the General Investigative Division.

5. The select committee recommends that regulations be promulgated that tie the investigation of activities of terrorist groups closely to specific violations of criminal law within the investigative jurisdiction of the FBI and that charge the Department of Justice with determining when a domestic political action group may be appropriately targeted for investigation of terrorist activities.

RECOMMENDATIONS OF THE MURPHY COMMISSION ON CONGRESSIONAL ORGANIZATION AND PROCEDURES ([90], pp. 205–215)

The Murphy Commission report combined its specific congressional oversight recommendations with those concerning Legislative-Executive relations generally. The intelligence-related items remain in the context in which they were presented; therefore, no deletions have been made in the Murphy recommendations reprinted below.

In the.............we have addressed the changing relation of the Congress to the executive in foreign affairs. The effect of our recommendations—as of the inevitable trend of events—is to place a greater burden on the Congress. But new responsibilities may require improved capabilities. We turn now, therefore, to consideration of changes in the organization and procedures of the Congress which might assist the Congress to meet its growing foreign affairs responsibilities. We begin with three aspects of the roles and functions of

Congressional committees.

MODIFICATIONS OF COMMITTEE JURISDICTION

Since economic relations seem certain to constitute a growing proportion of future foreign policy, the Commission has considered at some length how to improve the ability of the Congress to consider economic questions in the light of their foreign implications. We conclude that some further adjustment in Committee jurisdictions may be helpful.

In the House we propose that the Committee on International Relations be accorded "special oversight functions" over reciprocal tariff agreements, in addition to its other responsibilities for trade policy issues.

Moreover, we believe it important that, with increasing reliance on foreign trade instead of aid, and with greater use of international financial organizations to dispense foreign aid funds:

The House Committee on International Relations should exercise concurrent legislative oversight over international financial organizations, together with the House Committee on Banking and Currency.

Two related recommendations appear in Chapter.... One proposes that the Foreign and International Relations Committees should have some opportunity to comment on estimates of the Appropriations Committees. The other suggests that, in both Houses, those two committees should be represented on the Budget Committees.

We believe that these changes will substantially improve the ability of the House to act on foreign economic issues with a greater awareness of their implications for our relations with other countries as well as of their domestic significance.

In the Senate, Committee jurisdictions in the foreign affairs field seem more nearly satisfactory. The Senate Foreign Relations Committee has considerably broader jurisdiction than the Committee on International Relations, including "measures to foster commercial intercourse" and international financial institutions. The rules of the Senate, furthermore, provide far greater jurisdictional flexibility allowing the referral of legislation to two or more committees. However, Senate committee jurisdiction and workloads have not been systematically reviewed for nearly 30 years (the last review culminated in the Legislative Reorganization Act of 1946). And despite the heavy workloads which spread Senators far too thin, the number of subcommittees has increased since then from 34 to more than 120—many with overlapping foreign policy responsibilities. This tendency to proliferate subcommittees, the Commission believes, defeats one of the main purposes of the Legislative Reorganization Act.

Moreover, while precise congruence between House and Senate jurisdiction is not essential, recent House changes affecting foreign policy matters may suggest useful adjustments in the Senate.

From the point of view of improving Congress' ability to consider foreign policy matters efficiently and effectively, therefore, a review by the Senate of its own committee system now seems appropriate. The Commission strongly recommends such a review.

THE USE OF SUBCOMMITTEES

The Commission has noted the increased use of foreign policy subcommittees in the Congress. Subcommittees have distinct advantages over full standing committees as working units. They can respond more quickly to changing developments. Their procedures can be relatively informal, facilitating the exchange of views among Members and between Members and witnesses. They present greater opportunities for Members to develop expertise and to establish direct relationships with executive branch officials. Finally, they facilitate the holding of joint hearings, both within and among committees of the House and Senate, thus improving coordination in the Congress, and at the same time reducing the multiple demands for testimony from key executive officials.

Even in the Senate, where competing demands make it especially difficult for Members to participate fully in all the subcommittees to which they are assigned, hearings and preliminary action by even two or three interested Senators in subcommittee may be preferable to less frequent and detailed deliberations at the full committee level. In short, despite practical limitations, particularly in the Senate, active subcommittees can increase both the scope and depth of Congressional consideration of foreign policy matters.

The Commission therefore recommends fuller utilization of subcommittees to strengthen the basis of committee action, and to provide greater interchange with working-level executive officials at the Assistant and Under Secretary levels. It also recommends increased use of joint hearings by subcommittees to meet part of the need, expressed clearly in Congressional responses to the survey, conducted by this Commission, for better coordination of the actions of the Congress in the foreign policy field.

In view of the growing links between nations, and the growing importance of problems—like resource access, arms sales, oceans policy, food and population—which affect many states, the Commission believes that subcommittees on foreign affairs may be most useful if organized on a functional rather than a regional basis. The Commission therefore commends the experimental use of such functional sub-committees by the Committe on International Relations, and the creation of a Foreign Assistance and Economic Policy Subcommittee by the Foreign Relations Committee.

A NEW JOINT COMMITTEE

However useful the recommendations above concerning committee jurisdictions may prove, and however powerfully they may be reinforced by the proposals made below concerning committee staffs and analytic support, those recommendations leave untouched at least two major problems. One is that since political, military and economic aspects of foreign policy have become interlocked—and since many foreign and domestic policy issues undoubtedly will become so—Congress should contain some forum in which those interrelations can be directly weighed. This is particularly true in time of crisis when specialized standing committees, pressed for action, might benefit from help in appreciating how particular aspects of policy decisions relate to those being considered by other committees.

The second is that the Congress is requiring increased consultation with senior foreign policy officials of the executive branch at the same time that an increasing number of specialized committees are necessarily concerning themselves with the foreign policy aspects of their responsibilities. The result is the potential for a burdensome and unsustainable demand on senior executive officials for multiple appearances before Congress—a problem particularly severe when fast-moving events require the full and direct attention of the same officials in the conduct of policy.

Neither speed nor policy coordination are Congress' particular strengths—nor can they be. The greatest strength of the legislative process is its unique ability to explore alternatives and to weigh and resolve widely disparate points of view. Its strength in deliberation however, does not relieve Congress of responsibility for reasonable efficiency and coordinating capacity. Indeed, if Congress is to play the greater foreign policy role which this Commission endorses, those capacities will increasingly be demanded of it. And as the staff survey of Congressional views indicates, most Members, while regarding policy coordination primarily as the responsibility of the executive, also favor changes to improve Congress' own efficiency in the coordination process.

With these problems in mind, the Commission considered a number of proposals. It concluded that a single innovation may be materially helpful.

In the Commission's view, a Joint Committee on National Security should be established. It should perform for the Congress the kinds of policy review and coordination now performed in the executive branch by the National Security Council, and provide a central

point of linkage to the President and to the officials at that Council.
In addition it should take responsibility for Congressional oversight
of the Intelligence Community.

We believe this Committee should serve as the initial recipient and reviewer of reports and information from the executive branch on matters of greatest urgency and sensitivity directly affecting the security of the nation. It should advise the party leaders and relevant standing committees of both Houses of Congress on appropriate legislative action in matters affecting the national security, and should assist in making available to them the full range of information and analysis needed to enable them to legislate in a prompt and comprehensive manner.

The existence and activities of such a Joint Committee should in no way substitute either for direct consultation between the President and Congressional party leaders, or for the regular legislative and investigative functions of the present standing committees in each House. Rather, it should supplement these—providing a more systematic and comprehensive exchange of information, analysis and opinion than has proved possible under the existing committee and leadership system.

For both operational and security reasons, the Joint Committee should be small—containing not more than 20 Members. It should include the leaders of the key foreign, military, and international economic policy committees from each House, and several Members-at-Large appointed by the party leaders to represent them and to enhance the Committee's representativeness of the Congress as a whole.

The Commission recommends that the Joint Committee be vested with the following specific jurisdictions and authorities:

—*Receipt, analysis and referral (along with any recommendations it may consider appropriate) of reports from the President under the War Powers Act.*

—*Receipt and review of analytic products of the intelligence community.*

—*Oversight (in conjunction with the executive branch) of the system of information classification discussed above.*

—*Establishment and maintenance of facilities and procedures for storage and handling of classified information and materials supplied to the Congress.*

—*Establishment of a code of conduct to govern the handling by Committee members of classified or sensitive information.*

The successful experience of the Joint Committee on Atomic Energy illustrates the usefulness of legislative authority in helping assure a Committee's effectiveness. The Commission does not recommend that the proposed Joint Committee be vested with broad authority to report proposed legislation to the House and Senate. In general, any legislative recommendations of the Joint Committee should be reported to relevant standing committees for their consideration. The Commission finds, however, two narrow and specific areas in which the Joint Committee might usefully have authority to report legislation directly to the floor of each House just as the Joint Committee on Atomic Energy is empowered to do.

We propose that the Joint Committee:

—*Consider the creation of a statutory system of information classification, and (if intelligence oversight is assigned to it).*

—*Be granted authority for annual authorization of funds for the intelligence community.*

The Commission believes strongly that more systematic arrangements for Congressional oversight of the intelligence community are needed on a permanent basis. It believes that such oversight should be conducted by a Joint Committee of the Congress, and preferably one capable of assessing intelligence products and activities in the context of our total foreign policy. The Commission therefore believes the proposed Joint Committee on National Security would be the appropriate body for that task.

In the event that this Committee is not established, however, the Commission recommends that a Joint Committee on Intelligence be established to assume the task of Congressional oversight of the intelligence community.

The Commission well understands that establishing a Joint Committee on National Security, and making it function effectively, would be difficult. While the Congressional survey indicates majority support among Members for greater joint efforts in Congress, it also suggests many doubts and practical problems. The Commission has carefully considered these difficulties. It concludes, nevertheless, that the likely impact of the Joint Committee upon Congress' capacity to play a more meaningful foreign policy role fully justifies the efforts and concessions necessary to create it and to make it work.

CAPACITIES FOR EVALUATION AND REVIEW

The Commission believes that the necessity for closer supervision of foreign programs and policies is not limited to the intelligence field. Many programs outlive the circumstances which made them useful, and we expect that in the future, as the world changes at increasing rates, many more will do so. We believe, therefore, that the Congress must meet far more systematically than before its responsibilities for the evaluation and review both of major programs and of the policies on which they are based. The expanded use of time-limit and report-back provisions, discussed in the previous chapter, should contribute to that end. We offer here several additional proposals.

More Effective Use of Reports. Increased efforts should be made to consolidate, rationalize, and improve the quality and use of written reports to Congress from executive branch agencies required by law. At a minimum, we believe that:

A central Congressional repository for such reports, efficient procedures for making them available to all interested Members, and convenient means for maintaining security of classified reports, should be developed, as proposed above, by the Joint Committee on National Security.

Attaining the Promise of CRS. Equally important is the availability of supporting analytic resources to supplement committee staffs. Over the last several years Congress has substantially expanded the Congressional Research Service, strengthened the General Accounting Office, and created the Office of Technology Assessment and the Congressional Budget Office to supplement its other facilities. But this rapid growth in research capability has still not provided Congress with adequate research and informational capacity on foreign policy issues. The central problem, we believe, is that the Congressional Research Service has never reached the levels of usefulness that either the Congress or CRS itself have sought. Despite more than a doubling in size since 1970, a substantial growth in committee requests for policy research, and the imaginative use by CRS of automated information systems, the relationship between CRS and the Congress is characterized on both sides by a certain amount of frustration. Researchers lack the freedom and support to address major policy issues in depth; the Congress lacks assurance that CRS will provide timely and useful studies of program alternatives.

The Commission finds that the major difficulty is that there exists no body representing the interests of the Congress as a whole and authorized to provide CRS with policy guidance, assistance in securing resources, and some measure of insulation against the lower priority concerns which deflect it from sustained work on major issues.

The Commission therefore recommends that Congress designate the Joint Committee on Congressional Operations as responsible for performing those functions, thus insuring that some part of the CRS staff is able to focus steadily on issues to which Congress as a whole accords high priority.

The General Accounting Office and International Organizations. The Commission believes that the GAO, working with executive officials, can usefully assist international organizations to develop more comprehensive capabilities for financial review and program evaluation. The objective review by the Congress of the work of international organizations should form the major basis for the support of such organizations as they come to play increasingly important roles. Meanwhile, the Congress should continue to press, through both executive branch representatives and GAO, for more adequate accounting of international programs to which the U.S. has contributed, and for better information on the work and effectiveness of international organizations.

More Effective Use of Analytic Resources. The remaining deficiencies in Congressional use of program information and research result, we believe, from insufficient central supervision of its own growing resources, and relatively low levels of Congressional use of independent non-governmental sources of analysis. Accordingly:

> *The Commission recommends that the House Commission on Information and Facilities, created as part of the Committee Reform Amendments of 1974, look with special care at the research support available to Congress when legislating in foreign policy. We also suggest that the Information Commission seek better management of Congressional use of research by designating the Joint Committee on Congressional Operations to oversee research organizations; and that it seek to facilitate wider use by the Congress of the policy research capabilities of universities and non-profit research centers.*

One ready means of helping to achieve this last goal would be for the Foreign and International Relations Committees periodically to publish a summary of their research interests and priorities. The summary should specify the major questions pertinent to future foreign policy determinations on which the Congress would most welcome assistance, and should note the major study requests from foreign policy committees to CRS. Such a document, we believe, would encourage many public and private research organizations to orient planned research toward Congressional interests and concerns, and thus to increase the availability of independent analysis and information useful to the Congress without need for additional research bureaucracies.

> *The Commission recommends the publication of such a summary of Congressional foreign affairs research interests.*

Congressional Staff Support. One of the most important developments on Capitol Hill since World War II has been the creation of a professional staff to help the Congress in its consideration of significant policy issues. Prior to Legislative Reorganization Act of

1946 the committees of Congress dealing with foreign policy had little or no professional assistance. Committee reports—as well as speeches and background materials for the Congress—were normally prepared in the executive branch of the government or by outside sources. As a result, Congress was simply not equipped to discharge its responsibilities effectively.

Since their inception in 1947, the professional staffs on Capitol Hill have grown considerably in size. This has been a necessary development for two reasons: the growing complexity of foreign policy problems; and the increasingly heavy legislative burdens that have fallen on all Members of Congress and the resultant need for staff help in all areas.

Both the Senate Foreign Relations Committee and the House International Relations Committee have by custom hired professional bipartisan staffs. The Commission notes, however, that this tradition has been eroded somewhat in recent years as divisions over foreign policy have developed both within the major political parties and between them. In particular, the authority of the committee staff directors has diminished as their ability to recruit their own staffs has been limited. The present practice is for members of the Committees to request that one staff member be assigned to them alone. Whatever the merits of this procedure, the Commission believes that committee staff members should be appointed because of their professional qualifications and be available to serve members of both parties as the need arises. This principle should prevail whether or not the committee chooses to designate minority and majority staff members.

The Commission understands the desire of many Members of Congress for more professional assistance. This is especially true of some junior members of the Senate and House whose status in those bodies does not entitle them to very much staff support. In this connection, we note the recent action of the Senate to enable junior members to employ the professional assistance they need to handle their major committee responsibilities. We caution that the benefits of this action will not be worth the costs in lowered professional standards if staff directors do not have some voice in the hiring of such staff.

The Commission has no general recommendations to make with respect to congressional staffing, but makes two further observations. First, in any further expansion of congressional staff the emphasis should be on quality rather than quantity. Clearly the Congress should not seek to duplicate the vast array of professional talent found in the executive branch; it should emphasize *good* staffs rather than *large* ones. Second, the Commission believes it advisable for the Congress to add some expertise in the fields of international economics and in the relationship between science and technology and foreign policy. These are fields which will engage the attention of Congress increasingly as the years go by.

Increasing Attentiveness to Foreign Affairs.

We conclude our observations on the Congress and foreign affairs with three proposals intended to better equip Congress and the public to deal knowledgeably with a world in which foreign affairs in all aspects will touch our lives more powerfully and directly than heretofore.

International Contact. The Commission believes that substantial international contacts, by familiarizing Members of Congress with overseas conditions and foreign perspectives, have a beneficial effect upon the making of U.S. foreign policy and on the ability of Members to perform their legislative responsibilities wisely.

In the judgment of the Commission, more extended travel by Members, the preparation of special reports based on staff travel abroad (particularly Foreign and International Relations Committees investigative staff), and increased travel by teams of Members rather than individuals are highly desirable.

Full, written reports by staff and Members prior to and following travel abroad, as currently required under Foreign Relations Committee rules, are particularly valuable in helping assure coordinated, purposeful travel and a broad sharing of findings among interested Members and staff.

Foreign travel reporting requirements should be extended to the entire Congress, and an improved system of circulating, monitoring, and evaluating these reports developed.

Policies issued in 1974 by each House regarding financing of staff travel might serve as a model and first step toward more comprehensive guidelines.

The Commission endorses detailed and timely financial disclosure, in a form conveniently accessible to the public and the press, of the costs of all foreign travel and the sources of travel funds, whether utilized by Members of Congress or other Government officials.

Congressional Participation in International Negotiations. Similarly, the Commission endorses greater participation by Members of Congress in international negotiations, particularly multilateral negotiations, as an important means of increasing the first-hand information available to Members on foreign policy and its conduct. With the possible exception of Congressional delegates to the annual meetings of the UN General Assembly, however, we believe the roles of Congressional participants in such negotiations should ordinarily be limited to those of observers and advisers rather than plenary participants, particularly in cases where agreements growing out of such negotiations may be subject to specific Congressional review or approval. Congress might usefully specify the appropriate degree of advisory participation of Members in important international negotiations in the legislation directing or authorizing such negotiations.

Public Understanding of Foreign Policy Issues. At many earlier points in this report we have stressed the importance we attach to the development and articulation of guiding conceptions of U.S. purpose and policy in the world. We have proposed a number of measures designed to encourage greater attention to this need in the executive branch. But Congress has an important parallel function to perform.

Through carefully organized hearings Congress can provide the critical review of U.S. purposes, and of their relation to shorter-term policy, necessary to test their soundness and coherence, and to generate the public understanding and support without which, in the end, they cannot succeed.

The Foreign and International Relations Committees have a special responsibility in this regard. History suggests, moreover, that the public will respond positively to the thoughtful and probing review of major foreign policy issues; the China Policy hearings of the Senate Foreign Relations Committee in 1966 provide an excellent model.

Those hearings, moreover, demonstrated the importance of television coverage. The Commission believes that public awareness of foreign policy questions requires television coverage of major foreign policy hearings and Committee deliberations.

We recommend that:

Recent trends toward opening the deliberations of Congress on major foreign policy issues be encouraged. Committee hearings should routinely be open for television. At the discretion of the House and Senate, under their respective rules, consideration should also be given to making floor debates on major foreign policy issues available to public and commercial television on a case-by-case basis.

The Commission believes that whatever strains on the normal functioning of Congress might occur as a result would be more than offset by increased public understanding of the foreign policy issues facing the nation, and by public support for some of the difficult choices ahead.

Oversight Legislation

HISTORY OF RECENT LEGISLATION ([26], pp. 2–10)

The 1976 Senate Government Operations Committee hearings on bills to create a new intelligence oversight committee heard from a distinguished body of witnesses, some of whose remarks appear in this chapter. The report of the committee, partially reprinted here, drew upon the testimony presented, as well as the experience and views of its own members and staff, in order to prepare its recommendations on the creation of an oversight committee. As that committee proceeded with its study of the legislation, the Senate Rules Committee (which has jurisdiction over the committee structure) pursued its own inquiry. The views of the two committees are set forth in this section; these recommendations led to the passage on May 19, 1976 of Senate Resolution 400, which established a Senate Select Committee on Intelligence.

During the 93rd Congress four bills or resolutions were referred to the Government Operations Committee creating a new intelligence oversight committee. In December 1974, 2 days of subcommittee hearings were held by Senator Muskie on the proposals but no further committee action was taken.

At the outset of the 94th Congress three bills or resolutions were referred to the committee establishing a permanent new unit of Congress to oversee the government's intelligence activities. These proposals were S. 189, S. 317, and S. Con. Res. 4. In 1976 three additional bills to create a new intelligence committee were introduced and referred to this committee. S. 2865 was referred to this committee on January 26; S. 2893 on January 29; and S. 2983 on February 17. S. 2893, introduced by Senator Church and seven other members of the Select Committee on Intelligence Oversight, was referred to the Government Operations Committee pursuant to a unanimous consent agreement with instructions that this committee report back to the full Senate on the legislation by March 1, 1976.

The committee held 9 days of hearings on proposals to create a new intelligence oversight committee in January and February of this year. The following is a list of the 26 witnesses who certified at these hearings, in order of their appearance:

N26

Senator Mike Mansfield, Democrat of Montana.
Senator Frank Church, Democrat of Idaho.
Senator John G. Tower, Republican of Texas.
Senator Howard H. Baker, Jr., Republican of Tennessee.
Dean Rusk, former Secretary of State.
Nicholas Katzenbach, former Attorney General of the United States, and Under Secretary of State.
David Phillips, President, Association of Retired Intelligence Officers.
William Colby, Director of the Central Intelligence Agency.
McGeorge Bundy, former Special Assistant to the President for National Security Affairs.
Clarence Kelley, Director of the Federal Bureau of Investigation.
John McCone, former Director of the Central Intelligence Agency.
Clark Clifford, former Secretary of Defense.
Ambassador Richard Helms, former Director of the Central Intelligence Agency.
Robert F. Ellsworth, Deputy Secretary of Defense.
Senator Gaylord Nelson, Democrat of Wisconsin.
Senator Alan Cranston, Democrat of California.
Morton H. Halperin, Director of the Project on National Security and Civil Liberties.
Raymond S. Calamaro, Executive Director, Committee for Public Justice.
Senator Barry M. Goldwater, Republican of Arizona.
Senator Ernest F. Hollings, Democrat of South Carolina.
Congressman Michael Harrington, Democrat of Massachusetts.
Congressman Robin L. Beard, Republican of Tennessee.
Senator Strom Thurmond, Republican of South Carolina.
Dr. Henry A. Kissinger, Secretary of State.
Senator Walter D. Huddleston, Democrat of Kentucky.
Attorney General Edward H. Levi.

Following completion of these hearings, the committee met on February 19, 20, and 24. The committee completed action on this legislation on February 24 and voted unanimously to approve this resolution.

BACKGROUND OF THE LEGISLATION

BRIEF HISTORY OF CONGRESSIONAL OVERSIGHT OF THE INTELLIGENCE AGENCIES

Since the passage of the National Security Act of 1947, establishing the National Security Council and the Central Intelligence Agency, Congress has tried in a number of different ways to achieve close congressional supervision of the intelligence activities of the Government.

Congressional efforts to restructure congressional oversight of the intelligence community, either through creation of a joint committee or a special intelligence committee in each House, began as early as 1948. In that year Representative Devitt introduced legislation to establish a Joint Committee on Intelligence. This effort was the first of nearly 200 bills introduced in both Houses since 1948.

Soon after the creation of the CIA, an informal arrangement in the Senate was worked out with Senators Vandenburg and Russell whereby small subcommittees of the Armed Services and Appropriations Committees assumed responsibility for the oversight of the CIA. By the early 1950's, congressional oversight was routinely conducted by separate subcommittees of the House and Senate Armed Services and Appropriations Committees.

Subsequently, the Senate Foreign Relations and House Foreign Affairs Committees expressed growing interest in participating in congressional oversight of the intelligence community because of the possible effect on this country's foreign relations.

In January 1955, Senator Mansfield introduced S. Con. Res. 2, which would have established a 12-member Joint Committee on Central Intelligence. It gave the new committee legislative authority over the agency and required that the CIA keep the new committee "fully and currently informed with respect to its activities." The Mansfield resolution, originally co-sponsored by 32 other Senators, was defeated by the full Senate.

In July 1966, the Foreign Relations Committee reported out Senate Resolution 283, calling for the creation of a new Committee on Intelligence Operations in the Senate. However, after floor debate, the Senate failed to take final action on the proposal.

In 1967, the chairman of the Senate Armed Services Subcommittee on Intelligence invited three members of the Foreign Relations Committee to attend the CIA oversight sessions of his committee. This ad hoc arrangement was discontinued in the early 1970's.

The recurring need for reexamining the way Congress monitors the activities of the intelligence agencies was again highlighted during the investigations in 1973 of the Senate Select Committee on Presidential Campaign Activities when questions were raised about the legality or propriety of certain intelligence activities of the Central Intelligence Agency, the Federal Bureau of Investigation, and other agencies.

In 1974 the chairman of the Senate Armed Services Subcommittee invited the majority and minority leaders to attend CIA oversight sessions of the subcommittee as nonvoting members.

The House took action in 1974 (H. Res. 988) to give "special oversight (of) intelligence activities relating to foreign policy" to its Foreign Affairs Committee. In 1975 the committee, renamed the International Relations Committee, created a Subcommittee on Investigations to handle its oversight responsibilities under H. Res. 988.

In December 1974 the New York Times charged that the Central Intelligence Agency, in direct violation of its statutory charter, conducted a "massive, illegal domestic intelligence operation during the Nixon Administration against the antiwar movement and other dissident groups in the United States." The article also charged that "intelligence files on at least 10,000 American citizens" had been maintained by the CIA and that the agency had engaged in "dozens of other illegal activities," starting in the 1950's "including break-ins, wiretapping and the surreptitious inspection of mail."

On January 15, 1975, testifying before the Senate Appropriations Committee, Mr. William Colby, Director of the Central Intelligence Agency, stated that officers of the CIA had spied on American journalists and political dissidents, placed informants within domestic protest groups, opened the mail of U.S. citizens, and assembled secret files on more than 10,000 American citizens.

In response to public allegations of abuses by the Central Intelligence Agency, in particular, both the Senate and the House moved rapidly in 1975 to create temporary committees to investigate possible abuses by the intelligence agencies.

On January 28, 1975 the Senate agreed to S. Res. 21, as amended, to establish a Select Committee to Study Governmental Operations with Respect to Intelligence Activities. On February 19, 1975 the House established a Select Committee on Intelligence by agreeing to H. Res. 138. On July 17, 1975 the House agreed to H. Res. 591, which replaced that committee with another having the same name and functions. Both Senate and House committees were temporary study committees, ordered to report finally by February 29, 1976, and January 31, 1976, respectively.

RECOMMENDATIONS OF COMMITTEES AND COMMISSIONS

The committees of Congress, as well as the special executive commissions, that have examined the matter of congressional oversight of the intelligence community have consistently concluded that a new intelligence committee should be established.

As long ago as 1955 the Hoover Commission recommended creation of a new congressional oversight committee.

The recommendation climaxed a period of 6 years during which special executive commissions studied the Central Intelligence Agency four times. The studies voiced criticisms of the agency and its failure to correct inadequacies and poor organization.

When recommending creation of a new congressional unit in 1956, the Senate Rules Committee stated that creation of a new committee would:

> Insure the existence of a trained, specialized, and dedicated staff to gather information and make independent checks and appraisals of CIA activities pursuant to the committee's directives and supervision. The effect should be to allay much of the suspicion already expressed in Congress concerning the activities and efficiency of CIA operations. (S. Rept. No. 1570. 84th Congress, 2d sess.)

When explaining the resolution reported by the Foreign Relations Committee in 1966 to create a new congressional unit, Chairman Fulbright stated that a new committee would bring about "a more efficient coordination of the various intelligence activities of the Government." He added that creation of a new committee "would contribute to the quieting of criticism, the allaying of public fears, and the restoring of confidence in the Agency." (Cong. Rec., July 14, 1966, at p. 15673.)

In recent years, as the activities of the intelligence agencies have become the subject of increased public scrutiny, recommendations for a new congressional oversight committee have been renewed. In June 1975 the Commission on the Organization of the Government for the conduct of Foreign Policy (the Murphy Commission), after an extensive study lasting almost 2 years, recommended that Congress create a new structure for overseeing the intelligence community.

In June 1975 the President's Commission on CIA Activities Within the United States recommended in its final report that a new intelligence committee be established in order to improve the operations of the intelligence agencies and help prevent abuses in the future. This special commission, under the direction of Vice President Rockefeller, was created by the President in January 1975 to investigate allegations of abuses committed by the CIA within this country.

The Commission noted "Congress has established special procedures for review of the CIA and its secret budget within four small subcommittees. Historically, these subcommittees have been composed of Members of Congress with many other demands on their time. The CIA has not as a general rule received detailed scrutiny by the Congress." (Report of the President's Commission on CIA Activities Within the United States, p. 14.)

Although the Senate Select Committee on Intelligence has not yet completed its final report and recommendations, Chairman Church and other members of the committee introduced legislation to create a permanent intelligence committee in the Senate. At the time Chairman Church introduced the legislation he commented, "The present situation is clearly inadequate and even verging upon the chaotic. Restructuring is clearly needed."

The House Select Committee on Intelligence recommended, upon completion of its study creation of a separate House committee similar in scope and nature to the Senate Committee on Intelligence proposed by most of the Senate select committee. (H. Report No. 94–833, 94th Cong., 2d sess.).

This resolution is thus preceded by years of debate and study concerning congressional oversight of the intelligence agencies. It is preceded by a substantial number of proposals that have been made over the years for creation of a new committee.

NATURE AND PURPOSE OF THE RESOLUTION

NEED FOR A NEW COMMITTEE

The work during the last year of the Senate select committee and the Rockefeller Commission, and the abuses that have been discovered or alleged, have served to reemphasize the long-standing need for Congress to act in the area of intelligence oversight. But proposals for a new intelligence committee first began to be made only a few years after the Central Intelligence Agency was created. Concern over the activities of the intelligence agencies and congressional control over them clearly predates the events of the last few years.

The need and advisability of a new intelligence committee rests on a few basic facts.

A new intelligence committee can mark a new start. It can provide a forum to begin restoring the trust and confidence the intelligence agencies must have to operate effectively. It can formalize in an open and definitive manner the Senate's intention to exercise close oversight over a very important part of the Government's activities. Oversight by Congress is essential under our constitutional system. By its actions it can help assure the public that the abuses of the past will not be repeated in the future. Until full trust and confidence in our intelligence agencies is restored, the country will be unable to conduct a fully effective intelligence program.

The intelligence functions of this Government are unique in their importance to this Nation's security. At the same time, however, executive branch responsibility for intelligence is now spread among a number of organizations whose primary responsibilities involve diplomatic, military, economic or other matters. No one agency or department is solely responsible for our intelligence program. Direction and evaluation comes from interagency committees, and ultimately the National Security Council and the President.

Jurisdiction in the Senate over intelligence matters is correspondingly spread between a number of committees. No one committee is able to bring together through its oversight or legislative functions all the divergent portions of the intelligence community. For instance, the Director of Central Intelligence, the intelligence arms of the three military services, the Treasury Department, the Bureau of Intelligence and Research in the Department of State, the National Security Agency, the Defense Intelligence Agency, the Federal Bureau of Investigation, the Central Intelligence Agency, and the Energy Research and Development Administration all have representatives on the U.S. Intelligence Board. In the Senate responsibility for the 11 agencies that sit on the board and for their intelligence activities is shared by five legislative committees—the Armed Services Committee, the Foreign Relations Committee, the Finance Committee, the Judiciary Committee, and the Joint Committee on Atomic Energy. Because responsibility for the intelligence community is distributed among a number of different committees, it is not the prime focus of any single committee. The committees with responsibilty in the area cannot devote te time, or develop the staff, necessary to oversee fully the Government's intelligence activities. Because the area of intelligence is so important and complex, effective congressional oversight requires that any oversight committee devote a large proportion of its time and resources to the subject.

The Senate's present organization for oversight of intelligence also means that when the executive branch wishes to brief the Congress, on its own initiative, or in response to general congressional interest in a matter, it must brief a number of committees. This may place unnecessary burdens on the time of agency officials. Centralizing oversight responsibilities in a single Senate committee will provide a more orderly working relationship between Congress and the executive branch.

Centralizing oversight of the intelligence community will also help to assure the preservation of necessary security of sensitive information. Inevitably, the security of sensitive information is sacrificed whenever a substantial number of people have access to it. A single committee will help alleviate this problem by establishing a single body to receive most of the information on intelligence provided by the executive branch.

Congress itself can never run the intelligence agencies. Day-by-day oversight and direction must come from within the executive branch. Congress must exercise oversight, however, over the agencies and their activities, including covert operations and make sure that before the President initiates important new activities or programs he knows the attitude Congress is likely to take towards them. Congress must examine the economy and efficiencies of the intelligence programs which cost billions of dollars each year, and eliminate any unnecessary duplication or fragmentation among the maze of agencies now involved in intelligence.

As Senator Church, chairman of the Select Committee on Intelligence, testified before this committee:

> The work cannot be done on a piecemeal basis or by a subcommittee of another standing committee which is primarily engaged in a different preoccupation. It will require a well-staffed committee directing all of its attention to the intelligence community.

A wide range of other witnesses who testified during the nine days of hearings held by the committee also supported the need for a new committee. Present or former Government officials who supported a new intelligence oversight committee included Dr. Kissinger, who stated that creation of a new committee would be in the interests of national security, and Mr. Colby. Additional officials who supported creation of a new oversight committee included two other former directors of the Central Intelligence Agency, Mr. John McCone and Mr. Richard Helms; Mr. Clark Clifford, former Secretary of Defense; and Mr. McGeorge Bundy, former National Security Adviser to the President. Mr. David Phillips, President of the Association of Retired Intelligence Officers, stated that 98 percent of the members of the association polled by him favored creation of a new oversight committee.

SCOPE OF NEW COMMITTEE'S AUTHORITY AND RESPONSIBILITIES

It is the intent of this committee to create a committee with the necessary power to exercise full and diligent oversight.

An essential part of the new committee's jurisdiction will be authorization authority over the intelligence activities of the Department of Defense, the Department of State, the Federal Bureau of Investigation, and the Central Intelligence Agency. Without this authority the new committee would not be assured the practical ability to monitor the activities of these agencies, to obtain full access to information which the committee must have, to exercise control over the budgets of the agencies in order to reduce waste and inefficiency, and to impose changes in agency practices.

The resolution expressly provides that the Senate does not expect the intelligence community just to respond to inquiries or proposals made by the new committee. To be effective the intelligence community must take an active part in initiating the exchange of views and information between Congress and the executive branch. The resolution accordingly provides that the intelligence agencies should on their own take whatever steps necessary to keep the new committee fully and currently informed of their activities. This includes informing the new committee of significant anticipated activities, including covert and clandestine activities, before they are initiated so that there may be a meaningful exchange of views before any final decision is reached. It is expected that the President will fully consider such views and reassess the wisdom of any proposed programs which is strongly oppose by the committee. By creating a new committee that consults frequently with the executive branch, the committee hopes that Congress, the President, and the public can be spared future instances where covert activities initiated by the executive branch are subsequently rejected by Congress.

The scope of the new committee's jurisdiction is intended to include both foreign and domestic intelligence.

Without jurisdiction over both the domestic and foreign intelligence activities of the government, the new committee could not act in the comprehensive way it must. Many domestic and foreign intelligence activities are now closely related. For example, responsibility for the covert collection of intelligence from foreign sources residing within the United States may be shared by the Central Intelligence Agency and the Federal Bureau of Investigation. These same agencies may both be involved as well in gathering information on whether domestic groups in the United States are under foreign control.

The new committee must be able to review such relationship and consider, where necessary, legislation readjusting the division of responsibility among agencies for domestic and foreign intelligence. Past abuses in the intelligence area have in part involved a confusion between the proper role and function of domestic and foreign intelligence agencies.

STRUCTURE OF NEW COMMITTEE

The resolution establishes a permanent standing committee of the Senate consisting of 11 members. The committee concluded that at this time there were a number of advantages to a Senate committee, rather than a joint committee, and that on balance, there were no compelling reasons requiring Congress to depart from the normal practice of creating separate Senate and House legislative committees.

A Senate committee is more consistent with the bicameral nature of the Nation's legislative system. The new committee will in all likelihood be considering very important legislation concerning the nature and effectiveness of the Government's entire intelligence community. A single joint committee should not write legislation for both Houses.

A Seante committee wil give better recognition of the unique role the U.S. Senate plays under its constitutional advise and consent powers in the area of foreign relations.

Separate Senate and House committees will better assure that each House is able to conduct its oversight of the intelligence community in the manner that seems most appropriate to that House, its concerns, its rules, and its existing committee structure.

Separate Senate and House committees will better promote coordination between the new committee and the other committees in each House with interests in the intelligence area.

Separate Senate and House committees will help reduce the danger that a single joint committee, by overlooking certain practices or becoming too wedded to a particular point of view, will miss important abuses or fail to consider important legislative reform proposals.

Because the very nature of the committee's work will require the committee to act without informing the full Senate in many instances, the resolution contains special provisions to assure that the committee membership remain representative of the Senate as a whole. No member will be able to serve on the new committee for longer than 6 years at a time. This will assure a continual rotation of members, new viewpoints, and new interests.

In creating a new Senate intelligence committee, the committee was also very aware of the need to reduce the proliferation of committees.

The resolution has been drafted with this concern in mind. In order to reduce the proliferation of committees now involved in overseeing the Government's intelligence activities, the new committee is given jurisdiction over the entire intelligence community. It will have authorization authority over all major expenditures for intelligence. The resolution expressly provides that other committees in the Senate will no longer have jurisdiction in these areas. The number of legislative or select committees involved in this area in the Senate will be reduced from four to one.

It is expected that after creation of the new committee, the Senate may also want to review the effect of other relevant laws with the possible aim of further reordering Senate oversight of the intelligence agencies. This could include, for example, the present law requiring the President to brief all appropriate committees on covert operations conducted by the Central Intelligence Agency, or the present division of responsibilities between the legislative committees and the appropriations committee. The new committee is required by this resolution to study some of these questions itself, and report its conclusions to the full Senate no later than July, 1977.

PROCEDURES FOR PROTECTING CONFIDENTIAL INFORMATION

The committee devoted considerable discussion to how best to assure that the new committee would protect the confidentiality of some of the information that will be in its possession, while assuring that the Senate and the public have access to information on intelligence in a manner consistent with the public interest. A very delicate balance must be struck between the right of the people in a democracy to know what their government is doing, and the need to protect some information in the interests of national security.

Both the Senate Select Committee on Intelligence and the standing committees of the Senate that have been extensively involved in the intelligence area in the past have had an excellent record in protecting the confidentiality of information. The past experience of these committees is evidence that the Senate can exercise effective congressional oversight without the unauthorized disclosure of sensitive information occurring. In order to assure that this continues in the future, the new committee will have all the authority it needs to establish necessary security and clearance procedures. The new committee will be expected, for example, to make special physical arrangements to safeguard material.

Provisions in the resolution will assure the full Senate the opportunity to determine whether in particular instances information should be disclosed if the President objects. Other security procedures established by the resolution will apply when the new committee provides other Senators information which the committee, or the Senate, has determined should not be made public. Finally, the resolution creates a special procedure requiring the Select Committee on Standards and Conduct to investigation allegations made by a certain number of Senators that a Member, officer, or employee of the Senate has engaged in the unauthorized disclosure of information.

The resolution requires the staff to receive appropriate security clearances from the committee before they are hired and to agree in writing, before beginning to work for the committee, that they will not divulge any information either during or after their employment, unless authorized by the committee.

The ability of the new committee to obtain the information it needs to do an effective job of oversight will depend in large part on its ability to protect information which should not be disclosed to the public. The committee is confident that the new intelligence committee will strike the necessary balance between the necessity of protecting the confidentiality of certain information, and the need to provide the public the information it must have in a democracy to participate in the basic policy discussions about the nature of this country's intelligence program.

COMMITTEE ACTION ([42], pp. 76–81)

The material that follows relates action taken by the Committees on Government Operations, the Judiciary, and Rules and Administration regarding Senate Resolution 400—to establish a standing Committee on Intelligence Activities.

(a) Government Operations Committee

The Government Operations Committee held nine days of hearings and heard 26 witnesses testify on legislative proposals designed to improve oversight of the intelligence community. Of the Senators, former and current Cabinet officials, and Directors of Central Intelligence who testified, most favored creation of a new oversight committee although three members of the Senate Armed Services Committee strongly opposed such an action. The Senators tended to favor a standing committee of the Senate, but executive branch officials advocated a joint committee which would concentrate oversight and reduce the number of committees involved.

Chairman Ribicoff opened the hearings by declaring that he strongly favored creation of a new committee. He suggested that the answers to the following questions should influence its structure:

First, should the committee be a joint committee of Congress or a permanent committee of the Senate, should Senators serve on the committee on a rotating basis, and should the legislation explicitly reserve seats on the committee for members of other committees?

Second, should the new committee have jurisdiction over legislation, including authorization legislation, involving the Government's national intelligence activities?

Should the entire intelligence activities of the Government be subject to annual authorization legislation reviewed by the new committee?

Third, should the committee have jurisdiction over domestic intelligence activities and, if so—what type of jurisdiction?

Fourth, to what extent should the legislation spell out the extent and nature of the duty of the executive branch to keep the new committee fully and currently informed of its activities and plans?

Fifth, should the bill amend the procedures now governing notice to Congress of any covert actions undertaken by the executive branch?

Sixth, what, if anything, should the legislation say about the standards and safeguards that should govern the committees disclosure of sensitive information to other Senators, and to the general public?

Senators Mansfield, Church, Baker, Nelson, Cranston and Huddleston testified in favor of a new Senate oversight committee. Both Senators Mansfield and Church emphasized the importance of having a committee with a comprehensive mandate which could "accommodate an integrated perception of national intelligence." They argued that the existing system of piecemeal, uncoordinated oversight had not worked and would not do so. Senator Mansfield asserted that intelligence community's excesses were "a direct result of congressional neglect and inattention," endorsed rotating membership and stated that an annual authorizing function was "essential to the question of accountability."

Senators Tower, Thurmond and Goldwater strongly opposed alteration of the existing oversight system. Senator Tower felt the proposed legislation was "hastily conceived and simplistic" and stated that the present oversight committees can and should continue to carry out their responsibilities. Senator Goldwater noted that "In the past, there was little oversight of the intelligence community . . . (but) . . . If the Congress wants more oversight, the existing committees can and should be required to perform." Goldwater asserted that the idea of rotating membership was an assault on seniority and expertise and noted that the present committees had good, experienced staffs. Senator Thurmond argued that the Church bill (S. 2893) divorced the intelligence functions of the Armed Services, Foreign Relations, Judiciary and Finance Committees from their substantive work and should therefore be opposed.

Most current and former executive branch officials who testified strongly endorsed creation of a new oversight committee. Secretary of State Kissinger and former CIA Director William Colby both urged prompt action on the matter; "the sooner the better," said Colby. Colby also emphasized that "reasonable limits" should be placed upon the matters made available to such a committee and endorsed sanctions against executive branch and congressional employees who violated secrecy agreements. Kissinger, Colby, former Secretary of State Dean Rusk and long-term Presidential advisor Clark Clifford all voiced a clear preference for a joint committee, indicating that one advantage of such an arrangement would be to facilitate executive-legislative relationships.

Providing information on covert operations to the Congress was one of the more delicate issues discussed during the hearings. Secretary of State Kissinger, representing the Administration viewpoint, indicated that "the proper constitutional perspective" would suggest that the existing system of informing the Congress "in a time y fashion" was "adequate for oversight," but that preferably this information should be "concentrated in the (proposed) oversight committee." Clark Clifford urged that the law require notification of Congress prior to the execution of a covert action project. If the committee disapproves, he continued, the President would be notified. If "the President is determined to proceed on the project, then he may have the constitutional power to make that decision. Also, under the Constitution, the Congress could decide, on recommendation of the Joint Committee, to withhold funds necessary to finance the activity in question." Senator Thurmond argued that "prior restraints on Executive action contemplated will not only stay the President's hand in the conduct of our foreign affairs, but will intrude the legislature into the sphere of the Executive." Senator Church's viewpoint was that if the new committee were to perform its role, "then constitutionally we must remember that the Senate of the United States is to advise as well as to consent in foreign policy matters, and if it is to give its advice, it must have advance notice of significant operations of this kind."

Attorney General Edward H. Levi, testified that the FBI's counterintelligence activities were directed towards law enforcement and its activities should be seen as different from those of the intelligence agencies. He urged that FBI oversight and authorization activities not be placed within the jurisdiction of a new oversight committee.

S. Res. 400

On February 24, 1976, the Government Operations Committee voted 12–0 in favor of S. Res. 400, which would amend Rule XXV of the Senate to establish a standing Committee on Intelligence Activities with primary legislative, authorization, and oversight jurisdiction over Federal intelligence agencies and activities, including (1) the Central Intelligence Agency, (2) the Defense Intelligence Agency, (3) the National Security Agency, (4) other national intelligence activities of the Department of Defense, and (5) the intelligence activities of the Department of State and the Federal Bureau of Investigation. The standing committee would also have legislative and oversight jurisdiction over the "intelligence activities of all other departments and agencies of the government . . ."

The committee would be composed of 11 members, six from the majority and five from the minority parties, selected in the same manner as are other standing committees. Membership would rotate, with no member permitted to serve for more than six consecutive years. No professional staff member or consultant could serve the committee for a period totaling more than six years.

Agency heads would be required to keep the committee "fully and currently informed with respect to intelligence activities, including any significant anticipated activities" and to report immediately any violations of the constitutional rights of any person and any violations of law or executive order.

The resolution would establish procedures to control the disclosure of information within the Senate and to the public. These procedures would (1) prohibit the unauthorized disclosure of information and (2) permit disclosure of information, with Senate approval, over the written objection of the President. Alleged, unauthorized disclosure of intelligence information would be investigated by the Select Committee on Standards and Conduct upon request of five members of the committee or 16 Members of the Senate. The Select Committee would "report its findings and recommendations to the Senate."

(b) Judiciary Committee

S. Res. 400 was referred to the Judiciary Committee on March 18, 1976, and hearings were held on March 25 and 30. S. Res. 400 was interpreted by most members of the Committee as stripping it of its jurisdiction over the intelligence activities of the Department of Justice, particularly those of the FBI's Intelligence Division.

Attorney General Edward H. Levi testified that oversight of the FBI and the Department of Justice should be viewed as a whole and that their activities should be seen from a law enforcement perspective with its criminal investigations nexus. He favored retention by the Judiciary Committee of oversight over the Department of Justice. FBI Director Clarence Kelly concurred with the Attorney General's position and expressed concern about the possibility of "conflicting directives" if oversight of his Bureau were exercised by more than one committee.

Senator Walter Mondale, Chairman of the Subcommittee on Domestic Intelligence of the Senate Select Committee on Intelligence noted that his subcommittee's investigations revealed that FBI abuses had occurred primarily in the areas of intelligence and not law enforcement. He argued that if law enforcement officers had the right to go beyond traditional civil and criminal violations of the law exceptional vigilance was needed, and suggested that S. Res. 400 be amended to provide for concurrent oversight jurisdiction and joint referral of bills to both Judiciary and the proposed committee.

Senator Charles McC. Mathias, a member of both the Judiciary Committee and the Select Committee on Intelligence, favored concurrent jurisdiction and pointed out that the two committees would be looking at Department of Justice's intelligence activities from differing perspectives; the proposed oversight committee would be concerned primarily with the success and effectiveness of intelligence and the manner in which it was carried out whereas the Judiciary Committee would oversee from a law enforcement viewpoint.

On March 30, 1976, the Judiciary Committee reported its recommendations on S. Res. 400 to the Committee on Rules and Administration after voting to delete those provisions of the resolution which would grant jurisdiction over the intelligence activities of the Department of Justice, including the FBI, to the Committee on Intelligence Activities. The Committee earlier rejected by voice vote an amendment proposed by Senator Kennedy which would have provided for the sharing of jurisdiction between the Judiciary Committee and the proposed Committee.

(c) Committee on Rules and Administration

The Senate Committee on Rules and Administration held four days of hearings on S. Res. 400, hearing testimony from the Director of Central Intelligence (DCI) George Bush and a number of Senators.

Chairman Cannon questioned the effect the resolution would have on certain rules and established procedures of the Senate, expressed doubt about the capability of the Armed Services Committee adequately to review the Department of Defense budget if authorization authority over DOD national intelligence activities were granted to the new committee, noted that the Senate Legislative Counsel had advised that under a Senate Resolution (as opposed to a statute) the executive departments might not feel compelled to comply with the provision to keep the proposed committee "fully and currently informed" and wondered if a joint committee might not provide a better oversight arrangement.

Senator Byrd asserted that S. Res. 400 could not pass as written and suggested the alternative of creating a standing committee with subpoena power but without legislative or authorization jurisdiction in order to meet the political necessity for creating some kind of committee. "The oversight committee, if it has the power of subpoena, can get whatever information it needs," he argues.

Senator Stennis, Chairman of the Armed Services Committee and of its CIA Subcommittee, noted that his committee had discussed S. Res. 400 at two meetings; he stated that "were the Armed Services Committee to be deprived of (its) legislative authority, the intelligence community could become a separate entity unresponsive to the needs of national defense." Stennis rejected any proposal that would deprive his committee of its legislative jurisdiction and authorization authority; instead he recommended creation of a Permanent Armed Services Subcommittee on Intelligence, separately funded and staffed, cooperating with the Foreign Relations Committee and including the elected leadership of the Senate.

Senator Byrd asked Senator Stennis how he would feel about creation of a joint committee, including as members the chairmen of of the Armed Services, Foreign Relations, and Government Operations Committees and appointees of the leadership. Senator Stennis found the idea of a joint committee with "some oversight and surveillance on a gentlemanly basis" acceptable but strongly rejected any transfer of jurisdiction because, although his committee would still be able to obtain intelligence information its "continuity of relationship" would be lost.

Senator Church, Chairman of the Senate Select Committee on Intelligence, supported S. Res. 400 and asserted that an intelligence oversight committee, in order to be an effective instrument, must have (1) jurisdiction over the entire national intelligence community, (2) jurisdiction over the national intelligence budget "authorized on an annual basis," and (3) access to information. "Neither the Armed Services Committee nor any other committee has the time, because of its other duties, or the necessary overall jurisdiction to attend to the nation's intelligence system" he stated, adding that "The Executive budgets for and organizes and directs the national intelligence effort in a way that draws together the various components, and unless the Congress establishes a committee that can do the same, it will continue to fail in its oversight responsibilities."

Senators Stennis, Tower and Taft argued that authorizations for DOD intelligence could not be separated from the overall Defense budget. Senator Stennis stated that it "won't work" to ask the Armed Services Committee to handle only the personnel and hardware of a $100 billion dollar budget "much of it founded, bottomed on, intelligence" unless authorization jurisdiction over defense intelligence were retained by the Committee. He added that Senate-House

Armed Services Committee conferences on defense authorization bills would be a "procedural nightmare" if his committee lost authorization jurisdiction over DOD intelligence.

Senator Nunn, believing that meaningful interchange between the intelligence community and the Armed Services and Foreign Relations committees would be difficult if another committee had authorization authority, proposed creation of an Oversight Panel composed of members of the Armed Services, Foreign Relations and Appropriations Committees as an alternative to S. Res. 400.

George Bush, Director of Central Intelligence, testified in favor of strong, concentrated oversight, noting that it permitted the intelligence community to gain the advice and counsel of knowledgeable members and to maintain the trust and support of the American people. Such popular support was dependent upon a political structure which provided clear accountability. Provisions of S. Res. 400 which the DCI found it difficult to accept, however, were Section 7, which would permit the disclosure by the Senate of classified information over the objection of the President, and Section 11, which would require periodic authorization of appropriations. Bush felt that disclosure permitted under Section 7 might conflict with the statute requiring the DCI to "protect intelligence sources and methods," and he noted that the Central Intelligence Agency Act of 1949 provided for a continuing authorization for the CIA. On the latter point Bush stated, "We would not oppose a requirement to brief the proposed Committee on the CIA budget, and a requirement that the intelligence committee file a classified letter containing its CIA budget recommendations with the Appropriations Committee."

Senator Church explained that Section 7 represented an attempt to accommodate both the speech and debate clause of the Constitution (providing immunity to Senators from being questioned in any other place while performing legislative functions) and the security of legitimate secrets. (Section 7 also provides for sanctions against the unauthorized release of classified information.)

The Secretary of Defense, in a letter placed in the record by Chairman Cannon, pointed to two major problems his department foresaw with the granting of authority to the new committee; one—the visibility of the intelligence budget would create problems of confidentiality, and two—if the Senate and House had different authorizing systems, different, and time consuming DOD budget formulations would be required.

Senator Hruska testified that the Legislative Reorganization Act of 1946 had set standards controlling committee jurisdiction, which included the "coordination of the congressional committee system with the pattern of the administrative branch of the National Government" and that under this guideline the Judiciary Committee should continue to exercise jurisdiction over the Department of Justice, including the FBI.

Senator Ribicoff, chairman of the committee which drafted S. Res. 400, testified that a standing committee with legislative jurisdiction was necessary but suggested that the resolution be amended so that committees with jurisdiction over intelligence activities retain oversight on a concurrent basis with the proposed committee and that jurisdiction over FBI domestic intelligence be removed from the proposed committees' mandate.

DEBATE AND PASSAGE OF SENATE RESOLUTION 400, PROPOSED STANDING COMMITTEE ON INTELLIGENCE ACTIVITIES (*CONGRESSIONAL RECORD,* DAILY EDITION, MAY 13 AND 19, 1976, pp. S7254–S7563)

As Senate debate on establishment of an intelligence oversight committee began in May 1976, the Congressional Research Service issue brief, [97], p. 4, set forth six key issues to be addressed:

"In considering the advisability of a new oversight committee(s), Members may want to address the following questions:

"1. Should the new committee be a joint committee or should each House make its own oversight arrangements?

"2. Should the new committee have jurisdiction over domestic intelligence and counterintelligence as well as foreign intelligence?

"3. How many Members should be appointed to a new committee? On what basis should they be chosen?

"4. What statutory requirements should the Congress impose upon the executive with respect to sharing intelligence information with these and other committees?

"5. Should the new committee have authority to authorize appropriations, and if so, should all intelligence activities be subject to annual authorizations or only certain specified ones?

"6. What provisions will most adequately provide for both the protection and the proper dissemination of sensitive information with respect to (a) Members of the committee and its staff, (b) other Members of the Senate and House, and (c) the public."

The bill that reached the floor of the Senate was Senate Resolution 400, creating the Senate Select Committee on Intelligence. There were four different versions of Senate Resolution 400, each reflecting the work of a different committee and/or a different sponsor. (These different versions are summarized in [97], p. 5.) An impasse had developed over the size of the committee, its jurisdiction over domestic intelligence agencies, and its involvement in the appropriations process. A compromise was worked out, referred to as the Cannon compromise, after Senator Howard Cannon, chairman of the Committee on Rules and Administration.

The Cannon compromise, as summarized by the Congressional Research Service ([97, p. 5]), would: ". . . create a Select Committee on Intelligence with 17 members, nine appointed upon recommendation of the majority leader and eight upon recommendation by the minority leader. Two members each would be selected from the Armed Services, Foreign Relations, Appropriations and Judiciary committees and the others from the rest of the Senate for terms of eight years. The Select Committee would have exclusive legislative and authorization (annually or at least biannually) jurisdiction over the CIA and the Director of Central Intelligence and would share sequentially concurrent jurisdiction over all other intelligence agencies with the committees now holding jurisdiction. The Select Committee would be kept 'fully and currently informed,' including prior notification of covert operations and could, over the objection of the President, disclose classified information after approval by the full Senate."

As floor debate began, it was clear that the Senate was going to have its committee. At the conclusion of the 94th Congress, the House had not yet established any new oversight arrangement, leaving that matter pending for possible consideration in the 95th Congress. The floor debate on Senate Resolution 400 was concentrated in the Senate proceedings of May 13 and 19, 1976, portions of which are reprinted here.* As can be seen from the reprinted debate, the issues raised and examined in the hearings resurfaced. An unsuccessful attempt was made by Senator John Tower to keep defense intelligence appropriations out of the new committee's jurisdiction. Senators with a strong civil liberties interest, such as Lowell Weicker and Edward Kennedy, stressed the need to protect against further abuse of domestic rights. At passage, the Cannon substitute was virtually intact, amended to call for a 15-member rather than a 17-member committee.

---

*Two days of debate are partially reprinted here, detailing some of the give and take between participating senators and illustrating the political climate in which the measure was considered. To follow the entire floor debate, see the *Congressional Record* (daily edition), vol. 122, 5/10/76, p. S6767; 5/12/76, pp. S7059 and S7081; 5/13/76, p. S7254; 5/17/76, p. S7339; 5/18/76, p. S7408; 5/19/76, p. S7533. The text of Senate Resolution 400, as amended and passed, appears on p. S7563 of the 5/19/76 *Congressional Record.*

PROPOSED STANDING COMMITTEE ON INTELLIGENCE ACTIVITIES

The ACTING PRESIDENT pro tempore. Under the previous order, the hour of 1 p.m. having arrived, the Senate will now resume consideration of the unfinished business, Senate Resolution 400, which the clerk will report.

The assistant legislative clerk read as follows:

Calendar No. 728, a resolution (S. Res. 400) to establish a Standing Committee of the Senate on Intelligence Activities, and for other purposes.

Mr. MANSFIELD. Mr. President, I suggest the absence of a quorum.

The ACTING PRESIDENT pro tempore. The clerk will call the roll.

The assistant legislative clerk proceeded to call the roll.

Mr. WEICKER. Mr. President, I ask unanimous consent that the order for the quorum call be rescinded.

The ACTING PRESIDENT pro tempore. Without objection, it is so ordered.

PRIVILEGE OF THE FLOOR

Mr. WEICKER. Mr. President, I ask unanimous consent that Barbara Clarke be granted privilege of the floor.

The ACTING PRESIDENT pro tempore. Without objection, it is so ordered.

Mr. WEICKER. Mr. President, as we proceed with consideration of Senate Resolution 400, let us not lose sight of why it is that we have again come so far, what it is we seek to accomplish by our actions, and what it is we will lose should we fail to act responsibly.

Neither "Watergate" nor the subsequent investigation of our intelligence community was an aberration. In my own individual views in the Senate Watergate report. I explained that Watergate was a "documented, proven attack on laws, institutions, and principles." The report enumerated 189 separate violations of the Constitution. Every major substantive part of the Constitution was violated, abused, and undermined during the Watergate period, and, indeed, subsequent to it.

The report of the Church committee has since documented abuses and violations of law and the constitutional rights of citizens committed by virtually every agency in our intelligence community. Together, the reports of these two select committees, and the report of the House Intelligence Committee, contain a composite history of national shame.

Over and over again, the record has established with facts governmental abuse of our laws, systems, and ideals.

Three years of fact upon fact upon fact—the Watergate Committee, Church committee, House Judiciary Committee, Special Prosecutors, House Intelligence Committee, grand juries, trials, press investigations, revelations, the Rockefeller Commission, Schlesinger report, and so on.

What did we learn from all of this?

How did it happen?

Well, it happened, Mr. President, because among other things nobody was looking.

When I say nobody, I mean particularly those of us in this Chamber and our compatriots across the way. Nobody in the Congress was looking.

Finger-pointing time is over insofar as it concerns people standing on this floor, looking down at Pennsylvania Avenue or at the agencies are concerned. The time has come to look at ourselves.

There were plots to assassinate foreign leaders, attempts to buy what were supposed to be democratic elections in Italy, weapons provided to aid the Kurdish fight for independence, massive campaigns launched to threaten, discredit, and harass Dr. Martin Luther King and other American citizens, et cetera, et cetera, et cetera.

The CIA alone was not at fault. The FBI and IRS, a tax collection agency, joined in the act.

One fact emerges clearly from this record. Call it what you will, we do not have oversight. We have had weak sight, we have had blind sight, we have had hindsight, we have had shortsight, but we have not had oversight.

I think it is time to draw the line.

Three years of factfinding have given us all the investigations, revelations, and studies necessary to act on the creation of real oversight in the Senate and move on to legislative reform.

Meaningful oversight has constancy, power, and legislative purpose. Intelligence is too important to our national interests and has been proven too dangerous to our individual freedoms to be relegated to an impotent, investigatory committee. Even greater is the potential for abuse when a committee investigates without legislative purpose.

Currently, oversight over the intelligence community is concentrated in no less than four standing committees. At best intelligence oversight is a collateral function, a secondary function, of these committees. At worst, it is an ignored responsibility. None is authorized to legislate for the intelligence community as the consolidated package we know it has become.

Yet, if we leave their jurisdictions intact, we would continue to receive a fragmented picture of intelligence operations and would be handicapped in developing legitimate legislative remedies.

For all too long this vital sector of our Government has gone unchecked and unsupervised. It has operated under a series of Executive orders, departmental directives, and guidelines. Until last year not one congressional committee had examined either the propriety or effects of this departure from the norm.

I think the time has come to say it again and again, Mr. President: We are a Government of laws. It is not enough to say we remember these things and so they will not happen again. We are not a Government of memories, we are a Government of laws.

It is not enough to get up after the abuses have taken place and say, "I apologize". We are a Government of laws, not a Government of apologies.

It is not enough to go ahead and issue an executive order. Here today, gone tomorrow. We are a Government of laws, not a Government of executive orders.

The examination of agency charters, the establishment of a statutory foundation for agencies like the National Security Agency, the efficiency and effectiveness of the Defense Intelligence Agency, and the legislative recommendations of the Church committee are functions which must be assumed by a new, permanent intelligence committee.

The proposal for strengthened intelligence oversight is neither new nor unique. More than 20 years ago the distinguished majority leader introduced similar legislation. Since 1948 nearly 200 bills have been introduced in both houses. Three commissions—beginning with the Hoover Commission in 1955—endorsed proposals calling for more effective oversight.

I would like to use this particular moment in my speech, Mr. President, to pay particular compliments to the majority leader (Mr. MANSFIELD) and to the chairman of the Senate Committee on Government Operations (Mr. RIBICOFF). Were it not for these two men, I have no doubt that Senate Resolution 400 would not be on the floor today.

The Senate majority leader, who is not a Johnny-come-lately, is not riding a bandwagon, but, rather, foresaw the dangers 20 years ago. Had his advice been followed, there would have been no necessity for the rather sensational revelations of the past few years.

As he retires from a fruitful and a very positive career in public service, I want to pay the credit that is due. Should this pass and this idea become law, then, indeed, it should be dedicated to this man, because nobody has been further out front on the issue than MIKE MANSFIELD and my colleague from the State of Connecticut.

This particular idea was one of several right after the Watergate. Over the course of 3 years I have seen those ideas of Watergate reform, tax privacy, intelligence oversight, nibbled to death by the power structure, either in the Congress or the executive or the bureaucracy.

The nibbling finally came to an end when two of these important measures came into the hands of the senior Senator from Connecticut (Mr. RIBICOFF). He used that knowledge gained over many years of public service, and that ability which he has demonstrated over the years, to insist that these measures no longer be nibbled to death or fade away into the mist, but, rather, become the law of the land. Were it not for the hard-nosed position which he has taken over the past several months, I know that these measures would not be before us for consideration by the Senate.

Mr. RIBICOFF. Will my distinguished colleague yield?

Mr. WEICKER. I yield.

Mr. RIBICOFF. I appreciate the gracious comments of my colleague from Connecticut, but I believe the record should be clear that no other Member of this body in many, many years has shown such a continued dedication to the preservation of individual rights and liberties. It has been the consistent policy and philosophy of my junior colleague from the State of Connecticut. When the history of this era is written, there will be a special place accorded to the junior Senator from Connecticut for his continued advocacy and fight in this cause.

Mr. WEICKER. I thank my friend and colleague from the bottom of my heart.

The crux of this issue is accountability of Government to the people—constitutional accountability. In the past, Members of this body have chosen not to know because there were things which gentlemen ought not to know. Well, it is our responsibility to assure that those things which gentlemen ought not to know, never reoccur.

We can no longer pass off illegal activities as the work of the White House, because we have learned the hard way that even the White House must be controlled. That was precisely what was intended by our forefathers when 200 years ago when they established a system of checks and balances to govern this Nation.

It is not a system of checks and balances which excluded the CIA, the FBI, the IRS, and the various intelligence-law enforcement agencies, but a system of accountability for all the Government, for all the people. It is not a system which was intended to have Senators, Presidents, or corporate executives at one level and everybody else at another. It is for all the people.

Through the past failure of Congress to demand to know about the activities of intelligence agencies—the people through the fault of their elected representatives lost a constitutional power—to control the excesses of the executive Plainly and simply, the elected representatives abbrogated their constitutional responsibility.

And, Mr. President, if I have been hardnosed insofar as our colleagues in the executive are concerned, I think the record should also show something else. At a time when we celebrate a Bicentennial in the middle of an election year, I see from the statistics fewer and fewer Americans participating in their democratic processes. I hear the comment from too many, "I am turned off by those politics."

Let us make it clear. If we have a job of oversight as representatives of the people, if the President has a job to conform the agencies to the Constitution, then the people of this country have a job, and it is specifically to get the best men and women to serve.

There will be no greater ethics or excellence on the floor of the Senate or in the White House, or anywhere in our Government, than in the voting booths of this country. So the finger-pointing cannot only stop from us on the Hill, but it can also stop from the American people until they themselves become active participants in this constitutional democracy.

Today we are here to regain that authority and start exercising it. When we vote in a few days, we will see whether a majority of Members of this body are willing to assume the responsibilities bestowed upon them by their constituents. The Senate must decide if the preservation of the status quo is more important than the resurrection of constitutional accountability.

Let me state clearly, there is no reason for anybody in this country to have to choose between effective law enforcement and effective intelligence and constitutionality. One can go along with the other. I am particularly appalled by those who would make the American people choose, and say, "You have to choose one or the other." No, you can have both.

There is not one man on the Government Operations Committee or in any other committee which discussed this matter on which I have been privileged to sit who does not believe in having an effective CIA and an effective FBI. They are clearly necessary to the security of the Nation. But there is no reason why, in the achieving of that effectiveness, the

Constitution has to be left in the dust. No way.

Sure, it is going to have to change from the old system, from the old practices. Democracy, which we say is exercised by 100 Senators, is going to have to be exercised by 10 Senators, not 2, 3, or 4.

Democracy and the Constitution, which we talk about as belonging to all Americans, are going to have to belong to all Americans, not just a few. Concerning the scare tactic and the scare talk that if we have accountability, if we have oversight, we will lose our intelligence or law enforcement effectiveness, how effective is it to be investigating Americans rather than conveying intelligence about our enemies abroad?

How effective is it to have these agencies involved in politics, on the domestic side, rather than intelligence gathering?

. . .

Mr. CHURCH.
In this Bicentennial Year, we have celebrated the durability of our system of government and quality of strength of the Constitution. Part of that enduring strength is based upon the ability to make changes when we have to of a pragmatic nature, while remaining within our basic principles of law and procedure.

The experience of secret government activities over the past 30 years argues indisputably for changes to be made in both the legislative and executive branches if we are to preserve our constitutional system of government.

Over the past 15 months, the Select Committee on Intelligence Activities has carefully examined the intelligence structure of the United States. Considerable time and effort have been devoted in order to understand what has been done by the U.S. Government in secrecy during the 30-year period since the end of World War II. It is clear to the committee that there are many necessary and proper governmental activities that must be conducted in secrecy. Some of these activities affect the security and the very existence of the Nation.

It is also clear from the committe's inquiry that intelligence activities conducted outside the framework of the Constitution and statutes can undermine the treasured values guaranteed in the Bill of Rights. Further, if the intelligence agencies act in ways inimical to declared national purposes, they damage the reputation, power, and influence of the United States abroad.

The Select Committee's investigation has documented that a number of actions committed in the name of "national security" were inconsistent with declared policy and the law.

It is clear that a primary task for the oversight committee, and the Congress as a whole, will be to frame basic statutes necessary under the Constitution within which the intelligence agencies of the United States can function efficiently under clear guidelines. Charters delineating the missions, authorities, and limitations for some of the most important intelligence agencies do not exist. For example, there is no statutory authority for the NSA's intelligence activities. Where statutes do exist, as with the CIA, they are vague and have failed to provide the necessary guidelines.

The committee's investigation has demonstrated, moreover, that the lack of legislation has had the effect of limiting public debate upon some important national issues.

The CIA's broad statutory charter, the 1947 National Security Act, makes no specific mention of covert action. The CIA's former General Counsel, Lawrence Houston, who was deeply involved in drafting the 1947 act, wrote in September 1947—

We do not believe that there was any thought in the minds of Congress that the CIA under [the authority of the National Security Act] would take positive action for subversion and sabotage.

Yet, a few months after enactment of the 1947 legislation, the National Security Council authorized the CIA to engage in covert action programs. The provision of the Act often cited as authorizing CIA covert activities provides for e Agenc * * * "to perform such other functions and duties related to intelligence affecting the national security as the National Security Council may from time to time direct."

Secret executive orders issued by the NSC to carry out covert action programs were not subject to congressional review. Indeed, until recent years, except for a few Members, Congress was not even aware of the existence of the so-called secret charter for intelligence activities. Those Members who did know had no institutional means for discussing their knowledge with their colleagues. The problem of how the Congress can effectively use secret knowledge in its legislative processes remains to be resolved. It is the Select Committee's view that a strong and effective oversight committee is an essential first step that must be taken to resolve this fundamental issue.

Since World War II, with steadily escalating consequences, many decisions of national importance have been made in secrecy, often by the executive branch alone. These decisions are frequently basesd on information obtained by clandestine means and available only to the executive branch. Until very recently, the Congress has not shared in this process. The cautions expressed by the Founding Fathers and the constitutional checks designed to assure that policymaking not become the proviince of a few men have been circumvented through the use of secrecy. John Adams expressed his concerned about the dangers of arbitrary power 200 years ago:

Whenever we leave principles and clear positive laws we are soon lost in the wild regions of imagination and possibility where arbitrary power sits upon her brazen throne and governs with an iron scepter.

Recent Presidents have justified this secrecy on the basis of "national security," "the requirements of national defense," or "the confidentiality required by sensitive, ongoing negotiations or operations." These justifications were generally accepted at face value. The Bay of Pigs fiasco, the secret war in Laos, the secret bombing of Cambodia, the anti-Allende activities in Chile, the Watergate affair, were all instances of the use of power cloaked in secrecy which, when revealed, provoked widespread popular disapproval. This series of events has ended, for the time being at least, passive and uncritical acceptance by the Congress of Executive decisions in the areas of foreign policy, national security and intelligence activities. If Congress had met its oversight responsibilities through the years, some of these excesses might have been averted.

The worth of the work done by the Select Committee on Intelligence Activities over the past 15 months will be judged by the outcome of the resolution now under consideration. A strong and effective oversight committee of the kind set forth in the resolution now under consideration is required to carry out the necessary reforms contained in the Select Committee's final report. In order to restore legitimacy to what are agreed to be the necessary activities of the intelligence community, a strong oversight committee with a well-trained staff is required.

This is a time for a new beginning. Fifteen months of investigation has revealed enough evidence of the dangers of permitting the intelligence agencies of the United States to undertake their necessary activities without the kind of legislative oversight contemplated by the Constitution. It is quite clear that the concerns expressed over 20 years ago by Senator MANSFIELD have proven to be correct.

There have been over 200 proposals to establish an oversight committee since Senator MANSFIELD introduced his resolution over two decades ago. Surely, we do not need further evidence of the necessity for an oversight committee with the powers required to do the job. It is quite clear that the oversight structures we have designed in the past have proven inadequate.

The creation of a new permanent intelligence oversight committee is an absolutely necessary first step toward establishing an agreed-upon procedure by which problems of national importance that are necessarily secret in character can be addressed within the constitutional framework.

The jurisdiction of an effective committee must include oversight over what is known as the "national intelligence community." Because of the limitations of present committee jurisdictions, no committee presently is able to exercise oversight over national intelligence. At the present time, the Committees on Armed Services, Foreign Relations, and Judiciary, have been faced with the problem of overseeing fragments of the intelligence community. No committee has had the scope to look at national intelligence as a whole.

The resolution now before the Senate provides that the oversight committee would have sole jurisdiction over the CIA, and concurrent jurisdiction over the NSA, the DIA, the "national intelligence" components in the Department of Defense budget, and the intelligence portions of the FBI. The Select Committee, over the past 15 months, has found that these agencies have worked so closely together, that unless there is the clear ability to look at all of them, oversight cannot be effectively carried out. The pending resolution would not exclude committees with existing jurisdictions over particular elements of the intelligence community that fall within their larger oversight duties. Obviously, it is necessary for the Armed Services Committee to know the requirements and, to some extent, the activities of the NSA and the DIA to be sure that the Department of Defense's activities are of a piece. On the other hand, the bulk of activities of the CIA, a civilian agency, are not concerned with military matters and require a different oversight focus than is now the case. For a variety of reasons, the counterintelligence activities of the FBI have not been the subject of adequate oversight in the past. The new oversight committee would create a new jurisdiction, which would bring together all these disparate elements of the national intelligence community which are now scattered among several Senate committees and some functions which are not covered by any committee.

National intelligence includes the collection, analysis, production, and dissemination and use of political, military, and economic information affecting the relations of the U.S. with foreign governments, and other activity which is in support of or supported by a collection, analysis, production, dissemination and use of such information. National intelligence also includes, but is not limited to clandestine activities such as covert action and some activities that take place within the United States such as counterintelligence. In general, these are the activities that would be supervised.

The main legislative tool required to effectively carry out oversight is annual authorization authority for the CIA, and the national intelligence portions of the NSA, DIA, the counterintelligence portion of the FBI, and some other national intelligence groups found in various departments and agencies. The power of the purse is the most effective means that the Legislature can have to assure that the will of Congress is observed. There has never been an annual authorization of the intelligence community budget. The proposed oversight committee, for the first time, under appropriate security safeguards, would be able to consider all budgetary requests of the national intelligence community on an annual basis.

The second legislative power required by an oversight committee to function effectively, is the right to acquire necessary information. It is absolutely vital that the oversight committee be kept "fully and currently informed" on all matters pertaining to its jurisdiction. The executive branch should also be obligated to answer any requests made by the Committee for information within its jurisdiction. In my view, the right to information provisions of the resolution which are based upon the existing language of the Atomic Energy Act, section 202(d), have served Congress well for more than a quarter century. The resolution has added a provision that, consistent with the intent of section 202(d) of the Atomic Energy Act, the oversight committee should also have the power to require information concerning activities of the intelligence community that the committee believes it should be informed of prior to the initiation of any such activity.

The effect of such a provision would be to require prior legislative authorization of intelligence activities in the normal way. This authority lies at the heart of vigilant legislative oversight. It is the power of the purse operating in full conformity with the Constitution.

Without full knowledge obtained in sufficient time, meaningful oversight cannot be exercised. It is clear from present concerns and recent history that the country would have been well-served had a committee of the Congress known in advance of certain actions, so that the advice of the Congress might have been given, and foolish, costly, and harmful courses of action might have been averted.

Another important provision in the pending resolution is the procedure which should be followed in the event that the committee wishes to disclose information obtained from the executive branch which the President wishes to keep concealed. The Select Committee has been involved in a number of instances over the past year in which there has been a dispute between the committee and the executive branch.

Almost all of these points of disagreements were resolved in a manner agreeable to both sides. However, there were a few instances in which agreement could not be reached. One such example was the question of the release of the assassination report. But in working toward the creation of a constitutional procedure for dealing with issues of a secret character, the larger question of the proper role secrecy should play in our democratic society must be carefully addressed. The constitutional system of the United States is best suited to make national decisions through open discussion, debate and the airing of different points of view. Those who advocate that a particular secret must be kept should have the burden of proof placed upon them. They must show why a secret should be withheld from public scrutiny. Inevitably, there will be differences between the Executive and the Legislature as to whether the national interest is served by maintaining secrecy in particular cases or whether the usual constitutional process of open debate and public scrutiny should prevail. It is my view that important questions of this kind should be brought to the full Senate for decision.

The resolution now before the Senate prescribes the following procedure: If the oversight committee decided that it would be in the national interest to disclose some information received from the executive branch, it would be required to inform the executive branch of its intention. It would then be required to enter into a full and considered consultation concernig the problems raised by disclosure. If, after such full and considered consultation, the oversight committee decided to disclose any information requested to be kept confidential by the President, the committee would be required to notify the President of that decision. The committee could then, after 5 days, disclose the information unless the President, in writing, informed the Senate through the committee that he opposed such disclosure and gave his views why he opposed the disclosure of such information. The oversight committee, after receiving the President's objections, and if it decided that the President's reasons did not outweigh the reasons for disclosure, may refer the question to the full Senate in closed session for a decision.

In my view, once the Senate accepts the kind of process set forth in this resolution, it would respect the injunction of secrecy. We must recognize that at this time there is no agreement as to what a valid national security secret is, and that the Senate does not now have the procedural means to make decisions concerning matters classified secret by the executive branch.

One further step is set forth in this resolution—sanctions for improper disclosure. In my view, if any member of the Senate or staff disclosed sensitive information of the committee outside of the committee, except in closed session of the Senate, such disclosure should be referred to the Committee on Standards and Conduct to investigate and recommend appropriate action including, but not limited to, censure or removal from office.

The Senate has never addressed this issue squarely. It is my firm belief that it should do so now. Once the Senate comes to agreement as to how secret material should be handled, it should also impose upon itself rules to assure that improper disclosure, as defined by the Senate, will be properly dealt with.

..... We cannot shy away from the necessity to develop effective procedures to make legislative decisions concerning necessarily secret activities of the United States, but such decisions must be done in ways consistent with the Constitution.

The history of the past 30 years and the revelations of the past 2 years are proof that we have much work to do. Let us equip ourselves in the Senate to do our part of the job in the most effective way. We need an oversight committee to oversee the activities of the entire intelligence community with the power, knowledge, and staff required.

The need to bring secret Government activities under constitutional control is clear, the means to do so are contained in the resolution now before the Senate. We have had 30 years of experience and 15 months of intensive inquiry. What further proof do we need? ....

Mr. RIBICOFF. Mr. President, I yield myself 10 minutes.

Mr. President, this amendment would deny the new committee any legislative, authorization, or oversight jurisdiction over the intelligence activities of the Department of Defense.

It would fundamentally alter the compromise language offered by Senator CANNON last Wednesday.

I must strongly oppose this proposed amendment.

The new committee must have concurrent legislative and authorization jurisdiction over the national intelligence activities of the Department of Defense for the following reasons:

The Department of Defense is the Nation's primary collector of intelligence information. It controls 80–90 percent of the Nation's spending on national intelligence programs, and most technical collection systems are developed, targeted, or operated by Department of Defense personnel. The Department also supplies a great deal of information to nonmilitary intelligence agencies. It provides critical information of national security policymakers on a multitude of issues including strategic arms limitations and peace in the Middle East.

Accordingly, the executive branch treats the DOD intelligence activities as an integral part of the entire national intelligence community. For example, in February, the President charged a new committee on Foreign Intelligence, chaired by the Director of Central Intelligence, with responsibility for overseeing and coordinating the Government's entire national foreign intelligence program, including DOD's intelligence program.

If the new committee did not have jurisdiction over the defense intelligence agencies, it would be denied jurisdiction over most of the intelligence community.

It is very important to achieve the proper relationship between the civilian intelligence agencies and the military intelligence agencies. The two different types of agencies must work closely together to assure as accurate and unbiased intelligence as possible for use by all military and civilian decisionmakers. It would be difficult to achieve this goal if responsibility in Congress for the intelligence community was split up so that one committee was responsible for the civilian intelligence agencies and one the military intelligence agencies.

The Department of Defense has an enormous technological capability that could be used to violate the rights of American citizens. Past disclosures of wrongdoing have included the DOD as well as the FBI, CIA, and other agencies.

For example, the select committee has pointed to the following abuses:

First. Millions of private telegrams sent from, to, or through the United States were obtained by the National Security Agency from 1947 to 1975 under a secret arrangement with three U.S. telegraph companies.

Second. An estimated 100,000 Americans were the subjects of U.S. Army intelligence files created between the mid-1960's and 1971.

Third. Army intelligence maintained files on Congressmen because of their participation in peaceful political meetings under surveillance by army agents.

Fourth. As part of their effort to collect information which related even remotely to people or groups in communities which had the potential for civil disorder, army intelligence agencies took such steps as: sending agents to a Halloween party for elementary school children in Washington, D.C. because they suspected a local dissident might be present; monitoring protest of welfare mothers' organizations in Milwaukee; infiltrating a coalition of church youth groups in Colorado, and sending agents to a priests' conference in Washington, D.C. held to discuss birth control measures.

Fifth. Army intelligence officers opened the private mail of American civilians in West Berlin and West Germany.

Sixth. The military joined other intelligence agencies in drafting the so-called Huston plan in 1970, and later participated in the Intelligence Evaluation Committee, an interdepartmental committee established by the Justice Department to analyze domestic intelligence information.

Just this past weekend the select committee released a 49-page report describing in detail abuses by the Defense Department intelligence activities. It describes how the DOD collected information about the political activities of private citizens and private organizations, monitored radio transmissions in the United States, investigated civilian groups considered threats to the military, and assisted law enforcement agencies in surveillance of private citizens and organizations.

The same expertise gained by the new committee through oversight of the CIA and FBI could and should be used to oversee the DOD's intelligence activities so that civil liberties are protected.

A committee with the necessary resources must closely examine the DOD intelligence agencies to avoid duplication and inefficiency and assure the best intelligence possible. The Defense Department spends billions on intelligence. Yet the Deputy Secretary of Defense, Mr. Ellsworth, testified before the Government Operations Committee in January that—

The problem that we have had with the Defense Intelligence Agency, as I see, is the same problem that we have generally with all intelligence in this Nation. That is, there are weaknesses in the quality of analysis and estimates that our intelligence community provides to us.

I do not think that there is anyone in the intelligence community that would take issue with that.

Our objective is, as far as the DIA is concerned, to very substantially improve the quality of the analysis and estimates that the DIA produces for the Secretary of Defense and the Joint Chiefs of Staff.

If we cannot achieve that objective, then we have got to think of some other way of structuring defense intelligence activity so that we can improve the quality of the finished intelligence product.

Problems with DIA exist despite the fact that DIA's problems have been recognized for a number of years. In 1970, the Fitzhugh report, containing the conclusions of a blue ribbon defense panel organized by the executive branch, criticized DIA's performance, concluding that "the principal problems of the DIA can be summarized as too many jobs and too many masters."

In order to avoid waste and duplication, and improve the quality of intelligence generally, the intelligence committee must have an overview of all national intelligence activities. It must be able to make choices between programs within and outside of DOD and to make changes in the way all the agencies operate and are organized. Without authority over DOD's national intelligence activities, the new intelligence committee's jurisdiction would be incomplete in a crucial respect.

The pending substitute to Senate Resolution 400 recognizes that, to be effective, the new committee must have legislative and authorization authority over the intelligence activities of the Defense Department. At the same time, it is written in such a way to protect fully the interest of the Armed Services Committee in intelligence matters.

Under section 3(b) the Armed Services Committee will share with the new committee legislative and authorization authority over bills involving DOD intelligence. Any legislation, including authorizations, reported by the new committee and involving DOD intelligence activities will be sequentially referred to the Armed Services Committee upon request of its chairman.

Section 3(c) of the resolution assures the Armed Services Committee the right to continue to investigate the national intelligence functions of DOD in order to make sure that the intelligence agencies are providing DOD the intelligence it must have to operate effectively.

Section 3(d) provides that the Armed Services Committee will continue to receive directly from all intelligence agencies the intelligence it must have to continue to carry out its other responsibilities. One of the responsibilities of the new committee will be in fact to make sure that the intelligence agencies are promptly providing the other committees of Congress the information they should have.

Section 4(a) requires the new committee to promptly call to the attention of other committees, such as the Armed Services Committee, any matters deemed by the select committee to require the immediate attention of such other committees. Section 8(c) provides the new select committee with the authority and responsibility to adopt regulations that will permit it to share sensitive information with other committees in a way that will protect the confidentiality of the information.

To assure that there is close cooperation between the new committee and the Armed Services Committee, the substitute reserves two seats on the committee for members of the Armed Services Committee.

The substitute does not give the new committee any legislative, authorization, or oversight responsibility for tactical intelligence. Responsibility for this type of intelligence will remain solely within the jurisdiction of the Armed Services Committee.

The new committee will only have jurisdiction over that portion of DOD's intelligence activities which provides national intelligence that DOD, the State Department, the President, and others in the executive branch need to make broad national policy decisions. The definition of intelligence in section 14(a) of the substitute to Senate Resolution 400 specifically excludes from the committee's jurisdiction tactical foreign military intelligence. The new committee will not have jurisdiction over tactical intelligence which seeks to meet the more specific technical interests of the weapons developers and field commanders.

As a practical matter, the national intelligence portion of the DOD budget may be authorized by the new committee, in conjunction with the Armed Services Committee, apart from the rest of the DOD budget.

The distinction between national and tactical intelligence is an accepted one in the executive branch.

The Defense Department already prepares a consolidated defense intelligence program which includes expenditures for intelligence of the type covered by this resolution, but excludes "intelligence related activities which belong in the combat force and other major programs which they are designed to support." The Director of Central Intelligence already prepares a national intelligence budget. Indeed, President Ford's recent executive order gives the executive branch's Committee on Foreign Intelligence—CFI—headed by the Director of Central Intelligence, responsibility to control "budget preparation and resource allocation" for the national foreign intelligence program. The President's directive provides, however, that the Committee on Foreign Intelligence will not have responsibility for tactical intelligence.

The final report of the Church Committee on Foreign Military Intelligence similarly indicates that it also was able to separate national from tactical intelligence and to arrive at separate figures for each.

Distinction between the different types of intelligence are in fact already being made for Congress by the Department of Defense as part of the budgetary process.

In September 1975 the chairman of the House Appropriations Committee wrote the Secretary of Defense as follows:

The committee is concerned about apparent attempts to lessen the visibility of intelligence funding. Therefore, the committee directs that the 1977 budget presentations include manpower and dollar amounts for intelligence, direct support, and intelligence-related activities.

The committee insists that the total cost of intelligence be presented to the Congress, and by requiring submission of justifications for these programs the committee hopes to assure the accomplishment of this goal.

Mr. Ellsworth testified before the Government Operations Committee concerning this letter that,

The Defense Department and agencies are following this directive and are supplying to the committee a thorough justification of intelligence and intelligence-related activities in the fiscal year 1977 budget.

Mr. Ellsworth indicated that in the material being prepared for the House Appropriations Committee, the Defense Department was in fact attempting to distinguished between tactical and national intelligence despite, his testimony that the distinctions were difficult to make precisely.

In discussing Senate Resolution 400 before the Armed Services Committee last Thursday, Mr. Ellsworth did not argue that it was impossible to authorize separately the type of national intelligence activities covered by Senate Resolution 400.

There may be gray areas where it is difficult to decide whether a particular activity belongs to tactical or national intelligence. It may take the new committee several years to finally settle, in consultation with other interested committees and the executive branch, the precise dimensions of the budget.

But these technical budgetary issues can be removed. The Comptroller General wrote the House select committee November 10, that—

Once the Congress has outlined the activities which it wants identified and reported in the intelligence budget, it will be possible to establish guidelines for the executive branch to follow in developing and submitting the budget.

The responsible committees of Congress have every right to know as exactly as possible how much DOD spends on intelligence. To the extent that this information is not available now, it should be one of the first jobs of the new committee to work with the executive branch to make sure it is available in the future.

The fact that it may take some study and work to settle all the questions is no reason to deny the new committee the crucial authorization power it must have to exercise effective oversight.

In summary, the proposed substitute to Senate Resolution 400 will assure the Armed Services the ability to have access to intelligence information, and the ability to consider legislation, including authorization legislation, involving DOD intelligence. The resolution creates a new committee that can work with the Armed Services Committee in this area so that the time-consuming and difficult work necessary to oversee the intelligence committee will not have to fall on the Armed Services Committee alone.

Mr. TOWER. Will the Senator yield for a question?

Mr. RIBICOFF. I am pleased to yield.

Mr. TOWER. I would like to suggest to the Senator from Connecticut that the Stennis-Tower amendment does not touch the question of oversight, only the question of legislation. It is addressed only to the legislative section of the resolution and not on the question of oversight.

It does not take away the authority for oversight on the part of the new select committee.

Mr. RIBICOFF. That may be true.

Mr. TOWER. The power to subpena or what have you.

Mr. RIBICOFF. But in order to do this job, and do it properly, we do believe that it is important that the new committee share with the Armed Services Committee the legislative functions involved, and I believe that this can be done. It should be kept in mind that we have provided for sequential review in such cases by both committees.

What puzzles the Senator from Connecticut is the hesitancy by the Armed

Services Committees to really trust the remainder of the Senate in this way.

It has been provided in the Cannon substitute that 8 members of this committee will be taken from Armed Services, Foreign Relations, Appropriations, and Judiciary.

These are four committees that in the past have had jurisdiction—legislative jurisdiction, oversight jurisdiction, of the intelligence community.

What we are doing is adding seven more members to the committee, four from the majority and three from the minority. These seven men will be chosen by the majority and minority leaders. I, for one, have complete confidence and trust in the majority and minority leaders. My feeling is that these seven men will represent a cross section of the Senate, especially the younger men of the Senate, who have just as much of a stake, and whose integrity I have just as much confidence in, as I do the eight members from the other committees.

I have high respect for the distinguished Senator from Mississippi. There is not another Member of this 100, may I say to the Senator from Mississippi, for whom I have a higher respect and higher regard. I think the Senator from Mississippi appreciates that from the past experiences we both have had. I have complete faith in him.

On the other hand, I think the Senator from Mississippi and the Senator from Texas should realize that there are other Members who have arrived in recent years, some of the most able Members this body has ever had, and who are as deeply concerned and as deeply committed as the senior Members of this body.

Consequently, I think it is absolutely necessary, in order to have the complete support and complete confidence of the Senate in basic decisions that will be made in the future, that the committee have 15 members, with 7 members chosen from the Senate at large and 8 from Appropriations, Judiciary, Foreign Relations, and Armed Services.

Mr. President, at this time, on my time, I would like to accord the distinguished Senator from Georgia a colloquy on some problems that are bothering him as a member of the Armed Services Committee. I think the colloquy will clarify some of the questions that other members of the Armed Services Committee do have.

Mr. NUNN. I thank the Senator from Connecticut. I express my gratitude and appreciation as a Member of the Senate to the Senator from Connecticut and the Senator from Illinois, on the Government Operations Committee, and to the Senator from Nevada and the Senator from West Virgina, on the Rules Committee, for all the diligent work which has gone into this.

I really have three separate lines of questioning, but I will start with the question of whether or not there is anything in the pending substitute to Senate Resolution 400 which would require public disclosure in any form of the amount spent on intelligence.

Mr. RIBICOFF. No. Senate Resoluiton 400 creates a new committee and defines its jurisdiction. It does not try to decide the important issue whether the intelligence budget should be disclosed publicly, and, if so, in what form. The new committee is encouraged by section 13(a)(8) to study this issue. I would expect the full Senate to give this difficult issue full consideration after the new committee submits any recommendations it may have on the matter no later than next July 1.

Section 12 establishes a procedure which assures that, for the first time, the intelligence activities subject to the select committee's jurisdiction will be authorized on an annual basis. The section constitutes a commitment, on behalf of the Senate, that funds will not be appropriated for these agencies before such an authorization. Approval of an authorization, however, may be given in a way that keeps the figures secret, just as now the Senate appropriates funds for intelligence in a way that maintains the secrecy of the figures.

Mr. NUNN. I thank the Senator from Connecticut.

Another question along that line:

When the select committee reports an authorization bill for intelligence funds, how will the full Senate then consider the matter, assuming that the Senate has decided to continue to keep these figures secret?

Mr. RIBICOFF. If the Senate decided to continue to keep the overall figures secret, the process could work this way:

In the case of authorizations for defense-related intelligence activities, any bill reported by the new committee would be sequentially referred to the Armed Services Committee. As in the case of sequential referral of other legislation, there would be no need for full Senate debate prior to this sequential referral. The authorization figure would then be disguised in the DOD authorization bill approved by the Armed Services Committee, as is the case now.

In the case of an annual authorization for the CIA, after the select committee approves an authorization, I would expect that the figure would be disguised in some other authorization measure.

Mr. NUNN. I thank the Senator. I think that is extremely important, and clarifies a point that has been of considerable concern to the Senator from Georgia and I think many other Senators.

Another question along the same line: How would the new committee bring a matter involving the intelligence authorization figure to the attention of the full Senate, assuming the figures are still secret?

Mr. RIBICOFF. In that event, the Senate could invoke the same procedure for a secret session now available to the Senate. Under rule XXXV, the Senate could go into closed session and debate the matter in secrecy, just as they could debate the intelligence budget now in secret session.

Mr. NUNN. A further question: Will the requirement in section 12 for an annual authorization of the intelligence budget interfere with the ability of the Appropriations Committee to appropriate funds for intelligence in a timely fashion?

Mr. RIBICOFF. The committee authorizing expenditures for intelligence activities would be subject, like other committees, to the requirements of the Budget Act. The committees will have until May 15 to complete action on authorizations for intelligence. At the same time, the Budget Act contemplates that the Senate will not act on approriation measures until after May 15. This would apply to appropriations for the intelligence community. Assuming that all the committees adhere to the Budget Act, the requirements in section 12 will not affect the schedule the Appropriations Committee would follow for the appropriation of intelligence funds.

Mr. NUNN. One clarifying question on that latter point: I understand the timetable and that we may have to revise that timetable as the budgeting process is reviewed; but suppose, for instance, in terms of the overall intelligence activities, that there is a sequential referral of the annual authorization from the Intelligence Committee to the Armed Services Committee. I understand that under the provisions of Senate Resoltuion 400, in the case of such a referral the Armed Services Committee would be allowed to have that bill for 30 days. Suppose the Intelligence Committee gives them the bill on, say, May 14. Then the Armed Service Committee would be right up against the May 15 deadline. I suppose the committees would just have to work together under those circumstances.

Mr. RIBICOFF. I would say so. I would assume that the Intelligence Committee would, on a basis of comity, adopt a schedule that would assure that the Armed Services Committee had the full 30 days to do its job.

It should be remembered that on the Intelligence Committee there will be two members of the Armed Services Committee, and I personally would be very disappointed in the Intelligence Committee if they did not make sure that any committee entitled sequentially to 30 days would have the full 30 days before May 15 to comply with the Budget Act.

Mr. NUNN. I thank the Senator. I have another line of questioning on this point: Under present law, the Committee on Armed Services has authorizing jurisdiction over all of the military personnel and all of the civilian personnel in the Department of Defense. The manpower requirements report indicates that there are 42,000 military personnel, 9,500 civilians, and 5,300 reservists in the overall manpower authorization for fiscal year 1976 for the intelligence and security category.

My question is, With the new Intelligence Committee having authorizing jurisdiction over Defense Department intelligence, how would the two committees handle the manpower authorization which relates to Defense Department personnel in general, but also includes intelligence personnel?

Mr. RIBICOFF. Let me respond to the distinguished Senator from Georgia and the distinguished Senators from Mississippi and North Dakota, who are so deeply involved in such matters: This is the type of situation where, in my opinion, it would first go to the Armed Services Committee and then, sequentially, to the Intelligence Committee. You would come first, in my opinion, where the bill is a general Defense Department manpower bill.

The Armed Services Committee would continue to have exclusive jurisdiction over all aspects of the legislation except for the portion affecting national intelligence. The portion of the legislation affecting national intelligence would be reviewed by both the Committee on Armed Services and the new committee, under section 3. It would be up to the new committee and the Armed Services Committee to work out the details on the procedure for actual consideration by both committees of the intelligence portion of this bill.

Mr. STENNIS. Mr. President, will the Senator yield to me and let me intervene on that same point?

If the Senator will yield, I appreciate the suggestion of the Senator from Connecticut, but the bill, as I understand it, provides to the contrary, that it would go to the Intelligence Committee first. Senators will understand that our hearings on manpower start in the fall of the year, before the budget even comes in.

Mr. RIBICOFF. Well, basically it is up to the Parliamentarian, in a sequential referral, on the basis of what is in the bill. If it is basically armed services, it goes to the Committee on Armed Services first. If it is basically intelligence, it goes to Intelligence first. It is my personal interpretation that if it provided for overall manpower, covering the entire Department of Defense, commonsense would dictate—and, of course, the Parliamentarian is the final judge—that that would go to armed services first.

The PRESIDING OFFICER (Mr. ALLEN). The allotted time has expired.

Mr. RIBICOFF. I yield myself 2 more minutes.

It would go to Armed Services first, because intelligence would be only a part of the overall Department of Defense manpower authorization.

Then out of that would be carved out only the intelligence portion, which would then be referred sequentially to the Intelligence Committee.

May I say for the benefit of the Senate that it is my feeling that there are a lot of gray areas in this legislation. It is impossible to answer all the questions. We are going to have to work it out between all the committees and the Intelligence Committee. All the interested committees will have to exercise a great deal of commonsense.

I would say much will depend upon the quality of that 15-member committee. Also, I think it should be pointed out that the reason why we have a resolution, and the advantage of the resolution, is that a resolution does not bind the executive branch. If this is to work, we will have to have comity between the executive branch and the Senate of the United States. I personally believe that the greatest problem America has today in the matter of foreign policy is not our problem with foreign governments or our prospective opponents, but the divisions between the executive branch and the legislative branch. I think the greatest problem we suffer as a nation in the field of foreign policy is the conflict, we have gone through in the last few years between the executive and legislative branches of the Government in the whole field of foreign policy.

The PRESIDING OFFICER. The Senator's additional time has expired.

Mr. RIBICOFF. I yield myself 2 more minutes.

Here is an opportunity for the Senate and the executive branch to work closely together with the Intelligence Committee, to work out the problems of broad policy, for the executive branch to gain a sense of what the Senate is going to do, and what the sentiment of the Senate is. I can think of no greater blow to the executive branch in our foreign policy than to find our Nation embarrassed over a matter like Angola. If the executive branch had gone before a committee like the Intelligence Committee and had obtained the sense of this 15-member committee that it just would not fly, it would never have developed into such a matter of conflict, to the embarrassment of our Nation.

I have confidence in the majority and minority leaders, that the men they will choose will make this committee work in a way that benefits the Senate and the United States.

Mr. NUNN. Mr. President, may I ask one further question on that manpower matter?

Mr. RIBICOFF. I yield.

Mr. NUNN. It is my interpretation, from what the Senator from Connecticut has said, that the overall manpower authorization, as it is now, would be submitted to the Armed Services Committee, the Armed Services Committee would act on that manpower request, just as it acts on other requests, and then the portion of the manpower proposal dealing with intelligence would be referred to the intelligence committee for their review. Is that correct?

Mr. RIBICOFF. That is the way I interpret it.

Mr. NUNN. If there were a difference between, say, what the Committee on Armed Services authorized in terms of manpower and what the intelligence community authorized in terms of manpower how would that difference be brought to the Chamber?

The PRESIDING OFFICER. The Senator's time has expired.

Mr. NUNN. I know the Senate would resolve it. But how would it be brought to the Chamber?

Mr. RIBICOFF. Mr. President, I yield myself 1 additional minute.

I suppose the Senate would have to resolve this as they resolve all other conflicts. There is no difference. The Senate eventually is going to decide, and they will have to make that decision. But again, looking at the makeup of the committee, with eight members coming from basic committees and seven from the remainder of the Senate, and the Committee on Armed Services being well represented by two members, personally I do not think we are going to have any problems. I do not think we are going to ble that jealous or that shortsighted in this body.

Mr. NUNN. I thank the Senator from Connecticut. . . .

Mr. PERCY. Mr. President, the question comes up as to whether or not a consolidated committee is desirable and whether or not defense intelligence should be included. My point simply is that because of the interlocking character of intelligence, the President's Executive order puts the DCI over all intelligence, including national intelligence, but excluding tactical intelligence.

The compromise substitute offered by the distinguished Senator from Nevada (Mr. CANNON) does exactly the same thing. The administration, as I understand the testimony that witnesses gave, supports the concept of placing all intelligence in one committee. The administration made it clear that to avoid the proliferation of testimony which Mr. Colby said consumed, in 3 years, 60 percent of his time, leaving him only 40 percent of his time to administer the Central Intelligence Agency, it would prefer a joint committee. But they have made it clear that if it is the wisdom of the Senate and the House to decide on separate committees, that is our decision. And it is the decision of the Committee on Government Operations, the Committee on Rules, and the compromise group that have worked together that the Senate of the United States should establish its own committee.

I wish to read to my distinguished colleagues the words of Mr. George Bush, Director of the Central Intelligence Agency. Mr. Bush said:

The Central Intelligence Agency welcomes strong and effective congressional oversight. We have a great deal to gain from it. We gain the advice and counsel of knowledgeable Members. Through it, we can maintain the trust and support of the American people. We will retain the support only so long as the people remain confident that the political structure provides clear accountability of our intelligence services, through effective executive and congressional oversight.

Good oversight will insure that the intelligence agencies operate as the government— and the Nation—wish them to. But in establishing this accountability; I believe the Congress must also insure that oversight enhances, rather than hinders, the vital operations of our intelligence agencies.

Certainly, the Senator from Illinois has been deeply concerned about this. I have been satisfied that the compromise resolution takes that into account.

I close the quotation from Mr. George Bush by quoting this sentence:

And so I urge concentrated oversight.

What he does not want is fractionalized oversight. The Director of Central Intelligence would like to have effective meaningful oversight, but concentrated oversight.

I turn to the testimony given before the Committee on Government Operations. I wish to point out several prominent people who have testified, first from the Senate itself. Senator MANSFIELD emphatically believes in the creation of a new committee that would provide consolidated oversight. Senator CHURCH said:

We need a new committee. The work cannot be done on a piecemeal basis or by a subcommittee of another standing committee which is primarily engaged in a different preoccupation. It will require a well-staffed committee directing all of its attention to the intelligence community.

Senator BAKER favors a new committee. He said:

The greater good would be the prompt creation of a new standing Senate committee on intelligence oversight, even if this leaves to another day resolving the questions of prior notification of sensitive operations and the authority of the Senate to disclose classified information.

In all fairness, I would like to point out that our distinguished colleague from Texas (Mr. TOWER) did come in and testify. He opposed the creation of a new committee. Senator TOWER made it clear that he wants to leave reforms to the existing standing committees. But certainly, the Committee on Rules and Administration and the Committee on Government Operations overwhelmingly decided that that course was not one that we would recommend that the Senate follow.

Secretary Rusk testified. He testified that he was shocked to find, as Secretary of State, how many things were being done by intelligence agencies, not under his direct, day-by-day jurisdiction, but that involved foreign policy. He was shocked later, when he left office, to find how much had been carried on. He also stated very clearly to us that he would like to see a committee as quickly as possible.

Former Attorney General Katzenbach favors a new committee.

David Phillips, the president of the Association of Retired Intelligence Officers, stated that 98 percent of his membership favors some form of a new committee.

Mr. Colby, the past Director of CIA, said that he is in favor of "'a new committee with exclusive jurisdiction for the oversight of foreign intelligence."

McGeorge Bundy, former Assistant to the President for National Security, favors a new committee.

Mr. John McCone strongly urged a new committee.

Mr. Clark Clifford, former Secretary of Defense, favored a new committee.

Mr. Richard Helms said, "It is up to the Congress whether or not to have a new comimttee," but he thinks a committee would be an improvement.

So, overwhelmingly, it seemed to the Senator from Illinois, and unanimously to the members of the Committee on Government Operations, a new committee was needed and is necessary. On whether defense intelligence should be included or not, we came to the unanimous judgment in the Committee on Government Operations, on a vote of 16 to 0, that is should be included. DIA plays a role in covert actions—for example, the Schneider killing during the Chile Track II operation. Army counterintelligence was found spying on innocent Americans, bugging, taping, and opening mail.

As I pointed out before, the 5th Army was discovered performing intelligence operations—following the activities and keeping dossiers on such distinguished Illinois citizens as my distinguished colleague, Mr. ADLAI STEVENSON, who I presume was just as shocked as anybody else to learn that he and many prominent people were being followed by the 5th Army and dossiers were being kept on them. Obviously, it has been revealed by our own intelligence committee how much spying on innocent Americans was engaged in without proper oversight.

Military clandestine intelligence activities were supervised by the CIA. When we consider that only half of what the CIA spends comes from its own appropriations—the other half comes out of Defense appropriations through transfers or advances—certainly, it is desirable and necessary, I think mandatory, to include defense intelligence.

The question can be raised, what would the compromise substitute do to the jurisdiction of the Committee on Armed Services? The compromise would give the new select committee concurrent jurisdiction over major intelligence agencies of national importance, NSA and DIA. It would also have concurrent jurisdiction over joint defense-CIA programs and over clandestine military intelligence activities now supervised by the CIA.

The Committee on Armed Services would continue to have jurisdiction in this area and would continue exclusive jurisdiction over the bulk of tactical military intelligence. It is not impossible, as has been pointed out, to sort out these national intelligence elements from the defense budget. We have identified the relevant program elements.

The new Committee on Foreign Intelligence is charged with this task and with the responsibility for a national intelligence budget.

Certainly, the members of the Committee on Armed Services have a perfect right to ask this question: Will they, in the grave responsibilities that they have assumed and undertaken and have so ably carried out for so many years for the defense and security of the United States of America, be able to fulfill that function if they do not have the legislative authority over defense intelligence?

Certainly, the bill that is before us, the compromise version before us, in every conceivable way guarantees and insures that the end product of intelligence shall always be available to the Committee on Armed Services. There are not any ifs, ands, or buts about that assertion. Everybody in this body will know and recognize that they must have that, and the concurrent responsibility that they have over the defense budget seems to have been worked out in the compromise in such a way that I hope the majority of our colleagues today would defeat the pending amendment. . . .

Mr. THURMOND. Mr. President, I rise in support of amendment 1649, authored by the distinguished Senator from Texas, Mr. TOWER, and cosponsored by the chairman of the Senate Armed Services Committee, Mr. STENNIS, and myself, the ranking minority member of Armed Services.

This amendment would, in effect, remove from the proposed Select Committee on Intelligence the joint jurisdiction over the Department of Defense Intelligence Agencies. These would include the intelligence programs of the three separate services and the Defense Intelligence Agency and the National Security Agency.

It might be well to offer an initial and brief explanation of the activities of the agencies addressed in this amendment.

1. DEFENSE INTELLIGENCE AGENCY

The Defense Intelligence Agency is directly responsible to the Secretary of Defense and is the focal point of the military intelligence community. It maintains a balance in assimilating and analyzing the intelligence gathered by the separate military departments as well as its own efforts, all designed to enables the Secretary of Defense to act wisely on requests and programs of the military intelligence community.

2. NATIONAL SECURITY AGENCY

The National Security Agency deals with national or strategic intelligence and its collection and production apparatus serves not only the military, but other agencies of the Government such as the State Department and Treasury Department. The NSA is also the principal source for the National Security

Council and ultimately the President because its work goes beyond strictly military applications. It is charged primarily with much of the electronic apparatus used in intelligence gathering.

3. SERVICE INTELLIGENCE

In addition, each of the three military departments has a limited intelligence apparatus which is directed primarily in those areas of concern to the particular department.

For instance, the intelligence service of the Air Force is targeted on foreign military aircraft and foreign activities related to the air power while the Navy's intelligence apparatus is concerned with intelligence gathering submarines and estimates of capability of the Soviet and other foreign navies.

Mr. President, the definition of the work of these military agencies shows this amendment is not a capricious effort to dilute the strength of the proposed select committee. It represents a well thought out proposal upon which I feel there is a solid basis for support. This amendment deals strictly with military intelligence by military or DOD agencies. It does not involve the Central Intelligence Agency. Therefore, I would like to list some points which I feel in support of adoption of amendment 1649.

1. OVERLAP WITH SERVICE BUDGETS

It will be extremely difficult to separate the expenses of the separate military departments from the defense budget and present it as a separate request to the select committee. It is now more an estimate, but if dealt with exclusively by a single committee, the problem of cost identification becomes most complex.

Practically all of the intelligence activities of the military departments are performed by military personnel. In any one fiscal year, an individual may be on an intelligence assignment for only a portion of that year. He may be in a school in which only a portion of that period of training involves his intelligence duties. How does one decide how much of his salary should go in the intelligence budget? How much of his training should be charged to the intelligence budget? How much of the support he receives in the way of vehicle use, air transportation, secretarial support would go into the intelligence budget?

These examples illustrate the difficulty in separating military intelligence activities from the defense budget.

Furthermore, there are certain intelligence support activities which do not require authorization, but are dealt with only as to appropriations. Here again we have the problem of separating these activities and in so doing, we come back to the often-stated problem of more disclosure and ultimately more danger to our intelligence people and the effectiveness of their missions. Before closing on that point, I would like to cite a few examples.

NAVY EXAMPLE

For instance, when a submarine goes out on a mission, a part of its work may involve intelligence gathering. However, it will have other missions and how DOD can separate the costs and expenses in such a situation is beyond my comprehension.

AIR FORCE EXAMPLE

As another example, one might take the case of a pilot flying an intelligence mission in a military aircraft. How much of the cost of the aircraft, his salary, or support costs would be charged to intelligence? This plane may be used once or twice a year on intelligence missions.

Also, our committee will still have authorization over research and development programs involving intelligence. Do we have to clear our actions with the select committee? The bill language is not clear on this point.

These are but some of the problems in separating such budgets. Others will reveal themselves if this separation is required by the Senate.

2. DISCLOSURE

Mr. President, there is no doubt in my mind that to support this new committee of 15 members and a staff whose size is not defined in this bill, will require much more disclosure on the simple basis the information is being spread among a greater number of people.

Here again we are putting another layer on top of the four responsible Defense committees and the very separation of the intelligence operations from defense operations is going to lead to much, much greater disclosure.

3. IMPROVING MILITARY INTELLIGENCE

Mr. President, this step, in my judgment, in no way improves military intelligence. It may well have just the opposite effect by making intelligence work less attractive for our more qualified people because of the threat of disclosure which results by proliferation of data.

There is nothing apparent to me in this bill which improves military intelligence. It merely inserts another layer of authority. The Senate must realize that those abuses in the past would be better corrected by passage of new laws rather than new layers of legislative oversight and authorization. I certainly favor strengthening the oversight of the past, but when a President tells the Army to augment the Secret Service at a political convention, the Army can hardly be blamed for obeying that order. Oddly enough, these orders were never revealed, even to the Joint Chiefs nor to the Congress so it would appear to me that a law to control the Chief Executive would answer this issue if such is the will of Congress.

4. ADDITIONAL EXPENSES

Also, it seems every time some problem arises in Government the solution is to reorganize, insert another layer of supervision, add 50 more GS–18's in the executive branch, set up a new committee in Congress with a large staff, and in general, throw money at the problem.

The fact is that allowing the select committee authorization and legislative jurisdiction over the Defense intelligence activities will mean that these agencies will have to add to their personnel strength in order to respond to the requests for information and data which will be forthcoming from these new layers of supervision.

The Senate appears to ignore the point that the abuses and problems of the past few years in military intelligence agencies represent only possibly 2 or 3 percent of the entire intelligence effort. Yet we are restructuring the entire authorization program in an attempt to deal with a problem representing only 2 or 3 percent of the total effort. These problems could be dealt with by laws to prevent such abuses rather than an attempt to manage military defense intelligence agencies. Military intelligence will no longer be an arm of the executive branch, but rather an arm of the Congress.

5. COORDINATION WITH HOUSE

Mr. President, another point favoring this amendment is that the best information available to me indicates the House of Representatives plans to demand from the Executive that the intelligence budget be submitted as in the past. This raises another problem in establishing a select committee in the Senate, especially when DIA, NSA and other military intelligence activities are involved. The CIA, being a civilian agency not answerable to DOD, could possibly be separated from the defense budget, but I fail to see how the military agencies could be realistically separated.

In summary, Mr. President, this amendment should be approved by the Senate for any one of the reasons I have mentioned: First, there is the overlap of service budgets in the Defense request. Second, the problem of disclosure through proliferation. Third, the fact that this offers no improvement of military intelligence, but rather weakens it. Fourth, additional expenses will result

with little promise of improved intelligence production. Fifth, the problem of coordination with the House is highly aggravated.

Mr. President, these are but a few of the reasons I am cosponsoring the proposed amendment. This amendment makes a great deal of sense and I urge my colleagues to give it their most careful consideration before casting their vote.

Mr. President, I yield back the remainder of my time.

Mr. STENNIS. I thank the Senator very much for his very timely remarks and very convincing argument. . . .

Mr. STENNIS. Mr. President, I yield 5 minutes to the Senator from Arizona.

Mr. GOLDWATER. Mr. President, I support the amendment.

I believe we have to divide intelligence, as we are discussing it here today, into many, many facets. The resolution that established the select committee, in my opinion, was a wise one. Our job, supposedly, was that of ferreting out wrongdoings so far as intelligence gathering was concerned with respect to the American citizen. That is one form of intelligence. We have intelligence gathered from embassies by tapping. We have intelligence gathered by mail.

Mr. President, I am anxious to support this amendment, and I call attention to the fact that the amendment would remove from the proposed new select committee legislative jurisdiction over the Department of Defense intelligence. Why is this important?

Last week, I read several books, with which hindsight always can provide us, as to what we actually knew about the intent of the Japanese before Pearl Harbor. It was amazing. Had we had a properly working intelligence agency at that time, with the information we had gathered from a number of sources, none related to the other, we almost could have predicted the attack on Pearl Harbor to the hour. We could have resisted it and defeated the Japanese without any trouble at all. But because we did not have an intelligence agency such as the CIA at that time, we depended upon the warring factions in the services and the civilians in the War Department and the President, himself. We got ourselves into a very costly war.

That is why I support this amendment—not to prevent the establishment of a committee to have so-called oversight, but to allow the Committee on Armed Services to have that sole jurisdiction because, Mr. President, I do not care if you have a committee of one, it is almost impossible to stop leaks. As hard as our special committee tried, we could not bottle them all up, and, of course, the House was a sieve. It leaked, leaked, and leaked.

Under the Committee on Armed Services, we would handle just that intelligence that applies to the military, nothing else—no interest in the FBI, no interest in anything except the intelligence that the military has to gather.

Mr. President, I remind my colleagues in this body who have had experience in war or experience with the military that the estimate of the situation is a little formula that we are taught almost before we know what the rest of the service is about. The primary part of the estimate of the situation is intelligence: What does the enemy have, what does the enemy intend to do with what he has, what does he know about what we have, and what does he know about what we intend to do with out intelligence? Then, by working the two against each other, we come up with some possible lines of action. But if this information is made public, as we watched it be made public from the other body and from leaks downtown, then the estimate of the situation gets to be pretty much of a joke.

I know Members of this body are concerned about covert action. I know that Members feel that we should disclose, among the oversight function, any covert action. Well, Mr. President, this is dangerous. Those of us on the Committee on Armed Services, in spite of what our colleagues might think, know of many, many covert actions that were practiced during the years, many of which prevented wars between other countries, many of which prevented ourselves from getting into trouble. So, military intelligence, to me, is a most sacred item and we should look on it as such; create a full committee to take care of the abuses upon the American people, but allow military intelligence to go as it has in the past. We have developed a very fine intelligence-gathering system. In fact, I just read on the ticker tape this morning that our old friend, Averell Harriman, has recommended to the Democratic Platform Committee that covert action not be stopped, that it be encouraged because, by covert action, properly done, we prevent wars; we do not get into them.

I am afraid if a 15-member committee is ever created and given the handle on military intelligence, covert action will become something that will be very overt and we will be fighting the battles on the floor of the Senate instead of doing it in a round-about, backward, sneaky way. Call it what you want, but by doing it that way, we will prevent American men and, now, American women from being called into battle.

I hope my colleagues will support this amendment. It is not an Earth-shaking amendment. It is not going to destroy the concept of the substitute Senate Resolution 400. It will, in my opinion, protect the best interests of our country.

Mr. RIBICOFF. Mr. President, I yield 1 minute to the distinguished Senator from North Carolina.

Mr. MORGAN. Mr. President, as I understand the amendment offered by Senators STENNIS and TOWER, it eliminates from the jurisdiction of the new select committee any jurisdiction over defense intelligence, which would include the Defense Intelligence Agency, the National Security Agency, and the intelligence activities of the three military departments.

Under the Cannon substitute,, the new select committee would have jurisdiction over defense intelligence, except for "tactical foreign military intelligence serving no national policymaking function."

Those Senators supporting the Stennis/Tower amendment argue that it is impossible, as a practical matter, to separate, for purposes of oversight, tactical intelligence activities from national intelligence activities. They therefore would opt for the Armed Services Committee to retain sole jurisdiction over all defense intelligence activities.

While I have great respect and admiration for the distinguished chairman of the Armed Services Committee, the findings of the Select Committee on Intelligence lead me to disagree with him on this point. I think that it is possible to separate those intelligence programs carried out by the Department of Defense which contribute to the national intelligence picture from those carried out to support tactical military units. The Department of Defense already distinguishes between tactical intelligence programs and national intelligence programs for purposes of its annual budget submissions to the Congress.

Furthermore, we have seen that the President's Executive order of February 17, 1976, places within the Director of Central Intelligence managerial responsibility for all national intelligence activities, including those of the Department of Defense. We have here, then, the executive branch distinguishing between "tactical" and "national" intelligence activities carried out by the Department of Defense, for purposes of managing the intelligence community. Should Congress not do the same?

I know this is a cloudy issue for a lot of Senators who are unfamiliar with how DOD conducts its intelligence activities, but I think that insofar as oversight is concerned, the dividing line would be quite clear. The new select committee, as I see it, would have concurrent jurisdiction over all DOD agencies and programs which were created primarily to collect and produce intelligence for our national intelligence estimates. The Armed Services Committee would retain sole jurisdiction over those agencies and programs of the Department of Defense designed primarily to produce intelligence for use by military commanders in the field. To be sure, there may be national intelligence activities which produce information useful to the military commander in the field, and, by the same token, tactical intelligence activities may produce information useful to the national intelligence picture. But insofar as oversight of these activities is concerned, the select committee would have concurrent jurisdiction over those activities designed to provide national intelligence, and the Armed Services Committee would have sole jurisdiction over those activities designed to produce tactical intelligence.

Unless the proposed intelligence committee does share jurisdiction over the national intelligence activities of the Department of Defense, I think its effectiveness will be seriously jeopardized. I say this for several reasons.

First, as several Senators have pointed out already, between 80 and 90 percent of the intelligence budget goes to the Department of Defense. To eliminate such a sizable amount of intelligence expenditures from the scrutiny of the new intelligence committee would be to make a mockery of it.

Second, I think it will be impossible for the new committee to study the performance of the intelligence community as a whole without looking at DOD. How, for instance, can we make a judgment about the performance of the intelligence community during a Mideast war or an Angolan crisis, unless we have military intelligence in to explain its role? And how will we have their cooperation in these studies unless we have some type of oversight authority?

Third, I fear that if, in the future, the Committee on Armed Services proves to be more favorable than the proposed select committee to intelligence activities or intelligence expenditures, we will see the intelligence community decide to have military undertake more and more cf its activities in order to avoid facing the tougher committee. In sohrt, I think that the Stennis/Tower amendment will not result in even-handed oversight of the intelligence community.

Finally, I am concerned that leaving military intelligence in the exclusive hands of the Committee on Armed Services will not result in the type of oversight we need to protect the rights and privacy of our citizens. I remind my colleagues of the Church committee findings which showed that numerous activities of the Department of Defense resulted in violations of individual rights, none of which were ever investigated by the Committee on Armed Services. I point to the existence of the NSA's Watch List and Project Shamrock, and the domestic surveillance activities of the Army during the late 1960's. In this latter case, the investigation of Army surveillance was undertaken not by the Committee on Armed Services but by a Judiciary subcommittee.

The Church committee report also found that there are approximately 5,000 military investigators still in the United States. Can we be satisfied that these 5,000 investigators are staying within legitimate bounds by depending on the Committee on Armed Services?

In short, Mr. President, I do not think we will have an effective committee or effective oversight if Defense intelligence is left out of the committee's jurisdiction. I urge my colleagues to vote against the amendment offered by Senators STENNIS and TOWER. . . .

Mr. CHURCH. Mr. President, I thank the Senator very much for his remarks.

Mr. President, the Stennis amendment would strip the oversight committee of all legislative authority over strategic intelligence agencies which operate under the aegis of the Pentagon.

The resolution, the substitute resolution, does not take anything away from the Armed Services Committee. It does not in any way intrude upon the legislative authority that that committee possesses.

All this resolution does is to establish concurrent legislative authority so that the oversight committee might have adequate power to do its job.

But the Armed Services Committee, speaking through its distinguished chairman, opposed sharing any legislative authority with respect to those agencies that operate under the Defense Department.

It ought to be made clear, Mr. President, that we are speaking here only of those agencies within the Defense Department that are primarily concerned with strategic or sometimes what is called national intelligence. We are not at all concerned with, and we are not even reaching for, the Army intelligence.

the Air Force intelligence, or the Naval intelligence, which is purely military and purely technical.

We are talking about those agencies within the Defense Department that deal with the collection, the dissemination, and the assessment of political and economic intelligence under the direction of the DCI, strategic intelligence, and that we must have if the oversight committee is to do its job.

Mr. President, I suggest that if this amendment is adopted it will deny the oversight committee the leverage it needs to deal effectively with those intelligence agencies which account for the great bulk of the spending. It has already been mentioned if this amendment is adopted what it means is that between 80 and 90 percent of the spending for intelligence is excluded from the legislative reach of the oversight committee, and I think that is no minor matter. In fact, instead of a club, the adoption of this amendment would leave the oversight committee with nothing more than a small stick, and would gut the committee.

Now, the substitute resolution, on the other hand, gives the oversight committee sufficient legislative reach to embrace the whole intelligence community. Thus, the oversight committee would be the congressional counterpart to the way the executive branch itself organizes and administers national intelligence.

This is a seamless web, Mr. President. If you look at the way the executive branch pulls it all together, you will see the so-called military agencies actually operate under the direction of the DCI; they operate under the direction of an overall intelligence board. This is all of a piece, and it has to be left of a piece, and if you do not give the oversight committee jurisdiction to handle as a piece then you, of course, deny the committee effective oversight authority.

Everyone who has served in the Senate knows that the power of the purse is the ultimate test. To deny the oversight committee the power of the purse where the intelligence community is concerned would be to effectively undermine its role.

Furthermore, Mr. President, if this amendment is adopted it gets us right back to the problem we are trying to solve. For years the problem has been there has been no committee in Congress that could reach out and embrace the entire intelligence community. Now we have one if this substitute resolution is adopted. But if the Stennis amendment is approved, we are right back to where we started from. The net, that seamless web, has been broken, and we are back

to piecemeal jurisdiction distributed among several committees of Congress no one of which can do the job.

So, Mr. President, I do hope that in consideration of the need that has been demonstrated during the past 15 months of investigation, and the abuse we found, some of which occurred within the Defense Department—the National Security Agency was one of those that, contrary to the laws of the land, intercepted hundreds of thousands of cables and read them in a massive fishing expedition for intelligence information, all contrary to the statutes of this country.

So these agencies need to be supervised, and the oversight committee needs to have such reach so it may deal with the overall national strategic intelligence community the same way that the executive branch deals with it. Only then will you have effective senatorial oversight. Only then will you be assured that the abuses that we found in the course of this investigation can be prevented from reoccurring in the future.

So I do hope that the Senate, in its wisdom, will reject the amendment.

Mr. MONDALE. Mr. President, will the Senator yield?

Mr. CHURCH. Yes.

Mr. MONDALE. The argument was made today that not much of the scope of the abuses that were uncovered occurred in this area of defense intelligence. So I asked the staff to bring over just the copies of the reports that deal in detail with abuses occurring exclusively in the defense intelligence areas: One dealing with surveillance of private citizens, one dealing with the National Security Agency, and each of these going into detail showing over many years in a broad and deep scope the abuse of human rights and legal rights by these agencies.

If we proceed as this amendment proposes, to exempt these agencies, not only do we exempt 80 percent of the intelligence budget but we will be creating a situation where if they wanted to repeat what has happened in the past they would simply shift these activities over into the defense intelligence agencies because these agencies can do and have done, as this record shows, precisely the things that we seek to prevent.

Mr. CHURCH. I agree wholeheartedly with the Senator. He is correct in everything he said.

Mr. President, I yield the floor.

The PRESIDING OFFICER. The time of the Senator from Connecticut has expired. The time the Senator from Mississippi has left is 10 minutes.

Mr. STENNIS. Mr. President, I yield 6 minutes to the Senator from Texas.

Mr. TOWER. Mr. President, the issue here is not whether or not we should have oversight. I think everybody agrees that we should have oversight. The question is whether or not we are proceeding on the presumption that a committee set up specifically for that purpose can do a more perfect job than the other committees having jurisdiction over various elements of the intelligence-gathering communities.

I submit that it cannot.

Now, inherent in the proposal of this resolution is the suggestion that the Armed Services Committee has been derelict in its duties for lo these 25-plus years since the Central Intelligence Agency has been in existence.

I reject that notion. If there has been any dereliction, then the entire U.S. Senate and the House of Representatives must bear the responsibility because this was the accepted way of doing business for so many years. Then when abuses were brought to our attention, we reacted, and quite properly, in mandating a special investigation.

That brings up a point, the Senator from Idaho says that without legislative jurisdiction the oversight committee would not have sufficient authority and power to deal with the business of oversight.

I reject that notion because the select committee which he so ably chaired actually got everything it wanted and it had absolutely no legislative authority. All it could do was make recommendations.

I submit that a better way to maintain oversight would be to allow the jurisdiction in terms of oversight of our various intelligence-gathering activities to continue to lodge in the committees that now exercise that jurisdiction.

I think that the process could be perfected by the creation of, in the case of the Armed Services Committee, a permanent subcommittee with a permanent professional staff required to report to the Senate on a regular basis.

The thing I fear about this oversight committee that is supposed to resolve all of our problems regarding the intelligence community is that it is going to create more problems than it solves. Certainly, it is going to create problems in terms of the effectiveness of our clandestine activities.

Now, already, the debate on this resolution preceding that investigation, the Senate-House committee, has undermined foreign confidence in the ability of the United States to carry on intelligence-related activities in a confidential way.

We have damaged our credibility with the intelligence services of allied nations and they feel less disposed to cooperate with us now, feeling that much might be disclosed about their own operations if they do cooperate with us.

So what we are doing here is engaging in an exercise that, in my view, has the potential for seriously undermining the intelligence-gathering capability of the United States.

I cannot see that the need for the creation of such a committee, whatever the merits in the proposal are, outweigh the potential dangers to the security of the United States in terms of the proliferation of disclosure of confidential, classified and sensitive information.

The fact of the matter is that in the creation of this new committee we do not solve the problem of the proliferation, we exacerbate that problem.

Now, we have a brand new committee of 15 members, we also have a staff, for every member plus the regular permanent staff, and this is an enormous undertaking, particularly when we consider all the security precautions this committee will have to take.

This means that the potential for disclosure of sensitive information increases geometrically rather than arithmetically and the potential is very much there.

Yes, the select committee had a pretty good record of not leaking that which it chose not to disclose. I think the committee chose to disclose more than it should have.

The PRESIDING OFFICER. The Senator's time has expired.

Mr. STENNIS. I yield the Senator a minute.

Mr. TOWER. But we can always expect this to be the case.

The experience in the House is that the House committee, investigating intelligence committee, did not leak; it poured.

There is a vast potential for mischief here. This is not a committee that is being established on the basis of popular demand. The popular fear in this country, by citizens generally, is not that the CIA and the FBI are going to invade their rights, because most people being law-abiding, have no such fears Their concern is that other agencies of the government have intruded much too much in their lives.

The preponderance of the American people believe, I feel, that we have disclosed too much, not too little, and the dangerous potential is here, that we shall disclose much more and that we will impact adversely against the security of the United States through such action.

Mr. STENNIS. Mr. President, I just have one point.

This effort about holding disclosure to a minimum, everyone understands that we are not trying to keep the information away from the Senators or from the American people. This means disclosures to our adversaries, those that are pitted against us, that are planning against us.

I am sorry that there has not been more said about better ways of getting intelligence. Everything here directed about disclosures, demand, everybody have access. Let us have some better ways of getting better intelligence, more accurate intelligence, better system, better method, better arrangement, better protection for our men and those we hire, better alternative methods, will bring better and more valuable results.

I hope that this little amendment—and it is small—for the protection of this part of the intelligence program will be passed.

Mr. ROBERT C. BYRD. Mr. President, I ask unanimous consent that it be in order, with one show of hands, to order the yeas and nays on the pending Stennis-Tower amendment, the Cannon substitute, and Senate Resolution 400, as amended.

The PRESIDING OFFICER. Is there objection?

Without objection, it is so ordered.

Mr. ROBERT C. BYRD. Mr. President, I ask for the yeas and nays.

The PRESIDING OFFICER. Is there a sufficient second? There is a sufficient second.

The yeas and nays were ordered.

Mr. STENNIS. Mr. President, a parliamentary inquiry.

The PRESIDING OFFICER. The Senator will state it.

Mr. STENNIS. What is the pending matter now before the Senate?

The PRESIDING OFFICER. The amendment No. 1649 to amendment No. 1643 to Senate Resolution 400.

Mr. STENNIS. Is that the amendment that has been referred to here as the Tower-Stennis-Thurmond amendment?

The PRESIDING OFFICER. The Senator is correct, the Tower-Stennis amendment. . . .

The PRESIDING OFFICER. All time has been yielded back. The question is on agreeing to the amendment. The yeas and nays have been ordered and the clerk will call the roll.

The legislative clerk called the roll.

Mr. ROBERT C. BYRD. I announce that the Senator from Michigan (Mr. HART), the Senator from Indiana (Mr. HARTKE), and the Senator from Wyoming (Mr. McGEE), are necessarily absent.

Mr. GRIFFIN. I announce that the Senator from Tennessee (Mr. BAKER), the Senator from North Carolina (Mr. HELMS), and the Senator from Delaware (Mr. ROTH), are necessarily absent.

On this vote, the Senator from North Carolina (Mr. HELMS) is paired with the Senator from Tennessee (Mr. BAKER). If present and voting, the Senator from North Carolina would vote "yea" and the Senator from Tennessee would vote "nay."

The result was announced—yeas 31, nays 63, as follows:

[Rollcall Vote No. 179 Leg.]

YEAS—31

Allen	Fong	Scott, Hugh
Bartlett	Garn	Scott,
Bellmon	Goldwater	William L.
Brock	Hansen	Sparkman
Buckley	Hruska	Stennis
Byrd,	Johnston	Stevens
Harry F., Jr.	Laxalt	Taft
Cannon	Long	Talmadge
Curtis	McClellan	Thurmond
Eastland	McClure	Tower
Fannin	Nunn	Young

NAYS—63

Abourezk	Gravel	Montoya
Bayh	Griffin	Morgan
Beall	Hart, Gary	Moss
Bentsen	Haskell	Muskie
Biden	Hatfield	Nelson
Brooke	Hathaway	Packwood
Bumpers	Hollings	Pastore
Burdick	Huddleston	Pearson
Byrd, Robert C.	Humphrey	Pell
Case	Inouye	Percy
Chiles	Jackson	Proxmire
Church	Javits	Randolph
Clark	Kennedy	Ribicoff
Cranston	Leahy	Schweiker
Culver	Magnuson	Stafford
Dole	Mansfield	Stevenson
Domenici	Mathias	Stone
Durkin	McGovern	Symington
Eagleton	McIntyre	Tunney
Ford	Metcalf	Weicker
Glenn	Mondale	Williams

NOT VOTING—6

Baker	Hartke	McGee
Hart, Philip A.	Helms	Roth

So the Tower-Stennis amendment (No. 1649) was rejected. . . .

ADDITIONAL STATEMENTS ON THE CANNON SUBSTITUTE AMENDMENT

Mr. ROBERT C. BYRD. Mr. President, as a member of the Committee on Rules, I have worked closely with other Senators in writing the substitute amendment offered by Mr. CANNON to Senate Resolution 400. I am keenly aware of the compelling need for effective oversight of the intelligence community, and I also recognize that the best interests of the United States demand that the intelligence community must be able to function effectively and that there are matters which, in the national interest, the Government must be able to keep from public disclosure.

I believe that the compromise substitute offered by Senator CANNON and myself and other Senators to Senate Resolution 400 will provide the best legislative response to these legitimate competing interests.

The membership of the new committee would be drawn from the entire Senate, while at the same time drawing from the substantive committees which have expertise in intelligence-gathering matters—recognizing that members from these committees not only must continue to work closely with intelligence matters to enable their committees to fulfill their responsibilities properly; but, also that these members bring a special understanding and knowledge of intelligence activity matters to the new select committee.

The new committee, in exercising exclusive jurisdiction over the CIA, will be able to deal with the complexities of intelligence activities, without the burden of responsibility over other large areas of legislation which the substantive committees now shoulder. Centralization of responsibility for the CIA in one committee, while providing for closer oversight, also decreases the risks of inadvertent publication of highly sensitive material on the part of the Senate. Conversely, responsibility to only one Senate committee demands and will allow full cooperation and candor with that committee on the part of the CIA.

At the same time, the compromise proposal offered as a substitute for Senate Resolution 400, recognizes that in other areas of the intelligence community, the working relationship of the intelligence arm of the respective departments and agencies are so closely intertwined with the other activities of the departments that isolated oversight of these intelligence activities by one Senate committee would be detrimental to the proper functioning of both the affected department and the Senate in carrying out its constitutional oversight responsibilities.

The compromise also provides adequate protection against unwarranted disclosure of sensitive material, I believe, thus correcting a serious deficiency in the original bill.

Mr. President, it is a most difficult task to shift jurisdiction in the Senate to allow for the changing priorities which the national interest demands. It is not that our present committee structure did not want, or try, to prevent abuses in the intelligence community—the fact is that the intelligence activities of our Government have grown so large and so complex that the substantive committees, with all of their other heavy responsibilities, could not hope to give the necessary time and develop the specialized expertise needed to constantly monitor and effectively control the intelligence community.

Recognizing the reality that an effective intelligence community is an absolute necessity for our country's security, but also realizing that past abuses by some segments of the intelligence community require the Senate to act to restructure itself in such a way as to be able to exert the necessary legislative oversight to prevent future abuses, I urge the Senate to adopt the Cannon substitute proposal and pass Senate Resolution 400 as so amended.

Mr. TAFT. Mr. President, after a thorough study of the issues involved, and after actively participating in the debate on Senate Resolution 400 as well as offering several amendments thereto, I am constrained to vote against the so-called Cannon compromise. This is not to say that I do not favor a central committee of the Senate which would have legislative and even perhaps appropriations jurisdiction over our intelligence activities. I believe we all agree on the objectives for creating such a body—more adequate and continuing control on the part of the Congress over our various intelligence functions. But I differ with the Cannon compromise with respect to the means employed to achieve these objectives.

I believe that the compromise in several ways is premature and hastily drawn. The compromise calls for the creation of a select committee of the Senate which in effect has the powers and authority of a standing committee of the Senate. The substitute establishes a wholly new intelligence committee with legislative, budgetary, and oversight jurisdiction wrapped up in one committee. It is my view that this is extremely serious undertaking and should not be approved until all of the implications of creating a committee like this have been thoroughly developed over an extended period of time.

I believe it is also proper to have an informed input from the select committee to study the Senate committee system prior to our adoption of the compromise resolution. It would certainly seem logical that any proposal to establish in effect a standing committee of the Senate should receive study by the committee which the Senate has authorized for that purpose in conjunction with its overall study of committee jurisdictions. I believe we are depriving our Select Study Committee of jurisdiction over a matter which the Senate has previously agreed is eminently within the jurisdiction of this body.

I have additional problems with the compromise resolution as it presently stands. I successfully offered two amendments during the debate on this measure which I feel will strengthen the resolution. However, one of my amendments dealing with the Senators' committee assignments was defeated yesterday and I believe that this was a crushing blow to the establishment of a new Select Committee on Intelligence. Without going into detail into this issue, which is a matter of record, I believe that we have not given this committee a realistic chance to succeed because there is no accommodation made for a Senators' work on this select committee with his normal activities in the conduct of other senatorial committee assignments.

I am also concerned that the pending substitute will cause a proliferation of committee involvement in intelligence matters and will unavoidably lead to greater disclosures of our intelligence activities. While I recognize that the bill does provide for controls over unauthorized disclosure of classified information and while there is a provision for the Senate to investigate unauthorized disclosures, I am still not satisfied that we have tightened this area sufficiently so as to fully protect our intelligence secrets. I will continue to monitor this area assuming the select committee comes into being and if there are violations and abuses, I am prepared to offer legislation to impose criminal sanctions on the violators in addition to the disciplinary rules contained in the Standing Rules of the Senate.

For all of these reasons, I would prefer the approach taken by the Rules Committee which would establish a Senate Select Committee on Intelligence with oversight jurisdiction over the intelligence community, but would leave within the various standing committees the legislative jurisdiction in respect to intelligence activities.

I believe that a separate oversight committee, fully and currently informed and having a subpena power, can provide effective oversight for the intelligence community without a grant of legislative jurisdiction. This statement is borne out by virtue of the experience of the Select Senate and House Intelligence Committees which have very successfully exposed the abuses while not having legislative authority.

Mr. President, it seems to me that in order for the Senate to succeed in this area, it must work with the House of Representatives in fashioning a joint committee of Congress acceptable to both bodies. Legislative activity as broad as what we are providing for in this select committee has got to be done in conjunction with the House of Representatives if we are to gain control over our intelligence area. The beauty of adopting the Rules Committee approach is that it would furnish us with sufficient time to further study this prospect while at the same time not diminish our inquiry into the status of our intelligence functions. I note that Congressman CEDERBERG has for himself and the minority leader of the House, introduced a joint resolution to provide for the establishment of a Joint Committee on Intelligence which I believe shows a willingness on the part of the House to engage in a constructive dialog on creating a committee of this kind.

I would like to have the opportunity and time to develop this aspect further and it appears to me that we are going to foreclose this possibility by approving this Senate Select Intelligence Committee today.

Mr. KENNEDY. Mr. President, I strongly support the compromise amendment to Senate Resolution 400, offered by Senator CANNON and others, which I am pleased to cosponsor. This proposed substitute, as amended, would establish a permanent Select Committee on Intelligence Activities composed of 15 Members of the Senate, appointed on a rotating basis.

The committee will have full oversight, legislative, and budgetary authority over the Government's national intelligence activities. Its jurisdiction will not only cover the Central Intelligence Agency, but also the Defense Intelligence Agency, the National Security Agency, and the intelligence activities of other agencies—including the Federal Bureau of Investigation.

Although we are considering this resolution in the wake of the reports recently issued by the Senate Select Committee on Intelligence Activities and the President's Commission on CIA activities, the need for such a permanent intelligence oversight committee was recognized by the Hoover Commission over 20 years ago. In 1956 the Senate Rules Committee recommended the creation of a new congressional unit "to gather information and make independent checks and appraisals of CIA activities." Numerous other studies and reports since that time have reemphasized the need for closer more continuous, and more sophisticated oversight of intelligence activities of the Federal Government.

Under the able leadership of Senator CHURCH, the Select Committee on Intelligence Activities explored for over a year the various intelligence programs, agencies, expenditures, and activities of the Federal Government. Whatever doubts may have existed before, the over 1,000 pages of final report recently issued by that committee make it imperative that we proceed with dispatch to set up a permanent committee with broad jurisdiction and adequate powers to keep a watch over and maintain a check on the activities of all the agencies of the Federal Government dealing with intelligence.

It has taken the Intelligence Committee seven volumes of hearings and two volumes of reports to uncover, document, and analyze the intelligence activities of various Federal agencies. It would be impossible to describe in any brief floor remarks the scope of the abuses of power contained in that record.

It is replete with descriptions of bugging, wiretapping, mail opening, surreptitious entry, infiltration, assassination plots, drug experimentation, clandestine military operations, character assassinations, and more, all carried out under the banner of intelligence gathering and the protection of our national security. And all were carried out secretly, without public or congressional knowledge, without adequate controls or checks from within or without.

The establishment of a permanent Senate committee to keep tabs on the Governments' intelligence community is only the first step. Congress must proceed to develop comprehensive charters for the intelligence agencies, and guidelines for their activities. We must reorganize portions of those agencies, establish firm chains of command within and constant reporting and approval mechanisms without.

We must establish a statutory classification system and enact laws governing national security electronic surveillance. The list goes on and on. But at its head is the need to put in place a committee to oversee and study the intelligence activities and programs of our Government, to develop and review legislation concerning them, and to insure that they are in conformity with the Constitution and laws of our land.

Senate Resolution 400 has been before various committees of the Senate for over 2 months. It has been studied and debated, revised and revised again. But until the introduction of the Cannon substitute last week. What had emerged from these studies and debates and revisions was a division of this body into two basic groups—those who would put in place a permanent strong committee, equipped with the authority and jurisdiction to do the immense and difficult job of overseeing Government intelligence operations, and those who would construct a committee of paper maché, having the appearance of solidity but remaining thin on the outside and hollow on the inside. The Stennis amendment, which would strip the new committee of its jurisdiction over Defense Department intelligence functions—including DIA and NSA—reflects this second choice.

If we choose the latter course, then we are saying that the Senate tradition of ignoring the use and abuse of immense power and perhaps billions of dollars in the intelligence field is to be continued. We are choosing to put our heads back in the sand, knowing nonetheless that what we do not know and will not know could hurt us, thousands of other Americans, and our democratic society.

The evidence we have makes the former course the only responsible one. The proposed substitute to Senate Resolution 400, as it stands now, would arm the Senate with the tools to fulfill our constitutional duty to provide the controls and guidance over executive branch intelligence activities. In taking this road we are not acting as if intelligence is unimportant to our Nation. We are not saying that we should drop our guard against genuine foreign challenges to our national security. But we are asserting that Congress intends to play a direct role, a firm role, in guiding the conduct of intelligence activities and in protecting the rights and liberties of all American citizens.

I would like to turn my attention for a moment to the matter of the jurisdiction of the new committee proposed to be established by the substitute to Senate Resolution 400, which I am joining in proposing. As a member of the Senate Committee on the Judiciary, I had the occasion to hear testimony and join debate over whether any new permanent Senate Intelligence Oversight Committee should have jurisdiction to oversee the intelligence activities of the Federal Bureau of Investigation. I came away convinced that while the Judiciary Committee must maintain its historic jurisdiction over every aspect of the Bureau's operations, the new committee should nonetheless be vested with authority over the FBI's intelligence activities.

There are two reasons for this conclusion: First, there have been a myriad of abuses by the FBI, under the guise of domestic intelligence and counterintelligence, which have basically gone unchecked and undisclosed, despite the Judiciary Committee's interest in and involvement with the Bureau. And second, setting aside the issue of abuses, there is a legitimate role which the FBI has—as a full member of the intelligence community—which takes it into realms that can often best be understood and guided by a committee with broader jurisdiction over foreign intelligence activities of other agencies of Government as well.

The abuses of authority by the Federal Bureau of Investigation in the intelligence area are by now all too well known. They are not limited to narrow timeframes or circumscribed geographic areas. Nor, more importantly, do they reflect the isolated acts of zealous agents out on a frolic of their own. Instead, those abuses were embodied in on-going bureaucratic programs, ordered and approved at the highest levels, spanning the country and continuing for years.

The Bureau's counterintelligence programs were, in its own words, designed to "expose, disrupt and otherwise neutralize" political groups in the United States. The Cointelpro program, targeted against five groups, extended over 15 years and was found by the Department of Justice itself to have involved practices "abhorrent to a free society." Attorney General Levi stated that many of the Bureau's activities in this field were not only "foolish," but were also "illegal."

The FBI's bag of intelligence tricks included wiretapping, burglaries, surveillance, and abusive disruptive practices. And it also included efforts to discredit and harass American citizens whose only offense was to provide leadership in the antiwar and civil rights movements.

But I do not want to dwell solely on the misuse and abuse of FBI power so thoroughly documented by the Church committee. Because, Mr. President, it is clear that even without straying from its lawful and legitimate course, the FBI retains responsibilities that are not directed primarily toward law enforcement, but which are aimed at collecting intelligence information for our Government and at blocking attempts by foreign governments from collecting information from us.

On February 18 of this year President Ford issued an Executive order governing U.S. foreign intelligence activities. In that order, the FBI was listed alongside the Central Intelligence Agency, the National Security Agency, and the Department of Defense as a full-fledged member of the "foreign intelligence community."

In fact, while the CIA was charged with carrying out "foreign counterintelligence activities," the FBI was charged with conducting "foreign counterintelligence activities within the United States." I stress, Mr. President, that the only difference in the characterization of the responsibilities between the CIA and the FBI is the use of the geographic limitation which sets the CIA's duties outside our country, the FBI's inside. Incidentally, the Executive order spells out the Bureau's responsibilities in some detail, but not once in that order is law enforcement or prosecution for violating Federal laws mentioned.

In short, the FBI, while fundamentally a law-enforcement agency, is also an intelligence-gathering agency. In its report on Senate Resolution 400, the Rules Committee observed that "the intelligence activity of the FBI is a means by which it detects and investigates violations of Federal criminal laws." In fact, as the President's Executive order, the Bureau's own guidelines and organization chart, and testimony before the Judiciary Committee make clear, this is simply not the case. The Intelligence Division of the Bureau performs activities in the United States similar in nature to what the CIA does abroad. No direct law-enforcement nexus is necessary in the conduct of the Bureau's intelligence and counterintelligence programs.

Finally, it is difficult, and often impossible, to draw clear lines between the law enforcement and the intelligence functions of the FBI. Nor is there any clear line dividing domestic-oriented from foreign-oriented activities.

Mr. President, I would also like to point out for the record that while the Rules Committee report on Senate Resolution 400 contains what are called "recommendations of the Committee on the Judiciary," 7 of the 15 members of that committee dissented from those recommendations. Those 7 members joined in a letter to the Rules Committee, which was not reflected in its report, urging that the new Intelligence Committee retain concurrent legislative jurisdiction over FBI intelligence activities.

It seems plain to me, Mr. President, that if there are two committees in the Senate—one predominately concerned with law enforcement and the protection of constitutional rights, as is the Judiciary Committee, and the other predominately concerned with foreign intelligence, as will be the new Intelligence Committee—then both must have continuing, full, and active oversight and legislative jurisdiction over the intelligence activities of the Federal Bureau of Investigation.

As strong as I believe the case is for providing the Select Intelligence Committee with jurisdiction over FBI intelligence activities, that case is even stronger regarding the Defense Intelligence Agency, the National Security Agency, and other units of the Department of Defense. The Defense Department must be kept in check as to its activities both at home and abroad.

The Subcommittee on Constitutional Rights of the Judiciary Committee has documented the extensive nature of military surveillance of American citizens in the United States. Likewise the Church committee found that the Army Chief of Staff in 1967 approved a recommendation for "continuous counterintelligence investigations" to obtain information on "subversive personalities, groups or organizations." As later revised, the Army extended its intelligence gathering program beyond "subversion" and "dissident groups" to prominent persons who were friendly with or sympathetic to leaders of domestic civil disturbances. And even in the face of a Defense Department directive prohibiting military spying on civilians in the United States—as narrow as that directive is—that is evidence that the military has continued domestic surveillance.

One notable example of the Army's domestic activities was the pervasive Army presence in 1973 at Wounded Knee, S. Dak., where the Directorate of Military Support in the Pentagon coordinated the Army's participation in what was clearly a domestic disturbance. And my own subcommittees turned up widespread military drug testing programs which were geared to intelligence gathering and frankly showed little respect for the human subjects of the tests.

DOD's domestic intelligence-related activities, however, are but the tiniest tip of the iceberg. In fact, it has been estimated that of the total national intelligence budget, the Defense Department controls or is allocated upward of 80 percent. Much of what goes on with that money is still not in the public domain. And if the Stennis amendment is adopted by this body, much of what goes on with it will never be brought under any coordinated, effective, broad-based legislative oversight.

To place the CIA under the jurisdiction of the new intelligence committee, and at the same time to leave the Defense Department outside its purview, is worse than telling a boxer that he cannot hit below his opponent's waist with his left fist only. Because as much as we scrutinize the CIA, we cannot adequately control, chart, guide, or check abuses in Federal intelligence programs if the Select Intelligence Committee is not given authority over Defense Department intelligence activities. We may well wake up one day to find that many CIA activities have in fact been transferred over to Defense to escape congressional control.

We cannot delude ourselves. We know full well that the standing committees have not always performed their oversight tasks with vigilance or vigor. That is why we set up the Church committee to begin with. And that is why we are going to set up a permanent Select Committee on Intelligence Activities.

The Judiciary Committee had not uncovered, much less put a stop to, the wide range of FBI activities which violated the law but which have only recently come to light. Likewise, the Armed Services Committee has hardly done better in keeping an eye on the CIA and other intelligence agencies. We must establish a committee whose full-time job it is to look at Federal intelligence activities. And we must give that committee full authority over each and every Federal agency engaged in such activities.

The new committee must be empowered to obtain all relevant information it needs to do its job.

Further, by vesting in this new committee the shared jurisdiction over authorizing appropriations for all those intelligence activities, we will be giving that committee the clout and the control it will need.

I believe that one of the first tasks of this new committee should be to develop comprehensive charters for the carrying out of intelligence activities by the intelligence agencies. This will surely take an extraordinary investment of time and energy—one which is hardly likely to be undertaken by any of the present standing committees of the Senate. But if we are going to learn any lessons from the disclosures of the past, we cannot afford to lose any time in first making the hard decisions necessary and then installing firm limitations and guidelines to govern intelligence activities in the future.

As I stated earlier in these remarks, Mr. President, the Senate is confronted with a critical choice in this debate. We can elevate the traditions of the Senate—not only the tradition of zealously guarding committee jurisdictions against even slight encroachment, but also the tradition of ignoring what our intelligence agencies are doing—above the real needs of this Nation for legislative leadership in the intelligence field. Or we can dispense with petty institutional jealousies and put in place a committee which embodies our best efforts to fashion the broadest jurisdiction, the most sophisticated safeguards, and the strongest authority.

We cannot fool ourselves, and we should not try to fool the public: Any committee equipped with less jurisdiction or authority than provided in this substitute will not be capable of obtaining information from and exercising checks over those agencies which exercise such extreme power themselves and which have for so long eluded control by either the Congress or the Executive. And any committee without full jurisdiction across the range of all Federal agencies would stand as a monument to this body's willingness to cave in and cop out in the face of real challenge.

That is why I oppose the Stennis amendment and urge my colleagues to adopt the Cannon substitute as it now stands.

The PRESIDING OFFICER (Mr. SCHWEIKER). Under the previous order, the Senate will now proceed to vote on the amendment in the nature of a substitute, as amended, of the Senator from Nevada. (Mr. CANNON). On this question, the yeas and nays have been ordered, and the clerk will call the roll.

The second assistant legislative clerk called the roll.

Mr. ROBERT C. BYRD. I announce that the Senator from Michigan (Mr. PHILIP. A. HART), the Senator from Indiana (Mr. HARTKE), and the Senator from Wyoming (Mr. McGEE) are necessarily absent.

Mr. GRIFFIN. I announce that the Senator from Tennessee (Mr. BAKER), the Senator from North Carolina (Mr. HELMS), and the Senator from Delaware (Mr. ROTH) are necessarily absent.

I further announce that, if present and voting, the Senator from Tennessee (Mr. BAKER), and the Senator from North Carolina (Mr. HELMS) would each vote "yea."

The result was announced—yeas 87, nays 7, as follows:

[Rollcall Vote No. 180 Leg.]

YEAS—87

Abourezk	Glenn	Moss
Bartlett	Goldwater	Muskie
Bayh	Gravel	Nelson
Beall	Griffin	Nunn
Bellmon	Hansen	Packwood
Bentsen	Hart, Gary	Pastore
Biden	Haskell	Pearson
Brock	Hatfield	Pell
Brooke	Hathaway	Percy
Buckley	Hollings	Proxmire
Bumpers	Huddleston	Randolph
Burdick	Humphrey	Ribicoff
Byrd,	Inouye	Schweiker
Harry F., Jr.	Jackson	Scott, Hugh
Byrd, Robert C.	Javits	Scott,
Cannon	Johnston	William L.
Case	Kennedy	Sparkman
Chiles	Laxalt	Stafford
Church	Leahy	Stennis
Clark	Long	Stevens
Cranston	Magnuson	Stevenson
Culver	Mansfield	Stone
Dole	Mathias	Symington
Domenici	McClellan	Talmadge
Durkin	McGovern	Tower
Eagleton	McIntyre	Tunney
Eastland	Metcalf	Weicker
Fong	Mondale	Williams
Ford	Montoya	Young
Garn	Morgan	

NAYS—7

Allen	Hruska	Thurmond
Curtis	McClure	
Fannin	Taft	

NOT VOTING—6

Baker	Hartke	McGee
Hart, Philip A	Helms	Roth

So Mr. CANNON's amendment (No. 1643), as amended, was agreed to. . . .

The PRESIDING OFFICER. Without objection, it is so ordered.

Under the previous order, the committee substitute, as amended, is considered as having been adopted, and the Senate will now proceed to vote on the question of agreeing to Senate Resolution 400, as amended.

On this question the yeas and nays have been ordered, and the clerk will call the roll.

The legislative clerk called the roll.

Mr. ROBERT C. BYRD. I announce that the Senator from Michigan (Mr. PHILIP A. HART), the Senator from Indiana (Mr. HARTKE), and the Senator from Wyoming (Mr. McGEE) are necessarily absent.

Mr. GRIFFIN. I announce that the Senator from Tennessee (Mr. BAKER), the Senator from North Carolina (Mr. HELMS), and the Senator from Delaware (Mr. ROTH) are necessarily absent.

On this vote, the Senator from Tennessee (Mr. BAKER) is paired with the Senator from North Carolina (Mr. HELMS). If present and voting, the Senator from Tennessee would vote "yea" and the Senator from North Carolina would vote "nay."

The result was announced—yeas 72, nays 22, as follows:

[Rollcall Vote No. 181 Leg.]

YEAS—72

Abourezk	Garn	Morgan
Bayh	Glenn	Moss
Beall	Gravel	Muskie
Bellmon	Griffin	Nelson
Bentsen	Hart, Gary	Nunn
Biden	Haskell	Packwood
Brooke	Hatfield	Pastore
Bumpers	Hathaway	Pearson
Burdick	Hollings	Pell
Byrd,	Huddleston	Percy
Harry F., Jr.	Humphrey	Proxmire
Byrd, Robert C.	Inouye	Randolph
Cannon	Jackson	Ribicoff
Case	Javits	Schweiker
Chiles	Kennedy	Scott, Hugh
Church	Leahy	Stafford
Clark	Magnuson	Stevens
Cranston	Mansfield	Stevenson
Culver	Mathias	Stone
Dole	McClellan	Symington
Domenici	McGovern	Tunney
Durkin	McIntyre	Weicker
Eagleton	Metcalf	Williams
Fong	Mondale	
Ford	Montoya	

NAYS—22

Allen	Hansen	Sparkman
Bartlett	Hruska	Stennis
Brock	Johnston	Taft
Buckley	Laxalt	Talmadge
Curtis	Long	Thurmond
Eastland	McClure	Tower
Fannin	Scott,	Young
Goldwater	William L.	

NOT VOTING—6

Baker	Hartke	McGee
Hart, Philip A.	Helms	Roth

So the resolution (S. Res. 400) was agreed to.

NOTES AND REFERENCES

1. A brief history of the handling of state secrets and Executive privilege, dating back to the early Republic, appears in [64], pp. 3–14.

2. President Richard M. Nixon's Executive Order 11652 is reprinted in the Appendix.

3. Since the 1972 hearings of Representative William Moorhead's House Foreign Operations and Government Information Subcommittee on security classification problems, the Freedom of Information Act has been amended. A Library of Congress report on the operations of FOIA was inserted into the *Congressional Record* of August 9, 1976 by Representative Bella Abzug, chairwoman of the House Subcommittee on Government Information and Individual Rights.

4. For a different estimate of the volume of classified documents, see the testimony of Deputy Under Secretary of State for Administration William Macomber. In his March 1972 hearing before the Senate Committee on Foreign Relations, he was also questioned on the overall problem of classification ([13]).

5. The government of Great Britain utilizes an "Official Secrets Act," which is reprinted in [28A], pp. 222 ff.

6. President Dwight D. Eisenhower's Executive Order 10501 refers to "Safeguarding Official Information in the Interests of the Defense of the United States." The text of this order appears in the *Federal Register*, November 9, 1953, vol. 18, pp. 7049 *et seq.*

7. Professor Raoul Berger's statement was preceded and followed by a colloquy with Senators Edward Kennedy and Edmund Muskie on the concept of Executive privilege, as articulated in testimony given earlier in the day by Attorney General Richard Kliendienst. While Berger questions the legal basis for a doctrine of Executive privilege, Kliendienst favored it and extended its use to include virtually anyone working within the Executive branch—if the president himself so wished it. (Consult [28A], pp. 10–52.) The Berger statement on Executive privilege issues is reprinted here, along with a portion of the discussion that followed.

8. Norman Dorsen prepared this statement on Executive privilege as a recommended policy for the American Civil Liberties Union (ACLU), in collaboration with ACLU staff counsel, John Shattuck. It was presented during his testimony before the 1973 joint hearings of the Senate Government Operations and Judiciary Committees.

9. Note also the seven parts of hearings held in 1971–1972 by the House Foreign Operations and Government Information Subcommittee on U.S. Information Policies and Practices—Administration and Operation of the FOIA (92nd Congress, 2nd session), of which this text is a small portion ([64]). Testimony referred to herein relates to those hearings.

10. President Richard M. Nixon's Executive Order 11652 (March 1972) called for automatic declassification of most classified documents within no more than ten years. As a result of this order, The New York *Times* initiated the first of a series of declassification requests within the Departments of Defense and State the CIA, and the NSC; by April 1973, only five of the *Times* 49 requests had been granted. For further details, see testimony of Harding Bancroft, executive vice-president of The New York *Times,* before joint Senate hearings in April 1973 ([28A], pp. 157 ff.).

11. On November 11, 1975, Representative Bella Abzug, chairwoman of the House Subcommittee on Government Information and Individual Rights, detailed her efforts to obtain from the National Archives (a part of GSA) declassification of the documents of the Warren Commission (President's Commission on the Assassination of President Kennedy). See hearings before the Abzug Subcommittee ([73]).

12. During the hearing on Executive privilege, in which Senator Sam Ervin presented this statement, Attorney General Richard Kliendienst testified for the Justice Department on behalf of the Nixon administration and set forth his view of Executive privilege. The exchange that followed involved Senators Edward Kennedy, William Fulbright, Edmund Muskie, and Kliendienst in a lengthy debate of the fundamental questions of Legislative-Executive relations. Space limitations prohibit reprint of that material here. Refer to [28A], pp. 1–88.

13. James Hamilton, assistant chief counsel to Senator Sam Ervin's Senate Select Committee, presented a negative viewpoint on the ability of Congress to enforce an order to obtain information from the Executive branch ([24B], pp. 126–127).

14. Comptroller General of the United States and head of GAO Elmer Staats furnished the Pike Committee with correspondence from both the CIA and NSA, citing statutory authority for their refusal to provide GAO access to certain appropriations and expenditures records for their agencies. Note [84A], pp. 418–424, 427–428.

15. The text of the Hughes-Ryan Amendment is reprinted in [84A], p. 429.

16. See reprinted material from the Commission on CIA Activities Within the U.S. in Chapter 4 for additional information on the role of the CIA's inspector general.

17. The subject of covert action is addressed in Chapter 11.

18. The separation of the congressional authorization of the DOD intelligence activities from the overall Defense authorization bills became a point of contention in the May 13–19, 1976 Senate debate on passage of Senate Resolution 400 (which established a Senate committee for overseeing intelligence activities). Note Senate floor debate reprinted later in this chapter.

19. The structure and operation of the Defense Department's DIA are described in Chapter 6. In its final report, the Pike Committee recommended the abolition of DIA ([85], p. 27).

20. On November 6, 1975, the Pike Committee issued a subpoena to Secretary of State Henry Kissinger, demanding that he deliver to the committee all documents relating to State Department recommendations for covert action that were made to the NSC and the 40 Committee from January 20, 1961 to date. For additional information, see [83].

21. See the Appendix for the text of President Gerald R. Ford's description of his Executive Order 11905 (February 18, 1976), pertaining to the organization and control of the foreign intelligence community.

22. A Congressional Research Service report by John Cost and Gary Evans summarizes legislation introduced, relating to intelligence agencies, from 1947 through 1972 ([100]). Another such "Issue Brief" on intelligence oversight, by William Raiford, provides an update on that report ([97]). The subject of oversight during the 93rd and 94th sessions of Congress is reviewed further in this chapter.

23. Rules set up by the House and Senate govern the Legislative branch's handling of classified material submitted to the Congress by the intelligence agencies. In 1974, Representative Michael Harrington violated those rules by releasing to the public classified testimony of William Colby before the House Subcommittee on Intelligence, concerning the CIA and Chile. Events surrounding the Harrington matter are documented in [55] and [60].

24. The involvement of the CIA in foreign assassination plots is treated in Chapter 11.

25. Chapter 11 of the Murphy Commission report has been deleted ([90], pp. 151–159).

26. The Senate Government Operations Committee conducted hearings on legislation to create a Senate intelligence oversight committee (January and February 1976). Among those offering their views on the proposed committee were ten senators, two representatives, and numerous current and former high-ranking members of the Executive branch. Individual testimony appears in [25]. Earlier hearings (December 1974) by the same committee on proposals to strengthen congressional oversight of intelligence activities appear in [31],

Chapter 11
Covert Action Abroad: The Ethical Limits

Covert action refers to those actions that influence the outcome of events by secret and unattributable means. It is the term most frequently associated with dubious ethical activities and failures of the U.S. intelligence community. Such operations in Cuba, Iran, Chile, the Belgian Congo, Brazil, and, of course, Southeast Asia have been discussed or alluded to in earlier chapters of this volume. Except in cases where the rights of American citizens are involved, few public documents contain discussion and debate on the official limits of gathering information ("spying" as opposed to "dirty tricks"; intelligence gathering as opposed to covert operations). Participants in the public debate on foreign intelligence (in the 1970s) have expressed concern regarding strictures to be imposed on covert intervention in the affairs of other nations.

Francis Winters, in an appendix to the Murphy Commission report, observed: "The only moral argument [on covert political action] . . . is the intensely interesting question of situations in which such activity would *not* be repugnant to most U.S. citizens" (vol. 7, p. 298). He went on to summarize a September 30, 1974 *Time* magazine review of U.S. leaders' views on the subject: "Ideas vary about what limits should be set. Harry Howe Ransom, professor pf political science and an intelligence specialist at Vanderbilt University, believes that 'covert operations represent an act just short of war. If we use them, it should be where acts of war would otherwise be necessary.' Ransom would permit covert actions only when U.S. security is clearly in jeopardy. William T. R. Fox, professor of international relations at Columbia University, would additionally permit them 'to undo the spread of Hitler and other like governments.' Dean Harvey Picker, of Columbia's School of International Affairs, would allow clandestine operations to prevent nuclear war. As Senator [Frank] Church points out, however, the 'national security considerations must be compelling' for covert action to be justified. For his part, [CIA Director William] Colby declines to say under what precise circumstances he would favor covert action."

The ethical limits of recent U.S. intelligence activities have been determined more by the circumstances involved in the management of the intelligence community than by any standard of conduct established by public opinion or by the guidance of Congress. Intelligence work has been conducted in secret by officials who subscribe to the belief that the survival of the nation (or freedom or democracy or all of these) depends significantly on their actions. Secrecy, combined with such notions, has led intelligence officials to strain the bounds of what might be considered ethical conduct.

Chapter 11 examines efforts to establish a system for defining the ethical limits and studies the desirability of covert operations. The documents presented in this portion of the text set forth the issues, examine historic and legal precedents, and summarize the findings of investigations into covert operations bearing on the Salvador Allende Gossens government in Chile and the assassination of foreign leaders.

THE PUBLIC POLICY ISSUES

Two prominent public policy analysts, Taylor Belcher and Paul Blackstock, addressed the issue of U.S. support for covert operations in the Murphy Commission report. They set the problem of covert action in a foreign policy context. Excerpts from their contributions to the commission's final report are reprinted here in rearranged and abridged form. This rearrangement of text, due to space restrictions, inevitably has violated the organization of these authors' works. It should also be noted that Belcher and Blackstock wrote in 1974, prior to President Gerald R. Ford's reorganization of the intelligence community and prior to issuance of the reports of the Pike and Church Committees.

Clandestine Operations ([90], pp. 67, 68, 99–102)

ISSUE SUMMARY (TAYLOR BELCHER, NOVEMBER 1974)

a. The term "covert action" involves the effort to influence the affairs of other nations by secret and unattributable means. The case for and against maintaining a capability for conducting covert action operations has been eloquently set forth by a number of observers, but it is extremely difficult to draw up a balance sheet comparing past successes and failures. Whatever the assessments may be, the United States will inevitably maintain a covert action capability and undertake operations when deemed necessary by the highest authorities.

b. The problem then becomes one of appropriate criteria for action, sufficient review in the process of seeking approval for proposed projects, appropriate monitoring of on-going operations, and ex post facto assessments of value gained or lost.

c. Covert action operations are generally believed to have been too widely used in the past, and they should be limited to those which are in the *vital* national interest as determined at the very highest level in government. Furthermore, the decision to act should include a recognition of what may be needed to follow up success or, in case of failure, to minimize the costs of disclosure. All overt alternatives must be thoroughly considered before opting for covert action.

d. The present image of the CIA's clandestine service is depressingly bad. Pejorative adjectives abound: omnipresent, powerful, operating under a debilitating cloud of suspicion. The CIA is widely believed to have too many of the resources and instruments of foreign policy under its control. Its successes have been as heralded as its failures. The CIA is too widely publicized for a secret service.

e. In addition to covert action, there are many other kinds of clandestine operations which are dangerous and politically risky. Some intelligence collection programs have involved the U.S. in extremely awkward situations, e.g., in Pakistan, Greece, and Turkey. Decision making for major collection activities should, therefore, be at least as exhaustive as for covert action, and responsibility should be carefully exercised by the 40 Committee, an interdepartmental review and coordination body for sensitive clandestine operations which is chaired by the Assistant to the President for National Security Affairs.

f. The clandestine collection and covert action functions should remain under the unified control and direction of the CIA, for otherwise too many wires would be crossed, and there would be considerable confusion and overlapping of operations. The problem of arranging appropriate cover for clandestine operators overseas would also be exacerbated if the U.S. had two clandestine services.

g. A good case can be made for separating the CIA's Directorates of Intelligence and Operations. The new research and analysis organization would not be associated in the public mind with clandestine operations, and, moreover, would have a role more closely approaching that of the CIA as described in the National Security Act of 1947. Nevertheless, there are certain advantages in having regular communication between collectors of intelligence information overseas and analysts in Washington, and it would be difficult to devise a more appropriate organizational alternative to having the clandestine service in the CIA. On balance, the advantages of separation do not appear to outweigh the disadvantages.

h. It is extremely important to have adequate control over covert action and other kinds of clandestine operations. The 40 Committee is an adequate control mechanism, but it must be properly used and staffed. The best course would be to tighten the existing procedures by widening the circle of people consulted during the review process and by broadening the membership of the 40 Committee and its staff.

i. The question of personality is vital in any system. If the people at the top do not care to use the machinery provided for them, or listen to the experts, then the system will not work. At the present time, the system is not functioning properly. In recent years, the 40 Committee has seldom met and has generally conducted its business on the telephone. We must give life to existing safeguards and require their use by key foreign policy makers insofar as possible.

j. Congressional oversight over clandestine operations can be considerably improved, especially if a joint Congressional committee on intelligence or national security is established. Since such a committee could write its own rules; tight security procedures could be devised. Congressmen, moreover, would have an appropriate forum for registering doubts and complaints about intelligence. The creation of a joint committee would also tend to counter the general assumption that the present Congressional oversight committees for intelligence are not performing adequately.

k. Ex post facto review by the President's Foreign Intelligence Advisory Board (PFIAB) should be improved, and Ambassadors and key country team members overseas should exercise greater vigilance over clandestine operations. Adequate control mechanisms exist, but they need to be revitalized and used. Their effectiveness depends largely on leadership by the President and Secretary of State, as well as on the vigilance of Congress and the media. Secret services are as effective or ineffective as the governmental entities that control them. . . .

Covert Operations (Paul Blackstock, November 1974)

Before being named DCI, Colby had been head of CIA's Directorate of Operations (formerly called Plans), the agency's single largest division, responsible for all clandestine collection and covert operations and for CIA's eighty-five overseas stations. Employing an estimated 6–7,000 people the Directorate has had a budget of about $350 million, nearly half the CIA total.

Since the beginning of the Cold War almost one half of clandestine personnel have been diverted from the primary task of collecting and processing information, as envisaged by those who established the CIA in 1947, to warfare, paramilitary or even covert military operations as in Laos and Vietnam. Following withdrawal of the United States from hostilities in Southeast Asia, many of CIA's local assets have been assigned to such tasks as reporting on the international drug traffic in the area, a traffic linked politically to Meo tribesmen and other elements formerly supported by the CIA. During his brief tenure as DCI, Schlesinger indicated interest in the intelligence aspects of the international drug traffic (handled by a new centralized intelligence division of the Bureau of Narcotics and Dangerous Drugs in the Department of Justice), and international terrorism, symbolized by spectacular airplane hijackings, kidnapings, and other acts of terror. Colby has kept a much lower profile with respect to both these international problems.

The basic assumptions underlying American intervention, both open and covert in the so-called "Third World," which has been the major target of our covert operations during the Cold War decades, have been false. They reflect a grossly-oversimplified, black and white view of international relations, exemplified by the so-called "domino theory", which since Vietnam has been throughly discredited.

In the developing areas of the world, nationalism and the drive for modernization have produced a series of recurrent political and social revolutions which have displaced traditional elites and various colonial and post-colonial ruling groups. As new ruling elites in the Third World consolidate their power and extend their privileges, the nepotism and corruption associated with traditional societies will almost certainly create burning political, economic, and social grievances. These in turn will lead to new revolutions. In spite of heroic, if belated, U.S. efforts to arrest the process, this is clearly what happened to the Diem regime in South Vietnam, and the pattern will repeat itself elsewhere. Naturally Soviet or Chinese Communist parties, or both, will seek to exploit such indigenous revolutionary movements, employing their separate strategies of subversion or political warfare. However, the traditional cold war assumption that Communists will automatically succeed in capturing and controlling such movements unless vigorously opposed by U.S. covert operations and counterinsurgency programs is patently false. The cycle of revolution in the developing areas is thus as open-ended as the process of modernization itself, from which it is inseparable. It bears little or no relationship to the frustrations and fears of political warriors on either side of the Bamboo and Iron Curtains, and even less relationship to their propaganda slogans about the struggle between the so-called forces of freedom (or "national liberation") and forces of slavery (or "neo-colonialism").

The first scholarly examination of the complex problems involved in the management and control of covert operations was my book, *The Strategy of Subversion*, subtitled "Manipulating the Politics of Other Nations" (Chicago: Quadrangle, 1964). In the ensuing decade, covert operations have come under increasingly sharp criticism, culminating in a two-day conference sponsored by the Fund for Peace on September 12–13 in a Congressional hearing room at which CIA Director Colby admitted that such operations have been only marginally effective, but insisted that the United States should have a reserve of stand-by capability in this area.

Beginning in 1971–72, I conducted a confidential Survey on Intelligence and Covert Operations: Changing Doctrine And Practice, and found considerable ambivalence toward covert operations even among professional clandestine operators. Most of the 30 respondents, (two-thirds of whom had served at the Directorate level of various intelligence agencies for an average of 24 years) regarded covert operations as an essential arm of diplomacy, but at the same time subscribed to the criterion that they should be used only as a last resort before the direct use of military force in a pre-war situation. There was also general agreement with the proposition that "clandestine operational agencies are capable of pre-empting a policy-making role through operations which create situations of fact to which national policy must later be readjusted, thus creating serious problems of management and control" —not to mention the acute national embarrassment which results when, as frequently happens, such operations are "blown" and become public knowledge. A heavy majority of the respondents also agreed that "covert operations have been oversold and overused as an instrument of policy to such an extent that on balance they have become counter-productive." For the most part professional analysts with long careers in collection, production, estimates, and dissemination took the view that these purely intelligence functions should be separated organizationally from politically oriented covert operations. On the other hand, clandestine operators with mainly civilian backgrounds favor the status quo, with covert operations housed under CIA. This is to be expected, given the strong institutional loyalties which develop in all clandestine organizations. Almost all respondents, however, agree that effective control at the policy-making level has been inadequate in the past and wherever they may be housed will present problems in the future. With few exceptions, Congressional monitoring and control was regarded as inadequate and ineffective.

In addition to the complex problems of management, monitoring, and control involved in covert operations, they also have a tendency to escalate above the covert threshold into open warfare as illustrated by the Bay of Pigs as early as 1961 and again repeatedly with operations in Southeast Asia during the last decade. Although like Helms most of Colby's professional career has been spent in clandestine operations, he publicly indicated a certain disenchantment with them in testimony before the Armed Services Committee on July 2, 1973, when he stated that it was "very unlikely" that the agency would again mount such wide-scale, covert military operations as its support of the Meo tribesmen in Laos.

Ever since the clandestine Gulf of Tonkin incidents opened the door to large scale military intervention in Vietnam, Congress has been painfully aware that covert operations can lead the nation unwittingly down the garden path to war. The decision to wage war, many Senators contend, should properly rest with Congress. As a result of the war in Vietnam and the Watergate affair, the CIA has come under heavier and more determined Congressional scrutiny than at any time in its history. No less than five committees, four in the Senate and one in the House, were stirred by the Watergate disclosures to inquire into various aspects of CIA's operations, and Chairman John C. Stennis of the Armed Services subcommittee on intelligence stated that hearings would eventually be held on revising the agency's charter, the National Security Act of 1947.

Ironically, although Congress was aware of the need for closer surveillance over CIA well before the Vietnam conflict, it failed to act decisively in this regard time and again. Since the National Security Act of 1947 and the 1949 Central Intelligence Act previously noted, nearly 200 bills calling for closer surveillance of intelligence agencies have been introduced. Most of them attempted to establish a Congressional Committee to oversee the activities of CIA. Only two of them ever reached the floor of Congress, where both were decisively defeated by more than two-thirds majorities.

But how seriously the Congress will follow-up on its renewed interest in controlling covert operations remains to be seen. Unless the historic confrontation triggered by Watergate between the Executive branch of government and Congress is resolved clearly in favor of Congress, no fundamen-

tal change in the role and functions of CIA is likely. This applies to the Presidential use of covert political and military operations as an instrument of foreign policy no matter how much "dirty tricks" may be publicly deplored when used to influence the electoral process at home. In this regard Nixon's secret bombing of Laos and Cambodia set a precedent which future presidents may be tempted to follow in similar circumstances.

Ever since Machiavelli, Western statesmen and politicians have been fascinated with the idea of combining the wiles of the fox with the strength of the lion. In the crusading atmosphere of the Cold War and in Vietnam, it was hoped that covert operations might provide such a winning combination. That hope was based on ignorance, which has always been a poor counselor. Nevertheless, as long as the clandestine services of the CIA remain intact and ready to serve again "as the President's loyal tool," the temptation to use them may prove as irresistible in the future as it has in the past.

Meanwhile, within the Intelligence Community under both Schlesinger and Colby there has been a revival of interest in classical espionage, now classed as the covert side of human intelligence (HUMINT). Espionage has often been held in low esteem as producing "uncertain information from questionable people," the comment of Admiral Wemyss, the British First Sea Lord at the end of World War I. With the advent of advanced technological means of surveillance, such as the U-2 and R-171 reconnaissance planes, traditional espionage sources have been reduced to where they provide only an estimated 5 percent of information collected. However, the very success of technical sensors has indicated critical gaps in the information they can supply. For example, overhead photography can show a missile on a launcher. Radar intelligence can track it when fired, and telemetry intelligence (Telint) can provide data on performance of the war-head. But only a well-placed espionage agent (read defector in place) can tell you what is in the war-head of an operational missile and what targets it is to attack. These now recognized short comings of technical sensors have revived interest in human espionage to such an extent that, as previously noted, an interagency Human Sources Committee of the U.S. Intelligence Board has recently been created to study the problem. It is also recognized that "agents in place" such as Stig Wennerstrom or Oleg Penkovsky result from "Acts of God" (or the devil depending on whose ox is being gored). This being the case, the standard response of the clandestine services to additional intelligence requirements is to talk about developing new sources and the need to conserve existing, largely imaginary, assets.

Recommendations as to what to do about covert operations cover a wide spectrum from pious appeals for the public to have "confidence in the men responsible for secret operations" (which after Watergate is somewhat unrealistic) to sweeping demands that they should be entirely abolished. Such demands are as unrealistic as appeals for immediate, total, and universal disarmament. Because covert operations have an intrinsic appeal to the activist, manipulative personality types who are attracted to centers of power, the United States like other powers will retain at least a standby capability in this area. However, due to both public and Congressional pressure, it seems likely that covert operations will be used much more sparingly in the future than in the past and are likely to be kept under much closer scrutiny by a joint Congressional Committee modelled after the Joint Committee on Atomic Energy.

Where organizationally covert operations will be housed is a thorny problem which will probably be decided less on the merits of the solution arrived at than as a result of bureaucratic politics. Unfortunately any solution is intimately tied to the problem of improving existing U.S. espionage capabilities, such as they are after a decade of heavy reliance on technical sensors. Since 1947 the clandestine service division of CIA has directed both espionage (the illegal collection through secret agents of information to which access is legally denied) and covert political operations, frequently using the same agents for both purposes. This practice has resulted inevitably in degrading the collection function since the "action" (and the rewards) have been largely in the covert operations sector. The careers of both Helms and Colby are illustrative in this regard.

For at least the last two decades, the CIA stations abroad have been interested primarily in political warfare operations and have sought to recruit agents or sources who can be used for such purposes, primarily political dissidents, or others willing to engage in the overthrow of existing governments or to provide information needed for more subtle forms of intervention. Then, after a given covert operation has been approved, the emphasis shifts to developing additional sources who can provide information which will insure its success. The main thrust of the station's efforts is directed toward what in military terms is called *tactical* intelligence, and has something, but actually very little, to do with classical espionage, which has been aimed mainly at collecting information of strategic importance. The collection requirements for espionage can be satisfied only by a radically different approach

and by the recruitment of entirely different sources than the disaffected political activists who gravitate toward covert operations. What is needed are well placed people who have access to plans, strategic dialogue, staff papers, decision-making, etc., sources who can provide information on strategic intentions rather than details with respect to hardware and capabilities. The latter kind of information can be provided by technical sensors. In addition, espionage must become responsive to Washington-based requirements rather than to the operational plans of local station chiefs. The station must recruit sources which can respond to specific requirements rather than merely reporting general news based on hearsay evidence. The emphasis on covert operations has produced an essential mismatch between what is collected and what is needed to fill the gaps in the information provided by technical sensors. Moreover, the sources recruited for political warfare purposes rarely if ever have access to such information.

Clearly current clandestine collection practices and recruiting practices will have to be radically altered if there is to be any substantial improvement in U.S. espionage capabilities. But such a reversal is unlikely given the bureaucratic clout of vested interests in the clandestine services with their stake in the preservation of the status quo. The need to separate the clandestine collection effort from covert political operations has been recognized by such non-establishment scholars as Harry Howe Ransom, as well as by dedicated professionals serving on the USIB Human Sources Committee. However, unless the need for such separation can be impressed on policy-making and executive levels within both the intelligence community and the government at large, the weight of vested interests will almost certainly perpetuate the present organizational structure. Probably only the President, working through the NSC channel, has enough clout to insure that this basic reform is carried out. . . .

Should the United States Maintain a Capability for Covert Action? (Taylor Belcher) ([90], pp. 68–76)

1. DEFINITION OF TERMS

It is generally accepted that "covert actions" overseas include (1) political advice and counsel; (2) subsidies to individuals; (3) financial support and technical assistance to political parties; (4) support of private organizations, including labor unions, business firms, and cooperatives; (5) covert propaganda; (6) private training of individuals and exchange of persons; (7) economic operations; and (8) para-military (or) political action operations designed to overthrow or to support a regime.[1]

2. SOME COMMENTS IN SUPPORT OF COVERT ACTION

Lord Chalfont has stated that "if the U.S. is disbarred from access to some of the less attractive instruments of secret diplomacy, while its enemies, unhampered by the pressures of public opinion, continue to use them, the power structures of the

world might gradually but irreversibly be changed; and the change is not likely to be one to delight those who believe in an open society." [2]

William Colby, the present Director of Central Intelligence, has said: "It is advocated by some that the U.S. abandon covert action. In light of current American policy, as I have indicated, it would not have a major impact on our current activities or the current security of the U.S. However, I can envisage situations in which the U.S. might well need to conduct covert activity in the face of some new threat that developed in the world. There have also been, and are still, certain situations in the world in which some discreet support can assist America's friends against her adversaries in their contest for control of a foreign nation's political direction." [3]

President Ford has said publicly that the United States will not forego this option. Furthermore, it is significant that the Senate, on October 2, 1974, voted 68 to 17 not to prohibit further covert opera-

---

[1] See speech by Richard M. Bissell, Jr. before the Discussion Group on Intelligence and Foreign Policy, run by the Council on Foreign Relations, Jan. 8, 1968; published as an appendix to Marchetti and Marks, *The CIA and the Cult of Intelligence*, Alfred A. Knopf, New York, 1974.

[2] *London Times*, Sept. 30, 1974.
[3] Speech by DCI Colby at "Conference on the CIA and Covert Action" sponsored by the Center for National Security Studies, Washington, D.C., September 13, 1974.

tions (the so-called Abourezk Amendment), and the House voted down a similar amendment.

3. SOME COMMENTS AGAINST COVERT ACTION

There is, however, a tenable position that covert political action is beneath the dignity of the United States and the moral standards of the American tradition. Indeed, former Under Secretary of State and Attorney General, Nicholas Katzenbach, has written: "Our foreign policy must be based on policy and factual premises which are accepted by the overwhelming majority of the American people . . . As one step toward reestablishing credibility, we should abandon publicly all covert operations designed to influence political results in foreign countries . . . We should confine our covert activities overseas to the gathering of intelligence information . . ." [4]

4. THE PROS AND CONS

It would be extremely difficult to produce a balance sheet with a bottom line showing a definite profit or loss resulting from covert action. Any such measurement must of necessity be subjective.

The failures have been widely publicized and subjected to hypercritical study, the successes much less so, even when known. The Iranian example is generally considered one of the successes, but how can the net gain be measured? In billions of dollars in oil and a seemingly promising future for an ancient state? The fact that the United States, in the early 1960s, helped to maintain a leftist liberal in power in one South American country is less well known. Did this covert action contribute to internal stability and hence to easy access to essential raw materials, an important export market, and not incidentally to the preservation of a liberal regime in Latin America? Could the U.S. have accomplished as much without using covert action?

Similarly, it is difficult to assess the long run advantages of giving discreet assistance to a trade union, a political party, or a rising political figure in an area of importance to the United States. Competition for influence in foreign countries is a fact of life in foreign affairs, and the United States must be in a position to act when acting is considered in the vital national interest. The crucial decision, therefore, involves some judgment of the likely risks of a given operation, followed by a determination whether a situation is of sufficient importance to warrant the risks involved.

The United States may not use the capability often, but to be without a capability even to attempt

[4]Quoted from "Self-Inflicted Wounds" by Anthony Lewis, *New York Times*, September 23, 1974.

to influence events abroad through the use of covert contacts would be folly in today's world. Many operations have involved financial support of individuals or organizations already committed to a policy or a cause with which we are in agreement. U.S. support is often covert simply because overt aid would be unacceptable for political reasons. Recipients of this sort of assistance would be too open to criticism, their futures ruined by the facts becoming public. Covert support of this kind is neither immoral nor beneath the dignity of the United States.

Furthermore, just as the United States has impressive military forces short of our nuclear capability, the United States needs a covert action capability for those purposes not served by traditional diplomacy or military action.

There are also occasions when we can embarrass or damage our adversaries abroad simply by using covert action. The temptation to play games of this sort, however, is often greater than is warranted, given the risks of exposure. Some career intelligence operators prefer playing "dirty tricks" on our adversaries to the often humdrum and trying responsibilities of routine diplomacy. This kind of covert action is seldom worth the trouble involved.

Assuming that the United States stays in the business of covert operations, we must consider the deleterious effects of exposure on our credibility as a nation basically interested in promoting the rule of law internationally. It is perhaps too easy to shrug off the matter by reference to past and present practices of all great powers. Somehow the world accepts and even expects "dirty tricks" from our adversaries, but we must be "Mr. Clean" in this respect. Some say that the United States should set an example for the Soviets or others to follow, but in the process the United States would be abdicating the field to those who do not even suffer from a guilty conscience in this area.

Recently much has been written regarding the damage which knowledge of covert actions does to our overall credibility, especially in the diplomatic field. Ambassador Moynihan's now well known complaint about leaks in Washington and their damaging effect on his relations with senior government officials in India poses a serious problem. But it would not by any means be solved merely by doing away with covert action. The propensity to leak is great in Washington, and the usual leaks have little or nothing to do with covert action. This is not to say that the image of our covert action capabilities does not complicate both diplomatic relations and the domestic scene. The propensity to believe the worst is widespread. Normal diplomatic tasks, however, are not markedly more complicated by this attitude of mind, except in certain particularly touchy countries. . . .

Criteria for Covert Action (Taylor Belcher)

1. SITUATIONS IN WHICH COVERT ACTION MIGHT BE CONSTRUCTIVE

Assuming a policy decision to maintain a covert action capability and given the means to do so, the criteria governing their use become critical.

One cannot delineate a rigid set of standards which must be adhered to before engaging in covert action. Each case is in a sense ad hoc, with advantages or disadvantages requiring expert evalua-

tion. For example, third party "x", in a mainly two party system, might be seen as playing a vital balancing role in any marginal issue. Limited covert support of such a party could surely be defended, if the party were to vote on the side of moderation. Since such political organizations are usually without adequate resources, there is not only relatively easy access, but sometimes leaders begging for help.

The same can apply to individuals with leadership potential—indeed, they may not even need to know the true source of their support. Subsidizing a potential leader is no sure thing; he may even turn against the United States over the years, but, if such gambles pay off from time to time, the United States will have many influential advocates abroad.

What are some of the problems in the present era which might seem to require covert actions of some sort? It would not be difficult to justify action directed against terrorist groups or the international traffic in narcotics. Indeed foreign countries are usually cooperative in these areas. Covert action might also be justified to protect our supply of certain strategic raw materials or sources of energy. There can also be advantages in giving assistance to dissident intellectuals in totalitarian countries or in giving discreet support to certain individuals or parties struggling against totalitarian groups.

Many informed observers, such as Ransom, have taken the position that covert operations should only be undertaken to prevent a direct threat to our national security and as an alternative to military action. Senator Fulbright has said in support of his contention that covert action should be used only in emergencies: "We are compelled, therefore, to lay down a qualified rule, a rule to the effect that the end almost never justifies the means." [7] Nevertheless, there are many situations in which discreet covert action can be extremely useful in situations that do not involve life or death, and it would be a mistake to rule out covert action altogether as one of the ways to further U.S. foreign policy interests.

2. THE NEED FOR FOLLOW-UP ACTION

Covert action can rarely achieve an important objective alone. It can, however, buy time, forestall a coup, and create conditions more conducive to the use of overt means to achieve an objective. If, for instance, a coup d'état is averted and no additional step is taken to correct the abuses or the socio-economic conditions which brought on the unrest in the first place, then the effort will have been in vain and the risks run even less justifiable.

An example of failure to follow through is Guatemala, where the long term objective in overthrowing Arbenz twenty years ago is still to be realized. The United States bought time, but stability and social justice are still elusive and unrest is endemic. The same can be said of U.S. efforts in Chile under Allessandri and Frei. (Of course it was not just failure of the United States to follow through; the Chileans did little to take advantage of the time bought for them!)

Covert actions are, therefore, best suited for tactical situations, where success can bring quick, short term gains upon which overt, longer term programs can capitalize.

3. RISKS OF EXPOSURE

In the period of detente, the risks inherent in a given covert action program are much greater than during the cold war era. Furthermore, the U.S. Government finds it extremely difficult to keep secrets these days. An individual, a political party, or indeed a government could be seriously compromised or damaged by a link to the CIA. Furthermore, disclosure is costly to the image of America that we wish to project. We are not only considered inept if caught but also immoral, even if successful. We also prejudice our efforts to promote a world in which respect for law is paramount. Important sectors of our society are, partly in consequence, alienated from the government.

Exposure of a given covert action operation may result in strained relations with the host country. Governments are usually extremely sensitive to outsiders tampering with their institutions or citizens. In addition, our adversaries are often quick to take advantage of U.S. fiascos. One must also consider what damage a subsidy may do to the very organization or individual the U.S. hopes to help and strengthen. Too often our help is a crutch which can only be thrown away with difficulty.

Once having determined that the risks are worth it, the United States must apply the same criteria on a continuing basis in order to insure that the situation still calls for the same sort of operation and that the costs are still worth the hoped for results. As Hilsman observes, most covert political action programs have "such a high potential for political disaster that every single program, no matter how innocuous it seems, should be the subject of the fullest coordination and consideration."

4. CONSIDERATION OF ALTERNATIVES

There should also be a full consideration of all overt alternatives—whether the operation is a clandestine intelligence gathering project or a covert political action program. A decision to proceed should only be taken when all overt means have failed or are judged to be impossible to apply in the circumstances. The executive must pay more attention to reviewing on-going projects to determine whether they continue to be worth the money and the risk. Throughout all the studies of this subject, the question of control has been considered basic and indeed can and must be greatly improved.

Furthermore, despite constant remonstrances to the contrary, there is no doubt that the CIA proposes action programs and chooses the channels to be used in presenting the proposals for wider executive consideration. When Hilsman proposed that State's Bureau of Intelligence and Research (INR) be the clearing house for covert action programs, Allen Dulles blocked the idea. Hilsman alleges that the CIA has too much money and too many people and there is a consequent temptation to think up things to do just to keep busy. This may not be a current problem, in view of budgetary limitations, but it should be kept in mind.

Other Clandestine Activity (Taylor Belcher)

Other clandestine operations, which are not defined as covert action, nevertheless have many of the characteristics and dangers of covert action. For instance, gathering intelligence by clandestine or secret means can be a risky process. A few examples suffice to prove the point: the U-2 incident in 1960, the Pueblo and Liberty actions later, the generally accepted (although not officially recognized) exis-

---

[7] *New York Times*, April 23, 1967.

tence of secret communications facilities in various countries.

It has been suggested that our need for facilities at Peshawar in Pakistan may have influenced our policy decisions in the India-Pakistan conflict. Our facilities in Greece carried a very high price when it came time to reach decisions in Cyprus. The initial decision to establish these facilities led the United States to a potentially hostile situation that had not been envisaged at the time the decision was made. The decision process regarding sensitive collection programs should, therefore, be at least as exhaustive as that applied to covert action and should take place at the 40 Committee level.

Furthermore, in the field of clandestine collection of information, is it really worth the risk involved in keeping senior officials of foreign governments on the U.S. payroll? Is it worth the risk even to try to place electronic surveillance devices in places which may or may not provide intelligence? It has been said that we have a massive capability for determining capabilities, but what we need is a greater ability to assess intentions. It is doubtful

that we can learn enough about intentions by this type of collection operation to warrant the risk of exposure. This type of operation requires the most thorough check-out before final approval.

In addition, clandestine operations may uncover information of great value which cannot be used openly because of the need to protect sources. Obviously we must protect our agents, yet this need must be balanced carefully against possible gains from usage. As Lockhart has noted: "There is no point in producing intelligence of any sort if it cannot be used. If the ultimate result of running an agent is to enable some staff officer to put another pin in a map and nobody takes any action, that does not do anybody any good—it must make some contribution to the national effort." [9] Here again we need a thorough review to determine usability— and by whom—by our services or by those of the host country. The CIA should have to present cogent reasons to prevent the use of information which the Ambassador or the Secretary of State believe to be in the national interest.

Organizational Alternatives (Taylor Belcher)

1. THE SEPARATION OF THE COVERT ACTION APPARATUS FROM THE REST OF THE CIA'S CLANDESTINE SERVICE

The splitting off of the structure for covert action from the rest of the Clandestine Service would not be practical. All clandestine activity tends to involve the same personnel and techniques for recruiting and handling foreign agents. The same personnel must serve two functions, for otherwise there would be considerable confusion and overlapping of operations. The British and U.S. experiments at separation failed, as did the one in Germany during World War II. As one retired CIA official put it, "A single organization can groom and position abroad a standing force of trained intelligence officers whose basic skill is the recruitment and handling of foreign agents and can send directions down command channels as to whether agents are to be used for collection, for action or for both."

2. THE SEPARATION OF THE CIA'S DIRECTORATE OF INTELLIGENCE FROM THE REST OF THE CIA

One way to improve both image and functioning might be to place the CIA's Research and Analysis Directorate (DDI) in a new institution which might also include State's Bureau of Intelligence and Research (INR), leaving the clandestine services (DDO) separate. The new research and analysis organization, whether including INR or not, would have a role more closely approaching that of the CIA as envisaged in the National Security Act of 1947. The proponents of this change say that such an organization would command much greater cooperation from the now alienated academic community as well as other intellectual circles whose contributions to intelligence analysis are of some significance.

Furthermore, it is suggested that recruitment possibilities would be enhanced, since the stigma of working in an organization oriented in an important degree to clandestine operations would have been removed. The image of a truly central agency for coordination, collation, and dissemination of

intelligence collected by all other agencies would be greatly enhanced. The functions of the Clandestine Service would be kept apart, either in an organization directly responsible to the President through the NSC or, as some suggest, still through the DCI, though physically separated from his other service organizations.

Halperin, after endorsing the concept of a split along the foregoing lines, suggests in addition that the Research and Analysis or intelligence evaluation organization have a role in decision-making on all covert operations, including especially an evaluation of the likelihood of success and the cost of failure. It should also provide an evaluation, ex-post facto, of the value of the information obtained through clandestine collection activities.[10] In other words, Halperin believes that the clandestine operations should be evaluated by the Research and Analysis group, and he recommends they be joined in this responsibility by policy-level review in State, DOD and the White House.

There are, however, cogent arguments in favor of the organizational status quo. DCI Colby has spoken of the many advantages of cross-fertilization between analysts and operators. Physical separation would render this virtually impossible. Agency representatives insist that there is a close and valuable association between the DDO and the DDI and that National Intelligence Officers capitalize on their physical proximity as well as the assessment of clandestine collection efforts made by the DDI.

Aside from the tremendous expense of separation, other important factors militate against such action. The Clandestine Service would hardly be less conspicuous, for organizational requirements would dictate that the administrative headquarters,

[9]John Bruce Lockhart, "The Relationship Between Secret Services and Government in a Modern State," *Journal of the Royal United Service Institute for Defence Studies*, England, June, 1974.

[10]Morton Halperin, "Implications of Decision-Making for Covert Operations," unpublished manuscript distributed at the "Conference on the CIA and Covert Action," *op. cit.*, September 1974.

mostly field and action oriented, plus the communications facilities, would be substantial. Furthermore, the proponents of the status quo claim that the academic and intellectual community would hardly be more receptive to what they would consider a mere change in facade. In addition it is alleged that, contrary to the statements of observers such as Halperin, the contacts with academics are effective and mutually appreciated, and that recruiting from this sector has not been a problem.

It would also be difficult to devise a more appropriate organizational alternative to keeping the Clandestine Service in the CIA. It could be turned into a semi-autonomous agency under the overall control of the DCI, much as the Agency for International Development is related to the Secretary of State, but critics of the CIA would consider this simply a change in facade. It could be placed under the Department of State or the Department of Defense, but neither Department would be overjoyed at this possibility. Finally, it could report directly to and take orders from the NSC or the President. Critics would complain that this shift would move clandestine-operations too close to the White House, and thus subject it to abuse reminiscent of Watergate.

The combining of INR with the CIA's Intelligence Directorate might produce minor budgetary savings, but the loss of INR's independent status as a check and balance on the CIA would be costly in other respects.

On balance then, it seems that the arguments in favor of a structural status quo are persuasive, and efforts to improve the situation should concentrate on applying adequate criteria for action, controls, and review of on-going clandestine operations.

Cover (Taylor Belcher)

In order to position abroad a standing force of trained intelligence officers, there must be a cover mechanism, usually inside the U.S. Embassy. This practice can on occasion be embarrassing. Not all CIA operations abroad, however, are located in Embassies and the more official cover can be avoided, the less risk to the official image.

N3

A case has been made for the greater use of unofficial, or private, cover, and this would be most desirable. It is, however, difficult to conceive of a time when some degree of official cover, with the access and protection it provides, will not be necessary. The CIA presence can certainly be cut down but the requirement remains despite the disadvantages.

Bissell suggested in 1968 that the CIA would "have to make use of private institutions on an expanding scale, bearing in mind the need to operate under deeper cover, with increased attention to the use of cut-outs. CIA's interface with the rest of the world needs to be better protected." [11] Bissell suggested a long term program designed to build an apparatus of unofficial cover, using private organizations and many more non-U.S. nationals. The use of private U.S. organizations presents problems, given the temper of the times (and the Katzenbach Report) but there are possibilities in enlarging the number of non-U.S. nationals. On balance, however, some official cover in U.S. Embassies will inevitably be required, no matter how much progress is made in arranging additional unofficial cover.

Control over Clandestine Activity (Taylor Belcher)

1. IS IT ADEQUATE?

Who should consider and decide upon clandestine operations (both collection and action programs)? The system in existence looks reasonably good on paper, but close examination reveals certain faults. Benjamin Welles observed that "Control over the CIA, which the Agency touts endlessly in self-justification, is a fiction." [12] While he overstates the case, Welles shares a generally held belief that the oversight function leaves much to be desired.

Roger Morris shares Welles' preoccupation and recommends that all covert action programs be certified by the President as in the *vital* national interest and be subject to prior consultation with the Congress. He suggests:

1. The Secretary of State should have supervisory role over *all* foreign intelligence activities.
2. All Chiefs of Station should have Congressional approval.
3. The 40 Committee should have a special independent staff to provide all members with a full review of all aspects and implications of a given covert action proposal.

4. A *fully* staffed Congressional Joint Committee for Intelligence Supervision should be created.
5. The 40 Committee should include two members from each house, and minutes should be read in executive session. [13]

Morris goes too far in several of his suggestions. Presidential certification and *prior* consultation with Congress would put both the President and Congress on the spot, in case any covert action operations are blown. The idea that chiefs of station should have Congressional approval is hardly feasible, if only for security and other reasons. The suggestion that the 40 Committee include Congressional Members raises constitutional problems.

Most critics at least recognize the fact that there are mechanisms for control in being. They are justified in calling for more effective use of these mechanisms.

[11] Bissell as quoted in Marchetti and Marks, *op cit.*
[12] *Christian Science Monitor*, September 12, 1974.
[13] Roger Morris, "Following the Scenario: Reflections on Five Case Histories in the Mode and Aftermath of CIA Intervention," unpublished manuscript circulated at "Conference on CIA and Covert Action," *op. cit.*, September, 1974.

2. BETTER USE OF EXISTING PROVISIONS

Let us now examine control in the sense of initiation and approval of projects. The existing system provides a means for review which, though limited as to input by interested and above all knowledgeable officers, should function well enough to protect the interests of the United States. Nevertheless, with some relatively minor changes, the system can be much improved.

The present system of initiatives, prepared and reviewed in the field (usually by the Ambassador and CIA Station Chief, but sometimes by the operations group of the Country Team) or through CIA/State agreement at the Bureau level, sounds fine in theory and in actuality provides a relatively good review prior to consideration by the 40 Committee. The weakness in this facet of the system is largely a function of the knowledge and experience of those who are cleared to receive such information or to be consulted on the subject.

Chiefs of Station can often wield a lot of influence over new Ambassadors, particularly political appointees. The same can be said of CIA counterparts to Assistant Secretaries or Deputy Assistant Secretaries in Washington. In other words, there exists the possibility, if not the probability, that the cards are stacked to favor the views of the CIA whenever a particular covert action is proposed.

To mitigate these difficulties, the need-to-know circle should be extended to include those officers with special knowledge and experience, e.g., the Deputy Chief of Mission, the Chief of the Political or Economic Section and Defense representatives as appropriate in the field, and country directors or desk officers in Washington. Obviously such a move increases the problem of security, but the value of input from these individuals would far outweigh any risk of an increase in the probability of leaks.

3. 40 COMMITTEE—WEAKNESSES AND SUGGESTIONS

In addition, the procedures of the 40 Committee should be revised. The fact that it, as well as the PFIAB, is served by Secretariats headed by present or former CIA officers may present more of a cosmetic than a substantive problem. Nevertheless, a change in this aspect of the system would provide additional protection. The fact that the now-defunct "Special Group-Counter Insurgency" had a State Department representative on the Secretariat served as an early warning system within the bureaucracy. An experienced Foreign Service Officer on loan to the staff could play a devil's advocate role, removed as he would be from parochial enthusiasms or even bemusements. Members of the committee as now constituted, however, are powerful and often egocentric men, and there are too many instances when they have silenced or ignored informed and experienced officers who foretold the problems involved in a given course of action.

It has been pointed out that, contrary to the procedures of its predecessors and of the Special Group, the Committee seldom meets, and most of its business is transacted by phone. Such a system is inherently weak. The fact of prior consultation among deputies or discussion at working group or expert levels may or may not insure adequate review. The present system certainly does not provide the insurance of substantive discussion among principals, perhaps leavened, if not enlightened, by the observations of two or three trustworthy, prestigious, and experienced individuals other than the interested parties who now participate in the telephone polls and rare meetings.

The 40 Committee itself should be enlarged through the addition of two or three prestigious ex-users of intelligence or ex-coordinators of covert operations (ex-Assistant Secretaries of State, ex-ambassadors, retired senior military or even ex-Cabinet members such as Melvin Laird).

Better use of the present machinery could go a long way toward the goal of adequate control before the fact. The same can be said of ex-post facto review or oversight. The Congress and Executive bodies such as PFIAB provide for a means of, but do not necessarily deliver, adequate control. In addition, the present, somewhat desultory annual review system should be improved by more rigorous requirements for review by Embassy Country Teams, Ambassadors' and Station Chiefs, as well as in the Washington Bureaus.

4. CONGRESSIONAL OVERSIGHT

DCI Colby's official position on Congressional oversight is that anything Congress wants will be provided. The Agency has worked with the specified subcommittees in the past and forcefully asserts that appropriate members have been appropriately briefed. Nevertheless, doubts have been expressed both in Congress and elsewhere as to the efficacy of this system of briefings.

The DCI notes that the CIA is responsible to the Armed Services and Appropriations Committees of Congress and that they, along with other interested Members of Congress, are briefed about covert action programs. While he has declined to offer suggestions for improvements in the oversight system, there is considerable support within the CIA and elsewhere in the Executive Branch and in Congress for a Joint Committee on Intelligence or National Security, similar to the Joint Committee on Atomic Energy.

Since such a Committee would write its own rules, security would be better than under the existing system whereby standing committee rules apply, and, therefore, briefings could be more detailed and candid. This view is strongly supported, inter alia, by Senators Humphrey and Baker, Congressman Zablocki and by Ray Cline, former Director of INR in the State Department.

Such a change would ease congressional and public concern over CIA activities. It would also provide a better "forum for registering Congressional doubts and/or complaints and the initiation of advisory action with respect to any errors which might become apparent." It would also tend to counter the rather general belief that the present committees are not doing the job adequately.

On the other hand there may be opposition to such change from within the existing oversight committees since a Joint Committee on Intelligence or National Security would probably want to oversee all Departmental Intelligence work, including military intelligence, which is now the responsibility of the Armed Services Committees. It has been suggested that an alternative to a new committee would be the revision of the House and Senate rules to preclude access by other members to papers or transcripts concerning intelligence.

In his dissenting view on Senator Mansfield's resolution in 1955 for a Joint Committee on Intelligence, Senator Hayden (Arizona) said that the existing system was adequate, that close studies of much secret "executive" acts might better be left to the FBI, and that the creation of the Joint Committee would raise constitutional questions. Only the latter point deserves a full study.

5. PFIAB

PFIAB's role in ex-post facto oversight is minimal. This fact is not a result of anything other than choice by the Chairman and other members of the Board and the limitations placed on·their activities by other demands on members' time. PFIAB meets only once every two months for two days. It has conducted ex-post facto, hit or miss reviews of some covert action programs. It could do much more, particularly in reviewing the viability of on-going projects in sensitive areas. Its membership of prestigious individuals from many different professions provides a unique, critical, and disinterested forum for airing the potential for danger of on-going actions.

Its post mortem studies should also result in more objective observations than would be expected of a politically or bureaucratically oriented body. The group may take on new vitality and value in this important task. In doing so, however, PFIAB needs a somewhat less parochial staff.

Various observers have suggested alternatives for improved control mechanisms. Benjamin Welles proposes an *independent* review panel of retired judges, academics, industrialists, scientists, and ex-consumers of intelligence such as Ambassadors, Admirals, and Generals—the latter preferably recently retired.[15] It should be a simple matter to modify the PFIAB to include this meritorious suggestion. The Killian Committee, established as a result of recommendations by the Hoover Commission (1953–55), was a similar body and acted as an early PFIAB. Such men as Robert Lovett, Benjamin Fairless, J. P. Kennedy, E. L. Reyerson, and senior military representatives reportedly did well in this role. This vital function is not being adequately performed now.

6. THE NEED FOR LEADERSHIP AND VIGILANCE

A serious control problem is inherent in the system. The efficient functioning of any or all of these control mechanisms depends *almost wholly* on the interests, wishes, and personality of the Very Important Persons who are in control. First, top policy makers must have the energy and determination to make control effective. Do they have the time or the attention span to carry out this essential leadership task? Second, the information or intelligence they receive is mainly supplied by the system they are supposed to be controlling. Can they be completely objective in such matters? Do they have the inclination to call upon knowledgeable members of their staffs for dissenting views, or do they consider themselves already adequately informed?

As long as key policy makers lack the time and inclination to use the expertise of the bureaucracy, control is not adequate. To insure against this weakness, we can only count on Presidential and Cabinet leadership, plus continued vigilance and questions by members of the control groups, by the Congress and the media.

Obviously, exhortation to a President or a Cabinet member is not sufficient by itself. But members of the various oversight and control groups can insist on special staff assistance and then present expert views to their colleagues.

John Bruce Lockhart commented as follows on the problem of control: "I believe the weaknesses in the whole intelligence set-up is that those in charge are inadequately educated about the whole problem of control . . . Secret Services are as competent or incompetent as the governments that control them." [16] Perhaps the word "effective" is a better choice than competent, but the point is crucial to any consideration of the problem of clandestine operations.

Protection of Sources and Methods (Taylor Belcher)

The overall question of security, whether in the Congress or in the Executive, is one which has received much attention, particularly since the Ellsberg-Pentagon Papers incident and the exposé by Congressman Harrington concerning CIA activities in Chile. There is no doubt that present provisions are inadequate. Given the virtual impossibility of obtaining any legislation as far-reaching as the British Official Secrets Act, the U.S. must try for something less, but more adequate than the protection (or lack of it) afforded by our present laws. Director Colby has made certain proposals which should be thoroughly considered by the Congress though there would seem to be constitutional problems involved. His position is that it is necessary "to impose penalties on those who take upon themselves the choice of which secrets to reveal, rather than relying on the established declassification procedures of our government." [17] This would not apply to news media or others who have not consciously assumed an obligation to respect secrecy. Colby argues cogently that even agricultural production statistics, census information, and tax returns are better guarded than many more significant government secrets.

15 *Christian Science Monitor, op. cit.*
16 John Bruce Lockhart, *op. cit.*
17 Colby, *op. cit.*

Recommendations (Taylor Belcher)

1. Limit covert operations to those certified by the Secretary of State and the President (as respresented on NSC) as of great importance to the national security.

2. Provide by regulation and regular reminders from INR for periodic review of all clandestine operations and covert actions and their respective disaster plans in the respective Embassies—with problems, if any referred to Washington for decision.

3. Action proposals from the field should have more than high Bureau clearance in State—desk officers, office directors, and INR should have the task of mandatory review, but without veto power.

4. Require by law and regulation that particularly sensitive operations be reviewed at specified intervals (i.e. more frequently than the present annual review) by the Ambassador and Chief of Station in the field and by the 40 Committee and that the President, through the NSC, report to the appropriate Congressional authority the results of these reviews.

5. Provide by law and regulation for systematic review of all other on-going programs—both in the field and in Washington, with the requirement of certification by the Ambassador and Chief of Station, as well as appropriate Washington entities; e.g., PFIAB for certain categories and the Under Secretary of State for Political Affairs for lesser categories.

6. Strengthen the control and approval mechanism in the 40 Committee. The President and Secretary of State should be required by law (amend the 1947 act as necessary) to monitor adequately the 40 Committee functioning. This requires an enlarged staff—which should have representatives of other agencies than CIA, e.g., senior representatives of INR and DIA.

The privileged circle in CIA, State, DIA, etc., must be enlarged to include more of the experts on a given subject being readied for presentation to the Committee. Seniority or position cannot insure either substance or security. Provide by regulation for regular meetings and discussions, and include a provision that any agency or non-government representative may object at cabinet level if the meetings are not held.

Provide by regulation that the 40 Committee include representatives from outside the bureaucracy (not from the Congress), perhaps retired former users of intelligence; i.e., ex-military, ex-Assistant Secretaries of State, or ex-ambassadors. Require that each covert action recommendation include a thorough examination of follow-up requirements to be provided by overt means to capitalize on successful operations, not just a disaster plan in the event of failure or disclosure.

7. Through Presidential initiative, revitalize the PFIAB. Include in its terms of reference a requirement to impress upon members their *independent* responsibilities and urge them to use the resignation weapon if not satisfied with the attitude of the chairman or reactions by NSC, State, or the White House. Provide for a secretariat which is not solely run by former CIA officers but which includes (as in the modified 40 Committee) officials from State and Defense.

8. Establish a Joint Congressional Committee for Intelligence or National Security or, failing that, modify House and Senate rules concerning access to intelligence matters.

9. Maintain the present link between clandestine intelligence collection and covert operations in its present form within the CIA.

10. Request a thorough Congressional consideration of DCI Colby's suggestions for the revision of laws covering disclosure of secrets.

11. Every effort must be made, perhaps through numerical limitations, to lessen CIA presence on Embassy rosters.

12. Intelligence information should be used wherever possible and when deemed appropriate by the Ambassadors in the field. The CIA should have to present cogent arguments to prevent the use of information which the Ambassadors or Secretary of State believe to be in the national interest.

13. While it may only be a gesture, the Commission should emphasize the fact that the best system will not work without Presidential and Cabinet interest, vigilance, and monitoring.

HISTORY OF U.S. COVERT ACTION ([45A], pp. 141–161)

COVERT ACTION

No activity of the Central Intelligence Agency has engendered more controversy and concern than "covert action," the secret use of power and persuasion. The contemporary definition of covert action as used by the CIA—"any clandestine operation or activity designed to influence foreign governments, organizations, persons or events in support of United States foreign policy"—suggests an all-purpose policy tool. By definition, covert action should be one of the CIA's least visible activities, yet it has attracted more attention in recent years than any other United States foreign intelligence activity. The CIA has been

accused of interfering in the internal political affairs of nations rang-
ing from Iran to Chile, from Tibet to Guatemala, from Libya to Laos,
from Greece to Indonesia. Assassinations, coups d'etat, vote buying,
economic warfare—all have been laid at the doorstep of the CIA. Few
political crises take place in the world today in which CIA involve-
ment is not alleged. As former Secretary of Defense Clark Clifford
told the Committee:

> The knowledge regarding such operations has become so
> widespread that our country has been accused of being re-
> sponsible for practically every internal difficulty that has
> occurred in every country in the world.[1]

Senate Resolution 21 authorized the Committee to investigate
"the extent and necessity of overt and covert intelligence activities in
the United States and abroad." [2]   In conducting its inquiry into covert
action, the Committee addressed several sets of questions:

—First, what is the past and present scope of covert action?
Has covert action been an exceptional or commonplace tool of
United States foreign policy? Do present covert operations
meet the standard—set in the Hughes-Ryan amendment to
the 1974 Foreign Assistance Act—of "important to the na-
tional security of the United States?"

—Second, what is the value of covert action as an instru-
ment of United States foreign policy? How successful have
covert operations been over the years in achieving short-range
objectives and long-term goals? What have been the effects of
these operations on the "targeted" nations? Have the costs of
these operations, in terms of our reputation throughout the
world and our capacity for ethical and moral leadership,
outweighed the benefits achieved?

—Third, have the techniques and methods of covert action
been antithetical to our principles and ideals as a nation?
United States officials have been involved in plots to assassi-
nate foreign leaders. In Chile, the United States attempted
to overthrow a democratically elected government. Many
covert operations appear to violate our international treaty
obligations and commitments, such as the charters of the
United Nations and Organization of American States. Can
these actions be justified when our national security interests
are at stake?

—Fourth, does the existence of a covert action capability
distort the decisionmaking process? Covert operations by
their nature cannot be debated openly in ways required by
a constitutional system. However, has this meant that, on
occasion, the Executive has resorted to covert operations to
avoid bureaucratic, Congressional, and public debate? Has
this contributed to an erosion of trust between the executive
and legislative branches of government and between the
government and the people?

---

[1] Clark Clifford testimony, 12/5/75, Hearings, Vol. 7, p. 51.
[2] Senate Resolution 21, Section 2, Clause 14. The CIA conducts several kinds of
covert intelligence activities abroad: clandestine collection of positive foreign
intelligence, counterintelligence (or liaison with local services), and covert
action. Although there are a variety of covert action techniques, most can be
grouped into four broad categories: political action, propaganda, paramilitary,
and economic action.

—Fifth, what are the implications of maintaining a covert action capability, as presently housed in the CIA's Directorate for Operations? Does the very existence of this capability make it more likely that covert operations will be presented as a policy alternative and be implemented? Has the maintenance of this standing capability generated, in itself, demands for more and more covert action? Conversely, what are the implications of *not* maintaining a covert action capability? Will our national security be imperiled? Will our policymakers be denied a valuable policy option?

—Sixth, is it possible to accomplish many of our covert objectives through overt means? Radio Free Europe and Radio Liberty may be instructive in this regard. For years RFE and RL were operated and subsidized, covertly, by the CIA. Today they operate openly. Could other CIA covert activities be conducted in a similar manner?

—Finally, should the United States continue to maintain a covert action capability? If so, should there be restrictions on certain kinds of activities? What processes of authorization and review, both within the executive and legislative branches, should be established?

Over the past year, the Committee investigated several major covert action programs. These programs were selected to illustrate (1) covert action techniques, ranging from propaganda to paramilitary activities, from economic action to subsidizing and supporting foreign political parties, media, and labor organizations; (2) different kinds of "target" countries, from developed Western nations to less developed nations in Africa, Asia and Latin America; (3) a broad time span, from 1947 to the present; and (4) a combination of cases that the CIA considers to be representative of success and failure. One of the Committee's case studies, Chile, was the subject of a

N6 publicly released staff report. It served as background for the Committee's public session on covert action.[4] During its covert action inquiry, the Committee took extensive testimony in executive session and received 14 briefings from the CIA. The staff interviewed over 120 persons, including 13 former Ambassadors and 12 former CIA Station Chiefs. The successor Senate intelligence oversight committee(s) will inherit the Committee's classified covert action case studies as well as a rich documentary base for future consideration of covert action.

In addition to the major covert action case studies, the Committee spent five months investigating alleged plots to assassinate foreign leaders. This inquiry led, inevitably, into covert action writ large. Plots to assassinate Castro could not be understood unless seen in the context of Operation MONGOOSE, a massive covert action program designed to "get rid of Castro." The death of General Schneider in Chile could not be understood unless seen in the context of what was known as Track II—a covert action program, undertaken by the CIA at the direction of President Nixon, to prevent Salvador Allende from assuming the office of President of Chile. During the assassination inquiry, the Committee heard from over 75 witnesses during 60 days of hearings.

---

[4] Senate Select Committee, Hearings, 12/4–5/75, Vol. 7.

The Committee has chosen not to make public the details of all the covert action case studies, with the exceptions noted above. The force of the Committee's recommendations on covert action might be strengthened by using detailed illustrations of what the United States did under what circumstances and with what results in country "X" or "Y." The purpose of the Committee in examining these cases, however, was to understand the scope, techniques, utility, and propriety of covert action in order to make recommendations for the future. The Committee concluded that it was not essential to expose past covert relationships of foreign political, labor and cultural leaders with the United States Government nor to violate the confidentiality of these relationships. Therefore, names of individuals and institutions have been omitted.

In addition, the Committee decided, following objections raised by the CIA, not to publicly release two sections of this Report—"Techniques of Covert Action" and "Covert Action Projects: Initiation, Review, and Approval." These two sections will be submitted to the Members of the Senate in a classified form. However, for a discussion of covert action techniques, as they were practiced in Chile, see the Committee Staff Report, "Covert Action in Chile: 1963–1973" (pp. 6–10, 14–40).

Evolution of Covert Action

Covert action was not included as one of the charter missions of the CIA. The National Security Act of 1947 (which established the Agency and the National Security Council) does not specifically mention or authorize secret operations of any kind, whether for intelligence collection or covert action. The 1947 Act does, however, contain a provision which directs the CIA to "perform such other functions and duties related to intelligence affecting the national security as the National Security Council may from time to time direct." [6] One of the drafters of the 1947 Act, former Secretary of Defense Clark Clifford, has referred to this provision as the "catch-all" clause. According to Mr. Clifford:

> Because those of us who were assigned to this task and had the drafting responsibility were dealing with a new subject with practically no precedents, it was decided that the Act creating the Central Intelligence Agency should contain a "catch-all" clause to provide for unforeseen contingencies. Thus, it was written that the CIA should "perform such other functions and duties related to intelligence affecting the national security as the National Security Council may from time to time direct." It was under this clause that, early in the operation of the 1947 Act, covert activities were authorized. I recall that such activities took place in 1948 and it is even possible that some planning took place in late 1947. It was the original concept that covert activities undertaken under the Act were to be carefully limited and controlled. You will note that the language of the Act provides that this catch-all clause is applicable only in the event that the national security is affected. This was considered to be an important limiting and restricting clause. [7]

---

[6] 50 U.S.C. 403 (d) (5).
[7] Clifford, 12/5/75, Hearings, pp. 50–51.

Beginning in December 1947, the National Security Council issued a series of classified directives specifying and expanding the CIA's **N7** covert mission. The first of these directives, NSC-4-A, authorized the Director of Central Intelligence (DCI) to conduct covert psychological operations consistent with United States policy and in coordination with the Departments of State and Defense.

A later directive, NSC 10/2, authorized the CIA to conduct covert political and paramilitary operations. To organize and direct these activities, a semi-independent Office of Policy Coordination (OPC) was established within the CIA. OPC took policy direction from the Departments of State and Defense.[9] The directive establishing OPC referred to the "vicious covert activities of the U.S.S.R." and authorized the OPC to plan and conduct covert operations, including covert political, psychological, and economic warfare. These early activities were directed against the Soviet threat. They included countering Soviet propaganda and covert Soviet support of labor unions and student groups in Western Europe, direct U.S. support of foreign political parties, "economic warfare," sabotage, assistance to refugee liberation groups, and support of anti-Communist groups in occupied or threatened areas.

Until a reorganization in June, 1950, OPC's responsibilities for paramilitary action were limited, at least in theory, to contingency planning. Networks of agents were trained to assist the escape of resistance forces and carry out sabotage behind enemy lines in the event of war. However, OPC did conduct some guerrilla-type operations in this early period against Soviet bloc countries, using neighboring countries as bases and employing a variety of "black" activities.[10]

The size and activities of the OPC grew dramatically. Many covert action programs initiated in the first few years as an adjunct to the United States policy of communist containment in Europe eventually developed into large-scale and long-term operations, such as the clandestine propaganda radios aimed at the Soviet bloc—Radio Free Europe and Radio Liberty.

Many early OPC activities involved subsidies to European "counterfront" labor and political organizations. These were intended to serve as alternatives to Soviet- or communist-inspired groups. Extensive OPC labor, media, and election operations in Western Europe in the late 1940's, for instance, were designed to undercut debilitating strikes by communist trade unions and election advances by communist parties. Support for "counterfront" organizations, especially in the areas of student, labor and cultural activities, was to become much more prevalent in the 1950s and 1960s, although they later became international rather than European-oriented.

Communist aggression in the Far East led the United States into war in Korea in June 1950. At the same time, Defense Department pressure shifted the focus of OPC activities toward more aggressive responses to Soviet and Chinese Communist threats, particularly military incursions. Large amounts of money were spent for guerrilla and propaganda operations. These operations were designed to support the United States military mission in Korea. Most of these diversionary paramilitary operations never came to fruition. For example, during

---

[9] The semi-independent status of OPC within the CIA created a rivalry with the existing CIA component responsible for clandestine intelligence, the Office of Strategic Operations.

[10] "Black" activities are those intended to give the impression that they are sponsored by an indigenous opposition force or a hostile power, rather than by the United States.

this period the CIA's Office of Procurement acquired some $152 million worth of foreign weapons and ammunition for use by guerrilla forces that never came into existence.

As a result of the upsurge of paramilitary action and contingency planning, OPC's manpower almost trebled during the first year of the Korean War. A large part of this increase consisted of paramilitary experts, who were later to be instrumental in CIA paramilitary operations in the Bay of Pigs, the Congo, and Laos, among others. In support of paramilitary activities the CIA had bases and facilities in the United States, Europe, the Mediterranean and the Pacific. OPC's increased activity was not limited to paramilitary operations, however. By 1953, there were major covert operations in 48 countries, consisting primarily of propaganda and political action.

Another event in 1950 affected the development and organizational framework for covert action. General Walter Bedell Smith became CIA Director. He decided to merge OPC with the CIA's Office of Special Operations.[11] Although the merger was not completed until 1954, the most important organizational step took place in August 1952—a single new directorate, entirely within the structure and control of the CIA, was established. Known as the Directorate for Plans (DDP),[12] this new directorate was headed by a Deputy Director and was assigned responsibility for all CIA covert action and espionage functions. The CIA's "Clandestine Service" was now in place.

By the time the DDP was organized, OPC had a large staff and an annual budget of almost $200 million. It dominated the smaller and bureaucratically weaker OSO in size, glamour, and attention. Yet, one of the original purposes of the merger, according to General Smith, was to protect the OSO function of clandestine intelligence collection from becoming subordinate to the covert action function of OPC. In 1952, Smith wrote that the merger was:

> designed to create a single overseas clandestine service, while at the same time preserving the integrity of the long-range espionage and counterespionage mission of the CIA from amalgamation into those clandestine activities which are subject to short-term variations in the prosecution of the Cold War.

Despite Smith's desires, the Cold War, and the "hot war" in Korea, increased the standing, and influence, of the covert "operators" within the CIA. This trend continued throughout the 1950s and 1960s.

The post-Korean War period did not see a reduction in CIA covert activities. Indeed, the communist threat was now seen to be worldwide, rather than concentrated on the borders of the Soviet Union and mainland China. In response, the CIA, at the direction of the National Security Council, expanded its European and crisis-oriented approach into a world-wide effort to anticipate and meet communist aggression, often with techniques equal to those of the Soviet clandestine services. This new world-wide approach was reflected in a 1955 National Security Council Directive which authorized the CIA to:

---

[11] In order to accomplish the merger, Smith first consolidated the OPC chain of command by ordering the Director of OPC to report directly to the DCI instead of through the Departments of State and Defense. Smith also appointed his own senior representatives to field stations to coordinate the covert activities of the OPC and the espionage operations of the OSO. The two offices were often competing for the same potential assets in foreign countries.

[12] The name was changed to the Directorate for Operations (DDO) in 1973.

—Create and exploit problems for International Communism;

—Discredit International Communism, and reduce the strength of its parties and organization;

—Reduce International Communist control over any areas of the world.

The 1950s saw an expansion of communist interest in the Third World. Attempts to anticipate and meet the communist threat there proved to be an easier task than carrying out clandestine activities in the closed Soviet and Chinese societies. Political action projects in the Third World increased dramatically. Financial support was provided to parties, candidates, and incumbent leaders of almost every political persuasion, except the extreme left and right. The immediate purpose of these projects was to encourage political stability, and thus prevent Communist incursions; but another important objective of political action was the acquisition of "agents of influence" who could be used at a future date to provide intelligence or to carry out political action. Through such projects, the CIA developed a world-wide infrastructure of individual agents, or networks of agents, engaged in a variety of covert activities.

By 1955, the CIA's Clandestine Service had gone through a number of reorganizations. It emerged with a structure for the support of covert action that remained essentially the same until the early 1960s. The Clandestine Service consisted of seven geographic divisions and a number of functional staffs—foreign intelligence, counterintelligence, technical support for covert action, and planning and program coordination. With the demise of paramilitary activities following the Korean War, the Paramilitary Operations Staff had been abolished and its functions merged with the staff responsible for psychological action. An International Organizations Division, created in June 1954, handled all programs in support of labor, youth, student, and cultural counterfront organizations.

Using the covert action budget as one measure of activity, the scope of political and psychological action during the 1950s was greatest in the Far East, Western Europe, and the Middle East, with steadily increasing activity in the Western Hemisphere. The international labor, student, and media projects of the International Organizations Division constituted the greatest single concentration of covert political and propaganda activities. Paramilitary action began to increase again in the late 1950s with large-scale operations in two Asian countries and increased covert military assistance to a third.[13]

The Bay of Pigs disaster in 1961 prompted a reorganization of CIA covert action and the procedures governing it. A new form of covert action—counterinsurgency—was now emphasized. Under the direction of the National Security Council, the CIA rapidly expanded its counterinsurgency capability, focusing on Latin America, Africa, and the Far East. After the Geneva agreements of 1962, the CIA took over the training and advising of the Meo army, previously a responsibility of

---

[13] In 1962 a paramilitary office was reconstituted in the CIA. Following the Bay of Pigs, a panel headed by Lyman Kirkpatrick, then the CIA's Executive Director-Comptroller, recommended that an office be created in the Clandestine Service to centralize and professionalize paramilitary action and contingency planning, drawing upon Agency-wide resources for large-scale operations. As a result, a new paramilitary division was established. It was to operate under the guidance of a new NSC approval group—the Special Group (Counterinsurgency).

U.S. military advisers. The Laos operation eventually became the largest paramilitary effort in post-war history. In 1962 the Agency also began a small paramilitary program in Vietnam. Even after the United States Military Assistance Command (MACV) took over paramilitary programs in Vietnam at the end of 1963, the CIA continued to assist the U.S. military's covert activities against North Vietnam.

The CIA's paramilitary effort continued to expand throughout the decade. The paramilitary budget reached an all-time high in 1970. It probably would have continued to climb, had not the burden of the Laos program been transferred to the Department of Defense in 1971.[14]

Paramilitary action was but one of the CIA's collection of tools during the early and middle 1960s. Outside the Far East the CIA mounted an increasing number of political, propaganda, and economic projects. This was the era of Operation MONGOOSE, a massive covert assault on the Castro regime in Cuba. The need to combat the "export of revolution" by communist powers stimulated a variety of new covert techniques aimed at an increasingly broad range of "targets." Covert action reached its peak in the years 1964 to 1967.

N8

In contrast to the period 1964 to 1967, when expenditures for political and propaganda action increased almost 60 percent, the period 1968 to the present has registered declines in every functional and geographic category of covert action—except for paramilitary operations in the Far East which did not drop until 1972. The number of individual covert action projects dropped by 50 percent from fiscal year 1964 (when they reached an all-time high) to fiscal year 1968. The number of projects by itself is not an adequate measure of the scope of covert action. Projects can vary considerably in size, cost, duration, and effect. Today, for example, one-fourth of the current covert action projects are relatively high-cost (over $100,000 annually).

No matter which standards are used, covert activities have decreased considerably since their peak period in the mid- and late 1960s. Recent trends reflect this decrease in covert action. In one country, covert activities began in the early years of the OPC and became so extensive in the 1950s and 1960s that they affected almost every element of that society. A retrenchment began in 1965; by 1974 there were only two relatively small-scale political action projects. The only covert expenditure projected for fiscal year 1976 is a small sum for the development of potential "assets" or local agents who may be used for covert action in the future. In a second country, covert action expenditures in 1975 were less than one percent of the total in 1971. A slight increase was projected for fiscal year 1976, also for the development of potential assets for future use. The CIA has thus curtailed its covert action projects in these two countries, although its current investment in potential assets indicates that the Agency does not want to preclude the possibility of covert involvement in the future.

Some of the major reasons for the decline of covert activities since the mid- and late 1960s include:

---

[14] Part of the Agency's interest in paramilitary activities stemmed from the Agency's view that these activities are interdependent with intelligence collection functions. DCI John McCone protested the transfer of paramilitary programs in Vietnam to MACV in 1963–1964 because he thought that a third of the intelligence reporting of the CIA's Vietnam station might be lost with such a reduction of CIA participation.

—a reduction of CIA labor, student, and media projects following the 1967 *Ramparts* disclosure and the subsequent recommendations of the Katzenbach Committee;

—the transfer of covert military assistance in Laos from the CIA budget to the Defense Department budget in 1971, and the termination of many other covert activities in that area with the end of the war in Indochina in 1975;

—reductions in overseas personnel of the Clandestine Service as a result of studies and cuts made by James Schlesinger, first when he was with the Office of Management and Budget and later during his brief tenure as Director of Central Intelligence in 1973;

—shifting U.S. foreign policy priorities in the 1970s, which have de-emphasized sustained involvement in the internal affairs of other nations; and

—concern among Agency officials and U.S. policymakers that publicity given to CIA covert activities would increase the chances of disclosure and generally decrease the chances of success of the kinds of large-scale, high-expenditure projects that developed in the 1960s.[15a]

Congressional Oversight

There is no reference to covert action in the 1947 National Security Act, nor is there any evidence in the debates, committee reports, or legislative history of the 1947 Act to show that Congress intended specifically to authorize covert operations. Since the CIA's wartime predecessor, the Office of Strategic Services, had conducted covert operations, Congress may have anticipated that these operations were envisioned.

Whether specifically authorized by Congress or not, CIA covert operations were soon underway. Citing the "such other functions and duties" clause of the 1947 Act as authority, the National Security Council authorized the CIA to undertake covert operations at its first meeting in December 1947. At that point Congress became responsible for overseeing these activities.

N9

Shortly after the passage of the 1947 Act, the Armed Services and Appropriations Committees of the House and the Senate assumed jurisdiction for CIA activities and appropriations. In the Senate, following an informal arrangement worked out with Senators Vandenberg and Russell, small CIA subcommittees were created within Armed Services and Appropriations. Over time, the relations between the subcommittees and the CIA came to be dominated by two principles: "need to know" and "want to know." [17] The "want to know"

[15a] The next two sections of this report "Covert Action Techniques" and "Covert Action Projects: Initiation, Review, and Approval," remain classified after consultation between the Committee and the executive branch.

[17] The Rockefeller Commission made a similar point in its Report:

"In sum, congressional oversight of the CIA has been curtailed by the secrecy shrouding its activities and budget. At least until quite recently, Congress has not sought substantial amounts of information. Correspondingly, the CIA has not generally volunteered additional information." (Report of the Commission on CIA Activities Within the United States, 6/6/75, p. 77.)

principle was best expressed in a statement made in 1956 by a congressional overseer of the CIA, Senator Leverett Saltonstall:

> It is not a question of reluctance on the part of CIA officials to speak to us. Instead, it is a question of our reluctance, if you will, to seek information and knowledge on subjects which I personally, as a member of Congress and as a citizen, would rather not have, unless I believed it to be my responsibility to have it because it might involve the lives of American citizens.[18]

From the beginning, the House and the Senate subcommittees were relatively inactive. According to information available to the Select Committee, the Senate Armed Services subcommittee met 26 times between January 1966 and December 1975. The subcommittee met five times in 1975, twice in 1974, once in 1973 and 1972, and not at all in 1971.

Relations between the CIA and the subcommittees came to be determined, in large part, by the personal relationship between the chairmen and the CIA Director, often to the exclusion of other subcommittee members. Staff assistance was minimal, usually consisting of no more than one professional staff member.

The two Senate subcommittees had somewhat different responsibilities.[19] The Appropriations subcommittee was to concentrate on the budgetary aspects of CIA activities. The Armed Services subcommittee had the narrower responsibility of determining the legislative needs of the Agency and recommending additional or corrective legislation. It did not authorize the CIA's annual budget.

The CIA subcommittees received general information about some covert operations. Prior to the Hughes-Ryan Amendment to the 1974 Foreign Assistance Act, however, the subcommittees were not notified of these operations on any regular basis. Notifications occurred on the basis of informal agreements between the CIA and the subcommittee chairmen.[20] CIA covert action briefings did not include detailed descriptions of the methods and cost of individual covert action projects. Rather, projects were grouped into broad, general programs, either on a country-wide basis or by type of activity, for presentation to the subcommittees.

Chile can serve as an example of how oversight of covert action was conducted. According to CIA records, there was a total of 53 congressional briefings on Chile by the CIA between April 1964 and December 1974. At 33 of these meetings there was some discussion of covert action; special releases of funds for covert action from the Contingency Reserve were discussed at 23 of them. Of the 33 covert action briefings, 20 took place prior to 1973, and 13 took place after.[21]

---

[18] Congressional Record—April 9, 1956, p. S.5292.

[19] Initially the Armed Services and Appropriations subcommittees met separately. However, in the 1960s, because of overlapping membership the two committees met jointly. For several years Senator Richard Russell was chairman of both subcommittees.

[20] In 1967, the House and Senate CIA appropriations subcommittees began receiving notifications of withdrawals from the CIA's Contingency Reserve Fund within 48 hours of the release. In 1975 the two Armed Service subcommittees began receiving the same notifications, at the initiative of Director Colby.

[21] The 13 briefings which occurred after 1973 (March 1973 to December 1974) included meetings with the Senate Foreign Relations Subcommittee on Multinational Corporations and the House Foreign Affairs Subcommittee on Inter-American Affairs. All these meetings were concerned with *past* CIA covert action in Chile.

Of the 33 covert action projects undertaken in Chile between 1963 and 1974 with 40 Committee approval, Congress was briefed in some fashion on eight. Presumably the 25 others were undertaken without congressional consultation.[22] Of the more than $13 million spent in Chile on covert action projects between 1963 and 1974, Congress received briefings (sometimes before and sometimes after the fact) on projects totaling about $9.3 million. Further, congressional oversight committees were not consulted about projects which were not reviewed by the full 40 Committee. One of these was the Track II attempt by the CIA, at the instruction of President Nixon, to prevent Salvador Allende from taking office in 1970.[23]

Congressional oversight of CIA covert operations was altered as a result of the Hughes-Ryan amendment to the 1974 Foreign Assistance Act. That amendment stated:

> Sec. 662. Limitation on Intelligence Activities.—(a) No funds appropriated under the authority of this or any other Act may be expended by or on behalf of the Central Intelligence Agency for operations in foreign countries, other than activities intended solely for obtaining necessary intelligence, unless and until the President finds that each such operation is important to the national security of the United States and reports, in a timely fashion, a description and scope of such operation to the appropriate committees of the Congress, including the Committee on Foreign Relations of the United States Senate and the Committee on Foreign Affairs of the United States House of Representatives.[24]

The Hughes-Ryan amendment had two results. First, it established *by statute* a reporting requirement to Congress on covert action. Second, the amendment increased the number of committees that would be informed of approved covert operations. The inclusion of the Senate Foreign Relations Committee and the House International Relations Committee was in recognition of the significant foreign policy implications of covert operations.

Despite these changes, the oversight role of Congress with respect to covert operations is still limited. The law does not require notification of Congress before covert operations are implemented. The DCI has not felt obligated to inform the subcommittees of approved covert action operations prior to their implementation, although in some cases he has done so. Problems thus arise if members of Congress object to a decision by the President to undertake a covert operation.

The recent case of Angola is a good example of the weaknesses of the Hughes-Ryan amendment. In this case, the Executive fully complied with the requirements of the amendment. In January 1975 the administration decided to provide substantial covert political sup-

---

[22] Among the 25 projects were a $1.2 million authorization in 1971, half of which was spent to purchase radio stations and newspapers while the other half went to support municipal candidates in anti-Allende political parties; and an additional expenditure of $815,000 in late 1971 to provide support to opposition political parties in Chile.

[23] With respect to congressional oversight of CIA activities in Chile, the Committee's Staff report on "Covert Action in Chile" concluded:

"Between April 1964 and December 1974, CIA's consultation with its congressional oversight committees—and thus Congress' exercise of its oversight function—was inadequate. The CIA did not volunteer detailed information; Congress most often did not seek it." (Senate Select Committee, "Covert Action in Chile," p. 49.)

[24] 22 USC 2422.

port to the FNLA faction in Angola.[25] In early February, senior members of the six congressional committees received notification of this decision.

In late July the 40 Committee and President Ford approved an additional expenditure to provide covert military assistance to the FNLA and a second Angolan faction, UNITA. Again senior members of the six committees were notified. The Chairman, the ranking minority member, and Chief of Staff of the Senate Foreign Relations Committee were briefed in late July. Under procedures established within that committee, a notice of the CIA briefing was circulated to all committee members. When Senator Dick Clark, Chairman of the Foreign Relations Subcommittee on African Affairs, learned that the covert action program was in Africa, he requested further details. On July 28, Clark's subcommittee was briefed on the paramilitary assistance program to the FNLA and, apparently, some members of the subcommittee objected.

In early September the Administration decided to increase its covert military assistance to Angola by $10.7 million, bringing the total amount to $25 million. Again, the required notifications were carried out.[26]

In early November, Senator Clark raised his objections to the Angola operation before the full Senate Foreign Relations Committee. The Committee in turn asked Director Colby and Secretary Kissinger to testify, in closed session, on U.S. involvement in Angola. At this meeting, several members of the Committee expressed their concern for the program to Director Colby and Undersecretary Joseph Sisco, who represented the State Department in Secretary Kissinger's absence. Despite this concern, in mid-November President Ford and the 40 Committee authorized the expenditure of another $7 million for covert military assistance to Angola. In early December, the congressional committees were notified of this new infusion of military assistance.

Finding opposition within the briefing mechanism ineffective, Senator Clark proposed an amendment to a pending military and security assistance bill. In January 1976 after a complicated series of legislative actions, additional covert military assistance to Angola was prohibited by Congress by an amendment to the Defense appropriations bill.

The dispute over Angola illustrates the dilemma Congress faces with respect to covert operations. The Hughes-Ryan amendment guaranteed information about covert action in Angola, but not any control over this controversial instrument of foreign policy. Congress had to resort to the power of the purse to express its judgment and will.

---

[25] There were three factions involved in the Angolan conflict: the National Front for the Liberation of Angola (FNLA), led by Holden Roberto; the National Union for the Total Independence of Angola (UNITA), led by Jonas Savimbi; and the Popular Movement for the Liberation of Angola, (MPLA) led by Agostinho Neto. The latter group received military and political support from the Soviet Union and Cuba.

[26] On September 25, 1975 the *New York Times* first reported the fact of U.S. covert assistance to the FNLA and UNITA. The article stated that Director Colby had notified Congress of the Angola operation in accordance with the Hughes-Ryan amendment, but "no serious objections were raised." There was little reaction to the *Times* article, either in Congress or by the public.

Findings and Conclusions

Covert action has been a tool of United States foreign policy for the past 28 years. Thousands of covert action projects have been undertaken. An extensive record has been established on which to base judgments of whether covert action should have a role in the foreign policy of a democratic society and, if so, under what restraints of accountability and control. The Committee's examination of covert action has led to the following findings and conclusions.

N10

The Use of Covert Action

Although not a specific charter mission of the Central Intelligence Agency, covert action quickly became a primary activity. Covert action projects were first designed to counter the Soviet threat in Europe and were, at least initially, a limited and ad hoc response to an exceptional threat to American security. Covert action soon became a routine program of influencing governments and covertly exercising power—involving literally hundreds of projects each year. By 1953 there were major covert operations underway in 48 countries, consisting of propaganda, paramilitary and political action projects. By the 1960s, covert action had come to mean "any clandestine activity designed to influence foreign governments, events, organizations or persons in support of United States foreign policy." Several thousand individual covert action projects have been undertaken since 1961, although the majority of these have been low-risk, low-cost projects, such as a routine press placement or the development of an "agent of influence."

That covert action was not intended to become a pervasive foreign policy tool is evident in the testimony of those who were involved in the drafting of the 1947 National Security Act. One of these drafters, Clark Clifford, had this to say about the transition of covert action from an ad hoc response to a frequently used foreign policy tool:

> It was the original concept that covert activities undertaken under the Act were to be carefully limited and controlled. You will note that the language of the Act provides that this catch-all clause is applicable only in the event that national security is affected.[28] This was considered to be an important limiting and restricting clause.
>
> However, as the Cold War continued and Communist aggression became the major problem of the day, our Government felt that it was necessary to increase our country's responsibilities in protecting freedom in various parts of the world. It seems apparent now that we also greatly increased our covert activities. I have read somewhere that as time progressed we had literally hundreds of such operations going on simultaneously. It seems clear that these operations have gotten out of hand.[29]

---

[28] The CIA, under the 1947 Act, is directed "to perform such other functions and duties related to intelligence affecting the national security as the National Security Council may from time to time direct."

[29] Clifford, 12/5/75, Hearings, p. 51.

Covert Action "Success" and "Failure"

The record of covert action reviewed by the Committee suggests that net judgments as to "success" or "failure" are difficult to draw.[30] The Committee has found that when covert operations have been consistent with, and in tactical support of, policies which have emerged from a national debate and the established processes of government, these operations have tended to be a success. Covert support to beleaguered democrats in Western Europe in the late 1940s was in support of an established policy based on a strong national consensus. On the other hand, the public has neither understood nor accepted the covert harassment of the democratically elected Allende government. Recent covert intervention in Angola preceded, and indeed preempted, public and congressional debate on America's foreign policy interest in the future of Angola. The intervention in Angola was conducted in the absence of efforts on the part of the executive branch to develop a national consensus on America's interests in Southern Africa.

The Committee has received extensive testimony that covert action can be a success when the objective of the project is to support an individual, a party, or a government in doing what that individual, party, or government wants to do—and when it has the will and capacity to do it. Covert action cannot build political institutions where there is no local political will to have them. Where this has been attempted, success has been problematical at best, and the risks of exposure enormously high.

The Committee's findings on paramilitary activities suggest that these operations are an anomaly, if not an aberration, of covert action.[31] Paramilitary operations are among the most costly and controversial forms of covert action. They are difficult, if not impossible, to conceal. They lie in the critical gray area between limited influence, short of the use of force, and overt military intervention. As such, paramilitary activities are especially significant. In Vietnam, paramilitary strategy formed a bridge between the two levels of involvement. Paramilitary operations have great potential for escalating into major military commitments.

Covert U.S. paramilitary programs have generally been designed to accomplish one of the following objectives: (1) subversion of a hostile government (e.g., Cuba); (2) support to friendly governments

---

[30] Former Attorney General and Under Secretary of State Nicholas Katzenbach had this to say about covert action "success" and "failure":

"I start from the premise that some of our covert activities abroad have been successful, valuable in support of a foreign policy which was understood and approved by the electorate and Congress . . . I also start from a premise that some of our activities abroad have not been successful, and have been wrong and wrongheaded. In some cases we have grossly over-estimated our capacity to bring about a desired result and have created situations unintended and undesirable." (Nicholas Katzenbach testimony, House Select Committee on Intelligence, 12/10/75, Hearings, Vol. 5, p. 1797.)

[31] The Committee studied, in detail, covert military operations in five countries, including Laos, Vietnam, and Angola. The Committee analyzed paramilitary programs in terms of (1) executive command and control; (2) secrecy and deniability; (3) effectiveness; (4) propriety; and (5) legislative oversight. The latter issue is vital because paramilitary operations are directly related to, and pose special problems for, Congress' authority and responsibilities in making war.

(Laos); (3) unconventional adjunct support to a larger war effort (Korea, Vietnam, Laos after the middle 1960s).

There are two principal criteria which determine the minimum success of paramilitary operations: (1) achievement of the policy goal; and (2) maintenance of deniability. If the first is not accomplished, the operation is a failure in any case; if the second is not accomplished, the paramilitary option offers few if any advantages over the option of overt military intervention. On balance, in these terms, the evidence points toward the failure of paramilitary activity as a technique of covert action.[32]

Of the five paramilitary activities studied by the Committee, only one appears to have achieved its objectives. The goal of supporting a central government was achieved—the same government is still in power many years later. There were a few sporadic reports of the operation in the press, but it was never fully revealed nor confirmed.

In no paramilitary case studied by the Committee was complete secrecy successfully preserved. All of the operations were reported in the American press to varying extents, while they were going on. They remained deniable only to the extent that such reports were tentative, sketchy, and unconfirmed, and hence were not necessarily considered accurate.

The Impact of Covert Action

Assessing the "success" or "failure" of covert action is necessary. Just as important, however, is an assessment of the impact of covert action on "targeted" nations and the reputation of the United States abroad.

The impact of a large-scale covert operation, such as Operation MONGOOSE in Cuba, is apparent. Less apparent is the impact of small covert projects on "targeted" countries. The Committee has found that these small projects can, in the aggregate, have a powerful effect upon vulnerable societies.

In some cases, covert support has encouraged a debilitating dependence on the United States. In one Western nation the covert investment was so heavy and so persistent that, according to a former CIA Station Chief in that country:

> Any aspiring politician almost automatically would come to CIA to see if we could help him get elected . . . They were the wards of the United States, and that whatever happened for good or bad was the fault of the United States.

Cyrus Vance, a former Deputy Secretary of Defense, cited another such example:

> Paramilitary operations are perhaps unique in that it is more difficult to withdraw from them, once started, than covert

---

[32] For example, the covert paramilitary program in Laos certainly ceased to be plausibly deniable as soon as it was revealed officially in the 1969 Symington hearings of the Senate Foreign Relations Committee (it was revealed unofficially even earlier). If U.S. policy was the preservation of a non-communist Laotian government, the program obviously failed. Some administration witnesses, nevertheless, including DCI Colby, cited the war in Laos as a great success. Their reasoning was based on the view that the limited effort in Laos served to put pressure on North Vietnamese supply lines, and therefore was a helpful adjunct of the larger U.S. effort in Vietnam.

operations. This is well illustrated by the case of the Congo, where a decision was taken to withdraw in early 1966, and it took about a year and a half before the operation was terminated. Once a paramilitary operation is commenced, the recipient of the paramilitary aid tends to become dependent upon it and inevitably advances the argument that to cut back or terminate the aid would do the recipient great damage. This makes it especially difficult to disengage.[34]

In other cases, covert support to foreign political leaders, parties, labor unions, or the media has made them vulnerable to repudiation in their own society when their covert ties are exposed. In Chile, several of the Chilean nationals who had been involved in the CIA's anti-Allende "spoiling" operation had to leave the country when he was confirmed as President.

In addition, the history of covert action indicates that the cumulative effect of hidden intervention in the society and institutions of a foreign nation has often not only transcended the actual threat, but it has also limited the foreign policy options available to the United States Government by creating ties to groups and causes that the United States cannot renounce without revealing the earlier covert action.

The Committee also found that the cumulative effects of covert action are rarely noted by the operational divisions of the CIA in the presentation of new projects or taken into account by the responsible National Security Council review levels.

The Committee has found that certain covert operations have been incompatible with American principles and ideals and, when exposed, have resulted in damaging this nation's ability to exercise moral and ethical leadership throughout the world. The U.S. involvement in assassination plots against foreign leaders and the attempt to foment a military coup in Chile in 1970 against a democratically elected government were two examples of such failures in purposes and ideals. Further, because of widespread exposure of covert operations and suspicion that others are taking place, the CIA is blamed for virtually every foreign internal crisis.

The Executive's Use of Covert Action

In its consideration of covert action, the Committee was struck by the basic tension—if not incompatibility—of covert operations and the demands of a constitutional system. Secrecy is essential to covert operations; secrecy can, however, become a source of power, a barrier to serious policy debate within government, and a means of circumventing the established checks and procedures of government. The Committee found that secrecy and compartmentation contributed to a temptation on the part of the Executive to resort to covert operations in order to avoid bureaucratic, congressional, and public debate. In addition, the Committee found that the major successes of covert action tended to encourage the Executive to press for the use of covert action as the easy way to do things and to task the CIA with difficult requirements, such as running a large-scale "secret" war in Laos or

---

[34] Cyrus Vance testimony, 12/5/75, Hearings, Vol. 7. p. 85, footnote.

attempting to overturn the results of a national election in Chile—
within a five-week period.

The Committee found that the Executive has used the CIA to con-
duct covert operations because it is less accountable than other gov-
ernment agencies. In this regard, Secretary of State Henry Kissinger
told the Committee:

> I do not believe in retrospect that it was good national policy
> to have the CIA conduct the war in Laos. I think we should
> have found some other way of doing it. And to use the CIA
> simply because it is less accountable for very visible major
> operations is poor national policy. And the covert activities
> should be confined to those matters that clearly fall into a
> gray area between overt military action and diplomatic activi-
> ties, and not to be used simply for the convenience of the
> executive branch and its accountability.[35]

Under questioning, Secretary Kissinger went on to say that in Laos
there were two basic reasons why the CIA was used to fight that war:
"one, to avoid a formal avowal of American participation there for
diplomatic reasons, and the second, I suspect, because it was less
accountable."[36]

The Committee has found that the temptation of the Executive to
use covert action as a "convenience" and as a substitute for publicly
accountable policies has been strengthened by the hesitancy of the
Congress to use its powers to oversee covert action by the CIA. Much
of this hesitancy flowed from the legitimate desire on the part of con-
gressional oversight committees to maintain the security of covert
action projects. But it also resulted from a reluctance on the part of
the appropriate committees to challenge the President or to become
directly involved in projects perceived to be necessary for the national
security. Congressional hesitancy also flowed from the fact that con-
gressional oversight committees are almost totally dependent on the
Executive for information on covert operations. The secrecy needed
for these operations allows the Executive to justify the limited provi-
sion of information to the Congress.

Maintaining a Covert Capability

Former senior government officials have testified to their concern
that the use and control of covert action is made more difficult by a
strong activism on the part of CIA operational officers. McGeorge
Bundy, a former Special Assistant for National Security Affairs to
Presidents Kennedy and Johnson, has stated:

> While in principle it has always been the understanding of
> senior government officials outside the CIA that no covert
> operations would be undertaken without the explicit approval
> of "higher authority," there has also been a general expecta-
> tion within the Agency that it was its proper business to gen-
> erate attractive proposals and to stretch them, in operation,
> to the furthest limit of any authorization actually received.[37]

---

[35] Henry Kissinger testimony, 11/21/75, p. 54.
[36] Ibid., p. 56.
[37] McGeorge Bundy testimony, House Select Committee on Intelligence,
12/10/75, Hearings, Vol. 5, pp. 1794–1795.

Clark Clifford, in testimony before the Select Committee, reinforced this view:

> On a number of occasions a plan for covert action has been presented to the NSC and authority requested for the CIA to proceed from point A to point B. The authority will be given and the action will be launched. When point B is reached, the persons in charge feel that it is necessary to go to point C and they assume that the original authorization gives them such a right. From point C, they go to D, and possibly E, and even further. This led to some bizarre results, and, when investigation is started, the excuse blandly presented that the authority was obtained from the NSC before the project was launched.[38]

The activism referred to by Bundy and Clifford is reflected in part, in the maintenance of a standing covert action capability and a worldwide "infrastructure." The Committee found that one of the most troublesome and controversial issues it confronted in evaluating covert action was the question of the utility and propriety of the CIA's maintaining a worldwide "infrastructure" (e.g., agents of influence, assets, and media contacts). Are these "assets" essential to the success of a major covert action program? Or does this standby capability generate a temptation to intervene covertly as an alternative to diplomacy?

There is no question that the CIA attaches great importance to the maintenance of a worldwide clandestine infrastructure—the so-called "plumbing"—in place. During the 1960s the Agency developed a worldwide system of standby covert action "assets," ranging from media personnel to individuals said to influence the behavior of governments.[39] In recent years, however, the Agency has substantially reduced its overseas covert action infrastructure even to the point of closing bases and stations. A limited infrastructure is still maintained, however. For example, although the United States has no substantial covert action program in the Western Hemisphere today, the CIA does continue to maintain a modest covert action infrastructure consisting of agents of influence and media contacts.

The CIA's infrastructure is constructed in response to annual Operating Directives. These directives set station priorities for both clandestine collection and covert action.[40] The Operating Directives are developed and issued by the CIA and informally coordinated with concerned CIA geographic bureaus and the Department of State. Therefore, the infrastructure that is in place at any given time is there at the direction of the CIA.

The Committee finds several troublesome problems with the CIA's development and maintenance of covert action infrastructures

---

[38] Clark M. Clifford testimony 12/5/75, Hearings, Vol. 7, pp. 51–52.

[39] During its assassination inquiry, the Committee found that certain CIA assets, with the cryptonyms QJ/WIN, WI/ROGUE and AM/LASH were involved, or contemplated for use in, plots to assassinate foreign leaders.

[40] For example, the Chilean Operating Directive for FY 1972 directed the Santiago Station to: "Sponsor a program which will enable the Chilean armed forces to retain their integrity and independent political power. Provide direct financial support to key military figures who can be expected to develop a meaningful following in their respective services to restrain and, perhaps, topple the Allende government." The Select Committee found no evidence to indicate that this "direct financial support" was provided.

throughout the world: (1) The operating decisions are made by the CIA, although infrastructure guidelines are cleared with the State Department; the Agency's Operating Directives are rarely seen outside the CIA and (2) the actual covert action projects which build and maintain these infrastructures rarely, if ever, go to the NSC for approval.

The Committee finds that the independent issuance of Operating Directives, and the fact that most covert action projects which establish and maintain the CIA's infrastructure around the world do not go to the NSC, combine to shield this important clandestine system from effective policy control and guidance. The Committee believes that all small so-called "non-sensitive" projects which do not now go to the NSC level for approval should, at a minimum, be aggregated into appropriate country or regional programs, and then brought to the NSC level for approval.

Covert action should be the servant of policy. Secretary Kissinger made this point before the Committee when he testified:

> If the diplomatic track cannot succeed without the covert track, then the covert track was unnecessary and should not have been engaged in. So hopefully, if one wants to draw a general conclusion, one would have to say that only those covert actions can be justified that support a diplomatic track.[41]

Conclusions

Given the open and democratic assumptions on which our government is based, the Committee gave serious consideration to proposing a total ban on *all* forms of covert action. The Committee has concluded, however, that the United States should maintain the option of reacting in the future to a grave, unforeseen threat to United States national security through covert means.

The Hughes-Ryan amendment to the 1974 Foreign Assistance Act restricts the CIA from undertaking "operations in foreign countries, other than activities intended for obtaining necessary intelligence, unless and until the President finds that each such operation is important to the national security of the United States." The Committee has concluded that an even stricter standard for the use of covert action is required than the injunction that such operations be "important to the national security of the United States."

The Committee's review of covert action has underscored the necessity for a thoroughgoing strengthening of the Executive's internal review process for covert action and for the establishment of a realistic system of accountability, both within the Executive, and to the Congress and to the American people. The requirement for a rigorous and credible system of control and accountability is complicated, however, by the shield of secrecy which must necessarily be imposed on any covert activity if it is to remain covert. The challenge is to find a substitute for the public scrutiny through congressional debate and press attention that normally attends government decisions. In its consideration of the present processes of authorization and review, the Committee has found the following:

[41] Henry Kissinger testimony, 11/21/75. p. 38.

(1) The most basic conclusion reached by the Committee is that covert action must be seen as an exceptional act, to be undertaken only when the national security requires it and when overt means will not suffice. The Committee concludes that the policy and procedural barriers are presently inadequate to insure that any covert operation is absolutely essential to the national security. These barriers must be tightened and raised or covert action should be abandoned as an instrument of foreign policy.

(2) On the basis of the record, the Committee has concluded that covert action must in no case be a vehicle for clandestinely undertaking actions incompatible with American principles. The Committee has already moved to condemn assassinations and to recommend a statute to forbid such activity. It is the Committee's view that the standards to acceptable covert activity should also exclude covert operations in an attempt to subvert democratic governments or provide support for police or other internal security forces which engage in the systematic violation of human rights.

(3) Covert operations must be based on a careful and systematic analysis of a given situation, possible alternative outcome, the threat to American interests of these possible outcomes, and above all, the likely consequences of an attempt to intervene. A former senior intelligence analyst told the Committee:

> Clearly actions were taken on the basis of some premises, but they seem not to have been arrived at by any sober and systematic analysis, and tended often, it appeared, to be simplistic and passionate. In fact, there was often little or no relationship between the view of world politics as a whole, or of particular situations of threat held by operators on the one hand, and analysts on the other. The latter were rarely consulted by the former, and then only in partial disingenious and even misleading ways.
>
> It says something strange about successive DCIs that they allowed this bifurcation, even contradiction, to obtain.[43]

The Committee has concluded that bringing the analysts directly into the *formal* decision process would be a partial remedy to the problem of relating analysis to operations. More important would be the insistence of the Director of Central Intelligence that the political premises of any proposed covert operation be rigorously analyzed.

(4) The Committee also concludes that the appropriate NSC committee (e.g., the Operations Advisory Group) should review *every* covert action proposal. The Committee also holds strongly to the view

---

[43] John Huizenga testimony, 1/26/76, pp. 6–7. The Committee found, in its case study of Chile, that there was little or no coordination between the intelligence analysts and the covert operators, especially in politically sensitive projects, which were often restricted within the Clandestine Service and the 40 Committee. The project files for Chile gave no indication of consultation with the Intelligence Directorate from 1964 to 1973. The exclusion of expert analytic advice extended to the DCI's staff responsible for preparing National Intelligence Estimates. Today, however, the Deputy Director for Intelligence (DDI) is informed by the DDO of new covert activities. The DDI has an opportunity to comment on them and offer recommendations to the DCI, but he is not in the formal approval process.

that the small nonsensitive covert action proposals which, in the aggre-
gate, establish and maintain the Agency's covert infrastructure around
the world should be considered and analyzed by the appropriate NSC
committee. The Committee also believes that many of the small covert
action proposals for projects would fall away when forced to meet the
test of being part of a larger covert action operation in support of the
openly avowed policies of the United States.

(5) With respect to congressional oversight of covert action, the
Committee believes that the appropriate oversight committee should
be informed of all significant covert operations *prior* to their initia-
tion and that all covert action projects should be reviewed by the com-
N11 mittee on a semi-annual basis. Further, the oversight committee should
require that the annual budget submission for covert action programs
be specific and detailed as to the activity recommended. Unforeseen
covert action projects should be funded only from the Contingency
Reserve Fund which could be replenished only after the concurrence
of the oversight and any other appropriate congressional committees.
The legislative intelligence oversight committee should be notified
N12 prior to any withdrawal from the Contingency Reserve Fund.

Reported Foreign and Domestic Covert Activities of the U.S. Central Intelligence Agency: 1950–1974 ([103], CRS 1–13)

In 1974, Richard Grimmett, an analyst in the Foreign Affairs Division of the Congressional
Research Service, prepared a summary of major covert operations that had come to public
attention over the past 15 years. The Grimmett report, which follows, provides a glimpse at the
scope and type of covert operations with which the U.S. government has been associated.

The report which follows consists of abstracts of note-
worthy foreign and domestic covert activities reportedly
engaged in by the United States Central Intelligence Agency
from 1950 to 1974. The abstracts are arranged in chrono-
logical order from the earliest event to the most recent,
and are based upon information made public in newspapers,
magazines, books, testimony before Congressional committees,
or in other publications. Although the last date noted is
March 1974, the events described are based upon an exami-
nation of materials available during the first week of
February, 1975. No judgment is made herein concerning the
validity of any of the reports that were abstracted. Every
effort was made, however, to summarize them in a manner that
did not distort their substance.

1950 – The CIA began operating on Formosa in 1950
under the cover of Western Enterprises, Inc.,
training Nationalist Chinese commandos for
raids on the mainland of China.1/

1/ David Wise and Thomas B. Ross, The Invisible Government (New
York: Random House, 1964), pp.109–110.

1950 –   Beginning in 1950 until 1966, the Congress for
               Cultural Freedom, a private cultural organi-
               zation that was strongly anti-Communist, was
               subsidized by the CIA. The Congress received
               over $1,000,000 in grants during the above
               period.2/

1950 –   The Center for International Studies at Mas-
               sachusetts Institute of Technology was established
               in 1950, receiving a CIA grant of $300,000.
               Additional grants in substantial amounts were
               provided by the CIA to the Center until 1966.3/

1951 –   CIA Director William E. Colby stated that from
               1951 until 1965, the CIA "employed telephone
               wiretaps directed against twenty-one residents
               of the United States." All but two of the
               individuals tapped were either current or
               former CIA employees. The purpose of the taps
               was "to check on leaks of classified information."4/

1951-1952 –   Thomas Braden, head of the CIA's Division of
               International Organization from 1951 to 1954,
               stated that in 1951 or 1952 he gave Walter
               Reuther of the United Auto Workers $50,000
               in CIA funds, which were ultimately spent
               by Reuther's brother Victor in West Germany to
               support anti-Communist labor unions there.5/

1952 –   Since 1952 the CIA provided a subsidy to George
               Papadopoulos, the Greek colonel who later led
               the military coup in Greece in 1967. The CIA
               also gave subsidies to many Greek military and
               political figures for years after 1952. The
               subsidies apparently ended in 1972.6/

2/ Jerrold L. Walden, "Proselytes for Espionage -- The CIA and
      Domestic Fronts," Journal of Public Law 19, No.2 (1970),
      pp.195-196. The New York Times, May 14, 1967, p.32.

3/ The New York Times, April 14, 1966, pp.1-2. Victor Marchetti
      and John D. Marks, The CIA and the Cult of Intelligence
      (New York: Alfred A. Knopf, 1974), p.175. The New York
      Times, April 27, 1966, p.1.

4/ William E. Colby, "Statement before the Senate Armed Services
      Committee," January 16, 1975, p.30. (Hereafter cited as
      Colby, "SASC Statement," January 16, 1975).

5/ Thomas W. Braden, "I'm Glad the CIA is 'immoral'," The Satur-
      day Evening Post, (May 20, 1967), pp.10,12,14. The New
      York Times, May 8, 1967, pp.1,36. It was revealed in 1975
      that in order to monitor the flow of covert money to Euro-
      pean trade unions in the manner described above, the CIA
      secretly read the mail of AFL-CIO President George Meany
      and two of his key aides, Jay Lovestone and Irving Brown,
      during the 1950's. The Washington Post, January 10, 1975,
      pp.A1,A10.

6/ The New York Times, August 2, 1974, pp.1,3.

1952 -   In the early 1950's, CIA Special Operations Divi-
                  sion agents made attempts to develop resistance
                  movements inside Communist China. On November 9,
                  1952, CIA agents John Thomas Downey and Richard
                  George Fecteau were captured on the Chinese main-
                  land where they had been organizing and training
                  two teams of Nationalist Chinese agents to stir up
                  mainland Chinese against their Communist govern-
                  ment.7/

1952 -   From 1952 until 1966, the CIA gave the National
                  Student Association some $3.3 million to support
                  the organization's operations. During certain
                  years as much as 80 percent of the Association's
                  budget came from CIA funds. As the result of
                  its support of NSA in this manner, the CIA gained
                  and exercised considerable influence over the
                  activities and policies of the student
                  organization.8/

early 1950's -   Radio Free Europe and Radio Liberty, purportedly
                  "non-profit, privately managed" American radio
                  stations, which were established in the early
                  1950's, received the vast bulk of their financ-
                  ing from the CIA. The combined budget of the two
                  stations was between $30 and $35 million annually,
                  with the CIA providing over 95 percent of this
                  amount.9/

early 1950's -   From the early 1950's until 1953 Air Force
                  Colonel Edward Lansdale, under CIA auspices,
                  gave advice and assistance to Philippine leader
                  Ramon Magsaysay in his struggle against the
                  local Communist Huk guerrillas. Millions of
                  American dollars were provided by the U.S.
                  secretly for Lansdale's use in this program.
                  The program was instrumental in bringing about
                  the ultimate defeat of the guerrillas.10/

1953 -   Thomas W. Braden, head of CIA's Division of
                  International Organization, from 1951 to 1954,
                  stated that by 1953 the CIA was "operating or
                  influencing international organizations in
                  every field where Communist fronts had seized
                  ground, and in some where they had not even

---

7/ David Wise, "Colby of CIA -- CIA of Colby," The New York
        Times Magazine (July 1, 1973), p.9. Marchetti and Marks,
        op. cit., pp.113-114. Wise and Ross, op. cit., pp.106-107.

8/ Sol Stern, "NSA and the CIA," Ramparts 5, (March 1967),
        pp.29-38. Walden, op. cit., pp.185-189. The New York
        Times, February 18, 1967, p.14.

9/ Walden, op. cit., p.199. Marchetti and Marks, op. cit.,
        pp.162,167-168. The New York Times, March 14,1967, p.12.

10/ Marchetti and Marks, op. cit., pp.27-28. The New York Times,
        September 22, 1974, section 4, p.1.

begun to operate." The activities noted by
Braden were conducted through private,
"legitimate, existing organizations."11/

1953 -   The CIA directed and organized the coup that on
            August 19, 1953, successfully overthrew the gov-
            ernment of Iranian Premier Mohammed Mossadegh,
            who had connived with the Iranian Communist
            party and nationalized certain foreign oil hold-
            ings in his country. Kermit "Kim" Roosevelt,
            grandson of former U.S. President Theodore
            Roosevelt was the CIA agent who masterminded the
            downfall of Mossadegh and enabled Shah Mohammed
            Reza Pahlevi to keep his throne.12/

1953 -   CIA Director William E. Colby stated that from 1953
            until February 1973, the CIA "conducted several
            programs to survey and open selected mail between
            the United States and two Communist countries."
            According to a secret Senate memorandum the CIA
            survey focused on mail sent to and received from
            the Soviet Union and China and was centered in New
            York City and San Francisco. Colby stated that the
            purposes of the programs were "to identify individ-
            uals in active correspondence with Communist coun-
            tries for presumed counter-intelligence purposes,"
            to attempt "to learn the foreign contacts of a
            number of Americans of counterintelligence inter-
            est," and "to determine the nature and extent of
            censorship techniques."13/

1953 -   After the election of Jose (Pepe) Figueres as
            President of Costa Rica in 1953, the CIA worked
            with opposition forces in the country in attempts
            to overthrow the government. Of particular concern
            to the CIA was Figueres policy of granting asylum
            in Costa Rica to Communists and non-Communists
            alike. Figueres, a moderate Socialist, stepped
            down from power after his candidate lost the
            Presidential election in 1958.14/

1954 -   The CIA, on June 18, 1954, led the coup in Guate-
            mala that overthrew the Communist-dominated
            regime of President Jacobo Arbenz Guzman. Frank
            G. Wisner, CIA Deputy Director for Plans, had the
            major responsibility for carrying out the opera-
            tion. CIA agents trained and supported the forces

---

11/ Braden, op. cit., p.14. The New York Times, May 8, 1967, p.1.

12/ Wise and Ross, op. cit., pp.110-114. Marchetti and Marks, op.
        cit., pp.28-29. Andrew Tully, CIA: The Inside Story (New
        York: William Morrow and Company, 1962), pp.88-89,93,97.

13/ The Washington Post, January 16, 1975, pp.A1,A18. Colby,
        "SASC Statement, January 16, 1975, pp.31-32.

14/ Wise and Ross, op. cit., pp.119-120.

of Colonel CarJos Castillo-Armas who assumed power after the defeat of Arbenz. Agency support included the provision of CIA-piloted World War II fighter-bombers, as well as guns and ammunition.15/

1955 -   From 1955 until 1959 Michigan State University was utilized by the CIA to conduct a covert police-training program for the South Vietnamese. Five CIA operatives were concealed in the staff of the program, and were carried on the University's pay-roll as its employees. Originally, the University had entered into a $25,000,000 contract for its participation in the program, but in 1959 refused to continue to provide a cover for the operation and it was transferred out. In the period from 1955-1962, Michigan State received $5,354,352.75 for the services that it had rendered.16/

1958 -   In early 1958 the CIA gave direct aid to rebel groups on the island of Sumatra that were attempting to overthrow Indonesian President Sukarno. CIA pilots flew B-26 bombers on missions in support of the insurgents. On May 18, 1958, during such a bombing mission, CIA pilot Allen Lawrence Pope was shot down and captured by the Indonesians.17/

1958 -   In 1958 the CIA established a secret base at Camp Hale near Leadville, Colorado where the agency gave training to troops of the Dalai Lama, the temporal and religious ruler of Tibet. The Tibetan guer-rillas were trained and re-equipped by the CIA in order to support the struggle of the Dalai Lama's forces against the Communist Chinese. Guerrilla raids into Tibet by these forces did occur, some-times led by CIA contract mercenaries and supported by CIA planes. The training program appears to have ended in December, 1961.18/

1960 -   Beginning in 1956, CIA pilots began flying high-altitude U-2 spy planes over the Soviet Union to

---

15/ Tully, op. cit., pp.60-67. Wise, op. cit., p.9. Wise and Ross, op. cit., pp.165-183.

16/ Walden, op. cit., pp.181-183. David Wise and Thomas B. Ross, The Espionage Establishment (New York: Random House, 1967), p.152. The New York Times, April 14, 1966, p.1. Marchetti and Marks, op. cit., p.234. The New York Times, April 15, 1966, p.11.

17/ Marchetti and Marks, op. cit., pp.29,114. Wise and Ross, Invisible Government, pp.136-139. Wise, op. cit., p.9.

18/ The New York Times, April 19, 1973, p.2. Marchetti and Marks, op. cit., pp.114-116,143. Wise, op. cit., p.9.

photograph a variety of missile and defense related installations. On May 1, 1960, Francis Gary Powers, a CIA pilot, had his U-2 plane shot down over Sverdlovsk in the Soviet Union, prompting Soviet Premier Nikita Khrushchev to cancel his scheduled conference at Paris with President Dwight Eisenhower.19/

1960 -   In early 1960 President Dwight Eisenhower gave his approval to a CIA-sponsored project to train Cuban exiles for the purpose of overthrowing Cuban leader Fidel Castro. The Guatemalan President, Miguel Ydigoras Fuentes, permitted the CIA to use his country for its training camp. In November 1960 a rebellion broke out in Guatemala against President Ydigoras. Because of his assistance to the CIA to that point the agency secretly came to his aid, sending its B-26 bombers against the rebels. The insurgency was crushed and Ydigoras kept in power.20/

1961 -   Prior to the scheduled invasion of Cuba by Cuban exiles in April 1961, the CIA attempted to have Cuban leader Fidel Castro assassinated. To help set up the assassination, the CIA enlisted Robert Maheu, a former FBI agent, who was later to direct billionaire Howard Hughes' Nevada businesses. Maheu recruited John Roselli to arrange for the murder attempt. The CIA assigned two operatives, James O'Connell and William Harvey, to accompany Roselli on his trips to Miami to put together the assassination teams. The first attempt to kill Castro, made in March or early April 1961, was a failure. Five more assassination teams were subsequently sent against the Cuban leader in the next two years. All ended in failure. The last attempt was made in late February or early March 1963.21/

1961 -   A force of Cuban exiles that had been trained and equipped by the CIA made an unsuccessful invasion of Cuba at the Bay of Pigs in mid/April 1961 in an attempt to overthrow the regime of Fidel Castro. The person responsible for overall supervision of the operation was Richard M. Bissell, Jr., the CIA's Deputy Director for Plans. Four Americans flying CIA planes, and nearly 300 Cubans died during the invasion. Over 1,200 survivors were captured by Castro's forces.22/

19/ Wise and Ross, Invisible Government, pp.122-124. Wise, op. cit., p.9.

20/ Marchetti and Marks, op. cit., pp.298-299. Wise and Ross, Invisible Government, pp.24-29,33,182.

1961 -   Following the Bay of Pigs invasion of 1961, Cuban
             exiles were directed and paid by CIA agents to
             compile secret files on and watch over other
             Cubans and Americans "who associated with individ-
             uals under surveillance." By the late 1960's such
             activities were being supported by the CIA in
             several key American cities -- including Los An-
             geles, New York and San Juan. Southern Florida
             was also covered by these Cuban operatives. It
             was estimated that at the height of these activi-
             ties, roughly 150 informants were on the payroll
             of a Cuban "counterintelligence" office located
             in Florida.23/

1961 -   Former CIA agent Philip Agee stated that the agency
             began efforts in 1961 to bring down the regime of
             President Jose Velasco Ibarra of Ecuador after he
             refused to sever diplomatic relations with Cuba.
             Iberra was overthrown in November, 1961. His suc-
             cessor, Carlos Julio Arosemena, soon fell out of
             favor with the United States and once again the CIA
             used "destabilizing tactics" to overthrow his gov-
             ernment in July 1963. Agee noted that while on as-
             signment in Ecuador, he and five other CIA agents
             managed to gain economic and political control
             over Ecuador's labor movement. His CIA team, said
             Agee, ultimately "owned almost everybody who was
             anybody."24/

1961-1964 -   In the early 1960's the CIA became involved in the
             political struggle in the Congo. The agency paid
             cash to selected Congolese politicians and gave arms
             to the supporters of Joseph Mobutu and Cyril
             Adoula. Eventually the CIA sent mercenaries and
             paramilitary experts to aid the new government. In
             1964 CIA B-26 airplanes were being flown in the
             Congo on a regular basis by Cuban-exile pilots who
             were under CIA contract. These pilots and planes
             carried out bombing missions against areas held
             by rebel forces.25/

21/ The Washington Post, January 18, 1971, p.B7.

22/ Tully, op. cit., pp.243-256. Wise and Ross, Invisible Gov-
       ernment, pp.9-11,70-71. Wise, op. cit., p.9. Marchetti
       and Marks, op. cit., pp.33-34.

23/ The New York Times, January 4, 1975, p.8.

24/ Newsweek 84 (September 30, 1974), p.37. The New York Times,
       September 22, 1974, section 4, p.1.

25/ Newsweek 78 (November 22, 1971), p.37. The New York Times,
       September 22, 1974, section 4, p.1. Marchetti and Marks,
       op. cit., pp.31,117.

1962 – Beginning in 1962, the CIA became involved in a "secret war" in Laos against the Communist forces there. The CIA recruited and trained a private army of at least 30,000 Meo and other Laotian tribesmen. This group was known as L'Armee Clandestine. Pilots hired by the CIA flew supply and bombing missions in CIA-owned airplanes in support of this secret army. Expenditures by the U.S. to assist this army amounted to at least $300 million a year. Forty or fifty CIA officers ran this operation, aided by several hundred contract personnel.26/

1964 – E. Howard Hunt, former CIA agent, stated that during his tenure with the CIA's Domestic Operations Division he was ordered, in 1964, to arrange for the pick-up, on a daily basis, of "any and all information" that might be available at Senator Barry Goldwater's Presidential campaign headquarters. Hunt said that the documents obtained about Goldwater were delivered to Chester L. Cooper, a White House aide who formerly worked for the CIA.27/

1964 – The CIA, with the cooperation of the Agency for International Development and the State Department, secretly funneled up to $20 million into Chile to aid Eduardo Frei in his successful attempt to defeat Marxist Salvador Allende for the Presidency of the country. Richard Helms, as chief of the Clandestine Services (Directorate of Plans), was actively involved in the planning of the secret efforts by the CIA to defeat Allende. Cord Meyer, Jr. was also one of the CIA's key directors of the operation.28/

mid-1960's – During the mid-1960's the CIA secretly aided the government of Peru in its fight against rebel guerrilla forces. The agency flew in arms and other equipment. Local Peruvian troops were trained by personnel of the Special Operations Division of the CIA as well as by Green Beret instructors loaned by the U.S. Army. Because of the assistance the Peruvian Government was soon able to crush the revolt against it.29/

1965 – It was reported that in 1965, John M. Maury, the CIA station chief in Athens, became directly involved in Greek politics. He was reported to have helped King Constantine buy Deputies of the Greek Center Union Party, thus bringing about the downfall of the Government of George Papandreou.30/

26/ Marchetti and Marks, op. cit., pp.31–32,297. Wise, op. cit., p.9. Time 104 (September 30, 1974), pp.19–20.

1966, 1969, 1971	In 1966, and 1969 and 1971, the CIA conducted three separate domestic break-ins into premises occupied by CIA employees or ex-employees. All three of the entries were made because the agency believed that security concerns warranted such actions.31/
1967 -	The CIA gave assistance to Bolivian soldiers in 1967 in their successful effort to track down and capture Ernesto "Che" Guevara, the revolutionery who was stirring up rebellion against the government. Guevara was captured on October 8, 1967 by CIA-advised Bolivian rangers. He was executed shortly thereafter.32/
1967 -	It was reported that the CIA engineered the Greek military coup of 1967 that brought Colonel George Papadopoulos to power. It was further reported that the CIA was able to maintain control of the military regime because it had documentation of Papadopoulos's "wartime collaboration with the Nazis."33/
1967 -	In the wake of the revelation in 1967 that the CIA had subsidized the National Student Association, it was disclosed that the CIA had funded many other labor, business, church, university and cultural organizations through a variety of foundation conduits. It was estimated that at least $12,422,925 had been secretly spent in this manner by the CIA.34/

27/ The New York Times, December 31, 1974, p.1.

28/ The Washington Post, April 6, 1973, pp.A1,A12. Marchetti and Marks, op. cit., pp.15-16. Wise, op. cit., p.9. The New York Times, September 8, 1974, p.1.

29/ Marchetti and Marks, op. cit., pp.124-125.

30/ The New York Times, August 2, 1975, pp.1,3.

31/ Colby, "SASC Statement," January 16, 1975, p.28-29.

32/ Marchetti and Marks, op. cit., pp.126-131. The New York Times, September 22, 1974, section 4, p.1.

33/ The New York Times, July 1, 1973, p.14.

34/ Congressional Quarterly, February 24, 1967, pp.271-272. Jerrold L. Walden's article in the Journal of Public Law in 1970 provides a comprehensive discussion of the various domestic fronts utilized by the CIA. Walden, op. cit., pp.179-207. Congressional Quarterly, March 10, 1967, p.355. Wise, op. cit., pp.9,29.

1967 -　　　　In 1967 the CIA's Far East Division of Clandestine
　　　　　　　Services developed a program that came to be known
　　　　　　　as Phoenix. The program entailed a coordinated
　　　　　　　attack by all South Vietnamese and American mili-
　　　　　　　tary, police and intelligence units against the
　　　　　　　infrastructure of the Viet Cong. CIA funds served
　　　　　　　as the catalyst for the project. William E. Colby
　　　　　　　played the key supervisory role in its implementa-
　　　　　　　tion. In 1971, Colby revealed that between 1968
　　　　　　　and May 1971, the Phoenix program led to the death
　　　　　　　of 20,587 persons in Vietnam.35/

1967 -　　　　On August 15, 1967, Richard Helms, Director of the
　　　　　　　CIA set up a unit within the Counterintelligence
　　　　　　　office of the agency "to look into the possibility
　　　　　　　of foreign links to American dissident elements."
　　　　　　　This unit, "periodically thereafter," drew up re-
　　　　　　　ports "on the foreign aspects of the anti-war,
　　　　　　　youth, and similar movements, and their links to
　　　　　　　American counterparts."36/

1967 -　　　　In 1967 the CIA's Office of Security "inserted ten
　　　　　　　agents into dissident organizations operating in
　　　　　　　the Washington, D.C. area" in order to collect "in-
　　　　　　　formation relating to plans for demonstrations,
　　　　　　　pickets, protests, or break-ins that might endanger
　　　　　　　CIA personnel facilities and information." The
　　　　　　　program was terminated in December 1968.37/

1969 -　　　　The CIA in 1969 reportedly directed that a Special
　　　　　　　Forces team in South Vietnam should execute a man
　　　　　　　named Thai Khac Chuyen, on the grounds that he was
　　　　　　　a double-agent. The man was executed by the Spe-
　　　　　　　cial Forces unit.38/

1970 -　　　　CIA Director, Richard Helms joined with the direc-
　　　　　　　tors of NSA, DIA and FBI in recommending to Presi-
　　　　　　　dent Nixon "an integrated approach to the coverage
　　　　　　　of domestic unrest," which came to be known as the
　　　　　　　Huston Plan.39/

1970-　　　　 To secure "access to foreign circles" the CIA,
　　　　　　　after the Huston Plan was rescinded, "recruited or
　　　　　　　inserted about a dozen individuals into American
　　　　　　　dissident circles." It was believed that in this
　　　　　　　manner these individuals would "establish their
　　　　　　　credentials for operations abroad." In the course
　　　　　　　of their work some of these individuals "submitted
　　　　　　　reports on the activities of the American dissi-
　　　　　　　dents with whom they were in contact." This in-
　　　　　　　formation was kept in CIA files and reported to
　　　　　　　the FBI. In 1973 the program of information gath-
　　　　　　　ering was limited to collections made abroad.40/

35/ Marchetti and Marks, op. cit., p.246. Wise, op. cit., pp.8,
　　33-35. Newsweek 78 (November 22, 1971), p.39.

1970-73 – Under CIA direction over $8 million was channeled into Chile from 1970 to 1973 to "destabilize" the government of President Salvadore Allende. The money was used to support various groups within Chile who were opposed to Allende. CIA agents infiltrated the Socialist Party in Chile, and organized street demonstrations against the regime. Ultimately a coup was produced in September 1973. Allende died within hours after its start.41/

1971 – At the request of the White House the CIA provided a psychological profile of Dr. Daniel Ellsburg in 1971.42/

1971 – The CIA's Technical Services Division supplied technical equipment to White House aide E. Howard Hunt in 1971 which he later utilized in connection with the break-in and burglary of the office of Dr. Daniel Ellsburg's psychiatrist.43/

1971-1972 – In 1971 and 1972 the CIA employed physical surveillance against "five Americans who were not CIA employees." This was done because the CIA had "clear indications" that the five "were receiving classified information without authorization." It was hoped that the surveillance would "identify the sources of the leaks." A secret Senate memorandum indicates that four of the five subject to CIA surveillance were columnists Jack Anderson and Les Whitten, Washington Post reporter Michael Getler, and author Victor Marchetti.44/

36/ Colby, "SASC Statement," January 16, 1975, pp.19-20. The New York Times, December 29, 1974, pp.1,22.

37/ Colby, "SASC Statement," January 16, 1975, pp.23-24.

38/ The New York Times, August 14, 1969, p.1. Ibid., August 15, 1969, p.1, August 16, 1969, p.1, Ibid., September 26, 1969, p.10. Ibid., September 27, 1969, p.1. Ibid., September 30, 1969, p.1.

39/ Colby, "SASC Statement," January 16, 1975, p.20. The Washington Post, June 8, 1973, p.A15.

40/ Colby, "SASC Statement," January 16, 1975, pp.20-22.

41/ The New York Times, September 8, 1974, pp.1,26. Time 104 (September 30, 1974), p.21.

42/ Time 104 (September 30, 1974), p.19. Colby, "SASC Statement," January 16, 1975, pp.33-34.

43/ Wise, op. cit., pp.9-10. Time 104 (September 30, 1974), p.19. Colby, "SASC Statement," January 16, 1975, pp.33-34.

44/ The Washington Post, January 16, 1975, pp.A1, A18. Ibid., January 29, 1975, p.A1. Colby, "SASC Statement," January 16, 1975, p.31.

1971-1972 –   It was revealed that the CIA, from roughly 1971
               through 1972, had secretly provided training to
               about 12 county and city police forces in the
               United States on the detection of wiretaps, the
               organization of intelligence files and the handling
               of explosives. The training program, involving
               "less than 50 policemen," was reported to have in-
               cluded representatives from the police forces of
               New York City, Washington, D.C., Boston, Chicago,
               Fairfax County, Virginia and Montgomery County,
               Maryland. John M. Maury, legislative counsel for
               the CIA, stated that the program, in his view, did
               not "violate the letter or the spirit" of the Na-
               tional Security Act of 1947. Further, said Maury,
               the CIA's actions were "entirely consistent with
               the provisions of the Omnibus Crime Control and
               Safe Streets Act of 1968."45/

1973 –   It was revealed in late 1973 that the CIA had ap-
               proximately 40 American journalists "working abroad
               on its payroll as undercover informants, some of
               them as full-time agents." Roughly 25 of these
               journalists were "free lance magazine writers,
               part-time 'stringers' for newspapers, news maga-
               zines and news services." Eight were writers for
               "small, limited circulation specialty publications,"
               while "no more than five" were "full-time staff
               correspondents with general circulation news or-
               ganizations."46/

March 1974 –   After having compiled files on "about 10,000"
               American citizens since 1967, the CIA ended its
               formal program of collecting domestic counter-
               intelligence information.47/

45/ The New York Times, December 17, 1972, p.23. Congressional
    Record, February 6, 1973, pp.H3558-H3559. The New York
    Times, February 6, 1973, pp.1,25. Marchetti and Marks, op.
    cit., pp.224-225. Marchetti and Marks maintain that the
    training program had been conducted by the CIA "at least
    since 1967." (op. cit., p.225.)

46/ The New York Times, December 1, 1973, p.1. The Washington
    Post, December 1, 1973, p.3.

47/ Colby, "SASC Statement," January 16, 1975, pp.19-22.

CONSTITUTIONAL BASIS FOR COVERT ACTION

The Constitution does not explicitly address the need for or the legality of covert action. The extent to which it grants powers to the Executive branch to engage in such an operation is unclear and subject to varying interpretations. The heretofore secret memorandum, reprinted below, addresses the constitutional and legal basis for clandestine operations generally, as does the reprinted report from the Church Committee, which follows immediately thereafter. The authorship of the secret memorandum is not clear. It was obtained from the CIA under a 1976 FOIA request and the agency would not divulge the author's name or title. The Church Committee used the same document, but gave differing attributions as to its authorship. In its analysis of the 1947 National Security Act, the Church Committee report referred to it as a memorandum from the CIA's general counsel to the director. Earlier in the same Church Committee report ([45A] p. 36), authorship was credited to the Office of Legislative Counsel at the Justice Department and its preparation is attributed to a review of CIA covert operations following the 1961 Bay of Pigs operation. Markings on the copy received indicate it was given to the CIA's general counsel, Lawrence Houston, on January 17, 1962, suggesting perhaps that he was not the author. The memorandum was declassified by the CIA on August 2, 1976, after portions were deleted.

[*Publisher's Note:* The copy of the memorandum obtained by the editors, although poor, is reproduced here in its original form in the interest of providing the essence of the document.]

copie (Hughes S. Lawrence
Houston, Gen. Counsel, C.I.A.
Jan. 17, 1962
j 2 kj

SECRET

Memorandum Re:

Constitutional and Legal Basis for So-Called Covert Activities of the Central Intelligence Agency.

This memorandum will discuss the constitutional and legal authority for the Central Intelligence Agency to engage in covert activities

It is understood that certain cold-war activities of a covert nature,

have been engaged in by CIA almost from its inception, pursuant to an express directive of the National Security Council, and that the Congress has repeatedly appropriated funds for the support of such activities. *(Secret -- Unclassified, if bracketed matter is deleted. ᴄhm. Ford: Aug. 2, 1976)*

I.   Constitutional Powers of the President.

"As a nation with all the attributes of sovereignty, the United States is vested with all the powers of government necessary to maintain an effective control of international relations." Burnet v. Brooks, 288 U.S. 378, 396. These powers do not "depend upon the affirmative grants of the Constitution," but are "necessary concomitants of nationality." United States v. Curtiss-Wright Corp., 299 U.S. 304, 318.

SECRET

"In the preservation of the safety and integrity of the United

States and the protection of its responsibilities and obligations

as a sovereignty" the constitutional powers of the President are

broad. 30 O.A.G. 291, 292. "The very delicate, plenary and

exclusive power of the President as the sole organ of the federal

government in the field of international relations . . . does

not require as a basis for its exercise an act of Congress",

although, like all governmental powers, it must be exercised

in subordination to any applicable provisions of the Constitution.

United States v. Curtiss-Wright Corp., supra, at p. 320. His

duty to take care that the laws be faithfully executed extends

not merely to express acts of Congress, but to the enforcement

of "the rights, duties, and obligations growing out of the

Constitution itself, our international relations, and all of

the protection implied by the nature of the government under

the Constitution." In Re Neagle, 135 U.S. 1, 64. (1890). $\left(\bigcup\right)$

Examples of the exercise of these broad powers are

numerous and varied. Their scope may be illustrated by the

following: The President may take such action as may, in

his judgment, be appropriate, including the use of force, to

protect American citizens and property abroad. Durand v. Hollins,

- 2 -

Fed. Cas. No. 4186 (C.C.S.D.N.Y. (1860)); In Re Neagle, supra,

135 U.S. at 64; Hamilton v. M'Claughry, 136 Fed. 445, 449-50

(D. Kansas, 1905); II Hackworth, Digest of International Law,

327-334; VI Id., 464-5. Notwithstanding the exclusive power

of Congress to declare war, the President may repel armed

attack and "meet force with force". Prize Cases, 2 Black 635,

668 (1862). He may impose restrictions on the operation of

domestic radio stations which he deems necessary to prevent

unneutral acts which may endanger our relations with foreign

countries.   30 O.A.G. 291. (U)

Congress' grants of powers to executive agencies in

areas relating to the conduct of foreign relations and preser-

vation of the national security from external threats are

generally couched in terms which neither limit the powers of

the President nor restrict his discretion in the choice of the

agency through which he will exercise these powers. Thus, in

establishing a Department of State in 1799, Congress directed

that the Secretary should perform duties relating to "such . . .

matters respecting foreign affairs as the President of the

United States shall assign to the Department", and should

- 3 -

"conduct the business of the department in such manner as the
President shall direct." 1 Stat. 28; R.S. § 202, 5 U.S.C. 156.
More recently, in establishing the National Security Council,
Congress gave it the function of advising the President "with
respect to the integration of domestic, foreign, and military
policies relating to the national security." 50 U.S.C. 402 (a). (U)

From the beginning of our history as a nation, it has
been recognized and accepted that the conduct of foreign affairs
on occasion requires the use of covert activities, which might
be of a quasi-military nature. See, e.g., the acts of July 1,
1790, 1 Stat. 128, and Mar. 1, 1810, sec. 3, 2 Stat. 609. In
a message to the House of Representatives declining to furnish
an account of payments made for contingent expenses of foreign
intercourse, President Polk reviewed that practice and stated:

> "The experience of every nation on earth has
> demonstrated that emergencies may arise in which
> it becomes absolutely necessary for the public
> safety or the public good to make expenditures
> the very object of which would be defeated by
> publicity."

President Polk continued:

> "Some governments have very large amounts
> at their disposal, and have made vastly greater

- 4 -

Fin.

expenditures than the small amounts which have
from time to time been accounted for on Presi-
dent's certificates. In no nation is the
application of such sums ever made public.
In time of war or impending danger the situation
of the country may make it necessary to employ
individuals for the purpose of obtaining infor-
mation or rendering other important services
who could never be prevailed upon to act if
they entertained the least apprehension that
their names or their agency would in any
contingency be divulged. So it may often
become necessary to incur an expenditure
for an object highly useful to the country;
for example, the conclusion of a treaty with
a barbarian power whose customs require on
such occasions the use of presents. But this
object might be altogether defeated by the
intrigues of other powers if our purposes
were to be made known by the exhibition of
the original papers and vouchers to the
accounting officers of the Treasury. It
would be easy to specify other cases other
cases which may occur in the history of a
great nation, in its intercourse with other
nations, wherein it might become absolutely
necessary to incur expenditures for objects
which could never be accomplished if it were
suspected in advance that the items of ex-
penditure and the agencies employed would be
made public." 4 Richardson, Messages and
Papers of Presidents, 431, 435 (April 20,
1846)

- 5 -

Compare also Stuart, American Diplomatic and Consular Practice (1952) p. 196, (commenting on prevailing diplomatic practice of all countries), "actual cases of interference in the internal affairs of states to which the envoys are accredited are very numerous." (U)

An early example of such a secret operation is afforded by the Lewis and Clark expedition of 1803. That expedition was authorized prior to the Louisiana Purchase by a statute providing

> "That the sum of two thousand five hundred
> dollars be, and the same is hereby appropriated
> for the purpose of extending the external
> commerce of the United States (2 Stat. 206)."

Congress used this cryptic language at the request of President Jefferson because, in the words of a present-day judge, the "expedition, military in character, would enter into lands owned by a foreign nation with which the United States was at peace and . . . the utmost secrecy had to be observed." / First Trust Co. of St. Paul v. Minnesota Historical Soc., 146 F. Supp. 652, 656 (D.C. Minn. (1956)), aff'd sub. nom. United States v. First Trust Co. of St. Paul, 251 F. 2d 686 (C.A. 8). (U)

/ In his message to the Congress, President Jefferson stated:
"* * * The appropriation of $2,500 'for the purpose of
extending the external commerce of the United States,'
while understood and considered by the Executive as
giving the legislative sanction, would cover the under-
taking from notice and prevent the obstructions which
interested individuals might otherwise previously prepare
in its way." (1 Richardson, Message and Papers of the
Presidents, 352 at 354.)

- 6 -

Under modern conditions of "cold war", the President can
properly regard the conduct of covert activities
                                             as necessary to
the effective and successful conduct of foreign relations and
the protection of the national security. When the United
States is attacked from without or within, the President may
"meet force with force", <u>Prize Cases</u>, <u>supra</u>, In waging a world
wide contest to strengthen the free nations and contain the
Communist nations, and thereby to preserve the existence of
the United States, the President should be deemed to have
comparable authority to meet covert activities with covert
activities if he deems such action necessary and consistent
with our national objectives. As Charles Evans Hughes said
in another context, "Self-preservation is the first law of
national life and the constitution itself provides the necessary
powers in order to defend and preserve the United States." War
Powers Under the Constitution, 42 A.B.A. Rep. 232 (1917). Just
as "the power to wage war is the power to wage war successfully,"
<u>id</u>. 238, so the power of the President to conduct foreign relations
should be deemed to be the power to conduct foreign relations
successfully, by any means necessary to combat the measures taken
by the Communist bloc, including both open and covert measures.

(Secret -- Unclassified if bracketed matter is deleted (JithJal. 8/2/76)

- 7 -

SECRET

The exclusive power of Congress to declare war has been held
not to prevent use by the President of force short of war to
protect American citizens and property abroad. _A fortiori_, it
does not prevent his use of force short of war for other
purposes which he deems necessary to our national survival.
In either case the magnitude and possible grave international
consequences of a particular action may be such as to render
it desirable for the President to consult with, or obtain   :
the approval or ratification of, the Congress if circumstances
permit such action. But the necessity for obtaining such
approval does not depend on whether the action is overt or
covert. (U)

- 8 -

SECRET

II. Statutory Authority

There is no specific statutory authorization to any
agency to conduct covert cold war activities. Nor is there
any statutory prohibition, except to the extent, if any, that
the prohibitions of the Neutrality Acts, 18 U.S.C. Chapter 45,
against performance of certain acts by persons within the
United States might be deemed applicable to such activities
in particular circumstances. Hence the President is not re-
stricted by act of Congress in authorizing such acts, or in
assigning responsibility for them to such agency as he may
designate. (U)

Congress has authorized the Central Intelligence
Agency, "for the purpose of coordinating the intelligence
activities of the several government departments and agencies
in the interest of the national security," to perform, _inter_
alia,

> "such other functions and duties related to
> intelligence affecting the national security
> as the National Security Council may from time
> to time direct." 50 U.S.C. 403 (d).

As previously noted, the National Security Council, which
includes in its membership the President, the Vice President,
the Secretary of State and the Secretary of Defense, has over-
all responsibility for advice to the President respecting all
matters "relating to the national security." (U)

SECRET

We understand that in 1947, Secretary of Defense
Forrestal asked the Director of Central Intelligence if CIA
would be able to conduct covert cold-war activities,

CIA advised at that time that it would
conduct such activities if the National Security Council
developed a policy that the United States would engage in
such covert activities and assigned their conduct to CIA,
and if the Congress appropriated funds to carry them out.
In the latter part of 1947 the National Security Council
developed a directive (NSC 10/2) setting forth a program
of covert cold-war activities and assigned that program to
the Office of Policy Coordination under the Director of
Central Intelligence, with policy guidance from the Depart-
ment of State. The Congress was asked for and did appropriate
funds to support this program, although, of course, only a
small number of congressmen in the Appropriations Committees
knew the amount and purpose of the appropriation. The Office
of Policy Coordination was subsequently combined with the
clandestine intelligence activities in the Office of the
Deputy (Plans) of CIA and the cold-war charter was assigned

- 10 -

SECRET

SECRET

to CIA in coordination with the Department of State and Defense
by NSC Directive 54/12. *(Secret -- Unclassified if bracketed matter is deleted. (C.L. /cal: 8/2/76)*
A significant part of the strictly intelligence and

counter-intelligence functions of CIA are clandestine in nature.

It could perhaps be argued that many if not all of the covert

activities assigned to CIA by the directives referred to above

are at least "related" to intelligence affecting the national

security within the scope of 50 U.S.C. 403 (d) (5) in the

sense that their performance may need to be intimately dove-

tailed with clandestine intelligence operations, may involve

use of the same or similar contacts, operatives and methods,

and may yield important intelligence results.[_/]   Alternatively,

it would appear that the executive branch, under the direction

of the President, has been exercising without express statutory

authorization a function which is within the constitutional

powers of the President, and that the CIA was the agent

selected by the President to carry out these functions. *(U)*

_/ The historic relationship between the two types of activity
is indicated by the fact that the Office of Strategic Services,
CIA's predecessor during World War II, engaged both in
intelligence work, and in assistance to and coordination
of local resistance activities. See Alsop and Braden, Sub
Rosa, The O.S.S. and American Espionage (1946) p. 7.

- 11 -

SECRET

Congress has continued over the years since 1947 to
appropriate funds for the conduct of such covert activities.
We understand that the existence of such covert activities
has been reported on a number of occasions to the leadership
of both houses, and to members of the subcommittees of the
Armed Services and Appropriations Committees of both houses. _/
It can be said that Congress as a whole knows that money is
appropriated to CIA and knows generally that a portion of
it goes for clandestine activities, although knowledge of
specific activities is restricted to the group specified
above and occasional other members of Congress briefed for
specific purposes.   In effect, therefore, CIA has for many
years had general funds approval from the Congress to carry

_/ See letter dated May 2, 1957, from Mr. Allen W. Dulles,
Director, CIA to Senator Hennings, Freedom of Information and
Secrecy in Government, Hearing before the Subcommittee on
Constitutional Rights of the Senate Committee of the Judiciary,
85th Cong., 2d Sess., p. 376 at 377:

"The Director of the Central Intelligence Agency
appears regularly before established subcommittees
of the Armed Services and Appropriation Committees
of the Senate and of the House, and makes available
to these subcommittees complete information on
Agency activities, personnel and expenditures. No
information has ever been denied to their subcommittees."

on covert cold-war activities, which the Executive Branch
has the authority and responsibility to direct. $\left(\bigcup\right)$

It is well-established that appropriations for
administrative action of which Congress has been informed
amount to a ratification of such action. [or acquiescence in] Brooks v. Dewar,
313 U.S. 354, 361; Fleming v. Mohawk Co., 331 U.S. 111, 116;
see also Ivanhoe Irrig. Dist. v. McCracken, 357 U.S. 275,
293-294; Power Reactor Co. v. Electricians, 367 U.S. 396, 409.
Since the circumstances effectively prevent the Congress from
making an express and detailed appropriation for the activities
of the CIA, the general knowledge of the Congress, and specific
knowledge of responsible committee members,_/ outlined above,
are sufficient to render this principle applicable. $\left(\bigcup\right)$

_/ Compare the cases of veiled, or contingent fund, appro-
priations referred to in Part I. And note the importance
placed on the close contact between an agency and "its"
committees. E.g., Panama Canal Co. v. Grace Line Inc., 356
U.S. 309, 319.

Congressional Authorization for the Central Intelligence Agency to Conduct Covert Action ([45A], pp. 475–509)

The CIA's legal staff expressed confidence as to that agency's authority to engage in covert operations, but the Church Committee questioned the legal bases for such CIA authority. The Pike Committee, in its hearings, closely examined similar views by special counsel to the director of Central Intelligence, Mitchell Rogovin, and former NSC director, McGeorge Bundy ([84E], pp. 1729–1738, 1746–1757).

In recent years the CIA has spent millions of dollars in countries all over the world for "covert action." Covert action, as the Central Intelligence Agency has defined it, is any "clandestine activity designed to influence foreign governments, events, organizations, or persons in support of the United States foreign policy conducted in such a manner that the involvement of the U.S. Government is not apparent." [1] In its purpose to influence events, covert action is distinguished from clandestine intelligence gathering—often referred to as espionage.[2]

In the last several years controversy has surrounded the conduct of covert action by the Central Intelligence Agency. Since covert action is not listed as a mission of the CIA in either its basic charter, the National Security Act of 1947, or in the Central Intelligence Agency Act of 1949, questions arise regarding the authority by which the Agency undertook it. This report addresses the question of congressional authorization for covert action. It does not attempt to analyze the inherent power of the President to make covert action the responsibility of one of the executive branch agencies.

At the outset, it should be noted that Congress is, in part, responsible for the ambiguity which clouds the CIA's authority. The National Security Act was designed to provide flexibility to the newly created CIA so that it could meet unforeseen challenges. Flexibility was provided through an undefined and apparently open-ended grant of authority to the National Security Council, and through it, to the CIA. Without any indication in the Act's history that the Congress anticipated covert action or intended to authorize it, and without any executive branch attempt to obtain from Congress specific authority for the conduct of covert actions such as sabotage or paramilitary activities, the NSC directed CIA to undertake these activities. Until 1974, Congress did not attempt to clarify the Agency's authority in this area, even after learning about such well-publicized covert actions as the invasion of the Bay of Pigs.

An analysis of congressional authorization for the conduct of covert action goes far beyond the study of 30-year-old legislative debates. It provides evidence of changes in the roles of the President and the Congress in the formulation, implementation, and review of foreign policy.

---

[1] Testimony of Mitchell Rogovin, Special Counsel to the Director of Central Intelligence, House Select Intelligence Committee, 12/9/75, p. 1730. Covert action was originally defined by the National Security Council as "secret action to influence events in foreign countries which is so designed that, if discovered, official U.S. Government participation can be plausibly denied."

[2] Covert action also differs from clandestine collection and espionage in that the latter are designed to obtain intelligence without affecting the source or revealing the fact that the information has been collected.

It examines the procedures by which the President and the Congress have delegated power to the NSC and the CIA and the effect of those procedures. It illuminates the way the executive branch has interpreted undefined provisions of law. It raises questions about congressional oversight of covert action and particularly the ability of Congress, in the interest of security, to deny itself information. The result of the denial has been to allow small numbers of senior members to exercise the oversight function and to determine how much money the CIA was to receive and for what purposes.

Hopefully, this report will not only be useful to those interested in the past. An examination of the question of congressional authorization for the conduct of covert action may contribute to a better understanding of the relationship between the need for secrecy and the processes of constitutional government. Such an understanding is necessary as the United States moves into its third century.

Before turning to the National Security Act of 1947, two caveats are in order. The first and most important is that any attempt to understand the relationship between Congress and the executive branch in this area must be based on the evidence available, which is often quite sparse. For example, the Select Committee was able to locate the transcript of only one executive session of a congressional committee considering the National Security Act of 1947, although weeks of such sessions were held on this important legislation.

Covert action is now a well-defined and understood term. The second caveat is for the reader to remember that although the U.S. did undertake what would now be called covert action during World War II, the term, and its possible scope, were not clearly understood in the late 1940's.

A. The National Security Act of 1947

Although it has been cited as authority for the CIA to engage in covert action, the National Security Act of 1947 does not specifically
N13   mention covert action. A review of the hearings, committee reports and floor debates on the Act reveals no substantial evidence that Congress intended by passage of the Act to authorize covert action by the CIA. In addition, a contemporaneous analysis of the Act by the General Counsel of the CIA concluded that Congress had no idea that, under the authority of the National Security Act, the CIA would undertake covert action such as subversion or sabotage.

Congress did intend to provide the newly created CIA with sufficient flexibility so that it would be able to respond to changing circumstances. There is no evidence, however, that that flexibility was intended to allow the creation of a peacetime agency engaged in activities such as paramilitary action or attempted assassination.

Although the evidence strongly suggests that the executive branch did not intend through the language of the National Security Act to obtain authorization from Congress for the conduct of covert action, the record is not absolutely clear. Whether it did or did not so intend, the executive branch soon seized upon the broad language of the National Security Act. Facing what was perceived as an extraordinary threat from the Soviet Union and her allies, coming to believe that the only possible course of action for the United States was to respond to covert action with covert action, the NSC authorized the CIA to conduct covert action.

1. Textual Analysis

Nowhere in the National Security Act is covert action specifically authorized. Section 102(d)(5) of the Act, however, has been cited as authority for covert action.[4] That clause authorizes the CIA to "perform such other functions and duties related to intelligence affecting the national security as the National Security Council may from time to time direct." [5]

This clause was cited in NSC—4—A and NSC 10/2, the early directives from the National Security Council to the Central Intelligence Agency which directed the CIA to conduct covert action.[6] The Director of the CIA has cited the same section in claiming authorization for covert paramilitary activity.[7]

On its face, the clause might be taken to authorize an enormous range of activities not otherwise specified in the National Security Act.[8] An important limitation on the authorization, however, is that

---

[4] Section 102(d)(4), which authorizes the CIA to "perform for the benefit of existing intelligence agencies, such additional services of common concern as the National Security Council determines can be more efficiently accomplished centrally," appears on its face to be applicable to covert action to the same extent as Section 102(d)(5). Both represent an effort to provide the Agency with some flexibility in intelligence matters. Section 102(d)(4), however, has not been cited by either the NSC or the CIA as authorizing covert action.

A provision similar to Section 102(d)(4) in the Presidential Directive establishing the Central Intelligence Group, the CIA's predecessor agency, was cited as the CIG's authority to engage in clandestine collection of intelligence; Section 102(d)(4) was cited by the National Security Council in directing the CIA to engage in the same activity.

[5] 50 U.S.C. 403(d)(5).

[6] While the CIA has consistently invoked the President's power to authorize covert action, neither NSC 4–A or NSC 10/2 mentioned that power; both referred to the authority conveyed by the National Security Act.

[7] The General Counsel of the CIA wrote the DCI commenting on his testimony before the Subcommittee on Security Agreements and Commitments Abroad of the Senate Committee on Foreign Relations as follows:

"As for the authority of this Agency to engage in [covert paramilitary activity], I think you were probably exactly right to stick to the language of the National Security Act of 1947, as amended, particularly that portion which says that the Agency shall 'perform such other functions and duties related to intelligence affecting the national security as the National Security Council may from time to time direct.' Actually, from 1947 on my position has been that this is a rather doubtful statutory authority on which to hang our paramilitary activities." (Memorandum from the CIA General Council to the Director, Subject: Symington Subcommittee Hearings, 10/30/69.)

[8] One of the witnesses appearing before the executive session of the House Committee on Expenditures in the Executive Departments on June 27, 1947, described the function of section (d)(5) as being to allow the CIA to go beyond its enumerated functions during an emergency. (Peter Vischer testimony, House Committee on Expenditures in the Executive Departments, Hearings on H.R. 2319, 6/27/47, p. 78.)

the activities must be "related to intelligence affecting the national security." As Clark Clifford told the Senate Select Committee:

> You will note that the language of the Act provides that this catch-all phrase is applicable only in the event that the national security is affected. This was considered to be an important and restricting clause.[9]

Some covert actions are at least arguably "related to intelligence affecting the national security." As an individual in the CIA's Office of the General Counsel noted in a memorandum to the General Counsel:

> . . . it can be argued that many covert activities assigned to the Agency by the National Security Council are at least "related" to intelligence affecting the national security . . . in the sense that their performance often is intimately dovetailed with clandestine intelligence operations, use the same operations and methods and yield important intelligence results.[10]

Not all covert actions, however, have the characteristics suggested in the above quotation. Many covert operations, such as the invasion of the Bay of Pigs, have, at best, only the most limited relationship to intelligence affecting the national security.[11] As the General Counsel of the CIA wrote in 1947:

> Taken out of context and without knowledge of its history, these Sections [102(d)(4) and (5)] could bear almost unlimited interpretation, provided that the services performed could be shown to be of benefit to an intelligence agency or related to national intelligence.
>
> Thus black propaganda, primarily designed for subversion, confusion, and political effect, can be shown incidentally to benefit positive intelligence as a means of checking reliability of informants, effectiveness of penetration, and so forth. Even certain forms of S.O. [special operations] work could be held to benefit intelligence by establishment of W/T [wireless telegraph] teams in accessible areas, and by opening penetration points in confusion following sabotage or riot. *In our opinion, however, either activity would be an unwarranted extension of the functions authorized in Sections 102(d)(4) and (5).* This is based on our understanding of the intent of Congress at the time these provisions were enacted.[12] [Emphasis added.]

The General Counsel concluded again in 1962 that certain forms of covert action are not "related to intelligence." In a memorandum to the DCI he wrote, "some of the covert cold war operations are related to intelligence within a broad interpretation of Section 102(d)(5). It

---

[9] Clark Clifford testimony, 12/4/75, Hearings, Vol. VII, p. 51.
[10] Memorandum from the CIA Office of the General Counsel to the General Counsel, 2/6/74, p. 1.
[11] The secrecy which surrounded the invasion of the Bay of Pigs may well have interferred with the CIA's mission to correlate and evaluate intelligence related to the national security. Analysts in the Directorate of Intelligence were neither informed about, nor asked to evaluate, the invasion plans.

would be stretching that section too far to include a Guatemala or a Cuba even though intelligence and counterintelligence are essential to such activities." [13] In this same memorandum, the General Counsel suggested that, in order for the National Security Act to provide authority for the conduct of the wide range of covert action engaged in by the CIA, Section 102(d)(5) would have to read, "perform such other functions and duties related to the national security" as the NSC might from time to time direct, and not "perform such other functions and duties related to intelligence affecting the national security." [14] After this interpretation was given by the General Counsel, no attempt was made by the executive branch to have the National Security Act amended. [15]

Only the most strained interpretation of "intelligence affecting the national security" would allow certain covert actions by the CIA such as paramilitary activities or the attempted assassination of foreign leaders to come under Section 102(d)(5). As some covert actions are more directly "related to intelligence affecting the national security," however, it is important to examine the legislative history [16] of the Na-

---

[12] Memorandum from the CIA General Counsel to the Director, 9/25/47, p. 1.

[13] Memorandum from the CIA General Counsel to the Director, 1/15/62, p. 2. While the CIA has recently stated that "intelligence" was intended to have a broader interpretation than the General Counsel indicated in the memorandum, (See Rogovin, HSIC 12/9/75, p. 175) there is no evidence that Congress intended the phrase "related to intelligence" to cover such activities as the attempted assassination of foreign leaders. Under the CIA's expansive interpretation even this would be authorized as the agents involved in the assassination attempt might have previously provided intelligence to the CIA.

[14] General Counsel memorandum, 1/15/62, p. 2.

[15] In the same memorandum the General Counsel argued that the CIA was authorized by Congress to conduct covert action as "Congress as a whole knows that money is appropriated to CIA and knows that generally a portion of it goes for clandestine activities." Given presidential direction and congressional appropriation he advised that additional statutory authority is "unnecessary and, in view of the clandestine nature of the activities, undesirable." (*Ibid.* p. 3.)

[16] Legislative history includes review of the pre-enactment history, including a history of the predecessor agencies, the history of the enactment, and subsequent interpretation of the act. Legislative history is used as an aid to statutory construction where the language of the statute is unclear [*United States* v. *Donrus Co.*, 393 U.S. 297 (1965); *United States* v. *Public Utilities Commission California*, 345 U.S. 295 (1953)], where placing the "plain language" of a particular provision in the context of the whole statute creates an ambiguity [*Mastro Plastic Corp.* v. *National Labor Relations Board*, 350 U.S. 270 (1956); *Richards* v. *United States*, 369 U.S. 1 (1962)], or where it can be shown that an application of the literal words would bring about a result plainly at variance with their purpose [*Johansen* v. *United States*, 343 U.S. 427 (1952); *United States* v. *Dickerson*, 310 U.S. 554 (1940)]. It is pertinent only to show legislative intent and, thus, the various kinds of legislative history—hearings, reports, floor debates—are considered significant according to the likelihood that they indicate the purpose of the legislature as a whole. For instance, if Congress as a whole is not, or cannot be, aware of the evidence that a bill would have a particular effect, or remedy a particular evil, it cannot be assumed that Congress intended the statute to have that effect. In construing statutes courts will, therefore, consider whether the history manifested in the hearings, reports and floor debates was made available to the legislators, whether they were actually aware of it, and the credence which the legislators themselves may have given to it.

In certain instances, an examination of executive sessions may illuminate the intent of individual members of Congress. Such testimony might also clarify the Executive's interpretation of a particular piece of legislation.

tional Security Act to determine if these forms of covert action were within the range of activities which Congress intended to authorize or whether they represent what the CIA's former General Counsel called "an unwarranted extension of the functions authorized in Sections 102 (d) (4) and (5)." Congressional intent is particularly important in this instance as Congress required the language of Section 102 to be written into law rather than incorporating an earlier Presidential Directive by reference. This was done because several Members of Congress believed that if the CIA's missions were not set out in the statute, the President could change them at any time simply by amending the Directive.[17]

Before turning to the legislative history of the National Security Act, however it is important to note that Section 102(d) (5) sets out a second condition—the CIA must be directed by the NSC to perform the "other functions and duties." The authority of NSC to direct the CIA to undertake activities has recently come under attack.[18] The question of whether the NSC must specifically approve each covert action or whether it can delegate its authority or provide approval in advance for whole categories—or programs—of covert action has also been raised. General Vandenberg, who headed the Central Intelligence Group, the CIA's predecessor body, expressed to the drafters of the National Security Act his belief that the CIA should not have to come continually to the NSC for approval for action. According to a CIA legislative history of the Act, Vandenberg was told that the CIA would need to come to the NSC only on such specific matters as the NSC required.[19]

Over time the practice developed that all politically risky or costly covert action projects would be brought before the 40 Committee of the National Security Council, or its predecessors, for approval. However, low-risk projects could be approved within the CIA. During some periods of time only a quarter of all covert action projects undertaken by the CIA—the high-risk, high-cost covert actions—were approved by the NSC 40 Committee.[20] In at least one instance, the 40

---

[17] Hearings before the House Committee on Expenditures in the Executive Department on H.R. 2319, National Security Act of 1947 April–July, 1947, p. 171. See also Transcript, House Committee on Expenditures in the Executive Departments, Hearings on H.R. 2319, 6/27/47, pp. 57–58. Another reason given for enumerating the CIA's purpose was that the public would not have access to the *Federal Register* and thus would be ignorant of the Agency's missions.

[18] See Committee on Civil Rights and the Committee on International Rights of the Association of the Bar of the City of New York, "Central Intelligence Agency: Oversight and Accountability," p. 13; and Central Intelligence Agency response to "Central Intelligence Agency: Oversight and Accountability," p. 21. . . .

[19] See CIA Legislative Counsel memorandum, "Legislative History of the Central Intelligence Agency: the National Security Act of 1947," 5/25/67, p. 30 (hereinafter cited as "CIA's Legislative History".)

[20] A 1963 study showed that of the 550 existing covert action projects of the CIA, which according to the CIA's own internal instruction should have been submitted to the Special Group (the 40 Committee's predecessor), only 86 were separately approved (or reapproved) by the Special Group between January 1 and December 1, 1962. Memorandum for the Record, C/CA/PEG, Subject: "Policy Coordination of CIA's Covert Action Operations," 2/21/67.

Committee was not informed about a major covert action—the Track II attempt in Chile to foment a coup.

If Congressional authorization is claimed then the procedures established by Congress must be honored. If Congress intended covert actions to be undertaken on an ad hoc basis as specifically directed by the NSC then that procedure must be followed. As Chief Justice Marshall wrote, once Congress has "prescribed . . . the manner in which the law shall be carried into execution" the President is bound to respect the limitation.[22]

N14   *2. Preenactment History [23] of the National Security Act of 1974: The CIA's Predecessor Agencies*

Some of the language of the National Security Act, in particular Section 102(d)(5), closely resembles provisions of the Presidential Directive which established the CIA's predecessor agency, the Central Intelligence Group, in 1946. The CIG in turn grew out of the wartime experience with the Office of Strategic Services and its predecessor, the Office of Coordinator of Information.

The evolution from the Office of the Coordinator of Information to the Central Intelligence Agency may indicate what the Executive intended to accomplish through submission of the Central Intelligence Agency section of the National Security Act of 1947. To the extent to which Congress was familiar with this evolution, and with the roles played by the Coordinator of Information, the OSS, and the CIG, it could be said that Congress understood the meaning of the legislation which the Executive proposed and shared in the Executive's expectation of what the legislation would accomplish.

The Office of the Coordinator of Information was established by a Presidential Directive of July 11, 1941. The Directive was preceded by a memorandum to the President by William J. Donovan on June 10, 1941, proposing a centralized intelligence organization with psychological warfare among its functions.[24] The Directive did not

---

[22] *Little* v. *Barreme*, 2 Cranch 170, 178 (1805). If it is Presidential power which is delegated, then the procedures established for the delegation cannot be disregarded.

[23] Preenactment history is the term given to events occurring prior to the introduction of legislation, Sutherland, *Statutory Construction*, § 48.03 (4th ed. 1973). It encompasses events to which the legislation in question was apparently a response.

Preenactment history is considered by the courts, in some cases, to be significant in determining legislative intent. The challenge is to determine the mischief which particular legislation is meant to remedy. Generally, the courts look to events or patterns of abuse which were well publicized and which Congressmen would most likely know about and have in mind when they enacted a particular law: See *e.g. Clark* v. *Uebersee Fianz-Korp.*, 322 U.S. 459 (1947).

Thus the relaitonship between poor coordination of intelligence and the successful bombing of Pearl Harbor by the Japanese could be considered as extrinsic evidence of Congressional intent in passing the National Security Act of 1947.

[24] Memorandum from William J. Donovan to the President, 6/10/41. Physical subversion and guerrila warfare were not mentioned in Donovan's memorandum, but they were discussed with Cabinet officers involved and were felt by Donovan to be implicit with his plan.

mention psychological warfare, but authorized the Coordinator of Information to "collect and analyze all information and data which may bear upon national security" and to "carry out when requested by the President such supplementary activities as may facilitate securing of information important for national security." Like the National Security Act of 1947, the 1941 Directive was designed for flexibility.

The Presidential Directive establishing the COI made no distinction betwen overt and clandestine collection. Within the month, the COI established a unit to collect intelligence from overt sources, and by October the COI had begun the collection of information by undercover agents outside the Western Hemisphere.[25] On October 10, 1941, the "Special Activities" unit was established in COI to take charge of sabotage, subversion, and guerrilla warfare. Thus a Directive which authorized the collection and analysis of information, together with supplementary activities "to facilitate securing of information important for national security" was interpreted within the executive branch as authorizing what is now known as covert action.

All of these events preceded the outbreak of World War II. Following the outbreak of hostilities. President Roosevelt established the Office of Strategic Services (OSS) by military order dated June 13, 1942. Among the functions assigned to the OSS was to "collect and analyze such strategic information as may be required by the United States Joint Chiefs of Staff" and to perform "such special services as may be directed by the Joint Chiefs of Staff." Pursuant to this order, the OSS undertook both clandestine collection of intelligence and covert action.[27] The assignment of both these functions to the OSS was opposed by various branches of the Armed Services.

In 1944, William Donovan, then head of OSS, wrote to the President proposing a permanent peacetime intelligence service. He suggested that the service should collect, analyze, and disseminate "intelligence on the policy or strategy level," and that it should be responsible for "secret activities," such as "clandestine subversive operations." [28] At roughly the same time that General Donovan made his recommendations, General Doolittle proposed an intelligence agency which would collect intelligence either directly or through existing agencies and perform subversive operations abroad. The Joint Chiefs of Staff and the Department of State eventually responded to the Donovan proposal.[30] The debate focused on the extent of the new agency's independence, to whom it should report, and its responsibility for clandestine collection of intelligence.

In September 1945, OSS was disbanded amid the struggle over the future shape of American intelligence activities. By an Executive Order dated September 20, 1945, the responsibility for the clandestine

---

[25] The FBI was responsible for information collected by overt and covert means in the Western Hemisphere.

[27] See generally R. Harris Smith. *OSS* (Berkeley: University of California Press, 1972).

[28] Memorandum from William Donovan to the President, October 1944, as cited in CIA Legislative History, pp. 12–13.

[30] CIA Legislative History, pp. 14–17.

collection of intelligence was transferred to the War Department, where the Strategic Services Unit (SSU) was established.[31]

Also transferred to SSU were the OSS sections responsible for covert psychological and paramilitary activities. In a significant break with wartime operations, however, these latter sections were to be liquidated, leaving only such assets as were necessary for peacetime intelligence.[32]

In the absence of agreement among his advisers, President Truman directed Admiral Sidney Souers to prepare a plan for the establishment of a central intelligence organization. On January 22, 1946, President Truman issued a Presidential Directive [33] which established the National Intelligence Authority under the direction of the Director of Central Intelligence. The NIA was to include the Secretary of State, the Secretary of War, the Secretary of the Navy, and the personal representative of the President. Under the Directive, the NIA was to be "assisted by" the Central Intelligence Group, a coordinating body which drew funds and personnel from other agencies of the executive. The CIG was to collect, evaluate, and disseminate intelligence relating to the national security, plan for the coordination of intelligence agencies, and perform "such services of common concern" as the National Intelligence Authority determines can be more efficiently accomplished centrally.[34] The CIG was also to perform "such other functions and duties related to intelligence affecting the national security as the President and the National Intelligence Authority may from time to time direct."

Although the House Select Intelligence Committee was told in 1975 that the CIG was assigned the "function of conducting covert action" [35] the former General Counsel of the CIA noted that at the time of the CIG draft directive "there was really . . . no contemplation whatsoever of a program of what might be called covert action." [36] In fact, the CIG does not appear to have been engaged in any covert action abroad.[37] The covert action capability of the government which had been lodged in OSS and then transferred to SSU in the War Department had been, in early 1946, almost totally liquidated.[38] The absence of a covert action program and the decline of the capability

---

[31] For the following nine months, until the clandestine intelligence function was transferred to the Central Intelligence Group, SSU was responsible for clandestine intelligence gathering.

[32] Testimony of Lawrence Houston, former CIA General Counsel, 6/17/75, p. 6.

[33] Presidential Directive, 1/26/46; 11 *Fed Reg.* 1337, 2/5/46.

[34] The Presidential Directive made no explicit mention of clandestine collection of intelligence. It has been suggested that this function was omitted solely to avoid mention of intelligence collection in a published document. (See CIA's Legislative History, 7/25/67, p. 19.)

On July 8, 1946, the NIA issued NIA-5 authorizing the CIG to conduct clandestine intelligence collection outside the United States under the authority of the CIG to perform "services of common concern." NIA-5 resulted in the transfer of SSU to the CIG and the establishment within the CIG of the Office of Special Operations (OSO) to conduct espionage abroad.

[35] Rogovin, HSIC Hearings, 12/9/75, p. 1733.

[36] Houston, 6/17/75, p. 7.

[37] See interviews with Arthur Macy Cox and Lawrence Houston on file at the Center for National Security Studies.

[38] Houston, 6/17/75, p. 8.

suggests that a covert action mission for the CIA was not clearly anticipated by either the executive or the Congress.

3. The Enactment of the National Security Act of 1947

Efforts to draft legislation for a central intelligence organization began almost immediately after the Presidential Directive of January 22, 1946. Statutory authorization was required by the Independent Offices Appropriation Act of 1944, which provided that no office could receive funding for more than one year without specific authorization and appropriation by Congress. A June 7, 1946 report to the NIA by Admiral Souers, who drafted the 1946 Presidential Directive and who was the first Director of Central Intelligence, indicated the CIG's need for its own budget and personnel as well as for the authority to make certain kinds of contracts.

Lawrence Houston and John Warner,[39] both then with the CIG, began to work on a draft which would have established an organization far removed from the coordinating group concept of the CIG. The draft included provisions for an independent budget, direct hiring of personnel, and other administrative authorities which would allow the new agency to be autonomous and flexible. The provisions were drawn up after Houston and Warner had analysed the problems encountered by the OSS during the war, and were designed to avoid these difficulties.[40] As Houston noted, there was "no specific [covert action] program" under consideration at that time [41] but the aim of the draft was to "provide the Agency with the maximum flexibility for whatever it would be asked to do." [42]

In January 1947, another drafting group consisting of Clark Clifford, Charles Murphy, Vice Admiral Forest Sherman, and Major General Lauris Norstad, began to consider proposals for an agency to supercede the CIG, this time in the context of a proposal which would unify the Armed Services. On February 26, 1947, President Truman submitted to the Congress a draft entitled, "The National Security Act of 1947." Title 2 of Section 202 provided for a Central Intelligence Agency (CIA), which would report to a National Security Council (NSC). The NSC was to take over the duties of the NIA while the CIA was to have the functions, personnel, property, and records of the CIG.

The section in the draft legislation dealing with the CIA did not spell out, in any detail, its relationship to the rest of the executive branch or its functional responsibilities. As the framers were primarily concerned with the unification of the armed services,[43] the draft legislation, according to a memorandum from General Vandenberg to Clark Clifford, eliminated "any and all controversial material insofar as it referred to central intelligence which might in any way

---

[39] Both individuals later served as General Counsel to the CIA. Mr. Houston occupied that post from 1947 until 1974, and Mr. Warner has occupied it since.
[40] Houston, 6/17/75, p. 9.
[41] Ibid., p. 10.
[42] Ibid.
[43] CIA's Legislative History, p. 25.

hamper the successful passage of the Act." [44] The legislation incorporated by reference the functions of the CIG as set out in the Presidential Directive of January 22, 1946.[45]

S. 758, the Senate version of the draft legislation was referred to the Armed Services Committee, while H.R. 4214 was referred to the House Committee on Expenditures in the Executive Department. The Senate Committee held hearings for ten weeks, went into executive session on May 20, 1947, and reported out an amended version which was approved by voice vote. The House Committee held hearings from early April until July 1. On July 19, the House approved the amended bill and upon receipt of S. 758, amended it in accordance with the language of H.R. 4214. S. 758 emerged from Conference Committee with the functions of the CIA spelled out rather than incorporated by reference; the bill was approved by the Senate on July 24, 1947, and by the House on July 25, 1947.

There is little in the public record of this process to indicate congressional intent with respect to the CIA's authority to engage in covert action. The records of public hearings and floor debates on the National Security Act, as well as the proceedings of a committee meeting in executive session, support the view that Congress as a whole did not anticipate that the CIA would engage in such activities.

The record is ambiguous, however, in part because the legislators and witnesses were concerned that United States security might be compromised by too full and frank a discussion of American intelligence needs on the floor of Congress. As Representative Manasco stated:

> Many witnesses appeared before our Committee. They were sworn to secrecy. I hesitate to even discuss this section, as I am afraid that I might say something because the *Congressional Record* is a public record, divulge something here that we received in that Committee that would give aid and comfort to any potential enemy we have.[46]

Related to this point is the possibility that ambiguous language was expressly chosen in order not to offend world opinion. The former General Counsel of the CIA recalled that some Members of Congress sought to put in the statutory language the authorization to conduct espionage and counterespionage. But this we defeated, in "light

---

[44] Memorandum from General Vandenberg to Clark Clifford, cited in CIA's Legislative History, p. 27.

Administrative provisions for the CIA were omitted from the proposed legislation in order that unification of the armed services would not be stalled and because there was some concern that the drafting of these could not be completed in time. (*Ibid.*, pp. 26, 32.)

According to the CIA's Legislative History, "There was a general feeling that any unnecessary enlargement of the CIA provision would lead to controversy" and would affect the legislative processing of the National Security Act of 1947. (*Ibid.*, p. 32.)

[45] These functions had been expanded by NIA-5 to include the clandestine collection of intelligence.

[46] 93 Cong. Rec. 9605 (1947).

of the argument that they didn't want it advertised that this country was going to engage in such activities." [47]

An additional problem in interpreting the available evidence is that in 1947 no term was clearly understood to mean covert action as the term is used today. Members of Congress and witnesses used terms such as "operational activities," "special operations," or and "direct activities," but these remarks were as likely to have meant clandestine collection of intelligence as covert action. The following exchange between Representative Busbey and Secretary Forrestal in public hearings before the House Committee on Expenditures in the Executive Departments illustrates this problem:

> Mr. BUSBEY. Mr. Secretary, this Central Intelligence Group, as I understand it under the bill, is merely for the purpose of gathering, disseminating, and evaluating information to the National Security Council, is that correct?
>
> Secretary FORRESTAL. That is a general statement of their activity.
>
> Mr. BUSBEY. I wonder if there is any foundation in the rumors that have come to me to the effect that through the Central Intelligence Agency, they are contemplating *operational activities?*
>
> Secretary FORRESTAL. I would not be able to go into the details of their operations, Mr. Busbey. The major part of what they do, their major function, as you say, is the collection and collation and evaluation of information from Army Intelligence, Navy Intelligence, the Treasury, Department of Commerce, and most other intelligence, really. Most intelligence work is not of a mystical or mysterious character; it is simply the intelligence gathering of available data throughout this Government. . . . As to the nature and extent of any *direct operational activities,* I think I should rather have General Vandenberg respond to that question.[48] [Emphasis added.]

Another example is contained in a letter, printed in the hearing record, from Allen Dulles, then a private citizen but later Director of Central Intelligence, to the Senate Armed Services Committee. Dulles recommended that the CIA have its own appropriations, but be able to supplement these with funds from other agencies, "in order to carry on *special operations* which may, from time to time, be deemed necessary by the President, the Secretary of State, and the Secretary of National Defense." [Emphasis added.] [49]

---

[47] Houston, 6/17/75, p. 17. See also, memorandum from the CIA General Counsel to the Director, 5/7/48. In 1974, an individual in the CIA's Office of General Counsel wrote that additional statutory authority for covert action was "unnecessary and in view of the delicate nature of the activities, undesirable," (Memorandum from Stephen Hale to the General Counsel, 2/6/74.)

[48] James Forrestal testimony. House Expenditures in the Executive Departments Committee Hearings on H.R. 2319, 1947, p. 120. There is no record of any later statement by General Vandenberg on the subject.

[49] Letter from Allen Dulles to the Senate Armed Services Committee, Senate Armed Services Committee, Hearings on S. 758, 1947, p. 521.

Finally, Representative Patterson stated during the floor debates that while he clearly wanted "an independent intelligence agency working without direction by our armed services, with full authority in operation procedures," he knew that it was "impossible to incorporate such broad authority in the bill now before us. . . ." [50]

These exhaust the statements in open session—in hearings or on the floor—which arguably deal with covert action—although as was previously noted, they may also be read to refer to clandestine intelligence gathering. There is no clear explanation of or proposal for covert action. No justification for covert action was presented by the Executive.[51] It would be difficult, based upon these statements, to argue that Congress intended to authorize covert action by the CIA.

The legislating committees met extensively in executive session to consider the bill and to discuss the Central Intelligence Agency portions of it. The Select Committee has been able to locate a transcript for only one of these sessions, a June 27, 1947 meeting of the House Committee on Expenditures in the Executive Departments. At that meeting the wisdom of centralizing the clandestine intelligence collection function in the CIA was discussed in some detail. Although the Members and witnesses could put aside the security constraints which might have inhibited them in open session, this record too is ambiguous. It does, however, tend to support the proposition that Congress did not intend to authorize covert action by the CIA.

The CIA has cited two exchanges at this executive session for the proposition that the House Committee on Expenditures "had full knowledge of the broad implications" of the Presidential Directive and understood it to authorize the CIG to engage in covert action. Therefore, according to the CIA, by adopting the National Security Act, which contained the same broad language as the Directive, Congress was authorizing the CIA to conduct covert action.[52]

The first exchange quoted was between Representative Clarence Brown and General Hoyt S. Vanderberg, Director of Central Intelligence. The full context of the remarks which the Agency quoted, however, clearly indicates that the broad language of the 1946 Directive had been read to authorize clandestine collection of intelligence.[53]

---

[50] 93 Cong. Rec., H9447 (1947).

[51] "In none of the formal . . . explanations or justifications did we, so far as I can recall, set forth any program for covert action." (Houston, 6/17/75, p. 10.)

[52] Rogovin, HSIC, 12/9/75, p. 1734–35.

[53] The exchange quoted by the CIA's Special Counsel is italicized in the following quote:

"General VANDENBERG. In 'd' of the President's letter (the Presidential Directive of January 22, 1946), which you read, is the following:

'Perform such other functions and duties related to intelligence affecting the national security as the President and the National Intelligence Authority may from time to time direct.'

That was the basis. The Intelligence Advisory Board, which consists of the Chief of the three departmental intelligence organizations, State, War and Navy, in consultation with the Director of Central Intelligence, made an exhaustive study of the best way to centralize, both from the point of view of efficiency of operations and cost, certain phases of the national intelligence.

Continued

The CIA also cited the executive session testimony of Peter Vischer, who opposed the "other functions and duties" clause. He urged its defeat, calling it a loophole "because it enabled the President to direct the CIG to perform almost any operations." [54] The CIA notes this opposition, implies that Vischer opposed the clause as it authorized covert action, and claims congressional authorization for covert action because the clause was included in the National Security Act.[55] The full record shows, however, that Vischer spoke specifically in opposition to centralizing clandestine collection in the CIA. He objected to the "other functions and duties" language as it would authorize such collection.[56] His objection might have alerted the Committee to "broad implications" in the language, but not to its potential as authorization for covert action.

The only clear reference to the activities which are now referred to as covert action took place in the executive session during an exchange between Representative Rich and General Vandenberg. Representa tive Rich asked, "Is this agency [the CIG] used in anyway as a prop aganda agency?" General Vandenberg responded, "No, sir." [57]

Continued

They all felt, together with myself, who was Director at that time, that a very small portion, but a very important portion, of the collection of intelligence should be centralized in one place. Now, the discussion went on within the Intelligence Advisory Board as to where that place should be.

Mr. BROWN. May I interrupt just a moment there? In other words, you proceeded under the theory that this Central Intelligence Agency was authorized to collect this information and not simply to evaluate it?

General VANDENBERG. We went under the assumption that we should inform the National Intelligence Authority, with the setting up of the Central Intelligence Group, on an efficient basis, as was required from us from time to time to advise, because we were the Advisory Board for the National Intelligence Authority; and that part that says that we should "perform such other functions and duties as the President and the National Intelligence Authority may from time to time direct" and "recommend to the National Intelligence Authority the establishment of such overall policies and objectives as will assure the most effective accomplishment of the National Intelligence mission" gave us that right.

Mr. BROWN. Then, you did not consider that the word "evaluate" was a limitation on your duty, but *this other section was so broad that you could do about anything that you decided was either advantageous or beneficial, in your mind?*

General VANDENBERG. *Yes, sir.*

Mr. BROWN. *In other words, if you decided you wanted to go into direct activities of any nature, almost, why, that would be done?*

General VANDENBERG. *Within the Foreign Intelligence field, if it was agreed upon by all the three agencies concerned.*

Mr. BROWN. And that you were not limited to evaluation?

General VANDENBERG. That is right, sir.

(Transcript, House Committee on Expenditures in the Executive Department, Hearings on H.R. 2319, 6/27/47, pp. 9–11.)

Walter Pforzheimer has told one interviewer that General Vandenberg testified in the executive session about intelligence collection because Army Intelligence opposed any intelligence gathering by the CIA. Covert action, according to Pforzheimer, was not mentioned. Interview on file at the Center for National Security Studies.

In addition, as was noted earlier, there is no evidence that the Central Intelligence Group did engage in covert action.

[54] Rogovin, HSIC, 12/9/75, p. 1735.

[55] *Ibid.*

[56] Transcript,. House Committee on Expenditures in the Executive Departments, Hearings on H.R. 2319, 6/27/47, p. 37.

[57] *Ibid.*, p. 37.

These statements and the discussions in the executive session about the CIA's role in clandestine intelligence gathering suggest that the ambiguous references in the public hearings referred to clandestine collection operations.

Because the Select Committee has been unable to locate transcripts of the other executive sessions, it is impossible to state conclusively that covert action was not explicitly mentioned during these meetings. However, none of the participants queried recalled any such discussions and none of the committee reports contain any references to covert action.

A memorandum by the CIA's General Counsel, written soon after the passage of the Act, noted that "We do not believe that there was any thought in the minds of Congress that the Central Intelligence Agency, under this authority, would take positive action for subversion and sabotage." In that September 25, 1947 memorandum to the Director, the General Counsel wrote:

> A review of debates indicates that Congress was primarily interested in an agency for coordinating intelligence and originally did not propose any overseas collection activities for CIA. The strong move to provide specifically for such collection overseas was defeated, and, as a compromise, Sections 102(d)(4) and (5) were enacted, which permitted the National Security Council to determine the extent of the collection work to be performed by CIA. We do not believe that there was any thought in the minds of Congress that the Central Intelligence Agency under this authority would take positive action for subversion and sabotage. A bitter debate at about the same time on the State Department's foreign broadcast service tends to confirm our opinion. Further confirmation is found in the brief and off-the-record hearings on appropriations for CIA. ... It is our conclusion, therefore, that neither M.O. [morale operations] nor S.O. [special operations] should be undertaken by CIA without previously informing Congress and obtaining its approval of the functions and the expenditure of funds for those purposes.[58]

All of this is not to suggest that Congress or any Members of Congress specifically intended that covert action should be excluded from the authorized missions of the CIA. The issue of covert action simply was not raised in the course of the legislation's enactment. As the CIA's former General Counsel told the Senate Select Committee there is "no specific legislative history supporting covert action as part of the functions assigned" to the CIA.[59] Rather than authorizing covert action, the broad language of 102(d)(5) appears to have

---

[58] Memorandum from the CIA General Counsel to the Director, 9/25/47.
This memo may have been the result of an inquiry by Admiral Hillenkoetter, who had been asked by Secretary Forrestal if the CIA would be able to conduct covert and cold war activities such as black propaganda and sabotage in support of guerrilla warfare. Admiral Hillenkoetter, who had doubts about the CIA's authority to undertake such activities, asked his General Counsel for his opinion. (Houston, 6/17/75, p. 13–15.)
[59] Houston, 6/17/75, p. 10.

been intended to authorize clandestine collection of intelligence [60] and to provide the CIA with the "maximum flexibility" [61] necessary to deal with problems which, due to America's inexperience with a peacetime intelligence agency, might not be foreseen.

D. Post Enactment History

As previously noted, the executive branch presented no justification to the Congress for the conduct of covert action by the CIA. Yet even while the National Security Act of 1947 was being drafted, introduced, debated, and passed the Coordinating Committee of the Departments of State, War, and the Navy (SWNCC) prepared a paper establishing procedures for psychological warfare during peacetime as well as wartime. On April 30, 1947, SWNCC established a Subcommittee on Psychological Warfare to plan and execute psychological war.

These plans took on new importance as the United States became concerned over the course of events in Western Europe and the Near East. Tension soon became so high that in December of 1947, the Department of State advised the NSC that covert operations mounted by the Soviet Union and her allies threatened the defeat of American foreign policy objectives. The Department recommended that the U.S. supplement its own foreign policy activity with covert action.

At its first meeting in December, 1947, the National Security Council approved NSC–4, which empowered the Secretary of State to coordinate information activities designed to counter communism. A top secret annex took cognizance of the "vicious psychological efforts of the USSR, its satellite countries, and Communist groups to discredit and defeat the activities of the U.S. and other Western powers." The NSC determined that "in the interests of world peace and U.S. national security the foreign information activities of the U.S. government must be supplemented by covert psychological operations."

The CIA was already engaged in clandestine collection of intelligence and, as the NSC put it, "The similarity of operational methods involved in covert psychological and intelligence activities and the need to ensure their secrecy and obviate costly duplication renders the CIA the logical agency to conduct such operations." Therefore, acting under the authority of section 102(d)(5) of the National Security Act of 1947, the NSC instructed the Director of Central Intelligence to initiate and conduct covert psychological operations that would counteract Soviet and Soviet-inspired covert actions and which would be consistent with U.S. foreign policy and overt foreign information activities.[62]

In the following months the CIA was involved in a number of covert actions. As the Soviet threat loomed larger and larger, the need for covert action, beyond psychological operations, seemed more pressing. On June 18, 1948, the NSC issued NSC–10/2 which superseded NSC–4–A, and vastly expanded the range of covert activities. The CIA was

---

[60] Memorandum from the CIA General Counsel to the Director, 5/7/48.

[61] Houston, 6/17/75, p. 10.

[62] Pursuant to the NSC's instruction, the Special Procedures Group was established in the Office of Special Operations (OSO) of the CIA to conduct covert psychological operations.

authorized to undertake economic warfare, sabotage, subversion against hostile states (including assistance to guerrilla and refugee liberation groups), and support of indigenous anti-communist elements in threatened countries.

The NSC noted that CIA was already charged with espionage and counterespionage abroad.[63] Because of this, according to the NSC, it was "desirable" for "operational reasons" to assign covert action authority to the CIA rather than to create a new unit. Therefore, under the authority of 50 U.S.C 403(d)(5), the NSC ordered the establishment in CIA of the Office of Special Projects (OSP), to conduct covert action. The Chief of OSP was to receive policy guidance from the Secretary of State and the Secretary of Defense. OSP (later, OPC) was to operate independently of all components of the CIA to the maximum degree consistent with efficiency.[64]

Thus even though the CIA's General Counsel could find no authority in the legislative history of the National Security Act, the NSC relied upon the Act to direct the CIA to initiate covert actions. Language intended to authorize clandestine intelligence gathering and to provide flexibility for unforeseen circumstances was broadened by the executive to cover sabotage, subversion and paramilitary activities. The executive branch did not heed the advice offered by the CIA's General Counsel in 1947 that congressional authorization was still "necessary." [65] This may well have been due to a belief in the power of the President to direct such activities.[66]

It is impossible to prove conclusively that Congress intended or did not intend to authorize covert action by the CIA through the passage of the National Security Act of 1947. It is possible, however, after reviewing the hearings, committee reports, and floor debates, to say that there is no substantial evidence supporting the existence of Congressional intent to authorize covert action by the CIA through the enactment of the National Security Act.

This conclusion is supported by the following:

(1) The absence of any explicit provision in the Act itself.

(2) The absence of any reference to covert action in the committee reports.

(3) The absence of any clear statement by a Member of Congress, in the hearings or debates, which demonstrates the intent to authorize covert action.

(4) The absence of any reference to a program of covert action in the justifications and explanations by the executive branch of the Act.

---

[63] The CIA had also been charged with conducting covert psychological operations under the authority of NSC 4–A.

[64] Both NSC–4–A and NSC 10/2 cited 50 U.S.C. (d)(5); neither invoked the President's authority, if any, to order covert action in the absence of congressional authorization.

[65] Memorandum from the CIA General Counsel to the Director, 9/25/47, p. 2.

[66] The General Counsel of the CIA noted his belief that "if [the CIA got] the proper directive from the executive branch and the funds from the Congress to carry out that directive, these two together are the true authorization." (Memorandum from the General Counsel of the CIA to the Director, 10/30/69, at p. 2.)

(5) The absence of any discussion in the hearings or debates of the threats which would suggest the need for a covert action capability.

(6) The conclusion of the CIA's General Counsel, immediately following the Act's passage, that the CIA lacked statutory authority for covert action and that sections (d) (4) and (5) were intended by Congress to authorize clandestine intelligence gathering by the CIA.

B. The CIA Act of 1949

Passage of the CIA Act of 1949 has also been cited as support for the view that Congress has authorized covert action by the CIA. A careful analysis of the Act's legislative history does not support this view.

Two years after the enactment of the National Security Act and after the NSC had directed the CIA to engage in various covert activities, Congress passed the Central Intelligence Agency Act of 1949.[68] The 1949 legislation was an enabling act containing administrative provisions necessary for the conduct of the Agency's mission.[69] As such, it did not add to the missions of the Agency. The events surrounding its passage, however, may shed light upon what Congress believed it had authorized in the National Security Act of 1947.

The Act included a number of administrative provisions which clearly were designed to assure the security of some sort of clandestine activity by the CIA. These included the waiver of normal restrictions placed on governmental acquisition of materiel, hiring and, perhaps more important, accounting for funds expended. The General Counsel of the Central Intelligence Agency wrote that:

Provision of unvouchered funds and the inviolatability of such funds from outside inspection is the heart and soul of covert operation.[70]

The Central Intelligence Agency has argued that passage of the Central Intelligence Agency Act of 1949 "clearly reflects Congress' determination that the Agency be able to conduct activities such as covert action, similar to those conducted by the OSS." [71] Although members of the House Armed Services Committees were aware that the Central Intelligence Agency was conducting covert operations and that the administrative provisions would be "essential to the flexibility

---

[68] 50 U.S.C. 403a–403j.

[69] The administrative provisions had been included in a draft of the National Security Act of 1947 shown to Members of the House of Representatives. In order to avoid having to detail administrative provisions for all of the organizations set up under the National Security Act, these provisions were removed from the draft to be presented later as a separate act.

[70] Memorandum from the CIA General Counsel to the Director, 5/25/49, p. 2.

[71] Rogovin, HSIC, 12/9/75, p. 1735.

and security" [72] of these operations, there is no evidence that Congress as a whole knew the range of clandestine activities, including covert action, which was being undertaken by the CIA. The committee reports on the Central Intelligence Agency Act include no reference to covert action. The floor debates contain only one reference to covert action, and strongly suggest that the Congress knew only that clandestine intelligence gathering was going on.

In addition, the provisions of the 1949 Act are not uniquely designed to facilitate covert action. They would serve the needs of an organization performing espionage equally well; Members of Congress, in fact, described the Act as an "espionage bill." [73] Thus even a careful reader of the Act would not infer from its provisions that the Agency was conducting covert action.

Given these facts, it is difficult to find in the Act's passage congressional intent to authorize covert action or a congressional belief that the National Security Act of 1947 had authorized it.

The bill which was to become the Central Intelligence Agency Act of 1949 was first introduced in Congress in 1948. The Director of Central Intelligence appeared before the House Armed Services Committee on April 8, 1948, to discuss the bill. The Director noted:

> It was thought when we started back in 1946, that at least we would have time to develop this mature service over a period of years—after all, the British, who possess the finest intelligence in the world, have been developing their system since the time of Queen Elizabeth. Unfortunately, the international situation has not allowed us the breathing space we might have liked, and so, as we present this bill, we find our-

---

[72] The CIA General Counsel described the provisions of the Central Intelligence Agency Act of 1949 as follows:

"Administrative authorities of the Agency are contained in the Central Intelligence Agency Act of 1949, as amended. This has provided us with all the authorities and exemptions needed to carry out the wide variety of functions assigned to the Agency during the past twenty years. It enables us to have an effective and a flexible personnel program, ranging from the normal desk officer in headquarters to persons in a relationship so remote that they do not know they are working for the Agency. It enables us to exercise all the techniques required for clandestine activities, from traditional agent operations through proprietary and other more sophisticated types of machinery. It has enabled us to undertake major unforeseen projects, such as the U-2 operation.

"Two provisions of the Act are particularly important. The unique authority in Section 5 to transfer to and receive from other government agencies sums as may be approved by the Bureau of the Budget. This has given us great flexibility and security in our funding. The other, Section 8, with its wide authority for utilization of sums made available to the Agency, particularly subsection (b) thereof which allows us to make any expenditures required for confidential, extraordinary, or emergency purposes, and these expenditures will be accounted for solely on the certificate of the Director. This has been essential to the flexibility and security of our covert activities." (Memorandum from the CIA General Counsel to the Deputy Director for National Intelligence Programs Evaluation 10/9/68, p. 3.)

[73] 95 Cong Rec. 1946 (1949).

selves in operations up to our necks, and we need the authorities contained herein as a matter of urgency.[74]

It is clear that the operations that the Director referred to were understood by the executive branch to include covert action. In describing the provision of the bill which would eliminate the normal government advertising requirements, the Director stated that there were urgent requests from overseas which required immediate operational response. As an example, he provided: "Any possible action in connection with the Italian election." [75] In later remarks on the same section,[76] the Director cited the need to avoid advertising for contracts for the production of certain materiél, listing among his examples explosives and silencers.[77] Such materiél was clearly not for the purposes of clandestine intelligence gathering and reporting.

In his 100-page statement, the Director also explained the provision for unvouchered funds, the provision which the General Counsel of the Central Intelligence Agency described as the "heart and soul of covert operations." The Director stated:

> In view of the nature of the work which must be conducted by the CIA under the National Security Act and applicable directives of the National Security Council, it is necessary to use funds for various covert or semi-covert operations and other purposes where it is either impossible to conform with existing government procedures and regulations or conformance therewith would materially injure the national security. It is not practicable, and in some cases impossible, from either a record or security viewpoint to maintain the information and data which would be required under usual government procedures and regulations. In many instances, it is necessary to make specific payments or reimbursements on a project basis where the background information is of such a sensitive nature from a security viewpoint that only a general certificate, signed by the Director of CIA, should be processed through even restricted channels. To do otherwise would obviously increase the possibilities of penetration with respect to any specific activity or general project. The nature of the activities of CIA are such that items of this nature are recurring and, while in some instances the confidential or secret aspects as such may not be of primary importance, the extraordinary situations or the exigencies of the particular transaction involved warrant the avoidance of all normal channels and procedures.[78]

On the basis of this presentation, it can be concluded that at least the House Armed Services Committee, one of the committees which had jurisdiction over the CIA, knew that the CIA was conducting or would in the future conduct covert action. The Committee also knew that

---

[74] Statement of Adm. Roscoe Hillenkoetter, Director of Central Intelligence, House Armed Services Committee, 4/8/48, pp. 6–7 (statement on file at the CIA).

[75] *Ibid.*, p. 21.

[76] Sect. 3(s) of H.R. 5871, 80th Cong., 2d Session.

[77] Hillenkoetter, 4/8/48, p. 27. These examples were drawn by the Director from the history of the OSS.

[78] *Ibid.* pp. 111–113.

the administrative provisions would enhance the Agency's covert action capability.[79]

The evidence, however, is not entirely clear. While the present day reader may interpret "covert or semicovert operations" to mean covert action, the Members had had little exposure to these terms. Covert or semicovert operations could easily have been interpreted to mean clandestine intelligence gathering operations; the CIA's role in clandestine intelligence gathering had been discussed in a hearing before the same committee,[80] as well as in the press.[81]

Even if it were assumed, moreover, that the House and Senate Armed Services Committees fully understood that the CIA was engaging in covert action, there is no evidence that the Congress as a whole knew that the CIA was engaged in covert action or that the administrative provisions were intended to facilitate it. The hearings on the CIA Act of 1949 were held almost entirely in executive session. The committee reports on the Act did not mention covert action at all. They were bland and uninformative—the provision to provide the secret funding of the CIA through transfers from appropriations to other government agencies was described as providing "for the annual financing of Agency operations without impairing security." [82] They were strikingly incomplete. As the House Armed Services Committee report itself noted, the report:

> does not contain a full and detailed explanation of all of the provisions of the proposed legislation in view of the fact that much of such information is of a highly confidential nature.[83]

The floor debates contain only one indication that covert action, as opposed to clandestine intelligence gathering, was being, or would be undertaken by the CIA.[84] The debates strongly suggest that rather than approving covert action by the CIA, Congress was attempting to facilitate clandestine intelligence gathering by the Agency.

Prior to the passage of the Act there had been discussion in the press of CIA involvement in clandestine intelligence gathering. Clandestine intelligence gathering was mentioned on the floor; as noted previously, Members referred to the CIA Act of 1949 as an "espionage bill." [85] Senator Tydings, the Chairman of the Senate Armed Services Committee, stated, "The bill does not provide for new activity, but what it does particularly is to seek to safeguard information procured by

---

[79] It is quite likely that the Senate Armed Services Committee was presented with a similar statement from the Director, although the Senate Select Committee has been unable to locate any transcripts of executive sessions held by the Senate Armed Services Committee.

[80] Testimony of Gen. Hoyt S. Vandenberg before House Armed Services Committee Hearing on H.R. 5871, 4/8/48 (statement on file at the CIA).

[81] "The X at Bogatá," The Washington Post, 4/13/48; Hanson W. Baldwin, "Intelligence—II," The New York Times, 7/22/48.

[82] S. Rep. No. 725, 81st Cong., 1st Sess. 4 (1949).

[83] H. Rep. No. 160, 91st Cong., 1st Sess. 6 (1949). See also 95 Cong. Rec. 1946 (1949), remarks of Rep. Marcantonio.

[84] It was remarked in the House debates, in the context of a discussion of intelligence gathering that "in spite of all our wealth and power and might we have been extremely weak in psychological warfare, notwithstanding the fact that an idea is perhaps the most powerful weapon on this earth." (95 Cong. Rec. 1047 (1949).)

[85] 95 Cong. Rec., 1946 (1949).

agents of the government so that it will not fall into the hands of enemy countries or potential enemy countries who would use the information to discover who the agents were and kill them." [86] Thus there is ample evidence to suggest that the full legislature knew that the functions of the CIA included espionage; but there is no evidence to suggest that more than a few Members of Congress knew that the CIA was engaged in covert action. Without such knowledge Congress could hardly be said to have authorized it.[87]

Another factor undercutting the theory that passage of the CIA Act constituted congressional authorization for covert action is that the argument confuses implementing authority with statutory authority. Congress had set out the CIA's statutory authority in the National Security Act of 1947. The CIA Act of 1949 did not provide any additional non-administrative or non-fiscal powers to the CIA.[88] It simply provided the means for the CIA to implement the authorities already granted it.

N15

C. The Provision of Funds to the CIA by Congress

There is no evidence that Congress intended, by the passage of the National Security Act of 1947, to authorize covert action by the CIA. Passage of the Central Intelligence Agency Act of 1949 did not add the covert action mission to those already authorized by the National Security Act. Nevertheless, the National Security Council had in 1947 directed the CIA to engage in covert activities; by the early 1950s the Central Intelligence Agency was involved in covert action around the world.

In 1962 the General Counsel summarized the early developments in the CIA's undertaking of covert action : [91]

> The National Security Council did develop a Directive (NSC 10/2) setting forth a program of covert cold-war activities and assigned it to the Office of Policy Coordination under the Director of Central Intelligence with policy guidance from the Department of State. The Congress was asked for and did appropriate funds to support this program, although, of course, only a small number of Congressmen in the Ap-

---

[86] 95 Cong. Rec. 6955 (1949). This quote, indicating Chairman Tydings' interpretation of the Act, seems to undercut the argument that he and the Senate Armed Services Committee understood that the CIA was conducting covert action and that the provisions of the CIA Act of 1949 were designed to facilitate this.

[87] Without such knowledge a Member reading the Act would not be likely to infer that it was designed to facilitate covert action. As the provisions of the Act were not uniquely designed for covert action but were equally applicable to clandestine intelligence gathering, an activity which Congress knew about and approved, Members would be unlikely to realize from reading the Act that the CIA conducted covert action.

[88] S. Rep. No. 106, 81st Cong., 1st Sess. 1 (1949).

[91] In a September 25, 1947 memorandum to the Director, the General Counsel advised that no covert action "should be undertaken by CIA without previously informing Congress and obtaining its approval of the functions and expenditure of funds for those purposes." He further noted that even if the NSC were to assign the covert action function to the CIA it would still be necessary for the CIA to "go to Congress for authority and funds." (Memorandum from the CIA General Counsel to the Director, 9/25/47).

propriations Committees knew the amount and purpose of the appropriations.[92]

The Office of Legislative Counsel of the Department of Justice argued in 1962 that this provision of funds for covert action, even though known only to a few members of Congress, constituted con-

N16 gressional ratification of the CIA's conduct of covert action.

> Congress has continued over the years since 1947 to appro-
> priate funds for the conduct of such covert activities. We
> understand that the existence of such covert activities has
> been reported on a number of occasions to the leadership of
> both houses, and to members of the subcommittees of the
> Armed Services and Appropriations Committees of both
> houses. It can be said that Congress as a whole knows that
> money is appropriated to CIA and knows generally that a
> portion of it goes for clandestine activities, although knowl-
> edge of specific activities is restricted to the group specified
> above and occasional other members of Congress briefed for
> specific purposes. In effect, therefore, CIA has for many years
> had general funds approval from the Congress to carry on
> covert cold-war activities, which the Executive Branch has
> the authority and responsibility to direct.
>
> It is well-established that appropriations for administrative
> action of which Congress has been informed amount to a rati-
> fication of or acquiescence in such action. *Brooks* v. *Dewar*, 313
> U.S. 354, 361; *Fleming* v. *Mohawk Co.*, 331 U.S. 111, 116; see
> also *Ivanhoe Irrig. Dist.* v. *McCracken*, 357 U.S. 275, 293–294;
> *Power Reactor Co.* v. *Electricians*, 367 U.S. 396, 409. Since
> the circumstances effectively prevent the Congress from mak-
> ing an express and detailed appropriation for the activities of
> the CIA, the general knowledge of the Congress, and specific
> knowledge of responsible committee members, outlined above,
> are sufficient to render this principle applicable. [Citations
> omitted.] [93]

And in December 1975 the House Select Committee on Intelligence was told by the CIA that given "CIA reporting of its covert action programs to Congress, and congressional appropriation of funds for such programs" the "law is clear that, under these circumstances.

---

[92] Memorandum from the CIA General Counsel to the Director, 1/15/62, p. 2.

[93] Memorandum re: "Constitutional and Legal Basis for So-Called Covert Activities of the Central Intelligence Agency," prepared by the Office of Legislative Counsel, Department of Justice, 1/17/62, pp. 12–13.

The Office of Legislative Counsel apparently placed considerable weight on the knowledge of the subcommittee members of the committees having jurisdiction over the CIA (*Ibid.*, p. 12 n. 4) and implied "close contact" between the CIA and "its committees," (*Ibid.*, p. 13 n. 5) For example, the memorandum cited a letter dated May 2, 1957, from Mr. Allen W. Dulles, Director, CIA, to Sen. Hennings, in *Freedom of Information and Secrecy in Government*, Hearing before the Subcommittee on Constitutional Rights of the Senate Committee of the Judiciary, 85th Cong., 2d Sess., pp. 376, 377:

"The Director of the Central Intelligence Agency appears regularly before established subcommittees of the Armed Services and Appropriations Committees of the Senate and of the House, and makes available to these subcommittees complete information on Agency activities, personnel and expenditures. No information has ever been denied to their subcommittees."

Congress has effectively ratified the authority of the CIA to plan and conduct covert action under the direction of the President and the National Security Council." [95]

In order to analyze the claim that congressional provision of funds to the CIA constitutes congressional ratification of the CIA's authority to conduct covert action, the general question of congressional ratification by appropriation must be examined. The general rule has been stated as follows: "Ratification by appropriation is not favored and will not be accepted where prior knowledge of the specific disputed action cannot be demonstrated clearly."[96] In the same opinion the Court noted that:

> ratification by appropriation, no less than ratification by acquiescence, requires affirmative evidence that Congress actually knew of the administrative policy. . . . Moreover, to constitute ratification, an appropriation must plainly show a purpose to bestow the precise authority which is claimed." [Citations omitted.]

Appropriations do not convey authority or ratify agency acts without proof that Congress knew what the agency was doing. For instance, in *Green* v. *McElroy*, 360 U.S. 474, the Supreme Court held that an appropriation to the Department of Defense for its security program did not constitute ratification of a procedure which denied the right of an individual to confront the witnesses against him. On the other hand, if appropriations are enacted after objections have been made to the appropriations committees that no legal authority exists to carry out a particular project, congressional acknowledgement or ratification of the authority to perform the specified act can be inferred.[97]

In sum, general appropriations for an agency cannot be deemed to be ratification of a specific activity of that agency in the absence of congressional knowledge of the specific activity and congressional intent that the specific activity be funded from the general appropriation.[98]

The argument that through the provision of funds to the CIA Congress has effectively ratified the authority of the CIA to conduct covert action rests on the assumption that since the founding of the Agency, Congress has known that CIA was engaged in covert action and has provided funds to the CIA with the knowledge and intent that some of the funds would be used for covert action.

The CIA's conduct of covert action was not known by Congress as a whole during the early years of the CIA. In the interest of security few Members were informed about covert actions—a situation which

[95] Rogovin, HSIC, 12/9/75, p. 1736.

[96] *D.C. Federation of Civic Associations* v. *Airis*, 391 F.2d 478, 482 (D.C. Circ. 1968).

[97] *United States ex rel Tennessee Valley Authority* v. *Two Tracts of Land*, 456 F.2d 264 (6th Cir. 1972). Appropriations for the Vietnam War, in combination with other congressional actions, were held by most courts to constitute congressional authorization for the war. See e.g., *Berk* v. *Laird*, 317 F. Supp. 715 (E.D. N.Y. 1970). *But see, Mitchell* v. *Laird*, 488 F. 2d 611 (D.C. Cir. 1973).

[98] *Thompson* v. *Clifford*, 408 F.2d 154 (D.C. Cir. 1968) ; Sutherland, *Statutory Construction* (Sands ed. 1974) sec. 49.10.

continued until Congress mandated disclosure to six congressional committees of CIA activities not intended solely for intelligence gathering.[99] Even prior to this mandate, many Members of Congress not briefed on covert action by the executive branch probably knew that the CIA had engaged in covert actions such as the Bay of Pigs; this knowledge was not official being based neither on declarations of official U.S. policy nor on briefings of the Congress as a whole, but rather on information gained from other sources.[100] One of the reasons offered for the 1974 Amendment to the Foreign Assistance Act was that it would ensure that Congress would have sufficient information about covert action to determine if such activities should continue.[101]

It is difficult to fix a point in time in the past when it could be said with assurance that Congress as a whole "clearly" had the knowledge of covert action required for congressional ratification.[102] Congress certainly has that knowledge today.

The first requirement, congressional knowledge of covert action by the CIA, is, at least now, met. In the future appropriation to the CIA without any provision prohibiting the use of funds for covert action would ratify the CIA's authority. But did the provision of funds to the CIA in the past, or will the provision of funds in the future under present arrangements constitute "appropriations" which "plainly show a purpose to bestow the precise authority which is claimed"?

The answer would be a clear yes if the funding had been or were to be by open appropriations to the CIA. The answer would be yes if Congress as a whole had voted the appropriations to the CIA in executive session. This has not been the case.

The funds provided to the CIA are concealed in appropriations made to other agencies. They are then transferred to the CIA, pursuant to the provisions of the CIA Act of 1949,[103] with the approval of

---

[99] 22 U.S.C. 2422.

[100] Under the system of plausible denial the U.S. Government would not officially confirm that it engaged in covert action and would seek to avoid acknowledging a U.S. Government role in any particular covert action. Therefore, the knowledge imputed to Members of Congress not officially briefed on the CIA's covert actions would have to be based on other sources.

[101] Cong. Rec., S18065, daily ed., 10/2/74 (remarks of Senators Baker and Symington).

[102] It might be argued that Congress chose to limit knowledge of covert action to selected Members and that *their* knowledge, combined with that congressional decision, would be sufficient. J. Edwin Dietel, of the Office of General Counsel of the CIA, in a 11/20/73 memorandum for the record, in fact wrote: "We would also note that, while the specific activities that the Agency's appropriations are used for is limited to only a few Members of Congress, the whole Congress chose to adopt that procedure for reviewing the Agency's activities and appropriations."

First, it must be noted that until Congress "knew" about covert action, Congress could not delegate to a small group of Members the responsibility for overseeing it. When Congress reached that point of knowledge—and as noted it is impossible to say when that was—it arguably could delegate although there may be limits to that delegation.

Given the presumption against ratification by appropriation, the difficulty in fixing a time when Congress "knew," as well as the small number of knowledgeable Members, and the question of whether Congress could delegate to these Members the congressional knowledge required for ratification, it cannot be concluded that the knowledge of these few Members met the test cited for ratification by appropriation.

[103] 50 U.S.C. 403 f.

the OMB and selected members of the Appropriations Committee. Congress, as a whole, never specifically votes on funds for the CIA. Congress, as a whole, does not know how much money the CIA will receive in a given year. This secret funding undercuts the argument that the Congress has notified the CIA's conduct of covert action by knowingly appropriating funds to be used for covert action. In fact, there is some doubt that the CIA is even "appropriated" funds pursuant to the constitutional requireemnt.[105]

Even if the provision of funds is constitutionally valid, in the absence of a vote by Congress on the funding, it can hardly be said to "plainly" demonstrate a congressional intent to ratify the CIA's authority to conduct covert action.

The CIA ignored the questionable nature of Congress' knowledge of covert action and the secret funding of the CIA in claiming that "the law is clear that, under these circumstances, Congress has effectively ratified the authority of the CIA to plan and conduct covert action under the direction of the President and the National Security Council."[106] In support of its position, the Central Intelligence Agency cited what was described as "the leading case on this point," *Brooks* v. *Dewar*, 313 U.S. 354 (1941). According to the Central Intelligence Agency, "the Brooks case requires the conclusion that Congress has ratified the CIA's authority to plan and conduct covert action."[107]

Brooks involved a challenge to a licensing scheme established by the Secretary of the Interior under a statute providing him with broad responsibility for the administration of livestock grazing districts. Although the act in question did not explicitly authorize him to require persons wishing to utilize the land to purchase licenses, the Court found congressional ratification of his actions. The Court, in upholding the Secretary's argument that Congress had ratified his action wrote, "The information in the possession of Congress was plentiful and from various sources."[108] The Court cited annual reports of the

---

[105] Article I, Sec. 9, Clause 7 of the Constitution provides that "No Money shall be drawn from the Treasury but in Consequence of Appropriations made by Law." Appropriations are, by definition, specific amounts of money set aside for designated purposes [*Geddes* v. *United States*, 39 Ct. Claims. 428. 444 (1903)] It is not required to particularize each item in order for an appropriation to be valid [*United States* v. *State Bridge Commission*, 109 F. Supp. 690 (E. D. Mich. 1953)] but the appropriation must be sufficiently identifiable to make clear the intent of Congress. [*Ibid.*] As Congress votes on appropriations for other agencies from which CIA funds are secretly transferred rather than setting aside a specific sum of money for the CIA for a specific purpose, it can be argued that there is no constitutionally valid appropriation to the Agency. If the public accounting required by Article 1, Sec. 9, Clause 7 is a necessary condition for a constitutionally valid appropriation, it would be even harder to argue the validity of the present funding scheme as the statement published pursuant to the constitutional requirements do not reflect receipts and expenditures of the CIA.

The argument might be made that congressional establishment of the transfer provisions of the CIA Act of 1949 manifested a congressional purpose to authorize the CIA to conduct covert action. However, nothing in the debates supports this argument. Moreover, the transfer provision was equally applicable to any clandestine activity, including the clandestine collection of intelligence.

[106] Rogovin, HSIC, Hearings, 12/9/75, p. 1736.

[107] *Ibid.*

[108] 313 U.S. at 360.

Secretary, testimony at Appropriation Committee hearings, and statements on the floor of Congress. The Court found that the "repeated appropriations of the fees thus covered and to be covered into the Treasury . . . constitutes a ratification of the action. . ." [109]

Given the special treatment of the CIA, the relevance of *Brooks* seems questionable. "Plentiful" information is not available. No annual reports are issued by the Director of Central Intelligence. Until recently there have been few open hearings or floor debates on the activities of the CIA. Congress as a whole has never voted on appropriations for the CIA, nor designated funds for covert action.

Brooks and several other cases are also cited by a Justice Department memorandum written in 1962 and presented to the House Select Committee on Intelligence in 1975. The memorandum argues that:

> Since the circumstances effectively prevent the Congress from making an express and detailed appropriation for the activities of the CIA, the general knowledge of the Congress, and specific knowledge of responsible committee members . . . are sufficient to render this principal [ratification] applicable. [110]

Given the presumption against ratification by appropriation, the small number of knowledgeable Members, the uncertainty as to whether congressional knowledge required for ratification could be imputed from the knowledge of these few Members, and the question of whether a congressional appropriation can be imputed from the approval of secret transfers of funds to the CIA by subcommittees of the House and Senate Appropriations Committees, there is substantial doubt as to the validity of this position.

As was previously noted, the actual state of congressional knowledge about covert action prior to the 1970s is unclear. Congress, however, now knows that the CIA conducts covert action. Congress also knows that the Executive claims Congress has authorized the Agency to do so. [111] Finally, Congress knows that the CIA receives its funds through secret transfers of funds appropriated to the Department of Defense [112] and that some of the transferred funds are used to finance cover action. In the future the failure by Congress to prohibit funds from being used for covert action by the CIA would clearly constitute congressional ratification of the CIA's authority, eliminating any ambiguity. [113]

---

[106] *Ibid.*

[110] Rogovin, HSIC, 12/9/75, p. 1736.

[111] Congressional acquiescence, with notice, of long-standing executive policy, creates a presumption in favor of that policy's validity (*United States* v. *Midwest Oil Co.*, 236 U.S. 459 (1915). See also, *Sibach* v. *Wilson & Co.*, 312 U.S. 1 (1941).]

[112] Cong. Rec., H9359–76, daily ed., 10/1/75.

[113] Congress clearly has the authority to attach conditions to the use of the funds appropriated by it. [*Ohio* v. *United States Civil Service Commission*, 65 F. Supp. 776 (S.D. Ohio 1946) ; *Spalding* v. *Douglas Aircraft Co.*, 60 F. Supp. 985, 988 (1945) *aff'd* 154 F. 2d 419 (9th Cir. 1946).]

Such ratification, however, like ratification by acquiescense,[114] would would still be disfavored.[115] As the Supreme Court has cautioned, "it is at best treacherous to find in congressional silence alone the adopting of a controlling rule of law." [116] It would seem that important activities of the United States Government deserve direct and specific authorization from Congress.

D. The Holtzman and Abourezk Amendment of 1974

In 1974 Congress directly addressed the issue of the Central Intelligence Agency's conduct of covert action. In September, the House of Representatives defeated an amendment which would have forbidden the Central Intelligence Agency to spend funds "for the purpose of undermining or destabilizing the government of any foreign country." In October, the Senate defeated an amendment to the Foreign Assistance Act of 1974, which would have forbidden any agency of the United States Government to carry out "any activity within any foreign country which violates or is intended to encourage the violation of, the laws of the United States or of such countries," except for activities "necessary" to the security of the United States and intended "solely" to gather intelligence.

While both amendments would have limited the ability of the Central Intelligence Agency to conduct covert action, the failure of Congress to adopt them does not clearly constitute congressional ratification of the CIA's authority to conduct covert action.[117] Neither dealt with covert action in general. Strong opposition to even their consideration prior to hearings and committee reports was voiced. The amendments, however, did signal an increasing congressional concern over covert action and marked the beginning of attempts by Congress as a whole to regulate and obtain information on covert action.

In September 1974, Representative Holtzman proposed a joint resolution which would have amended the Supplemental Defense Appropriations Act as follows:

> After September 30, 1974, none of the funds appropriated under this joint resolution may be expended by the Central Intelligence Agency for the purpose of undermining or destabilizing the government of any foreign country.

---

[114] The theory that congressional acquiescence constitutes ratification that can be easily stretched. J. Edwin Dietel, Assitant General Counsel of the Agency, wrote a memorandum for the record dated May 7, 1974. In it he described a question submitted by Senator Proxmire to Director Colby during Mr. Colby's nomination hearing which concerned the Agency's secret financing of political parties. Mr. Dietel wrote that in a classified response Mr. Colby stated that the CIA has, over the last twenty-five years of its existence, provided secret financial assistance to political parties in a number of foreign countries. "As there have been no reverberations from this statement, there is, at least, tacit approval for this type of activity."

[115] *Thomas* v. *Clifford*, 408 F. 2d 134, 166, (D.C. Cir. 1968). See also, Norman Dorsen testimony, House Select Intelligence Committee, Hearings, 12/9/75, p. 1741.

[116] *Girouard* v. *United States*, 328 U.W. 61. 69 (1946).

[117] For a contrary view See Rogovin, HSIC, 12/9/75, pp. 1736–1737.

Ms. Holtzman introduced the amendment in response to revelations about the efforts of the CIA to "destabilize and undermine the government in Chile" and as a "beginning" in "restoring congressional prerogatives over the activities of the Government of this country." [118] Ms. Holtzman stressed her opposition to such activities directed against foreign governments with whom the United States was not at war "especially in an atmosphere of virtually complete secrecy, without approval by the Congress, or approval by the people of this country." [119]

The amendment was supported by Representative Giaimo, who noted:

> Since we have been informed of the improper activities of the CIA in Chile, and perhaps in other countries—and we have certainly been informed of its wrongful activities in Chile—this is the first opportunity which we have had in Congress to voice either approval or disapproval of the actions of our Government as they relate to the CIA. This is the first bill before us which presents us that opportunity. It is too late for us as a practical matter to do anything in the defense appropriation bill, but it is not too late now for us to approve this amendment, and to show to the world that the U.S. Congress will not sanction these nefarious and covert activities of the CIA, that the people of the United States will not approve and ratify the improper and wrongful acts of the CIA in Chile." [120]

The amendment was opposed by Representative Mahon who argued that the bill was "irrelevant" because the defense appropriation bill would be signed into law within a few days.[121] and because the legislation contained no proposal to undermine or destabilize any government.[122] He described as "indefensible" the presentation of the amendment as there had not been sufficient hearing by any of the committees of the House.[123] He was joined in his opposition by Representative Cederberg, a member of one of the CIA oversight subcommittees in the House, who indicated his belief that U.S. activities in Chile were taken "in the best interest of the United States," [124] and by Representative Conlan who argued that the amendment would lead to the identification of all our intelligence agents throughout the world and the destruction of the "basic defenses" of the United States. A vote for the amendment. Representative Conlan cautioned, would "cut off our covert intelligence operations" and "would be a vote for national suicide." [125]

The proposal was defeated by the House of Representatives on September 30, 1974, by a vote of 291–108.

Given this debate the defeat of the amendment cannot be read as congressional ratification of the CIA's authority to conduct covert ac-

---

[118] Cong. Rec. H9492–9493, daily ed., 9/24/74. (remarks of Rep. Holtzman).
[119] Cong. Rec. H9492, daily ed., 9/24/74.
[120] *Ibid.*, p. H9493 (remarks of Rep. Giaimo).
[121] *Ibid.*, (Remarks of Rep. Mahon).
[122] *Ibid.*
[123] *Ibid.*
[124] *Ibid.*, p. H9494 (remarks of Mr. Cederberg).
[125] *Ibid.*, (remarks of Rep. Conlan).

tion. The absence of hearings, the possible "irrelevance" of the amendment noted by both supporters and opponents of the bill, and the fact that the amendment only dealt with activities the purpose of which was the "undermining or destabilizing the government of any foreign country," all undercut an expansive reading of Congress' failure to adopt it.

On October 2, 1974 Senator Abourezk introduced an amendment (#1922) to the Foreign Assistance Act of 1974 which read as follows:

> Illegal activities in foreign countries, —(a) no funds made available under this or any other law may be used by any agency of the United States Government to carry out any activity within any foreign country which violates or is intended to encourage the violation of, the laws of the United States or of such countries.
> (b) The provision of this section should not be construed to prohibit the use of such funds to carry out any activity necessary to the security of the United States which is intended solely to gather intelligence information.

The amendment triggered a more extended floor debate than that generated by the Holtzman amendment.[126] During the debate Senator Abourezk asserted that his amendment would "abolish all clandestine or covert operations by the Central Intelligence Agency." [127] He argued that even the Director of the CIA had indicated that the national security would not be endangered if covert action were abolished.[128] Some of the opponents of the amendment argued that improved congressional oversight would be preferable to banning covert action. Senator Church noted that he could envision situations where threats to the national security would require covert activities.[129]

The amendment failed of passage. It might be argued that this failure, like that of the Holtzman amendment, constituted congressional ratification for the CIA's conduct of covert action.

The logic of this is undercut by a number of factors. One is that the amendment was not directed to all covert action, although the comments of some of the members implied that it was.[130] It was directed to activity abroad "which violates or is intended to encourage the violation of, laws of the United States or of such country." Thus, if failure to pass the amendment is to be read as congressional ratification of the actions which the amendment sought to prohibit, the Congress would have ratified only those foreign activities by the CIA which are illegal or intended to encourage the violation of law.

---

[126] See Cong. Rec. S18051–18056, daily ed., 10/2/74.

[127] *Ibid.*, p. 18051 (remarks of Sen. Abourezk).

[128] *Ibid.*

[129] *Ibid.*, (remarks of Sen. Church).

[130] Senator Abourezk stated that the amendment would "abolish all clandestine or covert operations," while Senator Church argued that increased oversight would be better than a complete prohibition. On the other hand, Senator Hatfield opposed the amendment as it did not go far enough in merely prohibiting the use of funds to carry out illegal foreign covert action; he argued that the capacity for any covert action should be taken away from the CIA. Senator Metzenbaum argued for the amendment's passage precisely because it was aimed only at illegal activities abroad by the CIA.

Whether the amendment passed or failed, it left unchanged whatever authority, if any, the CIA then had to conduct covert actions abroad which were illegal neither at home nor overseas.

Finally, the question of whether the amendment's failure should be read as congressional ratification of the CIA's authority to conduct such activities as would have been banned must be viewed in the light of other, and telling, arguments raised by those opposed to the amendment. Several Senators including Senators Humphrey, Stennis, and Goldwater objected to the fact that the amendment had not had the benefit of analysis by the committees with proper jurisdiction. Without the benefit of consideration by the Armed Services Committee, the amendment would be, according to Senator Stennis, "a shot in the dark." [131]

Using a different argument in opposition, Senator Baker stated that there existed "an insufficient state of information" by which to judge whether covert operations were or were not properly conducted. In place of the amendment he suggested that a proposed joint committee on intelligence oversight be established; Congress could then be supplied with sufficient information on covert action to make a judgment as to whether it should be banned or controlled by some other device.[132]

Given the fact that the amendment would prohibit only those foreign activities by the CIA which were illegal, the lack of explicit authorization for the CIA to conduct any covert action, the opposition of a substantial number of Senators to the amendment's consideration before it was examined by the committees with appropriate jurisdiction, and the statements by certain Senators that not enough was known about covert action to take a position on its continuance, the amendment's failure can hardly be given much weight in determining whether Congress has ratified the CIA's authority to conduct covert action.

E. The Hughes-Ryan Amendment

In 1974 Congress passed a significant amendment to the Foreign Assistance Act. The amendment provided that no funds might be expended by the CIA for operations not intended solely for obtaining necessary intelligence, in the absence of a Presidential finding that the operation is important to the national security of the United States, and a timely report to the appropriate committees of the Congress.

The amendment does not specifically authorize covert action by the CIA or unambiguously demonstrate congressional intent to provide such authorization. It does provide support for the position that Congress has authorized the CIA to conduct covert action or, more specifically, activities that are not intended solely for intelligence gathering. The debates indicate, however, a desire on the part of some Senators to withhold a decision on whether to authorize covert action until the reporting requirement provided Congress with more information.

---

[131] See Cong. Rec. S–18052, daily ed., 10/2/74 (remarks of Sen. Stennis).
[132] Ibid., p. S18065 (remarks of Sen. Baker).

In December 1974, the Congress passed a set of amendments to the Foreign Assistance Act. The amendments provided inter alia:

> Limitations on intelligence activities—(a) no funds appropriated under authority of this or any other Act may be expended by or on behalf of the Central Intelligence Agency for operations in foreign countries, other than activities intended solely for obtaining necessary intelligence, unless and until the President finds that each such operation is important to the national security of the United States and reports, in a timely fashion, a description and scope of such operation to the appropriate committees of Congress, including the Committee on Foreign Relations of the United States Senate and the Committee on Foreign Affairs of the United States House of Representatives (b) the provisions of subsection (a) of this section shall not apply during military operations initiated by the United States under a declaration of war approved by the Congress or an exercise of powers by the President under the War Powers Resolution.[133]

The statute does not explicitly authorize covert action by the Central Intelligence Agency. On its face it leaves the question of congressional authorization for covert action by the Central Intelligence Agency in the same position as existed prior to its passage, with two exceptions:

(1) For the first time a statute passed by Congress and signed by the President acknowledges that the Central Intelligence Agency might, in fact, conduct operations which were not intended solely for intelligence-gathering purposes; and

(2) The statute required that if such operations were to be carried out the President must first find that they are important to the national security of the United States. If such a finding is made, the operations must then be reported in a "timely fashion" to the appropriate committees of Congress.[134]

The amendment does not on its face provide any new authority for the President or the CIA. Nowhere in the public record is there any suggestion that the amendment might, in itself, serve as a new delegation by Congress of authority to the President to order any action by the CIA. If the amendment were read as a new delegation of powers to the President, the delegation would cover an enormously wide range of activities—all those activities not intended solely for intelligence gathering.[135]

While there is no evidence in the public record that Congress intended to delegate new powers to the President or the CIA, it might

---

[133] Appendix D, Hearings, Vol. 7, p. 230.

[134] There is some question as to the meaning of a "timely fashion." It is not clear whether it means prior to, at the same time as, or within a reasonable time after, the initiation of such an operation. The Central Intelligence Agency has, on occasion, notified the appropriate congressional committees before initiation of a project. The Senate Select Committee has recommended that the appropriate congressional committees be notified prior to the initiation of any significant covert action projects.

[135] This would be limited, to some extent, by the requirement of a presidential finding.

be argued that passage of the amendment constitutes congressional acknowledgment that the CIA did have authority to conduct those covert actions consonant with the Presidential finding. The CIA has, in fact, taken the position that passage of the amendment "clearly implies that the CIA is authorized to plan and conduct covert action." [136] Two committees of the Association of the Bar of the City of New York concluded that passage of the amendment serves as a "clear congressional authorization for the CIA to conduct covert activities." [137] This argument has considerable merit.

While certain restrictions were placed on the conduct of covert action, it was not prohibited as it might have been. The amendment was described in the floor debates as permitting the CIA to engage in many activities and "authorizing" even covert activities such as those designed to "subvert or undermine foreign governments." [138]

Congressional ratification or authorization, however, as demonstrated by the floor debates, was hardly unambiguous. A substantial number of the proponents of the amendment saw it as a temporary measure. As Senator Hughes, its sponsor, stated:

> . . . the amendment I offer should be regarded as only a beginning toward the imperative of imposing some order and structure to the means by which the American people, through their elected representatives, can exercise a measure of control over the cloak-and-dagger operations of the intelligence agencies of the U.S. government.[139]

He went on to say that the amendment "provides a temporary arrangement, not a permanent one, recognizing that a permanent arrangement is in the process of being developed." [140]

The development of this "permanent arrangement" depended on the effectiveness of the reporting requirement. Senator Baker, who had opposed the Abourezk amendment because there existed "an insufficient state of information" by which to judge covert operations, and Senator Symington both described the Hughes amendment as an important step in providing Congress with much-needed information about the activities of the intelligence agencies.[141] Thus the amendment might be seen not as congressional authorization for the CIA to conduct covert action but as a temporary measure placing limits on what the CIA would do anyway, while at the same time requiring reporting to Congress so that Congress as a whole, traditionally deprived of knowledge about covert action, could determine what action to take with respect to this activity.[142]

---

[136] Rogovin, HSIC, 12/9/75, p. 1737.

[137] "The Central Intelligence Agency: Oversight and Accountability," prepared by the Committee on Civil Rights and the Committee on International Human Relations, of the Association of the Bar of the City of New York (1975) p. 15.

[138] Cong. Rec. H11627, daily ed., 12/11/74. (remarks of Rep. Holtzman.)

[139] Cong. Rec., S18062, daily ed., 10/2/74. (remarks of Sen. Hughes.)

[140] Ibid.

[141] Ibid., p. S18065 (remarks of Sen. Baker and Sen. Symington).

[142] There is no evidence to support the view that Congress intended the amendment to serve as a post hoc ratification for all previous CIA activities not intended solely for intelligence gathering.

Proponents of this interpretation of the amendment can argue that a measure designed to gather information about an activity cannot be construed as congressional ratification of that activity. If it were, Congress would be powerless to seek regular reports about a controversial subject on which it had been ill-informed without such action being cited as congressional ratification for the subject of the reports.

The amendment did not directly address the question of congressional authorization for the CIA to conduct covert action. Its passage did not unambiguously demonstrate a congressional intent to authorize covert action. However, its passage supports the position that Congress has either provided the CIA with implied authority or ratified whatever authority the CIA possessed.

Congress clearly could have eliminated covert action. It chose, instead, to place certain limits on the CIA and to require reporting on covert actions to Congress. The reports to Congress should facilitate an informed legislative response to the issues raised by covert action. They also have the effect of preventing Congress from plausibly denying its own knowledge of covert action by the United States if questions of congressional authorization of covert action arise in the future.

Given the passage of the amendment and subsequent developments, particularly the hearings and reports of the House Select Committee on Intelligence, and the Senate Select Committee on Intelligence, there is little doubt that Congress is now on notice that the CIA claims to have the authority to conduct, and does engage in, covert action. Given that knowledge, congressional failure to prohibit covert action in the future can be interpreted as congressional authorization for it.

F. CONCLUSION

There is no explicit statutory authority for the CIA to conduct covert action. There is no substantial evidence that Congress intended by the passage of the National Security Act of 1947 to authorize covert action by the CIA or that Congress even anticipated that the CIA would engage in such activities. The legislative history of the CIA Act of 1949 similarly provides no indication of congressional intent to authorize covert action by the CIA.

The 1974 Amendment to the Foreign Assistance Act recognizes that the CIA does engage in activities other than those solely for the purpose of intelligence-gathering, i.e. covert action. Enacted following disclosures of CIA covert action in Chile, the amendment does provide support to the argument that Congress has authorized covert action by the Agency or has ratified the Agency's authority. (One of the purposes of the amendment, however, was to assure Congress the information about covert action necessary to decide what to do about it.)

Additional support for the argument that Congress has ratified the CIA's authority to conduct covert action would be provided by the continuing provision of funds to the CIA when it is clear that such funds will be used, in part, for covert action. Some support for the position may also be found in the continuing acquiescence of Congress in the executive branch's claim that court action has congressional authorization. While neither ratification by appropriation nor ratification by acquiescence are favored by the courts, they cannot be disregarded. In the past such claims were weak. A few individual members of Congress were kept informed about covert action but there were doubts about the knowledge of Congress as a whole. The claims are now more powerful because of the notoriety of the executive branch's claim of authorization by Congress and because Congress, in part due to the reports required since 1974 and House and Senate investigations, can no longer claim ignorance of covert action.

Given the present state of congressional knowledge any remaining ambiguity will be resolved—whether Congress acts directly or not.

Views of the inherent power of the President and the rightful role for Congress in the formulation, initiation, and review of U.S. actions abroad have changed since the establishment of the CIA and the enactment of the National Security Act in 1947. These changes are reflected in such legislation as the 1974 amendment to the Foreign Assistance Act. Whatever role evolves for the Congress in the future it must now take responsibility for the CIA's conduct of covert action, and for its results.

CASE STUDIES OF COVERT OPERATIONS

The most thorough study of U.S. covert operations to date concerns CIA activity in Chile from 1963 to 1973, concentrating on the time when Salvador Allende Gossens was president. (Allende was a Marxist, whose election to the presidency in 1970 was opposed by the U.S. government and by American corporations with business ties in Chile. Allende died during a coup d'etat in September 1973.) This documentation is due largely to the investigation of the Senate Select Committee on Intelligence and the interest of its chairman, Frank Church, in Latin American affairs.* A summary of the Church Committee findings is reprinted, setting forth the public policy issue posed by U.S. covert involvement. It is followed by portions of transcriptions from the testimony of former CIA head Richard Helms as to the CIA role in Chile. The Helms' testimony, taken on separate occasions, is contradictory and clearly shows the willingness of CIA officials to conceal covert operations, even before a congressional committee. The section on Chile concludes with a dialogue between Senator Church and Secretary of State Henry Kissinger in which the senator asserts both the moral and the strategic failure of the CIA's covert operation in Chile.

*Senator Frank Church, as chairman of the Foreign Relations Committee's Subcommittee on Multinational Corporations, examined the role of the ITT Corporation in Chile's national elections of 1970. He was also chairman of the Western Hemisphere Subcommittee through 1972.

Covert Action in Chile: 1963–1973 ([44G], pp. 1–2, 198–209)

Two case studies of U.S. involvement in foreign covert operations are presented in this chapter: Chile, from 1963 to 1973, and assassination plots against foreign leaders. These are two areas in which the Church Committee sought to obtain documentation in connection with its inquiry into the nature and consequences of U.S. covert intelligence operations. The documents illustrate the extent to which covert foreign intelligence operations were conducted with little or no knowledge of the president or the Congress. The findings are inconclusive on specific U.S. involvement in a number of activities and will undoubtedly provoke further inquiry. This particular investigation began late in the 94th Congress, when a joint Senate committee was created to look further into the assassination of President John F. Kennedy.* The Church inquiry established motives for possible Cuban involvement in President Kennedy's assassination, while exploring CIA associations with plots to assassinate Cuban Premier Fidel Castro. The material reprinted here represents only a portion of the literature generated on the CIA's activities in Chile and in assassination attempts. Reference to additional sources are cited throughout the reprinted text.

*Book V of the Final Report of the Church Committee stated the committee's findings regarding the intelligence community's performance in the Kennedy assassination investigation. It found reason for further inquiry and so recommended to successor committees ([45E], p. 7).

OVERVIEW

Covert United States involvement in Chile in the decade between 1963 and 1973 was extensive and continuous. The Central Intelligence Agency spent three million dollars in an effort to influence the outcome of the 1964 Chilean presidential elections. Eight million dollars was spent, covertly, in the three years between 1970 and the military coup in September 1973, with over three million dollars expended in fiscal year 1972 alone.[1]

It is not easy to draw a neat box around what was "covert action." The range of clandestine activities undertaken by the CIA includes covert action, clandestine intelligence collection, liaison with local police and intelligence services, and counterintelligence. The distinctions among the types of activities are mirrored in organizational arrangements, both at Headquarters and in the field. Yet it is not always so easy to distinguish the effects of various activities. If the CIA provides financial support to a political party, this is called "covert action"; if the Agency develops a paid "asset" in that party for the purpose of information gathering, the project is "clandestine intelligence collection."

The goal of covert action is political impact. At the same time secret relationships developed for the clandestine collection of intelligence may also have political effects, even though no attempt is made by American officials to manipulate the relationship for short-run political gain. For example, in Chile between 1970 and 1973, CIA and American military attache contacts with the Chilean military for the purpose of gathering intelligence enabled the United States to sustain communication with the group most likely to take power from President Salvador Allende.

What did covert CIA money buy in Chile? It financed activities covering a broad spectrum, from simple propaganda manipulation of the press to large-scale support for Chilean political parties, from public opinion polls to direct attempts to foment a military coup. The scope of "normal" activities of the CIA Station in Santiago included placement of Station-dictated material in the Chilean media through propaganda assets, direct support of publications, and efforts to oppose communist and left-wing influence in student, peasant and labor organizations.

In addition to these "routine" activities, the CIA Station in Santiago was several times called upon to undertake large, specific projects. When senior officials in Washington perceived special dangers, or opportunities, in Chile, special CIA projects were developed, often as part of a larger package of U.S. actions. For instance, the CIA spent over three million dollars in an election program in 1964.

Half a decade later, in 1970, the CIA engaged in another special effort, this time at the express request of President Nixon and under the injunction not to inform the Departments of State or Defense or the Ambassador of the project. Nor was the 40 Committee [2] ever informed. The CIA attempted, directly, to foment a military coup in Chile. It passed three weapons to a group of Chilean officers who plotted a coup. Beginning with the kidnaping of Chilean Army Commander-in-Chief René Schneider. However, those guns were returned.

---

[1] Moreover, the bare figures are more likely to understate than to exaggerate the extent of U.S. covert action. In the years before the 1973 coup, especially, CIA dollars could be channeled through the Chilean black market where the unofficial exchange rate into Chilean *escudos* often reached five times the official rate.

[2] The 40 Committee is a sub-Cabinet level body of the Executive Branch whose mandate is to review proposed major covert actions. The Committee has existed in similar form since the 1950's under a variety of names: 5412 Panel, Special Group (until 1964), 303 Committee (to 1969), and 40 Committee (since 1969). Currently chaired by the President's Assistant for National Security Affairs, the Committee includes the Undersecretary of State for Political Affairs, the Deputy Secretary of Defense, the Chairman of the Joint Chiefs of Staff, and the Director of Central Intelligence.

The group which staged the abortive kidnap of Schneider, which resulted in his death, apparently was not the same as the group which received CIA weapons.

N19

When the coup attempt failed and Allende was inaugurated President, the CIA was authorized by the 40 Committee to fund groups in opposition to Allende in Chile. The effort was massive. Eight million dollars was spent in the three years between the 1970 election and the military coup in September 1973. Money was furnished to media organizations, to opposition political parties and, in limited amounts, to private sector organizations.

Numerous allegations have been made about U.S. covert activities in Chile during 1970–73. Several of these are false; others are half-true. In most instances, the response to the allegation must be qualified:

Was the United States *directly* involved, covertly, in the 1973 coup in Chile? The Committee has found no evidence that it was. However, the United States sought in 1970 to foment a military coup in Chile; after 1970 it adopted a policy both overt and covert, of opposition to Allende; and it remained in intelligence contact with the Chilean military, including officers who were participating in coup plotting.

Did the U.S. provide covert support to striking truck-owners or other strikers during 1971–73? The 40 Committee did not approve any such support. However, the U.S. passed money to private sector groups which supported the strikers. And in at least one case, a small amount of CIA money was passed to the strikers by a private sector organization, contrary to CIA ground rules.

Did the U.S. provide covert support to right-wing terrorist organizations during 1970–73? The CIA gave support in 1970 to one group whose tactics became more violent over time. Through 1971 that group received small sums of American money through third parties for specific purposes. And it is possible that money was passed to these groups on the extreme right from CIA-supported opposition political parties.

The pattern of United States covert action in Chile is striking but not unique. It arose in the context not only of American foreign policy, but also of covert U.S. involvement in other countries within and outside Latin America. The scale of CIA involvement in Chile was unusual but by no means unprecedented. . . .

PRELIMINARY CONCLUSIONS

Underlying all discussion of American interference in the internal affairs of Chile is the basic question of why the United States initially mounted such an extensive covert action program in Chile—and why it continued, and even expanded, in the early 1970s.

Covert action has been a key element of U.S. foreign policy toward Chile. The link between covert action and foreign policy was obvious throughout the decade between 1964 and 1974. In 1964, the United States commitment to democratic reform via the Alliance for Progress and overt foreign aid was buttressed via covert support for the election of the candidate of the Christian Democratic party, a candidate and a party for which the Alliance seemed tailor made. During 1970 the U.S. Government tried, covertly, to prevent Allende from becoming President of Chile. When that failed, covert support to his opposition formed one of a triad of official actions: covert aid to opposition forces, "cool but correct" diplomatic posture, and economic pressure. From support of what the United States considered to be democratic and progressive forces in Chile we had moved finally to advocating and encouraging the overthrow of a democratically elected government.

A. COVERT ACTION AND U.S. FOREIGN POLICY

In 1964, the United States became massively involved in covert activity in Chile. This involvement was seen by U.S. policy-makers as consistent with overall American foreign policy and the goals of the

Alliance for Progress. The election of a moderate left candidate in Chile was a cornerstone of U.S. policy toward Latin America.

It is unclear from the record whether the 1964 election project was intended to be a one-time intervention in support of a good cause. It is clear that the scale of the involvement generated commitments and expectations on both sides. For the United States, it created assets and channels of funding which could be used again. For the Chilean groups receiving CIA funds, that funding became an expectation, counted upon. Thus, when opposition to Allende became the primary objective of covert action in 1970, the structure for covert action developed through covert assistance to political parties in 1964 was well established.

A fundamental question raised by the pattern of U.S. covert activities persists: *Did the threat to vital U.S. national security interests posed by the Presidency of Salvador Allende justify the several major covert attempts to prevent his accession to power?* Three American Presidents and their senior advisors evidently thought so.

One rationale for covert intervention in Chilean politics was spelled out by Henry Kissinger in his background briefing to the press on September 16, 1970, the day after Nixon's meeting with Helms. He argued that an Allende victory would be irreversible within Chile, might affect neighboring nations and would pose "massive problems" for the U.S. in Latin America:

> I have yet to meet somebody who firmly believes that if Allende wins, there is likely to be another free election in Chile. . . . Now it is fairly easy for one to predict that if Allende wins, there is a good chance that he will establish over a period of years some sort of communist government. In that case, we would have one not on an island off the coast (Cuba) which has not a traditional relationship and impact on Latin America, but in a major Latin American country you would have a communist government, joining, for example, Argentine . . . Peru . . . and Bolivia. . . . So I don't think we should delude ourselves on an Allende takeover and Chile would not present massive problems for us, and for democratic forces and for pro-U.S. forces in Latin America, and indeed to the whole Western Hemisphere.

Another rationale for U.S. involvement in the internal affairs of Chile was offered by a high-ranking official who testified before the Committee. He spoke of Chile's position in a worldwide strategic chess game in 1970. In this analogy, Portugal might be a bishop, Chile a couple of pawns, perhaps more. In the worldwide strategic chess game, once a position was lost, a series of consequences followed. U.S. enemies would proceed to exploit the new opportunity, and our ability to cope with the challenge would be limited by any American loss.

B. Executive Command and Control of Major Covert Action

In pursuing the Chilean chess game, particularly the efforts to prevent Allende's accession to power or his maintaining power once elected, Executive command and control of major covert action was tight and well directed. Procedures within the CIA for controlling the programs were well defined and the procedures made Station officials accountable to their supervisors in Washington. Unilateral actions on the part of the Station were virtually impossible.

But the central issue of command and control is *accountability*: procedures for insuring that covert actions are and remain accountable both to the senior political and foreign policy officials of the Executive Branch and to the Congress.

The record of covert activities in Chile suggests that, although established executive processes of authorization and control were generally adhered to, there were—and remain—genuine shortcomings to these processes:

Decisions about *which* covert action projects are submitted to the 40 Committee were and are made within the CIA on the basis of the Agency's determination of the political sensitivity of a project.

The form in which covert action projects were cleared with Ambassadors and other State Department officials varied. It depended—and still depends—on how interested Ambassadors are and how forthcoming their Station Chiefs are.

Once major projects are approved by the 40 Committee, they often continue without searching re-examination by the Committee. The Agency conducts annual reviews of on-going projects, but the 40 Committee does not undertake a review unless a project is recommended for renewal, or there is some important change in content or amount.

There is also the problem of controlling clandestine projects not labeled "covert action." Clandestine collection of human intelligence is *not* the subject of 40 Committee review. But those projects may be just as politically sensitive as a "covert action"; witness U.S. contacts with the Chilean military during 1970–73. Similarly, for security reasons, ambassadors generally know CIA assets only by general description, not by name. That practice may be acceptable, provided the description is detailed enough to inform the ambassador of the risk posed by the development of a particular assets and to allow the ambassador to decide whether or not that asset should be used.

There remains the question of the dangers which arise when the very mechanisms established by the Executive Branch for insuring internal accountability are circumvented or frustrated.

By Presidential instruction, Track II was to be operated without informing the U.S. Ambassador in Santiago, the State Department, or any 40 Committee member save Henry Kissinger. The President and his senior advisors thus denied themselves the Government's major sources of counsel about Chilean politics. And the Ambassador in Santiago was left in the position of having to deal with any adverse political spill-over from a project of which he was not informed.

The danger was greater still. Whatever the truth about communication between the CIA and the White House after October 15, 1970— an issue which is the subject of conflicting testimony—all participants agreed that Track II constituted a broad mandate to the CIA. The Agency was given to believe it had virtual *carte blanche* authority; moreover, it felt under extreme pressure to prevent Allende from coming to power, by military coup if necessary. It was given little guidance about what subsequent clearances it needed to obtain from the White House. Under these conditions, CIA consultation with the White House in advance of specific actions was less than meticulous.

C. The Role of Congress

In the hands of Congress rests the responsibility for insuring that the Executive Branch is held to full political accountability for covert activities. The record on Chile is mixed and muted by its incompleteness.

CIA records note a number of briefings of Congressional committees about covert action in Chile. Those records, however, do not reveal the timeliness or the level of detail of these briefings. Indeed, the record suggests that the briefings were often after the fact and incomplete. The situation improved after 1973, apparently as Congressional committees became more persistent in the exercise of their oversight function. Furthermore, Sec. 662 of the Foreign Assistance Act should make it impossible for major projects to be operated without the appropriate Congressional committees being informed.

The record leaves unanswered a number of questions. These pertain both to how forthcoming the Agency was and how interested and persistent the Congressional committees were. Were members of Congress, for instance, given the opportunity to object to specific projects before the projects were implemented? Did they want to? There is also an issue of jurisdiction. CIA and State Department officials have taken the position that they are authorized to reveal Agency operations only to the appropriate oversight committees.

D. Intelligence Judgments and Covert Operations

A review of the intelligence judgments on Chile offered by U.S. analysts during the critical period from 1970–1973 has *not* established whether these judgments were taken into account when U.S. policymakers formulated and approved U.S. covert operations. This examination of the relevant intelligence estimates and memoranda has established that the judgments of the analysts suggested caution and restraint while the political imperatives demanded action.

Even within the Central Intelligence Agency, processes for bringing considered judgments of intelligence analysts to bear on proposed covert actions were haphazard—and generally ineffective. This situation has improved; covert action proposals now regularly come before the Deputy Director for Intelligence and the appropriate National Intelligence Officer; but the operators still are separated from the intelligence analysts, those whose exclusive business it is to understand and predict foreign politics. For instance, the analysts who drafted the government's most prestigious intelligence analyses—NIEs—may not even have known of U.S. covert actions in Chile.

The Chilean experience does suggest that the Committee give serious consideration to the possibility that lodging the responsibility for national estimates *and* conduct of operational activities with the same person—the Director of Central Intelligence—creates an inherent conflict of interest and judgment.

E. Effects of Major Covert Action Programs

Covert Action programs as costly and as complex as several mounted by the United States in Chile are unlikely to remain covert. In Chile in 1964, there was simply too much unexplained money, too many leaflets, too many broadcasts. That the United States was involved in the election has been taken for granted in Latin America for many years.

The involvement in 1964 created a presumption in Chile and elsewhere in Latin America that the United States Government would again be involved in 1970. This made secrecy still harder to maitain, even though the CIA involvement was much smaller in 1970 than it had been in 1964.

When covert actions in Chile became public knowledge, the costs were obvious. The United States was seen, by its covert actions, to have contradicted not only its official declarations but its treaty commitments and principles of long standing. At the same time it was proclaiming a "low profile" in Latin American relations, the U.S. Government was seeking to foment a coup in Chile.

The costs of major covert ventures which are "blown" are clear enough. But there may be costs to pay even if the operations could remain secret for long periods of time. Some of these costs may accrue even within the calculus of covert operations: successes may turn to failures. Several officials from whom the Committee took testimony suggested that the poor showing of the Chilean Christian

Democrats in 1970 was, in some part, attributable to previous American covert support. Of course there were many causes of that poor showing, but in 1964 the PDC had been spared the need of developing some of its own grass roots organization. The CIA did much of that for it. In 1970, with less CIA activity on behalf of the Christian Democratic Party, the PDC faltered.

Of course, the more important costs, even of covert actions which remain secret, are those to American ideals of relations among nations and of constitutional government. In the case of Chile, some of those costs were far from abstract: witness the involvement of United States military officers in the Track II attempt to overthrow a constitutionally-elected civilian government.

There are also long-term effects of covert actions. Many of those may be adverse. They touch American as well as foreign institutions.

The Chilean institutions that the United States most favored may have been discredited within their own societies by the fact of their covert support. In Latin America particularly, even the suspicion of CIA support may be the kiss of death. It would be the final irony of a decade of covert action in Chile if that action destroyed the credibility of the Chilean Christian Democrats.

The effects on American institutions are less obvious but no less important. U.S. private and governmental institutions with overt, legitimate purposes of their own may have been discredited by the pervasiveness of covert action. Even if particular institutions were not involved in covert action, they may have been corrupted in the perception of Latin Americans because of the pervasiveness of clandestine U.S. activity.

In the end, the whole of U.S. policy making may be affected. The availability of an "extra" means may alter officials' assessment of the costs and rationales of overt policies. It may postpone the day when outmoded policies are abandoned and new ones adopted. Arguably, the 1964 election project was part of a "progressive" approach to Chile. The project was justified, if perhaps not actually sustained, by the desire to elect democratic reformers. By 1970, covert action had become completely defensive in character: to prevent the election of Allende. The United States professed a "low profile" but at the same time acted covertly to ensure that the Chilean elections came out right, "low profile" notwithstanding.

A special case for concern is the relationship between intelligence agencies and multinational corporations.

In 1970, U.S. Government policy prohibited covert CIA support to a single party or candidate. At the same time, the CIA provided advice to an American-based multinational corporation on how to furnish just such direct support. That raised all of the dangers of exposure, and eliminated many of the safeguards and controls normally present in exclusively CIA covert operations. There was the appearance of an improperly close relationship between the CIA and multinational companies when former Director John McCone used contacts and information gained while at the CIA to advise a corporation on whose Board of Directors he sat. This appearance was heightened because the contacts between the Agency and the corporation in 1970 extended to discussing and even planning corporate intervention in the Chilean electoral process.

The problem of cooperation is exacerbated when a cooperating company—such as ITT—is called to give testimony before an appropriate Congressional Committee. The Agency may then be confronted with the question of whether to come forward to set the record straight when it believes that testimony given on behalf of a cooperating company is untrue. The situation is difficult, for in coming forward the

Agency may reveal sensitive sources and methods by which it learned the facts or may make public the existence of ongoing covert operations.

This report does not attempt to offer a final judgment on the political propriety, the morality, or even the effectiveness of American covert activity in Chile. Did the threat posed by an Allende presidency justify covert American involvement in Chile? Did it justify the specific and unusual attempt to foment a military coup to deny Allende the presidency? In 1970, the U.S. sought to foster a military coup in Chile to prevent Allende's accession to power; yet after 1970 the government—according to the testimony of its officials—did not engage in coup plotting. Was 1970 a mistake, an aberration? Or was the threat posed to the national security interests of the United States so grave that the government was remiss in not seeking his downfall directly during 1970-73? What responsibility does the United States bear for the cruelty and political suppression that have become the hallmark of the present regime in Chile?

On these questions Committee members may differ. So may American citizens. Yet the Committee's mandate is less to judge the past than to recommend for the future. Moving from past cases to future guidelines, what is important to note is that covert action has been perceived as a middle ground between diplomatic representation and the overt use of military force. In the case of Chile, that middle ground may have been far too broad. Given the costs of covert action, it should be resorted to only to counter severe threats to the national security of the United States. It is far from clear that that was the case in Chile.

CHRONOLOGY: CHILE 1962–1975

1962

Special Group approves $50,000 to strengthen Christian Democratic Party (PDC); subsequently approves an additional $180,000 to strengthen PDC and its leader, Eduardo Frei.

1963

Special Group approves $20,000 for a leader of the Radical Party (PR); later approves an additional $30,000 to support PR candidates in April municipal elections.

April 8   Municipal election results show PDC has replaced PR as Chile's largest party.

1964

April   *Special Group approves $3,000,000 to ensure election of PDC candidate Eduardo Frei.*

May   *Special Group approves $160,000 to support PDC slum dwellers and peasant organizations.*

September 4   Eduardo Frei elected President with 55.7 percent of the vote.

N20   October 2   *Ralph A. Dungan appointed U.S. Ambassador to Chile.*

1965

303 Committee approves $175,000 to assist selected candidates in Congressional elections.

March 7   PDC wins absolute majority in Chamber of Deputies; becomes largest party in Senate.

November 15   Salvador Allende, in an interview reported in the *New York Times*, suggests the U.S. was among certain "outside forces" that had caused his defeat in the 1964 presidential election.

1967

N21   June 16   *Edward M. Korry replaces Ralph A. Dungan as U.S. Ambassador to Chile.*

303 Committee approves $30,000 to strengthen a faction of the Radical Party.

1968

July 12

303 Committee approves $350,000 to assist selected candidates in March 1969 congressional elections.

1969

March 1

Congressional elections reflect an increase in support for the National Party and a resulting loss in Christian Democratic strength.

April 15

At a meeting of the 303 Committee the question is raised as to whether anything should be done with regard to the September 1970 Presidential election in Chile. The CIA representative pointed out that an election operation would not be effective unless an early enough start was made.

October 21

Tacna and Yungay army regiments revolt, ostensibly for the purposes of dramatizing the military's demand for higher pay. The revolt, engineered by General Roberto Viaux, is widely interpreted as an abortive coup.

1970

March 25

40 Committee approves $125,000 for a "spoiling operation" against Allende's Popular Unity coalition (UP).

June

The possibility of an Allende victory in Chile is raised at an ITT Board of Directors meeting. John McCone, former CIA Director and, at the time, a consultant to the Agency and a Director of ITT, subsequently holds a number of conversations regarding Chile with Richard Helms, the current CIA Director.

June 27

40 Committee approves $300,000 for additional anti-Allende propaganda operations.

July 16

John McCone arranges for William Broe (CIA) to talk with Harold Geneen (ITT). Broe tells Geneen that CIA cannot disburse ITT funds but promises to advise ITT on how to channel its own funds. ITT later passes $350,000 to the Alessandri campaign through an intermediary.

August 18

National Security Study Memorandum (NSSM) 97 is reviewed by the Interdepartmental Group; the Group considers options ranging from efforts to forge amicable relations with Allende to opposition to him.

September 4

Salvador Allende wins 36.3 percent of the vote in the Presidential election. Final outcome is dependent on October 24 vote in Congress between Allende and the runner-up, Jorge Alessandri, who received 35.3 percent of the vote. Allende's margin of victory was 39,000 votes out of a total of 3,000,000 votes cast in the election.

September 8, 14

40 Committee discusses Chilean situation. The Committee approves $250,000 for the use of Ambassador Korry to influence the October 24 Congressional vote.

September 9

Harold Geneen, ITT's Chief Executive Officer, tells John McCone at an ITT Board of Directors meeting in New York that he is prepared to put up as much as $1 million for the purpose of assisting any government plan designed to form a coalition in the Chilean Congress to stop Allende. McCone agrees to communicate this proposal to high Washington officials and meets several days later with Henry Kissinger and Richard Helms. McCone does not receive a response from either man.

September 15

President Nixon instructs CIA Director Helms to prevent Allende's accession to office. The CIA is to play a direct role in organizing a military coup d'etat. This involvement comes to be known as Track II.

September 16

At an off-the-record White House press briefing, Henry Kissinger warns that the election of Allende would be irreversible, might affect neighboring nations, and would pose "massive problems" for the U.S. and Latin America.

1970—Continued

September 29	*A CIA official, at the instruction of Richard Helms, meets with a representative of ITT. The CIA officer proposes a plan to accelerate economic disorder in Chile. ITT rejects the proposal.*
October	*CIA contacts Chilean military conspirators; following a White House meeting, CIA attempts to defuse plot by retired General Viaux, but still to generate maximum pressure to overthrow Allende by coup; CIA provides tear gas grenades and three submachine guns to conspirators.*
October 14	*40 Committee approves $60,000 for Ambassador Korry's proposal to purchase a radio station. The money is never spent.*
October 22	After two unsuccessful abduction attempts on October 19 and 20, a third attempt to kidnap Chilean Army General René Schneider results in his being fatally shot.
October 24	The Chilean Congress votes 153 to 35 in favor of Allende over Alessandri.
November 3	Allende is formally inaugurated President of Chile.
November 13	*40 Committee approves $25,000 for support of Christian Democratic candidates.*
November 19	*40 Committee approves $725,000 for a covert action program in Chile. Approval is later superseded by January 28, 1971, authorization.*
December 21	President Allende proposes a constitutional amendment establishing state control of the large mines and authorizing expropriation of all foreign firms working them.

1971

January 28	*40 Committee approves $1,240,000 for the purchase of radio stations and newspapers and to support municipal candidates and other political activities of anti-Allende parties.*
February 25	*In his annual* State of the World *message, President Nixon states, "We are prepared to have the kind of relationship with the Chilean government that it is prepared to have with us."*
March 22	*40 Committee approves $185,000 additional support for the Christian Democratic Party (PDC).*
April 4	Allende's Popular Unity (UP) coalition garners 49.7 percent of the vote in 280 municipal elections.
May 10	*40 Committee approves $77,000 for purchase of a press for the Christian Democratic Party newspaper. The press is not obtained and the funds are used to support the paper.*
May 20	*40 Committee approves $100,000 for emergency aid to the Christian Democratic Party to meet short-term debts.*
May 26	*40 Committee approves $150,000 for additional aid to Christian Democratic Party to meet debts.*
July 6	*40 Committee approves $150,000 for support of opposition candidates in a Chilean by-election.*
July 11	In a joint session of the Chilean Congress, a constitutional amendment is unanimously approved permitting the nationalization of the copper industry. The amendment provides for compensation to copper companies within 30 years at not less than 3 percent interest.
August 11	*The Export-Import Bank denies a Chilean request for $21 million in loans and loan guarantees needed to purchase three jets for the national LAN-Chile airline.*
September 9	*40 Committee approves $700,000 for support to the major Santiago newspaper, El Mercurio.*
September 28	President Allende announces that "excess profits" will be deducted from compensation to be paid to nationalized copper companies.

1971—Continued

| September 29 | The Chilean government assumes operation of the Chilean telephone company (CHITELCO). ITT had owned 70 percent interest in the company since 1930. |

September 29 — *Nathaniel Davis replaces Edward Korry as U.S. Ambassador to Chile.*

October — *ITT submits to White House an 18-point plan designed to assure that Allende "does not get through the crucial next six months." The ITT proposal is rejected.*

November 5 — *40 Committee approves $815,000 support to opposition parties and to induce a split in the Popular Unity coalition.*

December 1 — The Christian Democratic and National Parties organize the "March of the Empty Pots" by women to protest food shortages.

December 15 — *40 Committee approves $160,000 to support two opposition candidates in January 1972 by-elections.*

1972

January 19 — *President Nixon issues a statement to clarify U.S. policy toward foreign expropriation of American interests. The President states that the United States expects compensation to be "prompt, adequate, and effective." The President warns that should compensation not be reasonable, new bilateral economic aid to the expropriating country might be terminated and the U.S. would withhold its support from loans under consideration in multilateral development banks.*

April 11 — *40 Committee approves $965,000 for additional support to El Mercurio.*

April 24 — *40 Committee approves $50,000 for an effort to splinter the Popular Unity coalition.*

May 12 — President Allende submits a constitutional amendment to the Chilean Congress for the expropriation of ITT's holdings in the Chilean telephone company.

June 16 — *40 Committee approves $46,500 to support a candidate in a Chilean by-election.*

August 21 — Allende declares a state of emergency in Santiago province after violence grows out of a one-day strike by most of the capital's shopkeepers.

September 21 — *40 Committee approves $24,000 to support an anti-Allende businessmen's organization.*

October 10 — The Confederation of Truck Owners calls a nationwide strike.

October 26 — *40 Committee approves $1,427,666 to support opposition political parties and private sector organizations in anticipation of March 1973 Congressional elections.*

December 4 — Speaking before the General Assembly of the United Nations, President Allende charges that Chile has been the "victim of serious aggression" and adds, "we have felt the effects of a large-scale external pressure against us."

1973

February 12 — *40 Committee approves $200,000 to support opposition political parties in the Congressional elections.*

March 4 — In the Congressional elections, Allende's Popular Unity coalition wins 43.4 percent of the vote.

March 22 — Talks between the U.S. and Chile on political and financial problems end in an impasse.

June 5 — Chile suspends its foreign shipments of copper as miners' strikes continue.

June 20 — Thousands of physicians, teachers, and students go on strike to protest Allende's handling of the 63-day copper workers' strike.

1973—Continued

June 21	Gunfire, bombings, and fighting erupt as government opponents and supporters carry out a massive strike.
	The opposition newspaper, *El Mercurio*, is closed by court order for six days following a government charge that it had incited subversion. The following day an appeals court invalidates the closure order.
June 29	Rebel forces seize control of the downtown area of Santiago and attack the Defense Ministry and the Presidential Palace before troops loyal to the government surround them and force them to surrender. This is the first military attempt to overthrow an elected Chilean government in 42 years.
July 26	Truck owners throughout Chile go on strike.
August 2	The owners of more than 110,000 buses and taxis go on strike.
August 20	*40 Committee approves $1 million to support opposition political parties and private sector organizations. This money is not spent.*
August 23	General Carlos Prats Gonzalez resigns as Allende's Defense Minister and Army Commander. General Pinochet Ugarte is named Army Commander on August 24. Prats' resignation is interpreted as a severe blow to Allende.
August 27	Chile's shop owners call another anti-government strike.
September 4	An estimated 100,000 supporters of Allende's government march in the streets of Santiago to celebrate the third anniversary of his election.
	The Confederation of Professional Employees begins an indefinite work stoppage.
September 11	The Chilean military overthrows the government of Salvador Allende. Allende dies during the takeover, reportedly by suicide.
September 13	The new military government names Army Commander Pinochet President and dissolves Congress.
September-October	The Junta declares all Marxist political parties illegal and places all other parties in indefinite recess. Press censorship is established, as are detention facilities for opponents of the new regime. Thousands of casualties are reported, including summary executions.
October 15	*40 Committee approves $34,000 for an anti-Allende radio station and travel costs of pro-Junta spokesmen.*

1974

June 24	*40 Committee approves $50,000 for political commitments made to the Christian Democratic Party before the coup.*
September 16	*President Ford acknowledges covert operations in Chile.*
October 25	The Inter-American Commission on Human Rights of the O.A.S. reports "grievous violations of human rights" in Chile.
December 30	*U.S. military aid is cut off.*

1975

June 20	Pinochet declares there "will be no elections in Chile during my lifetime nor in the lifetime of my successor."
July 4	Chile refuses to allow the U.N. Commission on Human Rights to enter the country.
October 7	The U.N. Commission on Human Rights reports "with profound disgust" the use of torture as a matter of policy and other serious violations of human rights in Chile.

Portions of the above chronology of events in Chile were extracted from chronologies prepared by the Congressional Research Service ("Chile, 1960–70: A Chronology"; "Chile Since the Election of Salvador Allende: A Chronology"; "Developments in Chile, March 1973 to the Overthrow of the Allende Government") and from material contained in the June 21, 1973, report of the Senate Foreign Relations Subcommittee on Multinational Corporations entitled "ITT and Chile."

EXPENDITURES IN CHILE, 1963–1973

The table of expenditures is from the exhibits section of the Church Committee transcript of hearings on covert action, held December 4 and 5, 1975. It was prepared as a supplement to testimony by William Bader, professional staff member of the Senate Select Committee. Bader's testimony elaborates on the covert action techniques employed and expenditures of CIA funds ([44G], pp. 7–10).

TECHNIQUES OF COVERT ACTION
Expenditures in Chile, 1963–1973 (to nearest $100,000)

Techniques

Propaganda for Elections and Other Support for Political Parties	$8,000,000
Producing and Disseminating Propaganda and Supporting Mass Media	$4,300,000
Influencing Chilean Institutions: (labor, students, peasants, women) and Supporting Private Sector Organizations	$ 900,000
Promoting Military Coup d'Etat	Less than $ 200,000

FEBRUARY 1973 TESTIMONY OF RICHARD HELMS ON OVERTHROW OF CHILEAN GOVERNMENT ([17], pp. 47–48)

Richard Helms was the director of Central Intelligence from June 1966 to February 1973. In 1973, he was appointed by President Richard M. Nixon to be ambassador to Iran, and on February 7 of that year, appeared before the Senate Foreign Relations Committee to testify on his fitness for confirmation by the Senate. At one point in the testimony, Senator Stuart Symington asked Helms specifically about CIA involvement in the overthrow of the government of Chile and received from Helms a categorical denial of involvement. Two years later, on January 22, 1975, Helms was asked to reappear before the committee. Involvement by the CIA in the Chilean coup had been uncovered by the Church Committee staff and the news media. Helms was queried further and eventually admitted CIA complicity in some of the Chilean activities resulting in the overthrow of the Allende government. While CIA officials may have previously lied or misled congressional committees to protect the cover of its clandestine projects, seldom is CIA documentation so thorough. Excerpts from the two Helms' testimonies are reprinted here.

OVERTHROW OF CHILEAN GOVERNMENT

Senator SYMINGTON. Did you try in the Central Intelligence Agency to overthrow the Government of Chile?

Mr. HELMS. No, sir.

Senator SYMINGTON. Did you have any money passed to the opponents of Allende?

Mr. HELMS. No, sir.

Senator SYMINGTON. So the stories you were involved in that war are wrong?

Mr. HELMS. Yes, sir. I said to Senator Fulbright many months ago that if the Agency had really gotten in behind the other candidates and spent a lot of money and so forth the election might have come out differently.

REASON FOR TALK ABOUT ITT AND CIA

Senator SYMINGTON. Why is there all this talk about the ITT and the CIA working together down there against a duly elected government?

Mr. HELMS. There were a lot of conversations between members of the Agency and members of ITT about political conditions in Chile, about the possibility of a Communist-Socialist government coming into power. As you well know, sir, the American companies have access to us, as they do to other people in the U.S. Government, and ITT was talking to a lot of people in the U.S. Government in those days and they didn't like the trends that were going on down there and were consulting with a host of people, including the Agency—a lot of this came out in the Anderson papers—but there was no exchange of money between us. We didn't collaborate with ITT except to exchange this information back and forth about the course of events.

There was, as I recall it, one occasion on which ITT asked one of our officers what they might do down there, what techniques they might use to sort of head off these eventualities. It was a conversation about this. To the best of my knowledge, the suggestions were never carried out. Nobody did anything about it. It was simply a conversation.

Senator SYMINGTON. Thank you.

JANUARY 1975 TESTIMONY OF RICHARD HELMS
([18], pp. 1–14)

The Senate Committee on Foreign Relations resumed questioning of Richard Helms on January 22, 1975 on the subject of Chile, focusing on Helms' statements regarding the CIA's funding of Salvador Allende Gossens' opposition. Allende was a Marxist who was elected president of Chile in 1970 and whose election was opposed by the U.S. government and by American corporations with ties in Chile.

The committee met, pursuant to notice, at 10:30 a.m., in room S–116, the Capitol Building, Senator John Sparkman [the chairman] presiding.

Present: Senators Sparkman, Church, Symington, Pell, McGee, McGovern, Humphrey, Case, Scott, and Biden.

Also present: Mr. Holt of the committee staff.

The CHAIRMAN. Mr. Ambassador, if you will take your seat we will get started.

As I understand it, it has been agreed that we will proceed in executive session.

Mr. Ambassador, we are glad to have you with us. Do you have a statement or do you want to make a statement?

Mr. HELMS. No, sir. I was invited to come before this committee and I am here and delighted to answer any questions to the best of my ability.

The CHAIRMAN. All right.

We do have a copy of your statement that was made before the Armed Services Committee. Each member has that before him.

We also have a statement here that Mr. Colby made before the Appropriations Committee.

MR. HELMS' TENURE AS HEAD OF CIA

How long were you head of the CIA?

Mr. HELMS. Six and a half years, sir, approximately.

The CHAIRMAN. That is a pretty long time.

Mr. HELMS. It looks as though it is turning out to be almost too long.

The CHAIRMAN. Were you there when the building was put up out there?

Mr. HELMS. Yes, sir. I joined the Central Intelligence Agency in 1947 when it was established by Statute.

The CHAIRMAN. As a part of the National Security Act?

Mr. HELMS. Yes, sir; that is right.

The CHAIRMAN. My former colleague, Senator Hill, was on the Armed Services Committee. He was very much interested and took a leading part in the development of the National Security Act at the time.

COMMITTEE'S CONCERN

As I conceive it, the Foreign Relations Committee is directly concerned with foreign aspects of the CIA. For my part I do not think the committee should be especially concerned, except individually, of course, as citizens of the country, with domestic operations.

The Armed Services Committee was given, I believe, oversight under the Security Act over the CIA. Is that not right?

Mr. HELMS. Yes, sir.

The CHAIRMAN. And they have exercised that oversight.

There is a resolution that is to be voted on, I believe, Monday to set up a select committee to go into the CIA matters. Of course, they would cover everything, and I am quite certain that some such resolution will be adopted.

COMMITTEE ATTENTION TO CIA OPERATIONS RESULTING FROM CHILEAN SITUATION

Our attention was brought to CIA operations as a result of our checking into the situation in Chile several years ago.

Were you head of CIA at that time?

Mr. HELMS. Yes, sir.

The CHAIRMAN. Acutally, Senator Church is the one who went into that more fully than anybody else. He was studying the ITT operation in Chile at that time and that is when we became involved with all of this.

At the time that we held the hearings on the ITT operations in Chile, and the CIA came up, we did not spend a great deal of time on the CIA side of the picture. We did say at that time, however, that we would at a future time hold hearings on the CIA. Actually, that accounts for the present session.

We did not anticipate at that time that there was going to be all of this hullaballoo that has developed over the last few months with reference to CIA.

I mentioned Chile as being the thing that really pinpointed our attention.

Since that time I have heard that there have been somewhat similar instances in other countries. I have nothing definite on them. I have heard the names of some of the countries, but I have no information with regard to that.

HOW CIA OPERATED IN ITS FOREIGN ACTIVITIES

Would you explain to us just how the CIA operated in its foreign activities?

Ambassador HELMS. Well, Mr. Chairman, the Agency as you know has been put under the National Security Council. In other words, it reports to the National Security Council which is effectively the President. The National Security Council in turn, in addition to what is stated in the National Security Act of 1974, has given the Agency two additional charters. One makes the Agency responsible for conducting intelligence collection and counterintelligence collection overseas, the other is a charter which gives the Agency responsibility for various types of what is referred to technically as covert actions, covert operations overseas. And encompassed in covert operations are covert political activities, black propaganda, military activities and paramilitary activities and a variety of things of this kind.

I would like to for a moment digress to say that I understand that this committee now under the new amendment to the Foreign Assistance Act will be responsible for monitoring various covert actions of the Agency and it might be helpful in that connection if the present Director were to show you the actual piece of paper, the National Security Council directive to which I refer, which is a top secret document, but which is the document and the charge under which these activities are carried out, because I do think that the authority for these things ought to be made clear, that this isn't something that certainly when I was Director of the Agency that we just did on our own, we had a clearance mechanism, we had an approval mechanism when we were asked to perform one of these actions or originated the idea ourselves, there was a National Security Council Committee called the 40 Committee to which we reported and which in turn either approved or disapproved whatever the proposal was. So that these actions throughout recent years have to the best of my knowledge been approved by other authorities in the U.S. Government, the White House, State Department, Defense Department and so forth.

Is that responsive to your question, sir?

The CHAIRMAN. Yes.

SEPTEMBER 4, 1970, CHILEAN RESIDENTIAL ELECTION

I have been reading the part of our transcript of your confirmation hearing which refers to the Chilean situation. You said that no money was used under your direction to influence that election.

Ambassador HELMS. Mr. Chairman, I don't recollect exactly what the language of Senator Symington's question was. My recollection of what he asked me at that time was whether we had given money to the political opponents of President Allende and I believe that I replied that we had not.

The CHAIRMAN. That is right.

Ambassador HELMS. I want to explain because there seems to have been some question about this response.

I thought at the time that Senator Symington was asking me a question to get a certain kind of information and that was this. That I had assumed that Senator Symington knew that in 1964, at the request of the White House, the CIA had given money to a political candidate [deleted] in Chile, in that election, that was [deleted] and we had given a considerable sum of money, I mean at least $2 or $3 million, as best I recall it. I am not sure whether it is that figure or slightly larger. Please don't hold me to that. But at least a significant sum of money was given to him in an effort to help him win the election against two other opponents who at that time were [deleted] and a third man, my mind is a little rusty on, [deleted] or something in 1964.

Mr. HOLT. In 1964 [deleted].

Ambassador HELMS. Does that conform with your recollection?

Mr. HOLT. Yes.

The CHAIRMAN. Here you use the name of Alesandri and another fellow named Tomic.

Senator CASE. That was in 1970.

Ambassador HELMS. What are you reading from?

The CHAIRMAN. I am reading from a committee memorandum which covers the questions presented to you when you were up for confirmation.

Ambassador HELMS. Well; sir, I just read the record yesterday when I was up for confirmation and I don't recall anyone mentioning Mr. Alessandri.

I have a printed record here of what I understand were my confirmation hearings.

Am I wrong about this?

The CHAIRMAN. No; the one about Alessandri, I think, came up in a hearing before Senator Church's multinational subcommittee.

Ambassador HELMS. I see. I have not seen that transcript. Would you be so kind as to read the portions of it because——

The CHAIRMAN. At your confirmation hearing, Senator Symington asked:

Did you try in the Central Intelligence Agency to overthrow the Government of Chile?

Your answer was "No, sir."

Senator Symington asked:

Did you have any money passed to the opponents of Allende?

You said "No, sir."

So that the stories that you were involved in that are wrong entirely.

That is Senator Symington.

You answered:

Yes, sir. I said to Senator Fulbright many months ago, that if the agency had really gotten in behind the other candidates and spent a lot of money and so forth, the election might have come out differently.

That is the extent of what we have in the questioning of Senator Symington.

1970 CHILEAN PRESIDENTIAL ELECTION

In order that we get the whole thing tied together, in 1973 before Senator Church's Multinational Corporations Subcommittee, Senator Church said:

Now, following the election, and up to the time that the Congress of Chile cast its vote installing Allende as the new President, did the CIA attempt in any way to influence that vote?

You asked, "Which vote?"

"Senator CHURCH. 'The vote of the Congress.' "

You answered, "No sir."

A few pages later, in the same transcript, the same subject recurs. Senator Church asked you:

Did the 40 Committee approve the commitment of funds for use in Chile for the purpose of influencing the outcome of the Chilean Presidential election of September 4, 1970?

You say, "Which funds are these?"

"Senator CHURCH. 'Any funds.' "

You say:

Well, the 40 Committee I know approved some funds for activities in Chile but that they were directed against the influence of the election, put that way, is not my recollection of it.

"Senator CHURCH. 'What were the funds used for?' "

You say, "I frankly don't remember very precisely any more."

Then later you said:

. . . there seems to be a feeling that the Agency put money into the political process, in other words, to back other, the other candidates in this election to defeat Allende, and this is about the only way I know that you influence elections. Maybe there are other ways, but I simply wanted to clear up the point that we did not back Alessandri, I forget the name of the other fellow, Tomic. We put no money in their campaign whatever and this has been haunting me that there seems to be a sensation that in saying we had not done this, that I have not been leveling. I mean we did not do it.

That is all I care to read. I thought I would do that in order that we could get started.

May I call on Senator Symington.

Senator SYMINGTON. Thank you, Mr. Chairman. I have no questions at this time.

The CHAIRMAN. Then I will swing to Senator Case.

IMPRESSION WE WERE NOT DOING ANYTHING TO INFLUENCE CHILEAN POLITICS

Senator CASE. Mr. Chairman, Mr. Ambassador, briefly, to follow up your lead on Chile. I must confess I am not now trying to put your statements against other people's statements made at different times, but the general impression we got both in your confirmation hearing and in the Multinational Subcommittee hearing, and not only from you but from Meyer, was that we were not doing anything to influence Chilean politics. This was obviously not true. Maybe we all should have known this as a matter of general knowledge.

N22

How come we keep getting this impression in the public record? I wish you would try and help.

MR. HELM'S FEBRUARY 1, 1973, TESTIMONY CONCERNING CHILE

Mr. HELMS. I would like to go back just a moment, because Senator Church has come back, to make it a little bit easier.

May I deal first with the testimony when I was up for confirmation, which was on February 7, I believe, in this printed record?

When Senator Symington asked me that question, or those two questions, I really thought that he and I were tracking, that he recalled that in 1964, at the request of the White House, the CIA had backed [deleted] in the election of 1964. There were two other candidates I believe at that time.

One of them was [deleted] and the other—Mr. Holt has helped me in my memory—a gentleman named [deleted].

When Senator Symington asked me this question, I thought that he was anxious to find out whether or not we had put money into Alessandri to make campaigns against Allende; in other words, the political opponents of President Allende, and we had not.

He also asked me a question there, and I thought that when I answered this, perhaps I should have answered it in a much more extensive way. May I say, right here and now, that I think I made one mistake in that testimony, maybe it is a serious mistake, but I should have probably asked either to go off the record or to have asked to discuss this matter in some other forum, because you will recall at that time Allende's government was in power in Chile and we did not need any more diplomatic incidents or any more difficulties than the United States and Chile already were having by 1973 when I testified.

As far as the earlier statement is concerned, whether the agency tried to overthrow the Government of Chile, I answered "No." I believe that is true. If it has been alleged differently by someone else, I would appreciate having it.

I know that the Nixon administration wanted it overthrown but there was no way to do it that anybody knew of and any probes that were made in Chile to ascertain whether there was any force there that was likely to bring this about produced no evidence that there was any such force.

The Agency, therefore, never tried. I believe that is true.

By the testimony I wish you gentlemen would help me because I have a sensation here sometimes I am walking onto a bog, that maybe somebody has come up and said something else, which makes it seem as through I am not being forthright.

Now the money, as I understand it, that went into the Chile operation went into civic action groups, supporting newspapers, radios, and so forth, in order to keep alive the [deleted] and the sort of Nationalist side of the Chilean spectrum, social spectrum. I did not realize that went into political parties, I did not think that it had, at least it was my understanding at the time. If somebody has said something else, I am prepared to stand corrected.

I want to be very responsive to Senator Case because I do not want there to be any question here any longer.

IMPORTANCE OF COMMITTEE'S GOOD OPINION

May I just disgress to say that the good opinion of this committee is very important to me, it always had been when I was Director and it is important to me this day.

I have been in the Government for 32 years. When you have been in Government that long, you get a pension when you are finished, and the only thing you have left is your reputation. If I do not have my reputation left when I leave the Government, I have lost 32 years effectively and I really am not a bit interested in seeing that happen.

So if the committee or Senator Case feels that you were deliberately misled here, I can only plead that I had no intention of lying, I had no intention of deliberately misleading this committee, and it is altogether possible that, as I was answering these questions, I was assuming a fund of knowledge on the part of you gentlemen which possibly you did not have.

Senator CASE. You must never assume that.

Really, that sounds a little bit like saying that we never asked the right questions.

Mr. HELMS. I am up against that problem.

Senator CASE. You are.

Mr. HELMS. It seems to me something Senator Fulbright once said to me, and I can only say that when it comes to here today, I will answer any possible questions in the Department that you want. If I have been guilty in the past of not having gone the whole way, all right, but at least——

Senator CASE. Since Chile is Senator Church's particular concern, I would like, Mr. Chairman, to yield to him.

The CHAIRMAN. Yes.

COMMITTEE'S PURPOSE

Let me interject right here, Mr. Helms, that I do not want you to feel that this committee is trying to get you or trying to embarrass you or anything like that. I want to say that I have known you throughout the years. I knew you when you were head of CIA; I never had any dealings with you, I knew you. I respected your leadership, and I always felt that you tried to do a good job.

You have read all of these statements in the press?

Mr. HELMS. Yes, sir.

The CHAIRMAN. I felt, and I am sure the members of this committee felt, that so far as covert actions in foreign countries were concerned, we more or less had an obligation to check into it. That is all we are trying to do. It is not to prosecute or persecute you.

Of course, you have had a long distinguished service in the Government and I think I can assure you that everyone on this committee wants to see you reach that time of retirement with your honor, and your reputation, intact and your head high.

Mr. HELMS. Thank you, sir.

Senator SYMINGTON. As long as my name has been mentioned in the testimony, may I make a short statement?

The CHAIRMAN. Yes, sir.

SUBJECT OF SENATOR SYMINGTON'S FEBRUARY 7, 1973, QUESTIONING

Senator SYMINGTON. When I was asking the question, I was not thinking about 1964 or any previous situation. That does not surprise me because I knew little about the CIA.

When I asked the question I was thinking of the Allende government, not of something that happened 6, 7, or 8 years ago.

I had been approached by people before about copper interests in Chile, but had not the faintest idea I was asking whether money had been given to Chile many years before.

Interest had to do primarily with the copper setup, so I fully sympathize with the witness when he says he thought my questioning had to do with what we had done to the Allende government in effort to bring it down.

The CHAIRMAN. Senator Church?

Senator CHURCH. Thank you, Mr. Chairman.

HARRINGTON LETTER'S ALLEGATIONS CONCERNING CIA ACTIVITY

What I would like to do, Mr. Ambassador, is to set out first of all, so that there are no traps or blind alleys in this, what we now have heard about the CIA activity in Chile, and I would like to refer to

the letter that the press got hold of, the Harrington letter. It was first
N23 revealed in "The New York Times," I think.

Since that time, we have checked the allegations in this letter
against testimony that Mr. Colby subsequently gave, that is, sub-
sequent to your testimony.

Mr. HELMS. Yes, sir.

Senator CHURCH. And, insofar as I can tell in making the com-
parison, although the Colby testimony was not as specific in all
particulars as the allegations in the letter, the Colby testimony
substantially confirmed these allegations. That is my impression of
N24 the Colby testimony.

In general, the letter alleges that the Nixon administration author-
ized more than $8 million for covert activities by the CIA in Chile
between 1970 and 1973. The purpose of these covert activities was
said to be an effort to make it impossible for President Salvador
Allende Gossens to govern; and second, that all of these activities
were specifically authorized by the Forty Committee, chaired by
Secretary of State Kissinger, which authorizes such clandestine
activities.

Again, according to the letter, the goal of these activities was to
destabilize, which is the term that the letter uses, the Allende govern-
ment; and further, it was considered a test of using heavy cash pay-
ments to bring down the government, viewed as antagonistic to the
United States.

Specifically, the forty Committee, chaired by Kissinger, is charged
with having authorized the following CIA activities and expenditures.

First. In 1969, $500,000 was expended to fund individuals who
could be nurtured to keep the anti-Allende forces active and intact.

Second. During the 1970 election, $500,000 was given to opposition
party personnel, and, third, that after the September 4, 1970 popular
election, $350,000 was authorized to bribe the Chilean Congress as
part of a scheme to overturn the results of the election in which
Allende gained a plurality, although that plan was later evaluated as
unworkable.

There are some other specifics. Let's take these first in order.

USE OF FUNDS AUTHORIZED IN 1969 AND 1970

Going back to your testimony on February 7, 1973, when Senator
Symington asked, "Did you have any money passed to the opponents
of Allende?" your answer was, "No, sir."

Now, first of all, were these sums that I have referred to authorized
in 1969 for use prior to the election and during the election of 1970?
What were they used for and how can these charges in the letter be
reconciled with your answer to the question that Senator Symington
put to you?

Ambassador HELMS. I understood Senator Symington to have asked
me if we had given money to Mr. Allende's opponents, which were
two, a man named Alessandri and a man named Tomic.

Senator MCGEE. You mean his actual opponents, not those opposing
him?

Ambassador HELMS. I understood the question to mean that because
in a previous election I had in mind we had actually given the money
to the candidates.

Senator McGEE. Senator Church; if you will yield on that, that seems to me an area where everybody has gotten off on a separate track.

Ambassador HELMS. I obviously did.

Senator CHURCH. To confirm what did in fact happen, going back to the specifics, in 1969, was $500,000 expended to fund individuals who could be nurtured to keep anti-Allende forces active and intact?

Could you tell us what the money was used for—whether this characterization is a fair one?

Ambassador HELMS. I cannot, I am sorry; at this late date, I don't recall any more; and I didn't realize that this testimony was going to be before us today, so I have not reviewed it before. I am hearing it now for the first time, and I am not going to be in the position of misleading you; and whatever the Agency records show as against maybe Congressman Harrington's record, I am quite prepared to accept, and they can be put in the record at this time.

Senator CHURCH. May I ask during the 1970 election, maybe part of this you can recall——

Ambassador HELMS. I will do my best.

Senator CHURCH [continuing]. During the 1970 election, the charge is made that $500,000 was given to opposition party personnel. Now, we have not been told that it was given directly to Alessandri or to the other opponent.

Ambassador HELMS. Senator Church, my recollection, and that is only to the best of my recollection, I didn't think this was being given to political parties, I thought it was being given to civic action groups. That was my recollection at that time. Whether these civic action or social groups might, by perfectly normal extrapolations, be tied to certain political parties, it may well be, but it was not my impression at the time that these were actually going into people in the political apparatus, as we would have it in this country in the Democratic or Republican Parties.

ALLEGED PLAN TO BRIBE CHILEAN CONGRESS

Senator CHURCH. The third of these charges is that after the September 4, 1970, popular election, $350,000 was authorized to bribe the Chilean Congress, as part of a scheme to overturn the result of the election in which Allende gained a plurality, although that plan was later evaluated as unworkable.

Now, what do you know about that proposition?

Ambassador HELMS. Well, as I say again, my recollection is not very clear. I know that there was a lot of planning going on about various ways, if possible, to upset the result; in other words, to have a vote in the Assembly when it came down to the two candidates that had won, that would be against Allende, that there was planning and work and thought given to how one might upset that, I think there is no doubt.

Senator CHURCH. Do you recall whether or not that planning was set aside, whether a finding was made that such plans were unworkable?

Ambassador HELMS. I think so.

Senator CHURCH. Did it go beyond the planning stage?

Ambassador HELMS. I think so, because as I think back to that period, there was obviously a lot of pressure from the Administration to see if something could be done about this, but I believe when it was examined, it was found it was quite unworkable, Allende had this all wrapped up, it was put in the bag, and there was nothing that was going to change it.

Senator CHURCH. Do you recall at this time whether or not any bribes were attempted?

Ambassador HELMS. That I do not remember.

May I say, Senator, I am not trying to mislead you. Maybe there were.

Senator CHURCH. I understand. I accept the fact that these details are difficult to remember.

OBTAINING INFORMATION CONCERNING HARRINGTON CHARGES FROM CIA SUGGESTED

Ambassador HELMS. May I say, sir, in an effort to put my memory in perspective at this particular time, there were a lot of other things going on, and I was not as intimately involved in these things as perhaps I might have been at any time in history, but I would like to invite you, because I realize the Foreign Relations Committee is going to have a key role now in all of these covert actions, to actually get somebody to come up here with the files and tell you very specifically what happened rather than what Congressman Harrington thinks happened.

Senator CHURCH. I was just about to make this proposal to the chairman, that following our hearing here, Mr. Chairman, we do obtain for our own record the full information from the CIA with respect to the particulars of these charges, so that we have directly from the Agency all of the facts concerning the charges, as I recognize you may not be able to recall particulars.

Senator HUMPHREY. You want all of the covert activities against all countries?

Senator CHURCH. No.

Senator HUMPHREY. Let me make it clear we are speaking now only with regard to the letter and the specific charges that have been made, a letter that was made public and became really the cause of this hearing today.

The reason I bring this up is that we do have general authority over covert activities.

Senator CHURCH. Yes.

POLICY QUESTION CONCERNING OBTAINING CIA INFORMATION

Senator HUMPHREY. I have very mixed feelings about this. I just put a note down here, "Do we want the CIA to tell us what they have been doing in some other countries?" because I think some of these things are a good deal cheaper than the Bay of Pigs. There are so many countries in which these covert activities take place that I think there is a real general policy question whether we ought to have them or not. If we do, how much do we want to know about them, and whom are we going to trust with the information?

I went over to the State Department Saturday and sat down with only the Secretary of State, and I saw it all in the paper the next morning. There is no way you can talk to anybody about anything that they won't report it, except perhaps that you love your mother.

The CHAIRMAN. Just the two of you talking?

Senator HUMPHREY. Just two of us.

The CHAIRMAN. Which one of you leaked it?

Senator HUMPHREY. I do not know which one, but I am telling you what happened. The memorandum to a lady who had set up the meeting had been given to the New York Times. On the day after I left, the New York Times editor called me up and said he wanted to read me a memorandum which precipitated my meeting over there, about which I knew nothing. I did not even know there was a memo.

I get back again to what is happening in Chile. I have to go now. I am trying to get jobs for 400 people in Minnesota today. That is a great deal more important to me right now than Chile.

Senator SCOTT. You better take that back unless you want it in the Times.

Senator HUMPHREY. I will leave it. I hope it gets printed because I have two towns out home, one with 300 people laid off and one with 270. That is 570 people with no jobs this morning, and I am really in trouble.

Let me say that I do think that we have a problem here. I am interested in getting this Chile question cleared up, but I would be interested to find out what we have done in other countries.

I have to say these things because to me I think there is a real policy question here of how far we go and what we do in terms of record.

Senator CHURCH. I agree that is one policy question we have to resolve in light of the provisions of the new law.

If it is reassuring at all, I had lunch privately with the Secretary yesterday.

Senator HUMPHREY. I saw you go out.

Senator CHURCH. So far I have not seen anything in the New York Times about it. [Laughter.]

Senator HUMPHREY. But I do think, if I may say, that we are fastened on the Chile question because it got to be a part of the general testimony but, interestingly enough to me, while we are concerned about Chile, and I am, I have yet to hear anybody really examining what we did in other places. And do not think we did not do a lot.

I am just worried about the trend we are following.

NEED FOR GUIDELINES IN OBTAINING CIA INFORMATION

Senator CHURCH. I would hope that if a select committee is chosen and approved by the Senate, some guidelines can be developed for the future with respect to covert operations because there is, I would suggest, a difference between an elected government and a government imposed by force of arms.

Senator HUMPHREY. Absolutely.

Senator SCOTT. And a difference between invasion, too, and action short of invasion.

Senator CHURCH. There are all kinds of differences, but this makes the need for some guidelines all the more important.

May I get back to the question of Chile?

NOT DIFFERENTIATING BETWEEN EVENTS QUESTIONED

Senator McGEE. May I inject one thought. These things most of us went through here, and the testimony that was presented, really were triggered by two things: Senator Church's very telling ITT hearings and the disclosures which began to unfold, and, secondly, the overthrow of the Allende government, the military coup, in September 1973.

Things, which happened at quite different times historically, often get merged. As I read the testimony again, questions that were provoked by events of an earlier time led to answers that were then directed at the coup which had just occurred. I generally feel now, more so than before as I reread this, that is where the double tracking occurred.

When the Western Hemisphere Subcommittee had the CIA, Ambassador Davis, Mr. Kubisch and the Secretary of State here, we came back to this again and again, They laid out very candidly for us in most instances what had transpired in the election of 1964 and how much it must have been toned down by 1970, even though there was still participation. But by the time of the coup, which is what brought all of .this to a very emotional head, there had been nothing in Harrington's letter or letters, or his memo or in the subsequent memos, that contradicted the Colby assessment given before our subcommittee after the coup, in November of 1973, namely: The CIA was not involved in any direct way with the coup; they had been warned that it was coming, once a week for several months. There was money being circulated but not in the dimension as before, because after the ITT hearings everybody learned a lot of lessons. The commitment was on a very modest scale, which was to keep opposition voices alive through newspapers or radio stations or individuals who were doing this sort of thing. But at no time was money given to the truckers' strike. No money was given to any group or encouragement to any group to overthrow the government. It was all pitched toward the 1976 election.

That is quite a different policy goal than triggering the defeat of Allende, or even the bribing question at the time that Allende and his opponent were to be voted on by the congress, which is very serious. That is why I think in hindsight it is awfully important, for me at least, to sort out which were the disastrous things that were undertaken earlier from which, hopefully, all have learned. Those ought to be included in the ultimate guidelines as ways not to do it, but we have been guilty of not differentiating between the events and kind of generalizing on them, particularly Congressman Harrington.

COMMITTEE KNOWLEDGE OF COVERT ACTIVITY

The CHAIRMAN. May I interject a thought at this point?

I agree with what Senator McGee has said and I have said time and again that we ought to establish guidelines. I think we must be very careful to avoid the idea that covert activity in foreign countries is something totally unknown to us. We have known of it.

Senator McGEE. Or unwarranted.

The CHAIRMAN. We have been told about it from time to time.

I believe we recognize the necessity still of having covert actions in foreign countries, but I think Senator McGee touches it properly when he says there ought to be guidelines. We ought not to run wild with them, but, nevertheless, I do not think we can just shake our heads and say, "The very idea of covert action in that country."

Senator CHURCH. I appreciate what you have said, and of course, we have known in the past in a general way of covert activities by the

CIA. The Chilean incident was not the first revelation of this kind but we had testimony on it—with apparent discrepancies—and that is what I am trying to get at.

PLAN TO BRIBE CHILEAN CONGRESS

Now, I just questioned you, to pick up the track again, Mr. Ambassador, about what happened after the popular election in September of 1970, when, according to our information, $350,000 was authorized to bribe the Chilean Congress as part of a scheme to overturn the results of the election, and it was later judged that such a plan was unworkable, and, you have testified that, as I understand your answer, that though you can't recall all of the particulars, that some attention was given to such a scheme, at least.

Isn't that correct?

Ambassador HELMS. Yes, sir.

Senator CHURCH. That being the case, let me refer to a question that I asked you on March 6, 1973, during the executive session of the Multinational Corporation, Subcommittee. I asked at that time, I quote from the record, "Now, following the election"—we were discussing the Chilean election—"and up to the time that the Congress of Chile cast its vote installing Allende as the new President, did the CIA attempt in any way to influence that vote?"

And you responded "Which vote?" And I said "the vote of the Congress." And you said, "No, sir."

Now do you see any discrepancy in your answer to my question at that time with what you have just told us?

Ambassador HELMS. Sir, I think that what is involved here is this. That as best I recall it thought was given to trying to upset this election but there was no way found to do it. In other words, when the situation was calculated and observed it was found that this was in the bag, that the money would certainly not get the votes necessary to overturn the election.

I realize, sir, even in light of that that my answer was narrow, but I would like to say something here.

I didn't come into the Multinational Committee hearing to mislead you, but I have had as Director, or did have as Director in 6½ years a lot of problems, and one of the principal problems was who in the Congress was really to divulge all of the details of covert operations to, and I must say this has given me a great deal of difficulty over the years and I just want to say once a real oversight committee is set up in the Congress it will make a great difference to any future Director because many times I have wanted to be able to go to somebody and say what do you think.

Senator CHURCH. I can appreciate that.

Ambassador HELMS. I must say this was very difficult for me.

Senator CHURCH. I can appreciate that. That has been an ambiguity which must have been difficult for every CIA Director.

Ambassador HELMS. It has been.

Senator CHURCH. And an ambiguity that should be cleared up.

Ambassador HELMS. If I was less than forthcoming it wasn't because I was being bloody minded, it was simply because I was trying to stay within what I thought was the congressional guidelines.

Senator CHURCH. I see.

POSSIBILITY OF OBLIGATION TO MISLEAD CONGRESSIONAL COMMITTEES

Senator McGOVERN. Mr. Helms, one thing that I think bears on this whole subject, including the line of questioning that Senator Church has developed, is something that has bothered me. Some years ago, an administration official was quoted publicly as saying he thought there are times when Government officials had a patriotic obligation to lie.

Senator SYMINGTON. I think Sylvester was his name.

Senator CASE. I thought it was Allen Dulles.

Senator McGOVERN. Maybe they both did.

Senator CASE. We are not joking at all and I am not saying that these people don't have the most honorable intentions in everything they do, including lying.

Senator McGOVERN. What I wanted to ask Ambassador Helms is this: Is it possible that a person, either the Director of CIA or someone high in the Agency, would feel that he had either a right, maybe an obligation, on certain occasions, to mislead congressional committees?

Is there a rationalization that you might go through—"Well, with the national interest in mind I am going to deliberately give a misleading answer on this, not because I want to be a liar but because I am concerned about the security of the country and, therefore, I am not going to give a truthful answer?"

Ambassador HELMS. Well, Senator McGovern, I could understand something like that going through any Director's mind. I would like to say the way I guided myself during the 6½ years I was Director, I made up my mind that I wasn't going to lie to any congressional committees, that I was going to be as forthcoming as I thought I could under the circumstances existing at the hearing, whether I was before an oversight committee or someplace else, and I must say I always had the alternative of going to the Senator privately and say please will you pull back on that, we are getting into a very sensitive area, and I realize against that background that these discrepancies or misinterpretations and so forth, maybe what I should have done at the time was to go to Senator Church's office and sit down with him and go over these things in a much more extensive way simply so he would know where the pitfalls were. But at that time the Allende government was still in power. I felt obliged to keep some of this stuff, in other words, not volunteer a good deal of information because my oversight committee wanted to hear it. I would have volunteered it, but my understanding had been that that was where I was going to give all of the covert information. I don't want to seek refuge and say I lied in the national security interest. I didn't run into any situation where I thought that was required.

COVER STORY FOR CIA COVERT OPERATION

Senator CHURCH. I don't know whether there is any basis of truth in it or not, but I have heard, when a covert operation is launched by the CIA, that, as a part of the planning for the execution of the operation, a cover story is agreed upon to be used in connection with any questions that might arise, and that the cover story is to apply wherever necessary, including its use in connection with questions that may be raised by congressional committees.

QUESTIONING OF HENRY KISSINGER WITH REGARD TO U.S. INTERVENTION IN CHILE ([19], pp. 271–272)

Compromised "cover" in operations of foreign espionage can be as damaging as a failure to achieve the objective of the mission itself. The U.S. intelligence community was unsuccessful in both these areas with regard to Chile, and Senator Frank Church did not hesitate to stress this point in his handling of the witnesses who testified on this matter. One of them was Henry Kissinger, secretary of state and an accomplished spokesman before congressional committees. Senator Church led Kissinger into a defense of the CIA Chilean operations and then confronted him with indignation. This testimony, brief as it is, illustrates the tenor of the Church inquiry as it drew to a close. Many members of Congress were incredulous as to the blunders committed in covert operations and outraged that they had occurred at all. Those attitudes influenced the political climate that led to the establishment of congressional oversight procedures in covert operations.

N25

Senator CHURCH. Nevertheless, Mr. Chairman, the practice of this committee has been to give members of this committee an opportunity to ask questions of this character, and I would like the Secretary to tell me how we can reconcile this kind of intervention with moral law which we are supposed to respect, with treaty law, with international law, or with any law other than the law of the jungle.

Secretary KISSINGER. Well, Senator, the period you are talking about is the period between 1970 and 1973. The beginning of the period to which you refer was in a period of still considerable hostility and acute cold war, so in 1970 the perception of the administration was not how to reconcile certain actions with détente because détente was something that we were still trying to establish.

May I please finish my answer and then—I am trying to explain in reference to your question.

Second, when the leadership and the President have worked out a fuller discussion of these issues, I think fairness would have to require that this be discussed, not just in terms of any one event in Chile but of a history that antedated by a considerable number of years, 1970.

But let me now deal with the specific issue that was posed by Allende. According to the Chilean Constitution, a president is elected in two ways, either by a majority vote of the population, or failing a majority vote, by a majority vote of the Congress among the candidates that were running; and by tradition the Congress has voted for the candidate that had the largest number of votes, however narrow that margin might have been.

In 1970, Allende received a 1 percent margin over his nearest competitor but, nevertheless, only 36 or 37 percent of the vote, which meant that 63 percent of the population had not voted for Allende. This in itself was not unusual in Chile because almost every modern president of Chile has been elected by relatively narrow margins of this kind.

What gave the Allende situation a particular character was that, having been elected by 36 percent, he then set about to establish what appeared to be a one-party government and systematically set about to throttle all opposition parties, all opposition press, so that the issue that was raised here was not an intervention in the democratic process. The issue that was raised was whether somebody elected with 36 percent and frankly, pursuing policies that we considered hostile to the United States, should then be able to establish a one-party government.

As the President pointed out, the intent of the U.S. Government was not to destabilize or to subvert him but to keep in being those political parties that had traditionally contested the elections. Our concern was with the election in 1976 and not at all with a coup in 1973 about which we knew nothing and which we had nothing to do with as I testified to in 1973, and as the President reaffirmed.

Senator CHURCH. Mr. Secretary, I have just one comment to make about this and then I am through. The present Government of Chile is a military government which seized power in an awful blood bath, and there is no opposition anymore, and there is no dissent anymore, and there is no covert plan any more—of this I am certain—either to assist the dissidents or encourage opposition. That makes your excuse for our intervention pretty weak. I cannot square this policy with what I regard as traditional American principles and I think it is a sad episode. I am finished.

Assassinations

The Church Committee concluded its interim report on alledged assassination plots of foreign leaders with an epilogue ([43], p. 285).

"The Committee does not believe that the acts which it has examined represent the real American character. They do not reflect the ideals which have given the people of this country and of the world hope for a better, fuller, fairer life. We regard the assassination plots as aberrations.

"The United States must not adopt the tactics of the enemy. Means are as important as ends. Crisis makes it tempting to ignore the wise restraints that make men free. But each time we do so, each time the means we use are wrong, our inner strength, the strength which makes us free, is lessened.

"Despite our distaste for what we have seen, we have great faith in this country. The story is sad, but this country has the strength to hear the story and to learn from it. We must remain a people who confront our mistakes and resolve not to repeat them. If we do not, we will decline; but, if we do, our future will be worthy of the best of our past."

FINDINGS AND CONCLUSIONS OF THE CHURCH COMMITTEE WITH REGARD TO ASSASSINATIONS
([43], pp. 255–284)

The role of the United States in various assassination plots was examined by the staff of the Church Committee and through its hearings (see Bibliography). The committee compiled over 8,000 pages of testimony from some 75 different witnesses and examined raw files in the presidential libraries of Dwight D. Eisenhower, John F. Kennedy, and Lyndon B. Johnson, as well as within the Executive branch itself. The Church report of November 20, 1975 was approximately 350 pages and its findings and conclusions are reprinted here, along with a chronology of related events. Subsequent to the issuance of this report, the committee released another significant report entitled, "The Investigation of the Assassination of President John F. Kennedy: Performance of the Intelligence Agencies" ([45E]). Surfacing in that committee investigation was the notion that involvement by the United States in assassination plots of foreign leaders might induce other nations to plot the assassination of our own president ([45E], p. 3). No conclusions were reached on such a possibility, but enough concern was generated to provoke creation of a new joint congressional committee to reexamine the findings of the Warren Commission (President's Commission on the Assassination of President Kennedy, the original commission set up to investigate the Kennedy assassination).

In evaluating the evidence and arriving at findings and conclusions, the Committee has been guided by the following standards. We believe these standards to be appropriate to the constitutional duty of a Congressional committee.

1. The Committee is not a court. Its primary role is not to determine individual guilt or innocence, but rather to draw upon the experiences of the past to better propose guidance for the future.

2. It is necessary to be cautious in reaching conclusions because of the amount of time that has passed since the events reviewed in this report, the inability of three Presidents and many other key figures to speak for themselves, the conflicting and ambiguous nature of much of the evidence, and the problems in assessing the weight to be given to particular documents and testimony.

3. The Committee has tried to be fair to the persons involved in the events under examination, while at the same time responding to a need to understand the facts in sufficient detail to lay a basis for informed recommendations.

With these standards in mind, the Committee has arrived at the following findings and conclusions.

A. FINDINGS CONCERNING THE PLOTS THEMSELVES

1. OFFICIALS OF THE UNITED STATES GOVERNMENT INITIATED PLOTS TO ASSASSINATE FIDEL CASTRO AND PATRICE LUMUMBA

The Committee finds that officials of the United States Government initiated and participated in plots to assassinate Patrice Lumumba and Fidel Castro.

N26

The plot to kill Lumumba was conceived in the latter half of 1960 by officials of the United States Government, and quickly advanced to the point of sending poisons to the Congo to be used for the assassination.

The effort to assassinate Castro began in 1960 and continued until 1965. The plans to assassinate Castro using poison cigars, exploding seashells, and a contaminated diving suit did not advance beyond the laboratory phase. The plot involving underworld figures reached the stage of producing poison pills, establishing the contacts necessary to send them into Cuba, procuring potential assassins within Cuba, and apparently delivering the pills to the island itself. One 1960 episode involved a Cuban who initially had no intention of engaging in assassination, but who finally agreed, at the suggestion of the CIA, to attempt to assassinate Raul Castro if the opportunity arose. In the AM/LASH operation, which extended from 1963 through 1965, the CIA gave active support and encouragement to a Cuban whose intent to assassinate Castro was known, and provided him with the means of carrying out an assassination.

2. NO FOREIGN LEADERS WERE KILLED AS A RESULT OF ASSASSINATION PLOTS INITIATED BY OFFICIALS OF THE UNITED STATES

The poisons intended for use against Patrice Lumumba were never administered to him, and there is no evidence that the United States was in any way involved in Lumumba's death at the hands of his Congolese enemies. The efforts to assassinate Castro failed.

3. AMERICAN OFFICIALS ENCOURAGED OR WERE PRIVY TO COUP PLOTS WHICH RESULTED IN THE DEATHS OF TRUJILLO, DIEM, AND SCHNEIDER

American officials clearly desired the overthrow of Trujillo, offered both encouragement and guns to local dissidents who sought his overthrow and whose plans included assassination. American officials also supplied those dissidents with pistols and rifles.

American officials offered encouragement to the Vietnamese generals who plotted Diem's overthrow, and a CIA official in Vietnam gave the generals money after the coup had begun. However, Diem's assassination was neither desired nor suggested by officials of the United States.

The record reveals that United States officials offered encouragement to the Chilean dissidents who plotted the kidnapping of General Rene Schneider, but American officials did not desire or encourage Schneider's death. Certain high officials did know, however, that the dissidents planned to kidnap General Schneider.

As Director Colby testified before the Committee, the death of a foreign leader is a risk foreseeable in any coup attempt. In the cases we have considered, the risk of death was in fact known in varying degrees. It was widely known that the dissidents in the Dominican Republic intended to assassinate Trujillo. The contemplation of coup leaders at one time to assassinate Nhu, President Diem's brother, was communicated to the upper levels of the United States Government. While the CIA and perhaps the White House knew that the coup leaders in Chile planned to kidnap General Schneider, it was not anticipated that he would be killed, although the possibility of his death should have been recognized as a foreseeable risk of his kidnapping.

4. THE PLOTS OCCURRED IN A COLD WAR ATMOSPHERE PERCEIVED TO BE OF CRISIS PROPORTIONS

The Committee fully appreciates the importance of evaluating the assassination plots in the historical context within which they occurred. In the preface to this report, we described the perception, generally shared within the United States during the depths of the Cold War, that our country faced a monolithic enemy in Communism. That attitude helps explain the assassination plots which we have reviewed, although it does not justify them. Those involved nevertheless appeared to believe they were advancing the best interests of their country.

5. AMERICAN OFFICIALS HAD EXAGGERATED NOTIONS ABOUT THEIR ABILITY TO CONTROL THE ACTIONS OF COUP LEADERS

Running throughout the cases considered in this report was the expectation of American officials that they could control the actions of dissident groups which they were supporting in foreign countries. Events demonstrated that the United States had no such power. This point is graphically demonstrated by cables exchanged shortly before the coup in Vietnam. Ambassador Lodge cabled Washington on October 30, 1963, that he was unable to halt a coup; a cable from William Bundy in response stated that "we cannot accept conclusion that we have no power to delay or discourage a coup." The coup took place three days later.

Shortly after the experience of the Bay of Pigs, CIA Headquarters requested operatives in the Dominican Republic to tell the dissidents to "turn off" the assassination attempt, because the United States was not prepared to "cope with the aftermath." The dissidents replied that the assassination was their affair and that it could not be turned off to suit the convenience of the United States Government.

6. CIA OFFICIALS MADE USE OF KNOWN UNDERWORLD FIGURES IN ASSASSINATION EFFORTS

Officials of the CIA made use of persons associated with the criminal underworld in attempting to achieve the assassination of Fidel Castro. These underworld figures were relied upon because it was believed that they had expertise and contacts that were not available to law-abiding citizens.

Foreign citizens with criminal backgrounds were also used by the CIA in two other cases that we have reviewed. In the development of the Executive Action capability, one foreign national with a criminal background was used to "spot" other members of the European underworld who might be used by the CIA for a variety of purposes, including assassination, if the need should arise. In the Lumumba case, two men with criminal backgrounds were used as field operatives by CIA officers in a volatile political situation in the Congo.

B. CONCLUSIONS CONCERNING THE PLOTS THEMSELVES

1. THE UNITED STATES SHOULD NOT ENGAGE IN ASSASSINATION

We condemn the use of assassination as a tool of foreign policy. Aside from pragmatic arguments against the use of assassination supplied to the Committee by witnesses with extensive experience in covert operations, we find that assassination violates moral precepts fundamental to our way of life.

In addition to moral considerations, there were several practical reasons advanced for not assassinating foreign leaders. These reasons are discussed in the section of this report recommending a statute making assassination a crime.

(a) *Distinction between targeted assassinations instigated by the United States and support for dissidents seeking to overthrow local governments*

Two of the five principal cases investigated by the Committee involved plots to kill foreign leaders (Lumumba and Castro) that were instigated by American officials. Three of the cases (Trujillo, Diem, and Schneider) involved killings in the course of coup attempts by local dissidents. These latter cases differed in the degree to which assassination was contemplated by the leaders of the coups and in the degree the coups were motivated by United States officials.

The Committee concludes that targeted assassinations instigated by the United States must be prohibited.

Coups involve varying degrees of risk of assassination. The possibility of assassination in coup attempts is one of the issues to be considered in determining the propriety of United States involvement in coups, particularly in those where the assassination of a foreign leader is a likely prospect.

This country was created by violent revolt against a regime believed to be tyrannous, and our founding fathers (the local dissidents of that era) received aid from foreign countries. Given that history, we should not today rule out support for dissident groups seeking to overthrow tyrants. But passing beyond that principle, there remain serious questions: for example, whether the national interest of the United States is genuinely involved; whether any such support should be overt rather than covert; what tactics should be used; and how such actions should be authorized and controlled by the coordinate branches of government. The Committee believes that its recommendations on the question of covert actions in support of coups must await the Committee's final report which will be issued after a full review of covert action in general.

(b) *The setting in which the assassination plots occurred explains, but does not justify them*

The Cold War setting in which the assassination plots took place does not change our view that assassination is unacceptable in our society. In addition to the moral and practical problems discussed elsewhere, we find three principal defects in any contention that the tenor of the period justified the assassination plots:

First, the assassination plots were not necessitated by imminent danger to the United States. Among the cases studied, Castro alone posed a physical threat to the United States, but then only during the period of the Cuban missile crisis. Attempts to assassinate Castro had begun long before that crisis, and assassination was not advanced by policymakers as a possible course of action during the crisis.

Second, we reject absolutely any notion that the United States should justify its actions by the standards of totalitarians. Our standards must be higher, and this difference is what the struggle is all about. Of course, we must defend our democracy. But in defending it, we must resist undermining the very virtues we are defending.

Third, such activities almost inevitably become known. The damage to American foreign policy, to the good name and reputation of the United States abroad, to the American people's faith and support of our government and its foreign policy is incalculable. This last point—the undermining of the American public's confidence in its government—is the most damaging consequence of all.

Two documents which have been supplied to the Committee graphically demonstrate attitudes which can lead to tactics that erode and could ultimately destroy the very ideals we must defend.

The first, document was written in 1954 by a special committee formed to advise the President on covert activities. The United States may, it said, have to adopt tactics "more ruthless than [those] employed by the enemy" in order to meet the threat from hostile nations. The report concluded that "long standing American concepts of American fair play must be reconsidered."[1]

---

[1] The full text of the passage is as follows:
"* * * another important requirement is an aggressive covert psychological, political, and paramilitary organization far more effective, more unique, and, if necessary, more ruthless than that employed by the enemy. No one should be permitted to stand in the way of the prompt, efficient, and secure accomplishment of this mission.

Although those proposals did not involve assassinations, the attitudes underlying them were, as Director Colby testified, indicative of the setting within which the assassination plots were conceived. (Colby, 6/4/75....)

We do not think that traditional American notions of fair play need be abandoned when dealing with our adversaries. It may well be ourselves that we injure most if we adopt tactics "more ruthless than the enemy."

A second document which represents an attitude which we find improper was sent to the Congo in the fall of 1960 when the assassination of Patrice Lumumba was being considered. The chief of CIA's Africa Division recommended a particular agent—WI/ROGUE—because:

> He is indeed aware of the precepts of right and wrong, but if he is given an assignment which may be morally wrong in the eyes of the world, but necessary because his case officer ordered him to carry it out, then it is right, and he will dutifully undertake appropriate action for its execution without pangs of conscience. In a word, he can rationalize all actions.

The Committee finds this rationalization is not in keeping with the ideals of our nation.

2. THE UNITED STATES SHOULD NOT MAKE USE OF UNDERWORLD FIGURES FOR THEIR CRIMINAL TALENTS

We conclude that agencies of the United States must not use underworld figures for their criminal talents [2] in carrying out Agency operations. In addition to the corrosive effect upon our government,[3] the use of underworld figures involves the following dangers:

a. The use of underworld figures for "dirty business" gives them the power to blackmail the government and to avoid prosecution, for past or future crimes. For example, the figures involved in the Castro assassination operation used their involvement with the CIA to avoid prosecution. The CIA also contemplated attempting to quash criminal charges brought in a foreign tribunal against QJ/WIN.

b. The use of persons experienced in criminal techniques and prone to criminal behavior increases the likelihood that criminal acts will occur. Sometimes agents in the field are necessarily given broad discretion. But the risk of improper activities is increased when persons of criminal background are used, particularly when they are selected precisely to take advantage of their criminal skills or contacts.

"The second consideration, it is now clear that we are facing an implacable enemy whose avowed objective is world domination by whatever means at whatever cost. There are no rules in such a game. Hitherto acceptable norms of human conduct do not apply. If the U.S. is to survive, long standing American concepts of American fair play must be reconsidered."

[2] Pending our investigation of the use of informants by the FBI and other agencies, we reserve judgment on the use of known criminals as informants. We are concerned here only with the use of persons known to be actively engaged in criminal pursuits for their expertise in carrying out criminal acts.

[3] The corrosive effect of dealing with underworld figures is graphically demonstrated by the fact that Attorney General Robert Kennedy, who had devoted much of his professional life to fighting organized crime, did not issue an order against cooperating with such persons when he learned in May 1961 that the CIA had made use of Sam Giancana in a sensitive operation in Cuba.

In May, 1962, the Attorney General learned that the operation—which was described to him as terminated—had involved assassination. According to a CIA witness, the Attorney General was angered by the report and told those briefing him that he must be consulted before underworld figures were used again. He did not, however, direct that underworld figures must never again be used.

c. There is the danger that the United States Government will become an unwitting accomplice to criminal acts and that criminal figures will take advantage of their association with the government to advance their own projects and interests.

d. There is a fundamental impropriety in selecting persons because they are skilled at performing deeds which the laws of our society forbid.

The use of underworld figures by the United States Government for their criminal skills raises moral problems comparable to those recognized by Justice Brandeis in a different context five decades ago:

Our government is the potent, the omnipresent teacher. For good or for ill, it teaches the whole people by its example. Crime is contagious. If the Government becomes a law-breaker, it breeds contempt for law; it invites every man to become a law unto himself. To declare that in the administration of the criminal law the end justifies the means—to declare that the Government may commit crimes in order to secure the conviction of the private criminal—would bring terrible retribution. Against that pernicious doctrine this Court should resolutely set its face. [Olmstead v. U.S., 277 U.S. 439, 485 (1927)]

e. The spectacle of the Government consorting with criminal elements destroys respect for government and law and undermines the viability of democratic institutions.

C. Findings and Conclusions Relating to Authorization and Control

In the introduction to this report, we set forth in summary form our major conclusions concerning whether the assassination plots were authorized. The ensuing discussion elaborates and explains those conclusions.

The Committee analyzed the question of authorization for the assassination activities from two perspectives. First, the Committee examined whether officials in policymaking positions authorized or were aware of the assassination activities. Second, the Committee inquired whether the officials responsible for the operational details of the plots perceived that assassination had the approval of their superiors, or at least was the type of activity that their superiors would not disapprove.

No doubt, the CIA's general efforts against the regimes discussed in this report were authorized at the highest levels of the government. However, the record is unclear and serious doubt remains concerning whether assassination was authorized by the respective Presidents. Even if the plots were not expressly authorized, it does not follow that the Agency personnel believed they were acting improperly.

1. THE APPARENT LACK OF ACCOUNTABILITY IN THE COMMAND AND CONTROL SYSTEM WAS SUCH THAT THE ASSASSINATION PLOTS COULD HAVE BEEN UNDERTAKEN WITHOUT EXPRESS AUTHORIZATION

As emphasized throughout this report, we are unable to draw firm conclusions concerning who authorized the assassination plots. Even after our long investigation it is unclear whether the conflicting and inconclusive state of the evidence is due to the system of plausible denial or whether there were, in fact, serious shortcomings in the system of authorization which made it possible for assassination efforts to have been undertaken by agencies of the United States Government without express authority from officials above those agencies.[1]

Based on the record of our investigation, the Committee finds that the system of Executive command and control was so inherently ambiguous that it is difficult to be certain at what level assassination activity was known and authorized. This creates the disturbing prospect that assassination activity might have been undertaken by officials of the United States Government without its having been incontrovertibly clear that there was explicit authorization from the President of the United States. At the same time, this ambiguity and imprecision leaves open the possibility that there was a successful "plausible denial" and that a Presidential authorization was issued but is now obscured.

Whether or not assassination was authorized by a President of the United States, the President as the chief executive officer of the United States Government must take ultimate responsibility for major activities during his Administration. Just as these Presidents must be held accountable, however, their subordinates throughout the Government had a concomitant duty to fully disclose their plans and activities.

As part of their responsibility, these Presidents had a duty to determine the nature of major activities and to prevent undesired activities from taking place. This duty was particularly compelling when the Presidents had reason to believe that major undesired activities had previously occurred or were being advocated and might occur again. Whether or not the Presidents in fact knew about the assassination plots, and even if their subordinates failed in their duty of full disclosure, it still follows that the Presidents should have known about the plots. This sets a demanding standard, but one the Committee supports. The future of democracy rests upon such accountability.

2. FINDINGS RELATING TO THE LEVEL AT WHICH THE PLOTS WERE AUTHORIZED

(a) Diem

We find that neither the President nor any other official in the United States Government authorized the assassination of Diem and his brother Nhu. Both the DCI and top State Department officials did know, however, that the death of Nhu, at least at one point, had been contemplated by the coup leaders. But when the possibility that the coup leaders were considering assassination was brought to the attention of the DCI, he directed that the United States would have no part in such activity, and there is some evidence that this information was relayed to the coup leaders.

(b) Schneider

We find that neither the President nor any other official in the United States Government authorized the assassination of General Rene Schneider. The CIA, and perhaps the White House, did know

---

[1] As noted above, there are also certain inherent limitations in the extensive record compiled by the Committee. Many years have passed, several of the key figures are dead, and while we have been assured by the present Administration that all the relevant evidence has been produced, it is always possible that other more conclusive material exists, but has not been found.

that coup leaders contemplated a kidnapping, which, as it turned out resulted in Schneider's death.

(c) Trujillo

The Presidents and other senior officials in the Eisenhower and Kennedy Administrations sought the overthrow of Trujillo and approved or condoned actions to obtain that end.

The DCI and the Assistant Secretary of State for Inter-American Affairs knew that the Dominican dissidents viewed the removal of Trujillo as critical to any plans to overthrow his regime and that they intended to assassinate Trujillo if given the opportunity. It is uncertain precisely when officials at higher levels of government with responsibility for formulating policy learned that the dissidents equated assassination with overthrow. Clearly by early May 1961 senior American officials, including President Kennedy, knew that the dissidents intended to assassinate Trujillo. The White House and State Department, as well as the CIA, knew that the United States had provided the dissidents with rifles and pistols and that the dissidents had requested machine guns which they intended to use in connection with an assassination effort.

Thereafter, on May 16, 1961 President Kennedy approved National Security Council recommendations that the United States not initiate the overthrow of Trujillo until it was known what government would succeed the dictator. That recommendation was consistent with earlier attempts initiated by the CIA to discourage the planned assassination and thereby avoid potential problems from a power vacuum which might arise. After deciding to discourage the planned assassination, the DCI directed that the machine guns not be passed to the Dominican dissidents. That policy was reconfirmed by the State Department, the Special Group, and, in a cable of May 29, 1961, by President Kennedy himself.

The day before the assassination, President Kennedy cabled the State Department representative in the Dominican Republic that the United States "as [a] matter of general policy cannot condone assassination." However, the cable also stated that if the dissidents planning the imminent assassination of Trujillo succeeded, and thereby established a provisional government, the United States would recognize and support them.

The President's cable has been construed in several ways. One reading stresses the President's opposition to assassination "as a matter of general policy." Another stresses those portions of the cable which discuss pragmatic matters, including the risk that the United States' involvement might be exposed, and suggests that the last minute telegram was designed to avoid a charge that the United States shared responsibility for the assassination. A third construction would be that both of the prior readings are correct and that they are not mutually exclusive. However the cable is construed, its ambiguity illustrates the difficulty of seeking objectives which can only be accomplished by force—indeed, perhaps only by the assassination of a leader—and yet not wishing to take specific actions which seem abhorrent.

(d) Lumumba

The chain of events revealed by the documents and testimony is strong enough to permit a reasonable inference that the plot to assassinate Lumumba was authorized by President Eisenhower. Nevertheless, there is enough countervailing testimony by Eisenhower Administration officials and enough ambiguity and lack of clarity in the records of high-level policy meetings to preclude the Committee from making a finding that the President intended an assassination effort against Lumumba.

It is clear that the Director of Central Intelligence, Allen Dulles, authorized an assassination plot. There is, however, no evidence of United States involvement in bringing about the death of Lumumba at the hands of Congolese authorities.

Strong expressions of hostility toward Lumumba from the President and his National Security Assistant, followed immediately by CIA steps in furtherance of an assassination operation against Lumumba, are part of a sequence of events that, at the least, make it appear that Dulles believed assassination was a permissible means of complying with pressure from the President to remove Lumumba from the political scene.

Robert Johnson's testimony that he understood the President to have ordered Lumumba's assassination at an NSC meeting does, as he said, offer a "clue" about Presidential authorization. His testimony, however, should be read in light of the fact that NSC records during this period do not make clear whether or not the President ordered Lumumba's assassination and the fact that others attending those meetings testified that they did not recall hearing such a Presidential order.

Richard Bissell assumed that Presidential authorization for assassinating Lumumba had been communicated to him by Dulles, but Bissell had no specific recollection concerning when that communication occurred. The impression shared by the Congo Station Officer and the DDP's Special Assistant Joseph Scheider that the President authorized an assassination effort against Lumumba was derived solely from conversations Scheider had with Bissel and Bronson Tweedy. However, the impression thus held by Scheider and the Station Officer does not, in itself, establish Presidential authorization because neither Scheider nor the Station Officer had first-hand knowledge of Allen Dulles' statements about Presidential authorization, and because Scheider may have misconstrued Bissell's reference to "highest authority."

(e) Castro

There was insufficient evidence from which the Committee could conclude that Presidents Eisenhower, Kennedy, or Johnson, their close advisors, or the Special Group authorized the assassination of Castro.

The assassination plots against Castro were clearly authorized at least through the level of DDP. We also find that DCI Allen Dulles approved "thorough consideration" of the "elimination" of Castro. Further, it is also likely that Dulles knew about and authorized the actual plots that occurred during his tenure. Bissell and Edwards testified that they had briefed Dulles (and Cabell) on the plot involving underworld figures "circumlocutiously," but that they were certain that he had understood that the plot involved assassination. Their testimony is buttressed by the fact that Dulles knew about the plot to assassinate Lumumba which was being planned at the same time, and which also involved Bissell. We can find no evidence that McCone was aware of the plots which occurred during his tenure. His DDP, Richard Helms, testified that he never discussed the subject with McCone and was never expressly authorized by anyone to assassinate Castro.

The only suggestion of express Presidential authorization for the plots against Castro was Richard Bissell's opinion that Dulles would have informed Presidents Eisenhower and Kennedy by circumlocution only after the assassination had been planned and was underway. The assumptions underlying this opinion are too attenuated for the Committee to adopt it as a finding. First, this assumes that Dulles himself knew of the plot, a matter which is not entirely certain. Second, it assumes that Dulles went privately to the two Presidents—a course of action which Helms, who had far more covert action experience than Bissell, testified was precisely what the doctrine of plausible denial forbade CIA officials from doing. Third, it necessarily assumes that the Presidents would understand from a "circumlocutious" description that assassination was being discussed.

In view of the strained chain of assumptions and the contrary testimony of all the Presidential advisors, the men closest to both Eisenhower and Kennedy, the Committee makes no finding implicating Presidents who are not able to speak for themselves.

Helms and McCone testified that the Presidents under which they served never asked them to consider assassination.

There was no evidence whatsoever that President Johnson knew about or authorized any assassination activity during his Presidency.

3. CIA OFFICIALS INVOLVED IN THE ASSASSINATION OPERATIONS PERCEIVED ASSASSINATION TO HAVE BEEN A PERMISSIBLE COURSE OF ACTION

The CIA officials involved in the targeted assassination attempts testified that they had believed that their activities had been fully authorized.[1]

In the case of the Lumumba assassination operation, Richard Bissell testified that he had no direct recollection of authorization, but after having reviewed the cables and Special Group minutes, testified that authority must have flowed from Dulles through him to the subordinate levels in the Agency.

In the case of the assassination effort against Castro, Bissell and Sheffield Edwards testified they believed the operation involving underworld figures had been authorized by Dulles when they briefed him shortly after the plot had been initiated. William Harvey testified he believed that the plots "were completely authorized at every appropriate level within and beyond the Agency," although he had "no personal knowledge whatever of the individuals' identities, times, exact words, or channels through which such authority may have passed." Harvey stated that he had been told by Richard Bissell that the effort against Castro had been authorized "from the highest level," and that Harvey had discussed the plots with Richard Helms, his immediate superior. Helms testified that although he had never discussed assassination with his superiors, he believed:

* * * that in these actions we were taking against Cuba and against Fidel Castro's government in Cuba, that they were what we had been asked to do. * * * In other words we had been asked to get rid of Castro and * * * there were no limitations put on the means, and we felt we were acting well within the guidelines that we understood to be in play at this particular time.

The evidence points to a disturbing situation. Agency officials testified that they believed the effort to assassinate Castro to have been within the parameters of permissible action. But Administration officials responsible for formulating policy, including McCone, testified that they were not aware of the effort and did not authorize it. The explanation may lie in the fact that orders concerning overthrowing the Castro regime were stated in broad terms that were subject to

---

[1] The lower level operatives, such as the AM/LASH case officers, are not discussed in this section, since they had clear orders from their immediate superiors within the CIA.

differing interpretations by those responsible for carrying out those orders.

The various Presidents and their senior advisors strongly opposed the regimes of Castro and Trujillo, the accession to power of Allende, and the potential influence of Patrice Lumumba. Orders concerning action against those foreign leaders were given in vigorous language. For example, President Nixon's orders to prevent Allende from assuming power left Helms feeling that "if I ever carried a marshall's baton in my knapsack out of the Oval Office, it was that day." Similarly, General Lansdale described the Mongoose effort against Cuba as "a combat situation," and Attorney General Kennedy emphasized that "a solution to the Cuba problem today carries top priority." Helms testified that the pressure to "get rid of Castro and the Castro regime" was intense, and Bissell testified that he had been ordered to "get off your ass about Cuba."

It is possible that there was a failure of communication between policymakers and the agency personnel who were experienced in secret, and often violent, action. Although policymakers testified that assassination was not intended by such words as "get rid of Castro." Some of their subordinates in the Agency testified that they perceived that assassination was desired and that they should proceed without troubling their superiors.

The 1967 Inspector General's Report on assassinations appropriately observed:

> The point is that of frequent resort to synecdoche—the mention of a part when the whole is to be understood, or vice versa. Thus, we encounter repeated references to phrases such as "disposing of Castro," which may be read in the narrow, literal sense of assassinating him, when it is intended that it be read in the broader figurative sense of dislodging the Castro regime. Reversing the coin, we find people speaking vaguely of "doing something about Castro" when it is clear that what they have specifically in mind is killing him. In a situation wherein those speaking may not have actually meant what they seemed to say or may not have said what they actually meant, they should not be surprised if their oral shorthand is interpreted differently than was intended.

Differing perceptions between superiors and their subordinates were graphically illustrated in the Castro context.[1] McCone, in a memorandum dated April 14, 1967, reflected as follows:

> Through the years the Cuban problem was discussed in terms such as "dispose of Castro," "remove Castro," "knock off Castro," etc., and this meant the overthrow of the Communist government in Cuba and the replacing of it with a democratic regime. Terms such as the above appear in many working papers, memoranda for the record, etc., and, as stated, all refer to a change in the Cuban government.[2]

Helms, who had considerable experience as a covert operator, gave precisely the opposite meaning to the same words, interpreting them as conveying authority for assassination.

Helms repeatedly testified that he felt that explicit authorization

---

[1] Senator MATHIAS. Let me draw an example from history. When Thomas Becket was proving to be an annoyance, as Castro, the King said, "who will rid me of this troublesome priest?" He didn't say, "go out and murder him". He said, "who will rid me of this man," and let it go at that.
   Mr. HELMS. That is a warming reference to the problem.
   Senator MATHIAS. You feel that spans the generations and the centuries?
   Mr. HELMS. I think it does, sir.
   Senator MATHIAS. And that is typical of the kind of thing which might be said, which might be taken by the Director or by anybody else as presidential authorization to go forward?
   Mr. HELMS. That is right. But in answer to that, I realize that one sort of grows up in tradition of the time and I think that any of us would have found it very difficult to discuss assassinations with a President of the U.S. I just think we all had the feeling that we were hired out to keep those things out of the oval office.
[2] It should be noted, however, that this memorandum was prepared several years after the assassination plots when a newspaper article alleged CIA involvement in attempts on Castro's life.

was unnecessary for the assassination of Castro in the early 1960's, but he said he did not construe the intense pressure from President Nixon in 1970 as providing authority to assassinate anyone. As Helms testified, the difference was not that the pressure to prevent Allende from assuming office was any less than the pressure to remove the Castro regime, but rather that "I had already made up my mind that we weren't going to have any of that business when I was Director."

Certain CIA contemporaries of Helms who were subjected to similar pressures in the Castro case rejected the thesis that implicit authority to assassinate Castro derived from the strong language of the policymakers. Bissell testified that he had believed that "formal and explicit approval" would be required for assassination, and Helms' assistant, George McManus, testified that "it never occurred to me" that the vigorous words of the Attorney General could be taken as authorizing assassination. The differing perceptions may have resulted from their different backgrounds and training. Neither Bissell (an academician whose Agency career for the six years before he became DDP had been in the field of technology) nor McManus (who had concentrated on intelligence and staff work) were experienced in covert operations.[3]

The perception of certain Agency officials that assassination was within the range of permissible activity was reinforced by the continuing approval of violent covert actions against Cuba that were sanctioned at the Presidential level, and by the failure of the successive administrations to make clear that assassination was not permissible. This point is one of the subjects considered in the next section.

4. THE FAILURE IN COMMUNICATION BETWEEN AGENCY OFFICIALS IN CHARGE OF THE ASSASSINATION OPERATIONS AND THEIR SUPERIORS IN THE AGENCY AND IN THE ADMINISTRATION WAS DUE TO: (A) THE FAILURE OF SUBORDINATES TO DISCLOSE THEIR PLANS AND OPERATIONS TO THEIR SUPERIORS; AND (B) THE FAILURE OF SUPERIORS IN THE CLIMATE OF VIOLENCE AND AGGRESSIVE COVERT ACTIONS SANCTIONED BY THE ADMINISTRATIONS TO RULE OUT ASSASSINATION AS A TOOL OF FOREIGN POLICY; TO MAKE CLEAR TO THEIR SUBORDINATES THAT ASSASSINATION WAS IMPERMISSIBLE; OR TO INQUIRE FURTHER AFTER RECEIVING INDICATIONS THAT IT WAS BEING CONSIDERED

While we cannot find that officials responsible for making policy decisions knew about or authorized the assassination attempts (with the possible exception of the Lumumba case), Agency operatives at least through the level of DDP nevertheless perceived assassination to have been permissible. This failure in communication was inexcusable in light of the gravity of assassination. The Committee finds that the failure of Agency officials to inform their superiors was reprehensible, and that the reasons that they offered for having neglected to inform their superiors are unacceptable. The Committee further finds that Administration officials failed to be sufficiently precise in their directions to the Agency, and that their attitude toward the possibility of assassination was ambiguous in the context of the violence of other activities that they did authorize.

(a) *Agency officials failed on several occasions to reveal the plots to their superiors, or to do so with sufficient detail and clarity*

---

[3] Of course, this analysis cannot be carried too far. In the Lumumba case, for example, Johnson and Dillon, who were Administration officials with no covert operation experience, construed remarks as urging or permitting assassination, while other persons who were not in the Agency did not so interpret them.

Several of the cases considered in this report raise questions concerning whether officials of the CIA sufficiently informed their superiors in the Agency or officials outside the Agency about their activities.

(i) *Castro*

The failure of Agency officials to inform their superiors of the assassination efforts against Castro is particularly troubling.

On the basis of the testimony and documentary evidence before the Committee, it is not entirely certain that Dulles was ever made aware of the true nature of the underworld operation. The plot continued into McCone's term, apparently without McCone's or the Administration's knowledge or approval.

On some occasions when Richard Bissell had the opportunity to inform his superiors about the assassination effort against Castro, he either failed to inform them, failed to do so clearly, or misled them.

Bissell testified that he and Edwards told Dulles and Cabell about the assassination operation using underworld figures, but that they did so "circumlocutiously", and then only after contact had been made with the underworld and a price had been offered for Castro's death.

Perhaps Bissell should have checked back with Dulles at an earlier stage after having received approval to give "thorough consideration" to Castro's "elimination" from Dulles in December 1959.

Bissell further testified that he never raised the issue of assassination with non-CIA officials of either the Eisenhower or Kennedy Administration. His reason was that since he was under Dulles in the chain of command, he would normally have had no duty to discuss the matter with these Presidents or other Administration officials, and that he assumed that Dulles would have "circumlocutiously" spoken with Presidents Eisenhower and Kennedy about the operation. These reasons are insufficient. It was inexcusable to withhold such information from those responsible for formulating policy on the unverified assumption that they might have been "circumlocutiously" informed by Dulles.[1]

The failure either to inform those officials or to make certain that they had been informed by Dulles was particularly reprehensible in light of the fact that there were many occasions on which Bissell should have informed them, and his failure to do so was misleading. In the first weeks of the Kennedy Administration, Bissell met with Bundy and discussed the development of an assassination capability within CIA—Executive Action. But Bissell did not mention that an actual assassination attempt was underway. Bissell appeared before the Taylor-Kennedy Board of Inquiry which was formed to report to the President on the Bay of Pigs and the Cuban situation, but he testified that he did not inform the Board of the assassination operation.[2] As chief of the CIA directorate concerned with clandestine operations and the Bay of Pigs, Bissell frequently met with officials in the Eisenhower and Kennedy Administrations to discuss Cuban operations, and his advice was frequently sought. He did not tell them that the CIA had undertaken an effort to assassinate Castro, and did

---

[1] Even assuming that Bissell correctly perceived that Dulles understood the nature of the operation, it was also inexcusable for Bissell not to have briefed Dulles in plain language. Further, even if one accepts Bissell's assumption that Dulles told the Presidents, they would have been told too late, because Bissell "guessed" they would have been told that the operation "had been planned and was being attempted."

[2] Dulles was also a member of the Board.

not ask if they favored proceeding with the effort. He was present at the meeting with Dulles and President Kennedy at which the new President was briefed on covert action in Cuba, but neither Dulles nor Bissell mentioned the assassination operation that was underway. Dulles himself may not have always been candid. On December 11, 1959, he approved the CIA's giving "thorough consideration to the elimination of Fidel Castro," but told the Special Group in a meeting the following month that "we do not have in mind the quick elimination of Castro, but rather actions designed to enable responsible opposition leaders to get a foothold."

The failures to make forthright disclosures to policy-makers continued during the time that Richard Helms was DDP. Helms' failure to inform McCone about the underworld operation (when it was reactivated under Harvey and poison pills were sent to Cuba) was a grave error in judgment, and Helms' excuses are unpersuasive. In May 1962 the Attorney General was told that the CIA's involvement in an assassination plot had terminated with the Bay of Pigs. Not only did Edwards, who had briefed the Attorney General, know that the operation had not been terminated, but Helms did not inform the Attorney General that the operation was still active when he learned that the Attorney General had been misled. Helms did not inform McCone of the plot until August 1963, and did so then in a manner which indicated that the plot had been terminated before McCone became Director. Helms' denial that AM/LASH had been involved in an assassination effort in response to Secretary of State Rusk's inquiries was, as Helms conceded, not factual.

When Helms briefed President Johnson on the Castro plots, he apparently described the activities that had occurred during prior administrations but did not describe the AM/LASH operation which had continued until 1965. Helms also failed to inform the Warren Commission of the plots because the precise question was not asked.[1]

Helms told the Committee that he had never raised the assassination operation with McCone or other Kennedy Administration officials because of the sensitivity of the matter, because he had assumed that the project had been previously authorized, and because the aggressive character of the Kennedy Administration's program against the Castro regime led him to believe that assassination was permissible, even though he did not receive an express instruction to that effect. He added that he had never been convinced that the operation would succeed, and that he would have told McCone about it if he had ever believed that it would "go anyplace."

Helms' reasons for not having told his superiors about the assassination effort are unacceptable; indeed, many of them were reasons why he should have specifically raised the matter with higher authority. As Helms himself testified, assassination was of a high order of sensitivity. Administration policymakers, supported by intelligence estimates furnished by the Agency, had emphasized on several occasions that successors to Castro might be worse than Castro himself. In addition, the Special Group (Augmented) required that plans for covert actions against Cuba be submitted in detail for its approval. Although the Administration was exerting intense pressure on the CIA to do something about Castro and the Castro regime, it was a serious error

---

[1] John McCone was Director of the CIA and at least knew about the pre-Bay of Pigs plot during the Warren Commission's inquiry. McCone failed to disclose the plot to the Commission. Allen Dulles was on the Warren Commission. He did not inform the other members about the plots that had occurred during his term as DCI.

to have undertaken so drastic an operation without making certain that there was full and unequivocal permission to proceed.

William Harvey, the officer in charge of the CIA's attempt using underworld figures to assassinate Castro, testified that he never discussed the plot with McCone or officials of the Kennedy Administration because he believed that it had been fully authorized by the previous Director, because he was uncertain whether it had a chance of succeeding, and because he believed that it was not his duty to inform higher authorities.

Nonetheless, the Committee believes there were occasions on which it was incumbent on Harvey to have disclosed the assassination operation. As head of Task Force W, the branch of the CIA responsible for covert operations in Cuba, Harvey reported directly to General Lansdale and the Special Group (Augmented). The Special Group (Augmented) had made it known that covert operations in Cuba should be first approved by it, both by explicit instruction and by its practice that particular operations be submitted in "nauseating detail". Yet Harvey did not inform either General Lansdale or the Special Group (Augmented) of the assassination operation, either when he was explicitly requested to report to McCone, General Taylor, and the Special Group on his activities in Miami in April 1962, or when the subject of assassination was raised in the August 1962 meeting and McCone voiced his disapproval. Harvey testified that a matter as sensitive as assassination would never be raised in a gathering as large as the Special Group (Augmented).

The Committee finds the reasons advanced for not having informed those responsible for formulating policy about the assassination operation inadequate, misleading, and inconsistent. Some officials viewed assassination as too important and sensitive to discuss with superiors, while others considered it not sufficiently important. Harvey testified that it was premature to tell McCone about the underworld operation in April 1962, because it was not sufficiently advanced; but too late to tell him about it in August 1962, since by that time Harvey had decided to terminate it. On other occasions, officials thought disclosure was someone else's responsibility; Bissell said he thought it was up to Dulles, and Harvey believed it was up to Helms.

The Committee concludes that the failure to clearly inform policymakers of the assassination effort against Castro was grossly improper. The Committee believes that it should be incumbent on the DDP to report such a sensitive operation to his superior, the DCI, no matter how grave his doubts might be about the possible outcome of the operation. It follows that the DCI has the same duty to accurately inform his superiors.

(ii) Trujillo

In the Trujillo case there were several instances in which it appears that policymakers were not given sufficient information, or were not informed in a timely fashion.

At a meeting on December 29, 1960, Bissell presented a plan to the Special Group for supporting Dominican exile groups and local dissidents, and stated that the plan would not bring down the regime without "some decisive stroke against Trujillo himself." At a meeting on January 12, 1961, the Special Group authorized the passage of "limited supplies of small arms and other materials" to Dominican dissidents under certain conditions.

At this time, the fact that the dissidents had been contemplating the assassination of Trujillo had been known in the State Department at least through the level of the Assistant Secretary of State for Inter-American Affairs, and by senior officials of the CIA, including the DCI. Yet the internal State Department memorandum which was furnished to Undersecretary Livingston Merchant, and which was said to have been the basis for the Special Group's agreeing to the limited supply of small arms and other material (i.e., explosive devices), did not mention assassination. Instead, it spoke of "sabotage potential" and stated that there "would be no thought of toppling the [government] by any such minor measure [as the supplying of small arms and explosives]."

At a meeting of the Special Group on February 14, 1961, representatives of the CIA briefed the new members of the Group on outstanding CIA projects. The Dominican Republic was one of the briefing topics. The minutes of that meeting indicate that Mr. Bundy requested a memorandum for "higher authority" on the subject of what plans could be made for a successor government to Trujillo. Bissell had no clear recollection as to the details of the February 14 briefing and was unable to recall whether or not the method of overthrow to be attempted by the dissidents was discussed. It is not known, therefore, whether the new members of the Special Group learned, at that time, of Bissell's assessment that overthrow of the regime required a decisive stroke against Trujillo himself. Robert McNamara recalled no mention at that meeting of any dissident plans to assassinate Trujillo.

On February 15 and 17, 1961, memoranda were prepared for the President by Secretary of State Rusk and by Richard Bissell respectively. Although both the Department of State and the CIA then had information concerning the dissidents' intent to assassinate Trujillo if possible, neither memorandum referred to such a contingency. Rusk disclaimed any knowledge of the dissidents intent to assassinate Trujillo until shortly before the event occurred, but Bissell admitted personal awareness of the assassination plans.

Bissell's February 17 memorandum indicated that dissident leaders had informed the CIA of "their plan of action which they felt could be implemented if they were provided with arms for 300 men, explosives, and remote control detonation devices." Various witnesses testified that supplying arms for 300 men would, standing alone, indicate a "non-targeted" use for the arms. One possible method of assassinating Trujillo which had long been discussed by the dissidents and which was the favored approach at the time of Bissell's memorandum envisioned assassination by means of a bomb detonated by remote control. But the memorandum made no reference to the use to which the explosive devices might be put. (There is no record of any query from recipients of the briefing paper as to the nature of the dissidents' "plan of action" or the uses for which the arms and explosives were intended.)

The passage of the carbines was approved by CIA Headquarters on March 31, 1961. Although the State Department's representative in the Dominican Republic concurred in the decision to pass the carbines, he was requested by the CIA not to communicate this information to State Department officials in Washington, and he complied with that request. Accordingly, neither the State Department nor the White House was aware of the passage for several weeks. Similarly, there was no contemporaneous disclosure outside the CIA, other than to the State Department representative in the Dominican Republic, that machine guns had been sent to the Dominican Republic via the diplomatic pouch.

A memorandum prepared by Adolph Berle, the State Department official from whom the CIA sought permission to pass the machine guns, states that "on cross-examination it developed that the real plan was to assassinate Trujillo and they wanted guns for that purpose." (Berle, Memorandum of Conversation, 5/3/61) Berle's memorandum states that he informed the CIA officials that "we did not wish to have anything to do with any assassination plots anywhere, any time." The CIA official reportedly said he felt the same way, even though on the previous day he had been one of the signers of a draft CIA cable which would have permitted passage of the machine guns to the dissidents for "* * * their additional protection on their proposed endeavor." (Draft HQs to Station Cable, 5/2/61)

Although the report of a new anti-Trujillo plot was discussed at a meeting of the Special Group on May 4, 1961, there is no indication that Berle, who was the Chairman of the Inter-Agency Task Force having responsibility for contingency planning for Cuba, the Dominican Republic, and Haiti, disclosed to higher authority the assassination information which he discovered by "cross-examination." The National Security Council met the next day and noted the President's view that the United States should not initiate the overthrow of Trujillo before it was known what government would succeed him. That National Security Council Record of Action was approved by the President on May 16, 1961. There is no record indicating whether Berle communicated to the President, or to members of the National Security Council, his knowledge as to the lethal intent of the dissidents who would be carrying out the overthrow of Trujillo.

(iii) *Schneider*

The issue here is not whether the objectives of the CIA were contrary to those of the Administration. It is clear that President Nixon desired to prevent Allende from assuming office, even if that required fomenting and supporting a coup in Chile. Nor did White House officials suggest that tactics employed (including as a first step kidnapping General Schneider) would have been unacceptable as a matter of principle. Rather, the issue posed is whether White House officials were consulted, and thus given an opportunity to weigh such matters as risk and likelihood of success, and to apply policy-making judgments to particular tactics. The record indicates that up to October 15 they were; after October 15 there is some doubt.

The documentary record with respect to the disputed post-October 15 period gives rise to conflicting inferences. On the one hand, Karamessines' calendar shows at least one White House contact in the critical period prior to the kidnapping of General Schneider on October 22. However, the absence of any substantive memoranda in CIA files—when contrasted with several such memoranda describing contacts with the White House between September 15 and October 15—may suggest a lack of significant communication on the part of the CIA as well as a lack of careful supervision on the part of the White House.

The standards applied within the CIA itself suggest a view that action which the Committee believes called for top-level policy discussion and decision was thought of as permissible, without any further consultation, on the basis of the initial instruction to prevent Allende from assuming power. Machine guns were sent to Chile and delivered to military figures there on the authority of middle level CIA officers without consultation even with the CIA officer in charge of the program. We find no suggestion of bad faith in the action of the middle level officers, but their failure to consult necessarily establishes that there was no advance permission from outside the CIA for the passage of machine guns. And it also suggests an unduly lax attitude within the CIA toward consultation with superiors. Further, this case demonstrates the problems inherent in giving an agency a "blank check" to engage in covert operations without specifying which actions are permissible and which are not, and without adequately supervising and monitoring these activities.

(b) *Administration officials failed to rule out assassination as a tool of foreign policy, to make clear to their subordinates that assassination was impermissible or to inquire further after receiving indications that assassination was being considered*

While we do not find that high Administration officials expressly approved of the assassination attempts, we have noted that certain agency officials nevertheless perceived assassination to have been authorized. Although those officials were remiss in not seeking express authorization for their activities, their superiors were also at fault for giving vague instructions and for not explicitly ruling out assassination. No written order prohibiting assassination was issued until 1972, and that order was an internal CIA directive issued by Director Helms.

(i) *Trujillo*

Immediately following the assassination of Trujillo, there were a number of high-level meetings about the Dominican Republic attended by the policymakers of the Kennedy Administration. All relevant facts concerning CIA and State Department support of the Dominican dissidents were fully known. No directive was issued by the President or the Special Group criticizing any aspect of United States involvement in the Dominican affair. Similarly, there is no record of any action having been taken prohibiting future support or encouragement of groups or individuals known to be planning the assassination of a foreign leader. The meetings and discussions following the Trujillo assassination represent another missed opportunity to establish an administration policy against assassination and may partially account for the CIA's assessment of the Dominican operation as a success a few years later. They may also have encouraged Agency personnel, involved in both the Trujillo and the Castro plots, in their belief that the Administration would not be unhappy if the Agency were able to make Castro disappear. No such claim, however, was made in testimony by any agency official.

(ii) *Schneider*

As explained above, there is no evidence that assassination was ever proposed as a method of carrying out the Presidential order to prevent Allende from assuming office. The Committee believes, however, that the granting of *carte blanche* authority to the CIA by the Executive in this case may have contributed to the tragic and unintended death of General Schneider. This was also partially due to assigning an impractical task to be accomplished within an unreasonably short time. Apart from the question of whether any intervention in Chile was justified under the circumstances of this case, the Committee believes that the Executive in any event should have defined the limits of permissible action.

(iii) Lumumba

We are unable to make a finding that President Eisenhower intentionally authorized an assassination effort against Lumumba due to the lack of absolute certainty in the evidence. However, it appears that the strong language used in discussions at the Special Group and NSC, as reflected in minutes of relevant meetings, led Dulles to believe that assassination was desired. The minutes contain language concerning the need to "dispose of" Lumumba, an "extremely strong feeling about the necessity for straightforward action," and a refusal to rule out any activity that might contribute to "getting rid of" Lumumba.

(iv) Castro

The efforts to assassinate Fidel Castro took place in an atmosphere of extreme pressure by Eisenhower and Kennedy Administration officials to discredit and overthrow the Castro regime. Shortly after Castro's ascendancy to power, Allen Dulles directed that "thorough consideration" be given to the "elimination" of Castro. Richard Helms recalled that:

I remember vividly [that the pressure] was very intense. And therefore, when you go into the record, you find a lot of nutty schemes there and those nutty schemes were borne of the intensity of the pressure. And we were quite frustrated.

Bissell recalled that:

During that entire period, the Administration was extremely sensitive about the defeat that had been inflicted, as they felt, on the U.S. at the Bay of Pigs, and were pursuing every possible means of getting rid of Castro.

Another CIA official stated that sometime in the Fall of 1961 Bissell was:

* * * chewed out in the Cabinet Room in the White House by both the President and the Attorney General for, as he put it, sitting on his ass and not doing anything about getting rid of Castro and the Castro Regime.

General Lansdale informed the agencies cooperating in Operation MONGOOSE that "you're in a combat situation where we have been given full command." Secretary of Defense McNamara confirmed that "we were hysterical about Castro at the time of the Bay of Pigs and thereafter."

Many of the plans that were discussed and often approved contemplated violent action against Cuba. The operation which resulted in the Bay of Pigs was a major paramilitary onslaught that had the approval of the highest government officials, including the two Presidents. Thereafter, Attorney General Kennedy vehemently exhorted the Special Group (Augmented) that "a solution to the Cuban problem today carried top priority * * * no time, money, effort—or manpower is to be spared." [1] Subsequently, Operation MONGOOSE involved propaganda and sabotage operations aimed toward spurring a revolt of the Cuban people against Castro. Measures which were considered by the top policymakers included incapacitating sugar workers during harvest season by the use of chemicals; blowing up bridges and production plants; sabotaging merchandise in third countries—

---

[1] The Attorney General himself took a personal interest in the recruitment and development of assets within Cuba, on occasion recommending Cubans to the CIA as possible recruits and meeting in Washington and Florida with Cuban exiles active in the covert war against the Castro Government.

even those allied with the United States—prior to its delivery to Cuba; and arming insurgents on the island. Programs undertaken at the urging of the Administration included intensive efforts to recruit and arm dissidents within Cuba, and raids on plants, mines, and harbors. Consideration and approval of these measures may understandably have led the CIA to conclude that violent actions were an acceptable means of accomplishing important objectives.

Discussions at the Special Group and NSC meetings might well have contributed to the perception of some CIA officials that assassination was a permissible tool in the effort to overthrow the Castro Regime. At a Special Group meeting in November 1960, Undersecretary Merchant inquired whether any planning had been undertaken for "direct, positive action" against Che Guevara, Raul Castro, and Fidel Castro. Cabell replied that such a capability did not exist, but he might well have left the meeting with the impression that assassination was not out of bounds. Lansdale's plan, which was submitted to the Special Group in January 1962, aimed at inducing "open revolt and overthrow of the Communist regime." Included in its final phase an "attack on the cadre of the regime, including key leaders." The proposal stated that "this should be a 'Special Target' operation * * *. Gangster elements might provide the best recruitment potential against police * * *." Although Lansdale's proposal was shelved, the type of aggressive action contemplated was not formally ruled out. Minutes from several Special Group meetings contain language such as "possible removal of Castro from the Cuban scene."

On several occasions, the subject of assassination was discussed in the presence of senior Administration officials. Those officials never consented to actual assassination efforts, but they failed to indicate that assassination was impermissible as a matter of principle.

In early 1961, McGeorge Bundy was informed of a CIA project described as the development of a capability to assassinate. Bundy raised no objection and, according to Bissell, may have been more affirmative.[1] Bissell stated that he did not construe Bundy's remarks as authorization for the underworld plot against Castro that was then underway. But the fact that he believed that the development of an assassination capability had, as he subsequently told Harvey, been approved by the White House, may well have contributed to the general perception that assassination was not prohibited.[2]

Documents received by the Committee indicate that in May 1961, Attorney General Kennedy and the Director of the FBI received information that the CIA was engaged in clandestine efforts against Castro which included the use of Sam Giancana and other underworld figures. The various documents referred to "dirty business," "clandestine efforts," and "plans" which were still "working" and might eventually "pay off." The Committee is unable to determine whether Hoover and the Attorney General ever inquired into the nature of the CIA operation, although there is no evidence that they did so inquire. The Committee believes that they should have inquired, and that their failure to do so was a dereliction of their duties.

---

[1] The Inspector General's Report states that Harvey's notes (which no longer exist) quoted Bissell as saying to Harvey: "The White House has twice urged me to create such as capability."

[2] Bundy, as the National Security Advisor to the President, had an obligation to tell the President of such a grave matter, even though it was only a discussion of a capability to assassinate. His failure to do so was a serious error.

Documents indicate that in May 1962, Attorney General Kennedy was told that the CIA had sought to assassinate Castro prior to the Bay of Pigs. According to the CIA officials who were present at the briefing, the Attorney General indicated his displeasure about the lack of consultation rather than about the impropriety of the attempt itself. There is no evidence that the Attorney General told the CIA that it must not engage in assassination plots in the future.

At a meeting of the Special Group (Augmented) in August 1962, well after the assassination efforts were underway, Robert McNamara is said to have raised the question of whether the assassination of Cuban leaders should be explored, and General Lansdale issued an action memorandum assigning the CIA the task of preparing contingency plans for the assassination of Cuban leaders. While McCone testified that he had immediately made it clear that assassination was not to be discussed or condoned, Harvey's testimony and documents which he wrote after the event indicate that Harvey may have been confused over whether McCone had objected to the use of assassination, or whether he was only concerned that the subject not be put in writing. In any event, McCone went no further. He issued no general order banning consideration of assassination within the Agency.

One of the programs forwarded to General Lansdale by the Defense Department in the MONGOOSE program was entitled "Operation Bounty" and envisioned dropping leaflets in Cuba offering rewards for the assassination of Government leaders. Although the plan was vetoed by Lansdale, it indicates that persons in agencies other than the CIA perceived that assassination might be permissible.

While the ambivalence of Administration officials does not excuse the misleading conduct by Agency officials or justify their failure to seek explicit permission, this attitude displayed an insufficient concern about assassination which may have contributed to the perception that assassination was an acceptable tactic in accomplishing the Government's general objectives.

Moreover, with the exception of the tight guidelines issued by the Special Group (Augmented) concerning Operation MONGOOSE, precise limitations were never imposed on the CIA requiring prior permission for the details of other proposed covert operations against Cuba.

No general policy banning assassination was promulgated until Helms' intra-agency order in 1972. Considering the number of times the subject of assassination had arisen, Administration officials were remiss in not explicitly forbidding such activity.

The committee notes that many of the occasions on which CIA officials should have informed their superiors of the assassination efforts but failed to do so, or did so in a misleading manner, were also occasions on which Administration officials paradoxically may have reinforced the perception that assassination was permissible.

For example, when Bissell spoke with Bundy about an Executive Action capability, Bissell failed to indicate that an actual assassination operation was underway, but Bundy failed to rule out assassination as a tactic.

In May 1962, the Attorney General was misleadingly told about the effort to assassinate Castro prior to the Bay of Pigs, but not about the operation that was then going on. The Attorney General, however, did not state that assassination was improper.

When a senior administration official raised the question of whether assassination should be explored at a Special Group meeting, the assassination operation should have been revealed. A firm written order against engaging in assassination should also have been issued by McCone if, as he testified, he had exhibited strong aversion to assassination.

5. PRACTICES CURRENT AT THE TIME IN WHICH THE ASSASSINATION PLOTS OCCURRED WERE REVEALED BY THE RECORD TO CREATE THE RISK OF CONFUSION, RASHNESS AND IRRESPONSIBILITY IN THE VERY AREAS WHERE CLARITY AND SOBER JUDGMENT WERE MOST NECESSARY

Various witnesses described elements of the system within which the assassination plots were conceived. The Committee is disturbed by the custom that permitted the most sensitive matters to be presented to the highest levels of Government with the least clarity. We view the following points as particularly dangerous:

(1) The expansion of the doctrine of "plausible denial" beyond its intended purpose of hiding the involvement of the United States from other countries into an effort to shield higher officials from knowledge, and hence responsibility, for certain operations.

(2) The use of circumlocution or euphemism to describe serious matters—such as assassination—when precise meanings ought to be made clear.

(3) The theory that general approval of broad covert action programs is sufficient to justify specific actions such as assassination or the passage of weapons.

(4) The theory that authority granted, or assumed to be granted, by one DCI or one Administration could be presumed to continue without the necessity for reaffirming the authority with successor officials.

(5) The creation of covert capabilities without careful review and authorization by policymakers, and the further risk that such capabilities, once created, might be used without specific authorization.

(a) *The danger inherent in overextending the doctrine of "plausible denial"*

The original concept of "plausible denial" envisioned implementing covert actions in a manner calculated to conceal American involvement if the actions were exposed. The doctrine was at times a delusion and at times a snare. It was naive for policymakers to assume that sponsorship of actions as big as the Bay of Pigs invasion could be concealed. The Committee's investigation of assassination and the public disclosures which preceded the inquiry demonstrate that when the United States resorted to cloak-and-dagger tactics, its hand was ultimately exposed. We were particularly disturbed to find little evidence that the risks and consequences of disclosure were considered.

We find that the likelihood of reckless action is substantially increased when policymakers believe that their decisions will never be revealed. Whatever can be said in defense of the original purpose of plausible denial—a purpose which intends to conceal United States involvement from the outside world—the extension of the doctrine to the internal decision-making process of the Government is absurd. Any theory which, as a matter of doctrine, places elected officials on the periphery of the decision-making process is an invitation to error, an abdication of responsibility, and a perversion of democratic government. The doctrine is the antithesis of accountability.

(b) The danger of using "Circumlocution" and "Euphemism"

According to Richard Bissell, the extension of "plausible denial" to internal decision-making required the use of circumlocution and euphemism in speaking with Presidents and other senior officials.

Explaining this concept only heightens its absurdity. On the one hand, it assumes that senior officials should be shielded from the truth to enable them to deny knowledge if the truth comes out. On the other hand, the concept assumes that senior officials must be told enough, by way of double talk, to grasp the subject. As a consequence, the theory fails to accomplish its objective and only increases the risk of misunderstanding. Subordinate officials should describe their proposals in clear, precise, and brutally frank language; superiors are entitled to, and should demand, no less.

Euphemism may actually have been preferred—not because of "plausible denial"—but because the persons involved could not bring themselves to state in plain language what they intended to do. In some instances, moreover, subordinates may have assumed, rightly or wrongly, that the listening superiors did not want the issue squarely placed before them. "Assassinate," "murder" and "kill" are words many people do not want to speak or hear. They describe acts which should not even be proposed, let alone plotted. Failing to call dirty business by its rightful name may have increased the risk of dirty business being done.

(c) The danger of generalized instructions

Permitting specific acts to be taken on the basis of general approvals of broad strategies (e.g., keep Allende from assuming office, get rid of the Castro regime) blurs responsibility and accountability. Worse still, it increases the danger that subordinates may take steps which would have been disapproved if the policymakers had been informed. A further danger is that policymakers might intentionally use loose general instructions to evade responsibility for embarrassing activities.

In either event, we find that the gap between the general policy objectives and the specific actions undertaken to achieve them was far too wide.

It is important that policymakers review the manner in which their directives are implemented, particularly when the activities are sensitive, secret, and immune from public scrutiny.

(d) The danger of "Floating Authorization"

One justification advanced by Richard Helms and William Harvey for not informing John McCone about the use of underworld figures to attempt to assassinate Fidel Castro was their assertion that the project had already been approved by McCone's predecessor, Allen Dulles, and that further authorization was unnecessary, at least until the operation had reached a more advanced stage.

We find that the idea that authority might continue or "float" from one administration or director to the next and that there is no duty to reaffirm authority inhibits responsible decision-making. Circumstances may change or judgments differ. New officials should be given the opportunity to review significant programs.

(e) The problems connected with creating new covert capabilities

The development of a new capability raises numerous problems. Having a capability to engage in certain covert activity increases the probability that the activity will occur, since the capability represents a tool available for use. There is the further danger that authorization for the mere creation of a capability may be misunderstood as permitting its use without requiring further authorization.

Finally, an assassination capability should never have been created. ...

V. RECOMMENDATIONS

The Committee's long investigation of assassination has brought a number of important issues into sharp focus. Above all stands the question of whether assassination is an acceptable tool of American foreign policy. Recommendations on other issues must await the completion of our continuing investigation and the final report, but the Committee needs no more information to be convinced that a flat ban against assassination should be written into law.

N27

We condemn assassination and reject it as an instrument of American policy. Surprisingly, however, there is presently no statute making it a crime to assassinate a foreign official outside the United States. Hence, for the reasons set forth below, the Committee recommends the prompt enactment of a statute making it a Federal crime to commit or attempt an assassination, or to conspire to do so.

A. GENERAL AGREEMENT THAT THE UNITED STATES MUST NOT ENGAGE IN ASSASSINATION

Our view that assassination has no place in America's arsenal is shared by the Administration.

President Ford, in the same statement in which he asked this Committee to deal with the assassination issue, stated:

I am opposed to political assassination. This administration has not and will not use such means as instruments of national policy. (Presidential Press Conference, 6/9/75, *Weekly Compilation of Presidential Documents*, Vol. II, No. 24, p. 611.)

The witnesses who testified before the Committee uniformly condemned assassination. They denounced it as immoral, described it as impractical, and reminded us that an open society, more than any other, is particularly vulnerable to the risk that its own leaders may be assassinated. As President Kennedy reportedly said: "We can't get into that kind of thing, or we would all be targets." (Goodwin, 7/18/75, p. 4)

The current Director of Central Intelligence and his two predecessors testified emphatically that assassination should be banned. William Colby said:

With respect to assassination, my position is clear, I just think it is wrong. And I have said so and made it very clear to my subordinates. (Colby, * * * 5/21/75, p. 89)

Richard Helms, who had been involved in an assassination plot before he became DCI, said he had concluded assassination should be ruled out for both moral and practical reasons:

As a result of my experiences through the years, when I became Director I had made up my mind that this option * * * of killing foreign leaders, was something that I did not want to happen on my watch. My reasons for this were these:

There are not only moral reasons but there are also some other rather practical reasons.

It is almost impossible in a democracy to keep anything like that secret * * *. Somebody would go to a Congressman, his Senator, he might go to a newspaper man, whatever the case may be, but it just is not a practical alternative, it seems to me, in our society.

Then there is another consideration * * * if you are going to try by this kind of means to remove a foreign leader, then who is going to take his place running that country, and are you essentially better off as a matter of practice when it is over than you were before? And I can give you I think a very solid example of this which happened in Vietnam when President Diem was eliminated from the scene. We then had a revolving door of prime ministers after that for quite some period of time, during which the Vietnamese Government at a time in its history when it should have been strong was nothing but a caretaker government * * *. In other words, that whole exercise turned out to the disadvantage of the United States.

* * * there is no sense in my sitting here with all the experience I have had and not sharing with the Committee my feelings this day. It isn't because I have lost my cool, or because I have lost my guts, it simply is because I don't think it is a viable option in the United States of America these days.

Chairman CHURCH. Doesn't it also follow, Mr. Helms—I agree with what you have said fully—but doesn't it also follow on the practical side, apart from the moral side, that since these secrets are bound to come out, when they do, they do very grave political damage to the United States in the world at large? I don't know to what extent the Russians involved themselves in political assassinations, but under their system they at least have a better prospect of keeping it concealed. Since we do like a free society and since these secrets are going to come out in due course, the revelation will then do serious injury to the good name and reputation of the United States.

Would you agree with that?

Mr. HELMS. Yes, I would.

Chairman CHURCH. And finally, if we were to reserve to ourselves the prerogative to assassinate foreign leaders, we may invite reciprocal action from foreign governments who assume that if it's our prerogative to do so, it is their prerogative as well, and that is another danger that we at least invite with this kind of action, wouldn't you agree?

Mr. HELMS: Yes, sir. (Helms, 6/13/75, pp. 76–78)

John McCone said he was opposed to assassinations because:

I didn't think it was proper from the standpoint of the U.S. Government and the Central Intelligence Agency. (McCone, 6/6/75. p. 15)

B. CIA DIRECTIVES BANNING ASSASSINATION

Helms in 1972 and Colby in 1973 issued internal CIA orders banning assassination. Helms' order said:

It has recently again been alleged in the press that CIA engages in assassination. As you are well aware, this is not the case, and Agency policy has long been clear on this issue. To underline it, however, I direct that no such activity or operation be undertaken, assisted or suggested by any of our personnel * * *. (Memo, Helms to Deputy Directors, 3/6/72)

In one of a series of orders arising out the CIA's own review of prior "questionable activity," Colby stated:

CIA will not engage in assassination nor induce, assist or suggest to others that assasination be employed. (Memo, Colby to Deputy Directors, 8/29/73)

C. THE NEED FOR A STATUTE

Commendable and welcome as they are, these CIA directives are not sufficient. Administrations change, CIA directors change, and someday in the future what was tried in the past may once again become a temptation. Assassination plots did happen. It would be irresponsible not to do all that can be done to prevent their happening again. A law is needed. Laws express our nation's values; they deter those who might be tempted to ignore those values and stiffen the will of those who want to resist the temptation.

The Committee recommends a statute which would make it a criminal offense for persons subject to the jurisdiction of the United States (1) to conspire, within or outside the United States, to assassinate a foreign official; (2) to attempt to assassinate a foreign official, or (3) to assassinate a foreign official.

N28

Present law makes it a crime to kill, or to conspire to kill, a foreign official or foreign official guest while such a person is in the United States. (18 U.S.C. 1116–1117). However, there is no law which makes it a crime to assassinate, to conspire to assassinate, or to attempt to assassinate a foreign official while such official is outside the United States. The Committee's proposed statute is designed to close this gap in the law.

Subsection (a) of the proposed statute would punish conspiracies within the United States; subsection (b) would punish conspiracies outside the United States. Subsection (b) is necessary to eliminate the loophole which would otherwise permit persons to simply leave the United States and conspire abroad. Subsections (c) and (d), respectively, would make it an offense to attempt to kill or to kill a foreign official outside the United States.

Subsections (a), (b), (c), and (d) would apply expressly to any "officer or employee of the United States" to make clear that the statute punishes conduct by United States Government personnel, as well as conduct by private citizens. In addition, subsection (a), which covers conspiracies within the United States, would apply to "any other person," regardless of citizenship. Non-citizens who conspired within the United States to assassinate a foreign official would clearly come within the jurisdiction of the law. Subsections (b), (c), and (d), which deal with conduct abroad, would apply to United States citizens, and to officers or employees of the United States, regardless of their citizenship. Criminal liability for acts committed abroad by persons who are not American citizens or who are not officers or employees of the United States is beyond the jurisdiction of the United States.

"Foreign official" is defined in subsection (e)(2) to make clear that an offense may be committed even though the "official" belongs to an insurgent force, an unrecognized government, or a political party. The Committee's investigation—as well as the reality of international politics—has shown that officials in such organizations are potential targets for assassination.[2] Killing, attempting to kill, or conspiring to kill would be punishable under the statute only if it were politically

---

[2] For example. Lumumba was not an official of the Congolese government at the time of the plots against his life, and Trujillo, even though the dictator of the Dominican Republic, held no official governmental position in the latter period of his regime.

motivated. Political motivation would encompass acts against foreign officials because of their political views, actions, or statements.

The definition of "foreign official" in section (e)(2) also provides that such person must be an official of a foreign government or movement "with which the United States is not at war pursuant to a declaration of war or against which the United States Armed Forces have not been introduced into hostilities or situations pursuant to the provisions of the War Powers Resolution." This definition makes it clear that, absent a declaration of war or the introduction of United States Armed Forces pursuant to the War Powers Resolution, the killing of foreign officials on account of their political views would be a criminal offense.

During the Committee's hearings, some witnesses, while strongly condemning assassination, asked whether assassination should absolutely be ruled out in a time of truly unusual national emergency. Adolf Hitler was cited as an example. Of course, the cases which the Committee investigated were not of that character. Indeed, in the Cuban missile crisis—the only situation of true national danger considered in this report—assassination was not even considered and, if used, might well have aggravated the crisis.

In a grave emergency, the President has a limited power to act, not in violation of the law, but in accord with his own responsibilities under the Constitution to defend the Nation. As the Supreme Court has stated, the Constitution "is not a suicide pact." (*Kennedy* v. *Mendoza-Martinez, 372* U.S. 144, 160 (1963))

During an unprecedented emergency, Abraham Lincoln claimed unprecedented power based on the need to preserve the nation:

> * * * my oath to preserve the Constitution to the best of my ability, imposed upon me the duty of preserving, by every indispensable means, that government—that nation—of which that Constitution was the organic law. Was it possible to lose the nation, and yet preserve the Constitution? By general law, life and limb must be protected; yet often a limb must be amputated to save a life; but a life is never wisely given to save a limb. I felt that measures, otherwise unconstitutional, might become lawful, by becoming indispensable to the preservation of the Constitution, through the preservation of the nation * * *. (*The Complete Works of Abraham Lincoln*, Vol. X, pp. 65–66.) (Nicolay and Hay, Eds. 1894.)

Whatever the extent of the President's own constitutional powers, it is a fundamental principle of our constitutional system that those powers are checked and limited by Congress, including the impeachment power. As a necessary corollary, any action taken by a President pursuant to his limited inherent powers and in apparent conflict with the law must be disclosed to Congress. Only then can Congress judge whether the action truly represented, in Lincoln's phrase, an "indispensable necessity" to the life of the Nation.

As Lincoln explained in submitting his extraordinary actions to Congress for ratification:

> In full view of his great responsibility he has, so far, done what he has deemed his duty. You will now, according to your own judgment, perform yours. (Abraham Lincoln, Message to Congress in Special Session, July 4, 1861.)

CHRONOLOGY OF MAJOR EVENTS CONCERNING ASSASSINATION PLOTS ([43], pp. 291–295)

The following capsule summary sets forth in chronological sequence major events covered in this Report. The purpose of the chronology is to remind the reader that the assassination plots and related events, which are organized in the Report around attempts against various leaders, often occurred during the same time frame, and can only be fully understood by considering the entire picture.

This chronology necessarily abbreviates and characterizes events, and does not indicate when certain things should have happened but did not. It is not a substitute for the full discussion of the events which appears in the body of the Report at the pages indicated in brackets. The Committee's interpretation of what occurred is fully set forth in the Findings and Conclusion of this Report.

1959

December 11—Dulles approves "thorough consideration be given to the elimination of Fidel Castro." (p. 92)

N29

1960

January 13—Special Group meeting considers Castro's overthrow. (p. 92)

Spring 1960—Meetings on covert action against Cuba at levels of CIA, Special Group, and NSC. (p. 93)

Sometime in Spring 1960—Ambassador Farland establishes links with Dominican Republic dissidents. (p. 193)

April 1960—President Eisenhower approves contingency plan for Dominican Republic—if situation deteriorates, U.S. to take action to remove Trujillo when successor regime lined up. (p. 192)

Late Spring-Early Summer—Bissell discusses assassination capabilities with Scheider. (pp. 20–21)

June 30—Congolese independence declared. Lumumba is Premier. Kasavubu is President.

July 1—CIA memo recommending delivery of sniper rifles to Dominican dissidents approved. (p. 194)

July 11—Tshombe declares Katanga independent.

July 13—UN Security Council calls for Belgian troop withdrawal from Congo and sends UN peacekeeping force.

July 14—Kasavubu and Lumumba suggest Soviet aid may be requested.

July 27—Lumumba visits Washington and receives aid pledge from Secretary Herter.

Event involving CIA request that a Cuban arrange an "accident" involving Raul Castro. (pp. 72, 93)

August 1960—U.S. interrupts diplomatic relations with Dominican Republic.

August 1960—Bissell and Edwards have discussion concerning use of underworld figures to aid in assassination of Castro. (p. 74)

August 18–26—NSC and Special Group discusses action against Lumumba and Dulles cables Congo station that Lumumba's "removal must be an urgent and prime objective . . ." (p. 52)

Early September—Scheider is ordered by Bissell to make preparations for assassination of an African leader. (p. 21)

Late September—Bissell and Edwards brief Dulles and Cabell about operation against Castro. (p. 194)

Late September—Initial meeting between Rosselli, Maheu, and CIA support chief. A subsequent meeting takes place in Florida. (p. 76)

September 5—Kasavubu dismisses Lumumba; power struggle ensues.

September 14—Mobutu, Chief of Staff of Congolese Army, takes over government by coup.

September 15—Lumumba seeks protective custody of UN guard.

September 16–20—CIA cables indicate Lumumba is seen as a continued threat while in custody—as capable of mounting a counterattack or appealing to the public. (p. 18)

September 17–19—Tweedy and Tweedy's Deputy tell Scheider to go to Congo to deliver poisons to Hedgman and instruct him to assassinate Lumumba if possible. (p. 21)

September 19—Tweedy cables Hedgman that Scheider will come to Congo on sensitive mission. (p. 22)

September 21—NSC meeting in which it is noted that Lumumba, although deposed, remains a threat. (p. 62)

September 26—Scheider goes to Congo. (p. 24)

October 3—CIA memo sets forth plans to support Dominican dissidents.

October 5—Scheider leaves Congo. (p. 24)

October 18—Memo from Hoover to intelligence agencies detailing Giancana's statements about an imminent Castro assassination but not mentioning CIA. (p. 79)

October 31—Bissell asks Mulroney to go to Congo. (p. 37)

Las Vegas wiretap discovered. (p. 77)

November 3—Special Group discusses covert action against Castro regime. (p. 98)

November 3—Mulroney arrives in Congo. (p. 40)

Sometime after November 8—Dulles and Bissell jointly brief President-elect Kennedy on details of planned invasion of Cuba. (p. 196)

December 1—Mobutu's troops capture Lumumba.

December 3—Lumumba imprisoned at Thysville.

December 29—Special Group approves plan of covert assistance to internal and external Dominican dissidents. (p. 196)

1961

January 12—Special Group meeting approved "limited supply of small arms and other material" to Dominican dissidents. (p. 196)

January 17—Lumumba transferred by Congolese government to Elizabethville where he is killed at hands of Katanga authorities.

January 22—President Kennedy succeeds President Eisenhower.

Sometime between January 22 and April 15 (sequence unknown)—Bissell and Bundy have discussion concerning an "executive action" capability. (p. 181)

President raises with Smathers subject of assassination, indicating his disapproval. (p. 123)

Rosselli passes pills to a Cuban in Miami. (p. 80)

January 25–26—Harvey discusses Executive action with CIA subordinates. (p. 183)

February 10 and February 15—Meeting in New York City between Dominican dissidents and CIA officials. (p. 198)

February 13—Lumumba's death announced by Katanga Interior Minister Munungo.

February 14—Special Group meeting at which new members are briefed by Dulles and Bissell on "specific actions taken by the predecessor group during the past year. (p. 202)

February 15—Rusk memo to President on Dominican Republic. (p. 203)

February 17—Bissell memo to Bundy speaks of Dominican dissident "plan of action". (p. 204)

March 13—Requests for arms and explosives made by Dominican dissidents to CIA and passed on to Washington. (p. 198)

March 15—Request by Station to Headquarters for three pistols for Dominican dissidents. (p. 199)

March 20—Station raises with Headquarters the Dominican dissident request for machine guns. (p. 201)

March 24—Cable advises pistols are being pouched for the Dominican dissidents. (p. 200)

March 31—Headquarters approves passing of carbines to Dominican Republic. (p. 100)

April 7—Carbines passed to "action group" and eventually to one of the assassins. (p. 200)

April 10—Bissell approves shipping machine guns to Dominican Republic by pouch. (p. 202)

April 15–17—Bay of Pigs invasion fails.

April 17—CIA order not to pass machine guns to Dominican dissidents without Headquarters approval. (p. 205)

April 18—Maheu tells FBI of CIA involvement in Las Vegas wiretap. (p. 126)

April 19–20—The Cuban involved in the underworld assassination plot and the Bay of Pigs invasion attends meeting at which the President, other Cubans, and high Administration officials not witting of the plot are present. (p. 124)

April 20—Headquarters advises Station not to pass machine guns to Dominican dissidents. (p. 206)

April 22–June 19—Taylor/Kennedy Board of Inquiry into Bay of Pigs invasion. (pp. 121, 135)

April 25—Cable advises Headquarters of imminent assassination attempt against Trujillo and possible use of U.S.-supplied weapons. (p. 206)

April 26—Headquarters orders Dominican Republic Station that there is no authority to pass additional arms and tells Station to advise dissidents that U.S. not prepared to cope with aftermath of assassination. (p. 206)

May 3—Berle determines Dominican dissidents seek machine guns to assassinate Trujillo and speaks against involvement in such an effort. (p. 207)

May 4—Special Group meeting at which DCI reports new anti-Trujillo plot. (p. 208)

May 5—NSC notes President's view that the U.S. should not initiate the over-throw of Trujillo until it knows what government will succeed him. (p. 209)

May 16—President approves Record of Actions of May 5, 1961, NSC meeting. (p. 209)

May 16—State Department is told that assassination attempt against Trujillo is imminent. (p. 208)

May 18—Special Group stands by decision not to pass machine guns being sought by Dominican dissidents. (p. 126)

May 22—Hoover memo to Attorney General Kennedy noting CIA had used Giancana in "clandestine efforts" against Castro. (p. 126)

May 29—President advises State Department official in Dominican Republic that U.S. "must not run risk of U.S. association with political assassination, since U.S. as a matter of general policy cannot condone assassination". This principle is "overriding" and "must prevail in doubtful situation." (p. 213)

May 30—Trujillo ambushed and assassinated near San Cristobal. Dominician Republic.

June 1 and period shortly thereafter—State Department and CIA review of actions taken in dealing with dissidents in Dominican Republic. (p. 214)

October 5—National Security Action Memorandum 100 directs assessment of potential courses of action if Castro were removed from the Cuban scene. CIA makes intelligence estimate. (p. 136)

November 9—President tells Tad Szulc that he is under pressure from advisors to order Castro's assassination, but does not name advisors. (p. 138)

November 15—Bissell asks Harvey to assume control of underworld operation on stand-by basis. (p. 83)

November 16—President Kennedy gives speech mentioning opposition to assassination. (p. 139)

November 29—John McCone succeeds Allen Dulles as Director, CIA.

November 1961—Operation MONGOOSE created. (p. 139)

1962

January 18—Lansdale assigns 32 planning tasks against Castro regime. (p. 142)

January 19—MONGOOSE meeting at which Attorney General says solution to Cuban problem today carries top priority. (p. 141)

January 29—CIA objects to prosecution of Maheu for Las Vegas wiretap. (p. 129)

February 19—Richard Helms succeeds Richard Bissell as Deputy Director, Plans, CIA.

Early April—Harvey establishes contact with Rosselli. (p. 83)

Late April—Harvey passes poison pills to Rosselli in Miami. (p. 84)

May 7—Houston and Edwards brief Attorney General on pre-Bay of Pigs underworld assassination plot. Thereafter decision made not to prosecute. (p. 131)

August 8—Special Group (Augmented) adopts a stepped-up plan designed to inspire internal revolt in Cuba. (p. 147)

August 10—The subject of assassination is raised at a meeting of the Special Group (Augmented). (p. 161)

September 7—Rosselli tells Harvey the pills are still in Cuba. (p. 84)

October 4—Attorney General advises Special Group (Augmented) that President wants more priority given to operations against Castro regime. (p. 147)

October 22–28—Cuban Missile Crisis.

November—Operation MONGOOSE ends.

Early 1963—CIA Technical Services Division explores exploding seashell and contaminated diving suit schemes. (p. 85)

April 1963—Special Group discusses the contingency of Castro's death. (p. 170)

May 8—South Vietnamese troops in Hue fire on Buddhists, triggering nation-wide Buddhist protest. (p. 217)

May 18—U.S. Ambassador Nolting meets with Diem to outline steps to redress Buddist grievances. (p. 217)

June 19—Special Group authorizes sabotage program against Cuba. (p. 173)

July 4—Vietnamese General Minh, Don, Kim, and Khiem agree on necessity of coup. (p. 218)

August 16—McCone is given memorandum detailing pre-Bay of Pigs assassination plot against Castro. (p. 107)

August 24—DEPTEL 243 is sent to Ambassador Lodge in Saigon telling him to press for dramatic actions to redress Buddhist grievances, including removal of Nhu and his wife. (p. 218)

August 26—CIA officers advise Vietnamese Generals Khiem and Khanh of DEPTEL 243. (p. 219)

August 29—A White House message authorizes Saigon to confirm that U.S. will support a coup if it appears it will succeed. (p. 219)

August 31—Attempted generals' coup in South Vietnam fails. (p. 220)

Fall 1963—Atwood explores possible accommodation with Castro. (p. 173)

October 2—McNamara and Taylor return from fact-finding mission in Vietnam and report that, although the war is progressing favorably, there is political turmoil. (p. 220)

October 3—General Minh outlines to Saigon Station a course of action which includes assassinating Diem's brothers, Nhu and Can. (p. 220)

October 5–6—CIA Headquarters directs Saigon that Minh's course of action not acceptable. (p. 221)

November 2—Diem is assassinated following a coup. (p. 223)

November 22—President Kennedy assassinated.

Vice President Johnson becomes President.

AM/LASH given poison pen device for assassinating Castro. (pp. 89, 175)

1964

March–May—Caches of arms delivered to AM/LASH in Cuba. (pp. 89, 175)

April 7—Special Group discontinues CIA-controlled sabotage raids against Cuba. (p. 177)

1965

Early 1965—AM/LASH put in contact with leader of anti-Castro group and receives weapon with silencer from him. (p. 89)

1966

1966—Helms reports to Rusk that CIA not involved with AM/LASH in Castro assassination plot. (p. 178)

1967

May 1967—Helms briefs President on 1967 Inspector General's Report. (p. 179)

1968

January 20—President Johnson leaves office, President Nixon inaugurated.

1970

September 4—Dr. Allende wins a plurality in Chile's Presidential election. (p. 225)

September 8 and 14—40 Committee discusses Chilean situation. Question of U.S. involvement in a military coup against Allende raised. (p. 229)

September 15—President Nixon instructs CIA Director Helms to prevent Allende's accession to office. The CIA is to play a direct role in organizing a military coup d'etat. This involvement comes to be known as Track II. (p. 227)

September 28—U.S. Military Attache in Santiago instructed to assist CIA in promoting coup. (p. 235)

October 5—CIA makes first contact with Chilean military conspirators. (p. 240)

October 13—CIA Station informs Headquarters that retired General Viaux intends to kidnap General Schneider to precipitate a coup. Viaux's plan is reported to Headquarters as part of a coup plot that includes General Valenzuela. (p. 242)

October 15—Karamessines meets with Kissinger and Haig at the White House. A decision is made to defuse the Viaux coup plot, at least temporarily. (pp. 242, 250)

October 16—Headquarters informs CIA Station of Viaux decision and instructs it to continue to generate maximum pressure to overthrow Allende by coup. (p. 243)

October 17—CIA informs Viaux associate of decision. Agent told that Viaux would proceed with coup in any case and that the abduction of Schneider is first link in chain of events. (p. 243)

U.S. Military Attache meets with Chilean Army officer and Navy officer. They request tear gas, grenades, and three sterile submachine guns, with ammunition. (p. 243)

October 18—General Valenzuela informs U.S. Military Attache that he and senior military officers prepared to sponsor a coup. (p. 244)

October 18—Tear gas grenades delivered to Chilean Army officer and Navy Captain. (p. 244)

October 19—Weapons sent from CIA Headquarters by diplomatic pouch to Santiago. (p. 244)

First Schneider abduction attempt fails. (p. 244)

October 20—Second Schneider abduction attempt fails. (p. 244)

October 22—Three submachine guns delivered to Chilean Army officer by U.S. Military Attache. (p. 245)

General Schneider is shot in kidnap attempt. (p. 245)

October 24—Dr. Allende confirmed by Chilean Congress. (p. 246)

October 25—General Schneider dies. (p. 246)

1972

Helms issues directive against assassination.

1973

Colby issues directive against assassination.

NOTES AND REFERENCES

1. The 40 Committee, chaired by assistant to the president for National Security Affairs, was previously known as the 303 Committee and the 54/12 Group; its existence was considered classified information until the early 1970s. This committee is currently known as the Operations Advisory Group and is charged with evaluating recommended covert action for presidential approval ([104], Congressional Research Service, p. 8).

2. Roger Hilsman, *To Move a Nation* (New York: Doubleday, 1967).

3. "Cover" refers to the use of a false identity to hide (cover) an intelligence agent's true activities. It can range from the extreme cases associated with spy novels—where the agent's name and even physical identity are changed—to the more common use of diplomatic or consular titles to cover the identity of a CIA official. Former CIA agent Philip Agee's cover when he operated out of the U.S. embassy in Mexico during the mid-1960s was "olympics attache." David Phillips, head of the Association of Retired Intelligence Officers, once used "nonofficial cover" in South America, where he published an English-language newspaper.

4. Harry Howe Ransom, *The Intelligence Establishment* (Cambridge, Mass.: Harvard University Press, 1970).

5. Background on early U.S. covert activities is found in [45A], pp. 48 ff.

6. A discussion of covert action in Chile is detailed later in this chapter.

7. The NSC is reviewed in Chapter 2.

8. Additional data on covert action in Cuba appears in [43], pp. 139 ff.

9. For treatment of the statutory authority for CIA activities and congressional authorization of covert action, see [45A], pp. 127–139.

10. Summaries of the Church Committee's recommendations regarding covert action are contained in [45A], Appendix II.

11. The subject of congressional oversight is addressed in Chapter 10.

12. The future of covert action is commented upon in significant dialogues of the Church Committee hearings ([44G], pp. 49–79).

13. The National Security Act of 1947 and the CIA Act of 1949 are reprinted in the Appendix.

14. The National Security Act was established in 1947, not in 1974.

15. For reprinted copies of congressional documents bearing on the CIA's legislative history, see Library of Congress, Congressional Research Service, "Legislative History of the CIA as Documented in Published Congressional Sources," January 8, 1975.

16. Chapter 10 addresses the issue of congressional budgetary oversight.

17. Chapter 4 includes information on the budget of the intelligence community.

18. Details of the techniques and effects of covert action in Chile are found in [44G], pp. 150–197. Overall U.S.-Chile relations during the Allende years are reviewed in [61].

19. Details on incidents involving Chilean army commander-in-chief, René Schneider, are provided later in this chapter and in [45D], pp. 121–128.

20. See testimony of Ralph Dungan, ambassador to Chile ([44G], pp. 23 ff.).

21. See testimony of Edward Korry, who succeeded Ralph Dungan as ambassador to Chile ([44G], pp. 29 ff., and [61], pp. 2–31).

22. Charles Meyer was the assistant secretary of state for Inter-American Affairs during 1969–1973. Refer to the testimony in [44G], pp. 35 ff.

23. In 1974, Representative Michael Harrington released the classified testimony of DCI William Colby (before the House Subcommittee on Intelligence), relating to the CIA and Chile. For hearings regarding his release of this information, see [55] and [60].

24. The testimony of CIA Director William Colby, referred to in this portion of the text, was taken in executive session and, therefore, is not available.

25. The material presented in this section of the text has been extracted from lengthy testimony on Chile. Additional testimony regarding Chile appears in [16], pp. 301–304, 320.

26. Details of alledged assassination plots are available in [43], pp. 13–254.

27. Additional views and recommendations from individual members of the Church Committee, with regards to assassination plots appear in an appendix to the Church report ([43], pp. 297–346).

28. The recommended statute of the Church Committee concerning conspiracies, attempts of assassination, and acts of assassinations by American citizens, is reprinted in [43], Appendix A, p. 289.

29. The parenthetical page citations appearing in this portion of reprinted text refer to pages in document [43].

Chapter 12
Intrusion into Domestic Affairs
and the Rights of Citizens

THE HUSTON PLAN ([44B], pp. 141–188)

"The right of the people to be secure in their persons, houses, and papers and effects against unreasonable searches and seizures shall not be violated, and no warrant shall issue, but upon probable cause, supported by oath or affirmation, and particularly describing the place to be searched and the persons or things to be seized." This is the right of the people, as guaranteed by the Fourth Amendment of the Constitution. Implicit, also, in this statute is a circumscription of domestic intelligence activities.

As the revelations associated with the Watergate scandal began to unfold and as the investigations of the intelligence community progressed, there was deepening concern that the capabilities of the U.S. foreign intelligence community were in danger of being diverted from their international purpose and applied instead to domestic situations.* The most explicit documentation of such a danger appears in the so-called "Huston Plan." This plan was a prescription for the use of the entire intelligence community in a coordinated covert operation to stifle dissent and muffle protest by U.S. citizens who were exercising rights granted by the Constitution.

Tom Charles Huston, a young attorney on the White House staff in the early 1970s, participated in a group called the Ad Hoc Interagency Committee on Intelligence. Chaired by FBI Director J. Edgar Hoover, this group included DCI Richard Helms; head of NSA Admiral Noel Gaylor; and DIA head Donald Bennett. (A description of this committee was given by Huston in his testimony before the Church Committee [44B], pp. 4 ff.) The committee was formed by President Richard M. Nixon at a June 5, 1970 meeting he held with those officials, plus White House aides H. R. Haldeman and John Erlichman; Huston, an assistant to Haldeman, was also present. Committee members met only twice and inconclusively, leaving day-to-day work to second-level staff, such as Huston. He was not a member of the committee, which was more akin to a temporary task force, without staff, rules, structure, or offices. Judging from his testimony, he recognized an opportunity within the intelligence bureaucracy and exploited his White House position to pursue it.

Huston prepared a draft "plan," which he submitted to his counterparts and eventually to three or four intelligence agency directors. Hoover was not given a copy at first, because FBI staff members working with Huston had counseled against showing the report to him—assuming he would be opposed to it because it contained proposals that would weaken FBI autonomy in domestic intelligence. The plan was approved by three intelligence agency directors and then submitted to Hoover. He, or his staff (it is not clear which), added some footnotes, which dissented from various proposals, and returned it to Huston. The plan was then submitted by Huston, through Haldeman, for approval by the president on June 25, 1970; it was approved and committee members were so advised. Ten days later, President Nixon revoked his approval of the plan, reportedly at the urging of both Hoover and Attorney General John Mitchell. The attorney general had not been aware the plan was being prepared, according to Mitchell's testimony ([78], Book VII, pp. 476 ff.), and registered his objections on hearing of it.

The Huston Plan had a brief history, but is a highly significant document in the history of the U.S. intelligence community. It was an unprecedented, coordinated, illegal effort to use the weapons of the U.S. espionage establishment against American citizens. It was authored in the White House, endorsed by the directors of the intelligence community, and approved by the president. The Huston Plan, which appeared in the Church Committee documentation as the "Special Report: Interagency Committee on Intelligence (Ad Hoc)," is reprinted here in its entirety.

*The Watergate scandal was triggered by an illegal break-in of the Democratic party's national headquarters, housed in the Watergate building in Washington. This break-in was accomplished by burglars hired by President Richard M. Nixon's Committee for the Re-election of the President. Following this incident were two years of turmoil for the government and the people of the United States. There were revelations about other political scandals, arising out of Watergate, as well as revelations of the efforts of the Nixon administration to cover up its role. This scandal paralyzed and eventually destroyed the Nixon administration. President Nixon resigned on August 9, 1974—before the House of Representatives could take action on the three articles of impeachment, which had been recommended by its Judiciary Committee. Seven of Nixon's closest advisers were indicted by a federal grand jury on Watergate-related criminal charges, and Nixon, himself, was named as an unindicted co-conspirator. Gerald R. Ford acceded to the presidency, and on September 8, 1974, he issued Nixon a presidential pardon.

SPECIAL REPORT
INTERAGENCY COMMITTEE ON
INTELLIGENCE (AD HOC)

CHAIRMAN J. EDGAR HOOVER

JUNE, 1970

---

[1] Under criteria determined by the Committee, in consultation with the White House, the Department of Defense, the Department of Justice, the Central Intelligence Agency, and the Federal Bureau of Investigation, certain materials have been deleted from those documents, some of which were previously classified, to maintain the internal operating procedures of the agencies involved, and to protect intelligence sources and methods. Further deletions were made with respect to protecting the privacy of certain individuals and groups. These deletions do not change the material content of these exhibits.

June 25, 1970

This report, prepared for the President,
is approved by all members of this committee
and their signatures are affixed hereto.

_____
Director, Federal Bureau of Investigation
                Chairman

_____
Director, Central Intelligence Agency

_____
Director, Defense Intelligence Agency

_____
Director, National Security Agency

PREFACE

The objectives of this report are to: (1) assess the current internal security threat; (2) evaluate current intelligence collection procedures; identify restraints under which U. S. intelligence services operate; and list the advantages and disadvantages of such restraints; and (3) evaluate current interagency coordination and recommend means to improve it.

The Committee has attempted to set forth the essence of the issues and the major policy considerations involved which fall within the scope of its mandate.

i

TABLE OF CONTENTS

PART ONE

SUMMARY OF INTERNAL SECURITY THREAT

I. MILITANT NEW LEFT GROUPS

A. Assessment of Current Internal Security Threat

The movement of rebellious youth known as the "New Left," involving and influencing a substantial number of college students, is having a serious impact on contemporary society with a potential for serious domestic strife.//The revolutionary aims of the New Left are apparent when their identification with Marxism-Leninism is examined// They pointedly advertise their objective as the overthrow of our system of government by force and violence. Under the guise of freedom of speech, they seek to confront all established authority and provoke disorder. They intend to smash the U. S. educational system, the economic structure, and, finally, the Government itself. New Left groups do not have a large enough number of rank-and-file followers, nor do they have a unity of purpose to carry out massive or paralyzing acts of insurrection. They do, on the other hand, have the will to carry on more militant efforts in local situations and an inclination to utilize more extreme means to attain their objectives.

1. Student Protest Groups. The Students for a Democratic Society (SDS) has, in the past year, split into several factions, including the Revolutionary Youth Movement (RYM), which has control over 30 chapters; and the Worker Student Alliance (WSA), which consists of 63 chapters. The WSA faction,//dominated by the Progressive Labor Party (PLP)// aims to build a worker-student movement in keeping with the PLP's aim of developing a broad worker-based revolutionary movement in the United States.

There are some 85 unaffiliated SDS chapters generally sympathetic to revolutionary tactics and goals. The trend of increased radical campus organizations is noticeable at campuses where recognition of SDS has been refused or rescinded and SDS members have banded together, with or without sanction, under a new title to attract student support. In addition, numerous ad hoc groups have been established on campuses and elsewhere to exploit specific issues.

The National Student Strike (NSS), also known as the National Strike Information Center, was formed following the entry of the United States forces into Cambodia and the deaths of four students at Kent State University. NSS, which helped to coordinate the nationwide student strike in May, 1970, has three regional centers and includes

among its leadership SDS members and other New Left activists. The
NSS has established a nationwide communications system of "ham" radio
stations on campuses to encourage student demonstrations and disruptions.
This communications capability may have a significant impact on campus
stability in the coming school year.

The Venceremos Brigade (VB), established to send United States
youth to Cuba to aid in the 1970 harvests, has continually received favorable
publicity in Cuban propaganda media. To date, over 900 members of
the VB have visited Cuba and another group of approximately 500 members
are expected to follow suit. While in Cuba, VB members were individually
photographed and questioned in detail about their backgrounds. Because
of their contacts with Cuban officials, these individuals must be considered
as potential recruits for Cuban intelligence activities and sabotage in the
United States.

The greatest threat posed to the security of the country by
student protest groups is their potential for fomenting violence and unrest
on college campuses. Demonstrations have triggered acts of arson by
extremists against war-oriented research and ROTC facilities and have
virtually paralyzed many schools. There has been a growing number of
noncampus, but student-related, acts of violence which increase tensions
between "town and gown" and which constitute a marked escalation of the
scope and level of protest activities. Few student protests are currently
related to exclusively campus issues; virtually all involve political and
social issues. Increasingly, the battlefield is the community with the
campus serving primarily as a staging area.

The efforts of the New Left aimed at fomenting unrest and
subversion among civil servants, labor unions, and mass media have met
with very limited success, although the WSA and its parent, the PLP,
have attempted through their "Summer Work-Ins" to infiltrate and
radicalize labor. The inability of these groups to subvert and control
the mass media has led to the establishment of a large network of under-
ground publications which serve the dual purpose of an internal communi-
cation network and an external propaganda organ.

Leaders of student protest groups have traveled extensively
over the years to communist countries; have openly stated their sympathy
with the international communist revolutionary movements in South Vietnam
and Cuba; and have directed others into activities which support these
movements. These individuals must be considered to have potential for

- 2 -

recruitment and participation in foreign-directed intelligence activity.

        2.   Antiwar Activists.   The impetus and continuity for the antiwar movement is provided by the New Mobilization Committee to End the War in Vietnam (NMC) and the Student Mobilization Committee to End the War in Vietnam (SMC).   The NMC is a coalition of numerous antiwar groups and individuals including communist "old left" elements. The SMC is under the control of the Trotskyist Socialist Workers Party (SWP).

        The NMC and SMC have announced a policy of "nonexclusion" which places no limitation on the type of individuals allowed to participate in demonstrations.   This policy opens the door for violence-prone individuals who want to capitalize on the activities of these groups. Both groups profess to follow a policy of nonviolence; however, the very nature of the protests that they sponsor sets the stage for civil disobedience and police confrontation by irresponsible dissident elements. Various individuals in NMC and SMC are calling for more militant protest activities, a subject to be discussed at national meetings by both groups in late June, 1970.

        Although antiwar groups are not known to be collecting weapons, engaging in paramilitary training, or advocating terrorist tactics, the pro-Hanoi attitude of their leaders, the unstable nature of many NMC advocates and their policy of "nonexclusion" underscore the use of the antiwar movement as a conduit for civil disorder.   This is further emphasized by the NMC leadership's advocacy of civil disobedience to achieve desired objectives.

        There is no indication that the antiwar movement has made serious inroads or achieved any more than a slight degree of influence among labor unions, the mass media, and civil servants.   One group, however, the Federal Employees for a Democratic Society (FEDS), offers a means of protest for recent radical graduates employed by the Federal Government.

- 3 -

The military and educational institutions are the prime
targets of the antiwar movement. In addition to vandalism, arsons, and
bombings of ROTC facilities, there has been stepped-up activity to
spread antiwar sympathy among American servicemen from within
through sympathetic members in the military and from without through
such programs as "GI Coffeehouses" and the proposed National GI
Alliance. The increasing access by members of the military to the
underground press, the establishment of servicemen's unions, and
organizations which facilitate desertions, have contributed significantly
to the increasing instances of dissent in the military services.

NMC and SMC leaders are constantly speaking before student
groups and endeavoring to use student radicals to further the antiwar
movement. They have called for an end to the ROTC and have demon-
strated, often violently, to force universities to halt war-related research
projects.

[The NMC maintains close contact with the
World Council for Peace and Stockholm Conference on Vietnam] A new
organization dominated by NMC leaders, the Committee of Liaison with
Families of Servicemen Detained in North Vietnam, emerged in January,
1970, after contacts with North Vietnamese representatives. It attempts
to present a favorable picture of North Vietnamese treatment of American
prisoners of war.

NMC leaders have frequently traveled abroad. It is therefore
necessary to consider these individuals as having potential for engaging
in foreign-directed intelligence collection.

[The Central Intelligence Agency (CIA), in its analysis of bloc
intelligence, is of the view that the Soviet and bloc intelligence services
are committed at the political level to exploit all domestic dissidents
wherever possible] This attack is being conducted through recruited
agents, agents of influence, and the use of front groups. It is established
bloc policy to deploy its forces against the United States as "the main
enemy" and to direct all bloc intelligence forces toward ultimately
political objectives which disrupt U. S. domestic and foreign policies.

3. New Left Terrorist Groups. The Weatherman terrorist
group, which emerged from a factional split of SDS during the Summer of
1969, is a revolutionary youth movement which actively supports the

- 4 -

revolutionary leadership role of the Negro in the United States. It has
evolved into a number of small commando-type units which plan to
utilize bombings, arsons, and assassinations as political weapons.

There has been evidence of Weatherman involvement in
terrorist tactics, including the accidental explosion of a "Weatherman
bomb factory" in New York City on March 6, 1970; the discovery of two
undetonated bombs in Detroit police facilities on the same date; and the
blast at New York City police installations on June 9, 1970.

While Weatherman membership is not clearly defined, it is
estimated that at least 1,000 individuals adhere to Weatherman ideology.
In addition, groups such as the White Panther Party, Running Dog, Mad Dog,
and the Youth International Party (Yippies) are supporters of Weatherman
terrorism but have no clearly definable ideology of their own.

Adherents to Weatherman ideology are also found within
radical elements on campuses, among those living in off-campus communes,
among New Left movement lawyers and doctors, and the underground press.
Individuals who adhere to the Weatherman ideology have offered support
and aid to hard-core Weatherman members, including 21 Weatherman
members currently in hiding to avoid apprehension.

They identify themselves politically with North Vietnam,
Cuba, and North Korea and consider pro-Soviet and pro-Chinese organi-
zations as being aligned with imperialist powers. In addition, some of the
Weatherman leaders and adherents have traveled to communist countries
or have met in Western countries with communist representatives.

Weatherman leaders and other members of terrorist groups
are not known at this time to be involved in foreign-directed intelligence
collection activity. The fugitive and underground status of many of these
people, as well as their involvement in activities which would likely bring
them to the attention of American authorities, would be a deterrent to
contacts by foreign intelligence organizations.

B. Assessment of Current Intelligence Collection Procedures

1. Scope and Effectiveness of Current Coverage. Although
New Left groups have been responsible for widespread damage to ROTC
facilities, for the halting of some weapons-related research, and for the
increasing dissent within the military services, the major threat to the
internal security of the United States is that directed against the civilian
sector of our society.

- 5 -

Coverage of student groups is handled primarily through live informants and it is generally effective at the national level or at major meetings of these groups where overall policy, aims, and objectives of the groups are determined.

The antiwar movement's activities are covered through the FBI by live informants in all organizations of interest. This is supported by information furnished by all members of the intelligence community and other Federal, state, and local agencies. Key leaders and activists are afforded concentrated and intensified investigative coverage on a continuing basis and, in situations where there are positive indications of violence, electronic surveillances have been implemented on a selective basis. Informant and electronic coverage does not meet present requirements.

Although several SDS chapters on college campuses which adhere to Weatherman ideology have been penetrated by live informants, there is no live informant coverage at present of underground Weatherman fugitives. There is electronic coverage on the residence of a Weatherman contact in New York City and on the residence of an alleged Weatherman member in San Francisco; however, no information has been developed concerning the whereabouts of the 21 Weatherman fugitives.

2. Gaps in Current Coverage. Established, long-term coverage is not available within student protest groups due to the fact that the student body itself changes yearly, necessitating a constant turnover in the informants targeted against these groups. His idealism and immaturity, as well as the sensitive issues of academic freedom and the right to dissent, all serve to increase the risk that the student informant will be exposed as such.

Generally, day-to-day coverage of the planned activities of student protest groups, which are somewhat autonomous and disjointed, could be strengthened. [Advance notice of foreign travel by student militants is particularly needed.] Campus violence is generally attributable to small, close-knit extremist groups among radical students. Coverage of these latter groups is minimal.

The antiwar movement is comprised of a great many organizations and people which represent varied political, moral and ethnic beliefs. Current manpower commitments preclude optimum coverage of all antiwar activities on a day-to-day basis.

Existing coverage of New Left extremists, the Weatherman group in particular, is negligible. Most of the Weatherman group has gone underground and formed floating, commando-type units composed of three to six individuals. The transitory nature of these units hinders the installation of electronic surveillances and their smallness and distrust of outsiders make penetration of these units through live informants extremely difficult.

Financially, the Weatherman group appears to be without a centralized source of funds. Wealthy parents have furnished funds to some of these individuals, including those in a fugitive status. Many members have also been involved in the thefts of credit and identification cards, as well as checks, and have utilized them for obtaining operating expenses.

3. Possible Measures to Improve Intelligence Collection. To establish effective coverage of student protest groups would require the expansion of live informant coverage of individual campus chapters of these organizations. This would entail extensive use of student informants to obtain maximum utilization of their services for the periods of their college attendance.

Because of the great number of individuals and groups in the antiwar movement, an increase in the manpower assigned to these investigations would facilitate more intensive coverage. In addition, there are several key leaders involved in virtually all antiwar activities, including international contacts, against whom electronic surveillances and mail covers would be particularly effective.

Improvement of intelligence gathering against New Left terrorists depends on a combination of live informant coverage among key leaders and selective electronic surveillances. Because of the nature of the Weatherman groups, live informant coverage will most likely result through the defection of a key leader.

- 7 -

Extensive efforts have been undertaken which should produce a live informant capable of furnishing information as to the location of Weatherman fugitives and planned terrorist acts. In the event a commune is located, prompt installation of electronic coverage should produce similar results. Utilization of additional resources to expand and intensify this collection would be beneficial.

II. BLACK EXTREMIST MOVEMENT

A. Assessment of Current Internal Security Threat

1. Black Panther Party. The most active and dangerous black extremist group in the United States is the Black Panther Party (BPP). Despite its relatively small number of hard-core members-- approximately 800 in 40 chapters nationwide--the BPP is in the forefront of black extremist activity today. The BPP has publicly advertised its goals of organizing revolution, insurrection, assassination and other terrorist-type activities. Moreover, a recent poll indicates that approximately 25 per cent of the black population has a great respect for the BPP, including 43 per cent of blacks under 21 years of age.

The Panther newspaper has a current circulation of approximately 150,000 copies weekly. Its pages are filled with messages of racial hatred and call for terrorist guerrilla activity in an attempt to overthrow the Government. The BPP has been involved in a substantial number of planned attacks against law enforcement officers, and its leadership is composed in large part of criminally inclined, violence-prone individuals.

Weapons are regularly stockpiled by the Party. During 1968 and 1969, quantities of machine guns, shotguns, rifles, hand grenades, homemade bombs, and ammunition were uncovered in Panther offices.

2. New Left Support for BPP. The BPP has received increasing support from radical New Left elements. During 1970, the BPP formed a working relationship with radical student dissenters by injecting the issue of Government "repression" of Panthers into the antiwar cause. Students for a Democratic Society (SDS) supported the BPP in a 1969 "united front against fascism." The probability that black extremists, including the BPP, will work closely with New Left white radicals in the future increases the threat of escalating terrorist activities. It would be safe to project that racial strife and student turmoil fomented by black extremists will definitely increase.

3. BPP Propaganda Appearances. Despite its small member-ship, the BPP has scored major successes in the propaganda arena. In

- 9 -

1969, BPP representatives spoke at 189 colleges throughout the Nation, while in 1967 there were only 11 such appearances. Although no direct information has been received to date indicating that the BPP has initiated any large-scale racial disorders, the year 1970 has seen an escalation of racial disorders across the Nation compared to 1969. This fact, coupled with an increasing amount of violent Panther activity, presents a great potential for racial and civil unrest for the future.

4. Appeal to Military. The BPP has made pointed appeals to black servicemen with racist propaganda. High priority has been placed on the recruitment of veterans with weapons and explosives training. The BPP has also called for infiltration of the Government. These activities, should they achieve even minimum success, present a grave threat.

5. BPP Philosophy and Foreign Support. The BPP relies heavily on foreign communist ideology to shape its goals. Quotations from Mao Tse-tung were the initial ideological bible of the BPP. Currently, the writings of North Korean Premier Kim Il-sung are followed and extensive use of North Korean propaganda material is made in BPP publications and training. The Marxist-oriented philosophy of the BPP presents a favorable environment for support of the Panthers from other communist countries.

BPP leaders have traveled extensively abroad including visits to Cuba, Russia, North Korea, and Algeria. International operations of the BPP are directed by Eldridge Cleaver, a fugitive from United States courts. Cleaver has established an international staff in Algeria, from where communist propaganda is constantly relayed to the BPP headquarters in Berkeley, California. He has also established close ties with Al Fatah, an Arab guerrilla organization, whose leaders have reportedly extended invitations to BPP members to take guerrilla training during 1970. Cleaver, in a recent conversation, indicated that North Koreans are conducting similar training for BPP members. Radical white students in Western Europe and the Scandinavian countries have organized solidarity committees in support of the BPP. These committees are the sources of financial contributions to the Party and provide outlets for the BPP newspaper.

6. Other Black Extremist Groups. The Nation of Islam (NOI) is the largest single black extremist organization in the United States with an estimated membership of 6,000 in approximately 100 Mosques. The NOI

- 10 -

preaches hatred of the white race and advocates separatism of the races.
The NOI as a group has, to date, not instigated any civil disorders;
however, the followers of this semi-religious cult are extremely
dedicated individuals who could be expected to perform acts of violence
if so ordered by the NOI head, Elijah Muhammed. When Muhammed,
who is over 70 years of age, is replaced, a new leader could completely
alter current nonviolent tactics of the organization. For example,
Muhammed's son-in-law, Raymond Sharrieff, now among the top
hierarchy of NOI, could rise to a leadership position. Sharrieff is
vicious, domineering, and unpredictable.

There are numerous other black extremist organizations,
small in numbers, located across the country. There is also a large
number of unaffiliated black extremists who advocate violence and
guerrilla warfare. One particular group, the Republic of New Africa
(RNA), headquartered in Detroit, Michigan, calls for the establishment
of a separate black nation in the South to be protected by armed forces.
These groups, although small, are dedicated to the destruction of our
form of government and consequently present a definite potential for
instigating civil disorder or guerrilla warfare activity.

7.   Black Student Extremist Influence. Black student extremist
activities at colleges and secondary schools have increased alarmingly.
Although currently there is no dominant leadership, coordination or
specific direction between these individuals, they are in frequent contact
with each other. Consequently, should any type of organization or
cohesiveness develop, it would present a grave potential for future
violent activities at United States schools. Increased informant coverage
would be particularly productive in this area. Black student extremists
have frequently engaged in violence and disruptive activity on campuses.
Major universities which made concessions to nonnegotiable black
student demands have not succeeded in calming extremist activities.
During the school year 1969-70, there were 227 college disturbances
having racial overtones. There were 530 such disturbances in secondary
schools compared with only 320 during the previous school year.

8.   Foreign Influence in the Black Extremist Movement.
Although there is no hard evidence indicating that the black extremist
movement is substantially controlled or directed by foreign elements,
there is a marked potential for foreign-directed intelligence or subversive
activity among black extremist leaders and organizations. These groups
are highly susceptible to exploitation by hostile foreign intelligence
services.

- 11 -

Currently the most important foreign aspect of the black extremist movement is the availability of foreign asylum, especially with regard to black extremists subject to criminal prosecution in the United States. Some foreign countries, such as Cuba, provide a temporary safe haven for these individuals. [Information has been received that passports and funds for travel have also been furnished by countries such as Cuba, North Korea, and   Communist intelligence services do not, at present, play a major role in the black extremist movement; however, all such services have established contact with individual black militants. Thus, the penetration and manipulation of black extremist groups by these intelligence services remain distinct possibilities. Communist intelligence services are capable of using their personnel, facilities, and agent assets to work in the black extremist field. The Soviet and Cuban services have major capabilities available.]

B. Assessment of Current Intelligence Collection Procedures

There are some definite gaps in the current overall intelligence penetration of the black extremist movement. For example, although there appears to be sufficient live informant coverage of the BPP   additional penetration
                                        is needed.
High echelon informant coverage could conceivably prevent violence, sabotage, or insurrection if such activity was planned by BPP leadership. Insufficient coverage of   BPP is offset
to some extent by technical coverage
            Penetration of leadership levels has been hindered in part by current BPP policies which prevent rank-and-file members from advancing to leadership roles.

Improvement in coverage of BPP financial activities could be made, particularly with regard to sources of funds and records. Information received to date indicates that financial support for the BPP has been furnished by both foreign individuals and domestic sources. Thus, a deeper penetration and correlation of foreign and domestic information received is essential to a full determination of BPP finances. Coverage of BPP finances has been hampered by fact that BPP leaders handle financial matters personally.

In view of the increased amount of foreign travel and contacts by BPP leaders abroad, there is a clear-cut need for more complete coverage of foreign involvement in BPP activities.

- 12 -

1. Other Black Extremist Organizations. Informant coverage of the NOI is substantial, enabling its activities to be followed on a current basis. Coverage of militant black student groups and individuals is very limited because of the sensitive areas involved. An effective source of such coverage would be reliable, former members of the Armed Forces presently attending college. Live informant coverage, particularly with respect to the activities and plans of unaffiliated black militants, needs to be increased. More sources both in the United States and abroad in a position to determine the amount of foreign involvement in black extremist activities need to be developed. Maximum use of communication interceptions would materially increase the current capabilities of the intelligence community to develop highly important data regarding black extremist activities.

III. INTELLIGENCE SERVICES OF COMMUNIST COUNTRIES

A. Assessment of Current Internal Security Threat

The threat posed by the communist intelligence services must be assessed in two areas: (1) direct intervention in fomenting and/or influencing domestic unrest; (2) extensive espionage activities.

Taken in complete context, these services constitute a grave threat to the internal security of the United States because of their size, capabilities, widespread spheres of influence, and targeting of the United States as "enemy number one." The largest and most skilled of these services is the Soviet Committee for State Security (KGB) which has roughly 300,000 personnel of whom some 10,000 are engaged in foreign operations.

1. Intervention in Domestic Unrest. There have been no substantial indications that the communist intelligence services have actively fomented domestic unrest. Their capability cannot, however, be minimized and the likelihood of their initiating direct intervention would be in direct relationship to the deterioration of the political climate and/or imminence of hostilities. The ingredients for a first-rate capability are present, including both the personnel and the ingrained philosophy and know-how for using such tactics.

Communist intelligence has shown a real capability to foment disorder in a number of trouble spots. The dissidence and violence in the United States today present adversary intelligence services with opportunities unparalleled for forty years. While fostering disorder and rebellion through communist parties and fronts is a potent weapon in the communist arsenal, their past success has been evident in clandestine recruitment efforts on campuses during times of unrest. H.A.R. (Kim) Philby, Guy Burgess, and Donald Maclean were all students at Cambridge during the depression period of the 1930's and were in the vanguard of what was then the New Left. Their recruitment and cooperation with Soviet intelligence wreaked havoc on British intelligence and also compromised U.S. security in those sectors where they had authorized access.

- 14 -

For instance, about 900
members of the Venceremos Brigade, a group of American youths,
recently completed a round trip to Cuba. This travel was financed
by the Cuban Government. While in Cuba, they were exhorted to
actively participate in United States revolutionary activities upon
their return to the United States.

A sabotage manual, prepared in   turned up in the
hands of individuals responsible for recent bombings
While the potential for widespread, well-organized
incidents of violence generated and controlled by the Cuban intelligence
service is considered minimal. isolated occurrences of this nature must
be considered probable. The   services appear to have assumed the
passive roles of observers and reporters.

The communist intelligence services maintain contacts
and exert influence among a variety of individuals and organizations
through the exploitation of ideological, cultural, and ethnic ties.
Most of these liaisons are maintained with some degree of openness
with individuals associated with the Communist Party, USA, various
of its front groups, other pro-Soviet organizations, nationality groups,
and foreign-language newspapers. These contacts are exploited as
sources for and propaganda outlets of communist intelligence services.
Regarded individually, these efforts cannot be considered a major
threat to our internal security; however, in total, they represent a
sizable element of our population which can be influenced in varying
degrees by communist intelligence service operations.

2. Intelligence Operations. Persistent and pervasive
intelligence operations which have their inspiration and direction supplied
by communist intelligence services represent a major threat to the
internal security.

- 15 -

(DELETED)

B. Assessment of Current Intelligence Collection

1. Scope and Effectiveness. The scope of overall intelligence
efforts is encompassed in the threefold goals of penetration, intelligence,
and prosecution. Domestic implementation of these goals is delimited
by agreement among United States intelligence agencies. Intelligence
components of the United States military services are immediately
concerned with protecting the integrity of their personnel and instal-
lations.

Methods used in these endeavors, employed in varying
degrees by U.S. intelligence agencies dependent upon their specific
tasks are: penetrations; defectors; double agent operations; physical,
technical, and photographic surveillances; examination and analysis
of overt publications; information supplied by friendly intelligence
services; and COMINT.

- 17 -

(DELETED)

2. Gaps in Current Coverage

(DELETED)

IV. OTHER REVOLUTIONARY GROUPS

A. Assessment of Current Internal Security Threat

1. Communist Party. The Communist Party continues
as a distinct threat to the internal security because of its extremely
close ties and total commitment to the Soviet Union. There are many
thousands of people in the United States who adhere to a Marxist
philosophy and agree with the basic objectives of the Communist
Party although they do not identify themselves specifically with the
organization. The Party receives most of its finances from the Soviet
Union, adheres to Soviet policies explicitly, and provides a major out-
let for Soviet propaganda. The Party will without question continue to
implement whatever orders it receives from the Soviets in the future.

There is little likelihood that the Communist Party, USA,
will instigate civil disorders or use terrorist tactics in the foreseeable
future. Its strong suit is propaganda. Through its publications and
propaganda it will continue its efforts to intensify civil disorders, and
foment unrest in the Armed Forces, labor unions, and minority groups.
The Party is on the periphery of the radical youth movement and is
striving to strengthen its role in this movement and to attract new
members through a recently formed youth organization, but it does
not appear this group will achieve any substantial results for the
Party in the future.

2. Socialist Workers Party and Other Trotskyist Groups.
These organizations have an estimated membership of   The
major Trotskyist organization, the Socialist Workers Party, has
attained an influential role in the antiwar movement through its
youth affiliate, the Young Socialist Alliance, which dominates the
Student Mobilization Committee to End the War in Vietnam and which
has more than doubled its size on college campuses in the past year.
Trotskyist groups have participated in major confrontations with
authorities both on and off campuses and have consistently supported
civil disorders. At this time they do not pose a major threat to
instigate insurrection or to commit terrorist acts. The propaganda
of these groups, while emphasizing student unrest, is also aimed at
creating dissatisfaction in labor organizations and in the Armed Forces.
The Trotskyist organizations maintain close relations with the Fourth
International, a foreign-based worldwide Trotskyist movement.

- 20 -

4. <u>Puerto Rican Nationalist Extremist Groups</u>. The
radical Puerto Rican independence movement has spawned approximately
ten violently anti-American groups committed to Puerto Rican self-
determination. Revolutionary violence is a major aim of the estimated
members of these groups and if sufficiently strong, they would
not hesitate to mount armed insurrection. Since July, 1967, some
130 bombings in Puerto Rico and in the New York City area have been
attributed to these extremists. American-owned businesses have
been the main targets, but there has been a recent upsurge of violence
against U.S. defense facilities in Puerto Rico.

B. <u>Assessment of Current Intelligence Coverage</u>

1. <u>Scope and Effectiveness</u>. Coverage of the Communist

Coverage of the Trotskyist and   groups

Current live informant coverage can furnish information on the general activities of these groups and it should serve to warn of policy changes in favor of insurrection or sabotage.

Informant penetration of the Puerto Rican independence groups provides information on the objectives of most of these organizations as well as the identities of their members. However, these sources have limited ability to provide advance information regarding violence committed by these groups or by individual members.

2. Gaps in Current Coverage.

Closer coverage at the policy-making levels of the Puerto Rican independence groups is needed to obtain more comprehensive information on persons involved in terrorist activities. The small memberships of many of these organizations is a major reason for the limited coverage.

3. Possible Measures to Improve Intelligence Collection. The selective use of electronic surveillances would materially enhance the intelligence coverage of the policy-making levels of these organizations. A particular benefit of electronic surveillance in the Puerto Rican field could be the development of information identifying persons involved in terrorist activities. Communications intelligence coverage and travel control measures could be improved to provide greater awareness of the travel and other activities of individuals of security interest. Through the establishment of additional informant coverage on college campuses, the involvement of these organizations in the radicalization of students could be assessed with increased accuracy.

- 22 -

PART TWO

RESTRAINTS ON INTELLIGENCE COLLECTION

The Committee noted that the President had made it clear that he desired full consideration be given to any regulations, policies, or procedures which tend to limit the effectiveness of domestic intelligence collection. The Committee further noted that the President wanted the pros and cons of such restraints clearly set forth so that the President will be able to decide whether or not a change in current policies, practices, or procedures should be made.

During meetings of the Committee, a variety of limitations and restraints were discussed. All of the agencies involved, Defense Intelligence Agency (DIA), the three military counterintelligence services, the Central Intelligence Agency (CIA), the National Security Agency (NSA), and the Federal Bureau of Investigation (FBI), participated in these considerations.

In the light of the directives furnished to the Committee by the White House, the subject matters hereinafter set forth were reviewed for the consideration and decision of the President.

I. SPECIFIC OPERATIONAL RESTRAINTS

A. Interpretive Restraint on Communications Intelligence

Preliminary Discussion

- 23 -

Nature of Restriction

Advantages of Maintaining Restriction

 Advantages of Relaxing Restriction

(DELETED)

-24-

(DELETED)

B.   Electronic Surveillances and Penetrations

Preliminary Discussion

The limited number of electronic surveillances and penetrations substantially restricts the collection of valuable intelligence information of material importance to the entire intelligence community

Nature of Restrictions

Electronic surveillances have been used on a selective basis. Restrictions, initiated at the highest levels of the Executive Branch, arose as a result of the condemnation of these techniques by civil rights groups, Congressional concern for invasion of privacy, and the possibility of their adverse effect on criminal prosecutions.

Advantages of Maintaining Restrictions

1. Disclosure and embarrassment to the using agency and/or the United States is always possible since such techniques often require that the services or advice of outside personnel be used in the process of installation.

2.

3. Certain elements of the press in the United States and abroad would undoubtedly seize upon disclosure of electronic coverage in an effort to discredit the United States.

4. The monitoring of electronic surveillances requires considerable manpower and, where foreign establishments are involved, the language resources of the agencies could be severely taxed.

- 26 -

Advantages of Relaxing Restrictions

1. The U. S. Government has an overriding obligation to use every available scientific means to detect and neutralize forces which pose a direct threat to the Nation.

2. Every major intelligence service in the world, including those of the communist bloc, use such techniques as an essential part of their operations, and it is believed the general public would support their use by the United States for the same purpose.

3. The President historically has had the authority to act in matters of national security. In addition, Title III of the Omnibus Crime Control and Safe Streets Act of 1968 provides a statutory basis.

4. Intelligence data from electronic coverage is not readily obtainable from other techniques or sources. Such data includes information which might assist in formulating foreign policy decisions, information leading to the identification of intelligence and/or espionage principals and could well include the first indication of intention to commit hostile action against the United States.

5. Acquisition of such material from COMINT without benefit of the assistance which electronic surveillance techniques can provide, if possible at all, would be extremely expensive. Therefore, this approach could result in considerable dollar savings compared to collection methods.

<u>DECISION:</u> Electronic Surveillances
and Penetrations

_____ Present procedures on electronic coverage should
continue.

_____ Present procedures should be changed to permit
intensification of coverage of individuals and
groups in the United States who pose a major
threat to the internal security.

_____ Present procedures should be changed to permit
intensification of coverage

_____ More information is needed.

<u>NOTE:</u> The FBI does not wish to change its present procedure of
selective coverage on major internal security threats as
it believes this coverage is adequate at this time. The
FBI would not oppose other agencies seeking authority of
the Attorney General for coverage required by them and there-
after instituting such coverage themselves.

- 28 -

C. Mail Coverage

Preliminary Discussion

The use of mail covers can result in the collection of valuable information relating to contacts between U. S. nationals and foreign governments and intelligence services. CIA and the military investigative agencies have found this information particularly helpful in the past. Essentially, there are two types of mail coverage: routine coverage is legal, while the second--covert coverage--is not. Routine coverage involves recording information from the face of envelopes. It is available, legally, to any duly authorized Federal or state investigative agency submitting a written request to the Post Office Department and has been used frequently by the military intelligence services. Covert mail coverage, also known as "sophisticated mail coverage," or "flaps and seals," entails surreptitious screening and may include opening and examination of domestic or foreign mail. This technique is based on high-level cooperation of top echelon postal officials.

Nature of Restrictions

Covert coverage has been discontinued while routine coverage has been reduced primarily as an outgrowth of publicity arising from disclosure of routine mail coverage during legal proceedings and publicity afforded this matter in Congressional hearings involving accusations of governmental invasion of privacy.

Advantages of Maintaining Restrictions

Routine Coverage:

1. Although this coverage is legal, charges of invasion of privacy, no matter how ill-founded, are possible.

2. This coverage depends on the cooperation of rank-and-file postal employees and is, therefore, more susceptible to compromise.

- 29 -

Covert Coverage:

1. Coverage directed against diplomatic establishments, if disclosed, could have adverse diplomatic repercussions.

2. This coverage, not having sanction of law, runs the risk of any illicit act magnified by the involvement of a Government agency.

3. Information secured from such coverage could not be used for prosecutive purposes.

Advantages of Relaxing Restrictions

Routine Coverage:

1. Legal mail coverage is used daily by both local and many Federal authorities in criminal investigations. The use of this technique should be available to permit coverage of individuals and groups in the United States who pose a threat to the internal security.

Covert Coverage:

1. High-level postal authorities have, in the past, provided complete cooperation and have maintained full security of this program.

2. This technique involves negligible risk of compromise. Only high echelon postal authorities know of its existence, and personnel involved are highly trained, trustworthy, and under complete control of the intelligence agency.

3. This coverage has been extremely successful in producing hard-core and authentic intelligence which is not obtainable from any other source. An example is a case involving the interception of a letter to a   establishment in   The writer offered to sell information to the   .nd enclosed a sample of information available to him. Analysis determined that the writer could have given   information which might have been more damaging

- 30 -

DECISION: Mail Coverage

_____ Present restrictions on both types of mail coverage should be continued.

_____ Restrictions on legal coverage should be removed.

_____ Present restrictions on covert coverage should be relaxed on selected targets of priority foreign intelligence and internal security interest.

_____ More information is needed.

NOTE:

The FBI is opposed to implementing any covert mail coverage because it is clearly illegal and it is likely that, if done, information would leak out of the Post Office to the press and serious damage would be done to the intelligence community. The FBI has no objection to legal mail coverage providing it is done on a carefully controlled and selective basis in both criminal and security matters.

- 31 -

D. Surreptitious Entry

Preliminary Discussion

Nature of Restrictions

Use of surreptitious entry, also referred to as "anonymous sources: and "black bag jobs, " has been virtually eliminated.

Advantages of Maintaining Restrictions

1. The activity involves illegal entry and trespass.

2. Information which is obtained through this technique could not be used for prosecutive purposes.

3. The public disclosure of this technique would result in widespread publicity and embarrassment. The news media would portray the incident as a flagrant violation of civil rights

Advantages of Relaxing Restrictions

1. Operations of this type are performed by a small number of carefully trained and selected personnel under strict supervision. The technique is implemented only after full security is assured. It has been used in the past with highly successful results and without adverse effects.

2. Benefits accruing from this technique in the past have been innumerable

3. In the past this technique, when used against subversives, has produced valuable intelligence material.

DECISION: Surreptitious Entry

_____ Present restrictions should be continued.

_____ Present restrictions should be modified to permit procurement

_____ Present restrictions should also be modified to permit selective use of this technique against other urgent and high priority internal security targets.

_____ More information is needed.

NOTE: The FBI is opposed to surreptitious entry

- 33 -

E. Development of Campus Sources

Preliminary Discussion

Public disclosure of CIA links with the National Student Association and the subsequent issuance of the Katzenbach Report have contributed to a climate adverse to intelligence-type activity on college campuses and with student-related groups. It should be noted that the Katzenbach Report itself does not specifically restrain CIA from developing positive or counterintelligence sources to work on targets abroad.

Restrictions currently in force limit certain other elements of the intelligence community access to some of the most troublesome areas: campuses, college faculties, foreign and domestic youth groups, leftist journalists, and black militants. It is recognized that these are prime targets of communist intelligence services and that the opportunity for foreign communist exploitation increases in proportion to the weakness of a U.S. counterintelligence effort.

Nature of Restrictions

The need for great circumspection in making contacts with students, faculty members, and employees of institutions of learning is widely recognized. However, the requirements of the intelligence community for increased information in this area is obvious from the concern of the White House at the absence of hard information about the plans and programs of campus and student-related militant organizations. At the present time no sources are developed among secondary school students and, with respect to colleges and universities, sources are developed only among individuals who have reached legal age, with few exceptions. This policy is designed to minimize the possibility of embarrassment and adverse publicity, including charges of infringement of academic freedom.

Advantages of Maintaining Restrictions

1. Students, faculty members, and others connected with educational institutions are frequently sensitive to and hostile towards any Government activity which smacks of infringement on academic freedom. They are prone to publicize inquiries by governmental agencies and the resulting publicity can often be misleading in portraying the Government's interest.

2. Students are frequently immature and unpredictable. They cannot be relied on to maintain confidences or to act with discretion to the same extent as adult sources.

Advantages of Relaxing Restrictions

1. To a substantial degree, militant New Left and antiwar groups in the United States are comprised of students, faculty members, and others connected with educational institutions. To a corresponding degree, effective coverage of these groups and activities depends upon development of knowledgeable sources in the categories named. In this connection, the military services have capabilities which could be of value to the FBI.

2. Much of the violence and disorders which have occurred on college campuses have been of a hastily planned nature. Unless sources are available within the student bodies, it is virtually impossible to develop advance information concerning such violence.

3. The development of sources among students affiliated with New Left elements affords a unique opportunity to cultivate informant prospects who may rise to positions of leadership in the revolutionary movement or otherwise become of great long-range value.

4. The extraordinary and unprecedented wave of destruction which has swept U.S. campuses in the past several months and which in some respects represents a virtual effort to overthrow our system provides a clear justification for the development of campus informants in the interest of national security.

- 35 -

5. Contacts with students will make it possible to obtain information about travel abroad by U.S. students and about attendance at international conferences.

DECISION: Development of Campus Sources

_____ Present restrictions on development of campus and student-related sources should be continued.

_____ Present restrictions should be relaxed to permit expanded coverage of violence-prone campus and student-related groups.

_____ CIA coverage of American students (and others) traveling abroad or living abroad should be increased.

_____ More information is needed.

NOTE: The FBI is opposed to removing any present controls and restrictions relating to the development of campus sources. To do so would severely jeopardize its investigations and could result in leaks to the press which would be damaging and which could result in charges that investigative agencies are interfering with academic freedom.

- 36 -

F. Use of Military Undercover Agents

Preliminary Discussion

The use of undercover agents by the military services to develop domestic intelligence is currently limited to penetration of organizations whose membership includes military personnel and whose activities pose a direct threat to the military establishment. For example, although the Navy has approximately 54 Naval ROTC units and numerous classified Government contract projects on various campuses across the country, the Naval Investigative Service conducts no covert collection on college campuses. The same is true of the other military services.

Nature of Restrictions

The use of undercover agents by the military investigative services to develop domestic intelligence among civilian targets is believed beyond the statutory intent of the Congress as expressed in Title 10, U. S. Code, and in current resource authorizations. The Delimitations Agreement (1949 agreement signed by the FBI, Army, Navy and Air Force which delimits responsibility for each agency with regard to investigations of espionage, counter-espionage, subversion and sabotage) reflects the current missions of the FBI and the military services. Further, there is a lack of assets to undertake this mission unless essential service-related counterintelligence missions are reduced. There is also concern for morale and disciplinary reactions within the services should the existence of such covert operations become known.

Advantages of Maintaining Restrictions

1. If the utilization of military counterintelligence in this mission is contrary to the intent of the Congress, discovery of employment may result in unfavorable legislation and further reductions in appropriations.

2. Lacking direct statutory authority, the use of the military services in this mission could result in legal action directed against the Executive Branch.

3. The use of military personnel to report on civilian activities for the benefit of civilian agencies will reduce the ability of the military services to meet service-connected intelligence responsibilities.

- 37 -

4. If expansion of the mission of the military services with regard to college campuses is to provide coverage of any significance, it will require corollary increases in resources.

5. Prosecutions for violations of law discovered in the course of military penetration of civilian organizations must be tried in civil courts. The providing of military witnesses will require complicated interdepartmental coordination to a much greater extent than the present and will serve, in the long run, to reduce security.

6. Disclosure that military counterintelligence agencies have been furnishing information obtained through this technique to nonmilitary investigative agencies with respect to civilian activities would certainly result in considerable adverse publicity. The Army's recent experience with former military intelligence personnel confirms this estimate. Since obligated service officers, first enlistees and draftees are drawn from a peer group in which reaction is most unfavorable, morale and disciplinary problems can be anticipated.

Advantages of Relaxing Restrictions

1. Lifting these restrictions would expand the scope of domestic intelligence collection efforts by diverting additional manpower and resources for the collection of information on college campuses and in the vicinity of military installations.

2. The use of undercover agents by the military counterintelligence agencies could be limited to localized targets where the threat is great and the likelihood of exposure minimal. Moreover, controlled use of trusted personnel leaving the service to return to college could expand the collection capabilities at an acceptable risk.

3. The military services have a certain number of personnel pursuing special academic courses on campuses and universities. Such personnel, who in many instances have already been investigated for security clearance, would represent a valuable pool of potential sources for reporting on subversive activities of campus and student-related groups.

- 38 -

DECISION: Use of Military
Undercover Agents

_____ Present restrictions should be retained.

_____ The counterintelligence mission of the military
services should be expanded to include the active
collection of intelligence concerning student-
related dissident activities, with provisions for
a close coordination with the FBI.

_____ No change should be made in the current
mission of the military counterintelligence
services; however, present restrictions
should be relaxed to permit the use of trusted
military personnel as FBI assets in the
collection of intelligence regarding student-
related dissident activities.

_____ More information is needed.

NOTE: The FBI is opposed to the use of any military undercover agents
to develop domestic intelligence information because this would
be in violation of the Delimitations Agreement. The military
services, joined by the FBI, oppose any modification of the
Delimitations Agreement which would extend their jurisdiction
beyond matters of interest to the Department of Defense.

- 39 -

II. BUDGET AND MANPOWER RESTRICTIONS

The capability of member agencies, NSA, CIA, DIA, FBI, and the military counterintelligence services, to collect intelligence data is limited by available resources, particularly in terms of budget and/or qualified manpower. For some agencies fiscal limitations or recent cutbacks have been acute. Budgetary requirements for some agencies, other than the FBI, are reviewed and passed upon by officials who, in some instances, may not be fully informed concerning intelligence requirements.

The military services noted that cuts in budget requirements for counterintelligence activities have the effect of severely hampering the ability of these services to accomplish missions relating to coverage of threats to the national security. Budgetary deficiencies have occurred at a time when investigative work loads are increasing significantly.

Manpower limitations constitute a major restriction on the FBI's capabilities in the investigation of subversive activities. The problem is further complicated by the fact that, even if substantial numbers of Agents could be recruited on a crash basis, the time required to conduct background investigations and to provide essential training would mean several months' delay in personnel being available for use against the rapidly escalating subversive situation.

In the event, as a result of this report, additional
collection requirements should be levied on the agencies involved,
it would be necessary to provide for essential funding. For example,

DECISION: Budget and Manpower Restrictions

_____   Each agency should submit a detailed estimate as
to projected manpower needs and other costs in the
event the various investigative restraints herein are
lifted.

_____   Each agency must operate within its current
budgetary or manpower limitations, irrespective
of action required as result of this report.

_____   More information is needed.

PART THREE

EVALUATION OF INTERAGENCY COORDINATION

I. CURRENT PROCEDURES TO EFFECT COORDINATION

There is currently no operational body or mechanism specifically charged with the overall analysis, coordination, and continuing evaluation of practices and policies governing the acquisition and dissemination of intelligence, the pooling of resources, and the correlation of operational activities in the domestic field.

Although a substantial exchange of intelligence and research material between certain of the interested agencies already exists, much remains to be done in the following areas: (1) the preparation of coordinated intelligence estimates in a format useful for policy formulation; (2) the coordination of intelligence collection resources of the member agencies and the establishment of clear-cut priorities for the various agencies; and (3) the coordination of the operational activities of member agencies in developing the required intelligence.

II. SUGGESTED MEASURES TO IMPROVE THE COORDINATION OF DOMESTIC INTELLIGENCE COLLECTION

It is believed that an interagency group on domestic intelligence should be established to effect coordination between the various member agencies. This group would define the specific requirements of the various agencies, provide regular evaluations of domestic intelligence, develop recommendations relative to policies governing operations in the field of domestic intelligence, and prepare periodic domestic intelligence estimates which would incorporate the results of the combined efforts of the entire intelligence community.

Membership in this group should consist of appropriate representatives named by the Directors of the Federal Bureau of Investigation, the Central Intelligence Agency, the National Security Agency, the Defense Intelligence Agency, and the counterintelligence agencies of the Departments of the Army, Navy, and Air Force. In addition, an

- 42 -

appropriate representative of the White House would have membership.
The committee would report periodically to the White House, and a
White House staff representative would coordinate intelligence originating
with this committee in the same manner as Dr. Henry Kissinger, Assistant
to the President, coordinates foreign intelligence on behalf of the
President. The chairman would be appointed by the President.

   This interagency group would have authority to determine
appropriate staff requirements and to implement these requirements,
subject to the approval of the President, in order to meet the
responsibilities and objectives described above.

DECISION: Permanent Interagency Group

   _____ An ad hoc group consisting of the FBI, CIA, NSA,
DIA, and the military counterintelligence agencies
should be appointed and should serve as long as the
President deems necessary, to provide evaluations
of domestic intelligence, prepare periodic domestic
intelligence estimates, and carry out the other
objectives indicated above. The ad hoc group should
be tasked to develop a permanent organization to
carry out the objectives of this report.

   _____ A permanent committee consisting of the FBI, CIA,
NSA, DIA, and the military counterintelligence
agencies should be appointed to provide evaluations of
domestic intelligence, prepare periodic domestic
intelligence estimates, and carry out the other
objectives indicated above.

   _____ No further action required.

   _____ More information is needed.

NOTE: The FBI is opposed to the creation of a permanent committee
for the purpose of providing evaluations of domestic intelligence,
however, the FBI would approve of preparing periodic domestic
intelligence estimates.

- 43 -

Memorandum from Huston to Haldeman ([78], pp. 480–484)

25.7 TOM CHARLES HUSTON MEMORANDUM, AUGUST 5, 1970

THE WHITE HOUSE

WASHINGTON

August 5, 1970

TOP SECRET
HANDLE VIA COMINT CHANNELS ONLY

EYES ONLY

MEMORANDUM FOR H. R. HALDEMAN

FROM: TOM CHARLES HUSTON

SUBJECT: DOMESTIC INTELLIGENCE

In anticipation of your meeting with Mr. Hoover and the Attorney General, I would like to pass on these thoughts:

1. More than the FBI is involved in this operation. NSA, DIA, CIA, and the military services all have a great stake and a great interest. All of these agencies supported the options selected by the President. For your private information, so did all the members of Mr. Hoover's staff who worked on the report (he'd fire them if he knew this.)

25.7   TOM CHARLES HUSTON MEMORANDUM, AUGUST 5, 1970

TOP SECRET
HANDLE VIA COMINT CHANNELS ONLY

-2-

3.   We are not getting the type of hard intelligence we need at the White House. We will not get it until greater effort is made through community-wide-coordination to dig out the information by using all the resources potentially available. It is, of course, a matter of balancing the obvious risks against the desired results. I thought we balanced these risks rather objectively in the report, and Hoover is escalating the risks in order to cloak his determination to continue to do business as usual.

4.   At some point, Hoover has to be told who is President. He has become totally unreasonable and his conduct is detrimental to our domestic intelligence operations. In the past two weeks, he has terminated all FBI liaison with NSA, DIA, the military services, Secret Service -- everyone except the White House. He terminated liaison with CIA in May. This is bound to have a crippling effect upon the entire community and is contrary to his public assurance to the President at the meeting that there was close and effective coordination and cooperation within the intelligence community. It is important to remember that the entire intelligence community knows that the President made a positive decision to go ahead and Hoover has now succeeded in forcing a review. If he gets his way it is going to look like he is more powerful than the President. He had his say in the footnotes and RN decided against him. That should close the matter and I can't understand why the AG is a party to reopening it. All of us are going to look damn silly in the eyes of Helms, Gayler, Bennett, and the military chiefs if Hoover can unilaterally reverse a Presidential decision based on a report that many people worked their asses off to prepare and which, on its merits, was a first-rate, objective job.

5.   The biggest risk we could take, in my opinion, is to continue to regard the violence on the campus and in the cities as a temporary phenomenon which will simply go away as soon as the Scranton Commission files its report. The one statement that Rennie Davis made at HEW which I thought made sense was that the Attorney

TOP SECRET

25.7 TOM CHARLES HUSTON MEMORANDUM, AUGUST 5, 1970

-3-

General was kidding himself when he said the campuses would be quiet this fall. Davis predicted that at least 30 would be closed down in September. I don't like to make predictions, but I am not at all convinced, on the basis of the intelligence I have seen, that we are anyway near over the hump on this problem, and I am convinced that the potential for even greater violence is present, and we have a positive obligation to take every step within our power to prevent it.

6. Hoover can be expected to raise the following points in your meeting:

(a) "Our present efforts are adequate." The answer is bullshit! This is particularly true with regard to FBI campus coverage.

(b) "The risks are too great; these folks are going to get the President into trouble and RN had better listen to me." The answer is that we have considered the risks, we believe they are acceptable and justified under the circumstances. We are willing to weigh each exceptionally sensitive operation on its merits, but the Director of the FBI is paid to take risks where the security of the country is at stake. Nothing we propose to do has not been done in the past -- and in the past it was always done successfully.

(c) "I don't have the personnel to do the job the President wants done." The answer is (1) he has the people and/or (2) he can get them.

(d) "I don't object to NSA conducting surreptitious entry if they want to." The answer is that NSA doesn't have the people, can't get them, has no authority to get them, and shouldn't have to get them. It is an FBI job.

25.7   TOM CHARLES HUSTON MEMORANDUM, AUGUST 5, 1970

TOP SECRET
HANDLE VIA COMINT CHANNELS ONLY

-4-

(e) "If we do these things the 'jackels of the press and the ACLU will find out; we can't avoid leaks." Answer: We can avoid leaks by using trained, trusted agents and restricting knowledge of sensitive operations on a strict need to know basis. We do this on other sensitive operations every day.

(f) "If I have to do these things, the Attorney General will have to approve them in writing." This is up to the AG, but I would tell Hoover that he has been instructed to do them by the President and he is to do them on that authority. He needn't look for a scape goat. He has his authority from the President and he doesn't need a written memo from the AG. To maintain security, we should avoid written communications in this area.

(g) "We don't need an Inter-Agency Committee on Intelligence Operations because (1) we're doing fine right now -- good coordination, etc. -- and (2) there are other existing groups which can handle this assignment." The answer is that we are doing lousy right now and there aren't other groups which can do the job we have in mind because: (1) they don't meet; (2) they don't have the people on them we want or have some people we don't want; (3) they don't have the author ity to do what we want done; (4) ultimately this new operation will replace them; and (5) they aren't linked to the White House staff.

There are doubtless another dozen or so specious arguments that Hoover will raise, but they will be of similar quality. I hope that you will be able to convince the AG of the importance and necessity of getting Hoover to go along. We have worked for nearly a year to reach this point; others have worked far longer and had abandoned hope. I believe we are talking about the future of this country, for surely domestic violence and disorder threaten the very fabric of our society. Intelligence is not the cure, but it can provide the diagnosis that makes a cure possible. More importantly, it can provide us with the means to prevent the

25.7 *TOM CHARLES HUSTON MEMORANDUM, AUGUST 5, 1970*

TOP SECRET
HANDLE VIA COMINT CHANNELS ONLY

-5-

deterioration of the situation. Perhaps lowered voices and peace
in Vietnam will defuse the tense situation we face, but I wouldn't
want to rely on it exclusively.

There is this final point. For eighteen months we have
watched people in this government ignore the President's orders,
take actions to embarrass him, promote themselves at his
expense, and generally make his job more difficult. It makes
me fighting mad, and what Hoover is doing here is putting
himself above the President. If he thought the Attorney General's
advice should be solicited, he should have done so before the
report was sent to the President. After all, Hoover was chairman
of the committee and he could have asked the AG for his comments.
But no, he didn't do so for it never occurred to him that the
President would not agree with his footnoted objections. He
thought all he had to do was put in a footnote and the matter was
settled. He had absolutely no interest in the views of NSA,
CIA, DIA, and the military services, and obviously he has
little interest in our views, or apparently even in the decisions
of the President. I don't see how we can tolerate this, but
being a fatalist, if not a realist, I am prepared to accept the
fact that we may have to do so.

Tom

TOM CHARLES HUSTON

TOP SECRET

FINDINGS AND RECOMMENDATIONS OF THE CHURCH COMMITTEE WITH REGARD TO DOMESTIC INTELLIGENCE OPERATIONS ([45B], pp. 265–341)

The Huston Plan is perhaps shocking in its magnitude and by its association with the highest levels of government, but as Senator Church pointed out, it "must be viewed as but one episode in a continuous effort by the intelligence agencies to secure the sanction of higher authority for expanded surveillance at home and abroad" ([44B], p. 2). The Church Committee seemed determined to place the Huston Plan in proper perspective—mindful, perhaps, that preoccupation with this incident might divert attention from other threats to civil liberties and political institutions.

COINTELPRO, operating before, during, and after the Huston Plan and unknown to Huston himself, was one such program. It and others, with acronyms such as CHAOS, MKULTRA, and SHAMROCK, were administered by various elements of the intelligence community and were either directed at American citizens or spilled over into the domain of domestic civil liberties. These programs were subjected to close scrutiny in congressional hearings and Executive branch investigations during the 1970–1975 period. The most thorough inquiry was conducted by Senator Church's Select Committee on Intelligence. The findings and recommendations of the final Church report, regarding domestic intelligence operations, are reprinted here.

Major Finding

The Committee finds that those responsible for overseeing, supervising, and controlling domestic activities of the intelligence community, although often unaware of details of the excesses described in this report, made those excesses possible by delegating broad authority without establishing adequate guidelines and procedural checks; by failing to monitor and coordinate sufficiently the activities of the agencies under their charge; by failing to inquire further after receiving indications that improper activities may have been occurring; by exhibiting a reluctance to know about secret details of programs; and sometimes by requesting intelligence agencies to engage in questionable practices. On numerous occasions, intelligence agencies have, by concealment, misrepresentation, or partial disclosure, hidden improper activities from those to whom they owed a duty of disclosure. But such deceit and the improper practices which it concealed would not have been possible to such a degree if senior officials of the Executive Branch and Congress had clearly allocated responsibility and imposed requirements for reporting and obtaining prior approval for activities, and had insisted on adherence to those requirements.

N1

Subfindings

(a) Presidents have given intelligence agencies firm orders to collect information concerning "subversive activities" of American citizens, but have failed until recently to define the limits of domestic intelligence, to provide safeguards for the rights of American citizens, or to coordinate and control the ever-expanding intelligence efforts by an increasing number of agencies.

(b) Attorneys General have permitted and even encouraged the FBI to engage in domestic intelligence activities and to use a wide range of intrusive investigative techniques—such as wiretaps, microphones, and informants—but have failed until recently to supervise or establish limits on these activities or techniques by issuing adequate safeguards, guidelines, or procedures for review.

(c) Presidents, White House officials, and Attorneys General have requested and received domestic political intelligence, thereby contributing to and profiting from the abuses of domestic intelligence and setting a bad example for their subordinates.

(d) Presidents, Attorneys General, and other Cabinet officers have neglected until recently to make inquiries in the face of clear indications that intelligence agencies were engaging in improper domestic activities.

(e) Congress, which has the authority to place restraints on domestic intelligence activities through legislation, appropriations, and oversight committees, has not effectively asserted its responsibilities until recently. It has failed to define the scope of domestic intelligence activities or intelligence collection techniques, to uncover excesses, or to propose legislative solutions. Some of its members have failed to object to improper activities of which they were aware and have prodded agencies into questionable activities.

(f) Intelligence agencies have often undertaken programs without authorization with insufficient authorization, or in disregard of express orders.

(g) The weakness of the system of accountability and control can be seen in the fact that many illegal or abusive domestic intelligence operations were terminated only after they had been exposed or threatened with exposure by Congress or the news media.

Elaboration of Findings

The Committee has found excesses committed by intelligence agencies—lawless and improper behavior, intervention in the democratic process, overbroad intelligence targeting and collection, and the use of covert techniques to discredit and "neutralize" persons and groups defined as enemies by the agencies. But responsibility for those acts does not fall solely on the intelligence agencies which committed them. Systematic excesses would not have occurred if lines of authority had been clearly defined; if procedures for reporting and review had been established; and if those responsible for supervising the intelligence community had properly discharged their duties.

The pressure of events and the widespread confidence in the FBI help to explain the deficiencies in command and authorization discovered by the Committee. Most of the activities examined in this report occurred during periods of foreign or domestic crisis. There was substantial support from the public and all branches of government for some of the central objectives of domestic intelligence policy, including the search for "Fifth Columnists" before World War II; the desire to identify communist "influence" in the Cold War atmosphere of the 1950s; the demand for action against Klan violence in the early 1960s; and the reaction to violent racial disturbances and anti-Vietnam war activities in the late 1960s and early 1970s. It was in this heated environment that President and Attorneys General ordered the FBI to investigate "subversive activities". Further, the Bureau's reputation for effectiveness and professionalism, and Director Hoover's ability to cultivate political support and to inspire apprehension, played a significant role in shaping the relationship between the FBI and the rest of the Government.

With only a few exceptions, the domestic intelligence activities reviewed by the Committee were properly authorized *within* the intelligence agencies. The FBI epitomizes a smoothly functioning military structure: activities of agents are closely supervised; programs are authorized only after they have traveled a well-defined bureaucratic circuit; and virtually all activities—ranging from high-level policy considerations to the minutia of daily reports from field agencies—are reduced to writing. These characteristics are commendable. An efficient law enforcement and intelligence-gathering machine, acting consistently with law, can greatly benefit the nation. However, when used for wrongful purposes, this efficiency can pose a grave danger.

It appears that many specific abuses were not known by the Attorney General, the President, or other Cabinet-level officials directly responsible for supervising domestic intelligence activities. But whether or not particular activities were authorized by a President or Attorney General, those individuals must—as the chief executive and the principal law enforcement officer of the United States Government—bear ultimate responsibility for the activities of executive agencies under their command. The President and his Cabinet officers have a duty to determine the nature of activities engaged in by executive agencies and to prevent undesired activities from taking place. This duty is particularly compelling when responsible officials have reason to believe that undesirable activity is occurring, as has often been the case in the context of domestic intelligence.

The Committee's inquiry has revealed a pattern of reckless disregard of activities that threatened our Constitutional system. Intelligence agencies were ordered to investigate "subversive activities," and were then usually left to determine for themselves which activities were "subversive" and how those activities should be investigated. Intelligence agencies were told they could use investigative techniques—wiretaps, microphones, informants—that permitted them to pry into the most valued areas of privacy and were then given in many cases the unregulated authority to determine when to use those techniques and how long to continue them. Intelligence agencies were encouraged to gather "pure intelligence," which was put to political use by public officials outside of those agencies. This was possibly because Congress had failed to pass laws limiting the areas into which intelligence agencies could legally inquire and the information they could disseminate.

Improper acts were often intentionally concealed from the Government officials responsible for supervising the intelligence agencies, or undertaken without express authority. Such behavior is inexcusable. But equally inexcusable is the absence of executive and congressional oversight that engendered an atmosphere in which the heads of those agencies believed they could conceal activities from their superiors. Attorney General Levi's recent guidelines and the recommendations of this Committee are intended to provide the necessary guidance.

Whether or not the responsible Government officials knew about improper intelligence activities, and even if the agency heads failed in their duty of full disclosure, it still follows that Presidents and the appropriate Cabinet officials *should* have known about those activities. This is a demanding standard, but one that must be imposed. The future of democracy rests upon such accountability.

Subfinding (a)

Presidents have given intelligence agencies firm orders to collect information concerning "subversive activities" of American citizens, but have failed until recently to define the limits of domestic intelligence, to provide safeguards for the rights of American citizens, or to coordinate and control the ever-expanding intelligence efforts by an increasing number of agencies.

As emphasized throughout this report, domestic intelligence activities have been undertaken pursuant to mandates from the Executive branch, generally issued during times of war or domestic crisis. The directives of Presidents Roosevelt, Truman, and Eisenhower to investigate "subversive activities," or other equally ill-defined targets, were echoed in various orders from Attorneys General, who themselves encouraged the FBI to undertake domestic intelligence activities with vague but vigorous commands.

Neither Presidents nor their chief legal officers, the Attorneys General, have defined the "subversive activities" which may be investigated or provided guidelines to the agencies in determining which individuals or groups were engaging in those activities. No reporting procedures were established to enable Cabinet-level officials or their designees to review the types of targets of domestic investigations and to exercise independent judgment concerning whether such investigations were warranted. No mechanisms were established for monitoring the conduct of domestic investigations or for determining if and when they should be terminated. If Presidents had articulated standards in these areas, or had designated someone to do the job for them, it is possible that many of the abuses described in this report would not have occurred.

Considering the proliferation of agencies engaging in domestic intelligence and the overlapping jurisdictional lines, it is surprising that no President has successfully designated one individual or body to coordinate and supervise the domestic intelligence activities of the various agencies. The half-hearted steps that were taken in that direction appear either to have been abandoned or to have resulted in the concentration of even more power in individual agency heads. For example, in 1949 President Truman attempted to establish a control mechanism—the Interdepartmental Intelligence Conference—to centralize authority for supervising domestic intelligence activities of the FBI and military intelligence agencies in a committee chaired by the Director of the FBI. The Committee reported to the National Security Council, and an NSC staff member was assigned responsibility for internal security.[1] The practical effect of the IIC was apparently to increase the power of the FBI Director and to remove control further from the Cabinet level. In 1962, the functions of the IIC were transferred to the Justice Department, and the Attorney General was put in nominal charge of domestic intelligence.[2] While in theory supervision resided in the Internal Security Division of the Justice Department, that Division deferred in large part to the FBI and provided little oversight.[3] The top two executives of the Internal Security Division were former FBI officials. They

---

[1] National Security Council memorandum 17/5, 6/15/49.
[2] National Security Action memorandum 161, 6/9/62.
[3] For example, the FBI continued an investigation of one group in 1964 after the Internal Security Division told the Bureau there was "insufficient evidence" of any legal violations. (Memorandum from Yeagley to Hoover, 3/3/64.) Two years later, an FBI intelligence official suggested that it would be "in the Bureau's best interest to put the Department on record again." The Department approved the FBI's request for permission to continue the investigation even though there had been "no significant changes as to the character and tactics of the organization." The FBI did not request further instructions in this investigation until 1973. (Memorandum from Baumgardner to Sullivan, 7/15/66; memorandum from Yeagley to Hoover, 7/28/66.)

appeared sympathetic to the Bureau, and like the Bureau, emphasized threats of Communist "influence" without mentioning actual results.[4]

Another opportunity to coordinate intelligence collection was missed in 1967, when Attorney General Ramsey Clark established the Interdivisional Intelligence Unit (IDIU) to draw on virtually the entire Federal Government's intelligence collecting capability for information concerning groups and individuals "who may play a role, whether purposefully or not, either in instigating or spreading civil disorders, or in preventing or checking them."[5] In the rush to obtain intelligence, no efforts were made to formulate standards or guidelines for controlling how the intelligence would be collected. In the absence of such guidelines and under pressure for results, the agencies undertook some of the most overly broad programs encountered by the Committee. For example, the FBI's "ghetto" informant program was a direct response to the Attorney General's broad requests for intelligence.

The need for centralized control of domestic intelligence was again given serious consideration during the vigorous demonstrations against the war in Vietnam in 1970. The intelligence community's program for dealing with internal dissent—the Huston Plan—envisioned not only relaxing controls on surveillance techniques, but also coordinating intelligence collection efforts. According to Tom Charles Huston's testimony, the President viewed the suggestion of a coordinating body as the most important contribution of the plan.[8] Although the President quickly revoked his approval for the Huston Plan, the idea of a central domestic intelligence body had taken root. Two months later, with the encouragement of Attorney General John Mitchell, the Intelligence Evaluation Committee was established in the Justice Department. That Committee, like its precursor, the IDIU, compiled and evaluated raw intelligence; it did not exercise supervision.[9]

The growing sophistication of intelligence collection techniques underscores the present need for central control and coordination of domestic intelligence activities. Although the Executive Branch has recognized that need in the past, it has not, until recently, faced up to

---

[4] For example, the annual report of Assistant Attorney General J. Walter Yeagley for Fiscal Year 1959 emphasized Communist attempts to wield influence, without pointing out the lack of tangible results:

"Despite the 'thaw,' real or apparent, in the Cold War, and despite [its] losses, the [Communist] Party has continued as an organized force, constantly *seeking to repair* its losses and *to regain* its former position of influence. In a number of fields its activities are directed ostensibly toward laudable objectives, such as the elimination of discrimination by reason of race, low cost housing for the economically underprivileged, and so on. These activities are pursued in large part *as a way of extending* the forces and currents in American life, and *with the hope of being able* to 'move in' on such movements when the time seems propitious." [Emphasis added.] (Annual Report of the Attorney General for Fiscal Year 1959, pp. 247–248.)

The same executives headed the Internal Security Division from 1959 until 1970, through the administrations of five Attorneys General and four Presidents. In 1971 a new Assistant Attorney General for the Internal Security Division, Robert Mardian, actively encouraged FBI surveillance and collaborated with FBI executive William C. Sullivan in transferring the records of the "17" wiretaps from the Bureau to the Nixon White House.

[5] Memorandum from Attorney General Clark to Kevin Maroney, et al., 11/9/67.

[8] Tom Charles Huston deposition, 5/23/75, p. 32.

[9] Staff summary of interview of Colonel Werner E. Michel, 5/12/75.

its responsibilities. President Gerald Ford's joint effort with members of Congress to place further restrictions on wiretaps is a welcome step in the right direction. Congress must act expeditiously in this area.

Subfinding (b)

Attorneys General have permitted and even encouraged the FBI to engage in domestic intelligence activities and to use a wide range of intrusive investigative techniques—such as wiretaps, microphones, and informants—but have failed until recently to supervise or establish limits on these activities or techniques by issuing adequate safeguards, guidelines, or procedures for review.

The Attorney General is the chief law enforcement officer of the United States and the Cabinet-level officer formally in charge of the FBI.[10] The Justice Department, until recently, has failed to issue directives to the FBI articulating the grounds for opening domestic intelligence investigations or the standards to be followed in carrying out those investigations. The Justice Department has neglected to establish machinery for monitoring and supervising the conduct of FBI investigations, for requiring approval of major investigative decisions, and for determining when an investigation should be terminated. Indeed, in 1972 the Attorney General said he did not even know whether the FBI itself had formulated guidelines and standards for domestic intelligence activities, was not aware of the FBI's manual of instructions, and had never reviewed the FBI's internal guidelines.[11]

The Justice Department has frequently levied specific demands on the FBI for domestic intelligence, but has not accompanied these demands with restrictions or guidelines. Examples include the Justice Department's Civil Rights Division's requests for reports on demonstrations in the early 1960's (including coverage of a speech by Governor-elect George Wallace [11a] and coverage of a civil rights demonstration on the 100th anniversary of the Emancipation Proclamation [12]): Attorney General Kennedy's efforts to expand FBI infiltration of the Ku Klux Klan in 1964; [13] Attorney General Clark's sweeping instructions to collect intelligence about civil disorders in 1967; [14] and the Internal Security Division's request for more extensive investigations of campus demonstrations in 1969.[15] While a limited investigation into some of these areas may have been warranted, the improper acts committed in the course of those investigations were possible because no restraints had been imposed.

The Justice Department also cooperated with the FBI in defying the Emergency Detention Act of 1950 by approving the Bureau's Security Index criteria for the investigation of "potentially dangerous"

---

[10] Despite the formal line of responsibility to the Attorney General, Director J. Edgar Hoover in fact developed an informal channel to the White House. During several administrations beginning with President Franklin Roosevelt the Director and the President circumvented the Justice Department and dealt directly with each other.

[11a] Memorandum from St. John Barrett to Marshall, 6/18/63.

[11a] Memorandum from Director, FBI to Assistant Attorney General Burke Marshall, 12/4/62.

[12] Memorandum from Director, FBI to Assistant Attorney General Burke

[13] Annual Report of the Attorney General for Fiscal Year 1965, pp. 185–186.

[14] Memorandum from Attorney General Clark to Hoover, 9/14/67.

[15] Memorandum from Assistant Attorney General Yeagley to Hoover, 3/3/69.

persons.[16] Even after Congress repealed the Detention Act, the Justice Department allowed the Bureau to continue listing "potentially dangerous" persons on a new Administrative Index. The Department stopped reviewing the names on the FBI's index, and apparently endorsed the FBI's view that the list could, contrary to law, be used for detention purposes in an "emergency."

The FBI's autonomy has been a prominent and long-accepted feature of the Federal bureaucratic terrain. As early as the 1940s the FBI could oppose Justice Department inquiries into its internal affairs by raising the specter of "leaks." [17] The Department acquiesced in the Bureau's claim that it was entitled to withhold its raw files, conceal the identities of informants, and, in a number of cases, refuse to give the Justice Department evidence supporting broad allegations and characterizations. Former Attorney General Katzenbach has pointed out that there were both positive and negative sides to the Bureau's autonomy:

> Keeping the Bureau free from political interference was a powerful argument against efforts by politically appointed officials, whatever their motivations, to gain a greater measure of control over operations of the Bureau. . . . [Director Hoover also] found great value in his formal position as subordinate to the Attorney General and the fact that the FBI was a part of the Department of Justice. . . . In effect, he was uniquely successful in having it both ways; he was protected from public criticism by having a theoretical superior who took responsibility for his work, and was protected from his suprior by his public reputation.

As a consequence of its autonomy, the Bureau could plan and implement many of the abusive operations described in this report. Former Attorneys General have told the Committee that they would never have permitted the more unsavory aspects of the New Left or Racial COINTELPROs if they had been aware of the Bureau's plans. To the extent that Attorneys General were ignorant of the Bureau's activities, it was the consequence not only of the FBI Director's independent political position, but also of the failure of the Attorneys General to establish procedures for finding out what the Bureau was doing and for permitting an atmosphere to evolve in which Bureau officials believed that they had no duty to report their activities to the Justice Department, and that they could conceal those activities with little risk of exposure.[20]

N2

---

[16] Memorandum from Belmont to Ladd, 10/15/52.

[17] Memorandum from Hoover to L. M. C. Smith, Chief, Neutrality Laws Unit, 11/28/40.

[20] The Justice Department's investigation of the FBI's COINTELPRO illustrates the reluctance of the Justice Department to interfere in or even inquire about Internal Bureau matters. Although the existence of COINTELPRO was made public in 1971, the Justice Department did not initiate an investigation until 1974. The Department's Committee, headed by Assistant Attorney General Henry Petersen, which conducted the investigation, agreed to use only summaries of documents prepared by the Bureau instead of examining the Bureau documents themselves.

Those summaries were often extremely misleading. For example, one summary stated:

"It was recommended that an anonymous letter be mailed to the leader of the Blackstone Rangers, a black extremist organization in Chicago. The letter would

(Continued)

Attorneys General have not only neglected to establish procedures for reviewing FBI programs and activities, but they have at the same time granted the FBI authority to employ highly intrusive investigative techniques with inadequate guidelines and review procedures, and in some instances with no external restraints whatsoever. Before 1965, wiretaps required the approval of the Attorney General in advance, but once the Attorney General had authorized wiretap coverage of a subject, the Bureau could continue the surveillance for as long as it judged necessary.

This permissive policy was current in October 1963 when Attorney General Robert Kennedy authorized the FBI to wiretap the phones of Dr. Martin Luther King, Jr. "at his current address or at any future address to which he may move" and to wiretap the New York and Atlanta SCLC offices.[21] Reading the Attorney General's wiretap authorization broadly, the FBI construed Dr. King's "residence" so as to permit wiretaps on three of his hotel rooms and the homes of friends with whom he stayed temporarily.[22] The FBI was still relying on Attorney General Kennedy's initial authorization when it sought reauthorization for the King wiretaps in April 1965 in response to new procedures formulated by Attorney General Katzenbach. Although Attorney General Kennedy's authorizing memorandum in October 1963 said that the FBI should provide him with an evaluation of the wiretaps after 60 days, he failed to complain when the FBI neglected to send him the evaluation. Apparently the Attorney General never mentioned the wiretaps to the FBI again, even though he received FBI reports from the wiretaps until he resigned in September, 1964.[23]

The Justice Department's policy toward the use of microphones has been even more permissive than for wiretaps. Until 1965, the FBI was free to carry out microphone surveillance in national security cases without first seeking the approval of the Attorney General or notifying him afterward. The total absence of supervision enabled the FBI to hide microphones in Dr. Martin Luther King's hotel rooms for nearly two years for the express purpose of not only determining whether he was being influenced by allegedly communist advisers, but to "attempt" to obtain information about the private "activities

---

(Continued)
hopefully drive a wedge between the Blackstone Rangers and the Black Panthers Party. The anonymous letter would indicate that the Black Panther Party in Chicago blamed the leader of the Blackstone Rangers for blocking their programs."

The document from which this summary was derived, however, stated that the Blackstone Rangers were prone to "violent type activity, shooting, and the like." The anonymous letter was to state that "the Panthers blame you for blocking their thing and there's supposed to be a hit out for you." The memorandum concluded that the letter "may intensify the degree of animosity between the two groups" and "lead to reprisals against its leadership." (Memorandum from Chicago Field Office to FBI Headquarters, 1/18/69.)

[21] Memorandum from J. Edgar Hoover to Attorney General Robert Kennedy, 10/7/63; memorandum from J. Edgar Hoover to Attorney General Robert Kennedy, 10/18/63.

[22] Letter from FBI to Senate Select Committee, 7/24/75, ...

[23] See M. L. King Report: "Electrtronic Surveillance of Dr. Martin Luther King and the Christian Leadership Conference." It should be noted, however, that President Kennedy was assassinated a month after the wiretap was installed which may account for Attorney General Kennedy's failure to inquire about the King wiretaps, at least for the first few months.

of Dr. King and his associates" so that Dr. King could be "completely discredited." [24] Attorney General Kennedy was apparently never told about the microphone surveillances of Dr. King, although he did receive reports containing unattributed information from that surveillance from which he might have concluded that microphones were the source.[25]

The Justice Department imposed external control over microphones for the first time in March 1965, when Attorney General Katzenbach applied the same procedures to wiretaps and microphones, requiring not only prior authorization but also formal periodic review.[26] But irregularities were tolerated even with this standard. For example, the FBI has provided the Committee three memoranda from Director Hoover, initialed by Attorney General Katzenbach, as evidence that it informed the Justice Department of its microphone surveillance of Dr. King after the March 1965 policy change. These documents, however, show that Katzenbach was informed about the microphones only after they had already been installed.[27] Such after-the-fact approval was permitted under Katzenbach's procedures.[27a] There is no indication that Katzenbach inquired further after receiving the notice.[28]

The Justice Department condoned, and often encouraged, the FBI's use of informants—the investigative technique with the highest potential for abuse. However, the Justice Department imposed no restrictions on informant activity or reporting, and established no procedures for reviewing the Bureau's decision to use informants in a particular case.

In 1954 the Justice Department entered into an agreement with the CIA in which the CIA was permitted to withhold the names of

---

[24] Memorandum from Frederick Baumgardner to William Sullivan, 1/28/64.

[25] The FBI informed the Committee that it has no documents indicating that Attorney General Kennedy was told about the microphones. His associates in the Justice Department testified that they were never told, and they did not believe that the Attorney General had been told about the microphones. (See memorandum from Charles Brennan to William Sullivan, 12/19/66; Courtney Evans testimony, 12/1/75, p. 20; Burke Marshall testimony, 3/3/76, p. 43.)

The question of whether Attorney General Kennedy suspected that the FBI was using microphones to gather information about Dr. King must be viewed in light of the Attorney General's express authorization of wiretaps in the King case on national security grounds, and the FBI's practice—known to the Attorney General—of installing microphones in such national security cases without notifying the Department.

[26] Memorandum from Director, FBI to Attorney General, 3/30/65, p. 2. The Attorney General's policy change occurred during a period of publicity and Congressional inquiry into the FBI's use of electronic surveillance.

[27] Memorandum from Director, FBI to Attorney General, 5/17/65; Memorandum from Director, FBI, to Attorney General, 10/19/65; Memorandum from Director, FBI, to Attorney General, 12/1/65.

[27a] Katzenbach advised Director Hoover in September 1965 that "in emergency situations [wiretaps and microphones] may be used subject to my later ratification." (Memorandum from Katzenbach to Hoover, 9/27/65.) Nevertheless, there is no indication that these microphone surveillances of Dr. King presented "emergency situations."

[28] Katzenbach testified that he could not recall having seen the notices, although he acknowledged the initials on the memoranda as in his handwriting and in the location where he customarily placed his initials. (Katzenbach, 12/3/75, Hearings, Vol. 6, p. 227.)

employees whom it had determined were "almost certainly guilty of violations of criminal statutes" when the CIA could "devise no charge" under which they could be prosecuted that would not "require revelation of highly classified information." [29] This practice was terminated by the Justice Department in January, 1975.[29a]

Despite the failure of Attorneys General to exercise the supervision that is necessary in the area of domestic intelligence, several Attorneys General have taken steps in the right direction. Of note were Attorney General Nicholas Katzenbach's review procedures for electronic surveillance in 1965; Ramsey Clark's refusal to approve electronic surveillance of domestic intelligence targets and his rejection of repeated requests by the FBI for such surveillance; Acting Deputy Attorney General William Ruckelshaus' inquiries into the Bureau's domestic intelligence program; Deputy Attorney General Laurence Silberman's inquiry into political abuses of the FBI in early 1975; and Attorney General Saxbe's decision to make the Justice Department's COINTELPRO report public.

During the past year, Attorney General Edward H. Levi has exercised welcome leadership by formulating guidelines for FBI investigations; developing legislative proposals requiring a judicial warrant for national security wiretaps and microphones; establishing the Office of Professional Responsibility to inquire into departmental misconduct; initiating investigations of alleged wrongdoing by the FBI; and cooperating with this Committee's requests for documents on FBI intelligence operations.[30] The Justice Department's concern in recent years is a hopeful sign, but long overdue.

Subfinding (c)

Presidents, White House officials, and Attorneys General have requested and received domestic political intelligence, thereby contributing to and profiting from the abuses of domestic intelligence and setting a bad example for their subordinates.

The separate finding on "political abuse" sets forth instances in which the FBI was used by White House officials to gather politically useful information, including data on administration opponents and critics. This misuse of the Bureau's powers by its political superiors necessarily contributed to the atmosphere in which abuses flourished.

If the Bureau's superiors were willing to accept the fruits of excessive intelligence gathering, to authorize electronic surveillance for political purposes, and to receive reports on critics which included intimate details of their personal lives, they could not credibly hold the Bureau to a high ethical standard. If political expediency characterized the decisions of those expected to set limits on the Bureau's conduct, it is not surprising that the FBI considered the principle of expediency endorsed.

---

[29] Memorandum from Lawrence Houston to Deputy Attorney General, 3/1/54.
[29a] Memorandum for the Record by General Counsel, CIA, 1/31/75.
[30] The Committee's requests also provided the Department of Justice with the opportunity to see most of these FBI documents for the first time.

Subfinding (d)

Presidents, Attorneys General, and other cabinet officers have neglected, until recently, to make inquiries in the face of clear indications that intelligence agencies were engaging in improper domestic activities.

Executive branch officials contributed to an atmosphere in which excesses were possible by ignoring clear indications of excesses and failing to take corrective measures when directly confronted with improper behavior. The Committee's findings on "Violating and Ignoring the Law" illustrate that several questionable or illegal programs continued after higher officials had learned partial details and failed to ask for additional information, either out of the naive assumption that intelligence agencies would not engage in lawless conduct, or because they preferred not to be informed.[31]

Some of the most disturbing examples of insufficient action in the face of clear danger signals were uncovered in the Committee's investigation of the FBI's program to "neutralize" Dr. Martin Luther King, Jr. as the leader of the civil rights movement. The Bureau informed the Committee that its files contain no evidence that any officials outside of the FBI "were specifically aware of any efforts, steps, or plans or proposals to 'discredit' or 'neutralize' King." [32] The relevant executive branch officials have told the Committee that they were unaware of a general Bureau program to discredit King. Former Attorney General Katzenbach, however, told the Committee:

> Nobody in the Department of Justice connected with Civil Rights could possibly have been unaware of Mr. Hoover's feelings [against Dr. King]. Nobody could have been unaware of the potential for disaster which those feelings embodied. But, given the realities of the situation, I do not believe one could have anticipated the extremes to which it was apparently carried.[34]

The evidence before the Committee confirms that the "potential for disaster" was indeed clear at the time. There is no question that officials in the White House and Justice Department, including President Johnson and Attorney General Katzenbach, knew that the Bureau was taking steps to discredit Dr. King, although they did not know the full extent of the Bureau's efforts.

—In January 1964 the FBI gave Presidential Assistant Walter Jenkins an FBI report unfavorable to Dr. King. According to a contemporaneous FBI memorandum, Jenkins said that he "was of the opinion that the FBI could perform a good service to the country if this matter could somehow be confidentially given to members of the press." Jenkins, in a staff interview, denied having made such a suggestion.[35]

---

[31] One cabinet official, when told that the CIA wanted to tell him something secret, replied, "I would rather not know anything about it." The "secret" matter was CIA's illegal mail opening program. (J. Edward Day testimony, 10/22/75, Hearings, Vol. 4, p. 45.)

[32] Letter from FBI to the Senate Select Committee, 11/6/75.

[34] Katzenbach, 12/3/75, Hearings, Vol. 6, p. 209.

[35] Memorandum from Cartha DeLoach to J. Edgar Hoover, 1/14/64; Staff summary of Walter Jenkins Interview, 12/1/75, pp. 1–2. Mr. Jenkins subsequently said that he was unable to testify formally because of illness and has failed to answer written interrogatories submitted to him by the Committee for response under oath.

—In February 1964 a reporter informed the Justice Department that the FBI had offered to "leak" information unfavorable to Dr. King to the press. The Justice Department's Press Chief, Edwin Guthman, asked Cartha DeLoach, the FBI's liaison with the press, about this allegation and DeLoach denied any involvement. The Justice Department took no further action.[36]

—Bill Moyers, an Assistant to President Johnson, testified that he learned sometime in early 1964 that an FBI agent twice offered to play a tape recording for Walter Jenkins that would have been personally embarrassing to Dr. King and that Jenkins refused to listen to the tape on both occasions.[36a] Moyers testified that he never asked the FBI why it had the tape or was offering to play it in the White House.[37] When asked if he had ever questioned the propriety of the FBI's disseminating information of a personal nature about Dr. King within the Government, he replied, "I never questioned it, no." When he was asked if he could recall anyone in the White House ever questioning the propriety of the FBI disseminating this type of material, Moyers testified. "I think . . . there were comments that tended to ridicule the FBI's doing this, but no." [38]

—Burke Marshall, Assistant Attorney General in charge of the Civil Rights Division, testified that sometime in 1964 a reporter told him that the Bureau had offered information unfavorable to Dr. King. Marshall testified that he repeated this allegation to a Bureau official and asked for a report. The Bureau official subsequently informed him "The Director wants you to know that you're a . . . damned liar." [39]

—In November 1964 the Washington Bureau Chief of a national news publication told Attorney General Katzenbach and Assistant Attorney General Marshall that one of his reporters had been approached by the FBI and offered the opportunity to hear some "interesting" tape recordings involving Dr. King. Katzenbach testified that he had been "shocked," and that he and Marshall had informed President Johnson, who "took the matter very seriously" and promised to contact Director Hoover.[40] Neither Marshall nor Katzenbach knew if the President contacted Hoover.[41] Katzenbach testified that, during this same period, he learned of at least one other reporter who had been offered tape recordings by the Bureau, and that he personally confronted DeLoach, who was reported to have made the offers.[42] DeLoach told Katzenbach that he had never made such offers.[43] The only record of this episode in FBI files is a memorandum by DeLoach stating that Moyers had informed him that the newsman was "telling

[36] Memorandum from John Mohr to Cartha DeLoach, 2/5/65; Edwin Guthman testimony, 3/16/76, pp. 20–23.
[36a] Bill Moyers testimony, 3/2/76, p. 19.
[37] Bill Moyers testimony, 3/2/76, p. 19; staff summary of Bill Moyers interview, 11/24/75.
In an unsworn staff interview, Jenkins denied that he ever received an offer to listen to such tapes. (Staff summary of Walter Jenkins interview, 12/1/75.)
[38] Moyers, 3/2/76, pp. 17–18.
[39] Marshall, 3/8/76, pp. 46–47.
[40] Katzenbach, 12/3/75, Hearings, Vol. 6, p. 210.
[41] Marshall, 3/3/76, p. 43; Katzenbach, 12/3/75, Hearings, Vol. 6, p. 210.
[42] Katzenbach, 12/3/75, Hearings, Vol. 6, p. 210.
[43] Katzenbach, 12/3/75, Hearings, Vol. 6, p. 210. DeLoach testified before the Committee that he did not recall conversations with reporters about tape recordings of Dr. King. (Cartha DeLoach testimony, 11/25/75, p. 156.)

all over town" that the FBI was making allegations concerning Dr. King, and that Moyers had "stated that the President felt that [the newsman] lacked integrity. . . ." [44] Moyers could not recall this episode, but told the Committee that it would be fair to conclude that the President had been upset by the fact that the newsman revealed the Bureau's conduct rather than by the Bureau's conduct itself.[45]

The response of top White House and Justice Department officials to strong indications of wrongdoing by the FBI was clearly inadequate. The Attorney General went no further than complaining to the President and asking a Bureau official if the charges were true. President Johnson apparently not only failed to order the Bureau to stop, but indeed warned it not to deal with certain reporters because they had complained about the Bureau's improper conduct.

In 1968 Attorney General Ramsey Clark asked Director Hoover if he had "any information as to how" facts about Attorney General Kennedy's authorization of the wiretap on Dr. King had leaked to columnists Drew Pearson and Jack Anderson. Clark requested the FBI Director to "undertake whatever investigation you deem feasible to determine how this happened." [45a] Director Hoover's reply, drafted in the office of Cartha DeLoach, expressed "dismay" at the leak and offered no indication of the likely source.[45b]

In fact, DeLoach had prepared a memorandum ten days earlier stating that a middle-level Justice Department official with knowledge of the King wiretap met with him and admitted having "discussed this matter with Drew Pearson." According to this memorandum, DeLoach attempted to persuade the official not to allow the story to be printed because "certain Negro groups would still blame the FBI, whether we were ordered to take such action or not." [45c] Thus, DeLoach and Hoover deliberately misled Attorney General Clark by withholding their knowledge of the source of the "leak."

Subfinding (e)

Congress, which has the authority to place restraints on domestic intelligence activities through legislation, appropriations, and oversight committees, has not effectively asserted its responsibilities until recently. It has failed to define the scope of domestic intelligence activities or intelligence collection techniques, to uncover excesses, or to propose legislative solutions. Some of its members have failed to object to improper activities of which they were aware and have prodded agencies into questionable activities.

Congress, unlike the Executive branch, does not have the function of supervising the day-to-day activities of agencies engaged in domestic

---

[44] Memorandum from Cartha DeLoach to John Mohr, 12/1/64.

[45] Moyers, 3/2/76, p. 9.

[45a] Memorandum from Clark to Hoover, 5/27/68. The story was published in the midst of Robert Kennedy's campaign for the Democratic presidential nomination.

[45b] Memorandum from Hoover to Clark, 5/28/68.

[45c] Memorandum from C. D. DeLoach to Mr. Tolson, 5/17/68. Four days later DeLoach had a phone conversation with Jack Anderson in which, according to partment official "had advised him concerning specific information involving an old wire tap on King." (Memorandum from C. D. DeLoach to Mr. Tolson, 5/21/68.) Both of these memoranda were initialed by Hoover.

intelligence. Congress does, however, have the ability through legislation to affect almost every aspect of domestic intelligence activity: to erect the framework for coordinating domestic intelligence activities; to define and limit the types of activities in which executive agencies may engage; to establish the standards for conducting investigations; and to promulgate guidelines for controlling the use of wiretaps, microphones, and informants. Congress could also exercise a great influence over domestic intelligence through its power over the appropriations for intelligence agencies' budgets and through the investigative powers of its committees.

Congress has failed to establish precise standards governing domestic intelligence. No congressional statutes deal with the authority of executive agencies to conduct domestic intelligence operations, or instruct the executive in how to structure and supervise those operations. No statutes address when or under what conditions investigations may be conducted. Congress did not attempt to formulate standards for wiretaps or microphones until 1968, and even then avoided the issue of domestic intelligence wiretaps by allowing an exception for an undefined claim of inherent executive power to conduct domestic security surveillance, which was subsequently held unconstitutional. [45d] No legislative standards have been enacted to govern the use of informants.

Congress has helped shape the environment in which improper intelligence activities were possible. The FBI claims that sweeping provisions in several vague criminal statutes and regulatory measures enacted by Congress provide a basis for much of its domestic intelligence activity.[45e] Congress also added its voice to the strong consensus in favor of governmental action against Communism in the 1950's and domestic dissidents in the 1960's and 1970's.

Congress' failure to define intelligence functions has invited action by the executive. If the top officials of the executive branch are responsible for failing to control the intelligence agencies, that failure is in part due to a lack of guidance from Congress.

During most of the 40-year period covered in this report, congressional committees did not effectively monitor domestic intelligence activities. For example, in 1966, a Senate Judiciary subcommittee undertook an investigation of electronic surveillance and other intrusive techniques by Federal agencies. According to an FBI memorandum, its chairman told a delegation from the FBI that he would make "a commitment that he would in no way embarrass the FBI," and acceded in the FBI's request that the subcommittee refrain from calling FBI witnesses.[46]

[45d] *U.S.* v. *U.S. District Court*, 407 U.S. 297 (1972).

[45e] These include the Smith Act of 1940 and the Voorhis Act of 1941. In addition to reliance on these statutes to buttress its claim of authority for domestic intelligence operations, the FBI has also placed reliance on a Civil War seditious conspiracy statute and a rebellion and insurrection statute passed during the Whiskey Rebellion of the 1790's. FBI Director Clarence Kelley, in a letter to the Attorney General, stated that these later statutes were designed for past centuries, "not the Twentieth Century." (Memorandum from Director, FBI, to Attorney General, Hearings, Vol. 6, Exhibit 53.) The Committee agrees.

[46] Memorandum from DeLoach to Clyde Tolson, 1/21/66.

Another example of the deficiencies in congressional oversight is seen in the House Appropriations Committee's regular approval of the FBI's requests for appropriations without raising objections to the activities described in the Director's testimony and off-the-record briefings. There is no question that members of a House Appropriations subcommittee were aware not only that the Bureau was engaged in broad domestic intelligence investigations, but that it was also employing disruptive tactics against domestic targets.

In 1958, Director Hoover informed the subcommittee that the Bureau had an "intensive program" to "disorganize and disrupt" the Communist Party, that the program had existed "for years" and that Bureau informants were used "as a disruptive tactic." [47] The next year, the Director informed the subcommittee that informants in 12 field offices

> have been carefully briefed to engage in controversial discussions with the Communist Party so as to promote dissention, factionalism and defections from the communist cause. This technique has been extremely successful from a disruptive standpoint.
>
> Under another phase of this program, we have carefully selected 28 items of anticommunist propaganda and have anonymously mailed it to selected communists, carefully concealing the identity of the FBI as its source. More than 2,800 copies of literature have been placed in the hands of active communists.[48]

Hoover described more aggressive "psychological warfare" techniques in 1962:

> During the past year we have caused disruption at large Party meetings, rallies and press conferences through various techniques such as causing the last-minute cancellation of the rental of the hall, packing the audience with anticommunists, arranging adverse publicity in the press and making available embarrassing questions for friendly reporters to ask the Communist Party functionaries.

The Appropriations subcommittee was also told during this briefing that the FBI's operations included exposing and discrediting "communists who are secretly operating in legitimate organizations and employments, such as the Young Men's Christian Association, Boy Scouts, civic groups, and the like." [49]

In 1966 Director Hoover informed the Appropriations subcommittee that the disruptive program had been extended to the Ku Klux Klan.[50]

The present Associate Director of the FBI, Nicholas Callahan, who accompanied Director Hoover during several of his appearances before the Appropriations subcommittee, said that members of the subcom-

---

[47] 1958 Fiscal Year Briefing Paper prepared by FBI for House Appropriations Committee.
[48] 1959 Fiscal Year Briefing Paper prepared by FBI for House Appropriations Committee.
[49] 1962 Fiscal Year Briefing Paper prepared by FBI for House Appropriations Committee.
[50] 1966 Fiscal Year Briefing Paper prepared by FBI for House Appropriations Committee.

mittee made "no critical comment" about "the Bureau's efforts to neutralize groups and associations." [51]

Subcommittee Chairman John Rooney's statements in a televised interview in 1971 regarding FBI briefings about Dr. Martin Luther King are indicative of the subcommittee's attitude toward the Bureau:

> Representative ROONEY. Now you talk about the F.B.I. leaking something about Martin Luther King. I happen to know all about Martin Luther King, but I have never told anybody.
> *Interviewer.* How do you know everything about Martin Luther King?
> Representative ROONEY. From the Federal Bureau of Investigation.
> *Interviewer.* They've told you—gave you information based on taps or other sources about Martin Luther King.
> Representative ROONEY. They did.
> *Interviewer.* Is that proper?
> Representative ROONEY. Why not? [52]

Former Assistant Attorney General Fred Vinson recalled that in 1967 the Justice Department averaged "fifty letters a week from Congress" demanding that "people like [Stokely] Carmichael be jailed." Vinson said that on one occasion when he was explaining First Amendment limits at a congressional hearing, a Congressman "got so provoked he raised his hand and said, 'to hell with the First Amendment.' " Vinson testified that these incidents fairly characterized "the atmosphere of the time." [53]

The congressional performance has improved, however, in recent years. Subcommittees of the Senate Judiciary Committee have initiated inquiries into Army surveillance of domestic targets and into electronic surveillance by the FBI. House Judiciary Committee subcommittees commissioned a study of the FBI by the General Accounting Office and have inquired into FBI misconduct and surveillance activities. Concurrent with this Committee's investigations, the House Select Committee on Intelligence considered FBI domestic intelligence activities.

Our Constitution envisions Congress as a check on the Executive branch, and gives Congress certain powers for discharging that function. Until recently, Congress has not effectively fulfilled its constitutional role in the area of domestic intelligence. Although the appropriate congressional committees did not always know what intelligence agencies were doing, they could have asked. The Appropriations subcommittee was aware that the FBI was engaging in activities far beyond the mere collection of intelligence, yet it did not inquire into the details of those programs.[54] If Congress had addressed the issues of domestic intelligence and passed regulatory legislation, and if it had probed into the activities of intelligence agencies and required them to

---

[51] Memorandum from FBI to Select Committee, 1/12/76.
[52] Interview with Congressman Rooney, NBC News' "First Tuesday," 6/1/71.
[53] Fred Vinson testimony, 1/27/76, p. 34.
[54] Director Hoover appears to have told the subcommittee of the House Appropriations Committee more about COINTELPRO operations and techniques than he told the Justice Department or the White House.

account for their deeds, many of the excesses in this Report might not have occurred.

Subfinding (f)

Intelligence agencies have often undertaken programs without authorization, with insufficient authorization, or in defiance of express orders.

The excesses detailed in this report were due in part to the failure of Congress and the Executive branch to erect a sound framework for domestic intelligence, and in part to the dereliction of responsibility by executive branch officials who were in charge of individual agencies. Yet substantial responsibility lies with officials of the intelligence agencies themselves. They had no justification for initiating major activities without first seeking the express approval of their superiors. The pattern of concealment and partial and misleading disclosures must never again be allowed to occur.

The Committee's investigations have revealed numerous instances in which intelligence agencies have assumed programs or activities were authorized under circumstances where it could not reasonably be inferred that higher officials intended to confer authorization. Sometimes far-reaching domestic programs were initiated without the knowledge or approval of the appropriate official outside of the agencies. Sometimes it was claimed that higher officials had been "notified" of a program after they had been informed only about some aspects of the program, or after the program had been described with vague references and euphemisms, such as "neutralize," that carried different meanings for agency personnel than for uninitiated outsiders. Sometimes notice consisted of references to programs buried in the details of lengthy memoranda; and "authorization" was inferred from the fact that higher officials failed to order the agency to discontinue the program that had been obscurely mentioned.

The Bureau has made no claim of outside authorization for its COINTELPROs against the Socialist Workers Party, Black Nationalists, or New Left adherents. After 1960, its fragile claim for authorization of the COINTELPROs against the Communist Party USA and White Hate Groups was drawn from a series of hints and partial, obscured disclosures to the Attorneys General and the White House.

The first evidence of notification to higher government officials of the FBI's COINTELPRO against the Communist Party USA consists of letters from Director Hoover to President Eisenhower and Attorney General William Rogers in May 1958 informing them that "in August of 1956, this Bureau initiated a program designed to promote disruption within the ranks of the Communist Party (CP) USA." [55] There is no record of any reply to these letters.

Later that same year, Director Hoover told President Eisenhower and his Cabinet:

> To counteract a resurgence of Communist Party influence in the United States, we have a . . . program designed to intensify any confusion and dissatisfaction among its members.

---

[55] Memorandum from the Director, FBI to the Attorney General, 5/8/58.

During the past few years, this program has been most effective. Selected informants were briefed and trained to raise controversial issues within the Party.... The Internal Revenue Service was furnished names and addresses of Party functionaries who had been active in the underground apparatus ... ; Anticommunist literature and simulated Party documents were mailed anonymously to carefully chosen members. . . .[56]

The FBI's only claim to having notified the Kennedy Administration about COINTELPRO rests upon a letter written shortly before the inauguration in January 1961 from Director Hoover to Attorney General-designate Robert Kennedy, Deputy Attorney General-designate Byron R. White, and Secretary of State-designate Dean Rusk. One paragraph in the five-page letter stated that the Bureau had a "carefully planned program of counterattack against the CPUSA which keeps it off balance," and which was "carried on from both inside and outside the party organization." The Bureau claimed to have been "successful in preventing communists from seizing control of legitimate mass organizations" and to have "discredited others who were secretly operating inside such organizations." [57] Specific techniques were not mentioned, and no additional notice was provided to the Kennedy Administration. Indeed, when the Kennedy White House formally requested of Hoover a report on "Internal Security Programs," the Director described only the FBI's "investigative program," and made no reference to disruptive activities.[58]

The only claimed notice of the COINTELPRO against the Ku Klux Klan was given after the program had begun and consisted of a partial description buried within a discussion of other subjects. In September 1965, copies of a two-page letter were sent to President Johnson and Attorney General Katzenbach, describing the Bureau's success in solving a number of cases involving racial violence in the South. That report contained a paragraph stating that the Bureau was "seizing every opportunity to disrupt the activities of Klan organizations," and briefly described the exposure of a Klan member's "kickback" scheme involving insurance company premiums.[59] More questionable tactics, such as sending a letter to a Klansman's wife to destroy their marriage, were not mentioned. The Bureau viewed Katzenbach's reply to its letter—which praises the investigative successes which are the focus of the FBI's letter—as constituting authorization for the White Hate COINTELPRO.[60]

The claimed notification to Attorney General Ramsey Clark of the White Hate COINTELPRO consisted of a ten-page memorandum captioned "Ku Klux Klan Investigations—FBI Accomplishments" with a buried reference to Bureau informants "removing" Klan officers and "provoking scandal" within the Klan organization [61] Clark

[56] Excerpt from FBI Director's Briefing of Cabinet, 11/6/58.
[57] Memorandum from Hoover to Attorney General Robert Kennedy, 1/10/61, copies to White and Rusk.
[58] Letter from J. Edgar Hoover to McGeorge Bundy, 7/25/61, and attached I.I.C. Report: "Status of U.S. Internal Security Programs."
[59] Letters from Hoover to Marvin Watson, Special Assistant to the President, and Attorney General Katzenbach, 9/17/65.
[60] Memorandum from Katzenbach to Hoover, 9/3/65.
[61] Memorandum from Hoover to Clark, 12/18/67.

told the Committee that he did not recall reading those phrases or interpreting them as notice that the Bureau was engaging in disruptive tactics[62] Cartha DeLoach, Assistant to the Director during this period, testified that he "distinctly" recalled briefing Attorney General Clark "generally . . . concerning COINTELPRO."[63] Clark denied having been briefed.[64]

The letters and briefings described above, which constitute the Bureau's entire claim to notice and authorization for the CPUSA and White Hate COINTELPROs, failed to mention techniques which risked physical, emotional, or economic harm to their targets. In no case was an Attorney General clearly told the nature and extent of the programs and asked for his approval. In no case was approval expressly given.

Former Attorney General Katzenbach cogently described another misleading form of "authorization" relied on by the Bureau and other intelligence agencies:

> As far as Mr. Hoover was concerned, it was sufficient for the Bureau if at any time any Attorney General had authorized [a particular] activity in any circumstances. In fact, it was often sufficient if any Attorney General had written something which could be construed to authorize it or had been informed in some one of hundreds of memoranda of some facts from which he could conceivably have inferred the possibility of such an activity. Perhaps to a permanent head of a large bureaucracy this seems a reasonable way of proceeding. However, there is simply no way an incoming Cabinet officer can or should be charged with endorsing every decision of his predecessor. . . .[65]

For example, the CPUSA COINTELPRO was substantially described to the Eisenhower Administration, obliquely to the Kennedy Administration designees, but continued—apparently solely on the strength of those assumed authorizations—through the Johnson Administration and into the Nixon Administration. The idea that authority might continue from one administration to the next and that there is no duty to reaffirm authority inhibits responsible decision making. Circumstances may change and judgments may differ. New officials should be given—and should insist upon—the opportunity to review significant programs.

The CIA's mail opening project illustrates an instance in which an intelligence agency apparently received authorization for a limited program and then expanded that program into significant new areas without seeking further authorization. In May 1954, DCI Allen Dulles and Richard Helms, then Chief of Operations in the CIA's Directorate of Plans, briefed Postmaster General Arthur Summerfield about the CIA's New York mail project, which at that time involved only the examination of envelope exteriors. CIA memoranda indicate that Summerfield's approval was obtained for photographing envelope exteriors, but no mention was made of the possibility of mail opening.[66]

---

[62] Clark, 12/3/75, Hearings, Vol. 6, p. 235.
[63] DeLoach, 12/3/75, Hearings, Vol. 6, p. 183.
[64] Clark, 12/3/75, Hearings, Vol. 6, p. 232.
[65] Katzenbach, 12/3/75, Hearings, Vol. 6, p. 202.
[66] Memorandum from Richard Helms, Chief of Operations, DDP, to Director of Security, 5/17/54.

The focus of the CIA's project shifted to mail opening sometime during the ensuing year, but the CIA did not return to inform Summerfield and made no attempt to secure his approval for this illegal operation.

Intelligence officers have sometimes withheld information from their superiors and concealed programs to prevent discovery by their superiors. The Bureau apparently ignored the Attorney General's order to stop classifying persons as "dangerous" in 1943; unilaterally decided not to provide the Justice Department with information about communist espionage on at least two occasions "for security reasons;" and withheld similar information from the Presidential Commission investigating the government's security program in 1947. More recently, CIA and NSA concealed from President Richard Nixon their respective mail opening and communications interception programs.

These incidents are not unique. The FBI also concealed its Reserve Index of prominent persons who were not included on the Security Index reviewed by the Justice Department; its other targeting programs against "Rabble Rousers," "Agitators," "Key Activists," and "Key Extremists;" and its use of intrusive mail opening and surrepititious entry techniques. Indeed, the FBI institutionalized its capability to conceal activities from the Justice Department by establishing a regular "Do Not File" procedure, which assured internal control while frustrating external accountability.

Subfinding (g)

The weakness of the system of accountability and control can be seen in the fact that many illegal or abusive domestic intelligence operations were terminated only after they had been exposed or threatened with exposure by Congress or the news media.

The lack of vigorous oversight and internal controls on domestic intelligence activity frequently left the termination of improper programs to the *ad hoc* process of public exposure or threat of exposure by Congress, the press, or private citizens. Less frequently, domestic intelligence projects were terminated solely because of an agency's internal review of impropriety.

The Committee is aware that public exposure can jeopardize legitimate, productive, and costly intelligence programs. We do not condone the extralegal activities which led to the exposure of some questionable operations.

Nevertheless two point emerge from an examination of the termination of numerous domestic intelligence activities: (1) major illegal or improper operations thrived in an atmosphere of secrecy and inadequate executive control; and (2) public airing proved to be the most effective means of terminating or reforming those operations.

Some intelligence officers and Executive branch administrators sought the termination of questionable programs as soon as they became aware of the nature of the operation—the Committee praises their actions. However, too often we have seen that the secrecy that protected illegal or improper activities and the insular nature of the agencies involved prevented intelligence officers from questioning their actions or realizing that they were wrong.

There are several noteworthy examples of illegal or abusive domestic intelligence activities which were terminated only after the threat of public exposure:

—The FBI's widesweeping COINTELPRO operations were terminated on April 27, 1971, in response to disclosures about the program in the press.[73]

—IRS payments to confidential informants were suspended in March 1975 as a result of journalistic investigation of Operation Leprechaun.[74]

—The Army's termination of several major domestic intelligence operations, which were clearly overbroad or illegal, came only after the programs were disclosed in the press or were scheduled as the subject of congressional inquiry.[75]

—On one occasion, FBI Director Hoover insisted that electronic surveillance be discontinued prior to his appearance before the House Appropriations Committee so that he could report a relatively small number of wiretaps in place.[76] Contrary to frequent allegations, however, no general pattern of temporary suspensions or terminations during the Director's appearances before the House Appropriations Committee is revealed by Bureau records.

—Following the report of a Presidential committee which had been established in response to news reports in 1967, the CIA terminated its covert relationship with a large number of domestically based organizations, such as academic institutions, student groups, private foundations, and media projects aimed at an international audience.[78]

Other examples of curtailment of domestic intelligence activity in response to the prospect of public exposure include: President Nixon's

---

[73] Memorandum from Brennan to Sullivan, 4/27/71; letter from Director, FBI, to all Field Offices, 4/28/71. Even after the termination of COINTELPRO, it was suggested that "counterintelligence action" would be considered "in exceptional instances" so long as there were "tight procedures to insure absolute secrecy" (Sullivan memorandum, 4/27/71; letter from Director, FBI to all Field Offices, 4/28/71.)

[74] See IRS Report: "Operation Leprechaun."

[75] The Army made its first effort to curb its domestic collection of "civil disturbance" intelligence on the political activities of private citizens in June 1970, only after press disclosures about the program which prompted two Congressional committees to schedule hearings on the matter. (Christopher Pyle, "CONUS Intelligence: The Army Watches Civilian Politics" *Washington Monthly*, January 1970.) Despite legal opinions, both from inside and outside the Army, that domestic radio monitoring by the Army Security Agency was illegal, the Army did not move to terminate the program until after the media revealed that the Army Security Agency had monitored radio transmissions during the 1968 Democratic National Convention (Memorandum from Army Assistant Chief of Staff for Intelligence to the Army General Counsel re: UPASA Covert Activities in Civil Disturbance Control Operations.) Department of Defense controls on domestic surveillance were not imposed until March 1971, after NBC News reported that the Army had placed Senator Adlai Stevenson III and Congressman Abner Mikva under surveillance. (NBC News, "First Tuesday", 12/1/70.)

[76] This involved nine of the so-called "17" wiretaps in February 1971. (Report of the Committee on the Judiciary, House of Representatives, 8/20/75, pp. 148, 149.)

[78] This included nine of the so-called "17" wiretaps in February 1971. In response to the storm of public and congressional criticism engendered by a press account of CIA support for a student organization, President Johnson appointed a Committee, chaired by then Under Secretary of State Nicholas Katzenbach, to review government activities that "endanger the integrity and independence" of United States educational and private voluntary organizations which operate abroad. In March 1967, the Committee recommended "that no federal agency shall provide any covert financial assistance or support, direct or

(Continued)

revocation of approval for the Huston Plan out of concern for the risk of disclosure of the possible illegal actions proposed and the fact that "their sensitivity would likely generate media criticism if they were employed;" [79] J. Edgar Hoover's cessation of the bugging of Dr. Martin Luther King, Jr.'s hotel rooms after the initiation of a Senate investigation chaired by Edward V. Long of Missouri; [80] and the CIA's consideration of suspending mail-opening until the Long inquiry abated and eventual termination of the program "in the Watergate climate." [81] More recently, several questionable domestic intelligence practices have been terminated at least in part as a result of Congressional investigation.[82]

(Continued)

indirect, to any of the nation's educational or private voluntary organizations." The CIA responded with a major review of such projects.

The question of the nature and extent of the CIA's compliance with the Katzenbach guidelines is discussed in the Committee's Foreign Intelligence Report.

[79] Response by Richard Nixon to Interrogatory Number 17 posed by Senate Select Committee.

[80] On January 7, 1966, in response to Associate Director Tolson's recommendation, Director Hoover "reserve[d] final decision" about whether to discontinue all microphone surveillance of Dr. King "until DeLoach sees [Senator Edward V.] Long." (Memorandum from Sullivan to DeLoach, 1/21/66.) The only occasion on which the FBI Director rejected a recommendation for bugging a hotel room of Dr. King's was January 21, 1966, the same day that Assistant Director De-Loach met with an aide to Senator Long to try to head off the Long Committee's hearings on the subject of FBI "bugs" and taps. (Memorandum from DeLoach to Tolson, 1/21/66.) When DeLoach returned from the meeting, he reported:

"While we have neutralized the threat of being embarrassed by the Long Subcommittee, we have not yet eliminated certain dangers which might be created as a result of newspaper pressure on Long. We therefore must keep on top of this situation at all times." (Memorandum, Executives Conference to the Director, 1/7/66.)

Another possible explanation for Hoover's cessation of the King hotel bugging is found in the impact of a memorandum from the Solicitor General in the Black case which Hoover apparently interpreted as a restriction upon the FBI's authority to conduct microphone surveillance. (Supplemental memorandum for the *United States*, *U.S.* v. *Black*, submitted by Solicitor General Thurgood Marshall, 7/13/66; Katzenbach, 10/11/75. p. 58.)

[81] In 1965, the Long Subcommittee investigation caused the CIA to consider whether its major mail opening "operations should be partially or fully suspended until the subcommittee's investigations are completed." When the CIA contacted Chief Postal Inspector Henry Montague and learned that he believed that the Long investigation would "soon cool off," it was decided to continue the operation. (Memorandum to the files by "CIA officer." 4/23/65.)

Despite continued apprehensions about the "flap potential" of exposure and repeated recognition of its illegality, the actual termination of the CIA's New York mail-opening project came, according to CIA Office of Security Director Howard Osborn because: "I thought it was illegal and in the Watergate climate we had absolutely no business doing this." (Howard Osborn deposition, 8/28/75, p. 89.) He discussed the matter with William Colby who agreed that the project was illegal and should not be continued, "particularly in a climate of that type." (Osborn deposition, 8/28/75, p. 90.)

[82] Shortly after the Senate Select Committee on Intelligence Activities held hearings on the laxity of the system for disclosure of tax return information to United States attorneys, the practice was changed. In October 1975, U.S. Attorneys requesting tax return information were required by the IRS to provide a sufficient explanation of the need for the information and the intended use to which it would be put to enable IRS to ascertain the validity of the request. Operation SHAMROCK, NSA's program of obtaining millions of international telegrams, was terminated in May 1975, according to a senior NSA official, primarily because it was no longer a valuable source of foreign intelligence and because the Senate Select Committee's investigation of the program had increased the risk of exposure. (Staff summary of "senior NSA official" interview, 9/17/75, p. 3.)

There are several prominent instances of terminations which resulted from an internal review process:

—In August 1973, shortly after taking office, Internal Revenue Service Commissioner Donald Alexander abolished the Special Service Staff upon learning that it was engaged in political intelligence activities which he considered "antithetical to proper tax administration." [83]

—An internal legal review in 1973 prompted the termination of the joint effort by NSA and CIA to monitor United States-South American communications by individuals named on a drug traffic "watch list." [84]

—On May 9, 1973, newly appointed CIA Director James Schlesinger requested from CIA personnel an inventory of all "questionable activities" which the Agency had undertaken. The 694 pages of memoranda received in response to this request—which became known at the CIA as "The Family Jewels"—prompted the termination or limitation of a number of programs which were in violation of the the Agency's mandate, notably the CHAOS project involving intelligence-gathering against American citizens. [85]

—In the early 1960s, the CIA's MKULTRA testing program, which involved surreptitiously administering drugs to unwitting persons,

N4

N5

---

[83] Donald Alexander testimony, 10/2/75, Hearings, Vol. 3, p. 8. Alexander testified, however, that in a meeting with IRS administrators on the day after he took office, the SSS was discussed, and "full disclosure" was not made to him. Prior to the Leprechaun revelations, Commissioner Alexander had also initiated a general review of IRS information-gathering and retrieval systems, and he had already suspended certain types of information-gathering due to discovery of vast quantities of non-tax-related material. (Alexander, 10/2/75, Hearings, Vol. 3, pp. 8–10.)

Another termination due to internal review, took place at IRS in 1968. The Chief of the Disclosure Branch terminated what he considered the "illegal" provision of tax return information to the FBI by another IRS Division. (IRS Memorandum, D. O. Virdin to Harold Snyder, 5/2/68.) During this same period, the CIA was also obtaining returns in a manner similar to the FBI (though in much smaller numbers), yet no one in the Intelligence Division or elsewhere in the Compliance Division apparently thought to examine that practice in light of the change being made in the practice with respect to the FBI. (Donald O. Virdin testimony, 9/16/75, pp. 69–73.)

[84] The CIA suspended its participation in the program as a result of an opinion by its General Counsel, Lawrence Houston, that the intercepts were illegal. (Memorandum from Houston to Acting Chief of Division, 1/29/73.) Shortly thereafter, NASA reviewed the legality and appropriateness of its own involvement in what was essentially a law enforcement effort by the Bureau of Narcotics and Dangerous Drugs rather than a foreign intelligence program, which is the only authorized province for NSA operations. ("Senior NSA official deposition," 9/16/75, p. 10.) In June 1973 the Director of NSA terminated the drug watch list, several months after the CIA had terminated its own intercept program. NSA's drug watch list activity had been in operation since 1970....

In the fall of 1973, NSA terminated the remainder of its watch list activity, which had involved monitoring communications by individuals targeted for NSA by other agencies including CIA, FBI, and BNDD. In response to the Keith case and to another case which threatened to disclose the existence of the NSA watch list, NSA and the Justice Department had begun to reconsider the propriety of the program. The review process culminated in termination. See NSA Report: Termination of Civil Disturbance Watch List.

[85] Schlesinger described his review of "grey area activities" which were "perhaps legal, perhaps not legal" as a part of "the enhanced effort that came in the wake of Watergate" for oversight of the propriety of Government activities. (Schlesinger testimony. Rockefeller Commission, 5/5/75, pp. 114, 116.) Schlesinger testified that his request for the reporting of "questionable activities" came after

(Continued)

N6   was "frozen" after the Inspector General questioned the morality and lack of administrative control of the program.[85a]

—Several mail-opening operations were terminated because they lacked sufficient intelligence value, which was often measured in relation to the "flap potential"—or risk of disclosure—of an operation. However, both the CIA and the FBI continued other mail-opening

N7   operations after these terminations.[86]

The Committee's examination of the circumstances surrounding terminations of a wide range of improper or illegal domestic intelligence activities clearly points to the need for more effective oversight from outside the agencies. In too many cases, the impetus for the termination of programs of obviously questionable propriety came from the press or the Congress rather than from intelligence agency administrators or their superiors in the Executive Branch. Although there were several laudable instances of termination as a responsible outgrowth of an agency's internal review process, the Committee's record indicates that this process alone is insufficient—intelligence agencies cannot be left to police themselves.

(Continued)

learning that "there was this whole set of relationships" between the CIA and White House "plumber" E. Howard Hunt, Jr., about which Schlesinger had not been briefed completely upon assuming his position. (Schlesinger, Rockefeller Commission testimony, p. 115.) "As a consequence," Schlesinger "insisted that all people come forward" with "anything to do with the Watergate affair" and any other arguably improper or illegal operations. (Schlesinger, Rockefeller Commission, 5/5/75, p. 116.)

[85a] After the Inspector General's survey of the Technical Services Division, he recommended termination of the testing program. (Earman memorandum, 5/5/63.) The program was then suspended pending resolution at the highest levels within the CIA of the issues presented by the program—"the risks of embarrassment to the Agency, coupled with the moral problem." (Memorandum from DDP Helms to DCI McCone, 9/4/65.) In response to the IG Report, DDP Helms recommended to DCI McCone that unwitting testing continue. Helms maintained that the program could be conducted in a "secure and effective manner" and believed it "necessary that the Agency maintain a central role in this activity, keep current on enemy capabilities in the manipulation of human behavior, and maintain an offensive capability." (Memorandum from Helms to DCI McCone, 8/19/63.) The Acting DCI deferred decision on the matter and directed TSD in the meantime to "continue the freeze on unwitting testing." (CIA memorandum to Senate Select Commitee, received 9/4/75.) According to a CIA report to the Select Committee:

"With the destruction of the MKULTRA files in early 1973, it is believed that there are no definitive records in CIA that would record the termination of the program for testing behavioral drugs on unwitting persons. . . . There is no record to our knowledge, that [the] freeze was ever lifted." (CIA memorandum to Senate Select Committee. received 9/4/75.)

Testimony from the CIA officials involved confirmed that the testing was not resumed. . . .

[86] Two FBI mail-opening programs were suspended for security reasons involving changes in local postal personnel and never reinstituted, on the theory that the value of the programs did not justify the risk involved. (Memorandum from San Francisco Field Office to FBI Headquarters, 5/19/66.) The CIA's San Francisco mail-opening project "was terminated since the risk factor outweighed continuing an activity which had already achieved its objectives." (Memorandum to Chief, East Asia Division, June 1973.) The lack of any significant intelligence value to the CIA apparently led to the termination of the New Orleans mail-opening program. (Memorandum from "Identity 13" to Deputy Director of Security, 10/9/57.) Three other programs were terminated because they had produced no valuable counterintelligence information, while diverting manpower needed for other operations.

Conclusions

The findings which have emerged from our investigation convince us that the Government's domestic intelligence policies and practices require fundamental reform. We have attempted to set out the basic facts; now it is time for Congress to turn its attention to legislating restraints upon intelligence activities which may endanger the constitutional rights of Americans.

The Committee's fundamental conclusion is that intelligence activities have undermined the constitutional rights of citizens and that they have done so primarily because checks and balances designed by the framers of the Constitution to assure accountability have not been applied.

Before examining that conclusion, we make the following observations.

—While nearly all of our findings focus on excesses and things that went wrong, we do not question the need for lawful domestic intelligence. We recognize that certain intelligence activities serve perfectly proper and clearly necessary ends of government. Surely, catching spies and stopping crime, including acts of terrorism, is essential to insure "domestic tranquility" and to "provide for the common defense." Therefore, the power of government to conduct *proper* domestic intelligence activities under effective restraints and controls must be preserved.

—We are aware that the few earlier efforts to limit domestic intelligence activities have proven ineffectual. This pattern reinforces the need for statutory restraints coupled with much more effective oversight from all branches of the Government.

—The crescendo of improper intelligence activity in the latter part of the 1960s and the early 1970s shows what we must watch out for: In time of crisis, the Government will exercise its power to conduct domestic intelligence activities to the fullest extent. The distinction between legal dissent and criminal conduct is easily forgotten. Our job is to recommend means to help ensure that the distinction will always be observed.

—In an era where the technological capability of Government relentlessly increases, we must be wary about the drift toward "big brother government." The potential for abuse is awesome and requires special attention to fashioning restraints which not only cure past problems but anticipate and prevent the future misuse of technology.

—We cannot dismiss what we have found as isolated acts which were limited in time and confined to a few willful men. The failures to obey the law and, in the words of the oath of office, to "preserve, protect, and defend" the Constitution, have occurred repeatedly throughout administrations of both political parties going back four decades.

—We must acknowledge that the assignment which the Government has given to the intelligence community has, in many ways, been impossible to fulfill. It has been expected to predict or prevent every crisis, respond immediately with information on any question, act to meet all threats, and anticipate the special needs of Presidents. And then it is chastised for its zeal. Certainly, a fair assessment must place a major part of the blame upon the failures of senior executive officials and Congress.

In the final analysis, however, the purpose of this Committee's work is not to allocate blame among individuals. Indeed, to focus on personal culpability may divert attention from the underlying institutional causes and thus may become an excuse for inaction.

Before this investigation, domestic intelligence had never been systematically surveyed. For the first time, the Government's domestic surveillance programs, as they have developed over the past forty years, can be measured against the values which our Constitution seeks to preserve and protect. Based upon our full record, and the findings which we have set forth...............above, the Committee concludes that:

> *Domestic Intelligence Activity Has Threatened and Undermined The Constitutional Rights of Americans to Free Speech, Association and Privacy. It Has Done So Primarily Because The Constitutional System for Checking Abuse of Power Has Not Been Applied.*

Our findings and the detailed reports which supplement this volume set forth a massive record of intelligence abuses over the years. Through a vast network of informants, and through the uncontrolled or illegal use of intrusive techniques—ranging from simple theft to sophisticated electronic surveillance—the Government has collected, and then used improperly, huge amounts of information about the private lives, political beliefs and associations of numerous Americans.

Affect Upon Constitutional Rights.—That these abuses have adversely affected the constitutional rights of particular Americans is beyond question. But we believe the harm extends far beyond the citizens directly affected.

Personal privacy is protected because it is essential to liberty and the pursuit of happiness. Our Constitution checks the power of Government for the purpose of protecting the rights of individuals, in order that all our citizens may live in a free and decent society. Unlike totalitarian states, we do not believe that any government has a monopoly on truth.

When Government infringes those rights instead of nurturing and protecting them, the injury spreads far beyond the particular citizens targeted to untold numbers of other Americans who may be intimidated.

Free government depends upon the ability of all its citizens to speak their minds without fear of official sanction. The ability of ordinary people to be heard by their leaders means that they must be free to join in groups in order more effectively to express their grievances. Constitutional safeguards are needed to protect the timid as well as the courageous, the weak as well as the strong. While many Americans have been willing to assert their beliefs in the face of possible governmental reprisals, no citizen should have to weigh his or her desire to express an opinion, or join a group, against the risk of having lawful speech or association used against him.

Persons most intimidated may well not be those at the extremes of the political spectrum, but rather those nearer the middle. Yet voices of moderation are vital to balance public debate and avoid polarization of our society.

The federal government has recently been looked to for answers to nearly every problem. The result has been a vast centralization of power. Such power can be turned against the rights of the people. Many of the restraints imposed by the Constitution were designed to guard against such use of power by the government.

Since the end of World War II, governmental power has been increasingly exercised through a proliferation of federal intelligence programs. The very size of this intelligence system, multiplies the opportunities for misuse.

Exposure of the excesses of this huge structure has been necessary. Americans are now aware of the capability and proven willingness of their Government to collect intelligence about their lawful activities and associations. What some suspected and others feared has turned out to be largely true—vigorous expression of unpopular views, association with dissenting groups, participation in peaceful protest activities, have provoked both government surveillance and retaliation.

Over twenty years ago, Supreme Court Justice Robert Jackson, previously an Attorney General, warned against growth of a centralized power of investigation. Without clear limits, a federal investigative agency would "have enough on enough people" so that "even if it does not elect to prosecute them" the Government would, he wrote, still "find no opposition to its policies". Jackson added, "Even those who are supposed to supervise [intelligence agencies] are likely to fear [them]." His advice speaks directly to our responsibilities today:

> I believe that the safeguard of our liberty lies in limiting any national police or investigative organization, first of all to a small number of strictly federal offenses, and secondly to nonpolitical ones. The fact that we may have confidence in the administration of a federal investigative agency under its existing head does not mean that it may not revert again to the days when the Department of Justice was headed by men to whom the investigative power was a weapon to be used for their own purposes.[1]

Failure to Apply Checks and Balances.—The natural tendency of Government is toward abuse of power. Men entrusted with power, even those aware of its dangers, tend, particularly when pressured, to slight liberty.

Our constitutional system guards against this tendency. It establishes many different checks upon power. It is those wise restraints which keep men free. In the field of intelligence those restraints have too often been ignored.

The three main departures in the intelligence field from the constitutional plan for controlling abuse of power have been:

(*a*) *Excessive Executive Power.*—In a sense the growth of domestic intelligence activities mirrored the growth of presidential power generally. But more than any other activity, more even than exercise of the war power, intelligence activities have been left to the control of the Executive.

For decades Congress and the courts as well as the press and the public have accepted the notion that the control of intelligence activities was the exclusive prerogative of the Chief Executive and his surrogates. The exercise of this power was not questioned or even inquired into by outsiders. Indeed, at times the power was seen as flowing not from the law, but as inherent in the Presidency. Whatever the theory, the fact was that intelligence activities were essentially exempted from the normal system of checks and balances.

---

[1] Robert H. Jackson, *The Supreme Court in the American System of Government* (New York: Harper Torchbook, 1955, 1963), pp. 70–71.

Such Executive power, not founded in law or checked by Congress or the courts, contained the seeds of abuse and its growth was to be expected.

(b) *Excessive Secrecy.*—Abuse thrives on secrecy. Obviously, public disclosure of matters such as the names of intelligence agents or the technological details of collection methods is inappropriate. But in the field of intelligence, secrecy has been extended to inhibit review of the basic programs and practices themselves.

Those within the Executive branch and the Congress who would exercise their responsibilities wisely must be fully informed. The American public, as well, should know enough about intelligence activities to be able to apply its good sense to the underlying issues of policy and morality.

Knowledge is the key to control. Secrecy should no longer be allowed to shield the existence of constitutional, legal and moral problems from the scrutiny of all three branches of government or from the American people themselves.

(c) *Avoidance of the Rule of Law.*—Lawlessness by Government breeds corrosive cynicism among the people and erodes the trust upon which government depends.

Here, there is no sovereign who stands above the law. Each of us, from presidents to the most disadvantaged citizen, must obey the law.

As intelligence operations developed, however, rationalizations were fashioned to immunize them from the restraints of the Bill of Rights and the specific prohibitions of the criminal code. The experience of our investigation leads us to conclude that such rationalizations are a dangerous delusion.

B. *Principles Applied in Framing Recommendations and The Scope of the Recommendations.*

Although our recommendations are numerous and detailed, they flow naturally from our basic conclusion. Excessive intelligence activity which undermines individual rights must end. The system for controlling intelligence must be brought back within the constitutional scheme.

Some of our proposals are stark and simple. Because certain domestic intelligence activities were clearly wrong, the obvious solution is to prohibit them altogether. Thus, we would ban tactics such as those used in the FBI's COINTELPRO. But other activities present more complex problems. We see a clear need to safeguard the constitutional rights of speech, assembly, and privacy. At the same time, we do not want to prohibit or unduly restrict necessary and proper intelligence activity.

In seeking to accommodate those sometimes conflicting interests we have been guided by the earlier efforts of those who originally shaped our nation as a republic under law.

The Constitutional amendments protecting speech and assembly and individual privacy seek to preserve values at the core of our heritage and vital to our future. The Bill of Rights, and the Supreme Court's decisions interpreting it suggest three principles which we have followed:

(1) Governmental action which directly infringes the rights of free speech and association must be prohibited. The First Amendment recognizes that even if useful to a proper end, certain governmental actions are simply too dangerous to permit at all. It commands that "Congress shall make *no* law" abridging freedom of speech or assembly.

(2) The Supreme Court, in interpreting that command, has required that any governmental action which has a collateral (rather than direct) impact upon the rights of speech and assembly is permissible only if it meets two tests. First, the action must be undertaken only to fulfill a compelling governmental need, and second, the government must use the least restrictive means to meet that need. The effect upon protected interests must be minimized.[2]

(3) Procedural safeguards—"auxiliary precautions" as they were characterized in the Federalist Papers [3]—must be adopted along with substantive restraints. For example, while the Fourth Amendment prohibits only "unreasonable" searches and seizures, it requires a procedural check for reasonableness—the obtaining of a judicial warrant upon probable cause from a neutral magistrate. Our proposed procedural checks range from judicial review of intelligence activity before or after the fact, to formal and high level Executive branch approval, to greater disclosure and more effective Congressional oversight.

The Committee believes that its recommendations should be embodied in a comprehensive legislative charter defining and controlling the domestic security activities of the Federal Government. Accordingly, Part i of the recommendations provides that intelligence agencies must be made subject to the rule of law. In addition, Part i makes clear that no theory, of "inherent constitutional authority" or otherwise, can justify the violation of any statute.

Starting from the conclusion, based upon our record, that the Constitution and our fundamental values require a substantial curtailment of the scope of domestic surveillance, we deal after Part i with five basic questions:

1. Which agencies should conduct domestic security investigations?

The FBI should be primarily responsible for such investigations. Under the minimization principle, and to facilitate the control of domestic intelligence operations, only one agency should be involved in investigative activities which, even when limited as we propose, could give rise to abuse. Accordingly, Part ii of these recommendations reflects the Committee's position that foreign intelligence agencies (the CIA, NSA, and the military agencies) should be precluded from domestic security activity in the United States. Moreover, they should only become involved in matters involving the rights of Americans abroad where it is impractical to use the FBI, or where in the course of their lawful foreign intelligence operations [4] they inadvertently collect information relevant to domestic security investigations. In Part iii the Committee recommends that non-intelligence agencies such as the Internal Revenue Service and the Post Office be required, in the course of any incidental involvement in domestic se-

---

[2] *De Gregory* v. *New Hampshire*, 383 U.S. 825, 829 (1966) ; *NAACP* v. *Alabama*, 377 U.S. 288 (1964) ; *Gibson* v. *Florida Legislative Investigation Commission*, 372 U.S. 539, 546 (1962) ; *Shelton* v. *Tucker*, 364 U.S. 479, 488 (1960).

[3] Madison, Federalist No. 51. Madison made the point with grace:

"If men were angels, no government would be necessary. If angels were to govern men, neither external nor internal controls on government would be necessary. In framing a government which is to be administered by men over men, the great difficulty lies in this: you must first enable the government to control the governed; and in the next place oblige it to control itself. A dependence on the people is, no doubt, the primary control on the government; but experience has taught mankind the necessity of auxiliary precautions."

[4] Directed primarily at foreigners abroad.

curity investigations, to protect the privacy which citizens expect of first class mail and tax records entrusted to those agencies.

2. When should an American be the subject of an investigation at all; and when can particularly intrusive covert techniques, such as electronic surveillance or informants, be used?

In Part iv, which deals with the FBI, the Committee's recommendations seek to prevent the excessively broad, ill-defined and open ended investigations shown to have been conducted over the past four decades. We attempt to change the focus of investigations from constitutionally protected advocacy and association to dangerous conduct. Part iv also sets forth specific substantive standards for, and procedural controls on, particular intrusive techniques.

3. Who should be accountable within the Executive branch for ensuring that intelligence agencies comply with the law and for the investigation of alleged abuses by employees of those agencies?

In Parts v and vi, the Committee recommends that these responsibilities fall initially upon the agency heads, their general counsel and inspectors general, but ultimately upon the Attorney General. The information necessary for control must be made available to those responsible for control, oversight and review; and their responsibilities must be made clear, formal, and fixed.

4. What is the appropriate role of the courts?

In Part vii, the Committee recommends the enactment of a comprehensive civil remedy providing the courts with jurisdiction to entertain legitimate complaints by citizens injured by unconstitutional or illegal activities of intelligence agencies. Part viii suggests that criminal penalties should attach in cases of gross abuse. In addition, Part iv provides for judicial warrants before certain intrusive techniques can be used.

5. What is the appropriate role of Congress:

In Part xii the Committee reiterates its position that the Senate create a permanent intelligence oversight committee.

The recommendations deal with numerous other issues such as the proposed repeal or amendment of the Smith Act, the proposed modernization of the Espionage Act to cover modern forms of espionage seriously detrimental to the national interest, the use of the GAO to assist Congressional oversight of the intelligence community, and remedial measures for past victims of improper intelligence activity.

Scope of Recommendations.—The scope of our recommendations coincides with the scope of our investigation. We examined the FBI, which has been responsible for most domestic security investigations, as well as foreign and military intelligence agencies, the IRS, and the Post Office, to the extent they became involved incidentally in domestic intelligence functions. While there are undoubtedly activities of other agencies which might legitimately be addressed in these recommendations, the Committee simply did not have the time or resources to conduct a broader investigation. Furthermore, the mandate of Senate Resolution 21 required that the Committee exclude from the coverage of its recommendations those activities of the federal government which are directed at organized crime and narcotics.

The Committee believes that American citizens should not lose their constitutional rights to be free from improper intrusion by their Government when they travel overseas. Accordingly, the Committee proposes recommendations which apply to protect the rights of Americans abroad as well as at home.

1. Activities Covered

The Domestic Intelligence Recommendations pertain to: the domestic security activities of the federal government; [5] and any activities of military or foreign intelligence agencies which affect the rights of Americans [6] and any intelligence activities of any non-intelligence agency working in concert with intelligence agencies, which affect those rights.

2. Activities Not Covered

The recommendations are not designed to control federal investigative activities directed at organized crime, narcotics, or other law enforcement investigations unrelated to domestic security activities.

3. Agencies Covered

The agencies whose activities are specifically covered by the recommendations are:

(i) the Federal Bureau of Investigation; (ii) the Central Intelligence Agency; (iii) the National Security Agency and other intelligence agencies of the Department of Defense; (iv) the Internal Revenue Service; and (v) the United States Postal Service.

While it might be appropriate to provide similar detailed treatment to the activities of other agencies, such as the Secret Service, Customs Service, and Alcohol, Tobacco, and Firearms Division (Treasury Department), the Committee did not study these agencies intensively. A permanent oversight committee should investigate and study the intelligence functions of those agencies and the effect of their activities on the rights of Americans.

4. Indirect Prohibitions

Except as specifically provided herein, these Recommendations are intended to prohibit any agency from doing indirectly that which it would be prohibited from doing directly. Specifically, no agency covered by these Recommendations should request or induce any other agency, or any person, whether the agency or person is American or foreign, to engage in any activity which the requesting or inducing agency is prohibited from doing itself.

5. Individuals and Groups Not Covered

Except as specifically provided herein, these Recommendations do not apply to investigation of foreigners [7] who are officers or employees of a foreign power, or foreigners who, pursuant to the direction of

---

[5] "Domestic security activities" means federal governmental activities, directed against Americans or conducted within the United States or its territories, including enforcement of the criminal law, intended to (a) protect the United States from hostile foreign intelligence activity, including espionage; (b) protect the federal, state, and local governments from domestic violence or rioting; and (c) protect Americans and their government from terrorist activity. See Part xiii of the recommendations and conclusions for all the definitions used in the recommendations.

[6] "Americans" means U.S. citizens, resident aliens and unincorporated associations, composed primarily of U.S. citizens or resident aliens; and corporations, incorporated or having their principal place of business in the United States or having majority ownership by U.S. citizens, or resident aliens, including foreign subsidiaries of such corporations, provided, however, Americans does not include corporations directed by foreign governments or organizations.

[7] "Foreigners" means persons and organizations who are not Americans as defined above.

a foreign power, are engaged in or about to engage in "hostile foreign intelligence activity" or "terrorist activity".

6. Geographic Scope

These Recommendations apply to intelligence activities which affect the rights of Americans whether at home or abroad, including all domestic security activities within the United States.

7. Legislative Enactment of Recommendations

Most of these Recommendations are designed to be implemented in the form of legislation and others in the form of regulations pursuant to statute. (Recommendations 85 and 90 are not proposed to be implemented by statute.

C. Recommendations

Pursuant to the requirement of Senate Resolution 21, these recommendations set forth the new congressional legislation [the Committee] deems necessary to "safeguard the rights of American citizens." [9] We believe these recommendations are the appropriate conclusion to a traumatic year of disclosures of abuses. We hope they will prevent such abuses in the future.

i. Intelligence Agencies Are Subject to the Rule of Law

Establishing a legal framework for agencies engaged in domestic security investigation is the most fundamental reform needed to end the long history of violating and ignoring the law set forth in Finding A. The legal framework can be created by a two-stage process of enabling legislation and administrative regulations promulgated to implement the legislation.

However, the Committee proposes that the Congress, in developing this mix of legislative and administrative charters, make clear to the Executive branch that it will not condone, and does not accept, any theory of inherent or implied authority to violate the Constitution, the proposed new charters, or any other statutes. We do not believe the Executive has, or should have, the inherent constitutional authority to violate the law or infringe the legal rights of Americans, whether it be a warrantless break-in into the home or office of an American, warrantless electronic surveillance, or a President's authorization to the FBI to create a massive domestic security program based upon secret oral directives. Certainly, there would be no such authority after Congress has, as we propose it should, covered the field by enactment of a comprehensive legislative charter.[10] Therefore statutes enacted pursuant to these recommendations should provide the exclusive legal authority for domestic security activities.

Recommendation 1.—There is no inherent constitutional authority for the President or any intelligence agency to violate the law.

Recommendation 2.—It is the intent of the Committee that statutes implementing these recommendations provide the exclusive legal authority for federal domestic security activities.

(*a*) No intelligence agency may engage in such activities unless authorized by statute, nor may it permit its employees, informants, or other covert human sources [11] to engage in such activities on its behalf.

---

[9] S. Res. 21, Sec. 5 ; 2(12).

[10] See, *e.g., Youngstown Sheet and Tube Company* v. *Sawyer*, 343 U.S. 579 (1952).

[11] "Covert human sources" means undercover agents or informants who are paid or otherwise controlled by an agency.

(*b*) No executive directive or order may be issued which would conflict with such statutes.

Recommendation 3.—In authorizing intelligence agencies to engage in certain activities, it is not intended that such authority empower agencies, their informants, or covert human sources to violate any prohibition enacted pursuant to these Recomendations or contained in the Constitution or in any other law.

ii. United States Foreign and Military Agencies Should Be Precluded from Domestic Security Activities

Part iv of these Recommendations centralizes domestic security investigations within the FBI. Past abuses also make it necessary that the Central Intelligence Agency, the National Security Agency, the Defense Intelligence Agency, and the military departments be precluded expressly, except as specifically provided herein, from investigative activity which is conducted within the United States. Their activities abroad should also be controlled as provided herein to minimize their impact on the rights of Americans.

a. Central Intelligence Agency

The CIA is responsible for foreign intelligence and counterintelligence. These recommendations minimize the impact of CIA operations on Americans. They do not affect CIA investigations of foreigners outside of the United States. The main thrust is to prohibit past actions revealed as excessive, and to transfer to the FBI other activities which might involve the CIA in internal security or law enforcement matters. Those limited activities which the CIA retains are placed under tighter controls.

The Committee's recommendations on CIA domestic activities are similar to Executive Order 11905. They go beyond the Executive Order, however, in that they recommend that the main safeguards be made law. And, in addition, the Committee proposes tighter standards to preclude repetition of some past abuses.

N8

General Provisions

The first two Recommendations pertaining to the CIA provide the context for more specific proposals. In Recommendation 4, the Committee endorses the prohibitions of the 1947 Act upon exercise by the CIA of subpoena, police or law enforcement powers or internal security functions. The Committee intends that Congress supplement, rather than supplant or derogate from the more general restrictions of the 1947 Act.

Recommendation 5 clarifies the role of the Director of Central Intelligence in the protection of intelligence sources and methods. He should be charged with "coordinating" the protection of sources and methods—that is, the development of procedures for the protection of sources and methods.[12] (Primary responsibility for investigations of security leaks should reside in the FBI.) Recommendation 5 also makes clear that the Director's responsibility for protecting sources and

---

[12] As noted in the Report on CHAOS, former Directors have had differing interpretations of the mandate of the 1947 Act to the Director of Central Intelligence to protect intelligence sources and methods. The Committee agrees with former Director William Colby that the 1947 Act only authorizes the Director to perform a "coordinating" and not an "operational" role.

methods does not permit violations of law. The effect of the new Executive Order is substantially the same as Recommendation 5.

Recommendation 4—To supplement the prohibitions in the 1947 National Security Act against the CIA exercising "police, subpoena, law enforcement powers or internal security functions," the CIA should be prohibited from conducting domestic security activities within the United States, except as specifically permitted by these recommendations.

Recommendation 5—The Director of Central Intelligence should be made responsible for "coordinating" the protection of sources and methods of the intelligence community. As head of the CIA, the Director should also be responsible in the first instance for the security of CIA facilities, personnel, operations, and information. Neither function, however, authorizes the Director of Central Intelligence to violate any federal or state law, or to take any action which is otherwise inconsistent with statutes implementing these recommendations.

CIA Activities Within the United States

1. *Wiretapping, Mail Opening and Unauthorized Entry.*—The Committee's recommendations on CIA domestic activities apply primarily to actions directed at Americans. However, in Recommendation 6 the Committee recommends that the most intrusive and dangerous investigative techniques (electronic surveillance; [13] mail opening; or unauthorized entry [14]) should be used in the United States only by the FBI and only pursuant to the judicial warrant procedures described in Recommendations 53, 54 and 55.

This approach is similar to the Executive order except that the Order permits the CIA to open mail in the United States pursuant to applicable statutes and regulations (i.e., with a warrant). The Committee's recommendations (see Parts iii and iv), places all three techniques—mail opening, electronic surveillance and unauthorized entry—under judicial warrant procedures and centralizes their use within the FBI under Attorney General supervision. The Committee sees no justification for distinguishing among these techniques, all of which represent an exercise of domestic police powers [15] which is inappropriate for a U.S. foreign intelligence agency within the United States and which inherently involve special dangers to civil liberties and personal privacy.

---

[13] The activity completely prohibited to CIA includes only the interception of communications restricted under the 1968 Safe Streets Act, and would not limit the use of body recorders, or telephone taps or other electronic surveillance where one party to the communication has given his consent. For example, electronic coverage of a case officer's meeting with his agent would not be included. The prohibition also is not intended to cover the testing of equipment in the United States, when done with the written approval of the Attorney General and under procedures he has approved to minimize interception of private communications and to prevent improper dissemination or use of the communications which are unavoidably intercepted in the testing process. Nor does the prohibition preclude the use of countermeasures to detect electronic surveillance mounted against the CIA, when conducted under general procedures and safeguards approved in writing by the CIA General Counsel.

[14] "Unauthorized entry" means entry unauthorized by the target.

[15] As part of the CIA's responsibility for its own security, however, appropriate personnel should be permitted to carry firearms within the United States not only for courier protection of documents, but also to protect the Director and Deputy Director and defectors and to guard CIA installations.

2. *Other Covert Techniques.*—The use of other covert techniques [16] by the CIA within the United States is sharply restricted by Recommendation 7 to specific situations.

The Committee would permit the CIA to conduct physical surveillance of persons on the premises of its own installations and facilities. Outside of its premises, the Committee would permit the CIA to conduct limited physical surveillance and confidential inquiries of its own employees [17] as part of a preliminary security investigation.

Although the Committee generally centralizes such investigations within the FBI, it would be too burdensome to require the Bureau to investigate every allegation that an employee has personal difficulties, which could make him a security risk, or allegations of suspicious behavior suggesting the disclosure of information. Before involving the FBI, the CIA could conduct a preliminary inquiry, which usually consists of nothing more than interviews with the subject's office colleagues, or his family, neighbors or associates, and perhaps confrontation of the subject himself. In some situations, however, limited physical surveillance might enable the CIA to resolve the allegation or to determine that there was a serious security breach involved.

Unlike the Executive Order, however, the Committee recommendations limit this authority to present CIA employees who are subject to summary dismissal. The only remedy available to the Government for security problems with past employees is criminal prosecution or other legal action. All security leak investigations for proposed criminal prosecution should be centralized in the FBI. Authorizing the use of any covert technique against contractors and their employees, let alone former employees of CIA contractors, as the Executive Order does, would authorize CIA surveillance of too large a number of Americans. The CIA can withdraw security clearances until satisfied by the contractor that a security risk has been remedied and, in serious cases, any investigations could be handled by the FBI.

The recommendation on the use of covert techniques within the United States also precludes the use of covert human sources such as undercover agents and informants, [18] with one exception expressly stated to be limited to "exceptional" cases. The Committee would authorize the CIA to place an agent in a domestic group, but only for the purpose of establishing credible cover to be used in a foreign intelli-

---

[16] "Covert techniques" means the collection of information including collection from records sources not readily available to a private person (except state or local law enforcement files) in such a manner as not to be detected by the subject. Covert techniques do not include a check of CIA or other federal agency or state and local police records, or a check of credit bureaus for the limited purpose of obtaining non-financial biographical data, i.e., date and place of birth, to facilitate such name checks, and the subject's place of employment. Nor do "covert techniques" include interviews with persons knowledgeable about the subject conducted on a confidential basis to avoid disclosure of the inquiry to others or to the subject, if he is not yet aware of CIA interest in a prospective relationship, provided the interview does not involve the provision of information from medical, financial, educational, phone or other confidential records.

[17] For purposes of this section employees includes those employees or contractors who work regularly at CIA facilities and have comparable access or freedom of movement at CIA facilities as employees of CIA.

[18] Recommendation 7(c) does permit background and other security investigations conducted with government credentials which do not reveal CIA involvement and, in extremely sensitive cases commercial or other private identification to avoid disclosure of any government connection.

gence mission abroad and only when the Director of Central Intelligence finds it to be "essential" to collection of information "vital" to the United States and the Attorney General finds that the operation will be conducted under procedures designed to prevent misuse.[19]

Apart from this limited exception, the CIA could not infiltrate groups within the United States for any purpose, including, as was done in the past, the purported protection of intelligence sources and methods or the general security of the CIA's facilities and personnel. (The Executive Order prohibits infiltration of groups within the United States "for purposes of reporting on or influencing its activities or members," but does not explicitly prohibit infiltration to protect intelligence sources and methods or the physical security of the agency.)

3. *Collection of Information.*—In addition to limiting the use of particular covert techniques, the Committee limits, in Recommendation 8, the situations in which the CIA may intentionally collect, by any means, information within the United States concerning Americans. The recommendation permits the CIA to collect information within the United States about Americans only with respect to persons working for the CIA or having some other significant affiliation or contact with CIA. The CIA should not be in the business of investigating Americans as intelligence or counterintelligence targets within the United States—a responsibility which should be centralized in the FBI and performed only under the circumstances proposed as lawful in Part iv.

The Executive Order only restricts CIA collection of information about Americans if the information concerns "the *domestic activities* of United States citizens." Unlike the Committee, the Order does not restrict CIA collection of information about foreign travel or wholly lawful international contacts and communication of Americans. As the Committee has learned from its study of the CIA's CHAOS opera-

---

It would also permit CIA investigators to check the effectiveness of cover operations, without revealing their affiliation, by means of inquiries at the vicinity of particularly sensitive CIA projects. If in the course of such inquiries, unidentified CIA employees or contractors' employees are observed to be endangering the project's cover, they may be the subject of limited physical surveillance at that time for the sole purpose of ascertaining their identity so that they may be subsequently contacted.

[19] Such action poses serious danger of misuse. The preparation may involve the agent reporting on his associates so that the CIA can assess his credentials and his observation and reporting ability. This could become an opportunity to collect domestic intelligence on the infiltrated group even when an investigation of that group could not otherwise be commenced under the applicable standards. Obviously, without restrictions the intelligence community could use this technique to conduct domestic spying, arguing that the agents were not being "targeted" against the group but were merely preparing for an overseas operation.

This was done, for example, in the use by Operation CHAOS of agents being provided with radical credentials for use in "Project 2," a foreign intelligence operation abroad. (See the CHAOS Report and the Rockefeller Commission Report.)

One alternative would be to let the FBI handle the agent while he is preparing for overseas assignment. On balance, however, that seems less desirable. The temptation to use the agent to collect domestic intelligence might be stronger for the agency with domestic security responsibilities than it would for the area division of the CIA concerned with foreign intelligence. Also, improper use of the agent to collect such information would be more readily identifiable in the context of the foreign intelligence operation run by the CIA than it would in the context of an agent operation run by the Intelligence Division of the FBI.

tion, in the process of gathering information about the international travel and contacts of Americans, the CIA acquired within the United States a great deal of additional information about the domestic activities of Americans.

The Executive Order also permits collection within the United States of information about the domestic activities of Americans in several other instances not permitted under the Committee recommendations:

(*a*) Collection of "foreign intelligence or counterintelligence" about the domestic activity of commercial organizations. (The Committee's restrictions on the collection of information apply to investigations of organizations as well as individuals.);

(*b*) Collection of information concerning the identity of persons in contact with CIA employees or with foreigners who are subjects of a counterintelligence inquiry. (Within the United States, the Committee would require any investigations to collect such information to be conducted by the FBI, *and* only if authorized under Part iv, and subject to its procedural controls.);

(*c*) Collection of "foreign intelligence" from a cooperating source within the United States about the domestic activities of Americans. "Foreign intelligence," is an exceedingly broad and vague standard. The use of such a standard raises the prospect of another Project CHAOS. (The Committee would prohibit such collection by the CIA within the United States, except with respect to persons presently or prospectively affiliated with CIA.);

(*d*) Collection of information about Americans "reasonably believed" to be acting on behalf of a foreign power or engaging in international terrorist or narcotic activities. (The Committee would require investigations to collect such information within the United States, to be conducted by the FBI, and only if authorized under Part iv.);

(*e*) Collection of information concerning persons considered by the CIA to pose a clear threat to intelligence agency facilities or personnel, provided such information is retained only by the "threatened" agency and that proper coordination is established with the FBI. (This was the basis for the Office of Security's RESISTANCE program investigating dissent throughout the country.) (The Committee would require any such "threat" collection outside the CIA be conducted by the FBI, *and* only if authorized by Part iv, or by local law enforcement.)

Recommendation 6.—The CIA should not conduct electronic surveillance, unauthorized entry, or mail opening within the United States for any purpose.

Recommendation 7.—The CIA should not employ physical surveillance, infiltration of groups or any other covert techniques against Americans within the United States except:

(*a*) Physical surveillance of persons on the grounds of CIA installations;

(*b*) Physical surveillance during a preliminary investigation of allegations an employee is a security risk for a limited period outside of CIA installations. Such surveillance should be conducted only upon written authorization of the Director of Central Intelligence and should be limited to the subject of the investigation and, only to the extent necessary to identify them, to persons with whom the subject has contact;

(*c*) Confidential inquiries, during a preliminary investigation of allegations an employee is a security risk, of outside sources concerning medical or financial information about the subject which is relevant to those allegations; [19a]

(d) The use of identification which does not reveal CIA or government affiliation, in background and other security investigations permitted the CIA by these recommendations, and the conduct of checks, which do not reveal CIA or government affiliation for the purpose of judging the effectiveness of cover operations, upon the written authorization of the Director of Central Intelligence;

(e) In exceptional cases, the placement or recruitment of agents within an unwitting domestic group solely for the purpose of preparing them for assignments abroad and only for as long as is necessary to accomplish that purpose. This should take place only if the Director of Central Intelligence makes a written finding that it is essential for foreign intelligence collection of vital importance to the United States, and the Attorney General makes a written finding that the operation will be conducted under procedures designed to prevent misuse of the undisclosed participation or of any information obtained therefrom.[20] In the case of any such action, no information received by CIA from the agent as a result of his position in the group should be disseminated outside the CIA unless it indicates felonious criminal conduct or threat of death or serious bodily harm, in which case dissemination should be permitted to an appropriate official agency if approved by the Attorney General.

Recommendation 8.—The CIA should not collect [21] information within the United States concerning Americans except:

(a) Information concerning CIA employees,[22] CIA contractors and their employees, or applicants for such employment or contracting;

(b) Information concerning individuals or organizations providing, or offering to provide,[23] assistance to the CIA;

(c) Information concerning individuals or organizations being considered by the CIA as potential sources of information or assistance;[24]

(d) Visitors to CIA facilities;[25]

(e) Persons otherwise in the immediate vicinity of sensitive CIA sites;[26] or

(f) Persons who give their informed written consent to such collection.

In (a), (b) and (c) above, information should be collected only if necessary for the purpose of determining the person's fitness for employment, contracting or assistance. If, in the course of such collection, information is obtained which indicates criminal activity, it

---

[19a] Any further investigations conducted in connection with (b) or (c) should be conducted by the FBI, and only if authorized by Part iv.

[20] In addition, the FBI should be notified of such insertions.

[21] "Collect" means to gather or initiate the acquisition of information, or to request it from another agency. It does not include dissemination of information to CIA by another agency acting on its own initiative.

[22] "Employees," as used in this recommendation, would include members of the employee's immediate family or prospective spouse.

[23] In the case of persons unknown to the CIA who volunteer to provide information or otherwise request contact with CIA personnel, the agency may conduct a name check before arranging a meeting.

[24] The CIA may only conduct a name check and confidential interviews of persons who know the subject, if the subject is unaware of CIA interest in him.

[25] The CIA may only collect information by means of a name check.

[26] The CIA may make a name check and determine the place of employment of persons residing or working in the immediate vicinity of sensitive sites, such as persons residing adjacent to premises used for safe houses or defector resettlement, or such as proprietors of businesses in premises adjacent to CIA offices in commercial areas.

should be transmitted to the FBI or other appropriate agency. When an American's relationship with the CIA is prospective, information should only be collected if there is a bona fide expectation the person might be used by the CIA.

CIA Activities Outside of the United States

The Committee would permit a wider range of CIA activities against Americans abroad than it would permit the CIA to undertake within the United States, but it would not permit the CIA to investigate abroad the lawful activities of Americans to any greater degree than the FBI could investigate such activities at home.

Abroad, the FBI is not in a position to protect the CIA from serious threats to its facilities or personnel, or to investigate all serious security violations. To the extent it is impractical to rely on local law enforcement authorities, the CIA should be free to preserve its security by specified appropriate investigations which may involve Americans, including surveillance of persons other than its own employees.

The Committee gives to the FBI the sole responsibility within the United States for authorized domestic security investigations of Americans. However, when such an investigation has overseas aspects, the FBI looks to the CIA as the overseas operational arm of the intelligence community. The recommendations would authorize the CIA to target Americans abroad as part of an authorized investigation initiated by the FBI.

The Committee does not recommend permitting the CIA itself to initiate such investigations of Americans overseas.[27] Present communications permit rapid consultation with the Department of Justice. Moreover, the lesson of CHAOS is that an American's activities abroad may be ambiguous, such as contact with persons who may be acting on behalf of hostile foreign powers at an international conference on disarmament. The question is who shall determine there is sufficient information to justify making an American citizen a target of his government's intelligence apparatus?

The limitations contained in Recommendation 9 only pertain to the CIA initiating investigations or otherwise intentionally collecting information on Americans abroad. The CIA would not be prohibited from accepting and passing on information on the illegal activities of Americans which the CIA acquires incidentally in the course of its other activities abroad.

The Committee believes that judgments should be centralized within the Justice Department to promote consistent, carefully controlled application of the appropriate standards and protection of Constitutional rights. This is the same position taken by Director Colby in setting current CIA policy for mounting operations against Americans abroad. In March 1974, Director Colby formally terminated the CHAOS program and promulgated new guidelines for future activity abroad involving Americans, which, in effect, transferred such responsibilities to the Department of Justice.[28]

---

[27] The counterintelligence component of the CIA would be able to call to the attention of the FBI any patterns of significance which the CIA thought warranted opening an investigation of an American.

[28] The guidelines state:

A. "Whenever information is uncovered as a byproduct result of CIA foreign targeted intelligence or counterintelligence operations abroad which makes

The Committee is somewhat more restrictive than the Executive Order with respect to collection of information on Americans. As mentioned earlier, the Order only restricts CIA collection of information about the "domestic activities" of Americans and does not prohibit the collection of information regarding the lawful travel or international contacts of American citizens. This creates a particularly significant problem with respect to CIA activities directed against Americans abroad.

The Order permits the CIA wider latitude abroad than do the Committee's Recommendations in two other important respects. The Order permits collection of information if the American is reasonably believed to be acting on behalf of a foreign power. That exemption on its face would include Americans working for a foreign country on business or legal matters or otherwise engaged in wholly lawful activities in compliance with applicable registration or other regulatory statutes. More importantly, the Order permits the CIA to collect "foreign intelligence" or "counterintelligence" information abroad about the *domestic activities* of Americans. The Order then broadly defines "foreign intelligence" as information about the intentions or activities of a foreign country or person, or information about areas outside the United States. This would authorize the CIA to collect, abroad, for example, information about the domestic activities of American businessmen which provided intelligence about business transactions of foreign persons.

The CIA does not at present specifically collect intelligence on the economic activities of Americans overseas. The Committee suggests that appropriate oversight committees examine the question of the overseas collection of economic intelligence.

Use of Covert Techniques Against Americans Abroad

Recommendation 11 requires the use of all covert techniques be governed by the same standards, procedures, and approvals required for their use by the Justice Department against Americans within the United States. Thus, in the case of electronic surveillance, unauthorized entry, or mail opening, a judicial warrant would be required. As a matter of sound Constitutional principle, the Fourth Amendment protections enjoyed by Americans at home should also apply to protect them against their Government abroad. It would be just as offensive to have a CIA agent burglarize an American's apartment in Rome as it would be for the FBI to do so in New York.

Requirements that a warrant be obtained in the United States would not present an excessive burden. Electronic surveillance and unauthorized entries are not presently conducted against Americans abroad without prior consultation and approval from CIA Headquarters in

Americans suspect for security or counterintelligence reasons . . . such information will be reported to the FBI . . . specific CIA operations will not be mounted against such individuals; CIA responsibilities thereafter will be restricted to reporting any further intelligence or counterintelligence aspects to the specific case which comes to CIA's attention as a byproduct of its continuing foreign targeted operational activity. If the FBI, on the basis of the receipt of the CIA information, however, specifically requests further information on terrorist or counterintelligence matters relating to the private American citizens . . . CIA may respond to written requests by the FBI for clandestine collection abroad by CIA of information on foreign terrorist or counterintelligence matters involving American citizens."

Langley, Virginia. Moreover, the present Deputy Director of CIA for Operations has testified that bona fide counterintelligence investigations are lengthy and time consuming and prior review within the United States, including consultation with the Justice Department, would not be a serious problem.[29] Indeed electronic surveillance of Americans abroad under present administration policy also requires approval by the Attorney General.

The Committee reinforces the general restrictions upon overseas targeting of Americans by recommending that the CIA be prohibited from requesting a friendly foreign intelligence service or other person from undertaking activities against Americans which the CIA itself may not do. This would not require that a foreign government's use of covert techniques be conducted under the same procedures, e.g., warrants, required by those Recommendations for the CIA and the FBI. It would mean that the CIA cannot ask a foreign intelligence service to bug the apartment of an American unless the circumstances would permit the United States Government to obtain a judicial warrant from a Federal Court in this country to conduct such surveillance of the American abroad.

The Committee places greater restrictions upon the CIA's use of covert techniques against Americans abroad than does the Executive Order. For example, the Order permits the CIA to conduct electronic surveillance and unauthorized entries under "procedures approved by the Attorney General consistent with the law." No judicial warrant procedure is required. In addition, the Order's restriction on CIA's opening mail of Americans is limited to mail "in the United States postal channels." In other words, under the Order the CIA is not prevented from intercepting abroad and opening a letter mailed by an American to his family, or sent to him from the United States.

The Order also contains no restrictions on the CIA infiltrating a group abroad, even if it were one composed entirely of Americans engaged in wholly lawful activities such as a political club of American students in Paris. Furthermore, the Order permits the CIA to conduct physical surveillance abroad of any American "reasonably believed to be" engaged in "activities threatening to the national security." On its face this language appears overly permissive and might be read to authorize a repetition of the CHAOS program in which Americans were targeted for surveillance because of their participation in international conferences critical of the U.S. role in Vietnam.

Recommendation 9.—The CIA should not collect information abroad concerning Americans except:

(*a*) Information concerning Americans which it is permitted to collect within the United States;[30]

(*b*) At the request of the Justice Department as part of criminal investigations or an investigation of an American for suspected ter-

---

[29] William Nelson testimony, 1/28/76, pp. 33–34. Mr. Nelson was not addressing procedures to obtain a judicial warrant; but the time required for an *ex parte* application on an expedited basis to a Federal Court in Washington, D.C., would not be excessive for the investigative time frames which Nelson described.

Furthermore, the present wiretap statute authorizes electronic surveillance (for 48 hours) on an emergency basis prior to judicial authorization.

[30] Recommendation 8. . . .

rorist,[30a] or hostile foreign intelligence [30b] activities or security leak or security risk investigations which the FBI has opened pursuant to Part iv of those recommendations and which is conducted consistently with recommendations contained in Part iv.[31]

Recommendation 10.—The CIA should be able to transmit to the FBI or other appropriate agencies information concerning Americans acquired as the incidental byproduct of otherwise permissible foreign intelligence and counterintelligence operations,[32] whenever such information indicates any activity in violation of American law.

Recommendation 11.—The CIA may employ covert techniques abroad against Americans:

(*a*) Under circumstances in which the CIA could use such covert techniques against Americans within the United States; [33] or

(*b*) When collecting information as part of Justice Department investigation, in which case the CIA may use a particular covert techniques under the standards and procedures and approvals applicable to its use against Americans within the United States by the FBI (See Part iv)'; or

(*c*) To the extent necessary to identify persons known or suspected to be Americans who come in contact with foreigners the CIA is investigating.

CIA Human Experiments and Drug Use

Recommendation 12 tracks similar restrictions in the Executive Order but proposes an additional safeguard—giving the National Commission on Biomedical Ethics and Human Standards jurisdiction to review any testing on Americans.

[30a] "Terrorist activities" means acts, or conspiracies, which: (a) are violent or dangerous to human life; and (b) violate federal or state criminal statutes concerning assassination, murder, arson, bombing, hijacking, or kidnaping; and (c) appear intended to, or are likely to have the effect of:

(1) Substantially disrupting federal, state or local government; or

(2) Substantially disrupting interstate or foreign commerce between the United States and another country; or

(3) Directly interfering with the exercise by Americans, of Constitutional rights protected by the Civil Rights Act of 1968, or by foreigners, of their rights under the laws or treaties of the United States.

[30b] "Hostile foreign intelligence activities" means acts, or conspiracies, by Americans or foreigners, who are officers, employees, or conscious agents of a foreign power, or who, pursuant to the direction of a foreign power, engage in clandestine intelligence activity, or engage in espionage, sabotage or similar conduct in violation of federal criminal statutes. (The term "clandestine intelligence activity" is included in this definition at the suggestion of officials of the Department of Justice. Certain activities engaged in by conscious agents of foreign powers, such as some forms of industrial, technological, or economic espionage, are not now prohibited by federal statutes. It would be preferable to amend the espionage laws to cover such activity and eliminate this term. As a matter of principle, intelligence agencies should not investigate activities of Americans which are not violations of federal criminal statutes. Therefore, the Committee recommends (in Recommendation 94) that Congress immediately consider enacting such statutes and then eliminating this term.)

[31] If the CIA believes that an investigation of an American should be opened but the FBI declines to do so, the CIA should be able to appeal to the Attorney General or to the appropriate committee of the National Security Council.

[32] Such information would include material volunteered by a foreign intelligence service independent of any request by the CIA.

[33] See Recommendation 7, ...

Recommendation 12—The CIA should not use in experimentation on human subjects, any drug, device or procedure which is designed or intended to harm, or is reasonably likely to harm, the physical or mental health of the human subject, except with the informed written consent, witnessed by a disinterested third party, of each human subject, and in accordance with the guidelines issued by the National Commission for the Protection of Human Subjects for Biomedical and Behavioral Research The jurisdiction of the Commission should be amended to include the Central Intelligence Agency and other intelligence agencies of the United States Government.

Review and Certification

Recommendation 13 ensures careful monitoring of those CIA activities authorized in the recommendations which are directed at Americans.

Recommendation 13—Any CIA activity engaged in pursuant to Recommendations 7, 8, 9, 10, or 11 should be subject to periodic review and certification of compliance with the Constitution, applicable statutes, agency regulations and executive orders by:

(*a*) The Inspector General of the CIA;

(*b*) The General Counsel of the CIA in coordination with the Director of Central Intelligence;

(*c*) The Attorney General; and

(*d*) The oversight committee recommended in Part xii.

All such certifications should be available for review by congressional oversight committees.

b. National Security Agency

The recommendations contained in this section suggest controls on the electronic surveillance activities of the National Security Agency **N9** insofar as they involve, or could involve, Americans. There is no statute which either authorizes or specifically restricts such activities. NSA was created by executive order in 1952, and its functions are described in directives of the National Security Council.

While, in practice, NSA's collection activities are complex and sophisticated, the process by which it produces foreign intelligence can be reduced to a few easily understood principles. NSA intercepts messages passing over international lines of communication, some of which have one terminal within the United States. Traveling over these lines of communication, especially those with one terminal in the United States, are the messages of Americans, most of which are irrelevant to NSA's foreign intelligence mission. NSA often has no means of excluding such messages, however, from others it intercepts which might be of foreign intelligence value. It does have, however, the capability to select particular messages from those it intercepts which are of foreign intelligence value. Most international communications of Americans are not selected, since they do not meet foreign intelligence criteria. Having selected messages of possible intelligence value, NSA monitors (reads) them, and uses the information it obtains as the basis for reports which it furnishes the intelligence agencies.

Having this process in mind, one will more readily understand the recommendations of the Committee insofar as NSA's handling of the messages of Americans is concerned. The Committee recommends first that NSA monitor only foreign communications. It should not monitor domestic communications, even for foreign intelligence purposes. Second, the Committee recommends that NSA should not select messages for monitoring, from those foreign communications it has intercepted, because the message is to or from or refers to a particular American, unless the Department of Justice has first obtained a search warrant, or the particular American has consented. Third, the Committee recommends that NSA be required to make every practicable effort to eliminate or minimize the extent to which the communications of Americans are intercepted, selected, or monitored. Fourth, for those communications of Americans which are nevertheless incidentally selected and monitored, the Committee recommends that NSA be prohibited from disseminating such communication, or information derived therefrom, which identifies an American, unless the communication indicates evidence of hostile foreign intelligence or terrorist activity, or felonious criminal conduct, or contains a threat of death or serious bodily harm. In these cases, the Committee recommends that the Attorney General approve any such dissemination as being consistent with these policies.

In summary, the Committee's recommendations reflect its belief that NSA should have no greater latitude to monitor the communications of Americans than any other intelligence agency. To the extent that other agencies are required to obtain a warrant before monitoring the communications of Americans, NSA should be required to obtain a warrant.[34]

Recommendation 14.—NSA should not engage in domestic security activities. Its functions should be limited in a precisely drawn legislative charter to the collection of foreign intelligence from foreign communications.[35]

Recommendation 15.—NSA should take all practicable measures consistent with its foreign intelligence mission to eliminate or minimize the interception, selection, and monitoring of communications of Americans from the foreign communications.[36]

Recommendation 16.—NSA should not be permitted to select for monitoring any communication to, from, or about an American without his consent, except for the purpose of obtaining information about hostile foreign intelligence or terrorist activities, and then only if a warrant approving such monitoring is obtained in accordance with procedures similar [37] to those contained in Title III of the Omnibus Crime Control and Safe Streets Act of 1968.

---

[34] None of the Committee's recommendations pertaining to NSA should be construed as inhibiting or preventing NSA from protecting U.S. communications against interception or monitoring by foreign intelligence services.

[35] "Foreign communications," as used in this section, refers to a communication between or among two or more parties in which at least one party is outside the United States, or a communication transmitted between points within the United States only if transmitted over a facility which is under the control of, or exclusively used by, a foreign government.

[36] In order to ensure that this recommendation is implemented, both the Attorney General and the appropriate oversight committees of the Congress should be continuously apprised of, and periodically review, the measures taken by NSA pursuant to this recommendation.

[37] The Committee believes that in the case of interceptions authorized to obtain information about hostile foreign intelligence, there should be a presumption that notice to the subject of such intercepts, which would ordinarily be required under Title III (18 U.S.C. 2518(8)(d)), is not required, unless there is evidence of gross abuse.

(This recommendation would eliminate the possibility that NSA would re-establish its "watch lists" of the late 1960s and early 1970s. In that case, the names of Americans were submitted to NSA by other federal agencies and were used as a basis for selecting and monitoring, without a warrant, the international communications of those Americans.)

Recommendation 17.—Any personally identifiable information about an American which NSA incidentally acquires, other than pursuant to a warrant, should not be disseminated without the consent of the American, but should be destroyed as promptly as possible, unless it indicates:

(*a*) Hostile foreign intelligence or terrorist activities; or

(*b*) Felonious criminal conduct for which a warrant might be obtained pursuant to Title III of the Omnibus Crime Control and Safe Streets Act of 1968; or

(*c*) A threat of death or serious bodily harm.

If dissemination is permitted, by (*a*), (*b*) and (*c*) above, it must only be made to an appropriate official and after approval by the Attorney General.

(This recommendation is consistent with NSA's policy prior to the Executive Order.[38] NSA's practice prior to the Executive Order was not to disseminate material containing personally identifiable information about Americans.)

Recommendation 18.—NSA should not request from any commercial carrier any communication which it could not otherwise obtain pursuant to these recommendations.

(This recommendation is to ensure that NSA will not resume an operation such as SHAMROCK, disclosed during the Committee's hearings, whereby NSA received for almost 30 years copies of most international telegrams transmitted by certain international telegraph companies in the United States.)

Recommendation 19.—The Office of Security at NSA should be permitted to collect background information on present or prospective employees or contractors of NSA, solely for the purpose of determining their fitness for employment. With respect to security risks or the security of its installations, NSA should be permitted to conduct physical surveillances, consistent with such surveillances as the CIA is permitted to conduct, in similar circumstances, by these recommendations.

c. *Military Service and Defense Department Investigative Agencies*

This section of the Committee's recommendations pertains to the controls upon the intelligence activities of the military services and Department of Defense insofar as they involve Americans who are not members of or affiliated with the armed forces.

In general, the restrictions seek to limit military investigations to activities in the civilian community which are necessary and pertinent to the military mission, and which cannot feasibly be accomplished by civilian agencies. In overseas locations where civilian agencies do not

---

[38] The Executive Order places no such restriction on the dissemination of information by NSA. Under the Executive Order, NSA is not required to delete names or destroy messages which are personally identifiable to Americans. As long as these messages fall within the categories established by the Order, the names of Americans *could* be transmitted to other intelligence agencies of the Government.

perform investigative activities to assist the military mission, military intelligence is given more latitude. Specifically, the Committee recommends that military intelligence be limited within the United States to conducting investigations of violations of the Uniform Code of Military Justice; investigations for security clearances of Department of Defense employees and contractors; and investigations immediately before and during the deployment of armed forces in connection with civil disturbances. None of these investigations should involve the use of any covert technique employed against American civilians. In overseas locations, the Committee recommends that military intelligence have additional authority to conduct investigations of terrorist activity and hostile foreign intelligence activity. In these cases, covert techniques directed at Americans may be employed if consistent with the Committee's restrictions upon the use of such techniques in the United States in Part iv.

Recommendation 20.—Except as specifically provided herein, the Department of Defense should not engage in domestic security activities. Its functions, as they relate to the activities of the foreign intelligence community, should be limited in a precisely drawn legislative charter to the conduct of foreign intelligence and foreign counterintelligence activities and tactical military intelligence activities abroad, and production, analysis, and dissemination of departmental intelligence.

Recommendation 21.—In addition to its foreign intelligence responsibility, the Department of Defense has a responsibility to investigate its personnel in order to protect the security of its installations and property, to ensure order and discipline within its ranks, and to conduct other limited investigations once dispatched by the President to suppress a civil disorder. A legislative charter should define precisely—in a manner which is not inconsistent with these recommendations—the authorized scope and purpose of any investigations undertaken by the Department of Defense to satisfy these responsibilities.

Recommendation 22.—No agency of the Department of Defense should conduct investigations of violations of criminal law or otherwise perform any law enforcement or domestic security functions within the United States, except on military bases or concerning military personnel, to enforce the Uniform Code of Military Justice.

Control of Civil Disturbance Intelligence

The Department of the Army has executive responsibility for rendering assistance in connection with civil disturbances. In the late 1960s, it instituted a nationwide collection program in which Army investigators were dispatched to collect information on the political activities of Americans. This was done on the theory that such information was necessary to prepare the Army in the event that its troops were sent to the scene of civil disturbances. The Committee believes that the Army's potential role in civil disturbances does not justify such an intelligence effort directed against American civilians.

Recommendation 23.—The Department of Defense should not be permitted to conduct investigations of Americans on the theory that the information derived therefrom might be useful in potential civil disorders. The Army should be permitted to gather information about geography, logistical matters, or the identity of local officials which is necessary to the positioning, support, and use of troops in an area where troops are likely to be deployed by the President in connection with a civil disturbance. The Army should be permitted to investigate Americans involved in such disturbances after troops have been deployed to the site of a civil disorder, (i) to the extent necessary to fulfill the military mission, and (ii) to the extent the information cannot be obtained from the FBI. (The FBI's responsibility in connection with civil disorders and its assistance to the Army is described in Part iv.)

Recommendation 24.—Appropriate agencies of the Department of Defense should be permitted to collect background information on their present or prospective employees or contractors. With respect to security risks or the security of its installations, the Department of Defense should be permitted to conduct physical surveillance consistent with such surveillances as the CIA is permitted to conduct, in similar circumstances, by these recommendations.

Prohibitions and Limitations of Covert Techniques

During the Army's civil disturbance collection program of the late 1960s, Army intelligence agents employed a variety of covert techniques to gather information about civilian political activities. These included covert penetrations of private meetings and organizations, use of informants, monitoring amateur radio broadcasts, and posing as newsmen. This provision is designed to prevent the use of such covert techniques against American civilians. The Committee believes that none of the legitimate investigative tasks of the military within the United States justified the use of such techniques against unaffiliated Americans.

Recommendation 25.—Except as provided in 27 below, the Department of Defense should not direct any covert technique (e.g., electronic surveillance, informants, etc.) at American civilians.

Limited Investigations Abroad

The military services currently conduct preventive intelligence investigations within the United States where members of their respective services are agents of, or are collaborating with, a hostile foreign intelligence service. These investigations are coordinated with, and under the ultimate control of, the FBI. The Committee's recommendations are not intended to prevent the military services from continuing to assist the FBI with such investigations involving members of the armed forces. They are intended, however, to place responsibility for these investigations, insofar as they take place within the United States, in the FBI, and not in the military services themselves. The military services, on the other hand, are given additional responsibility to conduct investigations of Americans who are suspected of engaging in terrorist activity or hostile foreign intelligence activity in overseas locations.

Recommendation 26.—The Department of Defense should be permitted to conduct abroad preventive intelligence investigations of unaffiliated Americans, as described in Part iv below, provided such investigations are first approved by the FBI. Such investigations by the Department of Defense, including the use of covert techniques, should ordinarily be conducted in a manner consistent with the recommendations pertaining to the FBI, contained in Part iv; however, in overseas locations, where U.S. military forces constitute the governing power, or where U.S. military forces are engaged in hostilities, circumstances may require greater latitude to conduct such investigations.

iii. Non-Intelligence Agencies Should Be Barred From Domestic Security Activity

a. Internal Revenue Service

The Committee's review of intelligence collection and investigative activity by IRS' Intelligence Division and of the practice of furnishing information in IRS files to the intelligence agencies demonstrates that reforms are necessary and appropriate. The primary objective of reform is to prevent IRS from becoming an instrumentality of the intelligence agencies, beyond the scope of what IRS, as the Federal tax collector, should be doing. Recommendations 27 through 29 are designed to achieve this objective by providing that IRS collection of intelligence and its conduct of investigations are to be confined strictly to tax matters. Moreover, programs of tax investigation, in which targets are selected partly because of indications of tax violations and partly because of reasons relating to domestic security, are prohibited where they would erode constitutional rights. Where otherwise appropriate, such programs must be conducted under special safeguards to prevent any adverse effect on the exercise of those rights.

These recommendations should prevent a recurrence of the excesses associated with the Special Services Staff and the Intelligence Gathering and Retrieval System.

Targeting of Persons or Groups for Investigations or Intelligence-Gathering by IRS [39]

Recommendation 27.—The IRS should not, on behalf of any intelligence agency or for its own use, collect any information about the activities of Americans except for the purposes of enforcing the tax laws.

Recommendation 28.—IRS should not select any person or group for tax investigation on the basis of political activity or for any other reason not relevant to enforcement of the tax laws.

Recommendation 29.—Any program of intelligence investigation relating to domestic security in which targets are selected by both tax and non-tax criteria should only be initiated:

(*a*) Upon the written request of the Attorney General or the Secretary of the Treasury, specifying the nature of the requested program and the need therefore; and

(*b*) After the written certification by the Commissioner of the IRS that procedures have been developed which are sufficient to prevent the infringement of the constitutional rights of Americans; and

(*c*) With congressional oversight committees being kept continually advised of the nature and extent of such programs.

---

[39] Based upon its study of the IRS, the Committee believes these recommendations might properly be applied beyond the general domestic security scope of the recommendations.

Disclosure Procedures

The Committee's review of disclosure of tax information by IRS to the FBI and the CIA showed three principal abuses by those intelligence agencies: (1) the by-passing of disclosure procedures mandated by law, resulting in the agencies obtaining access to tax returns and tax-related information through improper channels, and, sometimes, without a proper basis; (2) the failure to state the reasons justifying the need for the information and the uses contemplated so that IRS could determine if the request met the applicable criteria for disclosure; and (3) the improper use of tax returns and information, particularly by the FBI in COINTELPRO. Recommendations 30 through 35 are designed to prevent these abuses from occurring again.

While general problems of disclosure are being studied by several different congressional committees with jurisdiction over IRS, these recommendations reflect this Committee's focus on disclosure problems seen in the interaction between IRS and the intelligence agencies.

Recommendation 30.—No intelligence agency should request [40] from the Internal Revenue Service tax returns or tax-related information except under the statutes and regulations controlling such disclosures. In addition, the existing procedures under which tax returns and tax-related information are released by the IRS should be strengthened, as suggested in the following five recommendations.

Recommendation 31.—All requests from an intelligence agency to the IRS for tax returns and tax-related information should be in writing, and signed by the head of the intelligence agency making the request, or his designee. Copies of such requests should be filed with the Attorney General. Each request should include a clear statement of:

(*a*) The purpose for which disclosure is sought;

(*b*) Facts sufficient to establish that the requested information is needed by the requesting agency for the performance of an authorized and lawful function;

(*c*) The uses which the requesting agency intends to make of the information;

(*d*) The extent of the disclosures sought;

(*e*) Agreement by the requesting agency not to use the documents or information for any purpose other than that stated in the request; and

(*f*) Agreement by the requesting agency that the information will not be disclosed to any other agency or person except in accordance with the law.

Recommendation 32.—IRS should not release tax returns or tax-related information to any intelligence agency unless it has received a request satisfying the requirements of Recommendation 31, and the Commissioner of Internal Revenue has approved the request in writing.

Recommendation 33.—IRS should maintain a record of all such requests and responses thereto for a period of twenty years.

---

[40] "Request" as used in the recommendations concerning the Internal Revenue Service should not include circumstances in which the agency is acting with the informed written consent of the taxpayer.

Recommendation 34.—No intelligence agency should use the information supplied to it by the IRS pursuant to a request of the agency except as stated in a proper request for disclosure.

Recommendation 35.—All requests for information sought by the FBI should be filed by the Department of Justice. Such requests should be signed by the Attorney General or his designee, following a determination by the Department that the request is proper under the applicable statutes and regulations.

b. Post Office (U.S. Postal Service)

These recommendations are designed to tighten the existing restrictions regarding requests by intelligence agencies for both inspection of the exteriors of mail ("mail cover") and inspection of the contents of first class mail ("mail opening"). As to mail cover, the Committee's recommendation is to centralize the review and approval of all requests by requiring that only the Attorney General may authorize mail cover, and to eliminate unjustified mail covers by requiring that the mail cover be found "necessary" to a domestic security investigation. With respect to mail opening, the recommendations provide that it can only be done pursuant to court warrant.

Recommendation 36.—The Post Office should not permit the FBI or any intelligence agency to inspect markings or addresses on first class mail, nor should the Post Office itself inspect markings or addresses on behalf of the FBI or any intelligence agency, on first class mail, except upon the written approval of the Attorney General or his designee. Where one of the correspondents is an American, the Attorney General or his designee should only approve such inspection for domestic security purposes upon a written finding that it is necessary to a criminal investigation or a preventive intelligence investigation of terrorist activity or hostile foreign intelligence activity.

Upon such a request, the Post Office may temporarily remove from circulation such correspondence for the purpose of such inspection of its exterior as is related to the investigation.

Recommendation 37.—The Post Office should not transfer the custody of any first class mail to any agency except the Department of Justice. Such mail should not be transferred or opened except upon a judicial search warrant.

(*a*) In the case of mail where one of the correspondents is an American, the judge must find that there is probable cause to believe that the mail contains evidence of a crime.[41]

(*b*) In the case of mail where both parties are foreigners:

(1) The judge must find that there is probable cause to believe that both parties to such correspondence are foreigners, and one of the correspondents is an officer, employee or conscious agent of a foreign power; and

(2) The Attorney General must certify that the mail opening is likely to reveal information necessary either (i) to the protection of the nation against actual or potential attack or other hostile acts of force of a foreign power; (ii) to obtain foreign intelligence information deemed essential to the security of the United States; or (iii) to

---

[41] See recommendation 94 for the Committee's recommendation that Congress consider amending the Espionage Act so as to cover modern forms of espionage not now criminal.

protect national security information against hostile foreign intelligence activity.

iv. Federal Domestic Security Activities Should Be Limited and Controlled to Prevent Abuses Without Hampering Criminal Investigations or Investigations of Foreign Espionage

The recommendations contained in this part are designed to accomplish two principal objectives: (1) prohibit improper intelligence activities and (2) define the limited domestic security investigations which should be permitted. As suggested earlier, the ultimate goal is a statutory mandate for the federal government's domestic security function that will ensure that the FBI, as the primary domestic security investigative agency, concentrates upon criminal conduct as opposed to political rhetoric or association. Our recommendations would vastly curtail the scope of domestic security investigations as they have been conducted, by prohibiting inquiries initiated because the Bureau regards a group as falling within a vaguely defined category such as "subversive," "New Left," "Black Nationalist Hate Groups," or "White Hate Groups." The recommendations also ban investigations based merely upon the fact that a person or group is associating with others who are being investigated (e.g., the Bureau's investigation of the Southern Christian Leadership Conference because of alleged "Communist infiltration").

The simplest way to eliminate investigations of peaceful speech and association would be to limit the FBI to traditional investigations of crimes which have been committed (including the crimes of attempt and conspiracy). The Committee found, however, that there are circumstances where the FBI should have authority to conduct limited "intelligence investigations" of threatened conduct (terrorism and foreign espionage) which is generally covered by the criminal law, where the conduct has not yet reached the stage of a prosecuteable act.

The Committee, however, found that abuses were frequently associated even with such intelligence investigations. This led us also to recommend: precise limitations upon the use of covert techniques (Recommendations 51 to 60); restrictions upon maintenance and dissemination of information gathered in such investigations (Recommendations 64 to 68); and a statutory requirement that the Attorney General monitor these investigations and terminate them as soon as practical (Recommendation 69).

a. Centralize Supervision, Investigative Responsibility, and the Use of Covert Techniques

Investigations should be centralized within the Department of Justice. It is the Committee's judgment that if former Attorneys General had been held accountable by the Congress for ensuring compliance by the FBI and the intelligence agencies with laws designed to protect the rights of Americans, the Department of Justice would have been more likely to discover and enjoin improper activities. Furthermore, centralizing domestic security investigations within the FBI will facilitate the Attorney General's supervision of them.

Recommendation 38.—All domestic security investigative activity, including the use of covert techniques, should be centralized within the Federal Bureau of Investigation, except those investigations by the

Secret Service designed to protect the life of the President or other Secret Service protectees. Such investigations and the use of covert techniques in those investigations should be centralized within the Secret Service.

Recommendation 39.—All domestic security activities of the federal government and all other intelligence agency activities covered by the Domestic Intelligence Recommendations should be subject to Justice Department oversight to assure compliance with the Constitution and laws of the United States.

b. Prohibitions

The Committee recommends a set of prohibitions, in addition to its later recommendations limiting the scope of and procedural controls for domestic security investigations.

The following prohibitions cover abuses ranging from the political use of the sensitive information maintained by the Bureau to the excesses of COINTELPRO. They are intended to cover activities engaged in, by, or on behalf of, the FBI. For example, in prohibiting Bureau interference in lawful speech, publication, assembly, organization, or association of Americans, the Committee intends to prohibit a Bureau agent from mailing fake letters to factionalize a group as well as to prohibit an informant from manipulating or influencing the peaceful activities of a group on behalf of the FBI.

Subsequent recommendations limit the kinds of investigations which can be opened and provide controls for those investigations. Specifically, the Committee limits FBI authority to collect information on Americans to enumerated circumstances; limits authority to maintain information on political beliefs, political assocations, or private lives of Americans; requires judicial warrants for the most intrusive covert collection techniques (electronic surveillance, mail opening, and surreptitious entry); and proposes new restrictions upon the use of other covert techniques, particularly informants.

Recommendation 40.—The FBI should be prohibited from engaging on its own or through informants or others, in any of the following activities directed at Americans:

(*a*) Disseminating any information to the White House, any other federal official, the news media, or any other person for a political or other improper purpose, such as discrediting an opponent of the administration or a critic of an intelligence or investigative agency.

(*b*) Interfering with lawful speech, publication, assembly, organizational activity, or association of Americans.

(*c*) Harassing individuals through unnecessary overt investigative techniques [42] such as interviews or obvious physical surveillance for the purpose of intimidation.

Recommendation 41.—The Bureau should be prohibited from maintaining information on the political beliefs, political associations, or private lives of Americans except that which is clearly necessary for domestic security investigations as described in Part c.[43]

---

[42] "Overt investigative techniques" means the collection of information readily available from public sources or to a private person (including interviews of the subject or his friends or associates).

[43] Thus, the Bureau would have an obligation to review any such information before it is placed in files and to review the files, thereafter, to remove it if no longer needed. This obligation does not extend to files sealed under Recommendation 65.

c. Authorized Scope of Domestic Security Investigations

The Committee sought three objectives in defining the appropriate jurisdiction of the FBI. First, we sought to carefully limit any investigations other than traditional criminal investigations to five defined areas: preventive intelligence investigations (in two areas closely related to serious criminal activity—terrorist and hostile foreign intelligence activities), civil disorders assistance, background investigations, security risk investigations, and security leak investigations.

Second, we sought substantially to narrow, and to impose special restrictions on the conduct of, those investigations which involved the most flagrant abuses in the past: preventive intelligence investigations and civil disorders assistance. Third, we sought to provide a clear statutory foundation for those investigations which the Committee believes are appropriate to fill the vacuum in FBI legal authority.

Achieving the first and second objectives will have the most significant impact upon the FBI's domestic intelligence program and indeed, could eliminate almost half its workload. Recommendations 44 through 46 impose two types of restrictions upon the conduct of intelligence investigations and civil disorders assistance. First, the scope of intelligence investigations is limited to terrorist activities or espionage and the scope of civil disorders assistance is limited to civil disorders which may require federal troops. Second, the Committee suggests that the threshold for initiation of a full intelligence investigation be "reasonable suspicion." [44] Preliminary intelligence investigations—limited in scope, duration, and investigative technique—could be opened upon a "specific allegation or specific or substantiated information." A written finding by the Attorney General of a likely need for federal troops is required for civil disorders assistance.

The Committee's approach to FBI domestic security investigations is basically the same as that adopted by the Attorney General's guidelines for domestic security investigations. Both are cautious about any departures from former Attorney General Stone's maxim that the FBI should only conduct criminal investigations. For example, neither the Committee nor the Attorney General would condone investigations which are totally unrelated to criminal statutes (e.g., the FBI's 1970 investigation of all black student unions).

However, the Committee views its recommendations as a somewhat more limited departure from former Attorney General Stone's line than the present Attorney General's guidelines. First, the Committee would only permit intelligence investigations with respect to hostile foreign intelligence activity and terrorism. The Attorney General's guidelines have been read by FBI officials as authorizing intelligence investigations of "subversives" (individuals who may attempt to overthrow the government in the indefinite future). While the Justice Department, under its current leadership, might not adopt such an interpretation, a different Attorney General might. Second, the guidelines on their face appear to permit investigating essentially local civil disobedience (e.g., "use of force" to interfere with state or local government which could be construed too broadly).

---

[44] "Reasonable suspicion" is based upon the Supreme Court's decision in the case of *Terry* v. *Ohio*, 392 U.S. 1 (1968), and means specific and articulable facts which taken together with rational inferences from those facts, give rise to a reasonable suspicion that specified activity has occurred, is occurring, or is about to occur.

There are two reasons why the Committee would prohibit intelligence investigations of "subversives" or local civil disobedience. First, those investigations inherently risk abuse because they inevitably require surveillance of lawful speech and association rather than criminal conduct. The Committee's examination of forty years of investigations into "subversion" has found the term to be so vague as to constitute a license to investigate almost any activity of practically any group that actively opposes the policies of the administration in power.

A second reason for prohibiting intelligence investigations of "subversion" and local civil disobedience is that both can be adequately handled by less intrusive methods without unnecessarily straining limited Bureau resources. Any real threats to our form of government can be best identified through intelligence investigations focused on persons who may soon commit illegal violent acts. Local civil disobedience can be best handled by local police. Indeed, recent studies by the General Accounting Office suggest that FBI investigations in these areas result in very few prosecutions and little information of help to authorities in preventing violence.

The FBI now expends more money in its domestic security program than it does in its organized crime program, and, indeed, twice the amount on "internal security" informant operations as on organized crime informant coverage. "Subversive investigations" and "civil disorders assistance" represent almost half the caseload of the FBI domestic security program. The national interest would be better served if Bureau resources were directed at terrorism, hostile foreign intelligence activity, or organized crime, all more serious and pressing threats to the nation than "subversives" or local civil disobedience.

For similar reasons, the Committee, like the Attorney General's guidelines, requires "reasonable suspicion" for preventive intelligence investigations which extend beyond a preliminary stage. Investigations of terrorism and hostile foreign intelligence activity which are not limited in time and scope could lead to the same abuses found in intelligence investigations of subversion or local civil disobedience. However, an equally important reason for this standard is that it should increase the efficiency of Bureau investigations. The General Accounting Office found that when the FBI initiated its investigations on "soft evidence"—evidence which probably would not meet this "reasonable suspicion" standard—it usually wasted its time on an innocent target. When it initiated its investigation on harder evidence, its ability to detect imminent violence improved significantly.

The Committee's recommendations limit preventive intelligence investigations to situations where information indicates that the prohibited activity will "soon" occur, whereas the guidelines do not require that the activity be imminent. This limit is essential to prevent a return to sweeping, endless investigations of remote and speculative "threats." The Committee's intent is that, to open or continue a full investigation, there should be a substantial indication of terrorism or hostile foreign intelligence activity in the near future.

The Committee's restrictions are intended to eliminate unnecessary investigations and to provide additional protections for constitutional rights. Shifting the focus of Bureau manpower in domestic security investigations from lawful speech and association to criminal conduct by terrorists and foreign spies provides further protection for constitutional rights of Americans as well as serving the nation's interest in security.

1. Investigations of Committed or Imminent Offenses

Recommendation 42.—The FBI should be permitted to investigate a committed act which may violate a federal criminal statute pertaining to the domestic security to determine the identity of the perpetrator or to determine whether the act violates such a statute.

Recommendation 43.—The FBI should be permitted to investigate an American or foreigner to obtain evidence of criminal activity where there is "reasonable suspicion" that the American or foreigner has committed, is committing, or is about to commit a specific act which violates a federal statute pertaining to the domestic security.[45]

2. Preventive Intelligence Investigations

Recommendation 44.—The FBI should be permitted to conduct a preliminary preventive intelligence investigation of an American or foreigner where it has a specific allegation or specific or substantiated information that the American or foreigner will soon engage in terrorist activity or hostile foreign intelligence activity. Such a preliminary investigation should not continue longer than thirty days from receipt of the information unless the Attorney General or his designee finds that the information and any corroboration which has been obtained warrants investigation for an additional period which may not exceed sixty days. If, at the outset or at any time during the course of a preliminary investigation the Bureau establishes "reasonable suspicion" that an American or foreigner will soon engage in terrorist activity or hostile foreign intelligence activity, it may conduct a full preventive intelligence investigation. Such full investigation should not continue longer than one year except upon a finding of compelling circumstances by the Attorney General or his designee.

In no event should the FBI open a preliminary or full preventive intelligence investigation based upon information that an American is advocating political ideas or engaging in lawful political activities or is associating with others for the purpose of petitioning the government for redress of grievances or other such constitutionally protected purpose.

The second paragraph of Recommendation 44 will serve as an important safeguard if enacted into any statute authorizing preventive intelligence investigations. It would supplement the protection that would be afforded by limiting the FBI's intelligence investigations to terrorist and hostile foreign intelligence activities. It re-emphasizes the Committee's intent that the investigations of peaceful protest groups and other lawful associations should not recur. It serves as a further reminder that advocacy of political ideas is not to be the basis for governmental surveillance. At the same time Recommendation 44 permits the initiation of investigations where the Bureau possesses information consisting of a "specific allegation or specific or substantiated informa-

---

[45] This includes conspiracy to violate a federal statute pertaining to the domestic security. The Committee, however, recommends repeal or amendment of the Smith Act to make clear that "conspiracy" to engage in political advocacy cannot be investigated. (See Recommendation 93.)

tion that [an] American or foreigner will soon engage in terrorist activity or hostile foreign intelligence activity."

This recommendation has been among the most difficult of the domestic intelligence recommendations to draft. It was difficult because it represents the Committee's effort to draw the fine line between legitimate investigations of conduct and illegitimate investigations of advocacy and association. Originally the Committee was of the view that a threshold of "reasonable suspicion" should apply to initiating even limited preliminary intelligence investigations of terrorist or hostile foreign intelligence activities. However, the Committee was persuaded by the Department of Justice that, having narrowly defined terrorist and hostile foreign intelligence activities, a "reasonable suspicion" threshold might be unworkable at the preliminary stage. Such a threshold might prohibit the FBI from investigating an allegation of extremely dangerous activity made by an anonymous source or a source of unknown reliability. The "reasonable suspicion" standard requires that the investigator have confidence in the reliability of the individual providing the information and some corroboration of the information.

However, the Committee is cautious in proposing a standard of "specific allegation or specific or substantiated information" because it permits initiation of a preliminary investigation which includes the use of physical surveillance and a survey of, but not targeting of, existing confidential human sources. The Committee encourages the Attorney General to work with the Congress to improve upon the language we recommend in Recommendation 44 before including it in any legislative charter. If adopted, both the Attorney General and the appropriate oversight committees should periodically conduct a careful review of the application of the standard by the FBI.

The ultimate goal which Congress should seek in enacting such legislation is the development of a standard for the initiation of intelligence investigations which permits investigations of credible allegations of conduct which if uninterrupted will soon result in terrorist activities or hostile foreign intelligence activities as we define them. It must not permit investigations of consitutionally protected activities as the Committee described them in the last paragraph of Recommendation 44. The following are examples of the Committee's intent.

Recommendation 44 would prohibit the initiation of an investigation based upon "mere advocacy:"

—An investigation could not be initiated, for example, when the Bureau receives an allegation that a member of a dissident group has made statements at the group's meeting that "America needs a Marxist-Leninist government and needs to get rid of the fat cat capitalist pigs."

The Committee has found serious abuses in past FBI investigations of groups. In the conduct of these investigations, the FBI often failed to distinguish between members who were engaged in criminal activity and those who were exercising their constitutional rights of association. The Committee's recommendations would only permit investigation of a group in two situations: first, where the FBI receives information that the avowed purpose of the group is "soon to engage in terrorist activity or hostile foreign intelligence activity"; or second, where the FBI has information that unidentified members of a group are "soon to engage in terrorist activity or hostile foreign intelligence activity". In both cases the FBI may focus on the group to determine the identity of those members who plan soon to engage in such activity. However, in both cases the FBI should minimize the collection of information about law-abiding members of the group or any lawful activities of the group.

—Where the FBI has information that certain chapters of a political organization had "action squads," the purpose of which was to commit terrrorist acts, the FBI could investigate all members of a particular "action squad" where it had an allegation that this "action squad" planned to assassinate, for example, Members of Congress.

—An investigation could be initiated based upon specific information obtained by the FBI that unidentified members of a Washington, D.C., group are planning to assassinate Members of Congress.

The Committee's recommendations would not permit investigation of mere association:

—The FBI could not investigate an allegation that a member of the Klan has lunch regularly with the mayor of a southern community.

—The FBI could not investigate the allegation that a U.S. Senator attended a cocktail party at a foreign embassy where a foreign intelligence agent was present.

However, when additional facts are added indicating conduct which might constitute terrorist activity or hostile foreign intelligence activity, investigation might be authorized:

—The FBI could initiate an investigation of a dynamite dealer who met with a member of the "action squad" described above.

—Likewise, the FBI could initiate an investigation of a member of the National Security Council staff who met clandestinely with a known foreign intelligence agent in an obscure Paris restaurant.

Investigations of contacts can become quite troublesome when the contact takes place within the context of political activities or association for the purpose of petitioning the government. Law-abiding American protest groups may share common goals with groups in other countries. The obvious example was the widespread opposition in the late 1960's, at home and abroad, to America's role in Vietnam.

Furthermore, Americans should be free to communicate about such issues with persons in other countries, to attend international conferences and to exchange views or information about planned protest activities with like-minded foreign groups. Such activity, in itself, would not be the basis for a preliminary investigation under these recommendations:

—The FBI could not open an investigation of an anti-war group because "known communists" were also in attendance at a group meeting even if it had reason to believe that the communists' instructions were to influence the group or that the group shared the goals of the Soviet Union on ending the war in Vietnam.

—The FBI could not open an investigation of an anti-war activist who attends an international peace conference in Oslo where foreign intelligence agents would be in attendance even if the FBI had reason to believe that they might attempt to recruit the activist. Of course, the CIA would not be prevented from surveillance of the foreign agent's activities.

However, if the Bureau had additional information suggesting that the activities of the Americans in the above hypothetical cases were more than mere association to petition for redress of grievances, an investigation would be legitimate.

—Where the FBI had received information that the anti-war activist traveling to Oslo intended to meet with a person he knew to be a foreign intelligence agent to receive instructions to conduct espionage on behalf of a hostile foreign country, the FBI could open a preliminary investigation of the activist.

The Committee cautions the Department of Justice and FBI that in opening investigations of conduct occurring in the context of political activities, it should endeavor to ensure that the allegation prompting the investigation is from a reliable source.

Certainly, however, where the FBI has received a specific allegation or specific or substantiated information that an American or foreigner will soon engage in hostile foreign intelligence activity or terrorist activity, it may conduct an investigation. For example, it could do so:

—Where the FBI receives information that an American has been recruited by a hostile intelligence service;

—Where the FBI receives information that an atomic scientist has had a number of clandestine meetings with a hostile foreign intelligence agent.

Recommendation 45.—The FBI should be permitted to collect information to assist federal, state, and local officials in connection with a civil disorder either—

(i) After the Attorney General finds in writing that there is a clear and immediate threat of domestic violence or rioting which is likely to require implementation of 10 U.S.C. 332 or 333 (the use of federal troops for the enforcement of federal law or federal court orders), or likely to result in a request by the governor or legislature of a state pursuant to 10 U.S.C. 331 for the use of federal militia or other federal armed forces as a countermeasure; [45a] or

(ii) After such troops have been introduced.

Recommendation 46.—FBI assistance to federal, state, and local officials in connection with a civil disorder should be limited to collecting information necessary for

(1) the President in making decisions concerning the introduction of federal troops;

(2) military officials in positioning and supporting such troops; and

(3) state and local officials in coordinating their activities with such military officials.

4. Background Investigations

Recommendation 47.—The FBI should be permitted to participate in the federal government's program of background investigations of federal employees or employees of federal contractors. The authority to conduct such investigations should not, however, be used as the basis for conducting investigations of other persons. In addition, Congress should examine the standards of Executive Order 10450, which serves as the current authority for FBI background investigations, to determine whether additional legislation is necessary to:

(*a*) modify criteria based on political beliefs and associations unrelated to suitability for employment; such modification should make

---

[45a] This recommendation does not prevent the FBI from conducting criminal investigations or preventive intelligence investigations of terrorist acts in connection with a civil disorder.

those criteria consistent with judicial decisions regarding privacy of political association; [46] and

(b) restrict the dissemination of information from name checks of information related to suitability for employment.

5. Security Risk Investigations

Recommendation 48.—Under regulations to be formulated by the Attorney General, the FBI should be permitted to investigate a specific allegation that an individual within the Executive branch with access to classified information is a security risk as described in Executive Order 10450. Such investigation should not continue longer than thirty days except upon written approval of the Attorney General or his designee.

6. Security Leak Investigations

Recommendation 49.—Under regulations to be formulated by the Attorney General, the FBI should be permitted to investigate a specific allegation of the improper disclosure of classified information by employees or contractors of the Executive branch.[48] Such investigation should not continue longer than thirty days except upon written approval of the Attorney General or his designee.

d. Authorized Investigative Techniques

The following recommendations contain the Committee's proposed controls on the use of investigative techniques in domestic security investigations which would be authorized herein. There are three types of investigative techniques: (1) overt techniques (e.g., interviews), (2) name checks (review of existing government files), and (3) covert techniques (which range, for example, from electronic surveillance and informants to the review of credit records).

The objective of these recommendations, like the Attorney General's domestic security guidelines, is to ensure that the more intrusive the technique, the more stringent the procedural checks that will be applied to it. Therefore, the recommendation would permit overt techniques and name checks in any of the investigative areas described above.

With respect to covert technique, the Committee decided upon procedures to apply to the use of a particular covert technique based upon three considerations: (1) its potential for abuse, (2) the practicability of applying the procedure to the technique, and (3) the facts and circumstances giving rise to the request for use of the technique (whether the facts warrant a full investigation or only a preliminary investigation). The most intrusive covert techniques (electronic surveillance, mail opening, and surreptitious entry) would be permissible only if a judicial warrant were obtained as required in Recommendations 51 through 54. FBI requests to target paid or controlled informants, to review tax returns, to use mail covers, or to use any other covert techniques in domestic security investigations would be subject to review

---

[46] For example, *NAACP* v. *Alabama*, 357 U.S. 449 (1958) ; *Bates* v. *Little Rock*, 361 U.S. 516 (1960).

[48] If Congress enacts a security leak criminal statute, this additional investigative authority would be unnecessary. Security leaks would be handled as traditional criminal investigations as described in Recommendations 42 and 43 above.

and in some cases to prior approval by the Attorney General's office, as described in Recommendations 55 through 62.[49]

The judicial warrant requirement the Committee recommends for electronic surveillance is similar in many respects to the Administration's bill, which is a welcome departure from past practice. The Committee, like the Administration, believes that there should be no electronic surveillance within the United States which is not subject to a judicial warrant procedure. Both would also authorize warrants for electronic surveillance of foreigners who are officers, agents, or employees of foreign powers, even though the government could not point to probable cause of criminal activity.

However, while the constitutional issue has not been resolved, the Committee does not believe that the President has inherent power to authorize the targeting of an American for electronic surveillance without a warrant, as suggested by the Administration bill. Certainly, if Congress requires a warrant for the targeting of an American for traditional electronic surveillance or for the most sophisticated NSA techniques, at home or abroad, then the dangerous doctrine of inherent Executive power to target an American for electronic surveillance can be put to rest at last.[49a] The Committee also would require that no American be targeted for electronic surveillance except upon a judicial finding of probable criminal activity. The Administration bill would permit electronic surveillance in the absence of probable crime if the American is engaged in (or aiding or abetting a person engaged in) "clandestine intelligence activity" (an undefined term) under the direction of a foreign power. Targeting an American for electronic surveillance in the absence of probable cause to believe he might commit a crime is unwise and unnecessary.

In Part X, the Committee recommends that Congress consider amending the Espionage Act to cover modern forms of industrial, technological, or economic espionage not now prohibited. At the same time, electronic surveillance targeted at an American should be authorized where there is probable cause to believe he is engaged in such activity. Thus, the Committee agrees with the Attorney General that such activity may subject an American to electronic surveillance. But, as a matter of principle, the Committee believes that an American ought not to be targeted for surveillance unless there is probable cause to believe he may violate the law. The Committee's record suggests that use of undefined terms, not tied to matters sufficiently serious to be the subject of criminal statutes, is a dangerous basis for intrusive investigations.

The paid and directed informant was a principal source of excesses revealed in our record. However, we do not propose the application of a judicial warrant procedure to informants. Instead, we propose a requirement of approval by the Attorney General based upon a probable cause standard. Because of the potential for abuse, however, we believe the warrant issue should be thoroughly reviewed after two years' experience.

---

[49] Review of tax returns and mail covers would also be subject to the Post Office and IRS procedures described in earlier recommendations.

[49a] "When the President takes measures incompatible with the expressed or implied will of Congress, his power is at its lowest ebb. . . ." (*Youngstown Sheet & Tube Co.* v. *Sawyer*, 343 U.S. 579, 637 (1952), Justice Jackson concurring.)

There are some differences between the Attorney General and the Committee on the use of informants.[50] The Attorney General would permit the FBI to make unrestricted use of existing informants in a preliminary intelligence investigation. The Committee recognizes the legitimacy of using existing informants for certain purposes—for example, to identify a new subject who has come to the attention of the Bureau. However, the Committee believes there should be certain restrictions for existing informants. Indeed, almost all of the informant abuses—overly broad reporting, the ghetto informant program, agents provocateur, etc.—involved existing informants.

The real issue is not the development of new informants, but the sustained direction of informants, new or old, at a new target. Therefore, the restrictions suggested in Recommendations 55 through 57 are designed to impose standards for the sustained targeting of informants against Americans.

The Committee requires that before an informant can be targeted in an intelligence investigation the Attorney General or his designee must make a finding that he has considered and rejected less intrusive techniques and that targeting the informant is necessary to the investigation. Furthermore, the Committee would require that the informant cannot be targeted for more than ninety days [51] in the intelligence investigation unless the Attorney General finds that there is "probable cause" that the American will soon engage in terrorist or hostile foreign intelligence activity, except that if the Attorney General finds compelling circumstances he may permit an additional sixty days.

Other than the restrictions upon the use of informants, the Committee would permit basically the same techniques in preliminary and full investigations as the Attorney General's guidelines, although the Committee would require somewhat closer supervision by the Attorney General or his designee. Interviews (including interviews of existing informant's), name checks (including checks of local police intelligence files), and physical surveillance and review of credit and telephone records would be permitted during the preliminary investigation. The Attorney General or his designee would have to review that investigation within one month. Under the guidelines, preliminary investigations do not require approval by the Attorney General or his designee and can continue for as long as ninety days with an additional ninety-day extension. The remainder of the covert techniques would be permitted in full intelligence investigations. Under the Attorney General's guidelines, the Attorney General or his designee only become involved in the termination of such investigations (at the end of one year), while the Committee's recommendations would require the Attorney General or his designee to authorize the initiation of the full investigation and the use of covert techniques in the investigation.

1. Overt Techniques and Name Checks

Recommendation 50.—Overt techniques and name checks should be permitted in all of the authorized domestic security investigations

---

[50] The Attorney General is considering additional guidelines on informants.
[51] The period of ninety days begins when the informant is in place and capable of reporting.

described above, including preliminary and full preventive intelligence investigations.

2. Covert Techniques

a. Covert Techniques Covered

This section covers the standards and procedures for the use of the following covert techniques in authorized domestic security investigations:

(i) electronic surveillance;
(ii) search and seizure or surreptitious entry;
(iii) mail opening;
(iv) informants and other covert human sources;
(v) mail surveillance;
(vi) review of tax returns and tax-related information;
(vii) other covert techniques—including physical surveillance, photographic surveillance, use of body recorders and other consensual electronic surveillance, and use of sensitive records of state and local government, and other institutional records systems pertaining to credit, medical history, social welfare history, or telephone calls.[52]

b. Judicial Warrant Procedures (Electronic Surveillance, Mail Opening, Search and Seizure, and Surreptitious Entry)

The requirements for judicial warrants, set forth below, are not intended to cover NSA communication intercepts. Recommendations 14 through 18 contain the Committee's recommendations pertaining to NSA intercepts, the circumstances in which a judicial warrant is required and the standards applicable for the issuance of such a warrant.

Recommendation 51.—All non-consensual electronic surveillance, mail-opening, and unauthorized entries should be conducted only upon authority of a judicial warrant.

Recommendation 52.—All non-consensual electronic surveillance should be conducted pursuant to judicial warrants issued under authority of Title III of the Omnibus Crime Control and Safe Streets Act of 1968.

The Act should be amended to provide, with respect to electronic surveillance of foreigners in the United States, that a warrant may issue if

(*a*) There is probable cause that the target is an officer, employee, or conscious agent of a foreign power.

(*b*) The Attorney General has certified that the surveillance is likely to reveal information necessary to the protection of the nation against actual or potential attack or other hostile acts of force of a foreign power; to obtain foreign intelligence information deemed essential to the security of the United States; or to protect national security information against hostile foreign intelligence activity.

(*c*) With respect to any such electronic surveillance, the judge should adopt procedures to minimize the acquisition and retention of non-foreign intelligence information about Americans.

---

[52] The Committee has not taken extensive testimony on these "other covert techniques" and therefore, aside from the general administrative procedures contained in c. below, makes no recommendations designed to treat these techniques fully.

(*d*) Such electronic surveillance should be exempt from the disclosure requirements of Title III of the 1968 Act as to foreigners generally and as to Americans if they are involved in hostile foreign intelligence activity.[53]

As noted earlier, the Committee believes that the espionage laws should be amended to include industrial espionage and other modern forms of espionage not presently covered and Title III should incorporate any such amendment. The Committee's recomendation is that both that change and the amendment of Title III to require warrants for all electronic surveillance be promptly made.

Recommendation 53.—Mail opening should be conducted only pursuant to a judicial warrant issued upon probable cause of criminal activity as described in Recommendation 37.

Recommendation 54.—Unauthorized entry should be conducted only upon judicial warrant issued on probable cause to believe that the place to be searched contains evidence of a crime, except unauthorized entry, including surreptitious entry, against foreigners who are officers, employees, or conscious agents of a foreign power should be permitted upon judicial warrant under the standards which apply to electronic surveillance described in Recommendation 52.

N11

c. *Administrative Procedures (Covert Human Sources, Mail Surveillance, Review of Tax Returns and Tax-Related Information, and Other Covert Techniques)*

Recommendation 55.—Covert human sources may not be directed [54] at an American except:

(1) In the course of a criminal investigation if necessary to the investigation *provided* that covert human sources should not be directed at an American as a part of an investigation of a committed act unless there is reasonable suspicion to believe that the American is responsible for the act and then only for the purpose of identifying the perpetrators of the act.

(2) If the American is the target of a full preventive intelligence investigation and the Attorney General or his designee makes a written finding that [55] (i) he has considered and rejected less intrusive techniques; and (ii) he believes that covert human sources are necessary to obtain information for the investigation.

Recommendation 56.—Covert human sources which have been directed at an American in a full preventive intelligence investigation should not be used to collect information on the activities of the American for more than 90 days after the source is in place and capable of reporting, unless the Attorney General or his designee finds in writing

---

[53] Except where disclosure is called for in connection with the defense in the case of criminal prosecution.

[54] A "covert human source" is an undercover agent or informant who is paid or otherwise controlled by the agency. A cooperating citizen is not ordinarily a covert human source. A covert human source is "directed" at an American when the intelligence agency requests the covert human source to collect new information on the activities of that individual. A covert human source is not "directed" at a target if the intelligence agency merely asks him for information already in his possession, unless through repeated inquiries, or otherwise, the agency implicitly directs the informant against the target of the investigation.

[55] The written finding must be made prior to the time the covert human source is directed at an American, unless exigent circumstances make application impossible, in which case the application must be made as soon thereafter as possible.

either that there are "compelling circumstances" in which case they may be used for an additional 60 days, or that there is probable cause that the American will soon engage in terrorist activities or hostile foreign intelligence activities.

Recommendation 57.—All covert human sources used by the FBI should be reviewed by the Attorney General or his designee as soon as practicable, and should be terminated [56] unless the covert human source could be directed against an American in a criminal investigation or a full preventive intelligence investigation under these recommendations.

Recommendation 58.—Mail surveillance and the review of tax returns and tax-related information should be conducted consistently with the recommendations contained in Part iii. In addition to restrictions contained in Part iii, the review of tax returns and tax-related information, as well as review of medical or social history records, confidential records of private institutions and confidential records of Federal, state, and local government agencies other than intelligence or law enforcement agencies may not be used against an American except:

(1) In the course of a criminal investigation if necessary to the investigation;

(2) If the American is the target of a full preventive intelligence investigation and the Attorney General or his designee makes a written finding that [57] (i) he has considered and rejected less intrusive techniques; and (ii) he believes that the covert technique requested by the Bureau is necessary to obtain information necessary to the investigation.

Recommendation 59.—The use of physical surveillance and review of credit and telephone records and any records of governmental or private institutions other than those covered in Recommendation 58 should be permitted to be used against an American, if necessary, in the course of either a criminal investigation or a preliminary or full preventive intelligence investigation.

Recommendation 60.—Covert techniques should be permitted at the scene of a potential civil disorder in the course of preventive criminal intelligence and criminal investigations as described above. Non-warrant covert techniques may also be directed at an American during a civil disorder in which extensive acts of violence are occurring and Federal troops have been introduced. This additional authority to direct such covert techniques at Americans during a civil disorder should be limited to circumstances where Federal troops are actually in use and the technique is used only for the purpose of preventing further violence.

Recommendation 61.—Covert techniques should not be directed at an American in the course of a background investigation without the informed written consent of the American.

Recommendation 62.—If Congress enacts a statute attaching criminal sanctions to security leaks, covert techniques should be directed at Americans in the course of security leak investigations only if such

---

[56] Termination requires cessation of payment or any other form of direction or control.

[57] The written finding must be made prior to the time the technique is used against an American, unless exigent circumstances make application impossible, in which case the application must be made as soon thereafter as possible.

techniques are consistent with Recommendation 55(1), 58(1) or 59.
With respect to security risks, Congress might consider authorizing
covert techniques, other than those requiring a judicial warrant, to be
directed at Americans in the course of security risk [58] investigations,
but only upon a written finding of the Attorney General that (i) there
is reasonable suspicion to believe that the individual is a security risk,
(ii) he has considered and rejected less intrusive techniques, and (iii)
he believes the technique requested is necessary to the investigation.

(d) Incidental Overhears

Recommendation 63.—Except as limited elsewhere in these recom-
mendations or in Title III of the Omnibus Crime Control and Safe
Streets Act of 1968, information obtained incidentally through an au-
thorized covert technique about an American or a foreigner who is not
the target of the covert technique can be used as the basis for any au-
thorized domestic security investigation.

e. Maintenance and Dissemination of Information

The following limitations should apply to the maintenance and
dissemination of information collected as a result of domestic security
investigations.

1. Relevance

Recommendation 64.—Information should not be maintained except
where relevant to the purpose of an investigation.

2. Sealing or Purging

Recommendation 65.—Personally identifiable information on
Americans obtained in the following kinds of investigations should be
sealed or purged as follows (unless it appears on its face to be necessary
for another authorized investigation):

(a) Preventive intelligence investigations of terrorist or hostile for-
eign intelligence activities—as soon as the investigation is terminated
by the Attorney General or his designee pursuant to Recommendation
45 or 69.

(b) Civil disorder assistance—as soon as the assistance is termi-
nated by the Attorney General or his designee pursuant to Recom-
mendation 69, provided that where troops have been introduced such
information need be sealed or purged only within a reasonable period
after their withdrawal.

Recommendation 66.—Information previously gained by the FBI
or any other intelligence agency through illegal techniques should be
sealed or purged as soon as practicable.

3. Dissemination

Recommendation 67.—Personally identifiable information on Amer-
icans from domestic security investigations may be disseminated out-
side the Department of Justice as follows:

(a) Preventive intelligence investigations of terrorist activities—
personally identifiable information on Americans from preventive
criminal intelligence investigations of terrorist activities may be dis-
seminated only to:

---

[58] If Congress does not enact a security leak criminal statute, Congress might
consider authorizing covert techniques in the same circumstances as security risk
investigations either as an interim measure or as an alternative to such a statute.

(1) A foreign or domestic law enforcement agency which has jurisdiction over the criminal activity to which the information relates; or

(2) To a foreign intelligence or military agency of the United States, if necessary for an activity permitted by these recommendations; or

(3) To an appropriate federal official with authority to make personnel decisions about the subject of the information; or

(4) To a foreign intelligence or military agency of a cooperating foreign power if necessary for an activity permitted by these recommendations to similar agencies of the United States; or

(5) Where necessary to warn state or local officials of terrorist activity likely to occur within their jurisdiction; or

(6) Where necessary to warn any person of a threat to life or property from terrorist activity.

(b) Preventive intelligence investigations of hostile foreign intelligence activities—personally identifiable information on Americans from preventive criminal intelligence investigations of hostile intelligence activities may be disseminated only:

(1) To an appropriate federal official with authority to make personnel decisions about the subject of the information; or

(2) To the National Security Council or the Department of State upon request or where appropriate to their administration of U.S. foreign policy; or

(3) To a foreign intelligence or military agency of the United States, if relevant to an activity permitted by these recommendations; or

(4) To a foreign intelligence or military agency of a cooperating foreign power if relevant to an activity permitted by these recommendations to similar agencies of the United States.

(c) Civil disorders assistance—personally identifiable information on Americans involved in an actual or potential disorder, collected in the course of civil disorders assistance, should not be disseminated outside the Department of Justice except to military officials and appropriate state and local officials at the scene of a civil disorder where federal troops are present.[59]

(d) Background investigations—to the maximum extent feasible, the results of background investigations should be segregated within the FBI and only disseminated to officials outside the Department of Justice authorized to make personnel decisions with respect to the subject.

(e) All other authorized domestic security investigations—to governmental officials who are authorized to take action consistent with the purpose of an investigation or who have statutory duties which require the information.

4. Oversight Access

Recommendation 68.—Officers of the Executive branch, who are made responsible by these recommendations for overseeing intelligence activities, and appropriate congressional committees should

---

[59] Personally identifiable information on terrorist activity which pertains to a civil disorder could still be disseminated pursuant to (a) above.

have access to all information necessary for their functions. The committees should adopt procedures to protect the privacy of subjects of files maintained by the FBI and other agencies affected by the domestic intelligence recommendations.

f. Attorney General Oversight of the FBI, Including Termination of Investigations and Covert Techniques

Recommendation 69.—The Attorney General should:

(a) Establish a program of routine and periodic review of FBI domestic security investigations to ensure that the FBI is complying with all of the foregoing recommendations; and

(b) Assure, with respect to the following investigations of Americans that:

(1) Preventive intelligence investigations of terrorist activity or hostile foreign intelligence activity are terminated within one year, except that the Attorney General or his designee may grant extensions upon a written finding of "compelling circumstances";

(2) Covert techniques are used in preventive intelligence investigations of terrorist activity or hostile foreign intelligence activity only so long as necessary and not beyond time limits established by the Attorney General except that the Attorney General or his designee may grant extensions upon a written finding of "compelling circumstances";

(3) Civil disorders assistance is terminated upon withdrawal of federal troops or, if troops were not introduced, within a reasonable time after the finding by the Attorney General that troops are likely to be requested, except that the Attorney General or his designee may grant extensions upon a written finding of "compelling circumstances."

v. The Responsibility and Authority of the Attorney General for Oversight of Federal Domestic Security Activities Must Be Clarified and General Counsels and Inspectors General of Intelligence Agencies Strengthened

The Committee's Recommendations give the Attorney General broad oversight responsibility for federal domestic security activities. As the chief legal officer of the United States, the Attorney General is the most appropriate official to be charged with ensuring that the intelligence agencies of the United States conduct their activities in accordance with the law. The Executive Order, however, places primary responsibility for oversight of the intelligence agencies with the newly created Oversight Board.

Both the Recommendations and the Order recognize the Attorney General's primary responsibility to detect, or prevent, violations of law by any employee of intelligence agencies. Both charge the head of intelligence agencies with the duty to report to the Attorney General information which relates to possible violations of law by any employee of the respective intelligence agencies. The Order also requires the Oversight Board to report periodically, at least quarterly, to the Attorney General on its findings and to report, in a timely manner, to the Attorney General, any activities that raise serious questions about legality.

a. Attorney General Responsibility and Relationship With Other Intelligence Agencies

These recommendations are intended to implement the Attorney General's responsibility to control and supervise all of the domestic security activities of the federal government and to oversee activities of any agency affected by the Domestic Intelligence Recommendations:

Recommendation 70.—The Attorney General should review the internal regulations of the FBI and other intelligence agencies engaging in domestic security activities to ensure that such internal regulations are proper and adequate to protect the constitutional rights of Americans.

Recommendation 71.—The Attorney General or his designee (such as the Office of Legal Counsel of the Department of Justice) should advise the General Counsels of intelligence agencies on interpretations of statutes and regulations adopted pursuant to these recommendations and on such other legal questions as are described in b. below.

Recommendation 72.—The Attorney General should have ultimate responsibility for the investigation of alleged violations of law relating to the Domestic Intelligence Recommendations.

Recommendation 73.—The Attorney General should be notified of possible alleged violations of law through the Office of Professional Responsibility (described in c. below) by agency heads, General Counsel, or Inspectors General of intelligence agencies as provided in B. below.

Recommendation 74.—The heads of all intelligence agencies affected by these recommendations are responsible for the prevention and detection of alleged violations of the law by, or on behalf of, their respective agencies and for the reporting to the Attorney General of all such alleged violations.[60] Each such agency head should also assure his agency's cooperation with the Attorney General in investigations of alleged violations.

b. General Counsel and Inspectors General of Intelligence

The Committee recommends that the FBI and each other intelligence agency should have a general counsel nominated by the President and confirmed by the Senate. There is no provision in the Executive Order making General Counsels of intelligence agencies subject to Senate confirmation. The Committee believes that the extraordinary responsibilities exercised by the General Counsel of these agencies make it very important that these officials are subject to examination by the Senate prior to their confirmation. The Committee further believes that making such positions subject to Presidential appointment and senatorial confirmation will increase the stature of the office and will protect the independence of judgment of the General Counsel.

The Committee Recommendations differ from the Executive Order in two other important respects. The Recommendations provide that the General Counsel should review all significant proposed agency activities to determine their legality. They also provide a mechanism

---

[60] This recommendation must be read along with recommendations contained in Part ii, limiting the authority of foreign intelligence and military agencies to investigate security leaks or security risks involving their employees and centralizing those investigations in the FBI.

whereby the Inspector General or General Counsel of an intelligence agency can, in extraordinary circumstances, and if requested by an employee of the Agency, provide information directly to the Attorney General or appropriate congressional oversight committees without informing the head of the agency.

The Committee Recommendations also go beyond the Executive Order in requiring agency heads to report to appropriate committees of the Congress and the Attorney General on the activities of the Office of the General Counsel and the Office of the Inspector General. The Committee believes that the reporting requirements will facilitate oversight of the intelligence agencies and of those important offices within them.

Recommendation 75.—To assist the Attorney General and the agency heads in the functions described in a. above, the FBI and each other intelligence agency should have a General Counsel, nominated by the President and confirmed by the Senate, and an Inspector General appointed by the agency head.

Recommendation 76.—Any individual having information on past, current, or proposed activities which appear to be illegal, improper, or in violation of agency policy should be required to report the matter immediately to the Agency head, General Counsel, or Inspector General. If the matter is not initially reported to the General Counsel, he should be notified by the Agency head or Inspector General. Each agency should regularly remind employees of their obligation to report such information.

Recommendation 77.—As provided in Recommendation 74, the heads of the FBI and of other intelligence agencies are responsible for reporting to the Attorney General alleged violations of law. When such reports are made, the appropriate congressional committees should be notified.[61]

Recommendation 78.—The General Counsel and Inspector General of the FBI and of each other intelligence agency should have unrestricted access to all information in the possession of the agency and should have the authority to review all of the agency's activities.[62] The Attorney General, or the Office of Professional Responsibility on his behalf, should have access to all information in the possession of an agency which, in the opinion of the Attorney General, is necessary for an investigation of illegal activity.

Recommendation 79.—The General Counsel of the FBI and of each other intelligence agency should review all significant proposed agency activities to determine their legality and constitutionality.

---

[61] The Inspector General and General Counsel should have authority, in extraordinary circumstances, and if requested by an employee of the agency providing information, to pass the information directly to the Attorney General and to notify the appropriate congressional committees without informing the head of the agency. Furthermore, nothing herein should prohibit an employee from reporting on his own such information directly to the Attorney General or an appropriate congressional oversight committee.

[62] The head of the agency should be required to provide to the appropriate oversight committees of the Congress and the Executive branch and the Attorney General an immediate explanation, in writing, of any instance in which the Inspector General or the General Counsel has been denied access to information, has been instructed not to report on a particular activity or has been denied the authority to investigate a particular activity.

Recommendation 80.—The Director of the FBI and the heads of each other intelligence agency should be required to report, at least annually, to the appropriate committee of the Congress, on the activities of the General Counsel and the Office of the Inspector General.[63]

Recommendation 81.—The Director of the FBI and the heads of each other intelligence agency should be required to report, at least annually, to the Attorney General on all reports of activities which appear illegal, improper, outside the legislative charter, or in violation of agency regulations. Such reports should include the General Counsel's findings concerning these activities, a summary of the Inspector General's investigations of these activities, and the practices and procedures developed to discover activities that raise questions of legality or propriety.

c. Office of Professional Responsibility

Recommendation 82.—The Office of Professional Responsibility created by Attorney General Levi should be recognized in statute. The director of the office, appointed by the Attorney General, should report directly to the Attorney General or the Deputy Attorney General. The functions of the office should include:

(*a*) Serving as a central repository of reports and notifications provided the Attorney General; and

(*b*) Investigation, if requested by the Attorney General of alleged violations by intelligence agencies of statutes enacted or regulations promulgated pursuant to these recommendations.[64]

d. Director of the FBI and Assistant Directors of the FBI

Recommendation 83.—The Attorney General is responsible for all of the activities of the FBI, and the Director of the FBI is responsible to, and should be under the supervision and control of, the Attorney General.

Recommendation 84.—The Director of the FBI should be nominated by the President and confirmed by the Senate to serve at the pleasure of the President for a single term of not more than eight years.

Recommendation 85.—The Attorney General should consider exercising his power to appoint Assistant Directors of the FBI. A maximum term of years should be imposed on the tenure of the Assistant Director for the Intelligence Division.[64a]

---

[63] The report should include: (a) a summary of all agency activities that raise questions of legality or propriety and the General Counsel's findings concerning these activities; (b) a summary of the Inspector General's investigations concerning any of these activities; (c) a summary of the practices and procedures developed to discover activities that raise questions of legality or propriety; (d) a summary of each component, program or issue survey, including the Inspector General's recommendations and the Director's decisions; and (e) a summary of all other matters handled by the Inspector General.

The report should also include discussion of: (a) major legal problems facing the Agency; (b) the need for additional statutes; and (c) any cases referred to the Department of Justice.

[64] The functions of the Office should not include: (a) exercise of routine supervision of FBI domestic security investigations; (b) making requests to other agencies to conduct investigations or direct covert techniques at Americans; or (c) involvement in any other supervisory functions which it might ultimately be required to investigate.

[64a] It is not proposed that this recommendation be enacted as a statute.

vi. Administrative Rulemaking and Increased Disclosure Should Be Required

a. Administrative. Rulemaking

Recommendation 86.—The Attorney General should approve all administrative regulations required to implement statutes created pursuant to these recommendations.

Recommendation 87.—Such regulations, except for regulations concerning investigations of hostile foreign intelligence activity or other matters which are properly classified, should be issued pursuant to the Administrative Procedures Act and should be subject to the approval of the Attorney General.

Recommendation 88.—The effective date of regulations pertaining to the following matters should be delayed ninety days, during which time Congress would have the opportunity to review such regulations: [65]

(*a*) Any CIA activities against Americans, as permitted in ii.a. above;

(*b*) Military activities at the time of a civil disorder;

(*c*) The authorized scope of domestic security investigations, authorized investigative techniques, maintenance and dissemination of information by the FBI; and

(*d*) The termination of investigations and covert techniques as described in Part iv.

b. Disclosure

Recommendation 89.—Each year the FBI and other intelligence agencies affected by these recommendations should be required to seek annual statutory authorization for their programs.

Recommendation 90.—The Freedom of Information Act (5 U.S.C. 552(b)) and the Federal Privacy Act (5 U.S.C. 552(a)) provide important mechanisms by which individuals can gain access to information on intelligence activity directed against them. The Domestic Intelligence Recommendations assume that these statutes will continue to be vigorously enforced. In addition, the Department of Justice should notify all readily identifiable targets of past illegal surveillance techniques, and all COINTELPRO victims, and third parties who had received anonymous COINTELPRO communications, of the nature of the activities directed against them, or the source of the anonymous communication to them.[65a]

vii. Civil Remedies Should Be Expanded

Recommendation 91 expresses the Committee's concern for establishing a legislative scheme which will afford effective redress to people who are injured by improper federal intelligence activity. The recommended provisions for civil remedies are also intended to deter improper intelligence activity without restricting the sound exercise of discretion by intelligence officers at headquarters or in the field.

As the Committee's investigation has shown, many Americans have suffered injuries from domestic intelligence activity, ranging from deprivation of constitutional rights of privacy and free speech to the loss of a job or professional standing, break-up of a marriage, and impairment of physical or mental health. But the extent, if any, to

---

[65] This review procedure would be similar to the procedure followed with respect to the promulgation of the Federal Rules of Criminal and Civil Procedure.

[65a] It is not proposed that this recommendation be enacted as a statute.

which an injured citizen can seek relief—either monetary or injunctive—from the government or from an individual intelligence officer is far from clear under the present state of the law.

One major disparity in the current state of the law is that, under the Reconstruction era Civil Rights Act of 1871, the deprivation of constitutional rights by an officer or agent of a state government provides the basis for a suit to redress the injury incurred; [66] but there is no statute which extends the same remedies for identical injuries when they are caused by a federal officer.

In the landmark *Bivens* case, the Supreme Court held that a federal officer could be sued for money damages for violating a citizen's Fourth Amendment rights.[67] Whether monetary damages can be obtained for violation of other constitutional rights by federal officers remains unclear.

While we believe that any citizen with a substantial and specific claim to injury from intelligence activity should have standing to sue, the Committee is aware of the need for judicial protection against legal claims which amount to harassment or distraction of government officials, disruption of legitimate investigations, and wasteful expenditure of government resources. We also seek to ensure that the creation of a civil remedy for aggrieved persons does not impinge upon the proper exercise of discretion by federal officials.

Therefore, we recommend that where a government official—as opposed to the government itself—acted in good faith and with the reasonable belief that his conduct was lawful, he should have an affirmative defense to a suit for damages brought under the proposed statute. To tighten the system of accountability and control of domestic intelligence activity, the Committee proposes that this defense be structured to encourage intelligence officers to obtain written authorization for questionable activities and to seek legal advice about them.[68]

To avoid penalizing federal officers and agents for the exercise of discretion, the Committee believes that the government should indemnify their attorney fees and reasonable litigation costs when they are held not to be liable. To avoid burdening the taxpayers for the deliberate misconduct of intelligence officers and agents, we believe the government should be able to seek reimbursement from those who willfully and knowingly violate statutory charters or the Constitution.

Furthermore, we believe that the courts will be able to fashion discovery procedures, including inspection of material in chambers, and to issue orders as the interests of justice require, to allow plaintiffs with substantial claims to uncover enough factual material to argue their case, while protecting the secrecy of governmental information in which there is a legitimate security interest.

The Committee recommends that a legislative scheme of civil remedies for the victims of intelligence activity be established along the

---

[66] 42 U.S.C. 1983.

[67] *Bivens v. Six Unknown Fed. Narcotics Agents*, 403 U.S. 388 (1971).

[68] One means of structuring such a defense would be to create a rebuttable presumption that an individual defendant acted so as to avail himself of this defense when he proves that he acted in good faith reliance upon: (1) a written order or directive by a government officer empowered to authorize him to take action; or (2) a written assurance by an appropriate legal officer that his action is lawful.

following lines to clarify the state of the law, to encourage the responsible execution of duties created by the statutes recommended herein to regulate intelligence agencies, and to provide relief for the victims of illegal intelligence activity.

Recommendation 91.—Congress should enact a comprehensive civil remedies statute which would accomplish the following: [69]

(a) Any American with a substantial and specific claim [70] to an actual or threatened injury by a violation of the Constitution by federal intelligence officers or agents [71] acting under color of law should have a federal cause of action against the government and the individual federal intelligence officer or agent responsible for the violation, without regard to the monetary amount in controversy. If actual injury is proven in court, the Committee believes that the injured person should be entitled to equitable relief, actual, general, and punitive damages, and recovery of the costs of litigation.[72] If threatened injury is proven in court, the Committee believes that equitable relief and recovery of the costs of litigation should be available.

(b) Any American with a substantial and specific claim to actual or threatened injury by violation of the statutory charter for intelligence activity (as proposed by these Domestic Intelligence Recommendations) should have a cause of action for relief as in (a) above.

(c) Because of the secrecy that surrounds intelligence programs, the Committee believes that a plaintiff should have two years from the date upon which he discovers, or reasonably should have discovered, the facts which give rise to a cause of action for relief from a constitutional or statutory violation.

(d) Whatever statutory provision may be made to permit an individual defendant to raise an affirmative defense that he acted within the scope of his official duties, in good faith, and with a reasonable belief that the action he took was lawful, the Committee believes that to ensure relief to persons injured by governmental intelligence activity, this defense should be available solely to individual defendants and should not extend to the government. Moreover, the defense should not be available to bar injunctions against individual defendants.

viii. Criminal Penalties Should Be Enacted

Recommendation 92.—The Committee believes that criminal penalties should apply, where appropriate, to willful and knowing

---

[69] Due to the scope of the Committee's mandate, we have taken evidence only on constitutional violations by intelligence officers and agents. However, the anomalies and lack of clarity in the present state of the law (as discussed above) and the breadth of constitutional violations revealed by our record, suggest to us that a general civil remedy would be appropriate. Thus, we urge consideration of a statutory civil remedy for constitutional violations by any federal officer; and we encourage the appropriate committees of the Congress to take testimony on this subject.

[70] The requirement of a substantial and specific claim is intended to allow a judge to screen out frivolous claims where a plaintiff cannot allege specific facts which indicate that he was the target of illegal intelligence activity.

[71] "Federal intelligence officers or agents" should include a person who was an intelligence officer, employee, or agent at the time a cause of action arose. "Agent" should include anyone acting with actual, implied, or apparent authority.

[72] The right to recover "costs of litigation" is intended to include recovery of reasonable attorney fees as well as other litigation costs reasonably incurred.

violations of statutes enacted pursuant to the Domestic Intelligence Recommendations.

ix. The Smith Act and the Voorhis Act Should Either Be Repealed or Amended

Recommendation 93.—Congress should either repeal the Smith Act (18 U.S.C. 2385) and the Voorhis Act (18 U.S.C. 2386), which on their face appear to authorize investigation of "mere advocacy" of a political ideology, or amend those statutes so that domestic security investigations are only directed at conduct which might serve as the basis for a constitutional criminal prosecution, under Supreme Court decisions interpreting these and related statutes.[73]

x. The Espionage Statute Should be Modernized

As suggested in its definition of "hostile foreign intelligence activity" and its recommendations on warrants for electronic surveillance, the Committee agrees with the Attorney General that there may be serious deficiencies in the Federal Espionage Statute (18 U.S.C. 792 et seq.). The basic prohibitions of that statute have not been amended since 1917 and do not encompass certain forms of industrial, technological, or economic espionage. The Attorney General in a recent letter to Senator Kennedy (Reprinted on p. S3889 of the Congressional Record of March 23, 1976) describes some of the problem areas of the statute, including industrial espionage (e.g., a spy obtaining information on computer technology for a foreign power). The Committee took no testimony on this subject and, therefore, makes no specific proposal other than that the appropriate committees of the Congress explore the necessity for amendments to the statute.

Recommendation 94.—The appropriate committees of the Congress should review the Espionage Act of 1917 to determine whether it should be amended to cover modern forms of foreign espionage, including industrial, technological or economic espionage.

xi. Broader Access to Intelligence Agency Files Should be Provided to GAO, as an Investigative Arm of the Congress

Recommendation 95.—The appropriate congressional oversight committees of the Congress should, from time to time, request the Comptroller General of the United States to conduct audits and reviews of the intelligence activities of any department or agency of the United States affected by the Domestic Intelligence Recommendations. For such purpose, the Comptroller General, or any of his duly authorized representatives, should have access to, and the right to examine, all necessary materials of any such department or agency.

xii. Congressional Oversight Should Be Intensified

Recommendation 96.—The Committee reendorses the concept of vigorous Senate oversight to review the conduct of domestic security activities through a new permanent intelligence oversight committee.

xiii. Definitions

For the purposes of these recommendations:

A. "Americans" means U.S. citizens, resident aliens and unincorporated associations, composed primarily of U.S. citizens or res-

---

[73] E.g. *Yates* v. *United States*, 354 U.S. 298 (1957) ; *Noto* v. *United States*, 367 U.S. 290 (1961) ; *Brandenburg* v. *Ohio*, 395 U.S. 444 (1969).

ident aliens; and corporations, incorporated or having their principal place of business in the United States or having majority ownership by U.S. citizens, or resident aliens, including foreign subsidiaries of such corporations provided, however, "Americans" does not include corporations directed by foreign governments or organizations.

B. "Collect" means to gather or initiate the acquisition of information, or to request it from another agency.

C. A "covert human source" means undercover agents or informants who are paid or otherwise controlled by an agency.

D. "Covert techniques" means the collection of information, including collection from record sources not readily available to a private person (except state or local law enforcement files), in such a manner as not to be detected by the subject.

E. "Domestic security activities" means governmental activities against Americans or conducted within the United States or its territories, including enforcement of the criminal laws, intended to:

1. protect the United States from hostile foreign intelligence activity including espionage;

2. protect the federal, state, and local governments from domestic violence or rioting; and

3. protect Americans and their government from terrorists.

F. "Foreign communications," refers to a communication between, or among, two or more parties in which at least one party is outside the United States, *or* a communication transmitted between points within the United States if transmitted over a facility which is under the control of, or exclusively used by, a foreign government.

G. "Foreigners" means persons and organizations who are not Americans as defined above.

H. "Hostile foreign intelligence activities" means acts, or conspiracies, by Americans or foreigners, who are officers, employees, or conscious agents of a foreign power, or who, pursuant to the direction of a foreign power, engage in clandestine intelligence activity,[74] or engage in espionage, sabotage or similar conduct in violation of federal criminal statutes.

I. "Name checks" means the retrieval by an agency of information already in the possession of the federal government or in the possession of state or local law enforcement agencies.

J. "Overt investigative techniques" means the collection of information readily available from public sources, or available to a private person, including interviews of the subject or his friends or associates.

K. "Purged" means to destroy or transfer to the National Archieves all personally identifiable information (including references in any general name index).

---

[74] The term "clandestine intelligence activity" is included in this definition at the suggestion of officials of the Department of Justice. Certain activities engaged in by the conscious agents of foreign powers, such as some forms of industrial, technological, or economic espionage, are not now prohibited by federal statutes. It would be preferable to amend the espionage laws to cover such activity and eliminate this term. As a matter of principle, intelligence agencies should not investigate activities of Americans which are not federal criminal statutes. Therefore, the Committee recommends..............................that Congress immediately consider enacting such statutes and then eliminating this term.

L. "Sealed" means to retain personally identifiable information and to retain entries in a general name index but to restrict access to the information and entries to circumstances of "compelling necessity."

M. "Reasonable suspicion" is based upon the Supreme Court's decision in the case of *Terry* v. *Ohio*, 392 U.S. 1 (1968), and means specific and articulable facts which taken together with rational inferences from those facts, give rise to a reasonable suspicion that specified activity has occurred, is occurring, or is about to occur.

N. "Terrorist activities" means acts, or conspiracies, which: (a) are violent or dangerous to human life; and (b) violate federal or state criminal statutes concerning assassination, murder, arson, bombing, hijacking, or kidnapping; and (c) appear intended to, or are likely to have the effect of:

(1) Substantially disrupting federal, state or local government; or

(2) Substantially disrupting interstate or foreign commerce between the United States and another country; or

(3) Directly interfering with the exercise by Americans, of Constitutional rights protected by the Civil Rights Act of 1968, or by foreigners, of their rights under the laws or treaties of the United States.

O. "Unauthorized entry" means entry unauthorized by the target.

NOTES AND REFERENCES

1. Additional findings of the Church Committee regarding the involvement of intelligence agencies in domestic activities appear in [45B] and [84C].

2. The FBI's program, COINTELPRO, directed at American citizens, is further taken up in [44F], [80], and [45B], pp. 10–12, 65–67, 86–94.

3. The U.S. Army's military surveillance of civilians is detailed in [34] and [35].

4. The original intention of "watch list" activity seems to have been to investigate foreign influence on activities of particular significance to U.S. agencies and involving "presidential protection" and U.S. civil disorder. Refer to the testimony of NSA Director Lt. Gen. Lew Allen, Jr. on watch list activity in Chapter 7 and to reprinted correspondence between NSA and other intelligence agencies in [44E], pp. 145 ff.

5. Operation CHAOS, whose purpose was to determine if American political dissidents were receiving foreign support, is considered further in this chapter and in Chapter 5, [25], [45C], pp. 688–721, and [124], pp. 130–150.

6. The subject of drug-testing programs of the intelligence agencies is taken up later in this chapter, as well as in [44A], [45A], pp. 385–422, [89], and [124], pp. 226–229.

7. Data on the intelligence agencies' mail opening projects is found in [44D] and in Chapter 5.

8. President Gerald R. Ford's message on Executive Order 11905 is reprinted in the Appendix.

9. The communications intelligence activities of the NSA are dealt with in Chapter 7 and [44E].

10. The Church Committee investigated the role of the IRS in connection with furnishing its files to intelligence agencies ([44C]).

11. There is a significant body of congressional material concerning wiretapping and electronic surveillance, as well as pertinent court cases. Note [24B], [33], [38], [41], [44F], [81], [82A], and [82B].

Bibliography

CONGRESSIONAL COMMITTEE HEARINGS AND REPORTS REGARDING FOREIGN INTELLIGENCE— ARRANGED BY COMMITTEE (ITEMS 1–85)

Senate

COMMITTEE ON APPROPRIATIONS

1. Department of Defense appropriations for fiscal year 1972. Hearings. Part 1. 1971.
2. Treasury, U.S. Postal Service, and general government appropriations for fiscal year 1973. Hearings. Part 2. 1972.
3. Treasury, Postal Service and general government appropriations for fiscal year 1974. Hearings. Part 2. 1973.
4. Treasury, Postal Service and general government appropriations for fiscal year 1975. Hearings. Part 2. 1974.

COMMITTEE ON ARMED SERVICES

5. Hearing on the nomination of Albert C. Hall to be an Assistant Secretary of Defense (Intelligence). . . . October 28; November 11, 1971.
6. Amending the Central Intelligence Agency Retirement Act; hearing on H.R. 6167 and S. 1494. April 5, 1973.
7. Transmittal of documents from the National Security Council to the Chairman of the Joint Chiefs of Staff. Hearing. Part 1. February 6, 1974.
8. Hearing on the nomination of George Bush to be Director of Central Intelligence. December 15 & 16, 1975.
9. Establish a Senate Select Committee on Intelligence; hearing on S. Res. 400. May 13, 1976.

SUBCOMMITTEE ON MILITARY CONSTRUCTION

10. Military Construction Authorization for fiscal year 1973; joint hearings [with] the Subcommittee on Military Construction of the Committee on Appropriations. 1972.

COMMITTEE ON FOREIGN RELATIONS

11. Public financing of Radio Free Europe and Radio Liberty. Hearing on S. 18 and S. 1936. May 24, 1971.

12. The Senate role in foreign affairs appointments. A study of the provisions of the Constitution and law requiring confirmation of nominations in the foreign relations field. August 1971. (Committee print)
13. Department of State appropriations authorization, fiscal year 1973. Hearings. March 8, 9 & 10, 1972.
14. National Security Act amendment. Hearings on S. 2224 . . . to keep the Congress better informed on matters relating to foreign policy and national security by providing it with intelligence information obtained by the CIA. March 28 & 30; April 24, 1972.
15. Funding of Radio Free Europe and Radio Liberty. Hearings on S. 3645. June 6 & 7, 1972.
16. Nomination of Henry A. Kissinger to be Secretary of State. Hearings. Parts 1 & 2. 1973.
17. Nomination of Richard Helms to be Ambassador to Iran and CIA international and domestic activities. February 5 & 7; May 21, 1973. (February 7 was declassified and published on March 5, 1974.)
18. CIA. Foreign and domestic activities. Hearings. January 22, 1974.
19. Detente. Hearings on United States relations with Communist countries. August 15, 20 & 21; September 10, 12, 18, 19, 24 & 25; October 1 & 8, 1974.

SUBCOMMITEE ON UNITED STATES SECURITY AGREEMENTS AND COMMITMENTS ABROAD

20. United States Security Agreements and Commitments Abroad. Hearings. Vols. 1 & 2. 1971.

SUBCOMMITTEE ON WESTERN HEMISPHERE AFFAIRS

21. U.S. relations with Latin America. Hearings. February 21, 26, 27 & 28, 1975.

COMMITTEE ON GOVERNMENT OPERATIONS

22. Requiring certain officers in the Executive Office of the President be subject to confirmation by the Senate. Report to accompany S. 590. February 26, 1973. (Report 93-47)
23. Assuring information to Congress. Report to accompany S. Con. Res. 30. December 11, 1973. (Report 93-613)
24. Watergate Reorganization and Reform Act of 1975. Hearings on S. 495 and S. 2036. Parts 1 & 2. July 29, 30 & 31; December 3, 4 & 8, 1975; March 11, 1976.
25. Oversight of U.S. Government intelligence functions. Hearings. January & February 1976.
26. Senate Committee on Intelligence Activities. Report to accompany S. Res. 400, resolution to establish a standing committee of the Senate on intelligence activities and for other purposes. March 1, 1976. (Report 94-675)

AD HOC SUBCOMMITTEE ON PRIVACY AND INFORMATION SYSTEMS

27. Privacy: the collection, use and computerization of personal data. Joint hearings [with] the Subcommittee on the Judiciary. Parts 1 & 2. June 18, 19 & 20, 1974.

SUBCOMMITTEE ON INTERGOVERNMENTAL RELATIONS

28. Executive privilege, secrecy in government, freedom of information. Joint hearings [with] the Subcommittees on Separation of Powers, and on Administrative Practice and Procedure of the Committee on the Judiciary. Vols. 1 & 2. April, May & June 1973.
29. Legislation on government secrecy. May 8, 1974. (Committee print)
30. Government secrecy. Hearings. May 22, 23, 29, 30 & 31; June 10, 1974.
31. Legislative proposals to strengthen Congressional oversight of the Nation's intelligence agencies. Hearings. December 9 & 10, 1974.

SUBCOMMITTEE ON NATIONAL SECURITY AND INTERNATIONAL OPERATIONS

32. The National Security Council. Comment by Henry A. Kissinger. March 3, 1970. Submitted persuant to S. Res. 311. (Committee print)

COMMITTEE ON THE JUDICIARY

SUBCOMMITTEES ON ADMINISTRATIVE PRACTICE AND PROCEDURE AND ON CONSTITUTIONAL RIGHTS

33. Warrantless wiretapping and electronic surveillance—1974. Joint hearings [with] the Subcommittee on Surveillance of the Committee on Foreign Relations. April 3 & 8; May 8, 9, 10 & 23, 1974.

SUBCOMMITTEE ON CONSTITUTIONAL RIGHTS

34. Army surveillance of civilians. A documentary analysis. 1972. (Committee print)
35. Military surveillance of civilian politics. A report. 1973. (Committee print)
36. Military surveillance of civilian politics. Additional views of Senators Roman Hruska, Hiram Fong, Hugh Scott, and Strom Thurmond. 1973. (Committee print)
37. Criminal Justice Information and Protection of Privacy Act, 1975. Hearings. July 15 & 16, 1975.
38. Surveillance technology. Joint hearings [with] the Special Subcommittee on Science, Technology, and Commerce of the Committee on Commerce. June 23; September 9 & 10, 1975.
39. Privacy: the Collection, Use, and Computerization of Personal Data. Joint hearings with the Ad Hoc Subcommittee on Privacy and Information Systems of the Committee on Government Operations. S. 3418, S. 3633, S. 3116, S. 2810, S. 2542. June 18, 19 & 20, 1974. Part I.
40. Privacy: the Collection, Use, and Computerization of Personal Data. Joint hearings with the Ad Hoc Subcommittee on Privacy and Information Systems of the Committee on Government Operations. S. 3418, S. 3633, S. 3116, S. 2810, S. 2542. June 18, 19 & 20, 1974. Part II.

SUBCOMMITTEES ON CRIMINAL LAWS AND PROCEDURES, AND ON CONSTITUTIONAL RIGHTS

41. Electronic surveillance for national security purposes. Hearings. October 1, 2 & 3, 1974.

COMMITTEE ON RULES AND ADMINISTRATION

42. Proposed Standing Committee on Intelligence Activities; report of the Committee together with minority views and recommendations of the Committee on the Judiciary to accompany S. Res. 400 to establish a standing Committee of the Senate on Intelligence Activities. April 29, 1976. (Report 94-770)

SELECT COMMITTEE TO STUDY GOVERNMENT OPERATIONS WITH RESPECT TO INTELLIGENCE ACTIVITIES (CHURCH COMMITTEE)

43. Alleged assassination plots involving foreign leaders. An interim report. November 20, 1975. (Report 94-465)
44. Intelligence activities. Hearings. Vols. 1 & 7.
    44A. Vol. 1: Unauthorized storage of toxic agents. September 16, 17 & 18, 1975.
    44B. Vol. 2: Huston Plan. September 23, 24 & 25, 1975.
    44C. Vol. 3: Internal Revenue Service. October 2, 1975.
    44D. Vol. 4: Mail Opening. October 21, 22 & 24, 1975.
    44E. Vol. 5: The National Security Agency and the Fourth Amendment Rights. October 29; November 6, 1975.
    44F. Vol. 6: Federal Bureau of Investigation. November 18 & 19; December 2, 3, 9, 10 & 11, 1975.
    44G. Vol. 7: Covert Action. December 4 & 5, 1975.
45. Final Report. Books I–V. April 26, 1976. (Report 94-755)
    45A. Book I: Foreign and military intelligence.

45B. Book II: Intelligence activities and the rights of Americans.

45C. Book III: Supplementary detailed staff reports on intelligence activities and the rights of Americans.

45D. Book IV: Supplementary detailed staff reports on foreign military intelligence.

45E. Book V: The investigation of the assassination of President John F. Kennedy: Performance of the intelligence agencies.

House of Representatives

COMMITTEE ON APPROPRIATIONS

46. Department of Defense appropriations for 1976. Hearings. February 1975.

47. Department of Defense appropriations for 1977. Hearings. Parts 1–7. 1976.

48. Department of State. Appropriations for 1977. Hearings. Part 5. 1976.

SUBCOMMITTEE ON MILITARY CONSTRUCTION APPROPRIATIONS

49. Military construction appropriations for 1977. Hearings. Parts 1 & 2. 1976.

COMMITTEE ON ARMED SERVICES

50. Hearings on military posture for fiscal year 1973. January, February, March & April 1972. (H.A.S.C. 92-45)

51. Hearings on cost escalation in defense procurement contracts and military posture and H.R. 6722 to authorize appropriations during fiscal year 1974. Part 2. March, April, May & June 1973. (H.A.S.C. 93-9)

52. Hearings on military posture and H.R. 12564, Department of Defense authorization for appropriations for fiscal year 1975. Part 4. March & April 1974. (H.A.S.C. 93-43)

53. Full Committee consideration of H. Res. 72 directing the President to provide the House . . . full and complete information contained in the report of William E. Colby relating to certain activities of the CIA. . . . February 27, 1975. (H.A.S.C. 94-2)

54. Hearings on military posture and H.R. 3689: Department of Defense authorization for appropriations for fiscal year 1976. Parts 2 & 4. 1975. (H.A.S.C. 94-8)

55. Full Committee consideration of the inquiry into matters regarding classified testimony taken on April 22, 1974, concerning the CIA and Chile. Hearings. June 10 & 16, 1975. (H.A.S.C. 94-13)

SPECIAL SUBCOMMITTEE ON INTELLIGENCE

56. Hearings on the proper classification and handling of government information involving national security and H.R. 9853, a related bill. 1972.

57. Hearings on H.R. 6167 and S. 1494 to amend the Central Intelligence Act of 1964. March 30, 1973. (H.A.S.C. 93-7)

58. Inquiry into the alleged involvement of the Central Intelligence Agency in the Watergate and Ellsberg matters. Report. October 23, 1973. (H.A.S.C. 93-25)

59. Inquiry into the alleged involvement of the Central Intelligence Agency in the Watergate and Ellsberg matters. Hearings. May, June & July 1973. February, March, June & July 1974. (H.A.S.C. 94-4)

60. Inquiry into matters regarding classified testimony taken on April 22, 1974, concerning the Central Intelligence Agency and Chile. Hearing. September 25, 1974. (H.A.S.C. 94-12)

SUBCOMMITTEE ON INTER-AMERICAN AFFAIRS

61. United States and Chile during the Allende years, 1970–1973. Hearings. 1971–1974.

SUBCOMMITTEE ON NATIONAL SECURITY POLICY AND SCIENTIFIC DEVELOPMENTS

62. National security policy and the changing world power alignment. Report. October 25, 1972.

SUBCOMMITTEES ON INTERNATIONAL ORGANIZATIONS AND MOVEMENTS, AND ON INTER-AMERICAN AFFAIRS

63. Human rights in Chile. Hearings. Part 2. November 19, 1974.

COMMITTEE ON GOVERNMENT OPERATIONS

64. Executive classification of information; security classification problems involving exemption b. 1 of the Freedom of Information Act. May 22, 1973. (Report 93-221)
65. Amending the Freedom of Information Act to require that information be made available to Congress. Report to the Committee of the Whole House (to accompany H.R. 12462). April 11, 1974. (Report 93-990)
66. Privacy Act of 1974; report to the Committee of the Whole House. October 2, 1974. (Report 93-1416)

SUBCOMMITTEE ON FOREIGN OPERATIONS AND GOVERNMENT INFORMATION

67. U.S. Government information policies and practices. Hearings. Various parts. 1971 & 1972.
68. Availability of information to Congress. Hearings. April 3, 4 & 19, 1973.
69. The use of polygraphs and similar devices by Federal agencies. Hearings. June 4 & 5, 1974.
70. Security classification reform. July 11 & 25; August 1, 1974.

SUBCOMMITTEE ON GOVERNMENT INFORMATION AND INDIVIDUAL RIGHTS

71. [Hearings on the exemption of the CIA from the Privacy Act. Testimony by William Colby.] March & June 1975. [Publication pending, 1977]
72. Implementation of Privacy Act of 1974: Data banks. Hearings. June 3, 1975.
73. National Archives—Security classification problems involving Warren Commission file and other records. Hearings. November 1975.
74. Interception of non-verbal communications by Federal intelligence agencies. October 23, 1975; February & March 1976.
75. Authorization of appropriations for the Privacy Protection Study Commission. Hearing. June 9, 1976.

COMMITTEE ON INTERNATIONAL RELATIONS

76. Congress and foreign policy. Hearings. June 17, 22 & 29; July 1, 20, 22 & 28; August 24; September 16 & 22, 1976.

SUBCOMMITTEE ON INTERNATIONAL ORGANIZATIONS

77. Human rights in Chile. Hearing. December 1975.

COMMITTEE ON THE JUDICIARY

78. Hearings pursuant to H. Res. 803: a resolution authorizing and directing the Committee to investigate whether sufficient grounds exist for the House of Representatives to exercise its constitutional power to impeach Richard M. Nixon, President of the United States. 1974.
79. Nomination of Nelson A. Rockefeller to be Vice President of the United States. Hearings. November & December 1974. (Serial #45)

SUBCOMMITTEE ON CIVIL RIGHTS AND CONSTITUTIONAL RIGHTS

80. FBI counterintelligence programs. Hearings. November 20, 1974. (Serial #55)

SUBCOMMITTEE ON COURTS, CIVIL LIBERTIES, AND THE ADMINISTRATION OF JUSTICE

81. Wiretapping and electronic surveillance. Hearings. April 24, 26 & 29, 1974. (Serial #41)
82. Surveillance. Hearings on the matter of wiretapping, electronic eavesdropping and other surveillance. Parts 1 & 2. February, March, May, June, July & September 1975. (Serial #26)

SELECT COMMITTEE ON INTELLIGENCE (PIKE COMMITTEE)

83. Proceedings against Henry A. Kissinger. Report. December 8, 1975. (Report #94-693)
84. U.S. intelligence agencies and activities. Hearings. Parts 1–6.
   Part 1: Intelligence costs and fiscal procedures. July 31; August 1, 4, 5, 6, 7 & 8, 1975.
   Part 2: The performance of the intelligence community. September 11, 12, 18, 25 & 30; October 7, 30 & 31, 1975.
   Part 3: Domestic intelligence programs. October 9; November 13, 18, and the afternoon session of December 10, 1975.
   Part 4: Committee proceedings. September 10 & 29; October 1; November 4, 6, 13, 14 & 20, 1975.
   Part 5: Risks and control of foreign intelligence. November 4 & 6; December 2, 3, 9, 10, 11, 12 & 17, 1975.
   Part 6: Committee proceedings—II. January 20, 21, 24, 26, 27 & 28; February 3, 4, 5 & 10, 1976.
85. Recommendations of the Final Report of the Committee pursuant to H. Res. 591, establishing a Select Committee on Intelligence to conduct an inquiry into the organization, operations and oversight of the intelligence community. February 11, 1976. (Report 94-833)

U.S. GOVERNMENT PUBLICATIONS—ARRANGED BY ISSUING AGENCY (ITEMS 86–124)

Publications designated with asterisks are reprinted in the Appendix.

86. Central Intelligence Agency. *Memoranda Relating to Drug Experimentation, 1951–1975.* (Declassified July 1976)
87. _____. *New York Mail Intercept Program (HTLINGUAL): Report to the Director of Central Intelligence.* June 1976. 11 pp.
88. _____. *Presidents of the United States on Intelligence.* April 1975. 33 pp.
89. _____. *Statement Covering the Director's Report of December 24, 1974, to the President Covering Alleged CIA Involvement in Massive Illegal Domestic Intelligence Effort.* Washington, D.C., July 8, 1975.
90. *Commission on the Organization of the Government for the Conduct of Foreign Policy.* (Murphy Commission) Report. Washington, D.C.: GPO, 1975, 8 vols.
   Selected contents:
   Barnds, William J. "Intelligence Functions," Appendix U, pp. 7–20;
   _____. "Intelligence and Policymaking in an Institutional Context," Appendix U, pp. 21–40;
   Belcher, Taylor G. "Clandestine Operations," Appendix U, pp. 67–76;
   Blackstock, Paul W. "Intelligence, Covert Operations, and Foreign Policy," Appendix U, pp. 95–102;
   Macy, Robert M. "Issues on Intelligence Resource Management," Appendix U, pp. 52–66;
   McHenry, Donald F., with Fred K. Kirschstein. "Ethical Considerations and Foreign Policy," Appendix W, pp. 300–307;
   Ransom, Harry Howe. "Congress and American Secret Intelligence Agencies," Appendix U, pp. 87–94;
   Smith, Russell Jack. "Intelligence Support for Foreign Policy in the Future," Appendix U, pp. 77–86;
   Winters, Francis S., S.J. "Ethical Considerations and National Security Policy," Appendix W, pp. 293–299;
   Zablocki, Clement J. "Congress and National Security: A Look at Some Issues," Appendix V, pp. 207–209.
91. Department of State. Bureau of Intelligence and Research. *INR: Intelligence and Research in the Department of State.* Washington, D.C., 1973. 19 pp.
92. _____. *Research in Action: The Department of State's Bureau of Intelligence and Research.* Prepared by Allan Evans. Washington, D.C.: GPO, 1965. 21 pp.

93. Department of War. Strategic Services Unit. *War Report: Office of Strategic Services* (OSS). Washington, D.C., 1947. 3 vols.

94. Industrial College of the Armed Forces. *National Intelligence.* Jack Zlotnick. Washington, D.C., 1962. 73 pp.

95. _____. *National Security Management: Management of Defense Intelligence.* Charles Andregg. Washington, D.C., 1968. 52 pp.

96. Library of Congress. Congressional Research Service. *CIA and FBI Domestic Surveillance: Newspaper Reports and Commentary, December 22, 1974–February 13, 1975.* Keith, Robert, and William N. Raiford. 92 pp. (Multilith 75-47F)

97. _____. *Congressional Oversight of the Intelligence Community.* William N. Raiford. April 6, 1976. 20 pp. (Issue brief IB76024)

98. _____. *Intelligence Community: Reform and Reorganization.* Mark M. Lowenthal. May 7, 1976. 13 pp. (Issue brief IB76039)

99. _____. *Intelligence Community Investigation.* Richard F. Grimmett. May 28, 1975. 28 pp. (Issue brief IB75037)

100. _____. *Legislation Introduced Relative to the Activities of the Intelligence Agencies, 1947–1972.* John Cost. Revised and updated by Gary Lee Evans. December 15, 1972. 63 pp. (Multilith 73-22F)

101. _____. *Legislative History of the Central Intelligence Agency as Documented in Published Congressional Sources.* Grover S. Williams. January 8, 1975. 307 pp. (Multilith 75-5A 558/114)

102. _____. *Published Congressional Hearings and Reports concerning the Intelligence Community; Summary of Dates, Witnesses, and Topics, 1970–1975.* Lowenthal, Mark, and William N. Raiford. December 15, 1975. 34 pp. (Multilith 75-255F)

103. _____. *Reported Foreign and Domestic Covert Activities of the United States Central Intelligence Agency, 1950–1974.* Richard F. Grimmett. February 18, 1975. 13 pp. (Multilith 75-50F)

104. _____. *The United States Intelligence Community: A Brief Description of Organization and Functions.* Gary Lee Evans. Revised and updated by William N. Raiford. October 2, 1975. 75 pp. (Multilith 75-149F)

105. National Archives and Records Service. *The Origin of Defense-Information Markings in the Army and Former War Department.* Dallas Irvine. Washington, D.C., 1964. 49 pp.

106. National Security Council. *A Report to the Council by the Executive Secretary on Coordination of Foreign Information Measures.* Washington, D.C., December 9, 1947. 6 pp. (NSC-4) Declassified March 11, 1975.

107. _____. Memorandum to the Executive Secretary. *Interim Report No. 2: Relations between Secret Operations and Secret Intelligence.* May 13, 1948. 5 pp. (Dulles/Jackson/Correa Committee). Declassified July 1976.

108. _____. *A Report to the Council by the Executive Secretary on Office of Special Projects.* June 18, 1948. Washington, D.C. 3 pp.

109. _____. *The Central Intelligence Agency and National Organization for Intelligence: A Report to the National Security Council.* Allen W. Dulles, William H. Jackson, Matthias F. Correa. January 1, 1949. 193 pp. Declassified June 1976.

110. National Security Council. *A Report to the Council by the Executive Secretary on United States Objectives and Programs for National Security.* Washington, D.C., April 14, 1950. 66 pp. (NSC-68). Declassified February 27, 1975.

111. _____. *Intelligence Directives.*
No. 1: Duties and Responsibilities.
No. 2: Coordination of Collection Activities.
No. 3: Coordination of Intelligence Production.
No. 4: National Intelligence Objectives.
No. 5: Espionage and Counterespionage Operations.
No. 6: Foreign Wireless and Radio Monitoring (Declassified in part).
No. 7: Domestic Exploitation.
No. 8: Photographic Interpretation/Biographic Data on Foreign Scientific and Technological Personalities (Declassified in part).

No. 9: Communications Intelligence (Declassified in part).

No. 10: Collection of Foreign Scientific and Technological Data.

No. 11: Security Information on Intelligence Sources and Methods.

No. 12: Avoidance of Publicity concerning the Intelligence Agencies of the United States Government.

No. 15: Coordination and Production of Foreign Economic Intelligence.

No. 16: Foreign Language Publications.

No. 17: Electronic Intelligence (ELINT) (Declassified in part).

112. Office of Management and Budget. *The Budget of the United States Government, Fiscal Year 1977.* Washington, D.C.: GPO, 1976. 385 pp.

113. Office of the President. 1945–1952 (Truman). **[Presidential Letter Creating the Central Intelligence Group] to the Secretary of State, the Secretary of War, the Secretary of the Navy.* January 22, 1946.

114. _____. *Executive Order 10290, Prescribing Regulations Establishing Minimum Standards for the Classification, Transmission, and Handling by Departments and Agencies of the Executive Branch of Official Information Which Requires Safeguarding in the Interest of the Security of the United States.* September 24, 1951.

115. 1953–1960 (Eisenhower). *Executive Order 10501, Safeguarding Official Information in the Interests of the Defense of the United States.* November 5, 1953.

116. 1961–1963 (Kennedy). *Executive Order 10964, Amendment of Executive Order 10501.* September 20, 1961.

117. 1969–1974 (Nixon). **Executive Order 11652, Classification and Declassification of National Security Information and Material.* March 8, 1972.

118. _____. **Executive Order 11714, Amending Executive Order 11652 on Classification and Declassification of National Security Information and Material.* April 24, 1973.

119. _____. National Security Decision Memorandum 40. Washington, D.C., February 17, 1970. 2 pp. (To the Secretary of State, the Secretary of Defense, and the Director of Central Intelligence, Regarding the Responsibility for the Conduct, Supervision and Coordination of Covert Action Operations).

120. _____. *U.S. Foreign Policy for the 70's. A Report to the Congress.* Washington, D.C., February 18, 1970.

121. 1974–1976 (Ford) **The President's Message in Executive Order 11905,* United States Foreign Intelligence Activities. February 18, 1976.

122. _____. *The President's Message to the Congress Proposing Legislative Reforms.* February 18, 1976.

123. _____. Office of the White House Press Secretary. *The White House Fact Sheet: The President's Actions concerning the Foreign Intelligence Community.* February 18, 1976. 8 pp.

124. _____. President's Commission on CIA Activities within the United States. *Report of the Commission, June 1975.* Washington, D.C.: GPO, 299 pp. (Rockefeller Commission Report)

BIBLIOGRAPHIES AND ABSTRACTS (ITEMS 125–127)

Publications designated with asterisks are reprinted in the Appendix.

125. **Project on National Security and Civil Liberties. *Abstracts of Documents Released under the Freedom of Information Act Relating to Foreign Policy and National Defense.* Washington, D.C., September 1976. 18 pp.

126. United States. Congress. Senate. Committee on Government Operations. Subcommittee on National Policy Machinery. *Organizing for National Security: A Bibliography.* Washington, D.C.: GPO, 1959. 77 pp.

127. United States. Department of Defense. Defense Intelligence School. *Bibliography of Intelligence Literature: A Critical and Annotated Bibliography of Open-Source Intelligence Literature.* 4th edition. Washington, D.C., January 1976. 48 pp.

NONGOVERNMENT PUBLICATIONS RELATING TO THE INTELLIGENCE COMMUNITY (ITEMS 128–185)

128. Agee, Philip. *Inside the Company: CIA Diary*. New York: Bantam, 1975. 660 pp.
129. Alsop, Stewart. *Sub Rosa: The OSS and American Espionage*. New York: Harcourt, 1964. 264 pp.
130. Baker, Carol M., and Matthew H. Fox. *Classified Files: The Yellowing Pages*. New York: Twentieth Century, 1972. 115 pp.
131. Barnds, William J. "Intelligence and Foreign Policy: Dilemmas of a Democracy." *Foreign Affairs* 47 (January 1969), 281–295.
132. Blackstock, Paul W. *The Strategy of Subversion: Manipulating the Politics of Other Nations*. Chicago: Quadrangle, 1964. 351 pp.
133. Blum, Richard H., ed. *Surveillance and Espionage in a Free Society*. New York: Praeger, 1972. 319 pp.
134. Center for National Security Studies. *The Abuses of the Intelligence Agencies*. Washington, D.C.: The Center, 1975. Edited by Jerry J. Bermen and Morton H. Halperin.
135. Clark, Keith, and Lawrence J. Legere, eds. *The President and the Management of National Security*. New York: Praeger, 1968.
136. Cooper, Chester L. "The CIA and Decision-Making." *Foreign Affairs* 50 (January, 1972), 223–236.
137. Cutler, Robert. "The Development of the National Security Council." *Foreign Affairs* 34 (April 1956), 441–458.
138. Dulles, Allen W. *The Craft of Intelligence*. New York: Harper & Row, 1963. 277 pp.
139. Franck, Thomas, and Edward Weisband. *Secrecy and Foreign Policy*. New York: Oxford University Press, 1974.
140. Goulden, Joseph C. *Truth Is the First Casualty*. Chicago: Rand McNally, 1969.
141. Graham, Daniel O. "The Intelligence Mythology of Washington" *Strategic Review*, summer 1976, 59–66.
142. Green, James R. *The First Sixty Years of the Office of Naval Intelligence*. Washington, D.C.: American University, 1963.
143. Halperin, Morton. "Implications of Decision-Making for Covert Operations." Unpublished manuscript distributed at the Conference on the CIA and Covert Action. Washington, D.C., September 13, 1974.
144. Hilsman, Roger. *Strategic Intelligence and National Decisions*. Glencoe, Ill.: Free Press, 1956. 187 pp.
145. _____. *To Move a Nation*. Garden City, N.Y.: Doubleday, 1967.
146. Jackson, Henry M., ed. *The National Security Council*. New York: Praeger, 1965.
147. Jeffers, H. Paul. *The CIA: A Close Look at the CIA*. New York: Lion Press, 1970. 159 pp.
148. Kahn, David. *The Codebreakers: The Story of Secret Writing*. New York: Macmillan, 1967. 1164 pp.
149. Katzenbach, Nicholas deB. "Foreign Policy, Public Opinion and Secrecy." *Foreign Affairs* 52 (October 1973), 1–19.
150. Kennedy, Robert F. *Thirteen Days: A Memoir of the Cuban Missile Crisis*. Edited by Richard Neustadt and Graham Allison. New York: Norton, 1971.
151. Kent, Sherman. *Strategic Intelligence for American World Policy*. Princeton, N.J.: Princeton University Press, 1949. 226 pp.
152. Kim, Young Hum, *The Central Intelligence Agency: Problems of Secrecy in a Democracy*. Edited with an introduction by Young Hum Kim. Lexington, Mass.: Heath, 1968. 113 pp.
153. Kirkpatrick, Lyman B., Jr. *The Real CIA*. New York: Macmillan, 1968. 312 pp.
154. _____. *The U.S. Intelligence Community: Foreign Policy and Domestic Activities*. New York: Hill & Wang, 1973. 212 pp.
155. Leacacos, John P. *Fire in the In-Basket: The ABC's of the State Department*. New York: World, 1968.
156. MacCloskey, Monro. *The American Intelligence Community*. New York: Rosen, 1967. 190 pp.
157. McGarvey, Patrick J. *CIA: The Myth and the Madness*. New York: Saturday Review Press, 1972. 240 pp.

158. Marchetti, Victor, and John D. Marks. *The CIA and the Cult of Intelligence*. Introduction by Melvin L. Wulf. New York: Dell, 1974. 397 pp.
159. Morris, Roger. "Following the Scenario: Reflections on Five Case Histories in the Mode and Aftermath of CIA Intervention." Unpublished manuscript circulated at the Conference on CIA and Covert Action, Washington, D.C., September 1974.
160. Overstreet, Henry, and Bonaro Overstreet. *The FBI in Our Open Society*. New York: Norton, 1969.
161. Pacem in Terris, IV. *Proceedings*. Washington, D.C., December 1975. Santa Barbara, Calif.: Center for the Study of Democratic Institutions. 3 vols. (Publication pending, 1976) [Vol. 3: "Foreign Policy and American Democracy" contains papers presented by Senator Frank Church, William Colby, Morton Halperin, and others.]
162. Pettee, George S. *The Future of American Secret Intelligence*. Washington, D.C.: Infantry Journal Press, 1946.
163. Platt, Washington. *National Character in Action*. New Brunswick, N.J.: Rutgers University Press, 1961.
164. _____. *Strategic Intelligence Production: Basic Principles*. New York: Praeger, 1957. 302 pp.
165. Prouty, L. Fletcher. *The Secret Team: The CIA and Its Allies in Control of the United States and the World*. Englewood Cliffs, N.J.: Prentice-Hall, 1973. 496 pp.
166. Ransom, Harry Howe. *Central Intelligence and National Security*. Cambridge, Mass.: Harvard University Press, 1970. 309 pp.
167. Rowan, Richard W., with Robert G. Deindorfer. *33 Centuries of Espionage*. New York: Hawthorn, 1967.
168. Schlesinger, Arthur, Jr. "The Secrecy Dilemma." *New York Times Magazine*, February 6, 1972.
169. Schultz, Donald O., and Loran A. Norton. *Police Operational Intelligence*. Chicago: Charles C. Thomas, 1968. 204 pp.
170. Seth, Ronald. *Anatomy of Spying*. New York: Dutton, 1963.
171. Smith, R. Harris. *OSS: The Secret History of America's First Central Intelligence Agency*. Berkeley, Calif.: University of California Press, 1972. 458 pp.
172. Taylor, Maxwell D. *"The Legitimate Claims of National* Security." *Foreign Affairs* 52 (April 1974), 577–594.
173. Tully, Andrew. *CIA: The Inside Story*. New York: Morrow, 1962. 276 pp.
174. _____. *The Super Spies: More Secret, More Powerful than the CIA*. New York: Morrow, 1969. 256 pp.
175. *Village Voice*. "The CIA Report the President Doesn't Want You to Read: The Pike Papers." Introduction by Aaron Latham. February 16, 1976, pp. 69–92.
176. _____. "The Select Committee's Oversight Experience." February 23, 1976, pp. 59–69.
177. Watson, Douglas. "NSA: America's Vacuum Cleaner of Intelligence." *Washington Post*, March 2, 1975.
178. Whitehead, Don. *The FBI Story*. New York: Random House, 1956.
179. Whitehouse, Arch. *Espionage and Counterespionage: Adventure in Military Intelligence*. Garden City, N.Y.: Doubleday, 1964.
180. Wilensky, Harold L. *Organizational Intelligence*. New York: Basic Books, 1967. 226 pp.
181. Winterbotham, F. W. *The Ultra Secret*. New York: Harper & Row, 1974. 191 pp.
182. Wise, David. *The Politics of Lying: Government Deception, Secrecy and Power*. New York: Random House, 1973. 415 pp.
183. Wise, David, and Thomas B. Ross. *The Espionage Establishment*. New York: Random House, 1967. 308 pp.
184. _____. *The Invisible Government*. New York: Random House, 1964. 375 pp.
185. Wriston, Henry Merritt. *Executive Agents in American Foreign Relations*. Baltimore: Johns Hopkins Press, 1929. 872 pp. [Reprinted: Glouster, Mass: Peter Smith, 1967.]

Appendix 1
List of Acronyms

ACDA: Arms Control and Disarmament Agency.

ACS (I): Army Chief of Staff for Intelligence.

ACLU: American Civil Liberties Union.

ADDP: Assistant Deputy Director for Plans, second person in line of command of the DDP.

ADPC: Assistant Director for Policy Coordination, the senior administrative officer in the Office of Policy Coordination.

ADSO: Assistant Director for Special Operations, the senior administrative officer in the Office of Special Operations.

AFOSI: Air Force Office of Special Investigations.

AFSA: Armed Forces Security Agency.

ARC: Ad Hoc Requirements Committee, and interdepartmental group established in 1955 to coordinate intelligence collection requirements among the Departments for the U-2 program. Succeeded by COMOR in 1960.

ASA: Army Security Agency.

ADF/I: Assistant Secretary of Defense for Intelligence.

ASD/PA&E: Assistant Secretary of Defense for Program Analysis and Evaluation.

ASW: Antisubmarine Investigation.

BI: Background Investigation.

BID: Basic Intelligence Division, a component of ORR, responsible for production of National Intelligence Surveys. Became Office of Basic Intelligence in 1955.

BNDD: Bureau of Narcotics and Dangerous Drugs.

BNE: Board of National Estimates.

CA Staff: Covert Action Staff, a component of the DDP, responsible for review of covert action projects for the Directorate as well as management and control of some field operations.

CDIB: Consolidated Defense Intelligence Budget.

CDIP: Consolidated Defense Intelligence Program.

CFI: Committee on Foreign Intelligence.

CHAOS: Covert CIA operation directed at U.S. citizens and domestic activities.

CIA: Central Intelligence Agency.

CI&IA: Counterintelligence and Investigative Activity.

CIG: Central Intelligence Group, 1946-1947, predecessor of the CIA.

CIRL: Current Intelligence Reporting List.

CI Staff: Counterintelligence Staff, a component of the DDP, which until recently maintained virtual control over counterintelligence operations.

CJCS: Chairman, Joint Chiefs of Staff.

COINTELPRO: Covert FBI counterintelligence program directed at U.S. citizens and domestic activities.

COMINT: Communications Intelligence, technical and intelligence information derived from foreign communications, not including foreign press, propaganda, or public broadcasts.

COMIREX: Committee on Imagery Requirements and Exploitation, established in 1967 to succeed COMOR as the USIB subcommittee responsible for the management of collection planning.

COMOR: Committee on Overhead Reconnaissance, a USIB subcommittee established in 1960 to coordinate intelligence collection requirements among the Departments for the development and operation of all overhead reconnaissance systems.

COMSEC: Communications Security.

CONUS: Continental United States.

CRS: Central Reports Staff, a component of the CIG, responsible for correlation and evaluation of information drawn from other Departments.

CSS: Central Security Service.

DAS: Defense Attache System.

DCI: Director of Central Intelligence, chief officer of the CIG and the CIA.

DCID: Director of Central Intelligence Directive, a directive issued by the DCI which outlines general policies and procedures to be followed by the intelligence community. It is generally more specific than an NSCID.

DCII: Defense Central Index of Investigations.

DCS: Domestic Contact Service, a component of CIG, responsible for soliciting domestic sources for foreign intelligence information. Renamed the Domestic Contact Division in 1951; became a component of the DDI in 1952; renamed the Domestic Contact Service in 1965; transferred to DDO in 1973 and renamed the Domestic Collection Division.

DDA: Directorate for Administration, established in 1950, responsible for personnel, budget, security, medical services and logistical support for overseas operations.

DDCI: Deputy Director of Central Intelligence, second person in line of command of CIA.

DDI: Directorate for Intelligence, created in 1952, responsible for production of finished intelligence (excluding scientific and technical intelligence since 1963) and for collection of overt information.

DDO: Deputy Director for Operations, CIA, or Directorate for Operations.

DDP: Directorate for Plans, created in 1952 from the inte-
    gration of OSO and OPC, also known as the "Clandestine
    Service." Responsible for clandestine collection,
    counterintelligence, and covert operations. Renamed
    the Directorate for Operations in 1973.

DDR: Directorate for Research, created in 1962, immediate
    predecessor to the Directorate for Science and Tech-
    nology.

DDS: Deputy Director for Support, CIA.

DDS&T: Directorate for Science and Technology, organized in
    1963, combining OSI, the Data Processing Staff, the
    Office of ELINT, the DPD, and a newly created Office of
    Research and Development. Responsible for research
    development and operation of technical collection
    systems and for production of finished scientific and
    technical intelligence.

DIA: Defense Intelligence Agency, created by Secretary
    of Defense Robert McNamara in 1961, responsible for
    production of military intelligence.

DIOP: Defense Intelligence Objectives and Priorities.

DIPO: Defense Investigative Program Office.

DIRC: Defense Investigative Review Council.

DIRDIA: Director of the Defense Intelligence Agency.

DIRNSA: Director of the National Security Agency.

DIS: Defense Investigative Service.

DKIQs: Defense Key Intelligence Questions.

DMA: Defense Mapping Agency.

DOD: Department of Defense.

DOJ: Department of Justice.

DPD: Development Projects Division, a component of the
    DDP, responsible for overhead reconnaissance. Trans-
    ferred to DDS&T in 1963.

EIC: Economic Intelligence Committee, a subcommitte of
    the IAC created in 1951, charged with interdepart-
    mental coordination of economic intelligence activities
    and the production of publications. Continued under
    USIB.

ELINT: Electronic Intelligence, technical and intelligence
    information derived from the collection (or inter-
    ception) and processing of foreign electromagnetic
    radiations such as radar.

ERA: Economic Research Area, established in 1950 as a
    component of ORR, responsible for production of
    economic intelligence. Eventually developed into OER.

ERDA: Energy Research and Development Administration.

EXCOM: Executive Committee, established in 1965 for the
    management of overhead reconnaissance, giving the CIA
    and the Department of Defense decisionmaking authority
    over the national reconnaissance program.

FBI: Federal Bureau of Investigation.

FBID: Foreign Broadcast Information Division, an element
    of CIG which monitored overseas broadcasts. Became
    a component of the DDI in 1952; renamed the Foreign
    Broadcast Information Service in 1965.

FBIS: Foreign Broadcast Information Service.

FOIA: Freedom of Information Act.

FSO: Foreign Service Officer.

FYDP: Fiscal Year Defense Plan.

GAO: General Accounting Office

GDIP: General Defense Intelligence Program.

GMAIC: Guided Missiles and Astronautics Intelligence
  Committee, a USIB subcommittee established in 1958,
  responsible for interdepartmental coordination of
  intelligence related to guided missiles.

GMIC: Guided missiles Intelligence Committee, an IAC
  subcomittee created in 1956, responsible for inter-
  departmental coordination of intelligence related
  to guided missiles. Succeeded by GMAIC in 1958.

GRA: Geographic Research Area, created in 1950 as a
  component of ORR; in 1965 transferred to OBI, which
  was renamed Office of Basic and Geographic Intelligence;
  IBGI became the Office of Geographic and Cartographic
  Research in 1974.

GRU: Soviet Military Intelligence Service.

GSA: General Services Administration.

HUMINT: Human Intelligence.

IAB: Intelligence Advisory Board, an advisory group to the
  DCI, composed of the heads of the military and civilian
  intelligence agencies. Existed for the life of CIG.

IAC: Intelligence Advisory Committee, created in 1947 to
  serve as a coordinating body in establishing intel-
  ligence requirements among the Departments. Merged
  with USCIB in 1958 to form USIB.

IC Staff: Intelligence Community staff, established in 1972
  as a replacement for the NIPE staff. Responsible for
  assisting the DCI in the management of intelligence
  community activities.

ICAPS: Interdepartmental Coordinating and Planning Staff,
  a component of the CIG, which handled the administrative
  aspects of CIG's contacts with the Departments.

INR: Bureau of Intelligence and Research, the State Depart-
  ment's intelligence analysis component.

IRAC: Intelligence Resources Advisory Committee, an inter-
  departmental group established in 1971 to advise the
  DCI in preparing a consolidated intelligence program
  budget for the President. Members included representa-
  tives from the Departments of State, Defense, OMB, and
  CIA.

IR&DC: Intelligence Research and Development Council.

IRS: Internal Revenue Service.

ISA: International Security Affairs, DOD.

J-2: Joint Staff Director for Intelligence, DOD.

JAEIC: Joint Atomic Energy Intelligence Committee, a sub-
  committee of USIB, responsible for interdepartmental
  coordination of intelligence relating to atomic energy.

JAG: Joint Analysis Group, an interdepartmental body
  established in 1962, to provide regular assessments
  on Soviet and Chinese future military strengths.

JCS: Joint Chiefs of Staff.

JRC: Joint Reconnaissance Center.

JSOP: Joint Strategic Objectives Plan.

KGB: Soviet National Intelligence Organization.

KIQs: Key Intelligence Questions, initiated in 1974 and
     designed to produce intelligence on topics of par-
     ticular importance to national policymakers, as defined
     by the DCI.
MBFR: Mutual and Balanced Force Reduction.
MBO: Management by Objectives, a system established in
     1974 to measure performance against explicitly stated
     goals.
MKNAOMI: The first CIA operation associated with the use of
     biological weapons.
MONGOOSE: Operation MONGOOSE, a program conducted between
     1961 and 1962, aimed at discrediting and ultimately
     toppling the Castro government.
NFIP: National Foreign Intelligence Program.
NIA: National Intelligence Authority, supervisory body of
     the Central Intelligence Group (CIG), comprised of the
     Secretaries of State, War, and Navy, and the personal
     representative of the President.
NIB: National Intelligence Bulletin.
NID: National Intelligence Daily.
NIE: National Intelligence Estimate, a predictive judgment
     on the capabilities, vulnerabilities, and courses of
     action of foreign nations. It represents the composite
     view of the intelligence community.
NIOs: National Intelligence Officers, a senior group of
     analysts, organized in 1973 to replace ONE. Responsible
     for the management of intelligence collection and pro-
     duction.
NIPE Staff: National Intelligence Programs Evaluation Staff,
     established in 1963 under the DCI to serve as a coordi-
     nating body in the management of interdepartmental
     intelligence activities. Replaced by IC Staff in 1971.
NIPP: National Intelligence Projections for Planning, inter-
     agency assessments on Soviet and Chinese future mili-
     tary strengths, produced by the JAG.
NIRB: National Intelligence Review Board, established in
     1968, to advise the DCI in making judgments on foreign
     intelligence resource needs. Replaced in 1971 by IRAC.
NIS: National Intelligence Survey, a compendium of factual
     information on foreign countries drawn from throughout
     the intelligence community. The program was terminated
     in 1974.
NKVD: Predecessor to the KGB.
NPIC: National Photographic Interpretation Center, estab-
     lished in 1961 under the direction of the DCI to
     analyze photography derived from overhead reconnaissance.
NSA: National Security Agency.
NSA/CSS: National Security Agency/Central Security Service.
NSAM: National Security Action Memorandum.
NSC: National Security Council, the senior decisionmaking
     body in the Executive branch. Established in 1947,
     comprised of the President, the Vice President, the
     Secretaries of State and Defense with representatives
     of the JCS, Special Assistant to the President and
     other officials attending as required.
NSCIC: National Security Council Intelligence Committee.

NSCID: National Security Council Intelligence Directive, a directive issued by the NSC to the intelligence agencies. NSCIDs are often augmented by more specific DCIDs and by internal departmental or agency regulations.

NSDM: National Security Decision Memorandum.

NSSM: National Security Study Memorandum.

OAG: Operations Advisory Group.

OCB: Operations Coordinating Board, established in 1953 to replace the PSB as a senior review body for covert operations. Its members included deputy-level officials from the Departments of State, Defense, the office of the President, and from the foreign aid program.

OCD: Office of Collection and Dissemination, a component of the DDI charged with the dissemination of intelligence and the storage and retrieval of unevaluated intelligence. Renamed the Office of Central Reference in 1955; renamed the Central Reference Service in 1967.

OCI: Office of Current Intelligence, a component of the DDI, established in 1951. Responsible for the production of current intelligence in numerous areas.

OER: Office of Economic Research, a component of the DDI, established in 1967. Responsible for production of economic intelligence.

OMB: Office of Management and Budget.

ONE: Office of National Estimates, organized in 1950, to produce National Intelligence Estimates. Dissolved in 1973.

ONI: Office of Naval Intelligence.

OO: Office of Operations, a component of the DDI, charged with the collection of overt information. Dissolved in 1965.

OPC: Office of Policy Coordination, a component attached to the CIA but reporting to the Departments of State and Defense. Established in 1948 with responsibility for the conduct of covert operations. Merged with OSO in 1952 to form the DDP.

OPEC: Organization of Petroleum Exporting Countries.

OPR: Office of Political Research, established in 1974 as a component of the DDI. Responsible for long-term political research.

ORE: Office of Research and Evaluation, a component of CIG and CIA, established in 1946. Responsible for intelligence production and interagency coordination. Dissolved in 1951.

ORR: Office of Research and Reports, established in 1950, became a component of DDI in 1952. Responsible primarily for economic and strategic research. Dissolved in 1967.

OSD: Office of the Secretary of Defense.

OSI: Office of Scientific Intelligence, created in 1949. Responsible for basic science and technical research. Became a component of the DDI in 1952. Transferred to the DDS&T in 1963.

OSO: Office of Special Operations, a component of CIG
  and CIA, established in 1946, responsible for espionage
  and counter-espionage. Merged with OPC in 1952 to
  form the Directorate for Plans.
OSO: Office of Special Operations, DOD.
OSR: Office of Strategic Research, established in 1967 as
  a component of the DDI, combining military intelli-
  gence units in OCI and ORR.
OSS: Office of Strategic Services, U.S. intelligence
  agency from 1942-1945. Responsibilities included
  research, analysis, espionage and overseas operations.
PBCFIA: President's Board of Consultants on Foreign Intel-
  ligence Activities, an advisory body created in 1956 by
  President Eisenhower. Renamed President's Foreign
  Intelligence Advisory Board (PFIAB) in 1961
PCG: Planning and Coordination Group, NSC.
PFIAB: President's Foreign Intelligence Advisory Board.
PNIOs: Priority National Intelligence Objectives.
PSB: Psychological Strategy Board, a subcommittee of NSC
  established in 1951, charged with directing psycho-
  logical warfare programs. Its members included
  departmental representatives and Board staff members.
  Replaced by OCB in 1953.
R&D: Research and Development.
R.D.T.&E.: Research, Development, Test & Evaluation.
SALT: Strategic Arms Limitation Talks.
SCAs: Service Cryptologic Agencies.
SEC: Scientific Estimates Committee, a subcommittee of the
  IAC, established in 1952, charged with interagency
  coordination of scientific intelligence and the
  production of publications. Renamed the Scientific
  Intelligence Committee in 1959.
SIGINT: Signals Intelligence, which involves the inter-
  ception, processing, analysis and dissemination of
  information derived from foreign electrical communi-
  cations and other signals.
SNIE: Special National Intelligence Estimate, request by
  policymakers for a judgment on a particular question.
SOD: Special Operations Division, Fort Detrick, Maryland.
SPG: Special Procedures Group, a component of SOS,
  established in 1947. Responsible for the conduct
  of covert psychological operations.
SSU: Strategic Services Unit, a component of the War
  Department charged with clandestine collection and
  counterespionage. Transferred to CIG in 1946.
SWNCC: State, War, Navy Coordinating Committee, established
  in 1944, the predecessor body to the NSC.
TELINT: Telemetry Intelligence.
TOA: Technical Services Division, CIA.
TSD: Technical Services Division, a component of the DDP,
  engaged in research and development to provide opera-
  tional support for clandestine activities. Transferred
  to DDS&T in 1973.
USAINA: United States Army Intelligence Agency.

USCIB: United States Communications Intelligence Board,
    established in 1946 to advise and make recommendations
    on communications intelligence to the Secretary of
    Defense.

USIB: United States Intelligence Board, an interdepart-
    mental body established in 1958, through the merger of
    the IAC and the USCIB. Responsible for coordinating
    intelligence activities among the Departments.

WSAG: Washington Special Action Group.

Appendix 2
Glossary

Ad Hoc Requirements Committee: An interagency group established in 1955 by the Special Assistant to the DCI to coordinate collection requirements for the U-2 reconnaissance program.

Agent: An individual who acts under the direction of an intelligence agency or security service to obtain, or assist in obtaining, information for intelligence or counterintelligence purposes.

Agent of Influence: An individual who can be used to influence covertly foreign officials, opinion molders, organizations, or pressure groups in a way which will generally advance United States Government objectives, or to undertake specific action in support of United States Government objectives.

Analysis: A stage in the intelligence processing cycle whereby collected information is reviewed to identify significant facts; the information is compared with and collated with other data, and conclusions, which also incorporate the memory and judgment of the intelligence analyst, are derived from it.

Armed Forces Security Agency (AFSA): The predecessor to NSA; it was created in 1949 to consolidate the crytologic effort.

Army Security Agency (ASA): One of the Service Cryptologic Agencies; its collection activities are under the authority of the Director of NSA (DIRNSA) in his dual role as Chief of the Central Security Service (CSS).

Asset: Any resource—a person, group, relationship, instrument, installation, or supply—at the disposition of an intelligence agency for use in an operational or support role. The term is normally applied to a person who is contributing to a CIA clandestine mission, but is not a fully controlled agent of CIA.

Assessment: Part of the intelligence process whereby an analyst determines the reliability or validity of a piece of information. An assessment could also be a statement resulting from this process.

Backstopping: A CIA term for providing appropriate verification and support of cover arrangements for an agent or asset in anticipation of inquiries or other actions which might test the credibility of his or its cover.

Basic Intelligence: Factual, fundamental, and generally permanent information about all aspects of a nation—physical, social, economic, political, biographical, and cultural—which is used as a base for intelligence products in support of planning, policymaking, and military operations.

Note: This Glossary is reprinted from [45A], pp. 617–629.

Bigot Lists: Using the term bigot in the sense of "narrow," this is a restrictive list of persons who have access to a particular, and highly sensitive class of information.

Biological Agent: A micro-organism which causes disease in humans, plants, or animals, or causes a deterioration of materiel.

Biological Operations: Employment of biological agents to produce casualties in humans or animals, and damage to plants or material; or a defense against such an attack.

Biological Warfare: Use of living organisms, toxic biological products, or plant growth regulators to cause death or injury to humans, animals, or plants; or a defense against such action.

Biological Weapon: A weapon which projects, disperses, or disseminates a biologial agent.

Black: A term used to indicate reliance on illegal concealment of an activity rather than on cover.

Black Bag Job: Warrantless surreptitious entry, especially an entry conducted for purposes other than microphone installation, such as physical search and seizure or photographing of documents.

Black List: An official counterintelligence listing of actual or potential hostile collaborators, sympathizers, intelligence suspects, or other persons viewed as threatening to the security of friendly military forces.

Black Propaganda: Propaganda which purports to emanate from a source other than the true one.

Blow: To expose—often unintentionally—personnel, installations, or other elements of a clandestine activity or organization.

Board of National Estimates (BNE): Established in 1950 by DCI Walter Bedell Smith. The Board was composed of individuals who had responsibility for receiving National Intelligence Estimates for the Director of Central Intelligence. The Board was dissolved in 1973.

Bug: A concealed listening device or microphone, or other audiosurveillance device; also, to install the means for audiosurveillance of a subject or target.

Bugged: A room or object which contains a concealed listening device.

Case: An intelligence operation in its entirety; the term also refers to a record of the development of an intelligence operation, how it will operate, and the objectives of the operation.

Case Officer: A staff employee of the CIA who is responsible for handling agents.

Central Intelligence Group (CIG): The direct predecessor to CIA; President Truman established it by executive order on January 22, 1946. It operated under the National Intelligence Authority (NIA), which was created at the same time.

Chemical Agent: A chemical compound which, when disseminated, causes incapacitating, lethal, or damaging effects on humans, animals, plants, or materials.

Chemical Operations: Using chemical agents—excluding riot control agents—to kill, or incapacitate for a significant period, humans or animals, or to deny the use of facilities, materials, or areas.

Cipher: Any cryptographic system in which arbitrary symbols or groups of symbols represent units of plain text.

Clandestine Intelligence: Intelligence information collected by clandestine sources.

Clandestine Operations: Intelligence, counterintelligence, or other information collection activities and covert political, economic, propaganda and paramilitary activities, conducted so as to assure the secrecy of the operation.

Code: A system of communication in which arbitrary groups of symbols represent units of plain text. Codes may be used for brevity or for security.

Code word: A word which has been assigned a classification and a classified meaning to safeguard intentions and information regarding a planned operation.

Collation: The assembly of facts to determine the relationships among them in order to derive intelligence and facilitate further processing of intelligence information.

Collection: The acquisition of information by any means and its delivery to the proper intelligence processing unit for use in the production of intelligence.

Committee on Imagery Requirements and Exploitation (COMI-REX): One of three intelligence collection committees formerly under the United States Intelligence Board (USIB), dealing with photographic intelligence.

Communications: A method or means of conveying information from one person or place to another; this term does not include direct, unassisted conversion or correspondence through nonmilitary postal agencies.

Communications Center: A facility responsible for receiving transmitting and delivering messages; it normally contains a message center section, a cryptographic section, and a sending and receiving section, using electronic communications devices.

Communications Intelligence (COMINT): Technical and intelligence information derived from foreign communications by someone other than the intended recipient. It does not include foreign press, propaganda, or public broadcasts. The term is sometimes used interchangeably with SIGINT.

Communications Security (COMSEC): The protection of United States telecommunications and other communications from exploitation by foreign intelligence services and from unauthorized disclosure. COMSEC is one of the mission responsibilities of NSA. It includes cryptosecurity, transmission security, emission security, and physical security of classified equipment, material, and documents.

Compartmentation: The practice of establishing specials channels for handling sensitive intelligence information. The channels are limited to individuals with a specific need for such information and who are therefore given special security clearances in order to have access to it.

Compromise: A known or suspected exposure of clandestine personnel, installations, or other assets, or of classified information or material, to an unauthorized person.

Concealment: The provision of protection from observation only.

Confusion Agent: An individual dispatched by his sponsor to confound the intelligence or counterintelligence apparatus of another country rather than to collect and transmit information.

Consumer: A person or agency that uses information or intelligence produced by either its own staff or other agencies.

Continental United States (CONUS): A military term which refers to United States territory, including adjacent territorial waters, located within the North American continent between Canada and Mexico.

Control: Physical or psychological pressure exerted on an agent or group to ensure that the agent or group responds to the direction from an intelligence agency or service.

Counterespionage: Those aspects of counterintelligence concerned with aggresesive operations against another intelligence service to reduce its effectiveness, or to detect and neutralize foreign espionage. This is done by identification, penetration, manipulation, deception, and repression of individuals, groups, or organizations conducting or suspected of conducting espionage activities in order to destroy, neutralize, exploit, or prevent such espionage activities.

Counterguerrilla Warfare: Operations and activities conducted by armed forces, paramilitary forces, or nonmilitary agencies of a government against guerrillas.

Counterinsurgency: Military, paramilitary, political, economic, psychological, and civic actions taken by a government to defeat subversive insurgency within a country.

Counterintelligence: Activities conducted to destroy the effectiveness of foreign intelligence operations and to protect information against espionage, individuals against subversion, and installations against sabotage. The term also refers to information developed by or used in counterintelligence operations. See also counterespionage, countersabotage, and countersubversion.

Counterreconnaissance: Measures taken to prevent observation by a hostile foreign service of an area, place, or military force.

Countersabotage: That aspect of counterintelligence designed to detect, destroy, neutralize, or prevent sabotage activities through identification, penetration, manipulation, deception, and repression of individuals, groups, or organizations conducting or suspected of conducting sabotage activities.

Countersubversion: That part of counterintelligence designed to destroy the effectiveness of subversive activities through the detection, identification, exploitation, penetration, manipulation, deception, and repression of individuals, groups, or organizations conducting or capable of conducting such activities.

Courier: A messenger responsible for the secure physical transmission and delivery of documents and material.

Cover: A protective guise used by a person, organization, or installation to prevent identification with clandestine activities and to conceal the true affiliation of personel and the true sponsorship of their activities.

Covert Action: Any clandestine activity designed to influence foreign governments, events, organizations, or persons in support of United States foreign policy. Covert action may include political and economic action, propaganda and paramilitary activities.

Covert Operations: Operations planned and executed against foreign governments, installations, and individuals so as to conceal the identity of the sponsor or else to permit the sponsor's plausible denial of the operation. The terms covert action, covert operation, clandestive operation and clandestine activity are sometimes used interchangeably.

Critical Intelligence: Information or intelligence of such urgent importance to the security of the United States that it is transmitted at the highest priority to the President and other national decisionmaking officials before passing through regular evaluative channels.

Cryptanalysis: The breaking of codes and ciphers into plain text without initial knowledge of the key employed in the encryption.

Cryptography: The enciphering of plain text so that it will be unintelligible to an unauthorized recipient.

Crytology: The science that includes cryptoanalysis and cryptography, and embraces communications intelligence and communications security.

Cryptomaterial: All material—including documents, devices, equipment, and apparatus—essential to the encryption, decryption, or authentication of telecommunications.

Cryptosecurity: That component of communications security which results from the provision of technically sound cryptosystems and their proper use.

Cryptosystems: The associated items of cryptomaterial which are used as a unit and provide a single means of encryption and decryption.

Current Intelligence: Summaries and analyses of recent events.

Cut-out: A CIA term referring to a person who is used to conceal contact between members of a clandestine activity or organization.

Deception: Measures designed to mislead a hostile person or entity by manipulating, distorting, or falsifying evidence to induce a reaction prejudicial to his or its interests.

Decrypt: To convert encrypted text into plain text by use of a cryptosystem.

Defector: A person who, for political or other reasons, has repudiated his country and may be in possession of information of interest to the United States Government.

Defense Intelligence Agency (DIA): Department of Defense agency for producing military intelligence, created by directive of the Secretary of Defense in 1961.

Defense Intelligence Objectives and Priorities (DIOP): A single statement of intelligence requirements compiled by DIA for use by all DOD intelligence components.

Departmental Intelligence: The intelligence which government departments and agencies generate in support of their own activities.

Directive: Basically any executive branch communication which initiates or governs departmental or agency action, conduct, or procedure.

Director of Central Intelligence Directive (DCID): A directive issued by the DCI which outlines general policies and procedures to be followed by intelligence agencies under his direction; it is generally more specific than an NSCID.

Dissemination: The distribution of information or intelligence products (in oral, written, or graphic form) to departmental and agency intelligence consumers.

Domestic Emergencies: Emergencies occurring within the United States, its territories, or possessions, which affect the public welfare. Such emergencies may arise from an enemy attack, insurrection, civil disturbances, natural disasters (earthquakes, floods), fire, or other comparable emergencies which endanger life and property or disrupt the normal processess of government.

Domestic Intelligence: Intelligence relating to activities or conditions within the United States which threaten internal security (in general or to a governmental department, agency, or official) and which might require the employment of troops.

Double Agent: A person engaging in clandestine activity for two or more intelligence or security services who provides information to one service about the other, or about each service to the other, and who is wittingly or unwittingly manipulated by one service against the other.

Economic Intelligence: Intelligence regarding foreign economic resources, activities, and policies.

Electromagnetic Spectrum: The frequencies (or wave lengths) present in a given electromagnetic radiation (radiation made up of oscillating electric and magnetic fields and propagated with the speed of light—such as radar or radio waves). A particular spectrum could include a single frequency, or a broad range of frequencies.

Electronic Intelligence (ELINT): Technical and intelligence information derived from the collection (or interception) and processing of foreign electromagnetic radiations (noncommunications) emanating from sources such as radar. ELINT is part of the NSA/CSS Signals Intelligence mission.

Electronic Line of Sight: The path traveled by electromagnetic waves which is not subject to reflection or refraction by the atmosphere.

Electronics Security: The detection, identification, evaluation, and location of foreign electromagnetic radiations.

Electronic Surveillance: Surveillance conducted on a person, group, or other entitly by electronic equipment which is often highly sophisticated and extremely sensitive.

Elicitation: The acquisition of intelligence from a person or group which does not disclose the intent of the interview or conversation. This is a HUMINT collection technique, generally of an overt nature, unless the collector is other than what he or she purports to be.

Emission Security: That component of communications security which results from all measures taken to deny unauthorized persons any information of value which might be derived from the interception and analysis of compromising emanations from crypty-equipment or telecommunications systems.

Encipher: To convert a plain text message into unintelligible form by the use of a cipher system.

Encrypt: To convert a plain text message into unintelligible form by means of a cryptosystem; this term covers the meanings of encipher and encode.

Entity: A company, form, corporation, institution, bank, or foundation.

Espionage: Clandestine intelligence collection activity. This term is often interchanged with "clandestine collection."

Estimating: An effort to appraise and analyze the future possibilities or courses of action in a situation under study and the various results or consequences of foreign or United States actions relating to that situation. This analysis of such a foreign situation would consider its development and trends to identify its major elements, interpret the significance of the situation, and evaluate the future possibilities and prospective results of various actions which might be taken, including clandestine operations.

Evaluation: The process of determining the value, credibility, reliability, pertinency, accuracy, and use of an item of information, an intelligence product, or the performance of an intelligence system.

Executive Action: This term is generally an euphemism for assassination, and was used by the CIA to describe a program aimed at overthrowing certain foreign leaders, by assassinating them if necessary.

Exploitation: The process of getting information from any source and taking full advantage of it for strategic or tactical purposes.

Foreign Intelligence: Intelligence concerning areas outside the United States.

Grey Propaganda: Propaganda which does not specifically identify a source.

Guerrilla: A combat participant in guerrilla warfare.

Guerrilla Warfare: Military and paramilitary operations conducted in hostile or enemy-held territory by irregular, generally indigenous forces.

Guidance: The general direction of an intelligence effort, particularly in the area of collection.

Imagery: Representations of objects reproduced electronically or by optical means on film, electronic display devices, or other media.

Indications Intelligence: Intelligence in various degrees of evaluation which bears on foreign intentions regarding a course of action.

Infiltration: The placing of an agent or other person in a target area within hostile territory or within targeted groups or organizations.

Informant: A person who wittingly or unwittingly provides information to an agent, a clandestine service, or police. In reporting such information, this person will often be cited as the source.

Information: Raw, unevaluated data at all levels of reliability and from all kinds of sources, such as observation, rumors, reports, and photographs, which, when processed, may produce intelligence.

Informer: One who intentionally discloses information about other persons or activities to police or a security service (such as the FBI), usually for a financial reward.

Insurgency: A condition resulting from a revolt or insurrection against a constituted government which falls short of civil war.

Intelligence: The product resulting from the collection, collation, evaluation, analysis, integration, and interpretation of all collected information.

Intelligence Collection Plan: A plan for gathering information from all available sources to meet an intelligence requirement.

Intelligence Contingency Funds: Appropriated funds to be used for intelligence activities which are unforseen at the time of the budget and when the use of other funds is not applicable or would jeopardize or impede the task of an intelligence unit. Such funds are almost invariably used for covert activities.

Intelligence Cycle: The steps by which information is assembled, converted into intelligence, and made available to consumers. The cycle is composed of four basic phases: (1) *direction:* the determination of intelligence requirements, preparation of a collection plan, tasking of collection agencies, and a continuous check on the productivity of these agencies; (2) *collection:* the exploitation of information sources and the delivery of the collected information to the proper intelligence processing unit for use in the production of intelligence; (3) *processing:* the steps whereby information becomes intelligence through evaluation, analysis, integration, and interpretation; and (4) *dissemination:* the distribution of information or intelligence products (in oral, written, or graphic form) to departmental and agency intelligence consumers.

Intelligence Data Base: All holdings of intelligence data and finished intelligence products at a given department or agency.

Information Data Handling Systems: Information systems that process and manipulate raw information and intelligence data. The systems are characterized by application of general-purpose computers, peripheral data processing equipment, and automated storage and retrieval equipment for documents and photographs.

Intelligence Estimate: An appraisal of intelligence elements relating to a specific situation or condition to determine the courses of action open to an enemy or potential enemy and the probable order of their adoption.

Intelligence Process: Those steps by which information is collected, converted into intelligence, and disseminated.

Intelligence Requirement: A consumer statement of information needed which is not already at hand.

Intelligence Resources Advisory Committee (IRAC): Established in 1971 to advise the DCI in preparing a consolidated intelligence program budget for the President. It was abolished by President Ford's Executive Order, No. 11905, 2/18/76.

Interception: This term generally refers to the collection of electromagnetic signals (such as radio communications) by sophisticated collection equipment without the knowledge of the communicants for the production of certain forms of signals intelligence.

Interdepartmental Intelligence: The synthesis of departmental intelligence which is required by departments and agencies of the United States Government for performance of their missions; such intelligence is viewed as transcending the exclusive production competence of a single department or agency.

International Lines of Communication (ILC): Commercial telecommunications links.

Interrogation: A systematic effort to procure information by direct questioning of a person under the control of the questioner.

Interview: The gathering of information from a person who knows that he or she is giving information, although not often with awareness of the true connection or purposes of the interviewer.

This is generally an overt collection technique, unless the interviewer is not what he or she purports to be.

Joint Intelligence: Intelligence produced by elements of more than one military service.

Joint Intelligence Estimate for Planning (JIEP): A worldwide series of strategic estimates prepared annually by DIA for the Joint Chiefs of Staff; it is intended to be used as a base for developing intelligence annexes for JCS plans.

Key Intelligence Question (KIQ): Topics of particular importance to national policymakers, as defined by the DCI.

Link Encryption: The application of on-line crypto-operations to a communications system link so that all information passing over it is totally encrypted.

Links of Communication: "Links" is a general term used to indicate the existence of a communications facility between two points.

Microwave Relay: A process for propagating telecommunications over long distances by using radio signals relayed by several stations within "line of sight" from one another.

Monitoring: The observing, listening to, or recording of foreign or domestic communications for intelligence collection or intelligence security (e.g., COMSEC) purposes.

Multiplexing: A technique which allows one signal to carry several communications (e.g., conversations, messages) simultaneously.

National Intelligence: Intelligence produced by the CIA which bears on the broad aspects of United States national policy and national security. It is of concern to more than one department or agency.

National Intelligence Authority (NIA): An executive council created by President Truman's executive order of January 22, 1946, which had authority over the simultaneously created Central Intelligence Group (CIG). The NIA was a predecessor to the National Security Council.

National Intelligence Estimate (NIE): An estimate authorized by the DCI of the capabilities, vulnerabilities, and probable courses of action of foreign nations. It represents the composite views of the intelligence community.

National Security Agency (NSA): Established by President Truman, October 24, 1952, to replace the Armed Forces Security Agency (AFSA).

National Security Council Intelligence Directive (NSCID): Intelligence guidelines issued by the NSC to intelligence agencies. NSCIDs are often augmented by more specific DCIDs and by internal departmental or agency regulations.

Net Assessment Group: The group within the NSC staff that was responsible for reviewing and evaluating all intelligence products and producing net assessments. It was abolished in June 1973.

Notionals: Fictious, private commercial entities which exist on paper only. They serve as the ostensible employer of intelligence personnel, or as the ostensible sponsor of certain activities in support of clandestine operations.

Office of Policy Coordination (OPC): An office in CIA, established in 1948, to carry out covert action missions assigned to CIA by the National Security Council.

Office of Special Operations (OSO): Prior to 1952, OSO was a CIA component responsible for espionage and counterespionage. It merged with CIA's Office of Policy Coordination to form the Directorate for Plans.

Office of Strategic Services (OSS): The United States Intelligence service active during World War II. It was established by President Roosevelt in June 1942, and disbanded October 1, 1945.

Operational Intelligence: Intelligence produced to support the planning and execution of operations.

Operational Use: This term refers to using a person, group, organization, information, etc. in a clandestine operation or in support of a clandestine activity.

Operations Coordinating Board (OCB): This replaced the Psychological Strategy Board of the NSC on September 2, 1953.

Order of Battle: This term refers to information regarding the identity, strength, command structure, and disposition of personnel, units, and equipment of any military force.

Overt Intelligence: Information collected openly from public or open sources.

Paramilitary Forces: Forces or groups which are distinct from the regular armed forces of a nation, although they may resemble regular forces in organization, equipment, training, or mission.

Paramilitary Operation: An operation undertaken by a paramilitary force.

Penetration: The recruitment of agents within, or the planting of agents or technical monitoring devices within, a target organization to gain access to its secrets or to influence its activities.

Photographic Intelligence (PHOTINT): Information or intelligence derived from photography through photographic interpretation.

Plain Text: Unencrypted communications; specifically, the original message of a cryptogram, expressed in ordinary language.

Planning and Coordination Group (PCG): A committee of the Operations Coordinating Board of the National Security Council. PCG became the normal channel for policy approval of covert operations under NSC directive 5412/1 in 1955.

Plausible Denial:

Plumbing: A term referring to the development of assets or services supporting the clandestine operations of CIA field stations—such as safehouses, unaccountable funds, investigative persons, surveillance teams.

Political Intelligence: Originally, arranging, coordinating and conducting covert operations so as to "plausibly" permit official denial of United States involvement, sponsorship or support. Later this concept evolved so that it was employed by high officials and their subordinates to communicate without using precise language which would reveal authorization and involvement in certain activities and would be embarrassing and politically damaging if publicly revealed.

Processing: The manipulation of collected raw information to make it usable in analysis or to prepare it for data storage or retrieval.

Product: Finished intelligence reports disseminated by intelligence agencies to appropriate consumers.

Production: The preparation of reports based on an analysis of information to meet the needs of intelligence users (consumers) within and outside the intelligence community.

Propaganda: Any communication supporting national objectives which is designed to influence opinions, emotions, attitudes, or behavior of any group in order to benefit the sponsor, either directly or indirectly.

Proprietaries: A term used by CIA to designate ostensibly private commercial entities capable of doing business which are established and controlled by intelligence services to conceal governmental affiliation of intelligence personnel and/or governmental sponsorship of certain activities in support of clandestine operations.

Psychological Strategy Board (PSB): An NSC subcommittee established in 1951 to determine the desirability of proposed covert action programs and major covert action projects.

Psychological Warfare: The planned use of propaganda and other psychological actions to influence the opinions, emotions, attitudes, and behavior of hostile foreign groups so as to support the achievement of national policy objectives.

Reconnaissance: A mission undertaken to obtain, by observation or other detection methods, information about the activities and resources of foreign states.

Requirement: A general or specific request for intelligence information made by a member of the intelligence community.

Safe House: An innocent-appearing house or premises established by an intelligence organization for conducting clandestine or covert activity in relative security.

Sanitize: The deletion or revision of a report or document so as to prevent identification of the intelligence sources and methods that contributed to or are dealt with in the report.

Scan: In electromagnetic or acoustical contexts, a scan is one complete rotation of an antenna. With regard to ELINT, it refers to the motion of an electronic beam through space which is searching for a target.

Scientific and Technical Intelligence: Information or intelligence concerning foreign progress in basic and applied scientific or technical research and development, including engineering R&D, new technology, and weapons systems.

Security Measures: taken by the government and intelligence departments and agencies, among others, for protection from espionage, observation, sabotage, annoyance, or surprise. With respect to classified materials, it is the condition which prevents unauthorized persons from having access to official information which is safeguarded in the interests of national defense.

Sensitive: Something which requires special protection from disclosure, which could cause embarrassment, compromise, or threat to the security of the sponsoring power.

Service Cryptologic Agencies (SCAs): These are the Army Security Agency, Naval Security Group Command, and Air Force Security Service. Their signals intelligence-collection functions were brought under the operational control of the Director of NSA when the SCAs were confederated into the Central Security Service in 1971, and the Director of NSA was given extra responsibility as Chief of the CSS.

Sheep Dipping: The utilization of a military instrument (e.g., an airplane) or officer in clandestine operations, usually in a civilian capacity or under civilian cover, although the instrument or officer will covertly retain its or his military ownership or standing. The term is also applied to the placement of individuals in organizations or groups in which they can become active in order to establish credentials so that they can be used to collect information of intelligence interest on similar groups.

Signal: As applied to electronics, any transmitted electrical impulse.

Signals Intelligence (SIGINT): The general term for the foreign intelligence mission of the NSA/CSS; SIGINT involves the interception, processing, analysis, and dissemination of information derived from foreign electrical communications and other signals. It is composed of three elements: Communications Intelligence (COMINT), Electronics Intelligence (ELINT), and Telemetry Intelligence (TELINT). Most SIGINT is collected by personnel of the Service Cryptologic Agencies.

Source: A person, thing, or activity which provides intelligence information. In clandestine activities, the term applies to an agent or asset, normally a foreign national, being used in an intelligence activity for intelligence purposes. In interrogations, it refers to a person who furnishes intelligence information with or without knowledge that the information is being used for intelligence purposes.

Special Agent: A United States military or civilian who is a specialist in military security or in the collection of intelligence or counterintelligence information.

Special Group (Augmented): A NSC subcommittee established in 1962 to oversee Operation MONGOOSE, a major CIA covert action program designed to overthrow Fidel Castro.

Special Group (CI): The Special Group on Counter Insurgency, established by NSAM 124 on 1/18/63 to ensure the design of effective interagency programs to prevent and resist insurgency. Paramilitary operations were a prime focus.

5412/Special Group: An NSC subcommittee that was the predecessor to the 40 Committee.

Special Operations Division (SOD): A facility at Fort Detrick, Maryland that was the site for research and some testing and storage of biological and chemical agents and toxins.

Sterilize: To remove from material to be used in covert and clandestine actions any marks or devices which can identify it as originating with the sponsoring organization or nation.

Strategic Intelligence: Intelligence required for the formation of policy and military plans and operations at the national and international levels.

Subversion: Actions designed to undermine the military, economic, political, psychological, or moral strength of a nation or entity. It can also apply to an undermining of a person's loyalty to a government or entity.

Surreptitious Entry:

Surveillance: Systematic observation of a target.

Tactical Intelligence: Intelligence supporting military plans and operations at the military unit level. Tactical intelligence and strategic intelligence differ only in scope, point of view, and level of employment.

Target: A person, agency, facility, area, or country against which intelligence operations are directed.

Targeting: In regard to COMINT, the intentional selection and/or collection of telecommunications for intelligence purpose.

Target of Opportunity: A term describing an entity (e.g., governmental entity, installation, political organization, or individual) that becomes available to an intelligence agency or service by chance, and provides the opportunity for the collection of needed information.

Task: A term connoting the assignment or direction of an intelligence unit to perform a specified function.

Telecommunications: Any transmission, emission, or reception of signals, signs, writing, images, and sounds or information of any nature by wire, radio, visual, or other electromagnetic systems.

10/5 Panel: A predecessor to the 40 Committee of the NSC.

303 Committee: A predecessor to the 40 Committee of the NSC.

Toxin: Chemicals which are not living organisms, but which are produced by living organisms and are lethal.

Traffic: Messages carried over a telecommunications network.

United States Country Team: The senior, in-country, United States coordinating and supervising body, headed by the Chief of the United States diplomatic mission (usually an ambassador) and composed of the senior member of each represented United States department or agency.

United States Intelligence Board (USIB): Until it was abolished by Executive Order No. 11905 2/18/76, USIB was the NSC's central coordinating committee for the intelligence community.

Watch List: A list of words—such as names, entities, or phrases—which can be employed by a computer to select out required information from a mass of data.

Appendix 3
Legislation

NATIONAL SECURITY ACT OF 1947 ([84A], pp. 403–408)

NATIONAL SECURITY ACT OF 1947,
as amended

(61 Stat. 495, P.L. 80-253, July 26, 1947;
63 Stat. 578, P.L. 81-216, August 10, 1949;
65 Stat. 373, P.L. 82-165, October 10, 1951;
67 Stat. 19, P.L. 83-15, April 4, 1953;
68 Stat. 1226, P.L. 83-779, September 3, 1954;
70A Stat. 679, P.L. 84-1028, August 10, 1956;
78 Stat. 484, P.L. 88-448, August 10, 1964)

TITLE I—COORDINATION FOR NATIONAL SECURITY

NATIONAL SECURITY COUNCIL

SECTION 101. (a) There is established a council to be known as the National Security Council (hereinafter in this section referred to as the "Council").

50 U.S.C.A. 402(a)

The President of the United States shall preside over meetings of the Council: *Provided,* That in his absence he may designate a member of the Council to preside in his place.

The function of the Council shall be to advise the President with respect to the integration of domestic, foreign, and military policies relating to the national security so as to enable the military services and the other departments and agencies of the Government to cooperate more effectively in matters involving the national security.

The Council shall be composed of—

(1) the President;
(2) the Vice President;

September 1970

(3) the Secretary of State;

(4) the Secretary of Defense;

(5) the Director for Mutual Security [now abolished];

(6) the Chairman of the National Security Resources Board [now the Director of the Office of Emergency Preparedness]; and

(7) the Secretaries and Under Secretaries of other executive departments and of the military departments, the chairman of the Munitions Board [now abolished]; and the Chairman of the Research and Development Board [now abolished], when appointed by the President by and with the advice and consent of the Senate, to serve at his pleasure.

CENTRAL INTELLIGENCE AGENCY

SEC. 102. (a) There is established under the National Security Council a Central Intelligence Agency with a Director of Central Intelligence who shall be the head thereof, and with a Deputy Director of Central Intelligence who shall act for, and exercise the powers of, the Director during his absence or disability. The Director and the Deputy Director shall be appointed by the President, by and with the advice and consent of the Senate, from among the commissioned officers of the armed services, whether in an active or retired status, or from among individuals in civilian life: *Provided, however,* That at no time shall the two positions of the Director and Deputy Director be occupied simultaneously by commissioned officers of the armed services, whether in an active or retired status.

50 U.S.C.A. 403

(b)(1) If a commissioned officer of the armed services is appointed as Director, or Deputy Director, then—

(A) in the performance of his duties as Director, or Deputy Director, he shall be subject to no supervision, control, restriction, or prohibition (military or otherwise) other than would be operative with respect to him if he were a civilian in no way connected with the Department of the Army, the Department of the Navy, the Department of the Air Force, or the armed services or any component thereof; and

(B) he shall not possess or exercise any supervision, control, powers, or functions (other than such as he possesses, or is authorized or directed to exercise, as Director, or Deputy Director) with respect to the armed services or any component thereof, the Department of the Army, the Department of the Navy, or the Department of the Air Force, or any branch, bureau, unit, or division thereof, or with respect to any of the personnel (military or civilian) of any of the foregoing.

(2) Except as provided in paragraph (1) of this subsection, the appointment to the office of Director, or Deputy Director, of a commissioned officer of the armed services, and his acceptance of and service in such office, shall in no way affect any status, office, rank, or grade he may occupy or hold in the armed services, or any emolument, perquisite, right, privilege, or benefit incident to or arising out of any such status, office, rank, or grade. Any such commissioned officer shall, while serving in the office of Director, or Deputy Director, continue to hold rank and grade not lower than that in which serving at the time of his appointment and to receive the military pay and allowances (active or retired, as the case may be, including personal money allowance) payable to a commissioned officer of his grade and length of service for which the appropriate department shall be reimbursed from any funds available to defray the expenses of the Central Intelligence Agency. He also shall be paid by the Central Intelligence Agency from such funds an annual compensation at a rate equal to the amount by which the compensation established for such position exceeds the amount of his annual military pay and allowances.

(3) The rank or grade of any such commissioned officer shall, during the period in which such commissioned officer occupies the office of Director of Central Intelligence, or Deputy Director of Central Intelligence, be in addition to the numbers and percentages otherwise authorized and appropriated for the armed service of which he is a member.

(c) Notwithstanding the provisions of section 652 [now 7501] of Title 5, or the provisions of any other law, the Director of Central Intelligence may, in his discretion, terminate the employment of any officer or employee of the Agency whenever he shall deem such termination necessary or advisable in the interests of the United States, but such termination shall not affect the right of such officer or employee to seek or accept employment in any other department or agency of the Government if declared eligible for such employment by the United States Civil Service Commission.

(d) For the purpose of coordinating the intelligence activities of the several Government departments and agencies in the interest of national security, it shall be the duty of the Agency, under the direction of the National Security Council—

(1) to advise the National Security Council in matters concerning such intelligence activities of the Government departments and agencies as relate to national security;

(2) to make recommendations to the National Security Council for the coordination of such intelligence activities of the departments and agencies of the Government as relate to the national security;

(3) to correlate and evaluate intelligence relating to the national security, and provide for the appropriate dissemination of such intelligence within the Government using where appropriate existing agencies and facilities: *Provided,* That the Agency shall have no police, subpoena, law-enforcement powers, or internal-security functions: *Provided further,* That the departments and other agencies of the Government shall continue to collect, evaluate, correlate, and disseminate departmental intelligence: *And provided further,* That the Director of Central Intelligence shall be responsible for protecting intelligence sources and methods from unauthorized disclosure;

(4) to perform, for the benefit of the existing intelligence agencies, such additional services of common concern as the National Security Council determines can be more efficiently accomplished centrally;

(5) to perform such other functions and duties related to intelligence affecting the national security as the National Security Council may from time to time direct.

(e) To the extent recommended by the National Security Council and approved by the President, such intelligence of the departments and agencies of the Government, except as hereinafter provided, relating to the national security shall be open to the inspection of the Director of Central Intelligence, and such intelligence as relates to the national security and is possessed by such departments and other agencies of the Government, except as hereinafter provided, shall be made available to the Director of Central Intelligence for correlation, evaluation, and dissemination: *Provided, however,* That upon the written request of the Director of Central Intelligence, the Director of the Federal Bureau of Investigation shall make available to the Director of Central

September 1970

Intelligence such information for correlation, evaluation, and dissemination as may be essential to the national security.

(f) Effective when the Director first appointed under subsection (a) of this section has taken office—

(1) the National Intelligence Authority (11 Fed. Reg. 1337, 1339, February 5, 1946)   shall cease to exist; and

(2) the personnel, property, and records of the Central Intelligence Group are transferred to the Central Intelligence Agency, and such Group shall cease to exist.   Any unexpended balances of appropriations, allocations, or other funds available or authorized to be made available for such Group shall be available and shall be authorized to be made available in like manner for expenditure by the Agency.

TITLE III—MISCELLANEOUS

ADVISORY COMMITTEES AND PERSONNEL

SEC. 303. (a) The Secretary of Defense,   the Director of the Office of Defense Mobilization [now abolished],   the Director of Central Intelligence, and the National Security Council, acting through its Executive Secretary,   are authorized to appoint such advisory committees and to employ, consistent with other provisions of sections 171-171n, 172-172j, 181-1, 182-1, 411a, 411b, and 626-626d of Title 5,   and sections 401-403, 404, and 405 of this title,   such part-time advisory personnel   as they may deem necessary in carrying out their respective functions and the functions of agencies under their control. Persons holding other offices or positions under the United States for which they receive compensation, while serving as members of such committees, shall receive no additional compensation for such service. Other members of such committees and other part-time advisory personnel so employed may serve without compensation or may receive compensation at a rate not to exceed $50   for each day of service, as determined by the appointing authority.

50
U.S.C.A.
405

(b) Service of an individual as a member of any such advisory committee, or in any other part-time capacity for a department or agency hereunder, shall not be considered as service bringing such individual within the provisions of sections 281 [now 203], 283 [now 205], or 284 [now 207] of Title 18,   unless the act of such individual, which by such section is made unlawful when performed by an individual referred to in such section, is with respect to any particular matter which directly involves a department or agency which such person is advising or in which such department or agency is directly interested.

EFFECTIVE DATE

Sec. 310. (a) The first sentence of section 202(a) and sections 1, 2, 307, 308, 309, and 310 shall take effect immediately upon the enactment of this Act.

(b) Except as provided in subsection (a), the provisions of this Act shall take effect on whichever of the following days is the earlier: The day after the day upon which the Secretary of Defense first appointed takes office, or the sixtieth day after the date of the enactment of this Act.

CENTRAL INTELLIGENCE AGENCY ACT OF 1949 ([84A], pp. 409–417)

CENTRAL INTELLIGENCE AGENCY ACT OF 1949, as amended

(63 Stat. 208, P.L. 81-110, June 20, 1949;
64 Stat. 450, P.L. 81-697, August 16, 1950;
65 Stat. 89, P.L. 82-53, June 26, 1951;
68 Stat. 1105, P.L. 83-763, September 1, 1954;
72 Stat. 327, P.L. 85-507, July 7, 1958;
74 Stat. 792, P.L. 86-707, September 6, 1960;
78 Stat. 484, P.L. 88-448, August 19, 1964)

AN ACT

To provide for the administration of the Central Intelligence Agency, established pursuant to section 102, National Security Act of 1947, and for other purposes.

Be it enacted by the Senate and House of Representatives of the United States of America in Congress assembled,

DEFINITIONS

Section 1. When used in sections 403b-403j of this title, the term—

(a) "Agency" means the Central Intelligence Agency;

(b) "Director" means the Director of Central Intelligence;

(c) "Government agency" means any executive department, commission, council, independent establishment, corporation wholly or partly owned by the United States which is an instrumentality of the United States, board, bureau, division, service, office, officer, authority, administration, or other establishment, in the executive branch of the Government.

50
U.S.C.A.
403a.

September 1970

SEAL OF OFFICE

SEC. 2. The Director of Central Intelligence shall cause a seal of office to be made for the Central Intelligence Agency, of such design as the President shall approve, and judicial notice shall be taken thereof.

50 U.S.C.A. 403b.

PROCUREMENT AUTHORITIES

SEC. 3. (a) In the performance of its functions the Central Intelligence Agency is authorized to exercise the authorities contained in sections [2(c)(1), (2), (3), (4), (5), (6), (10), (12), (15), (17), and sections 3, 4, 5, 6, and 10 of the Armed Services Procurement Act of 1947 (Public Law 413, Eightieth Congress, second session)].

50 U.S.C.A. 403c.

(b) In the exercise of the authorities granted in subsection (a) of this section, the term "Agency head" shall mean the Director, the Deputy Director, or the Executive of the Agency.

(c) The determinations and decisions provided in subsection (a) of this section to be made by the Agency head may be made with respect to individual purchases and contracts or with respect to classes of purchases or contracts, and shall be final. Except as provided in subsection (d) of this section, the Agency head is authorized to delegate his powers provided in this section, including the making of such determinations and decisions, in his discretion and subject to his direction, to any other officer or officers or officials of the Agency.

(d) The power of the Agency head to make the determinations or decisions specified in [paragraphs (12) and (15) of section 2 (c) and section 5 (a) of the Armed Services Procurement Act of 1947] shall not be delegable. Each determination or decision required by [paragraphs (12) and (15) of section 2 (c), by section 4 or by section 5 (a) of the Armed Services Procurement Act of 1947], shall be based upon written findings made by the official making such determinations, which findings shall be final and shall be available within the Agency for a period of at least six years following the date of the determination.

TRAVEL, ALLOWANCES, AND RELATED EXPENSES

SEC. 4.   Under such regulations as the Director may prescribe, the Agency, with respect to its officers and employees assigned to duty stations   outside the several states of the United States of America, excluding Alaska and Hawaii, but including the District of Columbia, shall—

50 U.S.C.A. 403e.

(1) (A) pay the travel   expenses of officers and employees of the Agency, including expenses incurred while traveling pursuant to authorized   home leave;

(B) pay the travel expenses of members of the family of an officer or employee of the Agency when proceeding to or returning from his post of duty; accompanying him on authorized home leave; or otherwise traveling in accordance with authority granted pursuant to the terms of sections 403a-403j of this title or any other Act;

(C) pay the cost of transporting the furniture and household and personal effects of an officer or employee of the Agency to his successive posts of duty and, on the termination of his services, to his residence at time of appointment or to a point not more distant, or, upon retirement, to the place where he will reside;

(D) pay the cost of packing and unpacking, transporting to and from a place of storage, and storing the furniture and household and personal effects of an officer or employee of the Agency, when he is absent from his post of assignment under orders, or when he is assigned to a post to which he cannot take or at which he is unable to use such furniture and household and personal effects, or when it is in the public interest or more economical to authorize storage; but in no instance shall the weight or volume of the effects stored together with the weight or volume of the effects transported exceed the maximum limitations fixed by regulations, when not otherwise fixed by law;

(E) pay the cost of packing and unpacking, transporting to and from a place of storage, and storing the furniture and household and personal effects of an officer or employee of the Agency in connection with assignment or transfer to a new post, from the date of his departure from his last post or from the date of his departure from his place of residence in the case of a new officer or employee and for not to exceed three months after arrival at the new post, or until the establishment of residence quarters, whichever shall be shorter; and in connection with separation of an officer or employee of the Agency, the cost of packing and unpacking, transporting to and from a place of storage, and storing for a period not to exceed three months, his furniture and household and personal effects; but in no instance shall the weight or volume of the effects stored together with the weight or volume of the effects transported exceed the maximum limitations fixed by regulations, when not otherwise fixed by law;

(F) pay the travel expenses and transportation costs incident to the removal of the members of the family of an officer or employee of the Agency and his furniture and household and personal effects, including automobiles, from a post at which, because of the prevalence of disturbed conditions, there is imminent danger to life and property, and the return of such persons, furniture, and effects to such post upon the cessation of such conditions; or to such other post as may in the meantime have become the post to which such officer or employee has been assigned.

(2) Charge expenses in connection with travel of personnel, their dependents, and transportation of their household goods and personal effects, involving a change of permanent station, to the appropriation for the fiscal year current when any part of either the travel or transportation pertaining to the transfer begins pursuant to previously issued travel and transfer orders, notwithstanding the fact that such travel or transportation may not all be effected during such fiscal year, or the travel and transfer orders may have been issued during the prior fiscal year.

(3) (A) Order to any of the several States of the United States of America (including the District of Columbia, the Commonwealth of Puerto Rico, and any territory or possession of the United States) on leave of absence each officer or employee of the Agency who was a resident of the United States (as described above) at time of employment, upon completion of two years' continuous service abroad, or as soon as possible thereafter.

(B) While in the United States (as described in paragraph (3) (A) of this section) on leave, the service of any officer or employee shall be available for work or duties in the Agency or elsewhere as the Director may prescribe; and the time of such work or duty shall not be counted as leave.

(C) Where an officer or employee on leave returns to the United States (as described in paragraph (3) (A) of this section), leave of absence granted shall be exclusive of the time actually and necessarily occupied in going to and from the United States (as so described) and such time as may be necessarily occupied in awaiting transportation.

(4) Notwithstanding the provisions of any other law, transport for or on behalf of an officer or employee of the Agency, a privately owned motor vehicle in any case in which it shall be determined that water, rail, or air transportation of the motor vehicle is necessary or expedient for all or any part of the distance between points of origin and destination, and pay the costs of such transportation. Not more than one motor vehicle of any officer or employee of the Agency may be transported under authority of this paragraph during any four-year period, except that, as a replacement for such motor vehicle, one additional motor vehicle of any such officer or employee may be so transported during such period upon approval, in advance, by the Director and upon a determination, in advance, by the Director that such replacement is necessary for reasons beyond the control of the officer or employee and is in the interest of the Government. After the expiration of a period of four years following the date of transportation under authority of this paragraph of a privately owned motor vehicle of any officer or employee

who has remained in continuous service outside the several States of the United States of America, excluding Alaska and Hawaii, but including the District of Columbia, during such period, the transportation of a replacement for such motor vehicle for such officer or employee may be authorized by the Director in accordance with this paragraph.

(5) (A) In the event of illness or injury requiring the hospitalization of an officer or full time employee of the Agency, not the result of vicious habits, intemperance, or misconduct on his part, incurred while on assignment abroad, in a locality where there does not exist a suitable hospital or clinic, pay the travel expenses of such officer or employee by whatever means he shall deem appropriate and without regard to the Standardized Government Travel Regulations and section 73b [now section 5731 (a)] of Title 5, to the nearest locality where a suitable hospital or clinic exists and on his recovery pay for the travel expenses of his return to his post of duty. If the officer or employee is too ill to travel unattended, the Director may also pay the travel expenses of an attendant;

(B) Establish a first-aid station and provide for the services of a nurse at a post at which, in his opinion, sufficient personnel is employed to warrant such a station: *Provided,* That, in his opinion, it is not feasible to utilize an existing facility;

(C) In the event of illness or injury requiring hospitalization of an officer or full time employee of the Agency, not the result of vicious habits, intemperance, or misconduct on his part, incurred in the line of duty while such person is assigned abroad, pay for the cost of the treatment of such illness or injury at a suitable hospital or clinic;

(D) Provide for the periodic physical examination of officers and employees of the Agency and for the cost of administering inoculations or vaccinations to such officers or employees.

(6) Pay the costs of preparing and transporting the remains of an officer or employee of the Agency or a member of his family who may die while in travel status or abroad, to his home or official station, or to such other place as the Director may determine to be the appropriate place of interment, provided that in no case shall the expense payable be greater than the amount which would have been payable had the destination been the home or official station.

(7) Pay the costs of travel of new appointees and their dependents, and the transportation of their household goods and personal effects, from places of actual residence in foreign countries at time of appointment to places of employment and return to their actual residences at the time of appointment or a point not more distant: *Provided,* That such appointees agree in writing to remain with the

United States Government for a period of not less than twelve months from the time of appointment.

Violation of such agreement for personal convenience of an employee or because of separation for misconduct will bar such return payments and, if determined by the Director or his designee to be in the best interests of the United States, any money expended by the United States on account of such travel and transportation shall be considered as a debt due by the individual concerned to the United States.

GENERAL AUTHORITIES

SEC. 5. In the performance of its functions, the Central Intelligence Agency is authorized to

(a) Transfer to and receive from other Government agencies such sums as may be approved by the Bureau of the Budget, for the performance of any of the functions or activities authorized under sections 403 and 405 of this title, and any other Government agency is authorized to transfer to or receive from the Agency such sums without regard to any provisions of law limiting or prohibiting transfers between appropriations. Sums transferred to the Agency in accordance with this paragraph may be expended for the purposes and under the authority of sections 403a-403j of this title without regard to limitations of appropriations from which transferred; _{50 U.S.C.A 403f.}

(b) Exchange funds without regard to section 543 of Title 31;

(c) Reimburse other Government agencies for services of personnel assigned to the Agency, and such other Government agencies are authorized, without regard to provisions of law to the contrary, so to assign or detail any officer or employee for duty with the Agency;

(d) Authorize couriers and guards designated by the Director to carry firearms when engaged in transportation of confidential documents and materials affecting the national defense and security;

(e) Make alterations, improvements, and repairs on premises rented by the Agency, and pay rent therefor without regard to limitations on expenditures contained in the Act of June 30, 1932, as amended: *Provided,* That in each case the Director shall certify that exception from such limitations is necessary to the successful performance of the Agency's functions or to the security of its activities.

SEC. 6. In the interests of the security of the foreign intelligence activities of the United States and in order further to implement the proviso of section 403(d)(3) of this title[36] that the Director of Central Intelligence shall be responsible for protecting intelligence sources and methods from unauthorized disclosure, the _{50 U.S.C.A. 403g.}

Agency shall be exempted from the provisions of section 654 of Title 5,[37] and the provisions of any other law which require the publication or disclosure of the organization, functions, names, official titles, salaries, or numbers of personnel employed by the Agency: *Provided,* That in furtherance of this section, the Director of the Bureau of the Budget shall make no reports to the Congress in connection with the Agency under section 947(b) of Title 5.

SEC. 7. Whenever the Director, the Attorney General, and the Commissioner of Immigration shall determine that the entry of a particular alien into the United States for permanent residence is in the interest of national security or essential to the furtherance of the national intelligence mission, such alien and his immediate family shall be given entry into the United States for permanent residence without regard to their inadmissibility under the immigration or any other laws and regulations, or to the failure to comply with such laws and regulations pertaining to admissibility: *Provided,* That the number of aliens and members of their immediate families entering the United States under the authority of this section shall in no case exceed one hundred persons in any one fiscal year.

50 U.S.C.A. 403h.

APPROPRIATIONS

SEC. 8. (a) Notwithstanding any other provisions of law, sums made available to the Agency by appropriation or otherwise may be expended for purposes necessary to carry out its functions, including—

50 U.S.C.A. 403j.

(1) personal services, including personal services without regard to limitations on types of persons to be employed, and rent at the seat of government and elsewhere; health-service programs as authorized by section 150 [now section 7901] of Title 5; rental of news-reporting services; purchase or rental and operation of photographic, reproduction, cryptographic, duplication and printing machines, equipment and devices, and radio-receiving and radio-sending equipment and devices, including telegraph and teletype equipment; purchase, maintenance, operation, repair, and hire of passenger motor vehicles, and aircraft, and vessels of all kinds; subject to policies established by the Director, transportation of officers and employees of the Agency in Government-owned automotive equipment between their domiciles and places of employment, where such personnel are engaged in work which makes such transportation necessary, and transportation in such equipment, to and from school, of children of Agency personnel who have quarters for themselves and their families at isolated stations outside the continental United States where adequate public or private trans-

portation is not available; printing and binding; purchase, mainte-
nance, and cleaning of firearms, including purchase, storage, and
maintenance of ammunition; subject to policies established by the
Director, expenses of travel in connection with, and expenses inci-
dent to attendance at meetings of professional, technical, scientific,
and other similar organizations when such attendance would be
a benefit in the conduct of the work of the Agency; association and
library dues; payment of premiums or costs of surety bonds for
officers or employees without regard to the provisions of section 14
of Title 6; payment of claims pursuant to Title 28; acquisition of
necessary land and the clearing of such land; construction of build-
ings and facilities without regard to sections 259 and 267 of Title
40; repair, rental, operation, and maintenance of buildings, utili-
ties, facilities, and appurtenances; and

(2) supplies, equipment, and personnel and contractual services
otherwise authorized by law and regulations, when approved by the
Director.

(b) The sums made available to the Agency may be expended
without regard to the provisions of law and regulations relating to
the expenditure of Government funds; and for objects of a con-
fidential, extraordinary, or emergency nature, such expenditures to
be accounted for solely on the certificate of the Director and
every such certificate shall be deemed a sufficient voucher for the
amount therein certified.

SEPARABILITY OF PROVISIONS

SEC. 9. If any provision of this Act, or the application of
such provision to any person or circumstances, is held invalid, the
remainder of this Act or the application of such provision to persons
or circumstances other than those as to which it is held invalid, shall
not be affected thereby.

SHORT TITLE

SEC. 10. This Act may be cited as the "Central Intelligence
Agency Act of 1949."

Approved June 20, 1949.

Appendix 4
Executive Actions

PRESIDENTIAL DIRECTIVE: COORDINATION OF FEDERAL FOREIGN INTELLIGENCE ACTIVITIES ([113], HARRY S. TRUMAN, JANUARY 22, 1946)

To the Secretary of State, The Secretary of War, and The Secretary of the Navy.

1. It is my desire, and I hereby direct, that all Federal foreign intelligence activities be planned, developed and coordinated so as to assure the most effective accomplishment of the intelligence mission related to the national security. I hereby designate you, together with another person to be named by me as my personal representative, as the National Intelligence Authority to accomplish this purpose.

2. Within the limits of available appropriations, you shall each from time to time assign persons and facilities from your respective Departments, which persons shall collectively form a Central Intelligence Group and shall, under the direction of a Director of Central Intelligence, assist the National Intelligence Authority. The Director of Central Intelligence shall be designated by me, shall be responsible to the National Intelligence Authority, and shall sit as a non-voting member thereof.

3. Subject to the existing law, and to the direction and control of the National Intelligence Authority, the Director of Central Intelligence shall:

    a. Accomplish the correlation and evaluation of intelligence relating to the national security, and the appropriate dissemination within the Government of the resulting strategic and national policy intelligence. In so doing, full use shall be made of the staff and facilities of the intelligence agencies of your Departments.

    b. Plan for the coordination of such of the activities of the intelligence agencies of your Departments as relate to the national security and recommend to the National Intelligence Authority the establishment of such over-all policies and objectives as will assure the most effective accomplishment of the national intelligence mission.

    c. Perform, for the benefit of said intelligence agencies, such services of common concern as the National Intelligence Authority determines can be more efficiently accomplished centrally.

d. Perform such other functions and duties related to intelligence affecting the national security as the President and the National Intelligence Authority may from time to time direct.

4. No police, law enforcement or internal security functions shall be exercised under this directive.

5. Such intelligence received by the intelligence agencies of your Department as may be designated by the National Intelligence Authority shall be freely available to the Director of Central Intelligence Authority, the operations of said intelligence agencies shall be open to inspection by the Director of Central Intelligence in connection with planning functions.

6. The existing intelligence agencies of your Departments shall continue to collect, evaluate, correlate and disseminate departmental intelligence.

7. The Director of Central Intelligence shall be advised by an Intelligence Advisory Board consisting of the heads (or their representatives) of the principal military and civilian intelligence agencies of the Government having functions related to national security, as determined by the National Intelligence Authority.

8. Within the scope of existing law and Presidential directives, other departments and agencies of the executive branch of the Federal Government shall furnish such intelligence information relating to the national security as is in their possession, and as the Director of Central Intelligence may from time to time request pursuant to regulations of the National Intelligence Authority.

9. Nothing herein shall be construed to authorize the making of investigations inside the continental limits of the United States and its possessions, except as provided by law and Presidential directives.

10. In the conduct of their activities the National Intelligence Authority and the Director of Central Intelligence shall be responsible for fully protecting intelligence sources and methods.

EXECUTIVE ORDER 11652 ([117], MARCH 8, 1972)

CLASSIFICATION AND DECLASSIFICATION OF NATIONAL SECURITY INFORMATION AND MATERIAL

The interests of the United States and its citizens are best served by making information regarding the affairs of Government readily available to the public. This concept of an informed citizenry is reflected in the Freedom of Information Act and in the current public information policies of the executive branch.

Within the Federal Government there is some official information and material which, because it bears directly on the effectiveness of our national defense and the conduct of our foreign relations, must be subject to some constraints for the security of our Nation and the safety of our people and our allies. To protect against actions hostile to the United States, of both an overt and covert nature, it is essential that such official information and material be given only limited dissemination.

This official information or material, referred to as classified information or material in this order, is expressly exempted from public disclosure by section 552(b)(1) of title 5, United States Code. Wrongful disclosure of such information or material is recognized in the Federal Criminal Code as providing a basis for prosecution.

To insure that such information and material is protected, but only to the extent and for such period as is necessary, this order identifies the information to be protected, prescribes classification, downgrading, declassification, and safeguarding procedures to be followed, and establishes a monitoring system to insure its effectiveness.

Now, therefore, by virtue of the authority vested in me by the Constitution and statutes of the United States, it is hereby ordered:

SECTION 1. SECURITY CLASSIFICATION CATEGORIES

Official information or material which requires protection against unauthorized disclosure in the interest of the national defense or foreign relations of the United States (hereinafter collectively termed "national security") shall be classified in one of three categories, namely, "Top Secret," "Secret," or "Confidential," depending upon the degree of its significance to national security. No other categories shall be used to identify official information or material as requiring protection in the interest of national security, except as otherwise expressly provided by statute. These classification categories are defined as follows:

(A) *"Top Secret."*—"Top Secret" refers to that national security information or material which requires the highest degree of protection. The test for assigning "Top Secret" classification shall be whether its unauthorized disclosure could reasonably be expected to cause exceptionally grave damage to the national security. Examples of "exceptionally grave damage" include armed hostilities against the United States or its allies; disruption of foreign relations vitally affecting the national security; the compromise of vital national defense plans or complex cryptologic and communications intelligence systems; the revelation of sensitive intelligence operations; and the disclosure of scientific or technological developments vital to national security. This classification shall be used with the utmost restraint.

(B) *"Secret."*—"Secret" refers to that national security information or material which requires a substantial degree of protection. The test for assigning "Secret" classification shall be whether its unauthorized disclosure could reasonably be expected to cause serious damage to the national security. Examples of "serious damage" include disruption of foreign relations significantly affecting the national security; significant impairment of a program or poliyc directly related to the national security; revelation of significant military plans of intelligence operations; and compromise of significant scientific or technological developments relating to national security. The classification "Secret" shall be sparingly used.

(C) *"Confidential."*—"Confidential" refers to the national security information or material which requires protection. The test for assigning "Confidential" classification shall be whether its unauthorized·disclosure could reasonably be expected to cause damage to the national security.

SECTION 2. AUTHORITY TO CLASSIFY

The authority to originally classify information or material under this order shall be restricted solely to those offices within the executive branch which are concerned with matters of national security, and shall be limited to the minimum number absolutely required for efficient administration. Except as the context may otherwise indicate, the term "Department" as used in this order shall include agency or other governmental unit.

(A) The authority to originally classify information or material under this order as "Top Secret" shall be exercised only by such officials as the President may designate in writing and by:

(1) The heads of the Departments listed below;

(2) Such of their senior principal deputies and assistants as the heads of such Departments may designate in writing; and

(3) Such heads and senior principal deputies and assistants of major elements of such Departments, as the heads of such Departments may designate in writing.

Such offices in the Executive Office of the President as the President may designate in writing.

Central Intelligence Agency.
Atomic Energy Commission.
Department of State.
Department of the Treasury.
Department of Defense.
Department of the Army.
Department of the Navy.
Department of the Air Force.
United States Arms Control and Disarmament Agency.
Department of Justice.
National Aeronautics and Space Administration.
Agency for International Development.

(B) The authority to originally classify information or material under this order as "secret" shall be exercised only by:

(1) Officials who have "top secret" classification authority;

(2) Such subordinates as officials with "top secret" classification authority under (A)(1) and (2) above may designate in writing; and

(3) The heads of the following named departments and such senior principal deputies or assistants as they may designate in writing.

> Department of Transportation.
> Federal Communications Commission.
> Export-Import Bank of the United States.
> Department of Commerce.
> U.S. Civil Service Commission.
> U.S. Information Agency.
> General Services Administration.
> Department of Health, Education, and Welfare.
> Civil Aeronautics Board.
> Federal Maritime Commission.
> Federal Power Commission.
> National Science Foundation.
> Overseas Private Investment Corp.

(C) The authority to originally classify information or material under this order as "confidential" may be exercised by officials who have "top secret" or "secret" classification authority and such officials as they may designate in writing.

(D) Any department not referred to herein and any department or unit established hereafter shall not have authority to originally classify information or material under this order, unless specifically authorized hereafter by an Executive order.

SECTION 3. AUTHORITY TO DOWNGRADE AND DECLASSIFY

The authority to downgrade and declassify national security information or material shall be exercised as follows:

(A) Information or material may be downgraded or declassified by the official authorizing the original classification, by a successor in capacity or by a supervisory official of either.

(B) Downgrading and declassification authority may also be exercised by an official specifically authorized under regulations issued by the head of the Department listed in sections 2(A) or (B) hereof.

(C) In the case of classified information or material officially transferred by or pursuant to statute or Executive order in conjunction with a transfer of function and not merely for storage purposes, the receiving Department shall be deemed to be the originating Department for all purposes under this order including downgrading and declassification.

(D) In the case of classified information or material not officially transferred within (C) above, but originated in a Department which has since ceased to exist, each Department in possession shall be deemed to be the originating Department for all purposes under this order. Such information or material may be downgraded and declassified by the Department in possession after consulting with any other Departments having an interest in the subject matter.

(E) Classified information or material transferred to the General Services Administration for accession into the Archives of the United States shall be downgraded and declassified by the Archivist of the United States in accordance with this order, directives of the President issued through the National Security Council and pertinent regulations of the Departments.

(F) Classified information or material with special markings, as described in section 8, shall be downgraded and declassified as required by law and governing regulations.

SECTION 4. CLASSIFICATION

Each person possessing classifying authority shall be held accountable for the propriety of the classifications attributed to him. Both unnecessary classification and overclassification shall be avoided. Classification shall be solely on the basis of national security considerations. In no case shall information be classified in order to conceal inefficiency or administrative error, to prevent embarrassment to a person or Department, to restrain competition or independent initiative, or to prevent for any other reason the release of information which does not require protection in the interest of national security. The following rules shall apply to classification of information under this order:

(A) *Documents in general.*—Each classified document shall show on its face its classification and whether it is subject to or exempt from the general declassification schedule. It shall also show the office of origin, the date of preparation and classification and, to the extent practicable, be so marked as to indicate which portions are classified, at what level, and which portions are not classified in order to facilitate excerpting and other use. Material containing references to classified materials, which references do not reveal classified information, shall not be classified.

(B) *Identification of classifying authority.*—Unless the Department involved shall have provided some other method of identifying the individual at the highest level that authorized classification in each case, material classified under this order shall indicate on its face the identity of the highest authority authorizing the classification. Where the individual who signs or otherwise authenticates a document or item has also authorized the classification, no further annotation as to his identity is required.

(C) *Information or material furnished by a foreign government or international organization.*—Classified information or material furnished to the United States by a foreign government or international organization shall either retain its original classification or be assigned a U.S. classification. In either case, the classification shall assure a degree of protection equivalent to that required by the government or international organization which furnished the information or material.

(D) *Classification responsibilities.*—A holder of classified information or material shall observe and respect the classification assigned by the originator. If a holder believes that there is unnecessary classification, that the assigned classification is improper, or that the document is subject to declassification under this order, he shall so inform the originator who shall thereupon reexamine the classification.

SECTION 5. DECLASSIFICATION AND DOWNGRADING

Classified information and material, unless declassified earlier by the original classifying authority, shall be declassified and downgraded in accordance with the following rules:

(A) *General declassification schedule.*

(1) *"Top secret."*—Information or material originally classified "top secret" shall become automatically downgraded to "secret" at the end of the second full calendar year following the year in which it was originated, downgraded to "confidential" at the end of the fourth full calendar year following the year in which it was originated, and declassified at the end of the tenth full calendar year following the year in which it was originated.

(2) *"Secret."*—Information and material originally classified ' secret" shall become automatically downgraded to "confidential" at the end of the second full calendar year following the year in which it was originated, and declassified at the end of the eighth full calendar year following the year in which it was originated.

(3) *"Confidential."*—Information and material originally classified "confidential" shall become automatically declassified at the end of the sixth full calendar year following the year in which it was originated.

(B) *Exemptions from general declassification schedule.*—Certain classified information or material may warrant some degree of protection for a period exceeding that provided in the general declassification schedule. An official authorized to originally classify information or material "top secret" may exempt from the general declassification schedule any level of classified information or material originated by him or under his supervision if it falls within one of the categories described below. In each case such official shall specify in writing on the material the exemption category being claimed and, unless impossible, a date or event for automatic declassification. The use of the exemption authority shall be kept to the absolute minimum consistent with national security requirements and shall be restricted to the following categories:

(1) Classified information or material furnished by foreign governments or international organizations and held by the United States on the understanding that it be kept in confidence.

(2) Classified information or material specifically covered by statute, or pertaining to cryptography, or disclosing intelligence sources or methods.

(3) Classified information or material disclosing a system, plan, installation, project or specific foreign relations matter the continuing protection of which is essential to the national security.

(4) Classified information or material the disclosure of which would place a person in immediate jeopardy.

(C) *Mandatory review of exempted material.*—All classified information and material originated after the effective date of this order which is exempted under (B) above from the general declassification schedule shall be subject to a classification review by the originating department at any time after the expiration of 10 years from the date of origin provided: (1) A department or member of the public requests a review; (2) the request describes the record with sufficient particularity to enable the department to identify it; and (3) the record can be obtained with only a reasonable amount of effort.

Information or material which no longer qualifies for exemption under (B) above shall be declassified. Information or material continuing to qualify under (B) shall be so marked and, unless impossible, a date for automatic declassification shall be set.

(D) *Applicability of the general declassification schedule to previously classified material.*—Information or material classified before the effective date of this order and which is assigned to group 4 under Executive Order No. 10501, as amended by Executive Order No. 10964, shall be subject to the general declassification schedule. All other information or material classified before the effective date of this order, whether or not assigned to groups 1, 2, or 3 of Executive Order No. 10501, as amended, shall be excluded from the general declassification schedule. However, at any time after the expiration of 10 years from the date of origin it shall be subject to a mandatory classification review and disposition under the same conditions and criteria that apply to classified information and material created after the effective date of this order as set forth in (B) and (C) above.

(E) *Declassification of Classified Information or Material After 30 Years.*—All classified information or material which is 30 years old or more, whether originating before or after the effective date of this order, shall be declassified under the following conditions:

(1) All information and material classified after the effective date of this order shall, whether or not declassification has been requested, become automatically declassified at the end of 30 full calendar years after the date of its original classification except for such specifically identified information or material which the head of the originating department personally determines in writing at that time to require continued protection because such continued protection is essential to the national security or disclosure would place a person in immediate jeopardy. In such case, the head of the department shall also specify the period of continued classification.

(2) All information and material classified before the effective date of this order and more than 30 years old shall be systematically reviewed for declassification by the Archivist of the United States by the end of the 30th full calendar year following the year in which it was originated. In his review, the Archivist will separate and keep protected only such information or material as is specifically identified by the head of the department in accordance with (E)(1) above. In such case, the head of the department shall also specify the period of continued classification.

(F) *Departments Which Do Not Have Authority for Original Classification.*—The provisions of this section relating to the declassification of national security information or material shall apply to departments which, under the terms of this order, do not have current authority to originally classify information or material, but which formerly had such authority under previous Executive orders.

SECTION 6. POLICY DIRECTIVES ON ACCESS, MARKING, SAFEKEEPING, ACCOUNTABILITY, TRANSMISSION, DISPOSITION, AND DESTRUCTION OF CLASSIFIED INFORMATION AND MATERIAL

The President, acting through the National Security Council, shall issue directives which shall be binding on all departments to protect classified information from loss or compromise. Such directives shall conform to the following policies:

(A) No person shall be given access to classified information or material unless such person has been determined to be trustworthy and unless access to such information is necessary for the performance of his duties.

(B) All classified information and material shall be appropriately and conspicuously marked to put all persons on clear notice of its classified contents.

(C) Classified information and material shall be used, possessed, and stored only under conditions which will prevent access by unauthorized persons or dissemination to unauthorized persons.

(D) All classified information and material disseminated outside the executive branch under Executive Order No. 10865 or otherwise shall be properly protected.

(E) Appropriate accountability records for classified information shall be established and maintained and such information and material shall be protected adequately during all transmissions.

(F) Classified information and material no longer needed in current working files or for reference or record purposes shall be destroyed or disposed of in accordance with the records disposal provisions contained in chapter 33 of title 44 of the United States Code and other applicable statutes.

(G) Classified information or material shall be reviewed on a systematic basis for the purpose of accomplishing downgrading, declassification, transfer, retirement, and destruction at the earliest practicable date.

SECTION 7. IMPLEMENTATION AND REVIEW RESPONSIBILITIES

(A) The National Security Council shall monitor the implementation of this order. To assist the National Security Council, an Interagency Classification Review Committee shall be established, composed of representatives of the Departments of State, Defense, and Justice, the Atomic Energy Commission, the Central Intelligence Agency, and the National Security Council staff and a chairman designated by the President. Representatives of other departments in the executive branch may be invited to meet with the committee on matters of particular interest to those departments. This committee shall meet regularly and on a continuing basis shall review and take actions to insure compliance with this order, and in particular:

(1) The committee shall oversee department actions to insure compliance with the provisions of this order and implementing directives issued by the President through the National Security Council.

(2) The committee shall, subject to procedures to be established by it, receive, consider and take action on suggestions and complaints from persons within or without the Government with respect to the administration of this order, and in consultation with the affected department or departments assure that appropriate action is taken on such suggestions and complaints.

(3) Upon request of the committee chairman, any department shall furnish to the committee any particular information or material needed by the committee in carrying out its functions.

(B) To promote the basic purposes of this order, the head of each department originating or handling classified information or material shall:

(1) Prior to the effective date of this order submit to the Interagency Classification Review Committee for approval a copy of the regulations it proposes to adopt pursuant to this order.

(2) Designate a senior member of his staff who shall insure effective compliance with and implementation of this order and shall also chair a departmental committee which shall have authority to act on all suggestions and complaints with respect to the department's administration of this order.

(3) Undertake an initial program to familiarize the employees of his department with the provisions of this order. He shall also establish and maintain active training and orientation programs for employees concerned with classified information or material. Such programs shall include, as a minimum, the briefing of new employees and periodic reorientation during employment to impress upon each individual his responsibility for exercising vigilance and care in complying with the provisions of this order. Additionally, upon termination of employment or contemplated temporary separation for a 60-day period or more, employees shall be debriefed and each reminded of the provisions of the criminal code and other applicable provisions of law relating to penalties for unauthorized disclosure.

(C) The Attorney General, upon request of the head of a department, his duly designated representative, or the chairman of the above described committee, shall personally or through authorized representatives of the Department of Justice render an interpretation of this order with respect to any question arising in the course of its administration.

SECTION 8. MATERIAL COVERED BY THE ATOMIC ENERGY ACT

Nothing in this order shall supersede any requirements made by or under the Atomic Energy Act of August 30, 1954, as amended. "Restricted data," and material designated as "formerly restricted data," shall be handled, protected, classified, downgraded and declassified in conformity with the provisions of the Atomic Energy Act of 1954, as amended, and the regulations of the Atomic Energy Commission.

SECTION 9. SPECIAL DEPARTMENTAL ARRANGEMENTS

The originating department or other appropriate authority may impose, in conformity with the provisions of this order, special requirements with respect to access, distribution and protection of classified information and material, including those which presently relate to communications intelligence, intelligence sources and methods and cryptography.

SECTION 10. EXCEPTIONAL CASES

In an exceptional case when a person or department not authorized to classify information originates information which is believed to require classification, such person or department shall protect that information in the manner prescribed by this order. Such persons or department shall transmit the information forthwith, under appropriate safeguards, to the department having primary interest in the subject matter with a request that a determination be made as to classification.

SECTION 11. DECLASSIFICATION OF PRESIDENTIAL PAPERS

The Archivist of the United States shall have authority to review and declassify information and material which has been classified by a President, his White House staff or special committee or commission appointed by him and which the Archivist has in his custody at any archival depository, including a presidential library. Such declassification shall only be undertaken in accord with: (i) the terms of the donor's deed of gift, (ii) consultation with the departments having a primary subject-matter interest, and (iii) the provisions of section 5.

SECTION 12. HISTORICAL RESEARCH AND ACCESS BY FORMER GOVERNMENT OFFICIALS

The requirement in section 6(A) that access to classified information or material be granted only as is necessary for the performance of one's duties shall not apply to persons outside the executive branch who are engaged in historical research projects or who have previously occupied policymaking positions to which they were appointed by the President; *Provided*, however, that in each case the head of the originating department shall: (i) determine that access is clearly consistent with the interests of national security; and (ii) take appropriate steps to assure that classified information or material is not published or otherwise compromised.

Access granted a person by reason of his having previously occupied a policymaking position shall be limited to those papers which the former official originated, reviewed, signed or received while in public office.

SECTION 13. ADMINISTRATIVE AND JUDICIAL ACTION

(A) Any officer or employee of the United States who unnecessarily classifies or overclassifies information or material shall be notified that his actions are in violation of the terms of this order or of a directive of the President issued through the National Security Council. Repeated abuse of the classification process shall be grounds for an administrative reprimand. In any case where the departmental committee or the Interagency Classification Review Committee finds that unnecessary classification or overclassification has occurred, it shall make a report to the head of the department concerned in order that corrective steps may be taken.

(B) The head of each department is directed to take prompt and stringent administrative action against any officer or employee of the United States, at any level of employment, determined to have been responsible for any release or disclosure of national security information or material in a manner not authorized by or under this order or a directive of the President issued through the National Security Council. Where a violation of criminal statutes may be involved, departments will refer any such case promptly to the Department of Justice.

SECTION 14. REVOCATION OF EXECUTIVE ORDER NO. 10501

Executive Order No. 10501 of November 5, 1953, as amended by Executive Orders No. 10816 of May 8, 1959, No. 10901 of January 11, 1961, No. 10964 of September 20, 1961, No. 10985 of January 15, 1962, No. 11097 of March 6, 1963, and by section 1(a) of No. 11382 of November 28, 1967, are superseded as of the effective date of this order.

SECTION 15. EFFECTIVE DATE

This order shall become effective on June 1, 1972.

RICHARD NIXON.

MARCH 8, 1972.

THE WHITE HOUSE

ORDER

Pursuant to section 2(A) of the Executive order of March 8, 1972, entitled Classification and Declassification of National Security Information and Material, I hereby designate the following offices in the Executive Office of the President as possessing authority to originally classify information or material "top secret" as set forth in said order:

The White House Office.
National Security Council.
Office of Management and Budget.
Domestic Council.
Office of Science and Technology.
Office of Emergency Preparedness.
President's Foreign Intelligence Advisory Board.
Council on International Economic Policy.
Council of Economic Advisers.
National Aeronautics and Space Council.
Office of Telecommunications Policy.

RICHARD NIXON.

EXECUTIVE ORDER 11714 ([118], APRIL 24, 1973)

AMENDING EXECUTIVE ORDER NO. 11652 ON CLASSIFICATION AND DECLASSIFICATION OF NATIONAL SECURITY INFORMATION AND MATERIAL

By virtue of the authority vested in me by the Constitution and statutes of the United States, the second sentence of section 7(A) of Executive Order No. 11652 of March 8, 1972, is amended to read as follows:

"To assist the National Security Council, an Interagency Classification Review Committee shall be established, composed of a Chairman designated by the President, the Archivist of the United States, and representatives of the Departments of State, Defense and Justice, the Atomic Energy Commission, the Central Intelligence Agency and the National Security Council Staff."

RICHARD NIXON.

The White House,
April 24, 1973.

PRESIDENTIAL MESSAGE ON EXECUTIVE ORDER 11905 ([121], FEBRUARY 18, 1976)

EXECUTIVE ORDER PERTAINING TO ORGANIZATION AND CONTROL OF THE U.S. FOREIGN INTELLIGENCE COMMUNITY—MESSAGE FROM THE PRESIDENT OF THE UNITED STATES (H. DOC. NO. 94-374)

The SPEAKER pro tempore laid before the House the following message from the President of the United States; which was read and, together with the accompanying papers, without objection, referred to the Committee of the Whole House on the State of the Union, and ordered to be printed:

To the Congress of the United States:

By virtue of the authority vested in me by Article II, Sections 2 and 3 of the Constitution, and other provisions of law, I have today issued an Executive Order pertaining to the organization and control of the United States foreign intelligence community. This order establishes clear lines of accountability for the Nation's foreign intelligence agencies. It sets forth strict guidelines to control the activities of these agencies and specifies as well those activities in which they shall not engage.

In carrying out my Constitutional responsibilities to manage and conduct foreign policy and provide for the Nation's defense, I believe it essential to have the best possible intelligence about the capabilities, intentions and activities of governments and other entities and individuals abroad. To this end, the foreign intelligence agencies of the United States play a vital role in collecting and analyzing information related to the national defense and foreign policy.

It is equally as important that the methods these agencies employ to collect such information for the legitimate needs of the government conform to the standards set out in the Constitution to preserve and respect the privacy and civil liberties of American citizens.

The Executive Order I have issued today will insure a proper balancing of these interests. It establishes government-wide direction for the foreign intelligence agencies and places responsibility and accountability on individuals, not institutions.

I believe it will eliminate abuses and questionable activities on the part of the foreign intelligence agencies while at the same time permitting them to get on with their vital work of gathering and assessing information. It is also my hope that these steps will help to restore public confidence in these agencies and encourage our citizens to appreciate the valuable contribution they make to our national security.

Beyond the steps I have taken in the Executive Order, I also believe there is a clear need for some specific legislative actions. I am today submitting to the Congress of the United States proposals which will go far toward enhancing the protection of true intelligence secrets as well as regularizing procedures for intelligence collection in the United States.

My first proposal deals with the protection of intelligence sources and methods. The Director of Central Intelligence is charged, under the National Security Act of 1947, as amended, with protecting intelligence sources and methods. The Act, however, gives the Director no authorities commensurate with this responsibility.

Therefore, I am proposing legislation to impose criminal and civil sanctions on those who are authorized access to intelligence secrets and who willfully and wrongfully reveal this information. This legislation is not an "Official Secrets Act", since it would affect only those who improperly disclose secrets, not those to

whom secrets are disclosed. Moreover, this legislation could not be used to cover up abuses and improprieties. It would in no way prevent people from reporting questionable activities to appropriate authorities in the Executive and Legislative Branches of the government.

It is essential, however, that the irresponsible and dangerous exposure of our Nation's intelligence secrets be stopped. The American people have long accepted the principles of confidentiality and secrecy in many dealings—such as with doctors, lawyers and the clergy. It makes absolutely no sense to deny this same protection to our intelligence secrets. Openness is a hallmark of our democratic society, but the American people have never believed that it was necessary to reveal the secret war plans of the Department of Defense, and I do not think they wish to have true intelligence secrets revealed either.

I urge the adoption of this legislation with all possible speed.

Second, I support proposals that would clarify and set statutory limits, where necessary, on the activities of the foreign intelligence agencies. In particular, I will support legislation making it a crime to assassinate or attempt or conspire to assassinate a foreign official in peacetime. Since it defines a crime, legislation is necessary.

Third, I will meet with the appropriate leaders of Congress to try to develop sound legislation to deal with a critical problem involving personal privacy—electronic surveillance. Working with congressional leaders and the Justice Department and other executive agencies, we will seek to develop a procedure for undertaking electronic surveillance for foreign intelligence purposes. It should create a special procedure for seeking a judicial warrant authorizing the use of electronic surveillance in the United States for foreign intelligence purposes.

I will also seek congressional support for sound legislation to expand judicial supervision of mail openings. The law now permits the opening of U.S. mail, under proper judicial safeguards, in the conduct of criminal investigations. We need authority to open mail under the limitations and safeguards that now apply in order to obtain vitally needed foreign intelligence information.

This would require a showing that there is probable cause to believe that the sender or recipient is an agent of a foreign power who is engaged in spying, sabotage or terrorism. As is now the case in criminal investigations, those seeking authority to examine mail for foreign intelligence purposes will have to convince a federal judge of the necessity to do so and accept the limitations upon their authorization to examine the mail provided in the order of the court.

Fourth, I would like to share my views regarding appropriate Congressional oversight of the foreign intelligence agencies. It is clearly the business of the Congress to organize itself to deal with these matters. Certain principles, however, should be recognized by both the Executive and Legislative Branches if this oversight is to be effective. I believe good Congressional oversight is essential so that the Congress and the American people whom you represent can be assured that the foreign intelligence agencies are adhering to the law in all of their activities.

Congress should seek to centralize the responsibility for oversight of the foreign intelligence community. The more committees and subcommittees dealing with highly sensitive secrets, the greater the risks of disclosure. I recommend that Congress establish a Joint Foreign Intelligence Oversight Committee. Consolidating Congressional oversight in one committee will facilitate the efforts of the Administration to keep the Congress fully informed of foreign intelligence activities.

It is essential that both the House and the Senate establish firm rules to insure that foreign intelligence secrets will not be improperly disclosed. There must be established a clear process to safeguard these secrets and effective measures to deal with unauthorized disclosures.

Any foreign intelligence information transmitted by the Executive Branch to the Oversight Committee, under an injunction of secrecy, should not be unilaterally disclosed without my agreement. Respect for the integrity of the Constitution requires adherence to the principle that no individual member, nor committee, nor single House of Congress can overrule an act of the Executive. Unilateral publication of classified information over the objection of the President, by one committee or one House of Congress, not only violates the doctrine of separation of powers, but also effectively overrules the actions of the other House of Congress, and perhaps even the majority of both Houses.

Finally, successful and effective Congressional oversight of the foreign intelligence agencies depends on mutual trust between the Congress and Executive. Each branch must recognize and respect the rights and prerogatives of the other if anything is to be achieved.

In this context, a Congressional requirement to keep the Oversight Committee "fully" informed is more desirable and workable as a practical matter than formal requirements for notification of specific activities to a large number of committees. Specifically, Section 662 of the Foreign Assistance Act, which has resulted in over six separate committee briefings, should be modified as recommended by the Commission on the Organization of the Government for the Conduct of Foreign Policy, and reporting should be limited to the new Oversight Committee.

Both the Congress and the Executive Branch recognize the importance to this Nation of a strong intelligence service. I believe it urgent that we take the steps I have outlined above to insure that America not only has the best foreign intelligence service in the world, but also the most unique—one which operates in a manner fully consistent with the Constitutional rights of our citizens.

GERALD R. FORD.
THE WHITE HOUSE, *February 18, 1976.*

Appendix 5
Abstracts

```
┌─────────────────────────────────────────────┐
│              ABSTRACTS OF                     │
│           DOCUMENTS RELEASED                  │
│                 UNDER                         │
│      THE FREEDOM OF INFORMATION ACT           │
│              RELATING TO                      │
│   FOREIGN POLICY AND NATIONAL DEFENSE         │
└─────────────────────────────────────────────┘
```

Contents

I.   Documents released as a result of requests from
       the Project on National Security and Civil
       Liberties

II.   Selected documents released to others

III.   Ordering copies of documents from federal agencies

IV.   Ordering copies of documents from the Project

V.   Project Publications (Addendum of Documents)

September 1976

The PROJECT ON NATIONAL SECURITY AND CIVIL LIBERTIES is
sponsored jointly by the American Civil Liberties Union
Foundation and the Center for National Security Studies
of the Fund for Peace.

122 Maryland Avenue, N.E., Washington, D.C. 20002 . . .
(202)544-5380

Note: These Abstracts are reprinted from [125].

I.   DOCUMENTS RELEASED AS A RESULT OF REQUESTS FROM THE PROJECT
     ON NATIONAL SECURITY AND CIVIL LIBERTIES

A.   Department of Defense

     A-1   Negotiating Volumes of the Pentagon Papers, Vols. VI.C.
           1-4, "Settlement of the Conflict," Vietnam Task Force,
           Office of the Secretary of Defense, (Top Secret, declas-
           sified with numerous deletions on March 10, 1975),
           c. 700 pgs.

           The Negotiating Volumes of the Pentagon Papers were not
           available to the New York Times and are not included in
           any of the published versions of the Papers (Bantam,
           Beacon, or Government Printing Office). The volumes
           contain documents and cables from 1965-1968 reporting
           on various negotiating tracks. There is some summary
           and analysis. Released with pages deleted.

     A-2   Secretary of Defense Annual Posture Statement Section
           regarding Soviet and Chinese Strategic Capability (De-
           fense Programs and Budgets, 1963-1977), (Secret, de-
           classified with certain data deleted on June 26, 1975),
           11 documents totaling 195 pgs. (illegible portion)

           The previously classified sections of the posture state-
           ments relate to the nuclear strike capability of China
           and the Soviet Union vis à vis the United States and her
           allies, including estimates of future capabilities and
           deployments. Statistics, charts and graphs are provided
           indicating American strategic capability (i.e. in terms
           of IBMs, bombers, MIRV, etc.) and assessments are given
           of the opponent's capabilities.

     A-3   The 1958 Taiwan Straits Crisis: A Documented History by
           Morton H. Halperin, Memorandum RM-4900 ISA, December
           1966, (Top Secret, declassified with numerous deletions
           on June 13, 1975), 619 pgs.

           An in-depth study of the Taiwan Straits crisis with an
           emphasis on the decision-making process in Washington
           and by the American military in the field.

B.   Department of State

     B-3   Secretary of State Kissinger "Backgrounders" on SALT

           1)   December 3, 1974, Washington D.C., (For background
                use only. Released with four deletions totalling 44
                lines), 28 pgs.

                A discussion prior to an upcoming press conference.
                The five major issues which Kissinger isolated were
                1) total aggregates 2) limitations on MIRV 3) is-
                sue of forward-bases 4) British and French nuclear
                forces 5) Soviet compensation for their more vul-
                nerable geographic position.

─────────────────────────────

     The letter designations of these documents are those of the
     Project on National Security and Civil Liberties.

2)   Backgrounders given to the travelling press on a
     Tokyo-Peking flight, reported in a Department of
     State telegram, Peking 02087, November 1974 (Limited
     Offical Use, declassified in toto), 4 pgs.

B-4   Secretary of State Kissinger "Backgrounders" on the
      Middle East since October 2, 1975:

a)   A January 17, 1975 Luncheon Speech by Secretary
     Kissinger, The Madison Hotel, sponsored by Time,
     Inc. News Tours, (Confidential -- NODIS, declassi-
     fied with deletions on June 17, 1975), 33 pgs.

     Kissinger presents anecdotes, incidents and obser-
     vations about the Middle East situation and his own
     shuttle diplomacy. He states that the overwhelming
     political issue is "the Arab-Israeli conflict and
     the eventual solution by means of negotiation," and
     indicates he prefers the "step by step approach"
     rather than "throwing all the issues into one grand
     negotiation." He refers to his remark about the
     possible use of force by the United States in the
     Middle East, explaining that he was only referring
     to a "case of actual strangulation of the indus-
     trialized (world)."

b)   January 25, 1974 Department of State Memorandum of
     Conversation, Secretary of State Kissinger to Wash-
     ington Star journalists, (Confidential, declassi-
     fied with deletions), 6 pgs.

     Kissinger reports on recent Middle East trip, where
     he saw for the first time "how a real settlement in
     the area could be achieved."

c)   February 5, 1974 Memorandum of Conversation, Kis-
     singer to Time magazine editors, (Confidential,
     declassified with deletions), 9 pgs.

     Kissinger discussed questions about the Middle East,
     the oil embargo, staffmember David Young and other
     Watergate-related issues, and China.

d)   February 28, 1974 Background briefing, (Confiden-
     tial, declassified with deletions), 20 pgs.

     Kissinger discusses the release of the list of
     Israeli prisoners from the Syrians, the oil embargo,
     and Red Cross arrangements in the Middle East.

B-5   Department of State, Briefing Paper, February 22, 1973,
      "Interpretations of the Agreement on Ending the War and
      Restoring Peace in Vietnam," (Secret, declassified in
      toto on May 6, 1975), 13 pgs.

The report presents a point-by-point clarification of
certain articles of the Vietnam Peace Agreements, dis-
cussing such issues as the halting of aerial reconnais-
sance, troop withdrawal, base dismantlement, prisoners

of war, etc. Several paragraphs originally marked "secret" consider 'grey areas' in the language of the agreements which might be open for varied interpretation, and suggest the position the United States should take. For example, our negotiators left vague those passages dealing with the transfer of title in taking equipment out of the country. They feared making their intentions clear for fear of "running an unacceptable risk that the North Vietnamese would object and make the issue a major one in the negotiations." They felt a reasonable case could be made for our point of view, but they anticipated that the other side would "press the issue."

B-8 Documents related to American assurances to the Government of South Vietnam regarding American responses to violations of the cease-fire agreement:

a) February 10, 1973 Department of State telegram (26126), "International Conference on Vietnam," (Secret/NODIS, declassified in toto on May 30, 1975), 2 pgs.

The telegram reports a conversation between Vietnamese Ambassador Phuong and Assistant Secretary Green in which the topics included the conference chairmanship and the conference's lack of punitive power should the agreements be transgressed by either party.

b) February 15, 1973 Department of State telegram (2295), "Sullivan's Meeting with Thieu, February 14, 1973," signed Sullivan and Bunker, (Secret/NODIS, declassified and released in toto on May 30, 1975), 4 pgs.

Sullivan, Bunker, and Thieu discuss economic assistance -- Thieu felt the United States should use it "as a lever" on North Vietnam; Sullivan warns Thieu to keep up his claim that the communists were the ones obstructing peace efforts, or United States public opinion would discourage further aid to Vietnam.

Also discussed were the questions of POWs, civilian detainees, North Vietnamese tank movements (which Thieu saw as their safeguard should the agreements not be implemented), and the creation of a National Council in South Vietnam. Sullivan notes that the "real guarantees for peace" were US air power, economic aid to North Vietnam and the Chinese/Russian split over Vietnam.

c) State Department Airgram, "Background Material on Vietnam Cease-fire Implementation," December 21, 1973 (Confidential), 4 pgs.

The memo details the areas in which the department believes the communists have transgressed the pro-

visions of the Paris Accords, specifically citing
the continued fighting, the non-cooperation of the
communists in the International Commission of Con-
trol and Supervision (CCS), the stalemate in a
political settlement, the illegal movement of mili-
tary men and material southwards, and their un-
willingness to cooperate in investigations of MIAs.

C.   Central Intelligence Agency

C-1   Colby Report: a letter to the President, December 24,
1974 (unclassified, released July 8, 1975) 6 pg. letter
with 58 pgs. of attachments.

The report is response to a December 22 article in the
New York Times revealing CIA domestic intelligence
activities, to which numerous appendices are attached:

Annex A: An August 15 memorandum establishing a counter-
intelligence office "to identify possible foreign links
with American dissident elements." 2 pgs.

Annex B: Cable of November 3, 1967 from CIA headquarters
to CIA addressees establishing an interagency program to
deal with the abovementioned links. 2 pgs.

Annex C: A memorandum of September 1969 stating that the
program of counterintelligence was deemed to be proper.
2 pgs.

Annex D: A CIA project (June 1, 1972) of coordination
with the FBI, CIA and NSA known as the Huston Plan,
which integrated the government's "coverage of domestic
unrest." More specifically the program was to collect
and disseminate information "on foreign exploitation of
domestic dissidence and extremism." Annex D contains
directives for the Special Operations Group of the CIA.
Though the plan was not carried out, an agency was
created, the Interagency Evaluation Committee, chaired
by Robert Mardian, through which the CIA continued "its
counterintelligence interest in possible foreign links
with American dissidents." 11 pgs.

Annex E: Colby internal memorandum of April 1972 clari-
fying the legal scope of CIA activity, reiterating that
the CIA's jurisdiction does not lie within the United
States. (For Distribution to Office/Division Chief Level
Only), 4 pgs.

Annex F: A May 9, 1973 bulletin from Director Schle-
singer requesting employees to report any activities
outside the CIA Charter (Administrative-Internal Use
Only), 2 pgs.

Annex G: An August 29, 1973 memo re-emphasizing that the
focus of the counterintelligence program was to be on
foreign organizations, 4 pgs.

Annex H: A March 5, 1974 memo from the Director terminating the counterintelligence program, and indicating that any future intelligence would only be gathered on Americans abroad, in coordination with the FBI. (unclassified, with deletions from original classified version), 3 pgs.

Annex I: Colby also included miscellaneous memoranda which were relevant in terms of the allegations in the New York Times article which prompted the release of the Colby Report. Some of the topics of the diverse memoranda include: "Questionable Activities," "Care in Relation to Significant Domestic Events," "Audio Surveillance," "CHAOS," "Restriction on Files of American Citizens," "Restrictions on Operational Lists on Americans," "U.S. Citizens Involved in Narcotics Abroad," "Testing of Equipment in U.S.," "Influencing Human Behavior," "Postal Service," "OEC Speech-Processing Assistance" plus numerous memoranda concerning unidentified "Cryptonymn Projects." (Most memoranda are 1 pg. in length, some are 2 pgs., total pgs. in Annex I: 25 pgs.

C-5   A series of files referenced in a statement by Director Colby before the Senate Appropriations Committee:

a) Organization and Functions, Domestic Operations and Station, February 11, 1963 (Secret, declassified in toto on April 22, 1975), 1 pg.

The mission of the DODS is described as directing, supporting and coordinating "clandestine operational activities . . . within the United States against foreign targets . . ."

b) Redesignation of Component, January 28, 1972 (Secret, declassified April 22, 1975), 1 pg.

An inner-agency memo from Thomas Karamessines, Deputy Director for Plans, which officially announces the change in the name of the Domestic Operations Division (D.O.) to Foreign Resources Division (F.R.)

c) A letter dated August 29, 1967 from David Ginsburg, Executive Director of the National Advisory Commission on Civil Disorders requests a meeting with a CIA representative who can brief the Commission on any civil disorder intelligence the Agency might have. Richard Helms, Director of the CIA, responds in a letter dated 1 September 1967 that a representative will be sent and that although the CIA does not "have direct responsibility for domestic security and therefore (does) not conduct . . . the kinds of activities (in the United States) which could produce (the needed) information." Some "limited material . . . from abroad" could, in Helm's opinion, "conceivably be of interest." (released March 8, 1975), 3 pgs.

d) "Restless Youth," September 1968, No. 0613/68, 41 pgs.

The report analyzes the youth movement of the late 1960s internationally, studies its sociological base, and attempts to understand its structure, purpose, goals and possible ramifications. The report cites the Civil Rights Movement of the early 1960s as proving to the young dissidents later in the decade that confrontation politics is the only means for political change. It notes that student demonstrations are "calculated to dramatize an issue and attract public notice" and that their issues are often amorphous and ad hoc. Significantly, the report states that "there is no convincing evidence of control, manipulation, sponsorship, or significant financial support of the student dissidents by any international Communist authority."

The report suggests that an attempt to marshall the Young Republicans and Young Democrats as a counterforce to the radical groups would prove ineffective. The report estimates that about 120,000 out of 6.3 million American college students are political activists---with 30,000 to 35,000 of the 120,000 described as "hard core." The "largest and most vocal" student group is the Students for Democratic Society (SDS), and the report studies this organization in some detail.

The report notes that SDS fell out of favor with journalists and academicians when it appeared it had developed "tolerant views of institutional communism." The report feels that the end of the Vietnam War would most probably "cause dissidence to subside, but not disappear." It concludes that there exists a new self-consciousness among youth as 'a group which will shape their political conduct.

e) Memorandum for all CIA Employees, May 9, 1973, from James R. Schlesinger, Director, (Administrative - Internal Use Only), 10 pgs.

The Director requests that all CIA personnel report to him any past or present activities which lie outside the Agency's charter, and also announces that if an order is given to a CIA employee in the future which is inconsistent with the charter, the employee should report this occurrence to the Director.

C-6 Delimitation Agreement of 1948, consisting of a letter dated 22 September 1948, from Frank G. Wisner, Assistant Director for Policy Coordination (CIA) to Mr. D. Milton Ladd, Assistant to the Director, FBI (sanitized copy); a letter from J. Edgar Hoover to Mr. Wisner dated October 2, 1948; and a memorandum for the Record "Cooperation and Liaison between Federal Bureau of Investigation and Office of Policy Coordination," CIA, dated 22 September 1948, (released May 8, 1975), 7 pgs.

The documents taken together constitute an agreement between the FBI and the CIA permitting the CIA to operate in the United States, particularly with certain emigre groups.

C-8 "Potential Flap Activities." Memo to William Colby from William V. Broe, Inspector General covering "activities that are or might be illegal or that could cause the Agency embarrassment if they were exposed." Memo dated 21 May 1973. (Released with numerous deletions), 26 pgs.

The first portion of the Memo includes contacts with Watergate figures CIA personnel detailed to other executive offices, and CIA participation on the Intelligence Evaluation Committee and Staff (IES), headed by John Dean, for evaluating domestic intelligence studies. The second portion of the Memo covers Support, Real Estate, Procurement, Cover, Activities Directed Against U.S. Citizens, and Collection Activities. "Support" includes police training by CIA; "Real Estate" concerns rental of the safehouse used in a July 1971 liaison between Hunt and a CIA representative. "Activities Directed Against U.S. Citizens" details studies on the SDS, student unrest (Restless Youth) and black radicalism. CIA Operations enumerated under "Collection," some dating to as early as 1963, include: MOCKINGBIRD, CELOTEX I and II, BUTANE, SRPOINTER, REDFACE I, MERRIMAC, CHAOS. Support to the Metropolitan Police Department, the Bureau of Narcotics and Dangerous Drugs, and other Government agencies are detailed.

D. National Security Council

D-1 National Security Council Intelligence Directives 1947–1972, 87 pgs., incomplete and some deletions.

The NSCID's form the basis of the intelligence agencies' "secret charter." They assign the operational duties and responsibilities not explicitly authorized in the 1947 National Security Act. A version of NSCID 7 (1948) for example, is entitled "Domestic Exploitation" and makes clear that soon after Congress was assured that the CIA would operate only abroad, it began operating at home. Other NSCID titles included are "Coordination of Intelligence Production," "Signals Intelligence," and "United States Espionage and Counter-Intelligence Activities Abroad."

Of the NSCID's now in effect, the texts of numbers 1,2,3,5, and portions of 6 and 8 are included.

D-2 "United States Objectives and Programs for National Security," A Report to the National Security Council, by James S. Lay, Jr., Executive Secretary, (NSC-68), April 14, 1950 (released February 27, 1975), 66 pgs.

A lengthy report commissioned by President Truman as "a re-examination of our objectives in peace and war and of the effect of these objectives on our strategic plans, in the light of the probable fission bomb capability and possible thermonuclear bomb capability of the Soviet Union." The report provides a background to the present world tensions, a discussion of the purpose of the United States and the Kremlin in dealing with these tensions, and their "intentions and capabilities--actual and potential." The final chapter proposes possible courses of action--negotiation, isolation, war or "a rapid build-up of political, economic, and military strength in the free world." After the outbreak of the Korean War, the report served as a blueprint for American rearmament.

D-3   "Skybolt and Nassau: American Policy Making and Anglo-American Relations," Richard E. Neustadt, November 15, 1963, Report to the President (Top Secret, released with deletions on April 23, 1975), 132 pgs.

The report is a discussion of the breakdown in relations between the United States and Britain centering on the American decision to cancel the Skybolt missile project. Neustadt blames the breakdown of communication on a failure "to seek and obtain feedback"; specifically, on "the failure to assure that Britain's defense posture and Anglo-American cooperation rested on a rationale which could be justified on technical and military terms . . . as well as in implicit terms of domestic and diplomatic politics." The study was prepared by Richard Neustadt at the personal request of the President.

II.   SELECTED DOCUMENTS RELEASED TO OTHERS

A.   Department of Defense

Report of the Chairman, Joint Chiefs of Staff, on the Situation in Vietnam and MACV Force Requirements, (a.k.a. The Wheeler Report), February 27, 1968 (Top Secret, released March 19, 1975), 82 pgs.

Report by General Earle Wheeler, Chairman Joint Chiefs of Staff, of his trip to Vietnam following the TET offensive of 1968. Includes General Westmoreland's recommendation for 206,000 additional troops.

B.   Department of State

Documents related to American Decision to Intervene in the Korean War (1950):

a)   Memorandum of Conversation: the President and Cabinet members and military leaders, Subject: "The Korean Situation," June 25, 1950 (Top Secret--Limited Distribution, declassified on August 18, 1972), 6 pgs.

A discussion of what should be done in Korea and Formosa, the possibility of war with the USSR & the military strength of the USSR. The following memorandum was also read to those assembled:

b)   Memorandum on Formosa, Douglas MacArthur, 14 June 1950, (Top Secret) 5 pgs.

McArthur notes the threat of the Chinese Communists vis
à vis the island of Formosa, and stresses that the stra-
tegic interests of the United States would be "in seri-
ous jeopardy" if Formosa were overtaken. Formosa is
vital, according to the memorandum, in terms of its geo-
graphic and strategic importance to our defense, its
location in our sphere of influence (Japan-Okinawa-
Philippines), its potential for base installations, and
its value to the USSR as "an additional fleet" to re-
place the expensive equivalent of ten or twenty air-
craft carriers. MacArthur also notes that Formosa is a
food exporter and therefore has an important role to
play in assisting the depressed economies of its Asian
neighbors.

MacArthur sees our interest in Formosa insofar as it is
the "line (which must) be drawn beyond which Communist
expansion will be stopped." He recommends that "an im-
mediate survey of the need and extent of the military
assistance required in Formosa in order to hold Formosa
against attack" must be undertaken in order to make a
realistic assessment of the area.

c)   "The Korean Situation," Department of State Memorandum
     of Conversation, between the President and Secretaries
     Acheson, Johnson, Pace and Finletter, and Generals
     Bradley, Vandenberg and Collins, and Admiral Sherman,
     June 26, 1950 (Top Secret - Limited Distribution, de-
     classified in toto on August 18, 1972), 8 pgs.

     A discussion held shortly before the outbreak of the
     Korean War which centered on the support the American
     forces should provide to the South Koreans, the orders
     to be given to the Seventh Fleet to prevent an attack
     on Formosa, the need to accelerate aid to the Philip-
     pines in order to "have a firm base there," the support
     we could expect from the international community in our
     pending actions in Korea, and the possibility of mobi-
     lizing the National Guard. Also discussed was the up-
     coming UN Security Council meeting and the possible
     Russian response.

d)   "Notes on Meeting in Cabinet Room at the White House,"
     Department of State Memorandum of Conversation, between
     the President and the Secretaries of State and Defense,
     June 27, 1950 (Top Secret, declassified in toto on
     August 8, 1972), 4 pgs.

     Discussed is what support can be expected from others
     with regard to the pending situation in the Far East--it
     is noted that no help from France could be expected.
     The President makes a statement which indicates that the
     United States was now committed to defend South Korea
     from invasion. The point is emphasized that the United
     States was acting in support of the U.N.

C.   Central Intelligence Agency

CC-9 National Intelligence Estimates relating to the Cuban
     Missile Crisis (1962):

   a   "The Military Build-up In Cuba," Special National Intel-
       ligence Estimate, Number 85-3-62, (CIA-sanitized copy),
       9 pgs.

       The paper perceives the problem as assessing the stra-
       tegic and political implications of the Soviet military
       buildup in Cuba, which it states is taking place so as
       to strengthen the Communist regime there against the
       threat of an American overthrow. The military implica-
       tions of the buildup are that the air and coastal defense
       capabilities of Cuba have been improved; the political
       significance is that Castro is assured of remaining in
       power. The conclusion the report draws from these fac-
       tors is that Cuba will become "emboldened" to foment
       revolutionary activity in Latin America.

       The report provides a history of the military build-up,
       discusses its implications, and notes that the possibil-
       ities exist for an expansion of the buildup. The assess-
       ment is that the establishment of Soviet nuclear strik-
       ing capability on Cuban soil aimed at the U.S. is "in-
       compatible with Soviet policy" as the report perceives
       it, though the possibility should not be entirely dis-
       counted. A Soviet submarine base in Cuba would be of
       enormous value to the U.S.S.R., the report indicates.

   b   "Soviet Reactions to Certain U.S. Courses of Action on
       Cuba," 19 October 1962, (sanitized copy), 11 pgs.

       The problem defined is "to estimate probable Soviet
       reactions to certain U.S. courses of action with respect
       to Cuba." The report states that the Soviet objective
       in their military buildup in Cuba is to prove that the
       U.S. can no longer prevent the Soviet presence in its
       hemisphere. If the U.S. accepts the strategic missile
       buildup, its influence would decline and there would be
       a "loss of confidence in U.S. power and determination."

       The report considers the effect of warning either the
       U.S.S.R. or Cuba about its knowledge of the MRBM deploy-
       ment, which would probably result in a demand for nego-
       tiations on their part, and "degrade the element of
       surprise in a subsequent U.S. attack." It predicts that
       a blockade would not bring down the Castro regime and
       states that the Soviets would exploit all adverse reac-
       tions to such a U.S. move.

       The Soviet reaction to the use of military force by the
       U.S. is also considered, as it would be a threat to
       U.S.S.R. prestige and might "escalate to general war."
       The Soviets could respond by pretending that the attack

does not directly involve them since their bases in Cuba
have been unacknowledged, but they most probably would
consider "retaliatory actions outside Cuba," most likely
in Berlin.

Annex A considers the "Difference between Soviet Re-
sponses to a Blockade and U.S. Measures of Force Against
Cuba." It posits that the chances are greater that the
Soviets would respond by use of force if the U.S. used
force in Cuba than if the Americans chose to retaliate
with a blockade, in which case the Soviet response would
be expected to "concentrate on political exploitation,
especially in the U.N." In the case of a blockade, the
appendix concludes that the Soviets would not "resort to
major force."

Annex B considers the "Military Significance of Ballistic
Missiles In Cuba," summarizing in its conclusion that
"Soviet gross capabilities for inital attack on (the
U.S.) can be increased considerably by Cuba-based mis-
siles." (one sentence deletion within Annex B)

c "Major Consequences of Certain U.S. Courses of Action on
Cuba," 20 October 1962, (sanitized copy), 10 pgs.

The report details the status of the Soviet military
build-up in Cuba, outlines its purpose, notes the re-
sults of acquiescence to the build-up (the Soviets will
continue it further, the loss of confidence in the U.S.)
and discusses the effect of warning (Soviets would pro-
pose negotiations). The two alternative forms of block-
ade are presented (total and selective), and the Soviet
response to the use of military force is discussed. (It
would be greater than in the case of the blockade.) The
report concludes that whatever course of action is taken,
the Soviets would not respond by deliberately initiating
general war.

D. National Security Council

DD-1 A Report to the National Security Council, by Sidney W.
Souers, Executive Secretary, "Coordination of Foreign
Information Measures," December 9, 1947, NSC 4 (Confi-
dential downgraded to restricted, declassified on March
17, 1975), 6 pgs.

The report defines the problem as a need to find ways
"to strengthen and coordinate all foreign information
measures of the U.S. government." To counter Soviet
anti-American propaganda, the report says that the U.S.
government should create a new position--an Assistant
Secretary of State for Public Affairs--to accomplish the
aforementioned. In the appendix, the existing facilities
in the field of foreign information in the Departments
of State, Army, Navy and Air Force are listed.

E.   National Archives

> The Gaither Committee Report: "Deterrence and Survival
> in the Nuclear Age," Report to the President, Security
> Resources Panel of the Science Advisory Committee, Of-
> fice of Defense Mobilization, November 7, 1957 (Top
> Secret, declassified January 29, 1973), 34 pgs.
>
> The report calls for a substantial increase in defense
> spending with first priority to reducing the vulnerabil-
> ity of strategic forces. Improvements in general pur-
> pose forces and a fall-out shelter program are
> recommended.

III. ORDERING DOCUMENTS FROM AGENCIES

Copies of the above documents can be obtained from the
agencies which released them (addresses below) by making a
request under the Freedom of Information Act. The Project on
National Security and Civil Liberties has published a pamph-
let explaining the procedures for making requests under the
Act; . . . . Agencies generally charge a fee for reproduc-
tion; some agencies will also charge a search fee.

> DEPARTMENT OF DEFENSE:
> Directorate of Freedom of Information
> Office of the Assistant Secretary of
>   Defense (Public Affairs)
> Room 2C757, The Pentagon
> Washington, DC 20301
>
> DEPARTMENT OF STATE:
> Director, Freedom of Information Staff TA/FOI
> Room 5835, Department of State
> Washington, DC 20520
>
> CENTRAL INTELLIGENCE AGENCY:
> Freedom of Information Coordinator
> Central Intelligence Agency
> Washington, DC 20505
>
> NATIONAL SECURITY COUNCIL:
> Staff Secretary
> National Security Council
> 374 Old Executive Office Building
> Washington, DC 20506
>
> NATIONAL ARCHIVES:
> Freedom of Information Act Request
> Office of the National Archives
> Washington, DC 20408

IV. ORDERING DOCUMENTS FROM THE PROJECT

Copies of the above documents are also available from the
Project on National Security and Civil Liberties; use the
order blank . . . . Orders are prepaid. Please don't forget
to fill out the mailing labels . . . .

ORDER BLANK

V. ADDENDUM OF DOCUMENTS

A-10 Delimination Agreement of February 23, 1949 Including
Amendments and Supplements To Date (8 pages)

This agreement spells out the boundaries of investigative
responsibilities of the F.B.I., The Office of Naval Intel-
ligence, Intelligence Division of The Army, and the Office
of Special Investigation, Inspector General, U.S. Air Force
over "espionage, counter-espionage, subversion and sabo-
tage." The documents specify how these agencies should
coordinate their efforts.

Appendix A is an agreement as to areas of responsibility
during a "Period of Martial Law."

Appendix B specifies the "investigative jurisdiction"
of these agencies during "periods of predominent mili-
tary interest, not involving martial law."

"Supplemental Agreements" among the "subscribing agencies"
concern investigative responsibilities over "Private Con-
tractors of the Armed Forces," and "Civilian Components
of the Armed Services."

CC-15 The C.I.A. and Local Police, (177 pages) (numerous
deletions of individual names and locations)

A series of memos and letters concerning direct CIA assis-
tance to 12 municipal and/or county police departments in-
cluding New York's, Los Angeles's, Boston's, and Washing-
ton's.

The documents, dating from 1967-1975, trace the history
of CIA training seminars in photo and audio surveillance,
narcotics and "radical terrorist" control, and in other
investigative skills such as "lock and pick" techniques.
There is, in addition, documentation of CIA loans of equip-
ment as well as personnel (posing as Federal Law Enforce-
ment Assistance "consultants") to local law enforcement
officials.

The documents are available, free, through the CIA.

CC-16 Secret Legislative History of The CIA (143 pages)

These documents reveal the secret Congressional testimony
of the first two Directors of Central Intelligence, Lt. Gen-
eral Hoyt S. Vandenberg and Rear Admiral R. H. Hillenkoetter.

The Hillenkoetter testimony was presented to the House Armed
Services Committee in April, 1948 in support of the CIA Act which
Congress passed in 1949.

Director Hillenkoetter's testimony presents a picture of the
problems which the fledgling intelligence agency faced in its
first two years. Yet the need to conceal the Agency's appropri-
ations and expenditures was foremost among the authorities which

the Director sought. Hillenkoetter also stated that the Agency
needed authority to contract for services without the usual re-
quirement that such contracts be advertised.

Mitchell Rogovin, Special Counsel to the CIA has recently told
Congress that the Hillenkoetter testimony dealt with the CIA's
need for statutory authority to do research in areas such as
explosives and psychological war fare. Presumably, this is dis-
cussed in the deleted portions.

The Vandenberg testimony was presented to the Senate Armed Serv-
ices Committee in April 1947 in support of the National Secur-
ity Act of 1947 which provided for unification of the armed serv-
ices and establishment of the CIA.

Most of the testimony had been made public in 1947, but this
newly released document contains several paragraphs which were dele-
ted from the published hearing records.

Vandenberg's testimony includes comments on the need for CIA
authorization to engage in clandestine foreign intelligence,
and an account of how the German, Japanese, and Italian war ef-
forts had been impaired by the failure of these nations to devel-
op centralized intelligence organizations.

DD-5 "Responsibility For Paramilitary Operations." National
Security Council Action Memorandum No. 57, June 28, 1961. (2
pages)

This memo, drawn up by National Security Advisor McGeorge Bundy
and approved by President Kennedy, sought to define the purpose
of and responsibility for conducting paramilitary operations
"with maximum effectiveness and flexibility within the context
of the Cold War."

Bundy defines a paramilitary operation as a "conventional mili-
tary operation" except that it may be conducted "overtly, covert-
ly, or by a combination of both methods." Paramilitary assis-
tance may vary from a simple "infiltration of guerillas" to a
Bay of Pigs type invasion, and may be offered to both pro-
U.S. governments as well as to pro-U.S. rebels "seeking
to overthrow a government."

The memo recommends that the Defense Department receive
responsibility fo overt paramilitary operations while the
CIA should handle any operation which is "wholly covert
or disavowable."

CC-17 The Death of Frank Olson

These are the documents provided by the CIA to the family
of Dr. Frank Olson, the government biochemist who died
in November, 1953 when he jumped from a tenth story win-
dow.

The documents trace the CIA's investigation of the Olson
death as well as its involvement over the years with
drug experimentation. Although previously classified

"secret" they were declassified before given to the Olsons
in 1975. The release followed the Rockefeller Commis-
sion's disclosure of an "LSD suicide" as the result of a
secret CIA test on unsuspecting persons.

The 66 memos, reports, and statements, including an affa-
davit by the CIA inspector general affirming their com-
pleteness, indicate the following:
  1. The CIA drug test was part of a program conducted
from 1953 to 1963, when it was discovered by the CIA
inspector general and stopped. Yet as late as 1973,
the CIA was still involved with drug related experiments
in the "influencing of human behavior."
  2. Frank Olson was experimented upon illegally and
negligently although the agency maintains that "the ex-
periment was (not) part of any formal project."
  3. The true nature of Olson's death was concealed
for 22 years; the official explanation for his "suicide"
being "the occupational hazard to his mental stabil-
ity" incurred in his work.

Copies are obtainable through the Olsons' counsel,
Kairys and Rudkovsky, 1427 Walnut St., Philadelphia, PA,
19102

CC-18 Oswald And The Cuban Connection (27 pages; portions,
including names, deleted)

This report represents a review of items in the CIA's
Lee Harvey Oswald File "regarding allegations of Castro
Cuban involvement in the John F. Kennedy assassination."
The analysis was requested by the Rockefeller Commission.

The report seek s, in part, to explain the background of
of Oswald's "feelings toward and relations with Castro's Cuba."
Attention is paid to the significance of a bitter anti-Kennedy
speech made by Castro in September, 1963, as well as of "enig-
matic threats" made by a Cuban official in the Netherlands just
prior to the assasination."

The report focuses on the testimony of Nelson Delgado, who alleged
that a Cuban contact with Oswald existed as early as 1959. Also
discussed are the allegations of "conspiratorial contacts" be-
tween Oswald and the Cuban Consulate in Mexico City.

While asserting that some of these allegations have "the cast
of credibility," the report concludes that "there is no incre-
ment of credible evidence...of Soviet and/or Cuban involvement
in the assassination." But it is clear that the CIA has never
considered this "aspect of the case" closed.

C-9 Studies In Intelligence (130 pages, 24 articles. Other
articles are currently under review and may become available
if released.)

This is a classified publication circulated throughout the intelligence community. This collection of 24 articles from the complete publication, 13 of which are book reviews, provides an interesting view of how the intelligence community regards outside debate on its role and its activities. The book reviews discuss, at times in some detail, how independent authors often misperceive the nature of CIA capabilities and its modus operendi. Other articles deal with the conflicting priorities of secret intelligence gathering and an open society, and react to public debates on other intelligence issues.

C-10 The CIA And Assassination Plots (183 pages; numerous deletions)

A series of 74 letters, cables, and memos concerning CIA analyses of or participation in assassination plots involving foreign leaders. Documents relating to plots against Trujillo, Sukarno, Castro and Che Guevara are included, as well as more recent CIA estimates of the Mafia-Cuban connection and the death of President Kennedy.

DD-6 "The Central Intelligence Agency and National Organization For Intelligence," The Dulles-Jackson-Correa Report of 1949. (193 pages with annexes; deletions)

This report was commissioned by President Truman and the National Security Council as a "comprhensive...study of the organization, activities, and personnel of the CIA," then in its second year of operation. The report, which is critical in tone, concludes that the crucial task assigned to the CIA - to coordinate and "nationalize" U.S. intelligence activities - had not been accomplished. It finds a failure to "develop coordinated national intelligence which would superscede independent departmental efforts to produce overall intelligence," an that the agency's national intelligence function "is largely diffused and dispersed..."

Significantly, the study recommends the agency begin to place more emphasis on domestic activities and coordination with the FBI, since "fifth column activities and espionage do not begin or end at our geographical fronteirs."

Other topics covered in the report include: the problem of public exposure of intelligence activities, the need for a secret operational budget, an analysis (largely deleted) of the agency's Contact Branch "responsible for exploitation of...non-governmental organizations and individuals in the U.S. as sources of foreign intelligence," and a description (largely deleted) of the agency's covert operations units, which the report concludes had not been properly "advised of the current needs of policy makers" or "guided toward the most meaningful targets."

Included among the annexes are the first eight National Security Council Intelligence Directives (NSCID's) from the 1947-49 period, which are still in effect as the operational charter of the CIA.

D-10 National Security Decision Memorandum 40, "Responsibility For the Conduct, Supervision and Coordination of Covert Action Operations" (2 pages; one passage deleted)

A memo written by President Nixon in February, 1970 which orders the continuation of "covert action operations" by the U.S. intelligence agencies. The memo clarifies the delegated responsibilities of the agency heads as well as the role of the 40 Committee which is responsible for approving "all major and/or politically sensitive covert action programs." The President defines covert operations as "any type of activity necessary to carry out approved purposes except that they will not include armed conflict by regular military forces, or cover and deception for active military operations by the armed forces of the United States."

INDEX OF
INCLUDED DOCUMENTS
Arranged by Issuing Agency

INDEX OF
SUBJECTS AND NAMES